"Required reading for serious Chinese Archaeology scholars worldwide. The author brought to light a significant part of world and New Zealand history few knew anything about … For readers interested in learning more about the Chinese in New Zealand he provides a readable narrative about their daily lives. This book is highly recommended for all who want to learn about Chinese immigration and lives in the southern Pacific during the nineteenth and early twentieth centuries."

Dr Dudley Gardner, Principal Investigator,
Western Anthropological and Archaeological Research Institute, Wyoming

"Neville Ritchie's intensive and long-awaited examination of the Chinese in southern New Zealand brilliantly intertwines historical research and archaeological excavation with meticulous artefact analysis to present a wonderfully detailed portrayal of the daily lives of the South Island's early Chinese pioneers."

Priscilla Wegars, Affiliate Assistant Professor and Volunteer Curator,
Asian American Comparative Collection (AACC), University of Idaho

"Neville Ritchie's PhD thesis initially set out to describe the diverse material culture of Chinese in the Otago region of New Zealand's South Island. It achieved far more than that and became the go-to reference for archaeologists and historians involved in the Pacific Rim Chinese diaspora. Its welcome, long-awaited, publication will make this invaluable resource readily available to all."

Gordon Grimwade, Heritage Consultant and Adjunct Senior Lecturer,
Flinders University and University of New England

Studies in Australasian Historical Archaeology

Martin Gibbs and Mary Casey, Series Editors

The Studies in Australasian Historical Archaeology series aims to publish excavation reports and regional syntheses that deal with research into the historical archaeology of Australia, New Zealand and the Asia-Pacific region. The series aims to encourage greater public access to the results of major research and consultancy investigations, and it is co-published with the Australasian Society for Historical Archaeology.

An Archaeology of Institutional Confinement: The Hyde Park Barracks, 1848–1886
Peter Davies, Penny Crook and Tim Murray

Archaeology and history of the Chinese in southern New Zealand during the Nineteenth century: A Study of Acculturation, Adaptation and Change
Neville A. Ritchie

Archaeology of the Chinese Fishing Industry in Colonial Victoria
Alister M Bowen

The Commonwealth Block, Melbourne: A Historical Archaeology
Tim Murray, Kristal Buckley, Sarah Hayes, Geoff Hewitt, Justin McCarthy, Richard Mackay, Barbara Minchinton, Charlotte Smith, Jeremy Smith and Bronwyn Woff

Flashy, Fun and Functional: How Things Helped to Invent Melbourne's Gold Rush Mayor
Sarah Hayes

Good Taste, Fashion, Luxury: A Genteel Melbourne Family and Their Rubbish
Sarah Hayes

Port Essington: The Historical Archaeology of a North Australian Nineteenth-Century Military Outpost
Jim Allen

Recovering Convict Lives: A Historical Archaeology of the Port Arthur Penitentiary
Richard Tuffin, David Roe, Sylvana Szydzik, E. Jeanne Harris and Ashley Matic

The Shore Whalers of Western Australia: Historical Archaeology of a Maritime Frontier
Martin Gibbs

ARCHAEOLOGY AND HISTORY OF THE CHINESE IN SOUTHERN NEW ZEALAND DURING THE NINETEENTH CENTURY

A Study of Acculturation, Adaptation and Change

Neville A. Ritchie

Studies in Australasian Historical Archaeology
Volume 9

SYDNEY UNIVERSITY PRESS

Published 2023 by Sydney University Press
In association with the Australasian Society for Historical Archaeology
asha.org.au

© Neville A. Ritchie 2023
© Sydney University Press 2023

Reproduction and communication for other purposes
Except as permitted under Australia's *Copyright Act 1968*, no part of this edition may be reproduced, stored in a retrieval system, or communicated in any form or by any means without prior written permission. All requests for reproduction or communication should be made to Sydney University Press at the address below:

Sydney University Press
Gadigal Country
Fisher Library F03
University of Sydney NSW 2006
AUSTRALIA
sup.info@sydney.edu.au
sydneyuniversitypress.com.au

 A catalogue record for this book is available from the National Library of Australia.

ISBN 9781743329313 paperback
ISBN 9781743329320 epub
ISBN 9781743328941 pdf

Cover image: 4 Seasons tablewares © Neville A. Ritchie

Some quotations from scholarly sources may contain terms or views that were considered acceptable within mainstream New Zealand society when they were written, but may no longer be considered appropriate. The wording in these quotes does not necessarily reflect the views of Sydney University Press or the author.

CONTENTS

List of figures	vi
List of tables	x
List of plates	xiii
List of appendices	xiv
Abbreviations and acronyms	xv
Acknowledgements	xvii
Foreword	xix
Some background to the Clutha Valley Archaeological Project and the genesis of this thesis	xxi
1. Introduction	1
2. Chinese settlement in New Zealand	5
3. The Chinese on the Central Otago goldfields	21
4. The archaeological evidence	55
5. The material culture of the Chinese in southern New Zealand	107
6. Dietary analysis	401
7. Summary and conclusions	443
References	453
Index	467

Space limitations necessitated not reproducing the Plates and Appendices from the original thesis in the print edition. They can be accessed on the SUP website. Please visit https://sydneyuniversitypress.com.au/archaeology-chinese-miners-nz.

LIST OF FIGURES

Figure 1.1. Chinese dynasties and marks.	xxiv
Figure 2.1. Canton Villages Mission (CVM) districts map.	17
Figure 2.2. "Our Chinese Mission Map".	18
Figure 2.3. Certificate of Exemption 1881.	19
Figure 3.1. The southern goldfields: main localities mentioned in the text.	54
Figure 4.1. Map of the study area.	73
Figure 4.2. Firewood Creek site plan (S133/424).	74
Figure 4.3. Firewood Creek profile (S133/424).	75
Figure 4.4. Caliche shelter site plan (S133/223).	76
Figure 4.5. Sheung Fong shelter site plan (S133/21).	76
Figure 4.6. Ha Fong shelter site plan (S133/22).	77
Figure 4.7. Chinatown (Cromwell Chinese Camp S133/48).	78
Figure 4.8a. Chinatown hut plans (S133/48 Hut 1).	79
Figure 4.8b. Chinatown hut plans (S133/48 Hut 4).	79
Figure 4.8c. Chinatown – the central hut area (S133/48 Hut 6 and Feature 7).	80
Figure 4.8d. Chinatown hut plans (S133/48 Hut 9).	81
Figure 4.8e. Chinatown – the spring and gardens (S133/48 Huts 12, 14, 16, 17, 18, 19 and Feature 15).	81
Figure 4.8f. Chinatown hut plans (S133/48 Hut 21 and Feature 22).	82
Figure 4.8g. Chinatown hut plans (S133/48 Hut 23).	82
Figure 4.8h. Chinatown hut plans (S133/48 Hut 24).	83
Figure 4.8i. Chinatown hut plans (S133/48 Hut 26).	83
Figure 4.8j. Chinatown hut plans (S133/48 Hut 27).	84
Figure 4.8k. Chinatown hut plans (S133/48 Hut 29, Spring and garden terrace).	84
Figure 4.8l. Chinatown hut plans (S133/48 Hut 33).	85
Figure 4.8m. Chinatown hut plans (S133/48 Hut 34).	85
Figure 4.9. The Terraces site plan (S133/48), part of Chinatown.	86
Figure 4.10. Queensberry II (QB2) hut site plan (S124/207).	87
Figure 4.11. Apple Tree site plan (S124/212).	87
Figure 4.12. Sandy Point site plan (S124/231).	88
Figure 4.13. Northburn site plan (S133/77).	88
Figure 4.14. Ah Wee's site plan (S115/54).	89
Figure 4.15. Layout of dams and races associated with Ah Wee's mining (S115/52–54).	90
Figure 4.16. The Poplars site plan (S113/44).	90
Figure 4.17. Hanging Rock site plan (S133/474).	91
Figure 4.18. Riverside Shelter site plan (S133/791).	92
Figure 4.19. Plan of Arrowtown Chinese Settlement.	93
Figure 4.20a. Arrowtown Chinese Settlement excavated hut plans.	94
Figure 4.20b. Arrowtown Chinese Settlement excavated hut plans.	95
Figure 4.20c. Arrowtown Chinese Settlement excavated hut plans: ACS/4 (hut 4).	96
Figure 4.20d. Arrowtown Chinese Settlement excavated hut plans: ACS/5 (hut 5).	96
Figure 4.20e. Arrowtown Chinese Settlement excavated hut plans (Arrowtown huts 6a, 6b).	97
Figure 4.20f. Arrowtown Chinese Settlement excavated hut plans: ACS/8 (hut 8).	98
Figure 4.20g. Arrowtown Chinese Settlement excavated hut plans: ACS/10 (hut 10).	98
Figure 4.20h. Arrowtown Chinese Settlement excavated hut plans: ACS/11 (hut 11).	99
Figure 4.21. Ah Lum's store, Arrowtown site plan.	100
Figure 4.22. Rapids site plan (S133/453).	101
Figure 4.23. Flax Grove site plan (S133/494).	102
Figure 4.24. Flax Grove shelter (S133/494).	103
Figure 4.25. The Willows site plan (S124/42).	104

List of figures

Figure 4.26. Platform site plan (S133/466).	104
Figure 4.27. Graph of hut dimensions.	105
Figure 5.1. Liquor bottles.	283–85
Figure 5.2. Black glass beer bottles.	285
Figure 5.3. Miscellaneous beer bottles.	286
Figure 5.4. Embossed beer bottles.	286
Figure 5.5. Beer bottle labels.	287
Figure 5.6. Domestic bottles.	287–90
Figure 5.7. Pharmaceutical bottles.	291–93
Figure 5.8. French perfume bottles.	293
Figure 5.9. Chinese glass bottles.	294–95
Figure 5.10. Aerated water bottles.	295–97
Figure 5.11. Clear glass essence(?) bottle containing mercury.	297
Figure 5.12. Celadon wares.	298–99
Figure 5.13. Celadon rice bowl base-marks.	300
Figure 5.14. 4 Seasons wares.	300–02
Figure 5.15. Miscellaneous rice bowls.	303–04
Figure 5.16. Miscellaneous Chinese tablewares.	305–08
Figure 5.17. Ng Ka Py bottles.	308
Figure 5.18. Spouted pots.	309
Figure 5.19. Brownware shouldered food jars.	310
Figure 5.19c. Bulbous brown-glazed food jar, post-1920.	311
Figure 5.20. Shouldered food jar lids.	311
Figure. 5.21. Tall shouldered food jars.	312
Figure 5.22. Brownware flat-rimmed food jars.	312
Figure 5.23. Brown-glazed jarlet (Mangos collection) found at upper Chinatown.	313
Figure 5.24. Brownware straight-sided jars and lids.	313–14
Figure 5.25a. Brownware barrel jar uncovered behind Ah Lum's store (base punched out).	314
Figure 5.25b. Brown-slipped large-size barrel jar lid in profile.	315
Figure 5.26. Globular jar.	315
Figure 5.27. Miscellaneous Chinese ceramic cooking vessels.	316
Figure 5.28. Green-glazed ginger jars.	316
Figure 5.29. Green-glazed narrow-necked ginger jars.	317
Figure 5.30. Green-glazed hexagon-sided ginger jars.	318
Figure 5.31. Green-glazed straight-sided pots.	319
Figure 5.32. Type A blue-beige ginger jar.	319
Figure 5.33. Type B blue-beige ginger jars with "muslin texture" on surface.	320
Figure 5.34. Type C blue-beige ginger jar.	320
Figure 5.35. Blue-grey ginger jar with lustrous grey glaze and pictorial scenes in blue underglaze.	321
Figure 5.36. Flanged ginger jar lids.	321
Figure 5.37. Wing Lee Wai medicinal wine bottle.	322
Figure 5.38. Ceramic terminology.	322
Figure 5.39. Manufacturer's marks.	323
Figure 5.40. The common pale blue "Asiatic Pheasant" motif and base mark.	324
Figure 5.41. Japanese teapot with coralene beading found at ACS/2 (E11).	325
Figure 5.42. Euro-ceramic containers.	325
Figure 5.42e. Bristol-glazed crock found at Ch/26 (C3 Ly.2).	326
Figure 5.43. Can types.	327–29
Figure 5.44. Wax vesta boxes.	330–41
Figure 5.45. Opium pipe terminology.	342
Figure 5.46. Opium pipe bowl terminology.	342
Figure 5.47. Opium pipe bowls from Central Otago sites.	343–44
Figure 5.48. Opium cans.	344
Figure 5.49. Opium can cartouche types.	345
Figure 5.50. Artefacts made from opium can metal.	345
Figure 5.51. Artefacts associated with opium smoking.	346
Figure 5.52. A lustrous dark brown-glazed opium pipe bowl.	347

Figure 5.53. Tablespoons. 347–48
Figure 5.54. Teaspoons. 348
Figure 5.55. Table forks. 349
Figure 5.56. Knives. 349
Figure 5.57. Wok spoons. 350
Figure 5.58. Strainers. 350
Figure 5.59. Wok, spoon and cleaver. 351
Figure 5.60. Miscellaneous European utensils. 351–54
Figure 5.61. Security artefacts. 354
Figure 5.62. Miscellaneous metal artefacts. 355
Figure 5.63. Tools. 355–56
Figure 5.63i. Handshear blade (half) impressed with US(?) manufacturer's mark. 357
Figure 5.64. Gardening Tools. 358
Figure 5.65. Nail types. 359
Figure 5.65q–w. Special purpose nails. 360
Figure 5.66. Modified nails. 360
Figure 5.67. Wire artefacts. 361
Figure 5.68. Cartridges. 362–63
Figure 5.69. 12-gauge cartridges. 364
Figure 5.70. Lead artefacts. 364
Figure 5.71. Eisenwerke Air Pistol. 365
Figure 5.72. Scales and weights. 365
Figure 5.72h. Chinese rule scale. 366
Figure 5.73. Clay tobacco pipes. 367–69
Figure 5.74. Wooden tobacco pipes. 369
Figure 5.75. Vulcanite pipe stems and shank bands. 370–71
Figure 5.76. Chinese brass tobacco pipe bowl found in a Chinese hut, Cardrona Valley (Dennison pers. comm.). 371
Figure 5.77. Chinese inkstones and writing brush, 372–73
Figure 5.78. Ceramic toothpaste pots and bases. 374
Figure 5.79. Bone toothbrushes. 375
Figure 5.80. Metal buttons: one-piece construction. 375–76
Figure 5.81. Metal buttons: two-piece construction. 377
Figure 5.82. Metal buttons: three-piece construction. 378
Figure 5.83. Metal–non-metal composite buttons. 378
Figure 5.84. Fabric-covered buttons. 379
Figure 5.85. Shell buttons. 380–81
Figure 5.86. Bone and horn buttons. 382
Figure 5.87. Wooden buttons. 383
Figure 5.88. Glass buttons. 384
Figure 5.89. Porcelain/ceramic buttons. 384
Figure 5.90. Plastic synthetic buttons. 385
Figure 5.91. Rubber buttons. 385
Figure 5.92. Slate button. 386
Figure 5.93. Worked shell toggle(?). 386
Figure 5.94. Frequency seriation of button types/materials: Cromwell's Chinatown. 387
Figure 5.95. Frequency seriation of button types/materials: Arrowtown Chinese Camp. 388
Figure 5.96. Frequency seriation of button types/materials: rural sites. 389
Figure 5.97. Miscellaneous clothing fasteners. 390
Figure 5.98. Clothing hardware: braces, suspenders, etc. 390–91
Figure 5.99. Buckles. 392–93
Figure 5.100. Chinese artefacts associated with grooming and personal hygiene. 394
Figure 5.101. Artefacts associated with gambling and recreation. 395–96
Figure 5.102. Chinese coins and amulet. 397
Figure 5.103. Medallion. 397
Figure 5.104. Slate artefacts. 398
Figure 5.105. Bank receipts for gold deposits and other paper artefacts. 399–400
Figure 6.1. Example of butchering analysis form. 437

List of figures

Figure 6.2. Chinatown beef meat cuts. 438
Figure 6.3. Arrowtown beef meat cuts. 438
Figure 6.4. Ah Lum's store beef meat cuts. 438
Figure 6.5. Rural sites beef meat cuts. 439
Figure 6.6. Chinatown (Cromwell Chinese Camp) pig meat cuts. 439
Figure 6.7. Arrowtown pig meat cuts. 439
Figure 6.8. Ah Lum's store pig meat cuts. 440
Figure 6.9. Rural sites pig meat cuts. 440
Figure 6.10. Chinatown (Cromwell Chinese Camp) sheep meat cuts. 440
Figure 6.11. Arrowtown sheep meat cuts. 441
Figure 6.12. Ah Lum's store sheep meat cuts. 441
Figure 6.13. Rural sites sheep meat cuts. 441

LIST OF TABLES

Table 2.1. Population of Guangdong 1787–1850.	15
Table 2.2. Populations of Chinese in Otago towns by early 1870.	15
Table 2.3. Chinese employed on road or railway construction or as general labourers 1874–86.	15
Table 2.4. Chinese arrivals and departures 1876–1901.	16
Table 3.1. Estimated costs of living for Chinese and Europeans on the goldfields.	49
Table 3.2. Condensed summary of occupations of Chinese in 1871.	49
Table 3.3 Chinese occupational trends in the nineteenth century.	50
Table 3.4. Inter-house movements of a group of miners at Round Hill.	51
Table 3.5. Estimated populations of Chinese miners in 1871.	51
Table 3.6. Chinese involved in different types of mining.	51
Table 3.7. Recorded earnings or amounts sent to China by Chinese miners, merchants and gamblers working on the Round Hill field 1882–89.	52–3
Table 3.8. Chinese exhumations.	53
Table 4.1. Summary details of the study sites.	68–9
Table 4.2. Occupation dates of the study sites.	69
Table 4.3. Rockshelter construction features.	70
Table 4.4. Summary of construction features.	70–1
Table 4.5. Hut dimensions.	72
Table 4.6. Hut door orientation.	72
Table 5.1. Liquor bottles, minimum numbers per site.	191
Table 5.2. Beer bottles, minimum numbers per site.	192
Table 5.3. Domestic bottles, minimum numbers per site.	193
Table 5.4. Pharmaceutical bottles, minimum numbers per site.	194
Table 5.5. Chinese glass bottles, minimum numbers per site.	195
Table 5.6. Aerated water bottles, minimum numbers per site.	196
Table 5.7. Bottled products: minimum numbers and percentages.	197
Table 5.8 Alcohol prices on the goldfields.	198
Table 5.9. Celadon wares: site distribution.	199
Table 5.10. 4 Seasons wares: site distribution and decoration.	199
Table 5.11. Rare and miscellaneous Chinese tablewares: site distribution.	200
Table 5.12. Brownwares: minimum numbers per site.	201
Table 5.13. Dimensions of straight-sided brownware jars.	202
Table 5.14. Chinese ginger jars: site distribution.	202
Table 5.15. Dimensions of green-glazed straight-sided pots.	203
Table 5.16. Chinese ceramics: frequency, temporal and areal distribution.	204–05
Table 5.17. Represented manufacturer's marks.	206–09
Table 5.18. Predominant Ceramic type (Euro-ceramic or Chinese) in each site.	210
Table 5.19. Euro-ceramic earthenware and porcelain vessels: site distribution.	210–211
Table 5.20. Earthenware types: site distribution and percentages per site.	211
Table 5.21. Euro-ceramic and Chinese ceramic vessels: site distribution and occupation date.	211
Table 5.22. Comparison of ware types: minimum numbers and percentages.	212
Table 5.23. Euro-ceramics composition (all sites).	213–14
Table 5.24. Euro-ceramics decoration (all sites).	215
Table 5.25. Euro-ceramics composition: rural sites.	216–17
Table 5.26. Euro-ceramics decoration: rural sites.	218
Table 5.27. Principal can types: site distribution.	219
Table 5.28. Embossed and painted can labels.	220
Table 5.29. Known or inferred date ranges of metal containers.	221
Table 5.30. Wax vesta boxes: site distribution.	222–24

List of tables

Table 5.31. Typology of opium pipe bowls from Chinese sites in Central Otago.	226
Table 5.32. Opium pipe bowls: minimum numbers per site.	227
Table 5.33. Opium can remains.	228
Table 5.34. Typology of opium can cartouches.	229–30
Table 5.35. Opium can cartouche types.	231
Table 5.36. Artefacts made from opium can metal.	232
Table 5.37. Artefacts associated with opium smoking.	233
Table 5.38. Domestic utensils from Chinese sites.	234–35
Table 5.39 Chinatown: household and domestic artefacts.	236–37
Table 5.40 Arrowtown: household and domestic artefacts.	238–39
Table 5.41. Rural sites: household and domestic artefacts.	240
Table 5.42. Chinatown tools: site distribution.	241
Table 5.43. Arrowtown tools: site distribution.	242
Table 5.44. Rural sites tools: site distribution.	243
Table 5.45. Ah Lum's store: nails.	244
Table 5.46. Chinatown: distribution of nails and screws.	245
Table 5.47. Arrowtown: distribution of nails and screws.	246
Table 5.48. Rural sites: distribution of nails and screws.	247
Table 5.49. Chinatown: non-ferrous metal artefacts.	248
Table 5.50. Chinatown: miscellaneous metal artefacts.	249
Table 5.51. Arrowtown: miscellaneous ferrous artefacts.	250
Table 5.52. Arrowtown: miscellaneous non-ferrous metal artefacts.	251
Table 5.53. Rural sites: miscellaneous ferrous artefacts.	252–53
Table 5.54. Rural sites: miscellaneous non-ferrous artefacts.	254
Table 5.55. Cartridge and projectile types: site distribution.	255
Table 5.56. Chinatown: cartridge types.	255
Table 5.57. Arrowtown: cartridge types.	256
Table 5.58. Rural sites: cartridge types.	257
Table 5.59. Details of recovered ammunition types.	258
Table 5.60. Scale components, weights and accounting devices.	260
Table 5.61. Tobacco pipes and shank bands: minimum numbers per site.	261
Table 5.62. Inkstones found in Chinese sites in Central Otago.	262
Table 5.63. Summary of paper artefacts with Chinese calligraphy.	263
Table 5.64. Ceramic toothpaste and ointment pots.	264
Table 5.65. Bone toothbrushes: site distribution.	265
Table 5.66. Chinatown: buttons.	266
Table 5.67. Arrowtown: buttons.	267
Table 5.69. Embossed buttons (brass studs).	268
Table 5.68. Rural sites: buttons.	268
Table 5.70. Embossed metal buttons: all types (2- and 4-hole).	269
Table 5.71. Buttons classified by kinds of garments they represent (all sites).	270
Table 5.72. Glass beads.	270
Table 5.73a. Chinatown: clothing fittings.	271
Table 5.73b. Arrowtown: clothing fittings	271
Table 5.74. Rural sites: clothing fittings.	272
Table 5.75. Provenance and types of fabric remnants.	273
Table 5.76. Footwear.	274
Table 5.77. Artefacts associated with grooming and personal hygiene.	275
Table 5.78. Artefacts associated with gambling and recreation.	276
Table 5.79. Distribution of Chinese coins.	276
Table 5.80. British and New Zealand coins.	277
Table 5.81. Distribution of coal and lignite.	278
Table 5.82. Summary of recovered wood and charcoal specimens.	279–80
Table 5.83. Stone artefacts and related structural materials.	281
Table 5.84. Paper artefacts of European origin.	282
Table 6.1. Numerical predominance and ratios of pork/beef/sheep elements (meat cuts).	418
Table 6.2. Cattle (*Bos taurus*) elements (meat cuts) at the Chinatown (Cromwell Chinese Camp) huts.	419

Table 6.3a. Cattle (*Bos taurus*) elements (meat cuts) at the Arrowtown Chinese Camp huts. 420
Table 6.3b. Cattle (*Bos taurus*) elements (meat cuts) at Ah Lum's store, Arrowtown. 421
Table 6.4. Cattle (*Bos taurus*) elements (meat cuts) at the rural sites. 422
Table 6.5. Pig (*Sus scrofa*) elements (meat cuts) at the Chinatown (Cromwell Chinese Camp) huts. 423
Table 6.6a. Pig (*Sus scrofa*) elements (meat cuts) at the Arrowtown Camp huts. 424
Table 6.6b. Pig (*Sus scrofa*) elements (meat cuts) at Ah Lum's store. 425
Table 6.7. Pig (*Sus scrofa*) elements (meat cuts) and minimum numbers (MNE) at the rural sites. 426
Table 6.8. Comparison of saw and cleaver chop cuts on bones. 427
Table 6.9. Cut-type distribution on bones. 427
Table 6.10. Sheep (*Ovis aries*) elements (meat cuts) at the Chinatown (Cromwell Chinese Camp) huts. 428
Table 6.11. Sheep (*Ovis aries*) elements (meat cuts) at the Arrowtown Chinese Camp huts. 429
Table 6.12. Sheep (*Ovis aries*) elements (meat cuts) at Ah Lum's store. 430
Table 6.13. Sheep (*Ovis aries*) elements (meat cuts) at the rural sites. 431
Table 6.14. Skeletal portion meat weights. 432
Table 6.15. Estimated meat weights of pig, sheep and beef. 432
Table 6.16. Butchering unit definitions. 433
Table 6.17. Rabbit bones at all sites. 434
Table 6.18. Bird remains: minimum number of individuals (MNI). 435
Table 6.19. Fowl bones distribution. 436
Table 6.20. Commodity prices in the nineteenth century. 436
Table 7.1. Foods and beverages imported from China and consumed by the Chinese on the southern goldfields. 451
Table 7.2. Foods/beverages/products of European/New Zealand origin definitely consumed/used by the Chinese on the southern goldfields. 452

LIST OF PLATES

Space limitations necessitated not reproducing the Plates from the original thesis in the print edition. They can be accessed on the SUP website. Please visit https://sydneyuniversitypress.com.au/archaeology-chinese-miners-nz.

Plate 1. Sheung Fong shelter (S133/21), Cromwell Gorge, pre-excavation.
Plate 2. Northburn shelter (S1233/77), pre-excavation.
Plate 3. Cromwell Chinese Settlement (Chinatown), c.1890.
Plate 4. An aerial view of Cromwell and the Kawarau River. Cromwell's Chinatown was located in the willows on the left bank of the river. Photo taken 1980.
Plate 5. The central part of the Chinatown settlement during excavation (February 1980).
Plate 6. The restored hut in Chinatown (hut 26).
Plate 7. Ah Wee's hut site (S155/54), excavation underway.
Plate 8. The Poplars hut site (S115/44), Upper Clutha, excavation underway.
Plate 9. The Arrowtown Chinese Settlement in 1887.
Plate 10. Ah Lum's store, Arrowtown, during the excavation.
Plate 11. Euro-ceramic cups.
Plate 12. Euro-ceramic cups and mugs.
Plate 13. Euro-ceramic saucers.
Plate 14. Euro-ceramic saucers.
Plate 15. Euro-ceramic saucers.
Plate 16. Euro-ceramic plates.
Plate 17. Euro-ceramic miscellaneous vessels.
Plate 18. Euro-ceramic miscellaneous vessels.
Plate 19. Euro-ceramic bowls.
Plate 20. Opium can labels.

LIST OF APPENDICES

Space limitations necessitated not reproducing the Appendices from the original thesis in the print edition. They can be accessed on the SUP website. Please visit https://sydneyuniversitypress.com.au/archaeology-chinese-miners-nz.

Appendix 1 Numbers of Chinese in New Zealand: 1867–1981.
Appendix 2 Recorded Chinese sites in Central Otago.
Appendix 3 Measurements of Chinese tablewares.
Appendix 4 Measurements of Chinese ceramic containers.
Appendix 5 Chinese supply stores on the southern goldfields.
Appendix 6 Quantities and revenue from duty on the importation of opium into New Zealand: 1867–1923.
Appendix 7 Enacted and failed New Zealand government legislation pertaining to the Chinese: 1879–1910.
Appendix 8 Chinese coins found in the study sites.

ABBREVIATIONS AND ACRONYMS

AACC	Asian American Comparative Collection
AACCN	Asian American Comparative Collection Newsletter
ACS	Arrowtown Chinese Settlement
CAC	Colonial Ammunition Company
CVD	Clutha Valley Development
CVM	Canton Villages Mission
HNZ	Heritage New Zealand
MHR	Member of the House of Representatives
MN	minimum number
MNE	minimum number of elements
MNI	minimum number of individuals
MNMC	minimum number of particular meat cuts
MWD	Ministry of Works and Development
NZHPT	New Zealand Historic Places Trust, now Heritage New Zealand Pouhere Taonga
UMC	Union Metallic Cartridge Company

ACKNOWLEDGEMENTS

My thanks to the ASHA Publications Committee for deeming my dissertation worthy of their monograph series, and Professor Martin Gibbs and Dr Peter Davies for digitising the thesis and liaising with me when this project was first mooted. But over the past two years it has been the energy, enthusiasm and input (help with tables and figures especially) of Martin Gibbs that has seen the Sydney University Press version through to completion. It has been a pleasure to liaise with Naomi van Groll, SUP Publishing Manager, via emails and video links, on all aspects of the design, formatting, proofing and finalising of the monograph. Her dedication and enthusiasm is infectious. A big thanks too, to Nathan Grice, SUP Production Officer, for reformatting all the figures and tables. The latter, especially, was a big job. Further thanks to Susan Murray, for overseeing this project, and to Marie-Louise Taylor, copyeditor extraordinaire.

Hundreds of people contributed to the dissertation, far too many to mention all by name. They included approximately 150 students who helped with survey, excavations and artefact analysis, eight "deputies" who did stints with me over the duration of the CVD archaeological project (1977–86), the people with graphic skills who drew the hundreds of artefact drawings, numerous local informants, the many specialists who identified everything from bird and fish bones to bullets and Chinese coins for me. I feel I must acknowledge the three main illustrators by name – Debbie Foster, Sandy McElrea and Fiona Cameron. As the old adage goes "a picture tells a thousand words". Their drawing skills enhanced the original thesis and this published version. Thank you all for your help in achieving the research objectives of the archaeological project and the work embodied in this thesis. I also acknowledge the useful discussions I had with many Australian and US archaeologists, especially Dr Priscilla Wegars, who then and now administers the Asian American Comparative Collection at the University of Idaho, Moscow, Idaho.

FOREWORD

This volume was originally intended for publication in 2009 as the second volume in the Studies in Australasian Historical Archaeology series, providing the first New Zealand PhD in historical archaeology to match Jim Allen's *Port Essington* as the first Australian PhD (published as Volume 1 in the series). However, life and then other projects got in the way and after a 14-year lapse I sent an email to Nev in early 2022 to see if he was still interested. Newly retired, he was keen to unearth the project. The question some might ask is why would we bother to publish a 1986 PhD, reporting on a series of excavations and analyses from the mid-1970s to the mid-1980s? The answer is that aside from being one of the seminal volumes of Australasian historical archaeology, it is also still internationally acclaimed as one of the most comprehensive archaeological studies of the archaeology of a mid-19th century Chinese diaspora goldmining settlement.

I first got hold of a photocopy of a photocopy of Nev's PhD thesis sometime in the early 1990s courtesy of Denis Gojak (then and now a renowned collector of archaeological resources and ever-generous in loaning them to others). Despite repeated reproduction, the sheer number of artefact drawings in Nev's volume, especially of the Chinese artefacts, was striking. Just as impressive was the extensive research that he had undertaken in the United States and elsewhere to identify the items in his assemblages, as well the comprehensive comparative analysis between the different sites he had excavated. Nev's thesis has remained in hot demand, enhanced by his body of papers and reports on the topic. However, the original dissertation remains undigitised, so copies have become hard to obtain and of progressively worse quality.

In discussions with Nev it was decided that (like Jim Allen's PhD) a comprehensive update to incorporate more recent scholarship on the Chinese diaspora, or indeed to upgrade the analyses to match more recent approaches, would be a monumental task and a PhD in its own right. Therefore, we have gone down the track of leaving much of the content intact, with Nev providing both an introduction to explain the genesis of the original work and the context in which it was done, as well as a postscript reflecting on the research and what it achieved. Aside from "OCRing" and editing the original typewritten text, the biggest challenge in producing this volume was re-creating the dozens of tables that underscored the comparative analysis, as well as upgrading the original images. In his original dissertation, Nev reproduced his images at a 1:1 scale so that other researchers could simply hold their artefacts against the artefact drawings for comparative purposes. However, to make this published volume a manageable size it has been necessary to go back and create scales for each image so that they can be reduced to allow more to be fitted on each page. The Appendices and Plates from the original research and dissertation have been made available on the SUP website.

Professor Martin Gibbs,
December 2022
University of New England, Armidale

SOME BACKGROUND TO THE CLUTHA VALLEY ARCHAEOLOGICAL PROJECT AND THE GENESIS OF THIS THESIS

In the early 1970s, New Zealand was governed by the National Party under Robert Muldoon. One of their policies was "Think Big", which involved several major infrastructure projects intended to stimulate the economy. This included a series of hydro-electric dams on the Upper Clutha and Kawarau Rivers that became known as the Clutha Valley Development (CVD) project. It was planned to build five (possibly six) dams on the Upper Clutha and Kawarau Rivers, the last major rivers in New Zealand that were not dammed.

The power project started just after the passing of the *Historic Places Act 1975* (which for the first time included archaeological site protection provisions), so the Ministry of Works and Development (MWD), on behalf of NZ Electricity Department, was obliged to fund archaeological surveys of the areas that would be threatened by the hydro project, starting with a survey of the Cromwell Gorge, which would eventually become Lake Dunstan. The survey was undertaken in the summer of 1975–76 by Professor Charles Higham (Higham et al. 1976) and Graeme Mason (1977) assisted by Otago anthropology department students. A further survey was conducted along the route of the new gorge highway by Historic Places Trust archaeologist Mary Newman (1977). The surveys revealed that over 150 sites (95% associated with goldmining) would be affected by the proposed dam(s) in the Cromwell Gorge. Although the anthropology department would have been well placed to run an archaeological mitigation project, its academic interests at the time were more focused on pre-European sites in New Zealand and working in South-East Asia and Oceania, so it passed up the opportunity.

If it hadn't been for the passing of the *Historic Places Act 1975*, there probably would not have been a funded survey of the Lake Dunstan reservoir, and certainly no Clutha Valley Archaeology Project – it was the first major beneficial outcome of the new site protection legislation. In early 1976, as an MA student, I was attending one of Professor Higham's tutorials when he told me he planned to advocate to the Historic Places Trust (NZHPT, now Heritage New Zealand Pouhere Taonga) that a full-time archaeologist should be employed to undertake archaeological investigations in the areas encompassed by the proposed Clutha dams, i.e. the Cromwell Gorge, Kawarau Gorge and the Upper Clutha Valley. He asked me if I was interested. I said I would be but had doubts that it would ever happen. But somehow Prof. Higham persuaded the Historic Places Trust that the best way to mitigate the impact of the dams on archaeological resources was to appoint an archaeologist to lead an archaeological and historic research project. Following discussions in 1976–77, an agreement was reached between NZHPT and the MWD. The main features were:

1. MWD/NZED would fund a five-year historic and archaeological research project.
2. The project, to be known as the Clutha Valley Archaeological Project, would be under the direction of a resident archaeologist seconded to MWD, Cromwell, but employed and overseen by NZHPT.

In late 1977, NZHPT advertised for an archaeologist to head the archaeological project. I applied for and got the position and managed to drag it out for a decade. Because of the general lack of knowledge about the sites in the area (most of the known ones were associated with goldmining), the job initially was loosely defined in terms of research objectives, but these gradually crystallised as the ground surveys progressed. The immediate objective was to conduct systematic surveys of the entire Upper Clutha Valley and its tributaries, possibly an important precedent being established in that there was informal agreement that the entire valley, from the floor to the mountain tops, would be surveyed (i.e. way beyond the extent of the proposed reservoirs) so that the real impact of the losses caused by the hydro project could be assessed and mining water systems thoroughly documented.

Initial fieldwork priorities were largely governed by the MWD's need to gain resource consents for the Clyde Dam. So, work was centred on the Cromwell Gorge and Lowburn areas where an extensive test-pitting program was conducted in the summer of 1978. The 44 recorded rockshelters in the gorge were the primary focus. From this work, two broad site types were considered to be worth further investigation and research – the sites associated with the activities of the Chinese miners, and the few pre-European sites.

By the end of 1979, eight rockshelters had been investigated, of which three were occupied in pre-European times (Rockfall 1, Italian Creek and Caliche shelters; Ritchie 1982c) and five occupied by Chinese miners between 1866 and 1890 (Ritchie 1986b). By this time, I was aware that most of the sites that would eventually go under Lake Dunstan were associated with Chinese mining, and their habitation sites were highly recognisable because of the presence of remnants of distinctive Chinese artefacts. As there were no archaeological reports on Chinese sites, I decided it would become a major research focus. At the time I had no idea it would lead to a PhD. During 1979, survey work was conducted in the area affected by the Queensberry and Luggate Dam proposals (Ritchie 1980, 1980d), the Shotover Valley and the Bendigo goldfield. These surveys enabled the production of a descriptive terminology for tailing sites, which has enabled their recording in a more meaningful way by facilitating comparison of key features (Ritchie 1981a).

Cromwell's Chinese Camp (locally known as "Chinatown") was targeted for excavation in the summer of 1980 (Ritchie 1980a, 1983a, 1986b). There is no doubt that the Chinatown excavation really brought the archaeological project to the attention of the public and researchers overseas, particularly in the United States where in the early 1980s there was a burgeoning interest in the history and archaeology associated with that nation's many Asian immigrant groups. Prior to the Chinese Camp excavation, the excavations had been relatively small, and although informative, had not provided a large volume of material to work on. Chinatown changed that and had a major influence on the direction of the project over the next few years.

In early 1981, a survey of the Roxburgh Gorge was conducted (Harrison 1982). This went some way to redressing a sorry situation. When Lake Roxburgh was formed in 1956, there had been no prior archaeological survey or archaeological investigations of any sort. During the survey, about 150 sites were recorded, including 87 rockshelters with occupation material (compared with 44 in the Cromwell Gorge and 25 in the Kawarau Gorge). The surviving sites in the gorge probably represent less than half the number that existed prior to the gorge's inundation.

The period 1982–83 saw further historic site excavations in the Upper Clutha and Kawarau Gorge (including the Hanging Rock and Riverside Chinese shelters, and a forge site; the latter two were excavated principally for interpretative purposes for the Otago Goldfields Park). By the end of 1982, the major surveys and associated reports were finished and the analysis of excavated materials and writing up began in earnest. In 1983, I realised I had a huge corpus of data from the Chinese site excavations and associated research. I decided to make it the subject of my PhD.

From the initiation of the Clutha project, a close working relationship was maintained with the Otago Goldfields Park administered by the Department of Lands and Survey, the forerunner to the Department of Conservation. After the Chinatown excavation, the department had somewhat reluctantly accepted responsibility for the management and maintenance of Cromwell's Chinatown site. It was understandably reluctant to spend money and energy on a site that would shortly be inundated. But the site, as I had argued, proved to be by far the most frequently visited unit in the park – even more so after one of the huts was restored. By early 1983, the Goldfields Park authorities needed little convincing that they needed a replacement for Chinatown.

The selection of the Arrowtown Chinese Settlement (ACS) was not difficult. The settlement was smaller than that at Cromwell but had two real advantages: a standing Chinese store and easy access to work on and for future visitors. Using funds provided by Lands and Survey, excavation of the Arrowtown Chinese Camp and the store became the major projects for the summer of 1983–84 (Ritchie 1984a, 1984c, 1986b), along with excavation of the Rapids, a Chinese miners' campsite in the Kawarau Gorge (Piper 1984; Ritchie 1986b). Other 1982–83 excavations focused on four Chinese hut and shelter sites in the Upper Clutha selected after assessment of the Luggate and Queensberry survey data (Ritchie 1986b).

About mid-1985, the first of a series of test excavations was conducted on former business sites in the old main street of Cromwell, including areas behind the former store sites associated with Cromwell's Chinatown. With the end of the project in sight, only one small investigation, on a Chinese hut at Horseshoe Bend, Upper Clutha, was conducted during the summer of 1985–86. Horseshoe Bend was the 21st Chinese site to be excavated as part of the project, while another 40 had been tested to some degree.

From the outset of the project, it was intended to achieve a lot more than just undertake rescue excavations and the associated reports. The duration of the project, the large number of sites excavated and the presence of a full-time archaeologist (with a full-time assistant) enabled much more in-depth research and comparative studies on the main artefact categories – glass and tin containers and European and Chinese ceramic containers and domestic wares) than had been possible on any project in New Zealand previously.

The detailed studies of various artefact types broke new ground in historic goldfields archaeology in New Zealand, particularly with regard to dating tin matchboxes (Anson 1983; Bedford 1985a), the analysis of glass and tin containers (Ritchie and Bedford 1983d, 1985b) and a wide range of both European and Chinese artefacts found in the Central Otago sites (Ritchie and Harrison 1982b; Foster 1983; Piper 1984, 1988; Bedford 1985c; Cameron 1985; Ritchie 1986a; Ritchie and McGovern-Wilson 1986d; Ritchie and Park 1988b) and tailings analysis (Ritchie 1981). In addition to these thematic studies, the artefacts from several major site assemblages were thoroughly documented, in part to provide baseline data for future studies (Ritchie 1985c, 1986b; Bedford 1985b, 1986).

The CVD project (December 1977–June 1986) was ground-breaking at the time. The 10-year duration of the project has only recently been surpassed by the Christchurch earthquake archaeological project for longevity (Ritchie 2021).

NOTES ON THIS EDITION

In the years since the CVD project and the publication of this thesis, much progress has been made in the the standardisation of terminology for artefact types found in nineteenth- and twentieth-century overseas Chinese sites. Much credit is due to Priscilla Wegars, Affiliate Assistant Professor and Volunteer Curator of the Asian American Comparative Collection (AACC) at the University of Idaho. Readers are advised to refer to the Artifact Identification resources available via https://www.uidaho.edu/class/anthrolab/collections/aacc/id for the most up-to-date standardised terminology of Chinese wares used by archaeologists today.

Some quotations from scholarly sources may contain terms or views that were considered acceptable within mainstream New Zealand society when they were written, but may no longer be considered appropriate. The wording in these quotes does not necessarily reflect the views of Sydney University Press or the author.

For any references to the Plates and Appendices, please visit https://sydneyuniversitypress.com.au/archaeology-chinese-miners-nz.

Neville Ritchie,
August 2023

Archaeology and history of the Chinese in southern New Zealand during the nineteenth century

Chinese dynasties and marks

Figure 1.1. Chinese dynasties and marks (Miller and Miller 1983:236).

Chapter 1
INTRODUCTION

1.1 THE FRAMEWORK, METHOD AND FOCUS OF THIS BOOK

New Zealand's present population is predominantly of Māori or British origin. However, many numerically smaller ethnic groups from continental Europe, China, India, South-East Asia, Polynesia and elsewhere have become established and made important contributions to the nation's heritage and development. Together they comprise 20% of the population. The social histories of some of these groups have been documented in popular books such as Petersen's (1956) *Forest Homes* (the story of Scandinavian settlement), Goldman's (1958) *The History of the Jews in New Zealand*, Pearce's (1976) *The Scots of New Zealand*, Butler's (1977) *Opium and Gold* (the story of the Chinese miners in New Zealand), Trlin's (1979) *Now Respected, Once Despised* (the story of Yugoslav settlement in New Zealand) and McGill's (1982) *The Other New Zealanders* (a summary account of all the established ethnic minorities in New Zealand).

However, at the time of writing the thesis that this book is based on (1983–86), the history of the Chinese, New Zealand's third-largest racial group after those of British and Polynesian stock, and their collective contributions to New Zealand society and its development, was virtually unknown to the average New Zealander.

During the 19th century, most references to Chinese people tended to be racist, self-serving, bigoted and aimed at curbing "the rising tide of Chinese immigration". In the 20th century, with a changing social climate and greater racial tolerance, the emphasis turned to academic socio-demographic, immigration and assimilation studies (e.g. Hall and Scholefield 1927; M.J. McNeur 1930; Mathews 1934; Borrie 1939; Fyfe 1948; Scurrah 1950; Fong 1959; Grief 1974; Sedgewick 1982).

The main published works on the New Zealand Chinese are as follows. *The Overseas Chinese in New Zealand: A Study of Assimilation* (Fong 1959a), which was based on thesis research (Fong 1959b). *The Overseas Chinese in New Zealand* (Grief 1974) is essentially an update on Fong's volume. Beginning in the early 1970s, Dr James Ng, a Dunedin doctor, published several popular articles on the history of the New Zealand Chinese, motivated, in part, by a desire to see historic distortions corrected or balanced (Ng 1972a, 1972b, 1981, 1984a, 1984b). Ng's earlier papers were superseded in the 1990s by his magnum opus, a four-volume series *Windows on a Chinese Past* (Ng 1991, 1993, 1995, 1999). These books, containing a wealth of information, did not exist when I completed my thesis in 1986.

In 1977, Butler's book *Opium and Gold* was published. Because of its modern format and photographic content, it was the most accessible of the published studies on the history and social place of the New Zealand Chinese (see the Postscript for a summary of significant publications on the New Zealand Chinese after 1986).

No study of the 19th-century New Zealand Chinese (especially their involvement in goldmining) would be complete without recourse to the abundant data contained in Reverend Alexander Don's prolific records compiled during his ministry to the Chinese in southern New Zealand between 1880 and 1911 and his founding of the Canton Villages Mission (CVM) of the Presbyterian Church in 1898 (it continued until 1951; see Ng 1984a). Without his recorded observations, the history of the first decades of Chinese settlement in New Zealand would be far less well documented (refer to Chapter 3 for expanded discussion). Don left four major published records of detailed socio-historical information, which are invaluable to the New Zealand Chinese researcher:

1. His regular columns published between 1882 and 1889 in the *New Zealand Presbyterian* magazine under the title "Our Chinese Mission".
2. The published diaries of his "Annual Inland Tours" of Southland, Central Otago (1891–1910) and Westland (1911) during which he visited as many Chinese communities and isolated Chinese as he was physically able to during his Christian missionary work.
3. A diary, maintained between 1896 and 1919, which lists by name and number the majority of the Chinese (over 1,000) with whom Don had contact during this period. He noted their county of origin, age, number of years residence in New Zealand, movements within New Zealand and duration of stay at each location, and finally what became of them (if known).
4. In 1936 he published *Memories of the Golden Road: A History of the Presbyterian Church in Central Otago*. His book also contains many useful comments on 19th-century Chinese settlement.

At the time of writing the thesis this book is based on, the most recently completed socio-historical study on the New Zealand Chinese was Sedgewick's (1982) PhD thesis titled "The Politics of Survival: A Social History of the Chinese in New Zealand".

This book involves an acculturation and material culture study of the Chinese mining community in southern New Zealand during the 19th century. It differs from any of the preceding research in that it is based for the most part on archaeological evidence derived from the excavation of Chinese sites. This data, supplemented by information from literary sources, is used to define the lifestyle of the Chinese miners and their responses to their situation in New Zealand. In Section 1.2, the role of "historical archaeology" and the limited previous work of this type in New Zealand is discussed. In the final part of the chapter (1.3), the theoretical basis of the research is outlined. The historical context of Chinese settlement in New Zealand is reviewed in Chapter 2. Chapters 3–6 are comprehensive documentation of the social history and material culture of the Chinese goldseekers in southern New Zealand in the 19th century. In the concluding chapter (Chapter 7), departures from traditional patterns are identified and the changes assessed.

1.2 HISTORICAL ARCHAEOLOGY: BACKGROUND AND ROLE

Allen's (1969) PhD on the archaeology and history of the Port Essington settlement on the north-central coast of Australia was a key contribution to the development of historical archaeology in Australia. The Australian Society for Historical Archaeology was formed the same year. When this writer's thesis was written, historical archaeology was still very much in its infancy in New Zealand. Prickett's (1981) PhD thesis, "The Archaeology of a Military Frontier, Taranaki, New Zealand, 1860–1881", was the first substantial study in historical archaeology to be completed. Two years later, Spring-Rice completed another military-orientated thesis (an MA) on the history and archaeology of Fort Galatea in the Bay of Plenty (Spring-Rice 1983), and Mitchell (1983) submitted a research essay (which involved archaeological investigations) titled "The History and Archaeology of the Armed Constabulary Sites along the Napier-Taupo Road, 1869–1885". Twohill (1984) presented an MA thesis on the industrial archaeology of the Mt Zeehan Goldmining Property on the Coromandel.

This writer's PhD, when presented in 1986, was only the fourth historical archaeology thesis to be produced in New Zealand. However, in the interval since Prickett's thesis was completed, several books, reports and papers on historical-industrial archaeology were produced (excluding survey reports), such as those of Hayward and Diamond (1979, 1980, 1982), Jones (1981), Rusden (1979, 1982), Thornton (1982), Anson (1983), Bedford (1985a, 1985b) and Wilson (1984 ed.), as well as papers by this writer.

Although both groups of data (archaeological and historical) can be used independently, they are complementary and when used in tandem tend to set in motion not only "an exponential information growth process", but also "a verifying procedure" because the independent bodies of data are either in general agreement or oppose each other, indicating that either the archaeological inferences are possibly wrong or the historical record is incomplete. A case in point, drawn from this study, concerns the question of alcohol consumption by the Chinese on the goldfields. Historical observations tend to suggest the Chinese only consumed alcohol in moderation and were models of sobriety, whereas, in terms of volumes and types consumed, the archaeological evidence suggests otherwise (see Section 5.1 and Chapter 7 for further details).

Given that there was no previous archaeological research on the Chinese miners in New Zealand, of necessity, the main emphasis has been on documenting the material culture of the study group. The theoretical basis of the study has involved an assessment of the degree of acculturation and explaining behaviour (i.e. responses) in terms of cultural stability, adaptation or change. In the following section, the process and dynamics of acculturation are discussed.

1.3 THE THEORETICAL BASIS

1.3.1 ETHNIC ENCOUNTERS AND THE DYNAMICS OF ACCULTURATION

Since the dawn of history, groups of people who have lived in relative isolation for long periods and developed their own distinctive lifestyles have come into contact through events such as invasions, (re)discovery and colonisation and immigration. However fleeting interactions may be at first, if contact between groups is prolonged, conflict and competition usually develop, especially if the interacting groups have different racial characteristics, habits, customs and ideals (Song 1959:7). Such a sequence of events occurred in the late 19th century between the established Anglo-European population and the Cantonese goldseekers in New Zealand.

When different racial groups come into contact, they tend to go through a process described by Park (1926:192–6) as the "race relations cycle". The stages of the process – contact, competition, accommodation and assimilation – are progressive, but can be delayed and even reversed by such things as the imposition of segregation policies and the efforts of minority groups to maintain their "ethnic identities".

To reach the stage of "being accepted" by a dominant host population, an ethnic minority must almost invariably adopt some of the cultural traits of the dominant ethnic group. The process of adopting cultural traits (be it voluntary or involuntary) is known as "acculturation". There is a huge body of literature on the subject, much of it directed towards the problems and processes of integrating or improving the situation of indigenous and immigrant minorities into Western societies.

One indicator of a minority group's degree of acculturation is its retention of traits or artefacts associated with its traditional cultural milieu. Conversely, the adoption of traits and items of material culture of the "host" population is assumed to mirror the degree and rate of acculturation of a minority group. Generally, during "ethnic contact" situations, technological innovations are more readily adopted than social or religious changes. This happens because the accepting group can see immediate advantages in borrowing technological innovations, whereas it takes much longer to see merit (if any) in changing deep-seated and conditioned social and philosophical beliefs.

Because of the tendency of immigrant groups to adopt material things (such as new foods) and technological innovations almost from the beginning of cultural contact, the process and rate of acculturation is often amenable to study through archaeology, so long as the group being studied is "archaeologically visible"; that is, there must be specific artefacts, food refuse or structural remains in sites that can be unequivocally associated with the group being studied (but see below).

The Cantonese goldseekers in New Zealand are one such group. During their sojourn they maintained strong socio-economic links with their homeland, including the importation of many items of traditional material culture. The remains of distinctive oriental artefacts (such as ceramic tablewares and food containers, opium-smoking paraphernalia and gambling pieces) make Chinese sites readily identifiable and ideally suited for studying the retention of traditional cultural traits and acculturative changes. By comparing the composition of archaeological assemblages against a "picture of traditional culture", it is possible to gain a measure of the nature and degree of acculturation of the studied population.

Since the thesis this book is based on was written, "acculturation" has become a controversial term because it has been associated with forced assimilation of minority/ traditional or First Nations cultures at the expense of their traditional ways, beliefs and language, leading to loss of cultural identity and pride. In the last three decades there has been a worldwide renaissance among colonised and minority groups. They now rightfully contest their rights and embrace their traditional cultures, languages and beliefs.

In this book, I use the term "acculturation" simply as a measure of the Chinese goldseekers' responses over time, both voluntary and involuntary, to the situation they found themselves in New Zealand. The first Chinese miners in New Zealand, having come from the Victorian goldfields, had already adopted many European ways with regard to mining methodology, food and clothing. But as this book will show, they also retained "their Chineseness" regarding personal and community values, clan allegiances, spiritual beliefs and other matters.

Chapter 2
CHINESE SETTLEMENT IN NEW ZEALAND

2.1 THE MIGRANTS' HOMELAND AND SOCIAL ORGANISATION

The 19th-century New Zealand Chinese came from Guangdong province (Kwangtung) in southern China, and in particular 12 of the 29 counties surrounding the city of Guangzhou (formerly Canton). These areas were studded with hundreds of villages with populations varying from 100 to 1,000, with a few exceeding 20,000. The map (Figure 2.1) of the Canton Villages Mission (CVM) districts gives an idea of the density of settlement. To the north of Canton, the land is hilly, while to the south lies the broad dissected plain of the Pearl River Delta. Waterways were the main mode of transport, while the numerous market towns were pivotal in trade networks.

The villages were populated by lineages and clans: a lineage is composed of families who trace their descent through the male line back to a common ancestor; a clan, on the other hand, is defined by surname. A lineage is related to other lineages and in this way draws people into a large kinship system, while the clan is a unit of exogamy, specifying who may or may not marry. Both these aspects are crucial to social organisation in China and placed varying pressures on the Chinese migrants. As a lineage would rarely migrate in total, they had little effect in overseas situations, whereas clan links became significant in overseas Chinese communities where the population was big enough to encourage the maintenance of such ties. For example, in Vancouver, Canada, Willmott (1964:34) recorded the existence of 23 clan organisations. Because of the relatively small size of the New Zealand Chinese population, clan links (synonymous with surname) were not important, except in a few instances where single surnames dominated locality or community associations in particular communities (e.g. Don 1/2/1884:148, 1901:25), or instances where two families happened to be in conflict with each other (Sedgewick 1982:64).

The county of origin became and still is the fundamental unit of identification in New Zealand. Most of the New Zealand Chinese originated from the northern part of Poon Yue county (c. 70% of the total number), with lesser numbers from the Seyip, Tsangshing and Heungshan counties (Ng 1984b). The locality associations that developed represented these groupings, including Poon Yue and Fa Yuen (Poon Fa Association), Jung Sing and Tung Goon (Tung Jung Association) and Toy San and Sun Wui (Seyip Association; Sedgewick 1982:65). The Seyip Cantonese, who formed the majority in California and Victoria, were in the minority in New Zealand.

Rev. William Mawson, one of the early CVM missionaries, described the houses in the nucleated villages of Guangdong as low, windowless, constructed of sun-dried and fired bricks held together with a mixture of sand, lime and clay (Mawson et al. 1926:12). The floors were either of clay or large tiles, while the roof was of light tiles laid on pine rafters. Little wood was used in construction to minimise damage caused by ants. Two-storied buildings were forbidden by clan elders, who would not tolerate roof levels violating custom by being higher than the ancestral hall. However, wealthier Chinese who had made enough overseas to rebuild their homes often built two-storied houses with balconies as a display of wealth and status, and also to serve as watchtowers for their vulnerable villages (Sedgewick 1982:64).

The market towns were the focal point of business and trade in the rural districts. Each market town had a regular number of market days that alternated to avoid clashes between adjacent towns. Besides being places where commodities were bought and sold, the market cycle also served as an information distribution system, linking the peasantry with events (such as the New World goldrushes) far beyond their geographical sphere. Later, the market towns became the place where Chinese who had done well overseas returned, acquired some land or established their own businesses. But this simple and orderly existence experienced considerable upheaval in the years immediately preceding the discovery of gold in California and later in Australia and New Zealand.

2.2 REASONS FOR THE EXODUS FROM GUANGDONG

The Cantonese goldseekers who came to New Zealand were but one component of an immense population diaspora from southern China throughout the latter half of the 19th and first three decades of the 20th century. Chinese migrants also went to South-East Asia, the Philippines, islands of the Pacific and Indian Oceans, the United States, Canada, South America and Australia.

The "push" causes of this mass migration were the result of several factors that made the Guangzhou delta area a very unpleasant place to live. Firstly, the area was extremely overpopulated with an overall density of 600 persons per square kilometre by the late 19th century. The typical peasant cultivated less than a third of a hectare of land, and most of the land had to be rented at usurious rates from landlords (Johnson 1980:8). Table 2.1, reproduced from Wakeman (1966:179), shows the phenomenal population growth rate, which resulted in land becoming less available and more expensive as the population grew. This in turn caused increasing impoverishment of the peasantry and many became landless or almost landless.

Hunger and the shortage of land were not the only causes of the migration. For centuries, Guangzhou had been the point of contact between the Chinese empire and the outside world. Thus the Cantonese were aware of the imperialist activities of the European powers in neighbouring countries and feared like treatment for themselves. Hong Kong, at the entrance to the Guangzhou River, had become a British fortress, while British merchants in Hong Kong had developed an addictive and destructive trade in opium (Collis 1946). Guangzhou and its immediate hinterland, from where the New Zealand Chinese originated, was the main source of opium distribution throughout the empire. The British merchants imported the drug in chests from India and slipped the illegal cargo into China by means of Chinese middlemen. The trade was so lucrative that officials were soon corrupted and turned a blind eye to the traffic. By the 1830s, the balance of trade was decidedly against the Chinese empire and the resultant outflow of silver, the monetary standard of the nation, had caused an inflationary spiral in land owing to the fragile nature of the traditional economy. Lawlessness became an increasing problem, with bandits operating freely in the mountainous areas and pirate-merchants engaged in selling opium. Villages were attacked and looted, often accompanied by rape and slaughter. The Court of Peking sent Commissioner Lin Tse-hsü to bring about law and order, but in one of the most sordid acts in the history of British imperialism, the English merchants used their influence in London to persuade the British government to use military force to maintain the opium trade. Chinese forces were speedily defeated and after a brief period of peasant resistance, organised by the local gentry against the British, the Manchu Court sued for peace. They feared a peasant uprising more than British domination. The Treaty of Nanking, which ended the First Opium War, mentioned nothing of the opium trafficking, and consequently the trade continued with an attendant rise in banditry and corruption (Grief 1974:7).

The banditry, endemic corruption and Peking's (Beijing's) refusal to support popular resistance movements against the British pushed many of the more desperate of the populace (the landless, uprooted, disenchanted and those in financial decline) into rebellious anti-dynastic secret society activities. The rebellion, which lasted from 1850 until 1864, bypassed Guangdong quite by chance, but still had deleterious effects. Although it had fermented in the Guangzhou delta, the Taiping rebels eventually passed northwards out of Kiangsi (Jiangxi) to capture the Yangzi Valley and the old Ming capital Nanking (now Nanjing). The path of the Taiping movement through south-central China cut Guangdong off from imperial influence and opened the way for anarchy, banditry and secret society activity. With bandits operating freely out of the mountains separating Guangdong from the rest of China, and pirates on the rivers leading to Guangzhou making water traffic hazardous at best, Guangdong was cut off from its traditional sources of supply. Food prices began to soar, adding to the discomfort of city and rural life (Grief 1974:9). Hundreds of boatmen and porters lost their livelihood through the transfer of trade from landed routes to the British-controlled sea trade.

It was this situation of overpopulation, poverty, changes in the social order and economic turmoil that induced threatened smallholders and landless peasants to assist their sons and brothers to emigrate. It seemed an attractive solution as it was widely thought that they would become rich and return quickly to improve the lives of their families and clans. Among the areas affected by the negative events described above were those counties from which most of the Chinese who came to New Zealand in the 19th century stemmed – Poon Yue, Nanhai, Zang-Sheng and Si Yap. However, they had an important detail in their favour – the Pearl River trading link to Hong Kong was a conduit for information about what was happening in other countries and particularly the discovery of gold in several Pacific Rim countries.

Migration was officially forbidden by the Chinese government until 1859, but voluntary migration was allowed from Guangdong. Women rarely accompanied their husbands abroad, for it was not within Confucian propriety for women to emigrate. Furthermore, while the Chinese government's ban on male immigration was rarely enforced, it was strictly applied with regard to women.

The onus on Chinese migrants was therefore a difficult one, being part of a social structure with rigid patterns of expected behaviour, yet at the same time they were under pressure to leave and earn sufficient money to upgrade their family's position. Once the migrants were established overseas, they were often goaded to send back money or return (Sedgewick 1982:123–4). The family at home, embroiled in their own hardships, could not understand the difficulties of finding gold or any problems their kin were experiencing.

2.3 THE MAIN PHASES OF CHINESE SETTLEMENT IN NEW ZEALAND

Chinese settlement in New Zealand can be divided into four phases, which are summarised below. However, as the main period of Chinese mining was pre-1900, this research is principally concerned with the first phase, which will be elaborated on in Section 2.3 and subsequent chapters.

2.3.1 PHASE 1

Phase 1 dates from the first casual Chinese arrivals in the early 1860s, and the subsequent mass influx of goldseekers after 1866, until about 1900. During this period the Chinese were overwhelmingly "sojourners" in outlook and goldmining was their chief occupation, although many also became market gardeners.

In 1868, there were 1,270 Chinese miners spread throughout Otago out of a total of 5,684 miners of all nationalities (*Otago Witness* 18/4/1868:1). The New Zealand Chinese population peaked at just over 5,000 between 1878 and 1881. Virtually all were men. The percentage of goldminers among their number ranged from 90% down to 45% (in 1901). The heyday of Chinese mining was in the 1870s and early 1880s. After the 1880s, the easily-worked gold had been largely won and it became the turn of the larger scale, generally European owned, sluicing and dredging companies. Many Chinese worked together in small sluice mining ventures, but with the notable exception of the prominent Dunedin merchant Sew Hoy, the Shotover River dredging pioneer, they did not take up the new dredging technology. From the outset, but particularly throughout the 1870s, there was increasing anti-Chinese agitation culminating in immigration restrictions in 1881, 1888, 1896 and 1908. But even before the first restrictive legislation, Chinese miner numbers were decreasing – the easily-won gold was gone and the largely all-male population was declining. Gradually, the numbers of Chinese on the goldfields began to diminish as the remaining ones moved to cities, adopted other occupations, returned to China or died.

2.3.2 PHASE 2

Phase 2 began well before the turn of the century, but really picked up momentum after 1900 and continued until c.1932. This phase was characterised by three demographic changes. For the reasons mentioned above, there was a steady decline in the Chinese population and the gradual abandonment of many goldfield areas that formerly had large Chinese populations. The decline of goldmining forced increasing numbers into other occupations, notably farm labouring, market gardening and businesses such as laundries. A steady northward drift developed after 1890. Wellington became the major Chinese population centre in New Zealand, superseding Dunedin. By 1910, there were few towns or counties in the country that did not have at least a few Chinese residents, and many had 100 or more.

In the early years of the 20th century, the Chinese population in New Zealand steadily declined, reaching a low point of 2,017 in 1916. Of this number, only 130 were females (NZ Census 1916). These people comprised a hard core. Despite continuing immigration restrictions and other impositions (outlined in Section 2.3), they were able to earn a living and lobby against the anti-Chinese legislative restrictions. During this period the New Zealand Chinese became increasingly established in small businesses, especially laundries, market gardens, fruiterers and greengrocers. Increasing numbers of New Zealand towns had at least one Chinese shop. In European eyes, their incomes were meagre, but they were several times greater than what they would have been able to earn in China (if they could get work). Those who established themselves in New Zealand were also able to avoid the chaotic situation that had developed in southern China following the collapse of the Manchu regime. With the immigration restrictions and poll tax, it became virtually impossible to bring whole families to New Zealand, so the Chinese continued to look back to their home villages. The remittances from the successful in New Zealand enabled kin to improve their lot at home. Through tenacity and saving, they managed to bring many sons to New Zealand to assist or continue the businesses. They mostly arrived in the years 1900–1930. However, Chinese were still treated as aliens despite an increasing desire to settle their families in New Zealand.

2.3.3 PHASE 3

After 1930, Chinese migrants were permitted to bring children into New Zealand on temporary student visas. As the 1930s progressed, public opinion of the Chinese became increasingly favourable. In 1932, the ultra-discriminatory poll tax was abolished. For the first time since 1881, resident Chinese were able to go to and from China without this massive burden in addition to the cost of the fares. But in terms of the development of the New Zealand Chinese community, a more significant event was to take place. Between 1939 and 1941, as the Sino–Japanese conflict continued and war was being fought in the Cantonese countryside, permission was granted to allow 249 wives and 244 children under the age of 16 to enter New Zealand on temporary war refugee permits and on payment of £200 bonds. For the first time, large numbers of Chinese children were growing up and being schooled in New Zealand. After WWII, the refugee families and 300 child students who had arrived earlier in the 1930s were allowed to stay after representations by the Presbyterian Church, led by the Rev. Dr G.H. McNeur, a pioneer missionary in the church's Cantonese Mission. In 1949, following the Communist takeover, China's doors were slammed shut, thus beginning a new phase of assimilation for the New Zealand Chinese.

2.3.4 PHASE 4

The Communist takeover in China led to new directions for the New Zealand Chinese. While the arrival of wives and children began the process of assimilation, the actual turning point for the Chinese community in New Zealand, when they chose or were involuntarily compelled to "become total New Zealanders", occurred between 1950 and 1952. In those years, the Communists destroyed the landlord class in Guangdong, among whom were some New Zealand Chinese, and effectively severed links with home villages. At the same time, the New Zealand Chinese community was becoming increasingly dominated by young confident Chinese who had grown up in New Zealand. In 1952, integration was moved another step closer when the Chinese were reallowed naturalisation.

2.4 A CHRONOLOGICAL OUTLINE OF 19TH-CENTURY CHINESE SETTLEMENT IN NEW ZEALAND

The identity of the first Chinese immigrant to come to New Zealand is not known. Serious immigration did not begin until 1866, but several reports, both speculative and confirmed, allude to the arrival of a few Chinese in the 1850s (Fong 1959a:15; Grief 1974:4; Sedgewick 1982:79–80). These first Chinese arrivals almost certainly came from Australia. Chinese labourers were brought into Australia as early as 1848 (Choi 1975:18). By 1854, there were an estimated 2,400 in New South Wales. Some may have escaped their indentured existence and found passage to New Zealand. A Chinese man with the unlikely name of "Hopton Appo" was reported to have been naturalised in Nelson in 1852 (*NZ Gazette*: Names of Alien Friends who have been naturalised in New Zealand 1911:190).

An 1862 Dunedin newspaper report titled "The Advent of the Chinese" described the story of "the first Chinaman that has ever paid Dunedin a visit…" (*Daily Telegraph* 2/6/1862). A Mr Lo Keong, later an elder in the Chinese Church in Dunedin, is reported to have arrived from Australia in 1865 to start a business (see Appendix 5). He is also credited with being the first Chinese man to bring his wife to New Zealand (from Melbourne after their marriage in 1873; McNeur 1951:28).

These few early "visitors" differed from the later Chinese arrivals in that they were not involved in goldmining. They appear to have come to settle, although (except for Lo Keong) it is not known how long they stayed. Even at this early stage, racial discrimination was voiced. In 1853, a group of landowners and merchants in Canterbury proposed the importation of Chinese labour, but there was strong anti-Chinese opposition from the workers in Canterbury (Sedgewick 1982:81). Four years later, a meeting was held in Nelson with the express purpose of submitting proposals to the provincial governments on how to keep the Chinese out of New Zealand. An anti-Chinese committee was set up to "fight the Mongolian filth" (*Nelson Examiner* 12 and 15/8/1857). A report from Victoria described how a group of "well dressed and obviously educated" Chinese were thrown off a ship they had boarded to come to Otago in 1862 (Millar 1972:23). Although the first request for anti-Chinese legislation was made to, and rejected by, the New Zealand government in 1861 (NZ Parliamentary Debates 1861:373), by this time anti-Chinese feeling and legislation was well established in Australia. In 1853, South Australia imposed a £10 poll tax for Chinese immigrants, followed by Victoria in 1855 and New South Wales in 1861. Although the legislation was temporarily repealed in 1855, 1861 and 1867 respectively, there is no doubt that it influenced anti-Chinese feeling in New Zealand (Choi 1975:20–1; Sedgewick 1982:81).

Despite the strong anti-Chinese attitudes expressed in some parts of New Zealand, there were some who thought otherwise. In 1865, the Dunedin Chamber of Commerce, mainly made up of local merchants and businessmen who were feeling the effects of the rapidly declining mining population in Otago, decided they would favour Chinese immigration. Their justifications included the fact that the province needed population, that the Chinese were well behaved, important consumers, and that all the things the Chinese had been accused of had not been proved (Millar 1972:26). Their amiable attitude might, in part, have been a response to an inquiry from Chinese residents in Victoria, who wanted to know if they would receive protection from harassment in New Zealand, as they were supposed to receive in Victoria (Choi 1975:20–21). The reply from the Chief Secretary of Otago stated that they would be in the same situation as Europeans on the goldfields (Sedgewick 1982:82).

For the Chinese in Victoria, the response from the Chamber of Commerce must have sounded quite attractive. In Victoria they were experiencing rapidly increasing anti-Chinese sentiment and violence. New Zealand appeared to offer a less hostile environment and, at that date, had not attempted to pass any discriminatory legislation. Also, favourable news of the New Zealand goldfields must have spread, even though by 1865 the initial rush was well in decline. In February 1864, there had been an estimated 22,000–24,000 European miners on the goldfields, but by 1866 the number had dropped to 6,000 (Forrest 1961:67–9).

In October 1865, a written statement from the Provincial Treasurer conferring the right of protection on the Chinese was conveyed by a Dunedin merchant to a Chinese merchant in Melbourne (*Otago Daily Times* 10/11/1865). However, not everyone was happy. There were angry public meetings of miners at Wetherstones and Tuapeka condemning the measure. Miners in the Dunstan district wasted no time in sending a petition to the Superintendent of Otago opposing the immigration of Chinese. Meetings held in other areas expressed the same sentiment (Millar 1972:27–8), although a meeting held in Dunedin unanimously supported the decision (Butler 1977:13).

On 23 December 1865 a Chinese "entrepreneur", Ho Ah Mei, arrived from Melbourne to inspect the goldfields. He was followed by other Chinese settlers to assist him in his task (*Otago Witness* 23/12/1865). In 1871, Ho Ah Mei wrote a long letter to the editor of the *Otago Daily Times* outlining the purpose of his visit.

The full text of his letter was published and revealed that his first intention was to secure the introduction of labour, and then establish a provisioning business (*Otago Daily Times* 8/6/1871:2). After he returned to Melbourne in early 1866, he issued placards for various areas of the Australian goldfields. He met with little success initially but eventually convinced 12 "practical miners" to leave Australia by advancing them £20 each for the passage and supplies (*Otago Daily Times* 8/6/1871:2). They arrived in Dunedin in February 1866 and left two days later for Tuapeka on the suggestion of Vincent Pyke, the Inspector-General of Goldfields. A second group arrived a few days later. They were sent to a different area to test it. Ho Ah Mei was to be disappointed with the initial reluctance of the Victorian Chinese to move to New Zealand en masse. He encountered other obstacles to his plans and by 1871 had ended up as a clerk and interpreter for the government in Hong Kong. While in this position, he wrote the abovementioned letter, which also included a request directed to the government for reimbursement for his services (for arranging Chinese labour) and made an offer to act as agent for the employment of Chinese to work in Fiji. He reported that two more ships were bound for New Zealand; the *Northwind* had left in January 1871 and the other ship was due to leave in April (*Otago Daily Times* 8/6/1871:2).

Throughout 1866, less than 200 Chinese entered New Zealand, mostly through the Port of Otago, but in the following years the numbers grew steadily; 1,270 had arrived by mid-1868 and in 1871, 1,596 landed – bringing the total Chinese population to 2,641 (NZ Census 1871; Appendix 1). The Seyip Cantonese, the most numerous Chinese group in Victoria, went inland from Dunedin via Waikouaiti, Palmerston and Macraes Flat to Naseby and beyond, whereas the Sanyi, the second most numerous Cantonese grouping in Victoria, went inland via Milton and the Manuka Gorge to the Lawrence camp and inland to the Wakatipu region (Ng 2017:104).

In the early years of Chinese migration there was regular reporting of new arrivals and Chinese activity on the goldfields. Much of the reporting had a strong anti-Chinese bias (Buckingham 1974:5). The Chinese, according to one John Ah Tong, liked Otago much better than Victoria (*Otago Witness* 8/12/1866), but in many areas the feeling was not mutual. In 1866, Chinese miners were forcibly driven out of the Nevis (Parcell 1976:148); a man was murdered near Lawrence in mid-1867, and there were reports of Chinese being forcibly evicted from Mt Ida, Dunstan Creek and Naseby (Sedgewick 1982:86–7).

In 1868, both the Superintendent of the Goldfields and the police were enjoined "to keep protective watch over the Chinese" as had been promised to them (*Otago Witness* 8/2/1868). In December of the same year a "Proclamation of Police Protection over Chinese Miners" was officially gazetted:

Whereas several instances have occurred wherein the Chinese have been made the subject of persecution by the Europeans and other residents of the goldfields – in one case a gross outrage being committed by a number of persons on a single Chinaman, and in another threats having been used to induce Chinese miners to remove from the locality they have selected in which to carry out their operation. Notice is hereby given, that the Chinese having come to Otago under a promise made by successive Superintendents, that those who come will be fully protected, the provincial government is determined to fulfil that promise, and the police are enjoined to keep protective watch over the Chinese population in their respective districts, and in case of their being made aware of any injury having been illegally inflicted on any of the Chinese population, to lose no time in bringing the perpetrators thereof to justice. The Superintendent relies upon the assistance of all right thinking, well disposed people to aid in affording that protection to the Chinese, which persons residing within a British Settlement have the right to rely on.

Dunedin, Signed by James MacAndrew 29/1/1868, Superintendent (*Otago Provincial Government Gazette* 1868: 39)

Despite the difficulties and harassment, the Chinese were beginning to settle in and establish themselves. Chinese in the Lawrence area offered a £200 reward for apprehension of the murderer in the case outlined above. Among the stated occupations of the petitioners were butcher, dealer and storekeeper (*Otago Witness* 15/6/1867). Here and elsewhere, Chinese businesses were being established, which of course partially defeated the Chamber of Commerce's hope that they would be good consumers (i.e. customers of the European stores). Throughout 1867, Chinese continued to arrive. In September, five Chinese men, possibly disenchanted with mining, leased some land in Great King St in Dunedin and established a garden (*Otago Witness* 7/9/1867). By April 1868, there were 1,270 Chinese miners in the province compared with a total of 4,414 European miners (*Otago Witness* 18/4/1868:1).

Once the Chinese arrived at their destination, it was the express purpose of most to earn at least £100 as fast as possible, so that they could return to China, discharge their debts and establish themselves in their homeland either by acquiring a plot of land or enhancing their families' economic situation. The system sounded simple and relatives at home definitely believed it to be so, as revealed by this statement made by a Chinese miner to Don (1911:8):

> I can see now that it is really hard. I used to think that it was only pretended; for we said in China that if their lot was really so grievous, they

would return home sooner and not remain so long away…the home folk rather think it is like digging for peanuts – that the ground is shallow and the gold in lumps.

Generally, the Chinese were in debt when they arrived. Don (1/7/1884:3) recorded that most of the Chinese in Riverton had paid 40 taels of silver (£8 to £13) for their passage from China. This money was borrowed from kin or fellow villagers at a considerable rate of interest, sometimes as much as 2% per month. Sometimes the ticket was paid through a credit system whereby the individual had to work off his passage before he was free to do what he wanted. This "contract passage" system operated in New Zealand, but there was never any form of unskilled labour system (Don 1906:16). Some Chinese had their passage paid by a relative in New Zealand, but this was generally limited to close kin such as brothers and sons, and of course, the benefactor had to be wealthy enough to be able to advance the fare. Initially, this limited the scheme to wealthy merchants, until such time as the Chinese in New Zealand were ensured of a regular income through being employed as labour or self-employed in their own shops, which became much more prevalent after 1900 (Sedgewick 1982:121). Sponsorship was also used after 1881 to get around the obstacle of the poll tax.

In 1869, the first group of Chinese arrived direct from China (via Melbourne). They were noted to have a different appearance (they wore Chinese rainhats and slippers) and almost immediately upon arrival they made their way to the goldfields (*Otago Witness* 8/5/1869:5). In September, another 228 arrived from China after a 100-day passage (*Otago Witness* 18/9/1869). In October, three Chinese women with bound feet arrived. They went directly to join their husbands in Lawrence (*Otago Witness* 2/10/1869:14). The few Chinese women who came out during this period came to join merchant husbands (this was almost certainly the case in the instance mentioned above). Bound feet were status symbols; as they made a woman practically immobile, only the wealthy could support such women (Levy 1967). Besides the Chinese government ban on female emigration, the miners could not afford to bring out their families.

By the end of 1869, Chinese camps, and later communities, had been established at Lawrence, Clyde, Cromwell, Arrowtown and Nevis. Many Chinese were reported to be arriving in the Alexandra district "and filling the back valleys". They were said to be good customers at the (European) stores and were working old ground and doing well (*Otago Witness* 18/4/1868:13). The establishment of a Chinese store at Arrowtown was viewed with concern by European shopkeepers (*Dunstan Times* 17/9/1869:2).

At Lawrence, the Borough Council passed a resolution that they did not want Chinese in the town area (not an outright prohibition as oft quoted; Chandler pers. comm.). It was probably instrumental in the decision by the Chinese to establish a camp just beyond the borough limits. Elsewhere, the Chinese voluntarily set up camps on the periphery of established towns. In 1868, the Lawrence correspondent for the *Otago Daily Times* described the Chinese Camp thus (the correspondent also noted that most spoke at least some English):

> It consists of a double row of houses built parallel to the government road and the Chinese there have subscribed, of themselves, £20 for the formation of the main street and two sidetracks connecting it with that thoroughfare. Their dwellings are sufficiently comfortable and are fitted up in a creditable manner. At the time the camp contained a gaming house, cook shop, several stores, one of which was called He Tie and Company.
>
> (*Otago Daily Times* 8/7/1868)

Later the same month the Chinese were reported to be forming a road through the camp at a cost of £130 for 200 yards (*Otago Witness* 18/7/1868:2). By early 1870, the Chinese population in Otago had expanded to 2,640 (*Otago Witness* (15/1/1870:4), see Table 2.2 and Figure. 2.2 for specific localities).

At the time it was estimated that the Chinese miners were making from 30/- to £2 per week and producing approximately 1,400 ounces of gold per week, which was equivalent to about one fifth of the total production (*Otago Witness* 15/1/1870:4).

By 1870, settlements, both dispersed and nucleated, had been established in all the main mining areas in Otago. Service activities included gardens (see Chapter 6) and a range of small businesses including shops that sold cooked food and provisions, a blacksmith, a butcher and opium and gambling houses. The newly arrived Chinese interpreter Mr John Aloo reported that 15 to 20 gambling houses were in existence by 1870 (*Otago Witness* 1/10/1870).

Two substantial merchant firms had been established in Dunedin. In 1869, a 32-year-old merchant, Choie Sew Hoy, arrived from Melbourne to establish one of the major merchant firms in Dunedin (Ng 1984b). He brought 10 people with him (all were from Sai Gong village, Poon Yue County). Sew Hoy's business employed local people and eventually diversified into goldmining activities. The company has continued to this day, operated by the fourth and fifth generation of males in the family (Sedgewick 1982:92–3; Agnew and Agnew 2020). Besides operating businesses and mining on their own account, some Chinese preferred to work for wages. They were employed by both Chinese and Europeans on the goldfields. One European employer reported that "you could pay the Chinese less and they worked harder" (*Otago Witness* 18/4/1863:13). Another stated that the Chinese working in his claim were paid £2 per week and because he had trouble recognising his employees they were issued with daily tickets that they handed in at the end of the week for wages (*Otago Witness* 12/6/1869:14).

By 1871, the Chinese on the goldfields were well organised but a little too much so for many Europeans. They were reported to "have established their own meeting place, since a 'Joss House' had already been opened in the Tuapeka area" (*Otago Witness* 25/9/1869) and were providing their own supplies and now even had a doctor, Leang Chum Wah, who had arrived from Hong Kong (*Tuapeka Times* 28/4/1871). The first Presbyterian Chinese missionary, Paul Ah Chan (Wan Ah Chan), had arrived in Lawrence (*Otago Witness* 4/2/1871:15; McNeur 1951:14).

Largely because of the increasingly competitive goldmining situation, hostility towards the Chinese was on the increase. There were accusations of deviance and not paying miners rights (they didn't have to until 1868). The latter claim was substantiated when after a police crackdown numerous Chinese miners paid a total of £980 in fines (*Otago Witness* 1/12/1871). European shopkeepers were also upset because their Chinese counterparts were thriving. The Chinese miners if they so chose were virtually independent from European-owned services. A Chinese merchant in Dunedin responded to the accusations that the Chinese patronised only their countrymen's stores by pointing out that the Chinese storekeepers benefitted the province because they paid customs and harbour dues. He claimed he had paid £2,000 in customs duty (and also mentioned that he had opened a branch store in the North Island and was collecting fungus for export to China). Prior to this he had been collecting scrap iron on the goldfields, which he sent to China (*Otago Witness* 8/7/1871). This merchant, Chew Chong, who settled in New Plymouth in 1870, later through his edible fungus collecting and export business based at Eltham, became one of the most well-known Chinese merchants in New Zealand (*Cyclopedia of New Zealand* 1897 Vol. 1:340–1; Lyon 1972:1416–18).

Much of the opposition to the Chinese in Central Otago seems to have been centred around the Wakatipu district and especially Arrowtown. In November 1870, one T.L. Shepherd gave a speech proposing the immediate imposition of a £50 poll tax on the Chinese and a heavy duty on rice (*Otago Witness* 12/11/1870:15). In August of the following year, C.E. Haughton, Member of the House of Representatives for Wakatipu, asked the government whether they were going to take any action over the growing number of Chinese in the colony and raised the question again two weeks later (Scholefield and Hall 1927:262–3).

On 29 August 1871 (Scholefield and Hall 1927:262–3), the government set up a nine-member Select Committee to examine "the Chinese Question". Initially, it only contained one Otago member, but later two more were added (Thomson and MacAndrew). The latter, who was involved with the expanded public works program, had written to the Dunedin newspaper earlier in the year, urging the use of Chinese labour on the Clutha railway because "they would provide a reliable work force at a cheaper rate" (*Otago Witness* 15/4/1871).

The 46-page report of the Select Committee was presented in three documents (AJHR 1871 H–5, H–5A, H–5B). They include 13 interviews with people invited to appear before the Committee (only one of whom was Chinese, John Ah Tong, at the time resident in Wellington and employed as a cabinet-maker). Their comments were generally personal opinions and ranged from extremely negative to ambivalent. Most were willing to tolerate Chinese immigrants if they were useful and in the minority. Accusations of polygamy, frugality, maltreatment of European women, avoidance of taxation and general dirtiness were presented totally without proof. In addition, they were accused (with some justification) of gambling, opium smoking and taking their wealth back to China. The only statistical evidence presented included occupations, residence in New Zealand and offences committed during 1871 in the goldfield districts.

Besides the interviews, there were replies to seven questions sent to each of the goldfields wardens querying the usefulness and social effects of the Chinese. The responses from the wardens of Lawrence, Switzers and Naseby were generally positive. In each of these places a "Chinese settlement" had been established. It seems that Europeans were more favourably disposed towards the inhabitants of "Chinese settlements" than they were to situations where the Chinese were more widely dispersed. The wardens of all three places were also of the opinion that no immediate action should be taken about the immigration of Chinese into New Zealand but felt a poll tax could be imposed later if necessary. The other responses were more negative and recommended restrictions should be brought into force promptly, ranging from mild forms of discouragement to a poll tax, or even an annual tax plus a levy on their basic foods such as rice and dried fish on top of the existing duties. Similar questions were asked of police officers in various areas, and in general the responses were similar. None of the officers in areas where there were Chinese found them to be any more of a burden than Europeans in the same areas. They considered that they required no extra police supervision and if there were problems, they revolved around the shortage of interpreters rather than police officers (AJHR 1871 H–5:24).

Other useful information in the report indicated that small numbers of Chinese had already become established in non-mining occupations elsewhere in New Zealand, in situations where they would have to depend largely on European customers for their income. Chinese had established two gardens and two were employed in storekeeping in Christchurch; there were two Chinese fancy goods stores, a carter and an old settler in Nelson; in Westland there were 14 working in gardens around Woodstock and Ross, and there was a Chinese cook in Hokitika (AJHR 1871 H–5:24–5). In all these places, there was no established Chinese community, so relations with Europeans must have been amicable enough to support their presence.

The summation of the Select Committee was forwarded to the House on 27 October 1871, only two months after its initiation. Its conclusions and recommendations were as follows:

1. That the Chinese are industrious and frugal.
2. That they are as orderly citizens as Europeans.
3. That there is no special risk to the morality or security of the community to be apprehended from their presence in the Colony.
4. That they are not likely to introduce any special infectious diseases.
5. That they are well adapted for menial and light mechanical work and for agricultural occupations.
6. But that nearly all those who come to this Colony do so for the purpose of mining for gold.
7. That, as a rule, they occupy and turn to good account ground which at present would not pay the European miner.
8. That, as a rule, they return to China as soon as they have amassed a net sum of £100 upwards.
9. That no considerable number of them are at any time likely to become permanent settlers in the country.
10. That they spend less per head than the European population.
11. That the presence of the Chinese in the country has not hitherto entailed any additional police expenditure.

In view of the foregoing the Committee are of the opinion that there are not sufficient grounds shown for the exclusion of the Chinese; and that no sufficient case has up to the present time been made out to require the Committee to propose that legislative action should be taken having for effect the exclusion of the Chinese or the imposition of special burdens upon them.

W. J Steward, Chairman.
27 October 1871. (AJHR H–5B)

Nine members voted, there being five "ayes" and four "noes". Those who voted against the conclusions included the representatives from Wakatipu, Dunedin, Waimea and Otago. C.E. Haughton, representing Wakatipu, registered a protest against the recommendations on the grounds that he believed they were inconsistent with the evidence (AJHR 1871 H–5B:8).

The question of Chinese immigration was broached again in 1871 when John Brogden and Sons, an English company that had secured several railway building contracts in New Zealand, sought permission to bring in Chinese labourers. While the Minister of Works, Mr Ormond, sought the views of the Provincial Superintendents on the issue, European labour groups expressed their total opposition to the proposal. Drifter miners, be they European or Chinese, were little threat to the working man, but the possibility of large-scale importation of cheap labour was totally unacceptable (Sedgewick 1982:102–5).

The *Otago Witness* newspaper, which only three years earlier had defended the rights of the Cantonese miners, now damned them:

> It is only necessary to look at our great prototype, America, to see with what feelings the white population regard the competition of their almond-eyed brethren... The labouring man who has come here prepared to make the Colony his home... will certainly be justified in regarding with an evil eye those birds of passage who most certainly only remain to reap the crop, and who will be off to the Flowery Land when the time comes to pay for it. (*Otago Witness* 7/12/1872)

Meanwhile, Brogden circumvented the opposition by enlisting John Ah Tong (mentioned earlier) to procure disaffected Chinese labour from the goldfields. Ah Tong later withdrew from the scheme after a court case involving pay arrangements (*Bruce Herald* 21/1/1873). By the middle of December 1872, 96 Chinese were reported to be working on the construction of the Clutha railway (*Otago Witness* 14/12/1872:15, 28/12/1872:15). Brogden's success in acquiring Chinese labour did nothing to lessen anti-oriental sentiment among European workers. Ironically, six months before the Brogden–Chinese labour dispute, Chinese had been subcontracted to form a portion of the road from Queenstown to Arrowtown (*Otago Witness* 4/5/1872:8). Arrowtown people were reported to be employing "Celestials" at 5/- a day. Their labour was used in the construction of the Presbyterian Church and by the Improvement Committee for street repairs. They were described as very efficient workers (*Otago Witness* 12/4/1873:15). Vocal opposition towards the Chinese abated a little between the years 1873 and 1878, probably due to the burgeoning economy, plus the fact that large numbers of assisted immigrants were also entering the country over this time. Despite anti-Chinese sentiments, many Chinese gained employment as construction labourers during this period as the statistics in Table 2.3 show.

Between 1870 and 1881, when the first restrictive legislation was passed, 6,077 Chinese entered New Zealand and 3,100 departed. The overall Chinese population increased by 2,363 to 5,004 over the same period (meanwhile, in Australia the Chinese population increased from 28,351 to 38,533 in the same period, and Queensland passed the *Chinese Immigration Restriction Act 1877*, which imposed a £10 poll tax; Choi 1975:22–5). However, during this relatively quiescent period several significant events occurred in New Zealand that drastically affected the fortunes of the resident Chinese and those who wished to come later.

The first recorded movement of Chinese to the West Coast of the South Island was reported in May 1868 when "seven or eight" arrived in Hokitika from Otago (*West Coast Times* 27/5/1868). Numbers remained low initially, there being only 24 Chinese recorded in 1871, but by 1874 the Chinese population of Westland had risen to 882 (NZ Census 1874:23). By 1879, the West Coast had become one of the "hot beds" of anti-Chinese agitation fostered by people like Richard Seddon. He was later to become Premier of New Zealand, but then as MHR for Westland he championed anti-Chinese sentiment and was strongly in favour of immigration restrictions. In addition to becoming established on the West Coast, after 1871 increasing numbers of Chinese left the South Island and began to settle in the North Island.

Changes in the political structure of New Zealand during the 1870s also worked against the Chinese. In 1876, the Provincial Councils were abolished giving way to a central government based in Wellington. The centralisation of government, in conjunction with the development of party politics and the increasing migration of Chinese to other areas of New Zealand left little room for the regional sympathies or ambivalence they had received in former years (Sedgewick 1982:74). By 1881, the Chinese settlement of the North Island was well underway with small concentrations established in Wellington and Auckland and a gradual spread of small numbers of Chinese into other communities. From now on, the mobility of the Chinese both within New Zealand and back and forth from China increased considerably (Sedgewick 1982:74).

The other much-publicised event of the 1870s was a petition from the Chinese to the Otago Provincial Council (in 1872) requesting that Warden Beetham of Queenstown be removed from office for alleged injustices towards the Chinese. A counter-petition was submitted by white miners requesting Beetham's retention. A Select Committee appointed to adjudicate on the matter completely exonerated Beetham and the Chinese case was dismissed (Sedgewick 1982:109–11). In fact, the Chinese petition probably rebounded against them because it was circulated in an area (the Wakatipu) where there was considerable anti-Chinese feeling and relations were strained (witness Haughton's demands cited earlier).

Throughout the 1870s, economic slumps tended to result in anti-Chinese agitation. The powerful Federation of Labour developed a stance of opposing Asiatic immigration and the immigration of those from other nationalities that it suspected provided cheap labour including Indian, Italian, Greek and Yugoslav (Grief 1974:24). The agitation spread to Parliament where increasing numbers of MPs called for some sort of immigration restrictions, the most determined being those representing the goldmining areas of Otago and Westland. The defenders of the Chinese tended to be representatives of the landed, professional and mercantile interests who usually had a financial interest in the Chinese as consumers or potential labour. They resented the working man's efforts to control the labour supply and thus keep wages high. By the end of the 1870s, attitudes towards the Chinese were changing dramatically for the worse, fueled by European "working class" opposition to the employment of Chinese as labourers, negative publicity over matters such as the Beetham petition, and their increasing appearance in many parts of New Zealand where they had not been established previously.

The miners and workers found support in the Colonial Governor, Sir George Grey. He had intellectual support from William Pember Reeves, who became Resident Minister for the Middle Island (South Island) during the Fox ministry (1871–72). With Grey's encouragement, a Bill was introduced into Parliament in 1878 calling for a poll tax and limitations on the number of Chinese any one ship could carry to New Zealand. The latter clause was intended to prevent the possibility of a labourer trade developing. However, the Bill was not acted upon in that session, it being considered that there were more important issues at hand (Grief 1974:25). With the worsening of economic conditions, declining gold prices and growing unemployment, the champion of the working class, the Westland MHR, Richard Seddon, reintroduced the Bill in 1880. However, he had to bow to British Colonial Office pressure and the Bill was not acted upon.

In 1878, and for several years thereafter, New Zealand underwent a continuous economic slump that was particularly injurious to the working class. The 1880s Depression became so severe that for a while more people were leaving the colony than entering it.

In 1881, the Bill was reintroduced and passed (*Chinese Immigrants Act 1881*) amid great debate, denunciation and recrimination. The Bill instituted a poll tax of £10 and imposed a limitation of one Chinese passenger per 10 tons of burden on any ship travelling to New Zealand. Seddon and those favouring restrictions on Chinese immigration achieved their ambition, but in some ways it was a hollow victory because the numbers of Chinese both in New Zealand and desiring to come had peaked. The attractiveness of New Zealand to the Chinese had declined as the easily-won gold was gone and with it the dream of making a quick and easy fortune. During the 10 years from 1877 until 1886, 3,325 Chinese entered New Zealand, while 2,611 departed; a net gain of only 71.4 per annum (NZ Census 1876, 1881, 1886). The Chinese already in the colony were exempted from the tax (Figure 2.3 is an example of an exemption certificate), but each entry or re-entry required payment of the tax. For those who were compelled to pay the tax, it only prolonged the stay necessary to earn enough before they felt able to return to Guangdong.

Fear of additional restrictive legislation and the widespread anti-Chinese sentiments being expressed in newspapers and at a personal level caused the Chinese considerable anxiety. Don recorded several instances where Chinese said "they would leave now if they had enough money" or asked him whether it was true "that the Chinese are to be driven out" of New Zealand (e.g. Don 2/10/1882:65; 1/11/1882:87).

Despite the imposition of the poll tax, the Chinese remained the focal point of worker protests. The *Chinese Mining Exclusion Act 1882* was introduced, but not acted upon, to bar the Chinese from goldmining (Bills Thrown Out 1882:245). In 1893, Seddon became prime minister and promptly initiated a Bill to bar Chinese and Asiatics entirely from the colony. This was rebuffed for three successive years despite his most strenuous efforts, but in 1896 the poll tax was raised from £10 to £100, an exorbitant figure in those days. The allowable ratio of Chinese to maritime cargo was raised to one Chinese per 100 tons. Seddon was not only strongly opposed to Chinese (and other Asiatic) immigration because he considered they would take up jobs of established New Zealanders, he also blamed their presence for causing conflict regarding (British) imperial foreign policy and between the Legislative Council and the House of Representatives in New Zealand, both of which had vested interests in different spheres of the economy (Sedgewick 1982:221).

During the 20 years following the 1896 Act, the average annual arrivals (less than 200) almost equalled the number of departures. Even though the Chinese population was obviously declining through departures, the deaths of old miners and the absence of a birth rate, anti-Chinese agitation and demand for further legislative restrictions continued. In 1898, Seddon submitted another Bill that allegedly concerned itself with the quality of prospective migrants rather than their race. The Bill, which required a literacy test, was passed and attached to it was a clause raising the cargo tonnage to 200 tons for each Chinese carried to New Zealand. The following year a rider to that Act was passed that banned further Chinese from being granted certificates of naturalisation (a prohibition that was not lifted until 1952).

Even with this Act and the departure of Seddon from the political arena (he died in 1906), the Chinese continued to be the centre of controversy. In 1907, the new prime minister, Sir Joseph Ward, introduced a Bill to stiffen the literacy test, which was soon passed. In commenting on the Bill, Ward followed Seddon's lead by declaring his desire to rid the colony of all Asiatics (Grief 1974:27). Table 2.4 shows the effect on Chinese immigration of the various restrictive Acts.

By 1908, the firm basis of a "white New Zealand" policy, in imitation of similar policies enacted in Australia, the United States and Canada, was established (Wakeman 1966; Grief 1974:74). In 1920, another Bill limited Asiatic immigration to an "application basis". Thus each application would be judged on its "merits" and accepted or refused. The only exemptions to this were for entry of wives or children of holders of permanent resident visas in New Zealand. The £100 poll tax still applied.

In the 19th century, most of the anti-Chinese agitation was directed towards the Chinese on the goldfields or borne out of fear that they would swamp the market with cheap labour. During the first three decades of the 20th century, it emanated mainly from small traders and labour groups who feared competition and price-cutting from the increasing number of Chinese businesses (particularly fruit and vegetable shops) that were being established in the cities and towns (Sedgewick 1982:238–44).

During the years of anti-Chinese agitation, a consciousness emerged among many of the Chinese in New Zealand "of a need to survive" (Fong 1959a:47; Sedgewick 1982:263–4). This consciousness was also influenced by the changing attitude of the Chinese government, which by 1887 had begun to be concerned about overseas Chinese communities and their problems. Some evidence of group cohesion among the Chinese in New Zealand was clear earlier with the establishment of the Ch'eung Shin Tong (a society set up to arrange occasional shipments of *sin yan* ("former men") for burial in China, and the Cherishing Virtue Union (an anti-opium society). Both organisations are discussed in subsequent chapters. The numerous petitions to Parliament from Chinese seeking the abolition of the poll tax and other impositions are further evidence of organisational development in New Zealand. Although the petitions resulted in no modifications to the various discriminatory Acts, they did draw the attention of the Chinese government to the plight of the Chinese in New Zealand. Chinese Commissions visited the country in 1887 and 1906 respectively, resulting in the appointment of a Chinese Consulate in New Zealand (Sedgewick 1982:264). From 1926 until 1946, no permanent visas were issued to Chinese, although the odious poll tax was dropped in 1932, enabling Chinese residents the freedom to travel to and from China without the exorbitant tax in addition to the cost of their fares.

Altogether, nearly 15,000 Chinese entered New Zealand between 1866 and 1916 (the total includes some multiple entries; see Appendix 1 for population figures). In the latter year, the Chinese population reached an all-time low point of 2,012, of which only 79 were females.

2 Chinese settlement in New Zealand

Table 2.1. Population of Guangdong 1787–1850 (Wakeman 1966:179).

Year	1787	1812	1842	1850
Millions	16	19	25	28
Percentage Increase	-	19	36	8
Density/Sq. Mile	160	192	264	284

Table 2.2. Populations of Chinese in Otago towns by early 1870 (*Otago Witness* 15/1/1870:4).

Location	Population	Location	Population	Location	Population
Queenstown	350	Arrowtown	70	Nevis	300
Bendigo	40	Cromwell	60	Bannockburn	300
Mt Ida	250	Blacks	50	Dunstan Creek	30
Macraes	150	Waipori	450	Waitahuna	150
Lawrence	300	Beaumont	40	Switzers	20
Dunedin	80				

Table 2.3. Chinese employed on road or railway construction or as general labourers 1874–86 (NZ Census 1874–1886).

Year	Construction labour	Unspecified labour
1874	159	99
1878	58	135
1881	77	56
1886	22	55

Table 2.4. Chinese arrivals and departures 1876–1901. Sources: *Mount Ida Chronicle* 9/2/1873, *Otago Witness* 24/6/1871, NZ Census, Hall and Scholefield 1937:231, Ng 1993: 348.

Year	Arrivals Males	Females	Departures	NZ Chinese Population	Poll Tax (£)
1867	1,213	6		1,213	
1868					
1869					
1870					
1871	2,637	4		2,637	
1872	475		190		
1873					
1874	1,123	2		4,814	
1875	776		384		
1876	112		453		
1877	162		443		
1878	1,025	15	299	4,427	
1879	329		396		
1880	296		386		
1881	1,029	9	371	4,995	
1882	25		168		150
1883	44		297		270
1884	84		306		770
1885	94		164		510
1886	239	15	181	4,527	530
1887	354		246		920
1888	308		211		2780
1889	16		104		70
1890	18		169		90
1891	5	18	160	4,426	50
1892	58		197		440
1893	116		134		1050
1894	278		143		2200
1895	214		170		1460
1896	173	26	122	3,685	3685
1897	13		123		430
1898	28		93		100
1899	26		184		1200
1900	27		181		800
1901	75	32	145	2,825	2300

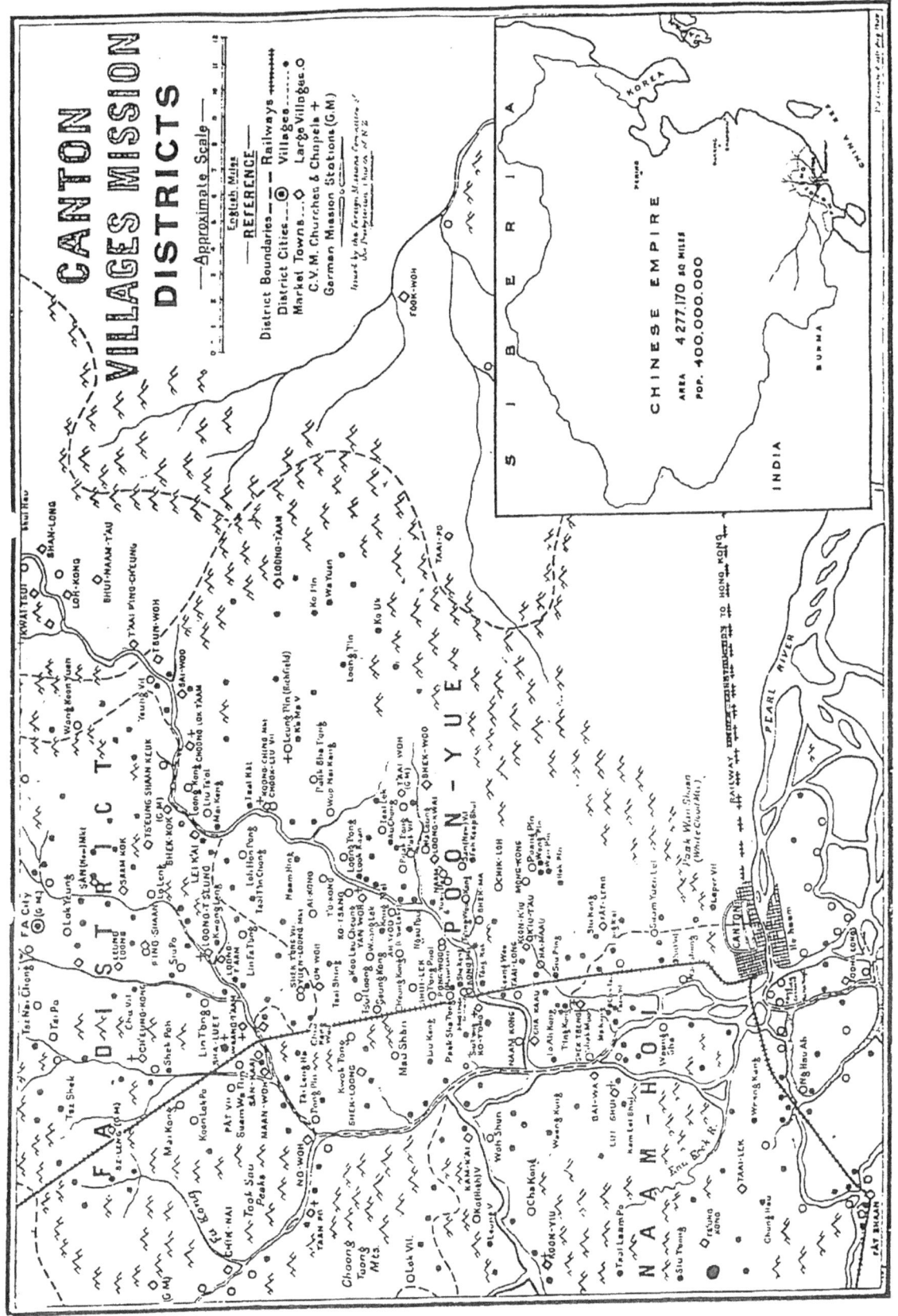

Figure 2.1. Canton Villages Mission (CVM) districts map (Davis 1916).

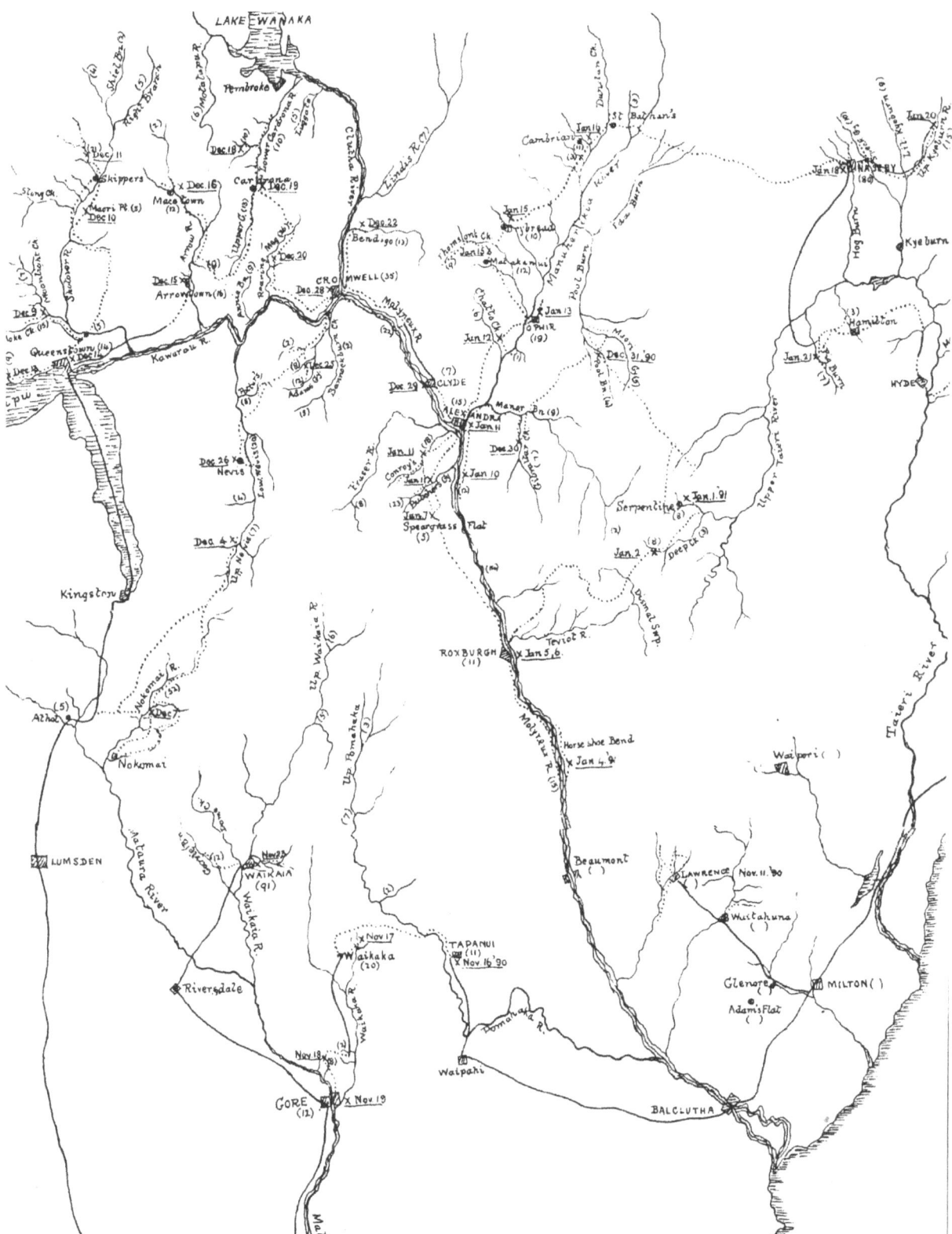

Figure 2.2. "Our Chinese Mission Map". Published in conjunction with Don's annual inland tour in 1890–91. There were three versions of this map published in the *New Zealand Presbyterian*. The numbers are the Chinese populations at each locality (originally published in Ng 1995: vol. 2, 191).

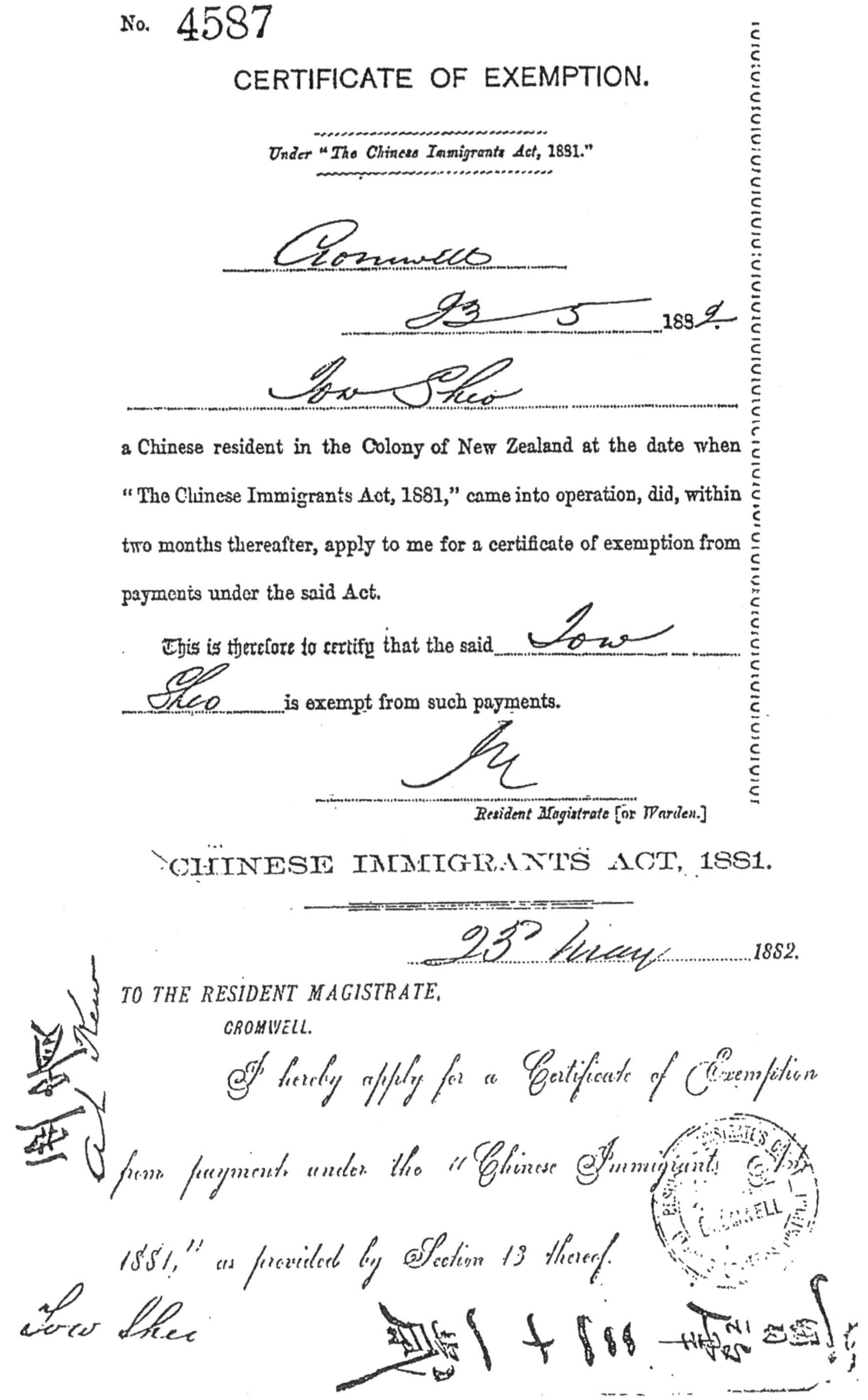

No. 4587

CERTIFICATE OF EXEMPTION.

Under "The Chinese Immigrants Act, 1881."

Cromwell

23 5 1882

Tow Sheo

a Chinese resident in the Colony of New Zealand at the date when "The Chinese Immigrants Act, 1881," came into operation, did, within two months thereafter, apply to me for a certificate of exemption from payments under the said Act.

This is therefore to certify that the said Tow Sheo is exempt from such payments.

Resident Magistrate [or Warden.]

CHINESE IMMIGRANTS ACT, 1881.

23rd May 1882.

TO THE RESIDENT MAGISTRATE,
CROMWELL.

I hereby apply for a Certificate of Exemption from payment under the "Chinese Immigrants Act 1881," as provided by Section 13 thereof.

Tow Shee

Figure 2.3. Certificate of Exemption 1881.

Chapter 3
THE CHINESE ON THE CENTRAL OTAGO GOLDFIELDS

The nature of Chinese settlement on the Central Otago goldfields is examined in this chapter. Although primarily based on contemporary records (notably newspaper articles and advertisements, the interim and final reports of the 1871 Select Committee on Chinese Immigration, and the numerous first-hand observations by the Rev. Alexander Don, the Presbyterian missioner to the Chinese on the southern goldfields), it begins to draw in archaeological evidence, which is discussed in detail in the subsequent chapters.

Don's writings contain such a wealth of social, demographic and historical information that is not recorded elsewhere that it is pertinent to provide some biographical notes and outline his relationship with the Chinese. Don was born in a digger's tent at Ballarat, Victoria, in 1857 and worked on the Australian goldfields from the age of nine. He returned to school in his late youth and became a teacher and missioner. He eventually went to New Zealand to pursue his missionary activity, thinking he would be sent to the New Hebrides. Finding that job filled, he volunteered for the job of "missioner to the Chinese", a position first established by the Presbyterian Church in New Zealand before 1870. At the time of his appointment, Don was acting as a master at Port Chalmers High School (Don 1/8/1879:33).

In 1879, he was sent to China and spent 18 months in Guangzhou learning to read and write Chinese. He returned to New Zealand and, after a period at the Theological Hall in Dunedin, was sent to the Riverton–Round Hill area in Southland, the largest Chinese mining centre at the time. During his time in Southland (from April 1882 until January 1886) he recorded his observations and dealings with the Chinese and contributed many articles about them and his work to the *New Zealand Presbyterian*, which was published monthly. His articles, under the title "Our Chinese Mission", although liberally interlaced with comments relating to his missionising objectives, are very detailed and contain a tremendous amount of information on just about any subject related to the Chinese in New Zealand between 1880 and 1920 that one would care to research (quotes from Don's "Round Hill period" are referenced thus, e.g. Don 12/3/1886:34). Although Don was unsuccessful in converting many of the Chinese to Christianity, he had the satisfaction of establishing the first Chinese church in New Zealand, and a mission centre at Round Hill in 1883.

A Chinese catechist from Guangzhou took over the Riverton–Round Hill parish in January 1886 and Don was transferred to Lawrence where there were 400 Chinese on the Tuapeka field (Butler 1977:82). In November of that year, he began a series of "annual summer tours" around the areas where Chinese miners were working in Otago. These trips involved about 1,000 miles of walking each year, during which he made every effort to visit as many of the Chinese miners as he was physically able to, no matter how remote their work sites. The tours continued after Don was transferred to Dunedin in 1889. His observations on each tour were published in a series of small booklets called *The NZ Presbyterian Chinese Mission Tour Reports* (Southland, Central Otago 1891–1910; Westland 1911). When quoted, they are referenced as follows: e.g. Don 1894:16.

Don also compiled a diary or list and brief life histories of 1,080 Chinese known as the "Roll of Chinese in New Zealand". It covers the years 1883–1913 and was established as "a list of contacts" to help facilitate the Canton Villages Mission project, which commenced in 1897. In the diary he listed their name, county of origin, age, number of years residence in New Zealand and what became of them (if known). James Ng reproduced the entire "Roll of Chinese" as the fourth and final volume of his *Windows on a Chinese Past* series (1993–99).

In 1897, Don revisited the areas in southern China from where the New Zealand Chinese had come. He was largely responsible for setting up the Canton Villages Mission in the "anti-foreigner" region north of Guangzhou (Ng 1984a). His success here, unlike his failure to attract many converts in New Zealand, was due in no small part to the many contacts he had established in New Zealand, and by being able to deliver letters and gold sovereigns from relatives in New Zealand. In 1900, he returned and recommenced the annual inland tours that he had undertaken every year since 1886. He died in 1934, leaving a matchless written legacy of first-hand observations about the Chinese mining experience in New Zealand.

As outlined in the previous chapter, the first real influx of Chinese miners into New Zealand did not occur until late 1866. They came initially from Victoria, in response to an invitation from the Otago Chamber of Commerce (prompted by depressed trading conditions) enjoining them to come and work on the Otago goldfields. By 1867, there were 1,185 Chinese widely distributed throughout the Otago goldfields (Forrest 1961:92). Generally, the miners among them only stopped long enough in the port of entry, Dunedin, to buy supplies and basic mining equipment before heading inland. These men knew what they were about, having gained experience on the Victorian goldfields.

3.1 THE CHINESE MINING CENTRES

The first year's immigration saw the Chinese widely distributed throughout Otago, but the main concentrations were centred on the Waipori–Tuapeka and Dunstan fields and around Naseby (Forrest 1961:92). By the year's end, they formed 5% of the province's population (Butler 1977:7). The landing of 390 Chinese in Dunedin in less than one month (September 1869) was reported by the *Otago Daily Times* (1/10/1869:7) as "a notable feature of the local mining scene". The Chinese were reported "to be in every part of the province" and according to the mining wardens "were doing well in all districts..." (*Otago Daily Times* 1/10/1869:7).

Seven years later there were 3,500 Chinese in Otago and 1,320 in Westland and Nelson (*Otago Daily Times* 1/10/1869:31). During the boom years (1870–85), the main Chinese settlements in Otago–Southland were established at Round Hill (population 400) near Orepuki, Lawrence (400), Alexandra (150), Naseby (150), Switzers (100) and Queenstown (150). Their populations were not static. They waxed and waned in response to mining fortunes, the annual winter/summer migrations caused by either too much or too little water, and a desire for a change of scene occasionally (these factors caused the European miners to relocate too).

Contemporary newspaper reports indicate the large Chinese Camp at Lawrence was well established within three years of the first Chinese arriving in the area:

> The Tuapeka has retained its prestige, and... is the only place in Otago that can boast of a Chinese Camp... In outward appearance it presents nothing that would be called imposing. Its architectural dignity is supported by sheets of galvanised iron and flitches of weatherboarding, and its brand is essentially that of a digging township in the early stage of existence. The buildings are wedged a trifle too closely together to suit modern ideas of good ventilation and sanitary improvement. Still the want of such scientific aids to domestic comfort is not unprecedented in the history of goldfields settlement... A closer inspection brings out the foreign element in its broadest aspect – the hieroglyphical tracings on the sign boards... The habitations are devoted to a variety of pursuits more or less intimately associated with the social and domestic instincts of the race... They include one or two general stores, with stocks as large and well-assorted as any establishment of the kind under European supervision... Among the other curiosities of the camp, the eating houses are, perhaps, the most inviting... Native artisans are few in number, still there are one or two ingenious tradesmen among them. There is a working jeweler, a carpenter, a baker and a hairdresser, all apparently doing a fair stroke of business. One building devoted to benevolent purposes is used as a refuge for new comers in destitute circumstances. Here lodgings and rations are provided, until such time as the inmate gets work, when he is expected to refund the cost... There is only one female resident, a good stout South of Ireland wench, who is reported to have espoused one of these sons of Shem some years ago while residing in Victoria... (*Otago Daily Times* 1/10/1869:7)

The *Tuapeka Times* described the Lawrence camp in 1883 as an area of less than an acre in extent, where there were from 60 to 70 habitations, "narrow, dark and dingy, constructed of boards, kerosene tins and sugar bags. Scattered around with fine disregard for sanitation there were ash-pits, cess-pools, pigsties, fowl houses and wells" (Mayhew 1949:90). The Chinese stores and "gambling dens" were also in this area. Nearby was the Chinese Empire Hotel, originally a wooden construction but replaced in the 1890s with a brick building. The latter was built by Sam Chew Lain, a giant Chinese man who was held in high regard by both the Chinese and European communities (Mayhew 1949). Part of his hotel, which has been used as a dwelling, still stands. It is the only standing structural remnant left of the Lawrence Chinese Camp (the original joss house has been moved back in recent years). Don described the settlement at Round Hill thus:

> The Chinese settlement of a hundred and twenty huts covers about five square miles of spur and gully; but like a sort of nucleus near the centre, is a collection of 38 houses, by Europeans called "Canton" – by Chinese called "The Street of Chinese Men"... of the 38 places, five are business houses, 24 are for gambling and opium smoking, whilst the use of most of the remainder is too easily guessed [presumably they were brothels]. (Don 1894:2)

Although the Round Hill settlement was much more spread out because of the terrain than the urban settlements in Central Otago, the nucleus at Round Hill played a similar role, supplying everyday needs and recreational services, and providing a sense of community for the Chinese miners in the area (in this case up to 400). Among the all-wooden structures at Round Hill there was a double-storied building, which was a tea shop owned by a Riverton firm; two hotels (the Peaceful Tower and the Universal Peace); and two restaurants (see Appendix 5). The Round Hill settlement also differed in that it was virtually a "Chinese town" (Orepuki being the European settlement although a few Chinese lived there too), whereas most of the other urban Chinese settlements were established within or adjacent to pre-existing European mining centres.

Besides the large settlements with their wide choice of supply and recreational services, numerous smaller Chinese settlements or camps grew on the periphery of established goldfield towns, e.g. those at Roxburgh, Clyde, Cromwell and Arrowtown. These smaller settlements offered a correspondingly lesser range of services; but like the larger centres, in addition to the resident Chinese, they serviced large numbers who lived and worked, often in remote gullies, in the surrounding hinterland. For example, Cromwell was the main centre for the 300 Chinese miners in the Upper Clutha district (*Otago Daily Times* 1/10/1869:7). In fact, far more Chinese lived in remote situations, mining in groups of one to eight, than lived in the "urban" centres. Their distribution reflects the discontinuous spread of the alluvial gold they sought and is typified by this quote from Don's records:

> This is the disposition of the 14 on the Cardrona: Near the head, 2 men; ½ mile lower, 1 man; three miles lower, 2; four miles still lower, 3; ½ mile further, 2; two miles further, 1; two miles yet, 2; one mile off, 1... Nearly as scattered are the 22 men in the Kirtleburn (the Roaring Meg). (Don 1893:8)

The Chinese were seldom the first on the scene, but occasionally large numbers moved into an area within a short space of time, creating the impression of a "Chinese rush", e.g. 70 established in the Motatapu Valley in such circumstances in 1873 (*Arrow Observer* 21/3/1873). Once the European miners felt outnumbered, they often sold out or left, leaving the Chinese with large areas to themselves, e.g. Don (1895:11) described the Upper Nokomai "as practically a Chinese River, there being 40 Chinese to 0 Europeans". But the Chinese settlements grew out of more than just a desire to live together. From the outset they were exposed to cool, if not hostile, attitudes from European miners and government officials and frequently were reviled in the newspapers. Most settlements had at least one person who could translate the local newspaper, interpret mining regulations and relay news. Thus they were well aware of the world around them, although often it must not have been what they desired. The earliest arrivals had minimal interaction with Europeans for several reasons:

1. The language barrier caused obvious difficulties.
2. Their initial contacts with the established European settlers were seldom warm and certainly not conducive to friendship.
3. The Chinese arrived with an inherent dislike and distrust of Europeans, who among other things had turned their home counties into a battlefield in the 1850s and actively encouraged opium smoking so that many of the male population had become habitual opium users to the detriment of their families (see Section 5.4).
4. They had their own ethnocentric biases and belief in the superiority of "things Chinese".
5. They had little need to interact because they could obtain most of their provisions from Chinese merchants. Despite this situation, collectively (see below) they did make significant purchases from European stores.

3.2 THE SUPPLY NETWORK

The inland Chinese settlements initially obtained their supplies from Chinese storekeepers in Dunedin, the main source of supply. The biggest storekeepers were known as merchants. Because they were the most literate, they tended to be regarded as leaders or spokesmen by the Cantonese goldseekers (Ng 1984b). In 1874, there were 89 Chinese (including one woman) living in Dunedin. By 1886, the number had risen to 256 (including 10 women), more than anywhere else in Otago (NZ Census 1886). The Dunedin Chinese were principally involved in supplying provisions and services such as accommodation to the Chinese in the interior. Each group of Cantonese favoured their own particular stores and merchant. In 1882, the three merchant premises in Walker St, the main Chinese enclave in Dunedin, were the Hip Fung Taai owned by Seyip merchant Wong Tape, the Kwong Shing Wing (the Tsangshing merchant business) and Sew Hoy's (the Poon Yue merchant). The latter was undoubtedly the most influential because of the numerical majority of the Poon Yue migrants (Ng 1984b). By 1889, there were an estimated 290 Chinese men in Dunedin, of whom 110 were gardeners, 70 shopkeepers, 66 hawkers and seven worked as hotel cooks (Don 1/7/1889:3).

As the Chinese became more established in the hinterland, a network of supply and "recreation" stores developed. Each community was served by as many stores as the market could bear:

> The official figure of the Chinese population of the Dunstan goldfields in September 1869 was 300, but by the end of the year more had arrived and there were 250 at Nevis alone, against a white miners population of 100. There were three Chinese storekeepers, one blacksmith, one shoemaker, two butchers, and sundry opium dens. At Nevis Crossing the population was practically all Chinese. By February 1870 their numbers had decreased to 160 but they still had a regular township of their own, a fact which caused great concern to the white miners. At Bannockburn – there was one Chinese store (Ah Chong's) on Shepherd's Creek, fully equipped with benches for opium smokers and tables for dominoes. By 1871 Ah Chong had a slaughter yard licence and ran a butchery as well as a store. (Parcell 1976:149)

This advertisement in the Lawrence newspaper illustrates the rapidity with which the Chinese storekeepers established their market:

> Mr John Ah Yeng, Chinese storekeeper has received a large consignment of teas directly from the Flowery Land. We recommend to all admirers of "the cup", this genuine article which is much improved on the dried manuka we are accustomed to. (*Tuapeka Times* 25/9/1869:3)

By the 1880s, there were at least 40 Chinese supply stores servicing the southern goldfields (Appendix 5). Most were established in settlements, as opposed to being isolated trading posts. In addition to their provisioning function, many also provided gambling and opium-smoking facilities. The population of the settlements usually swelled in winter when those who could afford not to work over the coldest months "would come in" and stay until the spring thaw.

Don specifically noted that the Chinese merchant stores imported foodstuffs "like rice and pickles from China and rice from Java and India" (Don 1/12/1882:104), but they also stocked a wide variety of other Chinese foods and delicacies (see Chapter 6), medicinal ingredients (Section 3.10), mining equipment, European hardware (Section 5.5) and occasional copies of Chinese newspapers (Section 5.6.2). A newspaper correspondent described the interior of a Chinese general store at Lawrence as follows:

> Hermetically sealed jars and glassware are perhaps, a trifle more numerous than we are accustomed to... Chests of tea are piled up against trusses of sugar. Bags of flour and other bread stuffs are propped by long handled shovels, picks and sluice forks, while the ceiling is literally draped with flitches of bacon, nests of American buckets, watertight boots, oilskins etc. The principal days for transacting business are Saturdays and Sundays... (*Otago Daily Times* 1/10/1869:7)

Thus far no 19th-century Chinese store stock records have come to light in New Zealand, but the range of goods available in the larger rural stores was probably something akin to the range of products recorded in a stock inventory of an up-country Chinese store in the United States, The Kwong Tai Wo Co. in Marysville, California. Food items included staples such as rice, oil, tea, vegetables, pork, fish, sauces, spices, fruit, wine, sugar, salt and flour. Tools included hoes, axes, shovels, rope and nails. Household items encompassed Chinese ceramic tablewares, a few "Barbarian" plates, soap, lanterns, wicks, brooms, kerosene, mahjong sets, scissors, door locks, mirrors, iron woks, tin teapots, scrub boards, dusters, measuring weights, dresser sets and chopsticks. Among the clothing carried were trousers, shirts, shawls, slippers, boots, silk ribbons, belts, padded jackets, vests, underclothes, shoes and Shanghai-style hats. Personal accessories ranged from fans and earrings to tobacco, guns and opium pipes (Sando and Felton 1984:3–4). The remains of many of these items were found in the study sites. They are documented and interpreted in Chapters 5 and 6. In the latter chapter, recourse is also made to the ledgers from two 19th-century European stores (in Roxburgh and Glenorchy). Both stores had a few Chinese clients whose purchases are recorded.

When the Chinese had money, they spent freely and initially their custom was welcomed by European traders as evidenced by these quotations:

> The European tradesmen [at Lawrence] are largely patronised by him, and one of the most powerful agencies that have operated towards the removal of the prejudice entertained against him, is the extent to which he has become the ready money customer. One of the most respectable firms in the Tuapeka is known to have admitted that the takings from Chinamen alone on a Saturday night averaged £30. (*Otago Daily Times* 1/10/1869:7)

> The Chinese are here [Upper Shotover] in abundance, Skippers Creek being the favourite place of Celestial resort. By some they are considered a nuisance, and a disadvantage to the place, while others are of the opposite opinion. There is one fact, however, the Chinese work for all they get, and when they have money expend it pretty freely; some [European] storekeepers' bills shown to me were highly satisfactory on this score. One barbarian dealer in grocery condiments let me see some Chinese accounts ranging from £40 to £120, and the items for luxuries such as lobster, sardines, jams, P.B. and old T. [Burnett's brandy] – sometimes amounting to cases of the latter – were something alarming. From what I learned, the Chinese are the best customers the storekeepers have for luxuries, which they consume in astonishing variety and quantity; with such facts before us they are not to be hastily despised. (*Otago Witness* 15/4/1871:15)

However, the attitude of European shopkeepers soon changed as the Chinese began setting up their own stores, e.g. the establishment of a Chinese store at Arrowtown was "viewed with concern" (*Tuapeka Times* 17/9/1869:2). A later report from the Upper Shotover states:

> The storekeepers are no longer the enthusiastic admirers of John. They find he competes with them in his stores, and is a keen, sharp trader. The latest move in this district is that the Chinese storekeepers pack out goods to their customers, and thus lessen the necessity of their resorting to town. They secure trade, and perhaps John saves time and money, but the town and local trade suffer. All classes agree that the Chinese are eating up an inheritance that we should leave for our race for the future. The miners feel so strongly on the subject that they are carefully noting the strong action which is being taken

in California. The continuous direct migration from China is also alarming the people... The Chinese storekeepers are preparing for a large influx of their countrymen, and in Queenstown a very large store is being erected, making three in all. The Chinese storekeeper is of course anxious to promote immigration. (*Otago Witness* 27/5/1871:15)

Although the Chinese stores were chiefly patronised by Chinese customers, some Chinese storekeepers actively sought European custom, as evidenced by this advertisement by Kum Goon Wa, a self-described "Chinese Storekeeper and Fancy Goods Warehouseman". He stated that he had "on Sale [in his Cromwell shop], at Prices which will command a ready market, Teas, Sugars and General Groceries for English as well, as Chinese customers, and of superior quality to any hitherto introduced into the district" (*Cromwell Argus* 17/5/1881). A year later he acquired a wholesale liquor licence (*Cromwell Argus* 8/8/1882:2).

Don (1/11/1882:89) estimated the average weekly cost of food was about 11/- to 12/- per man, of which about 3/6d was spent on rice and 5/3d on pork. Compare these figures with the estimates in Table 3.1 of Chinese and European living costs presented in the *Report of the Select Committee on Chinese Immigration 1871* (Buckingham 1974).

The wages and estimated costs of living for Europeans were twice as much as those of the Chinese. According to Don (1/12/1882:104): "Rice was the staff of life and occupied greater prominence than any dish among ourselves, being eaten at least twice and sometimes thrice a day; but the cost of rice is to the total cost of living as 1 to 3."

Since the rewards of mining were intermittent, merchants had to extend credit to insulate themselves against bankruptcy; mark-ups of 100% to 300% were common in the early days. In one case, where a Queenstown merchant went bankrupt (c.1894), his total liabilities amounted to nearly £5,000, of which over £3,000 was owed to two other Chinese firms. The book debts amounted to over £4,000. As gold became harder to find and local populations declined, the rates of mark-up and the amount of credit dwindled (Don 1895:14–15). Don commented that this notice in a Nokomai store where business was being discontinued "was characteristically Chinese": "As the business is being wound up, credit diminished and bank accounts reduced, our intimate friends should not show their auspicious countenances for loan or credit, as refusal is inelegant" (Don 1894:8).

Debts were a perennial problem to both miners and merchants. The latter had two main means of keeping track of their clients. Sometimes they would employ collectors who would travel around the mining areas and collect debts; otherwise, they were dependent on the long-established tradition of repaying debts before the Chinese New Year (in January/February) so as to begin the year "with a clean sheet" (Don 2/4/1882:184), or by trying to embarrass outstanding debtors by pasting bills on their hut or shop door setting forth their indebtedness for all to see (Don 2/4/1882:185). The only way to avoid repaying a debt in these circumstances was to leave one's residence over the New Year period and hope that one could obtain further credit upon one's return (Don 2/4/1882:185). William Aspinall observed that Wong Gong, the Chinese storekeeper at Māori Point in the Shotover, used to make Chinese debtors work off their debts by digging his market garden and doing other chores (Chandler pers. comm.).

There is little evidence that the Chinese merchants acted as bankers other than in extending credit for purchases of provisions and loaning money to clansmen. The Chinese generally shunned the European banks, although the banks were not opposed to their custom. Gold-buying was a profitable business for the banks during the goldrushes (Chappell 1961:56), and so long as it was the real thing they were not particularly concerned who offered it. A report in the *Tuapeka Times* (10/1/1883:2) described an occasion when some Chinese miners in Lawrence sold 35 ounces of nugget gold to the Bank of New Zealand. Further evidence of Chinese usage of European banks was found in one of the study sites (the Flax Grove shelter in the Kawarau Gorge). Here, seven fragmentary Bank of New Zealand receipts for gold dust deposits were recovered (Figure 5.105). The depositees were Chinese. The rationale expressed by one Chinese man for not using the European banks was not because he feared for the security of any money he deposited, but "if a man puts money in a bank, it is soon found out, and then he is continually applied to for loans", which he hardly dare refuse, especially if the would-be borrower was a respectable clansman (Don 1894:9).

Chinese stores provided other services for their clientele, including gambling and opium-smoking facilities (see Section 3.3), cooked meals and alcohol, a meeting place and an informal "news exchange" (there was usually someone there who could read local or Chinese newspapers), and usually services such as interpreting and letter writing. Several men at Round Hill and Riverton earned a living as scribes, writing letters for those unable to do so (Don 1/9/1882:45). In at least one instance, a local store (in Nokomai) collected the county rates from the local Chinese. All the notices would be sent to the store and distributed by the storekeeper who also collected the amount due. Don recorded that two men who had offended the storekeeper in the previous year had not received their rate demands and suspected him of withholding them, so that their holding would be forfeited and he would be avenged. They solved the problem by giving the money to Don so that he could pay their rates (Don 1895:12).

3.3 THE ROLE OF GAMBLING AND OPIUM STORES

Gambling and opium shops/saloons were in the same areas as the merchant stores but were more numerous. Don's records contain no less than 40 references to gambling being carried out while he was present, frequently in a room that formed part of a merchant store.

This newspaper reporter's description of a combination supply gambling and opium store (in the Greenstone River Valley on the West Coast) would appear to be typical of many in southern New Zealand:

> Not only is there a Chinese store where many Asiatic abominations are sold, but there is also a gambling and opium house in full swing. The first place visited was the store, where any number of strangely smelling packages are displayed for sale, of course, not including the inevitable "birds nest", but omitting that and pig, which John had not in stock, nearly everything else that delights the palate of a Chinaman can be obtained. In connection with this store there is accommodation for those who wish to indulge in opium smoking... There were some half dozen of the almond eyed either under the influence, or preparing to inhale the smoke... [he proceeds to describe the act of smoking, see Section 5.4]. The gambling was principally carried out in an adjoining tent, which in order that the opium inhalers should lose none of their opportunities, in the store there was displayed all the things needed for playing the game of Fan Tan or whatever... [a game in progress was apparently quickly concluded because there was a police officer with the reporter.]... [Further on he commented that] although a Boss-Chinaman has set up his emporium of nastiness in the locality, it by no means follows that all the Chinese patronise the store of their countrymen; on the contrary the European stores are largely patronised by the Chinese, and as far as could be learned they contrive to pay cash for all they purchase. (*West Coast Times* 29/7/1874)

The key factor in the establishment of a gambling saloon was a local Chinese population of sufficient size to support the business. A similar pattern was described in the United States by Culin (1887:10–11):

> The store is the centre around which life in a Chinese colony revolves. As soon as several men have collected in a town or city, one of them will send to the nearest place of supply and purchase such Chinese groceries and other wares as may be needed... Other opportunities for making money will not be lost sight of. The cellar will be fitted with bunks for opium smoking and tables covered with matting for the convenience of those desiring to play dominoes... The profit on the opium consumed and the [shop's] portion of the gambling winnings frequently constitute a more important source of revenue than the store itself.

Attracting custom does not seem to have been a problem. The numerous references throughout Don's writings attest to the fact that many of the Chinese miners enjoyed gambling. Don saw it in a slightly different light: "When a Chinaman is in employment he is industrious and frugal. Out of work he is lazy and riotous, spending the time in sleeping, opium smoking and gambling" (Don 1/2/1883:148). Most men seem to have used gambling as a means of recreation – a break from the long, tedious hours of mining and as additional entertainment on festival days, before and after the feast. But others, despondent over low mining returns or their poor financial situation, turned to gambling as a last resort, hoping that a lucky break would alleviate their misery and/or pay their fare home. Some Chinese (both saloon operators and clientele) made a deliberate decision to chance their luck. They opted to risk what money they had saved on gambling. If they were successful (and some were, e.g. Don 1/2/1887:147), they were able to return to China that much sooner than they would otherwise have been able. They were well aware of the consequences if they were unlucky – debts, deprivation and a prolonged sojourn (e.g. Don 1897:25).

It was generally held by the Chinese that there were two types of wealth: that produced by one's own hands, which was honourable, and that gained through the misfortune of others, such as the gains from gambling (Sedgewick 1982). Despite the popularity of gambling, the saloons were often "decorated" with references to death; e.g. Don described one saloon door which bore a sign reading "Enter the Door of Slaughter", while inside were several inscriptions including "The Murderer's Star is Enthroned Here". All the inscriptions were on white paper, the symbol of mourning, as opposed to red, the colour of joy. He believed the inscriptions were intended to encourage the bankers at the *fan-tan* tables (Don 1/11/1889:85). The most popular Chinese gambling games were *paak kop piu* (pakapoo), *fan-tan* and dominoes (see Section 5.6.6). *Paak kop piu* was especially important to the merchant-saloon owners because it provided a means of keeping track of debtors thus: a *paak kop piu* lottery commenced when a saloon issued a series of tickets, each bearing 80 Chinese words. The purchaser struck off 20. Each ticket cost 6d. The saloon retained one copy of the ticket while the buyer kept another copy. On a set day, 10 words were drawn which were the winning words. If one had struck off five of the winning words, one received 1/-; for 6, 9/6; for 7, £4; for 8, £21 10/-; for 9, £40; and with 10 words correct £80. Since the "bank" had only a limited amount, in instances where large wins were made, a proportionate division was made (Don 2/10/1882:67).

Each saloon employed collectors (generally ex-miners) who would hawk the lottery tickets from claim to claim and then go around again and collect the tickets after they were marked up. Once all the tickets were returned to the gambling saloon, the lottery was drawn, then the collectors would revisit the work sites and deliver the winnings to the lucky recipients (Don 1/2/1883:147). For each ticket sold, they got half a penny from the saloon proprietor and they took one tenth of what each winner received (Don 1/2/1883:147).

The collectors played a vital role in keeping stores and lottery operators solvent. As the gambling operation involved regular contact with the surrounding mining population, storekeepers and saloon operators were able to "keep tabs" on the miner's movements and prosperity. Don noted an instance at Round Hill where some claim-mates of a man who was killed in a rockfall in their claim became *paak kop piu* collectors rather than return to the claim after the accident (Don 1/2/1883:146).

The other major gambling games were undertaken in saloons, which depended on their clientele coming to them. Mahjong, dominoes and *fan-tan* saloons were especially busy during the weekends when miners took time off to go to the nearest settlement (*Otago Daily Times* 1/10/1869:7). Don recorded an instance where "fully 150 men" were in the various gambling houses at Round Hill one weekend (1/12/1882:105). Those who tended the tables got an average of 1/- for every pound spent and were sometimes described as "*lo ka*", "one who does not look for work but waits for work to turn up" (Don 1/12/1882:105).

Don's observations confirm gambling establishments were located in virtually every place where there was a Chinese store, and there were even more specialised "gambling houses". In towns like Lawrence, Cromwell and Alexandra, there were from two to seven gambling places operating at any one time. Don noted that their numbers fluctuated with the prosperity or poverty of the local miners and the willingness of a few individuals to set up such establishments. Usually, it required three or four men to pool their capital to start a gambling saloon and it would operate until one or more of the partners withdrew their capital or the local mining population declined to a point where the venture was no longer profitable. In one instance, a Chinese miner at Waitahuna (who had made a substantial gambling win at Lawrence), sold the share he had in a claim and bought a house in Waitahuna that he set up as the settlement's first gambling den (Don 1/10/1886:1). In Round Hill there were 12 gambling houses at one stage. To ensure business for all of them, they had worked out their own calendar in 12-day cycles, which ensured that at least one was open every day (Don 1895:4).

Undoubtedly, the possibility of a big win, which would provide the wherewithal to be able to return to China immediately (after having cleared one's debts), was a major incentive behind many of the miners' enthusiasm for gambling. For others, a win enabled them to "take it easy" for a while. Don recorded instances where miners "retired" to the nearest town or went on a holiday after a big win, leaving their claims to be worked by others (Don 1/10/1886:1).

Although gambling was illegal on the goldfields, the police, generally preoccupied with mining offences, infrequently arrested Chinese for gambling, although periodically the imposition of fines for gambling was reported in the Otago newspapers. The *Otago Daily Times* (1/10/1869:7) reported that "their proceedings (gambling at the Lawrence Chinese Camp) are conducted without the smallest attempt at disguise… despite the law of New Zealand defining gambling as a quasi-criminal offence". In fact, gambling was so tolerated that many Chinese felt free to describe their occupations as "gambling house operator" or "gambler" in the census returns (NZ Census 1874–1911).

However, some Chinese were critical of their countrymen's habits. In 1870, the Chinese interpreter John Aloo took it upon himself to announce that he was going to rid the goldfields of the 15 or 20 gambling houses then in existence (*Otago Witness* 1/10/1870:14). However, judging from their increasing numbers and prosperity, his campaign appears to have had little support. Similarly, the Chinese constable Wong Ngai, who was appointed to the Riverton–Round Hill area in September 1883 to catch gamblers, thieves and miners without licences, was singularly unsuccessful. He was too well known, and all the gambling houses closed for the duration of his presence (Don 1/12/1883:105).

3.3.1 OPIUM DISTRIBUTION

The role of opium smoking and associated artefacts is described in Section 5.4. Here, a brief discussion on the drug's importation and distribution is presented.

The opium habit arrived in New Zealand with the earliest Chinese migrants. Largely through the duplicity of British merchants based in Hong Kong, opium addiction had reached epidemic proportions among the male population of the Pearl River Delta in the years preceding the great efflux to the goldfields of California, Australia and New Zealand. Although early local newspapers seldom mention its presence, the distribution, sale and use of opium became an integral part of the Chinese way of life on the southern goldfields. Initially, it came into New Zealand as an unrestricted import. A duty of £1 per lb weight was imposed in 1866 (but it was not levied until 1869). The duty was increased to £2 after 1888 and a partial ban on its importation was passed in 1882 (NZHRS 1970:112).

The raw product was imported into China in 150-lb chests (Collis 1946:76). When re-exported, the prepared product was packed in small brass cans that contained 5 taels (c. 150 grams) of opium. In the absence of specific information, it is inferred that the Chinese merchants in Dunedin (and possibly the larger up-country businesses) regularly ordered opium along with other goods. After landing in Dunedin, the chests or other containers would have been "broken down" into smaller parcels in Chinese warehouses and freighted inland in response to anticipated demand or orders placed by the country stores. The opium was sold in the general stores and could also be bought and smoked in "opium shops/dens"; the latter were commonly associated with gambling saloons (*Otago Daily Times* 1/10/1869:7).

Many Chinese earned their livelihood or supplemented their income as "opium sellers". Because of its popularity as a recreational pastime and its addictive nature, opium smoking created a dependent supply situation, whereby regular users would be obliged to come to the stores/saloons frequently for more opium (and other supplies). After 1880, over 3,000 lb weight of opium was imported annually (Statistics of New Zealand, see Appendix 6). Consumption briefly declined in 1888, probably due to the efforts of a short-lived Chinese anti-opium society (the Cherishing Virtue Union) that was established the same year. The continued importation of opium in large quantities (besides its sought-after effects) undoubtedly revolved around the enormous profits to be made from dealing in it by those involved in every link in the distribution chain. In 1901, the *Opium Prohibition Act*, which specifically prohibited the smoking of opium by the Chinese, was passed. It made it an offence to import opium in any form suitable for smoking and required special permission from the Minister of Customs for its import in any other form (NZHRS 1970:113). Although the passing of the Act terminated the bulk importation of opium, supplies still got through by more circuitous means (discussed in Section 5.4).

3.4 OCCUPATIONS

From the first arrivals in 1866 until the turn of the century, mining was the predominant Chinese occupation. But the percentage of goldminers steadily fell from 85% in 1871 to 46% in 1901 (NZ Census 1901), while the numbers in non-mining occupations increased correspondingly. Most of the non-miners lived in Dunedin (until c.1900 when Wellington became the main centre of Chinese population) and the larger goldfield towns. They earned their livelihood by providing services to the miners; their occupations included storekeepers, hotel owners and workers, gardeners, carpenters and joiners, and gambling and opium house operators.

The Lawrence Chinese Camp was reported to have a jeweller, a carpenter, a baker and a hairdresser (*Otago Daily Times* 1/10/1869:7). Don described a few specialised occupations among the Chinese in Riverton and Round Hill: "There are several men here who earn a livelihood by writing letters for those unable to do so" (Don 2/10/1882:45). He also described Chinese "packers" who had their own horses for delivering supplies from the settlements to the workings, and a man who earned a living by drying and selling fish during the summer months (Don 2/10/1882:66–7). A condensed summary of the occupations of the Chinese in New Zealand in 1871 (i.e. five years after Chinese settlement commenced) is presented in Table 3.2.

Notable features of the table are that 3,570 (84.7%) of the Chinese population stated their primary occupation was mining. One hundred and three (2.4%) considered themselves to be store or hotel keepers, 49 (1.2%) were gardeners, and 11 (0.26%) carpenters and cabinet-makers. The *number* involved in the last category is interesting, for it is quite small compared with the numbers similarly employed in Australia where Chinese entered the cabinet-making trade on a large scale, in so doing generating considerable animosity from European cabinet-makers who found it difficult to compete (Yong 1977:44). The figures for labourers are also interesting – only 12 (a mere 0.3%) are described as labourers. Three years later, the 1874 census recorded that 258 Chinese were involved in labouring (principally as navvies and construction workers on public works contracts).

Table 3.3, compiled from information recorded in the NZ Census between 1871 and 1911, documents the broad trends and changes in the occupations of the Chinese in New Zealand during the 19th century. Each census reveals that disaffected miners were entering an increasingly diverse range of occupations but mining was still predominant until the turn of the century. In 1906, the census recorded for the first time that the numbers involved in market gardening (791) exceeded the numbers involved in mining (612). As gold became increasingly hard to find, many ex-miners began to work full- or part-time in the gardens of their more prosperous countrymen or worked as farmhands, rabbiters, gardeners or cooks for European landowners.

3.5 WOMEN

During the 19th century, the Chinese population in New Zealand was virtually all male (see Table 3.3). The first Chinese women (three, disguised in male attire) landed at Dunedin in October 1869. They were understood to be married and left almost immediately on the coach for Lawrence to join their husbands (*Otago Witness* 2/10/1869:14; Butler 1977:53). There were only officially nine Chinese women in New Zealand in 1878, i.e. 12 years after the first influx of Chinese miners (NZ Census 1878). By the turn of the 19th century, the number had risen to 78 (NZ Census 1902), which constituted less than 2.6% of the total Chinese population (2,963).

The lack of women, the consequent imbalanced sex ratio and strong prejudices (both Chinese and European) against intermarriage effectively ensured that the Chinese sojourner population in New Zealand would gradually decline as the old miners died or returned home without producing offspring. The general absence of women was an involuntary situation brought about by several factors. Until 1859, migration was officially forbidden by the Chinese government. After that date they allowed voluntary emigration from Guangdong, but the privilege was not readily extended to women. There appears to be three main reasons why female emigration was opposed: it was against Confucian propriety; it was believed if the women stayed in China, the young men would be more inclined to return quickly from their overseas sojourns; the women would maintain the traditional social organisation in the absence of the males.

According to John Ah Tong, the only Chinese man to be interviewed by the Select Committee on Chinese Immigration 1871, there was no law against women leaving China, but after the large exoduses to California, the "head men" (for reason 2 above) would only allow wives to go and join their husbands, or women who were sent for and had a definite promise of marriage upon arrival (AJHR 1871 H–5:5). At an individual level, however, undoubtedly the main constraint on bringing wives to New Zealand was the cost. Many of the Chinese miners had to borrow or have the fare advanced for their passage; consequently, they were in no position to bring dependents. A second but by no means insignificant consideration resulted from the Chinese practice of female footbinding. Although the practice was generally restricted to the upper classes, women whose feet were deformed in this manner had considerable difficulty walking far (Levy 1967), and without servants "to do their running around" they would have had great difficulty enduring the conditions likely to be encountered on the goldfields.

Don was told by one Chinese miner that "about 700 of the Chinese who came to New Zealand had wives in China". The deserted wives lived with their husbands' families (Don 1/9/1884:43). Some of the sojourners never saw their wives again.

Almost as soon as Chinese settlements were established, they tended to attract European women, who far outnumbered Chinese women. The European women were frequently described in contemporary accounts in terms such as "they are of the lowest type" or "women who would find it difficult to induce any respectable European to marry them" (AJHR 1871 H–5:14–22; Butler 1977:54). Probably, some of the resentment towards these women was because they chose to live with the Chinese rather than Europeans. It is difficult to quantify the incidence of prostitution. One might expect a demand for such services considering the virtually all-male nature of the Chinese mining communities, but there is no evidence that the Chinese resorted to it any more than the European miners on the goldfields. There is at least one record of a Chinese man being charged with keeping a brothel; "Qui Sing, was charged with keeping a brothel in Melmore Terrace, Cromwell and sentenced to two months hard labour" (Court News in *Cromwell Argus* 20/6/1896).

Relatively little intermarriage took place on the southern goldfields, so unions between a Chinese man and a European woman were usually noteworthy. Butler (1977:54) quoted some examples, for instance: "We understand that two marriages between European women and Chinamen will take place next week. Both the ladies are new chums, having arrived about eight months ago. They are young and blooming, though can scarcely be considered 'passing fair'. One of the expectant bridegrooms is a resident of Dunedin, and the other lives in the Tuapeka district. Of the ladies, one is a barmaid at Waipori, the other is at present a resident of the Chinese Camp, Lawrence." By 1888, there were 51 Chinese married to European women and they had produced a total of 101 children (AJHR 1888 H–29). A Chinese man at Round Hill named Wong was married to a Frenchwoman (Don 2/10/1882:66). He was generally opposed to intermarriages because he believed that the unions were usually made for reasons other than love. He believed the chief reason that some women married Chinese was to get possession of a marriage certificate to be produced when the police questioned their means of support and thus avoid vagrancy charges (Don 1893:11).

Because of the shortage of Chinese women, the marriage of Chinese couples in New Zealand was rare before 1920. One of the more renowned was that of the giant Chinese hotel keeper, Sam Chew Lain, at Lawrence and his diminutive wife:

> A gala day was held at the Tuapeka [i.e. Lawrence] Chinese Camp following the marriage of Mrs Chew Lain. The Chinese community assembled at the Chinese Empire Hotel [the building still stands] to compliment the woman and give her presents and cash. Apparently, she received gifts to the value of between two and three hundred pounds. (Butler 1977:53)

The absence of Chinese women on the goldfields led to many accusations by European anti-Chinese agitators that the Chinese were involved in immoral practices and that young children and girls were under particular threat. The Select Committee reviewing the question of Chinese immigration in 1871 asked the goldfield wardens for their views on the following question: "Is there any danger [posed by Chinese] to the morality of the community, especially young children and girls?" In its summation, the Committee concluded that the Chinese presented no special threat to the morality of the community (AJHR H–5B:4). As Butler (1977:57) noted: "The police records did not support the immorality claims… and there is no reason to believe that the Chinese miners indulged in child molesting to a greater degree, proportionately, than the rest of the population." The exaggerated claims were made by disgruntled Europeans who were only too keen to find a reason for decrying the Chinese.

3.6 HABITATIONS

Chinese houses in the nucleated villages around Canton were described by Mawson and others (1926:12) as low, windowless and constructed of sun-dried and fired bricks held together with a mixture of sand, lime and clay.

The floors were either of clay or large tiles, while the roofs were of light tiles laid on pine rafters. Little wood was used in construction because of the destruction caused by ants. Two-storied buildings were relatively uncommon and usually owned by those who had accumulated wealth overseas. Another description of a Cantonese village was provided by Yee (1975:9–10), who was brought up in the village of Loan Gon Doan. The (clearly more affluent) village consisted of 50 families all descended from one ancestor who established the community many hundreds of years ago. All the houses were symmetrical and exactly alike in design and materials. Each had brick walls, concrete floors, red tile roofs and mahogany doors "half a foot" thick. The central part of each house was two stories high, while the two side sections were divided into two rooms – a bedroom and a kitchen on each side (the second kitchen being for catering during festive occasions). There were no windows on the ground floor. The upstairs section consisted of four bedrooms and storage areas.

From these and other accounts it is evident that there was a high degree of uniformity within the vernacular architecture of the Guangzhou area, that sun-dried and baked earth constituted the main construction materials, and that most Chinese males knew the basics of house construction using these materials. Understandably, since few, if any, of the Chinese miners were accompanied by other family members, there was little need or desire to try to re-create replicas of contemporary Chinese villages in New Zealand, but from the outset they exhibited a remarkable adaptability and versatility in regards to "house" construction. According to Don (cited in the Butler quote below), they had a definite preference for huts rather than tents (but his assertion is contradicted to some extent by data recorded in the census returns, e.g. NZ Census 1874, 1878):

> He liked a home of finer stuff than calico. He built a hut of turf on the grassy plots, of slabs in the bush, of cobblestones on the shingle, of adobe where stones were scarce, of whatever stuff came handiest. And for roofing what better stuff than the bags that held his rice, or thatch of the great tussock of those days? (Butler 1977:32)

Field surveys, excavations, census data, contemporary accounts and photographs indicate that the range of construction techniques and materials (largely drawn from the local environment) was even wider and more varied than that outlined by Don. Potter (1890) provided this description of dwellings in the "Canton" at Round Hill, which he visited in 1888:

> The huts, hovels or houses are stuck up anyhow regardless of either line or order; the chimneys – huge piles of timber, sod and zinc cases – being placed in several instances where Europeans would put their front door... The (single) street is only seven feet wide and is thickly built upon on both sides, if buildings they can be called – canvas, fern tree and slabs entering largely into their construction...

The forested environment of the Round Hill area and the habitations the Chinese built there were more akin to those their countrymen constructed on the West Coast, which also has a wet climate and is forested. In the dry, virtually treeless environment of Central Otago, the Chinese resorted to many different methods of construction, including in one instance living in abandoned mine drives (Don 1911:14). The Chinese dwellings in the study area are described in detail in Section 4.5.

Labourers employed by Chinese mining companies sometimes lived in large dormitory-style huts such as those described below:

> Messrs Ah Kimm and Co form quite a little colony (23 men) by themselves, and are encamped in a small camp close to their claim... There is a large cookhouse and dining room... Ranged alongside is the Celestial abode or dwelling place. It is a very extensive building, and similarly constructed of sod walls with a thatched roof, the whole presenting a comfortable and warm appearance. The Celestial abode is 120 feet long and divided into four cottage-like compartments with their doorways facing towards the cookhouse. Each compartment is then subdivided again into sleeping places, some with only a narrow passage between the bunks or beds, while in others there is room for a table and a few seats, so that the inmates might enjoy the luxury of gambling or amuse themselves with a little music on their native fiddle, flute or guitar... (*Otago Witness* 9/10/1875)

> I should say there were about 200 [Chinese]. They seemed to work like one family, work, eat and sleep in the same hut... They had two big huts... Each was about 60 or 70 feet long, built with what we call wattle and dab [daub]. This consisted of stakes driven in the ground with saplings and tussocks in between, finished up with puddled mud. The roofs were thatched with tussocks tied on with flax... (McArthur 1945:11)

Many Chinese, especially those mining in the river gorges, lived full-time or temporarily in the natural "caves" that abound within the schist massifs of Central Otago. They formed shelters by selecting rock overhangs or open spaces under boulders and erecting walls of packed earth or rock, thus forming "homes" 4 to 20 square metres in area, the size being dependent on the space available under the overhang. In some locations, particularly in the main river gorges, suitable rocks for shelters were very numerous and the Chinese put them to good use, witness this quote from Don:

On January 9th 1901, we were a day among caves. We counted 21 – only six occupied – in 3 miles of the Molyneux River above Roxburgh [the Roxburgh Gorge]. In winter, when the great stream is low, the empty caves will have their occupants. Some of these caves are very roomy and comfortable – cool in summer and warm in winter. But there is absolutely no ventilation and when the door, usually a thick rice bag, is shut, it is almost pitch dark. (Don 1901:25)

There are 77 recorded rockshelters in the Roxburgh Gorge (Harrison 1982:24). Although this is the densest concentration in Central Otago, it is known that as many again were flooded when the gorge was inundated by the formation of Lake Roxburgh in 1956 (there was no prior recording). The 1874 census records indicate that by that date, 918 Chinese were living in semi-permanent houses built of brick, stone, wood or lathe and plaster (although the majority of these were probably small, if not, one-room dwellings), 2,288 lived in huts and 1,156 were living in tents or dwellings with canvas roofs. From that date, the census records show a steady decline in the numbers living in tents or canvas-topped structures.

The type of tenure is not recorded in early records. It appears "ownership" on unoccupied Crown land depended to some extent on who built or paid for the materials in a hut, e.g. during the course of a court case in Cromwell, Ah Kew (a gardener who lived and worked on the Cromwell Flat) stated that he owned three huts in the Chinese Camp at Cromwell (*Cromwell Argus* 24/9/1889). Presumably he leased or loaned the huts. In the Maniototo, only the Chinese (50) who "owned" huts were listed on the ratepayers roll (*Cromwell Argus* 1977:33). The Arrowtown Borough Council only levied a rate on Chinese commercial buildings up until 1883. After that date, hut owners or lessees in the Arrowtown Chinese Camp (on unsold Crown land) were rated too (Arrowtown Borough rate books). According to Don, "The Chinese at Round Hill usually lived three or four in one small house, but there is an exception in the case of the partners in a claim, who work together and eat together, but sleep each in separate houses, any one of which is large enough (by ordinary Chinese reckoning) for all three" (Don 1/8/1883:24). Don's records indicate that the normal occupancy of Chinese huts on the Central Otago goldfields varied between one and eight, depending on factors such as the date of occupation, the size of the structures, the amicability of the men and the nature of the claims. By the late 1880s, two was about the average number of occupants per hut. For instance, there were 21 men in 12 huts at Bendigo (Don 1/3/1887:164), 29 in 18 huts in the Lawrence–Tuapeka area (Don 1/10/1887: 63), 17 in 10 huts at Waikaia (Don 1/12/1888:106), 30 in 28 huts at Cromwell (Don 1/3/1887:164), 76 in 51 huts at Naseby (Don 1893:16) and 229 in the 110 inhabited huts at Round Hill (Don 1/8/1885:26).

Detailed descriptions of the size, orientation and structural details of Chinese huts and their significance are presented in Chapter 4. Here it will suffice to note that the "average 1–3 men Chinese hut" varied from 2.5–4.5m in length and 2–3m in width (internal dimensions). Don recorded a few exceptionally large Chinese huts. He considered the "finest Chinese hut on the goldfields, was a then abandoned cob dwelling at Blacks [Ophir] which measured 45 x 12 feet" (Don 2/4/1888:185). He also referred to a "six man hut at Round Hill". He did not state the dimensions, but the possibility was discussed of reducing it in length by 8 feet (2.4 metres), indicating it must have been a substantial structure. Eight men lived in a hut he visited at Waikaia, suggesting that it too was larger than the average Chinese dwelling (Don 1/3/1887:164).

In the situations where houses were occupied by two or more men, they usually had clan or locality of origin in common. Their mutual accommodation arrangements would endure so long as personality conflicts did not arise. Disputes resulted in one or more "hut mates" finding alternative accommodation. In the case of real or imagined "serious offences" or disease threats, individuals were ostracised and obliged to live alone. Houses were invariably abandoned after a death or suicide (Don 1/8/1884:25) and this was sometimes extended to the huts near one in which someone had died (Don 1/1/1885:126). Others abandoned huts "because of fear of demons" (rats, in this instance, according to Don 1/6/1887:225). Houses were also deliberately burnt down to make way for mining and to avoid the risk of the houses and occupants being swept away in potentially fatal landslips induced by mining (Don 1/2/1883:146, 148). These and other reasons meant that at times there was considerable mobility and changes in individuals' housing arrangements, even within a short space of time. By way of illustration, Don (1/9/1883:47) cited the inter-house movements of a group of miners at Round Hill within a period of less than one month, see Table 3.4.

C, H and J had moved to other areas. K, L and M had arrived at Round Hill recently. House 3 was destroyed to build house 7, only 200 yards (183 metres) away. Don (1/9/1883:47) believed that "the house may have been destroyed and rebuilt 'for luck' – the 'feng shui' of the locality of house 3 being bad". He also attributed the spate of movements as "reflecting the unsettledness of the men in the outlying districts and the consequent difficulty of work among them".

An indication of the amount of money the Chinese spent on houses was provided by Don when he recorded the following new house or hut costs after the Chinese at Alexandra re-established their settlement. They decided to abandon the old site following continual physical harassment from a group of Europeans "who wanted them out of the town proper: Canton is the name given by Europeans to the new settlement. Seven new places were built at outlays of from £26 to £210, the total being

"£563" (Don 1896:21), a considerable sum of money in those days.

The Chinese built their own dwellings and furnishings. Houses or huts were sparsely furnished, usually having only a chimney and fireplace, a sleeping platform, recesses or box-cupboards for food storage, a meat safe and wash-buckets. They almost invariably had some form of "chest" for storing bulk rice (Don 1/1/1883:128). He also noted another distinctive feature of the Chinese miners' dwellings:

> One can always tell a house in which Chinese have lived, by the sure presence of the "chop-block", on which meat and vegetables are cut small for eating with chopsticks. Some of the unoccupied houses here (at the Round Hill workings) are very old, and the existence of the chop block proves that the Chinese have been living years ago on ground which others are now working again. (Don 1/2/1883:147)

Frequently, houses were "decorated" inside and outside with auspicious inscriptions, usually on red paper or written in red. Some of these marked the occasion of building a new house, e.g. "Let prosperity come in the new house". An apparently almost universal door inscription stated: "May [the people at] this door become wealthy" (Don 1/1/1883:126). In some instances, houses were given names, e.g. Don noted that one of the miners at Round Hill had "christened" his house "The Mansion of the Followers of Equity" (Don 1/12/1882:103), while the three largest Chinese houses in Orepuki were called "Peace Harmony Hall", "Vast Harmony Hall" and "Sincere Harmony Hall" (Don 1901:17). House names were sometimes changed in the hope that it would bring a change of fortunes (Don 1/8/1883:25). Some inscriptions were more pragmatic, like this one pinned to the sack door of a cave-house beside the Molyneux River (the old name for the Clutha River below Cromwell): "Outsiders require not enter in; Things missing many suspicions begin" (Don 1892:12).

Keeping vegetable gardens was much more common among Chinese than European miners. Many of the Chinese established a small garden near their dwelling and often planted fruit trees such as apples and plums. Some also kept a few chickens and occasionally raised a pig. A detailed discussion on Chinese gardening and animal production is presented in Chapter 6.

3.7 CHINESE MINING IN NEW ZEALAND

3.7.1 GETTING ESTABLISHED

As outlined in the previous chapter, the first Chinese miners in New Zealand disembarked at Dunedin in 1866. Numbers remained low initially, but by 1871 the Chinese population had reached 4,215 (NZ Census 1871). It was a period of rapid change. The population of Otago (all nationalities) increased sixfold between 1861 and 1871 and the interior of the province was opened up for close settlement. Virtually all of the present-day towns in Central Otago owe their origin to this period. Dunedin became the business capital of New Zealand.

New Chinese arrivals quickly provisioned and headed inland. In most instances, the "new chums" made their way to the established Chinese camps where they could obtain further supplies, meet "brothers", and learn about potential mining sites. Initially, the Chinese concentrated on the Tuapeka, Dunstan and Naseby fields (Forrest 1961:92), the areas closest to Dunedin, but within three years (by the end of 1868) they were present in varying numbers on all the known alluvial fields in Otago. They were said to be earning 25/- to 40/- per week on the Dunstan (*Otago Witness* 19/1/1867:4).

The *Otago Witness* (18/4/1868:1) reported that the population of the Otago goldfields totalled 11,258 of whom 4,414 were European miners and 1,270 Chinese miners. The European and Chinese population figures given for the various mining centres indicate that at this stage, Europeans outnumbered the Chinese by three or more to one in most districts.

3.7.2 MINING LOCATIONS

Table 3.5 is a police estimate of the number of Chinese in Otago in 1871 (AJHR 1871 H–5:23). Although not stated, Chinese were also established in the Waipori, Manuherikia, Roxburgh, Arrowtown, Shotover, Cardrona, Nevis, Macraes, Upper Wakatipu and Waikaia areas (See Figure 3.1). Eighty-five percent of the Chinese were classed as miners in the 1871 census. The high number of Chinese in the Dunstan in that year is notable.

The Chinese seldom worked side by side with Europeans, but they often took up claims in neighbouring gullies or areas that had been abandoned by Europeans or were considered to have low gold values. The following newspaper report suggests that as Chinese numbers grew in a locality, Europeans tended to vacate the area:

> The rapid increase of the Chinese element on the goldfields in the Lakes District is viewed with great disfavour by the European miners. The Chinese are buying up claims on all sides, and the consequence is that as soon as the European miners find themselves outnumbered in any locality they clear out altogether and leave "John" in undisputed possession. (*Otago Witness* 15/10/1870:1)

Sometimes work areas were dictated by European "bans" on Chinese mining in certain localities: e.g. "At Orepuki the gold is got in the same manner as at Round Hill but no Chinamen are there, the Europeans having opposed all who attempted to gain a footing" (Don 1/6/1883:225). Ironically, two Europeans are credited with discovering gold at Round Hill, but they were unable to make the claim pay (Hall-Jones 1982:39). The Chinese moved in and within a short time established the Round Hill mining area and "Canton", the most concentrated and largest Chinese mining settlement and workings in New Zealand. Round Hill became and continued to be a virtually solely Chinese mining preserve.

This account of a localised ban on the Chinese (on the West Coast in this case) and the absence of condemnation of the move is probably typical of many such instances:

> Yesterday about a dozen Chinese who recently arrived here, made their way up to the Waimea. When they had proceeded as far as McLenn's store, between Stafford Town and the old Waimea, they were met by a large number of the diggers in that locality who requested them to proceed no further. On being told this the Chinamen returned. There was no attempt to offer violence. (*West Coast Times* 13/11/1868)

The following incident would appear to be an infrequent example of cooperation:

> The arrival of the Chinese at Clyde – an advance party of 10 men – was quite well received. The manager of Ovens Water Race Co. promised to let the Chinese have water free for a limited period to prospect with. The Chinese idea is for half to work for wages while the other half look around for ground which could support a large number of their countrymen. (Butler 1977:13)

3.7.3 MINING PREFERENCES AND METHODS

Although the Chinese miners were largely of peasant stock, they were heirs to at least a 4,000-year legacy of knowledge about mining, smelting and alloying of gold (and copper, tin and lead; Bernard and Tamatsu 1975:215–39). The use of nuggets of native gold and copper archaeologically predates these technological processes and suggests that alluvial mining goes back even further. They would also have been familiar with the basic principles of hydraulic engineering, for the Chinese have been organising large, labour-intensive projects for the procurement and distribution of sizeable volumes of water for wet rice farming for over two millennia (Bayard pers. comm.). It would not require radical changes to use these technologies for conveying and storing water for mining, rather than irrigation. Hydraulic innovations included the chain pump (*chin-chia*) and the water-powered wheel pump (*noria*) evolved for irrigation c. 200–300 AD (Triestman 1972).

The Chinese also have a long history of general engineering knowledge utilising simple labour-intensive technology, notably the method where men and women carry a bamboo pole with two balanced basket panniers or wooden buckets. Using large numbers of people, they could move huge volumes of material and build large, sturdy and inexpensive dams, canals and levees of tamped earth (Steeves 1984:14). In addition, a few among the Chinese had brothers, fathers or grandfathers who had mined in the United States (Don 1895:92) or South-East Asia (for tin or gold) and some had gained experience in Australia. Taken together then, the Chinese as a group were well prepared technologically and socially for mining in New Zealand.

By the time the Chinese arrived in southern New Zealand, European miners had discovered all the major alluvial goldfields and had been working the ground in most areas for between two and five years. In Otago the major rush was already over and hundreds of European miners had moved to the newly discovered fields on the West Coast, leaving many abandoned claims. The Chinese often moved into these areas (e.g. *Dunstan Times* 13/6/1884:2). Unlike the European miners who were generally motivated by the chance of making a big strike, the Chinese gained a reputation for patiently reworking old ground, content with a regular, if unspectacular, return (to some extent they could afford to because their cost of living was only about half that of Europeans). But the Chinese miners were not immobile. Don's records (particularly his 1896 diary) indicate that many moved periodically from one goldfield to another, often to return to one of their earlier locations years later. A consequence of their penchant for reworking old ground was that they seldom got the accolades reserved for discoverers of new goldfields, but in the circumstances, this was probably in their best interests because it was less likely to stir up European hostility. However, their reworking of old ground often drew criticism from European miners who considered the Chinese did not do any of "the hard work of prospecting" and were recovering all the gold that could be mined by Europeans at a later date. This so-called "deleterious effect of the Chinese" was emphasised by C.E. Haughton, the MHR for Wakatipu in his submission to the Select Committee (AJHR 1871 H–5:7).

Despite these criticisms, which became more vocal as anti-Chinese agitation grew, many Europeans, particularly the businessmen, considered that it was in everyone's interest that the Chinese reworked the old claims because they maintained mining returns and helped to keep local businesses viable:

> So far as persevering industry is concerned, the Mongolian is far ahead of his European neighbour. He lacks the enterprise, however, by which the other is characterised. He follows up an old scent closely, but he is nowhere at finding out a new lead. He re-works tailings, or scrapes out the refuse of an abandoned mine, and makes a good thing out of it, but it is very rarely indeed that he can be induced to venture upon untried ground. His principle appears to be that the certain prospect of small wages is better than the uncertain prospect of a large find. Even on these terms he is a valuable accession to the country. He has utilised the refuse of European mining, alike to the advantage of the place and his own personal benefit. (*Otago Daily Times* 1/10/1869:7)

An interesting insight into Chinese geomancy and their perception of the New Zealand mining environment is provided by this recorded statement. Early in his ministry to the Round Hill Chinese, Don expressed amazement to two men about the destruction of the landscape caused by sluicing. They replied that the damage was inconsequential because New Zealand had no feng shui, being *tei wan* (of earthly material), whereas China is of *tin wan* (heavenly material). They concluded that it would be improper to dig for gold in China (although China has a long goldmining tradition: see Steeves 1984:9–14), but it did not matter in New Zealand because it had been "opened" for only a few years (Don 2/10/1882:65–6).

In the early years of the Otago goldrushes, alluvial gold was easily won and it was practical for any miner to work a small claim with basic equipment such as a pan, cradle and long-handled shovel. But those bountiful times were short-lived. By about 1870, it was becoming increasingly necessary, for European and Chinese miners alike, to work the dry alluvial terraces by ground or hydraulic sluicing (refer Ritchie 1981 for descriptions of these techniques). Sluicing required cutting water races from a distant creek to bring water to a point above a claim. Usually, it was accumulated in a storage dam overnight from where it was conveyed to the work site by canvas or steel pipes. The simplest technique, ground sluicing, involved disaggregating alluvial terrace margins by saturating the ground then breaking it up with picks and shovels. Hydraulic sluicing required considerably more head (water pressure). Here the work face in a claim was broken down by the impact of a high-pressure water jet directed from a moveable nozzle. In both instances the gold was recovered by directing the water-borne mixture of soil, stones and freed gold down a channel. The gold was collected in sluice boxes or riffles in the base of the channel while the detritus was discharged downslope or into an adjacent river or stream.

A study of alluvial mining tailings showed that although the Chinese appear to have preferred some methods of working alluvial ground and stacking the waste rock (tailings) more than others, there is little evidence to indicate that the methods were used exclusively by them (Ritchie 1981). Steeves (1984), in a most useful study of Chinese mining in Oregon, USA, identified several features of mining dam construction that he considered were indicative of the Chinese building technique known as *hang-tu*, which utilises tamped earth within a wooden frame. To date, no investigations have been undertaken in New Zealand to determine if the same construction patterns are evident here. The absence of recognisable Chinese mining equipment in contemporary photographs and in museum collections points to an almost total adoption of Euro-American mining techniques and equipment by the Chinese, but appearances may be deceiving. For example, the simple pumps described earlier are small (and therefore probably difficult to recognise in photographs) and relatively fragile. It is likely their component parts would decay rapidly or be unrecognisable (as a pump) shortly after abandonment. Don described the extensive use of waterwheels by the Chinese for draining the claims at Round Hill (discussed below), but in no instance does he give an unequivocal indication of their size or capacity.

A regular supply of water was vital for mining. Study of the Cromwell Warden's Court applications for Water Rights (and Protection of Mining Claims) revealed that the first Chinese applications were processed in February 1868 for a group of four working in the Nevis (Cromwell Wardens, Court Records). Don recorded many times during his numerous visits to the Round Hill field between 1882 and 1889 that the Chinese there were either depressed or rejoicing depending on the availability of water. During dry spells, mining was either limited to a few hours per day or curtailed altogether. If the water was supplied by others, its cost varied depending on demand and the available supply. He cited an instance where a group at Round Hill paid 10/- a week for their water, which enabled nine hours of sluicing a day (Don 1/2/1883:197). In Central Otago, freezing conditions in winter often prevented mining for weeks on end, but on the other hand the lower river levels in winter provided better access to riverine deposits.

Sluicing claims were usually worked by groups of three to eight men (evidenced by numerous comments in Don's records and Wardens' Court Water Right applications submitted by groups of Chinese miners). Riverbed leases of 2–5 acres (0.8–2 hectares) extent, such as those on Big Beach in the lower Shotover, were systematically worked by small groups and companies of Chinese (OPG 1870–76). Working in groups shared the workload, provided companionship, enabled economies of scale and lessened the likelihood of theft, provocation or claim jumping. Usually, a party would be from one clan or village in China, and often shared the same hut. This was particularly so in the early days of Chinese mining, but after the 1880s, when gold was more difficult to find, there were more individual efforts.

Small parties usually rostered the job of cooking. Larger companies generally employed a cook, the food being prepared and consumed in a specialised cookhouse (see *Otago Witness* 9/10/1875). Most companies employed 10–30 men (see *Otago Witness* 9/10/1875), but 100 were reported to be working for one Chinese on the Waipori diggings (*Tuapeka Times* 1/5/1869:2) and "about 200" at Big Beach on the Lower Shotover in the 1870s (McArthur 1945:11). Although relations were generally peaceful between adjacent parties of Chinese miners, a vicious fight occurred between two rival companies at Big Beach in 1872 (*Tuapeka Times* 30/5/1872:5). Newspaper reports suggest the number of large parties who worked together declined in the mid-1870s, presumably a response to falling returns (e.g. *Arrow Observer* 19/9/1873:2–3). There were no indentured Chinese miner-labourers in New Zealand, although many had their fares paid, which they had to pay back with interest, from income earned by "self employment" or working for one of the Chinese mining companies. The solidarity built up through kin and clan links and the fact they were an oft-despised minority group resulted in a group cohesion among the Chinese that worked to their advantage – a factor that some Europeans appreciated:

> They apparently possess a spirit of organisation which enables them to overcome the many difficulties in their way, and accomplish results which would under ordinary circumstances, lie beyond them. It is the common experience of European miners that, when organisation is attempted among them, it ends in failure. European miners associated together in large numbers rarely show much discipline; if they are successful, they are apt to neglect their work and dissipate their money; if they are unsuccessful, they become dissatisfied and long for other fields. The Chinese, on the other hand, display unlimited discipline, and their work is never interfered with, whether their fortune is good or bad. A large area of ground, which has proved ruinous to European association has been shown to yield excellent results to the Chinese. (Butler 1977:39)

Most contemporary observers of the Chinese were impressed with their industry and ability to work long and hard (e.g. *Otago Witness* 9/7/1870:11, 9/10/1875). They tended to be more patient and perservering than the European miners, in part attributable to their upbringing; most came from backgrounds where they would have been used to long hours of manual work. The fact that they had a specific goal – returning wealthy to China – undoubtedly also contributed to their zeal. Don (1895:16; 1906:26; 1911:42) observed that they tended to work much longer when they were doing well, and shorter hours when they were doing badly, but so long as they had water and were making a small return, they seldom gave up before a claim was virtually exhausted (Don 1/2/1888:146, 1891:8). One group of 11 Chinese miners at Round Hill worked "shifts" and worked through the night on their claim, but according to Don (1/11/1882:87) this was unusual.

These accounts of early Chinese mining ventures near Arrowtown (one of the study sites) typify the energy and single-mindedness with which the Chinese commenced work and give an indication of some of their techniques:

> At the Arrow River the Chinese are engaged in testing the gorge, which has been repeatedly tried and abandoned in consequence of the great difficulty in reaching bottom. I consider the Chinese population are a great benefit to the district. They exhibit an amount of energy and perseverance most creditable to themselves and benefit to the community of which they form a portion… (*Otago Witness* 19/3/1870:10)

Towards the end of the year, the paper reported that there were 20 to 30 Chinese working the Arrow Flat. Originally, they had a deep tailrace running down the creek. After it was flooded, they excavated a new race through solid rock and overlaid it with large flat stones, brush, earth and rocks. They reasoned that future floods would flow over the top of the race (*Otago Witness* 15/10/1870:11):

> The bed of the Arrow was said to be worked out long ago and with the exception of one leased claim was abandoned by Europeans. John Chinaman comes and delves among the mines and finds payable gold where other people have been working before and probably fancied they had taken it all away. The Celestials appear to have taken complete possession of the riverbed and intend to systematically work it again. To accomplish this, they have constructed a tailrace nearly a mile long, and to drain the ground more effectively have provided themselves a powerful waterwheel and pumps, which keep the workings comparatively dry. The whole of the machinery is elaborately fixed, much more care having been bestowed upon it than is usually the case with Europeans. (*Otago Witness* 9/7/1870:11)

The breakup of what is believed to be the same Chinese mining company (45 men involved) was reported in the *Arrow Observer* (19/9/1873). During its four years of operation, it was purported to have spent £1,200 and built a large dam across Bush Creek (no trace of it exists today). The Chinese were good handymen and quick to learn the skills necessary for profitable mining, including making and maintaining mining tools and adopting suitable methods for efficiently working various types of mining ground. Some of the Chinese settlements had their own blacksmiths. Don recorded an instance where a group of Chinese was amused by the fact that European miners working nearby did not even sharpen their own picks, instead taking them into Queenstown (Don 1891:8). The Chinese at Round Hill considered the chopping of firewood, cutting of mining timber, bailing water and other maintenance tasks was *haan* (trifling or leisure) work (Don 2/10/1882:67).

Table 3.6, devised from information in the NZ Census, outlines the types of mining the Chinese were involved in. "Alluvial mining" is believed to refer to riverine placer mining as opposed to "sluicing", which although it was often carried out on riverbanks, was more often undertaken on dry terraces using water conveyed considerable distances in races. Newspaper reports indicate the Chinese continued to work the banks of the major rivers, particularly around Cromwell, long after the European miners had abandoned them (e.g. *Dunstan Times* 4/9/1874:2; *Cromwell Argus* 22/5/1877:5, 22/10/1878:4; *Tuapeka Times* 12/5/1880:3; 14/7/1880:2).

As is apparent in Table 3.6, few Chinese were involved in quartz reef mining. The Canton claim at Waipori became the only established Chinese quartz mine in Otago, if not New Zealand (the Canton battery is a notable surviving relic), although there are records that Chinese companies took out claims but never worked them on the Carrick (Hangar pers. comm.) and at Macetown (*Arrow Observer* 27/9/1879). Sew Hoy invested in European reef claims at Macetown but was not actively involved in working them (Agnew and Agnew 2020).

There was only one major Chinese dredging venture, that of the Dunedin Chinese entrepreneur, Sew Hoy, in conjunction with European businessmen (Hearn and Hargreaves 1985:12). In 1889, his Shotover Big Beach Company, in an innovative move, placed four small gold dredges on the relatively shallow Lower Shotover River, which had previously not been dredged. He employed skilled European engineers and Chinese labourers (Ng 1984b). The initial success of the operation was exaggerated by the press. Within a year the company was in liquidation and the dredges sold (Salmon 1963:232), but his entrepreneurship stimulated the "first dredging boom" in Otago (Hearn and Hargreaves 1985:12). The resourceful Sew Hoy (possibly the most unrecognised entrepreneur in 19th-century New Zealand) also established a hydraulic sluicing claim on nearby Star Beach. Upon the winding up of this enterprise, he used the experience he had gained to found the longest lived of all Chinese mining ventures in New Zealand, the Nokomai Hydraulic Sluicing Company. This operation also started in 1889, initially working ground near Garston, then moved to the Lion Flat on Nokomai station in 1926 and "finally accepted defeat in 1943" (Hearn and Hargreaves 1985:273, 279; Ng 1984b; Agnew and Agnew 2020).

An advertisement for the Cromwell Gold Dredging Company lists six Chinese storekeepers (Won Kee, Wing Lee, Kum Wing, Chin Tack, Ah Wing and Chin Loon) among the shareholders (*Cromwell Argus* 23/12/1884:2). With money on their side, it was easier for Chinese merchants to straddle the gap between the European and Chinese "worlds". Ironically, the Directors of the Golden Reward Gold Dredging Company (Lower Clutha River) used the fact that "seven Chinamen had made enough profit from this place to go home to China" as one of their key justifications in support of the profitability of the claim (the prospectus is reproduced in Hearn and Hargreaves 1985:33).

In local histories and popular books that refer to Chinese mining in New Zealand (e.g. Butler 1977:40), it is oft quoted that the Chinese had a general aversion to tunnelling and invariably went to great lengths to avoid it by "daylighting", i.e. digging deep open-cut trenches rather than tunnelling into a seam. While it is true that the Chinese had minimal involvement in hard rock reef mining, necessity seems to have overcome whatever inherent fears they had about tunnelling in some areas such as Round Hill where the technique was used extensively:

On this part of the creek most of the mines are in the shape of tunnels into the side of the hill, the washdirt being brought out in wheelbarrows. A stream of water comes from some higher region and performs a double office, first turning a large waterwheel which keeps the mine dry by giving motion to a curious kind of pump. (Don 1/7/1882:7)

The traditional enmity between the Hakkas ("Strangers" who moved into southern China from northern areas c.1740) and the Poontis (who considered themselves the "Natives" although they too had come from the north earlier) was maintained in New Zealand and they seldom worked together (partly because most of the NZ Chinese were Poontis), but Don recorded an instance where some members of both groups had made a mutually beneficial accommodation:

There is near here [Adams Flat in the Tuapeka area] a claim worked by three of each. The Hakkas are famous for their deep-sinking skill; the Poontis like to work an open claim. Here the three Hakkas sink and drive, while their Poonti mates do the hauling and washing. (Don 1896:47)

Waterwheels were a common feature on the Ourawera Creek area of the Round Hill field. They were constantly at work dewatering the tunnels and claims (Don 2/10/1882:67, 1/12/1882:104). Most claimholders "washed up" once, if not twice weekly (Don 1/9/1883:46). Quicksilver (mercury) was widely used for gold recovery (Don 1/12/1882:105). Evidence of mercury was found in two of the study sites (see Section 5.5.5). Dynamite and rock drills were occasionally used to shift boulders, but large boulders were usually propped up and worked around. The Chinese used wing dams extensively to divert creeks and rivers (*Otago Witness* 9/10/1875; Don 1897;13). The wing dams, built of wood or stone or a combination of both (see Ritchie 1981), were used to divert a river's flow either against a bank so it could be broken down and worked or to dewater one side of a creek bed so that the other side could be dry-worked. Many of the Chinese wing dams in Central Otago, particularly those made from alignments of vertically placed schist slabs, are very durable and, although they are frequently buried and re-exposed, have survived numerous floods.

Some Chinese made their living by "scavenging" – rewashing the tailings from claims belonging to others (Don 1/12/1882:105). Those involved in "scavenging" either could not afford to buy a claim or were driven to it by economic necessity. In October 1883, several parties of two, three or four men were working the tailings at the lower end of the Round Hill field, "a sure sign of the decadence of a goldfield" (Don 1/10/1883:67). After riverine mining declined, "beachcombers" continued to work the banks when the rivers were low. In 1893–94, the "majority of the miners near Roxburgh were beachcombers" Don (1894:35).

Accidental deaths occurred occasionally, usually due to the collapse of over-steepened mining faces. If a miner was killed, his house and the claim were abandoned. Don recorded a few instances where houses were also burnt down because they were on auriferous ground, or they were considered unsafe because they were too close to working areas (e.g. Don 1/2/1883:146, 148).

3.7.4 MINING EARNINGS

According to the *Otago Daily Times* (1/10/1869:7), "Dunedin (and the Otago goldfields) enjoys the reputation (among the Chinese) of being the best spot in the Australasian Colonies for making money in a short time, the native agents impressing this idea on those of their countrymen wishing to immigrate". Although the claim smacks of propaganda and it took longer than most anticipated, the fact that over 60% of the Chinese returned home within 10 years suggests that Chinese mining in New Zealand was successful by any standards.

Most of the Chinese miners were under considerable familial pressure to send money home regularly (for examples of letters see Butler 1977:49, and discussion in Sections 2.3 and 5.6.2). Often these expectations were not fulfilled (or not regularly enough as far as the kin were concerned) because miners' incomes fluctuated widely depending on circumstances such as their energy, health, luck and personal competence, the availability of water and the nature of a claim. In addition to fulfilling their familial obligations, there was a general desire among the miners to earn £100 so they could return to China and improve their status by establishing a business, acquire a fine house or buy a small plot of land. An informative record of the Chinese miners' earnings was left by Don (see Table 3.7). While he was based at Riverton, he often acted as an intermediary in financial transactions for the Chinese and frequently commented on the amounts and nature of remittances in his "Our Chinese Mission" notes. They not only provide insights into the overall earnings of the miners but also those of merchants and gamblers.

3.7.5 MINING OFFENCES

Frequently alleged or substantiated crimes committed by the Chinese are discussed in Section 3.9.3. Here, discussion is limited to offences specifically associated with mining, which constituted the major area of Chinese crime. Interestingly, some offences were virtually peculiar to the Chinese, such as offering bribes to subvert the course of justice, calling bogus witnesses, swapping mining licenses and selling spurious or adulterated gold (*Otago Witness* 6/8/1870:3; Don 1/12/1883:106; *West Coast Times* 1/10/1889:18; Butler 1977:61–4) and the old perennial "robbing tailraces". The latter offence was not the sole preserve of the Chinese, and there were instances where one group of Chinese alleged other Chinese had robbed their tailrace (Don 1/12/1883:105). Many Chinese were prepared to take the gamble of being caught without a miner's right (*Otago Witness* 18/5/1867:7). Consequently, usually following agitation from European miners, the police would make periodic raids on the Chinese mining areas, usually resulting in the conviction of many Chinese miners for not having a mining right.

One investigation in 1871 resulted in the Chinese paying a total of £980 in fines (*Otago Witness* 2/12/1871:15). Only 47 out of 253 Chinese miners at Waikaia had mining rights (*Dunstan Times* 26/8/1881:2). A report in the *West Coast Times* (10/2/1882) indicated that of 394 Chinese known to be goldmining on the coast, only 120 (30%) had miners' rights. Don outlined why some men didn't have licences:

> Nine Chinese were summoned before the warden [on 5/6/1883 at Riverton] for mining without licenses. Seven appeared and were each fined 20/-, excepting "a poor, old, and out of work man" who was fined 10/-. The costs amounted to 13/4 each, and they were ordered to take out licenses at once, making a total disbursement of £2/13/4d each. This is a large sum under the circumstances, for all of the men, with one exception, are only prospectors or "scavengers", being out of regular employment. They said to me "If we had claims we wouldn't risk working without licenses for fear of our claim being "jumped". (Don 1/8/1883:25)

Some Chinese swapped miners' rights, it being difficult for the European police to determine if the Chinese claimant had actually paid for the right he presented. To get around such difficulties, a Chinese police constable was stationed on the Round Hill field for a short period in 1883 to catch thieves, gamblers and those without miners' rights, but his mission was singularly unsuccessful because he was too well known and the illegal activities ceased when he was around (Don 1/12/1883:105).

There are several recorded instances of Chinese attempting to sell spurious or adulterated gold (*Tuapeka Times* 18/4/1872:5; Butler 1977:61). One counterfeiter was reported to have arrived on the second shipload of Chinese in 1866 but was identified, apprehended and returned to Australia (*Otago Daily Times* 8/6/1871:3). The manufacture of spurious or adulterated gold was considered a serious offence on the goldfields and deterrent sentences were imposed, as, for example, this case from the West Coast illustrates:

> The spurious gold manufactured by the Chinaman [Ah Sung] at Blue Spur and exhibited in Court yesterday was most ingeniously wrought. He had broken off pieces of an old copper plate, a piece of steel, and some brassware, partially fused, then painted them with gold paint... If mixed with a quantity of other gold it is very easy to believe the fraud would never be discovered... The Bench sentenced the accused to six months imprisonment with hard labour, holding that the

offence, especially on a goldfield was a most serious one. (*West Coast Times* 1/10/1889:18)

The Chinese were frequently accused of trying to influence the decision of court hearings in their favour by offering bribes or calling false witnesses. These practices were apparently quite prevalent in southern China due to the breakdown in law and order during the 19th century. Although it was not a major problem in New Zealand, clearly some Chinese thought it would work here (see Butler 1977:62–3 for some instances). Such practices were often motivated by a desire to protect a fellow clansman (Don 1/2/1884:148).

Thefts from tailraces, either by persons driven through desperate circumstances or succumbing to the temptation of making "easy money", were a perennial problem on the goldfields and caused a lot of ill feeling. Although the practice was by no means restricted to members of the Chinese population, from the outset, suspected thefts were frequently blamed on them by Europeans. When Chinese were caught "red-handed", the ensuing court cases usually attracted considerable publicity. Some instances: the *Otago Witness* (2/12/1871:10) reported that Ho Chew was beaten up by a European (who was acquitted) after being caught stealing gold from the latter's tailrace. It was claimed in court "that very few tailraces had not been plundered by the Chinese". Butler (1977:64) outlined an incident at St Bathans where a Chinese miner, Ah Cheow, was shot by a European, John Ewing, while attempting to get away after being caught washing the gold-collecting cloths from the European's sluice boxes. The Chinese man was sentenced to three months in prison, the judge remarking that he would have passed a more severe sentence but he looked on the wound as some form of punishment. Ewing was charged with shooting with intent to cause grievous bodily harm. The European community at Naseby banded together to pay his fine.

However, this particular crime was not committed solely against Europeans. Don recorded an instance where he believed two "out of work" Chinese had pilfered an elderly Chinese man's sluice box and stolen the yield of three weeks' work (Don 1/10/1883:67). In another incident he was told by a group of Chinese (in the "Concord of Mankind" store at Round Hill) that the tail boxes of some of the Europeans had been robbed recently and they were blaming the Chinese. The Chinese expressed the wish that the offenders would be discovered because they claimed their own tail boxes had been robbed "over and over again" and they did not know whether the culprits were Chinese or Europeans (Don 2/10/1882:67).

Don considered that "thieving – in one form or another" was the cause of most imprisonments of Chinese in New Zealand (Don 1893:17) but that thieving and breaking and entering houses was much more common when there were "many out of work" (Don 1/10/1883:67). Occasionally, the Chinese miners lost their claims when they were ordered by the courts to be disposed of by public auction to repay creditors. Don expressed his concern that the placards advertising such sales were only printed in English and that consequently, neither debtors nor their friends could understand what was happening until it was too late (Don 1/1/1883:127).

3.8 SOCIAL AND RELIGIOUS EVENTS

3.8.1 TEMPLES AND RELIGION

The Chinese miners did not strictly subscribe to any particular religion, but most adhered to a complex mixture of beliefs and customs drawn from the three major religious doctrines in China – Confucianism, Buddhism and Taoism – as well as animism and spiritism (Don 1/11/1882:88). The latter were responsible for the Chinese's strong belief in the supernatural. Very few of the miners doubted the existence of evil spirits and demons and strictly maintained customs designed to placate them. Ancestor worship and obeisance to various other gods often represented by clay, wooden or stone figurines were important too (Butler 1977:75–9). For further insights into the all-pervasive role of religion in a South China village see Kulp (1972:284–314).

Many Chinese on the goldfields maintained small shrines in their huts, emulating those in the larger temples (discussed below) at Round Hill and Lawrence. Two gods, commonly represented by "images", were Kwan Ti (the god of war) and Hung Shing (the god of the South Seas), but there were also numerous others that Don observed in houses including the "Goddess of Mercy" and the "North God" as well as ancestral shrines with offerings (Don 1897:44–5; 1911:16). The presence of "images" and the selling of materials such as incense, candles and paper money upset Don because he considered them idolatrous practices (Don 1/2/1887:147). Don thought idolatry became more prevalent and had more active appeal as the Chinese population decreased. It may have been a response to increasing deprivation and loneliness. Evidence of the maintenance of traditional religious beliefs was documented by Don (1897:16) when he noted that a Chinese miner, on being told another had become a Christian, stated "If he has decided not to return to China, it will be alright", implying that if the convert did return his new religion would be unacceptable.

There were two major Chinese temples on the southern goldfields. The first was established in Lawrence in September 1869. Contemporary accounts described it as a "joss house" and noted its inauguration was celebrated with fireworks and mass brandy drinking. Many Europeans attended the party (*Tuapeka Times* 25/9/1869:3). The chief "joss house" at Lawrence differed in that it had a large "happiness character" and the inscription "The Seat of the Ancestor's Spirit" painted on one end wall rather than a painted or carved image (Don 1893:20). The other temple was established at Round Hill in 1883. It was dedicated to Kwan Ti, the god of war, and had an elaborate painting of the god with his two attendants as a centrepiece (Don 1891:5). The temples were built and maintained with money raised by subscriptions solicited from the miners in the area. Don recorded one occasion when subscriptions were sought for the repair of three temples in the village of Great Cypress Hill in China (Don 1/10/1887:63).

By 1889, Dunedin had the largest Chinese population (c. 240) of any centre in Otago and Don was transferred there. After eight years of operating from a rented hall, he had the satisfaction of seeing a (Presbyterian) Chinese church erected in Walker St, the heart of the Chinese enclave. European Christians contributed £444, while 887 Chinese contributed £174.

3.8.2 THE ROLE OF FESTIVALS AND CELEBRATIONS

The celebration of festivals, usually governed by important events in the lunar year, was and still is an important part of the Chinese way of life. Besides the obvious recreational and celebratory aspects, they are important socially as a time of markedly increased consumerism and mobility. On the goldfields, the main festival occasions involved short-term "migrations" to settlements where celebrations were being held.

Three main festivals were held each year. Although, like their European counterparts, they had religious significance, feasting and partaking of recreational activities such as gambling and opium smoking were the main activities. The Chinese New Year in February was the main festival in the annual cycle and involved several days of holiday. Big feasts were held in each of the Chinese settlements, pigs would be killed and eaten and Chinese delicacies consumed in abundance. Vast amounts of red paper were used during the festival to signify good luck. Red paper inscriptions were pasted on doors and walls, letters were written on red paper, delivered in red envelopes and stamped with red ink. Presents were wrapped in red paper. The New Year festival was the one time, according to Don, when Poonti and Hakka, Seyip and Sam Yap men were all friends. During the festival the Chinese visited each other as well as attending to the old tradition of paying one's debts. Firecrackers were often let off to discourage demons from entering houses, but local ordinances ensured that the amount of noise and revelry in the goldfield towns was very limited compared to the "commotion" during these festival celebrations in China (Don 2/4/1883:184).

A Dunedin newspaper (quoted by Butler 1977:80) gave the following description of a Chinese New Year celebration in Dunedin:

> The Chinese New Year was made the occasion of general rejoicing on Friday by the Celestials resident in Dunedin. The morning was ushered in with the beating of tom-toms and the firing-off of crackers. A great feast was then prepared in Flinders Lane, off Stafford Street, where the tables were laid out with "every delicacy of the season" in the way of fruits, jellies, wines etc and poultry without number… The guests did ample justice to the good things provided.

Festivals were a time for "letting off steam" and relaxing. At Round Hill, "the merry-making" consisted mainly of playing dominoes, cards, billiards or *fan-tan* (Don 1/3/1884:163). The following account, which reveals as much about European prejudices as the observed, provides some interesting insights. The event was the Chinese New Year celebration at Arrowtown:

> For the past week, Arrowtown has been the centre of attraction for about 200 Chinese (about five times the town's normal Chinese population), who have made the night hideous with their exploding crackers, and their disgusting presence felt in more ways than one. On Sunday night last, even Europeans, and we believe females at that, were to be seen playing "fan-tan", while every night for a week, the Chinese stores have been the scenes of indescribable vice and repulsive practices. The opium-pipe too, we hear, has been freely dispensed, even to little boys. Several people were seen under the influence of brandy, and altogether the Chinese Camp has been the sink of iniquity for days and nights past. It seems strange that Europeans should so far forget themselves as to mingle freely with almond eyed, leprosy tainted, filthy Chinamen, but the fact is disgusting and lamentable as it may appear. (*Tuapeka Times* 11/3/1885:2)

The second most important holiday after New Year was the summer solstice celebration ("Tung-chi", also known as Dongzhi or Xiazhi), which took place on the day the sun was the furthest south of the equator (c. 22 December). In China it is called the winter solstice. Don (quoted in Butler 1977:81) described a summer solstice celebration thus:

> Nearly all have roast duck or fowl with brandy and nicknacks to supplement their rice. Lonely diggers go to towns and keep the feast at the shops they patronise or call upon the nearest neighbors that are celebrating at home. As it occurred on the 21st or 22nd of December, the Europeans call it "Chinese Christmas" while Xmas is known to the Chinese as the "Foreign Winter Solstice Festival".

Most of the Chinese festivals were celebrated at Riverton where there were three major shops that provided lavish fare for their clients (Don 1/9/1882:43). For example, the "All Souls" (or Zhongyuan) festival was a slightly more religious event held in mid-December. Don (1893:2) described one:

Out of 140 Chinese at Round Hill in 1892, 91 were subscribers to the "All Souls' Feast". Each man subscribed 6/6d and obtained a set of clothing (pants, hat, shirt, socks, and a handkerchief costing a total of 3/16/6d) which were burnt at the graves of 15 men. The purpose of the feast [according to Don] was to feed and clothe the doubles of the dead; but beyond a bottle or two of brandy poured out, a dozen or two eggs broken, and some rice scattered over the graves, the balance of the 29/11/6d subscribed went to railway fares to Riverton and a big dinner…

Zhongyuan rituals were undertaken to pacify "unattended ghosts that might otherwise be maligned". The rituals involved burning paper clothes and money and making libations to satisfy the needs of the ghosts (Willmott 1970:93).

The Ching Ming (or Worship of the Tombs) was an annual pilgrimage undertaken on about 4 April to the graveyard of the ancestors. Relatives visit the graves and provide food, money and (paper) clothing, and clean the graves, if necessary. In one instance, Don observed (Don 1/8/1884:24) it seemed to be a relatively informal event: "The Chinese went to the cemetery in wagonettes", lit small bundles of incense, offered hard-boiled eggs and apples (which they later removed for human consumption) and poured out some brandy. It was all over in 10 minutes, the Chinese having re-entered the vehicles and returned to Riverton where they "interpreted T'sing Ming by eating, drinking and gambling" (Don 1/8/1884:24). The miners from Round Hill visited the Riverton cemetery too, although not all miners quit work on this day, since some had no tombs of friends to worship or clean, did not desire to go, or perhaps could not afford the 10/- per man for the feast (Don 1/8/1884:24). One shop at Riverton did some £50 worth of business during a Ching Ming celebration, entertaining 100 men who ate heartily and, according to the shopkeeper, drank considerable amounts of brandy.

The other main religious celebration was the "Autumnal Equinox" or "Moon Festival" (held from c. 23 September for a fortnight until the full moon). This was marked by consumption of "moon cakes", which continued and increased until the full moon. According to Don (1/11/1884:85): "The former delicate occupants of refreshment-house shelves: pork and sugar dumplings, bean curd cakes, bean jam pies etc. – must bow before this 'king', this 'mooncake'… a conglomeration of nice things – pork fat, sugar, melon seeds, sesamum, olive seeds, and almonds – the whole enclosed in a beautifully browned, crisp crust…" Other festivals were celebrated in a similar way, including Ch'ung Yeung (the "Kite Flying Festival"; Don 1/1/1883:128), the "Dragon Boat Festival" (Don 1/8/1883:25), the "Weaver Girl" Festival (celebrated mainly by women and girls in China but a good excuse for the miners to "knock off" work early; Don 1/11/1884:84) and Four-tea's (the land god's) birthday (Don 1/6/1883:225).

There seems to have been little variation from one mining area to another in the way the festivals were celebrated. All festivals involved feasting and drinking, usually letting off crackers, and sometimes food was offered at shrines in individuals' huts before being consumed. If they could afford to, most men took the day(s) off. The days for celebrating the various festivals were determined by reference to the Chinese Almanac, which was always imported and provided the dates for the following year's celebrations. It also indicated "auspicious days" for doing various activities (Don 1/1/1885:125; 1894:10).

3.9 DISCRIMINATION, INTERNAL WRANGLING AND CRIME

3.9.1 DISCRIMINATION

From the day the Chinese set foot in New Zealand, almost all would experience varying levels of harassment and verbal abuse from Europeans. Contemporary newspaper reports and Don's writings chronicle an almost continuous anti-Chinese sentiment that varied only in intensity, duration and nature from one place to another. Within a few years there were calls for, and the eventual passing of, a series of legislative restrictions (see Section 2.3) aimed at discouraging Chinese immigration. The main grounds were fear of economic competition and racial intolerance. However, the legislative restrictions were a relatively late event; intolerance and anti-Chinese sentiments were expressed in many forms right from the outset:

1. The Chinese frequently suffered jeering, name calling and revilement as they landed from ships or passed through established European communities on their way to the goldfields and were commonly ridiculed in cartoons and denigrated in reports in contemporary newspapers. Anti-Chinese behaviour by Europeans was often condoned by European society, or no effort was made to speak out against it. They were also made the butt of cruel practical jokes (Don 1896:20; Charteris 1973; Gilkinson 1978:129–30).
2. The Chinese were frequently excluded or strongly discouraged from establishing in certain towns or areas. Some examples follow. At Lawrence the council passed a resolution that they did not want Chinese in the borough (Chandler pers. comm.). They were not prohibited as is often claimed, although the council resolution encouraged the Chinese to "set up camp" just outside the borough boundary (*Otago Daily Times* 1/10/1869:7). The writer of the same report marvelled that they had established themselves in "the very heart of the disaffected (with the Chinese) country" (*Otago Daily Times* 1/10/1869:7). Europeans opposed all attempts by the Chinese to

acquire claims at Orepuki on the Foveaux coast (Don 1/6/1883:225), and although the Chinese in the Nevis were later to outnumber Europeans two to one, initially they received a hostile reaction:

> The most remarkable event that has transpired…has been the visit of a party of Chinamen who came to spy out the nakedness of the land. Having first inspected the lower portion of the district (the Nevis Valley), they proceeded to Upper Nevis en route to Switzers, via Nokomai. They camped the evening near Whetto's Creek… But their slumbers were of short duration; for no sooner did the news of Johns' arrival get to the ears of the resident miners, than they rose en masse at the dead hour of night and drove the unwelcome visitors down the gorge in the direction of the lower Nevis; but whether the Chinese were otherwise maltreated by the barbarians is more than your correspondent can state. Suffice, it is to say, that they passed here the following morning at break of day in a state of fear and trembling, and half drowned. When last seen the Celestials were retreating towards the Kawarau at a jog trot. (*Otago Witness* 8/12/1867:11)

3. Physical violence towards the Chinese miners in New Zealand did not reach the levels of brutality experienced in California and Victoria. On those goldfields there are several recorded instances of European miners going on rampages through Chinese settlements, often resulting in killings, arson or forced departures (Preshaw 1888: 38; Chinn et al. 1969; Gittins 1981:91–106; Wegars 1985). However, the Chinese in New Zealand still experienced considerable harassment, such that within two years of the first arrivals (see Section 2.3) the Superintendent of the Otago Provincial Council felt compelled to issue a proclamation enjoining the police to keep watch over the Chinese in their districts and reaffirm the council's promise of protection (*Otago Witness* 8/12/1867:5). But as increasing numbers of Chinese miners became established, harassment intensified, particularly in Otago. Some instances can be regarded as examples of goldfields justice, e.g. the beating up of Chinese caught or suspected of stealing gold from tailraces, but most recorded in the contemporary press had a clearly racist motive, e.g. the *Otago Witness* (2/4/1870:10) reported that a Chinese hut in Moonlight Creek (a tributary of the Shotover River) and its inhabitants had been bombarded with large rocks and an unsuccessful attempt was made to burn the structure (it failed because the thatch was green). But a new hut being built by the same Chinese party at a site about three kilometres away was burnt down.

In 1888, several Chinese were assaulted in Dunedin (*Otago Daily Times* 3/1/1888); a Chinese market garden was plundered in Auckland (*New Zealand Herald* 13 and 16/3/1888) and an estimated 300–400 Europeans jeered and jostled Chinese landing at Dunedin (*Otago Daily Times* 9/5/1888:2). This kind of anti-Chinese violence continued in Dunedin, but the courts seem to have taken a dim view of it and severely punishers offenders (Don 20/9/1892). In a rather unusual move, a European, after witnessing "about a dozen hoodlums set upon and throw stones at a lone Chinese man in Bradshaw Street, South Dunedin", suggested that Messrs Lo Keong and Sew Hoy (leading Chinese merchants in Dunedin) be made "Chinese magistrates" (*Otago Daily Times* 2/4/1898:6).

4. Possibly the most distressing anti-Chinese behaviour in some areas involved frequent instances of larrikinism perpetuated by young European males against the Chinese in their settlements and camps. It was a form of entertainment for the perpetrators and involved a group wandering through the local Chinese camp (or throwing missiles from a high vantage point) and smashing windows and doors and deliberately breaking their basic possessions. Alexandra and Cromwell were two of the worst areas for this type of behaviour (Roebuck pers. comm.). In Cromwell, vandals' attacks on the huts in the Chinese settlement occurred so often that even small windows were dispensed with and the settlement was never left unattended. All the huts had strong chains and padlocks on the doors (Roebuck pers. comm.). Don chronicled this series of particularly nasty attacks against the Chinese in Alexandra in 1896:

> The three principal Chinese houses in the town had twice been attacked by a mob of twenty to thirty Europeans, who with stones and shovels broke windows; twenty pounds worth of fluming belonging to one party of four had been smashed four times in a short space; a man on the very eve of intended return to China had gone 5 miles to collect a small debt and was not seen again; another living in a cave had been tied hand and foot, his bedding and clothing fired, and himself left to roast alive; an inoffensive old man working his cradle was asked to show some gold, and on refusal had his queue cut off close to the head with a pocket knife; another returned from 10 days prospecting on the Fraser to find his few belongings – bedding, clothing etc, some 5 pounds worth – burnt outright; three others at work some distance from their caves, found on return that these had been entered, and all the contents smashed or burnt; two others had several times been fired at from bullet-loaded

guns, and a number of smaller outrages had been committed. (Don 1897:18–19)

The persecution at this level usually lasted only a few months because the offenders were eventually apprehended by the police. But the harassment achieved one of its apparent objectives: "the majority of the Chinese in the township moved out and rebuilt some distance off, leaving the select Europeans in undisputed possession…" (Don 1897:21).

5. Another form of harassment involved the "jumping" of Chinese mining claims by Europeans. Don reported it was a common occurrence at Round Hill (Don 1/2/1888:106). However, in many of these incidents the Chinese could have had legal redress if they had a miner's licence, which many did not bother with or claimed they could not afford them.
6. Blaming or accusing the local Chinese whenever there was an unsolved crime reflected another aspect of the widespread anti-Chinese sentiment on the goldfields. They were convenient scapegoats because they were powerless to defend themselves from such accusations. When taken to trial, they were almost invariably acquitted because they were not guilty (Parcell 1976:149). Sometimes there was a collective response to serious crimes. For example, in 1867 Chinese storekeepers in Lawrence offered a reward if the murderer of a Chinese miner was brought to justice (*Otago Witness* 15/6/1867:9). When disputes went to court or a Chinese man was committed for trial, it was widely thought by Europeans that the Chinese pretended ignorance of the English language (although a Chinese interpreter was generally present) and consequently got off lightly. On the other hand, many Chinese felt that European courts were biased against them (Don 1/4/1885:184); this matter came to a head in 1872 with the well-publicised attempt by the Chinese in the Wakatipu area to have Warden Beetham dismissed (see Section 2.3).
7. News of the often volatile meetings of European miners and workers calling for restrictions on Chinese immigration did not escape the Chinese. After 1870 there was a growing concern and insecurity among the Chinese population because they feared they would be suddenly evicted from New Zealand, although at least one was "quite happy to go if the government paid his fare" (Don 1/11/1882:87). Besides the series of legislative restrictions on immigration that were eventually imposed, several other attempts were made to introduce legislation or petition the New Zealand Parliament for further impositions on the Chinese (see Appendix 7). They include the *Chinese Miners Exclusion Act 1882*, which was not passed; the *Old Age Pension Act of 1896*, which specifically excluded Chinese (and other Asiatics); and considerable lobbying in the 1890s and after the turn of the century by the Trades and Labour Council and the "Knights of Labour" movement, which maintained a close scrutiny on Chinese traders (particularly those in the Wellington area), supposedly "to keep an eye" on trading practices and unemployment but their activities were really directed at building a case for further anti-Chinese legislation (Sedgewick 1982:192).
8. In addition to the calls of the workers, several, generally short-lived, racist pressure groups were formed in the main cities in the latter part of the 19th century and added their own anti-Chinese propaganda. Foremost among them was the White Race League, which was unashamedly pro-white and among other things sought to educate the public to patronise European stores only ("whites should only trade with whites") and passed a resolution that intermarriage between Europeans and Chinese, or other Asiatics, should be prohibited by law. The League was in part motivated by a desire to stop the dominance of the fruit and vegetable trade by the Chinese (Sedgewick 1982:192).

3.9.2 INTERNAL WRANGLING

Although most of the difficulties experienced by the Chinese in New Zealand were not of their own making, some were. The overseas Chinese maintained strong affiliations with their home counties. The two largest and most organised groups were the Poon Yue and the Jung Sing. These groups formed most of the early Chinese settlers in New Zealand. Don found the Seyip people, a third group, the least friendly, both towards him and other Chinese, and for many years he was obliged to hold separate meetings for them in some localities, e.g. Roxburgh (Don 1901:25). However, as time went on and the numbers of Chinese on the goldfields declined, more peaceful relations were established between the groups (Don 1906:14).

Sedgewick (1982:151–2) outlined an instance where a Chinese man (the Chinese catechist at Lawrence in 1889, Kwok Wai-shang) gained unanimous disapproval by speaking out in public about his countrymen. Although he was misquoted, he had violated an unwritten rule among the Chinese here that one never spoke out on behalf of the community unless it was legitimised by a whole group, or unless one had status and wealth on one's side. This limited such voicing to merchants, and even they seldom spoke out on behalf of the whole community.

3.9.3 CRIMES

The anti-Chinese sentiment led to many extravagant claims by Europeans of "Chinese crimes and faults". The object of most of these claims was to further the cause of the anti-Chinese immigration lobby. Thus there were regular claims that the Chinese were "a dissolute race", "would not assimilate", "were robbing the nation's inheritance and taking it all back to China", "had low moral standards" (inferred because of the absence of women), "simply dogged the footsteps of Europeans to plunder their tailraces", "did not buy from European traders" and even "misappropriated cats for gastronomic purposes" (*Otago Daily Times* 1/10/1869:7). More objective reports, notably the submissions from the mining wardens and the police presented to the 1871 Select Committee on Chinese Immigration, indicate the claims were almost totally unfounded and that the Chinese were generally more law abiding than their European counterparts (AJHR 1871 H–5; for examples, see Butler 1977:65).

Of course, there were some "law breakers" among the Chinese (excluding gambling, which although unlawful was common practice among the Chinese and largely ignored by the police – see Section 3.3). As discussed in Section 3.7.5, Chinese individuals were convicted for a range of mining offences, some of which, like the selling of spurious gold, were almost unique to the Chinese. In addition, domestic squabbles, disputes over mining claims and other grievances occurred regularly between Chinese groups and individuals and were usually dealt with by the local warden's or magistrate's courts (e.g. Don 1/7/1884:3, 1/4/1886:182). Don considered theft was the most prevalent Chinese crime and documented several examples of dishonesty (Don 1/8/1883:25, 1/11/1884:44, 1893:17). Occasionally some "disputes" led to violence. In the Cromwell area, "they first made history with the arrest of Ah Chong for the murder of Ah Hang at Kawarau Gorge, although he was later found not guilty" (Parcel 1976:149). In a later incident, a Chinese man was convicted of trying to burn down another man's hut in the Chinese settlement at Cromwell (*Cromwell Argus* 24/9/1889).

3.10 CHINESE GOLDFIELD MEDICINE, HEALTH AND BELIEFS

The Chinese who came to New Zealand initially were generally young and in good health. Few with disabilities or known medical problems would want to leave their homeland and endure poor health in a remote and foreign land. But having to contend with cramped conditions and poor food on the voyage to New Zealand, some developed deficiency diseases and other complaints before they landed.

Calls that the Chinese were introducing "bad diseases" (especially leprosy) into New Zealand, upon investigation, proved largely unfounded (further ammunition in the clamour for immigration restrictions). The 1871 Select Committee asked three European doctors who were working on the goldfields to comment on "whether the introduction of Chinese is likely to prejudice the health of the people of the colony, by the introduction of infectious diseases, or... prejudicial moral effects". All replied with words to the effect that the Chinese were remarkably healthy, no infectious diseases had come to their notice (they considered the so-called "Chinese leprosy" was non-contagious), and as the Chinese and Europeans had so little social interaction, morality issues were not a problem (AJHR 1871 H–5:25).

Although the larger Chinese settlements on the goldfields were comparatively crowded and lacked "modern" hygiene facilities, there is little evidence that the Chinese miners were less concerned about personal hygiene or appearance than their European counterparts (see Section 5.6.5). This comment by a European observer puts the comparative degree of sanitation in perspective:

> The buildings [in the Lawrence Chinese Camp] are wedged a trifle too closely together to suit modern ideas of good ventilation and sanitary improvement. Still the want of such scientific aids to domestic comfort is not unprecedented in the history of goldfields settlement, consequently their absence in this case does not strike the mind as being at all unusual. (*Otago Daily Times* 1/20/1869:7)

There were no major disease outbreaks (like the 1890s typhoid outbreak in European Cromwell; Votes and Proceedings, OPG 1874:127) in any of the Chinese settlements on the Central Otago goldfields, which suggests that camp hygiene levels belied outward appearances. Negative descriptions of Chinese camp hygiene usually refer to the Lawrence Chinese Camp, e.g. "...scattered around with a fine disregard for sanitation there were ash-pits, cess-pools, pigsties, fowl houses and wells" (*Tuapeka Times* 1883, quoted by Mayhew 1949:90). However, the Lawrence camp was almost certainly an extraordinary case. It was the first Chinese settlement to be established in Central Otago and was by far the largest (300 plus residents). In the absence of a major river nearby (rivers and riverbanks were commonly used for effluent and rubbish disposal), it probably had more visible unsanitary situations than Chinese settlements elsewhere on the goldfields.

With their overriding distrust of European doctors and hospital treatment, the Chinese had four courses of response to medical afflictions:

1. The first can be summed up by the phrase "grin and bear it". Some Chinese just ignored or lived with disfiguring medical conditions which in Don's opinion could have been easily cured by European medicine. However, they often self-diagnosed and suppressed internal pains with European patent medicines (most of which were opiate and alcohol based; see Section 5.1).

2. Some among the Chinese had considerable knowledge or a pharmacopoeia of age-old traditional cures and medicine formulations unknown to Europeans. Although some have been disclaimed by European research, they often produced the desired result. Many of the Chinese stores stocked a large range of imported items for formulating medicines. Don described part of the contents of a Chinese medicine chest that he examined at Round Hill. While informative, his comments clearly reflect his

own sensibilities and the general Western ignorance of Chinese medicines:

> I looked through a medicine chest at the "Exalted Arrival" shop. The chest is 6 feet high and 12 feet long, containing 100 small drawers, each divided into two or four compartments. Here are complete tortoise and turtle shells, parts of a tiger's jaw, rhinoceros' horn scrapings, dried centipedes about 8 inches in length, gummed to slips of bamboo; three entire dried snakes, each from 3 to 4 feet long; a black sickening mess called "dried scorpions" out of which the claws and jaws of these animals may be picked; entire dried lizards, held together by neat bamboo frames; dried snails, fine yellow sea sand, cicada's cast-off skins, and sufficient strychnos nuts to poison all Round Hill. These examples give only a faint idea of the disgusting things which enter into Chinese pharmacopoeia. Among the "mythical" remedies in the same cabinet are "dragon's teeth" and "dragon's bones". These latter look as though they have been underground for years [they were probably fossilised mammalian bone or teeth]. (Don 1/4/1884:184)

3. Another course of action open to sick Chinese was to call upon the services of a Chinese doctor. However, this option was much more onerous than it sounds. There were few Chinese doctors (perhaps half a dozen) resident on the goldfields. Their fees compared with European medical services were very high and frequently involved paying for the doctor's opium, board and lodging. The Chinese doctor who came to the Round Hill field, if requested, resided in Lawrence, about 200 kilometres away. Don cited one exceptional case where two Chinese doctors were consulted by a Round Hill man who had a broken leg in March 1883. At the time his "brothers" thought it would cost £80 to effect a cure. In April 1884 (and the leg still had not properly healed), the cost had risen to £220 made up of the following expenses: fares for Dr Chow to and from Lawrence, £4; Dr Chow's contract, £32; medicines (including opium smoked by Dr Chow, £24), £64; food (doctor, patient and attendant) for 11 months, £65; Dr T'aam's contract, £37; Dr T'aam's medicines, £8; Ah Kow's board and lodging till cured, about £10 (Don 1/4/1884:184). Despite the large costs, the Chinese doctors claimed European doctors would have amputated the leg.

The arrival of a Chinese doctor was often considered noteworthy by local newspapers. For example, the *Tuapeka Times* (28/4/1871) reported the arrival of Leang Chun Wah, who had obtained his MD in Hong Kong. The newspaper correspondent suggested "it would be a step in the right direction if the medical faculty in Dunedin adopted the Chinese doctor's philosophy of "no cure, no pay" (Butler 1977:47). Sedgewick (1982:165) described another Chinese doctor, W.Y.K. Chan, who had worked on the goldfields. According to an advertisement in the Christchurch Press (19/11/1938), he arrived in New Zealand in 1887 to take over the directorship of the K.Y.L. Company from his grandfather. This firm of merchants and herbalists was started in Melbourne and later opened branches in New Zealand at Arrowtown, Cromwell and Lawrence during the goldrushes. His son, who had placed the advertisement, was a herbalist in Christchurch for many years.

4. A fourth response to chronic illness involved clansmen mounting a collection to send a sick man back to China. Don recorded several instances of this happening at Round Hill (e.g. Don 1/1/1883:127, 1/8/1883:24). In the latter incident, the clansmen and relatives subscribed to pay off the sick man's debts as well as his return passage. These seemingly charitable gestures were a pragmatic response. It was difficult for clansmen and relatives, especially, to refuse a face-to-face request for financial assistance to return home. However, they appreciated in the case of a chronically ill person that it was much cheaper to raise £20 or £30 to send a live person home, than to ignore his condition and eventually have to spend as much as £80 for a burial and the associated feast, plus the costs of disinterment and shipment of the remains at a later date (Don 2/11/1885:85).

3.10.1 OLD AGE, DEATHS, FUNERALS, BURIALS AND EXHUMATIONS

For some of the elderly Chinese who were unwell or thought that they would never be able to return home with dignity and wealth, there was a choice between appealing to kin for enough money to pay for the return passage, or just plan to die in New Zealand and hope that clansmen or relatives would feel obliged to send their body home as a *sin yan* (former man). In the case of the first alternative, Don documented a variety of responses: e.g. a poor man sought £20 for a fare home from rich kin folk but was refused, so he started collecting seaweed, which he planned to sell to pay for his passage (Don 1/3/1884:162). In other cases, approaches were made to kin elsewhere in New Zealand. If there was no response, this was an acceptable way to refuse the request (Don 2/11/1885:86). As described earlier, it was much more difficult for kin to refuse a face-to-face request, and they often opted for the cheaper option of paying a sick man's fare rather than refusing the request and eventually having to pay the much greater expenses (the burial, celebration, disinterment costs etc.) that would be incurred if he should die (Don 1/10/1883:67, 2/11/885:85).

Those that died from accident, suicide or old age were usually taken by clansmen to the local morgue and later buried. If a man had no direct kin, those from the same lineage would take responsibility and collect among themselves to defray the cost of a burial (Don 1/1/1883:126). For example, in 1883 a young man (17 years old and two years out of China) was killed in a claim at Round Hill. His clansmen (of the surname Wong) collected £62/14/6d from 156 people for the funeral expenses. Similarly, in 1884 a very poor old man, Ly Kye, committed suicide because he had been unable to pay his debts and join some of his clansmen on their homeward voyage. Again, the clansmen took up a collection, raising £30, which paid for the man who removed the body (he had hung himself in his hut), for other men who arranged the funeral and the post-burial feast (Don 1/4/1884:184, 1/7/1884:4). "Before the body was placed in the coffin it was dressed in new trousers, jacket, socks, shoes, and hat – all Chinese except the socks and hat which were not to be had in Riverton... Twenty seven of the clan accompanied the body by rail to Riverton. All the way... one man scattered paper money" (Don 1/4/1884:184). Some reasons were advanced by Don to explain the practice of scattering punched paper (representing Chinese coins) along the funeral procession route. The main objectives were to "buy the goodwill of the road" and discourage the intervention of evil spirits (Don 1/4/1884:184).

Chinese funerals in New Zealand often attracted media publicity because the rituals were so different. The following account of the funeral of a leading Chinese merchant at Lawrence documents many of the Chinese burial practices such as paper scattering, wearing white (the colour of mourning), the spilling of brandy and the traditional post-burial feasting, although the funeral is clearly more extravagant and ostentatious than that afforded to a lowly miner:

> From the moment that the body left the hospital in the usual vehicle, one of the deceased's relatives, who occupied a seat beside the driver, commenced throwing on the road small squares of paper, and continued doing so until arrival at the grave. Most of the Chinamen wore a strip of white gauze on their hats. When the coffin was placed over the grave, the attendants brought, on a large tray, a roasted pig (might weigh about 80 lbs) and some boiled pork and fowl, cakes, cigars and apples. All the white bands which were worn around the hats were gathered together at the foot of the grave and set fire to... The apples were handed around, as also the biscuits. They filled with wine and brandy some little cups, and then spilt the whole on the ground; this was done three times, and during all this time brandy, gin and "Old Tom" were served around ad libitum. There was a sprinkling of the fair sex in attendance. When passing through the gate, on the way home, there was a Chinaman standing, and gave each one a small packet neatly wrapped up in coarse paper. Upon being opened it was found to contain a 1/-. This was given to all and sundry, young and old, male and female. As is usual when a blow out is expected, there were a few of those who made the most of the occasion, and as there were several parties doling out they made a rich harvest... (Butler 1977:81)

Although a few isolated Chinese graves are known, most of the Chinese who died on the New Zealand goldfields were buried in the nearest European cemetery. But they were seldom buried among the European burials (which were in turn grouped according to religious denomination), usually being relegated to a corner area (this pattern is evident in the Clyde, Cromwell and Arrowtown cemeteries). At least 700 were later exhumed and returned to China as *sin yan* (see next section).

Suicides were not common, but when one occurred, it caused considerable consternation among the Chinese. Some could be blamed on economic misfortune, often following excessive gambling or opium consumption, but many cases were the result of loneliness, poverty and despair at never being able to return home. Suicide was considered by some, especially if they attributed their situation to someone else's wrongdoing, to be a form of revenge or redress. By committing suicide and letting others know why, the "wrongdoer" would forever after lead a miserable life (Don 1/8/1884:25). Hanging appears to have been the most popular method of taking one's life. Accidental deaths, usually from earth-falls in the claims, averaged almost one a year at Round Hill (Don 1/3/1884:162). Houses and claims were abandoned after a death. Everything in the houses was left exactly as it was. No one would occupy the abandoned structures in case the owner's spirit (ghost) returned or risk the possibility of incurring the bad luck that surrounded such events (Don 1/8/1884:25).

3.10.2 EXHUMATION AND SHIPMENT OF REMAINS BACK TO CHINA

Because of the Chinese's desire "to lie with the ancestors" and be assured of their children's respect, a committee or organisation was established in many overseas Chinese communities to periodically arrange the shipment of human remains back to China. During the first 20 years of Chinese settlement in New Zealand there were occasional reports of Chinese burials being disinterred for shipment. In these instances, the coffins were usually conveyed on the same ship as returning kin, who felt a responsibility to take their deceased relatives home. The first recorded *wui koon* (mass exhumation) was conducted at Lawrence in 1869 by a Poon Yue "exhumation association" (*Tuapeka Times* 25/9/1869). The only evidence that remains of this association are two plaques preserved in the Otago Early Settlers Association Museum, Dunedin.

In 1882, a more formalised association was established by a group of concerned merchants for the exhumation of Poon Yue *sin yan* ("former men") whose remains were becoming increasingly numerous in goldfield cemeteries. The new Association, the Ch'eung Shin Tong (or Effulgent Goodness Hall), was based in Dunedin. The Association posted notices in Chinese shops throughout the goldfields. The notices listed the rules and objectives of the Association. Briefly they were as follows. Each person was to contribute 30/- (the wealthy were expected to give more). Collectors were employed to go around the goldfields and collect the money, which in turn was given to the manager of Sew Hoy's store. After deducting the collectors' expenses, the rest would be deposited in a bank to gain interest. Friends of the dead were instructed to inform the Hall (in writing) of the surname and name of the deceased, their village of origin, the place of burial and to keep the "former friend's" grave plot cleared and marked "so that there would be no mistake by the openers" (Don 1/12/1883:103–4). Receipts for contributions were to be issued, and if one was intending to return to China, the receipt had to be presented for cancellation before departure. Those who absconded would be fined £5 (Don 1/12/1883:103–4).

A total of 230 *sin yan* were exhumed for shipment to China in this initial operation. When the steamer *Hoihow* left Port Chalmers for China on 9 August 1883, it carried the *sin yan* plus 46 living men. The *sin yan* had been placed in separate coffins at a cost of £4 for large ones and 10/- for small ones. Some £2,000–£3,000 remained in the hands of the Association after paying all expenses (Don 1/10/1883:68).

The Ch'eung Shin Tong organised a second operation in 1892, although it differed in that now the primary concern was for the growing number of elderly and infirm Chinese. The advertisement placed under the name "The Flourishing Virtue Society" (note the name change) stated that although 762 people had contributed £1,098/9/3d to the fund for the removal of the dead, the organisers considered that those over 60 years old should be returned to China first. The advertisement read:

> Having already favoured the bones of the departed (by their removal some years earlier), it is a primary duty to care for the aged. We, who do not reckon several thousand miles as far to come, have all as members of a family to make provision for the food and clothing of one another. When they [the old men] came they were vigorous in body, from east to west they rushed about, year followed year, they were unable to return home, in a twinkling of a cycle [60 years] and more passed away; now weak in body and feeble in mind, unable in the morning to reckon on the evening, finding it difficult to plan for food, what can they do? (Don 1893:10)

The organisers requested that the names of the elderly should be submitted to them, and more money donated. Once the old men had been sent back to China, the managers would meet again and if the remaining funds were sufficient, they would arrange for the *sin yan* to be "carried home" (Don 1893:10). It is not certain whether this second *sin yan* operation was completed (Sedgewick (1983:43).

Although there had been a few private exhumations in the intervening years (Sedgewick 1983:43), the next major shipment was initiated by the Ch'eung Shin Tong in 1899. The operation was under the supervision of the Health Department and had specific authorisation from the Colonial Secretary. Strict rules were laid down authorising when the bodies could be exhumed and how the coffins were to be sealed, disinfected and dispatched (NZPD 1902:122, 442–3). In all, 474 bodies were exhumed, described in the Dunedin paper, see Table 3.8.

Another report stated that 40 graveyards had been visited all over the country, including Auckland, Wellington, Palmerston North, Greymouth, Christchurch, Dunedin and other towns, and that 489 bodies had been exhumed (*The Press* 30/10/1902). *The Press* report described the exhumation and preparations of the remains for shipment in detail. Those that were recent deaths were placed in carefully sealed zinc-lined cases then placed in kauri coffins. Old coffins were put back in the graves before they were filled in. The late Mr Sew Hoy and Mr Ah Chung received rimu coffins befitting their status. Where the remains consisted of bones alone, they were dried and placed in small wooden coffins. The work was contracted to Mr Mos Chang, who subcontracted other Chinese as assistants. The cost of each exhumation and shipment was about £30.

Once readied, the coffins from various areas were sent to Wellington for shipment on the SS *Ventnor*. Her cargo also included nine aged Chinese "body attendants", £4,500 worth of Westport coal and a quantity of fungus that was insured for £320. The ship left Wellington on 26 October 1902, bound for Hong Kong, but struck a submerged rock off Cape Egmont. Although it managed to steam on for a while, it eventually sank on 28 October, off Hokianga Harbour, with the loss of 13 lives and its cargo (*Cyclopedia of New Zealand* 1897 Vol. 1:487–8; Ingram and Wheatley 1977). There were two main results of this tragedy: a heartfelt sense of loss on the part of all the Chinese whose relatives would never reach home (many considered the *sin yan* on the ship had "died twice"; Don 1906:8), and a protracted debate over how the approximately £4,000 of insurance money should be best spent. The managers of the Ch'eung Shin Tong had many meetings to resolve the problem, but more than three years elapsed before a compromise was worked out. According to Don, "most Otago men" favoured using the money to repatriate those who were over 65 years old, along with any recent *sin yan* who needed to be sent home. A contribution was also made to a fund to be spent on a mortuary temple and burial ground near Stone Gate (a Poon Yue village) for "friendless men who die abroad" (Don 1906:8).

Europeans freely expressed their views about the propriety and "health risks" of the operations, but they were of major importance for the "peace of mind" of the Chinese in New Zealand, be they miner or merchant. Don (2/4/1883:185) made the point that English settlers commonly expressed a desire to be buried in the "Old Country" and also pointed out that the *sin yan* operations were little different from the long-established European practice of returning the bodies of people who die overseas to their home countries.

3.11 THE DECLINE YEARS: POST-1900

In 1900, after four years away from the goldfields (setting up the Canton Villages Mission), Don returned to visit the areas he had visited annually since 1886. The situation he saw now, and which he documented until his last "tour of the goldfields" in 1910–11, was one of growing disillusionment, poverty and despair among the remaining Chinese. In 1881, at the peak of the mining period, there were 5,004 Chinese in New Zealand (of whom 3,856 were miners); by 1901, the numbers had dropped to 2,963 (and only 1,313 were mining). Over 68% of the miners were over 45 years old, and many were barely eking out a subsistence living. Once the large Chinese populations in and around the main mining centres had declined, there was no possibility of maintaining the many stores and opium and gambling saloons that had kept the Chinese miners supplied and entertained over the previous three decades. Don noted that the population of Round Hill had dropped from 92 in 1897 to 37 in 1901. In the same period, Alexandra's Chinese population dropped from 52 to 29, that of Cromwell from 77 to 42, and Arrowtown's from 15 to 12. In the following decade whole areas had become completely depopulated of Chinese, e.g. by 1911 there were no Chinese living permanently between Roxburgh and Beaumont (Don 1911:22), and there were only three left on the Tuapeka where there had been hundreds in the 1870s (Don 1911:38).

As the rural stores closed, it became increasingly difficult for the remaining Chinese in the "back blocks" to obtain supplies, or they had to travel considerably greater distances to obtain them. This situation, coupled with increasing loneliness as local populations declined, and the difficulty of eking a living through goldmining, compelled many miners and those who had formerly supplied them with provisions and services to seek new kinds of work elsewhere. Most were "getting on in years" and no longer capable of arduous physical work. Some moved to larger communities and towns where they could obtain work in laundries, hotels or market gardens, or cook for their clansmen. Others worked for Europeans, picking fruit, thinning turnips, shearing or fencing (Don 1901:24). But some soldiered on, enduring an increasingly lonely existence as their compatriots moved away, returned to China or died.

Many of those who left the goldfields moved to the North Island. There were 792 established there in 1901, of whom 288 were living in and around Wellington, and 75 lived in Auckland (NZ Census 1901:23). A northward drift had been underway since the early 1870s; by 1896, 1,208 of the total Chinese population (3,859) were scattered in 66 of the 95 boroughs in both main islands (NZ Census 1896:161–3). In Dunedin, on the other hand, the Chinese population (230) and the main enclave of Chinese businesses and houses centred around Stafford and Walker Streets were declining. In a 1901 report on housing conditions, this area was described as one of the worst slums in Dunedin (Clark 1961:86).

Sedgewick (1983:161–3), using data gleaned from Don's comprehensive 1896 diary record of the movements of 1,080 Chinese, presented the following insights into the situation of the Chinese in New Zealand c.1900. Of the 1,080, 362 had left New Zealand permanently, but during their sojourn in New Zealand, only 93 had been home for a visit, and only 11 of them more than once. The 362 men had spent a total of 1,677 years away from China, many having been away for over 30 years. Their average age at departure was 58. The 39 who had been home for visits had spent an average of 37 years away from home.

Many of the Chinese miners were married before they left home. One of the miners at Round Hill told Don that 70% of the Chinese there had wives at home who stayed with their husband's kin and looked after his parents and other family members in their husband's absence (Don 1/9/1884:43). Many of the men lost touch through time. If they were not married and never went home to get married, it was regarded as a sign of poverty, and it became a further disincentive to return or maintain communication. Letters were seldom received from China unless remittances had arrived home or kin wanted more money (Section 5.6.2). Don's records contain many histories of individuals who had been in New Zealand 20 or more years. In one such instance, he noted a man of 66, who had been in New Zealand 27 years, had not received a letter from home for 18 years. Although he could write, he had not sent any money home, so nobody wrote to him (Don 1901:25). To encourage the sending of more money (or the sons to return), stories were often made up about bad harvests, the high cost of living or ailing parents (Don 1906:22, 1911:10). Often letters from home, rather than being comforting, left their recipients feeling insecure as to the real situation at home.

But not all the Chinese wanted to return home. They were uncertain what effects the Boxer Rebellion (1900) was having in their home area and the impact of Western influences that had seen the development of railways, new villages and a changed market pattern (Don 1911:20). In New Zealand, despite the immigration restrictions and European harassment, they felt free to do what they liked with their money including having occasional holidays in places like Dunedin. They would never have been able to have "holidays" in China without being roundly condemned. Others who had gone home "got a hard time" for being lazy (Don 1911:17). In some instances, a miner's family had died, leaving no close kin in China. Rather than returning to an unpredictable retirement, they opted to eke out whatever sort of living they could manage in New Zealand.

Although Prime Minister Seddon had ensured that the Chinese (and other Asiatics) were specifically excluded from receiving pensions under the provisions of the *Old Age Pension Act 1898* (Statutes of New Zealand 1898:58), many were able to get 4/- a week from the county Charitable Aid Board. The money, which was obtained in the form of credit at a local store, enabled them to obtain basic food supplies (Don 1911:26). In 1901, the census recorded that there were two Chinese in hospitals, 14 in "benevolent asylums" and 23 in "lunatic asylums" (NZ Census 1901:396). Many ageing Chinese were removed to old people's homes. By 1910 there were 12 living in "the Home" in Dunedin (Don 1911:26).

The short-term stays that most of the Chinese miners anticipated became prolonged sojourns for about 30% of the approximately 10,000 who landed during the 19th century. Many spent more of their life in New Zealand than in China (Don 1908:14). For others it became a lifetime exile. Don gave his views on the effects on the Chinese of prolonged sojourns stemming from misfortune or "self-induced" poverty:

> My own experience of the Chinese in general is this: Shortly after they come from China they work very hard and are very saving so as to be able to return soon; but if after some years struggling they are unsuccessful they seem gradually to lose all hope of ever being able to return, become lazy, drift into the opium habit and spend every penny on opium or gambling. The most prosperous men are the most industrious – working hard because they are prospering, and thus adding to their prosperity; while the non-prosperous become lazy and loose, and thus add to their poverty. (Don 1/3/1888:166)

By 1906, the Chinese population was down to 2,570 (of which only 55 were females); an aged, dispirited and declining group. Many, besides having to combat failing health, poverty and loneliness, were poorly equipped to operate in an English language environment. They continued to be exposed to hostility and restrictions from New Zealand society and were increasingly uncertain of what was happening in their homeland following the Sino-Japanese War (1894–95) and the Boxer Rebellion. However, despite the gloomy outlook, some among them (mainly members of the small Chinese population established in the North Island) managed to articulate an opposition to the barrage of restrictions, so that by the 1930s public opinion was becoming increasingly favourable. The first barrier to fall was the ultra-discriminatory poll tax, which was abolished in 1932.

Some of the last Chinese on the southern goldfields are fondly remembered (in the 1980s) by a rapidly depleting number of elderly European citizens of the goldfield towns of Central Otago. In physical terms, the Chinese left a legacy of occupation sites (settlements, stores, camps, huts and rockshelters), workings (dams, races and mining sites) and a sprinkling of place names and lonely graves. Few who have seen their sites would be unmoved by the industry, perseverance and hardship they represent.

While this chapter has painted a picture based on historic research, archaeological research affords another insight. The study sites are described next, followed by the results and conclusions drawn from the analysis of the cultural deposits. The concluding chapter draws the evidence together and specifically examines the degree to which the Chinese adopted European ways or maintained aspects of their traditional culture.

Table 3.1. Estimated costs of living for Chinese and Europeans on the goldfields (AJHR 1871 H–5:14–22).

	Chinese wages	Chinese cost of living	European wages	European cost of living
Roxburgh		9/-		16/-
Queenstown	£1/0/-	8/-	£2/8/-	
Clyde	£1/10/-	10/-	£2/10/-	£1/0/-
Lawrence	15–25/-	4–5/-	£2/10/-	12–15/-

Note The estimates are based on a week.

Table 3.2. Condensed summary of occupations of Chinese in 1871 (NZ Census 1871).

Occupation	Number of people	Percentage of total (%)
Miners	3,570	84.7
Carpenters	5	0.1
Storekeepers	103	2.4
Hotelkeepers	1	0.02
Gardeners	49	1.2
Agents	3	0.1
Cooks	3	0.1
Labourers	12	0.3
Hawkers	12	0.3
Cabinetmakers	6	0.1
No return	451	10.7
Total	4,215	

Table 3.3 Chinese occupational trends in the nineteenth century (NZ Census 1871–1911).

Broad occupational group	1871	1874	1878	1881	1886	1891	1896	1901	1906	1911	Trend
Miners	2,310 87.6%	4,022 83.5%	3,397 76.8%	3,860 77.3%	3,115 68%	3,025 68.3%	2,168 58.8%	1,313 46.5%	612 24.3%	416 16%	decreasing
Labourers (public works)	12 0.5%	258 5.4%	194 4.4%	133 2.7%	77 1.7%	75 1.7%	59 1.6%	49 1.7%	105 4.2%	63 2.4%	steady (4)
Food producers (market gardeners and farm workers)	49 1.9%	149 3.1%	406 9.2%	478 9.6%	694 15.3%	607 14.3%	698 18.9%	711 25.2%	840 33.4%	1,015 39.2%	increasing (2)
Merchants/Service industries/ Self-employed	133 5%	250 5.2%	336 7.6%	358 7.2%	492 10.9%	578 13.7%	637 17.3%	644 22.8%	788 31.3%	861 33.3%	increasing (3)
Others (1)	133 5%	135 2.8%	91 2.0%	166 3.3%	149 3.3%	141 3.3%	123 3.5%	108 3.8%	170 6.8%	232 9%	increasing
Total	2,637	4,814	4,424	4,995	4,527	4,426	3,685	2,825	2,515	2,587	
No. of Chinese women at each census		2	9	9	15	18	26	32	55	88	(5)

Notes:

(1) "Others" includes rabbiters, retired persons, prisoners, inmates of institutions, fishermen, mariners, coal miners, sons, daughters and visitors.
(2) The rising trend reflects a) the growing development of Chinese market gardening b) older Chinese working as gardeners and farm labourers.
(3) This trend reflects a) the growing involvement of the Chinese in laundry businesses particularly after 1896 b) the growing involvement of the Chinese in the retail fruit and grocery trade.
(4) The post-1870 increase coincides with the Vogel-era expansion of road and railway network in NZ.
(5) Most of the Chinese women are described as "wifes" in the nineteenth century census occupation lists.

Table 3.4. Inter-house movements of a group of miners at Round Hill (Don 1/9/1883:47).

	9 June 1883	2 July 1883
House 1	occupied by A	empty
House 2	occupied by B and C	occupied by B only
House 3	occupied by D, E	broken down
House 4	occupied by F	occupied by F and G
House 5	occupied by G, H	occupied by A and M
House 6	occupied by I and J	occupied by I, K and L
House 7	Not yet constructed	(new) occupied by D and E

Table 3.5. Estimated populations of Chinese miners in 1871 (AJHR 1871 H–5:23).

Goldfield	Main centres	Approx. populations
Tuapeka	Lawrence	1,090
Dunstan	Alexandra, Clyde, Cromwell	2,000
Mt Ida	Naseby, Kyeburn	228
Round Hill	Round Hill, Riverton	350
Total		3,715

Table 3.6. Chinese involved in different types of mining (NZ Census).

Type of mining	1874	1878	1881	1886	1891	1896	1901	1906	1911
alluvial miners	1,506	1,361	1,767	1,748	2,938	2,162	1,295	612	416
sluicers	1,861	1,115	1,099	1,196	(1)	(1)	18*	-	-
goldminers (2)	655	917	990	170	82	-	-	-	-
quartz miners (3)	-	4	2	1	-	-	-	-	-
dredge workers	-	-	-	-	5	-	-	-	-
race caretakers	-	-	-	-	-	-	-	-	4
Totals	4,022	3,397	3,858	3,115	3,025	2,162	1,313	612	420

Notes

*now described as "goldminers, hydraulic".

(1) both categories (alluvial miners and sluicers) appear to be grouped in these censuses.

(2) believed to include prospectors and those who did not specify whether they were "alluvial miners" or "sluicers".

(3) totals include those who cited their occupations as "crushers".

Table 3.7. Recorded earnings or amounts sent to China by Chinese miners, merchants and gamblers working on the Round Hill field 1882–89.

No. men	Amount (£)	Years in NZ	Note no.
1	70	-	1
1	600	-	2
40	3,000	-	3
5	168	-	4*
4	240	6-	5
1	200	-	6
several	700	-	6
1	900	10–20	7
1	170	10–20	7
1	120	110–20	7
1	200	10–20	7
1	150	10–20	7
1	200	10–20	7
1	300	-	8
8	1,000	4–14	9
1	200	-	10*
1	300	-	11*
5	1,300	-	12
1	160	5	13
1	159	27	14*
1	16.5 sov.	11	15
2	98 oz. gold	-	16

Notes:

* Earnings rather than remittances.

1. A single man returning to China. Don commented that he had £70 of his own, but £20 would be required for the expenses of the voyage (Don 2/10/1882:65).

2. This sum, £600, was the largest taken home by a single miner (Don 2/10/1882:66).

3. Don commented that a party of 40 men who were returning to China were carrying £6,000. Half of this was their own earnings; the rest, consisting of sums varying between £1 and £10, was for delivery to other miners' families. The Chinese were always relieved to hear that the money had arrived in China safely (Don 2/10/1882:66).

4. A group of five men realised £168 when they sold their gold. It represented seven or eight weeks' work. Don commented "this means over £4 weekly to each – rare good wages on the Hill" (Don 1/11/1883:87).

5. A group of four "brothers" with the surname "Chan" about to return to China told Don they were taking back £60 each. They had been away six years and did not want to run the risk of losing what they had (Don 1/11/1882:89).

6. This man also carried £700 entrusted to him for delivery (Don 2/4/1883:183).

7. These sums represent the result of between 10 and 20 years of earnings (Don 2/4/1883:183). All these remittances were lost (but later salvaged) when the SS *Chariton* sank en route to China.

8. This man hoped to buy some land and build a house in his native village, then either return to New Zealand or go to the United States (Don 2/7/1883:3).

9. The figure of £1,000 is approximate. Don stated that the eight men, three of whom were in business in Riverton and Round Hill, were returning to China with sums ranging from £70 to £200. Two other sick men were sent home with them, their fares paid by their friends (Don 1/9/1883:47).

10. £50 of this sum was gained by selling a third share of his claim. Don said the claim was yielding each man £4 to £6 weekly, considerably better than the average return (Don 1/10/1883:67).

Table 3.7. (*continued*) Recorded earnings or amounts sent to China by Chinese miners, merchants and gamblers working on the Round Hill field 1882–89.

11. The reference refers to concern over four returning Chinese after news that the SS *Changchow* had been wrecked. One of the returnees had £300 won by gambling during one of the Chinese festivals (Don 1/12/1884:106). He was also carrying £400 for friends. Later it was learned that the gambler was drowned because of the upsetting of a boat (Don 1/1/1885:125).

12. The bodies of six Chinese drowned when the SS *Changchow* was wrecked were recovered. They had a total of £2,000 on their persons, of which £700 was carried by the gambler mentioned above (Don 1/4/1885:184).

13. Don cited this remittance to demonstrate filiality. It concerned a 24-year-old man who had been in New Zealand for five years. During this period, he sent his parents £160 "which would be about half enough to support them during this period" (Don 1/8/1885:27).

14. This man's return fare was paid by a fellow clansman after he won £159 in two lottery wins at Lawrence. The benefactor "in return for such good fortune wished to please the gods by paying the passage home of his poorer clansman" (Don 1/2/1887:147).

15. Don read a notebook found in the abandoned hut of a Tuapeka miner who had been killed in his claim. Entries in the notebook indicated he had sent 16.5 sovereigns home in 11 years (Don 1/12/1888:106).

16. Reference to one of two brothers taking 98 ounces of gold back to China from their joint claim on the Molyneux. However, a dispute over the division of it led to a boycott of the traveller when he returned to New Zealand (Don 1893:17). This is one of the few references indicating amounts of gold taken out of New Zealand by returning Chinese, but as gold would have been much easier to resell or exchange in China, it is likely to have been quite a common practice, especially for small amounts.

17. According to the *Lake Wakatipu Mail* (8/2/1884), three Chinese working a small claim in the Shotover were making £100 each per week. This seems a phenomenally high return and was certainly the exception rather than the rule at that late date.

Table 3.8. Chinese exhumations (*Otago Daily Times* 27/10/1902).

Dunedin	265 bodies (84 large, 181 small)
Greymouth	173 bodies (66 large, 107 small)
Wellington	36 bodies
Total	**474**

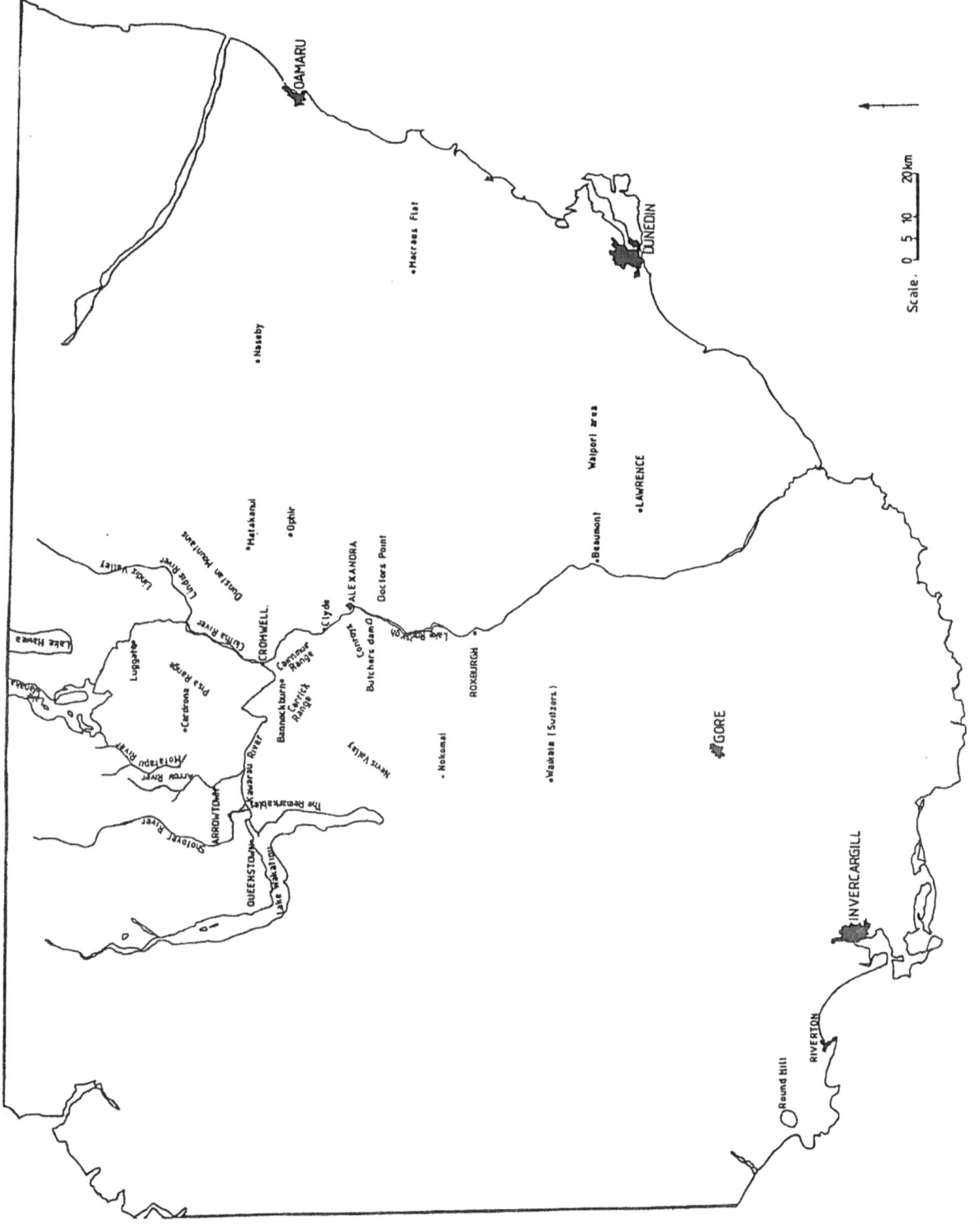

Figure 3.1. The southern goldfields: main localities mentioned in the text.

Chapter 4
THE ARCHAEOLOGICAL EVIDENCE

Thus far, archival and written records have been used to provide a social and historical picture of Chinese settlement in southern New Zealand. In this and the following chapters, archaeological evidence is used to establish another perspective on the social patterns and lifeways of the Chinese. Archaeological data not only corroborates (and sometimes refutes) historical observations, it also provides a considerable body of information that is not available from any literary source.

Archaeological information is derived primarily from two avenues of research – field surveys (i.e. the locating and recording of surviving field evidence) and systematic archaeological excavations backed by literature research. The archaeological investigations, which form the basis of this study, are outlined below.

4.1 THE FIELD SURVEYS

The large number of Chinese habitation sites and workings centred around Cromwell (see Appendix 2) constituted the primary source of field evidence and the incentive to embark on this research project. The sites were initially found and recorded during archaeological mitigation work associated with the Clutha Valley Development (CVD) project. The CVD project, designed initially to create three hydro dams and storage lakes and two feeder canals with powerhouses, also involved the partial inundation of part of Cromwell township (including the historic main street) and major re-routing of existing roads (Ritchie 1978, 1979). In the end, only one large hydro lake (Lake Dunstan) was formed behind the Clyde Dam. The two dams planned in the Kawarau Gorge were scrapped because of geological instability, and two powerhouses and feeder canals planned in the Upper Clutha Valley were not built because there was no need for them after a decision was made not to proceed with the proposed Aramoana aluminium smelter.

The surveys revealed approximately 250 sites would be impacted to some extent, of which around 70 were associated with the Chinese miners. The affected sites were recorded between 1976 and 1983 and are described in a series of survey reports – Cromwell Gorge (Higham, Mason and Moore 1976), Luggate area (Ritchie 1980b), Queensberry area (Ritchie 1980c), Roxburgh Gorge (Harrison 1982) and the Kawarau Gorge (Ritchie 1983b). Chinese sites were also recorded during surveys of the Shotover and Bannockburn Valleys, the Bendigo and Carrick goldfields, and the 12 Mile Creek catchment (Ritchie 1982a). Individual Chinese sites in the Motatapu (particularly S124/395), Cardrona and Nevis Valleys and in the areas around Lawrence, Macetown and Glenorchy were also examined. The primary and secondary study areas are depicted in Figure 4.1. The author has also examined Chinese sites and associated artefacts for comparative purposes in the following areas beyond Central Otago: the West Coast (Hokitika, Greymouth), Southland (the Round Hill goldfield, Nokomai and Waikaia Valley), Australia (the Palmer River goldfield), the United States (California, Oregon, Idaho, Montana, Arizona and Washington) and in British Columbia (Barkerville and Victoria); and participated in Chinese site excavations in Australia (Jack et al. 1984:51–8) and the United States (Miller 1983).

4.2 THE ARCHAEOLOGICAL INVESTIGATIONS

Between 1978 and 1985, 21 archaeological excavations, directed by this writer, were conducted on Chinese sites in the Upper Clutha and Wakatipu Basins, including two Chinese camps at Cromwell and Arrowtown. The assemblages from these sites form the data base for documenting the material culture and gaining an archaeological perspective on the lifestyle of the Chinese miners in southern New Zealand. Additional information was derived from field testing (involving test pitting and surface collecting) some 50 Chinese sites in the areas affected by the Clutha dams, and by examining and recording around 20 privately owned (generally fossicked) Chinese artefact collections, studying museum holdings, and through comparison with Chinese assemblages observed or reported from sites and collections in the United States, Canada, Australia, Hong Kong, Thailand and the Philippines. The sites, which form the primary data base (henceforth described collectively as "the study sites"), are summarised in Table 4.1. The letters "Ch" and "ACS" prefixing a number, e.g. Ch/14 or ACS/5, refer to the individual numbered hut sites in the Cromwell and Arrowtown Chinese Settlements.

4.2.1 THE EXCAVATED SITES: INTRODUCTORY NOTES

The study sites are described now. Discussions on construction techniques, materials, dimensions, layout and orientation of the structures are presented in the later sections of the chapter. Except for the Northburn, Willows and Platform sites, it was apparent before the excavations commenced (from surface exposures and construction characteristics) that the sites had been occupied by Chinese. The selection of the Cromwell Gorge shelters for excavating was based on a testing program undertaken in November 1978. This involved testing 40 sites, of which 34 were rockshelters, the others being open sites or huts. All the sites in the Cromwell Gorge are now under Lake Dunstan, except for the Firewood Creek and Caliche shelters, which were destroyed by the construction of the new Cromwell–Clyde highway.

The stratigraphy within the sites can be summarised as straightforward and uncomplicated. Unless otherwise stated, only one cultural layer was defined. A typical stratigraphic sequence consisted of an essentially sterile upper layer formed since the site's abandonment, beneath which lay the occupation layer, which in turn overlaid virtually sterile gravels, clay or hard rock. In two instances (in the Caliche and Hanging Rock shelters), moa bones were found below the cultural deposits. Moa eggshell was found in 60% (20) of the rockshelters in the Cromwell Gorge. A few rockshelters contained artefactual material from previous occupations (Māori) or subsequent usage by rabbiters or "depression miners", but in no instance was there a clear stratigraphic distinction between the successive occupations. This is attributed to the short time span between the occupations, micro-environmental conditions being unconducive to stratigraphic differentiation, and the often-considerable intermixing of the deposits by human and stock scuffage and rabbit burrowing. The difficulty of defining multiple occupations on stratigraphic grounds placed extra emphasis on using the recovered assemblages to this end. Dates of occupation for each site have been derived from analysis of the bottle glass and wax vesta boxes found within each (see Table 4.2). The artefacts from the sites are described in Chapter 5, and the faunal and floral components in Chapter 6.

1. Firewood Creek S133/424 rockshelter (now G41/124)

Location: S133 033697 near Cromwell
Excavated: Nov. 1978 (destroyed by highway construction Dec. 1978)

The Firewood Creek site (Figures 4.2, 4.3) was located near the mouth of Firewood Creek on the true left bank of the Clutha River, at a point about 400 m upstream of its junction with the Kawarau River. From the shelter, one looked across the town of Cromwell. The shelter consisted of a covered area, about 2 m wide and 3 m deep, beneath a large boulder (Figure 4.2). A stone-revetted water race, which conveyed water from the creek to workings upstream of the site and across to the opposite bank of the Clutha River, passed 2 m in front of the shelter. The water was conveyed across the river in a suspended pipeline. Here, there were extensive herringbone tailings, known as the Deadman's Point tailings. They were obliterated by lakeshore pre-formation work. It has not been ascertained whether they were of Chinese or European formation (I suspect the area was reworked by the Chinese). Inside the shelter the maximum standing height was 1.5 m. Six nails in the rock above the entrance attest to the hanging of bags or canvas as a draft screen. This is relatively unusual because most of the shelters in the area have, or had, substantial stone walls enclosing the "living chamber". The shelter did not have a fireplace, although a large rock to the left of the entrance was fire blackened. These factors suggest it was not occupied for any length of time. The back right corner was quite damp from seepage.

The entire interior of the shelter was excavated. There was little artefactual material in the front three-quarters but up to 30 cm accumulation in the back portion. Part of this was fossicked by unknown persons towards the end of the excavation. The bulk of the material from the site was found in the "throw zone" (i.e. the area within throwing range of the entrance) down the steep slope below the shelter. Here, scattered on the surface and up to 10 cm into the stony ground, there were numerous fragments of bottle glass, opium pipe bowls and cans, Chinese ceramics (notably celadon rice bowls), European ceramics (henceforth called Euro-ceramics), nails, cans, charcoal, bones and two Chinese coins. A sequence of squares was excavated down the slope below the shelter and widened out where surface evidence or excavation revealed concentrations of artefactual material (Figure 4.2). Analysis of the glass bottles and wax vesta matchboxes found in the shelter indicate that it was occupied from c.1880 until about 1895, although it was probably occupied earlier.

This small site was particularly notable for the large amount of opium-smoking refuse (opium pipe bowl and can fragments) it contained (see Section 5.4). The absence of a fireplace and a front wall of any substance suggest the shelter was not used for extended periods. It possibly served as a "crib hut-smoking venue" for Chinese miners working in the area. It was located about halfway (2 km) between the Cromwell Chinatown settlement and what became known during the dredging era as the Shine Basin, a broad open area of the Clutha River above Deadman's Point. The basin was worked extensively by the Chinese before it was completely modified by dredging. It is now under Lake Dunstan.

2. Caliche S133/223 rockshelter (now G41/498)

Location: S133 056661 Cromwell Gorge
Excavated: Feb. 1979 (destroyed by highway construction Feb. 1983)

Caliche shelter (Figure 4.4) was located about 30 m above the old Cromwell–Clyde highway, at a point about 6 km from Cromwell. The shelter consisted of a relatively dry area underneath a large boulder. The front was walled-up with large pieces of caliche (a pumice-like rock formed by the precipitation of leached $CaSO_4$, calcium sulphate – hence the site's name). This is the only known site where caliche was used for wall construction rather than the ubiquitous schist. Caliche is very light, large pieces weighing only a few kilograms. The stone, in this instance, was obtained from within the channel of a small creek where it had precipitated in shallow pools. The creek also served as the shelter's water source. At the time of the excavation, the wall stood 1 m high leaving about a 30 cm gap between the top of the wall and the overhanging rock. Large pieces of caliche lying in front of the wall and inside the shelter suggested that the wall was originally full height. At the western end, a gap in the rock allowed access (by crawling) to a smaller chamber, which was recorded by Higham, Mason and Moore (1976) as site S133/223.

At the front of the shelter, the roof was 1.7 m high, sloping to 0.7 m at the rear. The floor had been excavated before occupation to give greater head room, resulting in the living surface being about 30 cm below the ground level outside the shelter. A fireplace, made of earth-filled kerosene cans and slabs of schist, is believed to have been associated with a later occupation by rabbiters c.1930. No clear stratigraphic distinction could be discerned between the Chinese and rabbiter's occupations, the remains being intermixed. Four small waste flakes of silcrete were also found in the cultural layer, suggesting that the shelter was briefly used by a Māori party at some stage. The neck (vertebrae and tracheal rings) of a moa was found under 75 cm of sterile loess below the human occupation debris (Figure 4.4). These bones, which almost certainly predate human occupation in the area, were in situ and apparently undisturbed. No other bones were evident.

The entire floor area was excavated, as well as a chequerboard pattern of units on the revetted terrace in front of the shelter. No concentrated deposits of midden were located, just sparse scatters. The excavation revealed the base of a wall, also made of caliche, running diagonally across part of the terrace. It may have served as a windbreak.

3. Sheung Fong S133/21 rockshelter (now G41/373)

Location: S133 033674 Cromwell Gorge
Excavated: Nov. 1979 (inundated by the creation of Lake Dunstan in 1992)

The Sheung Fong shelter (literally "upper cave") is located on the true right bank of the Clutha River opposite Hartley and Reilly Beach, about 1.5 km below Cromwell. It is one of a group of four Chinese shelters (the others being sites S133/20, 22 and 23). S133/22, which is about 4 m below the Sheung Fong shelter, was also excavated. The shelter (Figure 4.5; Plate 1) is situated under a large boulder at the top of a colluvial slope. Immediately behind the shelter there is a steep schist face. The west and north sides of the L-shaped structure are enclosed by a wall of split schist extending from ground level to the overhanging rock. The chimney and fireplace are built into the north wall. The narrow doorway (30 cm wide) is typical of this type of Chinese dwelling.

Before excavation, there was no cultural material visible in the shelter, although odd fragments of glass and celadon ceramic were lying on the surface downslope. The entire interior of the shelter was excavated, as well as random squares on the steep slope below, to a point adjacent to the doorway of the lower shelter (Ha Fong S133/22).

4. Ha Fong S133/22 rockshelter (now G41/374)

Location: S133 033674 Cromwell Gorge
Excavated: Dec. 1979 (inundated by the creation of Lake Dunstan in 1992)

Ha Fong shelter (literally "lower cave") is situated about 4 m below the Sheung Fong shelter (upper cave) described above. The natural shelter was formed when a large schist slab came to rest on two large schist boulders, creating a roofed cavity. The shelter (Figure 4.6; Plate 2) was fully enclosed by the construction of mud-mortared, split schist walls along the north and west sides. The floor at the western end is approximately 40 cm below the outside ground level. Excavation revealed the floor of the western half had been covered with large schist slabs. At the eastern end, the silt and clay deposit had been partially excavated to extend the usable area, but enough had been left in situ to form a raised area that probably served as the sleeping platform. The lowest part of the roof is 1.2 m above the floor. The fireplace and chimney are built into the wall, immediately to the left of the entrance.

A notable feature of the excavation was the recovery of 11 large rubber gumboots buried beneath the surface in one square. It was concluded the boots may have been buried there by rabbiters (or a gumboot fetishist), but the boots are not stylistically different from others found in Chinese sites in the area (see Section 5.6.4). An intact Chinese green ginger jar was found buried in an upright position about a metre in front of the 70 cm wide entrance.

5. Chinatown S133/48 (the Cromwell Chinese Camp) (now G41/390)

Location: S133 022695 Cromwell
Excavated: Jan.–Feb. 1980 (destroyed by lakeshore pre-formation before being inundated by the creation of Lake Dunstan in 1992)

Cromwell's Chinese Camp (locally known as "Chinatown" according to an old identity and the Rev. Don) was established in the late 1860s. It is not certain whether it owes its origins to the arrival of the first Chinese storekeepers in Cromwell, who established a small business area on the undeveloped upper end of Melmore Terrace, the main street of Cromwell, or whether the storekeepers set up shop there because there was already a small Chinese settlement nearby. Regardless of who was first, the residential part of the settlement developed on the already mined-over terrace beside the Kawarau River, while the Chinese merchants established their businesses on the terrace above. The two areas were separated by a steep 30 m high bank. The residential part is depicted in Figure 4.7. One of the six known photographs of the settlement is reproduced in Plate 3 (also Plates 4–6).

The settlement's population averaged about 40 for most of the 19th century, the greatest number (67) being present in 1886 (NZ Census); but the census figures almost certainly include a few Chinese who lived within about a 5 km radius of Cromwell, and a few who lived in huts 500–1,000 m upstream of the settlement (see Ritchie 1983a:10 for population figures).

The residential part was excavated in Jan–Feb. 1980. The site and the excavation were described in an interim report (Ritchie 1980a) and in an information paper on Chinese site archaeology in the Cromwell area (Ritchie 1983a). Consequently, only summary details are presented here. Sixty-five percent of the 20 well-defined structures in the settlement were single, isolated units. The other seven were massed back to back and formed a central cluster around a stone-walled enclosure (probably a garden, but possibly a pig pen). The huts were constructed of cobbles of greywacke and slabs of schist derived from tailings from earlier European mining along the riverbank (see Figure 4.7). Mud mortar was usually employed to bind the stones, but in one instance (hut 19) a lime mortar and plaster was used on a least one wall. The stone walls were surmounted by roofs consisting of corrugated iron sheeting supplemented by scrappy offcuts of zinc and iron sheeting and flattened kerosene cans. The few post butts that survived were made of milled timber. Saplings and driftwood were probably also used for framing. Some of the huts had flooring made of interlocking slabs of schist, while in others the floor consisted of the compacted river terrace gravels. In nearly every instance, the door was located on the left-hand side of the fireplace and chimney, at one end of the hut. The limited post butt evidence suggested that the bed or sleeping platform was built across the opposite end wall. Some huts had wooden or stone doorsteps, and in many instances short pieces of iron standards were used to support the door jambs. Both the structural remains and photographic evidence indicate that windows and vents were entirely absent.

In January 1985, two small terraces (S133/48a: Figure 4.9) on the slope above and slightly to the east of the residential area were tested by trenching. The terraces are believed to be natural terracettes that have been slightly widened. They were used for horticultural purposes by some of the last Chinese in the Cromwell settlement (Craig pers. comm.). The excavations confirmed that the terraces have been considerably modified by slumping and fossicking. Modern rubbish was frequently found in direct association with pre-1900 Chinese and European artefacts. No clear evidence of made soils was evident; the sandy soil on the terraces seemed virtually identical to the soil elsewhere on the slope, except that there was a deeper cover of leaf litter on the terraces. An old apple tree on the edge of the lower terrace was almost certainly planted by the Chinese, as were the overgrown remnants of a small grove of plum trees sited 35 m east of the terraces. No trace of a Chinese hut or shed known to have been in the vicinity of Trench D (Figure 4.9) was found either, other than a short, low earth alignment running at right angles across the terrace. According to an elderly informant, the walls of the structure were made of earth-filled kerosene cans (Sanders pers. comm.). The terraces appear to have been heavily modified and any trace of the structure destroyed by fossickers.

The private sections where the Chinese stores were located on upper Melmore Terrace were not available for archaeological excavations, but a large collection (the Mangos collection) had been "dug up" by the landowner. I was able to examine this collection. The range of artefacts was similar to that uncovered in the residential area of Chinatown, although there are much higher concentrations of food containers and alcohol bottles. Artefacts from the store sites that were considered unique or noteworthy for some other reason are described in Chapter 5.

6. Queensberry II (QB2) S124/207 hut sites (2) (now G40/179)

Location: S124 145967 Queensberry district, Upper Clutha
Excavated: Nov. 1981 (extant)

The Queensberry II site (abbreviated to QB2; Figure 4.10) is a small mud-mortared schist miner's hut located on the right bank of the Clutha River in the Queensberry district (about midway between Cromwell and Wanaka). Forty metres north of the hut, the sparse remains of another hut (QB1) were also uncovered, similarly sited within a dense stand of briar and regenerating manuka. Both huts were excavated. The investigation of the QB1 site produced negligible artefactual remains, and so little remained of the stonework that it seems likely it was used in the construction of the QB2 hut.

At the time of the excavation, the walls of QB2 stood over a metre high. The hut exhibits two features common to Chinese huts in the Cromwell area: parts of three walls are built into the adjacent bank, and the back part of the floor is at a higher elevation (30 cm higher) than the rest of the floor. The elevated area, retained by a low stone riser, appears to have served as the sleeping platform. The front half of the hut was paved with schist slabs. A stone-lined pit in the back left corner is a unique feature of this hut. It probably served as a "food safe". Cultural debris from the hut was scattered down the slope towards the river.

4 The archaeological evidence

7. Apple Tree S124/212 hut and associated tailings (now G40/184)

Location: S124 137975 Queensberry district, Upper Clutha
Excavated: Dec. 1981 (extant)

The Apple Tree site (Figure 4.11), so named because an old apple tree was growing beside the hut, is located on the right bank of the Clutha River, within an area of tailings (S124/213) that are believed to have been created by the hut's occupant(s). The site is about 800 m upstream of S124/207 (QB2). The hut is a lean-to style construction utilising mud-mortared schist slabs and river cobbles. At the time of the excavation, all the walls stood to full height, revealing that the structure had no windows. Two walls are built into the bank. The north wall extends beyond the hut to form a retaining wall. Judging from photographs of villages in South China, lean-to style construction is a feature of multi-room houses there, but it is not a common feature of Chinese huts in Central Otago. The hut has a fireplace and chimney built into the west wall. There is also an outdoor fireplace (Figure 4.11). All the interior of the hut was excavated, as well as the flat area between the hut and the apple tree and the sloping ground to the south of the doorway.

The last Chinese occupant (possibly the only one) is remembered by an elderly European resident of Queensberry, Mr R. Lawless. When he was a young boy (c.1910) he used to give rabbits to the old Chinese miner. Although he could not recall the Chinese man's name, he believes that he committed suicide. His body was found in the river: "All his possessions were tied to it [the body], including a pick, shovel, camp oven and two billies." Before his demise, the old miner would often say "the river's calling me" (Lawless pers. comm. 1979).

8. Sandy Point S124/231 hut site (now G40/203)

Location: S124 137999 (Queensberry district, Upper Clutha)
Excavated: Dec. 1981 (extant)

The Sandy Point hut site (Figure 4.12) is situated on a terrace riser about 10 m above the southern end of an extensive river flat. Nearby, at GR 135000, an extensive area of tailings is located. When first recorded, the site was overgrown with manuka; a fire had swept through it at some stage, blackening the rocks and scorching the surface of exposed cultural debris in and around the hut. Only the chimney and fireplace were intact; the remaining walls stood no higher than 80 cm. The west wall, which was built into the slope, had completely collapsed, allowing about 2 cubic metres of gravel to pour into the hut. The debris had to be shovelled out before the excavation could commence. A retaining wall of planks and iron standards was erected to prevent further collapses.

A small, cobble-lined channel had been formed down the slope below the hut doorway. The upper part of the channel served as the entrance way, while the lower part would have ensured that surplus runoff, or water from the sluice workings, was channelled past the hut. The excavation encompassed the interior of the hut and a random pattern of units northeast of the doorway. A useful surface collection of tin wax vesta boxes was made off the gravel fan below the hut.

9. Northburn S133/77 rockshelter (now G41/107)

Location: S133 053763 Quartz Reef Point, near Lowburn
Excavated: Jan. 1982 (sited above new Cromwell–Tarras highway)

The Northburn shelter (Figure 4.13; Plate 2) is located within a small schist outcrop below the Quartz Reef Point mining area, about 7 km from Cromwell. The site is believed to have been a habitation associated with a small area of amorphous tailings (now under Lake Dunstan) on the left bank of the Clutha River, about 100 m below the shelter. About 150 m south of the shelter, there are the sparse remains of some stone walls and one-room buildings. One building has been restored as a crib. These structures were described as "the remains of the Lowburn Chinese Camp" (Perriam pers. comm.), but no positive evidence of Chinese occupation was observed during an inspection of the area in 1982.

When the excavation was conducted in 1982, the shelter was within the boundaries of Northburn station. Now, because the highway has been realigned, it is within the National Roads Board reserve. Although it is only 10 m above the new highway, it is not visible from the road because it is located under the upper side of a schist outcrop. Outwardly, the structure appears in very good condition and is quite picturesque (Plate 2). The wall, made of mud-mortared schist slabs, still stands to full height, even though it had many inherent structural weaknesses such as the failure to overlap stones. Gaps in the wall were plugged with tussock and mud. Nine months after the excavation, the central section of the wall collapsed. This has been rebuilt using soil-cement as the bonding medium. Inside, the shelter is remarkably cramped, the one-level dirt floor having a total area of only 5 square metres. A fireplace is built into the stonework at the southern end.

About 30 m above the shelter, a water race (S133/688) traverses the slope. A side-diversion has been constructed to divert water down a channel that passes in front of the shelter. The primary purpose of the channel appears to have been to convey water down to the riverside workings, but it would also have provided a readily accessible domestic supply.

The investigation involved excavation of the interior of the shelter and the metre-wide terrace in front of it, plus random squares in and on either side of the channel. In terms of cultural remains, it was a very impoverished site.

10. Ah Wee's S115/54 hut site (now G40/100)

Location: S115 067104 Upper Clutha River, Luggate area
Excavated: Nov. 1982 (extant)

This mud brick hut (Figure 4.14; Plate 7) is situated within a small grove of poplar trees, at the upstream end of a river flat that has been sluiced and now consists of an extensive series of herringbone tailings (S115/53). The storage dams and supply races (S115/52) are located on the terrace above the hut. This complex of sites (Figure 4.15) is believed to have been formed in the 1890s by Ah Wee, a Chinese miner (Roxburgh 1957:177).

The mud brick construction of this structure differs from that of most of the Chinese huts in the Cromwell region, which are made of stone. The walls are freestanding and 40 cm thick, but only stand their full height (2 m) at the southern end. Parts of the east and west walls are still erect, but the north wall has completely disintegrated. The interior was fully excavated, as was a random pattern of units within the flat area around the hut. Three units were also excavated in the bank below the site. A small midden, largely consisting of tin wax vesta boxes and broken glass, was uncovered in the tailings on the north side of the hut. This material was collected as one unit.

11. The Poplars S115/44 hut site (now G40/90)

Location: S115 054116 Upper Clutha River, Luggate area
Excavated: Dec. 1982 (extant)

The Poplars site is on the right bank of the Clutha River, at the upstream end of an elongated grove of poplar trees. The site is about midway between two gold workings (S115/43, amorphous tailings, and S115/45, box tailings). Both sets of tailings are poor examples of their respective types.

The hut is a mud-mortared structure made of schist and greywacke river cobbles (Figure 4.16; Plate 8). The back wall is built into the adjacent bank. Behind the hut there is a flattened area contained by remnants of stone revetment. This appears to have been a storage annex. The interior of the hut and annex were excavated, while the ground around the hut was thoroughly tested, particularly the areas out from the door and behind the structure. About 5 m beyond the door, a midden concentration was uncovered in a slight depression.

12. Hanging Rock S133/474 rockshelter (now F41/123)

Location: S133 945712 Gees Flat, Kawarau Gorge
Excavated: Dec. 1982 (extant)

This shelter (Figure 4.17) is situated under a large overhanging rock outcrop, about 10 m from the right bank of the Kawarau River. There are remnants of ground sluice workings in the vicinity. The structure is made of mud-mortared schist slabs, which now stand no higher than one metre. The height of the overhanging rock (2.5 to 4 m) suggests that the dwelling was, in effect, a hut built under an overhang. Three of the walls are made of stacked schist, while the back of the overhang formed the south wall.

The interior was excavated, as well as a random pattern of squares on the steep sloping ground towards the river. The external units proved unproductive. It would appear, in the case of this site, that refuse was dumped either into the river or into the nearby sluiced area and subsequently washed away. Some very fragmentary moa bones were found immediately beneath the cultural material in the southwest corner of the structure. Six metres east of the shelter there is a narrow stone-lined channel running down to the river. It probably served as the water supply. The nearby Kawarau River is entrenched at this point, making it very difficult and dangerous to obtain water directly from the river.

13. Riverside S133/791 rockshelter (now F41/410)

Location: 5133 948708 Gees Fiat, Kawarau Gorge
Excavated: Jan. 1983 (in Otago Goldfields Park reserve)

The small Riverside rockshelter is sited under an overhang at the top of a 15 m slope above the Kawarau River. The front of the shelter, which overlooks the river, is walled with mud-mortared schist slabs enclosing an area 4 m long by 1.3 m wide. The wall varies in height from 1.3 to 2 m and has collapsed around the entrance. A chimney is located at the eastern end (Figure 4.18). The floor area of the shelter (c. 7 square metres) was excavated, along with a few square metres of gently sloping ground to the east of the shelter and random squares amid the large rocks littering the slope down to the river. The ground around the site is virtually all gravel with no soil development. A small (0.5 square metre) area of soil retained behind the chimney may have been a little garden plot. There are extensive areas of European workings on the terrace above the site. Parts of these may have been reworked by the Chinese occupant of the shelter because there is little scope for working the banks along this part of the river.

14. The Arrowtown Chinese Settlement S123/249 (now F41/435)

Location: S123 684824 beside Bush Creek, Arrowtown
Excavated: Nov.–Dec. 1983

The site is now a Goldfields Park reserve. The huts and Ah Lum's store have been faithfully restored.

The one-time Arrowtown Chinese Settlement is located on the south bank of Bush Creek, at a point approximately 100 m upstream from the creek's confluence with the Arrow River. The Chinese were well established there in 1869 (Ritchie 1984:7). The *Dunstan Times* (13/5/1870:2) reported: "these industrious people have erected a row of 20 comfortable sod huts, all with windows and doors, fit for any European to dwell in… and they possess a store and a restaurant upon an enormous scale". Both contemporary photographs (see Plate 9) and the archaeological evidence indicate that by 1880 the settlement consisted of about 10 cob and stone huts, and at least two stores. An extensive garden area had also been established on the sloping ground above the huts (Ritchie and Bedford 1983:9). By 1910, many of the huts had been abandoned and Ah Lum's store (S123/250) was the only one still operating. The settlement was abandoned shortly after his death in 1925. Rate books held by the Arrowtown Borough Council and Crown Titles and Registrars indicate that there were four Chinese shops operating at Arrowtown between about 1885 and 1895. They changed hands several times (Hangar pers. comm. from title research). One of these stores (Sui Sing's), an elongated wooden structure, was sited in the middle of the Chinese Camp. It was operating before 1873 (it was offered for sale then; *Arrow Observer* 30/5/1873:3). The store and garden were transferred to Chung Kee (a.k.a. Wong Chong) during the period 1891–93. It was closed by 1899 (Hangar pers. comm.). The large abandoned Chinese store appears to have become locally known as "the Chinese long house". It served as a "social hall" (Dudley pers. comm. 1983). However, its use for the latter purpose appears to have been short-lived; within a few years, there is no trace of the structure in photographs.

The archaeological investigation involved the systematic excavation of the interior of all the huts, exposed midden deposits, and testing the ground around the structures to detect other cultural deposits (see Figures 4.19 and 4.20a–h). The huts and other remains are described in detail in Ritchie (1984). Constructional details of the structures and other relevant information are discussed in the comparative analysis sections in the latter parts of this chapter.

15. Ah Lum's store S123/250 (now F41/436)

Location: S123 684824 on higher ground, adjacent to the Arrowtown Chinese Settlement
Excavated: Dec. 1983 (the store was partially restored in 1985)

Ah Lum's store was one of at least three Chinese stores located adjacent to the Arrowtown Chinese Settlement. It is believed to have been built c.1880 and closed upon the death of Ah Lum (its fourth Chinese owner/lessee) in 1925. Research by Mark Hangar on the titles and rate book entries pertaining to the section the store stands on suggest that the store was not opened until Ah Chung Bung took up occupancy in 1893, and its store function ceased possibly not long after Ah Lum leased it in 1908 (Hangar pers. comm.).

The store (Plate 10), described in detail in Ritchie (1984:49–56), is a mud-mortared, split schist construction measuring 8 by 5 m. The schist has been worked by a stone mason and its finish and overall appearance is clearly a cut above the standard miner's hut. The building is divided into five rooms (Figure 4.21). The entire interior was excavated, as well as a random pattern of units around the building. A large Chinese barrel jar found buried up to its rim behind the store may have been used for collecting rainwater. A midden deposit (F15) associated with the store was also excavated. Preliminary artefact analysis results were presented in Ritchie (1984). The complete results are presented in Chapter 5. The store is notable in that it is the only preserved Chinese store on the New Zealand goldfields.

16. The Rapids S133/453 camp and forge (now F41/103)

Location: S133 900740 lower Kawarau Gorge
Excavated: Jan. 1984 (extant, on the shoreline of Lake Dunstan)

The Rapids site (Figure 4.22) is on a small flat area among poplar trees, 50 m downstream of the old Cromwell Development Co. pumphouse building in the Kawarau Gorge. The site area is separated from the river by a large schist outcrop. The site consists of a presumed habitation demarcated by a rectangle of stones with a mud-mortared chimney base in the southeast corner. Excavation indicated that the walls were not substantial, suggesting that the habitation may have been a canvas-roofed structure. A stone forge, evidenced by scraps of worked iron and slag, is located 3 m west of the structure. Although sheltered to some extent by a 0.8 m high rock wall, the area around the forge showed no signs of being roofed. Midden was concentrated in a narrow gap between rocks and the poplar trees on the river side of the site. It appears to have been thrown in the general direction of the river, but a portion fell short and gradually accumulated. The interior of the "habitation" was excavated but proved rather unproductive.

17. Flax Grove S133/494 rockshelter (now F41/103)

Location: S133 927723 Kawarau Gorge
Excavated: Feb. 1985 (extant)

This well-sheltered site is located under a rock outcrop 10 m above the right bank of the Kawarau River, near the confluence of an unnamed creek. The site's name was coined because of the presence of a small flax grove at the mouth of the creek. The layout and surrounds are depicted in Figures 4.23 and 4.24.

The site is similar to the Hanging Rock site, in that it is unlikely that the stone walling along the front extended right to the top of the overhang (which is 4 m high in the central part). Again, it is inferred that a light roof structure surmounted the wall, in effect creating a hut under the overhang. The height of the remaining walls varies from 1.5 to 2.5 m. The interior of the shelter was excavated plus the external units marked on Figure 4.23. The recovery of several paper artefacts including receipts for gold dust deposits, a "shopping list" and a list of medicinal ingredients (the latter two were in Chinese) was a notable feature of the site assemblage. The paper had been used as caulking between the gaps in the shelter wall.

18. The Willows S124/42 hut site (now G40/37)

Location: S124 094068 Clutha River, Luggate area
Excavated: Jan. 1985 (extant)

The Willows site is 10 m from the left bank of the Clutha River, and adjacent to alluvial gold workings (Sl24/123). The layout and dimensions of this mud-mortared, cobble-walled hut are as depicted in Figure 4.25. Although the site is known to have been occupied by a Chinese miner (he cooked for the harvesters on Kane's farm c.1910; Kane pers. comm.), few artefacts were found during the excavation, and none of positively Chinese origin. However, the hut's dimensions, and construction features such as the partially paved floor and small fireplace, are indicative of Chinese occupation (see later discussion in this chapter).

19. Platform S133/466 rockshelter (now F41/116)

Location: S133 947708 Gees Flat, Kawarau Gorge
Excavated: Feb. 1985 (in Otago Goldfields Park reserve)

The Platform shelter is located at the base of a rock bluff behind an area of tailings beside the Kawarau River. The layout of the site is depicted in Figure 4.26. Although the site is suspected to be of Chinese origin, no positive evidence to support this contention was found during the excavation. The floor deposit in the shelter consisted of fine cloying dust mixed with up to 30 cm depth of sheep manure (a thoroughly unpleasant place to work). The most notable feature of the site is a rectangular bracken-covered platform (presumably the sleeping area) along the north wall of the shelter. This area is retained by a low stone border.

4.3 SECONDARY SITES

In addition to the fully excavated Chinese sites described thus far, materials uncovered by systematic excavations or private individuals from Chinese sites elsewhere in Central Otago have also been examined. The major additional sources are briefly described below.

1. The Rockfall 1 site S133/37 Cromwell Gorge (now under Lake Dunstan)

This site is one of six occupied rockshelters within a prominent rockfall in the Cromwell Gorge. The site is notable in that it contains evidence of occupations by three different groups: Polynesians in the 16th century, Chinese miners in the 19th century and rabbiters in the 20th century. The prehistoric deposits, site layout and stratigraphy have been discussed elsewhere (Ritchie 1982b).

2. The Kawarau rockshelter S133/72 Ripponvale

This rockshelter was located in an area of tailings on the left bank of the Kawarau River near the entrance to the river gorge. The site was badly fossicked in 1979, and totally obliterated in mid-1983 by MWD lakeshore pre-formation work associated with the Clyde Dam reservoir. However, a useful assemblage of items discarded by the fossickers was gathered in 1979.

3. The Motatapu hut S124/393 Motatapu Valley

This Chinese hut site was uncovered and destroyed during a small-scale, private mining operation in the Motatapu Valley between 1980 and 1983. The miner, Mr J. Aspinall of Wanaka, carefully collected all the material as it was exposed, and still retains it. The assemblage includes some Chinese ceramics that are not known, or are very rarely found, in the Cromwell area (see Section 5.2).

4. The Ledge site S133/868 Kawarau Gorge (now F41/421)

The Ledge site is in the Kawarau Gorge, about 500 m upstream of the Roaring Meg power station. The site consists of the remnants of a European house and associated midden scattered for 25 m down a cliff face in front of the structure. At a point about 20 m from the top of the cliff, the midden is concentrated on a ledge, which acted as a collection receptacle. The ledge was excavated in January 1984. Amid the predominantly European material, some Chinese artefacts were uncovered, including an octagonal teacup of a type not previously known from Central Otago (see Section 5.2). The site was also notable for the large number and variety of tin wax vesta matchboxes recovered, reflecting its long occupation (Bedford 1985a).

5. Halfway House Hotel site 5133/128 Cromwell Gorge

During the excavation of this European hotel site (c.1864–1917) in November 1984, some oriental ceramics were uncovered, including a Japanese teacup (Bedford 1985b, 1985c). The Chinese artefacts are possibly derived from the employment of a Chinese cook or gardener at the hotel at some stage. The site is now under Lake Dunstan.

4.4 DATES OF OCCUPATION OF THE STUDY SITES

The occupation dates were determined primarily by wax vesta matchbox dating (see Anson 1983; Bedford 1985a), bottle dating (Ritchie and Bedford 1983) and by recourse to historical records. The dates obtained by the various techniques are presented in Table 4.2. Although historic records enabled the urban settlements to be dated fairly precisely, the "occupation dates" of the rural sites (based on historical records) are less reliable. The dates of the first occupation are generally based on the dates when the first Chinese became established in a particular area, e.g. the Kawarau Gorge, while the terminal dates are estimates based, in part, on contemporary comments (such as those of Don) that indicate when the Chinese vacated an area. However, in some areas there were a few who stayed on long after most of their countrymen had left.

Dating based on the analysis of tin wax vesta matchboxes is discussed in detail in Section 5.3.6. Matchboxes can provide a good indication of when a site was occupied, but it is necessary to be mindful that natural degradation of matchbox metal and differential survival means there is an inherent bias towards the recovery of more recent boxes, simply because they have had less time to deteriorate in the ground. This tendency to date "late" is reflected in Table 4.2.

Bottle glass presents few problems regarding its longevity in sites, and certain bottles are particularly useful for dating (see Section 5.1), but their utility for precise dating (i.e. plus or minus five years) is often limited because the periods of production and usage of many bottle types were too long. So, while they confirm the general period of occupation (which can also be determined by other means such as by dating ceramics or tin cans), more specific information about the beginning or termination of an occupation or re-occupation can be wanting. Embossed or distinctive bottles with short periods of production and usage are the most useful for efficient dating. Table 4.2 details the known or determined dates of occupation of each of the study sites. The urban settlements at Cromwell and Arrowtown had the greatest longevity. They existed for over 50 years from c.1870 until after 1920 (Cromwell 1920, Arrowtown c.1925). Ah Lum's was established in the early 1880s and continued to be used as a residence, if not a store, until Ah Lum's death in 1925 (see Ritchie 1983a:56).

Although poorly reflected in the "matchbox dates", the dates deduced from "bottle dating" indicate that the Cromwell Gorge rockshelters were the first sites in the area to be occupied by the Chinese. This is in line with the documented historic pattern (Parcell 1976). There was little positive archaeological evidence of pre-1870 occupation in any of the study sites. According to contemporary accounts, the first Chinese came into the area in 1866. The Upper Clutha sites were not occupied until c.1880. This parallels the sparse historic record of Chinese settlement in this area (apart from Bendigo Creek, which was occupied in the late 1860s). The Upper Clutha sites appear to have been abandoned between 1900 and 1910.

The assemblages recovered from two rockshelters (Northburn and Platform) and one hut site (the Willows) were impoverished and contained no bottles or matchboxes. However, from analysis of the other residues in the sites, it is fairly certain that they were occupied between 1880 and 1920, and in the case of the Willows site, it is known to have been occupied by a Chinese miner c.1905–15 (Kane pers. comm.).

4.5 ARCHITECTURAL FEATURES

Ethno-historical insights into the nature and social role of Chinese dwellings on the goldfields were presented in Section 3.6. This section presents an archaeological perspective on Chinese living spaces. The "architectural evidence" presented here is from the Clutha study sites; it may not reflect "Chinese housing" further afield (especially beyond Central Otago, although there are certainly common threads). As noted previously, the Chinese exhibited considerable versatility in house construction, generally utilising whatever was at hand. Consequently, Chinese dwellings varied in appearance from one mining district to another. For example, most of the Chinese huts on the Waipori goldfield were built of mud brick or cob, whereas at Round Hill, wooden shingles, punga logs (fern tree trunks) and rough timber (possibly mill offcuts) were used extensively. Photographs of the Lawrence Chinese Camp show it was largely built of timber with corrugated iron roofs. In the Clutha and Wakatipu Basins, relatively little timber was readily available, so stone (cobbles and/or schist slabs) and paddled-mud, or a combination of mud and stone, were the principle materials used. The huts of poor men or temporary structures were often built of rice sacking. Natural rockshelters were used extensively in the river gorges and rocky side gullies.

4.5.1 THE ROCKSHELTERS

A typical Chinese rockshelter in the Cromwell area consists of a one-room chamber formed by erecting a wall along the front of a natural rock overhang or the cavity beneath one or more large boulders. In some instances, e.g. the Hanging Rock and Flax Grove sites, the height of the overhang (4 m) is such that it was not practical to "wall up" the whole height, so a light roof was constructed, in effect creating a hut under an overhang. In those shelters where it can be determined, the doorways were small – measuring between 35 and 60 cm in width and vary from 1.3 to 1.6 m high. Construction features of the excavated rockshelters are summarised in Table 4.3 and discussed below.

The table clearly shows the predominant usage of mud-mortared schist slabs for walling. Of over 100 Chinese rockshelter dwellings observed in Central Otago by the writer, approximately 70% have schist slab walls, while schist and cobbles were utilised in about another 10%. This pattern is not hard to understand. Schist is ubiquitous in Central Otago and pieces suitable for building are readily available where it has weathered from outcrops. The stone has natural flat surfaces making it easy to stack and overlap successive layers. Used in conjunction with mud mortar, cheap, durable and weatherproof walls and structures could be built rapidly.

Although materials such as packed earth, vegetation or canvas are less likely to have survived as well as stone walls, field observations indicate that if the Chinese built a shelter with any degree of permanence in the Cromwell area, they utilised stone, either schist slabs if they were readily available or cobbles recovered from the tailings in mining claims. The use of caliche in the Caliche shelter is an interesting exception, but understandable since there was a convenient source of the material to hand. Packed mud was used occasionally for walling-in rockshelters if there was no ready source of stone nearby. About 9% (4) of the Chinese shelters in the Cromwell Gorge had no apparent solid walling. Examination of the front of the overhangs often revealed nails (or nail holes) suggesting that canvas, calico or sacking had been hung over the entrance. In the absence of timber to build a door or door frame, the Chinese sometimes made a "wire netting mattress" the same size as the doorway. The netting mattress was stuffed with tussock and other vegetation and pulled into the entrance as a door and draught-stopper (Roebuck pers. comm.).

Initially, rockshelter habitations were widely used by the Chinese in the Cromwell area because the river gorges, where the main strikes were made, abounded with both gold and suitable overhangs and caves for constructing shelters. As the gold in the river gorges was worked out, their usage declined, but they continued to be used in some areas, e.g. the Molyneux (Roxburgh) Gorge and Conroy's Gully (Don 1906:28), long after they had been generally abandoned in other areas. Don described them as "cosy in winter and cool in summer" (Don 1906:28). Many of the former "cave-dwellers" built huts in the settlements or on claims that they had started working elsewhere, but some maintained rockshelter dwellings that they returned to at specific times of the year, to work the beaches when the rivers were low.

As can be seen from a perusal of the internal dimensions of the shelters listed in Table 4.3, they varied considerably in size, although it is difficult to quantify their relative degree of "creature comfort". Those at the bottom end of the scale are characterised by the following features: low head room (sometimes improved by digging out the floor); dampness and seepage; uneven, rocky floor surfaces; rock surfaces that are prone to spalling; difficult access, poor ventilation and generally cramped conditions. In addition, some had poor access to water and firewood, and little ground suitable for gardening in the vicinity. At the other end of the scale there are shelters that appear to be well sheltered, dry and spacious both inside and out and have a sunny aspect. These dwellings were probably at least as comfortable as huts of similar dimensions. Field observations and the volumes of occupation refuse recovered from the smallest and least comfortable shelters suggest that they were generally not occupied for long periods. However, the inverse is not true of the larger and seemingly more comfortable structures. The duration of their occupation varied considerably, probably being dependent to a large extent on the availability and accessibility of gold in the vicinity.

4.5.2 EXCAVATED CHINESE STRUCTURES: CONSTRUCTION FEATURES

As noted, most of the Chinese dwellings (mainly miners' huts) in Central Otago were made of stone or mud (both mud brick and cob). Most are simple, rectangular, ridge-beam constructions characterised by a door and chimney at one end. Frequently, one or more of the walls were built into an adjacent bank or slope. There appear to be few structural differences between the rural and urban huts, although, as elaborated in the following discussion, there are some interesting differences between the construction of the huts in the Cromwell and Arrowtown settlements. Structural features of the study sites are summarised in Table 4.4. The possibility that the construction of some of the described structures has changed over the years, particularly regarding roofing materials, cannot be totally ruled out. However, the use of the materials cited below was confirmed by archaeological investigations, or in the case of the structures in the urban settlements, through study of contemporary photographs. Following the discussion on materials and related aspects, the dimensions (Section 4.6) and orientation of the structures (Section 4.7) are examined. Section 4.8 documents some distinctive differences between Chinese and European dwellings in the study area.

4.5.2.1 Wall construction

The immediately discernible features of the table are the differences between the huts in the Cromwell and Arrowtown settlements. Whereas most of the huts at Cromwell were built of cobbles, those at Arrowtown are predominantly of mud construction or a mud/stone combination. The Cromwell settlement was established in an area that had already been mined by Europeans. Consequently, there was an abundant supply of cobbles among the tailings available for construction purposes. There was little consistency in the stacking of the cobbles within and between individual huts in Chinatown. They are often stacked horizontally, vertically or diagonally within a short section of wall. Elsewhere, the Chinese in the study area preferred to use detrital slabs of schist for construction if they were readily available, presumably because they have more inherent stability and were easier to stack than cobbles.

The procedure for creating the mud walls of many of the Arrowtown huts was observed first-hand by a now deceased Arrowtown resident (Dudley pers. comm.). The first step involved deciding on the size of the proposed hut. The "interior" was then dug over and puddled by the addition of water. This material was then dug out (up to 30 cm below the ground level) and packed to form the walls. If there was a shortage of mud (or for some other reason), some sections were built up with stone (e.g. ACS/3 and ACS/4).

Other construction techniques were used at Arrowtown (see Table 4.4). ACS/1 was a pre-built corrugated iron structure brought on to the site after 1900 (Dudley pers. comm.), but the use of pre-built huts was uncommon. Generally, construction materials, such as earth, clay, stone and tussock, were obtained from the environment near building sites. The main cost would have been in terms of one's labour input. Insights into the construction of two of the other former hut sites in the Arrowtown settlement are now available only from contemporary photographs because all trace of both sites has been completely obliterated: ACS/7 was a combination mud and wood construction, while ACS/14 had vertical wooden cladding. Ah Lum's store is included in the table because it also served as a habitation. From title and rate book research, the "stone and timber" building was erected for Wong Hop c.1883 (Hangar pers. comm.). Its size, shaped schist masonry and relative grandeur would have been beyond the means of the average miner. The construction of most of the rural hut sites listed in Table 4.4 is typical of those in the Upper Clutha area. However, the Rapids and 12 Mile Creek sites are interesting exceptions. The wall outline in the Rapids site is evidenced by a rectangle of schist slabs, seldom more than two stones deep. The stones may have secured a canvas structure. The 12 Mile Creek site was not excavated. It is included in the table because it possibly typifies Chinese hut construction in the few forested areas of Central Otago. The hut, one of several adjacent to the 12 Mile Creek, is in an area of beech forest. All that now remains of the sites are stone chimney bases and cultural debris scatters. It is likely that the Chinese used the timber to hand in construction, but as anyone familiar with the wood (*Nothofagus menziesii*) knows, it deteriorates very rapidly when exposed to damp conditions.

A common feature of the Chinese huts in the Cromwell area is that one or more walls are built into an adjacent bank or slope. Seventy percent of the huts in the Cromwell settlement have two walls built into an adjacent bank, the other huts being freestanding or built back to back (Table 4.4). The QB2, Apple Tree, Sandy Point, Poplars, ACS/5 and Willows huts are built into adjacent slopes. The common denominator seems to be that the walls of these structures are made of stone. Mud huts such as the majority of those at Arrowtown and Ah Wee's are freestanding. The rationale for constructing huts in this fashion is uncertain. While they may have been more sheltered and saved building at least one wall, it must have increased the likelihood of problems with water seepage.

The other major structural difference between the Cromwell and Arrowtown settlements is the central mass of huts built back to back at Cromwell (Figure 4.7). Although this form of construction has historical precedents for defensive and social reasons in China, there seems no clear-cut reason for resorting to it at Cromwell. There was no saving in construction materials because where the walls abut, they are double thickness.

4.5.2.2 Chimney construction

Both field observations and study of contemporary photographs indicate that most Chinese huts in Central Otago had mud-mortared stone chimneys, the main exception being "mud huts" where the chimneys were built of the same medium. The solid chimney bases, many complete with hearth stones (or bricks) and fire bars, are now the only visible remnant of many mud huts. During their heyday, the chimneys were often surmounted by a "chimney pot", such as kerosene cans with their ends cut out or a short piece of mining pipe. These fittings presumably improved the chimney draft and avoided smoke problems. On the Round Hill field, many of the huts were not only built of wood but also had wooden chimneys. Fire was a constant threat. Huts were frequently destroyed by fire (Don 1/1/1883:126, 1/3/1883:183) and in 1883, a fire threatened to destroy the business part of the Round Hill settlement (Don 2/4/1883:183).

The second column of Table 4.4 records the position of the chimney in the various structures. While it is difficult to ascertain precisely the sociological or physical significance of chimney placement, some points can be made:

1. The juxtaposition of the door and chimney in an end wall. In effect, this allowed one to tend the fire and "keep an eye on" what was happening in the area immediately outside the door. This positioning may in part have been influenced by deeply entrenched Chinese superstitions, motivating one to "be ready" or "not be taken by surprise" by either physical disturbances or evil spirits.

2. In all the Chinese structures in the Cromwell Chinese Camp, the chimneys are located on the right side of the doorway as you enter, whereas at Arrowtown and in the rural hut sites, the chimneys are located either right or left of the doorway in equal ratios. Why there should be such consistency in the positioning of hut chimneys in the Cromwell Chinese Camp is difficult to explain because it does not seem to be a response to a physical factor like the direction of the prevailing wind (see related discussion in Section 4.7). It seems beyond the bounds of chance that every hut builder at Cromwell would elect to build the chimney on the right-hand side of the doorway, unless there was some factor governing this construction behaviour. Possibly, new hut builders were advised by existing members of the community to build in such a fashion, or they just replicated the design of the existing huts.

3. In only two instances, ACS/5 at Arrowtown and in the Apple Tree site in the Upper Clutha, is a chimney

located other than in an end wall adjacent to the door. In ACS/5 (Figure 4.20d) the doorway is built into the side of the house, but still within clear view of the fireplace, which is built into the end wall. In the Apple Tree hut, the doorway is in the right-hand side of one end wall, but the fireplace is built into the opposite side wall (Figure 4.11). As mentioned in Section 4.1, the Apple Tree hut is rather unusual. It may not have been built by a Chinese miner.

4.5.2.3 Windows and doors

The recovery of European-style door hinges, padlocks, padbolts and handles, and study of contemporary photographs, indicate that most Chinese huts had a door made of wooden planking. Often the top was angled in line with the slope of the roof, to increase the clearance. Doors were hinged within a wooden frame, or in some instances, pivoted at the top and bottom. In ACS/4, a cart stub axle was set into the ground on one side of the doorway, and the door pivoted by using the concavity in the end of the axle. In the Poplars site, the "kick-up" of an upturned bottle was used in a similar fashion.

Contemporary photographs (e.g. see Butler 1977:28, 63) show that some Chinese huts (both stone and mud brick) had small square/rectangular vents or windows above the door. They appear to have been formed by setting wooden or metal boxes (with their bases and lids removed) into the wall. The role of these features is not clear, but they probably served as vents and allowed some natural light and fresh air into the often windowless structures (the Ha Fong shelter has a similar feature set into the wall).

In the absence of glass fragments, it is often difficult to ascertain whether a structure in a ruinous state had glazed windows. Study of contemporary photographs and the absence of window glass fragments in archaeological contexts indicates that most rural Chinese huts did not have windows or had very small ones. Window glass was found in only one of the rural sites (the Flax Grove shelter). It was present in six of the huts in the Arrowtown settlement, but in only two at Chinatown. The absence of glazed windows is probably attributable, in part, to the high incidence of European larrikinism and vandalism that was directed towards the Cromwell settlement and its inhabitants. They may have foregone windows, rather than put up with the expense and hassle of replacing broken panes and the risk of injury from breaking glass and stones.

4.5.2.4 Roofing materials

There is a discernible difference between the types of roofing utilised at Cromwell and Arrowtown (see Table 4.4). At the former, most of the huts were roofed with corrugated iron, whereas at Arrowtown, tussock thatch was the main roofing material. The thatch was replaced annually (Dudley pers. comm.). Many of the Chinese huts photographed by Don on his travels around the goldfields had tussock thatch overlaid with rice bags and canvas. In Don's opinion (1/20/1887:63), "huts with sod, walls, clay floors and a thatch roof had an air of mustiness". This factor, together with its greater durability, may partly explain the preference for corrugated iron at Cromwell, despite the capital outlay it involved. Other manufactured materials used for roofing included wooden shingles (used extensively at Round Hill), flattened kerosene cans and scraps of sheet iron or zinc.

4.6 HUT SIZES AND DIMENSIONS

Table 4.5 and Figure 4.27 show the floor areas of the Chinese huts and their internal dimensions. The average floor area of the 26 huts listed in Table 4.5 is 8.3 square metres.

The huts at Arrowtown are generally smaller than those at Cromwell. At Cromwell, the average floor area of the surviving structures is 8.1 square metres, whereas at Arrowtown it is 7.3 square metres, but only 6.25 square metres if the larger socialising hut (ACS/2) is omitted from the calculation. The size of two of the largest huts (7 and 14) was unable to be determined from the ground evidence. Consequently, one can only say that most of the Arrowtown huts are smaller than those excavated elsewhere in the Clutha catchment. Whatever the reason for the construction of generally smaller houses in the Arrowtown settlement, it is unlikely to be income-related. The Arrow was and still is one of the most productive gold-bearing rivers in the study area. As outlined in Section 3.6, Chinese miners seldom lived alone before the turn of the 19th century; usually between two and eight shared a hut together. Three was a common number judging from Don's numerous comments. Hut sizes varied accordingly. Study of contemporary photographs, dimensions of huts measured during field recording, and Don's comments indicate that the "standard" 2 to 4 men huts varied from 3 to 5 m in length and were 2 to 3 m wide. The width component (usually between 2 and 3 m) has considerably less variability than the length component, which varies from about 2 to 5 m (Figure 4.27). The length variability probably reflects notions such as:

a. ease or familiarity in building elongated structures;
b. an elongated structure provides better separation of sleeping and cooking areas, and generally better use of space;
c. an elongated structure enables better use of some materials, e.g. corrugated iron;
d. an elongated structure is easier to extend.

4.7 HUT ORIENTATION AND DOOR POSITIONS

While several consistencies in the materials and layout of the Chinese structures have been documented thus far, there are some interesting patterns evident in the

4 The archaeological evidence

orientation of the structures. These possibly reflect, to some extent, the maintenance of traditional Chinese concepts based on the cosmological principles of feng shui geomancy and demon spiritology (discussed below). The orientation of the huts (i.e. their doors) is documented in Table 4.6.

The table reveals a trend for hut doors at Chinatown and in most of the rural sites to be orientated in the easterly quarter, although on the ground there is considerable variation; few huts face in exactly the same direction. At Arrowtown, the dominant orientation is towards the northwest, and there is considerably more consistency between huts (most have a fairly similar door orientation). It is difficult to isolate a dominant motive for the varying orientation of the huts. Clearly, particularly in the Cromwell Camp, it is partly dependent on topographic restraints; the camp occupied about a 30 m wide flattish area between a steep slope and the Kawarau River. There seems to have been an inclination towards facing out onto open or lower land rather than towards a slope. While a desire "to obtain a view" is an understandable reason for orientating a structure or positioning a door in a particular place, there may have been a more practical reason, such as a defensive reaction to prevent European louts from throwing stones or other missiles through the open doorways from a higher vantage point.

At Arrowtown, a notable feature of the hut door orientation is that the majority face out to the northwest overlooking what would have been open creek bed. At Cromwell, approximately half of the hut doors face east or southeast towards the river, while a similar pattern holds for the rural sites. Orientation towards the water is understandable both in terms of "obtaining a good view" and "keeping an eye on the river". The latter reason might have been particularly influential because mining returns were affected both favourably and adversely by the level of the rivers. Most of the doorways in the gorge rockshelters face towards the rivers too, but their position was largely governed by the shape and orientation of the space under suitable overhanging rocks.

The easterly orientation of most of the Cromwell Camp huts may have been partly influenced by a desire "to maximise the morning sun", although it doesn't seem to have been an important consideration at Arrowtown. Placement so as to maximise privacy (with the door open) and avoid the prevailing wind (by orientating the door away from it) do not seem to have been overriding considerations either; again, at Arrowtown most of the hut doors are directly exposed to the north-westerlies.

A possible major but less tangible factor influencing the orientation of structures lies in Chinese concepts such as feng shui. Feng shui, literally "wind" and "water", is a long-established philosophical concept or art concerned with the orientation and placement of objects and structures so as to maximise good fortune (by selecting places with good "ch'i" – the life essence), and conversely minimising the deleterious effects of evil spirits (Rossbach 1985). Feng shui is a complex language of symbols, many of which are derived from the environment such as the imagery (e.g. dragons) conjured by the shape of hills (Rossbach 1985:31).

Locations with "good feng shui" tend to have or offer:

1. Shelter (from the north wind in China).
2. The surrounding hills or slopes form a "protective armchair" formation (Rossbach 1985:40).
3. The ground is fertile but not excessively flood prone or swampy (Rossbach 1985:37).
4. Watercourses that are "balanced", i.e. not flowing too fast or too slowly, and are not straight ("which threatens money, life and prosperity" (Rossbach 1985:38).
5. Trees improve a "feng shui landscape", protecting against malign winds (or killing ch'i) and fostering good growing ch'i (Rossbach 1985:39).
6. Good feng shui locations look out onto water or open ground. There is also complex feng shui lore concerned with the positioning and shape of structures and their internal fittings to maximise ch'i (Rossbach 1985:71–140).

The difficulty in less prosaic archaeological terms is to evaluate whether the varying orientation of structures was influenced primarily by feng shui considerations or other factors. The problem is compounded because successful application of the concept involves consideration of many factors that someone not aware or concerned about feng shui would also consider when establishing a new home, such as its orientation and position in relation to shelter from the wind, obtaining a view, having sufficient elevation to avoid flooding, and positioning to maximise the hours of sunlight especially in winter and minimising frost.

The Chinese sojourners are unlikely to have neglected the deeply entrenched notions of feng shui when they established their settlements and homes on the goldfields of southern New Zealand. But for the reasons noted above, it is virtually impossible to ascertain just how much effect adherence to feng shui principles had. Rossbach (1985) documented some considerations that seem to be pertinent:

1. There seems to have been a fairly conscious avoidance of having hut doorways directly facing each other (see Rossbach 1985:111).
2. The Chinese generally avoided settling on flat, waterless areas (traditionally recognised as being devoid of ch'i). Obviously, there are very practical reasons for avoiding such areas too.
3. They appear to have preferred to settle in locations that backed on to terrace risers or sloping ground and overlooked rivers or streams. These places are traditionally associated with "good feng shui".
4. Many Chinese miners established their huts at the confluence of rivers and streams. These locations are

also renowned for their good feng shui (Rossbach 1985:38).
5. As documented in Section 4.6, most of the Chinese miners' huts were rectangular. This is recognised as a shape with good feng shui (Rossbach 1985:71, 77).
6. In the settlements at Cromwell and Arrowtown, there seems to have been a conscious avoidance of erecting structures in straight lines (which facilitate the passage of evil spirits). Don (1908:11), who was familiar with Chinese superstitions, alluded to such a consideration when he described the Cromwell Chinatown settlement in 1908:

> I had two hours in the wonderful collection of huts called "Chinatown". The 21 dwellings are nearly all set at different angles, built of different materials, and are of different sizes. Long straight lines are "unlucky" since the demons can thus easily travel.

While the placement factors outlined above may have been influenced by feng shui notions to some extent, some important feng shui considerations appear to have been neglected by the Chinese miners at Cromwell's Chinatown, if not elsewhere. Several of the huts at Chinatown had doors with slanting tops (evident in contemporary photographs) and presumably angled roof beams. Such doors and angled timbers "can destroy good feng shui… and can bring on an unusual horrible, unimaginable occurrence" (Rossbach 1985:112). Mirrors are the aspirin of feng shui. The mystic appeal of mirrors runs deep in Chinese history. Whether a problem was weak or bad ch'i or a badly shaped or positioned structure, the cure was to hang mirrors or other shiny objects inside and outside a house to keep malign spirits at bay (Rossbach 1985:68–9). If the Chinese miners in Central Otago maintained this defensive practice, they either did not break many mirrors (or discard them) or they took them with them, although they may have used other shiny objects to divert evil spirits.

4.8 SOME COMPARISONS BETWEEN CHINESE AND EUROPEAN DWELLINGS

From site recording, excavations and study of early photographs, some differences between Chinese and European dwellings in the Upper Clutha area have been defined:

1. The Chinese made much more extensive and prolonged use of natural shelters such as rock overhangs and caves formed under rockfalls.
2. The majority of Chinese huts in the Cromwell–Arrowtown area (regardless of the construction materials) follow a simple model characterised by the following features: rectangular shape (almost square in the case of small huts), ridge-beam construction, no windows, and the chimney and door are built adjacent to each other in one end wall (neither in the central position). Placement of the door in one of the long side walls is uncommon. European huts exhibit considerably more architectural variety. Some Chinese huts have a small window-vent, built into the wall above the door.
3. Stone huts built by the Chinese are frequently built into adjacent banks or slopes.
4. Chinese huts are generally smaller than those of Europeans. Their construction tends to be lighter but at least the equal of European huts in terms of structural soundness.
5. There is less "concept of street" in the Chinese settlements. The huts tend to be built in relatively haphazard patterns, presumably influenced by the factors mentioned above (Section 4.5).

Table 4.1. Summary details of the study sites.

Site name	Site no.	Site type	Location	Excavated
Firewood Creek	S133/424	rockshelter	Cromwell	Nov 1978
Caliche	5133/223	rockshelter	Cromwell Gorge	Feb 1979
Sheung Fong	S133/21	rockshelter	Cromwell Gorge	Nov 1979
Ha Fong	S133/22	rockshelter	Cromwell Gorge	Nov 1979
Chinatown	S133/48	settlement	Cromwell	Jan–Feb 1980
Queensberry II (QB2)+	S124/207	stone hut	Queensberry	Nov 1981
Apple Tree+	S124/212	stone hut	Queensberry	Dec 1981
Sandy Point+	S124/231	stone hut	Queensberry	Dec 1981
Northburn+	S133/77	rockshelter	Lowburn area	Jan 1982
Ah Wee's+	S115/54	mud hut*	Luggate area	Nov 1982

Table 4.1. Summary details of the study sites (*continued*).

Poplars	S115/44	stone hut	Luggate area	Dec 1982
Hanging Rock+	S133/474	rockshelter	Kawarau Gorge	Dec 1982
Riverside +	S133/791	rockshelter	Kawarau Gorge	Jan 1983
Arrowtown+	S123/249	settlement	Arrowtown	Nov–Dec 1983
Ah Lum's+	S123/250	store	Arrowtown	Dec 1983
Rapids+	S133/453	hut and forge	Kawarau Gorge	Jan 1984
Willows+	S124/42	stone hut	Luggate area	Jan 1985
The Terraces +	S133/48a	gardens	Cromwell	Jan 1985
Platform +	S133/466	rockshelter	Kawarau Gorge	Feb 1985
Flax Grove +	S133/494	rockshelter	Kawarau Gorge	Feb 1985
upper Chinatown	S133/48b	stores 4	Cromwell	Aug 1985
Notes				
* Ah Wee's site also incorporates an extensive area of tailings.				
+ Indicates the site still exists. Because the original five dams were reduced to one, many of the threatened sites were not affected.				

Table 4.2. Occupation dates of the study sites.

Site Name	Location	Date Range
Firewood Creek shelter	near Cromwell	1870–1910
Caliche shelter	Cromwell Gorge	1870–1890
Sheung Fong shelter	Cromwell Gorge	1870–1905
Ha Fong shelter	Cromwell Gorge	1870–1930
Cromwell Chinese Camp	Cromwell	1875–1915
QB2 hut	Upper Clutha	1880–1915
Apple Tree hut	Upper Clutha	1875–1915
Sandy Point hut	Upper Clutha	1875–1915
Poplars hut	Upper Clutha	1880–1920
Ah Wee's hut	Upper Clutha	1875–1905
Northburn shelter	Northburn	1875–1915
Hanging Rock shelter	Kawarau Gorge	1880–1915
Riverside shelter	Kawarau Gorge	1880–1920
Arrowtown Chinese Settlement (ACS)	Arrowtown	1870–1925
Ah Lum's store	Arrowtown	1875–1925
Rapids hut site	Kawarau Gorge	1875–1920
Willows hut site	Upper Clutha	1890–1915
Platform shelter	Kawarau Gorge	1875–1895
Flax Grove shelter	Kawarau Gorge	1885–1905
Note Dates based on matchbox and bottle dating and historical records.		

Table 4.3. Rockshelter construction features.

Site Name	Wall Type	Door Pos.	Fire Pos.	Floor type	Features	Internal Dimensions (m)
Firewood Creek	a	–	none	o	–	3.0 x 2.0
Caliche	b	i	k	n p	t u	4.0 x 2.5
Sheung Fong	c	g	k	o p n	q	4.0 x 2.0
Ha Fong	c	i	j	n o q	r	5.5 x 2.5
Rockfall 1	a c	–	–	o	u	7.0 x 3.0
Northburn	c	l	k	p	–	3.0 x 1.5
Kawarau	e	g	j	o	–	2.5 x 2.5
Hanging Rock	c	h	k	o p	v	4.5 x 2.0
Riverside	c	g	k	o p	–	4.0 x 1.5
ACS/16	f	–	–	o	w	2.0 x 1.5
Flax Grove	c	g	–	o p	–	6.0 x 2.0
Platform	c	g	j	o p	x	2.5 x 2.0

Key

a canvas or sacking wall indicated by nails in rock above entrance
b wall made of large pieces of caliche, gaps plugged with mud
c wall made of mud-mortared schist slabs
d wall made of mud-mortared river cobbles
e wall made of cobbles and slabs
f wall has timber framing
g door in centre of wall
h door in left hand side of end wall
l door in right hand side of end wall
j fireplace built into wall beside doorway
k fireplace built into one end of shelter (by the door)
l outside fireplace
m floor deepened by excavation to increase head height
n floor "split-level" i.e. elevated sleeping area
o floor material: natural gravel
p floor material: natural clay or silt
q floor partially paved with schist slabs
r vent in wall (usually a bottomless tin box)
s fireplace made of schist slabs
t fireplace built of earth-filled kerosene cans
u evidence of earlier prehistoric occupation
v essentially a hut built under a natural overhang
w uncertain as to whether it was a dwelling
x bracken-covered sleeping platform

Note The square metreage of each shelter is based on an assessment of their useable area.

Table 4.4. Summary of construction features.

Name	Wall	Chimney/door Pos.	Roofing material	Free-standing or otherwise
Ch/1	b	m?	s	w
Ch/2	b		s	w
Ch/4	a b	k	s	v
Ch/6	b	j	o?	x
Ch/7	b		o?	y
Ch/12	b	j	o	w x
Ch/14	b	j?	o	w x
Ch/16	b	j	o	w x

4 The archaeological evidence

Table 4.4. Summary of construction features (*continued*).

Ch/18	b	j	o	w x
Ch/19	b		o	w x
Ch/21	b	j	o	w x
Ch/23	b	j	o	w
Ch/24	b	j	o	w
Ch/26	b z	j	o	w
Ch/27	b	j	o q?	w
Ch/33	b	j	s	w
Ch/34	b	j	s	v
QB2	a z	j	s	w
Apple Tree	a	y	s	w
Sandy Point	a z	k	s	w
Ah Wee's	d	?	s	v
Poplars	a	j	s	w
ACS/1	g	k?	o	v
ACS/2	a	k	p	v
ACS/3	e	j	p	w
ACS/4	e	k	p	v
ACS/5	a	l	s	w
ACS/6	a	k?	p	w
ACS/7	d	?	p	v
ACS/8	d	k?	p	v
ACS/11	d	?	p	v
ACS/14	f	?	s	v
ACS/long house	f	t	o	v
Ah Lum's store	a z	u	o	v
The Rapids	h?	?	r?	v
Willows	a	k	s	w
12 Mile Creek	i?	?	s	v

Key

a walls made of mud-mortared schist slabs
b walls made of mud-mortared cobbles from rivers or tailings
c walls a combination of schist and cobbles
d walls made of cob (puddled mud)
e walls a combination of mud and stone
f walls made of timber
g walls made of corrugated iron
h walls possibly made of canvas
i walls possibly made of beech trees
j chimney to right of door at one end of structure
k chimney to left of door at one end of structure
l door in side wall, chimey also in side wall, chimney at one end
m door and chimney in side wall

n no evidence of chimney
o roof made of corrugated iron
p roof made of tussock thatch
q roof partially covered with flattened cans
r roof partially covered with canvas
s roofing material not known
t door in one end, chimney at opposite end
u sole fireplace in kitchen
v structure free-standing
w structure built into bank or slope
x structure built onto adjacent structure
y door in end wall, chimney in side wall
z cupboards or shelves set into walls

Table 4.5. Hut dimensions (in descending order of size).

Name	Floor area (square metres)	Name	Floor area (square metres)
ACS/2	12.5	ACS/5	7.5
Poplars	12.0	Apple Tree	7.0
Ah Wee's	12.0	Ch/16	7.0
Ch/l	11.5	ACS/B	6.75
Ch/12	11.25	Ch/14	6.65
Ch/26	10.8	Ch/18	6.60
Rapids	10.5	Willows	6.25
Ch/34	10.4	Ch/24	6.20
Ch/33	9.5	ACS/3	6.0
Ch/23	9.25	ACS/6	6.0
Q92	8.2	Ch/19	5.7
Ch/21	7.9	Ch/27	5.25
Sandy Point	7.5	ACS/4	5.0

Table 4.6. Hut door orientation (to nearest major cardinal point).

Chinatown			Arrowtown			Rural Sites		
Ch/1	NW		ACS/1	W		QB2	E	(tr)
Ch/4	E	(tr)	ACS/2	NW	(tr)	Apple Tree	SE	
Ch/6	SE	(tr)	ACS/3	NW	(tr)	Sandy Point	NE	
Ch/12	NE		ACS/4	NW	(tr)	Ah Wee's	?	
Ch/14	NE		ACS/5	NW	(tr)	Poplars	NE	(tr)
Ch/16	E	(tr)	ACS/6	W?		Hanging Rock	E	
Ch/18	E	(tr)	ACS/7	NW	(tr)	Willows	W	(tr)
Ch/19	NW		ACS/8	NW	(tr)			
Ch/21	E	(tr)	ACS/11	S?				
Ch/23	NE		ACS/14	NW				
Ch/24	E	(tr)	Ah Lum's	E				
Ch/26	SE	(tr)	long house	NW	(tr)			
Ch/27	NE							
Ch/33	W							
Ch/34	W							
Note If the hut door faces towards the adjacent creek or river, it is indicated thus: (tr).								

4 The archaeological evidence

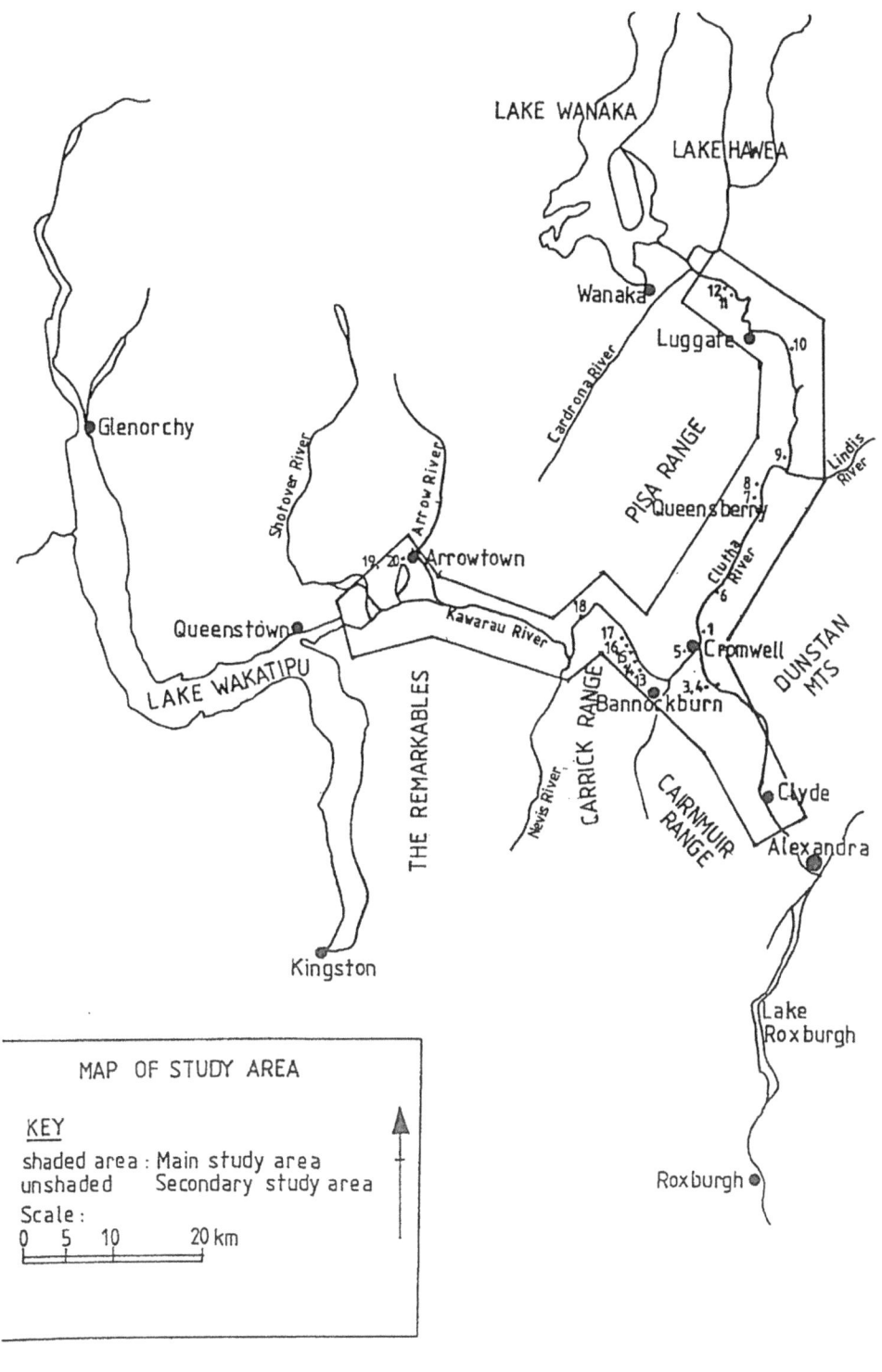

Key

1. Firewood Creek
2. Caliche
3. Sheung Fong
4. Ha Fong
5. Cromwell's Chinatown
6. Northburn
7. QB2
8. Apple Tree
9. Sandy Point
10. Willows
11. Ah Wee's
12. Poplars
13. Rapids
14. Riverside
15. Platform
16. Hanging Rock
17. Flax Grove
18. The Ledge
19. Arrowtown Chinese Settlement
20. Ah Lum's store

Figure 4.1. Map of the study area.

73

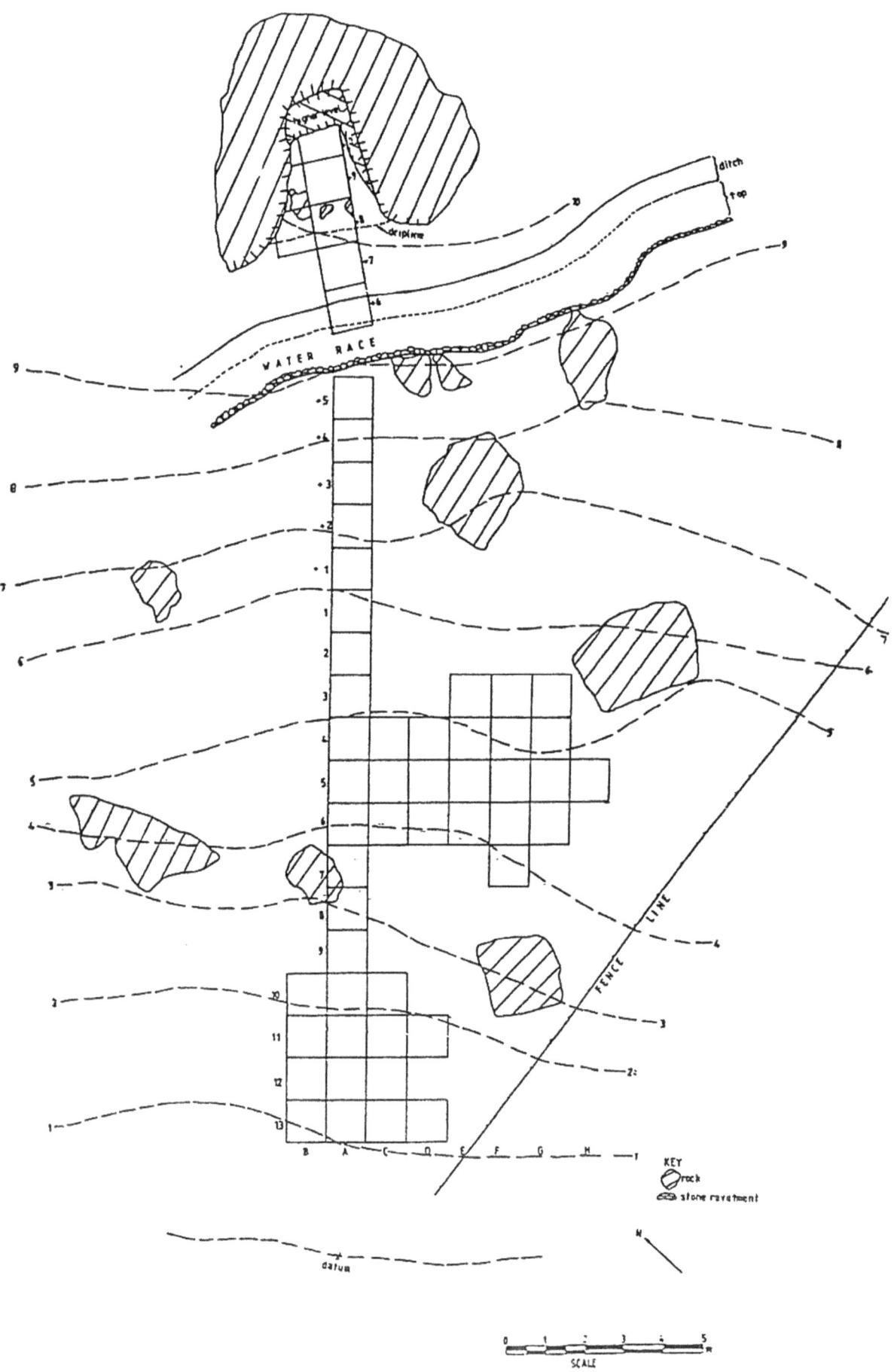

Figure 4.2. Firewood Creek site plan (S133/424).

4 The archaeological evidence

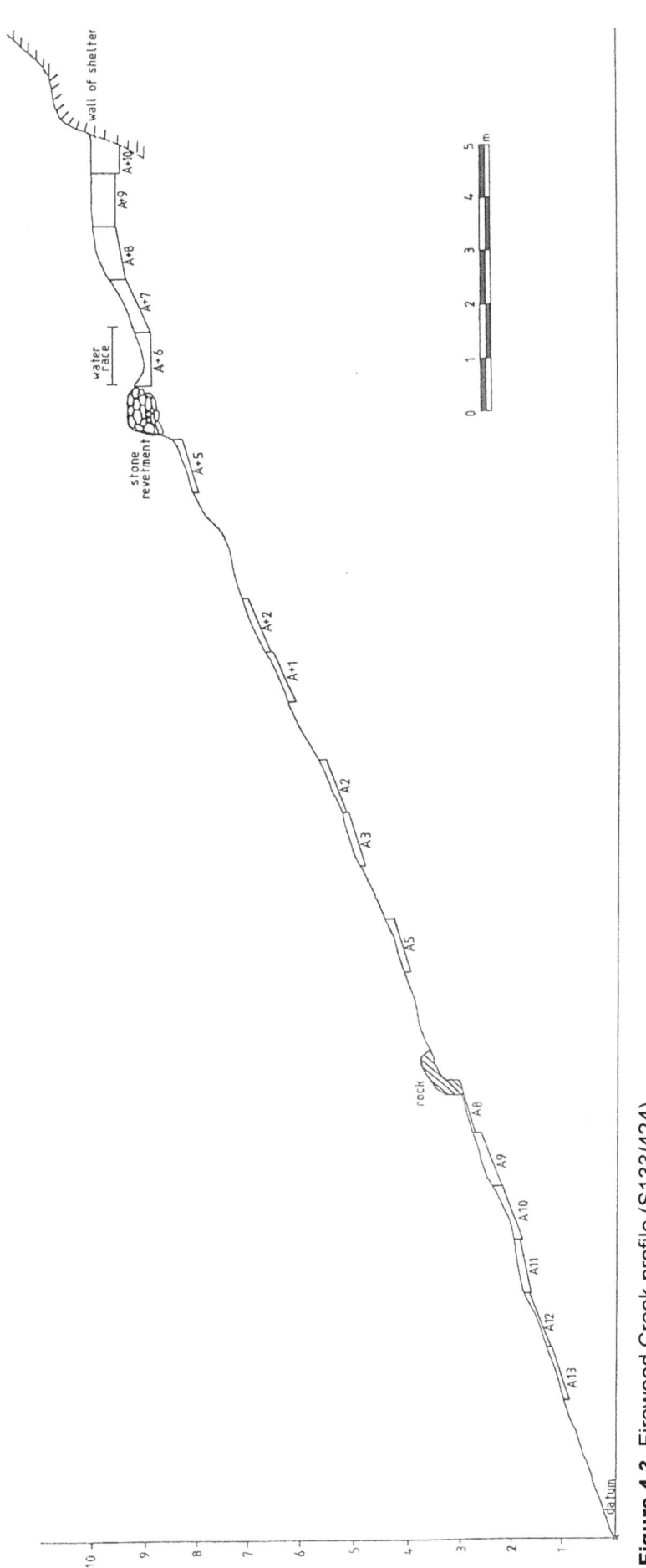

Figure 4.3. Firewood Creek profile (S133/424).

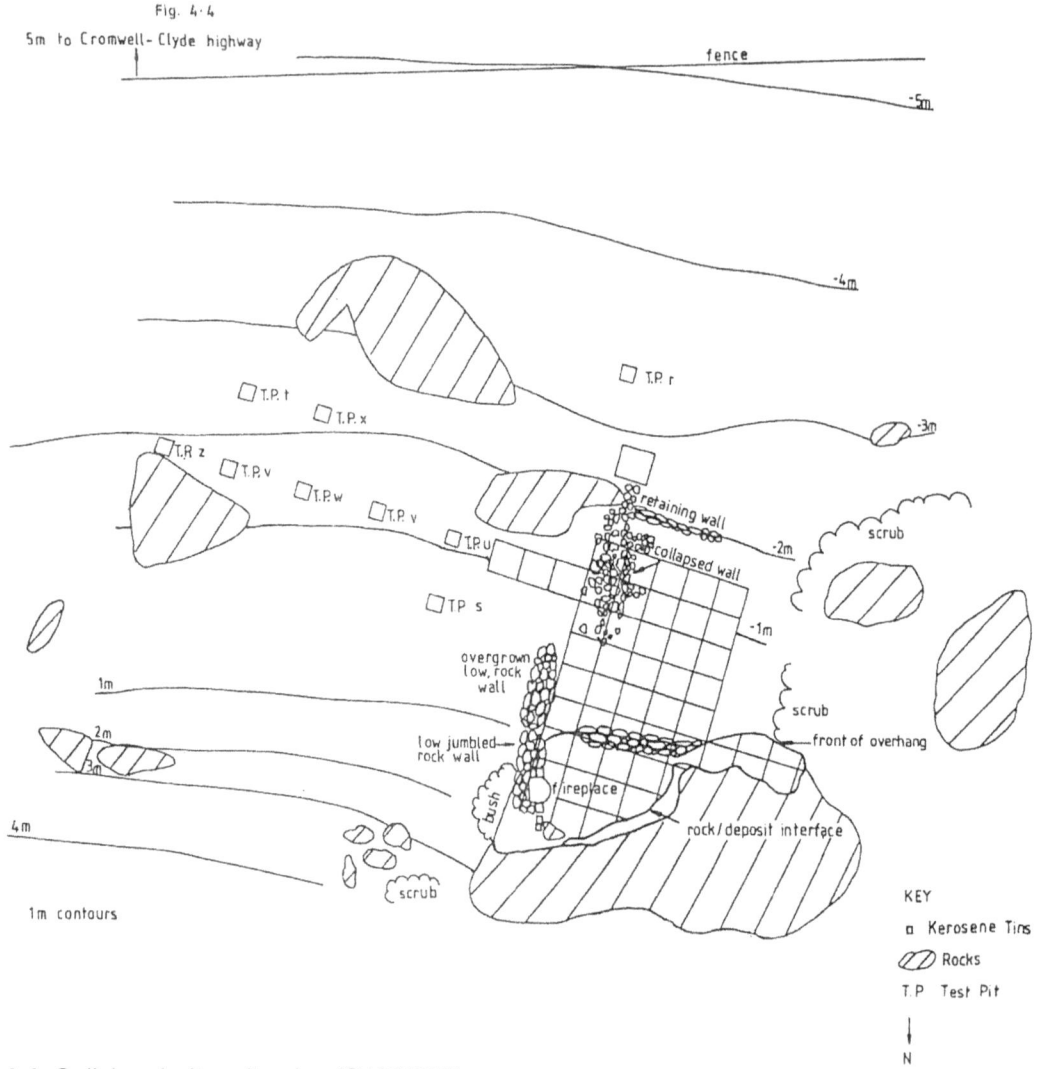

Figure 4.4. Caliche shelter site plan (S133/223).

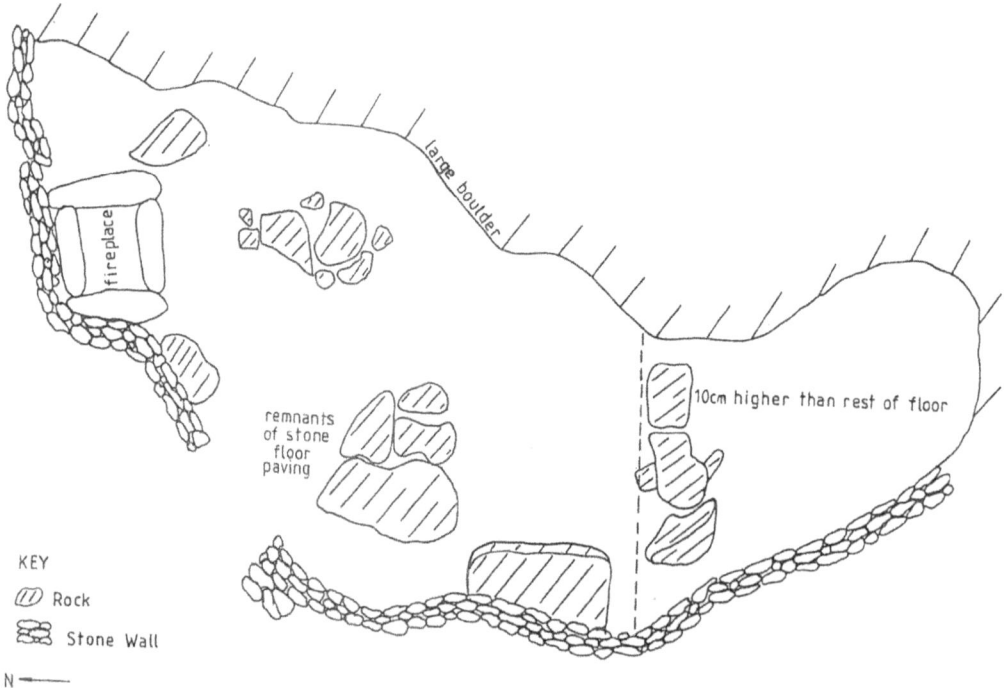

Figure 4.5. Sheung Fong shelter site plan (S133/21).

4 The archaeological evidence

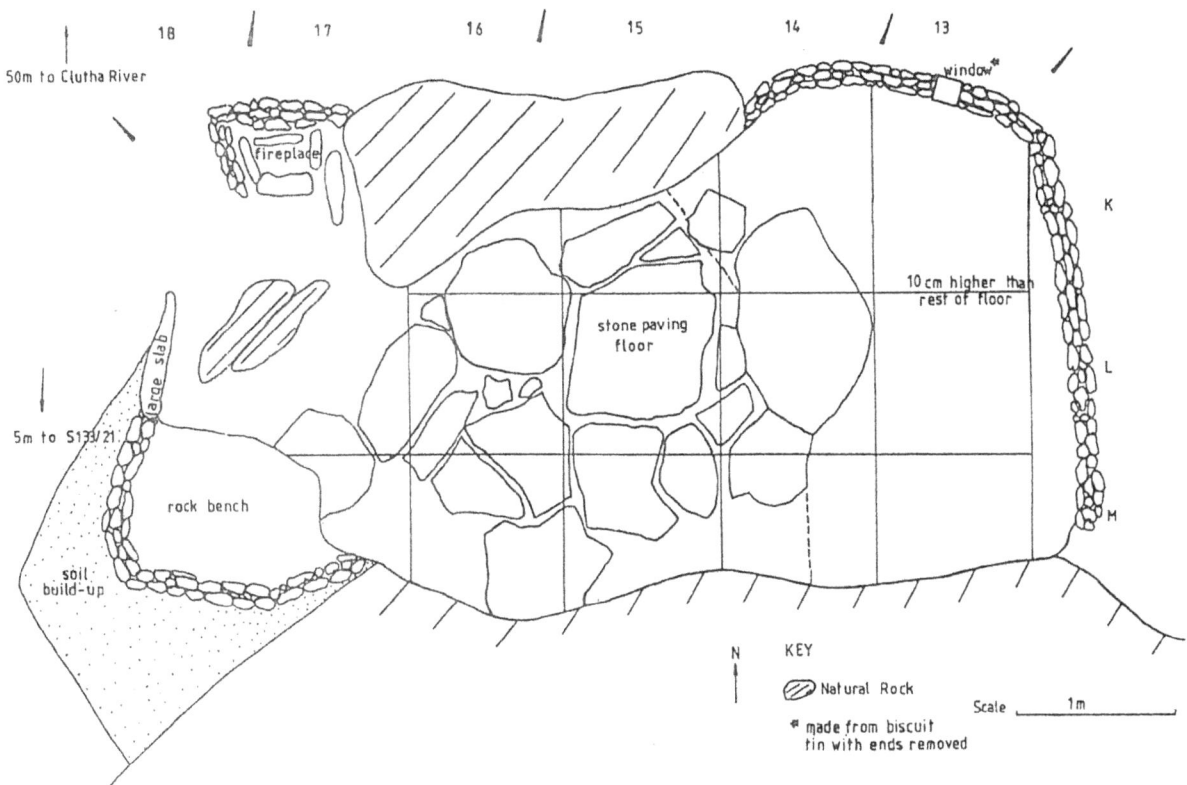

Figure 4.6. Ha Fong shelter site plan (S133/22).

Figure 4.7. Chinatown (Cromwell Chinese Camp S133/48).

4 The archaeological evidence

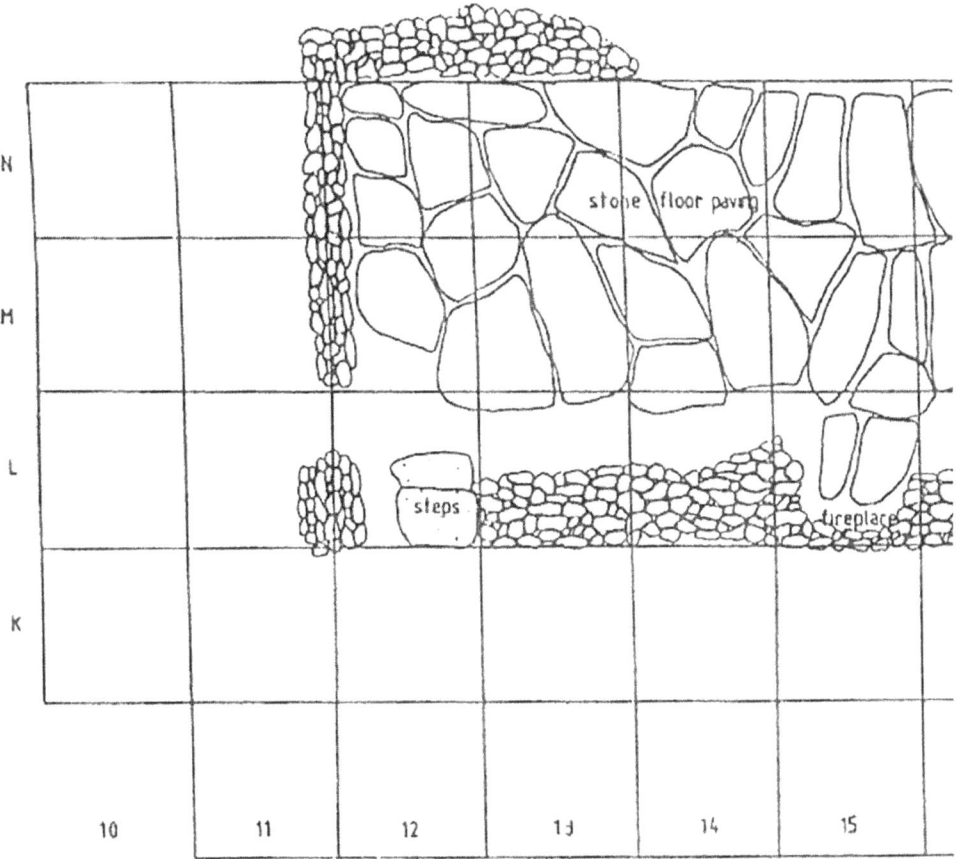

Figure 4.8a. Chinatown hut plans (S133/48 Hut 1).

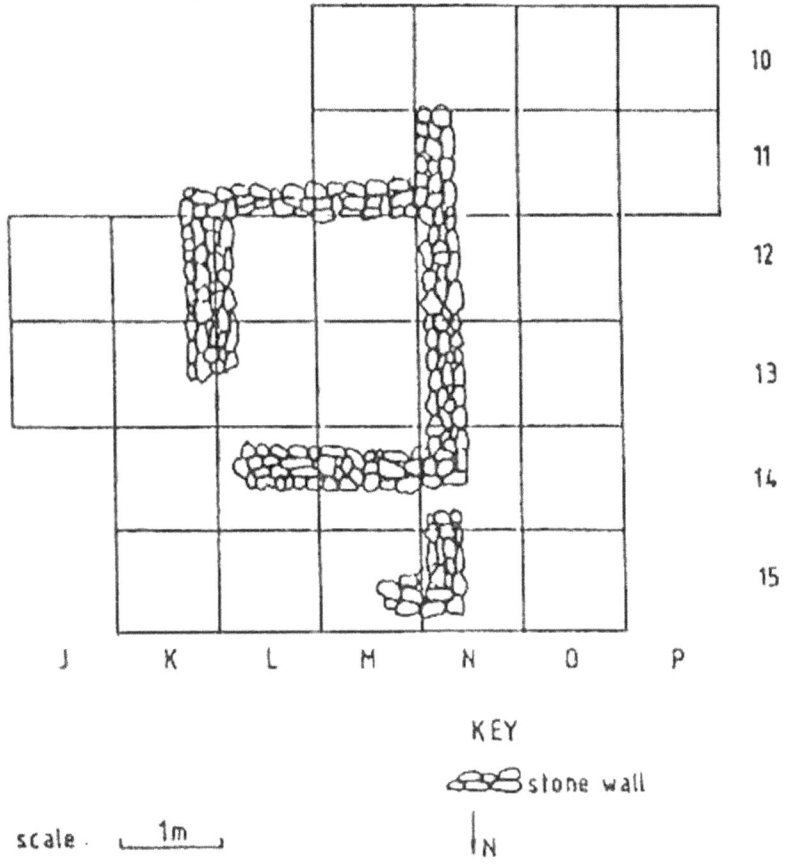

Figure 4.8b. Chinatown hut plans (S133/48 Hut 4).

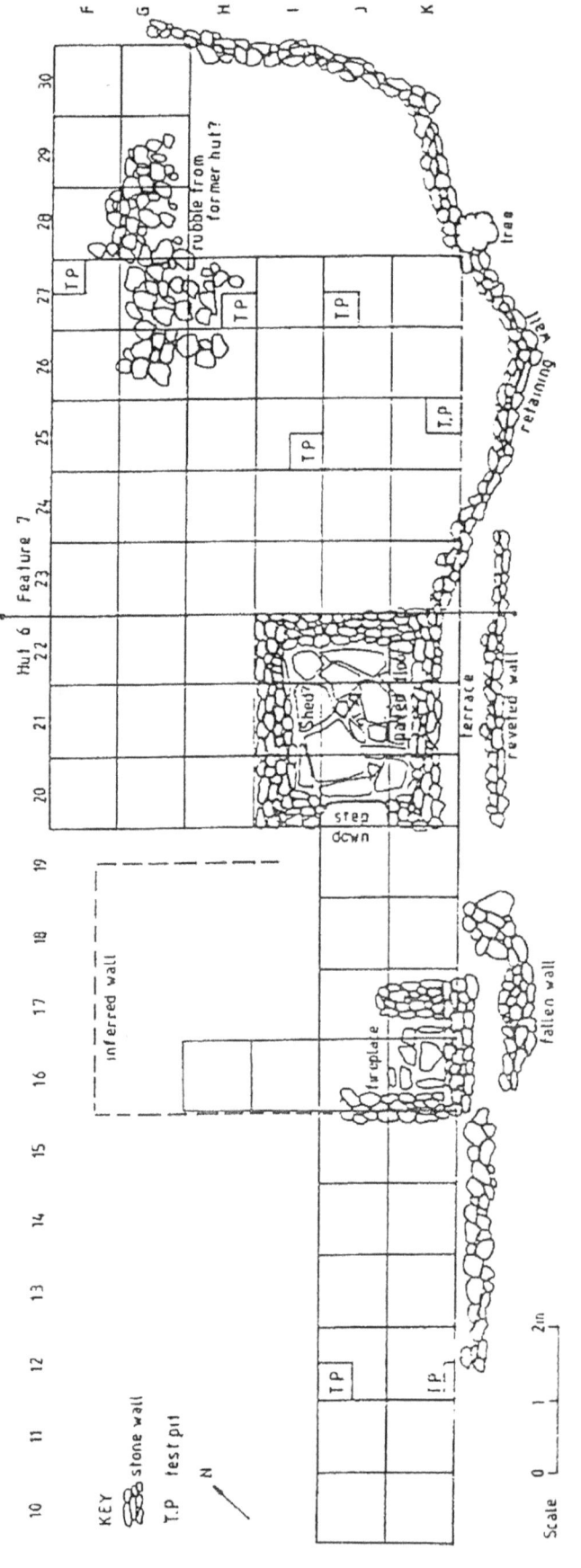

Figure 4.8c. Chinatown – the central hut area (S133/48 Hut 6 and Feature 7).

4 The archaeological evidence

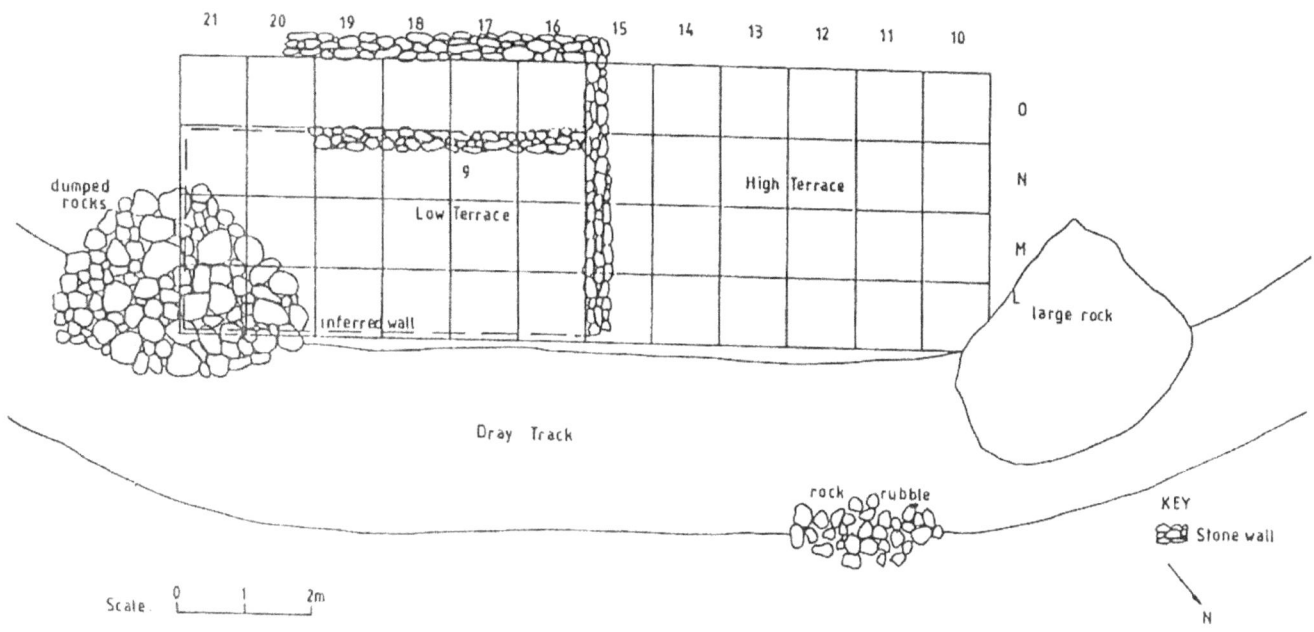

Figure 4.8d. Chinatown hut plans (S133/48 Hut 9).

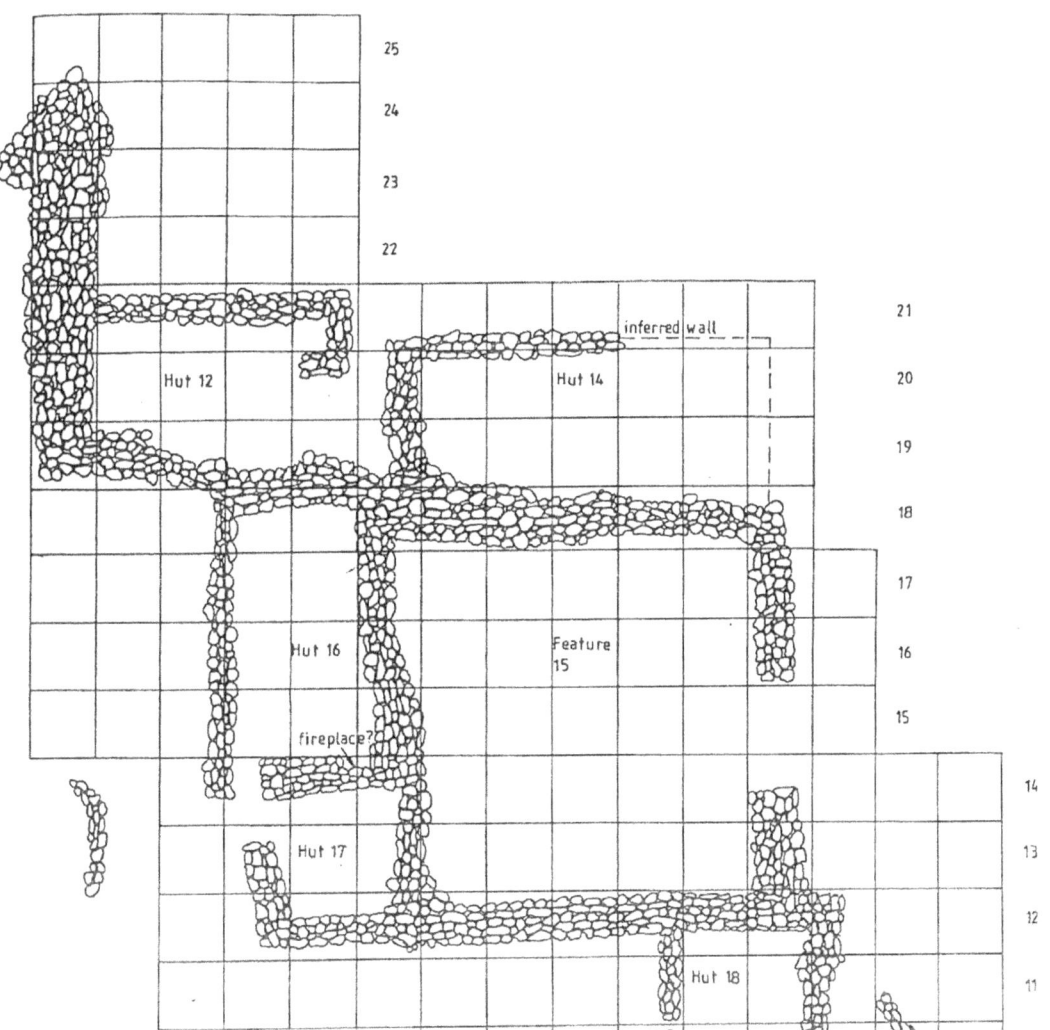

Figure 4.8e. Chinatown – the spring and gardens (S133/48 Huts 12, 14, 16, 17, 18, 19 and Feature 15).

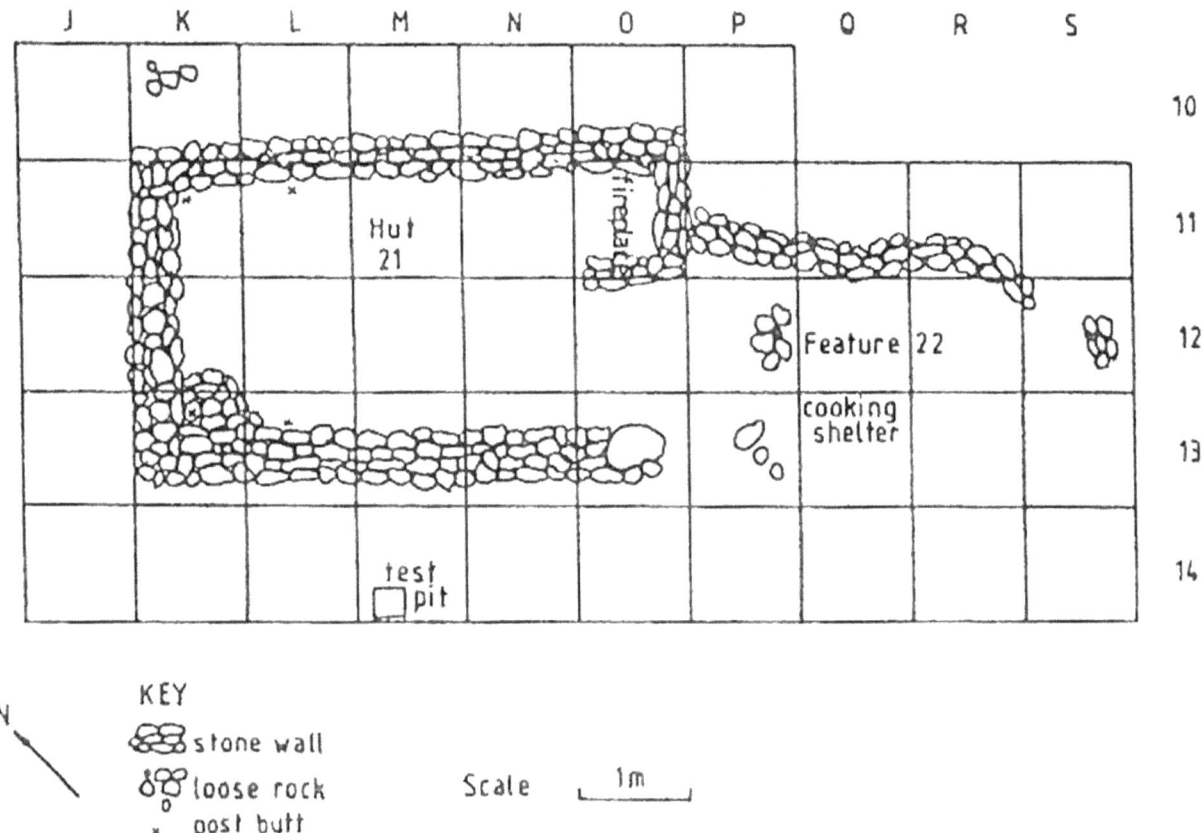

Figure 4.8f. Chinatown hut plans (S133/48 Hut 21 and Feature 22).

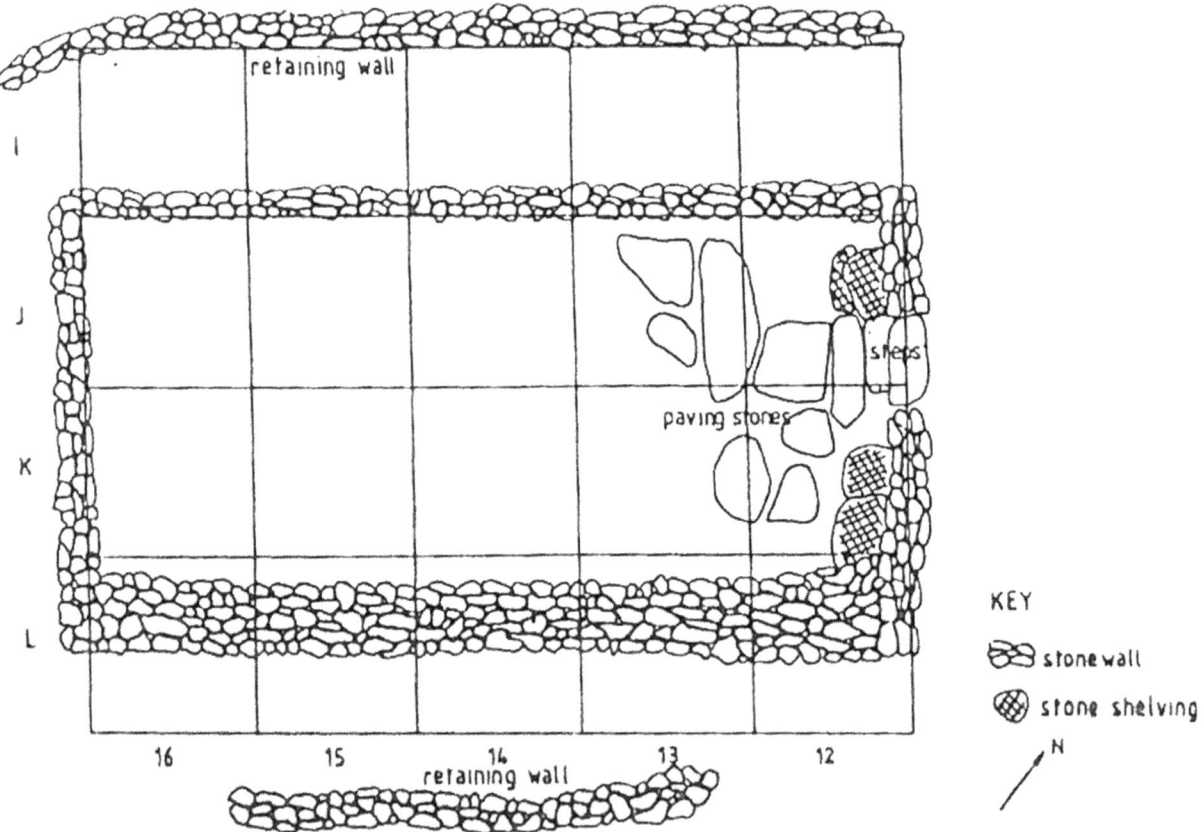

Figure 4.8g. Chinatown hut plans (S133/48 Hut 23).

4 The archaeological evidence

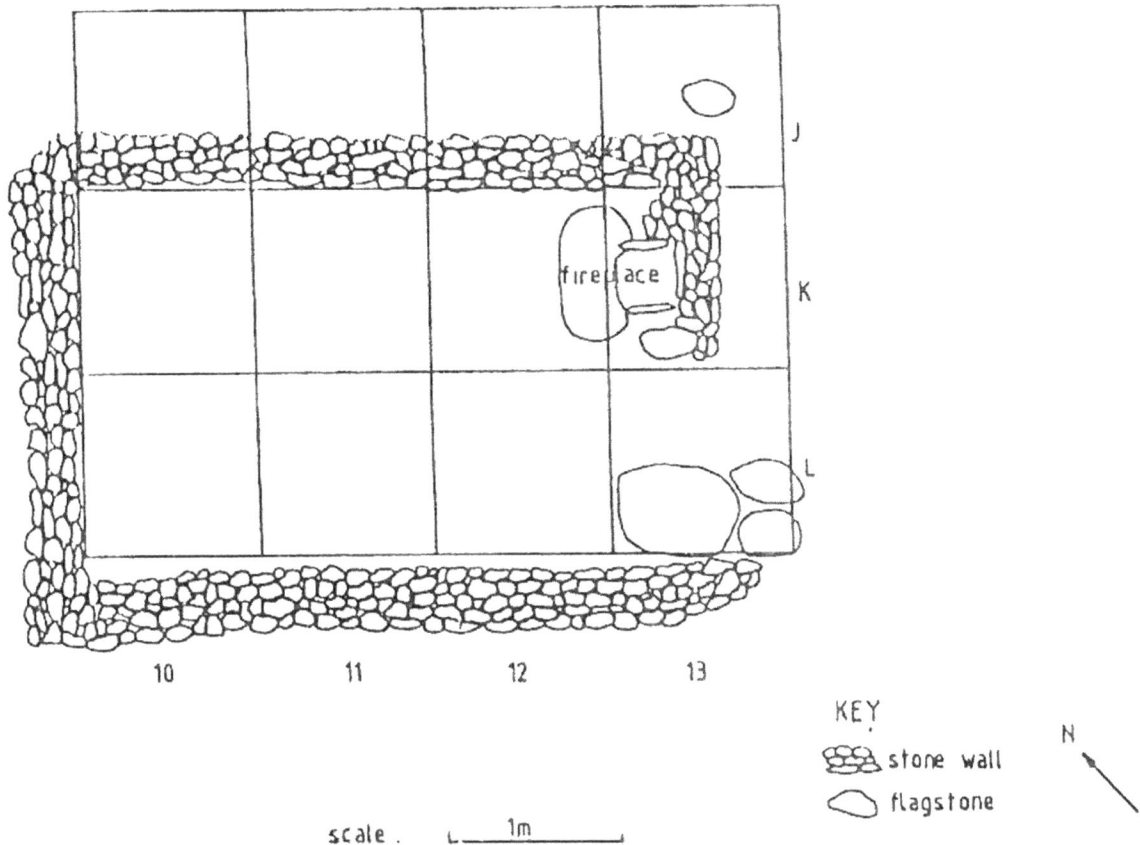

Figure 4.8h. Chinatown hut plans (S133/48 Hut 24).

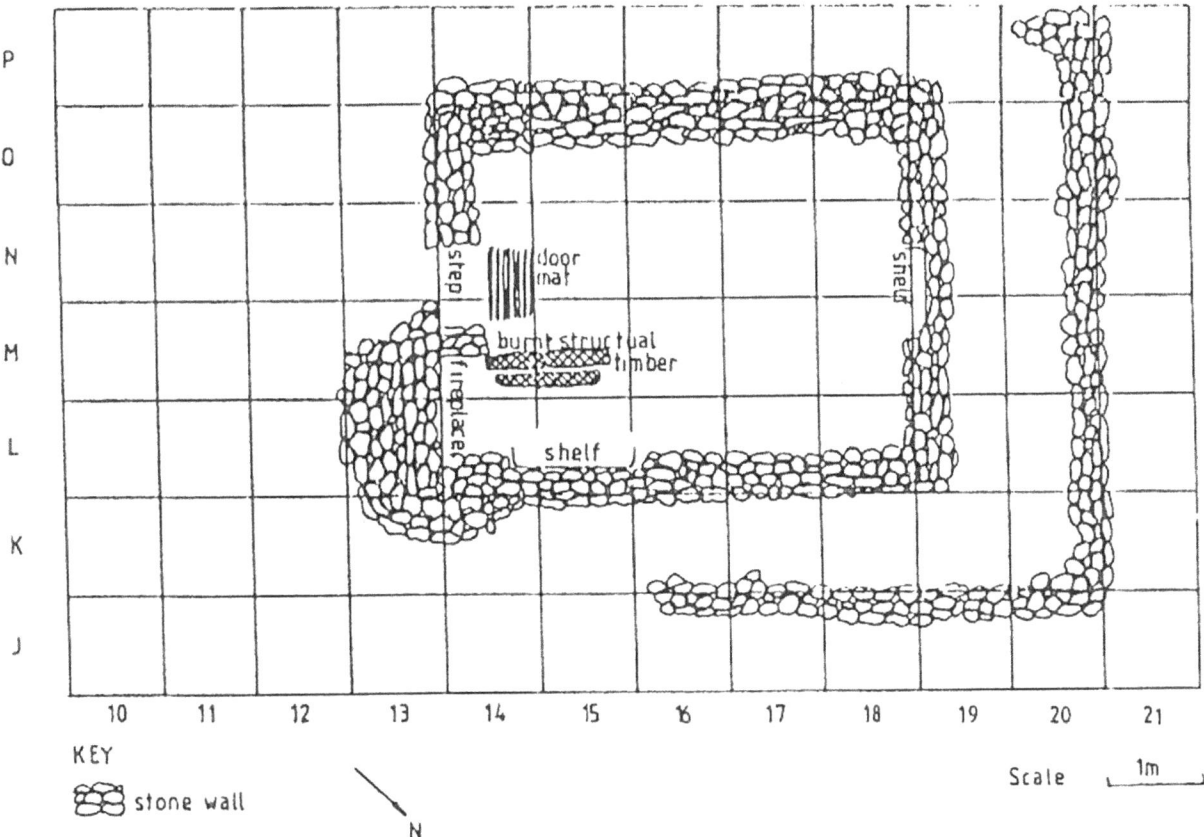

Figure 4.8i. Chinatown hut plans (S133/48 Hut 26).

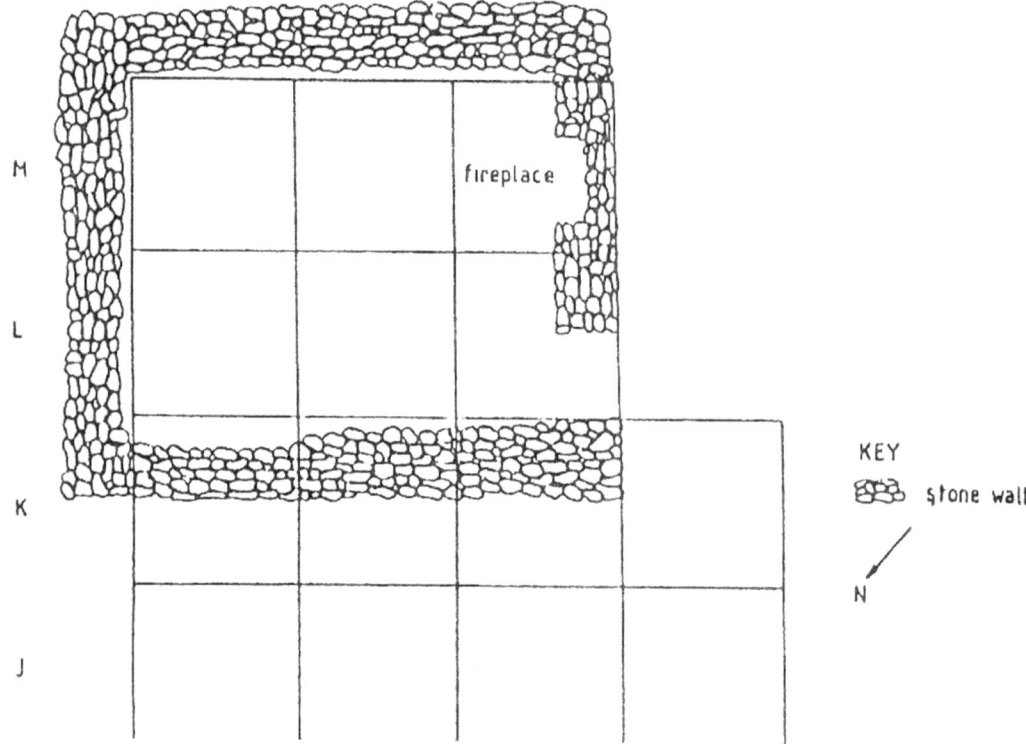

Figure 4.8j. Chinatown hut plans (S133/48 Hut 27).

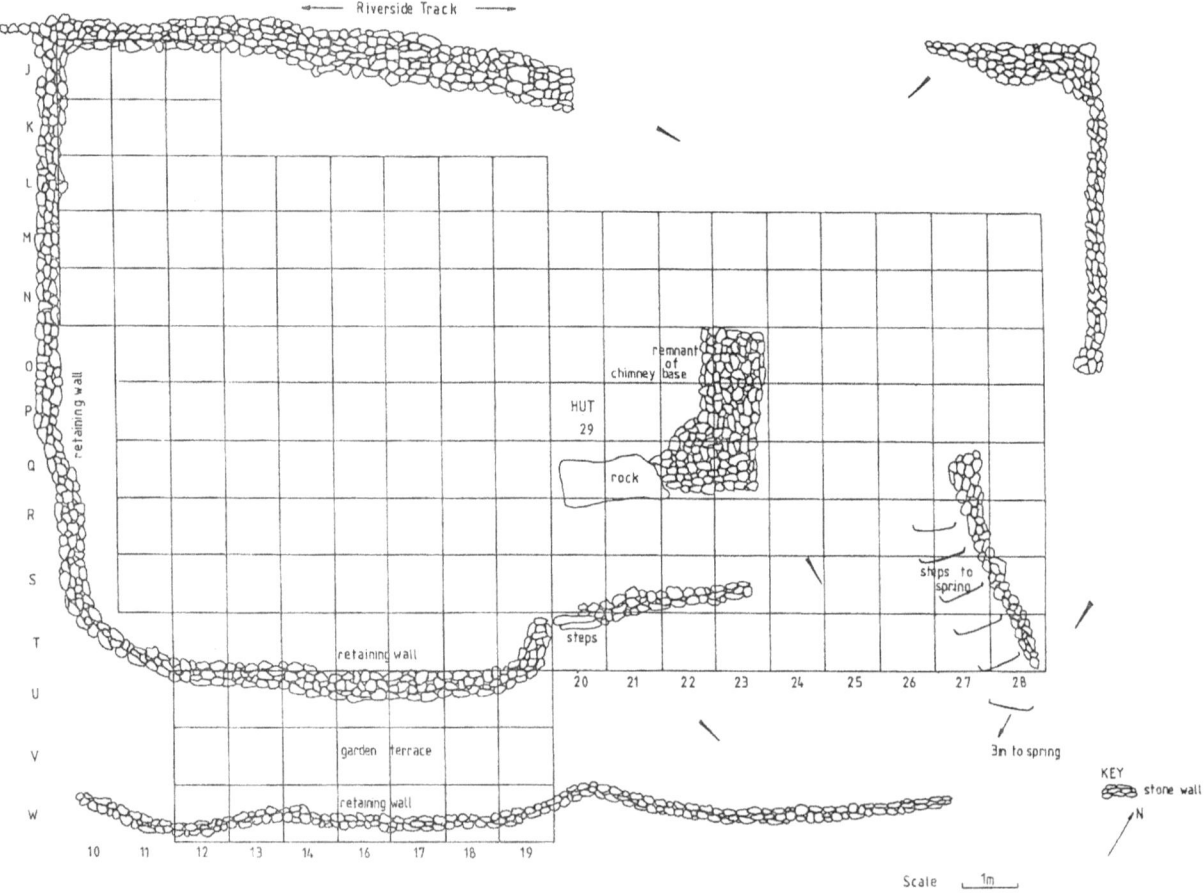

Figure 4.8k. Chinatown hut plans (S133/48 Hut 29, Spring and garden terrace).

4 The archaeological evidence

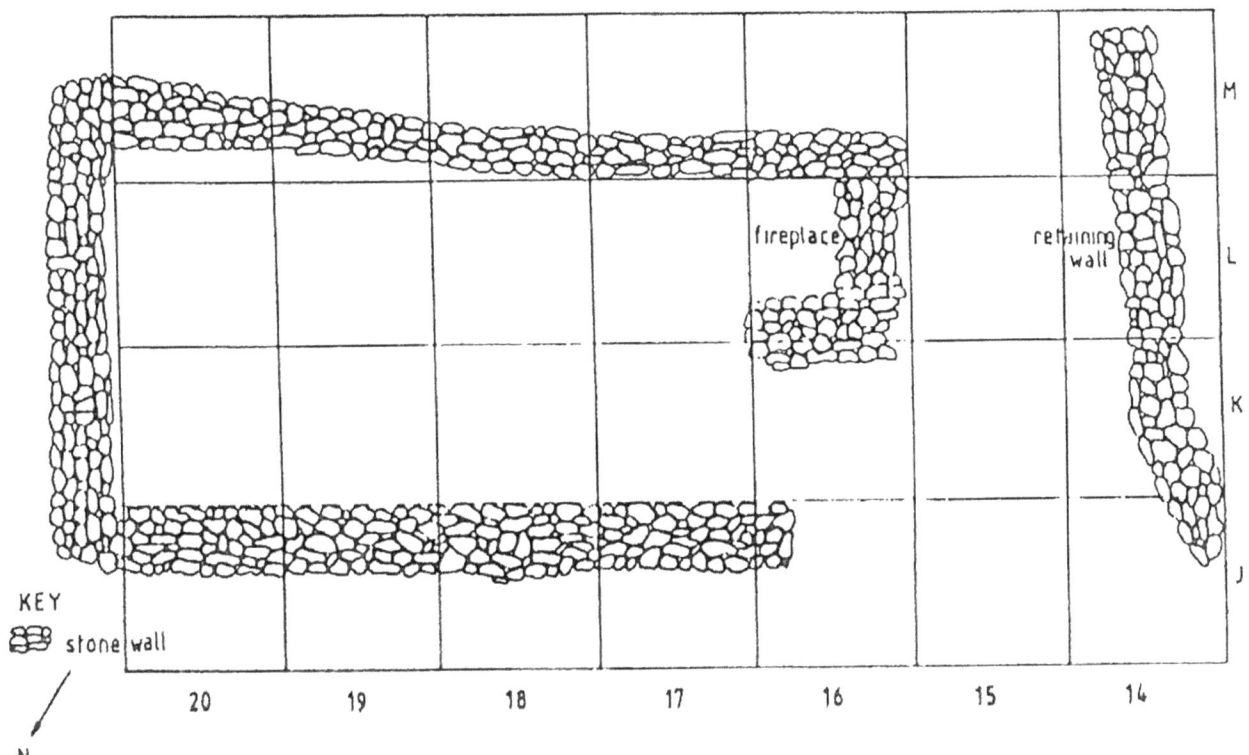

Figure 4.8l. Chinatown hut plans (S133/48 Hut 33).

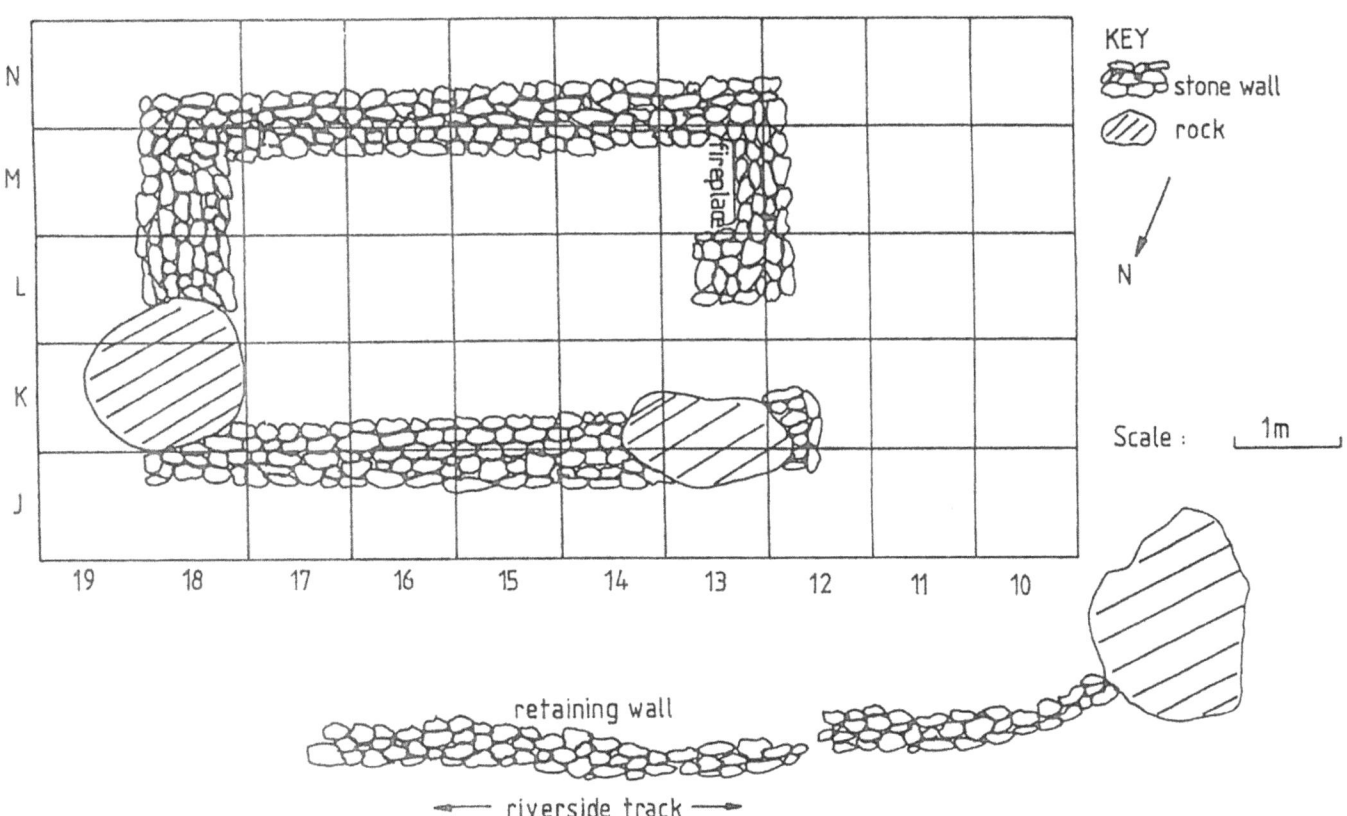

Figure 4.8m. Chinatown hut plans (S133/48 Hut 34).

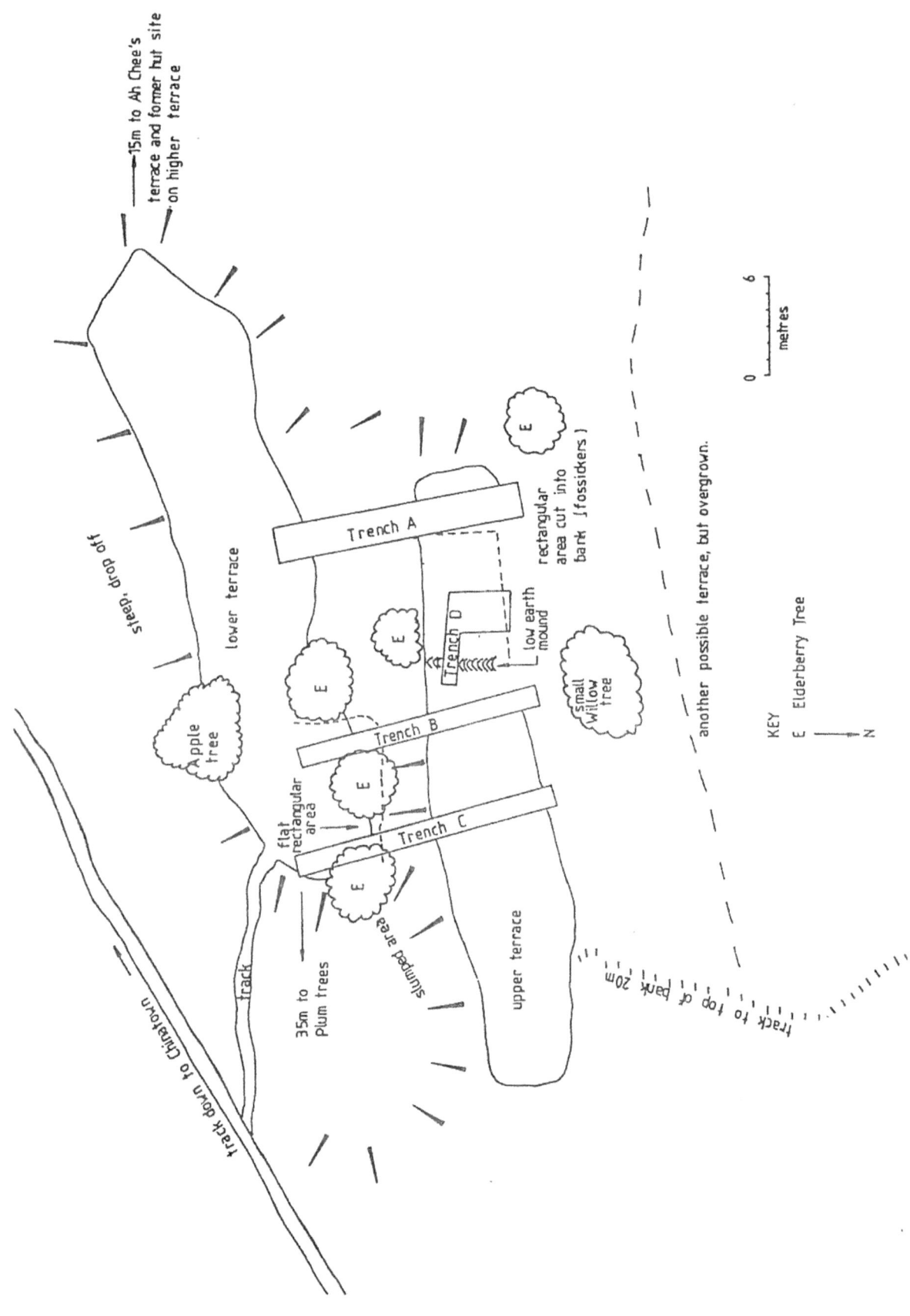

Figure 4.9. The Terraces site plan (S133/48), part of Chinatown.

4 The archaeological evidence

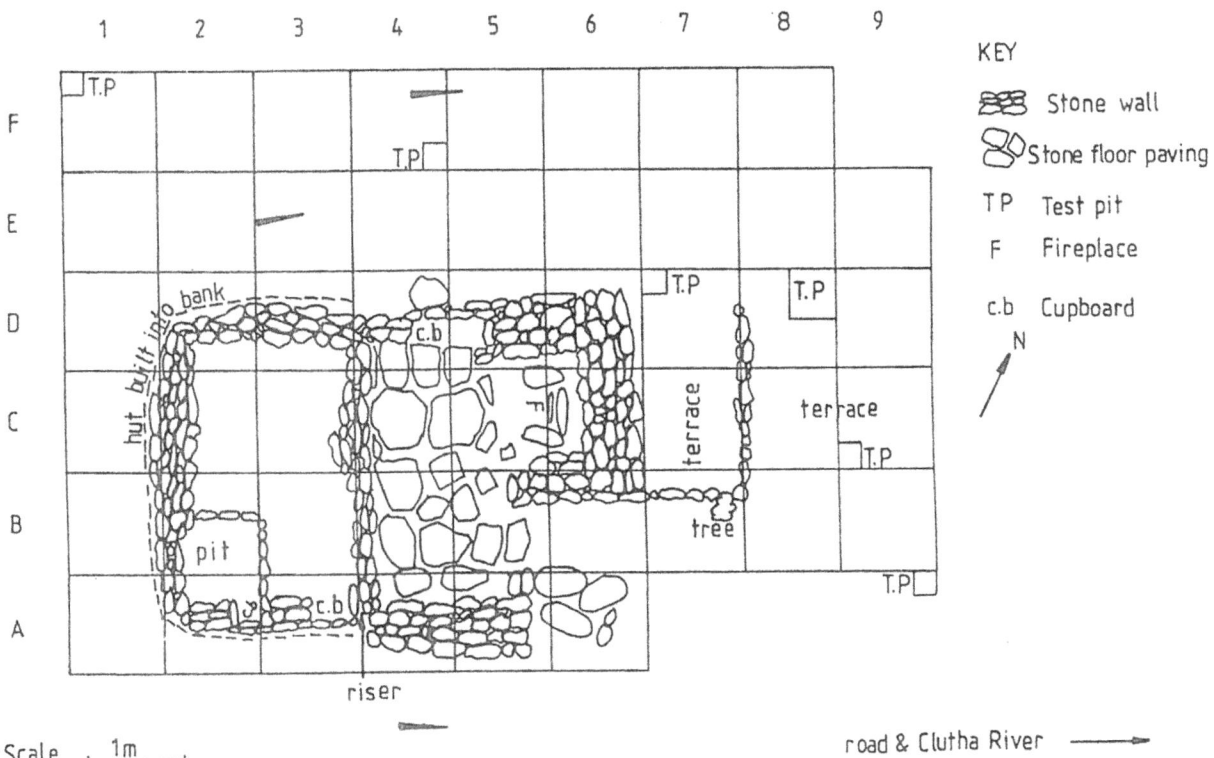

Figure 4.10. Queensberry II (QB2) hut site plan (S124/207).

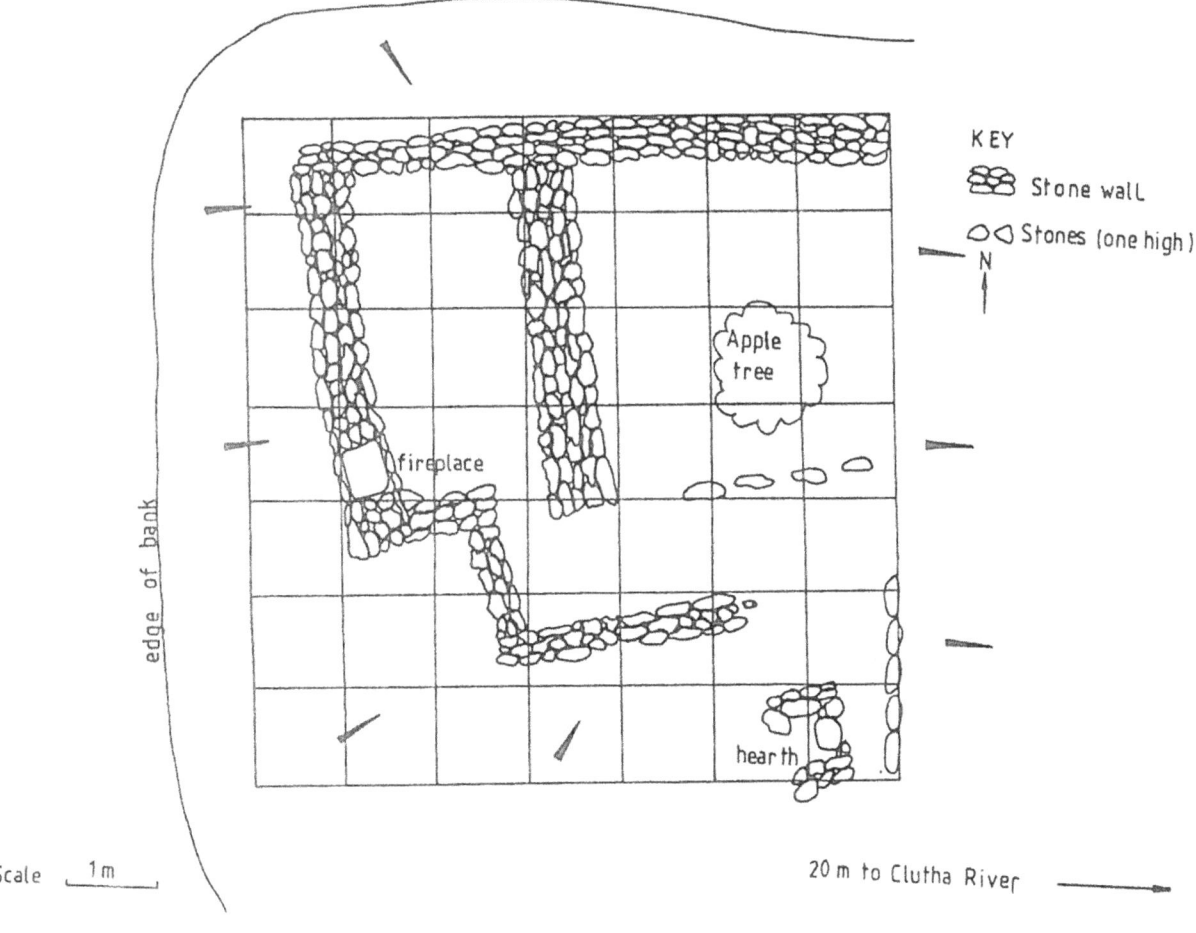

Figure 4.11. Apple Tree site plan (S124/212).

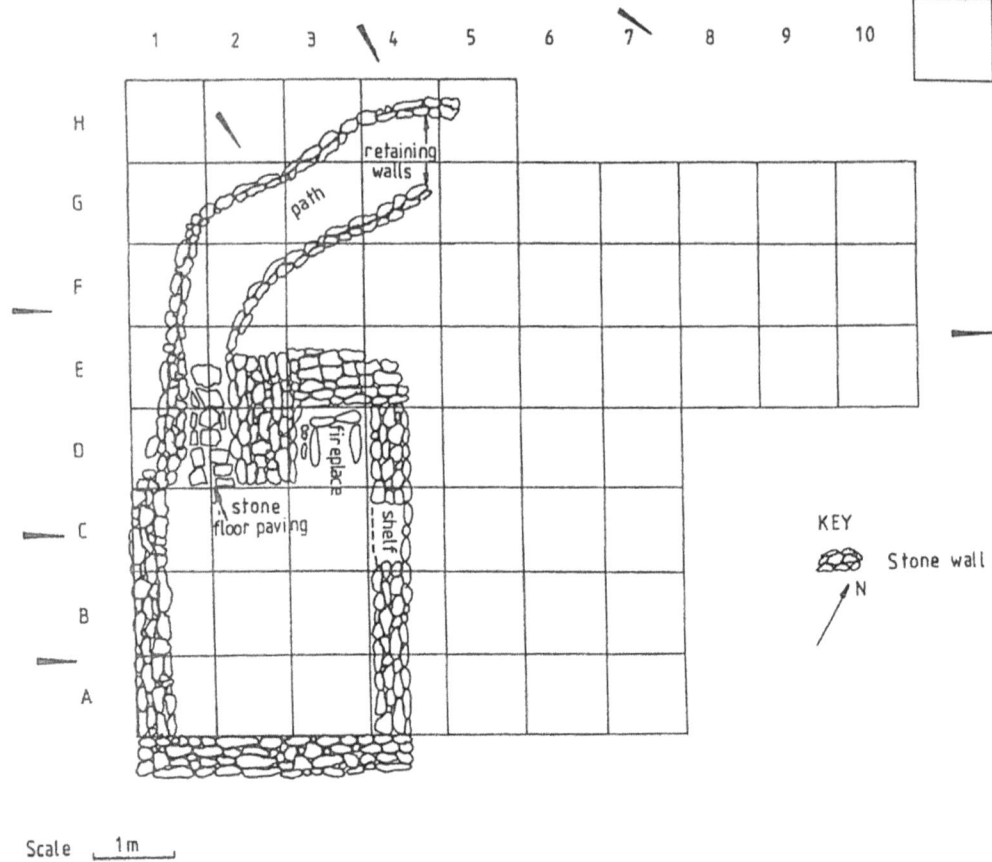

Figure 4.12. Sandy Point site plan (S124/231).

Figure 4.13. Northburn site plan (S133/77).

4 The archaeological evidence

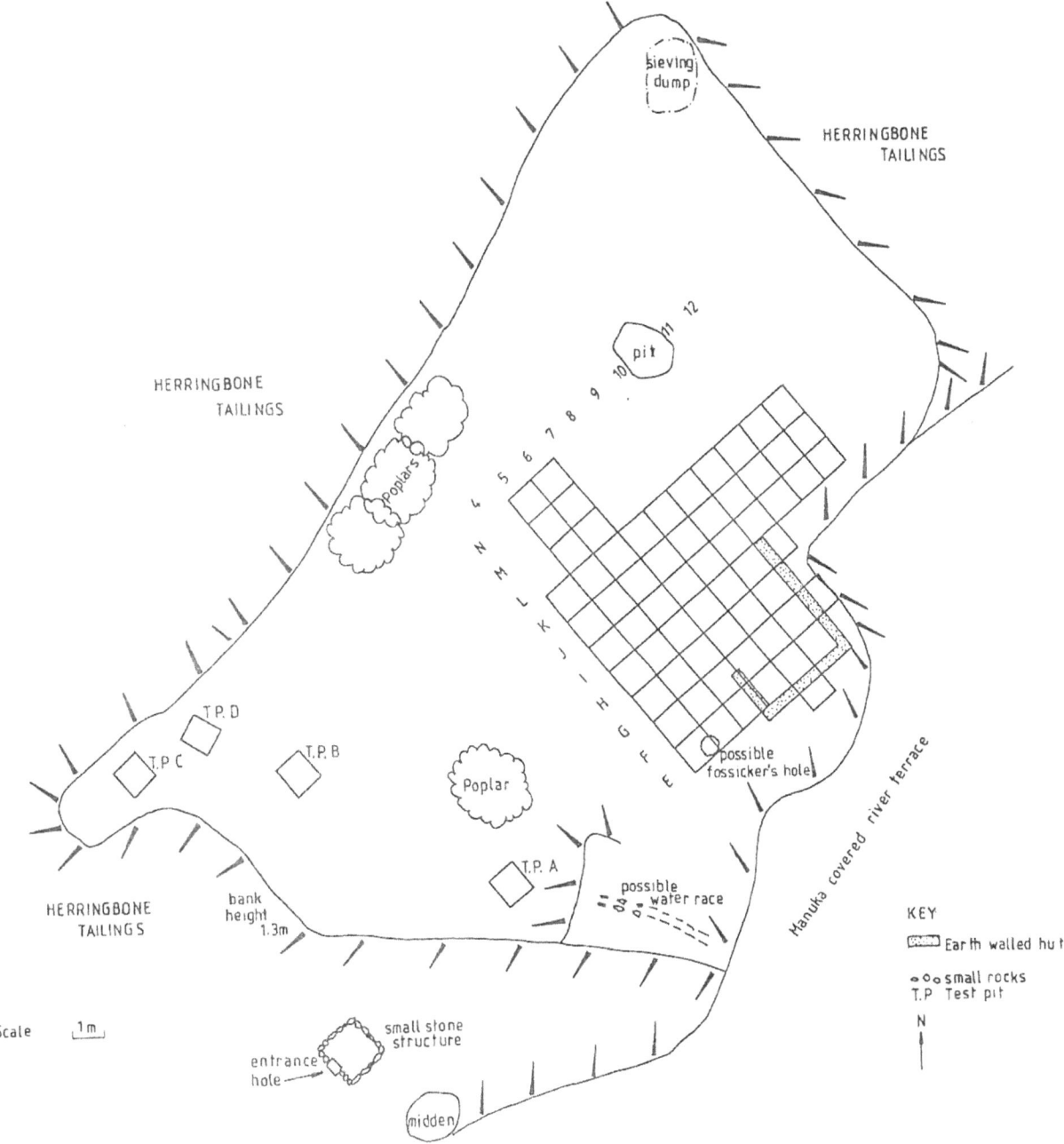

Figure 4.14. Ah Wee's site plan (S115/54).

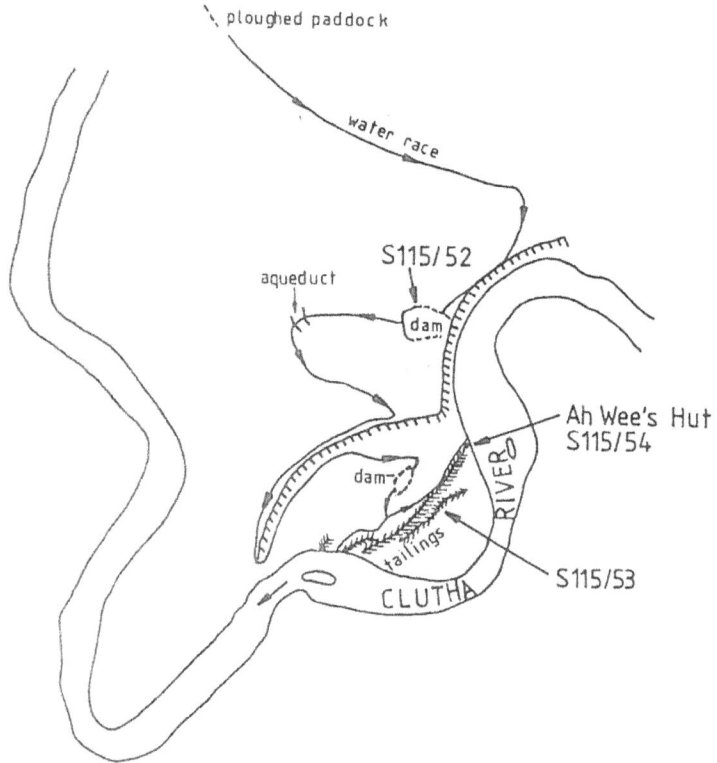

Figure 4.15. Layout of dams and races associated with Ah Wee's mining (S115/52–54).

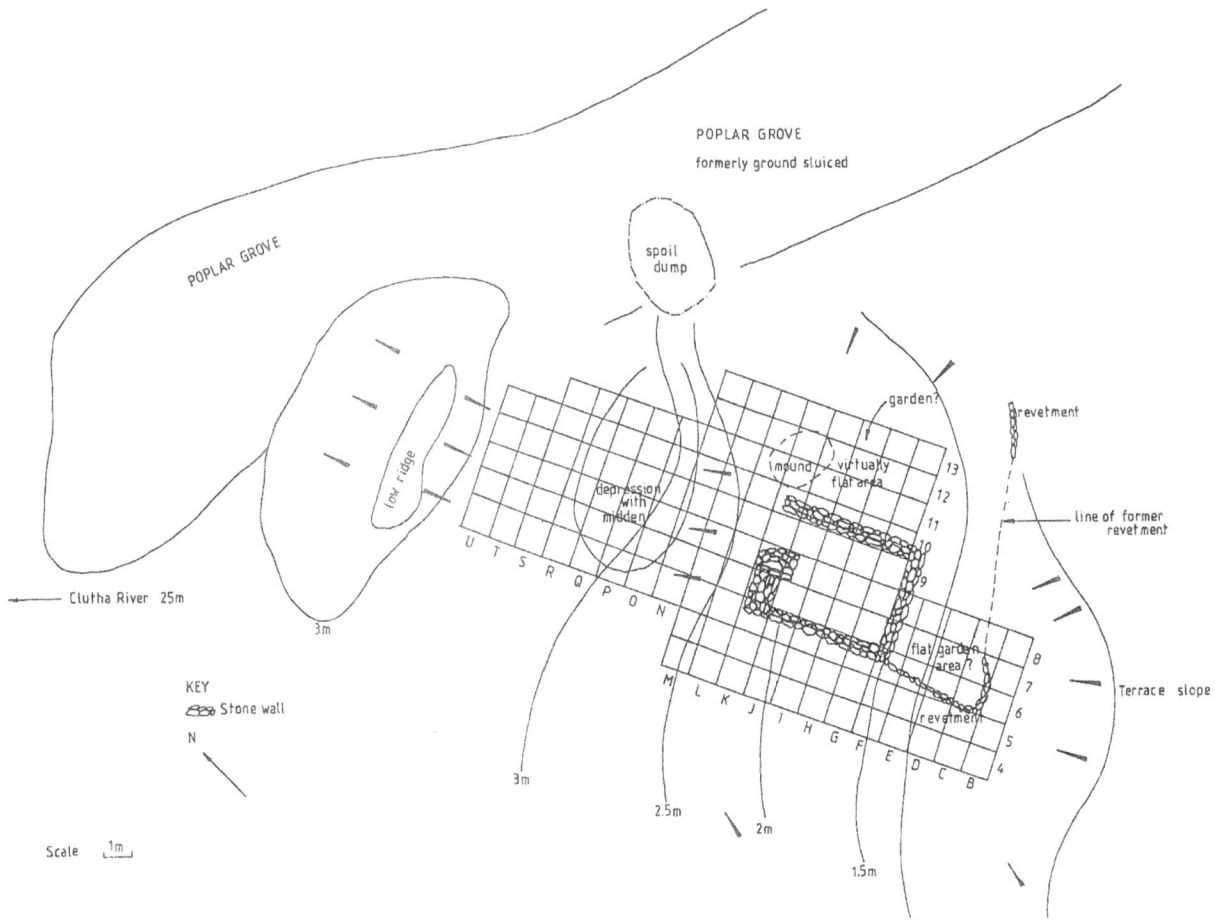

Figure 4.16. The Poplars site plan (S113/44).

4 The archaeological evidence

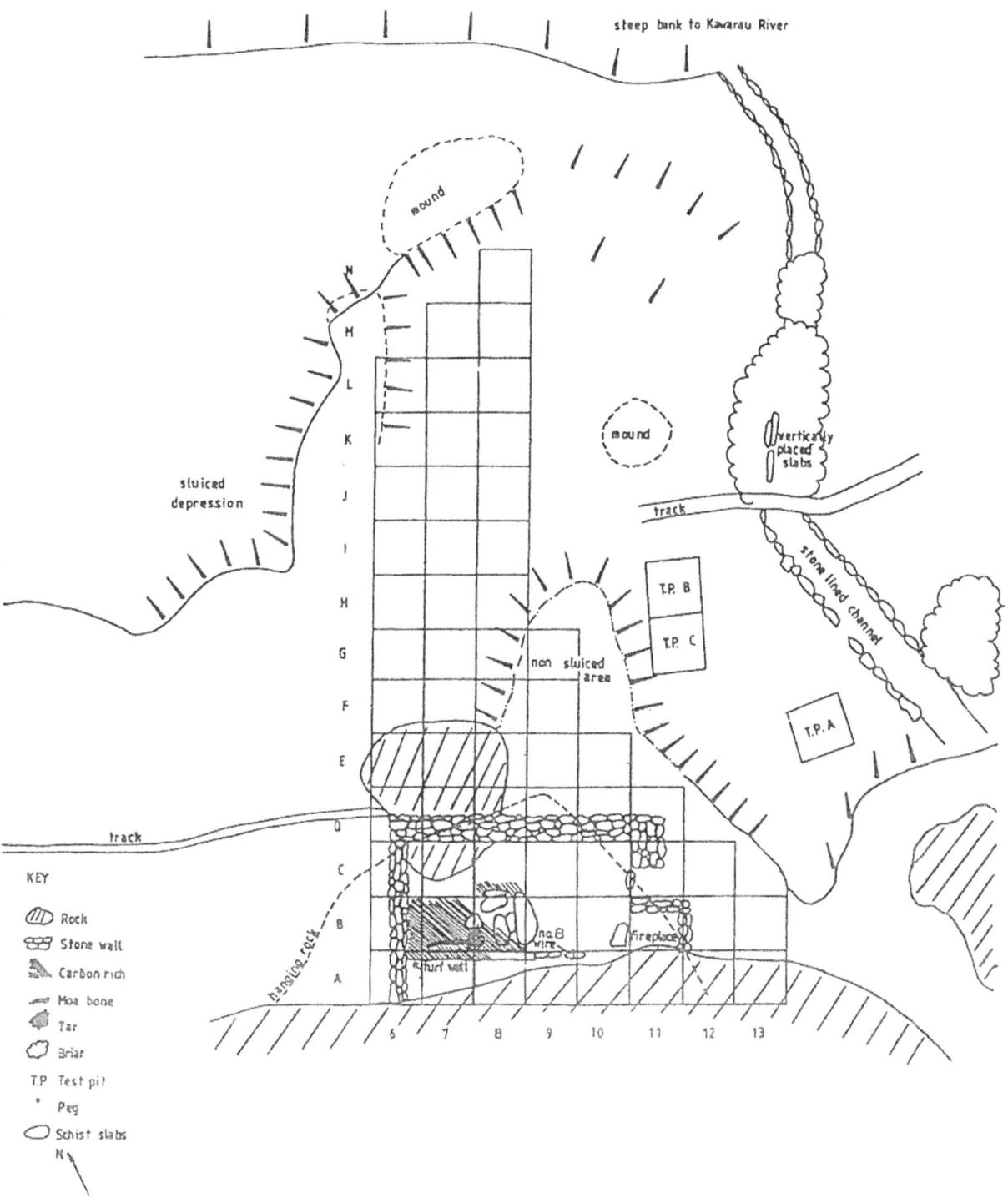

Figure 4.17. Hanging Rock site plan (S133/474).

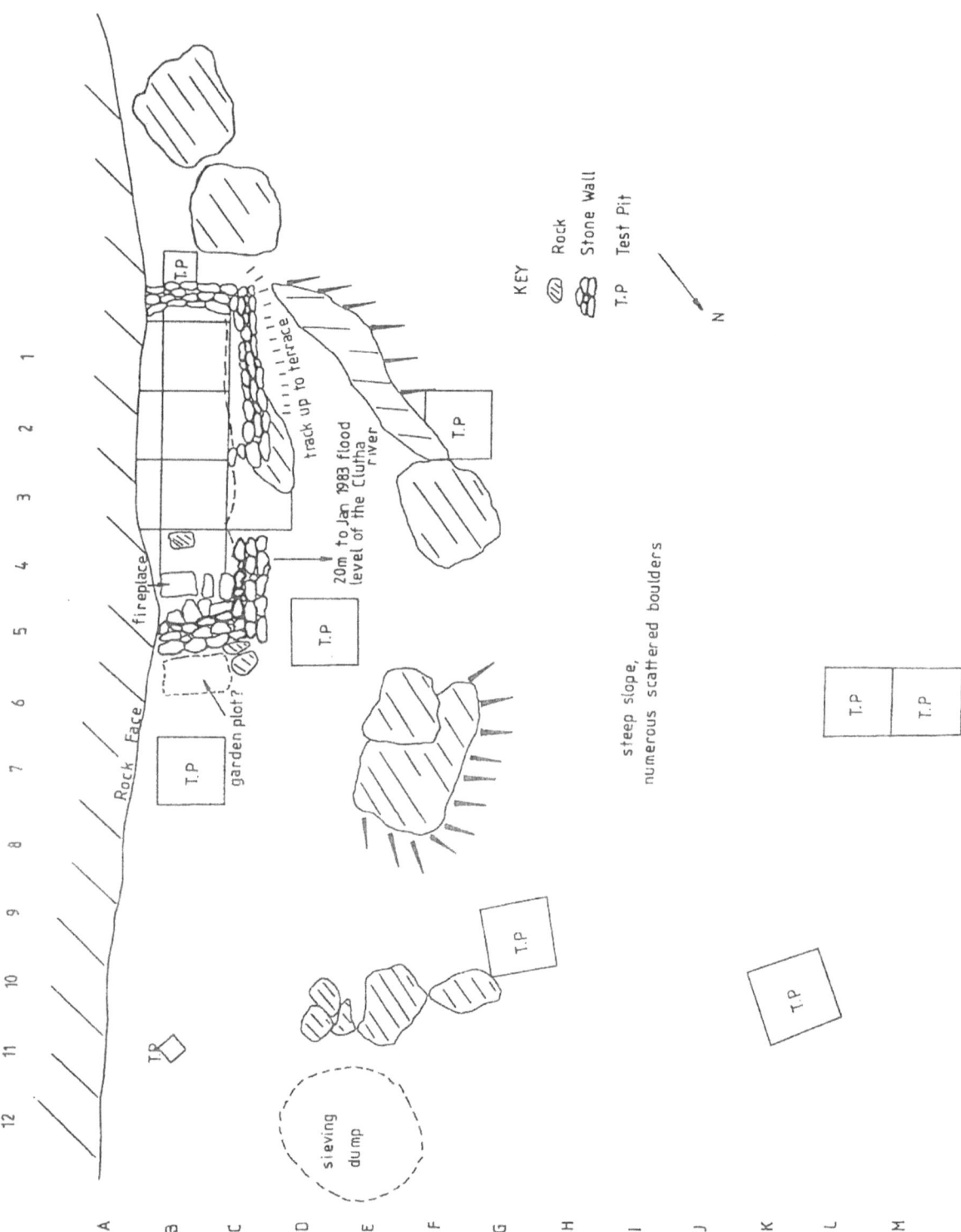

Figure 4.18. Riverside Shelter site plan (S133/791).

4 The archaeological evidence

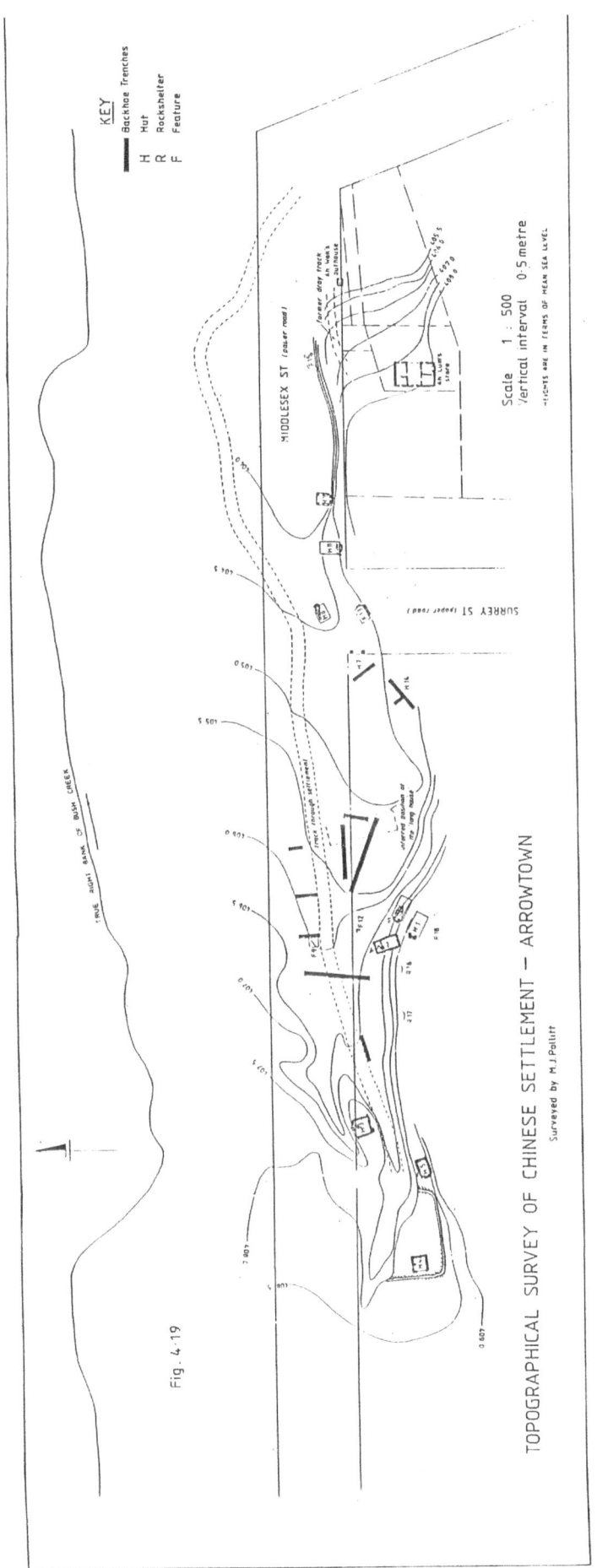

Figure 4.19. Plan of Arrowtown Chinese Settlement.

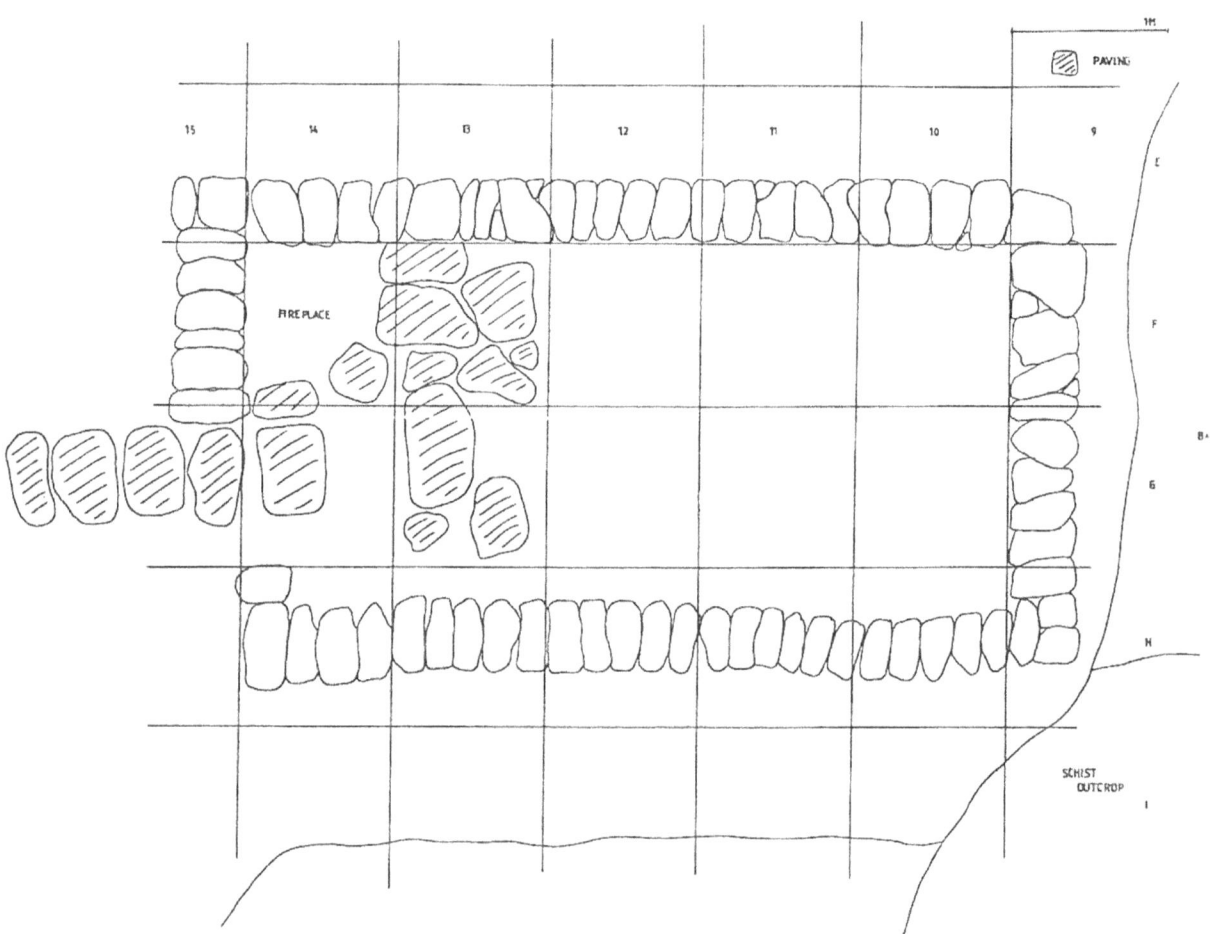

Figure 4.20a. Arrowtown Chinese Settlement excavated hut plans.

4 The archaeological evidence

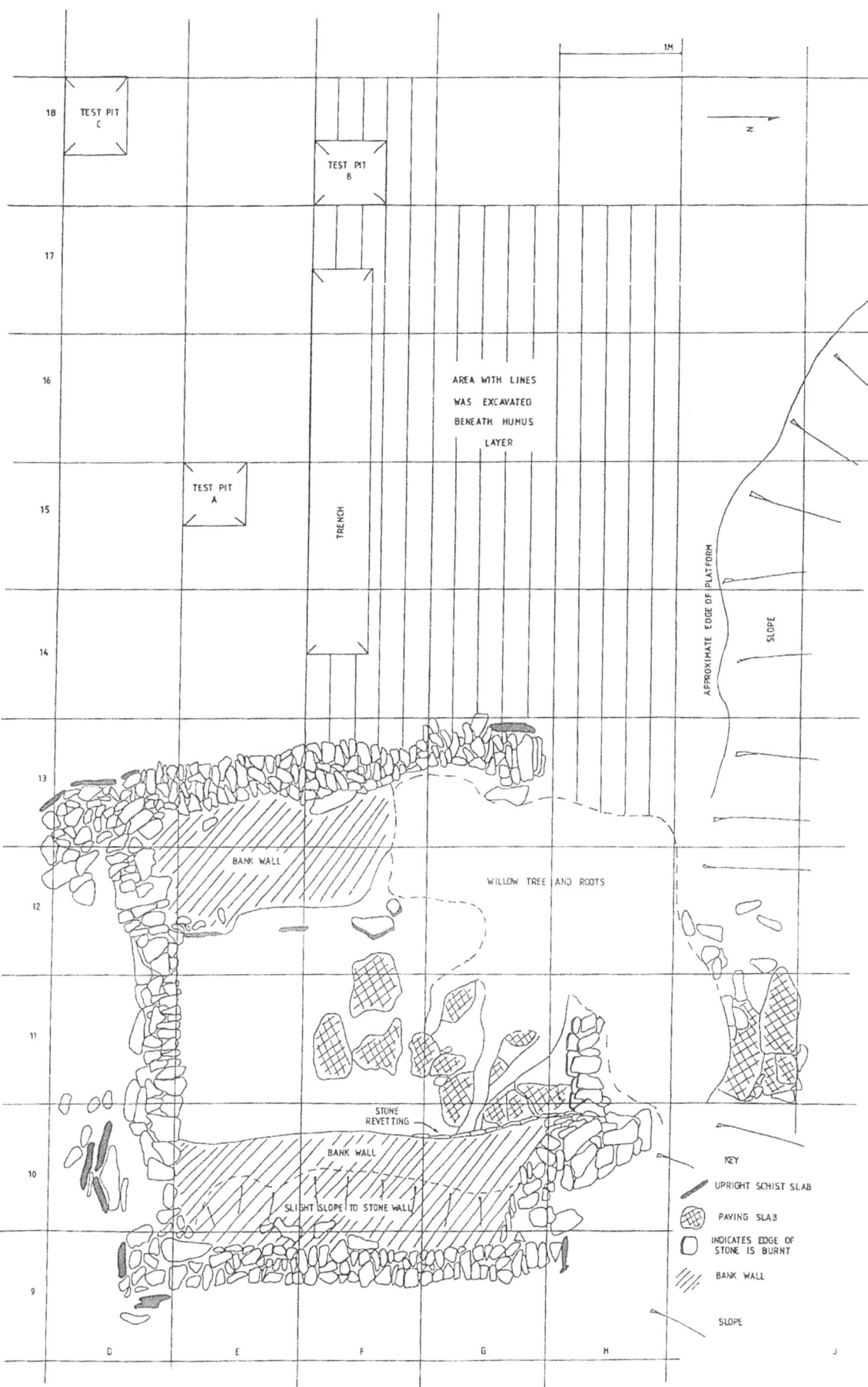

Figure 4.20b. Arrowtown Chinese Settlement excavated hut plans.

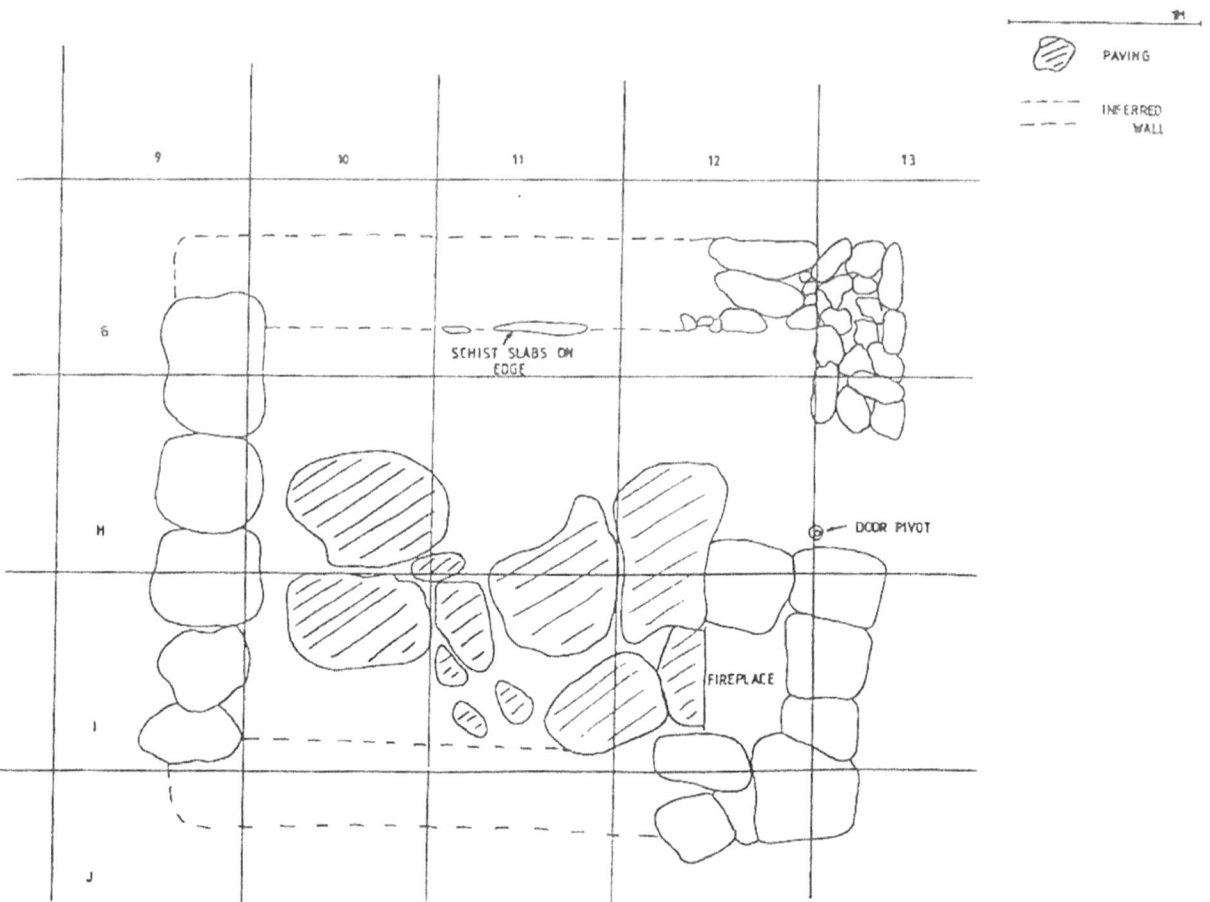

Figure 4.20c. Arrowtown Chinese Settlement excavated hut plans: ACS/4 (hut 4).

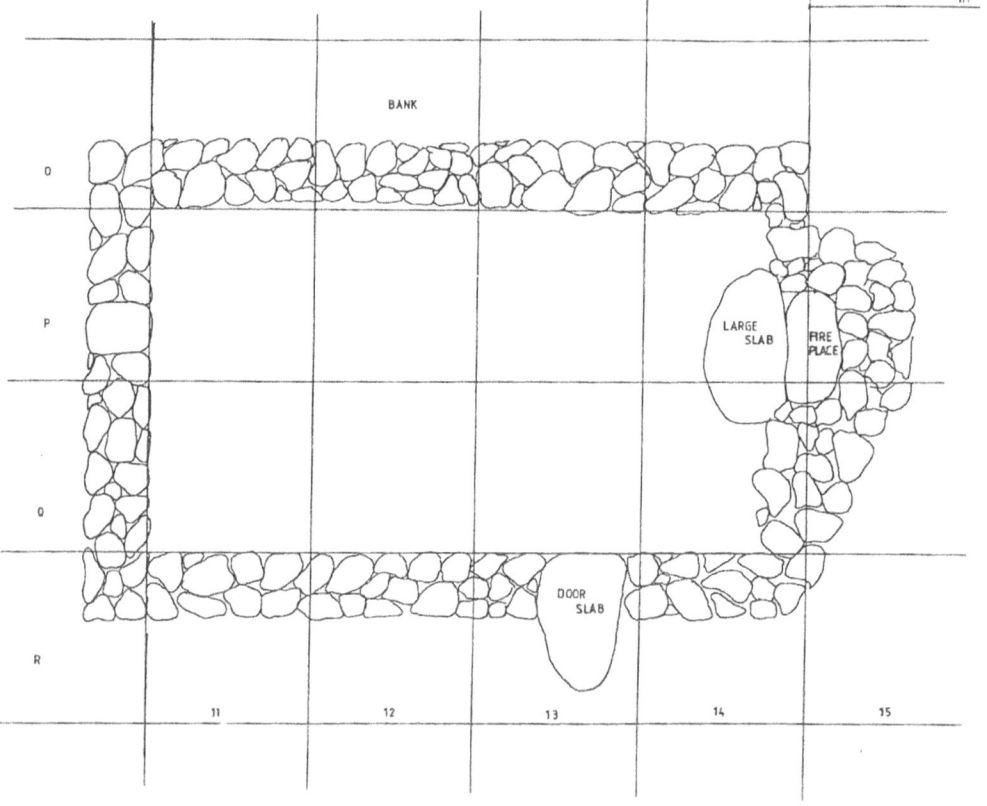

Figure 4.20d. Arrowtown Chinese Settlement excavated hut plans: ACS/5 (hut 5).

4 The archaeological evidence

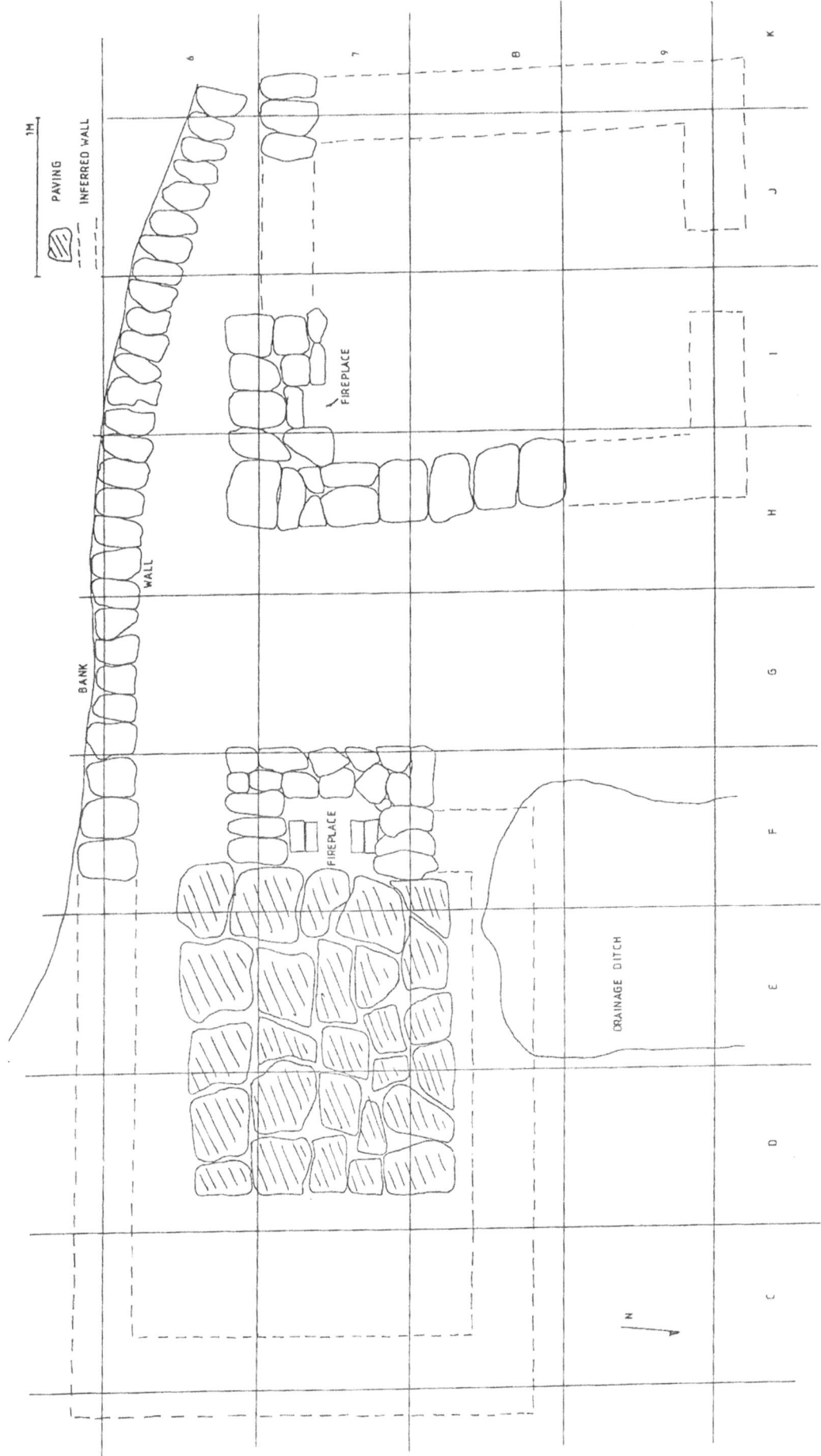

Figure 4.20e. Arrowtown Chinese Settlement excavated hut plans (Arrowtown huts 6a, 6b).

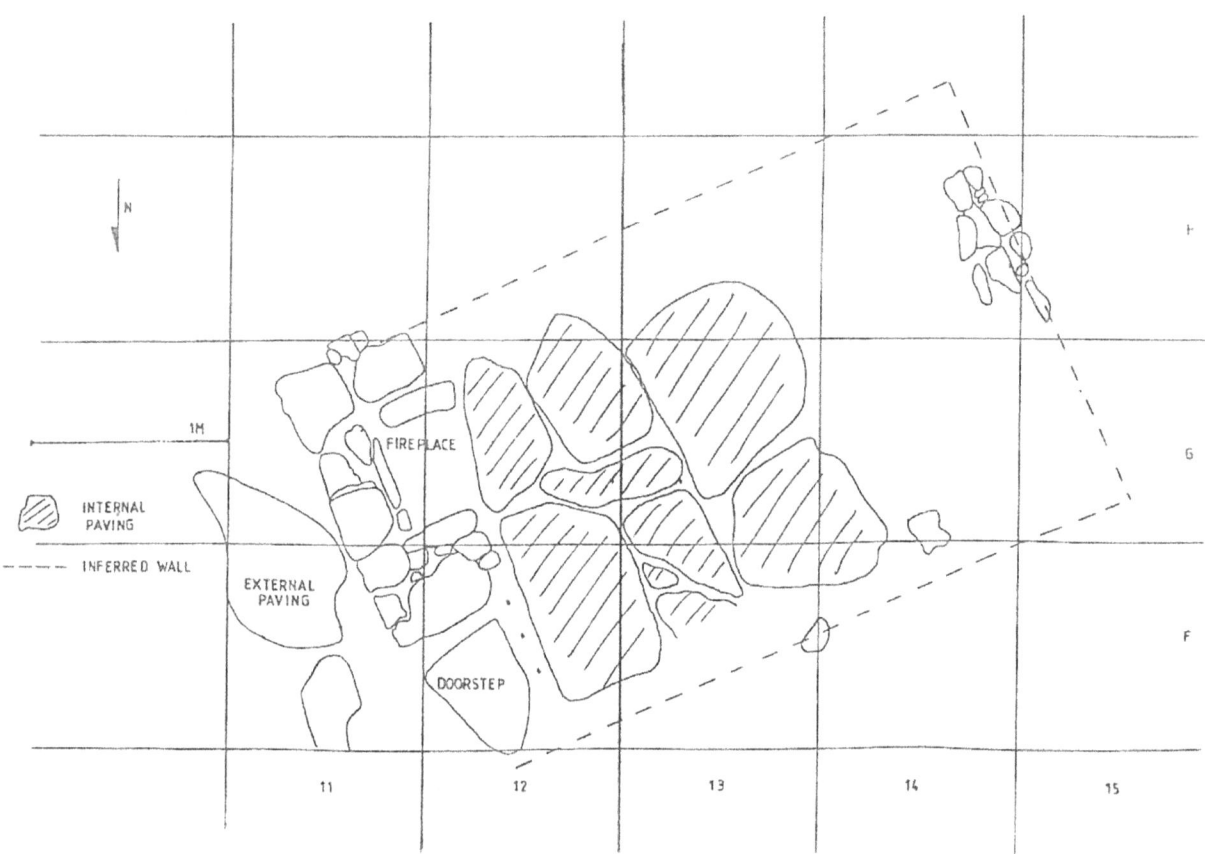

Figure 4.20f. Arrowtown Chinese Settlement excavated hut plans: ACS/8 (hut 8).

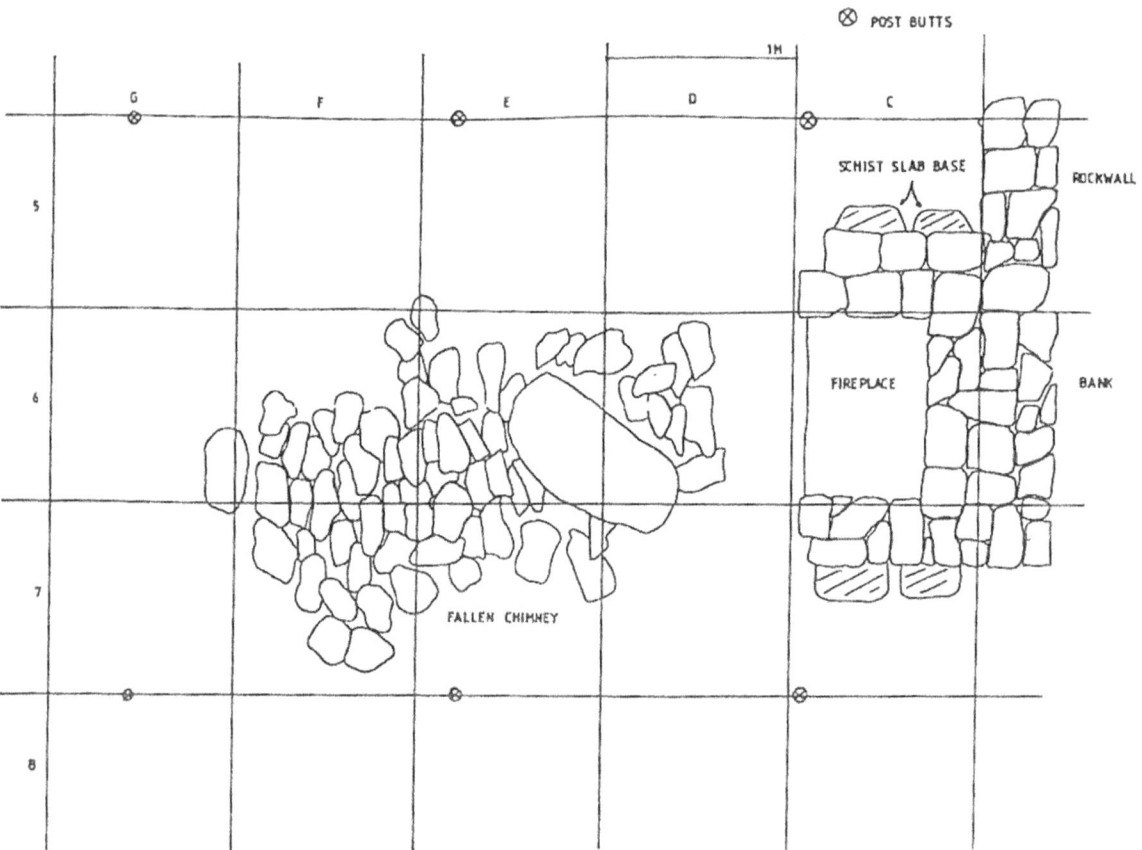

Figure 4.20g. Arrowtown Chinese Settlement excavated hut plans: ACS/10 (hut 10).

4 The archaeological evidence

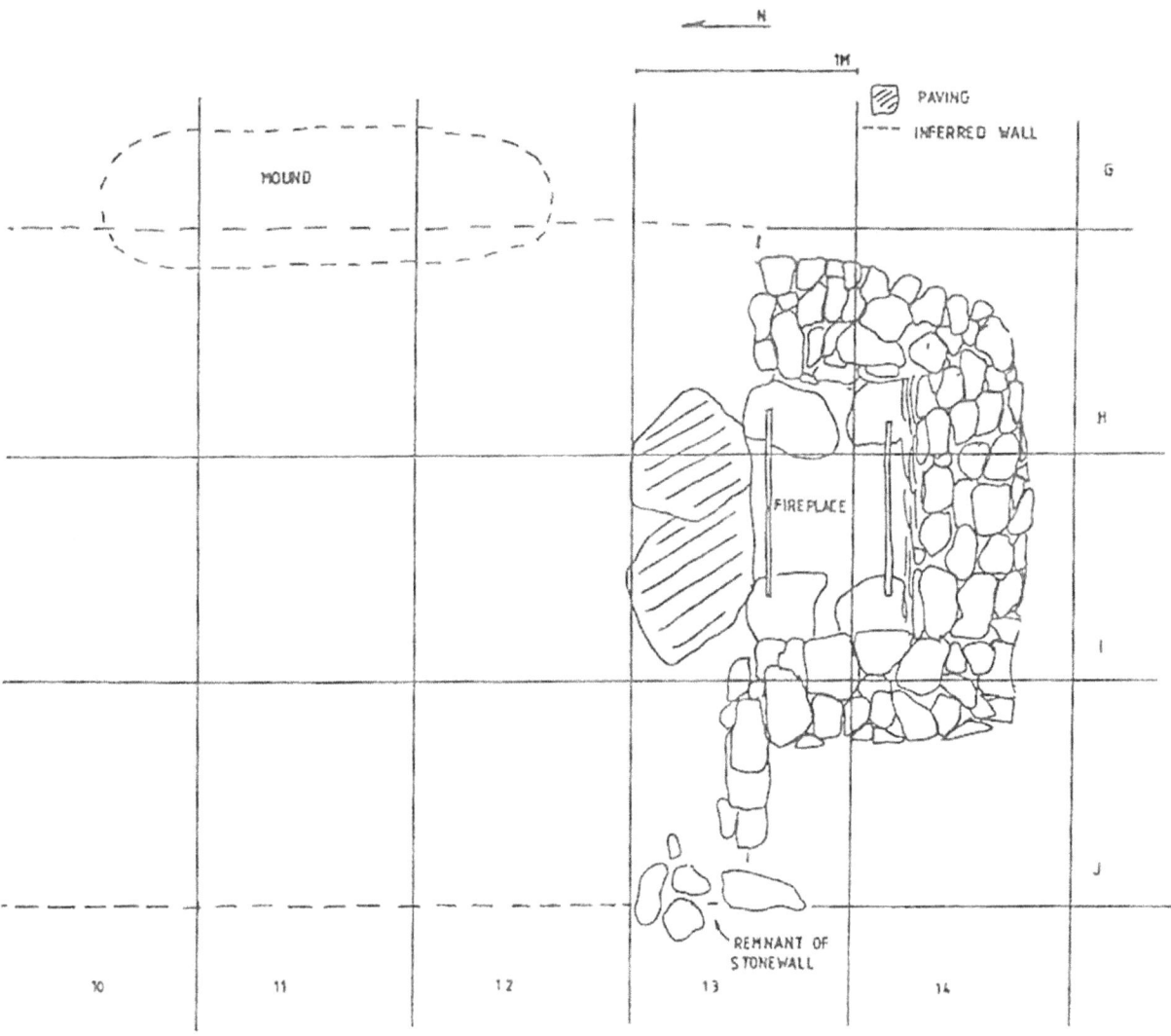

Figure 4.20h. Arrowtown Chinese Settlement excavated hut plans: ACS/11 (hut 11).

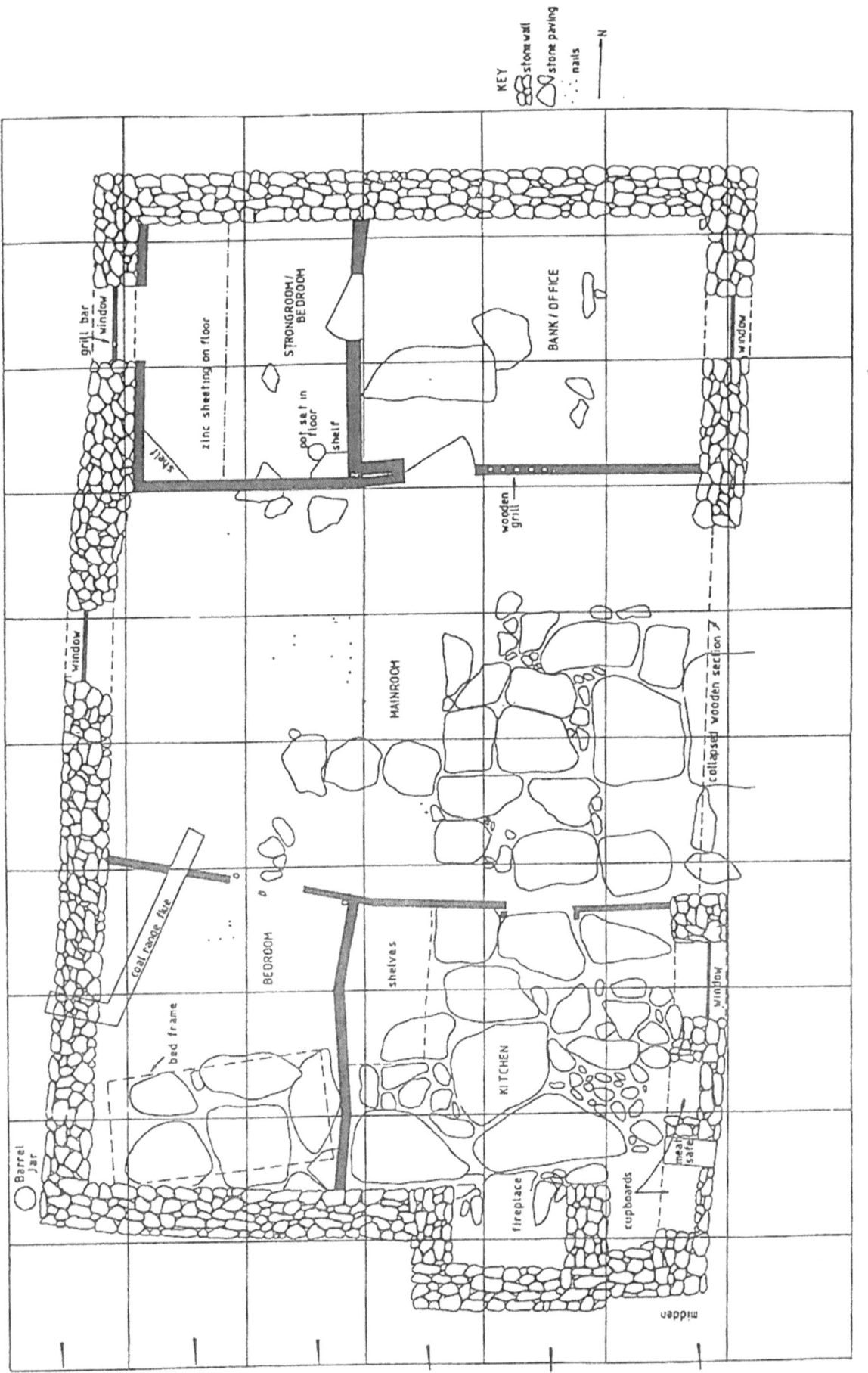

Figure 4.21. Ah Lum's store, Arrowtown site plan.

4 The archaeological evidence

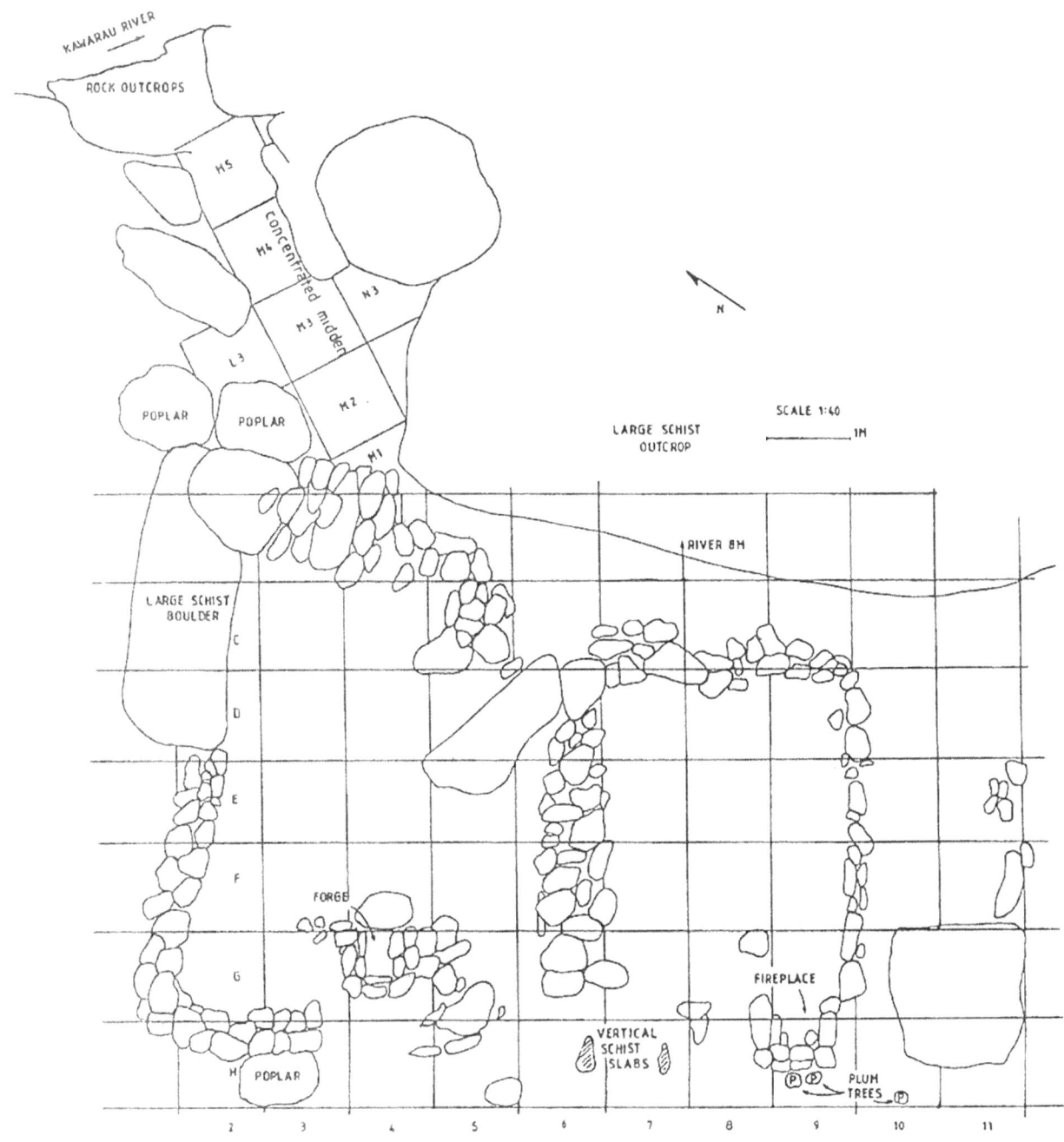

Figure 4.22. Rapids site plan (S133/453).

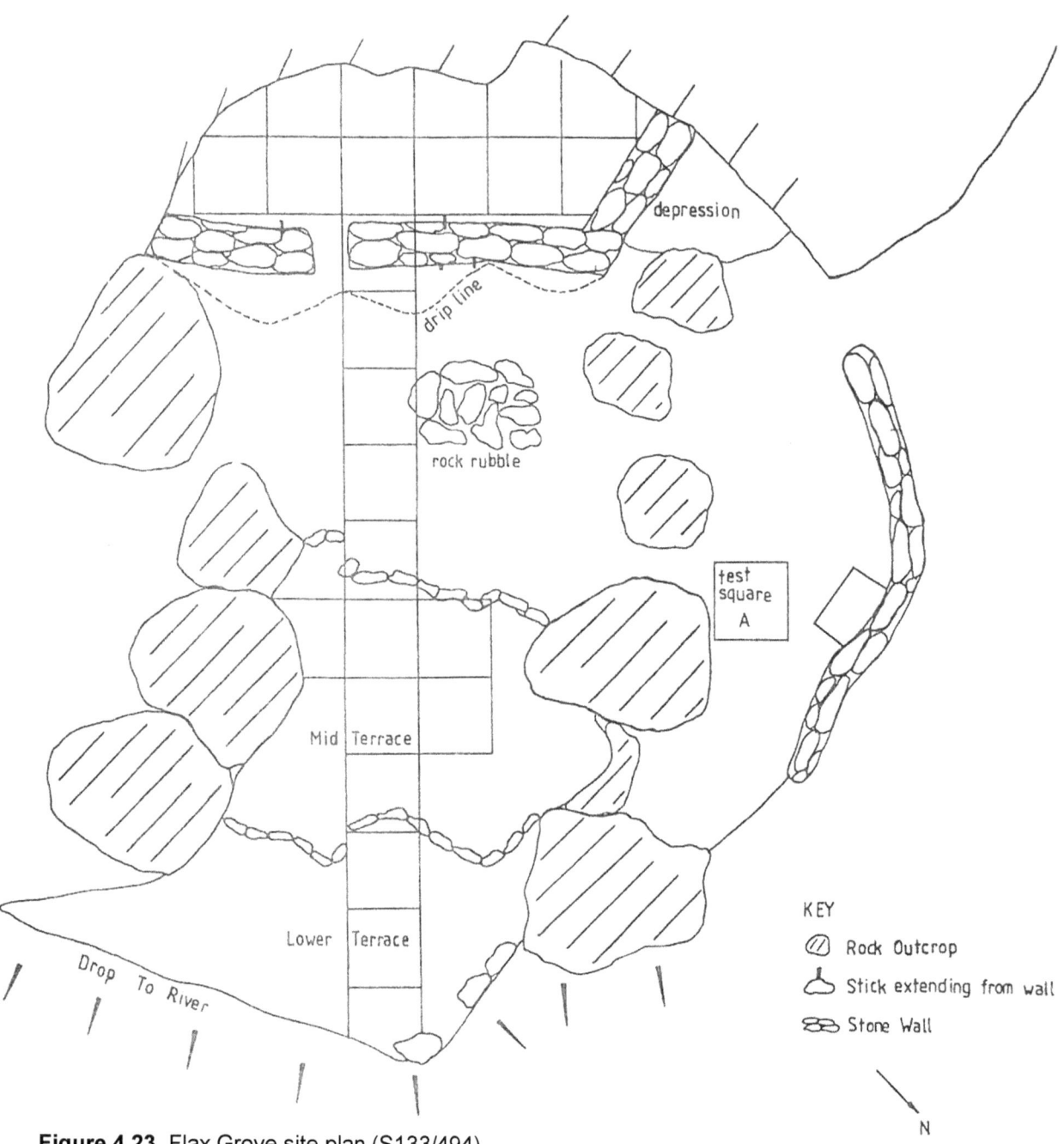

Figure 4.23. Flax Grove site plan (S133/494).

4 The archaeological evidence

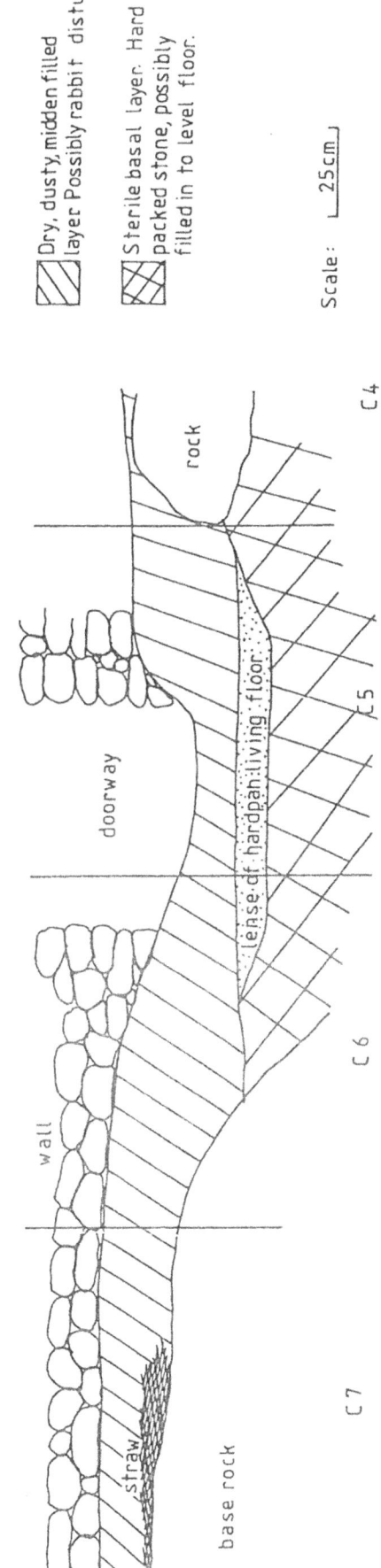

Figure 4.24. Flax Grove shelter (S133/494).

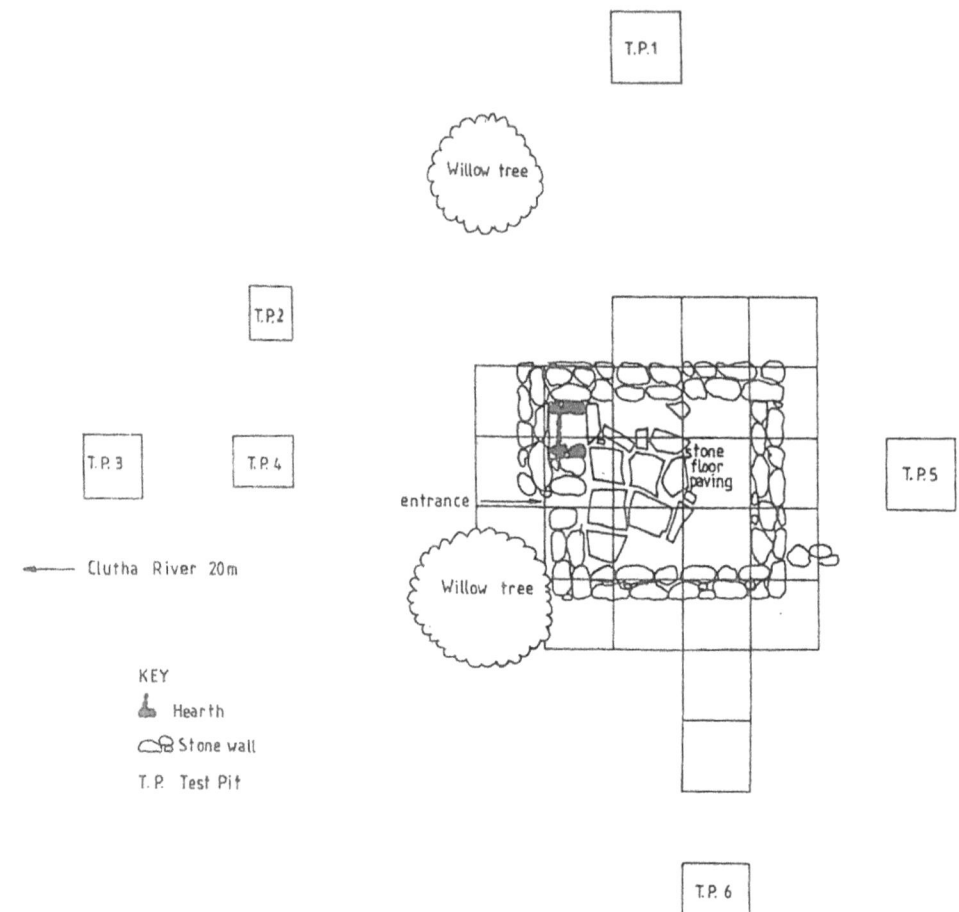

Figure 4.25. The Willows site plan (S124/42).

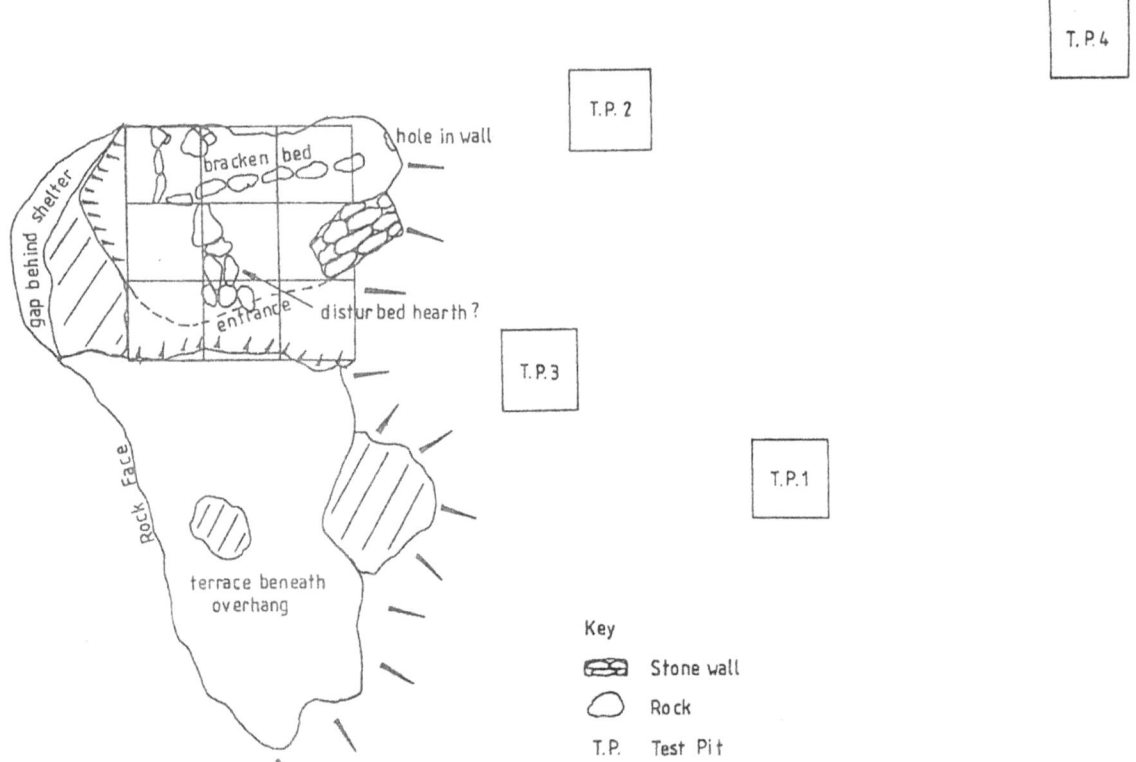

Figure 4.26. Platform site plan (S133/466).

4 The archaeological evidence

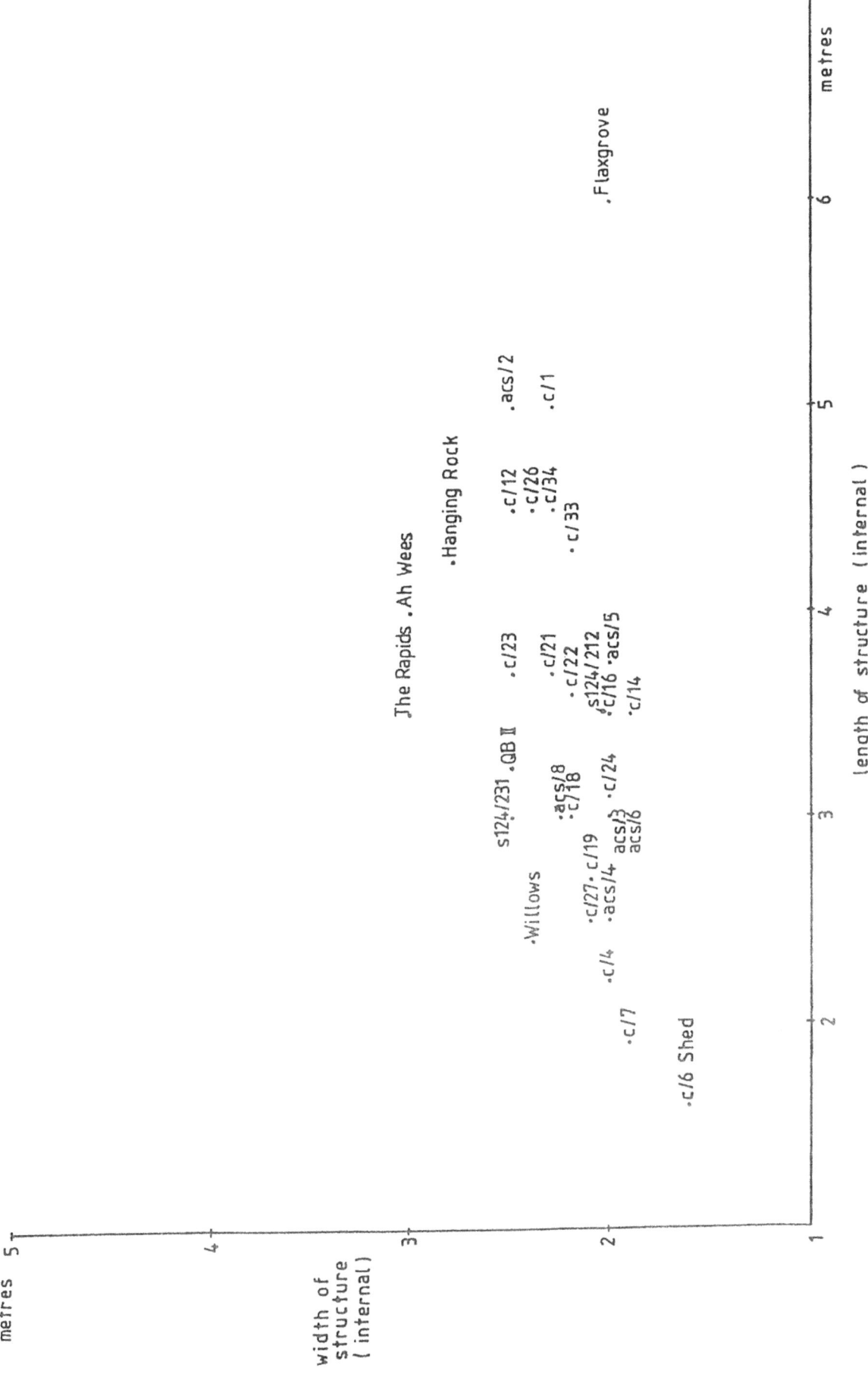

Figure 4.27. Graph of hut dimensions.

Chapter 5
THE MATERIAL CULTURE OF THE CHINESE IN SOUTHERN NEW ZEALAND

Given an almost complete lack of published details about overseas Chinese sites or artefacts in New Zealand, it was felt necessary to approach the study and analysis of the artefactual remains at the most basic level by defining types and describing and illustrating their variability. This provides a framework and corpus of information that future researchers can build on. In general, detailed description is restricted to artefacts found in the course of fieldwork, or uncovered by fossickers from sites in the study area. However, in some instances, Chinese artefacts found elsewhere in New Zealand, and in contemporary overseas sites, are described for comparative purposes or to draw attention to the possibility that similar types may be uncovered in New Zealand in the future.

The sheer quantity of excavated material necessitated extensive tabulation and abbreviation of some data. Provenance details are one area where this has been done. As most of the sites were "one layer" occupations, intra-site stratigraphy and provenance details have been kept to a minimum, but cultural and functional associations of artefacts have not been neglected.

At the time of writing the thesis that this book is based on, historical archaeology was still in its infancy in New Zealand and even basic classifications of common artefact categories had not been produced. One of the objectives of this work was to redress this imbalance. Functional categories have been used extensively in the subsequent discussion, but the predominant artefact types (glass, ceramic and metal containers) were grouped principally on their material of manufacture, partly because of the sheer volume of these materials, but the function and associations of these artefacts have not been overlooked. The data is presented in a form that is believed to have high comparability. The social and functional role of the artefacts is discussed in detail and extensively cross-referenced in this and the subsequent chapters.

Approximately 60% of the total volume of artefacts (and faunal material) was recovered from the two largest study sites, the Chinese camps at Cromwell and Arrowtown. These sites are used as the main database from which inferences are drawn regarding socio-economic patterns and behaviour. Reference is made to the assemblages from the outlying sites to highlight differences or similarities in material culture and explain the activities they represent within the Chinese social network.

A notable feature of all the excavations has been an absence, or at least a failure to find, major midden deposits despite considerable effort towards that end. Generally, the cultural debris was uncovered in small lenses, as scatters in and around habitations, or as small "caches" in adjacent banks or depressions. There are several factors that singly or collectively would explain the absence of concentrated midden deposits. These are examined below.

1. The Chinese produced little rubbish. This suggestion doesn't square with the archaeological evidence and historical observations. The Chinese consumed a wide variety of packaged foodstuffs, alcohols and medicines, as well as raising pigs and chickens and growing vegetables and fruits around their camps. Although they were frugal, they ate well when they could afford to and in consequence must have produced a lot of domestic refuse.

2. They dumped their rubbish a considerable distance from their dwellings. This makes good sense, particularly regarding smell and sanitation problems, but if they regularly dumped their rubbish at some distance, the pattern would have been recognised by now and the dumps duly located. Besides, there is usually enough debris scattered in and around the huts, albeit sometimes thinly spread, to indicate that long distance dumping was not a regular practice.

3. They dumped their rubbish into nearby rivers. The Chinese who were living on riverbank locations almost certainly dumped a lot of their inorganic refuse into the rivers, particularly the big-volume, fast-flowing rivers such as the Kawarau and Clutha. At the Rapids site, a trail of midden extended right to the edge of the steep drop into the Kawarau River. The same river further downstream at Chinatown would have quickly flushed away any rubbish dumped into it. At Ah Wee's site, a small refuse deposit was found in the adjacent tailings. It is likely that a similar pattern of disposal into workings was used at other sites, e.g. the Apple Tree and Hanging Rock sites.

4. They destroyed their rubbish by burning it, feeding it to livestock or composting it (including human wastes). These procedures were used and would destroy or re-utilise the bulk of organic wastes, but they would still leave substantial inorganic residues.

5. Most of the material in former concentrated middens has decomposed. Accepting that tin cans, paper, timber, clothing and food remains may have substantially rotted away, that still leaves a considerable volume of durable products such as iron, copper, glass and ceramics. Artefacts made from these materials and

butchered animal bones do in fact constitute the bulk of recovered materials, but the dry climate of Central Otago also favours the preservation of less durable materials such as tin and paper in some instances.
6. There is a high likelihood that the Chinese sites have been fossicked, but fossickers seldom take away all the broken and "valueless" material that constitutes the bulk of most dumps and usually leave unwanted materials scattered around their fossicking sites. Given this situation, a fossicked site or dump still contains much useful material from an archaeological perspective.
7. The Chinese regularly buried their rubbish in deep pits, which are not readily rediscovered. There is little evidence that the Chinese in Central Otago went to the trouble of digging rubbish pits. The "upper Chinatown" deposits (i.e. the rubbish from the Chinese stores above Chinatown) are the only instance where material has been found below a depth of 40 cm, and this can be attributed to the dumping of fill and the slumping of the bank over the midden.
8. Another possibility exists in Chinatown's case. The Chinese may have used Cromwell township's rubbish removal service. This involved the collection by horse and dray of loads of rubbish, its conveyance to the end of one of the town's streets, and dumping down the riverbank. Although a few Chinese artefacts have been found in these "town deposits", it is unlikely that the Chinese were invited or availed themselves of the service.

It can be accepted that the factors mentioned above have all worked to some degree against the formation or survival of concentrated middens. Nevertheless, some 20,000 artefacts and pieces of butchered bone were recovered from the many small lenses and scatters in the study sites. The various discussions and interpretations in this chapter are based principally on the analysis of this material. The term Euro is used to denote that an artefact is of known or suspected Western or occidental origin as opposed to being of known or suspected oriental manufacture or origin.

5.1 GLASS BOTTLES AND CONTAINERS

Glass was the most abundant artefactual material uncovered in the sites. The majority is derived from bottles, jars and vials, but window glass and glassware also make up a small part of the glass component. A minimum of 1,305 glass containers are represented by the remains from the study sites. Quantitative information about product types is presented in Tables 5.1–5.7. The glass from Cromwell's Chinatown has been extensively analysed and described previously (Ritchie and Bedford 1983). In that report the social role of the various bottled products was examined in detail. This discussion, an analysis of the glass containers from all the study sites, expands on the conclusions in the published report.

5.1.1 OBJECTIVES OF THE GLASS CONTAINER ANALYSIS

The glass containers were analysed with four primary objectives in mind:

1. to establish the dates of occupation of each structure where possible;
2. to determine differences in function or changing uses of structures;
3. to gain insights into socio-economic differentiation between sites;
4. to gain insights into subsistence and social behaviour.

5.1.2 ANALYTICAL PROCEDURE

The glass from each site or feature was analysed separately. After cleaning, the glass was identified and placed into categories based on a determination of the original contents of each vessel. Product identifications were facilitated by using well-established techniques: research into brand names, embossing and labels (where possible), comparative analysis of bottle morphology, glass characteristics and colour. A comparative collection of more than 300 units was established (largely from bottle collectors' duplicates and rejects) for direct comparison of fragments with suspected bottle types. Reference was also made to business directories (e.g. Stone's Directories, Wise's Directories and the NZ Post Office Directories), bottle club magazines, issues of the *New Zealand Antique Bottle Collector*, books on bottle identification, company histories, manufacturer's marks and bottle-collecting literature (*Cyclopedia of New Zealand* 1897–1908; Toulouse 1971; Fletcher 1972, 1975; Vader and Murray 1975; Aldridge and Aldridge 1978; Rusden 1979; White 1979; Tasker 1984) and excavation reports describing bottle remains (Herskovitz 1978; Armstrong 1979; Schulz et al. 1980).

Minimum numbers were achieved by counting only positively diagnostic pieces such as necks or bases and taking the greater of the two totals. The minimum number of common bottles, such as "green glass ring-seals" or "black beers", was compared to the number inferred by tallying the total weight of the same type of glass divided by the average weight of an intact bottle. This cross-check always resulted in a very high correlation (over 90%).

5.1.3 DERIVING OCCUPATION DATES FROM BOTTLES

Dating of bottles was achieved by utilising several well-recognised techniques involving the recognition of known (often patented, hence datable) changes in bottle manufacturing techniques over the last 150 years. These innovations are documented in several publications (e.g. Fletcher 1972; Morgan 1974; Vader and Murray 1975; White 1979). They include changes in shape, glass colour and purity, mould marks, sealing methods, neck forms, bases and deciphering maker's marks. Historical records such as histories of bottle manufacturers, business directories and newspaper advertisements are also very useful for dating purposes. The recovery of bottles of known short-term production or usage is essential for accurate and reliable dating of cultural deposits.

5.1.4 BOTTLE CATEGORIES BASED ON ORIGINAL CONTENTS

Glass containers, like many other forms of packaging (such as the shapes of tin cans), exhibit considerable conservatism through time. Consequently, particular and often well-recognised container types have been associated with specific products since they were first produced. Recognition of these groups or generic links is an important aid to the identification of a bottle's original contents. The main categories are detailed below. Examples of each type are depicted in Figures 5.1–5.11.

5.1.4.1 Alcohol bottles

Liquor bottles: (Table 5.1; Figure 5.1) These include brandy and whisky bottles and flasks (usually in aqua glass), schnapps and gin (in distinctive dark green, square cross-section bottles known as case bottles), a range of specialised spirit bottles (e.g. Dr. Townsend's Sarsaparilla, Gilbey's Gin, Silverstream Schnapps, Benedictine) and wine bottles (similar in form to modern wine bottles).

Beers and ales: (Table 5.2; Figures 5.2–5.4) This large group of bottles range from the earliest black glass applied-top forms made in three-piece moulds to post-1920s embossed crown-top beer bottles, usually of brown glass. A major sub-group within this category are the heavy green glass, ring-seal "beer" bottles (these bottles were also used for aerated waters). Other distinctive early types include blob and collar necks and the rarer skittle form.

5.1.4.2 Domestic/household bottles (Table 5.3; Figure 5.6)

Food bottles: This extensive group is dominated by the bottles that contained various food products such as sauces, pickles, salad oils, vinegars, essences and jams.

Non-food bottles: This group contained non-edible products such as blacking, leather dressing and inks.

5.1.4.3 Pharmaceutical and cosmetic bottles (Table 5.4; Figures 5.7–5.8)

This category includes prescription and patent medicines, poisons (often in blue glass), pill and ointment containers and perfume bottles.

5.1.4.4 Chinese glass

Chinese glass: (Table 5.5) Various glass containers that were probably made in China and contained products manufactured in China. The main types uncovered in the study area are small straight-sided vials (which contained various tinctures including laudanum, Figures 5.9a,b,d), teardrop-shaped vials (Figure 5.9f), tall cylindrical wide-mouthed clear glass bottles (Figure 5.9g) and small round and oval section bottles and vials that are often embossed with Chinese characters (Figures 5.9c,e). All these bottle forms are believed to have contained pharmaceuticals. Except for the tincture vials that are made of aqua glass, they are all made of clear glass.

Small "beer" bottles of presumed European manufacture: (Figures 5.9h,i) These have been found with remnants of Chinese language labels. They are believed to have been re-used by the Chinese. No examples have been recovered with labels that were legible enough to translate.

5.1.4.5 Aerated water bottles (Table 5.6; Figure 5.10)

This category includes some distinctive 19th-century bottle forms including the Hamilton patent (torpedoes), varieties of the Codd patent (marble bottles), ring-seals and the familiar crown-tops.

5.1.4.6 Undiagnostic fragments

In any archaeological glass assemblage, a certain proportion of the fragments are not positively ascribable to particular bottles or types. These can be divided into two groups:

a. Miscellaneous fragments of identified bottles. These are irrelevant in an analysis and can be put aside.
b. Fragments that appear to be from additional bottles. Although they add to individual site totals, they are too small or indistinctive to be positively ascribed to a particular bottle/product type.

Tables 5.1–5.7 detail the types of bottles and numbers recovered from the sites, the products they contained, and the date range for particular bottles as determined by the methods outlined earlier. For comparative purposes, emphasis has been placed on minimum numbers and types and their distribution, rather than the total weight of fragments of different glass types (see Prickett 1981; Spring-Rice 1982b). Illustrations of the vessels (Figures 5.1–5.11) and inferences on socio-economic behaviour are presented after the tables.

5.1.5 DISCUSSION AND CONCLUSIONS FROM THE GLASS ANALYSES

The four research objectives cited earlier are now addressed:

1. **Determining dates of occupation:** The dates of occupation of each of the study sites were summarised in Chapter 4 (Table 4.2) and are further outlined in Tables 5.1–5.6. Assuming that rubbish was disposed regularly during a site's existence, it is likely that most uncovered artefacts are temporally biased towards the latter part of the occupations. In fact, many probably result from the abandonment of individual huts and their contents when their owners departed. Notwithstanding this proviso, some spatial-temporal patterns were clear. In the Cromwell Chinese Camp, the earliest huts are located at the eastern end (huts 21, 22, 23, 26), beginning about 1870. Huts 6, 7 and 14 at the western end are of later date (post-1900), and some (e.g. hut 4) appear to have had predominantly European occupation. This is confirmed by historical accounts that indicate that the western end of the settlement was occupied, after it had been abandoned by the Chinese, by a few destitute Europeans during the 1930s Depression.

   Few unequivocal stratigraphic indications of successive re-occupations of sites were evident during the excavations. Analysis of the bottle remains (and other datable artefacts) found within and around most of the structures indicated a continuous dating sequence and suggest that in most instances there were no or only short breaks in occupancy between when a site was first occupied and when it was abandoned. However, the dates of the glass from huts 1, 6, 12 and 18 at Cromwell suggest these sites had two distinct periods of occupation: a pre-1900 occupancy evidenced by early forms such as black glass beer bottles, Sykes Macvay & Co stoppers (1860s–1888) and case gin bottles; and a later occupation evidenced by machine-made glass bottles of the 1930s.

2. **Hut functions:** Both the recovered bottle types and other artefacts indicate that most of the sites were humble living quarters, in and around which food was prepared and consumed. Only one site (hut 23 at Chinatown) appears to have been more specialised, judged on the presence of particular bottle and specialised artefact types. Among the artefacts in hut 23 were 90 bottles (predominantly alcohol), two kerosene lamp glasses, 18 tincture vials and various artefacts associated with opium smoking (560 of all the opium-smoking-related artefacts uncovered in the Cromwell Camp). Although the hut was similar in layout to the other habitations, the high incidence of alcohol bottles and opium-smoking equipment suggests it served as a smoking and social venue.

3. **Social differentiation:** Comparative analysis of the bottle remains and other artefact types from the various sites revealed no pronounced differences that might reliably indicate differences in social status or wealth. In fact, the site assemblages, including those from the Chinese store at Arrowtown, were remarkably egalitarian.

4. **Socio-economic insights based on the glass analysis:** Because of its inherent durability, glass, whether broken or intact, has a well-recognised longevity in archaeological contexts. If analysed in isolation, it would give a very misleading impression as to the socio-economic significance of glass-packaged products. To avoid this distortion, glass assemblages must be compared not only against other packaging remains, such as cans and ceramic containers, but also against the evidence of less durable packaging such as bamboo and paper, which are likely to have been present but decomposed. It is apparent from written records and the recovered assemblages that most of the large-volume products imported by the Chinese, e.g. tea, rice, soya oil, opium, preserved vegetables, sugared ginger, dried fish, fish pastes and Ng Ka Py (alcohol) were not packaged in glass. In the absence of a major indigenous glass container manufacturing industry in China, ceramic pots, sacks, metal containers (used for opium in particular), wooden boxes and wicker baskets continued to be the main forms for packaging and transporting foodstuffs until about 1910.

Pharmaceuticals, evidenced by distinctive small bottles and vials, are the only numerically significant glass-contained products of Chinese origin that were imported into New Zealand in the 19th century. The importation of Chinese medicines is understandable in light of the Chinese miners' general distrust of European doctors and medications (see Section 3.10). They preferred to use "tried and true" Chinese medicines and medical procedures such as acupuncture, but it is evident from the medicine bottle remains in the sites that they also started using many European medicines.

Although the Chinese continued to rely on a wide range of food and alcohol products imported from their homeland, almost from their first settlement in New Zealand, they adopted several European foodstuffs, alcoholic beverages and other products, many of which were packaged in glass. Some became virtual staples. This is well reflected in the remains from the study sites and in contemporary accounts such as those of Don.

Table 5.7 documents the numbers and percentage composition of the various glass-packaged products in the sites. The percentage calculations are rounded to the nearest whole number.

5.1.6 ALCOHOL CONSUMPTION

The popularity of alcoholic beverages on the goldfields is a well-established fact, so the high percentage of alcohol bottles (ranging from 50 to about 85% of the bottles in each site) is hardly surprising. Until the temperance movement gained ascendancy around the turn of the century, there were few laws governing the sale and distribution of alcohol. It was widely sold and consumed in large quantities. In early colonial New Zealand, alcohol was used as a food, a drink, a medicine and a pleasurable drug. Towards the end of the 19th century there was a spectacular drop in overall alcohol consumption, and most people were drinking it simply for pleasure (Eldred-Grigg 1984:211–12).

The Chinese do not appear to have been an exception to this drinking pattern. As indicated, large numbers of European alcohol bottles were found in the study sites. However, in addition to the consumption of European alcohol, the Chinese imported their own alcoholic beverages, particularly Ng Ka Py, which was bottled in distinctive globular ceramic bottles (Figure 5.17). The numbers of these vessels found in each of the study sites is documented in Table 5.12 for comparison with glass-packaged alcohols. Ng Ka Py was also used in a locally made medicine at Round Hill (Don 1/2/1884:147). The widespread use of opium by the Chinese must also be taken into account. The relative significance of these three mind-altering agents (European and traditional alcohols and opium) is difficult to quantify, but they all played a major role in Chinese recreation and social occasions. Later they appear to have increasingly served as solace to combat loneliness, poverty and despair.

The most common bottles (n=184) of any sort in the Chinese sites were large unembossed green glass ring-sealed bottles (Figure 5.3a). They were present in 15 of the 17 study sites. These bottles were generally used for brewed alcoholic drinks such as beers and stouts (many were imported English brews). But remnants of paper labels on bottles of this type (Figure 5.10) indicate that they were also used (probably recycled) by two local manufacturers, the Cromwell Brewery and Theyers & Beck of Alexandra (for their Champion trademark lemonade and ginger ale). Similar bottles may have been used by Buckham's, the Queenstown brewer and cordial manufacturer, but no labelled examples have been observed. Thus, it is not possible to comment categorically on the relative consumption patterns concerning the products bottled in these containers, but it is likely that most of those found in mining sites contained alcohol rather than aerated waters.

The beer bottles attest to the relative longevity of many of the Chinese sites. They range from the early black glass three-piece mould, applied-top forms (1860s–1870s; Figure 5.2) through skittle forms in dark green glass (pre-1890; relatively uncommon), green glass ring-seals (c.1880–1920; Figure 5.3a) and blob-top spun-mould forms (1910–20; Figures 5.3 b and c) to pictorially-embossed brown glass crown caps (post-1915–1930s; Figure 5.4). They constituted 10–30% of the glass containers from most of the sites (see Table 5.7). The earliest forms (the black glass bottles, n=41) were present in 13 of the 17 study sites.

Numerically, light green brandy bottles (n=136; Figure 5.1) were second only to beer bottles, and were present in 15 sites. Brandy was the most popular spiritous drink in New Zealand until the 1890s (Eldred-Grigg 1984:211). Hennessy's was a particularly popular brand (Eldred-Grigg 1984:211). and is well represented in the Chinese sites. Besides the archaeological evidence of its popularity among the Chinese, Don's numerous comments about brandy clearly show it became an important and integral part of socialising in the Chinese communities on the goldfields, and particularly so during festive and mourning occasions. The following quotes not only document the extensive consumption of brandy by the Chinese but also provide some interesting insights into alcohol-related behaviour. When Don (1/9/1892:43) visited the Round Hill goldfield he observed a list prepared by a storekeeper itemising the products consumed at a feast the previous night: "The total cost was about £50, the most prominent article being brandy, which seems to play the part here that samshoo [Ng Ka Py?] does at home." A few months later when he revisited the settlement, he entered a Chinese gambling house and "heard the familiar sound of voices associated with the Chinese drinking game *ch'aai mooi*. Six men were seated at a table literally covered with eatables, and besides a brandy bottle and small Chinese wine cups. In the next shop were about a score of men feasting and the brandy bottles and wine cups were prominent" (Don 1/12/1882:105). On another occasion he visited the hut of three men who shared the same dwelling. He noted (1/9/1883:47): "I counted 26 empty brandy, whisky and samshoo bottles lying outside – the accumulation of only a few months!" On another occasion he noted that "the festive components were two fowls, six pounds of pork bones with rice and brandy unstinted" (Don 1/2/1888:147). His recorded observations abound with numerous other comments about the prolific consumption of brandy (e.g. Don 1/5/1885:204, 1/8/1885:27, 1/5/1889:205).

In addition to its use as a social lubricant, brandy was used as a funerary offering. Don observed one occasion where the body of a Chinese miner, who had died the previous day on the Round Hill field, was being carried down to Riverton. His bearers "rested awhile on the way. When the body was lifted, several candles were lit and a bottle of brandy spilt to appease the wrath of the deceased's spirit at the removal of the body" (Don 1/8/1884:24).

Gin was only marginally less popular than brandy. One hundred and twenty-five bottles were recovered from 13 sites; the number recovered at Chinatown (55) being double that of brandy (28). Most of the gin was of Dutch origin, JDKZ being the post popular brand. Despite the obvious popularity of gin, there is a puzzling absence of observations about its consumption or social role in Don's records. His lack of comment is especially surprising because even fragments of the square-sectioned "case gin bottles" are very distinctive (see Figures 5.1 e and f).

Whisky, schnapps and cognac are other European alcohols that were popular with the Chinese (Table 5.1). Wine bottles were uncommon in the rural sites, but six were recovered at Chinatown and 10 at Arrowtown.

There are no records or archaeological evidence that any of the Chinese made wine, "home brews" or spiritous liquors.

It is difficult to quantify what effect prices might have had on alcohol preferences on the goldfields, but judging from the figures reproduced in Table 5.8, they appear to have had very little. Alcohol was a comparatively expensive commodity (compare the prices with the food prices in Table 6.20), but the miners, both Chinese and European, seem to have decided what alcohols they preferred and paid the going rate. Initially, alcohol prices were very high, but they gradually dropped as transport improved and as gold became harder to find with a consequent drop in the miners' spending power. The hotels also lowered their overheads by such things as forsaking "dancing girls" who were paid to entice the miners "to spend up large".

5.1.7 DOMESTIC PRODUCTS

Two hundred and twenty-six bottles (17.3% of the grand total from all sites) were categorised as "domestic bottles" (Table 5.3; Figure 5.6). All were of European origin, suggesting considerable acceptance or substitution of European processed and preserved foods by the Chinese. While the usage of European cooking and food products that were similar in appearance or composition to traditional Chinese products is readily understandable, it is evident from the archaeological evidence that the Chinese also adopted many of the processed European products that were widely available on the goldfields. These included Worcestershire sauce (notably the Lea & Perrins brand), salad oil, Champion's and other vinegars, pickles (particularly Hayward Bros' Flag brand, Stella [Pacific Preserving Works, Dunedin] and Military brand), and jams (St. George Preserving Works, Dunedin, and Kirkpatrick's of Nelson). Less numerous products include Nubian Blacking, essence of rennet, Carter's, Hollidge's and Antoine's inks, Hauthaway's Peerless Gloss (a leather dressing), fruit salts (e.g. J.T. Morton's), coffee and chicory (Symington & Co, Edinburgh), castor oil (in blue bottles) and cordials (Rose's Lime, and Lemos, a lemon-flavoured beverage). About 200 of the bottles and jars grouped in the "domestic category" were unembossed, but they can be reasonably reliably identified because their shapes are like embossed versions of the same bottle form. As outlined in Section 3.2, some Chinese storekeepers prided themselves on stocking European products as well as Chinese provisions.

5.1.8 PHARMACEUTICALS

The 74 pharmaceutical and "personal" bottles (Table 5.4; Figures 5.7) from the Chinese sites provide interesting insights into notions of sickness in the 19th century and the health concerns, real and imagined, of the Chinese. This category is dominated by patent and proprietary medicines such as Dr Sheldon's New Discovery, Perry Davis Vegetable Pain Killer (see Hayward and Diamond 1982:177; Sullivan 1984), Chamberlain's Pain Balm, Baxter's Lung Preserver (Christchurch), Barry's Tricophorous for the Skin and Hair, Woods' Great Peppermint Cure For Coughs & Colds, and Sanders and Sons' Eucalypti Extract. The alcohol and narcotic contents of these preparations were often incredibly high by today's standards (Herskovitz 1978:12). They were generally bought after self-diagnosis, influenced by extravagant claims (unfettered by government regulations) that the products would cure almost any sort of ailment. As an example, the formula of Perry Davis Vegetable Pain Killer, probably the biggest selling "quack" medicine in New Zealand in the 19th century, is given by Holbrook (1959:153) as follows: gum myrrh 2 1/4 lb, capsicum 10 oz, gum opium 8 oz, gum benzoine 6 oz, gum fuiaic 3 oz and 5 gallons of alcohol.

Other medicine bottles from the study sites include embossed chemists' bottles such as those of H. Hotop (Cromwell); L. Hotop (Queenstown), The Marshall Chemical Co (Princes Street, Dunedin), and Johnson and Haslett (Dunedin); screw-top vaseline jars (Chesebrough Manufacturing Company, New York), Lane's Emulsion (Oamaru), Ayer's Pills, unembossed ointment and pill jars, ENO's "Fruit Salt" (machine made), Tussicura (a cough medicine), laxative bottles, magnesia (Dinneford's, Ayer's and Kruse's), lavender water (green glass), blue glass poisonous product bottles and milk glass (hand or face) cream pots.

In addition to the medicines, nine French perfume bottles (Rimmel's in four styles, and Roger & Gallet) were found in five sites (of which three were found in isolated rural huts and rockshelters; Figure 5.8). Presumably, in the absence of women, these products were used for male cosmetic purposes.

5.1.9 BOTTLES OF CHINESE ORIGIN

While European medicine bottles were present in nine sites, glass bottles and vials (n=58), believed to have been manufactured in China and containing Chinese medicines were found in seven. The largest category (n=49) are small straight-sided vials (Figures 5.9a,b). These are known to have contained various medicinal products including tincture of opium (laudanum). The paper label on a specimen (Figure 5.9d) found in Ah Lum's store reads "U-I-Oil, Manufacturer, Cheung Wah, Canton, China". At least five other small medicinal vial forms in aqua glass (parallel and fluted-sided vials in two sizes, parallel sided vials with oval cross-sections, and teardrop-shaped vials in two sizes; Figures 5.9c,f) are known from Chinese sites in Central Otago, but only two of these forms have been found in the study sites. A single teardrop-shaped vial was found in the Cromwell Chinese Camp. It has three Chinese characters written in gilt paint on the front. This label was translated by Dr F. Lam. Although he found the Chinese characters difficult to anglicise, they stated a man's name (presumably the supplier) and indicated the product was some form of universal remedy. An oval cross-section vial (Figure 5.9c) found in Ah Wee's hut site in the Upper Clutha Valley bears the name of the same supplier. Two small, aqua rectangular-section bottles with sheared lips found at Arrowtown (Figure 5.9e) are also believed to be Chinese medicine bottles.

Figure 5.9g depicts a wide-mouthed, thin-walled, clear glass cylindrical bottle. These bottles have a fine roll lip and bear the remains of largely illegible Chinese labels. They too are believed to have contained a pharmaceutical product. Chinatown is the only site in which they have been found. Three were uncovered during the excavation of the residential part of the settlement and another three were found during excavations in deposits associated with the stores above the Chinatown settlement.

Three applied collar-top, spun-moulded bottles (10 oz size; Figure 5.9h) were found in the Chinatown site. These are similar in form to European beer bottles of comparable size. The archaeologically-recovered specimens are unembossed and have no traces of labels, but an identical specimen with a label bearing Chinese characters was donated for the comparative collection. The label on this bottle was largely illegible, but Dr Lam was able to determine that the label stated the contents were "a wine-based medicine", which he described as "a general remedy". Although the lower part of the label was worn, he thought it was a list of the ingredients.

Other glass bottles of Chinese origin have been found in Central Otago but have not been found in sites in the study area. They include small clear glass bottles of various shapes and sizes embossed with Chinese characters. These are believed to have contained medicinal preparations too. The known specimens (in a private collection) were found in the Nokomai Valley, an area where Sew Hoy's Hydraulic Mining Company continued operations until c.1945. The absence of these clear glass containers from the study sites suggests they were not imported before 1920.

Green glass crown-top bottles (Figure 5.9i) are another Chinese bottle type found in Central Otago. The bottles are similar to the modern clear glass 10 oz soft drink bottle but differ in that they have a distinctive raised band around the neck and frequently have Chinese characters on the base or sides. They are believed to have contained a medicinal wine (Wegars pers. comm.). Two of the more common ones are unembossed green glass bottles with Chinese characters on the base and brown glass bottles embossed with "Wing Lee Wai" (successors to earlier ceramic bottles of the same brand). None of these post-1910 bottles have been found in Chinese sites in the study area, but one of the unembossed green crown-tops was found (along with other Chinese artefacts) during the excavation of a European hotel site (the Halfway House Hotel) in the area (Bedford 1986).

None of the distinctive embossed Chinese glass "fruit jars" (see Peters 1981:94–104) are known from a New Zealand context. Archaeological specimens have been reported from Aptos, California (Whitlow 1981:51), and Lovelock, Nevada (Armstrong 1979:211).

5.1.10 AERATED WATERS

Only 39 aerated water bottles (Table 5.3; Figure 5.10a–g) were recovered, most being found in the urban sites (Chinatown n=15, Arrowtown n=10, Ah Lum's n=5). However, as mentioned earlier, some of the green glass ring-seal bottles may have contained aerated waters (see Figure 5.10h–i). Although aerated water bottles form a relatively insignificant portion of the total assemblage and therefore consumption patterns, they are often the most useful for dating because of regular and datable changes in the bottle forms (e.g. changes from Hamilton "torpedoes", through Maugham's patent "bomb" bottles to patented modifications of the Codd marble bottle).

This is certainly the case with the embossed bottles used by John McLoughlin, an early brewer and cordial maker in Cromwell. In 1912, McLoughlin ventured into aerated water production, but this activity only lasted until 1916 (Stone's Directories), thus providing a concise date range. During this brief span, he used two different versions of the Codd bottle (the Dobson, patented 1885, and the Reliance, patented 1886). Two different size ranges with three different embossings are known from excavated specimens and others observed in private collections.

Codd and other forms of aerated water bottles are usually embossed with the mark of various British bottle manufacturers. Research into the history of manufacturers can also assist with dating. For example, several of the excavated Codd bottles are embossed "Cannington and Shaw, St Helens, England". This firm was in business from 1875 until 1913 (Toulouse 1971:147).

Two torpedo bottles embossed with the wording "Theyers & Beck" and "Alexandra" were recovered. Canute Peterson Beck and Theyers are cited in Stone's Directories from 1888 until 1893 as brewers and maltsters, with Beck continuing on his own after that date. During the period of the brewing partnership, they also produced aerated waters. Thus, the Hamilton patent embossed Theyers & Beck torpedo bottles uncovered at Chinatown and Firewood Creek can be ascribed a similar date range (1888–93).

Aerated water bottles used by other Otago-Southland manufacturers are also represented. These include Reliance and Dobson patent Codd bottles from Thomson & Co (Dunedin), Moffet & Co (Invercargill), Lane & Co (Dunedin); crown-tops (Lane & Co) and Buckham's (Queenstown), and a blob-top (Thomson & Co). Two Puriri brand (Auckland) mineral water bottles were found in Ah Lum's store at Arrowtown. The consumption of mineral water became a bit of a fad among middle-class Europeans late in the 19th century (Bedford 1985b:18). The bottles may date from the initial European settlement of the site.

A small clear glass "essence" bottle (Figure 5.11) containing mercury was found in the Ha Fong site, a rockshelter in the Cromwell Gorge. Mercury was widely used to recover fine gold from sand and other mineral residues. The two elements, which amalgamate readily, were later separated by boiling off the mercury. Mercury globules were also found in the Poplars site.

5.1.11 RE-USE OF BOTTLES

The most notable area of re-use of glass containers involved the modification of light green, European brandy bottles to make opium-heating and reading lamps. These were formed by cutting off the top quarter and the basal third of the bottles (Figure 5.51c) to produce an artefact similar in appearance to a small lantern glass. Of the 51 recovered, 28 were found in the huts in the Arrowtown settlement. They are frequently found in Chinese sites in association with opium-smoking equipment (see Section 5.4; Table 5.37). Their use for this purpose was documented by Don (1/3/1887:163) when he preached a sermon in a gambling and opium shop in the Nevis:

> Picture us if you can! The preacher with an empty kerosene can laid flat on a table for a desk; ditto standing on end for his seat, the congregation seated and reclining on short stools and opium benches; the sacred page lighted by an opium lamp (a jam tin filled with tallow, a cotton wick and the upper part of a brandy bottle for a shade).

Another area of re-use of bottles involved cutting the upper third or half off bottles to make jars. This practice was quite common among Europeans in the 19th century but does not seem to have been so prevalent among the Chinese. Only one intact basal half of a bottle (a green glass ring-seal) was found in the study sites (in Chinatown), although another six were surface collected from a Chinese site in 12 Mile Creek (S132/65).

5.1.12 SOME COMPARISONS WITH EUROPEAN SITES

Although there are many similarities in the types and percentage composition of the bottles found in Chinese and European sites in Central Otago, the study of excavated assemblages and field observations has revealed some differences. The immediately obvious one is, of course, the presence of "Chinese glass" containers in the Chinese sites. These bottles, which almost without exception appear to be medicines, were discussed above and need no further comment here. But other differences in "medicines" are apparent too. Probably the most notable is the virtual absence of blue glass castor oil bottles (and blue glass in general) in the Chinese sites. The European practice of consuming castor oil as a health food does not seem to have appealed to the Chinese. Similarly, although some Chinese seem to have acquired a taste for European "quack medicines", the numbers of bottles of the most popular concoction, Perry Davis Vegetable Pain Killer, are considerably lower in Chinese sites than they are in contemporary European ones, suggesting it never reached the dizzy heights of popularity that it did among Europeans. The alcohol bottles from the study sites exhibit a pattern that has been found to be quite consistent in both Chinese and European assemblages. Rural sites' assemblages tend to be dominated by higher percentage alcohol bottles (spirits) rather than lower percentage alcohols such as beer. This pattern probably reflects a very practical response by most miners living in remote areas. It required less effort to carry in a small volume of high percentage alcohol rather than large volumes of lower percentage alcohols. Two European alcohols – brandy and gin – appear to have been particularly favoured by the Chinese miners. The high incidence of brandy bottles is in line with its general popularity during the 19th century (see Eldred-Grigg 1984:211).

5.2 CERAMICS

Ceramics of European (predominantly British) and oriental (predominantly Chinese) origin constituted about 20% of the artefactual material from the study sites. Oriental domestic tablewares (Section 5.2.1) and ceramic food containers (5.2.2) are described first, followed by a discussion on the European domestic crockery and the relatively small assemblage of Euro-ceramic containers (5.2.3). The latter section also incorporates a comparison of the roles of the Chinese and European ceramics. Two specialised categories of imported ceramics – opium pipe bowls and clay pipes – are discussed separately, in Sections 5.4 and 5.6.1 respectively.

5.2.1 CHINESE CERAMICS

There are many comprehensive reference works about the ceramics produced during the reigns of the various Chinese dynasties, but the ones that deal exclusively with ceramics of the late 19th and early 20th centuries almost invariably only describe the fine porcelains made principally for export. Most of these pieces were ornate and expensive. Artefacts of this quality are collectors' pieces, and are so rarely found in archaeological contexts that the publications that describe them are of little use to archaeologists.

The humble "peasant wares" found in the sites associated with overseas Chinese communities were not described in any detail until the latter half of the 1970s, when Chace (1976) outlined the ceramics uncovered from the Ventura site in California (Greenwood 1975) and Olsen (1978) published an account of the ceramics recovered from the former Chinatown in Tucson, Arizona. In the late 1960s to early 1970s, Chinese artefacts comparable to those found at Ventura and Tucson (generally described as "overseas Chinese artefacts" in the literature) were uncovered in the course of many archaeological projects in the western United

States, e.g. Chinese artefacts from railroad construction camps at Donner Pass, California, were described by Chace and Evans (1969), and Tunnell (1970) briefly discussed features of a railroad construction camp occupied by Chinese labourers in Texas. Since 1970, there has been a proliferation of North American (mainly US) site reports describing overseas Chinese sites and ceramics. The following are the most useful on Chinese ceramics: Quellmalz's (1972 and 1976) reports on Late Chinese Provincial Porcelain export wares from North American Pacific Coast sites; Jones, Davis and Ling's (1979) report on materials (including Chinese) uncovered during excavations in Idaho City; Jones' (1980) report on the Boise Chinatown excavations; Praetzellis and Praetzellis' (1979) report on the ceramics from Lovelock, Nevada (in Hattori et al. 1979) and their 1982 report on an early Chinese site in Sacramento; and Pastron, Gross and Garaventa's (1981) report on the ceramics uncovered during excavations on the San Francisco waterfront (in Pastron, Prichett and Ziebarth 1981). Another useful report is that by Willetts and Poh (1981) on the 19th–20th century Chinese ceramics found in Malaysia. Wegars (1983) presented a constructive conference paper highlighting unusual artefacts of Chinese manufacture. A report by Sando and Felton (1984), which describes ceramics and other items listed in the inventory records of a 19th-century Chinese store in the USA, is another very useful addition to the literature.

Prior to the research embodied in this book, no Chinese sites in New Zealand had been scientifically excavated or described, although bottle collectors have eagerly "dug up" the distinctive "Chinese pots" from Chinese sites in New Zealand for over a decade. The wide range of Chinese ceramics uncovered during the mitigation excavations necessitated by the Clutha power scheme, together with study of private and museum collections, and recourse to the burgeoning overseas literature, has enabled a comprehensive study of the Chinese ceramics in New Zealand to be undertaken for the first time. The descriptive sections and illustrations are intended to help researchers and lay-readers identify New Zealand Chinese ceramics and provide a corpus of baseline data for comparative purposes.

Like the overseas Chinese ceramics found in other countries, the Chinese ceramics found in New Zealand were made in China and imported by Chinese merchants principally for use by the resident Chinese population. Most Chinese ceramic vessels are associated with the packaging, transport, storage, preparation, cooking or consumption of food. Non-food related Chinese ceramics, principally opium pipes (discussed in Section 5.4), comprised about 10–20% of the Chinese ceramics from each of the study sites. It is, of course, difficult to prove that the Chinese were the only users of the imported ceramic wares, but historical records, and their association in sites with other distinctively Chinese artefacts such as coins and opium-smoking paraphernalia, indicate that Chinese were the principal users. There is no evidence that any ceramics were manufactured by Chinese in New Zealand.

The discussion on Chinese ceramics is divided into two parts. First, a typology, based on ceramic morphology and known (or inferred) function is presented to organise and classify the large number of individual vessels (n=482) represented in the site assemblages. Tables 5.9–5.16 document the numbers and types of ceramics and their site distribution. A minimum of 170 units of Chinese tableware and 312 containers have been recovered (see Table 5.22; these figures include artefacts found in excavations in the upper Chinatown site i.e. behind the Chinese stores on Melmore Terrace). The typology draws to some extent on and has cross-reference to the categories outlined by Chace (1976), Olsen (1978), Praetzellis and Praetzellis (1979) and Pastron, Gross and Garaventa (1981). It also incorporates Chinese ceramic types that were found elsewhere in New Zealand but that have not been uncovered in the Clutha area to date.

The second section examines the socio-economic role of the ceramics and addresses the following research concerns:

a. dietary patterns and subsistence behaviour (elaborated in Chapter 6 and Chapter 7);
b. importation patterns;
c. regional differences;
d. evidence of socio-economic differentiation and change.

5.2.1.1 A typology of Chinese ceramics found in Central Otago

Ceramics are usually divided into three body types: the relatively low-fired and porous earthenwares; the non-porous stonewares; and translucent, vitreous porcelains. These distinctions are used in the following discussion. Most of the ceramic forms are illustrated.

A few, now well-recognised, Chinese "tableware suites" are frequently found in overseas Chinese archaeological sites, but the proportions and variety of wares varies widely from one area to another and even between adjacent sites. The Chinese tablewares that are found most frequently in southern New Zealand are "Celadon wares" and the "4 Seasons" style. These, and less common wares, are described below. As the vessels were mass produced (probably at several kiln sites), there tends to be some variation, particularly in width and height measurements. Size ranges are given in the text. Specific dimensions of intact or virtually complete specimens of each type are listed in Appendix 3.

5.2.1.2 Celadon wares

Celadon ware is the term given to a suite of porcelain tablewares with a distinctive light blue-green glaze. Celadon-glazed porcelain is known from China from as early as 800 AD and was widely prized for its beauty and resemblance to jade by rulers and commoners alike

(Pastron, Gross and Garaventa 1981:432). A 19th-century Chinese store inventory from the United States lists celadon as "wintergreen wares" (Sando and Felton 1983:7). This name is also used in southern China (Olsen 1978:18). Celadon wares are believed to have been manufactured principally at Shantou (Swatow), north of Canton (Olsen 1978:39).

Celadon are by far the most common Chinese tablewares found in Central Otago. The 127 vessels of this type represent 76% of all the recovered Chinese table ceramics (see Table 5.9). Although celadon wares were available as individual pieces, collectively the various forms constitute a "dinner service".

Specimens of the following types of celadon have been found in the Clutha sites:

a. "standard" rice bowls (n=61, Figure 5.12a), mouth width (mw) 13.2–14.2 cm, base width (bw) 4.9–6.1 cm, height (ht) 6.1–7.0 cm.
b. large rice or serving bowls (n=17, Figure 5.12b), mw 16.0–16.6 cm; bw 6.2–6.4 cm, ht 7.2 cm.
c. small rice bowl (n=1), mw 11.0 cm, bw 4.4 cm, ht 5.9 cm.
d. shallow dishes (n=4, Figure 5.12f), mw 8.0–8.2 cm, bw 4.0–4.3 cm, ht 2.6–2.7 cm.
e. teacups (n=7, Figure 5.12e), mw 7.5–7.7 cm, bw 2.4–3.2 cm, ht 3.8–4.4 cm.
f. wine cups (n=13, Figure 5.12d), mw 4.2–4.8 cm, bw 1.7–2.1 cm, ht 2.2–2.6 cm.
g. spoons (n=31, Figure 5.12g), length 10.1–10.7 cm, width of "spoon" 4.6–5.5 cm.
h. large dish (n=1, Figure 5.12c). The dish (provenance S133/22, Ha Fong shelter, mw 18.5 cm, bw 11.0 cm, ht 3.4 cm) is similar in form to a European breakfast bowl. This celadon form appears to be relatively rare both in New Zealand and overseas. This is the only specimen of its type that the author is aware of in New Zealand. A vessel of similar form (N5-M-199) found during the San Francisco waterfront excavations was depicted by Pastron, Gross and Garaventa (1981:433).

The 148 units of celadon tableware uncovered during the San Francisco waterfront excavations constitutes the largest and most extensive assemblage recovered from a single 19th-century Chinese site to date. Besides the types outlined above, the San Francisco assemblage included a "medium size shallow dish" and "medium and large plates" (Pastron, Gross and Garaventa 1981:433) but does not appear to contain any celadon bowls corresponding to the "large" bowls described above. Their "large bowls" are the same size as the "standard size" rice bowls from the study sites.

All celadon wares consist of a white porcelain body with the celadon or wintergreen overglaze. The glaze varies in hue, depending on its thickness and the amount of iron in it. Generally, it is thickest at the base of the vessels, and almost invariably the interior and underside are distinctively lighter; the only exception is the spoons. Celadon bowls also have a distinctive white colouration and general thinning of the glaze around the rims, probably reflecting the viscosity of the glaze (i.e. it tended to run towards the base of an upright vessel). The foot rings (including the oval base ring of the spoons) were left unglazed to prevent the vessels from sticking together while stacked in the kiln. Two types of glaze irregularities are common: pitting and black speckling. The latter appears to be the result of the bowls being subject to intense heat such as that developed when a hut burnt down. A celadon rice bowl, found during the excavation of a store site on the terrace above Cromwell's Chinese Camp, has three concentric rings etched into the glaze on the inside rim. This has not been observed before or reported in the literature.

All celadon vessels have a mark or seal executed in cobalt blue underglaze in the centre of the underside of the base. On the larger vessels, the seals are more complete and informative, but there is some disagreement as to whether they contain useful cultural information that should, if possible, be routinely deciphered. Chace (1976:523) considered them to be "imaginary reign marks", while Olsen (1978:38) saw them as purely decorative. Praetzellis and Praetzellis (1979:143) concluded that they are generally written in "seal script" characters, which are not readily decipherable to untrained readers. Pastron, Gross and Garaventa's (1981:661–4) translators managed to decipher the marks on 99 out of the 148 celadon vessels in their assemblage. They concluded that "the marks were originally informative but have degenerated through repetitive production by illiterate craftspeople and have thus become unintelligible, illegible and confused" (Pastron, Gross and Garaventa 1981:435). Despite this, they stated that "the marks presented a variety of interesting information such as a date, a commendation, praise or good wishes, a potter's seal or hallmark including the name of the maker and the place of manufacture, a merchant's seal, a brand name, or possibly a special symbol or emblem" (Pastron, Gross and Garaventa 1981:434). A perusal of their translations and interpretations (Pastron, Gross and Garaventa:661–4) makes one question the utility of this rather vague and generalised information, but a few of the larger vessels bore marks invoking the Tongzhi period (1862–74) of the Qing dynasty, thus providing some definite chronological information. They also found the marks on the celadon wares were like those on other tablewares (Pastron, Gross and Garaventa 1981:434). Because no one was available locally to translate the marks on the Central Otago celadons, no translations are presented here, but a selection of base-marks on recovered celadon rice bowls have been reproduced in Figure 5.13. As has been found in the overseas studies, the marks on the smaller vessels (the tea and wine cups and spoons) are restricted to "single dots" or two or three, generally unintelligible, brush strokes.

5.2.1.3 "4 Seasons" wares (also known as "4 Flowers")

The "4 Seasons" pattern consists of crudely painted flowers of the four seasons of the year – the winter plum (winter), water lily (summer), peony (spring) and chrysanthemum (autumn) – painted in overglaze enamel in the four quadrants. The flowers are painted on the outside of bowls, tea and wine cups, and on the inside of the spoons and dishes. On all the forms, except the small wine cups, there is an additional round flower motif (usually in purple with small green leaves) painted on the inside centre of each piece. On the underside of the base of most of the larger 4 Seasons vessels there is a red-stamped grid or the "eternal knot" drawn in red. The glaze on this white porcelain generally has a slight greenish-blue hue and is rarely blemished.

In terms of numbers, this tableware is second to celadon in the Central Otago sites, but whereas celadons constitute about 76% of all the recovered Chinese tablewares, 4 Seasons (n=28) represent less than 16% and were only present in five of the study sites. Of the 28 vessels, 22 were from the three urban sites.

The 4 Seasons vessels of the following forms have been found (see Table 5.10 for distribution details). Again, the various types collectively constitute a "dinner service" although "rice bowls" are conspicuously absent from the combined Central Otago assemblage. The forms recovered in Central Otago are detailed below:

a. medium serving bowls (n=6, Figure 5.14a), mw 18.0–18.5 cm, bw 8.0–8.3 cm, ht 5.9–6.2 cm.
b. large serving bowls (n=5, Figure 5.14b), mw 20.5–22.0 cm, bw 9.0–9.1 cm, ht 6.8–7.5 cm.
c. teacups, circular (n=1), mw c.8.5cm, bw 4.0 cm, ht 4.0 cm.
d. teacups, octagonal (n=1, Figure 5.14e), mw (inferred) 8.3 cm, bw 2.5 cm, ht 4.7 cm.
e. wine cups (n=2, Figure 5.14c), mw 4.5 cm, bw 1.7–1.8cm, ht 2.4–2.5 cm.
f. spoons (n=9, Figure 5.14f), length c.5.2 cm, width 4.4–4.5 cm, ht 1.4. g. small dish with foot ring (n=1, Figure 5.14d) mw 8.5 cm, bw 3.8 cm, ht 3.9 cm (S143/61).
g. shallow dish (n=2, Figure 5.14g), mw 7.8 cm, bw 4.4 cm, ht 2.2 cm.
h. shallow dish (n=1, Figure 5.14h), mw 10.8 cm, bw 6.5 cm, ht c.2.2 cm.

Overseas reports indicate that the "4 Seasons suite" has the widest variety of vessel types. The following forms have also been reported:

a. rice bowls, small, mw 11.0 cm, bw 5.0 cm, ht 4.5 cm (Pastron, Gross and Garaventa 1981:665).
b. rice bowls, high sided, mw 10.0, bw 4.0–4.3 cm, ht c.5.8 cm (Pastron, Gross and Garaventa 1981:665).
c. shallow dishes, in three sizes: "medium" (mw 10.0 cm), "medium-large" (mw 12.9 cm) and "large" (mw c. 18.0–22.0 cm) (Pastron, Gross and Garaventa 1981:666).
4. flat dishes with upturned rims in three sizes (Chace 1976b:525).
5. another form of octagonal cup (Praetzellis and Praetzellis 1979:144, Figure 5).

The majority of the 4 Seasons tablewares found in Central Otago are medium and large serving bowls, small wine cups and spoons. Rice bowls are unknown, and "small" and "shallow" dishes and circular and octagonal teacups appear to be relatively rare. The single example of a "4 Seasons small dish with foot ring" (Figure 5.14d) was found in a rockshelter (S143/61) on Lake Roxburgh during a survey (Harrison 1982).

The small "shallow dishes" (Figure 5.l4g) appear to be more common, but none of the four observed specimens were found in the primary study area. Two were uncovered by a miner who destroyed a Chinese hut site (5124/393) in the Motatapu Valley during his mining operation (Aspinall collection, Wanaka) and another two are known from fossicked Chinese sites in the Eight Mile catchment, Wakatipu (Hamilton collection, Arrowtown). The two Hamilton collection specimens have a diameter of 8.1 cm and a height of 1.5 cm. A larger diameter "4 Seasons shallow dish" (Figure 5.14h) was found near hut 5 at Arrowtown during post-excavation site restoration. It is the only known New Zealand example of this size. These shallow saucer-like dishes were probably used for dipping food. The porcelain bodies are decorated with red and green handpainted floral designs over a white underglaze rather than the pale greenish-blue hue of most 4 Seasons wares. On the base of each vessel, the "eternal knot" is drawn in red.

The octagonal wine cup was found in the Ledge site (5133/868), a European house site dump in the Cromwell Gorge, which contained a small assemblage of Chinese artefacts. The San Francisco waterfront site (Pastron, Gross and Garaventa 1981:665) is the only other excavated site from which octagonal teacups have been reported, but they appear to be of smaller width.

5.2.1.4 "Bamboo" wares (or "3 Circles and Longevity")

This tableware (Figure 5.15a), which is common in US sites of the same period – e.g. Ventura (Chace 1976b:514), Tucson (Olsen 1978:16), Lovelock (Praetzellis and Praetzellis 1979:146) – is relatively uncommon (n=4) in the study sites (see Table 5.10) and appears to be uncommon elsewhere in New Zealand. The key elements in the design are three circles, a "dragonfly" and a highly stylised marsh pattern. The motif has been given various names in the US literature. It was originally termed "3 Circles and Dragonfly" by Chace (1976:514). The three circles can vary from being tightly enclosed circles to loosely scribbled irregular lines (Pastron, Gross and Garaventa 1981:426). The "dragonfly" has more recently been interpreted (Praetzellis and Praetzellis 1979:147) as a stylised form of the Chinese character "chin", which pictorially represents a mushroom (*ling chin*), the divine fungus and symbol of longevity or immortality (Praetzellis and Praetzellis 1979:147). Consequently, the design is now commonly called "3 Circles and Longevity". It is also known as "Blue Flower Ware" based on the Chinese name for these bowls, *qing hua wan*, which literally means "blue flower bowl" (Olsen 1978:16). Wegars (pers. comm. 1985) reported that the name "Bamboo" is now being widely adopted to describe this decorative motif. The pattern has been produced without major stylistic variations since the Ming dynasty (1368–1643 AD). It was extremely popular in Shantou (Swatow) where it was manufactured and from where it was shipped via Canton (Guangzhou) to numerous overseas destinations (Olsen 1978:15).

The clay body of the vessels is a form of porcelaneous stoneware ranging in colour from off-white to grey. It is semi-opaque, lacking the characteristic translucency of porcelains. The overglaze is clear with either a blue cast or a less common green cast. The cobalt blue underglaze designs were executed by hand on the exterior, with one and sometimes two rings circling the bottom of the vessels' interior. The entire vessels are glazed, but the glaze is often pitted or has gritty inclusions.

The only "Bamboo" vessel forms known in New Zealand are rice bowls. Of the three excavated specimens, those found in the Arrowtown Chinese Camp (hut ACS/5) and Cromwell's Chinatown have a blue cast, while the specimen found in the Firewood Creek site has a green cast. The vessel from upper Chinatown is the only one that is intact enough to measure. It has a mouth width of 12.2 cm, a base width of 5.4 cm and a height of 5.6 cm (Figure 5.15a). These vessels appear to be virtually identical to those described by Chace from the Ventura, California, site (Chace 1976:523), i.e. the sides angle abruptly near the base. Bowls of similar shape have been found at several post-1870 sites in the United States including Old Sacramento (Praetzellis and Praetzellis 1982), Tucson (Olsen 1978:16) and Woodlands (Felton, Lortie and Schulz 1984:40).

Chace (1976:523) uncovered Bamboo motif (which he called "3 Circles and Dragonfly") bowl fragments in Chinese railroad construction camps occupied during the 1860s at Donner Pass, California. These bowls had "curved unshouldered sides", but Pastron, Gross and Garaventa (1981:428) reported that both curved and straight-sided bowls were found in the N-5 dump site at San Francisco. This site dates from 1880–85. They concluded that since it was difficult to distinguish curved from straight-sided vessels among the 60 bowls in their assemblage, the shape differences are simply a result of variations inherent in mass manufacture (probably at several different sites) and not a deliberate design modification over time. They divided their bowls into "large" and "small". The smaller size (of which there were only three) ranged from 5.1 to 6.0 cm in height,

12–13 cm in mouth width and were 6.1 cm across the base. The larger bowls (n=57) varied from 6.3 to 7.3 cm in height, were 13.7 to 15.0 cm across the mouth and 6.8–7.4 cm in foot diameter. The dimensions of the one measurable specimen from the Central Otago sites most closely approximate those of their smaller size category. Although "Bamboo" rice bowls are common in North American sites, other vessel forms bearing this pattern are rare. Shallow dishes with a related pattern were found in the San Francisco site (mw 17.0 cm, bw 11.0 cm. ht 2.3 cm; Pastron, Gross and Garaventa 1981:428), and also in Malaysia (Willetts and Poh 1981:10, 62).

5.2.1.5 Other Chinese tablewares and vessels

Compared with ceramic assemblages found in Chinese sites in the United States, the range of Chinese tablewares uncovered thus far in southern New Zealand is restricted. However, many of the American assemblages are from sites that were occupied well past the turn of the 19th century. One might reasonably expect a greater range of styles in more recent Chinese sites in New Zealand. The ceramics discussed below fall into three categories: a. types that are rarely found; b. small fragments that appear to be representative of previously unencountered forms; c. specific ceramic forms that have been reported in contemporary overseas assemblages and might be expected to be found in New Zealand.

5.2.1.5.1 "Double Happiness" or "Swirl" tableware

"Double Happiness" was the name given by Chace (1976) to a cobalt blue, handpainted pattern found on bluish-grey porcelaneous stoneware rice bowls from pre-1870 sites in the Donner Pass area, California. He designated the ware "Double Happiness" because the "double happiness" symbol and other decorative features are repeated three times around the outer surface of the bowls. Praetzellis and Praetzellis (1979b:29) preferred to call the ware "Swirl" design (see Figure 5.15b) because the Chinese character for "double happiness" also appears on other wares. Chace (1976) proposed that the ware typified early sites (pre-1870) in the United States. This distinction seemed to hold true until the same wares were found in the 1880s N5 dump site at San Francisco (Pastron, Gross and Garaventa 1981:431). They suggested that the Bamboo design may have gradually replaced the Swirl design, accounting for its erratic spatial and chronological distribution in American sites.

At the time of writing, Double Happiness wares have not been reported in New Zealand. Judging from their temporal distribution in the United States, they are more likely to be found in the earliest Chinese sites here.

In addition to the rice bowls (which ranged in height from 5.5 to 5.8 cm, with an 11.0–14.0 m mouth width and 5.0–5.3 cm foot diameter), Pastron, Gross and Garaventa (1981:431) found porcelain bowl covers. They concluded that the rice bowls and covers were probably matched, since their fabric, size and double line execution were similar. Three of the bowls had paired Chinese characters on the bases. The translation proffered good wishes. Double Happiness wares are believed to have been manufactured near Canton (Guangzhou). Judging from illustrations in reports by Tjio (1973) and Tomlin (1978:14–16), they were also made at a kiln site near Tai Po in the northeastern New Territories, Hong Kong.

5.2.1.5.2 Bird and floral motif rice bowl

Two fragments of a handpainted rice bowl bearing a polychrome bird and floral motif on a white underglaze (Figure 5.15e) were found in the deposit associated with hut 6 at Arrowtown. This decorative style has not been observed before in New Zealand. They are possibly of the same type as that described by Chace (1976:527) as "Red Birds and Cherry Tree".

5.2.1.5.3 Crab motif rice bowl

A rim fragment (dm 11.0 cm) of a white-glazed, porcelain rice bowl (Figure 5.16f) bearing a handpainted crab motif was found during testing of the store sites above Cromwell's Chinatown. The crab is drawn in black, while the leaves are coloured in two shades of green. This decorative style has not been reported in the overseas literature. According to Yeo and Martin (1978:303), there is no Chinese symbolism attached to the crab. It was used in decoration in conjunction with fishes and water weed during the Ming period and later copied during the Qing era. They commented that the symbol may have had significance in the countries to which the ceramics were exported.

5.2.1.5.4 Brown-rimmed rice bowls

A pale blue rim sherd of a rice bowl (Figure 5.15d) with dark blue abstract (floral?) designs was also found during the site testing mentioned above. The bowl had a distinctive brown-coloured rim band. Smaller sherds with the same type of brown rim band were found singly in the residential part of the Chinese settlement during the 1980 excavation and in the Rapids site (Figure 5.15c). The only reported, archaeologically-recovered ceramics with a similar design are some equally small sherds found in the Cabinet Landing site near Clark Fork, Idaho, a railroad construction camp occupied for three months in 1882 (AACC Newsletter 1985 2/1:2). The New Zealand sherds have been examined by Priscilla Wegars, the curator of the Asian American Comparative Collection at the University of Idaho Laboratory of Anthropology. She believes them to be a transitional form of the Bamboo decorative style described earlier, and that they probably do not postdate 1882 (Wegars pers. comm. 1985).

5.2.1.5.5 Blue on grey-blue saucer-like dish

The only known New Zealand specimen of this type of dish is the example (Figure 5.16a) unearthed in hut 21 in the Cromwell Chinese Camp. These vessels were used for dim sim steaming (Wegars pers. comm. 1983). The Chinatown specimen has a grey-blue underglaze with dark blue abstract floral designs. It has a diameter of 10.5 cm, a base diameter of 5.0 cm and stands 1.6 cm high. The unglazed "stacking ring" (or biscuit band, see Willetts and Poh 1981:14, 82) on the inside centre is a distinctive feature.

5.2.1.5.6 Genre scenes

Chinese pottery with "genre scenes", also known as "Mandarin", are decorated with realistically-portrayed Chinese figures in everyday scenes. The painting is done in polychrome overglaze over a white underglaze. Only one of these vessels is known from an archaeological context in New Zealand, but several "genre scene" tablewares are held in museum and private collections. For example, the small Clyde Museum near Cromwell has several genre scene teacups and a large teapot and its holder (Clyde Museum C.V. 76.125a). It is believed to have been locally acquired and to date from the late 19th century. The "excavated" specimen (Figure 5.16d) is a European-style porcelain saucer decorated with detailed genre scenes. It has a diameter of 15.8 cm and a height of 1.9 cm. It was found after it had been discarded by someone who had been fossicking in the deposits associated with the Chinese stores above Cromwell's Chinatown (i.e. upper Chinatown). There are no reports of similar vessels found elsewhere. Genre scene vessels have been found in contemporary sites in the United States, such as Ventura (Chace 1976:527).

5.2.1.5.7 Shallow dish with "long tailed bird" motif

Figure 5.16b depicts a fragment of a shallow porcelain dish decorated with a handpainted bird and leaf motif that is outlined with a fine black line and coloured in orange, yellow, pink and green. The dish was found in 1978 (in similar circumstances to that mentioned above) adjacent to a fossicker's pit dug in the deposits associated with the Chinatown stores. It has a diameter of c. 15 cm and a height of 2.4 cm. No other specimens have been reported in the archaeological literature.

5.2.1.5.8 "Fish" motif spoon

The Chinatown hut 15 assemblage included a fragment of a porcelain spoon with a handpainted, orange-coloured fish design and green "waterweeds" that are ribbed with fine black lines (Figure 5.16c). This is the only reported archaeological specimen of this type.

5.2.1.5.9 Miniature floral decorated pot

A miniature, white-glazed pot (Figure 5.16e) was uncovered in upper Chinatown by the former landowner, Mr L. Mangos. The pot has overglaze enamel floral decorations in pink, green and orange. The flowers are reminiscent of the 4 Seasons style described earlier, but of necessity are condensed to fit on the small surface area. It has a shallow, inclined gallery, presumably to accommodate a close-fitting lid. The pot measures 2.5 cm high, has a base width of 2.0 cm, a mouth width of 1.9 cm and a maximum diameter of 2.2 cm. The Cromwell specimen is the only one of its type reported in the archaeological literature.

5.2.1.6 "Blue on white" wares

It is apparent from excavated and depicted Chinese tablewares that handpainted cobalt blue designs on a wide range of vessel types constitute another "Chinese ceramic suite". However, relatively few of these pieces, characterised by blue designs over a white underglaze (hence "blue on white"), have been found in New Zealand sites. Tableware forms that have been found in contemporary overseas sites or are known from New Zealand collections and which might be expected in 19th-century sites here include teapots, wine jugs, shallow dishes and ginseng steamers. These forms are described below.

5.2.1.6.1 Blue on white teapots

According to Quellmalz (1976:290): "Blue-on-white teapots were an indispensable item for a great many Chinese working people and it seems that every Chinese laundry must have had one on the North American Pacific Coast during the latter part of the 19th century. They are generally made of good quality white bodied porcelain and range in size from 1½ to 5½ quarts. The decoration may consist of figures sitting in a garden or a floral setting. The drawings often show signs of hasty execution."

Despite their abundance on the NW Pacific Coast and in the United States (Olsen 1978:29), only one provenanced specimen is known to the author from a southern New Zealand context (a fragment, see Figure 5.16g, from a Chinese hut site in Big Fuchsia Creek on the West Coast), but two unprovenanced examples of different sizes have been sighted. The first of these was observed in a Christchurch second-hand shop and was morphologically similar to the plain white excavated specimen described later (Figure 5.16k). It stands 14.0 cm high and has a base diameter of l0.0 cm. A larger specimen (18.5 cm high and 15.0 cm in diameter) forms part of the Redmond collection (Christchurch). This pot has blue floral designs on the sides and a decorative band around the rim between the handle lugs. Both specimens conform to a specific Chinese teapot configuration (typified by the specimen depicted in Figure 5.16k), which is characterised by the following features: cylindrical cross-section; tall straight sides, which angle in towards the mouth; protruding lugs above the shoulder for attachment of a wire or bamboo handle; curved spout emerging from a point about two-thirds up the side of the pot; recess around the inner lip on which the lid sits.

5.2.1.6.2 Blue on white wine jugs

Figure 5.16h depicts a blue on white porcelain wine jug of a type that initially appeared rarely in North American sites (Quellmalz 1976:291; Olsen 1978:27), but in recent years greater numbers have been found in sites near San Francisco including the San Francisco waterfront excavations (specimens observed in the Lowie Museum, Berkeley), San Jose (Roop and Flynn pers. comm.) and China Camp (State of California, Department of Parks and Recreation, Sacramento). They have also been found in Malaysia (Willetts and Poh 1981:35). Sando and Felton (1983:8), who translated a US Chinese storekeeper's stock inventory, believe this decorative style was known as "Simple Flower" design. No specimens are known from New Zealand contexts. The example described by Olsen (1978:27) stands 14.5 cm high and has a body diameter of 7.1 cm.

5.2.1.6.3 Blue on white ginseng steamers

Ginseng steamers are another blue on white vessel form that have not been uncovered in New Zealand to date. The only whole example known to the author is one found during the Tucson (Arizona) Urban Renewal excavations (Olsen 1978:38). This steamer (Figure 5.16i) consists of a metal rack, within which a cylindrical ceramic pot was used to steam ginseng. The ceramic portion is characterised by a blue on white landscape design and has a small lid that sits in the vessel's mouth. It stands 14.0 cm high and is 9.0 cm in diameter. The illustration (Figure 5.16i) is based on a photograph taken by the author of the Tucson specimen in the Arizona State Museum in 1981.

5.2.1.6.4 Blue on white bird feeders

Figure 5.16j depicts a Chinese bird feeder. The depicted specimen, an unprovenanced example in the Cromwell Museum, was until recently the only one of its type known to the author. In form and decoration, it is virtually identical to the blue on white specimen depicted by Willetts and Poh (1981:35, 79). Their specimen was acquired in Penang and is believed to date from the late 19th century. It stands 4.5 cm high, whereas the Cromwell specimen has a height of 2.8 cm, an internal mouth width of 2.0 cm and a base width of 2.8 cm. In November 1985, the author observed two of these bird feeders in an "oriental-looking" bamboo bird cage in a Christchurch antique shop. The feeders were secured to the bars of the cage by a short length of bamboo pushed through the protruding lug holes.

5.2.1.6.5 Other blue on white forms

Willetts and Poh (1981:35, 79) depict several blue on white tablewares including a stemmed cup, a jarlet, a teacup, a diamond-shaped sauce dish, a soup spoon, a covered bowl (rice bowl size) and a small covered pot. Although they date them as 19th–20th century, none of these forms have been reported from 19th-century archaeological contexts in the United States, and none are known in New Zealand. Some of the blue on white wares found in New Zealand and in other overseas locations may originate from a kiln at Wan-Yiu near the Taipo market in Hong Kong (Tjio 1973). Products from this kiln were transported overland by porters to Guangzhou and Dong Wan and sold to wholesalers who in turn sold them to retailers. Wan-Yiu was a private commercial kiln that operated during the Qing dynasty, "Its products being for the lower class of the public" (translated from Chinese: Tjio 1973).

5.2.1.7 Plain white wares

Only three forms of plain white-glazed, porcelaneous stoneware are known from Central Otago: rice bowls, teapots and spoons.

1. Plain white rice bowls. These (MN=2) are only known from surface-collected fragments found in Chinese hut sites near Bannockburn (S133/835) and in the 12 Mile catchment, Lake Wakatipu (S132/65).
2. Plain white teapots. The depicted specimen (Figure 5.16k), reconstructed from pieces recovered from the QB2 site (S124/207) in the Upper Clutha, is the only example of this vessel type that has been recovered archaeologically in Central Otago. It stands 14.0 cm high and measures 10.0 cm across the base. Its rusty wire handle was probably a replacement for an original bamboo or wicker handle. A smaller unprovenanced specimen (AV 76.477) in the Alexandra Museum stands 10.3 cm high, has a base diameter of 9.5 cm and has an internal mouth width of 5.0 cm. The lid is 6.5 cm wide.
3. Plain white spoons. Part of a plain white spoon of the traditional shape was found in Ah Lum's store at Arrowtown.

There are many illustrations of Chinese tablewares found in US sites with pecked or scratched symbols or names on the exterior of Chinese tablewares. None were found in the study sites in Central Otago.

5.2.1.8 Japanese ceramics

Only two Japanese "tablewares" have been found in the study sites; a brown-glazed teapot with white coralene beading (Figure 5.41) and a porcelain saucer believed to have been made by Noritake (Figures 5.39–3). These "non-Chinese" vessels, which were both recovered from deposits at the Arrowtown Chinese Settlement, are discussed further in Section 5.2.3. Some handpainted Japanese porcelain "dishes" were uncovered in a European hotel site (the Halfway House Hotel) in the Cromwell Gorge (Bedford 1985, 1986).

5.2.2 CHINESE CERAMIC FOOD CONTAINERS

The ceramics described here were principally utilitarian containers used for packaging, transporting and storing various foodstuffs and beverages. All the vessels were locally manufactured in southern China and exhibit relatively little change in style over the years, probably because the retention of a familiar container shape readily identifies a product. They are discussed in groups, based on vessel morphology, glaze and known and inferred uses. Dimensions of intact or substantially complete specimens are recorded in Appendix 4.

5.2.2.1 Brownwares

These include a wide range of brown-glazed stoneware containers (see Table 5.12), known by the Mandarin Chinese term *Jiàn yáo*. The vessels of this family have a distinctive glaze in various shades of brown, but most are dark brown in hue. The lustre of the glazes also varies considerably, ranging from dull to highly lustrous. They have a stoneware body fabric that varies from grey to buff. The larger vessels (the spouted pots, shouldered food jars, and barrel and globular jars) are of notably cruder construction. Whitlow (1981:38) describes these vessels as *Min Gei*, Cantonese for "folk art or people's art". *Min Gei* pottery was produced by many independent potters in China, and although the vessels conform rigidly to "an idealised form", few are identical, most differing slightly in dimensions, if not in glaze, clay quality or finish. As "common pottery" it has generally not warranted mention in references about Chinese ceramics.

The brownware containers were used for a wide range of traditional Chinese products such as Ng Ka Py (an alcoholic beverage), soy sauce, black vinegar, salted vegetables, pickled ginger, peanut oil, maltose sugar and fish pastes. The shape of the various containers was understandably influenced by the nature of the product it was desired to contain or transport, thus lighter, more runny liquids were packed in bulbous, narrow-necked vessels, while "viscous" foods such as preserved vegetables, food pastes and maltose sugar were packed in wide-mouthed jars so the contents could be extracted easily. Until c.1970 many of these products were still packed in virtually identical ceramic containers, but there has been an increasing tendency towards glass and plastic. Interestingly, some of the new containers retain the old body shape.

Typically, the clay bodies of larger brownware vessels contain numerous gritty inclusions. This is probably due to the addition of a sand-like temper to improve the malleability of the clay but could also be the result of using poorly refined clays. Glazing was accomplished by pouring the glazing liquid or slip into the interior, swirling it around and then pouring it out. The containers then appear to have been immersed in glazing liquid while held by the base. This results in a characteristic feature of the brownwares – unglazed bases and usually an unglazed strip extending 1–2 cm up the sides from the base. The pots were fired in an upright position evidenced by dribbles of the molten glaze that frequently ran right to the base of the pot. The various brownware container forms are documented below.

5.2.2.1.1 Ng Ka Py bottles

The traditional Chinese Ng Ka Py alcohol bottle is a flat-bottomed bulbous ceramic container with a flared neck (Figure 5.17a). They are variously described in the literature as "wine bottles" (Chace 1976:517 "because one term, translated as 'wine' is used in the Chinese language for all alcoholic beverages"), tiger whisky (or tiger jugs), Ny Ka Py, and by Pastron, Gross and Garaventa (1981:398) as "traditional shaped beverage bottles". Although the latter name is specific, because the bottles contained at least two different alcoholic drinks – a clear liquid called "Mei Kuei Lu Chiew" (Mui Kwe Lu) and amber-coloured Ng Ka Py – it is an unwieldy mouthful, so the widely-used term Ng Ka Py bottles is retained here. At the time of writing, Ng Ka Py is still available in more refined bottles of this type in North American and more rarely in New Zealand Chinese stores. It is an acquired taste!

Olsen (1978:49) promulgated the following seriation system for Ng Ka Py bottles found in the United States. The oldest are wheel thrown with a glassy, greenish-brown glaze that was not applied to the bottom of the vessels. During the next period the bottles were glazed all over. Bottles of the last period were manufactured in moulds and covered with a dark vitreous glaze. This group postdate 1933 and bear the words "Federal Law Forbids Sale for Re-use of this bottle. 4/5 Quart". Ng Ka Py bottles bearing any sort of embossed or impressed wording have not been found in archaeological contexts in New Zealand, nor have Olsen's "first period" bottles with unglazed bases. Chace (1976:517) reported that the Ng Ka Py bottles from the Ventura Chinatown site were hand thrown, whereas the Praetzellises reported that those from Lovelock, Nevada (Praetzellis and Praetzellis 1979) and Sacramento (Praetzellis and Praetzellis 1982:22) were formed in separate moulds and then assembled. The Ng Ka Py bottles found in Central Otago are similar in construction to those described by the Praetzellises. They were formed by joining three distinct parts (base, middle and neck sections). The joins are often visible through the glaze on intact specimens and are obvious when one examines the interior surface of broken fragments.

Ng Ka Py bottles were the most numerous Chinese brownwares in the study sites. A minimum of 80 were recovered, although there are few completely intact specimens. Because of their interesting shape and attractive appearance, they have considerable appeal to collectors. About 25% of the recovered specimens have moulded impressions of characters or abstract marks on the base or between the midline and neck of the vessels, e.g. of the 49 Ng Ka Py bottles in the Mangos collection (uncovered when Mangos was building a house on the site of the former Chinese stores "in upper Chinatown"), 13 have "marks" – nine on the side and four on bases. A typical "mark" is evident on the specimen depicted in Figure 5.17a.

Ng Ka Py bottles have a raised basal ring about 1–1.5 cm high. This ring, on which the vessels sit, must have been wiped clear of glaze after it was dipped in the glaze solution. In relatively rare instances, the basal ring is absent and replaced by three flat knobs or stub feet. Compared with other brownware vessels, Ng Ka Py bottles generally have a highly lustrous glaze and exhibit considerably more variation in colour. The colour range is dominated by specimens varying from orange-brown to dark brown, but some vessels (prized by collectors) have an appealing blue-black colouration. The colour variation appears to be largely uncontrolled, reflecting iron-rich impurities in the glaze and variable firing temperatures (Doo pers. comm.)

Measured specimens fall within the following dimension ranges: height 15.9–17.0 cm, mouth width 8.1–8.7 cm and base diameters of 12.5–13.0 cm (see Appendix 4). These dimensions fall within the same size range as those reported from many American sites. A neck of an Ng Ka Py bottle found at Chinatown was "corked", the only sealed specimen found in the study sites. A Christchurch collector, Mr D. Redmond, has an unusual flat-topped Ng Ka Py bottle that was found in Australia. Other than the flat lip, it is virtually identical to the specimens described above. It stands 15.0 cm tall and has two Chinese characters inscribed on the base.

According to Pastron, Gross and Garaventa (1981:402), Ng Ka Py bottles were available in three sizes in the United States, the largest being the same size as those commonly found in 19th-century cultural deposits. This writer has only observed one other size in New Zealand, again in the Redmond collection. There are two small Ng Ka Py bottles in the collection, both are 9.0 cm high, with an external mouth width of 4.0 cm and a maximum width of 8 cm (Figure 5.17b). One is a relatively modern bottle with a paper label stating "Wing Distillery, Gold Dragon, Tai Ho Yeong Distillery, Macao". The other specimen appears to be older and has two small holes drilled in it. It appears to have been modified into an opium pipe bowl (the provenance of this specimen is unknown; the labelled one was bought in Hong Kong). The same collector also has a modern glass version of this small sized Ng Ka Py bottle.

A 19th-century Ng Ka Py bottle in the Clyde Museum has a label that is virtually identical to that on a green glass crown-top bottle bought in a Chinese store in Dunedin in 1981. The pink label on the modern specimen depicts two long-legged birds facing each other, with the words "Wing Lee Wai, Wine Merchants, Trade Mark, Hong Kong and Macao, Mud Kwe Lu".

Evidence of a secondary re-use of Ng Ka Py bottles is clear on two of the specimens from the study sites. The upper half of the bottles has been broken off just above the joint between the base and mid sections of the vessels, in effect creating a crude bowl with a ragged edge. Three Ng Ka Py bottles with similar modifications have been reported from sites in Idaho (Wegars in *AACC Newsletter* 1985 2/1:2).

5.2.2.1.2 Spouted pots

Spouted pots are characterised by their squat dome shape, a high shoulder (which may be rounded or angled), a short neck with an outwardly rolled lip, and a short spout set on the upper part of the body (Figure 5.18a). These spouted containers were corked and used for transporting and storing liquid foodstuffs such as sweetened black vinegar and black molasses, in addition to soy sauce (Olsen 1978:36). Intact "spouted pots" are quite distinctive, but side and base fragments are often difficult to distinguish from pieces of shouldered food jars (described next).

The bases and lower sides appear to have been mass produced on hand wheels. Pastron, Gross and Garaventa (1981:405) suggested "that the sharp shoulder angle indicated the joining of separate upper and lower sections", but study of shoulder fragments of Central Otago specimens indicate the sides were formed in one piece. The pots have a characteristic shallow concave "kick-up" in the base. The spouts appear to be made from a short slab of clay worked around a stick. They vary considerably in internal diameter and length. After the spout was secured by pinching it on to the side of the vessels (often using an additional roll of clay), the opening was formed by pushing a stick about 8 mm in diameter down the spout and into the interior of a pot. In many instances little effort was made to smooth the ragged edge on the interior side of the opening.

Three sizes of circular spouted pots were described by Pastron, Gross and Garaventa (1981:405, 1983:298–9) from the N5 dump site. Their single "middle-sized" specimen is the only reported example of this size. All the soy pots described in the US literature to date are representative of their "largest size", which is also the only size (n=26) that has been archaeologically uncovered in the study sites. Measured Central Otago specimens fall within the following size ranges: height 12.1–14.0 cm, base width 14.0–14.8 cm, maximum body width 15.3 cm and internal mouth width 2.2–2.5 cm. These dimensions are similar to those outlined by Pastron, Gross and Garaventa (1981:406–7) for their "large size". The recorded dimensions of soy pots (Appendix 4) vary by up to 2.0 cm in their main dimensions, but the same basic shape is retained. This size variance is understandable in regards to their inferred manufacture, i.e. mass production in village or factory kilns without rigid standards or quality control. The variation in the dimensions and the degree of concavity of the basal kick-up must have also resulted in some variation in their capacity.

The writer has observed a large size spouted pot with a ceramic handle loop on the shoulder. This specimen from China Camp, a former Chinese shrimping village (dating from the 1860s) in San Francisco Bay, California, is the only known example with this feature (State of California, Department of Parks and Recreation archaeological laboratory, Sacramento). The San Francisco assemblage also contained 12 examples of a "small size spouted soy pot" (Pastron, Gross and Garaventa 1981:406). This was the first and only reported instance of small size spouted pots from an archaeological context. The only specimens of this size that the author has observed in New Zealand are two examples of unknown provenance in the Redmond collection, Christchurch (Figure 5.18b). These measure 8.0 cm in height, with a base width of 6.6 cm and an internal mouth diameter of 2.5 cm. The body of the vessels appears to be identical to those of the "jarlets" (described later; Figure 5.23), except the small spouted pots have a spout.

The interiors are generally glazed, the glaze being applied by pouring some in the mouth aperture and sloshing it around inside. This often produced a rather haphazard coverage. Usually, the lip area has a thick "double glaze", formed when the already glazed neck area received a second coating when the exteriors were glazed. All the spouted pots were probably corked, but one example found near feature 25 in the Cromwell Chinese Camp had an unglazed mushroom-shaped earthenware plug in the neck (Figure 5.18d). Such "stoppers" have not been reported from other sites. Pastron, Gross and Garaventa (1981:406) reported that many of the small spouted pots found in the N5 dump site, San Francisco, were stopped with truncated, cone-shaped corks.

About 12 examples of a very rare square form (Figure 5.18c) are known, mainly from sites on Vancouver Island, British Columbia, Canada (Quellmalz 1976:294; White 1979:162), although one was found at Warren, Idaho (Wegars pers. comm.). According to Quellmalz (1976:294): "each side has a design and characters moulded on the body. The top is rounded, and the mouth has a well defined lip. The brown glossy glaze stops short of the bottom which is not glazed." At least three design variants are known (described by Wegars in the *Asian American Comparative Collection Newsletter* 1984:1(4):2–3). The embossed characters on a specimen in the Otto collection, Boise, Idaho, have been translated and indicate the vessel contained pickles produced in Guangdong province, southern China (AACC, Wegars pers. comm.). About three examples of an even rarer "golden glazed" version of these square pots have been found in Canada. None of these square vessels are known from New Zealand contexts.

5.2.2.1.3 Squat-shouldered food jars

Squat-shouldered food jars, or fragments thereof, are one of the most frequently recovered Chinese artefacts both in New Zealand and overseas. Chace (1976:517) described these vessels as having a squat body with a high shoulder leading to a short neck and wide orifice. The rim is rolled outwards. The jars are entirely hand shaped on a wheel in two basic sizes (Figures 5.19a and b). Up to their shoulders, the large size jars are virtually indistinguishable from the large soy pots, and these portions may have been mass produced for both pot types.

Pastron, Gross and Garaventa (1981:410–13), after analysing the prolific San Francisco N5 dump assemblage, expanded the category "shouldered food jars" to include two distinctly different brownware vessel forms (although admittedly they are food jars too) – a tall angular-sided type and a small vase-like jar (called "jarlets" in this study). In this study, the term "shouldered food jars" is restricted solely to the squat form (in two sizes) as described by Chace (1976:517), Olsen (1978:31) and Praetzellis and Praetzellis (1979b:154) and many others. Shouldered food jars have been previously described in publications by this author as "DVCs" (dried vegetable containers), but this term is no longer used. The new body shapes, which Pastron, Gross and Garaventa have incorporated into "shouldered food jars", are described in this study as "tall shouldered food jars" and "jarlets". They are discussed after this section.

The dimensions of measured specimens (MN=71) of the large squat-shouldered food jars from local sites are: heights 12.2–13.8 cm, base widths 11.1–12.6 cm, widest points 14.1–15.5 cm and internal mouth widths of 7.9–8.8 cm. The size ranges of specimens of the small squat food jars (MN=38) are heights 9.7–10.3 cm, base widths 9.0–9.7 cm, maximum widths 10.8–11.1 cm and internal mouth widths 6.2–6.5 cm (see Appendix 4).

The glazing procedure involved swirling glaze around the interior and then pouring it out. The pots were then plunged "mouth first" into the glaze to cover the exterior. The slightly outward flare at the side/base interface would have enabled the vessels to be gripped more easily during the glazing process. These shouldered jars held a variety of products including preserved vegetables, sweet gherkins, soya bean cheese or curd, shrimp paste, salted garlic, salted radish, salted onion and pickled lemon (Chace 1976:519; Olsen 1978:32).

Both jar sizes had earthenware lids that were secured with soft unfired clay (remnants often adhere to the lids) and possibly with some form of adhesive tape as well. The lids are unglazed and handmade or simple-moulded. They appear to be made of a different type of clay from the jars themselves. When the lid-clay was fired it turned to a buff-red colour. Three different lid types, attributed to these jars, have been found in the Central Otago sites. The two most common forms are crudely made, fired discs of clay with the edges upturned to form saucer-like lids. The two sizes correspond to the two jar sizes. The larger ones (MN=71, Figure 5.20a) vary from 8.1–10.3 cm in diameter and are about 1.5 cm deep. The smaller ones (MN=38, Figure 5.20b) vary from 6.5–7.5 cm wide

and are about 1.0 cm deep. Four specimens of a rarer lid form, presumed to be associated with the larger jars, have also been recovered. These lids (Figure 5.20c) vary from 7.3–7.9 cm in diameter, have a depth of 1.2cm, and differ from those described above in that they are glazed (with a dark brown glaze) on the upper surface concavity. They also have a distinct inward bevel on the sides. Of the four recovered specimens, three were found in the Flax Grove site, the other in Cromwell's Chinese Camp.

About 40% of the bases of the large shouldered food jars unearthed in Central Otago are fire blackened (one small one from Chinatown also has a burnt base), indicating the containers were sometimes re-used as cooking pots. One specimen from Chinatown has remnants of rusty wire adhering to the neck, which suggests it was suspended.

5.2.2.1.4 Squat, bulbous shouldered food jars

Jars of this form (Figure 5.19c) are obtainable from Chinese stores today. They contain preserved vegetables (usually dried and finely sliced cabbage marinated in soy sauce). These vessels have not been found in archaeological sites in New Zealand, but specimens have been reported from two sites in the US: Tucson, Arizona (Olsen 1978:37) and Aptos, California (Whitlow 1981:41). Both sites were occupied well into the 20th century. These vessels appear to be a successor to the shouldered food jars described above and probably came on to the market c.1930. They have a smooth "modern-looking" lustrous brown glaze.

5.2.2.1.5 Tall shouldered food jars

Jars of this nature are unknown from archaeological contexts in New Zealand, but three slightly different variants of unknown provenance, in the Redmond collection, Christchurch, have been observed by this writer and measured. They are depicted in Figures 5.21a, b and c, which were drawn from a photograph. The only example of these jars that is described in the overseas archaeological literature is that reported by Pastron, Gross and Garaventa (1981:412) from the N5 dump site, San Francisco. It stands 17.5 cm tall, has a maximum width of 17.9cm, a base diameter of 11.5 cm, a mouth opening of 8.9 cm and a capacity of 70 oz (Pastron, Gross and Garaventa 1981:412).

The notable features of this type of shouldered food jar are their height, robust construction (in line with their greater capacity), and the fact that the sides angle out from the base until a point about midway up the sides, from where they angle sharply inwards towards the mouth. This gives them a distinctive profile.

The jar depicted in Figure 5.21a has a height of 15.0 cm, a base width of 10.0 cm, a maximum width of 17.5 cm and an internal mouth width of 6.5 cm. It is glazed on the inside and has an outward-rolled lip. It is burnt on the base suggesting it has been used as a cooking or water-heating vessel. The specimen illustrated in Figure 5.21b has a height of 17.5 cm, an internal mouth width of 7.5 cm, a base width of l0.0 cm, and is glazed both inside and out. It also has a roll lip. The specimen on the right (Figure 5.21c) is 19.0 cm high, with a base width of 11.5 cm and an internal mouth width of 9.0 cm. Unlike the others, it has a distinctive lip with a square cross-section. The variations in these three specimens typify the minor stylistic differences that might be expected in mass-produced, handmade ceramic containers. Like most of the brownware containers, their appearance is clearly secondary to their functional importance. These jars were probably used for liquid foodstuffs, their shape making them easy to hold and pour, and they had paper labels to distinguish different contents.

5.2.2.1.6 Brownware "flat rim" food pots

The depicted specimen (Figure 5.22b) is the only vessel of this type known from a New Zealand context. This example was reconstructed from pieces found in Ah Wee's hut site (S115/54) in the Upper Clutha Valley. It stands 8.5 cm high, has a base width of 7.5 cm, an internal mouth width of 6.5 cm, and is l0.0 cm wide at the broadest point. Its body shape is virtually identical to that of the "regular size" green-glazed "ginger" jars described later, except that this specimen has a light brown glaze covering the upper two-thirds of the body. It also has a notably different flat-topped rim.

Parts of a probable second vessel (Figure 5.22a) of this type were also found at Ah Wee's hut, but the diagnostic rim area was missing. This second vessel has the dark brown glaze found on most "brownwares". The contents of this vessel type are unknown. It is similar in profile to brownware containers (containing soya bean curd) that are sold in some Chinese stores in New Zealand, except that the latter are slightly taller and have four lugs with a string handle. No examples of this type of vessel have been reported in the overseas literature.

5.2.2.1.7 Brownware jarlets

These jars have a similar morphology to the small spouted pots described earlier, except they do not have a spout (Figure 5.23). Three have been found in the study sites (two in Cromwell's Chinatown, one at Arrowtown). The two measurable specimens (from Chinatown) stand 8.3 cm and 7.6 cm high, have base widths of 6.2 and 6.5 cm respectively, mouth widths of 2.2 cm (internal), and maximum body widths of 7.3 and 7.4 cm. An unprovenanced specimen in the Otago Museum has a 1 cm diameter hole drilled in the side of it. Like other ceramic vessels and small bottles modified in a similar fashion, it is believed to have been used as an improvised opium pipe bowl (see Section 5.4).

Brownware jarlets are relatively rare in overseas contexts too. Olsen (1978:34) described the one specimen uncovered at Tucson as a "small narrow-necked jug" and suggested it may have contained a thick syrup or jam, but in view of the narrowness of the aperture they are more likely to have contained a liquid or a product that could be easily poured like salt. One was recovered at the N5 dump site at San Francisco. The authors of that report also noted its similarity to their "small size spouted pots" (Pastron, Gross and Garaventa 1981:410). They were probably corked in a similar fashion.

5.2.2.1.8 Straight-sided jars

These, generally small, open-mouthed jars are characterised by their thin, relatively straight sides surmounted with an external gallery to accommodate a slightly domed, flanged lid. They are variously described in the overseas literature as "straight sided jars" (Chace 1976:519; Pastron, Gross and Garaventa 1981:413) and "small brownware jars" (Olsen 1978:33). Pastron, Gross and Garaventa have grouped the huge "barrel jars" into this category too, but here (as in most reports) they are treated separately.

At least four sizes of these small jars (MN=14; 11 bases, eight lids) have been uncovered in the study sites; the "sizes" being defined principally on the presence of five different lid diameters (Figures 5.24d–g). As can be seen from the dimensions recorded in Table 5.13, these pots vary considerably in height and diameter. Judging from examples described in overseas reports and specimens seen in private collections in New Zealand, there is virtually a continuum of sizes with base diameters varying from 3.0 to 15.0 cm and heights from around 3.0 to 14.0 cm, with a corresponding range of lid sizes. Furthermore, there is not a 1:1 relationship between basal diameter and side-wall height; pots of one base diameter were produced in more than one height. A cluster analysis of the dimensions of a larger sample of complete vessels might produce some meaningful size categories.

The lids of these pots are quite distinctive, being slightly domed and having vertical sides and sharp shoulders. Their exterior is covered with a dark brown glaze, which is usually smooth and glossy. The lids are designed so they fit snugly over the gallery-inset surmounting the side walls of the jars.

On a research visit to the United States in 1981, the author noted the most common "traditional" Chinese ceramic food container in several Chinese stores was a straight-sided jar containing "Tungoon Genuine Maltose – Packed in Kwangtung" (before the Chinese were introduced to white sugar, viscous maltose sugar was the main food sweetener they used). The modern malted sugar container (Figure 5.24c) is slightly larger than the largest of the straight-sided pots excavated in Central Otago. The bases of some of the excavated specimens bear one or two impressed Chinese characters. They have not been translated. They are said to have contained sweets, medicines, cosmetics and spices (Wegars 1983:2). A small pot of this type was observed by the writer in a reconstructed Chinese store display in Nevada City, Montana. Its label read: "MAN CHUN YUEN, Medicated orange peel, Made in Canton, China, Nett one ounce".

5.2.2.1.9 Barrel jars

Vessels of this type are large, heavy, straight-sided jars, but their construction characteristics (body fabric, tempering and glazes) are more allied to the shouldered food jars. Like the other brownware food containers, their bases are unglazed, but the interiors exhibit varying treatments. Some are fully dipped, or swirl glazed, others are slipped, and in rare instances they are unglazed.

Only one intact specimen has been found in the study sites. It was buried in an upright position behind Ah Lum's store at Arrowtown. It may have been recycled as a planter because most of the base had been punched out. This example (Figure 5.25a) is 43.0 cm high, 34.5 cm wide at the base and has an internal mouth diameter of 29.5 cm. The walls of the vessel are 1.6 cm thick. Fragments of 12 other barrel jars have been recovered; 11 of them were found in the Cromwell and Arrowtown Chinese Camps. The other one was unearthed in the Rapids site (see Table 5.12 for distribution details). The basal diameters of all except one vary between 33.0 cm and 37.0 cm. The exception is an obviously smaller specimen uncovered during a test excavation on the site of the former Cromwell Chinatown stores. This specimen has a basal diameter of 28.0 cm and proportionately thinner walls (0.5 cm).

The barrel jars had large, virtually flat, flanged lids (Figure 5.25b) that fitted over the gallery around the rim. Seven lids have been recovered – one in the Chinatown settlement, six in the adjacent store deposits. Again, two size ranges are apparent. The majority vary from 33.0 to 37.0 cm in diameter, with the single exception measuring 27.0 cm. The latter is likely to be the lid of the smaller barrel jar mentioned above. All the lids were slipped on the exterior; one was also slipped on the interior. While the lids are essentially flat, the central area usually has a slight concavity, possibly to enable jars of this type to be stacked on top of each other, with less risk of cracking the lids of the lower jars.

Barrel jars have been found in several overseas sites, e.g. Donner Pass, California and Langtry, Texas (Chace 1976:522), Old Sacramento (Praetzellis and Praetzellis 1979:78) and N5, San Francisco (Pastron, Gross and Garaventa 1981:417). Examples of the smaller size have been observed by the author in restored Chinese stores at Barkerville, British Columbia. They had a height of 30 cm. Several of the overseas specimens have brown-glazed rather than slipped lids.

Pastron, Gross and Garaventa (1981:415) concluded that due to the enormous and cumbersome proportions of these vessels and their weight when filled, they may have been used only in seaport or riverine locations where transport was not a great problem. Although this is borne out to some extent by the distribution of the specimens recovered from the study sites, most were found in the vehicle-accessible urban sites; their distribution must have been even more influenced by their function and size. They are massive, heavy, bulk-food jars, which one would not expect individual miners to buy and lug to their camps. The lack of interior glazing on some barrel jars suggests they were used to convey or store solid foods. Modern examples generally have a superior and more thorough glaze coverage, but they vary little in shape. They contain items such as "hundred-year-old" preserved duck eggs. Modern barrel jars are usually enclosed in a coarsely woven basketry carrier with handles. The heavy flat lids on the jars enable other jars and goods to be stacked securely on top.

Roebuck (pers. comm. 1983), a European who befriended the Chinese in Dunedin and worked in one of their stores c.1920, recalled that many products such as rice bowls, "other dishes" and foodstuffs came in "the big pottery barrels" and contained mixed lots packed in sawdust or straw. He said they were often put out in the shop until all their contents had been sold, then "they were put out the back". They were also re-used for storing rice and other foodstuffs. The glazed ones were probably used for water storage occasionally.

Another possible re-use of barrel jars was mentioned by Levine (1921:23). He noted "that large, vitrified clay jars, with straight sides, similar to jars used for fermenting beans in making soy bean sauce are the best jars for containing meat". The jars he alluded to were used for curing and were large enough "to conveniently hold the hams, shoulders and sides of two hogs" (barrel jars?).

5.2.2.1.10 Globular jars

These large brownware liquid containers have been variously described in the overseas literature as "huge globular jars" (Chace 1976:521–2; Praetzellis and Praetzellis 1979), "large brownware jars" (Olsen 1978:32–3) and "steep-shouldered" jars (Pastron, Gross and Garaventa 1981:407). The latter (Pastron, Gross and Garaventa 1981) documented the long history of this type of vessel. The earliest references date from the Tang dynasty about 800 AD. During the 18th century, containers of this form (in sizes up to a metre in height) were used in ships for storing opium, wine, rice and other foodstuffs, as well as drinking water. The primary distinguishing characteristic of these vessels is their distinctive globular shape (Figure 5.26b). They often, but not always, have four lugs sited approximately 3 cm below the rim to secure a lid, and the rim of most (but again not all) is triangular in profile. Study of intact specimens and fragments reveal that globular jars were formed in one action on a wheel. The glazes exhibit the typical range of brown hues one associates with the Chinese brownwares (i.e. from light to dark brown, and from matt to glossy). The exterior glaze usually ends just above the base. The interiors are usually, but not always, glazed. Some are coated with a brown slip, although not infrequently dribbles of glaze have run down the inside of the rim into the jars.

There is a virtual continuum of height sizes, varying from around 23.0 cm (Olsen 1978:33) to around 45 cm (Redmond collection, Christchurch), but most are between 32 and 38 cm high. They usually have a slight concavity in the base, which varies from 11.0 to 14.0 cm in diameter. The base and walls of these containers, like those of the barrel jars, often contain gritty inclusions. The walls vary from 0.7 to 1.2 cm thick. As is illustrated in Figure 5.26b, the side walls flare out from a relatively narrow base and curve inward at a point about two-thirds up the vessels to a constricted neck and rim. The mouth widths of measured specimens range from 9.8 to 10.3 cm.

Most globular jars have a distinctive triangular rim form, but one large unprovenanced example (in the Redmond collection, Christchurch) has a square-section rim with thread-like grooves. Two of the three globular jars in the collection do not have lugs. The lugs on the pots were formed by pushing on a short "sausage" of clay and leaving a raised section through which a cord could be threaded to tie down a lid. The form of lid on these vessels is uncertain, but they may have had unglazed, stepped, ceramic lids (Figure 5.26a) of which two specimens have been recovered (from Arrowtown and Chinatown). The portions that would fit into the necks of these jars are 9.5 cm wide. According to Olsen (1978:33), they had both wooden and ceramic lids.

Globular jars, as suggested by the fact that they are glazed/slipped both inside and out, were primarily used for holding liquids. Historic observations indicate they were specifically used for the conveyance and sale of products such as peanut oil, vinegar, bulk wine and bulk soy sauce. The narrow bases of the vessels would have facilitated the tipping of the vessels to pour from them. The small size of the mouth opening would have helped to prevent accidental spillage. Like the large barrel jars, globular jars and their contents were originally sold in a loosely woven basketry casing with handles to protect the containers and make them easier to transport. Similarly, they were used for conveying bulk supplies, and one would expect them to be more frequently encountered in urban or store sites. Of the nine fragmentary specimens in the study sites, six were from Cromwell's Chinatown, the others being found in the Arrowtown settlement. The vessel depicted in Figure 5.26b is an intact example found in the Cardrona Valley (Dennison pers. comm.). Its dimensions are cited in Appendix 4.

The Clyde Museum has a large globular jar on display. This "oil jar" was imported from Shanghai in 1927. A product description (?) is stencilled in glaze on a clear panel on the neck. The author observed modern examples of globular jars containing black vinegar in Chinese stores in the United States in 1981. They were smaller (28 cm high), with a highly lustrous, smooth light brown glaze and wire handles.

Tomlin (1978:14), following ethnographic and archaeological research at Tung O village on Lamma Island, Hong Kong, reported that many of the traditional provincial ceramic wares, such as large and small storage jars, wine jars, vinegar jars, cooking pots, mortars, tablewares (including "Swirl" design), incense burners, oil lamps and cooking stoves were still in use but were being rapidly replaced by plastic, tin and aluminium containers. He depicts (Tomlin 1978:15) five globular jars (three lugged, one unlugged and one relatively modern "vinegar jar"), which he states "were used in the village for storing dry foods such as rice and peanuts; for preserving home grown vegetables, bok-choi, cabbage etc., and for storing water. The large jars were usually obtained from shopkeepers… when they were emptied of their original contents, such as salted eggs, raw sugar and various types of preserved vegetables". It appears he is talking about more than one type of brownware storage jar in this last sentence, but globular jars are included.

5.2.2.2 Green-glazed stoneware food containers

Two types of green-glazed stoneware containers have been found in the Central Otago sites:

1. Rotund coarsely glazed pots, commonly called "ginger jars" although they contained a range of preserved foods, which according to Olsen (1978:35) included "preserved chopped garlic, sliced turnip, green onions, sweet gherkins, green plums, and preserved fish". Consequently, "ginger jars" should be regarded as a generic term.
2. Small straight-sided pots with insets or galleries for a snug-fitting lid. These pots, made in at least three sizes, are believed to have contained viscous foods such as fish pastes but may also have been used for products such as cosmetic or medicinal creams.

5.2.2.3 Green-glazed ginger jars

The three distinctive body forms (and variants) of green-glazed ginger jars known in New Zealand are:

5.2.2.3.1 Wide-mouthed ginger jars (two sizes)

These vessels are relatively common in Central Otago (and correspondingly rare in contemporary American sites). A minimum of 35 have been found in the study sites. Their profile is depicted in Figures 5.28a and b. They have a stoneware fabric overglazed with a smooth green glaze that is commonly flawed with pits and mineral inclusions. The glaze is usually lustrous and bright, but some recovered specimens are noticeably lighter or darker than the norm. When burnt, the glaze crazes and tends to turn red. It generally covers only the top two-thirds of the vessels, but most specimens have one or more dribbles running down to the base. The interiors are coated with a light brown slip.

The pots are wheel-made in one piece. Two sizes are recognised among the Central Otago assemblages: a "regular size" (n=33, Figure 5.28a) standing 7.7–8.4 cm high, with mouth widths of 7.3–8.2 cm, maximum widths of 9.4–9.8 cm and bases varying between 5.8 and 6.5 cm;

and a much rarer larger variant (n=2, Figure 5.28b). The only complete measurable specimen has a height of 9.4 cm, a mouth width of 8.2 cm, a base width of 7.1 cm and a maximum body width of 10.9 cm. It is possible the large specimens are just larger than usual aberrations of the "regular size". The "regular size" jars are uncovered in about equal proportions in both urban and rural sites (see Table 5.14 for distribution).

One "regular size" pot was found buried in an upright position (at a depth of 20 cm) about a metre out from the doorway of the Sheung Fong shelter (S133/21) in the Cromwell Gorge. Possibly it was used for a votive purpose. The mouth opening of the vessel in question was covered with a burnt cork plug and appeared to have been held in place by glued paper strips. The pot was empty.

5.2.2.3.2 Narrow-necked ginger jars

This vessel form (Figures 5.29a and b) is essentially a narrow-necked version of the jars described above, but they are considerably rarer (MN=2) in the study sites (and seem to be elsewhere in New Zealand and overseas). As shown in Table 5.14, their distribution in the study sites is restricted to the two urban settlements. They appear to be of later date (post-1900) than the wide-mouthed form described above. Twelve narrow-mouthed jars of this type were observed by the writer c.1984. They were recovered from a post-1890 European dump site at Logan Park, Dunedin (Knowles pers. comm.).

The dimensions of the sole intact excavated specimen (found in upper Chinatown) are height 8.8 cm, base 7.1 cm, internal mouth width 4.3 cm and maximum width l0.1 cm. The extra height of these vessels is attributable to their upward curving rims, which are designed to accommodate a flanged lid. The narrow neck opening suggests they contained a relatively free-flowing foodstuff. Three of the vessels from the Logan Park dump have four identical "crests" impressed on their shoulders (Figure 5.29b). This feature has not been reported previously. Unlike the bases of the wide-mouthed green ginger jars, the bases of the narrow-mouthed form often bear two Chinese characters in raised relief (occasionally they are in a rectangular frame).

Lids (n=4) of the type believed to have capped these vessels are also an uncommon survival in Central Otago. In no instance have they been recovered in direct association with the jars. A loose-fitting flanged lid was found about one metre from the intact jar (described above) from upper Chinatown, and is presumed to have been associated with it. The wheel-made lid (Figure 5.36b) is glazed on the top only, with the same green glaze as that on the pot. It has a diameter of 7.6 cm and a height of 2.l cm. The top is decorated with a distinctive "quarters" design, which is also a feature of some of the lids of the beige-coloured ginger jars described later. The other flanged lids are unglazed. They are quite loose fitting and must have been secured by traditional methods such as glued paper or material strips, or a loosely woven string or split bamboo outer covering. Continuity of the body form is evidenced by an ornate porcelain jar with the same basic shape (it contained ginger) purchased by the writer in a store in Dunedin in 1981.

5.2.2.3.3 Hexagonal-sided ginger jars (two sizes)

These distinctive ginger jars (Figures 5.30a and b) are unknown from any archaeological context in New Zealand, but several unprovenanced specimens of both sizes are held in museum and private collections, and they are often for sale in second-hand stores. Their appearance in New Zealand almost certainly postdates 1900, if not 1920. The dimensions of the two sizes are:

1. small: height l0.0 cm, base 8.2 cm, max. width 10.3 cm, mouth width 5.0 cm;
2. large: height 11.7 cm, base 10.5 cm, max. width 14.3 cm, mouth width 6.8 cm.

The larger size, at least, was still available in 1981; the writer purchased one containing "ginger in sweet syrup" in a Chinese store in Auckland in June 1981. The specimens in museums and private collections generally have a "noticeably older look" and much rougher glaze. No small size specimens have been observed in stores. This size may now be obsolete. The hexagonal-sided pots (both sizes) are decorated with cameo floral designs in relief, there being one on each of the six side panels. The pots are dip-glazed to a point just below the floral panels. The insides are sealed with a thin brown slip. Judging from specimens in collections, the pots were closed with unglazed, circular flanged lids, which were probably secured with split bamboo "netting" and glued paper in the past. Plastic "twine" was employed to secure the lid on the modern example. An adhesive paper label described the contents (see Olsen 1978:37–8).

5.2.2.4 Green-glazed straight-sided pots

These stoneware vessels (Figures 5.31a and b) virtually mirror the form and size ranges of the brownware straight-sided pots described earlier (this author has used the term "inset lid pots" to describe both these vessel forms in earlier writings). They are wheel-made, have a fine medium fabric, and have a light brown underglaze or slip on the interior, while the exterior, except the gallery, has an even covering of green glaze. The bases are unglazed and frequently have one or two Chinese characters in relief. The unmarked, flanged lids are slightly domed, glazed on the outside and slipped on the interior like the pots. The average height of the lids is 1.6 cm, but their diameters vary depending on the size of the associated pot. Although the lid-flanges fit snugly over the inset rims, they were probably additionally secured with glued tape, although none show clear evidence to this effect. A minimum of 11 plus six lids were found in the study sites. Their distribution is detailed in Table 5.14. The recovered specimens have considerably less size variability than the brown-glazed pots of the same shape (see Table 5.13).

The specific use of these pots is unknown. They probably contained foods of a creamy consistency such as fish or shrimp paste (these products are sold in plastic containers of the same shape in Chinese stores today), spices, condiments, flavourings, and possibly cosmetic and medicinal preparations.

5.2.2.5 "Blue-beige" and "blue-grey" stoneware containers

Two blue-beige stoneware ginger jar vessel forms are known from sites in southern New Zealand, but thus far only one specimen has been found in sites in the primary study area (Upper Clutha and Arrow Basins).

5.2.2.5.1 Blue-beige ginger jars

Type A jars (Figure 5.32b) are characterised by a medium clay fabric and patches of smudgy blue underglaze surmounted by a creamy-beige overglaze (see Olsen 1978:35). Bands around 2 cm wide were left unglazed below the rim and above the base. The latter area is often marked with dribbles of glaze.

A rim section of one of these vessels, from the Chinatown store deposits, represents the only vessel of this type found in the study area, but several jars of this type have been found in Chinese camps by collectors in the Motatapu Valley (S124/393; Aspinall collection), the Arrow River Valley (Hamilton collection) and elsewhere in Central Otago (see Table 5.14). Dimensions are recorded in Appendix 4. They have the following size ranges: height 13.0–15.0 cm, mouth widths 5.5–7.0 cm, base widths 11.5–12.0 cm, widest points 16.1–16.9 cm. Recently (c.1984), fragments of another of these vessels were uncovered in a European dump site (c.1890) near Logan Park, Dunedin.

The surfaces of the flanged lids (Figure 5.32a) are covered with the same beige-coloured glaze as the bodies of the jars. They are loose fitting but covered the unglazed area below the rim of the pots. Again, they were probably secured by a combination of glued cloth or paper and split bamboo netting.

Type B jars (Figures 5.33a and b) differ from those described as Type A by their different glaze, and being made in at least two sizes.

The glaze of Type B jars consists of abstract swirls and wavy linear bands of blue underglaze surmounted with a translucent overglaze that generally has considerably less lustre than the Type A glazes. The swirly effect is created by haphazardly applying cobalt blue with a brush while the pot is revolving on a wheel (Doo pers. comm.). Type B vessels appear to assume their beige colouration from refraction of light from the clay body, which has a grainy texture. This "surface appearance" is believed to be what Olsen (1978:45) describes as a "muslin texture". Gritty inclusions often cause bumps in the glaze.

Jars of this type have not been found in the immediate study area and none of those in private hands can be reliably related to archaeological contexts. They are believed to date from c.1910 so they may be uncovered in future. The dimensions of some unprovenanced specimens purchased from second-hand stores are recorded in Appendix 4. One is notable because it has only the faintest trace of blue colouration.

Like the Type A jars, Type B jars have a loose-fitting flanged lid. The lids are unglazed but are often decorated with a "quarters" design (Figure 5.36b) or a "square impression" enclosing a panel of Chinese characters (Figure 5.36a). Three sizes of lids with the "quarters" design are known. They have diameters of 5.0, 8.0 and 10.5 cm.

Type C (Figure 5.34) depicts a stoneware ginger jar given to the writer in 1981. It has the following dimensions: height 11.0 cm, base width 7.3 cm, mouth width 5.5 cm, maximum width 11.0 cm, and is decorated with blue underglaze swirls and overglazed with a translucent clear glaze producing the characteristic beige colouration due to refraction of light from the ceramic surface. The pot, which still contains its original contents, is closed with a cork and sealed with wax around the cork-rim interface. A paper label on the lid states "Tung Fong 'Lion Brand' Trade Mark, Finest Preserved Ginger, Made in Hong Kong". Such jars are not known from archaeological contexts and are almost certainly of post-1920 origin, possibly a successor to the small Type B, blue-beige ginger jars.

5.2.2.5.2 Blue-grey stonewares

These vessels conform to the typical ginger jar configuration (as depicted in Figure 5.35) but differ from those previously described because they have definite pictorial images (as opposed to swirls or abstract designs) in blue underglaze surmounted by a translucent cream-grey overglaze. The "pictures" range from simple plant representations to scenes depicting fishing, trees and lakes. The fabric and glaze are smooth with few impurities. A band extending up 2 cm below the mouth is unglazed, as are the bases.

Like the ginger jars described above, they have not been uncovered in the study area, but poorly provenanced specimens are held in museums and private collections. Their "better quality" appearance suggests they postdate 1900. The only specimen available for measuring (purchased in a second-hand store on the West Coast) has the following dimensions: height 15.0 cm, mouth width 6.0 cm, max. width 16.3 cm, base width 11.0 cm. The author has observed an exceptionally large pot of this type (in a bottle show display at Nelson c1982) featuring a lake, island, wharf and tree scene. This vessel, which stood 25 cm high, is believed to have been found in Australia and was for sale at $400. The form of the lids of these pots is unknown, but they were probably like the unglazed, flanged lids associated with the blue-beige ginger jars.

5.2.2.5.3 Miscellaneous ginger jar lids

It is often difficult to match isolated lids found in archaeological contexts with specific pots. The lids depicted in Figures 5.36a and c are believed to be from ginger jars, but it is not possible to definitively match them at this stage.

5.2.2.5.4 Blue on white ginger jars

Both handpainted and transfer-printed blue on white vessels with the classic rotund ginger jar body shape have been observed in collections and second-hand stores. Neither type is known from an archaeological context, and all the specimens observed so far look as though they postdate 1900 (i.e. they have a more refined appearance).

5.2.2.5.5 Wing Lee Wai alcohol bottles

None of these distinctive stoneware bottles (Figure 5.37) have been found in the study sites, but several, held in private collections, are known to have been removed from post-1900 (probably post-1920) Chinese sites in southern New Zealand, particularly in the Nokomai area, where a Chinese mining company operated until the 1940s.

The bottles are "Anglo" in shape; having a cylindrical lower section surmounted by a tall, narrow neck with three ridged grooves about 1.5 cm below the rim. The grooves were probably part of the bottle's closure system (corks and sticky paper?). Although no broken fragments were available for study, the body fabric appears to be relatively fine. The neck region is covered with a dark brown glaze, while the lower body has a translucent glaze through which the maker's (Wing Lee Wai) stencilled label (in blue underglaze) is legible. Three different variants of the label are known, but because of poor provenance information associated with the known specimens, it is not possible to seriate them.

The depicted specimen (Redmond collection, Christchurch) is 23.0 cm high and has a base width of 9.6 cm. Wing Lee Wai bottles with the other labels are of similar dimensions. The only other specimen available for measuring (Short collection, unprovenanced; Short pers. comm.) is 22.8 cm high and has a base width of 9.8 cm. It has a rather blurred label, but the following features were discernible within a shield: the words "Wing Lee Wai Herbal Fermentations" in a blue band; and several Chinese characters above and below the band.

These bottles appear to have been succeeded by a dark green, crown-capped bottle with a raised band around the neck. The bottles too bear the name "Wing Lee Wai (and again in Chinese characters; Wegars pers. comm.).

5.2.2.6 Missing ceramic links

This section documents five containers and cooking vessels that have been uncovered in contemporary overseas Chinese sites, but thus far, to this writer's knowledge, only one is known from a New Zealand site. In part, they are described to increase the likelihood of their recognition among fragmentary material from archaeological contexts in New Zealand.

5.2.2.6.1 Pans

Variously described in the overseas literature as "pans" (Chace 1976:521; Praetzellis and Praetzellis 1979a:186, Figure 2a; Pastron, Gross and Garaventa 1981:422) and "earthenware food vessels" or *shi ben tou* (Olsen 1978:34), these shallow bowls were, and still are, used for storage and preparation of food.

The vessel form is as depicted in Figure 5.27a, a drawing of a "pan" purchased by the writer in San Francisco Chinatown in 1981. Basically, the vessels are flat-bottomed, steep-sided, brown-glazed bowls. They are still available, in at least three sizes, in Chinese stores in North America. According to Chace (1976:521), they are favoured for cooking herbs and greens. The interiors of these bowls are covered with a thick, lustrous brown glaze, which may extend down the entire exterior or alternatively only down to the exterior ridge. The ridge runs around the midline of the vessels, enabling them to be stacked efficiently.

Pans have been found in several US sites, e.g. Ventura (two types; Chace 1976:520), Lovelock (Praetzellis and Praetzellis 1979:186) and Tucson (Olsen 1978:34). The average dimensions of the pans from the Tucson assemblage are height 4.5 cm and diameter 15.0 cm. This size is the one that is generally found in archaeological contexts. The only New Zealand "archaeological" example known to this author is a fragment of one uncovered in 1986 in a fossicker's hole on the slope below the Chinese store sites in Cromwell. No examples have been sighted or reported in NZ collections.

5.2.2.6.2 Thin brown jars

"Thin brown jars" is the name coined by Pastron, Gross and Garaventa (1981:418) to describe small, high-necked, ovoid, brownware bottles recovered in the 1880s N5 dump site, San Francisco. The type was unknown previously, but they have since been uncovered in excavations in a Chinese urban site in San Jose, California (Roop and Flynn pers. comm. 1985), and at China Camp, a Chinese shrimping village in Marin County, California (pers. comm. State of California, Department of Parks and Recreation, Sacramento). Both sites are near San Francisco. Vessels of similar form, containing alcohol, were available in San Francisco's Chinatown in 1980 (Pastron, Gross and Garaventa 1981:418).

They vary in colour from red to grey. The clay bodies are made from a fine stoneware paste and the interior of the archaeological specimens is unglazed. The exterior glaze is described as "extremely glassy and thin with numerous dribbles" (Pastron, Gross and Garaventa 1981:418). The pots were wheel produced, the translucency of the glaze tending to exaggerate the wheel-produced striations (Pastron, Gross and Garaventa (1981:419). The jars average 8.6 cm in height, have a rim diameter of 3.4 cm, a maximum diameter at the bulbous shoulder of 6.9 cm and are 3.9 cm across the base. Pastron, Gross and Garaventa (1981:420) surmised that their limited distribution may be due to the cost of the product they contained, or the vessel's fragility.

5.2.2.6.3 Medicinal teapots

Reports that parts of these vessels (Figure 5.27b) had been found in two sites in the United States (Praetzellis and Praetzellis 1979b:143, Figures 9a and d; Pastron, Gross and Garaventa 1981:420), have since been shown to be cases of mistaken identity (Wegars 1983:3). The recovered specimens lacked the diagnostically important spout and were, in fact, cooking pots (see Section 5.2.2.6.5).

Tomlin (1978:169) reported that during an excavation and ethnographic study at Tung O village, Lamma Island, Hong Kong, two types of teapot used for brewing tea and medicinal herbs were found in the village. He described the ware as being similar to brownware cooking pots, with a dark brown glaze on the interior. The ends of the handles were stamped with an untranslated trademark. A few fragments of spouts and handles were recovered (not illustrated) during the excavation and identified by the villagers as belonging to "old teapots". According to Praetzellis and Praetzellis (1979:143), ceramic herbal or medicinal teapots of this type can still be bought in the USS. No remains of this form of vessel are known in New Zealand.

5.2.2.6.4 Anglo-shaped ceramic beverage bottles

Again, the remarkable N5 San Francisco assemblage includes a previously-unreported new brownware beverage bottle form, executed in the shape of a Western beer or ale bottle. Five fairly similar specimens were recovered. The bottles are described in detail by Pastron, Gross and Garaventa (1981:402–4). They average 27.0 cm in height, 8.8 cm in maximum diameter, 2.7 cm in neck diameter and 8.2 cm in base width. Their specific usage is unknown. Presumably they contained some form of alcohol, but either the product or the bottle style gained little popularity, because on present evidence the bottles have a very limited chronological and areal distribution.

5.2.2.6.5 Ceramic cooking pots

Praetzellis and Praetzellis (1979b:138, 143, Figure 9a) illustrated an archaeologically rare form of thin-walled, fine-grained stoneware cooking pot of which an unstated number were found in a Chinese urban site in Sacramento, California. An 8 cm long handle, believed to be of a similar pot, was found in the N5 site at San Francisco (Pastron, Gross and Garaventa 1981:420, Figure 9.21). According to Wegars (1983:3), cooking pots "typically have a brown glaze over at least the lower portion of the interior and sandy beige unglazed exteriors". Although no pots of this type have been found in the study sites, an unglazed rim sherd (Figure 5.27c) believed to be from this type of vessel was found by the writer in 1979 on the surface of a probable post-1900 Chinese race warden's hut site (S151/3) in the Nokomai Valley.

Tomlin (1978:14) noted that traditional earthenware cooking pots (believed to be of this type) could still be bought in the markets in Hong Kong in the late 1970s. They are usually made of a thin, gritty clay with dark brown glaze on the interior. Passmore and Reid (1982:30) illustrate the modern equivalent of this form, which they describe as "casseroles" or "sandpots". On modern examples the base is usually reinforced within a wire basket. They are used for "braising, stewing, soup making, and a multitude of other cooking processes" (Passmore and Reid 1982:31).

5.2.2.7 Discussion: Chinese ceramics

In the preceding text, detailed descriptions of the various imported Chinese ceramic wares found in Chinese sites in Central Otago and overseas have been presented. Attention now is turned to interpretation. Analysis of the ceramics, both individually and collectively, provides two main bodies of information:

1. Inferences can be drawn about the wider socio-economic systems that affected the lifestyle and subsistence patterns of the Chinese community in Central Otago in the late 1800s–early 1900s.
2. The detailed descriptions provide a corpus of baseline data against which new material can be compared so that intra-site and inter-site and artefact variability can be determined, and national, regional and temporal differences defined. The information gained from the comparative process, in turn, generates new information or hypotheses that can be tested.

Although over half a century of occupation is embodied in the described assemblages, there is a clear stylistic continuity. The traditionalism that is a pervasive element in Chinese culture is expressed to a great extent in its ceramics, such as the retention of distinctive body shapes and glazes. Consequently, it is often possible to infer the contents of excavated Chinese food containers from modern examples, be they ceramic, glass or plastic, because the body shape has been retained. Similarly, the decorations and glazes employed on the tablewares can usually be traced back many centuries. The origin, distribution and role of these ware groups is discussed now. Opium pipe bowls, the other specialised type of Chinese ceramics that are commonly recovered, are addressed in Section 5.4.

5.2.2.8 Manufacture and importation

The major locations for the exportation of ceramics were, in descending order of importance, Guangzhou (Canton), Shantou (Swatow), Macao and Hong Kong (Olsen 1978:47). During the latter part of the Qing dynasty

(1644–1911 AD), Ching Te Chen in Jiangxi (Kiangsi) province was the major production centre for ceramic tablewares. A considerable portion of the wares made in Ching Te Chen were shipped unglazed to Canton to be decorated and glazed. Utilitarian wares, used primarily for the shipping and storage of foodstuffs, did not require a high degree of skill or quality and were mass produced at many smaller kiln sites closer to the major exportation ports on the eastern coast of South China. Despite some variation in dimensions, these often crudely made storage vessels were built for specific purposes and following long-established patterns. A degree of cooperation or standardisation is suggested by the fact that the bases and sides of the large shouldered food jars and spouted pots are identical. These portions could have been mass produced for both pot types.

5.2.2.9 New Zealand distribution

Most of the Chinese ceramics brought into New Zealand in the 19th century were landed at Dunedin. They were imported and distributed by a few major Chinese merchant businesses, of which Sew Hoy's is the most well known. The Dunedin merchants supplied both their own branch stores and other Chinese merchants who established stores in the goldfields' towns and mining areas (see Sections 3.2–3.3). Chinese miners regularly visited the stores and among other transactions purchased tablewares and ceramic-contained foodstuffs as required. Although some food containers were later re-purposed (discussed later), generally they were discarded after their contents were consumed.

Tablewares are likely to have been retained much longer, and in the largely male mining communities were probably not discarded until they were broken, or otherwise rendered unserviceable. An exception to this pattern possibly occurred in "restaurants", where remnants of once complete sets may have been periodically discarded and replaced with new sets. The presence of intact tablewares in some hut sites is probably attributable to factors such as the Chinese habit of abandoning huts and not interfering with their contents following a death, the contents of huts being abandoned after fires, or simply leaving surplus possessions when shifting to another location.

Table 5.16 summarises the frequency, and temporal and areal distribution, of Chinese ceramics in Central Otago. The categories are based on both numbers recovered from archaeological contexts and provenanced specimens in private and museum collections (see Tables 5.9–5.14 for site distribution details).

The Chinese ceramic assemblages are dominated (Groups 1 and 2 in Table 5.16) by brownware food containers (shouldered food jars, Ng Ka Py alcohol bottles, barrel and globular storage jars, and the small straight-sided pots) and celadon tableware (principally rice bowls, teacups, wine cups and spoons). The only other frequently recovered vessel is the "regular size" green-glazed ginger jar. Comparison with the ceramics reported in the American literature reveals some interesting differences in frequency and distribution in sites of approximate contemporaneity. Celadon tablewares are relatively uncommon in US sites compared to the overwhelming numbers of the 4 Seasons, Bamboo and Double Happiness tablewares. However, the absence of the Double Happiness style in Central Otago is not surprising because that suite is rarely found in post-1870 sites in North America. The differences are probably principally attributable to different suppliers servicing the American and New Zealand markets (most of the American Chinese are Seyip as opposed to Poon Yue, who were the majority in New Zealand). The frequency and distribution of the brownware storage vessels in rural sites in both countries exhibit much greater similarities with one major exception, the small wide-mouthed green-glazed ginger jars are relatively rare in US sites (see Evans 1981:91) whereas they are relatively common in New Zealand.

The Group 3 ceramics in Table 5.16, i.e. those of "less common occurrence" (3–10 known from Central Otago), also present some interesting comparisons. Firstly, the 4 Seasons suite, which are relatively common tablewares in contemporary US sites, are found infrequently in Central Otago sites in comparison with celadon. Similarly, Bamboo rice bowls are rarely found in New Zealand but are common in US sites dating between 1860 and 1900 (Evans 1981:92). The Double Happiness style, which is equally common in US sites, is not known from any archaeological context in New Zealand. Brownware jarlets are recovered infrequently in both countries; about five are reported in the overseas literature and only three (all recovered from the study sites) are known from New Zealand.

Of the wares listed in Group 4, several – such as the plain white rice bowls, spoons and teapots, and 4 Seasons teacups and shallow dishes – are uncommon in Central Otago sites compared with their US counterparts. However, the other cited wares seem to be equally rare, e.g. this author is unaware of the recovery of any of the following in US sites – brownware flat-rimmed pots (see Figure 5.22), miniature floral decorated pots, crab motif rice bowls and shallow blue-grey saucer-like dishes (see Table 5.16 for a guide to Figure numbers).

Despite their varying frequencies, chronologically the ceramics described thus far (excepting those that are rarely found) appear to have been in use for virtually the whole period of Chinese occupation in Central Otago (1866–1920s). Groups 5 and 6 ceramics are not only found infrequently but have an apparently restricted areal and temporal distribution in Central Otago, principally the Wakatipu Basin and the Nokomai Valley. Their presence in sites in these areas, particularly the Nokomai Valley, is attributed to their later occupation by Chinese. Inferred "earliest appearance" dates are outlined in Table 5.16. The distribution of these ceramics in the above areas may also be attributable, to some extent, to different sources of supply.

The ceramics listed in Group 7 are only known from museum or private collections. Although most are poorly provenanced, in most cases there is little evidence to suggest they were unearthed from local sites or obtained (pre 1930) from Chinese in New Zealand. Group 8 is a brief list of Chinese ceramic forms that have been recovered from contemporary archaeological contexts in North America but are presently unknown in New Zealand. They are listed to draw attention to the possibility of finding them in New Zealand sites.

5.2.2.10 Concluding comment

While it is possible to draw many inferences on the lifestyle of the Chinese from an analysis of the Chinese ceramic wares, the picture would be incomplete without recourse to the ceramics from other sources in the study sites.

In the next section, the ceramics of non-Chinese origin are examined. Inferences on lifestyle and acculturation, drawn from study of the combined assemblages, are presented at the end of the section. The questions of acculturation and adaptation by the Chinese and their responses to their situation in New Zealand are further discussed in Chapter 7 when all the historical, structural, artefactual and faunal evidence is considered.

5.2.3 EURO-CERAMICS

In the following discussion the term "Euro-ceramics" denotes any ceramics of non-oriental origin. Unless stated otherwise, the origin of most of the pieces is known or suspected to be the numerous potteries of Victorian England, which was the major supplier of manufactured goods to New Zealand throughout the 19th century. A few of the recovered pieces were made by potteries in New Zealand. The small, but not insignificant, ceramic industry that developed in New Zealand in the 19th century was briefly described by Park (1978) and is the subject of Lambert's (1985) *Pottery in New Zealand*.

Three main types of ceramics are widely recognised: earthenware, stoneware and porcelain, although there are many variations and some ceramics are considered transitionary. Earthenwares are fired to a point below where vitrification occurs, thereby rendering them light, and porous unless glazed. In the 19th century "white improved earthenwares" were produced, initially in England but later in the United States. These ceramics are dense, opaque, and relatively impervious because of their higher firing temperature and/or greater feldspar content (which acts as a flux). Their durability and relative cheapness were part of the reason for their popularity (Praetzellis and Praetzellis 1979:159). White earthenwares are archaeologically useful because they are commonly marked with details such as the manufacturer's name, place of business, brand or ware name. By recourse to a number of well-recognised ceramic reference works (e.g. Godden 1964), these marks often enable the ceramics to be precisely dated.

Stonewares are hard, high-fired ceramics which, because of their degree of vitrification, are generally strong and impermeable to liquids (Miller and Stone 1970:504). Consequently, specialised stoneware containers, such as crocks, storage jars and beverage bottles, found favour with many manufacturers of liquid products (e.g. ginger beer, ales, inks, blacking, jams etc.). They represent less than 10% of the ceramics from each site (Table 5.22). Porcelains are highly fired, fully vitrified and more or less translucent ceramics (Miller and Stone 1970). Generally, the uses of porcelain-ceramics were restricted to tablewares and ornaments. An absence of specific references or sales catalogues that describe the ceramics that were sold in New Zealand in the 19th century has necessitated a reliance on overseas literature, especially American historical archaeology ceramics analyses. Although various ceramic forms are unlikely to have had "identical periods of popularity", the overseas literature gives an indication of the date of the first appearance of (new) decorative features and their periods of predominance. The terminology cited in Figure 5.38 is used to describe various parts of vessels.

5.2.3.1 Objectives and methodology

A minimum of 290 Euro-ceramic vessels, ornamental pieces and containers are represented in the combined assemblage (Table 5.22). Only two (Sandy Point and Hanging Rock) of the 15 study sites did not contain any Euro-ceramics. The objectives of the ceramic analyses were to:

1. determine which types of Euro-ceramics were obtained by the Chinese and explain their usage;
2. elucidate the socio-economic role of Euro-ceramics;
3. compare the usage of Chinese versus Euro-ceramics;
4. determine dates of occupation where possible from datable pieces;
5. determine sources of origin where possible.

The analytical system used here is an adaptation of the methodology refined by Wegars (1981:115) after its initial application by Jones (1980) on the Euro-ceramics from the Boise Chinatown site, Idaho, USA. The ceramic fragments and intact vessels were first separated into groups based on whether their fabric or paste was earthenware, stoneware or porcelain. Once in these three categories, individual vessels (MNI) were determined by grouping sherds according to their decoration (plain, embossed or colour-decorated), glaze (presence or absence, crazed or not), marks (printed or impressed), shape (including panelling or scalloped rims), size (height, diameter or width of foot ring) and stratigraphy (archaeologically probable relationships).

Identifiable forms (Tables 5.19–5.22) included large and small plates, cups, saucers, small bowls, jugs, platters, mixing or serving bowls, teapots, egg cups, flowerpots, crocks, candleholders and a few ornamental pieces. A few fragments, while obviously unique, were too small to enable an accurate assessment of the particular vessel's size or shape. Selected sherds representative of the range of vessel forms and decorative techniques are depicted in Plates 11–19.

5.2.3.2 Earthenwares

Table 5.19 shows the breakdown of earthenware and porcelain vessels per site. The majority are utilitarian tablewares. They constitute 82–100% of each site's Euro-ceramic assemblage. The earthenwares were divided into three categories based on their decoration – plain white, embossed or colour-decorated. The 67 plain whiteware vessels constitute 29% of the total earthenware assemblage. Plain white wares, sometimes known as "hotel wares", were often bought for household use because they were relatively inexpensive and readily obtainable (Wegars 1981:119).

A relatively small number (MNI=9) of embossed white earthenware vessels were uncovered. "Embossed" is used to describe vessels that have embossed or moulded decoration but no added colour. To make this type of ware, clay slip was poured, or clay slabs pressed, into plaster of Paris moulds carved with decorative designs (Wegars 1981:119).

One hundred and sixty vessels were colour-decorated, representing 67.2% of the total earthenware assemblage. The term "colour-decorated" refers to the many methods of applying a coloured design or decoration to an otherwise plain or embossed ceramic body. They include transfer printing, handpainting, edge-banding, lithographic decoration (decals), handstamping, hairlining, gilding, and using coloured pastes or glazes. While often used alone, these techniques were often combined, such as using hairlining, gilding or edge decoration on the same vessel. The term "simple decorated" is used to collectively describe plain white vessels that are decorated with the most elementary decorative techniques such as hairlines, edge-bands and gilding (described below). The breakdown of decorative styles per site is tabulated in Tables 5.25, 5.27, 5.29 and 5.31. The techniques used on the study ceramics are outlined now.

5.2.3.3 Decorative techniques

5.2.3.3.1 Gilding

It is not known when gilding was first used as a decorative technique, but it was certainly in use in the United States by 1894 and became increasingly popular around the turn of the century (Wegars 1981:122). The method involved using a fine brush to apply powdered gold in liquid form to a vessel's rim or interior while it revolved on a potter's wheel. This produced concentric rings or bands. The gilded ceramics were then fired again to fix the gilding over the glaze. Sixteen otherwise plain, unembossed white wares from four sites were decorated solely by gilding. This represents only 5.5% of the total assemblage. Cups and saucers marked with one or two gilt hairlines on or near the rim were the principal vessel types decorated in this fashion.

5.2.3.3.2 Edge-banding

Edge-banding involves decorating the rim of vessels with a band of colour usually varying between 2 to 6 mm in width. This technique was used on 11 vessels from five sites. Maroon and blue were the most popular colours.

5.2.3.3.3 Hairlining

In this decorative technique a thin line in a contrasting colour was painted over or under the glaze, sometimes in combination with other decorative motifs. The method of applying the line was the same as for edge-banding; that is, a paint brush was held in a steady hand while the piece was rotated on a potter's wheel. The hairline was intended to be quite thin, often less than 1 mm in width, and was frequently placed inside a cup or around the rim area of saucers and small bowls. Hairlines are distinguishable from edge-banding by their width and placement. Only two colours, silver and gilt, were used for hairline decorations on the studied ceramics. Silver hairlining was evident on 10 vessels from three sites, while gilt hairlining was present on 16 vessels from four sites. Combined they represent 9% of the total Euro-ceramic assemblage, second only in terms of preference to plain white among the "simple decorated" wares (Tables 5.25, 5.27, 5.29, 5.31).

5.2.3.3.4 Handpainting

This term describes designs that were created by hand rather than decals or transfer prints. It does not include, in this context, the simpler processes of edge-banding, gilding or hairlining. Handpainting was evident on only two vessels, both jugs. Each had a handpainted blue stripe painted vertically down the handle. These matched blue edge-bands painted around the rim.

5.2.3.3.5 Transfer printing

Transfer printing was developed in England in the mid-18th century and quickly became the preferred means of decorating ceramics. It remained so until the early years of the 20th century, when it was superseded, but not completely replaced, by the decalcomania process (Wegars 1981:124). Briefly, this method involved engraving a design on a copper plate. The plate was then inked and wiped off. Next, a piece of tissue paper was pressed on to the plate. The inked paper was then placed on the vessel to be decorated and rubbed, causing the design to be transferred on to it. Following removal of the tissue paper, the piece was glazed and fired. The technique enabled very detailed designs and lettering to be applied relatively quickly and cheaply to table ceramics and containers. On tablewares, transfer printing is usually characterised by crisp floral or geometrical designs in a variety of colours, although only one primary colour was generally used on individual pieces. The technique also enabled the mass production of attractive lids for ceramic containers. These were used extensively by manufacturers in the 19th century as a means of advertising and labelling their products, e.g. toothpaste pots (Bedford 1985c).

Transfer-printed vessels were among the most common earthenware vessels in the Chinese sites; the 69 vessels representing some 23.8% of the combined assemblages. Transfer-printed wares were found in 11 sites and never represented less than 20% of the earthenwares in each site. They were absent from only two sites. Several transfer-printed vessels also bore maker's marks on the base. Information derived from them is detailed in Table 5.17. The transfer-printed vessels exhibit a range of colours including brown, maroon, mauve, green and blue. According to Kamm (1951:94), brown colours were particularly popular in the early 1880s but had passed their peak by the 1890s.

5.2.3.3.6 Flow blue

Two vessels incorporating a distinctive decorative technique known as "flow blue" were recovered. The effect is created by getting applied colours, usually blue, to run or flow by the addition of specific chemicals into the kiln during firing (Wegars 1981:124).

5.2.3.3.7 Lithographic transfers (decalcomania)

Patterns made by the lithographic process, as opposed to transfer printing, are supplied in the form of paper-backed sheets. These are cut up as required and the lithographs (or decals) pressed on to the vessels to be decorated. The process is known in the United States as "decalcomania" (Savage and Newman 1976:180; *Encyclopedia Britannica* 1979). This is now the most widely used form of printing for overglaze decoration. By about 1920 it had gained market supremacy over the transfer printing technique because decals were considerably cheaper to produce and faster to apply. The method also facilitated rapid application of multicoloured designs. Only five lithograph-decorated vessels (from the three urban sites) were uncovered.

The decorative techniques discussed above are those evident on the earthenware assemblages from the 13 sites that contained Euro-ceramics. They are particularly representative of the late 19th to early 20th century and correlate well with the dates derived from research into the maker's marks (see Table 5.17).

5.2.3.4 Porcelain

Fragments of 26 Euro-porcelain vessels were recovered during the excavations, comprising 9.8% of the total of 264 Euro-ceramic tablewares. The porcelains can be divided into three separate categories, like the divisions defined for the earthenwares:

1. plain white porcelain;
2. embossed white porcelain;
3. colour-decorated porcelain.

The colour-decorated porcelains exhibit many of the decorative techniques found in the earthenwares and include embossing, handpainting, hairlining, transfer printing and gilding. The numbers and types of Euro-porcelain artefacts are tabulated in Tables 5.20 and 5.22.

Two items of non-Chinese, oriental manufacture were uncovered; namely, a white porcelain saucer with a light gilt hairline probably made by the Japanese manufacturer Noritake (Figure 5.39–3; see Stitt 1974:201) and a brown-glazed teapot with imitation white coralene glass beading (Stitt 1974:126). Both artefacts were recovered from the Arrowtown Chinese Settlement (saucer: Ah Lum's store; teapot: ACS/2).

5.2.3.5 Stoneware

The usage of stoneware ceramics is largely restricted to containers and bottles. Fragments of 26 stoneware vessels, ranging from crocks through ink and ginger beer bottles, were recovered. They represent only 9.0% of the total number (290) of Euro-ceramic vessels of all types.

Stoneware vessels are glazed by one of two quite different techniques: salt-vapour or slip. In salt-vapour glazing (salt-glazing), salt is introduced into the kiln with the vessels to be fired. At 1204–1260°C, the salt vapourises and the free sodium combines with the silica in the clay to produce a glazed surface. A distinguishing characteristic of salt-glazed stoneware is a pitted "orange peel" appearance on the outside of the vessel. Salt-glazed vessels tend to be either unglazed on the interior or covered with a slip (Wegars 1981:126). Slip-glazing is achieved by dipping the vessel into liquid clay, which results in a smooth, even, glassy texture on the surface (Wegars 1981:126). "Bristol-glaze" is used to describe stoneware containers that have undergone a single firing and typically have a tan-glazed top and a clear-glazed base (Lambert 1985:160). Frequently, the sides of stoneware vessels bear impressed or stencilled underglaze company names or product descriptions, although in the studied assemblage, only two of the stoneware vessels are labelled and only one of these (see below) has been deciphered.

5.2.3.6 Manufacturer's marks

Twenty-two of the ceramic vessels were marked, including some duplication (4). Some of the marks or backstamps were able to be dated (Table 5.17), while others were indecipherable because they were fragmentary or illegible. Most of the marks are illustrated in Figures 5.39.1–11. Figure 5.39.12 depicts the common "Rouen" pattern, which was used by several manufacturers. Most of the ceramics were derived from the many kilns in Staffordshire, England (Table 5.17).

5.2.3.7 Discussion and conclusions

Euro-ceramic tablewares were present in 13 of the 15 site assemblages. The 13 assemblages contained a total of 264 units of Euro-ceramic tableware (238 earthenware and 26 porcelain) compared with a total of 141 units of tableware of Chinese origin (Tables 5.22 and 5.23). Euro-ceramic tablewares were numerically predominant in seven sites and equalled the number of Chinese pieces in two more. Of the two sites from which no Euro-ceramics were recovered, one (Sandy Point) contained three units of Chinese tableware, the other (Hanging Rock – a rockshelter) contained no ceramics of any kind. Several reasons can be advanced to explain the relatively high ratios of "Euro" (used henceforth to denote "non-Chinese") to Chinese table ceramics and to account for the types and variability of the vessels represented in the assemblages; namely, ethnic preferences, availability, prices, re-use of European discards, assumptions about the quality or durability of the goods, acculturative or assimilative changes, or the dictates of fashion. In the discussion (following Figures 5.39–5.42 and Tables 5.18–5.31) these factors are examined.

It is evident, assuming a relatively similar breakage and discard rate, that many of the Chinese miners acquired and used Euro-ceramic tablewares with little apparent concern about their origin; that is, there is no demonstrated preference for ceramics of Chinese origin. Moreover, over half of the sites' occupants used (or at least broke and discarded) considerably more Euro-ceramic tablewares than vessels of Chinese origin. Many Chinese storekeepers sold European foods and probably European tableware too; for example, Kum Goon Wah, a Cromwell merchant, stated that he had "On Sale,... Teas, Sugars, and General Groceries for English as well as Chinese customers..." (*Cromwell Argus* 17/05/1881).

Euro and Chinese ceramics were recovered in about equal volumes in the relatively isolated rural mining camps (see Table 5.18), but there was a considerably higher ratio of Euro-ceramics in the urban sites and the rockshelters (the latter are all located within 8 km from Cromwell), possibly reflecting pragmatic purchasing by Chinese who lived in or near the established towns.

Although the dates of occupation of each site were determined (from bottle and matchbox dating; Table 5.22) it was impossible to definitively document intra-site acculturative trends as reflected by changing ceramic ratios because most of the sites contained only a single discernible occupation layer. But it is likely that the usage of Euro-ceramics gradually increased, particularly after local Chinese stores closed. While tablewares can be readily dated through study of maker's marks, technological innovations etc., the dates can also give a false impression of the time of occupation of a site because, unlike product containers, tablewares are generally not discarded until they are broken (often several years after they were acquired). In an objective study of this problem, Adams and Gaw (1977) found that dates defined using ceramics from their study sites were some 20 years earlier than dates based on glass artefacts.

It is postulated that morphological and functional differences between Euro and Chinese tablewares account to some extent for the varying ratios in each site assemblage. Only five types of Chinese tablewares were commonly represented in the study sites; namely, serving bowls (2 sizes), rice bowls, teacups and wine cups and ceramic spoons, while cups, saucers and dinner plates are the predominant Euro-ceramic wares with lesser numbers of egg cups, teapots, small plates, bowls and other vessels (Table 5.19). As most of these vessel types have reasonably specific uses, it would suggest many Chinese acquired a mixture of European and Chinese vessels, depending on whatever they thought was best suited for particular foods or beverages, and possibly because they had broadened the range of foods and beverages consumed. Interestingly, Euro teacups (61) outnumber Chinese teacups (8) by a ratio of 8:1. They seem to have become the preferred drinking vessel with time, possibly because they were more readily available and have a much greater capacity.

There is a notable absence of Euro-ceramic "soup or breakfast-type" bowls in the assemblages; presumably the Chinese felt little need to substitute the multipurpose Chinese rice and serving bowls. The large number of Euro-ceramic dinner plates (n=39) may reflect increasing consumption of meat on the bone, a task made easier by using a large roomy plate. Compare this with the usage pattern deduced by Wegars after study of ceramic assemblages from the Boise, Idaho, Chinatown (see Jones 1980). Wegars (pers. comm. 1984) postulated that the poorer labourers at the site were using Euro-ceramics in a Chinese setting (bowls predominating), whereas the more well-to-do Chinese were using Euro-ceramics in a "European setting" (plates predominated). However, her postulation "does not fit" the situation in Central Otago, where Chinese bowls were being retained in preference to Euro-ceramic versions, and although European plates appear to have been widely adopted, there is no clear evidence that those who were using them were better off. The use of Euro-ceramic plates by the Chinese appears to be one of a number of "deliberate adoptions" of selected European items, which was not solely a response to a short term or permanent lack of availability of the Chinese equivalent.

Analysis of the Euro-ceramics revealed a distinct lack of "sets" of tableware, although some decorative styles were popular, particularly the "Rouen" pattern made by W H Grindley and other manufacturers (Figure 5.39–12). The absence of dinner sets is not surprising. There would have been little demand for dinner sets among the largely male Chinese mining population, most of whom lived in huts occupied by three or less, and they would have been relatively expensive and many of the vessels would have been poorly suited for eating Chinese meals. There was also a notable lack of matching cups and saucers in the recovered assemblages. Although more cups than saucers are likely to have been broken, possibly some Chinese bought cheap "odds and sods" or were unable or unconcerned about replacing broken crockery with identical pieces. Costs are likely to have had some bearing on the relative popularity or acceptance of Euro-ceramic tablewares, but this aspect cannot be assessed in the absence of local records that detail 19th-century Chinese and European tableware prices. Regarding the possibility of recycling, although there is ample evidence from the study sites that many Chinese collected and re-used discarded European items (Ritchie 1983a:19), there is no specific evidence indicating that they "collected" chipped or cracked but still functional ceramics that had been discarded by Europeans.

Euro-ceramic porcelain vessels are relatively uncommon and largely limited to cups, saucers and candleholders. The small number of porcelain pieces (26, 9.8%) probably reflects their higher cost compared to earthenwares, thus making their purchase less attractive. Porcelain vessels may also have proven less durable in mining contexts. This may be particularly pertinent regarding teapots. Only one distinctive straight-sided Chinese teapot was recovered (from QB2), whereas a total of 15 robust Euro-ceramic teapots were found, mostly in Cromwell's Chinatown and at Arrowtown. A porcelain doll-set cup and saucer were surprise finds in the Caliche site. Although the site was later occupied by rabbiters, both groups seem unlikely sources of the artefacts in question. Another porcelain doll-set saucer was uncovered in a small dump deposit associated with the Chinatown stores. Their presence remains an enigma.

Euro-ceramic assemblages have been reported from some overseas Chinese site excavations. Two of these, the Boise Chinatown, Idaho (Jones 1980; Wegars 1981:137) and Lovelock, Nevada (Praetzellis and Praetzellis 1979) were selected for comparative purposes. By comparing the ceramic assemblages, it might be possible to isolate regional variations, identify changes through time or generate new socio-cultural information.

Table 5.22 summarises the types of wares that were recovered from the various sites. The Cromwell and Arrowtown Chinese settlements are the oldest. They were occupied from c.1870 until 1920 and 1925 respectively. Ah Lum's store at Arrowtown operated from c.1880 until 1925, while the Central Otago rural Chinese sites were occupied from c.1870 until c.1910. The Boise Chinatown site existed from 1878 until 1920 (Jones 1980:5), and the Lovelock Chinese community was established c.1870 and died out in the 1940s (Hart 1979:11, 25).

The Euro-ceramic wares from the New Zealand and US sites, as tabulated in Table 5.22, show general consistencies in terms of the ratios of earthenwares, porcelains and stonewares. As might be expected, cheaper earthenwares predominate over the more expensive porcelain wares in all sites; in fact, by a ratio of 8:1. The inter-site percentages of porcelain vessels are remarkably consistent, representing 8–11% of each assemblage. Plain white and decorated porcelains occur in about equal volumes. Clearly, the Chinese preferred porcelain vessels of Chinese rather than Euro origin. Although, to some extent, it may reflect cultural conservatism, Chinese porcelain vessels were probably also perceived as better suited to or preferred for the serving and consumption of Chinese food.

An interesting inversion exists between the US and New Zealand sites regarding the plain white earthenwares. In the US sites they account for over 70% of the earthenwares, while in the New Zealand sites they represent less than 30% of each assemblage, colour-decorated wares being the predominant type. Why this inversion exists is unclear. It is unlikely that transfer-printed wares were cheaper in New Zealand or that the New Zealand Chinese were better off than their American counterparts and therefore tended to buy decorated rather than plain wares. The predominance of colour-decorated wares (particularly transfer prints) may be a function of fashion trends and the consequent mass importation and distribution of these vessels by Dunedin wholesalers during the period from c.1880 until 1910. In a study of the Euro-ceramics from a European site (Spalding, Idaho) in the United States, Wegars (1981:138) determined there was an increasing tendency with time towards the purchase of colour-decorated earthenwares. This trend appears to be replicated in Central Otago.

Gaw (1975:173) suggested that "decorated china" suggests a woman's presence at a site. While this may be true in many situations, particularly where excessively ornamental, decorated or higher quality ceramics are recovered, it does not fit the situation in this case. The study sites were virtually all male preserves, yet decorated wares, albeit relatively cheap transfer printed earthenwares, predominate. Although it probably reflects the available supply situation to a large extent, some of the Chinese miners may have opted for the higher outlay necessary to buy decorated wares because they preferred them over plain vessels. Furthermore, they are unlikely to have been totally immune from the dictates of fashion and possibly there was some element of "keeping up with the Joneses" among them.

To conclude, although the evidence is not unequivocal, as the years passed the Chinese miners increasingly used Euro-ceramics, while their use of Chinese ceramics gradually declined. This situation would come about, regardless of acculturative changes, through the increasing difficulty for the remaining Chinese to acquire Chinese goods as stores operated by their countrymen in rural areas gradually closed as local populations declined. The data tabulated in Table 5.18 suggests that the Chinese in and near the urban settlements were the main users of Euro-ceramics, while those living and working in more remote areas tended to retain and use predominantly Chinese wares. In the absence of contemporary price lists, it is impossible to assess how much price differentials are likely to have influenced the decision to buy either Euro or Chinese tablewares.

5.3 METAL CONTAINERS

Metal containers of various shapes and sizes have been used extensively in the Western world since the 1850s for packaging, preserving and distributing foodstuffs and other products. Although commonly called "tins" or "cans" (Old English canne – a vessel for liquids), most are made of rolled steel that is tin-plated to prevent rusting. Metal containers fall into two distinct categories: "metal boxes", which were made in a wide range of shapes and sizes for packaging; and "preserved canned goods", i.e. foods packed in hermetically sealed cans. Unless stated otherwise, all the containers described in the following discussion are made of tin (as defined above).

Once "tinned" products are consumed, the containers were usually discarded, sometimes in quite large quantities. Although their potential as sources of cultural information has been recognised by some overseas archaeologists (e.g. Busch 1981; Rock 1980), only a few "can reports" have been produced (e.g. Hunt 1959 – noteworthy for its time; Fontana and Greenleaf 1962; Rock 1984). The only detailed metal container studies undertaken in New Zealand to date are those by Anson (1983) and Bedford (1985a) on tin wax vesta boxes from the Clutha River study sites. The lack of specialised can studies is attributable to two factors:

1. Despite their extensive usage, cans have a relatively low durability compared with other cultural debris such as bottle glass and ceramics.
2. There is a general lack of understanding or inability to discern the cultural information that can be derived from the study of cans. Even those in very poor condition can be usefully analysed, provided they are studied carefully, construction and chronological features recognised, and the remains compared with control specimens.

The cans found in the Chinese sites were the subject of a specialised study by the writer and Stuart Bedford (Ritchie and Bedford 1985). This discussion is based on that work. The cans recovered from seven sites (those with substantial numbers of cans) – the Chinese urban enclaves at Cromwell (Chinatown; S133/48) and Arrowtown (S123/249); Ah Lum's store (S123/250 at Arrowtown); three Chinese hut sites in the Upper Clutha Valley – the Poplars (S115/44), Ah Wees (S115/54) and QB2 (S124/207); and a rockshelter in the Cromwell Gorge, Caliche shelter (S133/223) – formed the main data base of the study. Can remains from some 50 other Chinese and European sites in the Cromwell area were also used for comparative purposes. In addition, information was derived from the following sources:

a. research into canning history and technology;
b. the establishment of a comparative collection (about 200 units) comprising metal containers obtained from a wide range of sites and surface structures;
c. study of labelled metal boxes and cans in museums and private collections.

Analysis of the excavated assemblages revealed that a minimum of 1,099 metal containers are represented (587 cans and metal boxes and 512 tin wax vesta boxes). This number probably represents only a small percentage of the canned products actually used at each site, but it is assumed that each site assemblage is indicative of preferences and the main types of canned products that were bought and consumed. The relatively small can assemblages, particularly from the long-term occupation sites (the Cromwell and Arrowtown Chinese settlements), are attributable to decomposition of can remains in the relatively damp soil conditions of these two sites and, possibly, offsite disposal.

5.3.1 OBJECTIVES AND ANALYTICAL PROCEDURE

The objectives are:

1. to provide baseline data for future studies of metal containers in New Zealand;
2. to determine the utility of cans for dating historic deposits;
3. to examine the socio-economic role of canned products among the 19th-century southern Chinese.

The cans and metal boxes from each hut or site were analysed separately. After cleaning (brushing), the cans were placed into categories based on a determination of the original contents or product type of each container. If the original contents were unknown, the cans were categorised on morphological characteristics. Only cans in good condition were retained; all fragmentary and part cans, unless of rare or unusual form, were discarded after analysis. Product identifications were facilitated by research into company and brand names, by comparison of can morphology (using comparative, labelled museum or modern specimens) and through study of the constructional features of each can. Minimum numbers were ascertained by counting only positively defined can remains such as bases or lids. This system may have produced conservative calculations but avoided artificially maximising totals. Size variations in each basic can type were also recorded.

5.3.2 HISTORICAL BACKGROUND

Tin plate was first manufactured in Bohemia in the 14th century and for the next three centuries German tin plate predominated. Britain became the leading tin plate manufacturer after 1730 and dominated the market, particularly in tin box packaging, until the end of the 19th century.

5 The material culture of the Chinese in southern New Zealand

The first recorded use of hermetic sealing to preserve food was a method perfected in France in 1809 by Nicholas Appert, who won a 12,000 franc reward offered by Napoleon for the invention of a successful method of preserving foods. Appert's method, the foundation of modern canning, involved packing food in glass jars tightly sealed with cork and wire and cooking them in boiling water. A year later, an Englishman, Peter Durand, took out a patent for canning in tin canisters. The English firm of Donkin and Hall began commercial canning in 1812, the British Army being the first big consumer. Sir Joseph Banks, then president of the Royal Society, called them "embalmed provisions" (Davis 1967:80). Initially, there was considerable consumer reluctance to accept canned foods, but they soon became staples on military and exploratory expeditions. However, it was American canners who introduced several innovations after 1830, including automating the can-making process, which "really sold" preserved canned foods to the public for the first time (Clark 1977:6–10).

Despite the early innovations and dominance of the British tin-plate manufacturing industry, the British preserved food canning industry remained insignificant until after the First World War. In the interim, Britain had developed a dependence on a rising tide of preserved food supplies from Australasia, Argentina and the United States. However, the British tin box industry flourished, especially after 1830 when many home-based industries began using tin boxes for packaging products such as matches (wax vestas), biscuits, tobacco, cocoa, tea, coffee, pharmaceuticals, mustard, paints and varnishes, solvents and petroleum (Reader 1976:7–8). Each manufacturer developed their own distinctive tin box; for example, Huntley and Palmer introduced their well-known paper-labelled, returnable biscuit tins in 1830 (Davis 1967:71). Tin boxes dominated the packaging market until the introduction of cheaper cardboard packaging.

Soon after commercial food canning developed in Britain, English migrants introduced the technology into the United States, which became the major innovator. The major developments were as follows. In 1819, Thomas Kensett began canning oysters, meat and vegetables in New York, while in the same year William Underwood commenced canning fruit and vegetables in Boston. Initially both used glass containers, not changing over completely to tin canisters until 1837. In 1853, Bordon introduced canned condensed milk (patented in 1856). The tapered meat can was developed by Chicago meat packers in 1875 (Davis 1967:82). The major technical innovation, the introduction of the so-called "sanitary" can (discussed below), was developed in the 1890s and became the mainstay of the canning industry after the turn of the century (National Canners Association 1963; Clark 1977; Can Manufacturers Institute 1978; Busch 1981).

Other nations were quick to see the benefits of commercial canning. In Scotland, various kinds of fish were packed in cans in the 1820s, while the French introduced canned sardines in oil in the same decade. In Russia, powdered milk was first canned in 1842–43, as was salmon in Ireland in 1849. The Anglo-Swiss Condensed Milk Company (later Nestlé) established canneries in many countries after 1867. In Australia, two firms (in Sydney and Newcastle) began canning meat for export in 1848 (Davis 1967:81).

In New Zealand, several enterprising firms took up the new technology. Their efforts, like those of their Australian counterparts, were particularly directed towards the canning of meat, which promised a huge but unfulfilled overseas market prior to the advent of refrigerated shipping in 1882. The Woodlands Packaging and Canning Co. (initially a branch of the Glasgow Meat Preserving Co.), established at Woodlands near Invercargill, is claimed to be the first cannery in New Zealand (*Cyclopedia of New Zealand* 1905 Vol. 4:1064). An article in the *Southland News* (20/5/1870) indicates the company had begun boiling down meats and that "everything was in readiness to carry out the primary objective – the preservation of meat by the tinning process" (Trotter 1973:37). By 1900, the annual canned output of the works was 10,000 cases of canned rabbit meat and 4,000 cases of canned beef and mutton. A variety of other products were also canned from time to time, including corned beef, cheek soup, tail soup, bouilli, bovril, ox tongues and oysters (Trotter 1973:41). In 1870, the New Zealand Meat Preserving Co. (whose headquarters were in Glasgow) built an extensive plant at Kakanui in North Otago for the canning of meat for export. The factory had its own tin-making plant. However, the silting of the port at the Kakanui river mouth and the advent of refrigeration killed the enterprise (McDonald 1962:132–3).

The *Otago Witness* (15/4/1871:17) reported a large meat preserving works had commenced operations at Green Island near Dunedin in 1871. Meat was being preserved at the rate of 400 sheep or 25 head of cattle per day. The article describes the canning process thus:

> The manufacture of the tin canisters in which the meat is preserved is carried on upon an extensive scale... The tin is cut to the required size and the bottoms and lids are cut and shaped by means of two large dies. In the lids a small hole is perforated (to release the steam in the cooking process). The tins thus cut and shaped are passed into the Tinning room where they are soldered, and the meat put into canisters containing 6lbs, 4lbs and 2lbs respectively.

The article goes on to describe the rest of the canning and cooking process in detail. Significantly, in these three earliest New Zealand canneries the meat was being packed into handmade cans produced onsite. Other products were being canned in New Zealand in the 19th century, including fruit and vegetables at Nelson in 1881 (Kirkpatrick & Co.), whitebait at Greymouth in 1884

(*Cyclopedia of New Zealand* 1906 Vol. 5:100, 573) and condensed milk (the Underwood Milk Preserving Co. at Wallacetown near Invercargill) in 1892 (*Cyclopedia of New Zealand* 1905 Vol. 4:913).

5.3.3 CAN LABELLING

The labelling of metal containers has a history of its own. In the first half of the 19th century, labelling methods included handpainting, stencilling or embossing the container itself, attaching paper labels or soldering on embossed labels. Transfer printing on tin was pioneered in London in the 1860s. Metal lithography appeared in the 1880s, but it was the advent of the rotary offset lithographic press, patented in 1903, which saw the widespread acceptance of the method used in most tin-plate printing today (Clark 1977:11, 27–8). Metal lithography became the norm for cans that were not hermetically sealed, such as containers for tea, spices, gunpowder, drugs and tobacco. Can labels do not fare well in archaeological contexts and so their usefulness is limited. The only labels that consistently survive are those that are embossed (impressed) into the can body or lid (e.g. Figure 5.43j).

5.3.4 THE MAIN METAL CONTAINER FORMS

Although the methods of metal container manufacture (and, more recently, materials) have changed considerably over the years, there has been considerable conservatism in container forms. Thus, through study of a container's morphology, it is often possible to deduce the general product type, if not the original contents. Furthermore, the presence or absence of recognisable construction features also provides clues to a metal container's original use and its antiquity.

In the following discussion, the main metal container forms found in the study sites and their characteristics are described.

5.3.4.1 The standard cylindrical can

The mainstay of the canning industry since its inception has been the standard cylindrical can made in a range of sizes, for the preservation of a wide variety of foodstuffs, particularly vegetables, fruit, fish and meat. As a result of increased mechanisation, several innovations have occurred in cylindrical can manufacture, but one is particularly notable – the advent of the modern hermetically-sealed "sanitary" or "packers" can in the 1890s, which succeeded the "hole-and-cap" can.

5.3.4.1.1 The "hole-and-cap" can

Initially, cans were manufactured completely by hand. To make the body, a piece of metal (tin plate) was bent into shape on a roller and the overlapping seams soldered together. Two discs of tin plate were then cut for the ends, their edges being bent down or flanged to fit the "body" of the can. The "bottom disc" was soldered on to the can body immediately, but there were two commonly used techniques for "lidding" – the lid could be soldered on after the can had been filled, or the equally common "hole-and-cap" technique was employed. This involved soldering on a top with a centrally located circular hole in it (about 3 cm in diameter) before the can was filled. The food was pushed or poured through the hole, then a cap with a small venthole was soldered over the opening. During processing, when enough steam had escaped, the venthole was closed with a drop of solder (Busch 1981:96; Figure 5.43a). The hole-in-cap can changed little in style throughout the 19th century, although its manufacture was increasingly mechanised by innovations such as the modification of a drop press in the late 1840s to convert flat discs into flanged can ends (Rock 1984:100) and the development of a semi-automatic machine by the Norton Brothers in 1883 to solder side seams. This machine produced cans at the rate of 2,500 per hour, compared to 60 per hour in the 1870s, and five or six per hour in the early 19th century (Clark 1977:18).

5.3.4.1.2 The "sanitary" or "packers" can

The most far reaching innovation in canning history occurred in the late 1890s with the advent of the so-called "sanitary" can (Figure 5.43b), beginning the gradual demise of the hole-and-cap can. The sanitary or open-top can was initially developed in Europe where ends were attached by hand-crimping the edges, a seal being effected by a rubber gasket. In 1897, the Max Ams Machine Co. developed a machine that automatically crimped the ends to the body with a double-locked seam. The new can was considered more sanitary because it was soldered on the outside only. It appealed to canners because the process was fully automated, and the cans could hold larger pieces of food and be filled more easily. By the 1920s the sanitary can was totally accepted by the public and virtually replaced all other can types. The modern sanitary can is basically the same as it was at the beginning of the century, although the manufacturing process has been further automated, can weight has been reduced by cold-rolling the metal (steel) and the use of electrolytic tin plating (since 1937) has further reduced the tin content (National Canners Association 1963:18). The early canners soon developed a range of can types, both hermetically sealed and reclosable, for specific preserving or packaging purposes. The main variants and known or inferred products and brands are now discussed.

5.3.4.2 Fish cans

The flat oblong can used for packing seafood was developed at the outset of commercial canning (Fontana and Greenleaf 1962:72). The earliest fish cans were made in three pieces, then soldered. By 1880, the peak of mechanical automation, the base and body were being drawn in one piece. Fourteen years later, "open-top" double-seamed sardine cans were introduced.

5.3.4.2.1 Sardine cans

The flat, rectangular sardine can was in regular use before 1880. The popularity of canned fish led to experimentation with quick-opening devices. In 1895, the Norton Brothers of Chicago developed a key-method of roll-opening a scored strip on the lid of a sardine can. A refinement, the key opener for the "open-top" double-seamed sardine can, was patented in 1906 (Fontana and Greenleaf 1962:71). Although generally smaller than their predecessors (Figure 5.43c), modern sardine cans retain the same basic features, making them ideally suited for tightly packing, processing and marketing small fish such as sardines.

5.3.4.2.2 Oval fish cans

These cans (Figure 5.43d) were developed in the late 19th century (probably in England or Scotland) for packing and processing larger fish such as herrings. Again, the basic shape has been retained through the years, although can technology has progressed from soldered to crimped seams, to one-piece seamless cans bearing all the hallmarks of fully-automated production. As with many can styles, the modern versions tend to be smaller than their forerunners.

5.3.4.2.3 Squat cylindrical cans

Large-scale canning of salmon commenced on the Sacramento River in California in 1864 (Busch 1981:97). Initially, the fish were packed by hand, but the process was soon automated partly through the development of a squat cylindrical can (Figure 5.43g), a compact shape that was well suited for packaging fish meat and that continues to be widely used today for the same purpose.

5.3.4.3 Meat cans

Three types of cans were predominantly used for packaging meat.

5.3.4.3.1 Cylindrical meat cans

These were essentially larger versions of the form described above. Presumably it was found convenient to package meat in relatively wide, shallow cans, so the form became established. They were used extensively for packing red meat before the advent of refrigeration. Three types of squat cylindrical cans (Figure 5.43g) have been uncovered in the study sites: hole-and-cap, locked seams and the modern sealed seam type. In New Zealand, products such as corned beef, sheep tongues and rabbit meat have been canned in tins of this type.

5.3.4.3.2 Tall rectangular hole-and-cap cans

A few tall rectangular hole-and-cap cans (Figure 5.43f) have been uncovered. These are believed to have contained meat. The form seems to have been short-lived, probably being superseded by the tapered meat can.

5.3.4.3.3 The tapered meat can

The hole-and-cap tapered meat can was patented in 1875 by Chicago meat packers (Davis 1967:82). The design was intended to facilitate the easy removal of the processed cooked meat from the tin (Figure 5.43e). Again, the can form survives to the present day but modern examples tend to be smaller. The key-opening device developed by the Norton Brothers (Figure 5.43h) was rapidly adopted by meat packers after 1895 (Rock 1984:100).

5.3.4.4 Flanged-lid cans

Two types of flanged-lid cans were found.

5.3.4.4.1 Tall rectangular flanged-lid cans

This type of can (Figure 5.43i) has virtually gone out of existence, having been replaced by cheaper cardboard packaging. Cans of this type first appeared in quantity after about 1870. They were designed to contain dry products used in relatively small quantities. Thus a can could be opened and resealed as often as desired until the contents were consumed. Colman's Mustard (in four sizes) was probably the best known product in cans of this type in New Zealand. Most flanged-lid cans had paper labels (which seldom survive in archaeological contexts), but their lids (or bases) were often embossed with the user's name or brand of the product (Figure 5.43j). Many fancy imported cans of this type had transfer or lithographed labels.

5.3.4.4.2 Cylindrical flanged-lid cans

Like the rectangular flanged-lid cans, this form has also become virtually obsolete. Their use also dates from c.1870 and they also contained dry products, which were generally used in small quantities. Fry's chocolate and cocoa were common imported tins of this type, while the main products packed in this type of tin in New Zealand included Edmonds custard and baking powder (Figure 5.43l; the latter in three sizes), cigarettes and tobacco (described next), spices – e.g. W. Gregg & Co. (Figure 5.43k), Wilson's, Wilson, Balk & Co. and Strang's – and coffee and chicory (W. Gregg & Co.'s Club Coffee, Figure 5.43m; Strang's Coffee).

5.3.4.5 Tobacco and cigarette tins

Two major can forms were used for packaging tobacco and cigarettes: cylindrical flanged-lid tins (slip-lids) and rectangular small hinged-lid tins (pocket tobacco). Other can types were also used, including lever-lid (press-top) cans for bulk sales (e.g. Riverhead tobacco) and squat, rectangular flanged-lid cans with hinged lids (e.g. Cameron's Havelock Tobacco). In the 19th century, tobacco was also sold in soldered-top boxes (see below).

5.3.4.5.1 Cylindrical flanged-lid tobacco tins

This type of tin is no longer used for tobacco or cigarettes but was in vogue until c.1950. Two main size variants exist, standing 5 cm and 10 cm high respectively. Usually, the paper labels have decomposed on archaeological specimens but the brand or packer's name (e.g. W.D. & H.O. Wills, Figure 5.43q) is often discernible on the embossed lids. The "slip-lid", an ingenious modification of the basic cylindrical flanged lid, was patented in 1888 (Reader 1976:18). Before then, cigarette manufacturers were reluctant to use flanged-lid tins because they were not completely airtight. The problem was solved by the invention of the "slip-lid cutter" (Figure 5.43r). The tin had an inner cover made of tagger (tin foil) that was surmounted by a flanged lid with an inbuilt cutter. The cutter rested outside the tin (and under the label) until it was wanted, when it could be pushed inwards. This action pierced the tagger and by turning the lid, the cutter opened the airtight inner cover.

5.3.4.5.2 Rectangular hinged-lid tobacco and cigarette tins

Because of their convenience, rectangular pocket tobacco and cigarette tins (Figure 5.43s) gradually became the favoured packaging for these products, although they too have been largely superseded by cardboard packaging. Hinged pocket tobacco tins were first produced in 1892 (Jones n.d.:2).

5.3.4.6 Rectangular soldered-top boxes

This is another obsolete metal box form (Figure 5.43o). Rectangular tin boxes of this type were used in the 19th century to contain tobacco (and may also have contained other products). Usually, they are found with the soldered lid partly prised off to facilitate removal of the contents.

5.3.4.7 Hinged-lid boxes

These containers are essentially "tin boxes" with a hinged lid. Typical examples are the square biscuit tins (pioneered by Huntley and Palmer in the 1830s) and tea boxes (Figure 5.43p). Tea boxes usually measure about 30 cm long, 20 cm wide and 20 cm deep and have a hinged lid with a slight overlapping flange.

5.3.4.8 Press-top (or lever-lid) cans

This type was developed by the Self-Opening Tin Box Co. of London in 1895 (Tyrrell pers. comm). Cylindrical press-tops are the most common form (Figure 5.43n). Their easy opening yet airtight seal made them particularly attractive to paint manufacturers, but other products, such as viscous foods like treacle, syrup and honey, and dry products like baking powder, coffee and chicory (e.g. Strang's) were also packed in press-tops. Other forms of press-top cans (not excavated) include "internal press-tops", in which the lid fits snugly down the inside of the can body, and square press-top tins (e.g. Twinings tea tins).

5.3.4.9 Wax vesta boxes

Wax vestas (matches) were first sold in small rectangular tin boxes in the 1830s, the practice continuing until about 1940. The many types and utility of this container type for dating sites has been demonstrated by Anson (1983). An extended but simplified classification system was produced by Bedford (1985a). Because of their utility for dating, vesta boxes are discussed separately in Section 5.3.6.

5.3.4.10 Kerosene and oil cans

The ubiquitous "kerosene" cans appear in sites dating from c.1870 through to the present. They were produced in 2- and 4-gallon capacities. The cans are square in cross-section but have rounded corners. The main distinctive features are on the lid area where a screw-top pourer hole and occasionally an embossed product name are located. Early examples had a rigid bracket handle whereas later specimens have a wire handle that can be folded flat on the top of the can. Although cans of this type were primarily used for the conveyance and distribution of liquid fuels and solvents, cans of similar construction were also used for packing bulk supplies of viscous foods such as jam and fruit pulp. A variant, usually with a rectangular cross-section, was used for motor oil. It has a 1-gallon capacity.

5.3.4.11 Reinforced drum-cans

In the 19th century, some paints and varnishes (and perhaps nails) were imported into New Zealand in solid drum-like cans 42 cm high, 28 cm in diameter and with 3-cm wide reinforcing bands around their base and top. After their original contents were used, handles were often added to empty cans so they could be re-used for purposes such as coal and ash buckets and for kibbles (buckets suspended from a windlass over a mineshaft). Their robust construction made them ideally suited for these purposes.

5.3.4.12 Opium cans

Until 1901, opium was legally imported in large quantities from China for the Chinese migrant population. The opium resin was packed in distinctive brass rectangular flanged-lid containers (Figure 5.43u). Remnants of these cans are found in most Chinese sites in Central Otago. The construction and manufacture of these containers and the social role of the product they contained is examined in Section 5.4.

5.3.4.13 Opium antidote(?) cans

The small tin "box" depicted in Figure 5.43v is reputed to be an "opium antidote container" (Ritchie and Harrison 1982:20). The slide-lid covers a 1 cm diameter aperture. To date, six of these containers have been recovered (all from Cromwell's Chinatown and the Arrowtown Chinese Settlement), but it has not been possible to confirm their usage for the purpose stated above. These cans and other artefacts known or believed to be associated with opium usage are discussed in Section 5.4.

5.3.5 DISCUSSION

The can assemblages were analysed with two primary queries in mind:

1. gleaning insights into the role of canned products;
2. examining the utility of can dating and corroborating the dates of occupation of each site, where possible.

In the following discussion, the Chinatown assemblage is first treated separately and then compared with the assemblages from the other sites under review. The types of tin matchboxes from each site are listed in Tables 5.32 and 5.35 but are omitted from further consideration because they have been discussed in depth elsewhere (Anson 1983; Bedford 1984). Matchboxes are also omitted from the can type ratio calculations outlined in the text because their highly variable numbers cause an unrealistic distortion of the percentage frequency of the various can types per site.

5.3.5.1 The Cromwell Chinatown assemblage

Cans constituted approximately 20% (by volume and number) of the containers at Chinatown. This percentage is likely to have been higher, perhaps 40%, when the rapid degradation of tin cans is taken into account. Five types dominate the 173 can (minimum number) assemblage; namely, general food and circular flanged-lid cans, tobacco tins, opium cans and wax vesta boxes. Not surprisingly, "general food cans" were one of the most common can types uncovered (32 specimens, comprising 18.5% of the total assemblage). Analysis of the cans from each hut revealed that they span the occupation of Chinatown from c.1870 until 1920, but no hut could be positively described as "early" or "late", i.e. the cans reflected a broad time span. They are likely to have contained products such as preserved vegetables (beans and tomatoes?), soups and condensed milk. Some of the early cans (generally hole-and-cap) were found with their tops opened in the manner depicted in Figure 5.43t, a method of opening that we have found so far to be limited to Chinese sites (but not all of them). Presumably it enabled a can to be opened easily with a knife, the contents poured and the lid partially reclosed if desired. A related can type, the squat cylindrical form (nine specimens, 5.2%) probably contained meat products such as corned beef or sheep tongues. The four rectangular hole-and-cap cans also probably contained preserved beef. In addition, three keyed and two unkeyed tapered meat cans were recovered. These are the classic "bully beef" type. Collectively, meat cans comprise 10.4% (n=18) of the Chinatown assemblage. Five fish cans were recovered, two of which are the typical rectangular sardine can type, while the other three are oval, akin to the well-known "herring tins". Fish cans represent 2.9% of the can assemblage.

Cylindrical flanged-lid tins represent 17.3% (30) of the assemblage. This type was generally used for the packaging of dry powder products such as coffee, spices, chocolate and cocoa beverages and baking and custard powders. Four embossed tins bore the inscriptions "Gregg's Coffee and Spice Mills, Dunedin", "Strang's Chocolate and Cocoa", "Fry's Cocoa" and "Edmonds" (presumably baking or custard powder). Several small flanged-lid specimens, measuring 5.5 cm in diameter and standing 7.5 cm tall, are typical spice cans.

There were 10 circular press-tops (lever-lids) in the assemblage. These tins were widely used for viscous liquids such as paint and treacle, but they were also used by some dry product manufacturers (e.g. Strang's coffee). In the absence of labels or embossing, it is not possible to ascribe a specific product to these can remains with certainty, but they probably contained foodstuffs rather than paint (the Chinatown huts were built of stone and judging from remnants of corrugated iron the roofs were unpainted).

Tobacco tins of all types including cylindrical, hinged rectangular and soldered-top boxes constituted 15% (n=26) of the assemblage. Only two brand names could be positively determined from embossed or painted labels, namely W.D. & H.O. Wills' "Capstan Navy Cut" (in cylindrical flanged-lid cans, with and without slip-lid cutters) and Cameron's "Havelock Tobacco" (in squat, rectangular flanged-lid tins with hinged lids).

Seven 4-gallon capacity "kerosene cans" were uncovered. In most instances the top had been cut out and a handle added to facilitate their use as buckets. This type of can had many uses, which are discussed later, but few survive in archaeological contexts because they tend to degrade rapidly after being flattened and buried.

Twenty-two opium cans (12.8%) were found at Chinatown; only slightly fewer than the number and percentage of tobacco. The prevalence of opium cans in Chinese sites in Central Otago (and hence its widespread usage) is discussed in Section 5.4. However, the durability of the brass opium cans must be considered. It is likely they, or at least their component pieces, survive better in the ground than the tin-coated tobacco cans.

Other metal food containers uncovered at Chinatown are listed in Table 5.27. They include tea boxes (2) and biscuit tins (2).

5.3.5.2 Canned products' usage – all sites

Not surprisingly, tin wax vesta matchboxes dominate the site assemblages, constituting from 15.2% to 75.3%. Wax vestas were used extensively in the predominantly male mining communities for lighting fires, cigarettes, pipes, lamps and candles. Consequently, empty matchboxes were frequently discarded. Their primary archaeological significance is their utility for dating historic deposits (Anson 1983; Bedford 1984). They have been omitted from the can-type ratio calculations because the large numbers recovered from some sites cause considerable distortion in the inter-site ratios of the various can types, and they did not contain foodstuffs.

Table 5.27 details the numbers and percentage composition of the main can types found in the study sites. Because of problems associated with differential survival and precise determination of can contents, assumptions about specific products and the social role of canned goods have an inherent inaccuracy factor that is difficult to quantify. Some broad trends are outlined now, the comments being based on the ratios of the various can types (which reflect different food types and presumably their popularity). Specific brands as revealed by embossed lids are listed in Table 5.28.

The numerical data gives an indication of the role of hermetically-preserved foods such as vegetables, soups, meat and fish. Condensed milk cans were relatively rare (see below). Preserved food cans varied from 29.4% of the assemblage at Ah Lum's to 55.3% at the Poplars; however, the mean (of all seven sites) 37.3% is probably a more accurate indicator of the role of preserved canned foods relative to other tinned foodstuffs. Notwithstanding the fact that these figures may be partly attributable to differential survival, the percentage of preserved canned foods is noticeably higher at the sites most distant from the major service towns, Cromwell and Arrowtown.

"Dry food" cans (i.e. rectangular and cylindrical flanged-lid cans) contained products such as baking and custard powder, curry, spices, coffee and chicory, although judging from the few coffee essence bottles in the sites, the Chinese do not appear to have consumed much of the latter two products (see Table 5.3). A small percentage of these can forms (evidenced by embossed lids) contained non-foods such as washing blue and starch, but these products constitute less than 10% of these can types. The percentage of dry food cans in the sites shows an interesting reversal of the preserved food trend. Here the most distant sites, the Poplars and Ah Wee's, have the lowest percentages for this type of container (12.75% and 9.7% respectively), while at the closer-in sites, except Ah Lum's, percentages varied from 12.8% to 26.7%. The small number of dry food containers in Ah Lum's is not readily explainable. As "dry food" cans constituted on average 22% of the studied assemblages, their contents were obviously important components of the Chinese diet, but these products were used in lesser volumes than preserved canned foods in most instances.

Cans containing opium and tobacco varied from 21.9% (at QB2) to 52.9% (at Ah Lum's) of the total site can assemblages, although no allowance has been made for variation in can size. Two of the three tobacco cans at Ah Wee's were the bulk soldered-top tins, which have 10 times the volume of a pocket tobacco tin. Presumably, the varying proportions of tobacco and opium cans reflect individual preferences for either drug (except, of course, the combined Chinatown and Arrowtown assemblages). Opium was being smoked at all the sites, often in considerable quantities, reflecting its historically documented widespread usage by the Chinese. The absence of tobacco and cigarette cans in two of the seven sites was surprising, but alternative tobacco smoking evidence in the form of two clay pipes was found in each site. Contemporary accounts clearly indicate that tobacco smoking was an entrenched habit. For example, Don (1882:87), the Presbyterian missioner to the Chinese, noted: "After meals the Chinese almost to a man cut up some tobacco and make and smoke a small cigarette." A few years later he recorded: "Opium smokers pay for their own opium, but as a non-tobacco smoker is about as rare as a non-tea drinker, or a non-rice eater, partners in work include tobacco in the common account" (Don 1888:166). "Other cans" represent a miscellany of canned products such as kerosene, solvents, flea powder and opium antidote(?). Fragmentary, unidentified cans are also included in this category. They constituted from 2.1% to 13.9% of the site assemblages.

Between 1870 and 1910, production of and demand for canned foods expanded rapidly. Understandably, canned foods had a particular appeal to the mining community. In the absence of refrigeration, a stock of cans ensured a ready supply of rodent-proof provisions that also required minimal cooking time and effort. Although contemporary observations indicate the Chinese miners generally grew more fresh vegetables than their European counterparts, the number of canned products in the assemblages suggests they too appreciated the convenience of canned provisions. They appear to have purchased them frequently despite their cost (see Table 6.20). Although there were more "late" than "early" cans in the assemblages, suggesting that the consumption of canned food progressively increased, this cannot be demonstrated unequivocally because of the problem of differential survival. More recent cans are likely to have survived. No European site assemblages were included in this study, but a notable difference is apparent in surface scatters in that European sites have a much higher incidence of condensed milk cans. The archaeological evidence and contemporary observations suggest the Chinese were not great consumers of milk products.

5.3.5.3 Secondary uses of metal containers

The other major socio-economic use of cans involves their re-use for other purposes. This in turn can be divided into two categories:

1. empty, essentially unmodified containers used for storage;
2. the modification of empty containers for another purpose.

Empty reclosable tins were probably used extensively by the Chinese for holding small objects and as rodent-proof food containers. Wax vesta boxes have been uncovered containing small nails, a key, pumpkin seeds and a fragmentary piece of paper (possibly a gambling coupon). Empty general food tins were used for storing items such as nails, bar soap and utensils.

Modified can uses were considerably more varied. They range from fitting wire handles to topless kerosene cans or nail drums so they could be used for water and coal buckets or kibbles, to punching holes in the base of the same to enable their use as watering cans or, perhaps, showers. Kerosene cans were also used extensively for metal sheeting. A "sheet" was produced by cutting the ends out of a tin, cutting it up one side and flattening the metal to produce a sheet measuring about 1 m long and 30 cm wide. The tin sheets were used for roofing, patching, garden borders and lining the outer walls of mud huts to prevent rabbits from burrowing in (Ritchie 1984:34). A European but not definitely Chinese re-use of kerosene cans involved cutting them length-wise down the middle to produce two shallow trays. These were used as seed beds and usually had a few punched drainage holes.

Reclosable cylindrical flanged-lid cans (especially the small spice cans) are often found with numerous small holes (less than 1 mm in diameter) punched in the lid. They appear to have been used as "condiment shakers". Occasionally, food cans are uncovered with holes punched in their base (Figure 5.43x). They may have been used as soap containers. Another common re-use of general food cans involved cutting down one side of a can to make a candleholder and flame-guard. Larger tin tea boxes with numerous holes (of 2–3 mm diameter) punched in the base may have been used as colanders for draining foods or as "steamers".

Small cylindrical food cans were used as the fuel reservoir in Chinese opium and reading lamps. Don (1/3/1887:163) specifically noted the use of "jam tins" for this purpose when he preached a sermon in an opium and gambling shop in the Nevis Valley:

> Picture us if you can! The preacher with an empty kerosene tin laid flat on a table for a desk; ditto standing on end for his seat, the congregation seated and reclining on short stools and opium benches; the sacred page lighted by an opium lamp (a jam tin filled with tallow, a cotton wick and the upper part of a brandy bottle for a shade).

Usually, a metal bracket was fitted over the top of the reservoir (a tin can) to support the wick (Figure 5.43y). Two cans modified in this way were uncovered at Ah Wee's and Arrowtown.

The brass opium cans were extensively re-used by the Chinese. Several lids have been found with numerous small, punched holes suggesting they were being used as "salt shakers", while the many angular offcuts of can metal (particularly the body metal) found in most Chinese sites, as well as numerous complete artefacts, attest to regular artefact production from opium can metal.

Improvised artefacts include "washers", "discs" (game counters?), "funs trays" (i.e. small trays for holding deals of prepared opium; Figure 5.43w), "tie tags" (made of strips of can metal) and small gold blowing trays. These artefacts are described in Section 5.4.

5.3.5.4 Origins of canned products

The earliest New Zealand canners saw canning primarily as a means of packaging and preserving food surpluses (particularly meat) for export rather than supplying the local market. But by the 1880s there was increasing acceptance of and a growing local demand for preserved canned foods. A burgeoning reciprocal trade with Britain had developed; New Zealand traded farm produce in return for British manufactured goods including many products packed in metal boxes, e.g. Colman's mustard, starch etc., Fry's chocolate and cocoa, and wax vestas. The latter were first produced in England in 1832 and exported to the colonies in large volumes after that date. Other European countries, such as Belgium, also exported wax vestas to New Zealand (Anson 1983; Bedford 1984).

Gradually, New Zealand-manufactured goods began to displace imports. The first New Zealand-made wax vestas were produced in 1895 (Anson 1983:135). New Zealand food manufacturers appreciated the utility of metal containers too; some of the most prominent users were the manufacturers of coffee and chicory and spices, e.g. Gregg's, Wilson's and Strang's (Table 5.28). Their tins were made by local tinsmiths under contract or onsite using imported machinery. Advertisements like the following appeared frequently in Dunedin newspapers of the 1880s and 1890s:

> Tinsmiths Machines of every description made on the very latest approved principles for the rapid production of Canisters etc. Dies made to any pattern. Meat works supplied with complete outfits… Get Prices from the following before ordering elsewhere. F.J. Lake, Moray Place, Dunedin.
>
> (*Otago Daily Times* 1/1/1898:5).

5.3.5.5 Deriving occupation dates from cans

Dating cans involves the recognition of construction features that reflect changes or innovations in can manufacturing technology over time. In particular, it is necessary to determine the sealing or closing system of each can, the type of seam (particularly whether it is hand soldered, overlapped or double seamed) and ascertain the longevity of use of particular cans. Most of the major innovations were patented (hence datable) and are documented in a number of publications, e.g. National Canners Association 1963; Can Manufacturers Institute 1978; Busch 1981). A problem to be wary of is that sometimes several years elapsed between the granting of a patent and the widespread distribution of cans reflecting the innovation. The antiquity of a can may also be gleaned from research into product types or manufacturers if their names appear on the can remains.

Table 5.29 outlines the approximate known or inferred dates of usage of the main can types in New Zealand. The stated time spans are broad but they are able to be narrowed considerably, or specific can types seriated, by recognition of the "dating features" inherent in the construction of each can. Obviously, those that have short production (or user) spans are the most useful for dating, but most cans have some utility for dating in broad terms, so long as they are intact enough to enable one to recognise construction features.

All the can forms listed (except opium cans) have undergone constructional changes since their first appearance and their present form (or obsolescence), yet all have retained the same basic shape. The changes through time include the virtual abandonment of hole-and-cap cans after 1910, a progressive tendency to reduce both the size and the body weight of cans, machine soldering virtually eliminating hand soldering after about 1900, the introduction of the locked seam (which eliminated any soldering on the inside surfaces) and the development of seamless containers.

5.3.5.6 Conclusions

Cans are commonly-discarded artefacts that have considerable potential for more detailed analysis and hence the generation of new information on user groups. Their potential is at present unrealised, partly because of the focus by archaeologists on the analysis of more durable materials such as glass and ceramics. Although cans and metal boxes are "fragile" in the sense that their survival rate, due to oxidation, is a somewhat unknown factor, it is usually possible to determine both the form and approximate age of those that survive, even if the remains are in poor condition. There is also a difficulty in linking individual cans with specific contents, but it is still possible to generate meaningful cultural information by identifying particular can forms and deducing their likely contents, in a general rather than a specific sense.

This research soon revealed that not only are the earliest can manufacturers and users in New Zealand poorly documented (although from the outset they manufactured their own cans), there was little archaeologically-derived comparative material to draw on. Consequently, emphasis has been placed on defining can types, their construction features, changes through time and determining likely contents, to produce baseline data for New Zealand that other researchers can build on. Future studies will provide additional insights into the growing role of canned foods in New Zealand in the latter half of the 19th century and help confirm or refute some of the trends defined in this study (see Bedford 1985; Ritchie 1985). More product-specific analyses are needed to narrow or subdivide the broad date ranges which at present exist for some can types.

5.3.6 WAX VESTA MATCHBOXES

The two major research contributions on wax vesta boxes uncovered in New Zealand sites, Anson's (1983) pioneering typology and dating system and Bedford's (1984) streamlined classification, are both spin-offs from the Clutha archaeological project, of which this Chinese site research constitutes a major part. Furthermore, as some 700 of the boxes used in their respective studies were derived from the Chinese sites (i.e. the same data base), their results are particularly relevant.

Of the various artefacts that can be used for dating historic sites in New Zealand – e.g. bottles, coins, nails, buttons, ceramics and matchboxes – the latter may prove to be the most useful for "tight dating" because of their extensive usage (for fire, lantern, cigarette and pipe lighting), limited time of retention (most were discarded as soon as the matches were exhausted), wide range of brands, many (often subtle) constructional changes through time (documented by both Anson and Bedford) and their relative durability despite their tin composition. The solid and compact construction of wax vesta boxes and the fact that they were generally closed when discarded seems to aid their survival in sites, so that although they may be uncovered in a very fragile, encrusted or oxidised state, it is usually possible to determine the box type. Of the 1,191 boxes listed in Table 5.30, only 36 could not be identified because of their advanced state of deterioration.

Table 5.30 shows the types and site distribution of the matchboxes from the sites in the study area (the assemblage was used extensively in the formulation of Bedford's "simplified classification"). Only two of the listed sites are not specifically Chinese; namely, the Ledge, a European house dump; and a few surface-collected boxes recovered in the course of the Bendigo survey. The box types (i.e. Bedford's brand categories) are depicted in Figure 5.44:1–19.

5.3.6.1 Discussion

Although other studies are possible, e.g. determining the geographic distribution of brands and the origins of consumer goods, clearly the main utility of studying wax vesta boxes from archaeological deposits rests in their potential to assist in the dating of historic sites. In this regard, Anson (1983) produced both an absolute and a relative chronology for the matchboxes he studied, while Bedford, who had access to a much bigger sample, also took the known and inferred age of matchboxes into consideration in the formulation of his classification system.

Anson's relative chronology involved a multivariate cluster analysis based on matchbox-type percentages and the presence or absence of his defined constructional features. The results of the analysis indicated that the majority of the boxes with one-piece base and sides construction, flat smooth bases, side-added abrasive paste and vesta holding impresses were "early", i.e. pre-1885, whereas those with base and sides made from separate pieces of metal, heavily recessed and roughened bases and snap catches were "later", i.e. post-1885 (Anson 1983:133–4). In addition to being able to seriate the boxes, Anson worked towards absolute dating by researching the histories of wax vesta-producing companies and by cross dating some boxes by comparison with specimens from dated short occupation sites (British forts associated with the Māori Wars 1860s–1880s: (Prickett 1981; Spring-Rice 1982b).

As a result of Anson's and Bedford's work it is possible to suggest dates of occupation for most of the sites in this study. The dates and their validity are discussed now. Readers should be aware of two complicating factors. First, natural degradation of matchbox metal and differential survival means that there is an inherent bias in all matchbox assemblages towards the recovery of more recent boxes, simply because they have had less time to disintegrate in the ground compared to the earlier boxes. This in turn can lead to a tendency for sites to be dated "late". However, the problem of "late dating" will be gradually lessened as continuing historical research and cross dating progressively delimits the production and use spans of the various brands. The date of obsolescence of some brand categories is also poorly understood at present, consequently it is often difficult to suggest a terminal date for occupations. For the time being, we have a dating framework (Anson's system) and a flexible classification system (Bedford's) that can be expanded as more information comes to hand.

The second problem concerns sample size. As a rule of thumb, the larger and more varied a matchbox assemblage is, the better it is for determining probable dates of occupation. Small assemblages, say <10, can only be reliably used for dating in conjunction with other datable artefacts such as bottles.

5.3.6.2 Occupation dates of the study sites based on wax vesta box analysis

5.3.6.2.1 Firewood Creek, a rockshelter near Cromwell

Suggested date of occupation: mid-1880–1890s (Anson). This date is consistent with the occupation span as determined from glass analysis, but the site was probably occupied before 1880.

5.3.6.2.2 Caliche shelter, Cromwell Gorge

Occupied post-mid-1890s. This date is later than expected, but the box sample may be associated with a post-1900 occupation of the shelter by European rabbiters.

5.3.6.2.3 Sheung Fong and Ha Fong shelters, Cromwell Gorge

Suggested date of occupation: 1880s. Historical records suggest that these adjacent sites are likely to have also been occupied in the preceding decade.

5.3.6.2.4 Cromwell's Chinatown

A post-1895 date was suggested for Chinatown after study of 44 boxes from 11 box-bearing huts. The late date is inconsistent with the known occupation of the site from c.1870 until 1920, but only two huts produced definite pre-1895 boxes (Anson 1983), these boxes dating post-1870 into the 1880s. The problem here seems to be differential survival or discard (i.e. the earliest boxes in most hut assemblages have disintegrated or were discarded elsewhere).

5.3.6.2.5 Rockfall 1, a shelter in the Cromwell Gorge

Suggested date of occupation: 1870s–1880s. This date is consistent with other artefact dates and the historic settlement of the gorge.

5.3.6.2.6 QB2, Apple Tree, Sandy Point, Ah Wee's and the Poplars

Except for the Apple Tree site, analysis of the boxes from these widely separated hut sites in the Upper Clutha Valley suggested post-1895 occupations. Although these dates are internally consistent and tie in with the generally later mining of the Upper Clutha Valley, they probably date towards the end of the occupations rather than the beginning. Boxes recovered from the Apple Tree site date from the 1880s. It is known to have been occupied by an elderly Chinese miner in the first decade of the 20th century.

5.3.6.2.7 Hanging Rock and Riverside shelters, Kawarau Gorge

Only seven boxes were recovered in total from these sites. They suggest a pre-1885 date of occupation. The area is known from historic records to have been occupied from c.1870 on.

5.3.6.2.8 The Arrowtown Chinese Settlement

Some 210 boxes were recovered, reflecting occupation from the 1870s (see Table 5.30, types 1a, 5a) to post-1900. However, around 50% of the assemblage is composed of R. Bell & Co., New Zealand, stamped label boxes, dating post-1895. The dates suggested are consistent with the known occupation of the site, i.e. from c.1870 until the 1920s. As at Chinatown, the relatively small proportion of pre-1885 boxes may be attributable to degradation of the earlier boxes in the relatively damp (by Central Otago standards) site conditions.

5.3.6.2.9 Ah Lum's store, Arrowtown

Analysis of the 12 box assemblage suggested it was occupied post-1870 until post-1910, a date range that is consistent with the known dates of occupation from the late 1870s until the mid-1920s.

5.3.6.2.10 The Ledge, a large midden associated with a European house in the Kawarau Gorge

Of the 416 matchboxes recovered from the site, only five of Bedford's 19 brand categories were not represented. The vesta box assemblage from this site spurred Bedford to develop his classification system. This deposit clearly spans from c.1870 to post-1910. The volume and variety of boxes suggests the occupation was virtually continuous during this period.

5.3.6.2.11 Flax Grove, Kawarau Gorge

Twenty-one boxes of six types were found in this shelter (see Table 5.30). Their "dates" indicate the site was occupied from c.1880 until around the turn of the century. Some of the boxes, which had been poked into gaps between the stones in the shelter wall, were in pristine condition. Dates on pieces of newspaper that had been crumpled up and also poked into the wall (to prevent draughts) indicate the site was definitely occupied between 1893 and 1897.

5.4 OPIUM USAGE AND THE ASSOCIATED MATERIAL CULTURE

The narcotic and sleep-inducing qualities of the opium poppy (*Papaver somniferum*) have been known for many centuries. It is first mentioned on Sumerian tablets from the 4th millennium BC (Stanford University Museum 1979:2). From the Middle East, its usage spread to Greece, Persia and India. It was probably introduced into China in the 13th century (Holmes 1911:130). Opium was used principally as a medical panacea, relaxant, and to allay hunger pangs; uses not to be usurped until the 19th century when alternative drugs and painkillers became available (*Encyclopedia Britannica* 1979 Vol. 5:1,052). The drug was socially acceptable in most countries for "recreational purposes", because unlike alcohol, users were peaceable and did not disturb public order (Eldred-Grigg 1984:110).

Opium usage was not considered a serious problem in China until after 1773, when the British East India Company gained a monopoly on opium cultivation in India and began importing increasingly larger quantities of Indian opium into the country. The resultant drain of silver from China caused serious social and economic repercussions. The Chinese Court repeatedly attempted to stem the importation of opium, but the prohibition itself promoted corruption within the Chinese trading community, abetted by Hong Kong-based British merchant companies (Collis 1941). An attempt by the Chinese to curb opium imports was the direct cause of the First Opium War, which broke out in 1839. The British used "gunboat diplomacy" to protect their established opium trade and demanded and gained the ceding of Hong Kong to Britain as restitution. The Chinese government made many attempts between 1839 and 1858 to suppress the importation of opium but was thwarted because many of the provincial viceroys encouraged the trade, including home cultivation. The latter activity increased so rapidly that by 1900 opium was cultivated in every province in China (Holmes 1911:130).

By the mid-19th century there was widespread social turmoil in the southern provinces of China due to banditry, rebellion, land shortages, corruption and European imperialism. Opium usage flourished and was practised by many of the Chinese who left their homeland to work on the goldfields of the United States, Canada, Australia and New Zealand. In New Zealand it was introduced, along with traditional smoking paraphernalia, during the first substantial immigrations of Chinese into the Otago goldfields after 1866.

5.4.1 A SOCIO-HISTORICAL OUTLINE OF OPIUM SUPPLY AND USAGE IN NEW ZEALAND

Opium usage and the associated trade was an integral part of life among the Chinese on the southern goldfields. For the Chinese business community, it was a highly marketable commodity (and the most profitable), while smoking the drug, together with gambling, were important forms of relaxation for the Chinese miners. Three grades of opium were recognised in China:

1. "raw opium", as imported from India;
2. "prepared opium", raw opium that was purified by a boiling, maceration and filtering process;
3. "opium dross", the scrapings from opium pipes, which were reboiled and manufactured into a second-class prepared opium.

Prepared opium (also called boiled opium) has a thick treacle-like consistency and was usually exported in this form to America, Australia and elsewhere (Culin 1891a:498; Holmes 1911:136).

Bulk opium was shipped to New Zealand in "large chests" (Don 1/12/1888:106), probably like the wooden chests used for importing the raw product into China. They weighed 150 lb (Collis 1941:76). Lesser amounts were shipped in crates containing a range of products as ordered by individual merchants in New Zealand. Regardless of the size of the bulk shipment containers, each contained a number of small brass boxes of processed opium weighing 5 tael apiece (also referred to as *leung* or Chinese ounces). A tael weighed 1.33 ounces avoirdupois, so the contents of a single box weighed 6.65 ounces. No records have been found that itemise the types of opium that were sold in New Zealand, but a situation similar to that in the United States probably prevailed where several brands of varying qualities were available (Jones et al. 1979:43; Sando and Felton 1984:16–18). Pipe scrapings were also resold.

Culin (1891:499), who studied Chinese opium smoking in Philadelphia, noted that most of the opium brought into the United States was shipped via Hong Kong, where it was prepared. This was known as "superior opium". Two main brands were sold at US$9.00 per can/box. These were known by the producing company names Lai Un and Fuk Lung. A cheaper opium (prepared in Victoria, British Columbia) was sold at US$6.80 for a 5-tael can. The scrapings from opium pipes were always carefully preserved. These were reboiled with an admixture of fresh opium and sold as "number two opium" or "opium refuse mass" (Culin 1891:499). Holmes (1911:136) describes the exported opium as "being carefully sealed up in small pots having the name of the maker (i.e. *hong*) on each", whereas Culin (1891:498) noted that in China "(prepared) opium was put in white porcelain pots holding 5 *leung* (tael) for local use and in brass cans containing the same amount for export".

Don's writings indicate (see later discussion) that opium costs varied, presumably being dependent on the mark up, quality and volume purchased. He refers to "tins" and "pots" but in no instance does he mention the weight or size of the containers. Regarding the "tins", he is almost certainly referring to the standard 5 tael (6.65 oz) opium cans that are commonly found in sites (see Table 5.33 and related discussion). The "pots" he referred to may be the same type of vessels in which prepared opium was distributed in China. The presence of "pots" may also reflect processing of the drug locally – perhaps the preparation of a product similar to the "number two opium" described above.

According to Culin (1891:500), "opium was not sold (in Philadelphia) directly from the can by the retail merchant, but always from a large pottery vessel". Many of the purchasers had a small horn box to carry their opium or the merchant supplied them with "an ordinary playing card, ingeniously cut and folded into a small shallow box, which he balanced upon the pan of the hand scale. Opium is invariably sold in this manner... the customer watching the operation, solicitous of obtaining good weight" (Culin 1891:500). Although the archaeological evidence indicates that many of the Chinese miners in Central Otago purchased opium by the 5-tael can, presumably lesser amounts could be purchased and carried in a suitable container, possibly old opium cans supplied by the opium seller. A European observer who visited a Chinese miner's camp in the Shotover Valley noted that "two of the inmates had an ivory box of the prepared drug" (*Otago Witness* 9/10/1875); it was probably similar to the horn boxes described above.

Initially, opium could be imported into New Zealand with no restrictions, but it was not long before the government levied an importation duty. The first duty levied on the importation of opium was recorded in the Statistics of New Zealand in 1869. The rate of £1 sterling per lb weight was increased to £2 per lb in 1888. Initially, opium was imported from Victoria, New South Wales and the United Kingdom, but from 1878 it was shipped directly from China (Statistics of New Zealand; see Appendix 6).

Judging from the sparse references in contemporary newspapers, it appears the importation and sale of opium by the Chinese was initially of little concern to the European populace, although the *Report of the Select Committee on Chinese Immigration 1871* (Buckingham 1974) made several references to it. Don's articles make frequent reference to the habit. Like gambling, it was a social problem for Don and the Church since it hindered their work and very often caused financial hardship and deterioration of the health of regular users.

By 1880 there was an increasing amount of anti-Chinese agitation among some sectors of the New Zealand community, including demands for a ban on further Chinese immigration into New Zealand. This resulted, in 1881, in the first of a series of legislative restrictions on Chinese immigration (see Section 2.3), and gradually developed into a process of squeezing out the Chinese by making their lives miserable.

In 1882, the Customs Consolidation Law was passed, which placed a partial prohibition on the import of opium by decreeing that opium could not be imported "unless in ships of 40 registered tons burden at least, and in whole or complete packages, each containing not less than 45 lb nett weight; and only into such ports as are or may be approved by the Governor for the importing and warehousing of opium" (New Zealand Board of Health 1970:112). The objective of the legislation is unclear. It was possibly motivated by a concern that Chinese importers were getting small but regular opium supplies into the country duty free by shipping it in mixed consignments. However, the imposition in 1888 of an increased duty on rice, tea and opium was clearly part of the plan to discourage permanent Chinese settlement in New Zealand.

Chinese merchants in the principal ports of New Zealand responded to the anti-Chinese agitation by starting an anti-opium crusade. They formed the Cherishing Virtue Union and tried to enforce the following rules, which were distributed and posted on placards:

1. No opium is to be sold after October 4th (1888) at New Zealand ports and after December 2nd up country.
2. Anyone secretly importing is to be fined £120 for every large chest seized.
3. Anyone buying from a non-Chinese is to be fined £5 for every tin so bought.
4. In both of the above cases the opium will also be confiscated.
5. Anti-opium medicinal pills are to be distributed free to cure those having the opium habit

(Don 1/12/1888:106).

The objective of the Chinese merchants' crusade appears to have been principally retaliation rather than concern over the effects of opium usage among the Chinese. They sought to deprive the government of the sizeable duty on opium imports, which was stated to be £10,000 at the time (Don 1/12/1888:106).

The beneficial effects of the Association apparently lasted only a short time; smokers tried to quit the habit but often merely replaced it with gambling (Don 1/4/1889:185). The importation of opium declined in 1888, as evidenced by the £634 drop in duty revenue, but the following year it soared to over £7,000 (see Appendix 6). Many shops continued to sell it, and the cure was only distributed in very small quantities (Don 1/4/1889:185). Some deferred to older remedies. One "cure" that was popular was as follows: "2 mace of burnt alum, 4 mace of opium ashes, stir into milk or coconut and allow to stand for a week. Whenever craving occurs, take a Chinese wine cup full of the mixture" (Don 1/4/1889:185).

By the middle of 1889 the Association had been wound up. The organisers posted a public notice that said: "The former arrangements for the Cherishing Virtue Union with regard to the two matters of abstaining from opium and cherishing virtue have unavoidably come to naught through differences of opinion. Contributors, on application to the managers who have received their contribution, may have the same refunded" (Don 1/7/1889:3). Although Don did not specify the cause of the disagreement, it probably revolved around the loss to the merchants of the enormous profits from opium importation and distribution (although exact figures are not known). Merchants who stopped selling opium also probably suffered a decline in other business. Furthermore, by the late 1880s the habit was well entrenched and there was little desire on the part of most regular users to abstain from the drug. Over 3,000 lb of the drug were imported legally each year after 1880. Opium smoking became more prevalent as times became harsher.

In 1901, the *Opium Prohibition Act* was passed after persistent lobbying by New Zealand Chinese who viewed opium smoking as an unfilial pursuit, although Seddon, the then prime minister, was reluctant to pass the Bill because the government would lose the revenue hitherto collected on imported opium. Two petitions presented to the government in 1900 and 1901 "praying that an Act be passed prohibiting or limiting the importation of opium and controlling the sale or use thereof" had a total of 623 signatories (mostly Chinese supported by European ministers; see AJHR 1901 3 3–1:8; AJHR 1901 4 I-2:7. The Act had the stated intention of preventing the importation of opium by the Chinese. It made it an offence to import opium in any form suitable for smoking and required special permission for its import in any other form (New Zealand Board of Health 1970:113). The dramatic drop in opium importation (based on duties collected: 1901 £6,617, 1902 £270, 1903 £101; see Appendix 6) clearly indicates that most of the opium imported into New Zealand in the 19th century was imported for consumption by Chinese and the trade was in the hands of Chinese merchants.

Until 1901, opium was available off the shelf in Chinese grocery stores. More isolated miners received their supplies in the weekly mail (Don 1896:18). There was a common misconception at the time that the 1901 Act banned the sale of opium or related preparations to Chinese, but this was not so until 1910, when pharmacists were also compelled to keep an "opium sales register" (in part brought about by further petitions in 1904 seeking that more drastic measures be taken for the suppression of opium smoking and gambling among the Chinese). The 1901 restriction (consolidated with 1902 and 1906 amendments, it became the *Opium Prohibition Act 1908*) related solely to importation by the Chinese. It gave the police the right to search without warrant any premises occupied by Chinese where they had reasonable cause to suspect that opium smoking was going on, permitted or abetted (New Zealand Board of Health 1970:113).

The *Opium Prohibition Act* forced Chinese opium users to resort to more covert methods for obtaining their supplies. Some were able to procure tincture of opium (laudanum), which was still available to Europeans for medicinal purposes. In Roxburgh, for example, sympathetic Europeans are known to have regularly obtained tincture of opium for Chinese friends or employees by claiming to the pharmacist that the drug was required "to treat a sick horse". The last entry in the Roxburgh chemist's "opium register" is dated 1921. The register covers sales of tincture of opium which sold for 2/6 per ounce. On evaporation of the alcohol, it would yield a piece of opium about the size of a pea (Jeffrey, ex chemist, pers. comm.). An old account book from an orchard in the same area reveals that the European employer regularly docked 2/- or so from his Chinese employees' wages for opium purchases on their behalf. Again, the reason cited for the purchases was "veterinary purposes" (Chandler pers. comm). The use of subterfuges such as this was probably widespread. This so-called "Sunday trade" to the Chinese is acknowledged in a government report on drug abuse (New Zealand Board of Health 1970:115). The decline in availability of opium may also have led to an increase in consumption of opium-based medicines, although this is difficult to quantify archaeologically because opium derivatives formed the basis of many pain relief medications until relatively recently, c.1960s.

Some bowls may have been deliberately broken to enable the maximum recovery of any opium residues adhering to the inside surfaces. Possibly the craving for the narcotic outweighed any concern about the cost of a replacement bowl.

The prohibition also led to the small-scale but persistent smuggling of opium into New Zealand, the drug being primarily destined for elderly Chinese addicts, who had largely removed to dilapidated enclaves in Dunedin and Wellington. Despite the legislation, opium continued to be smoked by a few elderly Chinese up until at least the 1960s, their supplies being obtained from compassionate doctors in later years (Butler 1977:68). In Wellington, the houses of elderly Chinese in Haining Street were regularly raided by police in the late 1950s to early 1960s. The police seized opium, smoking equipment and gambling tickets (the two vices were often carried on together). Customs records of this period also indicate frequent opium seizures off foreign vessels in New Zealand ports (Hocken Library records).

5.4.2 THE SOCIAL EFFECTS OF OPIUM SMOKING

Many, if not most, of the Chinese stores on the goldfields offered opium smoking and gambling facilities (see Section 3.3.1), which often accounted for the lion's share of storekeeper's income. Opium smoking and gambling were also commonly carried out in "houses" especially set up for the purpose in most districts. The smoking houses were equipped with "bunks", a platform about 1.2 m wide and 60 cm off the floor (sometimes two tiered) on which the smokers lay. Rev. Don's writings abound with references to opium smoking and contain numerous insights into the social role and effects of the drug. In terms of numbers of venues, he noted that "the 5 opium houses serving a population of 90 at Waikaia was an unusually large number in relation to the population" (Don 2/4/1888:185). Although miners regularly smoked opium at their claims or camps, most enjoyed the service provided by an opium house keeper and the companionship of the other clientele. According to an authority on addiction, "the opium smoker wants company, is talkative, his mind turns in a philosophical direction… and he is at peace with everyone" (Courtwright 1982:27).

A European observer made these observations about an "opium den" located behind a gambling hall in the Lawrence Chinese Camp:

> There are… a number of ante-rooms, set apart for smoking opium. The largest is not much more capacious than an ordinary-sized packing case. They are neither lighted nor ventilated, and as each of them is supposed to accommodate six smokers, their noisome condition can be easily imagined. The floor is elevated a few inches above the ground. The opium board with the small lamp attached is placed in the centre, around which the occupants squat down in tailor-like fashion and blow away at the noxious vapour. By degrees it takes effect upon them, and they drop back into a wooden board, blocked out in the centre for the express purpose of securing their bodies in reclining posture… The ostensible object of these dens is to provide relaxation to those engaged in the play, and although anyone is admitted on the payment of 6d, the habitue of the gambling table is the most frequent occupant… Although a pernicious practice, it can scarcely be deemed a public scandal. It debases the individual but does not outrage public decency by exhibitions of pothouse pugilism and street brawling, therefore it becomes us not to be too severe in the strictures we put upon it. (*Otago Daily Times* 1/10/1869:10)

There were two sorts of users: casual smokers who enjoyed an occasional smoke, often after the evening meal (Don 2/4/1888:185); and habitual users who had developed a dependence and became very distressed if there was a shortfall in supply for any reason (Don 1896:18). In one instance, Don observed that "all the opium pipes are being scraped to the core to obtain 'ashes' where-with to take off the sharp points of the craving" (Don quoted in Butler 1977:68). Users often smoked in pairs, one preparing the pipe while the other savoured the effects of the drug (*Otago Witness* 9/10/1875).

Many opium users suffered progressively deteriorating health and poverty. Some claimed they could not work without it (Don 1891:8). The percentage of New Zealand Chinese who were habitually addicted is not known, but in the United States it has been estimated that between 15% and 30% were addicted (Courtwright 1982:26). I would estimate from Don's comments, other ethno-historical observations, the opium importation records (see Appendix 6) and the archaeological evidence that upwards of 60% of the Chinese smoked opium but less than 10% were seriously addicted.

Don noted that heavy smokers were ostracised and usually lived and worked alone because "without exception no one would partner someone who wouldn't pull their weight" (Don 1/6/1885:224). He noted heavy smokers smoked between 3/- and 14/- worth per week (Don 1/11/1884:85, 1/3/1888:166), whereas an average miner's income varied from 10/- to £4 a week. One worker at the Phoenix battery in the Shotover Valley smoked a tin (size unstated) every five weeks; tins at that time costing 35/- each (Don 1890:8). Obviously, if a miner was doing poorly, these outgoings would deplete his income fairly rapidly, and the associated physiological problems such as stomach ache and sleepiness would result in lost mining time, which in turn would lessen income. If one needed a Chinese doctor, of which there were several offering their expensive services on the goldfields, then he was confronted with an additional problem because it was customary to not only provide the doctor with room and board but also pay for his opium. Don recorded that one Dr Chow, called on by a man to tend his broken leg, consumed "ten pots of opium in four and a half months, costing a total of £15" (i.e. 30/- per pot; Don 1/9/1883:47).

5.4.3 OPIUM SMOKING: THE METHOD AND THE TECHNOLOGY

The narcotic effect of opium is obtained by inhaling smoke given off from a piece of heated opium resin. Opium is traditionally smoked in an "opium pipe", the antiquity of which is unknown but certainly precedes the upsurge of smoking in China during and after the late 18th century.

Opium pipes consist of three main components – a stem, a pipe bowl and a connecting saddle (Figure 5.45). The stems were usually made of bamboo cut to about 60 cm in length and 10 cm in circumference (Kane 1882:33). The bamboo was cut so that one end of the pipe was effectively sealed by one of the natural partitions in the stem of the bamboo. Good pipes were equipped with an ivory mouthpiece. At a point approximately two-thirds of the distance along the pipe from the mouthpiece, a hole was cut into the stem to accommodate a brass saddle to which a ceramic bowl was fitted. A scrap of cloth (known as the *gee* rag) was used to ensure a tight fit between the neck of the bowl and the brass connecting flange.

Although there are many stylistic differences between bowls, each conforms to the same general design, having a relatively flat under surface in the centre of which there is a small hole, c. 3 mm in diameter, through which the air-opium smoke mixture is drawn into the pipe. From this surface the sides of a pipe bowl rise to culminate in a neck flange that fits into the neck of a brass saddle to effect a connection to a pipe stem. Sometimes the bowl flanges were chipped off and replaced with a metal rim, which was fastened to the bowl with burnt alum (Kane 1882:35). Archaeological evidence of this practice is outlined later.

Other articles in a smoker's kit included a container (often a small box of buffalo horn) to keep the opium, a needle (*yen hauck*) on which the opium was positioned in the bowl (see below) and "cooked", an opium lamp (described later), a pair of scissors for trimming the wick, straight and curved knives for cleaning the bowl of the ash (*yen zi*) that collects and renders the pipe foul, a saucer to hold this ash, a sponge to wipe the surface of the bowl, and a tray to hold all of these items (Kane 1882:35–6).

There is some disagreement in the literature as to the exact smoking method. There are reasonable grounds (based on examination of various accounts of the opium-smoking procedure and study of the burn locations and residues on several hundred pipe bowl fragments from the study sites) to suggest that more than one technique was commonly employed. The act of smoking involved the following basic actions:

1. digging a small amount of opium (a viscous black material) out of a container;
2. rolling it on a flat surface to make it globous;
3. impaling it on an opium needle and "cooking" it over an opium lamp;
4. securing the heated opium to the outer surface of the bowl by pushing the needle through the small aperture in the smoking surface of the bowl. This left the opium mass surrounding the aperture;
5. inclining the pipe over an opium lamp and inhaling the smoke as soon as the flame contacted the opium.

This is essentially the method outlined by Kane (1882: 41–2) and Dobie (1936:254).

Two other methods have been described both involving placing the opium inside the bowl. Etter (1980:99) states that a heated opium pellet was inserted through the small aperture in the smoking surface of the bowl. The needle was then removed, leaving the smoking resin on the inside of the smoking surface. The user then inhaled, finishing the "smoke" in about 30 seconds (Etter 1980:99).

Etter (1980:99) appears to be describing the same method of opium smoking as that outlined by Kane (1882:41–2). Wylie (1980:3) suggested another possible technique: the opium was placed inside the bowl first and then heated by applying direct heat to the smoking surface. He considered use of this method would account for the recovery of many badly charred remnants of smoking surfaces. Since the same "damage pattern" would occur on smoking surfaces from the method outlined by Kane (1882) and Dobie (1936), Wylie's suggestion requires further research to confirm it as a definite smoking technique.

There are no ethnographic accounts detailing precisely how opium was smoked by the Chinese on the southern goldfields, but as some 50% of the 200-odd smoking surface fragments examined in this study are heavily charred on the exterior while others are relatively clean, it seems likely that more than one method was used, it being merely a matter of personal preference. Examination of bowl fragments shows that the small aperture in the smoking surface was often enlarged up to 1.2 cm in diameter by reaming it out with a file or grinding tool. Enlargement of the apertures would seem unnecessary for smoking by the method described by Kane, but would facilitate the insertion of an opium ball into the interior of a pipe bowl (for smoking by the methods outlined by Etter and Wylie) and/or the removal of ash residues.

5.4.4 ARCHAEOLOGICAL EVIDENCE OF OPIUM SMOKING

In New Zealand, physical evidence of Chinese opium smoking in the 19th century is almost totally limited to the discarded and broken artefacts found in archaeological contexts. Surprisingly few opium-related artefacts have found their way into museum collections, and there are relatively few written observations and no pictorial records of the practice of opium smoking.

This study of Chinese opium smoking in Central Otago is based substantially on the analysis of approximately 1,500 archaeologically-derived artefacts (often fragmentary) that are known to have been associated with opium smoking. These include the remains of ceramic pipe bowls (1,075 fragments), other pipe components (29), opium cans (182) and heating lamps (51), as well 43 auxiliary artefacts (described later). The numerical data presented here renders that presented by Ritchie and Harrison (1982) obsolete.

The artefacts were derived primarily from 16 of the 20 study sites (see Tables 5.31–5.37). Additional material for comparative analysis was obtained from examination of five private collections containing artefacts from the business area of Cromwell's Chinatown (upper Chinatown), the Nokomai and Cardrona Valleys, Macetown and the Wakatipu Basin. Small surface collections were also studied from a Chinese hut (S133/621) in the Roaring Meg Creek, a rockshelter (S133/72) near the mouth of the Kawarau Gorge, an unrecorded rockshelter in Conroy's Gully near Alexandra and a cache of opium cans uncovered near a Chinese hut (S133/430) sited some 500 metres upstream of Cromwell's Chinatown. In addition, material uncovered during a testing program in around 30 Chinese rockshelters in the Cromwell Gorge was incorporated into the analysis. The sites span the period from c.1870 until 1925.

5.4.4.1 Artefacts associated with opium smoking

The artefacts associated with opium smoking were made of several different materials. Consequently, their durability and survivability in archaeological contexts varies considerably. Broken fragments of the ceramic pipe bowls and the flattened remains of the brass opium cans are the most frequently uncovered "opium artefacts", followed by artefacts made from opium can metal (especially "funs trays", described later), metal connecting flanges and opium-heating lamps (made from modified glass bottles). Two fittings that are believed to be opium pipe mouthpieces have been recovered, but no evidence of the bamboo pipe stems has been found. This is understandable. A regular smoker is unlikely to have left his pipes behind when he moved. Bowls and stems that had been used and were well saturated with opium were highly prized by their owners. They acquired an "heirloom value" and commanded high prices (Culin 1891:499). In the unlikely event that a pipe (stem) was left in an abandoned Chinese dwelling, it is likely to have been removed, souvenired or decomposed.

The various opium-related artefacts are discussed now, beginning with a discourse on and presentation of a Central Otago opium pipe bowls typology. The widespread distribution and durability of bowl fragments make these artefacts particularly useful for comparative research. The bowl study is followed by a discussion on opium cans and artefacts made from can metal, followed by a review of the other artefacts associated with opium smoking. In the concluding discussion, behavioural interpretations based on the archaeological evidence are presented.

5.4.4.2 Introduction to opium pipe bowls

The discussion on opium pipe bowls is divided into three sections:

a. their manufacture;
b. the packaging, distribution and sale of opium pipe bowls and other smoking equipment;
c. a stylistic analysis and typology of the bowl forms recovered from Chinese sites in Central Otago.

5.4.4.2.1 Manufacture

The manufacturing techniques of the opium pipe bowls can be readily inferred from study of the bowl fragments. Without exception they are made from stoneware and earthenware clays. The upper part of the bowl and the smoking surface were made in separate moulds, then the latter component was slip-welded to the bowl proper. The delicate thinness of the bowls and fingerprints on the inside surface indicate the two portions were joined together while the clay was still fairly wet. In some cases, a brush or smoothing tool appears to have been inserted through the neck to further seal the bowl and smoking surface along their inside margin. Frequently, this joint proves to have fused poorly; many broken bowl fragments show a "clean break" along the rim.

Less is known or can be inferred about the bowl manufacturing sites or factories in South China. The prevalence of press moulding and the consistent form of opium pipe bowls suggests a reasonably organised production format, rather than large numbers of different village kilns "doing their own thing" and producing a wide range of distinctive styles of handmade pipe bowls. However, the latter possibility cannot be precluded, as several types of mass-produced, but standardised, ceramic wares, notably food containers and tablewares, were produced in widely scattered village kilns. It is also not certain whether the individual styles (refer the typology, Table 5.31) were produced by single or regional kiln sites, or if each "production centre" produced several styles. Press moulding would have facilitated relatively easy conversion from the production of one style to another so that a range of styles could have been produced either simultaneously or in a chronological sequence. Assuming there were several centres or factories manufacturing opium pipe bowls, some quality control is attested by the even standard of the finished products. Most bowl forms have been found in both slipped and unslipped variants. The differences may reflect either minor stylistic changes that developed through time or individual factory or kiln sites' responses to production contracts for certain bowl forms from Chinese entrepreneurs.

The use of at least two major fine clay types can be promulgated from an examination of the pipe bowl fragments uncovered in Central Otago. The differing clay types are evidenced by different firing colours: orange and grey. These clays must have been derived from two discrete but not necessarily unrelated clay sources in South China. Trace element analysis of the clays of the various bowl types may shed some light on the number of quarry sources for the pipe clays. This in turn might support inferences about multiple manufacturing centres.

5.4.4.2.2 The packaging, distribution and sale of opium-smoking equipment

Very little has been recorded about the packaging, distribution and sale of opium-smoking equipment. However, it is known that like the processed smoking opium, smoking equipment was manufactured in China and shipped out through the main ports of egress, Canton and Hong Kong, to overseas Chinese merchants who undertook the distribution and sale of the products at the market end. Culin (1891:499) observed that Chinese shops (in the United States) sold everything required by smokers. The bamboo pipe stems cost (in US currency) from $1.00 to $1.25 and upwards depending on their thickness, the connecting sockets (flanges) were 25c and bowls were 50c apiece. Old pipes were frequently offered for sale at $10 and upwards, while pipe stands cost 75c and opium lamps 75c to $1. The latter were said to be made in Birmingham, England, but imported via China (Culin 1891:499).

Thus far, no records have been found that detail the way opium-smoking equipment was sold in New Zealand, or its cost. Presumably, complete pipes could be obtained and replacement parts (particularly bowls) were freely available. The buyer probably had a choice of several bowl styles (as found in archaeological contexts). This may reflect different shipments or sources of origin (i.e. consignments from different kilns).

Opium pipe bowls are relatively fragile and would have had to be well packed to survive the long journey from China to the Central Otago goldfields intact. The shape of the bowls precludes nesting several units for transportation. Chinese ceramic wares (possibly including opium pipe bowls) were landed at Dunedin in mixed consignments packed in straw or rice chaff inside the large brownware barrel jars (Roebuck pers. comm. 1984). This may have been a common method of shipment. The recovery of clean broken bowl fragments suggests that sometimes pipe bowls were broken and discarded before they were used.

5.4.4.2.3 Opium pipe bowls: morphology and typology

The following comments on opium pipe bowl morphology and the typology are based on an analysis of a minimum of 127 pipe bowls (1,075 fragments) derived from the study sites in Central Otago. A further 17 pipe bowls (many reconstructed from fragments) held in private collections were also examined. Twelve basic types have been isolated; these have been further subdivided into 26 subgroups based on stylistic differences (Figure 5.47). Minimum numbers were determined by:

1. counts of intact neck-connecting flanges within each site or collection;
2. counts of the minimum number of identifiable types within a site or collection.

The greater of these two counts was taken as the minimum number for any one site or collection. Owing to the multiplicity of fragments that are usually created when a pipe bowl is broken, counts of side or smoking surface fragments are totally unreliable for minimum number purposes.

An examination of the available literature (mostly US reports) on opium pipe remains (e.g. Bente 1976; Hattori et al. 1979; Etter 1980; Jones et al. 1979; Jones 1980; Wylie 1980; LaLande 1981; Skinner pers. comm. 1982; Miller 1983; and Wylie and Fike 1985) indicates that the range of types detailed here is by no means exhaustive. However, it does incorporate all the presently known forms found in Central Otago (and elsewhere in New Zealand). Approximately 700 of the total sample of bowl fragments could be confidently ascribed to a particular type. To date, none of the higher quality stoneware and glazed porcelain pipe bowls that have been uncovered in some sites in the United States (Etter 1980:98; Miller 1983:5) have been found in New Zealand.

5.4.4.3 Bowl morphology

The basic terminology of an opium pipe bowl is depicted in Figure 5.46. Most bowls are 4–5 cm high (including the neck and connecting flange), while the smoking surfaces vary from 5 to 9 cm in diameter. According to Harney and Cross (1975:57), the design and dimensions of the bowl "were very carefully calculated to produce a maximum amount of distillation with a minimum amount of incineration of the opium in the process of smoking".

The recovered bowls occur in only two basic colour variations – orange and grey – although there is considerable variation (often within one type), particularly in the hue of the orange bowl sherds, due to handling, carbon deposits, opium residues and whether the sherds are slipped or unslipped. Bowls of both colours are made of fine-quality clay, the grey ones being made of a very fine stoneware clay or a grey firing earthenware.

All the Central Otago bowl forms are unglazed, but many grey and orange sherds have a high sheen. This is attributed to a "kiln glaze" formed during the firing process. Slipped (bearing a coating of a fine clear slip) and unslipped variants of many of the bowl types have been recovered. Underfiring is evidenced by a grey-black band in the cross-section of some bowl sherds. This feature indicates the bowls have only undergone a single firing (Doo pers. comm. 1979).

Many of the recovered bowl fragments have handwritten Chinese characters inscribed on their side facets. Translations indicate the calligraphy (usually between two and five characters) consists of euphoric phrases such as "Double Radiance" or "Moon over the Flowers". In addition, some bowls have a small, framed cartouche impressed into the side. These probably state the name of the kiln or village of origin of the pipe bowls, but the examples that have been translated have not obviously referred to particular locations.

5.4.4.4 A typology of opium pipe bowls

The shape of the smoking surface is the primary distinguishing criteria used in the typology presented here. Each pipe type is prefixed "C", "H" or "O", depending on whether its smoking surface is circular, hexagonal or octagonal. The letter is followed by a number that indicates a discrete type based on the bowl's morphology. The trailing letters (a, b, c etc.) indicate variants (subtypes). The characteristics of each type and known variants are outlined in the typology (Table 5.31) and they are depicted in Figure 5.47. The minimum numbers of each subtype found in the study sites are summarised in Table 5.32. Their distribution is examined in the concluding discussion in this section.

5.4.4.5 Opium cans

Remains of the small brass cans in which opium was imported are found in or on the surface of most Chinese sites in Central Otago. Only one size has been recovered – a straight-sided, rectangular, flanged-lid can standing 9.5 cm high, with basal dimensions of 6.6 cm by 4.1 cm (Figure 5.48a). They held 5 *leung* (taels), equivalent to 186.5g.

The cans consist of five components – a body, a top and base, and two "sealing" strips. The body was produced by placing a rectangular sheet of brass around a block and beating the metal into the required shape. The side seam was then overlapped and soldered. A small rectangular brass sheet was used for the base. Small notches were cut in the corners, enabling the edges to be bent up to form a lip. This was placed on one end of the body section and soldered on. The lids were made in a similar fashion, except that a 0.9–1.2 mm wide strip of brass (0.2 mm thick) was soldered to the lid section to form a flange. In addition, a heavier gauge (0.5 mm thick) "reinforcing strip" was fitted around the interior of the lip of the can. Thus, the can lids could be slipped off and on the cans easily and effected a tight seal.

In five of the study sites, half opium cans were recovered (Table 5.33). These were formed by cutting an intact can around the midpoint. One of the half cans, found within hut 6 at Chinatown, contained a sizeable block of opium resin (Figure 5.48a). The can also differed in that the label (largely illegible) was printed on green paper rather than the usual orange. The half cans may have been cut down for easier access to the contents, or sold in this manner (i.e. as half portions).

Due to the softness and thinness of the metal, opium cans are generally recovered in a flattened condition. Frequently, the five basic can components have come apart and are found widely dispersed. This presents a problem when determining minimum numbers because it is difficult to distinguish an opium can lid from a base if the lid-sealing strip is missing.

Most (if not all) opium can lids have an impressed cartouche (see Figures 5.48b and 5.49), while many bases also bear a cartouche. There are two common cartouche shapes, "coffin shaped" (in a frame) and "rectangular" (usually unframed), and a rarer elongate "octagonal" (framed) shape. Translation of cartouches indicates they state the names of manufacturers, brands or "general greetings" to the user. Because cartouche measurements may eventually prove useful for distinguishing between bases and lids, a typology of cartouche marks incorporating dimensions, shape, translations and other details is presented in Table 5.34, while Table 5.35 details the numbers and distribution of the various cartouche marks.

As noted above, opium cans originally had orange-coloured paper labels. Of the 182 cans examined in this study (Table 5.33) only three had partially legible labels. Two of these are depicted in Plate 20.

5.4.4.6 Artefacts made from opium can metal

The Chinese made many artefacts from the brass metal of spent opium cans (Table 5.36). The major usage, in numerical terms (116 from the study sites), was the production of small shallow trays known as "funs" (Figure 5.50a; Roebuck pers. comm. 1981). A "fan", pronounced "fun" (Wegars pers. comm.) is a Chinese unit of measure (c. five grains; Culin 1891:497). These trays appear to have served the same role as the folded playing cards commonly used by Chinese merchants in the United States for weighing out opium (Culin 1891:500). Despite their prevalence in Chinese sites in Central Otago, the only funs tray reported in the US literature is a single specimen from the Woodland Chinese site in California (Felton et al. 1984:68–9).

All the funs trays recovered from the study sites are made from the body metal of opium cans, except four from the Northburn shelter site that are made of tin but formed in the same fashion. No two are identical, but they generally measure about 3.0 cm by 2.3 cm with a depth of 0.4 cm. However, a few are quite small, measuring about 2 cm by 2 cm. Five suspected funs tray preforms have also been recovered. These appear to have been cut to shape but not actually folded into trays. A small "tray" made of can metal from the Poplars site has the appearance of a "double length" funs tray.

A total of 45 funs trays were recovered by excavation within the Cromwell Chinese Camp. Of this total, 43 were completed and two were preforms. One or two funs were found in most of the huts, but in huts 23 and 33, 18 and 14 were uncovered respectively. Hut 23, based on associated evidence, notably the can remains, clearly seems to have been a major opium-smoking venue, while the incidence of funs in hut 33 also suggests high usage.

In most sites several cut "scraps" of opium can metal were recovered (Table 5.36). Some of these probably represent offcuts formed during the production of funs trays, while others appear to have been produced during the formation of other artefacts from can metal, e.g. thin strips of metal were used to tie two items together, in a manner similar to the modern tie-tag (in Chinatown, a

Chinese coin was found attached to a piece of iron chain with a twisted strip of opium can metal). Occasionally, small disc-shaped pieces of can metal (15–20 mm across) are recovered. These possibly served as game counters or pan weights. Similar pieces were found in the Yreka and Woodlands sites in California (Helvey and Felton 1979; Felton et al. 1984:69–70). Other disc-like offcuts were used as washers or for enlarging the head of a nail in order to secure objects more effectively, e.g. the "blinds" covering two of the windows in the Chinese store at Arrowtown were secured with opium can "washers". Remnants of the original paper labels on the opium cans still adhered to the metal (Ritchie 1984:54).

Another frequently uncovered opium can metal artefact (Table 5.36) is miniature "gold blowing trays" (Figure 5.50b). Although these artefacts were to all intents and purposes used for "gold blowing", it is difficult to imagine their efficacy. "Corner brackets" made from can metal were found in six sites (Chinatown, Sheung Fong, QB2, Sandy Point, Apple Tree and the Rapids). Leaf designs cut from can metal were found in three sites (Chinatown, Arrowtown and the Rapids); their role is unknown.

Several one-off artefacts made from can metal were also uncovered. These include a candleholder (Figure 5.50c from QB2), a funnel (QB2) and a tubular mouthpiece(?) (Caliche).

The can body seems to have been the favoured component for making artefacts. This is understandable because the ends are smaller and modified to the extent that they have folded edges. The impressed cartouches also tend to weaken the metal (a few lids or bases have been found in which the cartouche has been so heavily impressed it has virtually punched right through the metal). The Chinese possibly avoided modifying the ends bearing cartouches because of superstitious beliefs. Only two can ends bearing cartouches have been cut, although a few have been recovered that have numerous fine holes (0.5–1.0 mm) punched in them, reminiscent of "salt shakers". As a consequence of this pattern of usage, the individual tallies of recovered lids, bases and both types of sealing strips are usually greater than the number of can bodies recovered per site, the "missing bodies" presumably having been used in artefact production.

Three opium can reinforcing strips (from three different sites) have been found with a hole (c. 2 mm diameter) drilled through the midpoint and the ends bent to form a flange. The specimen from Ah Wee's site was found in situ across the top of a small tin can (Figure 5.51e). The reinforcing strips appear to have been used to support the wicks in improvised opium-heating lamps in which cut-down bottles were used as globes and tin cans as the fuel reservoirs (see opium lamp discussion). As can be seen from a perusal of Table 5.33, three can reinforcing strips were recovered for every two lid strips. This is attributed to the greater durability of the reinforcing strips; the thinner lid strips tend to break up more readily. Although they bear no evidence of cuts or other modifications, around 20 of the recovered can reinforcing strips were flattened out "full length". There seems little likelihood that this could happen other than by intentional human actions.

5.4.4.7 Pipe bowl connecting pieces

Two types of fittings were found:

5.4.4.7.1 Saddles

These are the two-piece brass fittings (Figure 5.51d) that form the interface between an opium pipe stem and a pipe bowl. Their recovery pattern is detailed in Table 5.37.

5.4.4.7.2 Bowl connectors

These fittings are also made of brass. Two types (Figures 5.51a,b) have been recovered, with either circular or faceted flanges. They appear to be similar to the fittings described by Culin (1887:35). He stated that the ceramic neck of a pipe bowl was usually chipped off and replaced with a metal rim (i.e. a bowl connector), which was fastened to the pipe bowl with burnt alum. To make a tight fit, a flange was normally wrapped with a piece of soft cloth (a *gee* rag). This was held in place with a little smoking opium, which according to Culin formed an excellent glue. When uncovered, these fittings commonly have remnants of blackened calico-type material (the *gee*) wrapped tightly around the neck and are often blackened on the internal surfaces.

5.4.4.8 Pipe mouth and end pieces

Two "unusual" metal fittings were found in Caliche and ACS/6. Although both are flattened and deformed, judging from their inferred shape and diameter, they were opium pipe mouth or end fittings (most likely the latter). The Caliche specimen (made from a copper alloy) is too fragmentary to measure. The ACS/6 (Sq. I8, Ly.l) specimen is made from soft plated steel, has a diameter of 3.0 cm, an internal diameter of 2.0 cm and a length of 0.8 cm.

5.4.4.9 Opium-heating lamps

Opium-heating lamps were an essential part of a smoker's equipment. They minimally consist of a container (the fuel reservoir), a glass lamp globe, and a device across the top of the reservoir to support a wick. Two early American reports on opium usage (Kane 1882:37; Culin 1891:499) refer to the use by the Chinese "of opium lamps of glass, said to be made in Birmingham. They are designed so that air entering at the base emerged out the top and kept the flame constant" (Culin 1891:499).

Remains of manufactured lamp globes, such as those depicted by Culin (1891:498), have not been found in Central Otago sites. Instead, all the opium lamp globes (51) uncovered to date are improvisations made by modifying glass bottles. In most cases a light green, ring-seal, brandy or cognac bottle was selected, although bulbous-necked aqua-coloured alcohol bottles were also used. Green was probably preferred for its shading effect, although the predominance of lamp globes made from brandy bottles suggests that this type of bottle was preferred for other reasons, such as their ready availability and probably their ease of cutting. The top 5 cm was cut off (using a hot wire or a burning string soaked in kerosene), as was the bottom 12 cm, leaving a central portion shaped like an inverted glass funnel (Figure 5.51c). A small glass or tin container was placed in the bottom of the funnel. This contained the fuel, usually a vegetable oil or tallow. A wick was held in place over the reservoir by a metal bracket (often made from an opium can reinforcing strip). The ignited wick produced a constant flame over which the opium resin was heated (Figure 5.51e). Don, the Presbyterian missioner to the southern Chinese, specifically described an opium lamp used in an opium and gambling shop in the Nevis Valley. The lamp consisted of "a jam tin filled with tallow, a cotton wick and the upper part of a brandy bottle for a shade" (Don 1/3/1887:163). Two tin can "reservoirs" from opium lamps have been recovered; one each from Chinatown and QB2. The one from QB2 had an opium can reinforcing strip fitted across the top to secure the wick, while an old clock sprocket jammed into the top of the can served as the wick holder in the specimen from Chinatown.

5.4.4.10 Opium needles

Opium smoking involved heating a small piece of opium resin over a heating lamp. A small ball of opium was impaled on the end of a metal "needle" and heated until it gave off smoke. The smoking opium was then transferred to the pipe.

The needles were commonly made from short lengths of brass wire or rod, pointed at one end for holding the resin. Twenty, 15–20 cm lengths of 1.5 mm copper wire sharpened at both ends were found in hut 34 at Chinatown. Although the wire is relatively flexible, they may have served as opium needles (opium needles, seized by the police during raids on the residences of elderly Chinese in Wellington during the early 1960s, were made from hat pins).

5.4.4.11 Miscellaneous artefacts

Other artefacts found in the study sites that may have been associated with opium smoking include pocket knives (a knife was used for cutting the opium resin), scissors (used for trimming lamp wicks) and pieces of No. 8 wire with a flattened screwdriver-like tip (possibly for digging out the opium). Scissors are particularly numerous in some of the sites (see Tables 5.49–5.51, 5.53). Descriptions of opium smoking also indicate that old cups or small ceramic bowls were often used to contain prepared opium before it was smoked in pipes. All the cups and bowls from the study sites were examined for vestiges or stains suggestive of opium, but none were found. Nor was evidence found of the cylindrical horn boxes, often described in accounts of opium smoking (e.g. Kane 1882:35–6), which were used as containers for personal supplies of prepared opium.

5.4.4.12 Medicinal vials

Small square cross-section vials with snap-off necks (see Figures 5.9a,b) are frequently uncovered within Chinese sites in Central Otago. Although they are commonly reputed to have contained opium, this is a fallacy. The vials (in two sizes) contained a wide range of medicinal preparations including, but not exclusively, tincture of opium (laudanum). Similarly, two considerably rarer vial forms, teardrop-shaped (in two sizes) and vials with fluted sides, contained a range of medicinal preparations, some of which were almost certainly opiate based (Figure 5.9). After the sale of opium was prohibited to Chinese in New Zealand, in addition to acquiring supplies through friendly Europeans, it is likely that addicted Chinese who were unable to maintain their supply turned to opiate-based medicinal preparations. These were freely available, as they formed the base of most pain relief medicines until relatively recently.

5.4.4.13 Opium antidote(?) cans

Six examples of a small tin container about the size of a standard matchbox (4.3 cm tall by 3.3 cm wide) were found in the two urban Chinese settlements (see Table 5.37). These cans have a distinctive sliding lid at one end (which forms the top) of the can. The lid covers a 1.0 cm diameter aperture from which the contents were poured. The depicted specimen (Figure 5.51f) is one of two in the Cromwell Museum that have a stamped cartouche on the front surface. The poor condition of the excavated specimens precludes determining whether they are similarly marked.

An informant (Jeffrey pers. comm.), quoting information given to him by a New Zealand Chinese man, stated that they contained an "opium antidote". Although the cans are often found in close proximity to artefacts associated with opium smoking, until this ascription can be confirmed, other possible contents such as matches or snuff cannot be ruled out. The short-lived anti-opium organisation called the Cherishing Virtue Union set up by a group of Chinese merchants in Dunedin in 1888 had as one of its objectives the free distribution of "anti-opium medicine" (Don 1/12/1888:106). These cans possibly contained that medicine.

5.4.4.14 Improvised opium pipes

Three examples of what are believed to be improvised makeshift opium pipes have been uncovered from Chinese sites in Central Otago. Of these, two are held in a private collection, the other having been excavated at Arrowtown. The two privately held specimens (in the Short collection, Queenstown) consist of a small beige-coloured vase? (8 cm high) with two small protrusions in the form of lion heads on either side and a small clear glass medicine bottle (6 cm high). Both vessels have had a small hole drilled into the interior at about the mid-height point. The vase-like specimen is blackened internally, whereas the glass specimen is only blackened around the drill hole. The excavated specimen from Arrowtown consists of a modified ceramic "penny ink" bottle (Figure 5.51g; Ritchie 1984:63). The neck has been broken off (reminiscent of the removal of the neck of many opium pipe bowls) and a small hole has been drilled in the base. Attached to a pipe stem in the usual manner, it probably operated quite effectively. The Otago Museum holds an unprovenanced brownware jarlet (D25.2372; of the type depicted in Figure 5.23). It has a 1.5 cm hole drilled in the side of it and also appears to have been used as a smoking device.

5.4.4.15 A New Zealand-made opium pipe bowl

The Luke Adams pottery (1882–1965) made a wide variety of pottery vessels at Sydenham, Christchurch (Park 1978; Lambert 1985:62–70), including, according to a Christchurch bottle collector (Redmond pers. comm.), replicas of Chinese opium pipe bowls for the Chinese local market. The pipe bowls were manufactured between 1882–1918 (Redmond pers. comm.). The only example known to the author is a pristine condition specimen in the Redmond collection. It is depicted in Figure 5.52. The stoneware (?) bowl has a dark brown, highly lustrous glaze on both the interior and exterior. It most closely resembles the Chinese C6 type described earlier but is of more robust construction. The Adams bowl stands 4.0 cm high and has a diameter of 6.75 cm. The hole in the smoking surface, which has not been enlarged, is 0.9 cm wide. Another interesting feature is that the bowls were made without the narrow-neck section that the Chinese often broke off their own bowls and replaced with a metal flange. These construction features suggest the bowls may have been made in this fashion to comply with a specific order placed by a local merchant. It is not known why the pipe bowls were manufactured in New Zealand (assuming bowls of Chinese origin were available), but it would seem most unlikely that the pottery would have branched out into opium pipe bowl manufacture without having the production pre-sold or a guaranteed purchaser. The bowls appear to be quite rare and are not known from any archaeological context in New Zealand. This is, to my knowledge, the only recorded instance of non-Chinese manufacture of opium pipe bowls for an overseas Chinese population.

A book on the New Zealand domestic pottery industry (Lambert 1985:62) has a photograph captioned "blue glazed opium burner with a wide band of coggle decoration (Auckland Museum collection)". The artefact in question appears to be an opium pipe bowl of European manufacture. Although its manufacture appears to be attributed to the Luke Adams pottery, the accompanying text makes no reference to it.

5.4.4.16 Discussion: opium usage by the Chinese in Central Otago

Tables 5.31 to 5.37 summarise the distribution and numbers of "opium artefacts" found in the study sites. Opium pipe remains were uncovered in all but one of the 17 excavated sites (and even this site contained evidence of opium smoking – three opium cans), reflecting the widespread usage of the drug by the Chinese miners. However, some 80% of the total assemblage of 1,075 bowl fragments (including some fairly complete specimens) were derived from only three sites – the business and residential sections of the Cromwell Chinese settlement, the Rapids hut site and the Firewood Creek shelter. The latter site is especially remarkable, not only for its outstandingly large assemblage of opium pipe bowls (MN=40), but also for the fact that nine of the 12 defined styles are represented.

Overall, two bowl forms are clearly numerically dominant – type C1 (particularly the C1a variant) and type C3 (particularly the C3b form). Both types were co-present in seven and nine sites respectively. Other than subtypes C5b and H1b (both present in six sites), no other forms shared a remotely comparable frequency.

The four large site assemblages of opium-related artefacts are discussed now.

The remains from the residential and business parts of Cromwell's Chinatown are discussed as separate entities because the two areas are geographically discrete. The opium-related evidence from upper Chinatown (the business area) is principally derived from three private collections. One hundred and twenty fragments (of eight bowl subtypes) were available for study, nearly three times the number of fragments and twice the number of varieties found in the systematically excavated residential area, where 41 fragments (8 bowls of five types) were found. While the figures might give the impression that opium smoking was primarily undertaken in the stores, artefacts associated with opium smoking (pipe bowls, heating lamps and funs trays) were found in 13 of the residential structures.

Five hundred and sixty-four bowl fragments were recovered from the Firewood Creek shelter, representing a minimum of 40 bowls of nine types. The sample from this small site was obtained from only 30 square metres of excavation. By any standards, the number of bowl sherds from this site is disproportionately high, suggesting that it served a specialised role. The assemblage is also notable in that it is one of only three of the study sites that contained grey sherds (types C5e, C6a, C6b). Although the shelter (see the description in Chapter 4) contained subsistence artefacts, its small size, relative dampness and lack of artificial walling or a fireplace suggest it would not have been occupied for long periods. It possibly served as a smoking shelter for Chinese miners working in the area.

The opium pipe bowls from the residential part of the Arrowtown settlement and Ah Lum's store are treated separately. A minimum of 14 bowls (of six types) were found in the residential area, which is nearly three times the number found in the larger Cromwell Chinatown residential area. However, only two bowls were found in the single (excavated) store at Arrowtown, whereas a minimum of 17 were found in the deposits associated with the Chinese stores at Cromwell. The apparent higher incidence of opium smoking in the residential area at Arrowtown compared with that at Cromwell is difficult to substantiate, but in favour of such an argument, a proportionately higher number of "opium-related" artefacts (see Table 5.37) were found in the huts in the Arrowtown camp than at Cromwell.

The Rapids, a single hut campsite in the Kawarau Gorge, is another small site from which a relatively large assemblage of opium pipe remains were recovered – a minimum of 18 pipes of 13 subtypes (Table 5.32) including one of the relatively rare (in Central Otago) grey stoneware bowl forms (type C6a). The distribution of the bowl remains in the site (amid a shallow midden deposit on the edge of the riverbank; Figure 4.22) provided no real clues as to their contemporaneity or date of disposal (a pattern common to most of the site deposits). The site is believed to have been occupied from c.1880 until c.1910 (see Section 4.2). Although it may have been occupied by a single heavy user for only a short time, the variety of pipe types more likely reflects cumulative deposition from one or more users over several years.

Etter (1980:100) suggested that a higher percentage of the better quality stoneware pipe bowls are likely to be found in areas of more permanent settlement such as urban settlements. In terms of numbers and varieties, the Central Otago evidence does not support this hypothesis. There is no clear evidence of a quality differentiation between the urban and rural sites. On the contrary, the situation is reversed; all the (arguably) higher quality grey stoneware bowls were found in the rural sites.

Intact or substantially complete opium pipe bowls are rarely found in sites. The high incidence of breakage is attributable to several factors. Opium pipe bowls are relatively fragile. The recovery of many spotlessly clean fragments suggests they were often broken in use or transit and discarded before they were even "fired up". As Wylie (1980:5) suggested, a portion of the high incidence of breakage may be attributed to intoxicated smokers, who would fall asleep or otherwise accidentally "mishandle" their pipe and consequently break the bowl (see Dobie 1936:251). Another cause of breakage may have occurred during the periodic removal of the pipe bowls for cleaning or replacement. Don (quoted in Butler 1977:68) observed pipe bowls being scraped clean to obtain the last traces of opium during a shortfall in supply. Scraping and general pipe maintenance may have been easier if the bowls were removed from the pipe stem; the bowls may have been broken occasionally while trying to separate them.

Many pipe bowl necks bear testimony to the practice (described by Culin 1891a:35) of deliberately breaking off the ceramic neck and replacing them with metal connecting flanges. Some bowl "neck areas" not only have the original ceramic "necks" chipped off but also have hand-scored grooves across the break scar. The scoring appears to be an improvisation to facilitate attachment of the bowls to the metal connecting flanges. This trait does not appear to be idiosyncratic; it is present on several bowl types from the Chinatown, Firewood Creek, Arrowtown and Sheung Fong sites.

Scrutiny of the recovered bowl fragments revealed that the small hole in the smoking surface of opium pipe bowls was sometimes enlarged, presumably to facilitate placement of the prepared opium into the pipe. This trait (enlarging the hole) alluded to by Ritchie and Harrison (1982:33) had not been reported in the overseas literature until recently when Wylie and Fike (1985:1) described not only the same practice but also evidence of ceramic inserts being shaped and fitted into enlarged holes in the smoking surface. They found the practice was more common on "elaborate pipe bowls" and surmised that it was possibly done "to enhance the appearance of quality pipes". Some pipe bowls in the Asian American Comparative Collection, University of Idaho, Laboratory of Anthropology) have square and triangular holes (Wegars pers. comm. 1985). The level of opium smoking in some urban Chinese communities in the United States enabled some Chinese to make a living as "pipe menders" (Culin 1891:500; Tchen 1984:66). Repairs and modifications such as those outlined above were probably made by experienced "pipe menders" in New Zealand Chinese communities too.

Despite the number and areal distribution of the study sites, no clear geographic or localised trends stand out from the pipe bowl distribution (see Table 5.32). Similarly, no definite chronological trends could be determined as to whether certain bowl types were more or less common at different stages between 1870 and the 1920s. Some styles that appear to be relatively rare, and appear to have restricted distribution, may with further excavations and research prove to be more widespread. Although sub-regional and temporal differences are apparent in the distribution of Chinese artefacts such as tablewares and ceramic containers, it was concluded that the opium pipe assemblages from the study sites were not large enough to reliably define distribution patterns of the various types. However, the typology should serve as a foundation on which to build.

Minimum numbers analyses were performed on the can remains, based on separate counts of can bodies, can reinforcing strips and the lid strips from each site, the greatest number of the three components being accepted as the minimum number of cans represented. "Lids" and "bases" (i.e. the end pieces) were counted but not used for determining minimum numbers, because if they are in a crumpled condition or an advanced state of decay, it is virtually impossible to distinguish a lid from a base. The robust can reinforcing strips are the most durable component of the cans and hence their tally usually represents the minimum number of cans present.

Table 5.33 details the minimum numbers of the various can components from each site. These figures strongly support the contention that the Chinese regularly re-used can body metal. The assemblage from hut 23 at Chinatown is a case in point. Here, only three can bodies and four lids/bases were uncovered, yet 31 reinforcing strips and 27 lid strips were present. Eighteen funs trays and three offcuts of can metal were found in the same hut, suggesting the "missing" can body metal was used in the manufacture of the trays. By corollary, at the Firewood Creek site, can bodies (16), bases/lids (35), reinforcing strips (20) and lid strips (18) are in approximately equal numbers and there was little evidence of re-use of the can metal.

A minimum numbers analysis undertaken on the can remains from all the excavated Chinese dwellings (other than the Arrowtown and Cromwell settlements) revealed that, on average, the remains of nine opium cans were left in each site when it was abandoned.

A possible insight into covert consumption of opium was exposed in 1979 when a small cache of six opium cans was inadvertently uncovered by workmen removing sand near a former Chinese hut (S133/430), located 200 metres upstream of the Chinatown site. The cans were buried (with no other artefacts) in an excavated depression in the bank and may reflect a deliberate attempt to hide evidence of opium smoking.

To conclude this section, the archaeological evidence strongly reinforces historical observations by Don and others, that the practice of opium smoking was widespread among the Chinese on the southern goldfields. Remains of opium pipe bowls were present in all but one of the 17 primary study sites. Opium can components were found in all 17 sites, artefacts made of opium can metal were uncovered in 15, and other artefacts associated with opium smoking were present in eight of the sites. As the choice of sites for excavation was not based on whether they were known or suspected to contain evidence of opium smoking, there seems little reason to suppose that a similar high incidence of smoking evidence would not be found in Chinese sites elsewhere in Central Otago.

However, it is not contended that the Chinese were universally addicted to the drug; the cans and other remains are likely, in most instances, to be the result of casual but regular usage by successive occupants of the various structures. According to Kane (1891:501), the Chinese divided smokers into two groups; those who were addicted and those who were not. Most users were able to keep usage of the drug at a level consistent with getting on with the job at hand (that being mining for most). While the debilitating effects of advanced opium addiction are well known, the worst effects for many casual users would have been economic – lost time spent in visiting "opium dens" or preparing, smoking and recovering from the drug at "home". Opium was relatively expensive. Kane (1891:50) stated that a casual user (in the United States) used 25c worth a day, whereas an addict would consume $1.00–$1.50 worth during the same period. Although it is difficult to compare American and New Zealand opium prices because several brands and grades were available at different prices (see Sando and Felton 1984:15–19), Don's comments on opium costs suggest that similar consumption–cost ratios prevailed in southern New Zealand. For example, he noted: "there are some very heavy smokers up country. One smokes 4/6d and another 3/- worth weekly. One man on Skippers smokes a tin of opium which costs 28/- every two weeks, and several others smoke the same amount every three or four weeks" (Don 1/3/1888:166).

The Chinese used opium primarily as a "recreational drug" and generally smoked in the company of others. Some argued the drug was a defence against the effects of cold and exposure and was less injurious than alcohol (Culin 1891:501). While it is debatable whether prolonged usage of the drug or strong liquor is the more debilitating, contemporary accounts indicate that unlike alcohol, opium smoking caused few social problems beyond gradual impairment of the health and wealth of users. The Chinese were aware that one of the consequences of spending too much on opium was a prolonged sojourn in New Zealand or the very real possibility of never being able to raise enough money to return to China.

Opium usage was not, of course, the sole preserve of the Chinese. The drug was widely used in European society in the 19th century, particularly in liquid and powder forms, for health and pleasure (Eldred-Grigg 1984:110). However, the smoking of solid opium in New Zealand was largely a Chinese trait (see Eldred-Grigg 1984:112 for a contrary viewpoint) based on archaeological evidence, historic observations and the rapid decline in solid opium imports after the passing of legislation in 1901 prohibiting importation of opium by the Chinese (see Appendix 6). Some supplies were still smuggled in, but the massive decrease in legal imports after 1901 almost certainly reflects the declining demand among the Chinese as their population dwindled after the turn of the century. Although some Europeans smoked opium, frequented Chinese "opium dens" or obtained opium from Chinese (Chinese merchants were the main importers of solid opium during the 19th century), there is little evidence to suggest that the smoking of opium in the Chinese manner (using the traditional pipe; and smoking in specialised smoking venues, often described as "dens" in European accounts) was widely adopted by any level of European society. The fact that opium smoking was seen as a peculiarly Chinese habit, the time needed to prepare the drug, and the lack of the necessary paraphernalia and experience in its use are all likely to have worked against European adoption of the practice; besides, more convenient forms of the drug such as laudanum, "whiffing" powder and opiate-based "medicines" were readily available.

5.5 MISCELLANEOUS ARTEFACTS ANALYSIS

"Miscellaneous artefacts" of iron, non-ferrous metals, wood, stone, fabric and paper usually constitute a significant portion of the material remains found in Chinese sites. While they are obviously an important component and reflection of lifestyle, these artefacts are sometimes difficult to describe, categorise and interpret for several reasons:

a. limited numbers (often only single specimens);
b. the condition of the artefacts (particularly the ferrous ones);
c. differential survival;
d. a much reduced level of comparability and historical data compared with artefact categories such as ceramics and bottle glass;
e. even though they can be described in detail, it is often impossible to ascertain their precise function, e.g. that of a 20 cm diameter coil of copper wire.

Miscellaneous artefacts were divided into "metal" and "non-metal" categories, then further divided into groups depending on their known or inferred functions, or convenient material-type categories. Each category was examined with regard to functions, origins, dating potential, inferred social or economic role, and their intra- and inter-site distribution. The data for each category was tabulated. The illustrations are of selected artefacts that bear brand names or other interesting or diagnostic features.

5.5.1 FOOD PREPARATION AND COOKING UTENSILS

5.5.1.1 Domestic utensils

Domestic utensils constituted a large and varied assemblage, well suited for comparative purposes. They were analysed by Stuart Bedford and written up in an unpublished report (Bedford n.d.). The following discussion expands on that presented in his paper. Table 5.38 includes some additional artefacts from the Flax Grove site that were not considered in Bedford's manuscript.

5.5.1.2 The assemblages

A total of 238 domestic utensils were recovered from 18 sites (see Tables 5.38–5.41) and were divided into six groups based on function:

1. eating utensils such as table knives, forks and spoons (n=85). Chopsticks were notably absent.
2. cooking and food preparation utensils including carving and paring knives (n=12), cleavers, wok spoons and strainers (n=21).
3. cooking vessels such as frying pans, pots, billies and woks (n=52).
4. teapots (n=20).
5. pocket knives (n=21).
6. miscellaneous and multipurpose (n=27).

Knives were the most common utensils. There were several different types including food preparation knives (carving and paring, n=12), table knives and pocket knives (21). The latter are a multifunctional tool and could, on occasion, have been used for cutting, preparing or eating foods as well as other uses such as opening tin cans. All the knives were very corroded; consequently, no evidence of maker's marks was discernible. A carving knife blade found in ACS/3 was notably larger than most of those recovered. The blade portion measures 25.5 cm (Figure 5.60e). It was probably used for deboning meat.

Spoons were the next most common utensil and included table, dessert and teaspoons and one wooden example. All were made of inexpensive nickel or silver-plated steel. Many were embossed with maker's hallmarks. These have not been deciphered, but legible examples are depicted in Figure 5.53.

The least common European utensil was the fork. These too were made of plated steel and several bear maker's marks (Figure 5.55). Three had bone or wooden handles (grips).

Iron wok ladles and spatulas were the most common utensils of Chinese origin (Figure 5.57). They were grouped together as "wok spoons" because most of the excavated specimens are corroded, which makes it difficult to determine ladles from spatulas. Two appear to have been fabricated from pieces of scrap metal. Cleavers are represented by their blades only, the wooden handles having disintegrated. The cleaver blades are all "traditional Chinese narrow blade" types (like the "meat cleavers" from the Pierce Chinese mining site, Idaho, depicted by Stapp and Longenecker 1984:51–2). The New Zealand specimens are also of a similar size (c. 16 cm by 7 cm). One blade from Arrowtown (now on display in the Arrowtown Museum) bears impressed Chinese characters, presumably the manufacturer's mark.

Two flat strainers were recovered (Figure 5.58). Both are made of wire. One is crudely constructed and appears to be an improvisation. In Chinese cooking they are used for straining deep-fried or boiled foods (Yee 1975:3). Originally, they may have had bamboo handles.

Billies were the most numerous cooking vessels. Several sizes were represented, all made of tin-plated steel and of the same basic shape. As no kettles were found, it is inferred that billies were the main vessels used for boiling water, besides their traditional roles as all-purpose cooking and tea-brewing vessels. The Chinese also re-used empty ceramic shouldered food jars (mainly the large size) as billies on occasion. About 25% of the jar bases of this type recovered from sites in the Cromwell area are fire blackened. Judging by their clean interiors, they were probably used for boiling water. In a few instances the rusted remains of wire suspension or possibly handle loops have been found adhering to neck rims.

Cast iron pots of round or oval construction were the second most common form of cooking vessel. All were fragmentary; only the oval specimen was able to be measured. There were only two enamelled pots. They probably reflect later occupations, but their low numbers may possibly reflect a preference by the Chinese for the more solid and durable cast iron pots. Enamel wares appear to be relatively uncommon in pre-1900 European and Chinese sites in Central Otago (see O'Dell 1982).

Six large frying pans with distinctive long, flat iron handles (Figure 5.60g) were recovered. Five were of circular construction, the other being oval. The frying pans were probably used like woks, for stir-frying food.

A bowl-shaped improvised vessel was uncovered in hut 26 at Chinatown. Made from copper sheeting, it is fire blackened and may have been used as a wok. It was probably manufactured onsite.

Enamel "pie dishes" were found in three sites. Although these vessels are normally used for baking, the Chinese miners may have used them as bowls for mixing, heating or serving food.

There were 20 teapots of the following types: 15 Euro-ceramic (Figure 5.60a), three Euro-enamel, one Japanese ceramic (Figure 5.41) and one Chinese ceramic (Figure 5.16k). Tea was undoubtedly the main non-alcoholic beverage consumed by the Chinese. Its consumption is mentioned frequently in the writings of the Rev. Alexander Don. As in China, tea was drunk during most social occasions. It was considered rude not to offer a guest a cup of tea (Don 1895:50, 1911:18). Besides teapots, evidence of tea-drinking, in the form of European and Chinese teacups, is found in most Chinese sites in Central Otago. The relative paucity of oriental teapots may reflect the prevailing supply situation, a price differential, or a recognition of the greater durability of the more robust European ceramic and enamelled-steel teapots. Ten additional metal artefacts associated with food consumption or preparation were not included in Bedford's analysis. These included enamel mugs and saucers (6), tin mugs (2), a small pewter? scoop (from Ch/19) and the worm drive from a meat mincer (found outside Ah Lum's store in Arrowtown).

5.5.1.3 Discussion

Chinese cuisine has been described as "90% preparation and 10% cooking [time]" (Yee 1975:5), and the traditional Chinese kitchen characterised as one containing "few implements of great versatility" (Yee 1975:5). The traditional cooking implements are the wok, ladle and spatula, chopsticks (used in cooking for stirring and tasting), strainers, cleavers, steamers and the wok. Only two of these implements were not represented in the studied assemblages, namely the bamboo and wooden items – chopsticks and steamers (although some large tin cans found with holes punched in their bases may have been used as improvised steamers). Wooden artefacts (especially chopsticks) are likely to have been used extensively but have not survived in archaeological contexts. This may also have been the case with tin-plated vessels such as billies, which normally disintegrate rapidly in damp ground conditions.

There were two main sources of cooking and eating utensils used by the Chinese in Central Otago – England and China. England's role in supplying manufactured goods to the British Crown colonies during the 19th century is well known. Most, if not all, of the steel eating utensils (the knives, forks and spoons) are likely to have been of English origin, although corrosion had obscured maker's marks on many of them. Although the metal cooking pots bear no discernible manufacturer's marks, they too are likely to have been of English origin. Traditional Chinese cooking utensils, along with oriental foods, were imported in bulk shipments from China by Chinese merchant-entrepreneurs in Dunedin and then retailed through branch and other private stores on the goldfields (Ritchie 1983:9).

Food has always played an important part in Chinese culture and, if not at the centre, at least accompanies most social interactions (Chang 1977:15). Although most of the Chinese miners probably had little cooking experience before they left China (household cooking was done by the women there; Yee 1975:12), recorded observations and the archaeological evidence suggests they were generally more adept and imaginative cooks than their European counterparts. Don's records abound with comments about the effort the Chinese miners he visited put into food preparation. He also provided many insights into their culinary practices, such as this description of the foods laid out for a Chinese New Year feast: "…each table bore five or six bowls of accompaniments to the rice, one each of roast duck, roast fowl, roast and boiled pork and two of peas in pod, with cuttlefish and vermicelli" (Don 1/5/1885:204). Although Don did not describe the utensils, it is obvious that a wide variety of cooking techniques must have been employed. One Chinese cookbook lists 20 methods of cooking: boiling, steaming, roasting, red-cooking, clear-simmering, pot-stewing, stir-frying, shallow-frying, deep-frying, meeting, splashing, plunging, rinsing, cold-mixing, sizzling, salting, pickling, steeping, drying and smoking (Chao 1972:39).

The excavated domestic utensils and recent studies of butchered faunal remains from Chinese sites in Central Otago (Piper 1984; Chapter 6, this volume) show that both traditional foods and methods of cooking and preparation were retained to a large extent. But from the outset, European cooking vessels and eating utensils were obtained and used extensively too. As detailed in Table 5.38, at least five (and usually more) European domestic utensils were found in each of the excavated sites. Although reliance on European implements probably increased with time, it is not possible to demonstrate this unequivocally because of the susceptibility to decay of many of the traditional Chinese utensils and the difficulty of precisely dating the artefacts in question.

While their focus was on mining; food preparation, cooking and consumption were an important and social part of a Chinese miner's working day. It was a task often shared by two or three miners who worked together, taking turns (Don 1/9/1884:43). According to Anderson and Anderson (1977:370), only an individual who worked alone or was in abject poverty would eat alone. This pattern was described by Don too, but he also mentioned that eating and living alone was compelled on some individuals after they were ostracised by their fellows for some real or imagined grievance or suspected contagious medical condition (Don 1/4/1884:183). Towards the end of the Chinese mining era in Central Otago (c.1920–30), solo living became increasingly the norm for the by now elderly miners, most of whom were dependent on "the benefit" for subsistence. Many adopted simpler cooking methods, deduced from this observation about the remaining Chinese in the Lawrence Chinese Camp in the early 1930s: "They used to buy any old cut of meat and stew up all the ingredients in a pot until it was like a slurry" (Bell pers. comm. 1984).

5.5.1.4 Conclusions

The site assemblages examined in this study date from c.1870 until c.1925. Analysis of the utensils associated with cooking and eating shows that almost from their first appearance on the Central Otago goldfields, the Chinese acquired and used European utensils, notably knives, forks, spoons, billies, frying pans and pots, but they maintained many of the culinary practices of their homeland, evidenced by the presence of Chinese cleavers and wok spoons, data derived from meat butchering analyses and studies of imported Chinese food product containers. Although it is not possible to unequivocally demonstrate a change from almost exclusive reliance on traditional Chinese utensils to increasing usage of implements and vessels of European manufacture, this appears to have been the trend. Some changes would have been forced upon the Chinese as their supply stores gradually closed and items of Chinese manufacture became increasingly hard to obtain, but in many instances they appear to have quickly realised the usefulness of some European items, such as billies, and acquired them.

5.5.2 HOUSEHOLD ARTEFACTS

The household fittings are listed in Tables 5.40–5.41. Six functional categories were defined:

1. **Structural remnants.** These include angular offcuts of corrugated iron (all from Chinatown huts), window glass, fire bricks (used in hearths), galvanised downpipe (ACS/4) and door knobs and hinges. Most of the door knobs were the plain brass type, but a white porcelain specimen was found in hut 22 at Chinatown and a brown marled ceramic door knob came from ACS/6.

2. **Security fittings.** The number of door locks, lock fittings, padlocks, keys and short lengths of chain suggests that the Chinese miners were concerned about the security of their possessions, although it may have been a regional or urban problem because Don (1893:17) noted: "Scores of times the men here have spoken in admiration of the way they can leave doors unlocked or things about, which they dared not do in China." Despite the confidence of those who spoke to Don, he considered "that thieving in some form or other" (often from other Chinese) was the cause of most imprisonments of Chinese in New Zealand (Don 1893:17).

   Security-related artefacts found in Chinatown included five padlocks, six door keys, two cupboard keys, and the remains of at least four slide-latch (padbolt) door locks in various huts. A similar pattern was found in the Arrowtown assemblages although no padlocks were found. Security artefacts were less common in the rural sites, padlocks being restricted to the Caliche shelter and Poplars sites, and an improvised key was found in Ah Wee's hut. All the locks are believed to be of European manufacture. Some are depicted in Figure 5.61. No traditional Chinese padlocks, door hinges or fittings of the types depicted by Hommel (1969:292–5) were found. Further evidence that even isolated huts were generally locked when the owner was absent was recorded by Don (1906:25). He noted an instance where a Chinese miner (working in Bannockburn Creek near Cromwell) told him he would find his door key in a matchbox under a stone, if he wanted to stay the night. A small cupboard key was found in a matchbox just inside the doorway of the Poplars hut site.

3. **Internal fittings.** These included linoleum fragments (in three huts at Chinatown and five at Arrowtown), cup hooks, clothes hooks, cupboard door hinges (in some instances attached to pieces of light planking suggesting wooden boxes were used as cupboards) and remnants of rubber door mats. Single mattress springs were found in two huts in Chinatown, while fragments of wooden picture frames were found in ACS/6 and Ch/6.

4. **General-purpose domestic artefacts.** These included scissors (a total of 18 in three different sizes and evenly distributed among the sites), blue dye (Ch/23), clocks (represented by cogs only), a few crayons and lead and slate pencils (see Section 5.6.2), a full cotton reel (ACS/3), a sack needle (ACS/6), a watering can rosette (Ch/6), an iron bucket (the Rapids), a leather suitcase handle (Caliche), wooden pegs, canvas grommets, a bottle opener (Ch/23), a wooden handled scrubbing brush (Ch/16) and the ribs of an umbrella (Ch/33).

5. **Lighting, cooking and heating.** Artefacts associated with "fire places" or "heating" included fire bricks, fire grates, fire bars (pieces of iron rods and iron standards), fragments of cast iron coal ranges (in ACS/4 and Ch/6), a poker (outside Ah Lum's) and the name plate of an American-made "Perfection Smokeless Oil Heater" (Ch/27; Figure 5.62a). Lighting artefacts included two presumed candleholders (small blocks of wood with 2–4 nails in the top), blobs of melted candle wax, a torch bulb holder, battery remnants and the remains of nine kerosene lanterns from eight hut sites (eight of the nine lanterns were found in the "urban" huts at Chinatown and Arrowtown). A maker's name, "Juno", was discernible on only one of the lanterns (from Ch/34). Cuffley (1973:43) noted that "Juno" lamps are listed as "new" in the 1911 catalogue of American manufacturer, Miller's of Meriden, Connecticut. In addition, large numbers of tin wax vesta matchboxes were recovered from most of the sites. They were described in Section 5.3.6.
6. **Musical instruments.** These were represented by two items (both from ACS/6) – a mouth organ embossed "The Rainbow, M. Hohner, Germany" and the "finger control portion" of a tuba or similar instrument.
7. **Use unknown.** As in most excavations, a few artefacts were uncovered of which the use (or the categorisation) is not clear. They included a miniature syringe (from Ch/23; Figure 5.62d) and three identical curved tin spouts (Figure 5.62b) – single specimens being found in ACS/6 and the Firewood Creek and Ha Fong shelters near Cromwell. Fragments of painted glass (found in Ah Lum's store) depicting a woman and Chinese writing may have been part of an advertising panel.

5.5.3 TOOLS

The tools found in and around the Chinese sites are listed in Tables 5.42–5.44. They were divided into five categories based on inferred function – mining related, wood chopping, construction, maintenance and rabbiting, but obviously there are some overlaps in their usage. Nails, treated as a separate tool category, are discussed in Section 5.5.4.

From the outset, the Chinese miners in New Zealand were self-reliant. They built their own habitations, collected and cut their own fuel, maintained or improvised their mining equipment and repaired their possessions as required. The number of tools from each site varied considerably, but in some it reflects a considerable investment. However, none of the individual assemblages are large or specialised enough to suggest artisan roles such as carpenters or cabinet-makers. On the contrary, they indicate that most of the Chinese miners were "general handymen" and used their skills regularly.

Don (1891:8) recounted a discussion he had with a group of Chinese miners who were working in Seven Mile Creek near Queenstown. It is evident from the conversation that the Chinese considered themselves superior to Europeans in most things, particularly in cooking and carpentry, and he noted that one man said: "If a Chinese sees a thing done once he knows how to do it" (Don 1891:8). Don commented that this statement was generally true and added, "they laugh at European miners in the neighbourhood who are unable to sharpen their own picks and take them to Queenstown" (Don 1891:8).

The role of gardening in the southern Chinese economy is discussed in Chapter 6. The principal gardening tools used by the Chinese miners based on recovered remnants were the hoe (Figure 5.64) and rake, although the soil was probably turned initially with a shovel (probably the same as those used in mining operations). Kerosene cans (with wire handles added) were used for conveying water to the hut garden plots at Chinatown (Wishart pers. comm.) and probably elsewhere.

The assemblages contained five implements used principally for mining by the Chinese: miner's shovels (represented by rivetted shovel blades like a specimen recovered from the Pierce Chinese mining site, Idaho, depicted in Stapp and Longenecker 1984:48); sluice forks (for picking stones out of tailraces); picks (represented by pick heads only); perforated sheet-iron trays (the tray portions of gold cradles); and gold pans.

Small amounts of coal were found in many of the sites (Table 5.81), but historical records indicate that wood was the main fuel used by the Chinese despite its general paucity in Central Otago. They often spent half to one day a week to obtain their supplies (Don 1911:38). Remnants of a few carpenter's saws were recovered, but axes, tomahawks and splitting wedges appear to have been the main tools used for the acquisition and breaking down of firewood into manageable pieces. Contemporary observers noted that the Chinese collected driftwood if it was available and were extremely frugal with their wood supplies even if supplies were relatively abundant. At Arrowtown "they chopped every piece of wood up into kindling size pieces" (Dudley pers. comm.). Wood was principally used for cooking rather than heating.

General-purpose construction and maintenance implements represent the bulk of the recovered tools. They include hammers, mallets, nail punches, grindstones, whetstones, hacksaw blades, folding rulers, spanners, triangular-section and flat files, drill bits and screwdrivers. Although the uses of the tools is fairly self-evident, the role of two other commonly-recovered implements is poorly understood; namely, hand shears (often only represented by a single blade; Figure 5.63i) and short lengths (c. 15 cm long) of No. 8 wire of which one end has been flattened and squared off to produce a screwdriver-like tip (Figures 5.67d and e). The latter were possibly used to clean opium or tobacco pipes.

Analysis of the faunal remains (see Chapter 6) and contemporary observations confirm that many Chinese (particularly after c.1890) caught rabbits for sustenance and the income to be earned from treating and selling their skins (e.g. Don 1911:15). Rabbiting equipment is represented by the remains of gin traps, trap-securing pegs and chains, and U-shaped skin-stretching wires (length c. 35 cm) made of No. 8 wire. Smaller U-shaped wires (length c. 17 cm) were also frequently recovered and may also have been used for stretching skins. The triangular-sectioned files may have been used for trap maintenance.

The number of mining, gardening and rabbiting tools varied considerably between sites, but overall there is little difference in the numbers and distribution of the general-purpose construction and maintenance tools. One improvisation, the lengths of No. 8 wire with screwdriver-like tips, has already been mentioned; other modifications included a miner's fork in which the tines were cross-bound with No. 8 wire to produce a "grate-like" effect (Ha Fong shelter), and a bone knife handle in which the knife blade has been replaced with a screwdriver "end" (Figure 5.63b; Ah Lum's kitchen). Worn "mushroom-headed" dredge bucket link pins were found in the Caliche shelter and two huts at Chinatown. They may have been used as anvils or mortars, but it is difficult to distinguish whether use damage was done during their dredging or subsequent roles.

The recovered iron and steel tools are believed to be of Western origin, although few bear evidence of maker's marks. The majority were probably made by manufacturers in Great Britain (the main source of manufactured goods imported into New Zealand in the 19th century); the United States, Australia and New Zealand are likely to have been the main secondary sources. A saw blade from ACS/6 with an impressed "Kangaroo" trademark is likely to be of Australian origin. Although Chinese stores probably stocked some European tools, there is no New Zealand documentation to this effect. Tools would have been readily available from European ironmongers or hardware stores, and they were probably the primary source, but given the recognised frugality and adaptiveness of the Chinese, they are likely to have picked up or scavenged useful tools or other items if they found them in abandoned workings, habitations or European dumps. Chinese appreciation of the versatility of some European tools is evident in a comment recorded by Don (2/10/1882:65) when he noted that a Chinese man returning to China after working on the Round Hill field, was taking a shovel with him because "it would be most useful in China".

5.5.4 NAILS AND SCREWS

A minimum of 1,887 nails and screws were found in the study sites. Only those that could be reasonably positively assigned to specific types were tabulated (Tables 5.45–5.48); broken and corroded remnants were discarded. The large number and variety of nails and screws constitutes a considerable research resource. However, the generation of significant cultural information from "the nails" is presently thwarted by a lack of information on sources of origin, dates of introduction and main periods of popularity of specific types. As the undertaking of this research is a major task, it is beyond the scope of this work and, consequently, only summary details and limited discussion are presented here.

The nails were grouped based on inferred or known uses. A distinction was made between "spikes" (i.e. handmade nails with square or rectangular wedge-shaped shafts) and "nails" (i.e. machine-made nails with cylindrical shafts). Unless otherwise stated, the nails were "loose" (i.e. not found in pieces of timber).

5.5.4.1 Nail and screw types

5.5.4.1.1 Structural nails and spikes

a. Rosehead nails: Nails with distinctive "roseheads" (Figure 5.65a) are the most common type of nail found in the study sites. The style is now obsolete, but they were widely used for general construction purposes in New Zealand from c.1870 (or earlier) until at least the 1930s. The recovered specimens have mean lengths of 3.5, 4.0, 5.0, 5.5, 6.0, 6.5, 7.0, 7.5, 8.0, 8.5, 10.0 and 11.5 cm, indicating they were used for a wide range of structural framing and interior purposes.

b. Rosehead spikes: These are essentially rosehead nails with rectangular (mostly) or square-sectioned shafts (Figure 5.65b). They were handmade. Their introduction predates that of the rosehead nails, but periods of usage of the two types had considerable overlap before the usage of rosehead nails became predominant. The mean shaft lengths of the recovered specimens were as follows: 3.5, 4.0, 5.0, 5.5, 6.0, 6.2, 6.5, 7.0 and 10.0 cm, the majority being over 5 cm in length.

c. Flat-headed nails: These nails consist of a cylindrical shaft with a circular flathead (Figures 5.65c,d). The best known flat-headed nails are case nails (c. 4.5–5.5 cm long) used in wooden box and crate construction. Case nails are discussed further below. The nails defined here as flatheads are 5.5 cm-plus long, most being over 7.0 cm. They are machine-made.

d. Flat-headed spikes: Rectangular and square-sectioned flat-headed spikes (Figures 5.65e,f) were widely used for construction purposes around the turn of the 19th century. The recovered specimens have mean lengths of 4.7, 5.5, 5.7, 7.5, 10.0 and 13.0 cm. Those over 10 cm in length are generally known as "bridge spikes".

e. Jolthead nails: Nails with this distinctive head shape (Figures 5.65h,i) are relatively uncommon in the study sites. Their widespread usage for construction purposes in New Zealand postdates 1925. They are machine-made.

f. Rhomboid-headed nails: This term was coined to describe what appears to be an early version (Figure

5.65g) of the jolthead nail. Rhomboid-headed nails have an essentially square head and a cylindrical shaft.

g. Flarehead nails: This term was coined to describe large numbers of nails uncovered in the Chinatown huts that have a distinctive "flared head" like that depicted in Figure 5.65j.

5.5.4.1.2 Light construction nails

This category includes nails under 5 cm long that would have been used for interior and light construction purposes or are survivals from furniture or fittings.

a. Case nails: These are flat-headed nails (Figure 5.65k) that were and still are used for nailing together wooden packing crates and boxes. Some of these nails may have been salvaged from old packing case timber and re-used, or they may reflect the re-use of wooden supply boxes as shelves or furniture within the Chinese structures. The majority of the recovered case nails have cylindrical shafts (like modern case nails), but a few have square-section shafts (they were badly corroded). The latter almost certainly predate the nails with cylindrical shafts.
b. Offset head nails: A few nails (Figure 5.65l) were found with bent over or "offset" heads. They appear to be virtually identical to "Chinese nails" depicted by Hommel (1969:23, Figure 33d). According to Hommel (1969:22), they were made by hammering and flattening the centre point of a double-pointed spike on an anvil. By bending the metal back and forth, it was easily broken and furnished two nails. The recovered specimens are all lightweight nails (with lengths under 5 cm and shaft diameters of c. 1.5 mm), suggesting they were used for light construction purposes. They may have been recycled.

5.5.4.1.3 Roofing nails and screws

a. Flat-top leadheads: Flat-topped lead-headed nails (Figure 5.65m) were used for securing roofing iron (length c. 5.5 cm). They are believed to predate the introduction of the bell-top leadhead.
b. Bell-top leadheads: These are essentially the same shape (Figure 5.65n) as the modern leadhead nail, which was widely used for securing roofing iron until c.1990.
c. Dome-head nails: These galvanised nails (Figure 5.65p) were used in conjunction with a loose-fitting lead or zinc disc and used to secure sheet iron.
d. Dome-head roofing screws: These are essentially a threaded version of the above type and were used for the same purpose. The roof of Ah Lum's store is secured with this type of screw (Figure 5.65o).
e. Disc-head nails: This type consists of a flat-headed nail with a slightly curved disc of galvanised sheet iron immediately below the nail head. They are used for securing sheet iron and probably postdate the introduction of leadheads. Sometimes this type of nail was improvised by punching a flat-headed nail (or clout) through a disc of brass sheeting (e.g. opium can metal) or lead sheeting (Figure 5.65p).

5.5.4.1.4 Special purpose nails and screws

a. Horseshoe nails: These were found in ones and twos in several of the sites (Tables 5.45–5.48) together with horseshoes (see Table 5.50). As there is no evidence that any of the Chinese miners in Central Otago kept horses (but see Section 5.5.5), the nails were probably scavenged and re-used (Figure 5.65q).
b. Clouts: These are a specialised form of flat-headed nail (Figure 5.65r) with a wide head (c. 8 mm) and a relatively short shaft (20–40 mm). They were used for securing flat metal sheeting (e.g. sheet iron).
c. Fencing staples: Although only small numbers were recovered, wire fencing staples (3.0–3.5 cm long; Figure 5.65s) were found in many of the sites. In addition, some long (6.5 cm) square-sectioned staples were recovered. They may have been used for security in conjunction with chain and padlock.
d. Dome-head tacks: These specialised nails (Figure 5.65t) were found in a few sites. They are generally used for securing fabric onto furniture.
e. Tacks: These are a form of clout with a flat top and tapering, square-section shaft (Figure 5.65u). They are principally used for securing linoleum and carpet. Like the dome-head tacks, they have a limited distribution in the study sites.
f. Sole nails: These are small flat-headed nails (c. 1.5 cm) of which the head is only marginally bigger than the shaft. They were used for attaching the soles to the upper parts of footwear. They may have fallen out of decomposed footwear or been used for repairing soles. Some of the recovered boots were partially re-soled (see Table 5.76 and Section 5.6.4).
g. Hob nails: The recovered specimens are small knob-headed nails (similar to the "Hungarian shot heads" depicted in a catalogue of the George Lawrence Company of Portland, Oregon; Lawrence c.1926:57). Hob nails (Figure 5.65v) protruded from the sole of a boot and afforded additional traction.
h. Woodscrews: Only a few specimens (varying in length from 2 to 9 cm) were found in the study sites.

5.5.4.1.5 Nails and screws: discussion

Nails can be broadly used for dating, but their usefulness for this purpose is limited because of several factors including differential survival (i.e. there are likely to be less of the earliest nails), the long and often overlapping periods when the main nail types were in vogue, the possibility of salvage and re-use of old nails, and the possibility that "old style" nails were retained or acquired and used at a later date. Despite these problems, their potential as a source of cultural information has hardly been touched on in New Zealand. More research is required on the manufacture and importation of nails into New Zealand in the 19th century, with a focus on determining the main periods of popularity and uses of the various types.

The large numbers and wide range of nail types found in the sites suggests that the Chinese rapidly acquired European nails (and to a much lesser extent screws) and used them to build structures, furniture and equipment and for securing or hanging items. Many of the nails (particularly the flat-headed case nails) may have been salvaged from shipping boxes and re-used. In the absence of nails being recovered in timber remains, it is difficult to pin down specific uses. In the descriptions presented above, the predominant European uses were outlined for each nail type.

To relate the various nail types to specific uses, a study was made of the nails visible in Ah Lum's store, the only substantially complete structure among those studied. The types of nails and their uses are detailed in Table 5.45. As can be seen in the table, a wide variety of nails were used in the framing and interior subdivisions in the store. The selection of most of the nail types presents no surprises and they were used in a conventional manner. No types were specifically restricted to one area. The large number of nails protruding from the walls of the store (especially in the kitchen) is a notable feature. They would have been used for hanging things rather than construction purposes. Other evidence of a seemingly Chinese penchant for hanging things are the large numbers of wire hooks found in Chinese structures (see Section 5.5.5, Tables 5.50, 5.51, 5.53).

The offset head nails are the only nails of probable Chinese origin. The 18 examples of this type (Tables 5.45–5.48) represent less than 1% of the total nail assemblage. Thirteen of the 18 were found in the Flax Grove site, suggesting they may be derived from the same source (a packing case or furniture imported from China, perhaps).

Only three modified nails were recovered: a headless nail with a groove cut transversally across the blunt end like a needle (Figure 5.66a); a nail shaft with a barb-like notch cut near the point (Figure 5.66b); and a spike nail that had been cut transversally and the head splayed into a "Y" shape (Figure 5.66c). Candleholders made from blocks of wood with four protruding nails were found in Caliche shelter and ACS/6. The use of discs of opium can metal in conjunction with case nails to secure linen window blinds in Ah Lum's store represents an interesting adaptation.

5.5.5 MISCELLANEOUS METAL ARTEFACTS: FERROUS AND NON-FERROUS

Experience has shown that in any Chinese mining site excavation a large volume of often bulky miscellaneous ferrous artefacts can be expected, with lesser amounts of non-ferrous material. Those recovered from the study sites are listed in Tables 5.49–5.54. Their likely roles are discussed now, although they are often difficult to define because many of the artefacts in question were obviously multifunctional.

A total of 13 horseshoes were uncovered from four huts in Cromwell's Chinatown, and another nine in five huts at the Arrowtown settlement. They are unlikely to be derived from horses kept by the Chinese miners. Firstly, there are no historical records or archaeological evidence that Chinese miners kept horses on the Central Otago goldfields for carrying supplies, mining equipment or personnel (although Don recorded that some of the Chinese storekeepers in Riverton employed Chinese packers who kept horses for freight transport between the township and the Round Hill goldfield; Don 2/10/1882:66,67, 1/11/1884:85). By the time the Chinese arrived in Central Otago, the Cobb & Co. stagecoach company was well established, as were several European freight packers. From the outset, the Chinese storekeepers appear to have used these established services to convey their supplies rather than go to the expense themselves of maintaining horses, wagons and stables and growing oats and so on.

A few Chinese businessmen on the goldfields owned horses; for example, Lye Bow, who operated a market garden at Butcher's Creek near Alexandra, owned a horse and spring cart c.1910–1920; the *Tuapeka Times* (c. January 1875) reported that some Chinese gardeners lost their horse and cart when they toppled into a river; Mr Ah Hee, a Chinese storekeeper at Roxburgh, was reported to have been thrown while mounting his horse (Chandler pers. comm.). The *Otago Witness* (18/9/1875) reported that a Chinese storekeeper on the Shotover employed an "Irish-Mongolian" by the unlikely name of "Timothy O'Chee Chee" as a "storeman packer": "Everything is conveyed to them [the miners] on horseback, be it beef, bread, tea, matches or tobacco. The system of business pursued is that customers send back word by the storeman's packer, when he delivers one lot of goods, what he shall bring them on the next, and as the visits are made for the most part weekly, and upon stated days, no confusion arises." Don recorded at least two other references to Chinese owning horses; in one instance, a Chinese gardener in Milton had been severely injured by his horse and cart after it had bolted "due to a European waggoner's disobligingness" (Don 1895:65); in the other, a Chinese man in the Ida Valley had his dray horse spooked by a "ghost" (Don 1906:35).

Some Chinese (particularly market gardeners) kept packhorses on the goldfields, but the practice was uncommon; the storekeepers largely relied on European packers, while individuals carried their own supplies on their backs or shoulders using the traditional shoulder yoke. Consequently, the horseshoes in the Chinese mining camps are almost certainly not from horses owned by the miners. This contention is supported by the lack of associated evidence, such as horseshoe nails and harness gear, in the sites. As none of the worn shoes appear to have been modified, they may have been collected for their scrap metal value. In the case of Cromwell's Chinatown, a European blacksmith's business (Wishart's) located at the eastern end of the Chinese shops and above the residential part of the settlement would have provided a ready source. The slope behind the old smithy is still littered with horseshoes and other blacksmithing debris.

The remains of European-style fire grates and fire bars (made of 20–40 cm lengths of square-section iron bars, flat iron standards and cylindrical iron rods) were found in many of the sites. The wide range of lengths, thicknesses and shapes leads one to infer that Chinese miners acquired most of these items from discarded sources, e.g. blacksmiths, abandoned houses or European household dumps.

While tin and zinc sheeting were found in most of the sites, remnants of corrugated iron were limited almost solely to the Chinatown huts, many of which are known from early observers and historical photographs to have been roofed with it (see Ritchie 1984:40–2 for a comparison of the Cromwell and Arrowtown structures). It is not known whether the corrugated iron roofs of the Chinatown huts were made of new or recycled corrugated iron, but much of the iron visible in the early Chinatown photographs appears to be in very good condition. Corrugated iron was first produced by British steel mills in the 1830s. By the 1870s it was established as the dominant roofing material in New Zealand, being imported from Great Britain and Australia as well as being rolled from imported stock in New Zealand (Chapple et al. 1983:26–7). The Chinese at Cromwell appear to have appreciated its utility as a roofing material, despite the outlay. Possibly an element of "keeping up with the Joneses" set in, with one miner at Chinatown erecting a "tin roof" and others following. Although they may have acquired second-hand sheets, it was probably necessary to buy "new" rather than scavenge them because good quality iron was always in demand (see Section 4.5.2 for further elaboration on roofing materials).

Several short lengths of iron chain were recovered, on average about one per site. Some are the securing chains of rabbit traps (they still had the peg attached); other uses would have included securing doors, equipment and gates (in conjunction with a padlock).

Wire artefacts (Figure 5.67) comprised around 20% of the miscellaneous artefacts. Six main forms are represented: wire "S" hooks, wire pegs (usually with a "looped head"), double-ended hooks (15–20 cm long), lengths of No. 8 and lighter wire (usually about 30 cm long), improvised wire handles (particularly for kerosene can buckets) and short lengths of chain with a wire hook at one or both ends. The hooks clearly attest to a penchant for hanging things – whether it be billies over the fire, or foodstuffs, clothing and other gear – from rafters or on a wall. The roof area in the relatively compact huts and in Chinese stores was used for storing and suspending foodstuffs and other items to keep them from the ravages of rodents and free up the floor space.

Heavy bolts, nuts and washers were found in and around many of the Chinese sites (see Tables 5.50–5.51, 5.53). Their precise function will never be known. If they were used for structural purposes, in most instances they were probably larger than desired, but they may have been used (with appropriate spacers) if the price was right, i.e. free.

Lengths of barrel hoop iron and case strapping (usually 20–30 cm long) were found in several sites. Most were unmodified, other than being cut to the above lengths, but some had been made into right angle brackets, and others were bent into a "J" shape (Figure 5.63e). The role of the J-shaped pieces is uncertain.

Small octagonal tin discs with 2 mm sharp protrusions on one side (Figure 5.62c) were recovered in several sites. They are "tobacco tags", albeit plain ones. These artefacts were attached to "plugs" of chewing or smoking tobacco for brand identification. They were invented in 1870 by the Lorillard Tobacco Company, a leading manufacturer of plug tobacco. Their use reached a peak between 1890 and 1910, but some manufacturers continued to use them into the 1930s. A huge variety of plain, paper-coated, plated, galvanised, painted and lithographed tobacco tags were developed in a wide range of shapes and degrees of elaboration (Hubbard 1968; Umberger and Umberger 1971; Schild 1972; Sudbury 1980). If the recovered artefacts are, as they appear to be, tobacco tags, they are most likely to be off plugs of smoking tobacco (see Section 5.6.1) because the practice of chewing tobacco never become established in New Zealand, despite the presence of many American miners on the New Zealand goldfields in the 19th century.

The assemblages include a wide variety of iron rings – circular, oval and D-shaped. A few appear to be off harness gear (see horseshoe discussion) and two were the "loop handles" of kerosene cans. The role of the others is unclear.

A few short lengths of iron plumbing pipes were recovered. Most were less than 20 cm long. They appear to be discarded offcuts; why the Chinese brought them back to their huts is uncertain. A crumpled mass of galvanised downpipe was found adjacent to ACS/4. Possible explanations of its presence have been presented elsewhere (Ritchie 1983:35).

The non-ferrous metal artefacts are listed in Tables 5.49, 5.52 and 5.54. They constitute a highly varied assemblage dominated by four metals: zinc, copper/brass, lead and tin.

Zinc metal, in the form of perforated and unperforated sheeting, was found in and around several sites. Uses of the unperforated metal have already been mentioned in the discussion on the role of corrugated iron. The perforated metal was in two forms: remnants of pre-punched zinc sheeting identical to that used in "European" meat safes, and sheets folded into shallow trays with irregular patterns of hand-punched holes (2–4 mm) on the bottom surface. These appear to have been used as drainers or seeding trays (the metal is too light for these trays to have been used in gold cradles; see earlier "tool" discussion).

Cuprous metal was recovered in the form of rifle cartridges (Section 5.5.6), short lengths of copper wire and offcuts of copper and brass sheeting. Many of the latter are derived from the cutting up and re-use of spent brass opium cans (secondary uses of opium can metal were discussed in Section 5.4). A tapered gold-blowing tray made from heavier gauge copper sheeting was found in QB2, and nondescript brass rings, grommets, knobs, threaded fittings and pieces of light chain were uncovered in several sites (see Tables 5.52 and 5.54).

Lead artefacts are discussed in Section 5.5.6. The forms of the recovered lead artefacts clearly indicate that some of the Chinese in the urban settlements at Cromwell and Arrowtown were involved in salvaging and recycling lead. In addition, crumpled sheets of tinfoil (believed to be liners from cardboard tea packets) were found in ACS/2 and the Apple Tree site.

Although manufactured tin artefacts were limited to a few mugs and plates (discussed earlier under "domestic utensils"), the Chinese improvised many artefacts from tin cans (see more on the secondary uses of can metal in Section 5.3).

Two other metals were recovered, both definitive evidence of goldmining activity. A single gold nugget was found in a crevice in the floor of the Hanging Rock shelter, while mercury was found in two sites – in a small glass bottle (Figure 5.11) found in the Ha Fong shelter and as globules in the soil in two units in the Poplars hut site. Mercury, which readily amalgamates with gold, was used in the recovery of fine gold.

5.5.6 FROM BULLETS TO SOLDER: CHINESE LEAD SALVAGE

Although there is little historical or archaeological evidence that the Chinese miners regularly kept and used firearms, large numbers of fired "live" and "blank" cartridges and spent projectiles were found in some of the study sites, especially in huts in the Chinese camps at Cromwell and Arrowtown. Frequently, the bullets were in stratigraphic association with pieces of lead in the form of solidified masses, slag, tubular "ingots" and rolled rectangular slabs. The presence of the two artefact categories is clearly related, one seldom being present without some evidence of the other. This unusual combination of artefacts afforded an opportunity for a special study (Ritchie n.d.c). A condensed version is presented here.

5.5.6.1 Specific objectives

The specific objectives of the investigation were to:

1. identify the recovered munitions for comparative and dating purposes;
2. determine manufacturers and likely periods of usage;
3. account for the presence of the cartridges/projectiles in the sites, when there is little evidence that the Chinese kept firearms for hunting, recreation or self-defence;
4. explain the frequent association of bullet remnants and lead in various forms and determine what activities they reflect;
5. account for the recovery of a hand gun in one of the sites.

5.5.6.2 The assemblages

The cartridges and projectiles were identified and dated by Nelson Cross of Alexandra and Grant Sherriff of Dunedin, both of whom have a specialist knowledge of guns and cartridges. A minimum number of 1,047 cartridges and projectiles are represented in the combined assemblages. Their periods of manufacture span from c.1880 to the present day (c.1984). However, the two numerically dominant types – .577 calibre Snider (both brass foil and solid brass casings; n=55) and .303 calibre CAC Mk II C2 cartridges (n=371) and projectiles (n=572) – were primarily in use in the period between c.1870 and 1905. Their distribution is summarised in Table 5.55. Tables 5.56–5.58 provide details about the numbers and types of cartridges and associated artefacts from each site. Manufacturer's marks, main periods of use and other details about the recovered ammunition types are recorded in Table 5.59.

5.5.6.3 Dates of usage

It is relatively easy to determine the date of introduction and the principle period of usage for most late 19th and 20th century ammunition types, but it is much more difficult to determine the actual date of deposition of a cartridge in a site because ammunition can be acquired and kept for several years without being fired, cartridges can be reloaded and re-used at a later date, and the possibility always exists that spent ammunition was being collected at a later date for a secondary purpose. Consequently, cartridges can only be used to reliably establish dates to the extent that they are the earliest possible times that deposition could have occurred. However, some lines of inquiry can be pursued to narrow the time span within which a cartridge is likely to have been discarded:

a. some guns and/or types of ammunition had reasonably specific periods of popularity, e.g. the .303 calibre bullet largely superseded the .577 calibre after 1905;
b. technological changes, e.g. the change from brass foil to solid brass casings on .577 calibre ammunition (c.1895);
c. associations with other datable artefacts in sites;
d. local historical accounts of the usage of specific types of rifles and ammunition at various times.

5.5.6.4 Manufacturers

Ten ammunition manufacturers are represented in the combined assemblages and two calibres were predominant: .577 Snider ammunition (55 or 5.2%) and .303 cartridges (371, 35.4%) and .303 projectiles (572, 54.6%). The histories and usage of these cartridge types in New Zealand is discussed now (see Table 5.59 for historical data and technical details).

English-made Snider rifles that fired .577 calibre projectiles were used extensively by the British armed forces and colonists in New Zealand in the last third of the 19th century. Between 1866 and 1900, nine different Marks of cartridge and seven types of bullet were developed. The pre-1890 cartridge casings consisted of a lamination of brass foil and paper attached to a black-lacquered iron disc (brass in the Mk II) that held a percussion cap and anvil. In use, the different Marks were distinguished by the colour of the paper used and by markings on the outside (Temple 1977:34–8; Spring-Rice 1982:121), but these are usually undiscernible in cartridges from archaeological contexts. All Marks after 1895 had solid brass casings.

The Colonial Ammunition Company (CAC) is the only major cartridge manufacturing company that has operated in New Zealand. It commenced operation, under that name, in Auckland in 1888. It had previously operated (since 1886) under the name of Whitney and Sons. The first production calibre was the .577 Snider, followed later by the "bottleneck" .450/577 Martini–Henry cartridge (Harris 1980:49). Most Snider ammunition made by the Colonial Ammunition Company is likely to have been used not long after it was manufactured because prior to the advent of a full-time New Zealand Army in 1909, shooters would not have been able to acquire obsolete ex-Army ammunition (Sherriff pers. comm.).

The Lee-Metford magazine rifle, the first designed to fire the new higher velocity .303 calibre cartridges, was introduced into British military service in December 1888 (Barnes 1972:45; Harris 1980:7). Within a few years, rifles such as the Enfield, which fired .303 ammunition, were widely adopted in the British colonies, superseding .577 calibre firearms. In 1898, a new production line was installed in the Auckland factory of CAC to produce .303 cartridges. They became available later in the same year. The Mk II was the first version produced (Harris 1980:49).

5.5.6.5 Discussion and conclusions

As most of the recovered cartridges (both live and blanks) and bullets had been fired, it is evident that the Chinese were collecting them and bringing them back to their huts for "non-ballistic" purposes. The archaeological evidence outlined here clearly indicates that the principal Chinese interest in the cartridges and bullets was their metal value and in particular, the recovery of their lead content. To make the latter activity economic would require regular collections from concentrated sources of the raw materials.

The only possible and practical sources of this quantity of used live and blank cartridges (of the same batches) and spent projectiles during the period the Chinese were resident (late 1860s through to the mid-1920s) would have been European rifle ranges where there would have been high concentrations of discarded shells and bullets in and around the targets (Cross pers.comm.). The majority of the 572 .303 calibre cupro-nickel jacketed bullets had been fired. Although about 5% were virtually intact, most were ruptured and deformed indicating they had hit a hard target.

From 1865 on, the Volunteer Movement was flourishing in New Zealand (Sherriff 1983:73). Rifle clubs were formed at Cromwell and at Bannockburn 5 km to the south (Parcell 1976:118), and the Wakatipu Mounted Rifles unit was established in Arrowtown. These groups conducted regular exercises (using blanks) and inter-club competitive "shoots". For example, in 1901 the newly formed Bannockburn club competed against the Cromwell club. The Cromwell team, using their old Sniders, were soundly beaten by the Bannockburn team who were equipped with the New Enfield rifles. The Sniders were immediately discarded (Parcell 1976:119). The Bannockburn club had its range in the gullies behind the township. Similar sheltered locations were probably used by the Cromwell and Arrowtown clubs. These locations are the most likely source of the cartridges and bullets in the Chinese sites.

The lead was recovered by subjecting bunches of bullets to high temperatures and collecting the molten lead as it dripped out. This process is suggested by the fact that most of the .303 projectiles bear evidence of having been "cooked" (oxidation and metal deterioration); many pieces of lead-rich slag and casting spillage were recovered and in three instances (two from hut 26, Chinatown, and ACS/4) bullet jackets have been found in solidified lead masses. It is inferred from the latter that a handful of bullets were heated in a pot or similar container, the cupro-nickel jackets being picked out of the molten mass and discarded along with slag and impurities. The molten lead was then cast, evidenced by the recovery of elongated and tubular castings and several rolled slabs of lead.

The "tubular lead" was probably sold to both European and Chinese customers for use as solder. In the late 19th century, there were often shortages of solder in New Zealand (Cross pers. comm.). On the West Australian goldfield during this same period, impoverished settlers' families were earning 5/- a pound for solder recovered by heating piles of old tin cans found around prospectors camps (Facey 1984:13–14). I have found no evidence of Europeans or Chinese being involved in this practice on the Central Otago goldfields, but an early American observer (Mark Twain) noted that the Chinese in Virginia "gathered up… tin cans which the white people threw away and procured marketable tin and solder from them by melting" (Twain 1972:351). Similarly, the Chinese in

Woodland, California, were reported in the *Woodland Daily Democrat* (18/2/1879) to be engaged in "the lucrative enterprise of separating solder from tin in old cans for sale to Sacramento junk dealers" (Prazniak 1984:128).

The lead slabs were probably used primarily as flashing. It would appear from the recovered artefacts that the Chinese exploited other sources of lead too, such as offcuts from lead pipes and sheeting, battery electrodes, and possibly such things as the lead rosettes from horse harnesses (one was recovered in hut 33 at Chinatown). In two of the rural sites (Ah Wee's and QB2), fused lumps of lead alloy were recovered. The alloy from Ah Wee's is pewter and is probably derived from a partially melted down ornamental stand that was found in the site. The composition of the other specimen has not been determined.

The brass cartridges were probably being collected principally for their metal value too. There is less evidence of a demand for scrap brass, although they may have been hoarded in anticipation of a demand arising. A few lesser secondary uses were also defined. Figure 5.69h depicts the base of a 12 bore shotgun cartridge found in the Firewood Creek site (Sl33/424). It contained two circular mother-of-pearl discs, which are possibly *wei-qi* (also known as "go") counters. Although this was the only incidence of something being found in a cartridge, it suggests that sometimes they were used for storage or possibly for measuring things such as medicinal powders.

Figure 5.70a depicts a piece of lead found in the Hanging Rock shelter (S133/474). It bears numerous circular cut marks and would appear to have been used as a base for punching discs (in leather?) or possibly wads for shotguns. Although no cartridges of similar diameter were found in the shelter, a cartridge was possibly used as an improvised core punch. Lead is often used as a punching base because its malleable nature will not blunt tools.

I have suggested previously (Ritchie 1980:11) that the large volume of cartridges found in hut 26 at Chinatown may reflect their usage in the manufacture of Chinese fireworks. Analysis of the cartridges has effectively disproved this contention. All the cartridges had been fired. Furthermore, the majority are .303 cartridges, which originally contained cordite, a material that is totally unsuited for fireworks manufacture (Cross pers. comm.).

Cartridges were found in 13 of the 15 study sites, but large numbers (more than 20) of early cartridges/projectiles were found only in the urban settlements at Cromwell and Arrowtown. In each of these sites there was a definite internal distribution; the cartridges and projectiles were concentrated in two huts at Cromwell (Ch/7 and Ch/26) and four at Arrowtown (ACS/4, 5, 6 and 15). As reflected in Tables 5.56 and 5.57, numerous pieces of lead in various forms were recovered in these and other huts in the settlements.

It is concluded that the recovery of non-ferrous metals from cartridges/bullets and other materials was never a major economic activity but nevertheless was pursued by a few individuals in the urban settlements as an additional (or possibly their sole) source of income. Several factors point to this activity beginning after about 1885: the raw materials would not have been readily available before then; and after this date it was becoming increasingly difficult for many of the by now elderly Chinese to earn a living through small-scale mining or other hard, physical work such as labouring.

In terms of the metal salvage activity, the recovery of a hand gun (Figure 5.71) in hut 34 in Cromwell's Chinatown appears to be totally irrelevant – in fact, it was a rather unexpected find. The weapon, a cast iron push-in barrel air pistol, is identical to a specimen depicted by Gilbart (1979:613), although the breech plug screw is missing from the archaeological specimen. According to Gilbart, an acknowledged authority on air weapons (Sherriff pers. comm.), pistols of this type "almost certainly date from about 1897". They were described as very well made. The frame, cylinder and butt were cast in one piece and finished in black enamel. The barrel is 14 cm long and has a calibre of 4.5 mm (.177). The trigger guard is separate and, like the trigger, is nickel plated. Although the archaeological specimen bears no discernible marks, Gilbart's specimen (still in its original box) bears the letters "E.G.", indicating it was made by Eisenwerke of Gaggenau, Germany (Sherriff pers. comm.).

Although there are recorded instances of overseas Chinese bearing and using firearms, e.g. during interpersonnel disputes such as the Tong Wars in the United States (Hart 1979:31–3), there is little evidence that the Chinese in New Zealand kept firearms for hunting, recreation or self-defence. Even in the United States, Chinese weaponry was principally limited to blade weapons (Kildare 1972). I am aware of only one instance where a New Zealand Chinese kept a gun; a miner in the Shotover had a gun for shooting goats for food c.1900 (Chandler pers. comm. from information provided by Harry Helms). European youths occasionally took "pot shots" at the Chinatown huts from the steep slope behind it, but the Chinese were never known to return "the favour" (Wishart pers. comm. 1980). The air pistol recovered in Chinatown was probably manufactured between c.1897 and the First World War. It, along with many other types of cast iron air pistols, could have been readily purchased from hardware stores (Sherriff pers. comm.). It is conceivable that the (possibly inoperative) weapon was found or acquired by the Chinese inhabitant of hut 34 and used for "scaring harassers" rather than for shooting purposes.

5.5.7 SCALES, WEIGHTS AND ACCOUNTING DEVICES

According to Bartlett (1971:22), "before scales for weighing gold dust came into common usage (in

California), the tenet was a teaspoon of gold dust equalled one ounce of gold. Whether it did or not, the miners accepted it as "fair judgement". A similar rough estimate system almost certainly operated during the earliest days of the New Zealand goldrushes, but it was not long before merchants, bankers and miners started weighing gold and other products accurately on scales to ensure they were receiving fair measure. Two types of scales were used by the Chinese, the "rule scale" and the "balance scale". The typical Chinese rule scale (Figure 5.72h) consisted of a portable counterweight device made up of three main components: a graduated balance bar/arm, from one end of which a small brass or copper pan was suspended at four points by cotton or fine string. The weight was determined by moving a suspended brass counterweight (the recovered specimens are all ovoid brass discs) until the arm was in balance (i.e. horizontal). The weight was read off the gradations at the point where siting the counterweight placed the scales in balance. This type of scale was used widely by Chinese merchants and miners for measuring small volumes of various products.

Rule scales were carried in small wooden cases, not dissimilar in appearance to a small violin case. The case was made in two identical sections held together by a pivot pin at the narrow end. The scales fitted within hollowed-out chambers cut into both sides of the interior of the case. The pan and counterbalance fitted into the bulbous end, while the balance bar occupied the entire length of the case. Several rule scale components were found in the study sites (Table 5.60). The brass pans were flattened but clearly recognisable by their circular shape and the pattern of four small holes around the perimeter, the points of attachment to the balance bar. The two measurable specimens have a diameter of 7.3 cm (Figure 5.72b). The two balance bars were broken into small pieces and would have been difficult to distinguish from fragments of ivory chopsticks were it not for the incised gradation marks (Figure 5.72d). The recovered counterbalance discs (5) are made of brass and measure c. 2.8 cm by 2.2 cm by 0.25 cm thick (Figure 5.72c). They have a single hole near the edge from which they are suspended. A brass medallion found in hut 34 at Chinatown, and impressed "Opening of Covent Garden theatre, 1809", has a crudely drilled hole near its top edge. Although it was probably used as a neck ornament, it may have served as an improvised counterweight. The wooden cases, if discarded, would rapidly decompose in the ground. None are known from an archaeological context.

Balance scales, observed in museums and antique shops, show they were available in a range of sizes although the basic technology is the same. They consist of two identical pans suspended at the ends of a balance beam made of wood, steel or brass. In use, the balance beam was suspended at its centre point from a roof beam or other convenient suspensory location. "Weights" of known weight (usually made of brass or iron) were placed in one pan, while the gold or other items to be weighed were placed in the other. When the balance bar is perfectly horizontal, the weight of the product equals that of the brass weights in the opposing pan. Balance scale pans can be distinguished from rule scale pans because they have only three (rather than four) suspending holes. The versions used by merchants for weighing loose and bulky foodstuffs were often quite large and robust, the pans being 13–20 cm in diameter and capable of holding several pounds. Balance scales (particularly the smaller portable versions) were sold in partitioned wooden or tin carrying cases (Bartlett 1971:23). Although some brass weights were found in the study sites (see Table 5.60; Figures 5.72e–g), no other balance scale components were recovered.

Most of the scale components and weights were found in the residential part of Cromwell's Chinatown, and in particular, in hut 23 (Table 5.60). As this structure contained the majority of the artefacts associated with opium smoking evidence, it seems likely there was a direct relationship, i.e. the scales and weights were used for weighing opium, or gold for opium.

The iron weight (Figure 5.72a) found in the main room of Ah Lum's store is a European type that was widely used around the turn of the century. The groove enabled a stack of weights to be secured.

Four wooden abacus beads of 2 cm diameter (with an internal hole of 0.4 cm diameter) were found in the main room of Ah Lum's store. They are remnants of the only definite traditional accounting device found in the study sites. However, several artefacts described in Section 5.6.2 (artefacts associated with written communications), such as slate pencils, pieces of slate and a coloured pencil, may have been used for accounting purposes too.

5.6 MISCELLANEOUS ARTEFACTS

The artefacts discussed in this section usually constitute a small but significant portion of the materials recovered from Chinese sites in Central Otago. Although a few contain metal components, most of the artefacts reviewed in this section are "non-metal".

5.6.1 TOBACCO PIPES

Two specialised studies have been undertaken on the tobacco pipes from the study sites, that of Foster (1983) on "Clay Pipes from the Cromwell Area, Central Otago" and that by Pfeiffer (1985) on "Tobacco Pipes from the Arrowtown Chinese Settlement". This discussion draws on these studies. Foster's paper described all the pipes found in European and Chinese sites in the Cromwell area up until 1981, but her report is now outdated because several more pipe remains have been recovered from further excavations. A complete listing of numbers, types, brands and their distribution is presented in Table 5.61.

The tobacco pipe remains are of four basic types: clay pipe bowls and associated mouth-stem pieces (white ball clay and terracotta), wooden pipe bowls, synthetic vulcanite or amber stem-mouthpieces, and plain and embossed silver-plated brass or steel "shank bands" (see Table 5.61).

5.6.1.1 Clay pipe bowls

There is a considerable technical and historical literature on clay pipes, particularly those manufactured in Great Britain, which constitute the majority of those found in New Zealand (e.g. Walker 1971, 1977; Oswald 1975; Davey 1979, 1980), as well as useful Australasian reports on excavated assemblages (Dane and Morrison 1979; Prickett 1981; Rusden 1982).

Initial analysis of the clay pipe remains from the study sites was undertaken by Foster (1983). Clay pipes made by at least five manufacturers were present in the assemblages:

1. **Davidson, Glasgow**. The firm of Davidson, Glasgow (Caledonian Pipeworks) operated from 1861 (when Thomas Davidson, Jr, bought out William Murray) until 1910 (Walker 1971:25). Davidson and the earlier Murray firm may only have manufactured pipes for export, since they are the only major Scottish clay pipe manufacturers whose pipes are not represented in the National Museum of Antiquities of Scotland (Sharp 1984). Three Davidson pipes (Figures 5.73a,q,r) were found in the study sites. Figure 5.73p depicts a Davidson pipe stem found in a hut at Carricktown. The brand is well represented elsewhere in Australasia (Dane and Morrison 1979; Prickett 1981; Rusden 1982). See Section 5.6.1.1.1 and Foster (1983) and Pfeiffer (1985) for further details.
2. **W. T. Blake, London**. William Thomas Blake operated in City Road, London, from 1873 until 1898 (Foster 1983:98). Only one pipe (Figure 5.73j) made by this manufacturer was recovered – in the Rockfall 1 shelter in the Cromwell Gorge.
3. **Gambier & Co**. This company manufactured in Ardennes, France, and was famous for their "portrait head" pipes. From 1865 until 1895 they operated in Carter Lane, London (Oswald 1975:115). The sole Gambier pipe (Figure 5.73o) was found in hut 26 at Chinatown.
4. **William White** operated in Glasgow from 1908 until 1955, and in London between 1838 and 1879 and from 1884 until 1899. The firm claimed to be the largest manufacturer of clay pipes (Prickett 1981:444). Three "W. White" pipes were recovered – from the Apple Tree (1) and Sandy Point sites (2); (Figures 5.73h,l). One of the Sandy Point specimens was also marked "Ben Nevis Cutty" (see Foster 1983:96 for stylistic variations and Section 5.6.1.1.1).
5. **Pamplin**. A ribbed terracotta pipe (Figure 5.73f) was found in ACS/6. According to Pfeiffer (1985:6), this pipe was made in the Pamplin, West Virginia, area (Hamilton and Hamilton 1972:40, Plate 16j; Sudbury 1979: 303, Plate 44–4). It is the only clay pipe of definite American manufacture found in the study sites. The Pamplin clay pipe industry was established in the 1860s and continued until the 1950s (Sudbury 1977:3, 25; Pfeiffer 1985:6).
6. **Part marks**. Three pipes were recovered with illegible or parts of maker's marks:
471 WAS---/ GLASGOW (Chinatown)
---NTEER (Caliche)
-- – PIPE within a circle (Ah Lum's store, main room; Figure 5.73d).

5.6.1.1.1 Related discussion

a. **Ben Nevis Cutty** appears to have been used as a trademark by several Scottish clay pipe manufacturers. Pfeiffer (1985:2) commented in reference to a Davidson pipe from ACS/3 that it was "distinguished not only by the 'Ben Nevis Cutty' decoration on the rear of the bowl but also by its size". One of the White pipes from Sandy Point is impressed "W. White, Maker, Ben Nevis Cutty" and a pipe bowl from the Ledge site (S133/868, a European house dump with some Chinese material) is impressed "Ben [?] Nevis Cutty" (on the bowl) and "19 Chr[istie?], [Glas]gow" (on the stem). Pipes bearing only the words "Ben Nevis Cutty" have been found in several Chinese and European sites in Central Otago (Foster 1983:96, 98–9).

The pipe depicted in Figure 5.73b is impressed "Ben Nevis Cutty" and "McPhee, Dunedin". The words "Ben Nevis Cutty" suggest it is of Scottish origin, and McPhee was probably a distributor or pipe seller in Dunedin. *Cyclopedia of New Zealand* (Otago Vol. 4 1905), and Wise's, Stone's, the NZ Post Office and Harnett's annual business directories do not list any shopkeepers or distributors by that name in Dunedin, but recent research has proven that McPhee made pipes in Dunedin between c.1880 and 1908 and was New Zealand's first pipe maker (see White 2016). McDougall's c.1875 price list notes that pipes stamped with names on bowl or stem are 2d per gross extra (Pfeiffer 1985:5).

b. BEN NEVIS: A clay pipe found in the main room in Ah Lum's store at Arrowtown was impressed "Ben Nevis, No. 141" (Figure 5.73c). Pfeiffer (1985:5) stated "probably the only way to determine the maker of this pipe is to discover a manufacturer's list where a 'Ben Nevis' is No. 141". McDougall, the largest Scottish clay pipe exporter, lists a "Ben Nevis" as No. 39 in their c.1875 "Irish Price List" (Sudbury 1980:45–6). Pipes impressed with "Ben Nevis" are almost certainly of Scottish origin (Ben Nevis, in

Inverness-shire, Scotland, is the highest mountain in Great Britain).

c. DECORATED PIPES: a few of the recovered pipes have patterned bowls or decorative bands but no maker's name, e.g. the specimen with rouletting below the rim depicted in Figure 5.73g and the ridge pattern on the bowl in Figure 5.73m.

d. Pfeiffer (1985:2) suggested that "Scotland" marked on pipes may indicate a post-1891 date. At that time the United States made it mandatory for all imported items to have their country of origin marked on them and it is possible that shipments to other destinations were also marked. However, if pre-1891 pipes were being marked "Glasgow", it would seem unlikely that the pipe exporters would change to the less specific "Scotland".

e. Figure 5.73u depicts the flat stem of a clay tobacco pipe found during test excavations (August 1985) in deposits associated with the Chinatown stores. The stem is notably different from the other clay pipes because the mouthpiece has been dipped in a green glaze and it is also ovoid in cross-section rather than cylindrical.

5.6.1.2 Wooden pipe bowls

Seven wooden pipe bowls were found in the three urban sites: Arrowtown (1), Ah Lum's store (1) and Chinatown (5). The pipes from the Arrowtown sites were examined by Pfeiffer. Of the two wooden specimens, he concluded one (from ACS/6) is "a probable briar" pipe bowl (Figure 5.74b) but noted that although the dense, knurled appearance of the wood suggests briar, other tough burls or roots were also used to make smoking pipes. The Arrowtown specimen is in the "half bent billiard ball" shape (Pfeiffer 1985:6). Briar pipes originated in the St. Claude region of France in the mid-1850s. Within a decade they had become popular in the United States (Pfeiffer 1985:6). They were probably introduced into New Zealand by American miners and others after 1860 but may have taken another decade or so to become established in New Zealand, and particularly among the Chinese.

The other Arrowtown specimen (Figure 5.74a) was found in the kitchen of Ah Lum's store. It is made of cherrywood, the only type of softwood with commendable smoking attributes (Dunhill 1969:192). It still has bark around the exterior, which according to Pfeiffer (1985:6) helped to counter the tendency for the wood to split from heat and cake buildup. Judging from their knurled appearance, four of the five Chinatown bowls appear to be "briars". The fifth had been burnt, the wood being totally reduced to charcoal but retaining its pipebowl shape. The wood appears to be fine grained and smooth, unlike that of a briar pipe.

5.6.1.3 Synthetic pipe stems

Vulcanite or hard rubber pipe stems first appeared in the 1860s, yet a mere 10 years later, at least one catalogue depicted a variety of vulcanite stems for briar, meerschaum and even clay pipes (Demuth 1875:3–26). Thirty-one vulcanite pipe stems (Figure 5.75) were found in five of the study sites: Caliche (7), Chinatown (8), Arrowtown (9), Ah Lum's store (4) and the Flax Grove (3). None have maker's marks. Two main forms are represented: "friction-fit" and "threaded stem" types. In the latter form, the synthetic stem and the pipe bowl are connected by a tubular, threaded, wooden or plastic connecting piece. Those depicted (Figure 5.75) from Arrowtown and Ah Lum's are typical of the types recovered. Stylistically, the vulcanite stems from Arrowtown resemble those in "turn of the century" catalogues rather than those of the 1870s–90s (Pfeiffer (1985:9).

Amber mouthpieces and stems were most used for meerschaum pipes or cigar holders (Pfeiffer 1985:9). Five amber stems were recovered, one each from Caliche, QB2, Apple Tree, Flax Grove and Ah Lum's store (Figure 5.75f).

5.6.1.4 Shank bands

Shank bands are tubular metal ferrules of steel or silver-plated brass, typically between 1.2 and 1.9 cm long, which were used for both decoration and to strengthen the bowl shanks (where the stem is inserted). They are usually associated with friction-fit stems (Pfeiffer 1985:9). Some are embossed as decorative features (see Table 5.61; Figures 5.75g,o,q).

5.6.1.5 Discussion

Tobacco smoking has a long history in China among both men and women (Laufer 1924:22). It was usually smoked in the "traditional Chinese long pipe", which consisted of three separate pieces: a small round bowl of brass, white copper or tootnague (an alloy, peculiar to China, of copper, zinc, nickel and iron); a mouthpiece of stone, ivory or milk glass; and a bamboo or hardwood stem (Laufer 1924:22).

Although clay pipe bowls were an integral part of Chinese opium pipes, clay pipes were not used for smoking tobacco in China. The archaeological evidence indicates that if the Chinese miners arrived with traditional tobacco smoking pipes, the pipes were quickly superseded by the almost universal adoption of European smoking technology, i.e. either clay or wooden composite pipes. No remains of traditional Chinese tobacco smoking pipes have been found in the study sites. The only specimen known from Central Otago was found by a curio-hunter in a Chinese hut in the Cardrona Valley (Dennison pers. comm.). It measures 6.0 cm long and stands 2.25 cm high (Figure 5.76).

There appears to have been a gradual transition from clay pipes to the more durable pipes of composite construction (e.g. wooden bowls and vulcanite stems), but the archaeological evidence is not unequivocal. The heyday of the British clay pipe export industry was 1875–85 (Walker 1971:33), after which composite pipes gained the ascendancy. Why the Chinese abandoned their traditional smoking equipment is unclear – perhaps they preferred the larger capacity and greater compactness of the European pipes. Although the incidence of broken clay pipes is easy to understand given their fragility, it is not readily apparent why so many intact composite pipes (particularly the stems) were abandoned. One of the clay bowls from Arrowtown (ACS/7 Trench B) has been carved around the area where the stem had broken so that a new stem could be fitted. This is a common feature of pipes in Chinese frontier sites in the United States (Pfeiffer 1985:5), but it is the only example known from a Central Otago site.

Don provided several insights into the prevalence and social role of tobacco smoking among the Chinese on the southern goldfields. He noted that "Tobacco smoking is very popular among the Chinese. Opium smokers pay for their own opium, but as a non-tobacco smoker, is about as rare as a non-tea drinker, or a non-rice eater, partners in work include it [tobacco] in the common account" (Don 1/3/1888:166), although he mentioned an instance where two Chinese miners who worked together were now living apart because one objected to paying for tobacco that he did not use. While explaining his reasons for moving to Don, the man pointed to his partner's tobacco cutter (Don: 1/3/1888:166). Don's comments (e.g. Don 1/3/1888:165) clearly indicate that tobacco smoking, together with opium smoking and gambling, were the Chinese miners' chief forms of relaxation.

Both tobacco and opium smoking were habitual among the Chinese on the southern goldfields, but they were used in different social contexts. Although some opium smokers smoked alone (many in the later years), it is a "talk inducing" drug that most users prefer to smoke in the company of others (Courtwright 1982:27). Tobacco, on the other hand, is frequently smoked alone as a relaxant. The Chinese were aware of the deleterious effects of prolonged and excessive opium smoking in terms of both health and cost (it was much more expensive than tobacco). They ostracised those who "couldn't pull their weight" because they had incapacitated themselves with the drug.

5.6.2 WRITING AND COMMUNICATION ARTEFACTS

Many writing artefacts of Chinese origin were found in the study sites. Some are of types that are generally unfamiliar to non-Chinese. The discussion in this section is centred around one such artefact – Chinese inkstones. Recovered specimens, associated paraphernalia, their functions and the role of written communications are now examined.

5.6.2.1 Historical background

The earliest examples of Chinese writing are on ceramic sherds dating from c. 4000 BC. From the Shang dynasty onwards (1800–1200 BC), the evolution of Chinese writing is well documented. From the outset, Chinese writing and painting have been closely related, eventually evolving into various calligraphic scripts (Aero 1980:38–9).

The four main artefacts associated with Chinese writing – ink, inkstones (or slabs), brushes and paper – all have long histories. Collectively, they are often described as "the 4 precious things" (Jenyns 1982:232) or "the 4 treasures" (Yu 1981:7).

The ink, widely known today as "Indian Ink", is more accurately called "*encre de Chine*" by the French, for this rich black ink was developed in China towards the end of the Han dynasty (c. 200 AD; Aero 1980:139). From that date on, the literature on Chinese ink making is extensive (Jenyns 1982:229–30). Chinese ink differs from Western ink in its composition. Unlike Western ink, it does not fade when exposed to light for long periods, and it is sold in the form of solid inksticks or inkcakes rather than as a liquid. The inksticks and cakes are formed in moulds, enabling an infinite variety of shapes to be produced, ranging from simple square-sectioned sticks to elaborate sculptured inkcakes. The chief constituents of Chinese ink are lampblack and glue. The pigment was originally obtained by burning pine and other sappy woods in special furnaces and collecting the soot. The finer inks are made from the lampblack obtained by burning vegetable oils (Jenyns 1982:239). The glues were made by rendering animal products, e.g. horns. Sometimes the inks were perfumed or had other additives (Aero 1980:139). The production of good quality Chinese ink depends on good pigments, good glue (which imparts texture and longevity) and long grinding (Aero 1980:139).

When required, a portion of an inkstick is ground on a palette that is specially designed for the purpose. They are usually known as inkstones or inkslabs (although not all were made of stone; some were made of ceramic). The oldest known specimens date from the Han dynasty (Chang and Chang 1980:142). Although inkstones are made in many shapes and sizes and are often elaborately carved and decorated, they all have in common a flat or slightly concave surface for grinding the inkstick and a shallow "well" at one end for holding water (see Figure 5.77:1–6). The ground ink powder is mixed with water brushed up from the well to produce ink of whatever consistency the user wants. In their simplest and commonest form, inkstones consist of rectangular or circular slabs of fine-grained stone (c. 1.5 cm thick) with the abovementioned features carved into their surface. Even these basic forms may have floral or other decorations, usually carved in raised relief around the "well". Frequently, the owner's name or "literary sentiments" are incised into the base of the stone. They were usually sold and kept in a two-piece wooden "case" consisting of a base section (often footed) and a lift-off cover. The quality and decoration on the "cases" usually matched that of the inkstone inside. Inkstones were regarded as the most valued of the calligraphic tools. They have an inherent heirloom value related to their durability, antiquity and quality of workmanship, and unlike the other writing necessities (brushes, inksticks and paper), being made of stone and other durable materials, virtually never wear out. Both inkstones and inkcakes (the latter because of their scent and artistic modelling) are considered collectors' items (Jenyns 1982:231–2).

Several examples of another form of ink-grinding device, "ink mortars", are documented, but little is known about their antiquity. Ink mortars are essentially robust ceramic dishes with a broad flat base. Reported archaeological specimens (all from US and Canadian sites) are stoneware, vary between 10 and 16 cm in diameter, 7 to 9 cm in base diameter, 3 to 4 cm in height and have green-glazed rims (Bressie and Bressie 1972:101; Asian Artefact Inventory data). Although they may have had other uses such as for washing brushes and mixing shades of grey (Yu 1981:24), their robust construction suggests their primary purpose was for dry-grinding inksticks and cakes.

Like the other "writing artefacts", the Chinese writing (and painting) brush has a long history. The invention of the camel's hair brush is traditionally attributed to one Meng Tian in 250 BC, but brushes probably existed much earlier, as evidenced by the decorations on pottery from the Shang era (c. 1523–1028 BC; Yu 1981:10). The Chinese brush is unique, its distinguishing feature being the fact that the tips are always trimmed to a point. The brush part is made from animal hair, including that of weasels, rabbits, deer, foxes, wolves, sheep, and goats. The handle is usually made of bamboo, which imparts lightness and balance (Figure 5.77–7). Chinese brushes are made in at least 10 sizes and there are many different types of variable stiffness. They have been described by a Chinese painting teacher as "a superbly sensitive and responsive instrument, the pivotal point from which Chinese calligraphy and painting developed" (Yu 1981: 10–13).

The fourth "writing treasure", paper, was invented in China c.105 AD. The invention is attributed to one Cai Lun, a member of the Imperial household. Over a thousand years elapsed before this revolutionary discovery reached Europe. Prior to the development of paper, the Chinese used silk and bamboo as writing surfaces. The basic technique of paper making has changed little over the centuries. It involves macerating plant fibre, rolling the drained fibre into sheets which are then dried. The different qualities, weights and textures of paper are produced by mixing various combinations of wood pulp, plant fibres and bleaching chemicals. The most common additives in Chinese rice paper (which has become a generic name) are mulberry bark, bamboo, hemp and sandalwood. Rice stalks are seldom used today. Rice paper is delicate yet strong and noted for its absorbency (Yu 1981:26–7).

5.6.2.2 The archaeological evidence

Artefacts associated with traditional Chinese writing were recovered from three sites: Chinatown (S133/48; in four huts), the Flax Grove shelter (S133/494) in the Kawarau Gorge and the Sandy Point hut site (S124/231) in the Upper Clutha Valley; however, only two of the "4 traditional writing treasures" are represented, inkstones (described in Table 5.62 and illustrated in Figure 5.77:1–6) and a few pieces of paper bearing Chinese calligraphy. Other than remnants of paper labels on opium cans and bottles of Chinese origin, most of the paper artefacts were recovered from two sites, the Flax Grove and Rockfall 1 shelters (Table 5.64). They were preserved because they were used as caulking in the stone walling. The most notable are a list detailing various ingredients for a medicine to treat rheumatism and headaches, and a list citing various products, weights and prices. Both are written on rice paper. *Paak kop piu* gambling tickets were found in both shelters. Numerous scraps of plain red paper found in Ah Lum's store were also probably of Chinese origin. Red paper was used extensively on auspicious occasions (see Don 2/4/1882:184). Don (2/11/1885:84) noted that the Chinese usually burnt "waste lettered paper".

Several writing artefacts of European origin were also recovered, including stoneware and glass ink bottles (in several sites, e.g. Chinatown n=4, ACS n=6), a piece of chalk (ACS/2), a purple lead pencil (Ah Lum's store), a red crayon (Sheung Fong shelter), slate pencils (n=9, in Ch/16, Ch/18, ACS/5, Ah Lum's main room and bedroom, Caliche, Ah Wee's, the Rapids and the Flax Grove site) and several fragments of writing slates (Ch/19 and Ch/21, ACS/7, Firewood Creek, Ha Fong and the Rapids). Many of the latter have a grid of incised lines and some have chamfered edges (see Section 5.6.7; Figure 5.104). The piece of slate from ACS/7 has vertical columns incised on it with individual marks totalling 13 (written ⅢⅢ ⅢⅢ III). The fragments of gridded slate in four sites were possibly used in the game *wei-qi*, rather than for literary or accounting purposes. Fragments of unmarked building slate found in other sites, including rockshelters, may have been earmarked for the same purpose. The purple lead pencil may have been used by Ah Lum himself for accounting purposes.

5.6.2.3 Discussion and conclusions

Although the Chinese sojourners had access to many familiar things (particularly foods) through the network of Chinese stores on the goldfields, it is clear from contemporary records (notably those of the Rev. Alexander Don) that many gradually lost touch with kith and kin in China and events there because of a gradual communication breakdown, both voluntary and involuntary. The situation was exacerbated by the time lag between writing and receipt of letters, reluctance to write because individuals often did not have any spare money to send home, and the distancing effect created by the protracted sojourns of many of the miners.

Most of the letters the Chinese miners received in New Zealand, directly or indirectly, asked for money.

Relatives at home often did not understand the difficulties involved in goldmining and tended to think the miners spent most of their earnings on opium, gambling and high living (probably true in some cases) rather than saving to improve the standard of living of their family in China. Similarly, it was unusual for a Chinese miner to write home unless he had sent or was about to send some money (see Don's comments summarised in Butler 1977:49–50). The evidence suggests that as gold returns declined, so too did letter writing.

It is difficult to ascertain the degree of literacy, or at least the ability to read and/or write Chinese, among the Chinese miners. Again, Don provides insights. Regarding letter writing he noted that "as in China, several men in Round Hill and Riverton earned a living as scribes, writing letters for those unable to do so" (Don 1/9/1882:45). Don himself was often asked and offered payment to write letters (Don 1/9/1882:45). On the same visit he noted that "a group of men were clustering about an educated man in a store who was reading the news from the *Chinese Mail* (Don 1/9/1882:44). He advocated the *Chinese Illustrated News* to the Chinese miners as a means of keeping in touch with events at home; several of the miners at Round Hill subscribed (Don 1/7/1882:3). Chinese language books were highly valued: "They were removed from one hut to another by their owners until they literally fell apart" (Don 1/1/1885:124). These references indicate that at least in the early years, many of the Chinese were keenly interested in keeping up with events in their homeland, treasured reading material, and if they could not write, contracted someone to do so. Don (1894:22–3) also noted an incident where a Chinese miner, who had had his mining tools stolen by a European, waded through six volumes of a Chinese–English dictionary selecting "violent and abusive phrases and words". He practised on "sheet after sheet of paper (old grocery bags and account forms) and then composed a letter and gave it to the misappropriator". As a result, he got his tools back.

The archaeological evidence reflects the interest in written communications too, although some of the "traditional prerequisites", inksticks and writing brushes, have not been recovered. Presumably, most of the inkstones were owned by educated Chinese who could write their native script fluently, possibly "the scribes" as described by Don, but why so many intact inkstones were abandoned remains a mystery.

No clear pattern is evident from the distribution of the recovered inkstones. As might be expected, there was a relatively high proportion (4, or 66%) in the Cromwell Chinese Camp site (i.e. Chinatown), yet none were found in the Arrowtown settlement. Two of the Chinatown specimens were found within a metre of each other in hut 26. One of the two is the only example in the assemblage that could be considered "worn out" (Figure 5.77–5). The sparse rural distribution is more readily understandable, inkstones only being found in two sites – the Flax Grove shelter in the Kawarau Gorge and in the Sandy Point (Upper Clutha) hut site.

It is apparent from excavated specimens and descriptions in art books (e.g. Jenyns 1982) that inkstones have "tremendous individuality", perhaps greater than any other Chinese artefact. To date, few have been reported in the archaeological literature. Brown and Rusco (1979:624) described and depicted a complete example from Lovelock, Nevada, while a fragment, with an apparently identical design, found in the Cortez Mining District of the same state, was reported by Hardesty and Hattori (1983:43). Evans (1980:94) stated that a fragment of a black inkstone was recovered at Donner Summit, California. The Asian American Comparative Collection at the University of Idaho, Laboratory of Anthropology holds two donated specimens (Wegars pers. comm.).

There are three basic shapes of inkstone: rectangular with rounded corners, oval and circular, but there are wide variations in dimensions and decoration within these broad categories. There seems to be more consistency in the rock types selected for making inkstones. The Central Otago specimens (except the one from the Sandy Point site) are all composed of either grey or black phyllitic rock. This is consistent with the rock types of the overseas specimens described above. The fact that the Sandy Point specimen is of such markedly different petrology raises doubts about whether it is an inkstone.

The six inkstones from Chinese sites in Central Otago constitute a useful assemblage for comparative and typological purposes. Their presence reflects the long history of Chinese writing and the retention of its basic technology. The Euro ink bottles and other writing artefacts indicate the gradual adoption by many of the miners and storekeepers of Western writing technology, while the ethno-historical information suggests that overall there was a gradual decline in written communications between the Chinese miners in New Zealand and their families in China.

5.6.3 DENTARY ARTEFACTS

The two main dentary artefacts in the study sites, ceramic toothpaste pots and bone-handled toothbrushes, were studied by Bedford (1985c). The discussion and historical information presented here are based on his analysis and conclusions.

Earthenware pots were first used in the 18th century for retailing a wide variety of food and cosmetic products such as bear's grease ("for the growth of hair"), shaving creams and ointments, but by the end of the 19th century their main usage was for packaging toothpastes. Bedford's study concentrated on toothpaste containers because only one other product packaged in this type of container was represented in the study sites, the ubiquitous "Holloway's 'cure-all' Ointment".

5.6.3.1 The assemblages

Dentary artefacts were found in five sites – Ah Wee's (S115/54), QB2 (S124/207), both rural sites in the Upper Clutha area, Firewood Creek (S133/424), Caliche (S133/223) and Cromwell's Chinatown (S133/48). The latter three are within 5 km of Cromwell. Twelve ceramic pots were recovered in total. Seven were represented by pot lids (two being complete with bases). Of the seven, five are toothpaste lids while the other two were "Holloway's Ointment" containers (Table 5.64). The other ceramic pots (5) were represented by unmarked bases, so it is not possible to state for certain what product they contained.

Twelve toothbrushes, of three different styles, were defined by Bedford (1985c), including one from the Ledge site (S133/868), a European house dump that contained a small amount of Chinese material. Later, another toothbrush, incised "J. C. Oddie, Chemist, Timaru" (Figure 5.79d; Table 5.65), was found during test trenching of a small horticultural terrace area associated with Cromwell's Chinatown. A circular aluminium dentifrice can labelled "Cussons's Dentifrice, London and Manchester, Made in England" was found at the base of layer one in feature 25 (a mixed midden deposit) at Chinatown. Its deposition almost certainly postdates the Chinese occupation.

5.6.3.2 Historical background: ceramic pots and toothbrushes

5.6.3.2.1 Ceramic pots

Ceramic pots were first used for packaging products in the 18th century. The earliest pots were decorated with uniform blue rings or stripes and were sold to retailers who then applied their own paper labels. From 1750 a few retailers began to have their pots handpainted by potters who would add the trader's name. As time went on, addresses and short descriptions of the pot's contents were added (Davis 1967:39).

During the mid-1800s great changes were being made in the methods of industrial production and marketing (Prickett 1981:581). American manufacturers ushered in a new era of mass production and the standardisation of products and packaging. With these advances came an increasing range of manufactured goods and there was a demand for cheaper, more attractive and sales-stimulating containers. The establishment of large-scale manufacturers and wholesalers created a shift away from small shopkeepers who manufactured, packaged and sold locally, to large retailers who traded on a national level. Handpainted pots were totally unsuited to cope with the 19th-century boom in sales of packaged household products and their nationwide distribution.

Transfer printing was the answer to quantity production of attractive pot lids and other earthenware containers. By the beginning of the 19th century, underglaze transfer printing in one colour was developed. With this process (see Section 5.2.3 for details about the process) a single design could be used an almost unlimited number of times.

By the 1840s, multicoloured underglaze transfer printing had been perfected. The best known makers of these pot lids were F. & R. Pratt & Co. of Fenton, Staffordshire, who produced pot lids with elaborate scenes. Today these lids are called "Pratt Ware". Other firms used the underglaze colour printing process on pottery too. Their customers were the retailers who sold products to upper-class markets. Coloured pot lids had a limited period of manufacture and reached the peak of their popularity in the 1860s (Davis 1967:40). As they were relatively expensive to produce, companies recouped their cost in the price of the luxury products sold in the pots e.g. bear's grease or shrimp paste. It is no surprise then that no Pratt Ware pots have been found in early goldmining sites in Central Otago. The three excavated multicoloured toothpaste pot lids have litho-transfers, which was a cheaper and later process (Clarke 1970:299). The demise of the multicoloured lids was brought about by the combined effects of rising production costs, competition from other packaging materials and changing fashions. Production had virtually ceased altogether by 1900 (Fletcher 1975:9).

Black and white transfer printed pot lids remained popular well after coloured lids had fallen out of general use because they were cheaper to produce, could compete with other forms of packaging and were durable. Paper labels, no matter how inexpensive printers could make them, were rather inefficient on pots containing greasy creams and those that came into contact with water as often as toothpaste pots (Fletcher 1975:10).

The growth of large manufacturing and wholesale chemists who ordered thousands of lids a year to advertise their product also helped sustain the black and white pot lid market (and one or two litho-transferred, multicoloured lids such as the John Gosnell & Co. lid; Figure 5.78a). As public interest in health and hygiene grew, so too did the trade in quack medicines, ointments, cosmetics and toothpaste. During the last 20 years of the 19th century, the black and white pot lid market was sustained and even expanded. England exported large quantities to the United States and to all parts of the British Empire.

Transfer printed pots underwent several changes in shape and style. The earliest pots were straight-sided cylinders with flat lids. From the 1840s the domed lid became the standard shape. Circular pots were by far the most popular, although by the 1890s a few wholesale chemists began to favour square and rectangular pots in an attempt to solve the problem of insecure lids (a problem never satisfactorily resolved); a flat-sided pot could be more easily fastened with string (Fletcher 1975:27). Printing a transfer on the underside of a lid as well as on the top had brief popularity in the 1890s. Costs of production were kept down by mass producing pots with standardised designs advertising "toothpastes" or "cold creams". These had blank spaces for an individual chemist's name and address. After 1900, competition from other packaging materials became relentless – greaseproof cardboard, pots made of cork and, most significant of all, the adoption of the collapsible (squeezable) tube as a form of packaging for toothpaste. Collapsible tubes were invented in 1841 and were first used for artists' colours. The first record of toothpaste in tubes is 1892 (Davis 1967: 83).

5.6.3.2.2 Toothbrushes

The first implements associated with oral hygiene were probably twigs used as toothpicks to relieve the irritation of food stuck between the teeth. In some parts of Africa and Asia the separated end fibres of a twig are still used as a primitive form of toothbrush. The custom of chewing aromatic woods to give a pleasant odour to the breath has a long history in the Middle East and elsewhere (Beaver 1980:iv).

The first record of a brush specifically for cleaning the teeth occurs in a letter written in England in 1651. The brushes at this time were short stiff-haired tools resembling paintbrushes, but even then they were described as "toothbrushes" (Beaver 1980:iv).

In the 1780s an efficient and simple toothbrush was designed (the style is basically unchanged today) by a London tradesman, William Addis. It was made of bone and horse-tail hair. The making of these bone-handled brushes was an extremely labour-intensive process involving up to 53 separate processes, mostly concerned with shaping the handle.

Bone toothbrush handles (of the types recovered in the study sites; Figure 5.79) were made from ox thigh and buttock bones, the ends of the bones being sawn off and sold to button makers (Beaver 1980:3). The handles were shaped with planes, files and knives, and then drilled to take the tufts of hair. On the back of the brush, shallow grooves were cut for wires to secure the tufts in place. The handles were tumbled, to give them a smooth matt surface, polished, bleached and degreased before white horse-tail hair or pigs bristles were inserted. Adding the bristles required skill and dexterity as small bunches were drawn into the holes by wires in the back of the brush.

The first plastic-handled (celluloid) toothbrushes appeared in the 1920s and were produced alongside bone-handled brushes. Handmade bone-handled toothbrushes became obsolete in Western countries after the Second World War (Beaver 1980:33), but in 1981 the author purchased one in a Chinese store in San Francisco. This modern example, which was made in Hong Kong, is of basically similar construction to those depicted in Figure 5.79.

5.6.3.3 Discussion and conclusions

The appearance of these artefacts in Chinese sites supports other evidence showing that although the Chinese miners continued to rely on products imported from China, they were quick to adopt several European foodstuffs, beverages and other products, which are represented in the archaeological assemblages e.g. pipes (Foster 1983), tinned products (Ritchie and Bedford 1985) and bottled goods (Ritchie and Bedford 1983).

The industrial strength of England in the 19th century, its role in supplying manufactured goods to all areas under the British flag, and New Zealand's dependence on this trade is clearly demonstrated by these artefacts. Except for the one pot lid made for the Australian chemist Felton (Figure 5.78b), all the excavated lids and bases were made in England and used by large British chemical wholesalers. The Australian lid may have been made in Australia (Vader and Murray 1975:78) but is just as likely to have been made in England. No pot lids advertising a New Zealand chemist were excavated although over 40 are known, such as "Haynes Carbolised toothpaste", which was made in Dunedin and widely distributed within New Zealand (*Cyclopedia of New Zealand* 1905 Vol. 4; see Bedford 1985c).

All the excavated toothbrushes were made of bone. The process of manufacture has destroyed possible identification of the bone type (Kooyman pers. comm.). They were probably made in England, judging from incised toothbrushes found in a contemporary European site, the Logan Park dump, Dunedin (many toothbrushes were also imported from France). None of the excavated brushes bear maker's marks, but four have an identical impressed "bull's eye" design suggesting they were produced by the same firm (a similar mark has been observed on a toothbrush found in a Chinese site in the United States). A toothbrush with the retailer's name "J. C. Oddie, Chemist, Timaru" incised on the handle was uncovered during a test excavation on a small horticultural terrace associated with Cromwell's Chinatown. However, although the toothbrush is undoubtedly contemporaneous with the Chinese occupation (Oddie established his business in 1895; *Cyclopedia of New Zealand* 1903 Vol. 3), the terrace deposit was found to be disturbed and mixed, evidenced by the juxtaposition of 100-year-old artefacts alongside a frisbee and beer cans.

The relatively small number of pots and toothbrushes may be due to several factors. Even in 1900, after 120 years of toothbrush production, products for cleaning teeth were still not widely used, especially among the working class (Beaver 1980:15). Regular brushing of teeth may not have been a common practice among the miners, or less obvious methods may have been employed. The expense may have been a disincentive too; at a cost of sixpence or more per pot, toothpaste was probably considered a luxury or only purchased when a miner was well off.

The fact that 66% (8) of the toothbrushes and 50% (6) of the toothpaste pots were found in Cromwell's Chinatown suggests that the Chinese there may have adopted European teeth-cleaning practices and the associated artefacts more readily than their countrymen who lived further from "town".

The utility of toothpaste pots for dating sites is limited because they are relatively uncommon artefacts. None have been uncovered in the other major historic site excavations in New Zealand to date (Nichol 1979; Prickett 1981; Spring-Rice 1982), but it is likely a lot more will be found in future, particularly in urban sites. Pots that have a maker's mark or a company's name on the lid can be dated (particularly those advertising short-lived New Zealand chemists). Toothbrushes have limited utility for dating because of their long production span and lack of differentiation. Again, those that have a maker's mark on the handle should be datable (see Herskovitz 1978:129).

Artefacts associated with oral hygiene are a small and infrequently recovered component of historic archaeological sites in New Zealand thus far, yet they are the humble forbears of "everyday implements" that we take for granted. Although their archaeological potential in New Zealand may appear somewhat limited (because of the small site assemblages recovered to date), gradually, as more of these types of artefacts are recovered and reported, more significant cultural information and traits will be able to be defined.

5.6.4 BUTTONS, TEXTILES, CLOTHING HARDWARE AND FOOTWEAR

The buttons, textiles and clothing hardware (but not the footwear) from the study sites were the subject of a BA (Hons) dissertation by Fiona Cameron (1985). I acknowledge I have substantially drawn on her research in the following discussion. Cameron also drew all the button and clothing hardware illustrations reproduced in my thesis and here. These artefacts are of special significance because the adoption of European clothing was one of the areas where the Chinese sojourners made significant acculturative changes.

5.6.4.1 Buttons

Altogether, 519 buttons were recovered. The types and their distribution are detailed in Tables 5.66–5.72.

It is likely that most of the buttons were imported from the leading manufacturing countries, Great Britain (which was the main producer during the 19th century) and the United States. Button manufacturing (using synthetic plastics) did not begin in New Zealand until 1939, although small numbers of handcrafted buttons were made here before that date (Cameron pers. comm.).

A brief description and discussion of the main types is presented now. Minimal descriptions of manufacturing techniques are outlined here (see Cameron 1985 for further details). The buttons as classified by Cameron (1985) are depicted in Figures 5.80–5.92 and their site distribution is detailed in Tables 5.66–5.72. For specific details about each button type, refer to Cameron (1985).

5.6.4.1.1 Shell buttons

During the latter half of the 19th century, a major industry developed in the Pacific Islands revolving around the collection of pearl-oyster shell for button manufacture (Albert and Kent 1949). The British industry, centred around Birmingham, peaked in the 1870s (White 1977:67). According to Kirk (1975:326), shell buttons were more popular in the United States than elsewhere. The US industry differed too in that it also utilised large volumes of shell from freshwater species. In early 20th century American catalogues, "pearl buttons" are advertised as attractive features on many styles of clothing (Clerico 1979:442). They dominated button production in the United States from c.1890 until the late 1940s when synthetic buttons began to dominate the market (Clerico 1979:440), but in Britain their popularity had peaked by 1890 (White 1977:75).

Two basic styles were found in the study sites – plain 2 and 4 hole "sew through" types (Figure 5.85). These buttons are most associated with light garments such as shirts and underwear. They constitute 33% (n=170) of the assemblages from the study sites. Figure 5.93 depicts the remains of a piece of hand-worked shell found in the Rapids site. It may have been used as an improvised toggle.

5.6.4.1.2 Glass buttons

Glass buttons (10) constitute a mere 1.9% of buttons found in the study sites. Because it is difficult to distinguish them from porcelain buttons, Cameron (1985:113) used X-ray diffraction. All 10 proved to be of pressed glass manufacture. This type of button was used on the same type of garments as the pearl shell buttons, but their low representation may indicate they were used on higher-quality garments, which the miners seldom acquired. Most of the glass buttons are relatively plain "sew through" types (Figure 5.88; see Cameron 1985 for further details). Pressed glass buttons were especially popular between 1870–80 and 1910 (Epstein 1968:62; Peacock 1972:49).

5.6.4.1.3 Metal buttons

The 283 metal and metal-composite buttons (47.6%) constituted the largest type-group found in the sites. Metallic buttons include a wide variety of styles (Cameron 1985:20–69) and this is reflected in the site assemblages (Figures 5.80–5.83). According to Kirk (1976:388), machine-made buttons began to dominate the button market by 1850. Embossed metal buttons were particularly popular between 1880 and 1900 (Cameron pers. comm.). Most of those used on New Zealand-made clothing were imported from Britain. The Metal Stamping Company of London and Birmingham was the leading manufacturer. Two major manufacturing techniques are evident: one-piece construction (either by casting or stamping) and composite construction. The major variants are:

a. **recessed-metal buttons** (Figure 5.80). These were the most common metal buttons in the sites. The 183 buttons of this type represent 35% of the combined assemblages. They consist of a stamped or cast metal disc (one-piece construction) with a central depression or recess containing 2 or 4 holes for sewing the buttons on to garments. Most "sew through" metal buttons were used on men's trousers (Clerico 1979:460). Both plain and impressed buttons of this form were made, but the latter are particularly useful from an archaeological point of view because they bear brands, trademarks, manufacturer's names, and locations and other information that can be useful for dating or determining trade links etc. Concave "dish-shaped" variants were also recovered. The legible, embossed recessed-metal buttons are listed in Table 5.70.
b. **fabric-covered metal buttons** (Figure 5.84). This type constitutes only 5.6% (29) of the assemblages. The majority are linen-covered. There may have been more originally, but the fabric has decomposed. They have a depression in the reverse side, partly covered with a thin wire bar to enable the buttons to be sewn on to garments by means of a cloth shank. They were popular from the 1880s on. There are advertisements for imported button covering machines and button components in Stone's Directories from 1889 on (Cameron pers. comm.). According to Kirk (1976:387), these buttons were used on a wide range of clothing.
c. **metal studs** (Table 5.69) (n=29). These are essentially a variation of a rivet. They are not sewn on but are secured in place by hand or machine flaring of the back portion of the stud. They were and still are commonly used on trousers, especially jeans.
d. **collar studs** are a distinctive form of "button" that were used for securing men's dress shirt collars. Only one was found in the study sites (in hut 23 at Chinatown).

5.6.4.1.4 Bone buttons

Bone was one of the first materials utilised for making buttons and was also used as a filler in composite metal buttons. Cattle bone was the main type of bone used (Luscomb 1968:25), degreased and cleaned bone often being obtained as offcuts from toothbrush manufacturers (Beaver 1980:iv). By the 1930s they had virtually disappeared from the marketplace in the United States (Kirk 1975:301) and were probably declining in popularity in New Zealand too. They represent only 4% (22) of the buttons from the Chinese sites (Figure 5.86). Several of the bone buttons are over 2.5 cm in diameter, which suggests they are off overcoats. All are "sew through" styles. One of the "bone" buttons was made of horn (Cameron 1985:104).

5.6.4.1.5 Synthetic plastic buttons

Buttons of this type (n=5; Figure 5.90) constitute only 1.0% of the combined assemblages. The invention of bakelite, the world's first synthetic plastic, in 1907 was the foundation of the plastic industry (Luscombe 1968:154). Because they can be moulded into practically any shape or style, synthetic plastics are the dominant material used in button manufacture today, virtually replacing the use of natural materials such as rubber, bone, shell and ivory. However, as "plastics" were not widely adopted by button manufacturers until the 1930s (Luscomb 1968:154), it accounts for the relatively low incidence of plastic buttons in the study sites, which all predate 1925.

5.6.4.1.6 Wooden buttons

These are relatively uncommon (15, or 2.9%) and limited to "sew through" buttons of large diameter, probably off overcoats (Figure 5.87; see Cameron 1985:106).

5.6.4.1.7 Rubber buttons

Four (0.8%) vulcanite rubber buttons were recovered (Figure 5.91). According to Kirk (1975:347), the manufacture of rubber buttons was not commercially successful and lasted only a few years. Most rubber buttons postdate 1851, when Goodyear patented a technique for making rubber hard and inflexible and suitable for button making (Kirk 1975:347). The recovered specimens are all "sew through" types. They were generally used on coats and heavy outer wear (Clerico 1979:481).

5.6.4.1.8 Slate button

A single button (Figure 5.92) made of slate was found in hut 7 at Chinatown. Slate and clay buttons were produced by British and French manufacturers during the 19th century (Cameron pers. comm.). They never attained wide popularity.

5.6.4.1.9 Discussion on buttons

No clear patterns are evident in the inter-site distribution of the buttons; generally, those sites that contained relatively few artefacts also produced few buttons, whereas in the more productive sites such as huts 23 and 26 at Chinatown, large numbers of buttons were uncovered.

Shell and metal buttons are numerically dominant in the site assemblages, a pattern that corresponds with their main periods of production and popularity, but only the latter can be reasonably precisely dated. Dates are determined by changes in manufacturing techniques, production, popularity and availability (Kirk 1976:229). Embossed metal buttons are particularly useful from an archaeological perspective because information such as brands, manufacturer's names and locations can be used for dating or determining trade links.

Cameron (1985:136–48) seriated the buttons from the study sites (Figures 5.94–5.96). Generally, she found a close association with the known periods of occupation or dating achieved by other means (Cameron 1985:147). Certain button classes indicated inconceivably early dates for the initial occupation of the Chinatown site. This discrepancy could reflect the re-use of pearl/shell buttons or old clothing, but the buttons are more likely derived from earlier European activity in the area (the Chinatown area was mined by Europeans between 1862 and 1866), i.e. before the first Chinese arrived.

Most of the buttons are of types that were used on men's clothing, particularly trousers, shirts and underwear, with lesser numbers from coats, suits, cardigans etc. (see Table 5.71). The low numbers of glass buttons is because they were not used on "work clothes". Few, if any, of the recovered buttons are of types usually or specifically associated with women's or children's clothing. This is not surprising because the study sites are known from historical observations and records to have been occupied almost exclusively by adult male Chinese.

Clothing is one aspect of Western material culture that the Chinese miners appear to have readily accepted, probably for the very practical reason that Western garments were better suited for the rigours of mining and the climate of southern New Zealand. Only two of the recovered buttons were almost certainly associated with Chinese garments (and by inference made in China). These buttons are in the form of small brass balls with an attachment shank (Figure 5.81 Style A). Single specimens were recovered from the Firewood Creek and Ha Fong shelters (both sites date from c.1870). Buttons of this type are evident on men's jackets in contemporary photographs depicting scenes in China (see Cameron 1985). Although limited numbers of Chinese fasteners may have been lost or discarded at the sites and not survived, the most plausible explanation is that the Chinese miners adopted Western clothing from the outset. This contention is supported by contemporary observations and early photographs that depict the Chinese miners in European clothing, whether at work or leisure.

Initially some Chinese continued to wear items of traditional clothing around their settlements, in part as a means of "class distinction":

> Then there are the hook-nosed shoes, the nankeen breeches, and the broad brimmed hat, by which the claims of class distinction are adjusted among our Mongolian friends, all contributing to a scene sufficiently novel to make even an "Old Identity" feel as if he were a stranger in the land of his adoption. (a European observer's comments about the Lawrence Chinese Camp; *Otago Daily Times* 1/10/1869:7)

Well-to-do merchants were invariably photographed in ornate traditional (Mandarin) clothing in posed photographs (see Butler 1977 for examples). The Chinese probably acquired Western clothes from European stores initially, but in view of the potential market, the Chinese merchants are unlikely to have wasted much time before obtaining stock. Some of the European clothing may have been acquired from second-hand sources, but there is no documentary evidence that the Chinese miners acquired European "castoffs" and it may have been culturally offensive to do so.

The following observation by Don indicates that traditional Chinese clothing was available from Chinese stores at Riverton (and probably other locations on the goldfields) at least until the mid-1880s. The incident concerned the body of a Chinese miner who had committed suicide at Round Hill. Don (1/4/1884:184) stated: "Before being coffined, the corpse was dressed (by his clansmen) in new trousers, jacket, socks, shoes, and hat – all Chinese except the socks and hat, which were not to be had in Riverton." I have not been able to ascertain whether dressing corpses in traditional clothing was a standard funerary practice for those who died on the New Zealand goldfields, but it is likely such action and expense probably depended on the number, wealth and benevolence of fellow clansmen.

5.6.4.2 Clothing hardware

Like the buttons, the clothing hardware components were studied by Cameron (1985), consequently only limited discussion is presented here. However, this discussion also incorporates artefacts such as glass beads, which were not examined by Cameron. The types and their distribution are detailed in Tables 5.73a–5.74.

After buttons, buckles were the next most common and widespread clothing fittings, particularly iron and brass belt buckles classified by Cameron (1985) as types A and B respectively. The other subcategories she defined, C, D and E, cover small rectangular buckles that functioned as adjusters on waistcoats and trousers (Cameron 1985:154). By mutual agreement, her illustrations are reproduced here. Refer Cameron (1985) for specific details. Thirteen of the buckles are impressed either "Paris Solide", "Paris", "Prima Solide" or "Prima". Their similar construction and the style of the wording suggests they were all made by the same French manufacturer. A selection of the buckles is depicted in Figure 5.99. Only three ornate buckles were found, depicting a "Crossed Swords" trademark (Ch/23), a lion face (Ch/19; Figure 5.97–3) and crossed cricket bats (Apple Tree site; Figure 5.97–1).

Several braces adjusters (including the common D-shaped adjusters) and associated fittings such as leather loops were also recovered. Their limited distribution suggests that belts were the preferred means for securing trousers. This contention is supported by literature references (Cameron 1985:155). Other miscellaneous items of clothing hardware are depicted in Figure 5.98.

The eight spherical glass beads are detailed in Table 5.72. They are almost certainly of Chinese origin (see Fenstermaker and Williams 1979), but it is uncertain whether they were worn in the form of a necklace or as a clothing or hair adornment. Similar beads were also used as spacers in Chinese bamboo door curtains (Fenstermaker and Williams 1979).

The role of the other artefacts is self-explanatory. Except for a blue plastic suspender (which was found on the surface of Ch/19 and is unlikely to be very old), the clothing fittings reflect a masculine environment.

5.6.4.3 Textile analysis

The textile remains were studied by Cameron (1985). The dry climate of Central Otago and the protected environments of the rockshelters and some of the open sites enabled the recovery of many textile specimens, although there were few substantially complete garments. The recovered specimens were examined microscopically and burn-tested to identify fibres and permit an assessment of garment types (Cameron 1985:162). One site, the Flax Grove shelter, was especially productive (see Table 5.75); many of the textiles from this site have attached clothing fittings.

Fragments of woollen fabric (n=183) constituted the majority of the samples. Most were machine woven and are most likely remnants of garments of New Zealand or British manufacture (Cameron 1985:166). Woollen material was first manufactured in New Zealand in 1848, but a large-scale manufacturing industry was not established until the 1870s, when companies such as Kaiapoi Woollen Manufacturing commenced operation.

During the latter half of the 19th century, wool-growing was only a very small industry in China and exports of wool products were negligible (Pope 1984:143). These factors, plus the fact that wool is seldom mentioned in descriptions of traditional attire, led Cameron (1985:166) to conclude that the woollen remains found in the sites represent foreign items of clothing and bedding acquired and used by the Chinese.

Cotton materials formed the second-largest category of fibre fragments (n=119). Cotton has been cultivated in China since the 13th century. It became the most popular and widely used fabric for Chinese clothing, especially for the peasantry. The Chinese peasant's costume comprised versatile loose-fitting cotton garments (Pope 1984:143; Cameron 1985:171).

According to Cameron (1985:171), the recovered cotton fragments cannot be positively associated with Chinese or European clothing, but the patterns and textures on many of the fragments appear to this writer's inexperienced eye to be consistent with those on European garments. Lightweight cottons were used in shirts, while heavier grades such as denim, duck and corduroy were used primarily for trousers and to a lesser extent jackets (Hardingham 1978:57–8). Cotton knit material was used for lightweight summer underwear. Linseed oil-impregnated cotton (oilskin) was used for waterproof clothing (Cameron 1985:166).

Only two silk articles were found in the study sites. A cream-coloured silk ribbon tied in a bow was found in the Firewood Creek site (S133/424), and a black and cream combination bow tie was recovered from the Ha Fong shelter (8133/22). Although silk has been widely used in China for over 3,000 years, and was valued for its opulence, high tensile strength and superior insulating qualities (Cameron 1985:172), it is unlikely that the two recovered silk articles (bow ties) are of Chinese origin. According to Ebbett (1979:30), simple, knotted bow ties were popular items of men's dress from the 1850s onwards in New Zealand.

Two fragments of linen were recovered. Both were of plain weave and beige in colour (linen canvas). This type of material is commonly called "duck" (Hardingham 1978:98). Linen is not usually associated with Chinese garments. It was normally used as shirting and trouser material by European clothing manufacturers (Hardingham 1978:106). After studying the recovered fabric remains, Cameron (1985:172) concluded that there was no unequivocal evidence of traditional Chinese attire within any of the study sites. She concluded the predominance of woollen fragments indicates that most of the garments represented were of European origin (see Table 5.75). Heavy woollen materials such as tweeds, checks and plain twill were used for jackets, waistcoats and trousers (Hardingham 1978: Ebbett 1979:30). These materials were popular in the middle to late 1800s (Ebbett 1979:30). Finer plain weaves were often used for shirting, while knitted wool was used for cardigans and winter underwear (Ebbett 1979:32).

5.6.4.4 Footwear

Remnants of 31 pairs of footwear were found in the sites. Because most of the shoes and boots were deformed or in a fragmentary condition, it was often difficult to record length and other details; however, construction characteristics were defined where possible. The footwear was divided into "rights" and "lefts" in order to determine the minimum number of pairs. Their distribution is detailed in Table 5.76.

Square-toed leather work boots were the predominant type, a minimum of 21 pairs being represented. Typically, the boots consist of multi-layered soles (2–3 layers of leather) and heels (4–6 pieces of leather) held together with a dense pattern of nails; the sole units were attached to solid leather uppers by stitching. In all instances where the upper part of the boots survived, they were secured by bootlaces threaded through brass eyelets. Many of the boots had U-shaped steel heel plates and crescent-shaped steel toe plates, as well as small hob nails to provide traction. In seven instances, the boots had been repaired (partially re-soled) at some stage. One of the leather boots (from Ch/6) is of noticeably lighter construction and has soft leather uppers. Although it is similar in shape to the work boots, it may represent a dressier, going-out style.

Rubber gumboots (MN=5) were the next most common form of footwear. Like the leather boots, they would have been used as a general-purpose work boot. Unlike modern gumboots, the excavated specimens all have two-piece soles (i.e. the tread is nailed to the base of the boot). The large number of nails in the soles and the fact that the head of many protrude slightly from the surface of the leather suggests that the Chinese may have put extra nails into the soles of the rubber boots for additional traction. Five rubber boots, from the Sandy Point, Ha Fong and Poplars sites (Table 5.76), had hob nails in the heels and soles. Steeves (1984:141) reported that there were hob nails in rubber boots lying on the surface of Chinese sites he had studied in Oregon, USA, and proposed that the practice of putting them in the soles of European-made rubber boots was unique to the Chinese miners. No evidence has been found to refute his contention. An interesting composite boot with a rubber sole and leather uppers was recovered from the Rapids site.

Only four pairs of shoes are represented: a pair of "step-in" leather shoes (from Ch/6); a single large, pointed-toe, "step-in" style shoe (Ch/6); a rubber-soled shoe (Ah Lum's); and a buckled-style child's shoe (ACS/3). The deposition of the latter two almost certainly postdates the Chinese occupation.

Most of the boots and shoes were found as isolated units both within and outside the structures. The only notable concentration was the recovery of 14 boots (MN=8 pairs, both leather and rubber) in the space of one square metre in the floor of the Ha Fong shelter. They appear to have been deliberately buried there, although the reason for doing so is not clear. Excepting the Ha Fong "cache", little can be made of the distribution of the footwear remains, which is probably attributable as much to differential survival as it is to other factors.

None of the recovered footwear bear brands or marks indicating their source of origin. However, as heavy leather and rubber work boots are not a traditional form of Chinese footwear (Hommel 1969:204), they are almost certainly of European manufacture, and were most likely made in the United Kingdom, the United States or New Zealand, although other Western sources, such as Australia, cannot be discounted. Leather "miners boots" with hob-nailed soles similar to those recovered are depicted in 1890s American store catalogues (Israel 1968; Schroeder 1970).

According to Pearce (1982:155), very few 19th-century New Zealand towns were without a bootmaker and repairer. Machinery for sewing leather revolutionised the craft, but as far as New Zealand was concerned it was a revolution that was delayed for almost 40 years. The American inventors who patented the essential devices in the 1850s (see Anderson 1968:61) held such a tight monopoly over the machine manufacture of footwear that it was not until after the turn of the century that making boots and shoes with the help of machines became firmly established in New Zealand. The first footwear factory in the country was established in Greymouth in 1860 by Michael O'Brien to make boots for goldminers. By the 1870s several factories were operating throughout New Zealand (Anderson 1968:156; Appendix 5). John Switzer, "Manufacturer and Importer of Boots, Shoes and Grindery" of Princes Street, Dunedin, was advertising that he sold "the celebrated Cookham House (British) boots" in 1863 (Harnett & Co. 1863). Sargood, Son & Ewen are another possible local source of the boots. They established in Dunedin in the mid-1860s and were manufacturing their "Standard brand" boots and shoes well before the turn of the century (McKee & Co. 1902). The machine sewing and overall appearance of the two pairs of "step-in" style shoes (mentioned above) suggests they are also of European (as opposed to oriental) manufacture.

The adoption by the Chinese of European "working footwear" is readily understandable. Robust, waterproof footwear is virtually essential in an often very cold environment like that of Central Otago, and mining involves working in or near water. Except for the child's shoe, the size and width of the recovered boots and shoes suggests they were all menswear; a pattern that is consistent with the nature of Chinese settlement in New Zealand in the 19th century (i.e. almost exclusively male mining enclaves).

Some of the recovered leather boots had been partially re-soled. In China, footwear repairs, particularly re-soling, was usually undertaken by itinerant cobblers (Hommel 1969:212). There are no records of such services on the southern goldfields, but Chinese cobblers established businesses at Alexandra (Don 1893:15), Nevis (Parcell 1976:149) and Riverton–Round Hill (Don 1/2/1884:147). The latter was described as a "bootmaker" (Don 1/2/1884:147). Don (1/8/1884:24) mentioned that a Chinese miner he visited at Round Hill was mending his Chinese shoes, and in another instance he noted that the body of a Chinese miner was dressed by his clansmen in Chinese clothing, including shoes, before being placed in a coffin (Don 1/4/1884:1884). Although no remnants of traditional Chinese straw or cloth footwear have been recovered, these observations indicate that "Chinese shoes" and "shoes made or repaired by Chinese" were available on the goldfields until at least the mid-1880s. But despite their availability, the evidence suggests that from first settlement the use of traditional Chinese footwear declined and was probably largely restricted to the wealthy (merchants and the like) and for indoor use and special occasions such as that mentioned above.

The only evidence of re-use of discarded footwear was found in the Riverside shelter. Here, a rectangle of rubber had been cut out of the upper part of a discarded gumboot, possibly for use as a patch or as packing.

Because of the fragmentary condition of the footwear and a lack of specific references, no efforts were made to date the excavated footwear by analysis of their construction characteristics. However, the recovered specimens constitute a useful assemblage for future research on "dating footwear", as promoted by Anderson (1968) and others.

5.6.4.5 Concluding comments on clothing and footwear

From the analysis of the buttons, clothing hardware, textile remnants and footwear there is no doubt that the Chinese miners in southern New Zealand readily adopted European clothing. This conclusion is affirmed from study of the clothing worn by Chinese miners in early photographs. Although it could be argued their traditional clothing and footwear were totally unsuited to the rigours of mining and the Central Otago climate and that they were compelled rather than chose to adopt European clothing, the archaeological and historical evidence suggests a degree of acceptance of European clothing far beyond that necessary for mere creature comfort. Clothing is one area where the Chinese sojourners made a significant acculturative adaptation. They obviously appreciated the warmth, durability and practicality of contemporary European men's clothing (especially work clothes and boots) and decided to wear them in preference to traditional apparel. They may also have felt the wearing of European garments made them less conspicuous and therefore less likely to attract attention and harassment.

5.6.5 PERSONAL HYGIENE AND GROOMING

Despite the numerous mentions of 19th century Chinese goldfield settlements in New Zealand, there are few accounts of hut furnishings and the more intimate aspects of personal hygiene and grooming (see Section 3.10 for some insights). The Rev. Alexander Don was one of the few Europeans who regularly ventured into Chinese dwellings. His records contain a wealth of information on most aspects of the Chinese miners' lives, but he recorded surprisingly few observations on hygiene and grooming. This does not mean, of course, that they were unconcerned about such matters, they understandably spent little time on "cleaning" when Don was present. He noted when he observed a Tuapeka Chinese miner sweeping out his hut that such activity was unusual (Don 1/2/1884:147). According to Don, the Chinese dreaded cold water. They liked very hot water to wash themselves ("washing" was done by rubbing with a wet towel) and for washing clothing (Don 2/4/1883:185). During the Chinatown excavation, elderly residents of Cromwell recalled "the tidiness of the Chinamen", and the fact "they kept the area around their huts very neat" (only one informant entered one of the huts; he had been invited in for a meal).

Few artefacts associated with personal hygiene and grooming were uncovered (see Table 5.77). They comprise a small but interesting combination of traditional and European items, although the latter are predominant. Looking at the "Chinese" artefacts first, Figure 5.100a depicts a pair of brass "cleaning tools" that were found in the Ha Fong shelter. According to a Chinese tourist who observed them on display in the Ministry of Works Information Centre in Cromwell, they were used for cleaning nails, ears etc. An identical pair was found in a Chinese hut in the Cardrona Valley (Dennison pers. comm.). Figure 5.100b is part of a wooden comb found (along with a hair queue) in a Chinese hut site in the Nevis Valley many years ago (Murray pers. comm.). A burnt fragment of a similar wooden comb was found in hut 26 at Chinatown. Three unprovenanced "grooming artefacts" (Figures 5.100c,d,e) in the Cromwell Museum are also depicted (they are believed to have been owned by Chinese in the Cromwell area). Figure 5.100c depicts a "Chinese razor" (CR 77.703) consisting of a thick triangular steel blade that folds into a crudely made wooden handle. The back of the blade has two impressed Chinese characters. Figure 5.100d is a small brush (CR 77.781) with a flat spatula-shaped handle made of horn. Figure 5.100e is a double-sided wooden comb with fine teeth of a different wood. It has delicately incised Chinese characters and a floral design along the centre section.

The European artefacts associated with grooming and hygiene reflect barbering, dental hygiene and possibly some concern about body odour. Seven cut-throat razors were recovered (four from Chinatown, two from Arrowtown and one from the Apple Tree site). A buckle, believed to be off a shaving strop, was unearthed in hut 34 at Chinatown, a 6 cm long tube of "Jeyes' Antiseptic Shaving Cream" was found in the Ha Fong shelter, and a "Barry's Trichopherous for the Skin and Hair" bottle was in the Sandy Point site. A remnant of a possible bone comb (Chinese?) was found in the main room of Ah Lum's store. In addition, scissors that could have been used for hair cutting were found in most sites (see Table 5.39) and a clothes or hair brush was found in hut 16 at Chinatown. Artefacts associated with dental hygiene were discussed in Section 5.6.3. It is notable that all are of European origin.

Ten French perfume bottles were some of the most unexpected finds in the Chinese sites (Ha Fong (1), Chinatown (3), Apple Tree (1), Poplars (1), Arrowtown (4); Table 5.3). If women were present in the Chinese settlements, the presence of the perfume bottles would be more easily explained, but considering the well-documented absence of women (see Section 3.5), and particularly in the more remote mining sites, the existence of the perfume bottles cannot be readily attributed to their presence. A possible explanation is offered. The Chinese miners were presumably concerned with "smells", either their own, those of others or those in their dwellings, and used the perfumes on their bodies or as "deodorants" (liquid incense?) to mask them. According to Don, Chinese on three occasions had expressed amazement to him that Europeans had olfactory powers (Don 1/4/1885:183), and later he noted that the Chinese often considered that Europeans emitted a disagreeable body odour that they attributed to the extensive use of beef suet and butter (neither were used by the Chinese in cooking; Don 2/8/1886:22). These comments suggest the Chinese, rightly or wrongly, considered themselves to have a refined sense of smell, and perfumes, although they were French, may have been used by some to mask what they considered were unpleasant smells. A Chinese hairdresser set up shop almost as soon as the Lawrence Chinese Camp was established (*Otago Daily Times* 1/10/1869:7). One aspect of possible acculturative behaviour, the maintenance of the traditional custom of wearing the hair in a queue, has been very difficult to quantify. According to LaLande (1982:41), overseas sojourners maintained them as a "readmission pass" to the homeland, but judging from contemporary photographs (for examples, see Butler 1977), many of the Chinese miners in New Zealand seem to have dispensed with them by 1890, if not earlier (although it is difficult to be 100% certain because most were photographed face on and many are wearing hats). Don's records contain a surprising absence of comments about this socially significant aspect of Chinese grooming.

To conclude, the Chinese appear to have made some acculturative adaptations in the area of personal hygiene and grooming, particularly with regard to the acceptance of European methods of dental hygiene and to a lesser extent shaving technology, but overall, they appear to have maintained a level of personal cleanliness and regular barbering, which were important aspects of traditional grooming behaviour.

5.6.6 ARTEFACTS ASSOCIATED WITH GAMBLING

The Chinese miners' predilection for gambling is well documented through the recorded observations of the Rev. Alexander Don, which abound with references to the playing of *fan-tan*, *paak kop piu* and dominoes (e.g. Don 2/10/1882:66–67, 1/12/1882:105, 1/2/1883:147, 1911:9), with lesser numbers of references to cockfighting (e.g. Don 1/12/1882:104), card playing (e.g. Don 1/5/1889:204), "heads or tails" (e.g. Don 1/12/1884:105), dice games (Don 1893:2, 1895:4–5) and attending horse races (Don 1893:19). Several contemporary newspaper accounts describe gambling and associated facilities in the Chinese settlements (e.g. *Otago Daily Times* 1/10/1869:7; other references in Section 3.3). According to Don (1/8/1885:26), gambling was justified by custom "for everyone gambles in China", "gambling being instilled in childhood" (Don 1/11/1889:85). Some Chinese made or attempted to make a livelihood as professional gamblers (Don 1/11/1884:84).

Many Chinese stores provided gambling and opium-smoking facilities (e.g. Don 2/10/1882:66, 1/2/1886:148) and most of the Chinese settlements had one or more gambling places (see Sections 3.2 and 3.3; Don 1/10/1886:61, 1/3/1887:164, 1/5/1889:205; *Otago Daily Times* 1/10/1869:7). But gambling, particularly the lottery-style game *paak kop piu*, served as much more than just a means of recreation or a chance of getting rich quickly, for it also provided a means whereby storekeepers could attract customers and keep tabs on their credit worthiness. This important social role of the game was outlined in Section 3.3.

It is perhaps surprising then that few artefacts specifically associated with gambling were found during the excavations. Those recovered are detailed in Table 5.78. It is likely that the majority of the 311 Chinese coins ("cash") found in the study sites were used for gambling purposes (see Section 5.6.6.2 discussion on the role of Chinese coins).

5.6.6.1 Discussion

Although Don (1/3/1887:164) recorded the existence of a "lottery house" in the residential part of the Cromwell Chinatown settlement, no definitive gambling devices were recovered. However, it is likely that the large numbers of Chinese coins (discussed below), particularly those in hut 26, were used for gambling purposes, more specifically the playing of *fan-tan*, a game that was particularly popular among the Chinese at Cromwell (Don 1911:9). The game and associated paraphernalia were described in detail by Culin (1891b:1–7), who studied the game being played by Chinese in cities in the eastern United States. Briefly, it involves laying wagers on the number of counters between one and four (Chinese "cash" coins were often employed) left under a metal cover (*tan koe*) after groups of four are successively removed by a *tan kun* (the gamemaster, literally the "ruler of the spreading out"). According to Culin, players either put their money directly on the table or used counters or chips instead, a supply of which, of different denominations and assigned values, was usually heaped on the table. He noted that Chinese "cash" (or *zin*) coins usually represented US$0.10; *pak chu* "white pearls" (white glass counters; Figure 5.101c) US$1; *hak chu* "black pearls" (black glass counters; Figure 5.101d) US$5; chessmen US$10; and dominoes US$50 (Figure 5.101b). Dominoes were often covered with a piece of paper with an assigned value written on them (Culin 1891b:4). Similar "counters" may have been used in New Zealand (see below).

Two artefacts (Figures 5.101a and f) are believed to be *tan kei* (metal covers). The specimen depicted in Figure 5.101a, a steel lid with a brass knob, was found in the Rapids site, while that depicted in Figure 5.101f is an unprovenanced item (CR 77.788) from the Cromwell Museum. It is made of lead and has a "cash" coin inlaid in the top of the knob.

The presence of pieces of gridded slate in several sites (Table 5.83, Section 5.6.8) may be associated with the game of *wei-qi*. See Ball (1906) for rules of the game. The strongest evidence that *wei-qi* was played was found in the Firewood Creek site. Here fragments of gridded slate and two pearl-oyster shell discs (believed to be *wei-qi* counters) were found in close association. The shell discs were inside the base of a 12-bore shotgun cartridge (see Section 5.5.6, Figure 5.69h). Farris (1984:148) describes the glass counters (see below) as "go" pieces, but they were used as counters in several games including *fan-tan* (Culin 1891:4).

At Arrowtown, 11 of the glass gambling counters (10 white and one black) and the sole domino were found in the main room of the store. Their presence and the fact that this room was the most spacious in the building suggest it was utilised for gambling purposes, in addition to being a store and meeting place. Mr A. Dudley (pers. comm. 1983) recalled that "20 or 30 years ago, there used to be lots of boxes of dominoes and gambling pieces scattered on the floor. They have been souvenired over the years".

Six wooden discs, similar in size to "Chinese checkers", were found at Arrowtown; one was in ACS/2, the others in Ah Lum's bank room. They appear to have been formed by making transverse cuts across a wooden broom handle.

Evidence of the *paak kop piu* lottery system was found in the Flax Grove shelter in the Kawarau Gorge, where four tickets were crumpled up (along with many other scraps of paper) and used as caulking between the stones in the shelter wall. Remnants of another five tickets were found scattered among surface litter in the Rockfall I shelter in the Cromwell Gorge (as were two pages of the Bible written in Chinese).

Dice games are seldom mentioned in the contemporary literature in New Zealand, but Don recorded that they were played. In a brief observation about the decline of the Round Hill settlement, he noted: "The rattle of the dice and the clatter of dominoes are seldom heard (now); the jabbering and cursing of a crowd five deep around the gaming tables are no more" (Don 1893:2). Later he described a Chinese gambling game in which three die were tossed, the gambler winning if eight or nine spots turned up and losing if 11 or 12 were exposed. The other sums were neutral (Don 1895:4–5). The role of dice games among the Chinese miners in New Zealand appears to be like that recorded by Culin (1893:493) in the United States. He noted that the Chinese played several games involving die, but they were not a popular mode of gambling compared with *fan-tan* and Chinese dominoes (Culin 1893:493). No die were found in the study sites.

5.6.6.2 Chinese coins

Three hundred and eleven Chinese copper coins were found in the study sites. They are usually referred to as "cash" (Chinese *zin*). The "cash" were studied and identified by Mr G.S. Park, then Director of the Auckland Museum, using Coole's (1965) authoritative reference work. Their reign, mint and "Coole number" are detailed in Appendix 8.

"Cash" were cast in a standard form and weight with only the legend varying from about 200 BC until 1911 AD (Park 1980:55). They are renowned for being in circulation for centuries. The coins from the study sites were struck during the reigns of the Qing dynasty emperors from Shunzhi (1644–1662) to Guangxi (1875–1909); the majority being minted during the reign of Kangxi (1662–1723). Three examples are depicted in Figure 5.102. The site distribution of all the "cash" is outlined in Table 5.79.

The role of Chinese coins in New Zealand (and other contemporary overseas Chinese communities) is not fully understood. They were legal tender in China. Some Chinese may have landed in New Zealand with the expectation that any "cash" they brought with them would be negotiable, but several factors virtually preclude any possibility that they were used as currency in New Zealand (and probably elsewhere). Firstly, "cash" had a low intrinsic value. In 1907, approximately 10,000 cash were worth £1 sterling (Morse 1966:83). An economy using "cash" would require large numbers of the coins; in China they were routinely threaded together in strings of 100 or 1,000 (see King 1965:54–7).

If the coins were being used as currency in New Zealand (or within other overseas Chinese communities), one would expect the presence of substantial numbers in archaeological sites, especially since the European banking system would not accommodate them. Yet the 311 "cash" found in the Central Otago study sites represent the largest assemblage of such coins recovered archaeologically anywhere in the overseas Chinese world. Beals (1980) discussed 101 "cash" found in six aboriginal sites in the American Northwest. The yields of "cash" from reported Chinese site excavations (all in the United States) include 62 from Ventura (Kleeb 1976), 38 from Lovelock (Hattori 1979), one from Idaho City (Jones et al. 1979), 141 from Yreka (Farris 1979), 24 from Old Sacramento (Farris 1980), 10 from Weaverville (Brott 1982), 84 from Tucson (Olsen 1983), seven from Woodland (Farris 1984) and four from Pierce (Stapp and Longenecker 1984:41). Given the relative value of the coins, the low numbers imply they were not being used as currency.

The only massive cache of Chinese coins purported to have been found in an overseas Chinese context are a hoard of approximately 30,000 found c.1980 in an earthenware crock near Maytown on the Palmer River goldfield, Queensland, Australia. This cache, which included two pieces of "knife-money", contained coins dating from the Tang dynasty (618–906), was being sold under the auspices of the Palmer River Historic Preservation Society (Jack pers. comm.; Courtenay pers. comm.; advertisement in the *Australian* 7/2/1982). Recent research has confirmed this purported cache was a hoax (Zhu and Ritchie 2019).

The existence of closed internal trading systems utilising Chinese coins was suggested, but by no means unequivocally demonstrated, by Kleeb (1976), Hattori (1979), Farris (1979, 1980) and Olsen (1983) in their published studies of the Chinese coins found in the Ventura, Lovelock, Yreka, Sacramento and Tucson sites. Farris (1979:50, 1980:28) suggested, on the strength of a single report from an anonymous elderly Chinese informant, that an artificial or "token" value was assigned to "cash" in some overseas Chinese communities in the United States. However, if this were the case, the local economy would have been under continual threat of debasement by the possibility of someone importing large volumes of "cash" from China. In fact, Farris stated that his informant referred to the importation of large numbers of "cash", which would have seriously corrupted any form of local economy that utilised "cash" as coins or tokens.

A further consideration concerns the complexity of the money system in China. It is unlikely any overseas Chinese community could have replicated the complicated system of checks and balances that were an integral part of the Chinese money system (King 1965:51–68). Finally, contemporary observers, notably the Rev. Alexander Don, make no reference to the use of "cash" as currency in New Zealand. It is inconceivable that the Chinese could have operated closed money systems within the goldfields communities without someone commenting on such practices. If there was any evidence suggestive of such practices, anti-Chinese agitators would almost certainly have used it to arouse further opposition to Chinese immigration.

For the reasons cited above, it is unlikely that Chinese "cash" were used as trade tokens and there is no compelling evidence that any form of internal monetary systems using Chinese "cash" as the currency existed in the American, Australian or New Zealand Chinese communities. Although "lost" Chinese coins were quite common in areas where the Chinese lived (Wishart pers. comm.), they do not appear to be "common enough" to support contentions that they were used as currency or trading tokens or were hoarded in anticipation of returning home.

It seems much more likely that "cash" were imported into New Zealand (and the United States) for use as part of the equipment of playing *fan-tan* (Culin 1891), as well as being gambling tokens in the controlled setting of the game (1891:4; Farris 1984:148). According to Culin (1891:5–6), Qing dynasty coins were imported (into the United States) in large quantities expressly for gambling purposes. Only perfect pieces were selected and preferably lots from the same mint. Their wide distribution in Central Otago equates with the prevalence and location of Chinese gambling establishments on the goldfields. Although "cash" may have been used as gambling tokens, their principal role seems to be that of "counters" in the game of *fan-tan*. An observation by Don (1894:2) that "pence and small silver have supplanted the half-crown and half-sovereign stakes at fan-tan" suggests that European currency was generally used for stake money. At about the time Don was writing, a half sovereign represented some 5,000 "cash" (Morse 1966:83).

The use of small numbers of Chinese coins as good luck pieces, talismans or ornaments cannot be discounted, although there is no documentary evidence to this effect in New Zealand. Farris (1984:147) states they "also came to be used in fortune-telling (as in the I Ching)". Another possible use of "cash", and an explanation for their being scattered in Chinese sites, appears in a recent New Zealand historical novel (Kang 1985). One of the characters, unable to sleep through worry, scatters "cash" on the floor of her room and spends the night searching in the dark for all the coins, to take her mind off her troubles (Kang 1985:48). I have found no documentary evidence that scattering cash and searching for them in the dark was a means of taking one's mind off troubles.

A notable feature of the Chinese coin assemblage is their age. Two hundred and fifty (80%) were minted during the reign of Kangxi (1662–1723). This antiquity is not unusual in Chinese coins and is due to the fact that Chinese coins were not withdrawn from circulation, so large numbers coined during the reigns of some long-term emperors, such as Kangxi, stayed in the monetary system over the centuries. Since their monetary value depended on the value of the metal they contained, they retained the same value over long periods of time (Park 1980:58). While their antiquity is of interest, "cash" understandably have little utility for dating 19th–20th century archaeological contexts, except as a terminus ad quem.

The mints of origin are also of interest (see Appendix 8). For example, 166 (66.4%) of the 250 Kangxi reign "cash" were struck at the Quan and Yuan mints near Beijing (Coole 1965:66). Most of the Chinese who came to New Zealand came from Guangdong (c. 1,900 km south of Beijing), but only two coins from the Kuang mint in Guangdong are present. Some explanation is offered by the fact that considerably greater numbers of coins were produced by the mints in north China than those in the south (see Bushell 1880:195–308 for mint output figures). The presence of large numbers of coins from northern mints may also be attributable to the mid-17th century movement of people into southern China. But given the comparatively small numbers of coins involved, the importation, perhaps by a professional gambler, of only a few strings of northern coins would seriously distort the normal geographic distribution of the coins.

5.6.7 ANGLO-NEW ZEALAND COINS

Only 43 non-Chinese coins were found in the study sites; their distribution being limited to the urban sites and the Caliche and Sheung Fong shelters in the Cromwell Gorge. The low numbers, random distribution and the fact that most were found singly suggests they were lost, misplaced or left when a site was abandoned. The predominance of small size and denomination coins that were widely used in the 19th century also suggests their presence is attributable to unintentional loss.

The coins reflect the New Zealand coinage of the era, and its use by the Chinese. English currency was used exclusively in New Zealand until 1933 when the nation began minting its own coins, although British coins remained legal tender until 1967 (Hargreaves 1972). The numbers and denominations are detailed in Table 5.80. Taken collectively, the coins broadly span the main period of occupation of the sites, but other than that, their utility for dating is limited. The few post-1930 coins postdate the Chinese occupations and must have been lost after the last Chinese departed.

Contemporary Euro coins were found in six huts in both the Chinatown and Arrowtown settlements; however, only those in hut 26 at Chinatown are especially notable because this hut also contained 226 Chinese coins. The high incidence of both Euro and Chinese coins may indicate the gambling game *fan-tan* was played in the hut (see Culin 1891b; Park 1980; and discussion in Section 5.6.6 above). In my opinion, the association of Euro and Chinese coins in hut 26 is not proof or support of Kleeb's (1976:507) contention that the presence of mixed Euro and Chinese coin "hoards" may indicate that Chinese coins were used as currency. In the situation outlined above, the Chinese coins are more likely to have been used as non-monetary game pieces or counters rather than gambling tokens or money, and the European coins may represent lost "stake" money or simply lost coins.

Two points are made regarding the distribution of the coins at Arrowtown. The association of Euro and Chinese coins in Ah Lum's store is probably attributable to a gambling situation like that described above, and the higher than average number of coins might be expected considering the structure was used as a store for at least 25 years. There is a higher percentage of pre-1900 (especially pre-1880) Euro coins in the Arrowtown assemblage compared with that from Cromwell. This may reflect the slightly earlier establishment of the Arrowtown Chinese Settlement.

5.6.8 COAL, WOOD AND STONE

Several pieces or artefacts of coal, wood and stone were recovered. Their distribution is detailed in Tables 5.87–5.89.

5.6.8.1 Coal

The presence of lumps of lignite and sub-bituminous coal in many of the sites indicates that these subfossil fuels were used by the Chinese to supplement the limited wood supplies, either driftwood, wood from packaging or wood collected at considerable distances from the sites. Like their use of wood, they probably used coal sparingly. In most of the sites only a few lumps were found, but in hut 17 at Chinatown several distinct lenses of mixed lignite and sub-bituminous coal were exposed. The term "hut" is a misnomer; the structure was almost certainly used as a storage shed for the adjacent hut 16.

There are several small lignite seams in the Cromwell area (at Bannockburn) and at Gibbston, approximately 10 km east of the Arrowtown settlement. Although none are worked commercially today, many were mined between 1880 and 1910 to provide coal for the steam-powered gold dredges and domestic use. The Chinese may have purchased coal from the operators of the mines, but it is equally likely that they took a bag along with them and just helped themselves from exposed seams in the riverbanks. The nearest sources of the sub-bituminous coal are the Ohai fields in Southland and the Kaitangata field in South Otago, both more than 150 km away. This coal was probably brought into the area by European coal merchants and acquired from them or indirectly through users such as blacksmiths. Wishart's Smithy, located adjacent to the Chinatown settlement, is a possible source of the sub-bituminous coal used by the Chinese there. Later they may also have acquired small amounts "free", for example if they collected spillage from the unloading of wagons in the Cromwell railway yard or elsewhere.

5.6.8.2 Wood and charcoal

Table 5.82 summarises the wood remains. Owing to their fragmentary and often burnt nature, only a few could be positively ascribed to specific functions.

Structural timbers were evidenced by a few remnants of dressed 3 x 2 inch (and similar size) timber. These would have supported the roof and door framing. Post butts were found in only one hut (Ch/22). Their absence indicates that the roofs were abutted and secured directly on to the top of the stone or earth side walls. The layout of post butts in the back half of Ch/22 suggests they supported a sleeping platform (see Figure 4.8). Several of the structures had a "doorstep" composed of a plank set into the ground in the entrance way (many were still in situ).

Remnants of light planking and box wood (built into recesses in the walls in Ch/26 and in Ah Lum's store) indicate that wooden boxes were re-used for shelving and cupboards, and probably for other purposes such as seating. None of the planking or box wood bore marks indicating their origin or previous uses, but they are similar in appearance to European packing boxes of the era. Some of the boards used to form the partition between the main room and kitchen in Ah Lum's store are marked with Chinese characters written with black paint. These have not been translated, but the timbers in question have earlier nail holes and were probably derived from imported packing cases. During the Chinese occupation of the store, the partition was covered with wallpaper.

Single sides of three small wooden boxes, measuring c. 12 x 2 x 0.4 cm, were found in ACS/5, Ah Lum's and the Flax Grove shelter. The specimen from Ah Lum's has two scored recesses cut into the interior edge (for a sliding lid?). These remains are likely to be remnants of boxes (Figure 5.101g) for game pieces.

The recovered wood specimens have not been speciated, but none appear to be strikingly different from New Zealand timbers (other than the fragment of coconut shell found in ACS/2) and none were hard woods. Samples of charcoal were recovered from hearths or from concentrations in the floors of several sites, but they have not been identified. In some instances, particularly in the Caliche, Hanging Rock and Flax Grove shelters, the possibility that some of the charcoal may be derived from pre-European occupation cannot be discounted.

5.6.8.3 Stone artefacts and related structural materials

The stone materials fall into two categories: portable artefacts and structural materials. Their distribution is outlined in Table 5.83. Schist and greywacke cobbles derived from the abandoned European workings in the area were the main building materials used at Chinatown, while the huts in the Arrowtown settlement were built from either schist slabs or puddled clay (see Chapter 4).

Fire bricks, impressed with "Garnkirk" (believed to be of Scottish origin), were found in the hearths of two of the Chinatown huts (Ch/14 and Ch/18). The bricks were used to support the fire bars. They were probably scavenged from a European dump or building site. Small unmodified fragments of plain building bricks were found in three of the Arrowtown huts.

Small patches of plaster were evident on parts of the interior walls of two of the Chinatown huts (Ch/18 and Ch/34), while lumps of plaster were found within the area of hut 10 at Arrowtown. It may have been used as caulking.

Grindstones, inkstones and items made of slate constitute the main types of stone artefacts that were recovered. They were discussed in Sections 5.5.3 and 5.6.2 respectively. The patterns of lines on the pieces of incised slate vary and suggest that they were used for more than just making tallies or recording memos. Pieces of gridded slate (Figure 5.104) found in four sites (Table 5.83) may have been used in the game of *wei-qi*. The role of the two virtually identical marble slabs found in huts 23 and 26 at Chinatown is unclear (possibly small pallets for cutting or grinding materials).

Finally, mention is made of the four silcrete flakes and two heated stones found in the Caliche shelter. Although totally mixed among the Chinese occupation debris, they attest to a brief Māori usage of the shelter (Ritchie 1982).

The moa remains and eggshell found deep within the same shelter are believed to be a natural deposit.

5.6.9 PAPER ARTEFACTS OF EUROPEAN ORIGIN

Despite the dryness of the Central Otago climate, paper artefacts in the study sites have generally not fared well. The Flax Grove and Rockfall I sites were the only ones from which relatively large quantities were recovered. In both instances, the paper was preserved because it was used as caulking between the stones in the shelter walls. Paper artefacts and newspapers of European origin are listed in Table 5.84 with annotations below (paper artefacts bearing Chinese calligraphy or of presumed Chinese origin are detailed in Table 5.63 in Section 5.6.2).

5 The material culture of the Chinese in southern New Zealand

Table 5.1. Liquor bottles, minimum numbers per site.

Site key:
- A Firewood Creek
- B Caliche
- C Sheung Fong
- D Ha Fong
- E Chinatown
- F QB2
- G Apple Tree
- H Sandy Point
- I Northburn
- J Ah Wee's
- K Poplars
- L Hanging Rock
- M Riverside
- N Arrowtown
- O Ah Lum's
- P Rapids
- Q Flax Grove

Product	Brand/bottle type	A	B	C	D	E	F	G	H	I	J	K	L	M	N	O	P	Q	MN	Date Range
Schnapps	Udolpho Wolfe's, Schade & Buysing's, Gilbey's "Silverstream"	1	2			14		2							4	5			28	1880–1920
Cognac/Brandy	Hennessy Brandy, cognac, ring-seal aqua spun-mould bottle, Schade & Poplice (metal cap)	5	3	1	2	28	3		5		5	13	1	3	46	10	7	4	136	1880–1920
Gins	plain case gins, embossed "JDKZ", Boll & Dunlop Rotterdam	4	2		1	55	2	3			2	3	1		15	14	20	3	125	1880–1920
Spirit flasks	cognac/brandy, coffin-shaped flasks, whisky flasks	5	5	2	5	12	3	1							9	3	1	2	48	1880–1920
Whisky	aqua applied-top, some 3-piece mould, "Highland Whisky, Glasgow"	5	4	1	1	12	2	4			3	6	1	2	29	3	9	2	84	1880–1920
Miscellaneous Liquors	Benedictine, Johnnie Walker whisky, ring-seal wines, hocks, embossed examples: "Penfolds Wines" hock "Bonner Burger Vebein", Finsbury Distillery Co., Dr Townsend's Sarsparilla	1	1	1	1	31	1				4	6		1	33	8	9		97	
Total		21	17	5	10	152	11	10	5	0	14	28	3	6	136	43	46	11	518	

Table 5.2. Beer bottles, minimum numbers per site.

Site key:
A Firewood Creek B Caliche C Sheung Fong D Ha Fong E Chinatown
F QB2 G Apple Tree H Sandy Point I Northburn J Ah Wee's
K Poplars L Hanging Rock M Riverside N Arrowtown O Ah Lum's
P Rapids Q Flax Grove

Type of beer bottle	Brand/bottle type	A	B	C	D	E	F	G	H	I	J	K	L	M	N	O	P	Q	MN	Date Range
Black	3-piece mould applied-top, some embossed on base "A.B. & Co." also "N & Co."	2	1	1	1	10	5	5	1			3		1	6	2	3		41	1870–80
Ring-seal	dark green "champagne" type, beer and/or aerated water, some "Johnson, Liverpool"	1	3	1	1	61	2	3	3	1	5	12	2		57	17	15		184	1885–1920
Crown-top	brown glass (mostly), various companies often embossed e.g. "Powley & Keast", "Invercargill Bottle Co.", "R. Powley & Co, Moa Brand, Dunedin", "Crown Brewery, Christchurch"		1			14									2		2		19	1920–35
Blob-top	dark green spun-moulded	1				9													10	1910–20
Skittle	dark green collar-top					1													1	pre-1900
Green applied-top	dark green spun-moulded					8													8	
Miscellaneous	including 2 collar tops, "R & Co."	1													12	6	3	1	23	
Total		5	5	2	2	103	7	8	4	1	5	15	2	1	77	25	23	1	286	

5 The material culture of the Chinese in southern New Zealand

Table 5.3. Domestic bottles, minimum numbers per site.

Site key																		
A Firewood Creek				B Caliche			C Sheung Fong			D Ha Fong			E Chinatown					
F QB2				G Apple Tree			H Sandy Point			I Northburn			J Ah Wee's					
K Poplars				L Hanging Rock			M Riverside			N Arrowtown			O Ah Lum's					
P Rapids				Q Flax Grove														

Product	Brand/bottle type	A	B	C	D	E	F	G	H	I	J	K	L	M	N	O	P	Q	MN	Date Range	Figure #
salad oil	"twisty" neck aqua bottles, two sizes		1			2									3	2			8		5.6b
sauces	"Lea & Perrins" aqua Worcestershire Sauce, "Mellor & Co.", "Thompson & Hill, Auckland", "M.J. Heinz & Co" (patented 1890)	1	2			9		1	1						6	7		1	28	1880–1920	
sauce	"Lea & Perrins" shape, clear glass, machine-made				1	5													6		
vinegar	"Champions", others	1			1	6		1			5	6			6	3	2	2	33	1880–1920	5.6a
pickle jars	embossed Haywards"Flag" brand, "Stella Preserving Works, Dunedin", "Military" brand, unembossed; "Melhuish's Celebrated Pickles"	2		1	1	17									3	1		1	26		5.6c
jams/preserving jars	roll-top and screw-top jars, embossings: "St George Preserving Works, Dunedin", "S. Kirkpatrick & Co., Nelson", unembossed				1	18									3	2		1	25	1890–1910	5.6f
coffee and chicory	"Symington & Co, Edinburgh"														1	1			2		
essence			1			2	1								1				5		
cordial	"Roses Lime"																	1	1		
fruit salt jar	"J.T. Morton"	1																	1		
fruit salts	"Enos" aqua, machine-made		1			1									2				4		
ink	"Carters", "Hollidge", "N. Antoine, Paris No. 145", clear glass			1		2	1								2	3			6		5.6p, q
leather dressing	square wide-mouthed aqua bottles, embossed "Hauthaways Peerless Gloss (USA)"					2									1	3			6	1900–15	
blacking	"Nubian" wide-mouthed aqua pannelled bottle					3									2				5		5.6n
small crown-tops	use unknown, machine-made														6				6	post-1920	
miscellaneous household	"Lemos" lemon drink, unembossed rennet bottles from Chinatown	3	1		1	28		1					3		7	7	2		53		
perfumes (French)	embossed "Rimmel, Perfumer, Paris", four styles, "Roger & Gallet, Paris"				1	3		1					1		4				10	c. 1910	
disinfectant	embossed brown glass "Jeyes Fluid"					1													1		
blue castor oil							1												1		
bottle containing mercury	small clear glass bottle				1														1		
Total		8	6	2	7	99	3	4	1	0	5	6	4	0	47	26	4	6	228		

Table 5.4. Pharmaceutical bottles, minimum numbers per site.

Site key																				
	A Firewood Creek			B Caliche			C Sheung Fong			D Ha Fong			E Chinatown							
	F QB2			G Apple Tree			H Sandy Point			I Northburn			J Ah Wee's							
	K Poplars			L Hanging Rock			M Riverside			N Arrowtown			O Ah Lum's							
	P Rapids			Q Flax Grove																

Product	Brand/bottle type	A	B	C	D	E	F	G	H	I	J	K	L	M	N	O	P	Q	MN	Date Range	Figure #
medicine	Dr Sheldon's "New Discovery"					1													1		
medicine	"Davis" vegetable painkiller					1				1					3	1	1		7		5.7n
medicine	"Chamberlain's Pain-Balm"					1													1		
medicine	Lanes Emulsion		1																1		
medicine	"H. Hotop, Chemist, Cromwell"					2													2		5.7a, b
medicine	"Marshall Chemical Co., 86 Princes St, Dunedin"					1													1		
medicine	Baxters Lung Preserver, Christchurch					1													1		5.7i
medicine	Johnson & Haslett, Chemist, Dunedin					1													1		
misc. medicine	plain unembossed aqua glass	1				7									4	3			15		
misc. medicine	machine-made clear glass		1			5											1		1	1930s	
cough mixture	"Tussicura", made in Dunedin					1													1		5.7m
cough mixture	"Chamberlain's Cough Remedy"					1													1		
hair tonic	"Barry's Tricopherous for the Skin & Hair"							1											1		5.7l
pills	Marshall Chemical Co., Dunedin. brown glass		1			1													2	1910-1920	
pills	Ayers Pills		1																1		
vaseline	Chesebrough Mfg. Co., New York, clear glass, screw top					2														1887-1920	5.7d
magnesia	Dinnefords, Ayers, Kruses					4													4		5.7o, p
cream pots	milk glass, screw-top ointment pots. One from Chinatown with fluted sides					2													2		
extracts	embossed Eucalypti Extract, Saunders & Son vial					3													3		5.7f
jar	rect, screw top, embossed "Everetts"					1													1		5.7e
jars, ointment(?)	small clear glass screw tops					2												1	3		
vials	unembossed					4									1				5		5.7h
poison	blue glass, embossed "Not to be Taken"					2									1				3		
dressing(?)	embossed 'Farmers Friend', base 6 x 6cm															1			1		
dressing	H. Foerderer, Philadelphia														1				1		5.7g
lavender water(?)	green glass vial, no embossing					1													1		
Total		1	4	0	0	44	0	1	0	0	1	0	0	0	10	5	1	2	61		

5 The material culture of the Chinese in southern New Zealand

Table 5.5. Chinese glass bottles, minimum numbers per site.

Site key		A	Firewood Creek	B	Caliche	C	Sheung Fong	D	Ha Fong	E	Chinatown
		F	QB2	G	Apple Tree	H	Sandy Point	I	Northburn	J	Ah Wee's
		K	Poplars	L	Hanging Rock	M	Riverside	N	Arrowtown	O	Ah Lum's
		P	Rapids	Q	Flax Grove	R	Upper Chinatown				

Product and bottle type	A	B	C	D	E	F	G	H	I	J	K	L	M	N	O	P	Q	R	MN	Figure #
tincture vials																				
straight-sided, aqua		3			31	1		1		1				9	2		1		49	5.9a,b
tear drop shape, aqua					1														1	5.9f
oval cross-section										1									1	5.9c
medicine																				
small, rect, X-sect., range of sizes, aqua														1	1				2	5.9e
pharmaceutical																				
wide mouthed, clear glass cylindrical bottles with rolled lip, paper labels illegible					3													5	8	5.9g
dark green beers(?)																				
dark green applied collar top, spun-moulded fragments of labels bear indecipherable Chinese characters					3														3	5.9h
Total	0	3	0	0	38	1	0	1	0	2	0	0	0	10	3	0	1	5	64	

Table 5.6. Aerated water bottles, minimum numbers per site.

Site key		A Firewood Creek B Caliche C Sheung Fong D Ha Fong E Chinatown F QB2 G Apple Tree H Sandy Point I Northburn J Ah Wee's K Poplars L Hanging Rock M Riverside N Arrowtown O Ah Lum's P Rapids Q Flax Grove																	
Product	Bottle type	A	B	C	D	E	F	G	H	I	J	K	L	M	N	O	P	Q	MN	Date Range
Hamilton	torpedo type bottle, unembossed, aqua	1	1	1		2									1	1			7	
Hamilton	torpedo type aqua bottle, embossed "Theyers & Beck, Alexandra"	1				1													2	1888–93
Codd	Reliance & Dobson patents, unembossed		1			4										2	1			8	
Codd	embossed 'J McLoughlin Cromwell' (both patents)					2														2	
Codd	"Thomson & Co, Dunedin" ("1908" on base)					1										1				2	post-1908
Codd	Lane & Co, Dunedin (Dobson Patent)					1										1				2	
Crown-top	Lane & Co, Dunedin					4										1				5	1920–35
Crown-top	Buckham's, Queenstown															1				1	post–1930
Maugham flat base																1	1				
Blob-top	embossed "Thomson & Co."															1				1	
Blob-top	plain	2																1		3	
Maugham																1				1	
mineral water	"Puriri" brand																2			2	
Total		4	2	1	0	15	0	0	0	0	0	0	0	0	0	10	5	1	0	36	

5 The material culture of the Chinese in southern New Zealand

Table 5.7. Bottled products: minimum numbers and percentages.

Site key	A	Firewood Creek	B	Caliche	C	Sheung Fong	D	Ha Fong	E	Chinatown
	F	QB2	G	Apple Tree	H	Sandy Point	I	Northburn	J	Ah Wee's
	K	Poplars	L	Hanging Rock	M	Riverside	N	Arrowtown	O	Ah Lum's
	P	Rapids	Q	Flax Grove						

Product Type	A	B	C	D	E	F	G	H	I	J	K	L	M	N	O	P	Q	MN
Liquors	21	17	5	10	168	11	10	5	0	13	28	3	6	137	43	46	11	534
% of total/site	30	27	26	57	33	50	43	29	0	50	53	50	86	43	35	58	55	41%
Beers	5	5	2	2	103	7	8	4	1	5	15	2	1	77	25	23	1	286
% of total/site	7	8	10	10	20	32	35	24	100	19	28	33	14	24	23	29	5	
Domestic/Household	9	5	2	7	97	4	4	2	0	5	10	0	0	46	24	6	5	226
% of total/site	13	8	10	37	19	18	17	12	0	19	19	0	0	15	22	8	25	
Medicines/Grooming	1	4	0	0	44	0	0	1	0	1	0	0	0	14	6	1	2	74
% of total/site	1.4	6.3	0	0	9	0	0	6	0	4	0	0	0	5	6	1	10	
Chinese Glass	0	3	0	0	38	0	0	1	0	2	0	0	0	10	3	0	1	58
% of total/site	0	4.7	0	0	7	0	0	6	0	8	0	0	0	0.3	3	0	5	
Aerated Waters	4	2	2	0	15	0	0	0	0	0	0	0	0	10	5	1	0	39
% of total/site	5.7	3.1	10	0	3	0	0	0	0	0	0	0	0	0.3	4	1	0	
Undiagnostic	4	5	1	0	46	0	1	4	0	0	0	1	0	23	5	3	0	93
% of total/site	5.7	8	5	0	9	0	4	24	0	0	0	17	0	7	4	4	0	
Site total	44	41	12	19	511	22	23	17	1	26	53	6	7	317	111	80	20	1,310

Note: The percentages are rounded

Table 5.8 Alcohol prices on the goldfields.

Product	May 1863	December 1863	September 1870
brandy	30–36/- gallon	29–30/- gallon	3/6d bottle
brandy, Hennessy's		75–80/- case	4/9d bottle
brandy, Otard		72–75/- case	
Old Tom (Burnetts)			3/6d bottle
gin	90–95/- gallon		
geneva, JDKZ		65–70/- case	3/9d bottle
whisky		20–22/- gallon	3/- bottle
whisky, Stewards			3/3d bottle
whisky, Dunvilles			4/- bottle
rum, 10 over proof			3/6d bottle
wines		20–23/- case	
port wine, best			3/6d bottle
port wine, medium			3/- bottle
sherry, best			3/6d bottle
sherry, medium			2/6d bottle
claret			2/3d bottle
colonial wines			2/6d bottle
porter, Bloods			1/3d bottle
porter, Byass (Bass?)			1/3d bottle
porter, pints			10d bottle
porter, colonials			1/10d bottle
bottled beer	24–26/- dozen		
English Ale, Bass	17 pounds/hogshead*		
ale. Tennents			1/3d bottle
ale, Instone			1/3d bottle
ale, colonial			10d bottle

Sources

May 1863: "Queenstown Prices Current" *Lake Wakatipu Mail* 16/5/1863:4

December 1863: "Queenstown Prices Current" *Lake Wakatipu Mail* 23/12/1863

September 1870: "List of Hotel Prices, Southland Hotel, Hokitika as at Sept. 30th 1870", reproduced from *Southland Hotel Centenary booklet* (1984:13)

* A hogshead of beer contains 54 gallons. The beer in this instance was "Bass No. 3 bulk". By 1894, a hogshead of beer could be bought for 110/- (AJHR C3–A:62).

5 The material culture of the Chinese in southern New Zealand

Table 5.9. Celadon wares: site distribution.

Site key								
	A	Firewood Creek	B	Caliche	C	Sheung Fong	D	Ha Fong
	E	Chinatown	F	QB2	G	Apple Tree	H	Sandy Point
	I	Ah Wee's	J	Poplars	K	Hanging Rock	L	Riverside
	M	Arrowtown	N	Rapids	O	Ah Lum's	P	Flax Grove
	Q	Upper Chinatown						

Type	A	B	C	D	E	F	G	H	I	J	K	L	M	N	O	P	Q	Total
serving bowls					3								2				2	7
rice bowls	2	1	2	1	17	3	2	1	1	2		1	23	3	2			61
small bowl*																	1	1
tea cups		1			2								1	1			2	7
wine cups	1				9	1		1					2				1	15
shallow dishes		1			1	1							1					4
large dish				1														1
spoons					13	1	3		2			4	2	1	1	4		31
Total	3	3	2	2	45	6	5	2	3	2	0	5	31	4	4	4	6	127

*The bowl described as a "small bowl" is a smaller than average rice bowl (see Section 5.2.1.2).

Table 5.10. 4 Seasons wares: site distribution and decoration.

Site key										
	A	Firewood Creek	B	Caliche	C	Sheung Fong	D	Ha Fong	E	Chinatown
	F	QB2	G	Apple Tree	H	Sandy Point	I	Ah Wee's	J	Poplars
	K	Hanging Rock	L	Riverside	M	Arrowtown	N	Rapids	O	Ah Lum's
	P	Lake Roxburgh	Q	U. Ch'town	R	Ledge	S	Motutapu		

Artefact type	A	B	C	D	E	F	G	H	I	J	K	L	M	N	O	P	Q	R	S	Total
serving bowl (large)					1								3				1			5
serving bowl (medium)					1	1							2		2					6
tea cup														1						1
shallow dish with ring base																1				1
spoons					2								3	1	2		1			9
wine cups						1		1												2
octagonal tea cup																		1		1
shallow dish (small)																		2		2
shallow dish (large)													1							1
Total					5	1	1						9	1	5	1	2	1	2	28
"Bamboo" decoration																				
rice bowl (blue hue)					1								1		1					3
rice bowl (green hue)	1																			1
Total	1				1								1		1					4

Table 5.11. Rare and miscellaneous Chinese tablewares: site distribution.

Vessel Type	Site	Figure #	MN
Rice Bowls			
bird motif	ACS/6	5.15e	1
crab motif	Upper Chinatown	5.15f	1
brown rim	Ch/13, Rapids, upper Chinatown	5.15c, d	3
Small dishes			
blue on grey	Ch/26	5.16a	1
bird motif	Upper Chinatown surface	5.16b	1
Saucers			
genre scene	Upper Chinatown surface	5.16d	1
Japanese ("Noritake" symbol on base)	Ah Lum's store	5.39–3	1
Chinese spoons			
plain white	Ah Lum's store		1
fish motif	Ch/15	5.16c	1
Teapots			
plain white, Chinese style	QB2	5.16k	1
Japanese (with coralene beading)	ACS/2	5.41	1
Miniature floral pot	Upper Chinatown trench	5.16e	1
Unglazed cooking pot	Nokomai hut S151/3 surface	5.27c	1

5 The material culture of the Chinese in southern New Zealand

Table 5.12. Brownwares: minimum numbers per site.

Site key																			
A Firewood Creek		B Caliche		C Sheung Fong		D Ha Fong		E Chinatown											
F QB2		G Apple Tree		H Sandy Point		I Ah Wee's		J Poplars											
K Hanging Rock		L Riverside		M Arrowtown		N Rapids		O Ledge											
P Ah Lum's		Q Flax Grove		R Upper Ch'town															

Artefact type	A	B	C	D	E	F	G	H	I	J	K	L	M	N	O	P	Q	R	Total	Comments
Ng Ka Py bottles	1		2	1	32			1	1	1	1		27	3		6	1	3	80	
shouldered jars (large)	1	2		3	27	2	2	2	1	2	1		14	3	3	5	3	5	76	
lids for above	2	2	4	3	28	1	3	1	2	1			11	6		3	2	2	71	saucer-shaped, unglazed
shouldered jars (small)			2		9		1			1		1	3		1			1	19	
lids for above				2	18	1	1						5	3		4	8		38	saucer-shaped, unglazed
spouted pots					13								5	1		4		1	26	
barrel jar					1			1	1				3	1		3		5	13	
barrel jar lids					1													7	8	flanged and glazed
jarlets					2								1						3	
straight-sided pots	1				7								2					1	12	several sizes, see Appendix 4 and Table 5.13
lids for above					7													1	8	see Appendix 4
rolled-lip jars									2										2	ginger jar shape
globular jar					6								3						9	
unglazed lids for above(?)													1					1	2	stepped, unglazed
shouldered jar lid (glazed)					1												3		4	glazed on concave surface
plug for soya pots					1														1	unglazed, mushroom-shaped
Total	5	4	8	9	153	4	7	5	7	5	2	1	75	17	4	21	17	27	372	

201

Table 5.13. Dimensions of straight-sided brownware jars.

Jar height (cm)	Base diameter (cm)	Max. width (cm)	Lid diameter external (cm)	Notes
2.8	3.7	2.9		ACS post-excavation
3.0	3.8			Redmond collection
3.2	5.5			Ch/23, rim broken off
3.5	4.7	4.0		Redmond collection
3.9	5.6	4.8	5.8	Ch/23
4.1	5.3	4.7		Ch/17
4.2	5.7	4.6		Chinatown stores*
4.3	5.8	4.9		Redmond collection
c14.0	c14.0			Nelson Show

* This pot has the *Tung Lai* (Clever Company) mark on the base. An identical pot with the same mark is known from a Chinese site in Victoria, British Columbia (Keddie collection, Asian Artefact Inventory).

Table 5.14. Chinese ginger jars: site distribution.

Site key																
	A	Caliche		B	Sheung Fong		C	Ha Fong		D	Chinatown					
	E	Apple Tree		F	Ah Wee's		G	Arrowtown		H	Rapids					
	I	The Ledge		J	Ah Lum's		K	Flax Grove		L	Upper Chinatown					
	M	Arrow River		N	Motutapu											

	A	B	C	D	E	F	G	H	I	J	K	L	M	N	Total	Figure #
Green-glazed ginger jars																
wide mouth, standard	2	2	1	11	1	1	7	3	1		4				33	5.28a
wide mouth, large				2											2	5.28b
narrow-necked				2							2				4	5.29
lids for above				2		1					2				5	
straight-sided pots				5	1		2				2				10	5.31
lids for above				4						1	1				6	
Total (MN = 51)															**60**	
Blue-beige ginger jars																
blue-smudge pattern				1								2	2		5	5.32b
flanged lids for above				1			1								2	5.32a
Total (MN = 6)															**7**	
Flanged ginger jar lids																
square panel											1				1	5.36a
"quarters" design				1											1	5.36b
grey-glazed							1			1					2	5.36c
Total															**4**	

Table 5.15. Dimensions of green-glazed straight-sided pots.

Height (cm)	Base diameter (cm)	Mouth (cm)	Widest point (cm)	Lid diameter external (cm)	Provenance
4.3	4.2	3.2		-	Ch/23
4.5	4.1	2.9	4.7	-	Ch/23
5.2	4.9	2.9	5.4	5.4	Upper Chinatown (Mangos collection)
5.2	5	4.1	5.5	-	Ch/26

Table 5.16. Chinese ceramics: frequency, temporal and areal distribution.

Widely distributed and found in most Chinese sites	Site/location	Figure #
celadon rice bowls		5.12a
celadon wine cups		5.12d
celadon soup spoon		5.12g
Ng Ka Py bottles		5.17a
spouted pots (regular)		5.18a
brownware shouldered food jars (large)		5.19b
green-glazed ginger jar (wide mouth, standard size)		5.28a
Widely distributed and frequently uncovered (>20 known)		
celadon tea cups		5.12e
4 Seasons spoons		5.14f
brownware shouldered food jars (small)		5.19a
brownware straight-sided jars (various sizes)		5.24
barrel jars (largely restricted to urban sites)		5.25a
globular jars (largely restricted to urban sites)		5.26b
green-glazed straight-sided pots (various sizes)		5.31
Less common but wide areal distribution (3–10 known)		
celadon rice serving bowls (large)		5.12b
celadon shallow dishes		5.12f
4 Seasons serving bowls (medium)	QB2	5.14a
4 Seasons serving bowls (large)	Ch/26	5.14b
bamboo rice bowls (green and blue hues)		5.15a
brownware jarlets		5.23
green ginger jars (wide mouth, large)		5.28b
green ginger jars (narrow mouth)		5.29a
plain white rice bowls	S133/835, S132/65, 12 Mile Ck, Carrick	
Rare occurrence (1 or 2 known)		
celadon large dishes	Ha Fong	5.12c
4 Seasons shallow dish	Lake Roxburgh	5.14g
4 Seasons octagonal tea cup	The Ledge	5.14e
4 Seasons round tea cups	Ah Lum's, only small fragments	
bird and flower motif rice bowl	ACS/6	5.15e
crab motif rice bowl	Chinatown stores	5.15f
shallow blue on grey saucer-like dish	Ch/21	5.16a
miniature floral decorated pot	Chinatown stores	5.16e
blue on white teapots		5.16g
plain white teapots	QB2	5.16k
brownware flat-rimmed food jars	S115/54	5.22b
unglazed cooking pots	S151/3	5.27c

Table 5.16. Chinese ceramics: frequency, temporal and areal distribution (*continued*).

Seemingly restricted areal distribution; relatively rare	Site/location	Figure #
blue-beige "smudged blue" ginger jars	Wakatipu basin, Motutapu	5.32
Wing Lee Wai bottles	Nokomai	5.37
Seemingly restricted temporal distribution; relatively rare		
green hexagonal ginger jars (both sizes), post-1900(?)		5.30
Wing Lee Wai bottles, post-1920(?)	Nokomai	5.37
beige-blue ginger jars (smudge blue type), post-1880(?)		5.32
Only known from private collections; no excavated specimens		
blue on white bird feeders	Cromwell Museum	5.16j
Ng Ka Py bottle (small)	Redmond collection	5.17b
spouted pots (small)	Redmond collection	5.18b
tall, angular shouldered food jars	Redmond collection	5.21
green hexagonal ginger jars (both sizes)		5.30
ginger jars: blue swirls, glaze has "muslin texture" (two sizes), post-1900(?)		5.33
blue-grey ginger jars (pictorial)	only seen in collections and antique shops	5.35
No specimens observed in New Zealand		
Double Happiness rice bowls		5.15b
blue on white with simple flower motif wine jugs		5.16h
blue on white ginseng steamers		5.16i
square soy pots		5.18c
brown-glazed pans		5.27a
medicinal tea pots		5.27b
anglo-shaped ceramic beverage bottles (see Section 5.2.2.6.4)		not depicted
thin brown jars (see Section 5.2.2.6.2)		not depicted
4 Seasons rice bowls		not depicted

Table 5.17. Represented manufacturer's marks.

Manufacturer	Place of origin	Date	Product	Vessel type
Jackson and Gosling	Grosvenor Works, Longton, England	c.1914–20	earthenware, white	saucer
T Forester & Sons (Godden 1983:157)	Phoenix Works, Longton, England	post-1900	porcelain, plain white with silver fleur-de-lis on bottom interior	cup
unknown	England(?)	unknown	light brown paste earthenware	single fragment of a crock
Sampson Bridgwood & Son Ltd.	Anchor Pottery, Longton, England	post-1910 (Godden 1964:102)	white earthenware with black hairline around rim	cup
W H Grindley & Co.	Tunstall, Staffordshire, England	1891–1925 (Godden 1983:10; 1964:294).	white earthenware with "Rouen" transfer print design (Figure 5.39-12). The plate from Ch/26 is a plain white earthenware	serving plates
Jabez Blackhurst	Boston Works, Tunstall, England	1872–83 (Godden 1964:78)	blue on white transfer print on earthenware	serving plate (fire-blackened)
unknown	England	post-1867	black on white transfer-printed earthenware pot, 3.5 cm high, 3.6 cm diameter (internal)	Holloway's ointment pot (Figure 5.42b)
R Cochran & Co.	Glasgow, Scotland	c.1846–1918	blue-purple "Lorraine" pattern transfer-printed earthenware	serving plate
Pinder Bourne & Co.	Burslem, England	c.1862–82	black transfer-printed crest on creamy-white glazed earthenware	mug(?) (base only, 10.3 cm diameter)
Pinder Bourne & Co.	Burslem, England	c.1862–82	black-brown transfer-printed earthenware	plate (single base sherd)
Pinder Bourne & Co.	Burslem, England	c.1862–82	plain white earthenware	plate (12 body sherds, c.19 cm diameter)

Mark	Discussion	Provenance
Brown transfer print design reading "Jackson and Gosling, Grosvenor China, England RG. No. 643424" surmounted by a crown (Figure 5.39-6).	See Godden #2161. postdates 1914 (Godden 1964:350).	Chinatown hut 1, (M16 Ly.1)
"Phoenix English China" printed in black within an uncircumscribed circle (Figure 5.39-5)	According to Godden (1964:257), distinguishing names such as "Phoenix China" and "Phoenix Ware" postdate 1910.	Chinatown hut 7 (H28 Ly.1)
Stencilled "....and Co., ...PROOF, ... HERCULES"	–	Chinatown hut 14
"Anchor China, Bridgwood, Made in England" printed in black (Figure 5.39-7)	"Made in England" denotes a 20th century date (Godden 1983:10). Identical to Godden's # 597 (Godden 1964:102) except "S.B. & S." is replaced with "Bridgwood" and has "Made in England" rather than "England"	Chinatown hut 17 (K12 Ly.1)
"W H Grindley & Co, England" under the Royal Arms (Godden 1964:13) featuring a lion and a unicorn and surmounted by the words "Royal Ironstone China" (Figure 5.39-10)	The distinctive "Rouen" pattern was used by other manufacturers such as Doulton and P E & Co. The design constitutes the most common transfer print pattern on the studied Euro-ceramics. It appears on cups, saucers and plates. This particular mark is not depicted by Godden.	Chinatown huts 21, 26 and 33
A blue transfer print consisting of the word "Rhine" in a oval floral design above the name "Jabez Blackhurst" (Figure 5.39-11)	"Rhine" is the name of the design: a pictorial scene depicting a boat, a castle and trees.	Chinatown hut 26 (M16 Ly.2)
Transfer printed "Holloway's Ointment for the Cure of Gout and Rheumatism, Inveterate Ulcers, Sore Breasts, Sore Heads, Bad Legs Etc, 533 Oxford St"	Holloway moved his business from the Strand to the more fashionable Oxford St address in 1867 (Hosking 1978:9).	5133/48, Chinatown hut 33 (L17 Ly.1; 5124/207), QB2 (C5 Ly.1)
Printed Royal Arms under "R Cochra[n & Co]" (part only)	R Cochran and Co produced earthenwares (white, printed enamelled ware) at Glasgow, Scotland from c. 1846 until 1918 (Godden 1983:55). Their Verreville Pottery (also Brittania Pottery) operated until 1896 (Godden 1964:157).	Chinatown hut 33 (K20, Ly.1)
Black transfer-printed Royal Arms over the words "Stone China, Pinder Bourne & Co, Burslem" (Figure 5.39-4)	Pinder Bourne & Co. manufactured earthenwares at Nile St, Burslem from c. 1862 until 1882, at which time the works were taken over by Doulton and Co. (Godden: 1983:104).	Chinatown hut 34 (L14 Ly.2)
Black transfer-printed Royal Arms over "Stone China, Pinder Bourne & Co, Burslem". Same as above listing.	As above.	ACS/8 (G13, Ly.1)
Black transfer printed "Royal Arms over "Stone China, Pinder Bourne & Co, Burslem". Same as listings above.	As above.	ACS/9 (Unit 2)

Table 5.17. Represented manufacturer's marks (*continued*).

Manufacturer	Place of origin	Date	Product	Vessel type
Pinder Bourne & Co.	Burslem, England	January 1879 (Godden 1964:495)	Transfer-printed and handpainted earthenware	plate (30 sherds, 25 cm diameter)
Pinder Bourne & Co.	Burslem, England	c.1862–82	"Rouen" pattern transfer-printed earthenware	saucer (11 sherds, 16 cm diameter)
Noritake(?)	Japan	unknown	white porcelain with single gilt band on the interior	saucer, European style, 15.5 cm diameter
Hollinshead and Kirkham (Ltd)	Unicorn Pottery, Tunstall, England	1933–42	cream earthenware with multi-coloured decal and handpainted orange lines	jug
J Bourne and Sons	Denby, England	1870s	light brown slipped, stoneware bottle	ink bottle, height 24 cm (Figure 5.42d).
Milton Potteries	Milton, Otago, New Zealand	1900–15	cream glazed earthenware jar	jam jar, height 16 cm (Figure 5.42a)
T Forester and Sons	Phoenix Works, Longton, England	post-1910	plain white glazed earthenware	cup
John Edwards and Co.	England	Probably post-1891 (Godden 1983:10)	blue-green transfer print "Alva" pattern	plate (7 sherds, 23 cm diameter)
T Furnival and Sons	Cobridge, England	c.1871–90	plain white earthenware	plate (33 sherds, 26 cm diameter)

5 The material culture of the Chinese in southern New Zealand

Mark	Discussion	Provenance
Impressed "Pinder Bourne & Co 79-1"	Also bears a blue transfer-printed crest incorporating a crown and laurel design (part only) with the word "Cable" – other wording missing (Figure 5.39-8).	S133/453, Riverside (B3 Ly.1)
Brown transfer-printed circle surmounted by a crown with the letters "P.B. & [Co?]" on the underside of the circle (Figure 5.39-2)	Mark similar to Godden #3045 (1964:495) but last letters illegible. If the last letter is an "H", the manufacturer would be Pinder Bourne & Hope (Godden 1964:495).	5133/453, Rapids (M4 Ly.1)
A green decal bearing a symbolic design in a circle within a laurel of leaves (Figure 5.39-3)	The mark is similar, but without the wording, to the Noritake 'Tree Crest' design depicted by Stitt (1974:201).	5123/250, Ah Lum's store, half on surface in main room; matching other half found in "bank" room (E9 Ly.1)
Printed mark incorporating a unicorn	Mark same as Godden #2075 (Godden 1964:332). This ceramic must have been deposited after the Chinese occupation of the store, possibly during the short-term occupation by a European hermit in the late 1940s.	An Lum's store, main room, surface
Impressed "J Bourne and Sons, Patentees, Denby Pottery near Derby, 1878" (Godden #474 1964:90)	Joseph Bourne of Denby was one of the major British manufacturers of stoneware bottles, particularly for ginger beer.	ACS/2 (F12 Ly.2)
Impressed on one side "St George Jam Works, Dunedin". Impressed on other side "Milton Otago Potteries" in an oval circle	The Milton Potteries operated from 1873 until 1915. The oval Milton Potteries stamp is believed to date from 1900 until 1915 (Park 1978:21).	ACS/5 (P13 Ly.2)
Black printed "Phoenix Ware, Made in England, T F & S Ltd"	T Forester and Sons operated a pottery at Longton from c. 1883-1959 (Godden 1983:157). 'Made in England' denotes a post 1900 date. (ibid:10). 'Phoenix China' and 'Phoenix Ware' were used on the company's pottery after 1910 (Godden 1964:257).	ACS/8 (G12 Ly.1)
(part only) Blue-green transfer-printed heraldic shield design bearing the words "John Edwards, England, Alva" (Figure 5.39-9)	John Edwards & Co operated a pottery from 1880 until 1900 (Godden: 1964:231 #1452.).	ACS/9 trench
"T Furnival & Sons, Trade Mark, England" under printed Royal Arms mark incorporating a lion, a unicorn, an anchor, and "Dieu Et Mon Droit" (Figure 5.39-1)	Godden #1649 (1964:263). Thomas Furnival & Sons made "white granite and vitrified ironstone and decorated toilet wares" (Praetzellis and Praetzellis 1979:166). They operated at Cobridge between 1871 and 1890 (Godden 1983:177).	S133/223, Caliche (Y2 Ly.3)

Table 5.18. Predominant Ceramic type (Euro-ceramic or Chinese) in each site

Type	Rockshelters (n=7)	Huts (n=5)	Chinatown	Arrowtown	Ah Lum's store
Euro-ceramics predominant	3	1	yes	yes	yes
Chinese- ceramics predominant	2	4	no	no	no
equal numbers	1	0	0	0	0
Total units of euro-ceramics	37	17	100	65	37
Total units of Chinese ceramics	11	20	49	44	11

Table 5.19. Euro-ceramic earthenware and porcelain vessels: site distribution.

Site key				
	A	Firewood Creek 1880–95	B	Caliche 1870–1920	C	Sheung Fong 1875–1900
Note. Dates are based on artefact dating and historic records.	D	Ha Fong 1875–1900	E	Chinatown 1869–1920	F	QB2 post-1895
	G	Apple Tree 1885–95	H	Sandy Point 1885–95	I	Ah Wee's post-1890
	J	Poplars 1885–95	K	Hanging Rock 1880—900	L	Riverside 1870–1900
	M	Arrowtown 1870–1925	N	Rapids 1870–1900	O	Ah Lum's 1880–1925

Earthenware vessel type	A	B	C	D	E	F	G	H	I	J	K	L	M	N	O	Total
cups/mugs	1	3		1	25		1			2			9	4	11	57
saucers	1	3			15					3			10		3	35
large plates	3	4		1	5					2		2	12	2	8	39
side plates					4								2			6
other plates					7								3	4		14
egg-cups					2										1	3
bowls	2	2			5					1			1		3	14
teapots	2				9								4			15
food jars	1			1	2								1			5
miscellaneous	3				4	2				1			8		1	19
unk. vessel form		2			4	1	1			1			7		2	18
flower pots					4		1									5
jugs		1														1
Subtotal	13	15	1	2	86	3	3	0	6	4	0	2	57	10	29	231
% of total	93	82	100	100	91	100	100	0	86	100	0	100	88	100	90	

5 The material culture of the Chinese in southern New Zealand

Table 5.19. Euro-ceramic earthenware and porcelain vessels: site distribution.

Porcelain vessel Type	A	B	C	D	E	F	G	H	I	J	K	L	M	N	O	Total
cups/mugs					1								1		2	4
saucers					4								3		2	9
plates/dishes	1	2			4				1				1			9
miscellaneous		1											3			4
Subtotal	1	3	0	0	9	0	0	0	1	0	0	0	8	0	4	26
% of total	14	17	0	0	9	0	0	0	14	0	0	0	12	0	11	

Table 5.20. Earthenware types: site distribution and percentages per site.

Site key	A	Firewood Creek 1880–95	B	Caliche 1870–1920	C	Sheung Fong 1875–1900
	D	Ha Fong 1875–1900	E	Chinatown 1869–1920	F	QB2 post-1895
Note. Dates are based on artefact dating and historic records.	G	Apple Tree 1885–95	H	Sandy Point 1885–95	I	Ah Wee's post-1890
	J	Poplars 1885–95	K	Hanging Rock 1880–1900	L	Riverside 1870–1900
	M	Arrowtown 1870–1925	N	Rapids 1870–1900	O	Ah Lum's 1880–1925

	A	B	C	D	E	F	G	H	I	J	K	L	M	N	O	Total
Plain white	3	6	1	0	22	1	2	0	2	0	0	0	19	4	10	70
% of total	23	40	100		24	20	66		33				33	66	30	29%
Embossed white	1	0	0	0	2	0	0	0	0	1	0	0	2	0	3	9
% of total	8				2					25			3.5		9	4%
Colour-decorated	9	9	0	2	67	3	1	0	4	3	0	2	36	2	20	158
% of total	69	60		100	74	80	33		66	75		100	63	33	60	67%
Total	13	15	1	2	91	4	3	0	6	4	0	2	57	6	33	237

Table 5.21. Euro-ceramic and Chinese ceramic vessels: site distribution and occupation date.

Site key	A	Firewood Ck 1880–95	B	Caliche 1870–1920	C	Sheung Fong 1875–1900
	D	Ha Fong 1875–1900	E	Chinatown 1869–1920	F	QB2 post-1895
Note. Dates are based on artefact dating and historic records.	G	Apple Tree 1885–95	H	Sandy Point 1885–95	I	Ah Wee's post-1890
	J	Poplars 1885–95	K	Hanging Rock 1880–1900	L	Riverside 1870–1900
	M	Arrowtown 1870–1925	N	Rapids 1870–1900	O	Ah Lum's 1880–1925

	A	B	C	D	E	F	G	H	I	J	K	L	M	N	O	Total
Chinese ceramics (C)																
Celadon vessels	3	2	2	2	39	5	5	3	1	4	0	1	33	5	4	109
Bamboo vessels	1				1								1			3
4 Seasons					4		1						8		5	18
Others					5	1							2	1	2	11
Total	4	2	2	2	49	6	6	3	1	4	0	1	44	6	11	141
Euro-ceramics (E)																
earthenwares	13	15	1	2	91	4	3	0	6	4	0	2	57	7	33	238
porcelain	1	3	0	0	9	0	0	0	1	0	0	0	8	0	4	26
Total	14	18	1	2	100	4	3	0	7	4	0	2	65	7	37	264
Predominant Ceramic	E	E	C	eq.	E	C	C	C	E	eq.	eq.	E	E	C	E	

Table 5.22. Comparison of ware types: minimum numbers and percentages.

Type	Chinatown	Arrowtown	Ah Lum's	Rural Sites	Boise, ID (Wegars 1981:137)	Lovelock, ND (Praetzellis and Praetzellis 1979:179)
Euro-earthenwares						
plain white	22	19	10	17	124	603
embossed white	2	2	3	2	13	40
colour-decorated	48	37	19	33	28	45
others	21	6	1	4	13	1
Subtotal	93	64	33	56	178	689
% of total	83.8	78	84.6	83.6	84.7	67.3
Euro-porcelains						
plain white	3	4	3	4	10	Chinese and Euro not separated
embossed white	2	1	0	2	0	-
colour-decorated	4	2	1	0	8	-
others	0	1	0	0	0	-
Subtotal	9	8	4	6	18	-
% of total	8.1	9.8	10.3	8.9	8.6	-
Euro-stonewares	9	10	2	5	14	193
% of total	8.25	13.3	5.1	7.5	6.7	18.9
Euro-ceramics	111	82	39	67	210	882
Chinese ceramics	49	44	11	37	n/a	125

5 The material culture of the Chinese in southern New Zealand

Table 5.23. Euro-ceramics composition (all sites).

	Chinatown	Arrowtown	Ah Lum's	Rural sites	Total
Earthenware					
cups	24	6	10	12	52
large mugs	1	3	1	0	5
saucers	15	10	3	9	37
plates, side	4	2	3	0	9
plates, large	5	12	8	12	37
plates, indeterminate size	4	3	1	1	9
platters(?)	2	0	0	0	2
egg cups	2	0	1	0	3
basin(?)	0	1	0	0	1
bowls, steep-sided	2	1	2	3	8
small dishes/bowls	3	0	1	2	6
serving dish, oval	1	0	1	0	2
lid for bowl	0	1	0	0	1
soap dish	0	1	0	0	1
teapots, white paste	2	2	0	1	5
teapots, red paste	6	2	0	0	8
teapot lids, red paste	3*	1	0	0	1
jardiniere(?)	0	1	0	0	1
flower pots, red	4	0	0	1	5
chamber pot(?)	1	0	0	0	1
paste pots, straight-sided	2	0	0	0	2
Holloway's Ointment pots	1***	0	0	3	4
ink bottle, 1d ink	0	1	0	2	3
pot lids, decorated	1	0	0	2	3
bases for above	4	0	0	2	6
jam jars	0	1	0	0	1
small food jar	0	0	0	2	2
unidentified	4	7	2	1	14
Subtotal	**91**	**55**	**33**	**53**	**232**

Notes
* don't match teapots
** don't match food jars
*** 533 Oxford St address on pot, therefore post-1867.

Table 5.23. Euro-ceramics composition (all sites) (*continued*).

	Chinatown	Arrowtown	Ah Lum's	Rural sites	Total
Porcelain					
cups	1	1	2	0	4
saucers	4	3	2	0	9
plate with open work	0	1	0	0	1
serving plate	0	0	0	1	1
dish, scalloped	0	0	0	1	1
dish, 17 cm diameter	0	0	0	1	1
vase(?)	1	0	0	0	1
candle holders	2	0	0	0	2
door knobs	1	0	0	0	1
jugs, small fragments	0	1	0	0	1
chair castor	0	1	0	0	1
doll's set tea cup and saucer	0	0	0	2	2
form indeterminable	0	1	0	1	2
Subtotal	**9**	**8**	**4**	**6**	**27**
Stoneware					
tubular handle	1	0	0	0	1
bottles	2	2	0	0	4
jars, often salt glaze	2	0	0	1	3
jar lids**	2**	0	0	0	0
crocks	1	2	1	0	4
paste pots (straight-sided)	1	0	0	0	1
ink bottles	1	5	0	2	8
blacking bottle	0	0	1	0	1
form indeterminant	0	1	0	1	2
Subtotal	**10**	**10**	**2**	**4**	**26**
Total	**110**	**73**	**39**	**63**	**287**

Notes
* don't match teapots
** don't match food jars
*** 533 Oxford St address on pot, therefore post-1867.

Table 5.24. Euro-ceramics decoration (all sites).

	Chinatown	Arrowtown	Ah Lum's	Rural Sites
Earthenware				
plain white	22	19	10	19
white with silver hairlining	4	0	4	3
white with gilt hairlining or design	8	4	3	0
white with rim or edge banding	7	1	1	2
white with wording	1*	0	0	0
white with embossing or scalloping	2	2	3	2
white with combination of above features	3	3	2	2
handpainted design	1	1	0	0
transfer printed	19	18	7	24
flow blue transfer print	0	1	1	0
lithographed (decalcomania)	3	1	1	0
tea pots, white paste	0	0	0	2
earthenware teapots, red paste	9	3	0	1
red earthenware flowerpots	4	0	0	0
coloured glazes (bowls and jars)	4	3	0	0
cream earthenware	0	0	1	0
salt glazed earthenware food containers	4	1	0	0
Subtotal	91	57	33	55
% of total	83.50	76.0	84.60	83.60
Porcelains				
plain white	3	4	3	2
white with hairlining or edge banding	3	2	0	0
white with embossing	2	1	0	2
coloured	1	0	0	0
chair castor	0	1	0	0
Japanese "Noritake" saucer	0	0	1	0
doll's cup and saucer	0	0	0	2
Subtotal	9	8	4	6
% of total	8.25	10.70	10.30	8.90
Stonewares				
ink bottles	0	5	0	2
food jars and lids	6	2	0	0
bottles and crocks	2	2	2	3
tubular handle (vessel form unknown)	1	0	0	0
indeterminate vessel form	0	1	0	0
Subtotal	9	10	2	5
% of total	8.25	13.30	5.10	7.50
Total	109	75	39	66

* Wording reads "Might in the Right... European..." Design incorporates a picture of a battleship. The saucer appears to be a World War I Victory souvenir.

Table 5.25. Euro-ceramics composition: rural sites.

Site	Site no.	Vessel form	Earthenware	Porcelain	Stoneware	Total
Firewood Creek	S133/424					
		cup	1			1
		saucer	1			1
		large plates/platters	3			3
		dish c.17 cm diameter	1	1		2
		bowl(?)	1			1
		shallow bowl 18 cm diameter	1			1
		small dish 5 cm diameter	1			1
		teapot, white paste	1			1
		teapot lid, white paste	1			1
		Holloway's toothpaste pot	1			1
		small jar	1		1	2
Subtotal			13	1	1	15
Sheung Fong	S133/424	small food jar	1			1
Subtotal			1	0	0	1
Ha Fong	S133/22	cup	1			1
		plate, serving	1			1
Subtotal			2	0	0	2
Northburn	S133/77	small white food jar	1			1
		form indeterminate		1		1
Subtotal			1	1	0	2
Riverside	S133/791	plates, serving	2			2
Subtotal			2	0	0	2
Apple Tree	S124/212	cup	1			1
		toothpaste pot base	1			1
		small red paste flower pot	1			1
Subtotal			3	0	0	3
Caliche	S133/223	cups	3			3
		saucers	3			3
		plates, serving	4			4
		bowl	1			1
		scalloped dish		1		1
		sugar bowl	1			1
		jug	1			1
		form indeterminate	1			1
		Holloway's lid 9.7 cm diameter	1			1
		doll's set cup	0	1		1
		doll's set saucer	0	1		1
Subtotal			15	3	0	18

Table 5.25. Euro-ceramics composition: rural sites (*continued*).

Site	Site No.	Vessel form	Earthenware	Porcelain	Stoneware	Total
The Poplars	S115/44	saucers	3			3
		small bowl	1			1
Subtotal			**4**	**0**	**0**	**4**
QB2	S124/207	toothpaste pot (rect.)	1			1
		toothpaste pot lid (circ.)	1			1
		Holloway's Ointment pot (post 1867)	1			1
		penny ink bottle			1	1
Subtotal			**3**	**0**	**1**	**4**
Ah Wee's	S115/54	cups	2			2
		plates, serving	2	1		3
		Cherry toothpaste lid and base	1			1
		penny ink bottle			1	1
		form indeterminate	1			1
Subtotal			**6**	**1**	**1**	**8**
The Rapids	S133/463	cups	4			4
		saucers	2			2
		bottle			1	1
		form indeterminate	1			1
Subtotal			**7**	**0**	**1**	**8**
Total			**57**	**6**	**4**	**67**

Table 5.26. Euro-ceramics decoration: rural sites.

Site key	A	Firewood Creek	B	Sheung Fong	C	Ha Fong					
	D	Northburn	E	Riverside	F	Apple Tree					
	G	Caliche	H	Poplars	I	QB2					
	J	Ah Wee's	K	Rapids							
	A	B	C	D	E	F	G	H	I	J	K	Total
Earthenware												
plain white	3			1		2	6			2	5	**19**
white with gilt hairlining	1											**1**
white with silver hairlining							3					**3**
white with edge-banding	1								1			**2**
white with embossing	1								1			**2**
white with combination of above							1				1	**2**
transfer printed	4		2		2		5	2	3	3	3	**24**
teapots (white paste)	2											**2**
toothpaste pot base	1											**1**
flowerpot, red paste					1							**1**
Subtotal	**13**	**0**	**2**	**1**	**2**	**3**	**15**	**4**	**3**	**5**	**9**	**57**
% of total = 83.60												
Porcelains												
plain white				1						1		**2**
white with embossing	1						2					**3**
doll's cup and saucer							2					**2**
Subtotal	**1**	**0**	**0**	**1**	**0**	**0**	**4**	**0**	**0**	**1**	**0**	**7**
% of total = 8.90												
Stoneware												
ink bottles	1								1	1		**2**
jars, crocks and bottles		1								1		**3**
Subtotal	**1**	**1**	**0**	**0**	**0**	**0**	**0**	**0**	**1**	**1**	**1**	**5**
% of total = 7.50												
Total	**15**	**1**	**2**	**2**	**2**	**3**	**19**	**4**	**4**	**7**	**10**	**69**

5 The material culture of the Chinese in southern New Zealand

Table 5.27. Principal can types: site distribution.

Food category	Can type	Chinatown		Caliche		QB2		Ah Wee's		Poplars		ACS		Ah Lum's		Range
		Qty	%	Qty	%	Qty	%	Qty	%	Qty	%	Qty	%	Qty	%	
Preserved Foods	general foods	32	18.5	5	12.8	7	21	12	29.2	16	34	35	15.8	3	8.8	8.8–34.0
	oval fish/sardines	5	2.9	4	10.2	4	12.5	4	9.7	7	14.8	28	12.7	7	20.5	2.9–20.5
	squat cyl./tapered/rect. h/c/key cans	18	10.4	2	5.1	1	3.1	3	7.3	3	6.4	9	4.1	0	0	0–10.4
Subtotal M=37		55	31.8	11	28.1	12	36.6	19	46.2	26	55.2	72	32.6	10	29.3	29.4–55.3
Dry Products	circ. Flange	30	17.3	5	12.8	4	12.5	3	7.3	4	8.5	56	25.3	2	5.9	5.9–5.3
	rect. flange	5	2.9	0		3	9.4	1	2.4	2	4.25	3	1.4	1	2.9	0–9.4
	others (biscuit tins, tea boxes, press-top cans)	11	6.4	4	20.2	3	9.4	2	4.8	3	6.4	9	4.1	0		
Subtotal M=22		46	26.6	9	33	10	31.3	6	14.5	9	19.15	68	30.8	3	8.8	8.8–31.35
Smokables	tobacco cans (all types) M=14.3	26	15	12	30.8	0		3	7.3	0		26	11.8	12	35.3	0–35.3
	opium cans M=18	22	12.8	4	10.2	7	21.9	11	26.9	11	23.4	33	15	6	17.6	10.2–26.9
Subtotal		48	27.8	16	41	7	21.9	14	34.2	11	23.4	59	26.8	18	52.9	
Other cans	kerosene/solvents/ undiagnosed M=7.6	24	13.9	3	7.7	2	6.25	2	4.8	1	2.1	22	9.95	3	8.8	2.1–13.9
	opium antidote	2	1.2									4	1.8			
Match boxes	wax vestas	41	19.2	7	15.2	49	60.5	49	54.4	144	75.3	210	48.7	12	26	512
Site total	all cans	216		46		80		90		191		435		46		1,104

Table 5.28. Embossed and painted can labels.

Merchant's name	Location	Product	First appearance	Provenance	Type of can
W. Gregg & Co.	Coffee and spice mills, Lower Rattray St, Dunedin	Club Coffee	post-1861	CH/4, Poplars	circ. flanged lid
		spice tin		S133/22	circ. flanged lid
R. Wilson & Co.	General Merchants, coffee and spice manufacturers, Bond St, Dunedin	spice tin	est'd in 1861	QB2	rect. flanged lid
		spice tin		QB2	circ. flanged lid
Wilson Balk & Co	Spice merchants, Bond St, Dunedin	spice tin	post-1898	ACS/4	circ. flanged lid
Strangs	Invercargill, general merchants. Marketed their own cocoa, chocolate coffee and chicory and spices		post-1887	CH/7, Poplars, S133/21	circ. flanged lid
Edmonds	Christchurch, manufacturers of baking and custard powder		post-1880	CH/36	circ. flanged lid
WD & HO Wills	Wellington, cigarette makers and tobacco packers	"Capstan"	post-1880	CH/4, Ch/26	circ. flanged lid
				Ch/33, ACS/2	slip-lid cutters
Cameron's	England(?)	Havelock Tobacco	post-1890	Ch/34	rect. hinged, flanged lid
British/Australian Tobacco Co.	Australia(?)	Havelock Tobacco	post-1890	ACS/6 (2), Ah Lums	pocket tobacco
		mustard	c. 1870	Poplars	rect. flanged lid
		Azure Blue (no.1)	c. 1870	S133/69	rect. flanged lid
Colman's	England	starch	c. 1870	S123/144	rect. flanged lid
		mustard oil for rheumatism	c. 1870	S123/144	rect. flanged lid
		concentrated mustard oil	c. 1870	S133/69	rect. flanged lid
Robinson's	England(?)	groats	c. 1870	S133/69	rect. flanged lid
Fry's	London and Bristol	cocoa and chocolate	c. 1870	Ch/23, Poplars, QB2	circ. flanged lid
unkown	England	Bournville cocoa	c. 1870	Ah Wee's, Rapids	circ. flanged lid
unknown	England(?)	Blossom Ointment	unknown	Ah Lum's	circ. flanged lid

Table 5.29. Known or inferred date ranges of metal containers.

Type/product	Date range	Utility for dating
General food cans		
hole-and-cap	1840s-1930	good, most pre-1900
overlapped/single seam	1885-1900	good
double seam	1900-present	
Meat cans		
rect. hole-and-cap	1850s-1900	good
tapered cans	1875-present	good
squat cylindrical	1880s-present	
key-opening cans	1890-present	
Dry foods		
rectangular flange-lids	1830s-c1950	poor, unless embossed
circular flanged-lids	1830s-present	poor, unless embossed
Press-tops (lever lids)	1895-present	poor
Tobacco and cigarette cans		
circular flanged-lid	1870 -c1950	
slip-lid with cutter	1890-c1950	good
soldered-top box	pre 1900	good
pocket tobacco	1900-c1950	
Fish cans		
sardine	1880-present	good
oval cans	1880-present	good
Wax vesta matchboxes (see Anson 1983; Bedford 1984)	1830s-1940	excellent
Opium cans	pre-1910	
Kerosene cans	c1880-present	

Table 5.30. Wax vesta boxes: site distribution.

Site key		A Firewood Creek		E Chinatown		I Ah Wee's			
		B Caliche		F QB2		J Poplars			
		C Sheung Fong		G Apple Tree		K Hanging Rock			
		D Ha Fong		H Sandy Point		L Riverside			

Type	Brand	A	B	C	D	E	F	G	H	I
1A	Bell & Black									
1B										
1C		1								
1D		1								
1E										
1F		4		1				2		
1G		1				1		1	7	
1H										
2A	Palmer						1			
2B										
2C										
3A	Palmer & Sons						1			
3B										
4A	Letchford									
5A	Pace & Sons	3				1			2	
6A	Royal Patent								2	
7a	R Bell & Co., london									
7b										
7c						1				
7d										
7e										
8a	R Bell & Co., London. painted labels	4	2	3	1		4	1	3	11
8b										1
8c		2		1						
8d		2								
8e										
9a	R. Bell & Co., N.Z. stamped labels		3			14	9	1		3
9b						4				
9c										
9d										
9e										
10a	R. Bell & Co., N.Z. painted labels					4				
11a	Bryant & May, London									

5 The material culture of the Chinese in southern New Zealand

M	Arrowtown	Q	Motutapu	U	12 Mile Camp
N	Rapids	R	Ah Lum's	V	Bendigo
O	Ledge	S	Bonnie Jean	W	Flax Grove
P	12 Mile Track	T	QB1		

J	K	L	M	N	O	P	Q	R	S	T	U	V	W	Totals	Comments
			1											**1**	1870s
			3									1		**4**	
			2					1				1		**5**	1875
				12										**13**	
				1										**1**	
	2		1	3										**13**	
				24	3									**37**	1880
				29										**29**	
				1										**2**	
				7										**7**	
				5										**5**	
				8					1					**10**	
				1										**1**	
														0	
	10	1	1											**18**	post 1871
				1										**3**	
				3										**3**	
				5										**5**	
				2										**3**	
			1	1										**2**	
				1										**1**	
61			5	15	20		3		2		20		1	**156**	
1														**2**	
	1	1		1										**6**	
13		1	5	9				1						**31**	
				1										**1**	
			48	124				3					4	**209**	
			49	1	2			1		7				**64**	pre 1895
			22							6			5	**33**	post 1895
			3											**3**	
			3		1		3	1		21	1	1		**31**	c.1911 Anson
												2		**6**	
			2											**2**	

Table 5.30. Wax vesta boxes: site distribution (*continued*).

Type	Brand	A	B	C	D	E	F	G	H	I
11b			9		1	3	4	10	3	
11c										
11d										1
11e		2		1	1	4	33			17
11f										
11g										
11h										1
12a	Bryant & May, London	1			1					
12b	painted labels				1					
12c										1
13a	Mariotte & Co									
13b										
14a	Super Belgian									4
14b										
14c										3
14d										
15a	Lehman & Lehman									
16a	NZ Wax Vestas						1			
16b										
16c										
16d										
17a	Harlequin									
18a	London Wax Vestas									
19a	Patent Wax Vestas									
unidentified		3				10				
cardboard box R. Bell & Co.										
Totals		**33**	**5**	**6**	**4**	**41**	**52**	**9**	**24**	**45**

J	K	L	M	N	O	P	Q	R	S	T	U	V	W	Totals	Comments
27		1	24	17	56		6	2			30			**193**	1881 Anson
														0	
4			3		1						2			**11**	
1			17		61						5		2	**144**	1880?
					11						1			**12**	
											2			**2**	
					1			1						**3**	
					2									**4**	
					1									**2**	
														1	c1890
											2			**2**	
					1									**1**	
2			2		1						3			**12**	1887 Anson
2														**2**	
12														**15**	
1														**1**	
1														**1**	
														1	post 1895?
					37									**37**	post 1895?
					3									**3**	post 1895?
														0	
				2		1								**3**	1904 advt.
														0	
														0	1880
					24	1		2						**40**	
													1	**1**	cylindrical. Fig.5.105e
135	**3**	**4**	**209**	**64**	**317**	**5**	**4**	**10**	**14**	**3**	**66**	**2**	**15**	**1,085**	

Table 5.31. Typology of opium pipe bowls from Chinese sites in Central Otago.

	Smoking-surface	Rim	Sides	Comments	Variants
Type C: bowls with circular smoking surfaces					
C1	circular, diameter 7.2 cm	flaring	smooth with single raised ridge	32 specimens from 8 sites.	a. orange, clay slipped b. orange, unslipped
C2	circular, diameter 6.9 cm	rounded, flaring	smooth	sole specimen from Firewood Creek site.	orange, slipped
C3	circular	flaring, with scalloped facets	10 facets	31 specimens of types C3.a and C3.b from 11 sites. Type C3.c limited to single specimens from three sites.	a. orange, clay slipped, diameter 7.8–8.0 cm b. orange, unslipped, diameter 7.8–8.0 cm c. orange, clay slipped, diameter 6.5 cm
C4	circular, diameter 6.2 cm	vertical with raised double ridge	straight, double raised ridges at interfaces	10 specimens recovered from 6 sites. This is the only type in which a noticeable variation in height is evident between specimens (the distance between the double raised ridges varies at the interfaces from 2.5–3.5 cm in the measurable specimens).	a. orange, clay slipped with unslipped smoking surface b. orange, clay slipped all over c. orange, unslipped
C5	circular, diameter 6.1–6.3 cm	vertical, no raised ridges	straight, smooth	14 specimens recovered from 4 sites.	a. orange, unslipped with linear design impressed below rim b. orange, slipped, plain, undecorated c. orange, slipped, broken line design below rim d. orange, unslipped, plain, undecorated e. grey, unslipped, single incised line 2 mm below rim
C6	circular, diameter 6.1–6.6 cm	rounded	smooth	4 specimens from 3 sites.	a. grey, no decoration (apart from inscribed characters on sides) b. grey, with single scored line below rim
C7	circular, maximum diameter 5.8–c.6.1 cm	rounded inwards	bulbous, with broad midpoint decorative band bounded by single raised ridges	sole specimen of type C7.a from upper Chinatown. sole specimen of type C7.b from the Rapids site.	a. orange, unslipped, decorative band around the middle bears 2 impressed flowers (side by side) and diagonal and vertical lines b. orange, unslipped, similar pattern to above but decorative band contains 2 flowers only, spaced 2.2 cm apart
C8	circular, rim diameter 5.5 cm	rounded inwards	smooth, two parallel decorative ridges below rim impressed diamond pattern above neck	single specimens from Rapids and upper Chinatown.	orange, unslipped
C9	circular, diameter c.5.7 cm	not present on sole sherd	smooth, straight, angle out towards smoking surface	no decorations on sole sherd of this type from the Apple Tree site.	orange, unslipped
Type O: bowls with octagonal smoking surfaces					
O1	octagonal, width 6.2 cm	flaring	faceted, corresponding to the shape of the smoking surface	7 examples from 2 sites.	a. orange, slipped with a geometric pattern stamped below the rim b. orange, slipped with a dotted line below the rim c. orange, unslipped with a dotted line below the rim
O2	octagonal, width 6.7–6.8 cm	rounded slightly inwards	faceted, flaring	3 examples from 2 sites (1 is inscribed with Chinese characters, the others are plain).	a. grey, unslipped
Type H: bowls with hexagonal smoking surfaces					
H1	hexagonal, width 6.9–7.1 cm	flaring	faceted, each side of the hexagon is 3.3 cm wide at the rim	13 specimens from 7 sites.	a. orange, unslipped b. orange, slipped

Table 5.32. Opium pipe bowls: minimum numbers per site.

Site key		
A Firewood Creek	B Caliche	C Sheung Fong	D Ha Fong
E Chinatown	F QB2	G Apple Tree	H Sandy Point
I Ah Wee's	J Poplars	K Hanging Rock	L Riverside
M Arrowtown	N Rapids	O U. Chinatown	P Ah Lum's store
Q Northburn			

Type	A	B	C	D	E	F	G	H	I	J	K	L	M	N	O	P	Q	Total	No. sites where bowl type was present
C1a	8	1	1		2								5	2	3			22	7
C1b	5				1				1					1	2			10	5
C2	1																	1	1
C3a	4								1			1	3	2	3			14	6
C3b	5	1			2		1		1		1				6		1	19	9
C3c										1			1	1				3	3
C4a					1										1			2	2
C4b	1		1										1	1				4	4
C4c														2				2	1
C5a	1																	1	1
C5b	1		1			1	1						1	1				6	6
C5c	1						1						1					3	3
C5d							1											1	1
C5e	1																	1	1
C6a	1								1					1				3	3
C6b	1																	1	1
C7a															1			1	1
C7b														1				1	1
C8														1	1			2	2
C9							1											1	1
O1a	2																	2	1
O1b	2													2				4	2
O1c	1																	1	1
O2a	2													1				3	2
H1a	2									1				1				4	3
H1b	2				2	1	1				1	1		2				9	6
discrete but unidentifiable bowls				1						1			2			2	1	7	5
MN	41	2	3	1	8	2	6	0	4	4	1	2	14	19	17	2	2	128	79
No. variants per site	19	1	3	1	5	1	6	0	4	4	1	2	6	13	7	1	2		
No. fragments per site	565	8	20	1	41	18	59	0	12	19	4	23	911	46	120	9	4	1075	

Table 5.33. Opium can remains.

Site key																					
	A	Firewood Creek		B	Caliche			C	Sheung Fong			D	Ha Fong			E	Chinatown			
	F	QB2		G	Apple Tree			H	Sandy Point			I	Ah Wee's			J	Poplars			
	K	Hanging Rock		L	Riverside			M	Flax Grove			N	Rapids			O	12 Mile			
	P	Arrowtown		Q	Ah Lum's			R	cache			S	Rockfall 1			T	Kawarau			

	A	B	C	D	E	F	G	H	I	J	K	L	M	N	O	P	Q	R	S	T	Total
Can bodies																					
whole	16	3	1	3	14	6	5	3	12	13	0	5	3	15	7	28	3	7	0	3	147
halves	2				1	1				3						3					10
Bases and lids																					
bases	1				2	1			1	1			1	1	3	1		2			14
lids	3		2		5	1	1		7	3		3				8			1		34
base/lid	11	1	1	3	18	4	5	1	4	10		4	2	16	2	15	1	2		3	103
base/lid?	18	2	1	3	13	4	2	1	5	7		4		8	1	5		2		1	77
poc	1													1							2
pn		1			2				2					1		2		2			10
crest	34	3	4	6	38	10	8	2	17	22		10	3	22	2	28	1	2	1	4	217
plain	1	1			4				1			2		1	1	9	2				22
MN	35	4	4	6	42	10	8	2	18	22		12	3	23	3	37	3	2	1	4	239
Can strips																					
lid S.	18	2	3		27	4	4	2	6	9	1	2	2	16		19	1			2	118
Can R.	20	3	3	2	31	5	5	1	10	11	2	5	2	22	4	23	5	4		1	159
MN can strips	20	3	3	3	31	6	5	3	12	13	2	5	3	22	7	28	5	7	1	3	182

Key
- halves — an opium can that has been cut around the midpoint to create two half-cans
- bases — a definite base because it is attached to a can body
- lids — definitely a lid because it is still attached to a lid strip
- base/lid — a base or lid with a legible cartouche
- base/lid? — a base or lid with an illegible cartouche
- poc — a "punched out" cartouche from a lid or base
- pn — hand-painted numbers, e.g. "187" painted across can end, often across the cartouche
- crest — no. of bases/lids with legible or illegible cartouches
- plain — no. of bases/lids with no cartouche
- MN — minimum number of bases or lids per site

Notes

1. Although no unmodified opium can remains were found in the Northburn site, 13 "funs trays" made of opium can metal were recovered. They would minimally represent the metal from at least two opium cans. In addition, four tin "funs trays" were recovered. They are the only known tin examples.

2. One cartouche-marked can end from Sheung Fong has 6 holes punched in it, but it is not bent in the manner of a bracket.

3. The half-can from Chinatown contains a solidified mass believed to be opium resin.

4. One of the can bodies from Ah Lum's store has 6 holes drilled in it.

5 The material culture of the Chinese in southern New Zealand

Table 5.34. Typology of opium can cartouches.

Note This listing is of selected "type specimens" only. Unless otherwise indicated, several other specimens of each type have been recovered. The type specimens were selected for their clarity or evidence of "variations". The numbers of each type of cartouche per site are tabulated in table 5.35.

Key

c	coffin shaped cartouche	nf	unframed (generally found on bases)
f	framed (generally found on lids)	r	rectangular shaped cartouche
h	hand painted numbers or letters	Ch	Chinatown
o	elongate octagonal shaped cartouche	ACS	Arrowtown

Dimensions of cartouche: width followed by length.

Type specimen	Base or lid	Shape	Dimensions (cm)	Provenance
Type 1	Lid	c,f	1.10 x 2.15	Chinatown surface
Type 1	Lid	c,f	0.90 x 2.00	Ch/14 (B8 Ly.1)
Type 1	Lid	c,f	1.10 x 2.15	Ch/22 (M12) surface
Type 1	Lid	c,f	1.00 x 2.25	Rockfall 1 wall fill
Type 1	Lid	c,f	1.00 x 2.20	Opium can cache*
Type 1	Lid	c,f,h	1.05 x 2.15	ACS/2 (H14 Ly.1)
Type 1	Lid	c,f	0.95 x 2.15	Ch/21 (M13 Ly.3)
Type 1	Lid	c,f,h	1.05 x 2.15	ACS/2 (H16 Ly.1)

Comments on Type 1

1. The most common cartouche mark on the Central Otago cans. It appears on approximately 80% of the ends with legible marks.
2. The mark is identical to that on a pristine, intact can in the Short collection, Queenstown. Translation of the characters indicates these cans are products of the Zhao Long store, Shang Huan, a district in Hong Kong (Wegars pers.comm.).
3. The mark has only been found on lids in Central Otago.
4. This cartouche exists in at least three slightly different "impressions", the differences being clearly visible features such as: fine as opposed to robust characters; smaller dimensions; a more heavily defined frame.

* About eight opium cans buried in a bank c.200 upstream of Chinatown.

Type specimen	Base or lid	Shape	Dimensions (cm)	Provenance
Type 2	lid	c,f	1.10 x 2.35	Riverside (B2 Ly.1)
Type 2	lid/base	c,f	1.15 x 2.30	ACS/3 (F12 Ly.1)

Comments on Type 2

1. This framed mark appears to be on lids only.
2. The mark has several characters in common with Type 1.
3. This mark appears to be the same as that depicted in WCC-73 and WCC-75b ("Abundant Happiness"(?), Shang Huan; Asian Comparative Collection, University of Idaho; LaLande 1981:172, Figure II-6-49).

Type specimen	Base or lid	Shape	Dimensions (cm)	Provenance
Type 3	lid/base	c,f	0.95 x 2.10	Rapids (N3 Ly.1)
Type 3	lid/base	c,f	1.00 x 2.10	ACS/6 (H8 Ly.1)

Comments on Type 3

1. This framed mark appears to be on lids only.
2. This cartouche reads "Man Wo Fung, Hong Kong" (Jones, Davis and Ling 1979:45, Figure 19d). Man Wo Fung was affiliated with Jardine, Matheson & Co. (Jones, Davis and Ling 1979: 44).

Type specimen	Base or lid	Shape	Dimensions (cm)	Provenance
Type 4	base	r,nf	0.65 x 2.10	Chinatown surface
Type 4	lid/base	r,nf	0.65 x 2.10	Poplars (H8 Ly.1)
Type 4	base	r,nf	0.70 x 2.10	Rapids (N3 Ly.1)
Type 4	lid/base	r,nf	0.60 x 2.05	ACS/7 trench C

Comments on Type 4

1. This unframed mark appears to be on bases only.

Table 5.34. Typology of opium can cartouches (*continued*).

Type specimen	Base or lid	Shape	Dimensions (cm)	Provenance
Type 5a	lid/base	r,f	0.85 x 1.85	Ch/24 (M15 Ly.1)
Type 5a	lid/base	r,f	0.80 x 1.95	ACS/4 (K16) surface
Type 5b	lid/base	r,nf	0.70–0.75 x 2.20	Flax Grove (H6 Ly.1)
Type 5b	lid/base	r,nf	0.85–0.9 x 2.10	Riverside (A2 Ly.1)

Comments on Type 5

1. There are two quite distinct variations of this mark. The most noticeable difference is that it occurs in both framed and unframed "impressions", but they also differ in dimensions as is evident above. The sides of the unframed specimens also taper slightly, as indicated above.
2. ACC-84-133 appears to be the same as the Type 5a specimens "Yu Yuan Zao".
3. ACC-84-143 appears to be the same as the Type 5b specimens.
(ACC = Asian Comparative Collection, Lab of Anthropology, University of Idaho.)

Type specimen	Base or lid	Shape	Dimensions (cm)	Provenance
Type 6	lid/base	r,f	0.80 x 1.95	Apple Tree (I12 Ly.2)

Comments on Type 6

1. Almost certainly a lid: end has loose strip with it.

Type specimen	Base or lid	Shape	Dimensions (cm)	Provenance
Type 7	lid/base	r,f	1.00 x 3.00	Ah Lum's (B9 Ly.1)
Type 7	lid/base	r,f	1.00 x 2.90	Apple Tree (H7 Ly.2)
Type 7(?)	lid/base	r,f	1.10 x 2.95	Rapids (L3) surface

Comments on Type 7

1. This cartouche is "noticeably long".
2. The third specimen listed above has one illegible character.

Type specimen	Base or lid	Shape	Dimensions (cm)	Provenance
Type 8	lid/base	o,f	1.00 x 2.20	Ha Fong (I21 Ly.3)
Type 8	lid/base	o,f	0.95 x 2.20	ACS/5 E.wall (Ly.2)

Comments on Type 8

1. This cartouche is a distinctive "elongate octagonal" shape.
2. This framed cartouche appears to be on lids only.
3. These specimens appear to be identical to ACC-10-CW-159,10, from Pierce, Idaho, translated as "Golden Profit" (Wegars pers. comm.).

Type specimen	Base or lid	Shape	Dimensions (cm)	Provenance
Type 9	lid/base	r,nf	0.70 x 2.10	Sheung Fong (Q23) Lev.2
Type 9	lid/base	r,nf	0.65 x 2.15	Poplars (Q10 Ly.1)
Type 9	lid/base	r,nf	0.65 x 1.95	Rapids (C6) Lev.1

Comments on Type 9

1. This unframed mark appears to be on bases only.

Type specimen	Base or lid	Shape	Dimensions (cm)	Provenance
Type 10	lid/base	r,nf	0.65 x 1.70	Rapids (B5 Ly.1)

Comments on Type 10

1. This is the only recovered specimen of this type.
2. The cartouche is "noticeably short".

Type specimen	Base or lid	Shape	Dimensions (cm)	Provenance
Type 11	lid/base	r,nf	1.00 x 1.95	Poplars (P8 Ly.1)

Comments on Type 11

1. This is the only recovered specimen of this type.
2. The rectangular cartouche has slightly rounded corners.

Table 5.35. Opium can cartouche types.

Site Name	Cartouche types													Illegible cartouche	No cartouche	Total can bases/ lids per site
	1	2	3	4	5a (framed)	5b (unframed)	6	7	8	9	10	11				
Firewood Creek	12			1										18	1	35
Caliche	1								1	1				2	1	4
Sheung Fong	2							1						1		4
Ha Fong	2								1					3		6
Chinatown	21			3	1									13	4	42
QB2	5													4	1	10
Apple Tree	2	1					1	1	1					2	1	8
Sandy Point	1													1		2
Ah Wee's	7									1				10	1	18
Poplars	11			2									1	7		22
Hanging Rock																0
Riverside	3	1		1	1									4	2	12
Arrowtown	16		2	3	2									5	9	37
Rapids	11		1	2				1	1		1			9	1	27
Ah Lum's store															2	3
Flax Grove	1					1									1	3
12 Mile Creek						1								1	1	3
can cache				1						1?						2
Kawarau	1			1	1									1		4
Rockfall 1	1															1
Total	**97**	**3**	**3**	**14**	**5**	**2**	**1**	**2**	**4**	**3**	**1**	**1**		**81**	**25**	**243**

Table 5.36. Artefacts made from opium can metal.

Site key	A Firewood	B Caliche	C Sheung Fong	D Ha Fong
	E Chinatown	F Apple Tree	G QB2	H Sandy Point
	I Ah Wee's	J Poplars	K Riverside	L Rapids
	M Arrowtown	N Ah Lum's store	O Northburn	P Chinatown upper terraces

Artefact type	A	B	C	D	E	F	G	H	I	J	K	L	M	N	O	P	Total
funs trays		2			46				1	2		1	33	18	13	3	119
gold blowing trays				1	3	2	1			1	1	1	2				12
discs (1)					6								2				8
washers (2)	1	1	2				1						2	7			14
leaf designs (3)					1							1	1				3
candleholder							1										1
twist tags	5	1															6
funnel							1										1
corner brackets			1#		2	1	1	1					2				8
circular flange						1											1
tray (4)									1								1
opium lamp brackets	1*		2		2				1				1				7
Total	**7**	**4**	**5**	**1**	**60**	**4**	**5**	**1**	**2**	**4**	**1**	**5**	**39**	**27**	**13**	**3**	**181**
offcuts (body metal)	7	3	5	4	12				2	4		12	12				56
offcuts (end metal)	1											1					2

Notes

(1) <2 cm diameter

(2) <2.5 cm diameter

(3) The specimen from the Rapids site was made from can end metal; a cartouche is visible

(4) this appears to be a "double length" funs tray

\# made from can end metal; a cartouche is visible

* possibly two brackets, the second one evidenced by a 4 cm-long piece of reinforcing strip with a punched hole

Table 5.37. Artefacts associated with opium smoking.

Site key	A	Firewood Creek	B	Caliche	C	Chinatown				
	D	QB2	E	Apple Tree	F	Ah Wee's				
	G	Riverside	H	Poplars	I	Arrowtown				
	J	Ah Lum's	K	Northburn						

Artefact Type	A	B	C	D	E	F	G	H	I	J	K	Total
Connecting pieces												
saddles (2 piece)			3	1					4	1		9
circular flanges (1)	1	1	2		1		2		5			12
faceted flanges (2)			2						3		1	6
Mouth or end pieces												
copper alloy		1										1
plated steel									1			1
Opium lamp components												
large glasses (4)		3	6	5	1			4	28	4		51
reservoirs (cans) (5)			1	1								2
Opium antidote(?) cans (6)			2						4			6
Opium needles(?) (7)			20			1						21
Tincture vials (8)	4		31	1	1			1	10	1		49

Notes

(1) The circular flanges are of two sizes with diameters of 2.7 cm and 3.2 cm. One specimen has a groove around the circumference.

(2) The faceted flanges are of two sizes with diameters 2.7 cm and 3.0 cm.

(3) Both of these specimens are flattened and deformed. Their use is inferred from their shape and diameter. The specimen from ACS/6 is made from light soft-plated steel, diameter 3.0 cm, hole diameter 2.0 cm, thickness 0.8 cm.

(4) All the opium lamp globes are improvisations made by cutting off the bases and necks of bottles. Light green ring-seal brandy bottles were preferred followed by aqua 3-piece mould bottles. Clear glass bottles were generally not used (their widespread usage would postdate the sites in most instances).

(5) The opium lamp reservoirs consist of small tin cans with the top removed and a bracket fitted across the top to support a wick. The brackets were usually improvised by bending an opium can reinforcing strip to the required size and punching a hole through the centre point to retain the wick. In one instance (from Chinatown) an old clock cog was jammed in the top of a can, the wick apparently supported by feeding it through a hole in the centre of the cog.

(6) The contents of these cans has not been verified (see Section 5.3.4.13).

(7) The "opium needles" consist of lengths of copper wire with pointed ends (possibly umbrella struts). Their suggested use is unsubstantiated.

(8) These small glass vials, imported from China, contained a wide range of medicines, including tincture of opium (laudanum). The contents were distiquished by paper labels on the vials. Generally the labels seldom survive in archaeological contexts.

Table 5.38. Domestic utensils from Chinese sites.

Site key																	
	A	Firewood Creek			B	Caliche			C	Sheung Fong			D	Ha Fong		
	E	Chinatown			F	QB2			G	Apple Tree			H	Sandy Point		
	I	Ah Wee's			J	Poplars			K	Hanging Rock			L	Riverside		
	M	Arrowtown			N	Rapids			O	Ah Lum's			P	Flax Grove		

	A	B	C	D	E	F	G	H	I	J	K	L	M	N	O	P	Total
Knives																	
bone handles					3								8		1		**12**
wood handles					3								1				**4**
blades only					9		1		1				7				**18**
food preparation		1				1	2			1	1		5	1			**12**
Subtotal		**1**			**15**	**1**	**3**			**2**	**1**		**21**	**1**	**1**		**46**
Forks																	
bone/wood handles	1				5												**6**
all metal					11		1						1			1	**14**
Subtotal	**1**				**16**		**1**						**1**			**1**	**20**
Spoons																	
table			1		8				1						1	1	**12**
dessert					2												**2**
tea					12				1	1						2	**16**
wooden					1												**1**
Subtotal																	**31**
Billies (tin)																	
bodies								2	1				5		1	2	**11**
lids		1	1		2	1	1			2		2	6	1	2		**19**
handles	1		1	1	3	1		1	1	1	1		4	1		1	**17**
MN	**1**	**1**	**2**	**1**	**3**	**1**	**1**	**1**	**2**	**2**	**2**		**6**	**1**	**2**	**3**	**29**
Pocket knives	1	1	4		5		1				1	1	6	1			**21**
Pots																	
cast iron		1			3		1		1				2	1		3	**12**
enamel					1								1				**2**
Subtotal																	**14**
Fry pans (cast iron)				1	3								1	1	1	1	**8**
Teapots																	
enamel					1												**1**
lids only									1				1				**2**
Euro-ceramic	2				9								4				**15**
Japanese ceramic													1				**1**
Chinese ceramic						1											**1**
Subtotal	**2**				**10**	**1**			**1**				**6**				**20**

Table 5.38. Domestic utensils from Chinese sites (*continued*).

	A	B	C	D	E	F	G	H	I	J	K	L	M	N	O	P	Total
Enamel pie dishes																	
oval/rectangular		1	1		1											1	4
Strainers (improvised)			1			1											2
Cleavers (narrow blade)						1				2			1			1	5
Wok spoons		1	1	8	1					1			1	1			14
Woks				1													1
Toasting wire				1													1
Bottle opener				1													1
Bamboo skewer															1		1
Meat mincer															1		1
Metal funnel															1		1
Total	5	6	9	4	91	4	7	2	9	4	4	1	46	10	13	23	238

Comments

1a. The "bone and wood handles" and the "blades" are all parts of table knives.

1b. The "food preparation" knives include paring and carving knives.

2. Most of the tablespoons are plain. One ornate and one plain specimen are depicted.

3. The diameters of the billies varied from 13 to 21 cm. The stated minimum number is a conservative count.

4. All single-blade pocket knives have either wood or shell grips.

5. Most of the cast iron pots were fragmentary but had diameters of c.20 cm.

6. The diameter of the frypans varied from 21 to 30cm. All have distinctive long handles ranging from 30 to 36 cm.

7. One of the strainers is an improvisation made from wire.

8. Most of the wok spoons are one piece constructions and were generally in poor condition when uncovered. One has a brass handle. Two appear to be improvisations made up from scrap metal.

9. The cleavers are represented by the blades only. They vary in length from 15 to 17cm.

10. An additional wok spoon and a cleaver blade were found beside a fossick hole in the Kawarau shelter (S133/72), Kawarau Gorge.

11. The toasting wire found in the Ha Fong shelter is made from No. 8 wire. It is possibly of European origin.

12. One of the forks from Chinatown is a three-pronged meat fork from Ch/34.

13. The bamboo skewer was found in Ah Lum's bank room.

14. The meat-mincer was represented by the "worm drive" portion only. It was found outside Ah Lum's store, behind the south wall of the structure. It was probably not asssociated with the Chinese occupation.

15. One of the cast iron pots from the Flax Grove site was of the oval "dixie" type.

Table 5.39 Chinatown: household and domestic artefacts.

Artefact	6	7	14	16	18	19	21	22	23	26	27	33	34	Total
metal picture frame	1													1
watering can	1													1
iron offcuts (1)	1													1
piece of coal range	1												1	2
3-prong coat hook	1													1
ornate bracket	1													1
iron wall hook	1													1
iron coat hook			1											1
cup hook								1						1
fire grate pieces	1	1						1						3
brass cap (2)		1												1
padlocks		1						3					1	5
fragments of linoleum		1			1					1				3
door hinges			1							1			2	4
mattress springs			1										1	2
door keys								2	2	1				5
door lock fittings				1			1	2	1					5
keyhole faceplate							1	1						2
doorknob faceplate								1						1
brass door knob							1							1
white porcelain door knob										1				1
cupboard keys								2					1	3
cupboard door hinge										1				1
brass lamp base (?)				1										1
scissors (large)				1		1	1		1					4
scissors (medium)								1						1
scissors (small)							1	1	1					3
scrubbing brush				1										1
3 prong wire fork (3)				1										1
enamel candleholder						1							1	2
lantern parts				1*	1			1					1	4
faceplate off oil heater (4)										1				1
blue enamel saucer					1									1
tin plate			1											1
tin mug													1	1
enamel mug									1					1
clock parts					1					1		2		4

Table 5.39 Chinatown: household and domestic artefacts (*continued*).

Artefact	6	7	14	16	18	19	21	22	23	26	27	33	34	Total
pewter(?) scoop					1									1
rubber door mat fragments						1								1
improvised wire guard										2				2
miniature syringe(?)										1				1
bottle opener										1				1
push button off torch										1				1
brass ring and split pin (5)										1				1
blue dye										1				1
brass ball (6)												1		1
threaded knob (7)												1		1
iron rings (8)												4		4
umbrella struts												18		18
brass thimbles											2			2
Total	8	4	4	6	4	4	5	16	6	14	2	26	9	106

Notes

1. the iron offcuts were placed around the hearth in the hut.
2. probably off a fuel can, embossed "Gargoyle".
3. although no barbs are evident this may have been used for eeling.
4. embossed "Perfection Smokeless Oil Heater" (Figure 5.62a).
5. attached to fragment, appears to be off a drawer.
6. 3 cm diameter, 2-piece construction, use unknown.
7. conical with concave sides, appears to be a drawer knob.
8. of 28 cm diameter, internal diameter 21.cm, use unknown.

Table 5.40 Arrowtown: household and domestic artefacts.

Key to Ah Lum's store														
MR main room														
BA bank room														
BE bedroom														
ST strongroom														
KI kitchen														

	Hut #								Ah Lum's store					
Artefact	2	3	4	5	6	8	9	10	13	MR	BA	BE	ST	KI	Total
camp oven handles	1	1													2
iron grates	1			3*											4
linoleum (types)		2		1		1		1	1						6
cotton reel (full)		1													1
wooden handle (1)		1													1
scissors (large)		5	1		1				2						9
scissors (small)												1			1
enamel mug		1													1
enamel saucer			1		1										2
pot-lid knob		1			1										2
rivetted iron handle			1												1
lantern screw cap			1												1
lantern			1#											2	3
part of coal range			1												1
metal candkleholder							1								1
wooden candleholder (2)					1										1
wooden picture frame					1										1
mouth organ (3)					1										1
tuba stop					1										1
sack needle					1										1
ceramic door knob					1										1
iron door knob										2					2
door knob surround						1				1	1			1	4
brass keyhole surround										2				1	3
improvised keyhole facing										1					1
door latch slide												1			1
door hinges					1	1	1	1				1			5
cupboard hinges									1	1	1				3
window latch										1					1
metal bracket					1										1
galvanised downpipe			1		1										2

Table 5.40 Arrowtown: household and domestic artefacts.(*continued*).

Artefact	2	3	4	5	6	8	9	10	13	MR	BA	BE	ST	KI	Total
curved metal spout (4)					1										1
brass grometts						3									3
clock parts		2					1		1		1				4
alarm clock														1	1
poker				1										1	2
tin funnel	1												1		2
wire noose(?)											1				1
battery top plate											1				1
red pigment												1			1
wooden knob												1	1		2
wooden peg													1		1
lawn mower parts														1	1
pictorial glass panel												1			1
screw-on spout (brass)													1		1
light chain													1		1
Total	3	14	7	4	14	5	4	1	5	9	7	3	1	7	‹89

Notes

* one circular, one outside hut

\# "Juno" brand

1. the handle has a ferrule, possibly an awl
2. zinc-covered wooden block with group of nails to secure candle
3. embossed "The Rainbow, M. Hohner, Germany".
4. identical tin spouts were found in the Firewood Creek and Ha Fong sites.

Table 5.41. Rural sites: household and domestic artefacts.

Site key	A Caliche		B Sheung Fong		C Ha Fong				
	D Apple Tree		E Poplars		F Rapids				
	G Ah Wee's		H QB2		I Flax Grove				
Artefact	A	B	C	D	E	F	G	H	I	Total
threaded fitting	1									1
leather suitcase handle	1									1
brass gromett	1									1
top and base of battery	1									1
torch bulb holder	1									1
padlocks	1			1						2
brass door knob				1						1
improvised door key						1				1
candle wax		1	1							2
candle holder, wooden			1							1
brass thimbles		1	1					1		3
tin plates 22–24 cm			2	1	1		1	1		6
wooden peg			1							1
scissors (medium)									1	1
scissors (large)			1	1				1		3
iron bucket					1					1
nail drum hoops					2					2
perforated zinc sheeting					1					1
plastic threaded cap					1					1
screw cap off lantern						1				1
bone handle (off toothbrush?)						1				1
umbrella struts							2			2
broom head with horse hair(?)									1	1
ceramic castor off an iron bed									1	1
Total	6	2	7	4	6	3	3	3	3	37

5 The material culture of the Chinese in southern New Zealand

Table 5.42. Chinatown tools: site distribution.

Tool Types	6	11	12	14	16	18	19	21	22	23	26	27	33	34	Total	Comments
nail punch	1														1	
brass ferrules							2			2				2	6	
mallet head				1											1	
hand shears					1					1	1	1		1	5	
grindstones						1									1	circ. sect
grindstones						1	1							1	3	rect. sect.
files, triangular			1			1			3		1				6	
files, flat										1	1				2	
hacksaw blade							1								1	
folding rulers								1		1					2	hinge parts
knife(?)										1					1	
hammer head										1					1	claw type
handle										1					1	off tool
spanner, Stillson										1					1	
drill bit														1	1	
wire screwdriver						1									1	improvised from No. 8 wire
awl										1					1	
hoe blade	1														1	
garden rake									1						1	
socket										1					1	hoe(?)
axe heads		1									1				2	tomahawks
axe heads					1										1	regular
splitting wedge											1				1	
gold blowing tray												1			1	made of tin
pickhead													1		1	
miner's fork														1	1	tines only
gold cradle?	1														1	tray part
trap spring											1				1	not off rabbit trap
Total	3	1	1	1	1	5	4	1	4	11	6	2	1	6	47	

241

Table 5.43. Arrowtown tools: site distribution.

Tool Types	Hut #											Total	Comments
	2	3	4	5	6	7	8	10	11	13	15	Ah Lum's		
hand shears	1		1	1		1	1		3				8	all 1/2 blades
file, triangular	1		1		1		1						4	
file, flat		1			1					2		2	6	
carpenter's saw		1	1										2	blade only
prising bar		1											1	
"L" spikes		2											2	tools
grindstones		1	1		2								4	cylindrical, tapered
whetstone					1								1	
brass ferrules		1									1	3*	2	*in bank room, Ah Lum's
wire screwdriver			2		1							2	5	improvised
iron tongs				1					1				2	lightweight
mallet head					1								1	
pliers					1								1	
keyhole saw					1								1	marked "Kangaroo" brand
chisel												1	1	blade only
drill bit							1						1	
screwdriver												1	1	improvised bone handle
socket	1				1								2	off garden tools
hoe blade				1		1							2	
rabbit trap		2		1			1			1			5	
gold pan												1	1	found outside, behind chimney
shovel head			1					1	1				3	rivetted
improvised wedge		1											1	
Total	3	10	7	4	10	2	4	1	5	3	1	10	60	

Table 5.44. Rural sites tools: site distribution.

Site key	A Caliche		B Sheung Fong		C Ha Fong					
	D QB2		E Apple Tree		F A Wee's					
	G Rapids		H Poplars		I Flax Grove					

Tool Type	A	B	C	D	E	F	G	H	I	Total	Comments
shear blades	1				1					2	halves
files, triangular	3	2							1	6	
files, flat		1					1			2	
files, round			1							1	
carpenters saws	1				1					2	portions of blades
screwdrivers	1				1					2	improvised from No. 8 wire
drill bits		1				1			1	3	
pliers		1								1	
skewer?		1								1	26 cm long, twisted wire handle
brass ferrules	1*	2	2							4	*square section ferrule
nail punch			1	2						3	
scriber				1						1	
oilstone				1						1	
folding ruler				1						1	hinge only
plane blade					1					1	
screwdriver						1				1	
iron tongs				1						1	
axe head		1								1	small
axe wedge				1						1	
miners shovels			1	2	1		1			5	
miners forks		1							1	2	wire round tines to make a grate
gold cradles				1	1	1	1?		1	4	improvised perforated trays
pick heads				2					1	3	
rabbit traps	1			1			1			3	
skin stretching wires				5			10	9	6	30	
kero can bucket				1						1	
Total	8	10	5	17	8	3	14	9	11	85	

Table 5.45. Ah Lum's store: nails.

Nail type	Location	Use
Main room		
sq. sect. flathead	protruding from wall	used as hook
staple	over "bank window" sliding grill	securing slide(?)
roseheads	protruding from walls and beams	used as hooks
flatheads	protruding from walls and beams	used as hooks
roseheads	through framing timbers	structural
tacks	in roof frame timbers	securing scrim
screws	in roof beam at odd angles	unknown
screw-in hooks	in roof beam	for hanging things
Bedroom		
rhomboid heads	protruding from walls	used as hooks
roseheads	protruding from walls	used as hooks
flatheads	protruding from walls	used as hooks
roseheads	in wooden sleeping platform	structural
flatheads	in wooden sleeping platform	structural
Kitchen		
flatheads	protruding from walls	used as hooks
roseheads	protruding from walls	used as hooks
roseheads	in walls and shelves	to secure planking
screws	in door frame	to secure hinges
sq. sect. flathead	in door frame	unknown
Back bedroom/strongroom		
caseheads	in walls	used as hooks
tacks	in walls	securing scrim
roseheads	in walls	securing tongue and groove lining
sq. sect. roseheads	in 3 x 2 inch timber	structural
roseheads 3.8 cm	in walls	securing sacking
roseheads 10.5 cm	in wall	coat(?) hook
case nail	on slide	handle
domehead screw	back of door	coat hook
Bank room		
rhomboid heads	in walls	used as hooks
roseheads	in wall timbers	structural
roseheads	in window slide	structural
flathead	in wall	used as hook
rosehead spikes (hand made)	in door, ends bent over	structural
tacks	in door	used to secure notice
case nails	in window frame	used with opium can metal "washers"
Roof		
screw nails		used to secure corrugated iron
domeheads wih lead washers		used to secure corrugated iron

Table 5.46. Chinatown: distribution of nails and screws.

Nail Types	1	4	6	7	8	11	12	14	15	16	17	18	19	21	22	23	24	26	27	33	34	36	Total
roseheads	1	2	7	6	1	1	8	1	1	25	1	8	14	23	12	21	7	143	7	15	14	3	321
nail shafts		1	12	1			1			1			4	15	4	6		50	1	9	1	4	110
flareheads			2				7			5	2			20	13		1	19					70
rhomboid heads			2			2	1		1			2	6	2	1	2	13	5		1		1	39
flatheads			6	2		1		1		5			4	3	4	5	4	13	2	5	1		56
domeheads				1								1		1				3			1		7
wedge spikes (hand made)				1			1					2				5		9			7		25
round spikes																2					1		3
horseshoe nails				1															1				2
boot sole nails							1											26			2		29
tacks							1							1									2
flathead/flares							4			1		2						4					11
nails with leather washers										2			1										3
spikes				1						2			13	3	1	1		1		1	2	8	33
disc-head roofing nails													1	5	3								9
tapered clouts														4				1					6
"L" head nails														1									1
wood screws														1				1					2
jolt head nails														1		1							2
copper flarehead														1									1
lead heads														5		5	1	4	1				15
staples (fencing type)															1					3	2		7
sq. section flatheads																				6			6
sq. head/square shaft																1				2			3
square spikes																3							3
triangular sect. nails																1							1
sq. head with applied lead																1							1
Total	1	3	29	13	1	4	24	2	2	41	3	15	43	86	39	54	26	279	12	42	32	17	768

Table 5.47. Arrowtown: distribution of nails and screws.

Type	Ah Lum's	Hut # 1	2	3	4	5	6	7	8	9	10	13	15	Total
Structural														
rosehead nails	3	1	19	46	37	6	55	7	58	3	22	14	5	**276**
rosehead spikes			1	13	1	1	22	10	6	1	3	6	4	**68**
flathead nails			1		1		3		7					**12**
flathead, sq. section					4									**4**
flathead spikes	1			5			2	1			2		1	**12**
sq. sect. spikes				1		1	1							**3**
jolthead nails			1	1	1		6		1		1			**11**
Roofing														
lead flat-tops							1	1	1					**3**
lead bell-tops							1		1					**2**
domehead and disc							1		1		1			**3**
domehesd screws												7		**7**
Light construction														
case nails			4	1	4	3	13		6					**31**
offset head nails				1			1						1	**3**
offset head spikes							1							**1**
Special purpose														
horse shoe nails	3		1	2	2		7				1			**16**
clouts								4						**4**
fencing staples	1							4	1	1			3	**10**
sq. section staple										1				**1**
domehead tacks								3		1				**4**
wood screws	1											1		**2**
Total	**9**	**1**	**27**	**70**	**46**	**15**	**114**	**30**	**82**	**7**	**30**	**28**	**14**	**473**

Table 5.48. Rural sites: distribution of nails and screws.

Site key	A	Northburn		B	QB2	C	Sandy Point	
	D	Ah Wee's		E	Poplars	F	Hanging Rock	
	G	Flax Grove						

Type	A	B	C	D	E	F	G	Total
Structural								
roseheads	12	18	17	133	11	11	50	**252**
rosehead spikes	1	7	21	55	39	2		**125**
flatheads		1		16	6		1	**24**
flathead spikes (hand made)	1	1	3	2		1	6	**14**
sq. section spikes	1				9			**10**
jolthead nails					25		1	**26**
proto-joltheads					1			**1**
rhomboid heads				1				**1**
Light construction								
case nails	2	5	2	1		1	11	**22**
sq. section case nails		1	1		1			**3**
offset heads	1						13	**14**
Special purpose								
clouts	1		2					**3**
brads	2							**2**
tacks		6	1			1	1	**9**
domehead tack		1						**1**
screws					2		3	**5**
fence staples					20			**20**
headless nails				2				**2**
modified nail (groove across head)				1				**1**
horseshoe nails							1	**1**
improvised nails(?)							3	**3**
Total	**21**	**40**	**47**	**211**	**114**	**16**	**90**	**539**

Table 5.49. Chinatown: non-ferrous metal artefacts.

Artefact	Hut # 1	4	6	12	14	16	17	18	19	21	23	26	27	33	34	Total	Comments
copper wire		1			1					1		1*				4	*a coil
copper bead		1														1	
copper "U" section										1						1	possibly part of a picture frame
copper wire handle												1				1	
lead washer	1															1	
lead, tubular		1														1	
lead								3								3	car battery electrodes
tin(?) foil liners															2	2	one marked "Lipton's Gold Medal" liner from teabox
brass valve		1														1	off a primus or lantern
brass caps			1#	1	1							1			1	5	# threaded, others friction fit
brass knob								1							1	2	
brass ring								1								1	
brass link chain								1								1	
brass tubing												1				1	
brass washing															1	1	
zinc sheeting			1		1	1	1	1	1				1			7	
zinc sheeting, perforated								1				1				2	hole diameter 2 mm, probably off meat safe
threaded shaft							1									1	from a lantern
detonator(?)												1				1	6 mm cylindrical tube with wire extending from one end, hollow.
Total	1	4	2	1	3	1	2	8	1	2	0	6	1	0	5	37	

5 The material culture of the Chinese in southern New Zealand

Table 5.50. Chinatown: miscellaneous metal artefacts.

Artefact	Hut # 1	6	11	12	14	16	17	18	19	21	22	23	24	26	27	33	Total	Comments
iron bracket	1																2	
chain, short piece	1		1										1				3	
horseshoes		9					1							1			11	
dredge bucket pin		1															1	used as hammer or anvil
iron pegs/spikes		1	1	1			1				1	1	1			3	10	
wire pegs					1	1	1	2	2	1						2	10	
bolts		1	1	1	2		1									2	8	
nuts					1											2	3	
iron sheeting		1															1	
iron grating			1														1	
brackets (tin)				1													1	
coil of wire					1												1	
hoop iron					1		1										2	
hoop iron bracket						1											1	improvised
"J" shaped hoop iron						1	1		1								3	use unknown but common
rebar (firebar?)				1									1				2	
iron standard (firebar?)													1		1		2	
"U" shaped wire					1												1	
tobacco tags, octagonal							1			22	1		2				26	
threaded cap off can							1										1	
galvanised pipe							1			1							2	short lengths
wedge-shaped iron							1										1	
light wire loops								1		1		1	2				5	
wire "S" hooks									1	2		2	1	1	1		8	
wire hooks								1				1					2	
wire ring															1		1	10 twisted strands of light wire
wire netting															1		1	
improvised wire handle									1	1							2	
barrel iron hoop									1								1	cut into 20 cm length
steel hoop														1			1	
metal rings									2						1		3	
tin sheeting									1	2							3	
staple, 7.0 cm long										1							1	
iron "bomb shapes"													2				2	use unknown
phallic-shaped metal cap														1			1	
paint brush ferrule														1			1	
coil spring															1		1	
helical gear cog															1		1	
cart stub axle																1	1	possibly used as door pivot as in ACS/4
	2	13	3	4	7	4	10	4	8	30	3	5	7	10	5	12	128	

Table 5.51. Arrowtown: miscellaneous ferrous artefacts.

Key to Ah Lum's store
- **MR** main room
- **BE** bedroom
- **KI** kitchen
- **ST** strongroom
- **OU** outside

Artefact	Hut #													Ah Lum's store					Total	Comments
	1	2	3	4	5	6	7	8	9	10	11	13	15	MR	BE	KI	ST	OU		
"S" hooks	1	2	4	9		1	1				1								19	
wire hooks		2	1	1															4	
wire double hook				1		1								1		2			5	
washers	1						1							1	1				4	
bolts and nuts			2	1										7					10	
iron standards		1	3	1	1						1	1						1	9	
No. 8 wire		1																	1	
"L" hoop iron		2		1	1			1											5	
iron rings		1	2				1	1											5	
hoop iron		4				1		2											7	
oval hoop iron			1																1	
wire pegs		2	14	2	2	2		2						1	1			2	28	
iron sheeting			6	2										1					9	
light wire			9		1									1			1		12	
light wire loop				4	1		1					1		1					8	
"V" shaped wire			1																1	
iron chain			1					1											2	
chain and pegs			2																2	off rabbit traps
chain and hooks			2																2	30 cm long, hooks on both ends
chain and loop					1														1	probably billy hook
dog type chain			1																1	
tin cup			1																1	
light stub axle				1	1														2	ACS/4 specimen used as door pivot
tobacco tags, octagonal				4															4	
iron spike				1															1	
rebar c.40 cm long				2	1					1				2					6	
iron bars										1		1	1				1		4	
horse shoes							3		1		4	1							9	
iron plate																1			1	off stove or coal range
metal funnel																1			1	
tin box																		1	1	33 x 2 x 10 cm, cut longitudinally, possibly used for growing seedlings
Total	2	15	51	30	7	6	7	7	1	1	6	2	3	16	2	3	2	5	166	

Table 5.52. Arrowtown: miscellaneous non-ferrous metal artefacts.

Key to Ah Lum's store
BA　　bank room
ST　　strong room
OU　　outside

Artefact	Hut #								Ah Lum's			Total
	2	3	4	5	6	7	8	13	BA	ST	OU	
zinc sheeting, large pieces**	6		1	3	1	1		1				13
strip of zinc metal								1				1
square of zinc, 18 x 12 cm		1										1
zinc washer, improvised									1			1
brass ring, 3.5 cm diameter		1										1
tin foil, loops and small pieces***	2		1	1								4
copper spring, use unknown			1									1
threaded copper tubing									1			1
copper split pin									2	5		7
light brass chain							1					1
bottle foil		1*	1									2
ornate handle, of a poker(?)										1		1
Total	8	3	4	4	1	1	1	2	4	6	0	34

Notes

* reads "C E Morton Ltd, Leadenhall, London"

** the floor of the bank room and the strong room were covered with large pieces of zinc sheeting

*** The foil from ACS/5 was inside the crumpled remains of a square cardboard box, probably a tea packet. All the tin foil is probably from tea packets

Table 5.53. Rural sites: miscellaneous ferrous artefacts.

Site key														
A Caliche				**B** Firewood Creek			**C** Sheung Fong			**D** Ha Fong				
E QB2				**F** Apple Tree			**G** Poplars			**H** Ah Wee's				
I Sandy Pt.				**J** Northburn			**K** Riverside			**L** Rapids				
M Rapids Forge														

Artefact	A	B	C	D	E	F	G	H	I	J	K	L	M	Total	Comments
dredge bucket pin	1													1	
large iron washers	1	1		2								1		5	
tobacco tags	1			1		8						1		11	
iron pegs	3		1	2										6	
iron spikes	1		2	1										4	
iron offcuts	1	2											23*	26	*380 g weight
iron slag												4		4	bags full
steel cap	2													2	threaded
rebar c.30 cm	1		1											2	firebars?
iron bars	1			2										3	c. 50 cm length
iron rings	1			2		1	1							5	3-5cm dm.
iron standards	1			1				1	3	3				9	parts only, one from Ha Fong; "L" shaped
"L" hoop iron	1				1									2	
hoop iron		1	1		1	1	27		1					32	
box strapping						1	1							2	
No. 8 wire	1		1				6		4					12	loops and short lengths, various sizes
wire pegs		1	2	2	4	1	6	2	3	1	1	3		26	
light wire loop	1	1												2	
light wire												2		2	
wire "S" hooks	1		1	5	5	12	23	7	8	1	1			64	
wire hook and swivel				1										1	
"V" shaped wires		1		2			5	1			1			10	
wire handles					1	1			1					3	
toasting wire				1										1	
wire hook and chain							1							1	billyhook(?)
billy hook						1								1	found in hearth
iron chain	1							2				1		4	
chain and stirrup						1								1	
rivet	1													1	

Table 5.53. Rural sites: miscellaneous ferrous artefacts (*continued*).

Artefact	A	B	C	D	E	F	G	H	I	J	K	L	M	Total	Comments
metal spouts, small		1		1										2	identical spout found in ACS/6 (Figure 5.62b)
horse shoes			1											1	
bolts			2					1						3	
"U" bolt												1		1	
metal rim			1											1	from a wash basin
tin sheeting					1			1						2	
sheet iron							3	8	1			1		13	mostly irregular offcuts, various sizes
metal cap					1									1	2 x 2 cm
tin plate disc						1								1	
shallow tray							1							1	made of tin, 27 x 22 x 2.5 cm
metal lid							1							1	15 cm diameter, flat with no lip, use unknown
1/2 kerosene can								1						1	base perforated, watering can or shower(?)
iron bracket								1						1	
tin basin									1					1	
metal cap 1.9 cm diameter									1					1	off a shot flask(?)
fuel can screw cap												1		1	
Total	20	8	13	22	16	28	75	27	23	2	3	11	27	275	

Table 5.54. Rural sites: miscellaneous non-ferrous artefacts.

Site key	A QB2		B Caliche		C Firewood Creek		D Sheung Fong					
	E Ha Fong		F Apple Tree		G Poplars		H Ah Wee's					
	I Hanging Rock		J Riverside		K Rapids							
Artefact	A	B	C	D	E	F	G	H	I	J	K	Total	Comments
copper wire	1		1		1		2*			1	1	7	*a coil
copper disc				1								1	off battery(?)
copper cap					1							1	
copper eyelets										2		2	
brass rivets		1						2				3	
brass disc		1										1	crescent shaped
brass washer			1			1						2	
brass disc					1							1	3.3 cm diameter
brass grommet										1		1	
brass ring, light			1									1	
brass chain, light	1											1	with hook on one end
threaded brass handle		1										1	
threaded fitting			1									1	use unknown
hinged lid			1									1	4 x 4 cm, use unknown
zinc sheeting	5			1	3						6	15	see note 1
bracket made of above							1					1	
zinc screw cap					1							1	3.2 cm diameter
zinc disc					1							1	
zinc sheeting, perforated					1							1	probably tray off gold cradle
lead disc					1							1	2.1 cm diameter [see note 2]
gold blowing tray	1											1	5 x 5 cm, copper sheeting [see note 3]
tin foil					1							1	packet liner
mercury globs					1*		2					3	see note 4
gold nugget									1			1	
Total	8	3	5	2	11	2	5	2	1	3	8	50	

Notes

1. one piece from the Rapids impressed "W.S. Oberhausen"; some appear to have been formed into trays or boxes but only remnants remain.
2. 12 star-shaped holes punched in it
3. heavier gauge copper than opium can metal
4. the mercury found in Ha Fong was in a clear glass bottle; that in the Poplars was found in two discrete globs in the ground.

5 The material culture of the Chinese in southern New Zealand

Table 5.55. Cartridge and projectile types: site distribution.

Site	.577 foil	.577 brass	.303 case	.303 bullet	12 bore	Other calibres	Total
Chinatown	1	1	276	571	2	18	869
Arrowtown	42	4	92	1	0	4	143
Rural sites	4	3	3	0	13	12	35
Total	47	8	371	572	15	34	1,047

Table 5.56. Chinatown: cartridge types.

		Hut #											
Cartridge type	Dates	1	6	12	17	18	19	22	23	26	27	33	34	Total
.577 Snider Mk 9 foil	1871–95												1	1
.577 Snider Whitney CAC	1890–1900	1												1
.303 CAC Mk 2 C2	1900–05		273	1					1			1		276
.303 Cu-Ni bullet jackets	unknown									571				571
.450/577 "bottleneck"	1887–1900											1		1
.410 Remington UMC	post-1890	1												1
.410 unidentified	unknown						1							1
.366 (Dreyse) bullet	1880s(?)											1		1
.22 Remington UMC	1890–1980s	12									1			13
.22 Winchester	modern						1							1
12 G. CAC	1885–96					1	1							2
12 G. Eley Bros.	post-1900												1	1
Total		14	273	1		1	1	2	1	571	1	3	2	870
Lead														
lead battery electrodes					3									3
lead, melted masses										2				2
lead rosette													1	1
lead, cast, tubular		1												1
Total		1			3					2			1	7

Table 5.57. Arrowtown: cartridge types.

Cartridge type	Dates	Hut # 1	3	4	5	6	8	13	15	Ah Lum's	Total
.577 Snider Boxer Snider/Kynock	1890s								1		1
.577 Whitney brass	1895–1900			18	1						19
.577 Snider Mk 9 foil	1871–1900		1	5	1	1			13	2	23
.303 CAC Mk II C2	1898–1905	1				39			1		41
.303 Cu-Ni bullet jacket				1							1
.303 reloaded	pre-1914				50						50
.310 Kynock						1					1
Total		**1**	**1**	**24**	**52**	**41**			**15**	**2**	**136**
Lead											
slag residue				3							3
glob of solidified lead			1	1							2
pieces of lead pipe							1				1
lead slabs, "ingots'"							1	1			2
lead slabs, rectangular										5	5
cast lead, tubular										2	2
solidified lead masses containing bullets											
Total			**1**	**4**			**2**	**1**		**7**	**15**

Table 5.58. Rural sites: cartridge types.

Site key		A	Firewood Creek	B	Caliche		C	Sheung Fong		D	Ha Fong
		E	QB2	F	Apple Tree		G	Sandy Point		H	Ah Wee's
		I	Poplars	J	Hanging Rock		K	Riverside		L	Rapids

Cartridge Type	Dates	A	B	C	D	E	F	G	H	I	J	K	L	Total
.577 Mk 1 1st pattern	1879		2											2
.577 Mk 1 no base	1890		1											1
.577 lead bullet (impacted)		1												1
.577 Snider Whitney CAC	1895			1										1
.303 Mk 6	post-1904	2												2
.303 Mk 7 CAC NZ	post-1918													0
.410 brass foil case	pre-1900	1		1										2
.22 Remington UMC	pre-1890	2										1		6
.22 Remington brass	post-1890						1							0
.22 RWS nickel alloy	post-1920			1										1
.22 ICI	post-1920			5										5
12 G. CAC No. 12 NZ	post-1918			2	1									2
12 G. brand indeterminate				1										1
12 G. UMC "New Club"	1880–90							1						1
12 G. Eley Bros.	1880–90	1			1				1					3
12 G. Eley Bros.	post-1900	4			1									6
Total		7	4	3	12	1	2		1			1	3	34
Lead														
lead, cast, tubular						2								2
lead, rect slabs, "ingots"								1						1
lead round lump					1									1
lead alloy, melted					1									1
lead shot, chilled No.5									7					7
lead scraps, melted														0
lead with punch marks									1					1
pewter, melted stand								1						1
pewter, melted fragments								8						8
Total					2	2		10	8					22

Table 5.59. Details of recovered ammunition types.

Calibre	Description	Manufacturer	Type	Mark
.577	brass foil rifle cartridge, length : 4.6cm (Figure 5.68a)	Snider, English make	Mk 9 foil	none discernible
.577	brass foil, rifle cartridge (Figure 5.68a)	Snider-Kynock(?)	"boxer" primer	
.577	brass, rifle cartridge, length 4.6 cm (Figure 5.68c)	Snider		
.577	brass, rifle cartridge, length 4.6cm	CAC–Whitney		
.577	brass, rifle cartridge , length 4.6cm	CAC		
.303	drawn brass, rifle cartridge with cupro-nickel jacketed (Figures 5.68d and e)	CAC	Mk II C2	"C.A.C. II C" on base
.303	brass, rifle cartridge (Figure 5.68f)	CAC	Mk 6	"C.A.C. VI" on base
.303	brass, rifle cartridge (Figure 5.68g)	CAC	Mk 7	"C.A.C. VII Z" on base
.32	drawn brass, short and long rifle cartridges (Figures 5.68h and i)	Remington UMC		"U" on base
.310	drawn brass, cadet rifle cartridge (Figure 5.68j)	possibly Kynock, United Kingdom	"Cadet" cartridge	none discernible
.366	lead projectile (Figure 5.68k)	unknown		
.410	brass foil cartridge (Figure 5.68i)	various		none discernible
.410	brass cartridge	Remington UMC		"U" on base
.450/577	drawn brass Martini–Henry "bottleneck" cartridge (Figure 5.68m)	various		not head-stamped
.22	brass, short and long rifle cartridges (Figures 5.68n and o)	Remington UMC		"U" on base
.22	brass, long rifle cartridge (Figure 5.68p)	Winchester		"H" on base
.22	brass, short rifle cartridge (Figure 5.68q)	Imperial Chemical Industries, Great Britain		"I.C.I." on base
.22	nickel-alloy, rifle cartridge (Figure 5.68r)	Rheinisch-Westfälische Sprengstoff, Nürnberg		"R" in a shield
12 bore	brass shotgun cartridge base (Figure 5.69a)	Eley Brothers, London		"Eley No 12, London" on base
12 bore	brass shotgun cartridge base, early type. case construction (Figures 5.69b and c)	Eley Brothers, London		"Eley Bros, London" on base
12 bore	brass shotgun cartridge base (Figure 5.69d)	CAC Auckland		"C.A.C. No 12" on base
12 bore	brass shotgun cartridge base (Figure 5.69e)	CAC Auckland		"C.A.C. No 12 NZ"
12 bore	brass shotgun cartridge bases (Figures 5.69f and g)	Union Metallic Cartridge Co.		"U.M .C. New Club" on base

5 The material culture of the Chinese in southern New Zealand

Date of introduction	Main period of popularity	Notes
16/8/1871	mid 1870s–1895	
1880s(?)		
c.1880	c. 1880–95	
1887	late 1880s–1900	
1895	1895–1905	The Colonial Ammunition Company (CAC) was established in Auckland in 1888. They still produce ammunition.
1898	1898–1904	
1904 (Harris 1980:68)	1904–09	
post-1918	1918–c.1950	The Z signifies a nitre-cellulose rather than a cordite charge. After 1909 C.A.C. cartridges have the last 2 digits of the year of production stamped on the base.
c. 1900		This calibre was widely used in New Zealand.
c. 1900		The .310 Cadet cartridge first appeared in Australia and New Zealand in 1900. .310 calibre rifles were used extensively for cadet training; 14,150 were issued to cadet forces in NZ between 1903 and 1911 when they were phased out and replaced with .22 rifles (Edsall 1981:227–28; Skennerton 1975).
c. 1880		Chinatown hut 33 (LI7) surface. This projectile is a different calibre from that of any of the recovered cartridges. It is possibly a Colt mould (Sherriff pers. comm.).
pre-1900		Caliche shelter (S133/223; Z4 Ly.2).
post-1911		Chinatown hut 1 (M16, Ly.1). The Union Metallic Cartridge Co. (UMC) was founded in 1867. In c.19th century, UMC and Winchester were the major manufacturers of ammunition in the US. Remington, whilst a major manufacturer of firearms, did not produce ammunition during this period. Remington and the UMC merged in 1911 (Sherriff pers.comm; Remington publications).
1887–88 (if English); post-1895 (if CAC NZ)		Chinatown hut 6 (I–J20 Ly.3)
1890		
1870		The "H" stands for Henry Winchester, founder of the Winchester Repeating Arms Co.
post-1920		
post-1921		"R" brand .22 ammunition is cited in A. & W. McCarthy (of Dunedin) catalogues from 1905. The use of the "RWS" trademark became general after 1910–11.
1895–1919		See NZCCB No. 234 (1985).
1880–1919		See NZCCB No. 234 (1985).
c. 1885–96		
post-1918		
1891		Replaced the "Club Brand" (Herskovitz 1978:51).

259

Table 5.60. Scale components, weights and accounting devices.

Artefact	Provenance	Comments	Figure #
Rule scale components			
pan (4 hole)	Ch/18 (N17 Ly.2)	7.1cm diameter	5.72b
pan (4 hole)	Ch/23 (K16 Ly.2)	7.3cm diameter	
pan (4 hole)	Ch/23 (K15 Ly.2)	part only, circular	
balance arm	Ch/22 (R13 Ly.1)	4 pieces, incomplete	5.72d
balance arm	Ch/23 (K16 Ly.1)	2 pieces, incomplete	
brass counterweight	Ch/23 (K12) baulk	3.0 x 2.4 cm, oval	5.72c
brass counterweight	Ch/23 (K12 Ly.2)	2.9 x 2.4 cm, oval	
brass counterweight	Ch/22 (N12 Ly.2)	3.0 x 2.5 cm, oval	
brass counterweight	ACS/6 (D7 Ly.1)	2.6 x 2.1 cm, oval	
brass counterweight	Caliche (E2 Ly.2)	2.9 x 2.5 cm, oval	5.72c
Weights			
"standing" weight	Ch/23 (J15 Ly.4)	8 oz., brass	5.72e
"disc" weight	Ch/23 (J15 Ly.4)	8 g, brass	5.72f
container weight	Ch/14 (L7) surface	2 troy oz., brass	5.72g
slotted disc weight	Ah Lum's main room	1 lb, steel	5.72a
Abacus beads			
wooden (4)	Ah Lum's surface	c. 2 cm diameter	

5 The material culture of the Chinese in southern New Zealand

Table 5.61. Tobacco pipes and shank bands: minimum numbers per site.

Site key	A	Firewood Creek	B	Caliche	C	Sheung Fong
	D	Flax Grove	E	Chinatown	F	QB2
	G	Apple Tree	H	Sandy Point	I	ACS
	J	Rapids	K	Ah Lum's	L	Rockfall 1

	A	B	C	D	E	F	G	H	I	J	K	L	Total
Clay pipes													
471 WAT…					1								1
A. TABIS, GAMBIER					1								1
W.WHITE, GLASGOW							1	1					2
W.T. BLAKE												1	1
DAVIDSON, GLASGOW		1							2				3
BEN NEVIS CUTTY	1				1			1			1		4
BEN NEVIS									1				1
McPHEE, DUNEDIN									1				1
PAMPLIN, terracotta								1					1
part marks		1								1	1		3
repaired stem									1				1
rouletted rim									1				1
plain	2	1	1	1**	3	1	2	1	3		1	1	17
PAMPLIN, terracotta									1				1
Subtotal	3	3	1	1	6	1	3	3	10	1	3	2	38
Wooden bowls													
briar					4				1				5
cherrywood											1		1
unspecified					(1)*								1
Subtotal					5				1		1		7
Synthetic stems													
vulcanite		7		3	8				9		4		31
amber		1		1		1	1				1		5
other materials			1*										1
Subtotal		8	1	4	8	1	1	0	9	0	5	0	37
Total all pipes	3	11	2	5	19	2	4	4	19	1	9	2	81

Shank bands	A	B	C	D	E	F	G	H	I	J	K	L	Total
plain		1		1	2				2				6
embossed		4	1	1	3				2	1	1		13
Total shank bands		5	1	2	5				4	1	1		19

Notes

* bowl burnt, converted to charcoal

** relatively thick stem fragment, 1–1.25 cm, flattened on one side, no marks

(1) bone with brass shank

Table 5.62. Inkstones found in Chinese sites in Central Otago.

Description	Shape	Dimensions (cm)	Ornamentation	Marks
fine grained, grey slate-like stone (Figure 5.77-1)	circular, sides vertical	Dm. 7.2 Ht. 0.8	none	vague, illegible "scratches" on base
fine grained black stone (Figure 5.77-2)	rectangular with rounded corners, sides vertical	L. 6.5 W. 3.9 1.2	none	some poorly legible Chinese characters incised in base
fine grained black stone (Figure 5.77-3)	rectangular with rounded corners, s i des vertical	L. 13 W. 9.1 Ht. 1.3	raised relief floral decoration between grinding area	single Chinese character scratched on side
fine-grained black stone (Figure 5.77-4a and 4b)	cir cular, sides vertical	Dm. 5.8 Ht. 0.4	none	none
fine-grained grey stone, sides angle inwards (Figure 5.77-5)	oval	L. 10.7 W. 9.2 H. 1.0	none	several poorly legible Chinese characters incised in base. Some are written over the top of others
coarse-grained, creamy-white marble (Figures 5.77-6a and 6b)	rectangular, sides vertical	L 8.0 W. 5.8 Ht. 1.0	none	4 Chinese characters incised on base, originally inked in black

5 The material culture of the Chinese in southern New Zealand

Comments	Provenance
the surface is blackened with ink residue	Chinatown hut 18 (N16 Ly.2)
the stone has been used but is little worn	Chinatown hut 26 (M13 Ly.1)
the grinding area has a marked concavity from wear and is surrounded by ink residues	found by a Cromwell resident, Mr R. Hansen, on the terrace beside the Kawarau stream of the Cromwell Chinese settlement
found in association with part of its wooden base (Figure 5.77-4b). Both artefacts have been burnt, c.1/3 of the base has survived. The height of the stone and base is 0.9 cm. The diameter of the base is 6.8 cm.	Flax Grove shelter, Kawarau Gorge (C6 Ly.1)
reconstructed from 4 fragments found in the hut. The grinding area is very worn, to the point where the stone in the grinding area is less than 2 mm thick. This may have caused the stone to break and be discarded. The stone has a very shallow (0.5 mm) rim around the base	Chinatown hut 26 (M14 Ly.2)
the basic shape and form is identical to the other inkstones. However, its coarse grain and open texture would make it an inferior inkstone. It almost certainly has never been used to grind black ink. Some straw-coloured residues on the surface are believed to be decomposition products rather than grinding residues. May have been kept for talismanic rather than practical purposes. The characters have been translated but make little sense. They read "river", "times", "contain", the fourth character was indecipherable (Wegars pers.comm. 1985).	Sandy Point hut site, upper Clutha Valley (A1) surface

Table 5.63. Summary of paper artefacts with Chinese calligraphy.

1. A list of ingredients for a headache and rheumatism cure, written on rice paper.
2. *Paak kop piu* tickets (4; Figure 5.101e).
3. A shopping list (on rice paper) detailing products, volumes and prices.
4. Tea wrapper "Best Kooloo Tea, Canton", "1885" on wrapper.
5. Small fragments of squares of red paper, most have one or more Chinese characters written on them.
6. Two pages from a Bible (Ch.19) written in Chinese. Almost certainly obtained from Rev. Don or his successor (Figure 5.105d).
7. *Paak kop piu* tickets (5), four unmarked.
Note
Artefacts 1-5 were found in the wall of the Flax Grove shelter. 6–7 were found in the wall of the Rockfall 1 site (S133/37). In addition, poorly legible Chinese-language paper-labels have been found on opium cans and bottles.

Table 5.64. Ceramic toothpaste and ointment pots (MN=10).

Label	Components	Dimensions	Comments	Provenance
Pot lids				
"Alexandra Cherry Toothpaste, Prepared by Alfred Felton, Melbourne" (Figure 5.78b)	lid and base	Dm. 7.4 cm Ht. of lid and base 4.8 cm circular	A multi-coloured lid with a gold band featuring a woman's face. The lid has a diamond-shaped registration mark, dated 24/1/1865. This mark appeared on a wide range of ceramics between 1842 and 1883 (Bedford 1985c:173).	Ah Wee's (H9 Ly.1)
"Coralite Toothpaste, Prepared by Mess Gabriel, Dentists, Ludgate Hill, London" (Figure 5.78c)	lid and base	Ht. 3.1 cm L. 8.4 cm W. 5.1 cm rectangular	a black and white lid, embossed on base "B & Co" (Bates, Elliot & Co, Burslem 1870-75).	QB2
"Cherry Toothpaste, Prepared by John Gosnell & Co, London, Patronised by the Queen"	2 identical and intact lids	Dm. 8.0 cm Ht. 2.0 cm circular	A multi-coloured lid with gold band. World wide distribution. Excavated in USA (Herskovitz 1978)	Chinatown
"S Maw, Son and Thompson"(?)	lid fragment		black and white lid	QB2 (B10 Ly.2)
"Holloway's Ointment, 533 Oxford St, Late 244 Strand, London"	lid, intact	Dm. 9.6 cm Ht. 1.7 cm circular	single coloured lid (dark green). Thomas Holloway set up his business at 244 Strand in 1837.	Caliche (Y2 Ly.2)
"Holloway's Ointment, 244 Strand, London"	lid, fragments	circular	Holloway shifted his business to 533 Oxford St in 1867. The Firewood Creek site is believed to have been first occupied c.1870.	Firewood Creek (B13 Ly.1)
Bases				
		Dm. 7.8 cm Ht. 2.8 cm circular, fragment	embossed on base "BE & Co" (Bates Elliot & Co, 1870–75)	Chinatown hut 7 (K25 Ly.3)
		Dm. 6.5 cm Ht. 2.6 cm circular, intact	illegible embossing on base	Chinatown hut 7 (K25, Ly.2)
		Dm. 6.5 cm Ht. 2.65 cm circular, fragment	no marks	Chinatown hut 18 (N18, Ly.2)
		Dm. 6.5 cm Ht. 3.1 cm circular, intact	no marks	Chinatown hut 34, (M14 Ly.2)

Table 5.65. Bone toothbrushes: site distribution (n=13).

Components	Shape of Handle	Dimensions	Comments	Provenance
handle only (Figure 5.79a)	rounded	W. handle 1.4 cm		Chinatown hut 18 (M17 Ly.3)
intact (Figure 5.79b)	pointed	L .13.6.cm W. handle 1.4 cm		Chinatown hut 18 (M16 Ly.3)
handle and other fragments (Figure 5.79c)	rounded	W. handle 1.4 cm		Chinatown hut 34 (F12 Ly.2)
intact (Figure 5.79d)	rounded	L .16.4 cm W. 0.85 cm	incised "JC Oddie, Chemist, Timaru". Oddie established his business in 1895 (*Cyclopedia of New Zealand* 1903 vol. 3)	Chinatown horticultural terrace, test trench
handle only (Figure 5.79e)	pointed	W.1.4 cm	"Bull's Eyes" impressed in handle	The Ledge (D4 Ly.2)
handle only (Figure 5.79f)	pointed	W. 1.2 cm	small size, 3 "Bull's Eyes" impressed in handle	Chinatown hut 23 (J3 Ly.2)
handle only (Figure 5.79g)	pointed	W. 1.4 cm	there is a small loop of wire attached to the handle, 3 "Bull's Eyes" impressed in handle	Chinatown hut 18 (M16 Ly.2)
handle only, (Figure 5.79i)	rounded and ornate		3 "Bull's Eyes" on handle	Chinatown hut 14 (E9 Ly.1)
almost intact	rounded			Chinatown hut 18 (N12 Ly.1)
intact	pointed	L.13.6 cm W. handle 1.5 cm		Chinatown hut 18 (G7 Ly.1)
almost intact	pointed	L. 13.4 cm W. handle 1.5 cm		QB2 (FI2 Ly.1)
handle only	pointed	W. handle 1.4 cm		QB2 (D6 Ly.2)

Table 5.66. Chinatown: buttons.

Button types/materials	Hut # 4	6	7	12	14	16	17	18	19	21	22	23	24	26	27	33	34	36	Total
Mother-of-pearl																			
2-hole				2		4		1		2	2	6	3	8	8	2	1	1	40
4-hole	2		1		1	4		2	2	5	2	5		5	6	1	2		37
metal																			
recessed, embossed		2	1			3	1	2	1			4		6		1	1		22
plain or illegible				1						4		7		5					17
cloth covered metal		1				1				2		3			1				8
metal studs, Cu, Fe			1							3		3		4		1			12
metal studs, flat zinc					1	2	2			3									8
dish shaped metal								1		1									2
collar studs												1							1
poppet type														4					4
metal with pearl inlay														1					1
dome button														1			1		2
copper 2-hole														1		2			3
glass																			
milk glass				4								1		2					7
white glass stud														1					1
wooden												4							4
plastic			1													1			2
bone										1		1		4	1	1	1		9
vulcanite		1																	1
slate			1																1
Total	2	4	15	7	2	14	3	6	3	21	4	35	3	41	16	9	6	1	182

Table 5.67. Arrowtown: buttons.

Button types/materials	AL Ah Lum's store						NP no provenance – found in ground between huts							
	Hut #													
	AL	1	2	3	4	5	6	7	8	9	10	13	15	NP	Total
Mother-of-pearl															
2-hole	11									2				1	14
4-hole	11													4	15
metal															
recessed, embossed	3	2	1	7		2	3		1	3	1	1	4	2	30
recessed plain	5		1	2										2	10
cloth covered metal	5	9			3				1						18
metal studs, Cu, Fe	1												2		3
metal stud, embossed					2				1						3
dish shaped metal	2			1	2		2								7
metal ceramic	1														1
metal poppet type							3		2			1			6
milk glass													1	3	4
wooden	1					2								1	4
plastic/synthetic	1														1
porcelain ceramic								1	1						2
bone	1	1		1										3	6
rubber	1			1										1	3
Total	43	12	2	12	7	4	8	1	6	5	1	3	6	17	127

Table 5.68. Rural sites: buttons.

Site key	A Rapids	B Riverside	C Northburn	D Hanging Rock
	E Sandy Pt	F Poplars	G Apple Tree	H QB2
	I Ha Fong	J Sheung Fong	K Firewood Ck	L Caliche
	M Flax Grove			

Button types/materials	A	B	C	D	E	F	G	H	I	J	K	L	M	Total
Mother-of-pearl														
2-hole	2				1	1	1	2	2	9	13	12	4	**47**
4-hole									7	1		3	6	**17**
metal														
recessed, embossed	5	1		2	1		5	4	23		8	1	6	**56**
recessed plain	2		1		2		8	3	6	3	10	5	7	**47**
cloth covered metal			1							2				**3**
metal studs, Cu, Fe												1	1	**2**
metal stud, embossed							4	1						**5**
dish shaped metal											2			**2**
metal composite												1		**1**
brass balls									1		1			**2**
poppet type							1				1		5	**7**
milk glass											1		2	**3**
bone	2										3	4		**9**
wooden	1							1			2	3		**7**
plastic/synthetic			1											**1**
porcelain ceramic							1				1		5	**7**
Total	**12**	**1**	**3**	**2**	**2**	**3**	**20**	**11**	**39**	**15**	**40**	**29**	**39**	**216**

Table 5.69. Embossed buttons (brass studs).

Brand	Firewood Ck	Chinatown	Apple Tree	Arrowtown	Total	Origins
L.S. & Co., S.F.		1			1	USA
France		1			1	France(?)
Dowler & Sons, Birmingham				4	4	UK
Defiance	1		4	2	7	NZ(?)
W.M. & Co., Kaiapoi		1			1	NZ(?)
embossed design	1	4	4	6	15	unknown
Total	**2**	**7**	**8**	**12**	**29**	

Notes

"Dowler's of St Paul's Square, London" were established in the early 1800s. They were mass-producing metal buttons after 1880.

5 The material culture of the Chinese in southern New Zealand

Table 5.70. Embossed metal buttons: all types (2- and 4-hole).

Site key		A Firewood Creek		B Caliche		C Sheung Fong		D Ha Fong						
		E Chinatown		F QB2		G Apple Tree		H Sandy Point						
		I Hanging Rock		J Riverside		K Arrowtown		L Rapids						
		M Flax Grove												

Embossing	Dm. (cm)	A	B	C	D	E	F	G	H	I	J	K	L	M	Total	Origins
Ring Edge Best	1.2–1.3	1				2	1					2*		1	5	UK
Ring Edge Best	1.5–1.65				1	6	1	2			1	6			17	UK
Ring Edge Solid	1.6	1													1	UK
Double Ring Edge	1.3			1		1						2			4	US(?)
Excelsior	1.2				1	1						2			4	NZ(?)
Excelsior	1.5–1.7	1			9	8		1				5*		1	25	NZ?
Improved Patent	1.2											1			1	UK(?)
Improved Patent	1.5–1.6			1		1		1				1	3		7	UK(?)
Improved 4 Holes	1.2											1			1	UK(?)
Improved 4 Holes	1.45					1									1	UK(?)
Strange & Co. (1)	1.5					1									1	NZ
Suspender	1.4	2			2									1	5	UK(?)
Suspender	1.6				1	2								1	4	UK(?)
Our Own Mark	1,6					1		1				1			3	NZ(?)
W.M. & Co., Kaiapoi (2)	1.6					1						1			2	NZ
Milligan, Oamaru (3)	1.6					1						1			2	NZ
Ne Plus Ultra	1.5											2			2	UK(?)
Tottenham Court Rd.	1.3				1										1	UK
Tottenham Court Rd.	1.7				2										2	UK
……Oxford St	1.6				1										1	UK
The Miners Mole (4)	1.5												1		1	NZ
Ask for Crowns	1.5		1	1	1										3	UK
Cookson & Co., London	1.6	1													1	UK
Roslyn Mills (5)	1.6											1			1	NZ
NZ Clothing… (6)	1.6												2		2	NZ
illegible embossing	—	3				17	2	5	1			2*		2	32	
Total	—	9	1	3	19	43	4	10	1	1	1	28	6	6	131	

Notes

* includes one in each instance from Ah Lum's store (n=3). Full embossing reads "London, Tottenham Ct Rd S135".

(1) "Strange & Co." were clothing manufacturers in established in Christchurch in 1864.

(2) "W.M. & Co., Kaiapoi" established the Kaiapoi Woollen Mills near Christchurch in 1885.

(3) "Milligan, Oamaru" was a tailor and draper who established in Oamaru in 1865.

(4) "The Miners Mole" was a trademark of Sargood, Son & Ewen, clothing and footwear manufacturers who established in Dunedin in the mid 1860s.

(5) "Roslyn Mills" was the name of the Mill established by Ross and Glendening in Dunedin in 1879.

(6) "The New Zealand Clothing Factory" was established in Dunedin by Hallenstein Bros. in 1876.

(7) "Cookson & Co, London" operated from 1850 until 1925. They were lead smelters, manufacturers and antimony refiners based at 8 Cullum st., London.

Table 5.71. Buttons classified by kinds of garments they represent (all sites). Reproduced from Cameron (1985:152).

Button types/categories	MN of buttons	% of the sample
Underwear porcelain/ceramic linen/fabric-covered (sew through styles)	15	2.90
General utility (pants, jackets, waterproof clothing, cardigans) linen/fabric covered (shanked styles), bone, plastic/synthetic, rubber	81	15.60
Cuff, collar, shirt pearl/shell, glass, collar studs	182	35.50
Mens' work clothing (jackets, trousers, suspenders)metal	239	45.60
Chinese brass ball fasteners	2	0.40
Total	**519**	**100**

Table 5.72. Glass beads (n=8).

Colour	Dm. (cm)	Ht. (cm)	Hole Dm. (cm)	Provenance
blue				ACS/4 (J15 Ly.2)
blue				ACS/11 (E9 Ly.1)
blue	0.7	0.8	0.25	Ah Lum's store (C8 Ly.1) bedroom
blue	0.7			Ha Fong (H22 Ly.1)
yellow	0.7			Caliche (B5 Ly.2)
yellow	0.7			Caliche (G4 Ly.2)
black	0.8	0.5	0.3	Ah Lum's store (C6 Ly.1) main room
black	0.8	0.5	0.3	Ah Lum's store (B9 Ly.1) strong room

5 The material culture of the Chinese in southern New Zealand

Table 5.73a. Chinatown: clothing fittings.

Artefact	Hut # 7	12	16	18	19	21	23	26	27	33	34	Total	Comments
rectangular buckles	1			1	2		9	4			4	9	see Note 1
lion face buckle				1								1	
"swords" buckle							1					1	
oval brass buckle							1					1	
rectangular brass buckle							1					1	
brass clothing rivet								1				1	see Note 2
wire hook							1					1	
brass clothing hook								1				1	
clothing clasp			1				1					2	
safety pin							1					1	
braces adjusters							3					3	wire type
braces adjusters							1					1	snap type
spiral chain							1					1	necklace(?)
light chain							1			1		2	
suspender					1							1	blue plastic
spectacles	1						1#		2			4	# mesh on sides

Notes

1. Seven of the rectangular "waistcoat or trouser" adjuster-buckles found in hut 23 were impressed: "Paris Solide" (2), "Paris" (2), "Prima Solide" (2) and "Prima" (1). Two of the four rectangular buckles from hut 26 were impressed "Paris Solide". Their similar construction suggests they were made by the same French manufacturer.

2. The rivet is embossed "L.S. & Co, S.F. (Levi Strauss & Co, San Francisco)".

Table 5.73b. Arrowtown: clothing fittings

Artefact	Hut # 2	3	4	5	8	10	11	13	15	Ah Lum's MR	BE	Total	Comments
wire buckles	1		1	1								3	
rectangular buckles		1*		2		1		1	1	1		7	* "Prima" brand
"D" shaped buckles			1							1		2	off braces
buckles									2			2	form unclear
watch winder(?)			1									1	pocket watch
purse clasp			1									1	
braces parts			2	1							1	4	
braces clasps			2*									2	* "Climax Patent"
clothing stud			1									1	
brass rivet										1		1	
glass beads			1			1				1	2	5	3 blue and 2 black
pearl ear ring										1		1	

Table 5.74. Rural sites: clothing fittings.

Site key								
	A Flax Grove		B Rapids		C Riverside		D Northburn	
	E Hanging Rock		F Sandy Point		G Ah Wee's		H Poplars	
	I Apple Tree		J QB2		K Ha Fong		L Sheung Fong	
	M Firewood Creek		N Caliche					

Artefact	A	B	C	D	E	F	G	H	I	J	K	L	M	N	Total	Notes
rectangular buckles	1	1		1*	1*				1*		1		1		7	*
iron buckles		1	1		1	3#	3	1	3	4#	3		2		22	a
"D" buckles							4							1	5	b
wire buckles							2								2	
steel fastener		1													1	
ornate buckle									1						1	c
worked shell		1													1	d
wire clasps			2												2	
oval stud									1						1	e
braces adjuster										2	1		3		6	f
braces hook											1				1	
purse clasp											1				1	
beads											1			2	3	g
brass chain												1			1	
bone "washer"													1		1	h
copper belt(?) clasp													1		1	
brass ring and stud													1		1	
safety pin														1	1	
Total	1	4	3	1	2	3	7	3	6	7	7	1	6	7	58	

Notes

* "Paris" brand.

a. One of the buckles from the Sandy Point site is impressed "Brevete S.G.D.G."(Figure 5.99-S11). A buckle from QB2 was associated with serge material and two metal buttons impressed "Ring Edge Best".

b. The "D" shaped buckles are braces adjusters.

c. This solid brass buckle has a "crossed cricket bat" motif (Figure 5.97-1).

d. This artefact consists of a piece of oyster(?) shell formed in a hexagon shape with a 1 cm-diameter hole cut in centre of it (Figure 5.93).

e. The stud features an emu and a kangaroo, suggesting it is of Australian origin.

f. The 2 braces adjusters from QB2 are impressed "Brierley's Beau Ideal Patented" (Figure 5.98-1). One of the braces adjusters from Caliche is stamped "The Anglesey Bracer Patent" (Figure 5.98-8).

g. The 3 beads are spherical with flattened threading faces. The specimen from Ha Fong is blue glass; the 2 from Caliche are yellow glass.

h. The "bone washer" is threaded on the inside. Use unknown.

Table 5.75. Provenance and types of fabric remnants. Adapted from Cameron (1983:165).

Sites	Wool	Cotton	Silk	Linen	Oilskin	Total
Chinatown S133/48						
Hut 6	4					4
Hut 16	1					1
Hut 17	1					1
Hut 18	1					1
Hut 19	2					2
Hut 26	1	1				2
Hut 27	2					2
Hut 33	1					1
Arrowtown S123/249						
Hut 1	2					2
Hut 3	2					2
Hut 4	6					6
Hut 5	3	4				7
Hut 8	1					1
Ah Lum's store S123/250	7	2				9
Rural sites						
Firewood Creek S133/424	13	1	1			15
Sheung Fong S133/21	2	4				6
Ha Fong S133/22	16	6	1	1	1	25
Poplars S115/44					1	1
Hanging Rock S133/474	4					4
Northburn S133/77	4	6				10
Sandy Point S124/231	2	1				3
Caliche S133/223		3				3
Flax Grove S133/494	109	87		1	1	198
Total	**184**	**115**	**2**	**2**	**3**	**306**

Table 5.76. Footwear.

Arrowtown huts	Hut # 1	2	3	4	5	6	7	8	9	10	13	15	Total	Comments
leather workboots	1				7*			1			1		10	* 5 pairs
leather boot soles		2			2	3*		1			2		10	* 2 pairs
leather heel pieces					3	2			2		3		10	
leather boot uppers				1	1	1							3	
"U" shaped heel plates	1	1	1	2		2					1	2	10	
crescent-shaped toe plates			1		1					1			3	
child's leather shoe							1						1	buckled
sole of shoe							1						1	20 cm long
tapered strap							1						1	sandal(?)
black cotton bootlace					1								1	
rubber gumboot		1											1	
rubber boot sole		1											1	
rubber boot heel			1										1	
													MN (pairs) = 11	

Chinatown huts	1	6	16	22	23	24	Total	Comments
leather workboots	1	1					2	sole, multi-layered, nailed
leather heel pieces	2						2	of above type
light workboot		1					1	soft leather uppers
leather in-soles			1		1		2	
rubber gumboot		1					1	
shoes, step-ins		1					1	1 pair
shoe, pointed toe		1					1	soft uppers, c. 27 cm long
"U" shaped heel plates				3			3	
crescent-shaped toe plates				1			1	
							MN (pairs) = 6	

Ah Lum's store	1	Total	Comments
leather workboots	1	1	
"U" heel plates	2	2	
leather bootlace	1	1	
leather strap	1	1	
rubber shoe sole	1	1	
		MN (pairs) = 2	

Key for rural sites

- A Riverside
- B Sandy Point
- C Rapids
- D QB2
- E Sheung Fong
- F Ha Fong
- G Poplars

Rural sites	A	B	C	D	E	F	G	Total	Comments
leather workboots	2	1		1	1	7*		12	* MN 4 pairs
leather boot soles			1	1		1		3	
leather boot uppers	1				1			2	off workboots
"U" shaped heel plates		1	7	1		2		11	
crescent-shaped toe plates	2		3	2		1		8	
cork inner sole	1							1	
rubber gumboots		1				1		2	
rubber gumboot uppers	1*				1	2		4	* section cut out
rubber gumboot soles			1	1		2		4	
hobnailed rubber gumboot		2			2	1		5	
rubber boot with leather uppers			1					1	
leather offcut			1					1	5 mm thick
								MN (pairs) = 12	

Table 5.77. Artefacts associated with grooming and personal hygiene.

Artefact	Chinatown hut #											Total	Comments
	7	12	16	18	19	21	23	26	27	33	34		
shaving strop											1	1	buckle
cut throat razors		1			1*	1		1				4	* bakelite
wooden comb								1				1	burnt frag. Chinese origin(?) see Figure 5.100b
clothes brush		1										1	

Key for Ah Lum's store
MR main room
BE bedroom

	Arrowtown hut #								Ah Lum's		Total	
	2	3	4	5	8	10	11	13	15	MR	BE	
cut throat razors				1							1	2	
bone comb?										1		1	fragment

Key for rural sites A Apple Tree B Ha Fong C Sheung Fong D Caliche

	A	B	C	D	Total	Notes
cut throat razor	1				1	
shaving cream		1			1	A 6 cm-long tube of "Jeyes Antiseptic Shaving Cream"
plastic combs			1	1	2	Embossed "Featherlite". It appears to be of recent origin.
manicuring tools		1			1	A connected pair of Chinese manicuring tools (see Figure 5.100a)

Note. This table does not include the containers of grooming products such as skin and hair tonics and perfumes (see Section 5.6.5), and toothpastes.

Table 5.78. Artefacts associated with gambling and recreation.

Site key	A ACS/2	B Ah Lum's store	C Ah Wee's
	D Flax Grove	E Rockfall 1	F Rapids
	G Rapids		

Artefact	A	B	C	D	E	F	G	Total	Notes
white glass counters	2	14	1					17	
black glass counters		1						1	
wooden dominoes		1						1	
wooden checkers(?)	1	5						6	
paak kop piu tickets				4	5			9	
we-qi counters(?)						2		2	made of mother-of-pearl shell
fan tan cover							1	1	made of steel with brass knob (Figure 5.101a)
Total	3	21	1	4	5	2	1	37	

The following pieces of wood are possibly remnants of domino boxes:

a. side of small wooden box found at ACS/5 (O11 Ly.2), 12.2 x 1.4 x 0.4 cm

b. side of small wooden box found in Ah Lum's main room (E7, Ly.1), 12.2 x 1.5 x 0.4 cm

c. burnt lid or base fragments of a small wooden box with adhering fragments of red paper. The dimensions of the fragments suggest they are from a box similar to those mentioned above (see Section 5.6.6).

Table 5.79. Distribution of Chinese coins.

	Chinatown hut #												
	1	7	12	14	16	18	21	22	23	26	33	34	Subtotal
Number of coins	1	4	1	1	8	2	4	4	2	226*	2	3#	258

Notes

* 206 of the coins in hut 26 were found in a single fused mass. They appear to have been threaded on a string.

A Ya Sheung amulet (Figure 5.102d) was also found in hut 34.

	Arrowtown hut #					
	3	5	6	surface	Ah Lum's	Subtotal
Number of coins	1	3	2	2	14	22

Key for rural sites	A Poplars	B Ah Wee's	C QB2
	D Sheung Fong	E Firewood	F Rapids
	G Ledge		

	A	B	C	D	E	F	G	Subtotal
Number of coins	1	11	5	4	5	1*	4**	31
Total (all sites)	311							

Notes

* Although only one Chinese coin was found in the Rapids, a circular lid found in the site (Figure 5.101a) may have been used as a "spreading out" cover, a tan koe in the game of fan tan (Culin 1891:2–3).

** The Ledge (S133/868) is a European house dump site that contained a small amount of Chinese material.

5 The material culture of the Chinese in southern New Zealand

Table 5.80. British and New Zealand coins.

No.	Site	Date	Denomination	Comments	Notes
	Chinatown				
1	Ch/6	19--	British penny	Edward VII 1901–10	
2	Ch/6	1907	British halfpenny		2, 3 and 4 found together
3	Ch/6	1908	British halfpenny	Edward VII 1901–10	
4	Ch/6	?	British halfpenny	Edward VII 1901–10	
5	Ch/12	1902	British 3d	Edward VII 1901–10	
6	Ch/14	1887	British 3d	Victoria 1837–1901	
7	Ch/21	1896	British 6d	Victoria 1837–1901	
8	Ch/21	?	British 6d?		needs cleaning
9	Ch/21	1903	British 3d		
10	Ch/21	1889	British 3d	Victoria	
11	Ch/21	1902	British 3d	Edward VII 1901–10	
12	Ch/26	1891	British 3d	Victoria	On shelf in wall with Chinese coins
13	Ch/26	1883	British halfpenny	Victoria 1837–1901	
14	Ch/26	1904	British halfpenny	Edward VII 1901–10	
15	Ch/26	?	British 3d		No's 15–18 found together with buttons and nails
16	Ch/26	1908	British 3d	Edward VII 1901–10	
17	Ch/26	1890	British 3d	Victoria	
18	Ch/26	1907	British 6d	Edward VII 1901–10	
19	Ch/33	1913	British halfpenny	George V	
20	Ch/33	1882	British shilling	Victoria	
21	Ch/33	1906	British 6d	Edward VII 1901–10	
22	Ch/36	1946	NZ 6d	George VI 1936–56	
	Arrowtown				
23	ACS/1	1879	British florin	Victoria 1837–1901	
24	ACS/4	1889	British halfpenny	Victoria 1837–1901	
25	ACS/4	1904	British halfpenny	Edward VII 1901–10	
26	ACS/5	1875	British penny	Victoria 1837–1901	
27	ACS/6	1899	British penny	Victoria 1837–1902	
28	ACS/6	1912	British 3d	George V 1910–1936	
29	ACS/8	1906	British penny	Edward VII 1901–10	
30	ACS/10	1875	British penny	Victoria 1837–1901	
	Ah Lum's store				
31	bank/office	18--	British penny	Victoria – "bun head" issue 1860–95	
32	bank/office	?	British shilling	Victoria – broad range 1838–95	
33	bank/office	1891	British 3d	Victoria	
34	bank/office	?	British 6d	Victoria	
35	bank/office	1950	NZ 3d	George VI	
36	main room	1868	British 6d	Victoria	
37	main room	1868	British shilling	Victoria	
38	strong room	1902	British 6d	Edward VII 1901–10	
39	strong room	1908	British 3d	Edward VII 1901–11	
40	strong room	18?0	British 3d	Edward VII 1901–12	
	Sheung Fong				
41	U22 Ly.1	1907	British halfpenny	Edward VII 1901–12	
42	U22 Ly.1	1951	NZ florin	George VI	
	Caliche				
43	H4	?	British 3d	Victoria	

Table 5.81. Distribution of coal and lignite.

Arrowtown	hut							Ah Lum's store		
	1	2	4	6	8	10	15	main bedroom	bedroom	kitchen
coal	X		X		X			X	X	
lignite	X	X	X	X	X	X	X	X	X	
charcoal				X		X				X
Chinatown	hut									
	F11	14	17	22	27	36				
coal		X	X		X					
lignite	X		X	X		X				
Rural Sites	Sheung Fong		Apple Tree		Rapids					
coal	X		X(1)		X					
Note:										
In all instances the coal was limited to 15 or fewer pieces per site, except in hut 17 in Chinatown which had distinct lenses of coal dross. (1) the coal was in the hearth.										

Table 5.82. Summary of recovered wood and charcoal specimens.

	Provenance	Material
Chinatown		
CH/12	Sq. 4 Ly.2	wood on floor, fragments 2 cm thick
CH/14	M13 Ly.1	light plank, fragment
Ch/14	M16 Ly.3	plank with metal hinges, cupboard door(?)
Ch/16	K16 Ly.2	2.5 cm planking under matting
Ch/16	K16 Ly.2	curved plank, barrel stave(?)
Ch/16	L14 Ly.1	wood with adhering floral wallpaper near door
Ch/18	N18 Ly.1	burnt wood, form indetminate
Ch/21	N11 Ly.1	light plank in recess by fireplace
Ch/21	K12 Ly.2	2 x routed wood, window frame(?)
Ch/21	P13,surface	wood from doorstep
Ch/22	S13 Ly.1	post butt, squared, support for sleeping platform(?)
Ch/23	K16 Ly.2	pieces of burnt wood
Ch/23	J15 Ly.3	3 x 2 inch timber 40 cm, structural(?)
Ch/26	L16 Ly.2	dressed burnt wood
Ch/26	NE wall	shelf, box wood
Ch/26	M13 Ly.1	burnt wood and tin sheeting, overlying coin mass
Ch/26	M14 Ly.2	burnt stuctural wood 3 x 2 inches
Ch/26	M14 Ly.2	burnt floor boards, 3 cm thick, 17 cm wide
Ch/33	east wall	protruding shelf, plank 2 cm thick
Ch/34	L13 Ly.2	light split planking, kindling(?)
Arrowtown		
ACS/2	F16 Ly.1	coconut shell fragments
ACS/2	H17 H10 F10	3 pieces of cut wood: 14 x 4 cm, 18 x 4 cm, 11 x 4 cm
AC2/2	F16 Ly.1	burnt wood
ACS/3	various units	5 plank fragments
ACS/4	H9 and I12	charcoal
ACS/5	O11 Ly 2	side of small box, 12.2 x 1.4 x 0.35 cm domino box(?)
Ah Lum's	main room	side of small box, virtually identical to above
Ah Lum's	bank room	burnt wooden ball 3.0 cm diameter
Rural sites		
Caliche	various units	charcoal (6 bags)
Firewood Creek	A10	whittled points 3 and 5 cm long
Firewood Creek	A10	plank, fragment
Firewood Creek	various units	charcoal (4 bags)
Sheung Fong	U22	box wood with nails
Sheung Fong	R21 and V22	charcoal (2 bags)

Table 5.82. Summary of recovered wood and charcoal specimens (*continued*).

	Provenance	Material
Sheung Fong	U21	burnt wood
Ha Fong	J18 and K17	charcoal (2 bags)
Ha Fong	various units	wood scraps
QB2	B8	crescent shaped wood, use unknown
QB2	various units	charcoal (5 bags)
Apple Tree	F2	charcoal (1 bag)
Sandy Point	in fireplace	wood 35 cm long, chiselled at one end
Sandy Point	C4	shelf planking
Sandy Point	B2	burnt wood
Sandy Point	fireplace and B3	charcoal (2 bags)
Sandy Point	C1	burnt plank fragment
Hanging Rock	B10	charcoal
Hanging Rock	B11	misc wood fragments
Northburn	AII and C11	misc wood fragments
Northburn	A10	burnt wood
Riverside	B4	wood found in ash lens
Riverside	various units	charcoal (3 bags)
Riverside	B1	misc wood fragments
Riverside	A4	bracken, bedding(?)
Rapids	L3 surface	cut timber 5 x 3 inches
Rapids	F3	charcoal
Flax Grove	stuck in wall	joss stick remnants
Flax Grove	B8	burnt fragments of small box with paper adhering
Flax Grove	B7	burnt box wood fragments
Flax Grove	C6	wooden lid, diameter 13 cm
Flax Grove	E5	firewood(?)
Flax Grove	C8	piece of knotted bark, pre-European(?)
Flax Grove	D5	plank in doorway
Flax Grove	C8 and B9	dry grass/bracken (2 bags), bedding(?)

5 The material culture of the Chinese in southern New Zealand

Table 5.83. Stone artefacts and related structural materials.

Chinatown	Hut #								
	14	18	19	21	23	26	34	Total	Comments
firebricks	1	2						3	impressed "Garnkirk"
plaster		X					X	X	on interior walls
red ochre					X			X	less than 1 gram
marble slabs				1	1			2	small, use unknown, dimensions 10.2 x 10.4 x 2.2 cm, hole in centre 1.2 x 2.4 cm
slate, incised			9	3				12	pieces of slate
slate, unmarked				3				3	3 pieces with chamfered edges
inkstones		1				2		3	one found nearby

Arrowtown	Hut #						
	2	7	10	11		Total	
bricks			1	1		2	small fragments
plaster		X				X	lumps in ground
slate, incised		1				1	in Arrowtown Museum now
slate, unmarked	1		3			4	

Key to rural sites	A Caliche		B Firewood Creek		C Ha Fong		
	D Flax Grove		E Sandy Point		F Rapids		
	A	B	C	D	E	F	Total	
inkstones				1	1		2	
slate, plain			1				1	
slate, scored		10					10	pieces, from sharpening(?)
slate, incised		1				1	2	parallel lines
pebble, flat							1	smoothing stone(?)
greywacke cobble		1					1	chatter damage on one end
silcrete flakes	4						4	presumably pre-European (one found near moa egg shell, see Ritchie 1982)
heated stones	2						2	probably pre-European

Note
X indicates presence of artefact/material but impossible to quantify.

Table 5.84. Paper artefacts of European origin.

Site key	A	Flax Grove	B	Ch/6		C	Ch/34		
	D	Northburn	E	Poplars		F	ACS/5		
	G	Rockfall 1	H	Ah Lum's store					

Artefact	A	B	C	D	E	F	G	H	Total	Comments
gold receipts (1)	7						2		9	
newspaper remnants (2)	X	X	X	X				X	5	
tea wrappers (3)	1								1	
tea packet (4)					1				1	
brown paper wrapper (5)	1								1	
brown paper bags (6)	12						1		13	
cigarette papers (7)	1								1	
wax vesta wrapper (8)	1								1	
R Bell & Co vesta box (9)							3		3	Cylindrical cardboard
portion of a postage stamp (10)					1				1	
pages from a Bible (11)							2		2	Chinese language

Notes

1. The 7 receipts for gold dust from the Flax Grove site were issued by the Bank of New Zealand, Cromwell, in the mid-1890s. Examples are depicted in Figure 5.105c. The 3 fragmentary gold receipts found in the Rockfall 1 site were issued by the Colonial Bank of New Zealand. The bank branch and dates are not discernible.

2. Newspaper remnants:

   a. Chinatown hut 4: fragments of the *Otago Daily Times* 1914.

   b. Chinatown hut 34: fragments of the *Otago Daily Times* (5/10/1908).

   c. Northburn: fragments of the *Otago Witness*. No discernible dates.

   d. Flax Grove: fragments of the *Otago Witness* 1894–99.

   e. Ah Lum's store: fragments of the *Tuapeka Times* (late 1870s) and *Glasgow Weekly Herald* (14/1/1882) pasted on walls of kitchen.

3. The tea wrapper reads "Best Kooloo Tea, Canton", "1885" on wrapper.

4. Tea packet(?): a square cardboard box with foil liner. Fragments of illegible pink paper label.

5. Paper wrapper with part of original lettering. Wording suggests tea. Paper is brown, coarse and flecked.

6. The 13 paper bags, of various sizes, are made of soft brown paper (possibly of Chinese origin). They had no contents or residues.

7. A packet of cigarette papers of presumed French origin. Label reads "Repeater Brand, Le Meilleur Paper, Cigarette ----nique".

8. Wax vestas tin wrapper (possibly off a 6 pack). Label reads "R. Bell & Co Wax Vesta Matches, Established for more than half a century".

9. Cylindrical cardboard match boxes (3) labelled "R. Bell & Co". (Figure 5.105e). These are believed to postdate 1910 (Caldwell 1982:1).

10. The edge trim (selvege) and small fragment of a postage stamp.

11. The 2 pages (Ch.19, p.72) from a bible written in Chinese script (Figure 5.105d) are probably remnants of one of those distributed by the Rev. Alexander Don or his successors.

5 The material culture of the Chinese in southern New Zealand

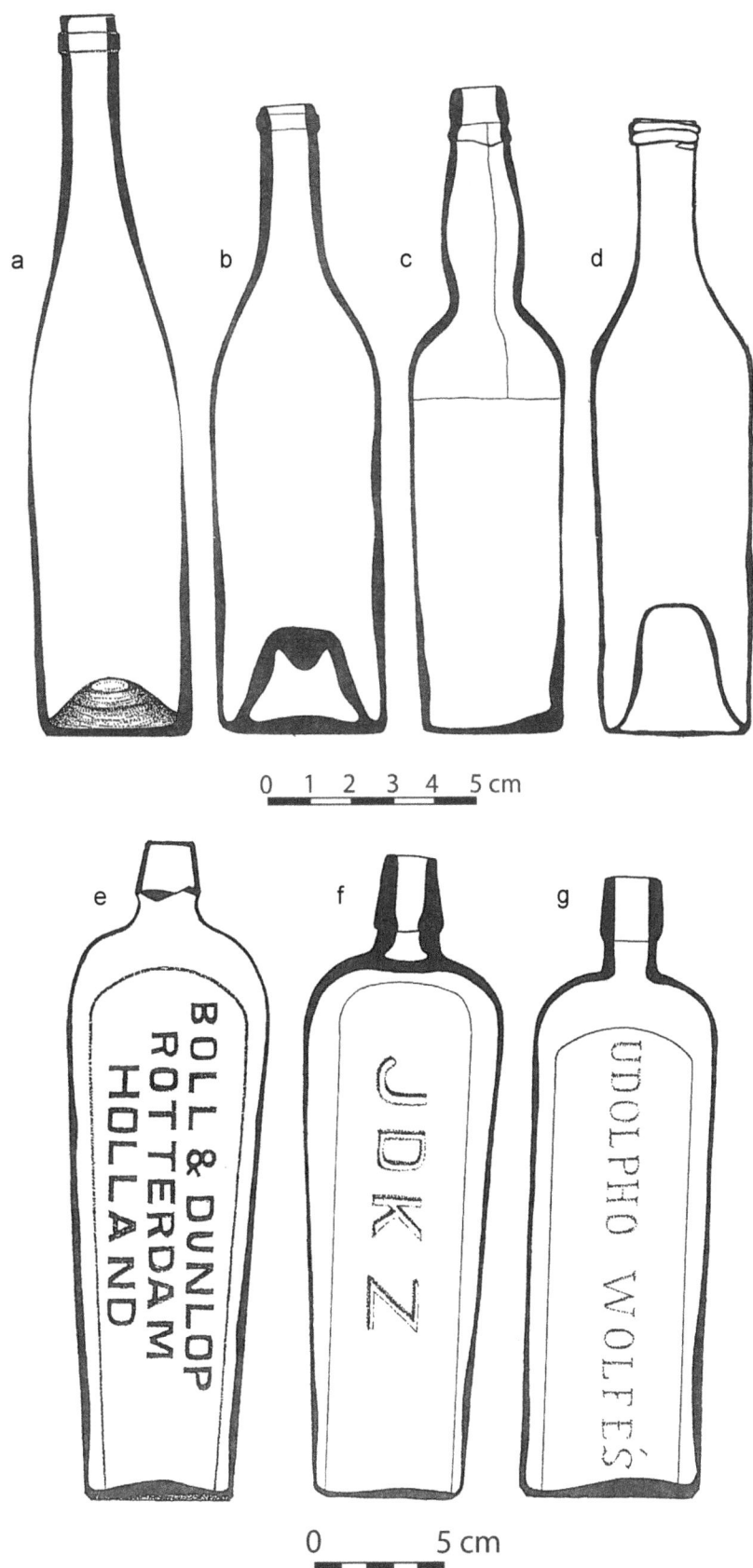

Figure 5.1. Liquor bottles. See Table 5.1 for distribution. **a.** Light green ring-seal wine bottle. **b.** Light green ring-seal brandy bottle 1890–1910. **c.** Aqua 3-piece mould whisky bottle. **d.** Light green wine bottle with hand-applied lip. **e.** "Boll & Dunlop" gin found behind Ah Lum's store. **f.** "JDKZ" Dutch gin found at various sites. **g.** "Udolpho Wolfe's" schnapps.

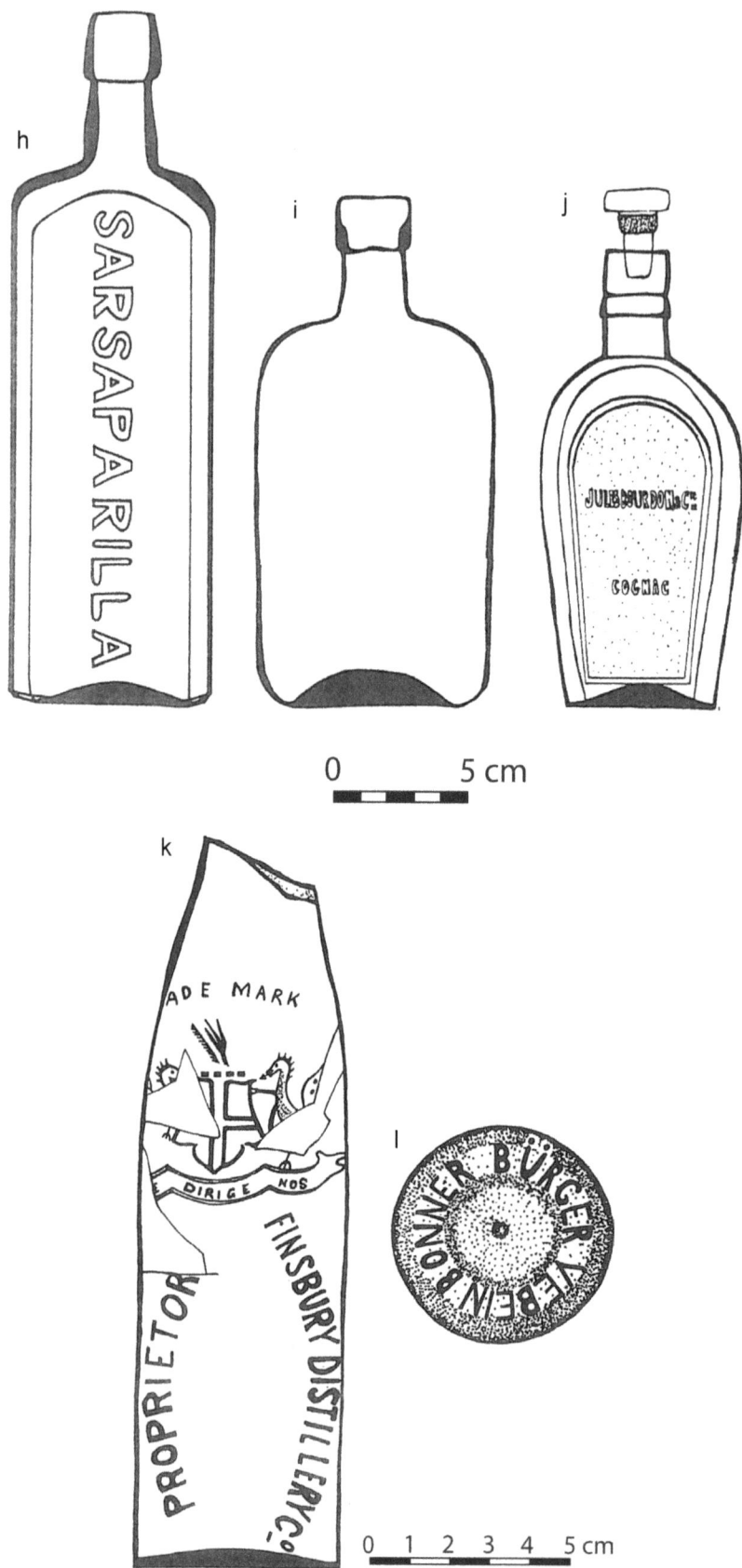

Figure 5.1. Liquor bottles (*continued*). See Table 5.1 for distribution. **h.** Dr Townsend's Sarsaparilla found at Ah Wee's (D7 Ly.1). **i.** Aqua whisky flask found at various sites. **j.** "Jules Bourdon & Co." cognac (coffin flask with paper label) from upper Chinatown trench. **k.** "Finsbury Distillery Co." bottle. Alcohol type not known, found on ACS/4 (H13) surface. **l.** "Bonner Burger Vebein" embossed on base of dark green ring-seal wine(?) bottle (Ch/26 F17 Ly. 2).

5 The material culture of the Chinese in southern New Zealand

Figure 5.1. Liquor bottles (*continued*). See Table 5.1 for distribution. **m.** "Boord & Son London, Old Jamaica Rum" (paper label on black glass) 3-piece mould bottle found in upper Chinatown.

Figure 5.2. Black glass beer bottles. See Table 5.2 for distribution. **a–d.** 3-piece mould, applied-top black glass beer bottles found at various sites.

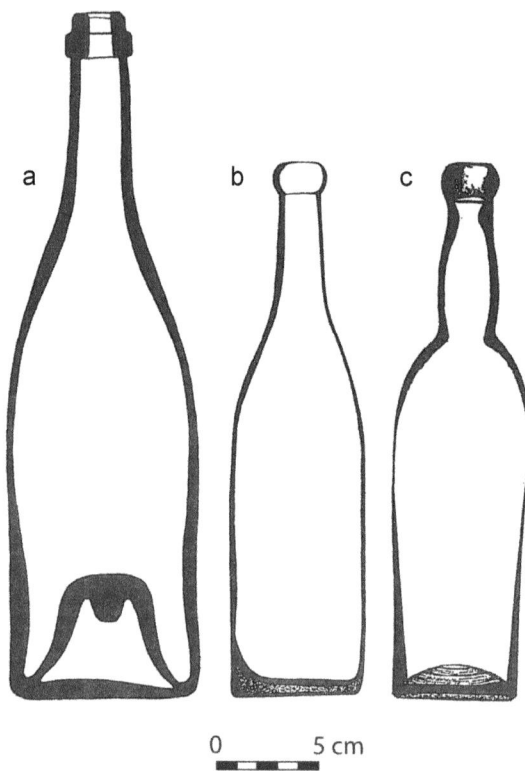

Figure 5.3. Miscellaneous beer bottles. See Table 5.2 for distribution. **a.** Large size green glass ring-seal beer bottle found at various sites. These bottles were also used for aerated waters (see Figure. 5.10h, i). **b.** Dark green spun-moulded blob-top beer bottle found at Chinatown and various sites. **c.** Dark green spun-moulded blob-top beer bottle with bulbous neck found at Chinatown and various sites.

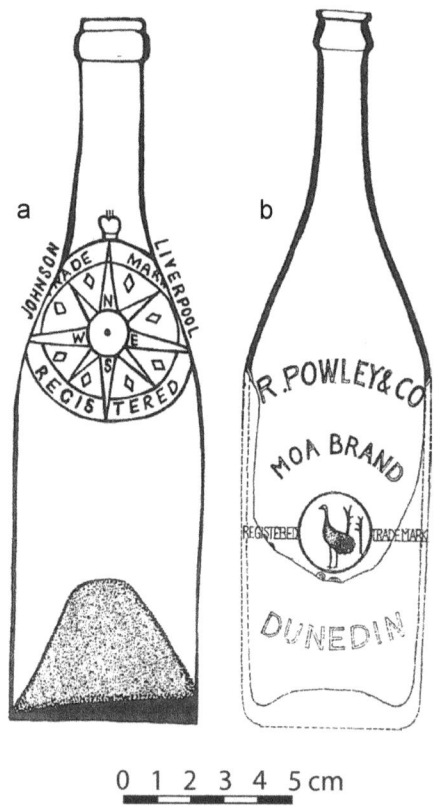

Figure 5.4. Embossed beer bottles. **a.** Dark green ring-seal "beer" bottle embossed with "Johnson, Liverpool, Trade Mark, Registered" found at the Poplars site (J17 Ly.2). **b.** Brown glass crown-top beer bottle embossed "R. Powley & Co, Moa Brand, Dunedin", found at Chinatown hut 19 (K13 Ly.2).

5 The material culture of the Chinese in southern New Zealand

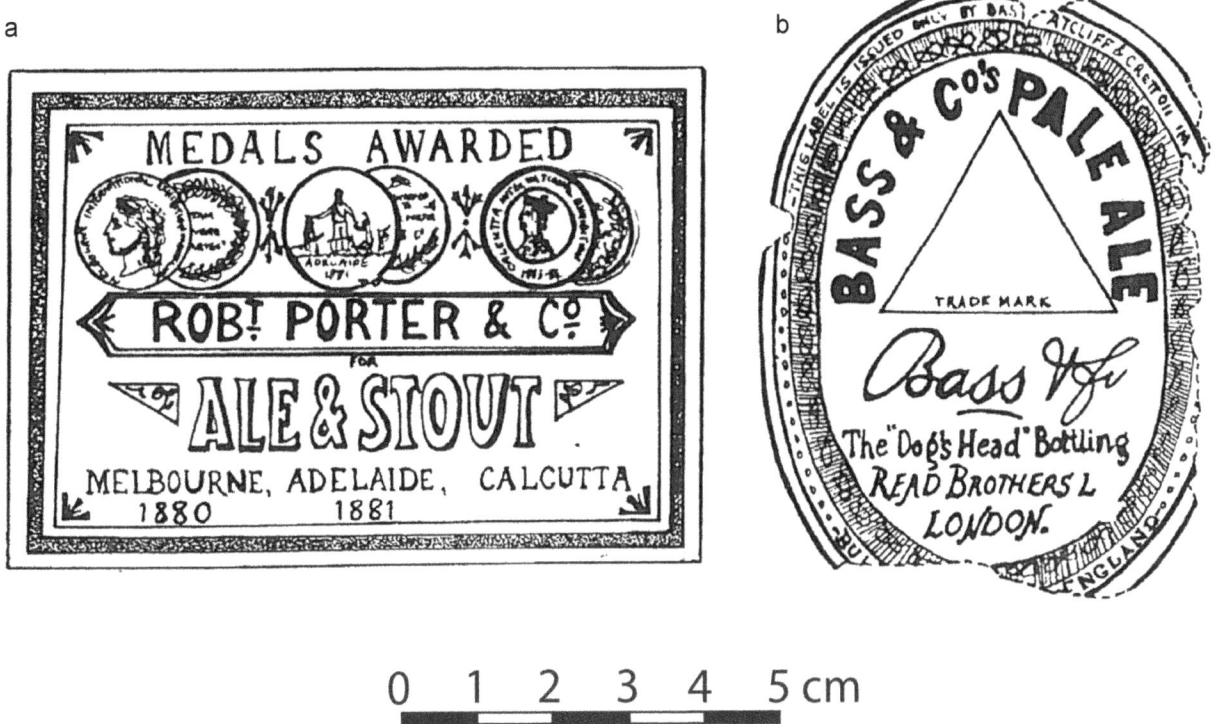

Figure 5.5. Beer bottle labels. **a.** "Rob't Porter & Co. Ale & Stout" label on large ring-seal beer bottle found at upper Chinatown store deposit (trench). **b.** "Bass & Co's Pale Ale" label on large ring-seal beer bottle found at upper Chinatown store deposit (trench).

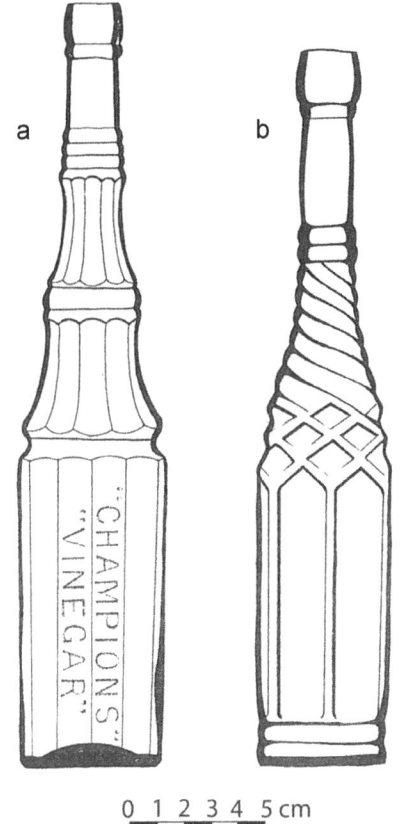

Figure 5.6. Domestic bottles. See Table 5.3 for distribution. **a.** "Champions Vinegar", aqua bottle. **b.** "Twisty" neck aqua bottle for salad oil.

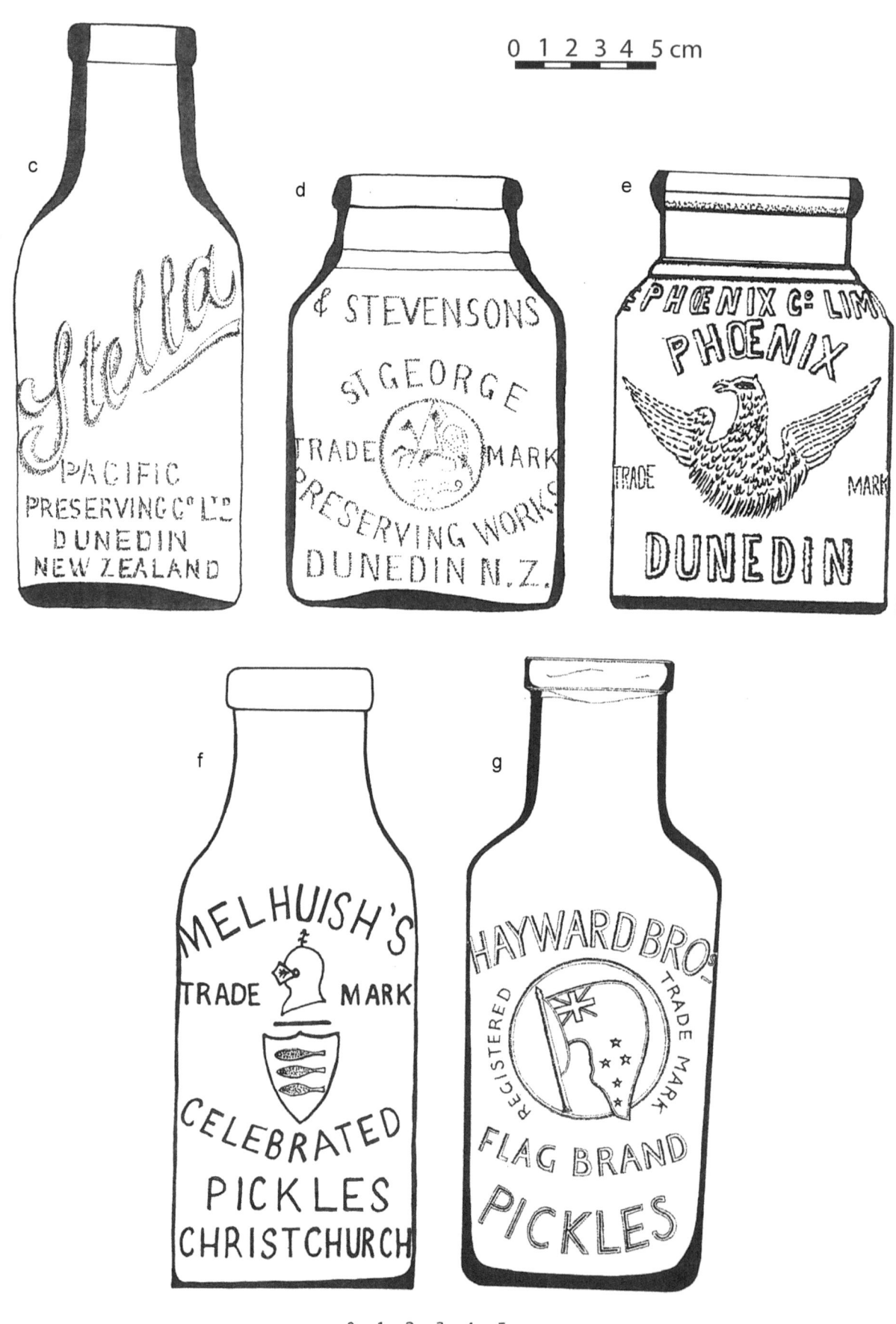

Figure 5.6. Domestic bottles (*continued*). See Table 5.3 for distribution. **c.** Clear glass "Stella" pickle bottle. **d.** "St George" jam jar. **e.** "Phoenix" jam jar. **f.** "Melhuish's" pickle jar. **g.** "Hayward Bros" pickle jar.

5 The material culture of the Chinese in southern New Zealand

Figure 5.6. Domestic bottles (*continued*). See Table 5.3 for distribution. **h.** Blue glass castor oil bottle found at QB2 (K13 Ly.2). **i.** Worcestershire sauce bottle, aqua. Found at various sites. **j.** Relish bottle, aqua. Found at various sites. **k.** "Symington & Co, Edinburgh" Coffee & Chicory Essence bottle, aqua. Found at the Rapids site (E12 Ly.2). **l.** Clear glass essence(?) bottle with glass stopper (and base mark), found at Ch/33 (A11 Ly.2). **m.** "Sykes Macvay & Co" glass stopper c. 1885 (see Section 5.15).

289

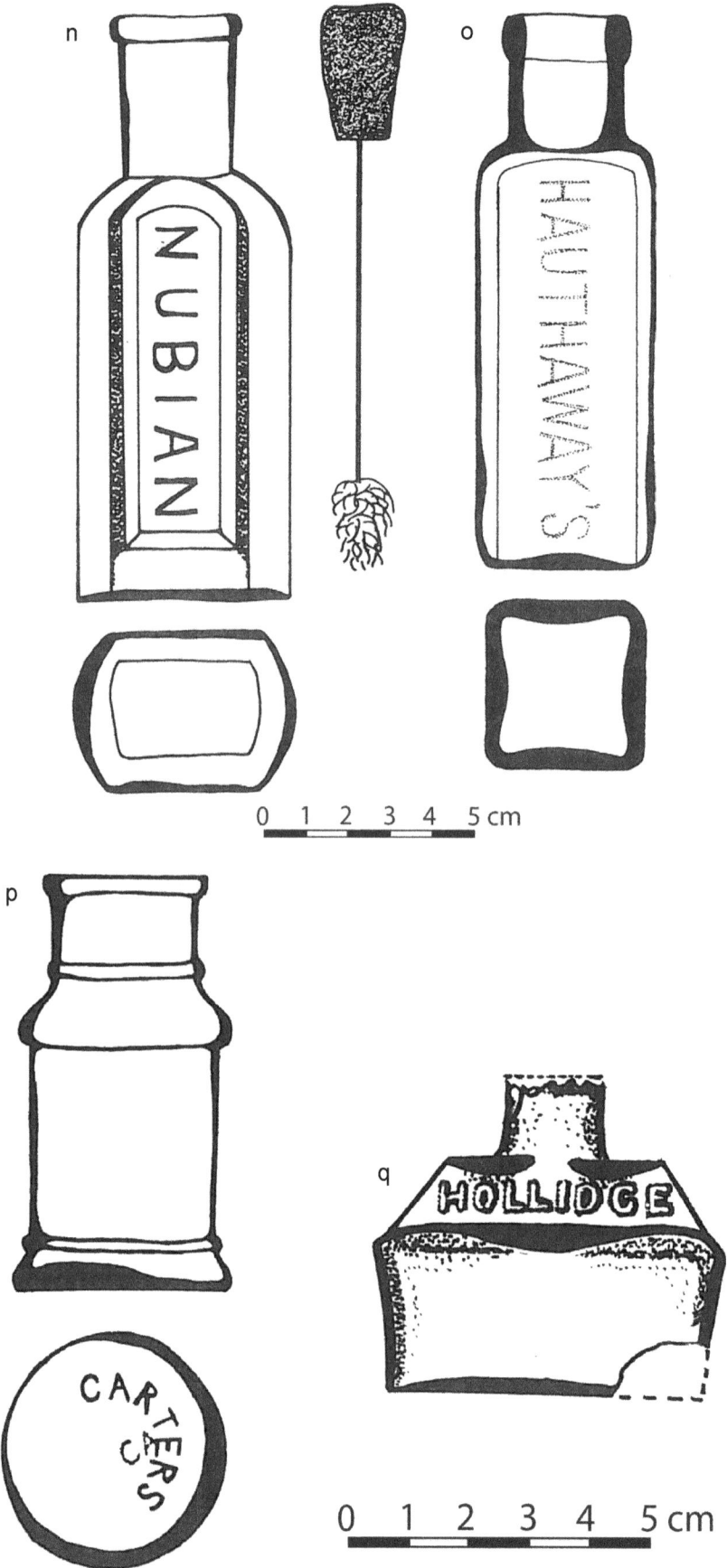

Figure 5.6. Domestic bottles (*continued*). See Table 5.3 for distribution. **n.** "Nubian" blacking. Aqua panelled bottle. **o.** "Hauthaway's Peerless Gloss (USA)" aqua leather dressing bottle. **p.** Light green-blue bottle embossed "Carter's" (ink) on base found at Ch/33 (K18 Ly.2). **q.** "Hollidge" ink aqua bottle found at Sheung Fong (J13 Ly.1).

5 The material culture of the Chinese in southern New Zealand

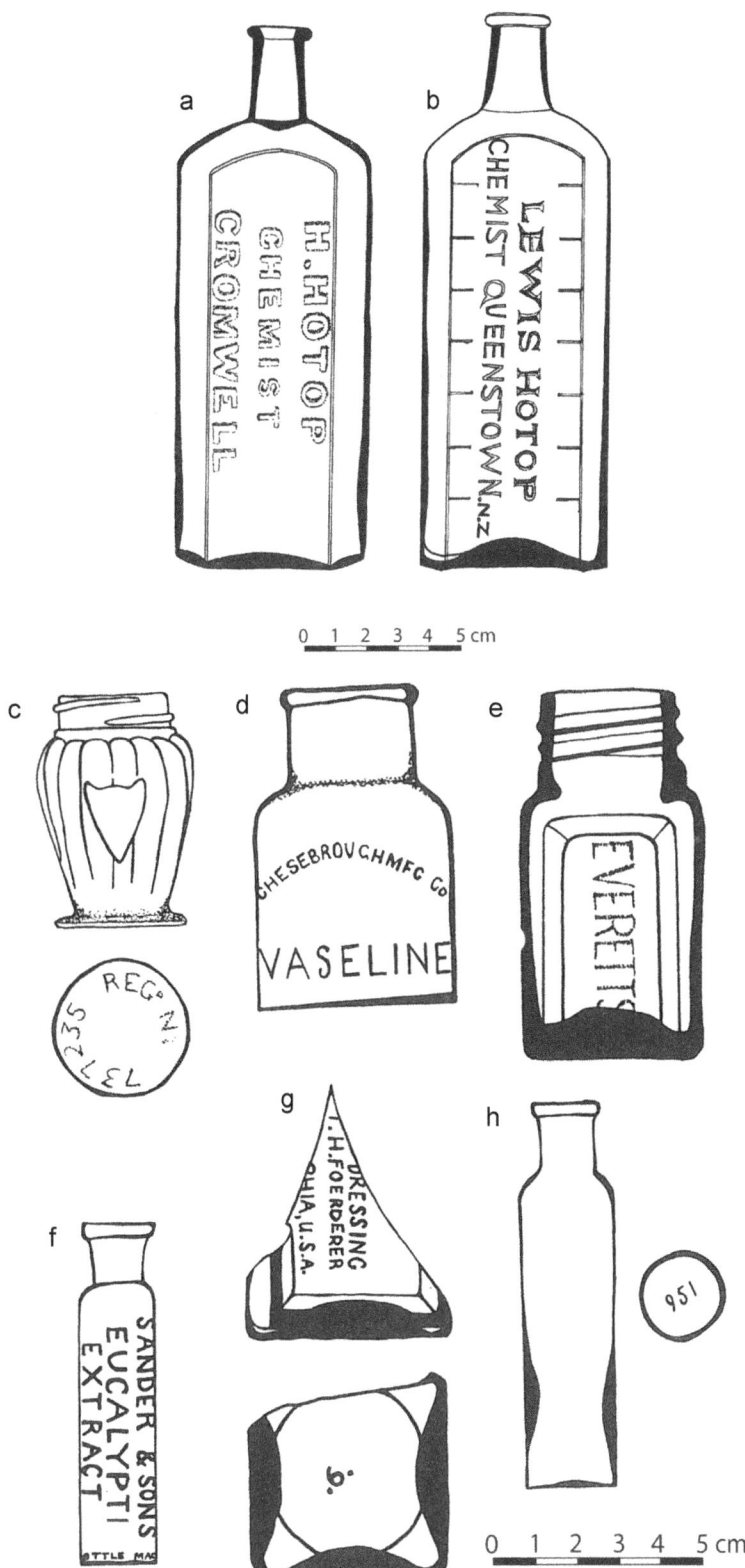

Figure 5.7. Pharmaceutical bottles. See Table 5.4 for distribution. **a.** "H. Hotop" of Cromwell (1880–1915), chemist bottle found in Chinatown, Ch/14 (J12 Ly.2). **b.** "Lewis Hotop" of Queenstown (c.1880–1906), chemist bottle found behind Ah Lum's store. **c.** Milk glass "skin cream" jar (and reg'n mark on base) found at Chinatown hut 33 (G12 Ly.1). **d.** "Chesebrough Mfg. Co." vaseline bottle, found at Chinatown. **e.** "Everetts" bottle found at Chinatown hut 6 (Ly.1). **f.** "Sander & Sons Eucalypti Extract" bottle found at Chinatown Hut 34 (J16 Ly.2). **g.** "I H Foerderer, (Philadel)phia, U.S.A." leather dressing bottle (and base) found at ACS/4 (E12 Ly.1). A bottle of this type is illustrated in Sellari and Sellari 1975: 396–7. **h.** Green glass lavender water(?) bottle (and base) found at Chinatown hut 26 (Ly.1).

Figure 5.7. Pharmaceutical bottles (*continued*). See Table 5.4 for distribution. **i.** "Baxter's Lung Preserver, Christchurch" aqua bottle found at Ch/23 (E7 Ly.2). **j.** "Chamberlain's Pain-Balm" aqua bottle found at Ch/27 (F2 Ly.2). **k.** "Woods' Great Peppermint Cure" aqua bottle found at upper Chinatown trench. **l.** "Barry's Tricopherous for the Skin and Hair" found at Sandy Point (H2 Ly.2). **m.** "Tussicura" cough remedy c. 1915–20. Rectangular bottle depicted side on. **n.** "Davis" vegetable painkiller aqua bottle.

5 The material culture of the Chinese in southern New Zealand

Figure 5.7. Pharmaceutical bottles (*continued*). See Table 5.4 for distribution. **o.** "Dinneford's Magnesia" aqua bottle. **p.** "Kruses Prize Medal Magnesia" aqua bottle. Distribution limited to Chinatown.

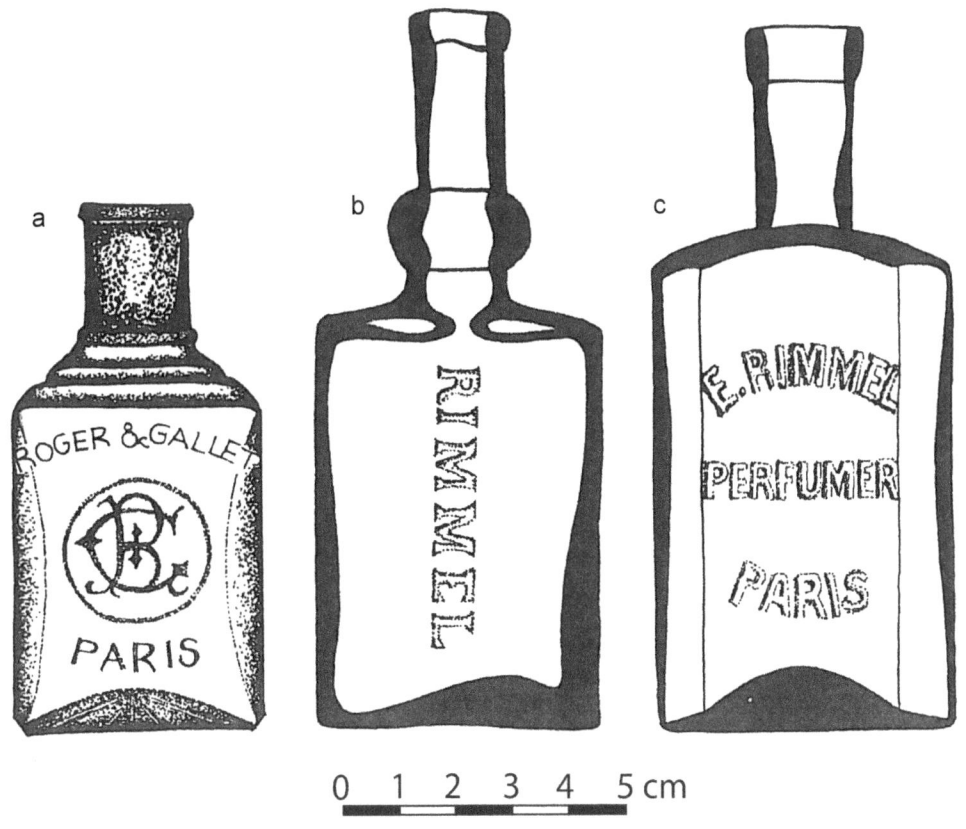

Figure 5.8. French perfume bottles. See Table 5.3 for distribution. **a.** "Roger & Gallet, Paris" found at ACS/6 (G11 Ly.2). **b.** "Rimmel" found at the Ha Fong shelter (R13 Ly.1). **c.** "E. Rimmel, Perfumer, Paris" found at Chinatown hut 26 (E11 Ly.2).

Figure 5.9. Chinese glass bottles. See Table 5.5 for distribution. **a.** Small tincture vial found at various sites. **b.** "Regular" tincture vial found at various sites. **c.** Oval vial with handpainted gilt lettering found at Ah Wee's (K16 Ly.1). **d.** Vial (paper label reads "U-I-OIL, Manufacturer, Cheung Wah, Canton, China". Found at Ah Lum's, in the bedroom. **e.** Rectangular-section shear-top bottle, found in Ah Lum's main room (E12 Ly.2). **f.** Tear-drop shaped vial found at Chinatown hut 23 (J15 Ly.2). **g.** Wide-mouthed clear glass cylindrical pharmaceutical(?) bottle with rolled lip and remnant of illegible paper label found at Chinatown and Chinatown stores.

5 The material culture of the Chinese in southern New Zealand

Figure 5.9. Chinese glass bottles (*continued*). See Table 5.5 for distribution. **h.** Spun moulded green glass collar-top "beer" bottle with remnants of paper label bearing Chinese writing. Medicinal wine bottle(?) found at upper Chinatown trench. **i.** Green glass crown-top bottle with raised band on neck. Medicinal wine bottle(?) found at Nokomai. One also found at Halfway House (Bedford pers.comm.).

Figure 5.10. Aerated water bottles. See Table 5.6 for distribution. **a.** "Thomson & Co., Dunedin', with "1908" on base. Found at Chinatown and Arrowtown. **b.** "J. McLoughlin, Cromwell", found at Chinatown. **c.** "Lane & Co., Dunedin", found at Chinatown and Arrowtown.

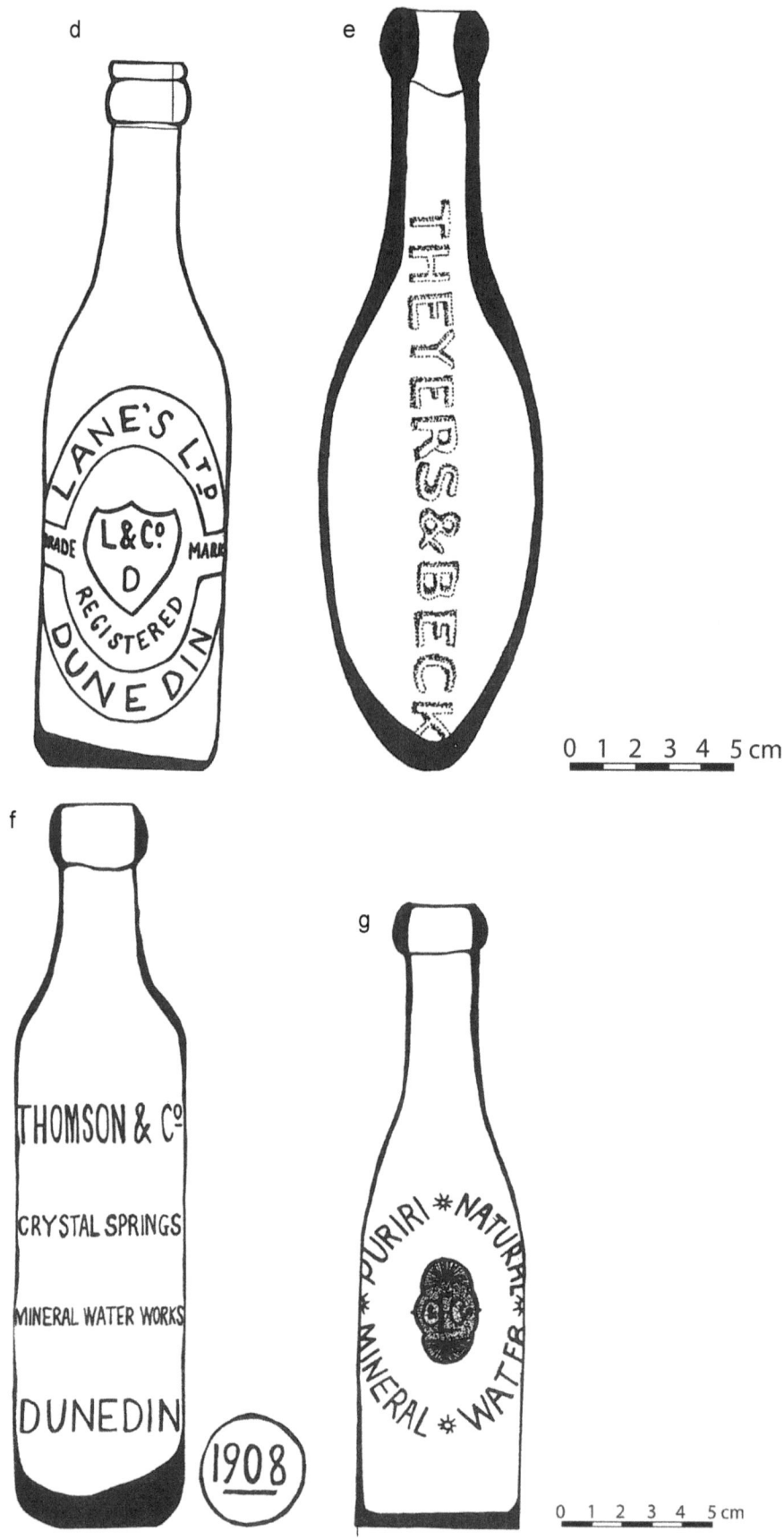

Figure 5.10. Aerated water bottles (*continued*). See Table 5.6 for distribution. **d.** "Lane's Ltd., Dunedin" clear glass crown-top found at Chinatown and Arrowtown. **e.** "Theyers & Beck" aqua "torpedo" type bottle, found at Chinatown and Firewood Creek. **f.** "Thomson & Co., Dunedin" blob-top aqua glass bottle, "1908" on base, found at Arrowtown. **g.** "Puriri Natural Mineral Water" blob-top bottle, dark green glass found at Ah Lum's kitchen.

Figure 5.10. Aerated water bottles (*continued*). See Table 5.6 for distribution. **h.** "Cromwell Brewery Co., Excel[sior] Ginger A[le]" label on fragment of dark green ring-seal bottle. **i.** "Theyers & Beck, Alexandra South, [C]hampion-era-" aerated water label on fragment of dark green ring-seal bottle. Both labelled fragments were found during renovations in the Victoria Hotel, Cromwell.

Figure 5.11. Clear glass essence(?) bottle containing mercury. Cylindrical cross-section found at Ha Fong shelter, Cromwell Gorge (S23 Ly.1).

Archaeology and history of the Chinese in southern New Zealand during the nineteenth century

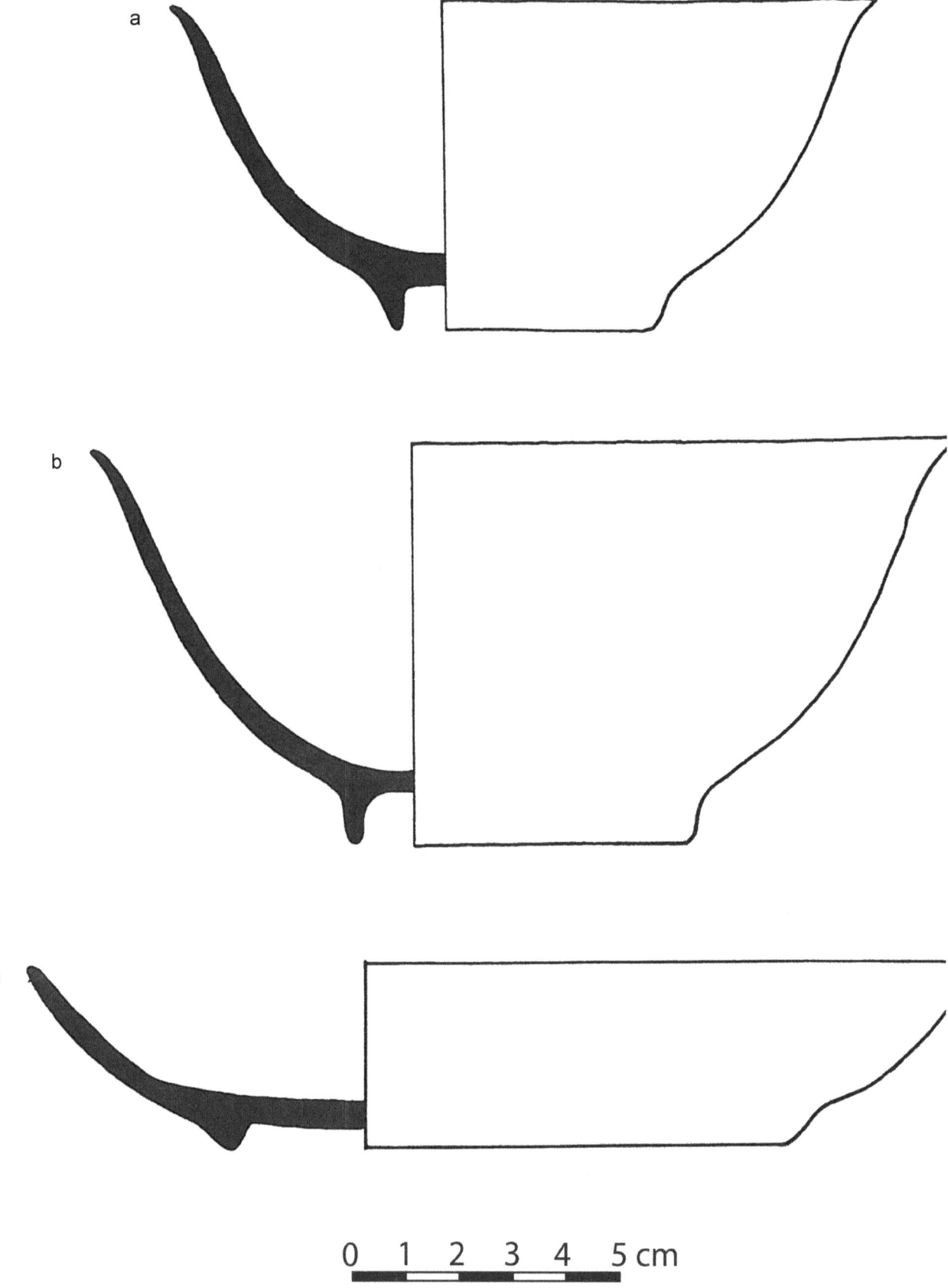

Figure 5.12. Celadon wares. See Table 5.9 for distribution. **a.** Rice bowl. **b.** Large rice-serving bowl. **c.** Large dish.

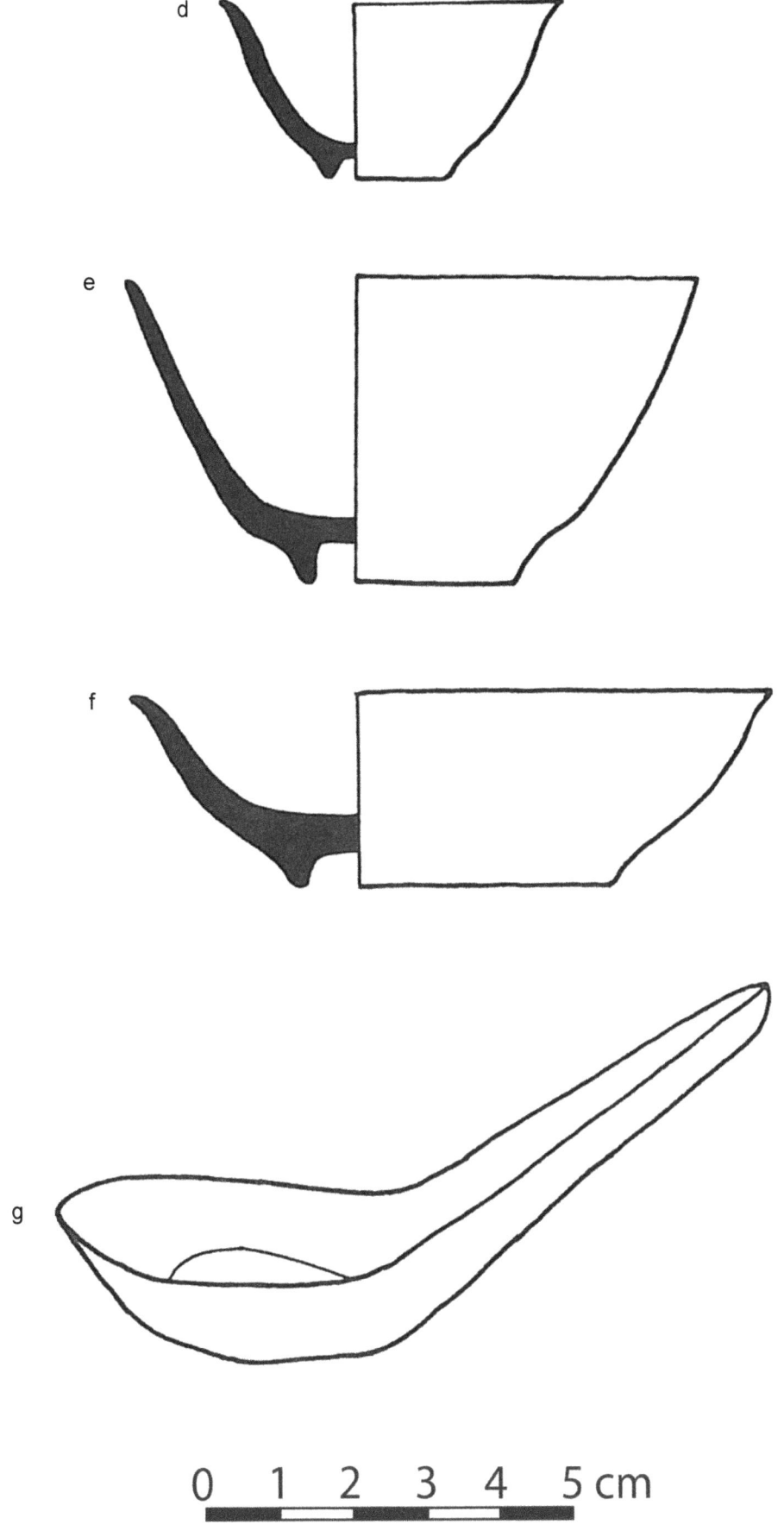

Figure 5.12. Celadon wares (*continued*). See Table 5.9 for distribution. **d.** Wine cup. **e.** Tea cup. **f.** Shallow dish. **g.** Spoon.

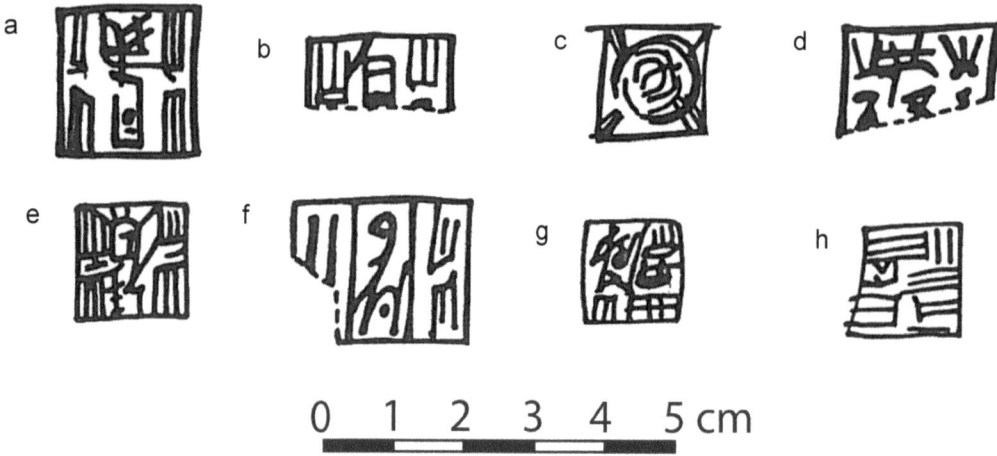

Figure 5.13. Celadon rice bowl base-marks. **a.** Ch/23 (J14 Ly.4). **b.** ACS/13 (E9 Ly.1). **c.** Ch/23 (J16 Ly.2). **d.** Ch/23 (I13 Ly.2). **e.** ACS/9 (B13 Ly.1). **f.** ACS/13 (F11 Ly.2). **g.** ACS/9 (B13 Ly.1). **h.** ACS/5 doorway, exterior.

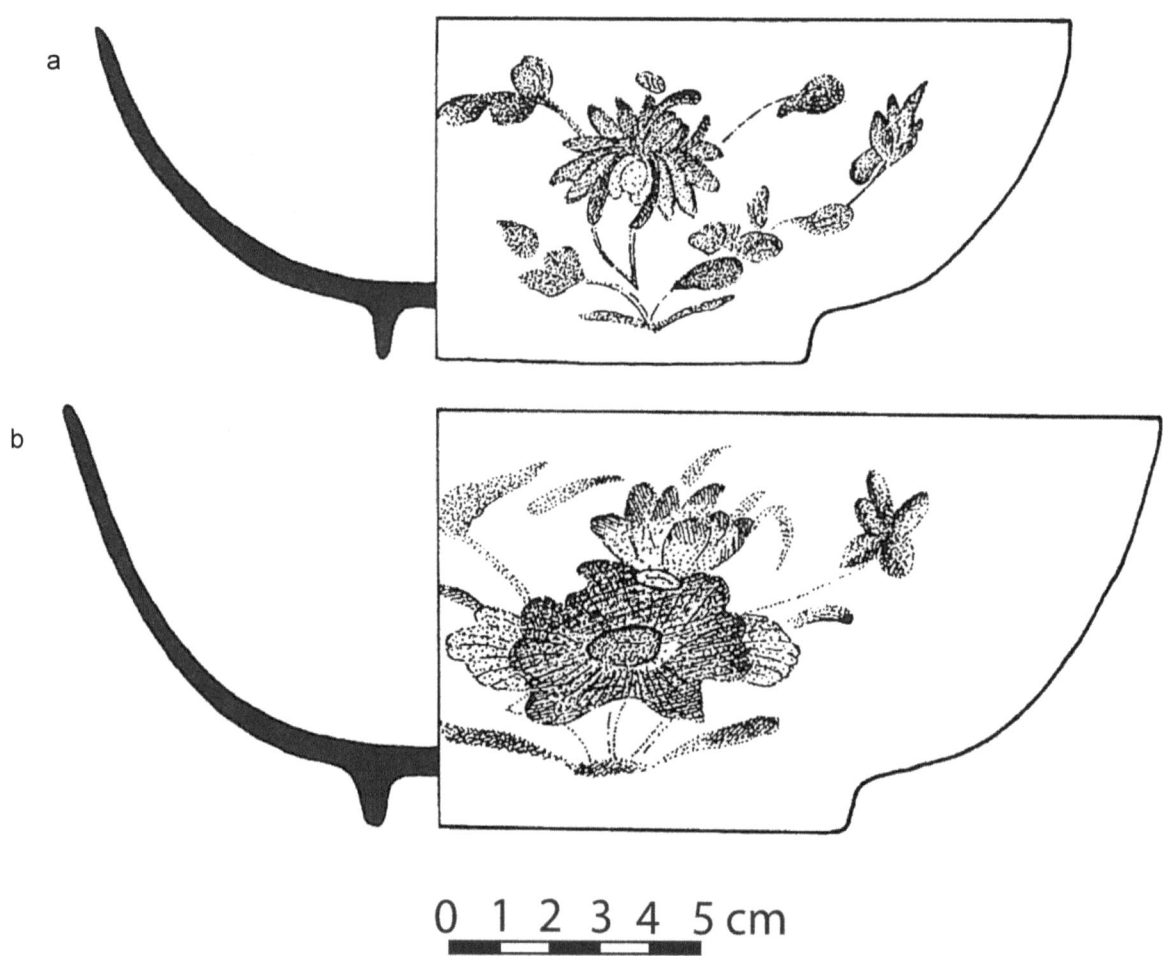

Figure 5.14. 4 Seasons wares. See Table 5.10 for distribution. **a.** Medium serving bowl. **b.** Large serving bowl.

5 The material culture of the Chinese in southern New Zealand

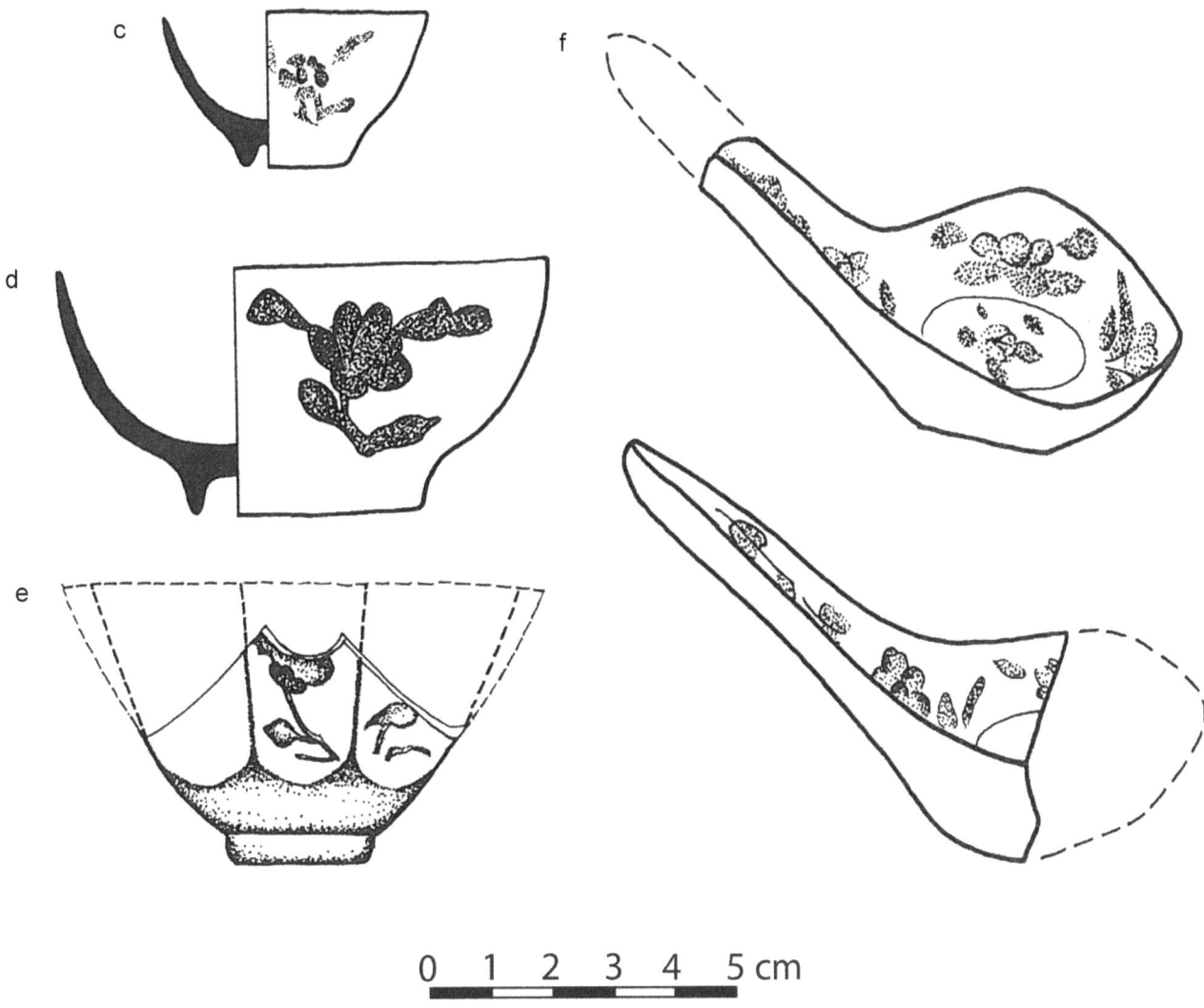

Figure 5.14. 4 Seasons wares (*continued*). See Table 5.10 for distribution. **c.** Wine cup. **d.** Tea cup. **e.** Octagonal tea cup. **f.** Two spoons.

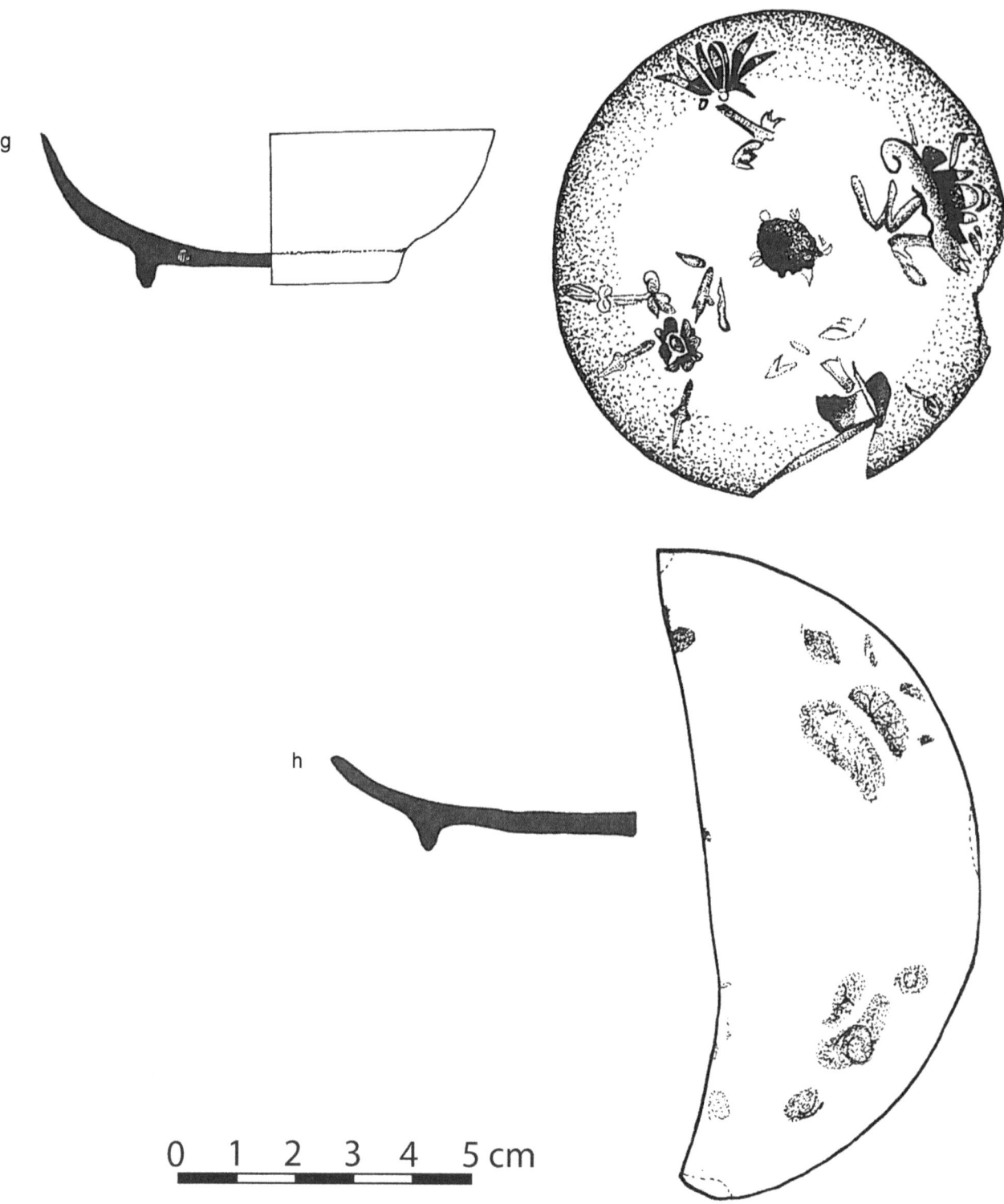

Figure 5.14. 4 Seasons wares (*continued*). See Table 5.10 for distribution. **g.** Shallow dish, plan view and section. **h.** Larger shallow dish, plan view and profile found at ACS/5 post excavation. See Section 5.2.1.3.

5 The material culture of the Chinese in southern New Zealand

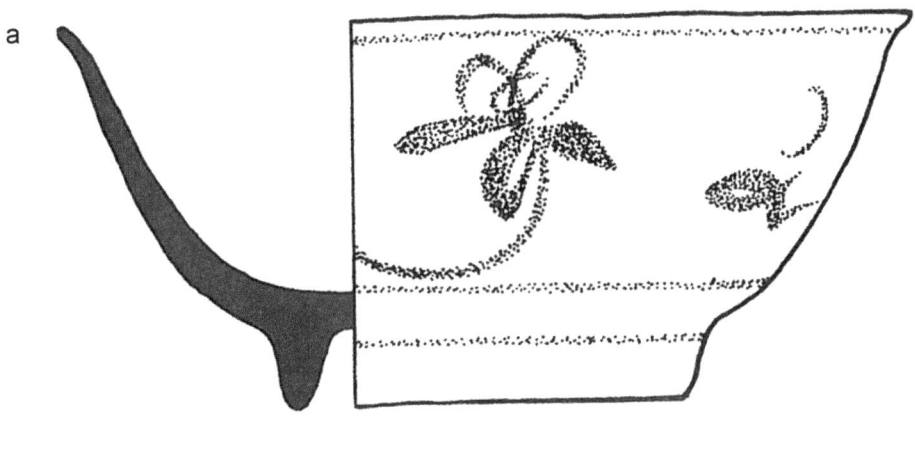

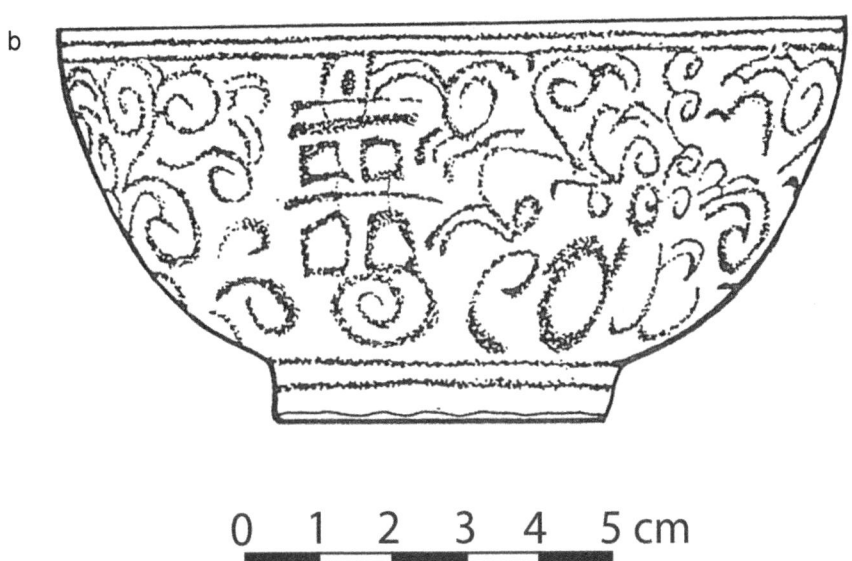

Figure 5.15. Miscellaneous rice bowls. **a.** Bamboo motif rice bowl found at upper Chinatown. **b.** Double Happiness or Swirl motif rice bowl. Drawing enlarged from an illustration in Sando and Felton (1983:8).

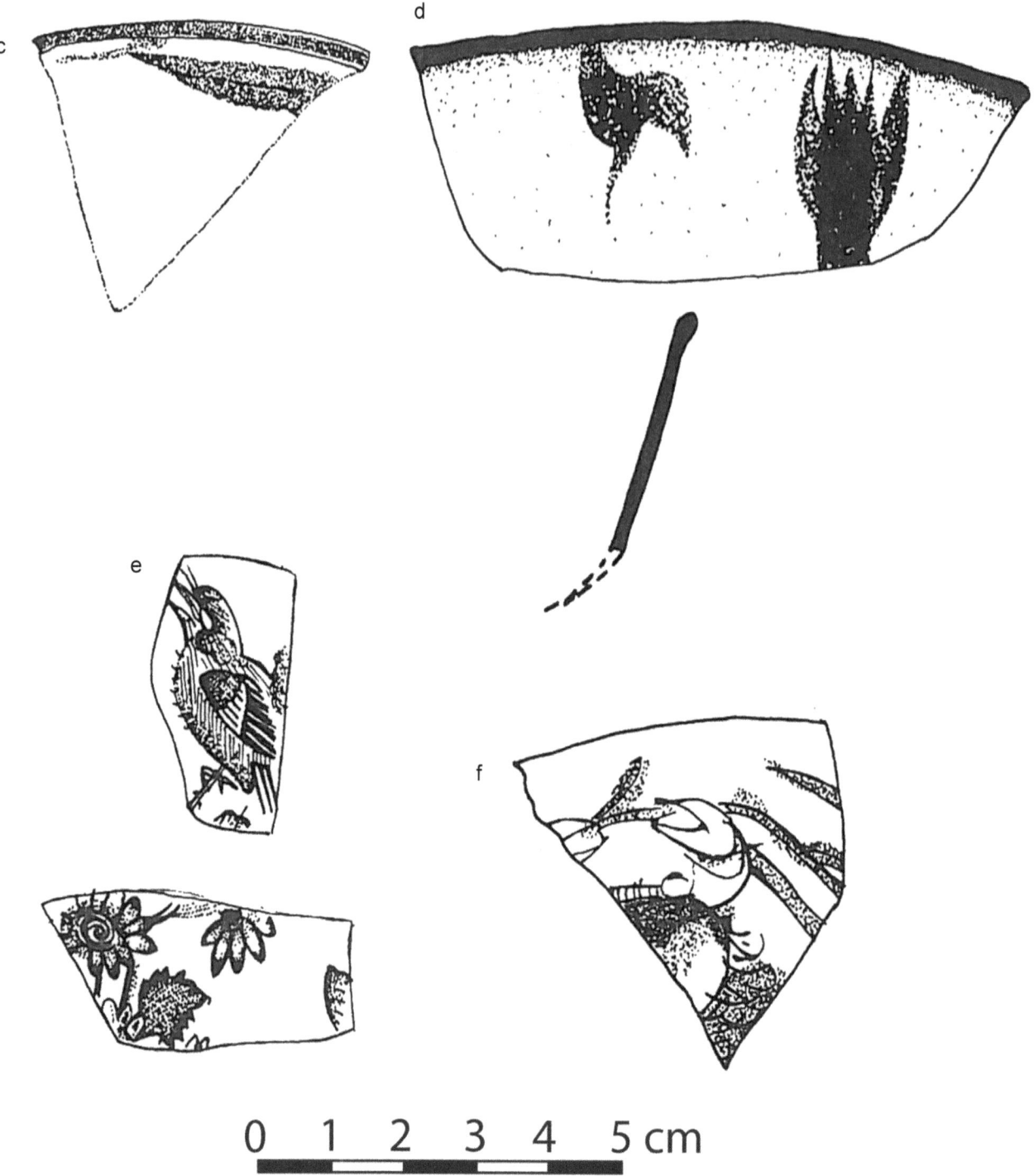

Figure 5.15. Miscellaneous rice bowls (*continued*). **c.** Brown-rimmed rice bowl with light blue body fragment. Found at Rapids site (E10 Ly.2). **d.** Brown-rimmed rice bowl with light blue body fragment and rim profile. Found at upper Chinatown, trench. **e.** Bird and flower motif rice bowl fragments found at ACS/6 (E9 Ly.2). **f.** Crab motif rice bowl fragment found at upper Chinatown surface.

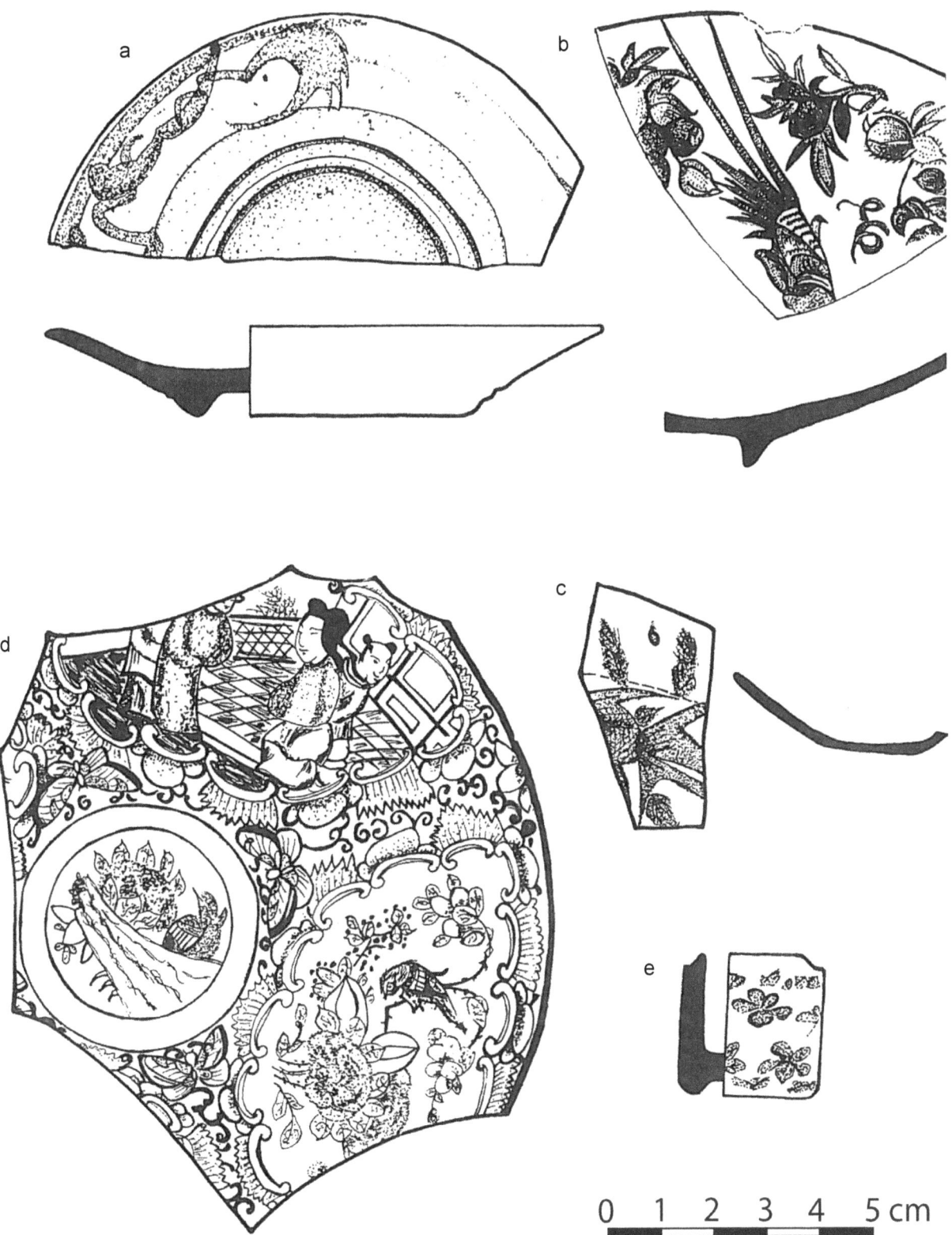

Figure 5.16. Miscellaneous Chinese tablewares. **a.** Blue on grey small dish, plan and profile view. Found at Ch/21 (P11) on wall shelf. **b.** Orange and green bird motif saucer, plan and profile view. Found at upper Chinatown. **c.** Orange and green fish motif spoon, plan and profile view. Found at Ch/15 (I16 Ly.2). **d.** Polychrome genre scene saucer found at upper Chinatown surface. **e.** Miniature floral decorated pot (4 Seasons?) found at upper Chinatown (Mangos collection).

Figure 5.16. Miscellaneous Chinese tablewares (*continued*). **f.** Base fragment of large blue on white teapot found at the Chinese camp, Big Fuchsia Creek, West Coast. **g.** Profile of Figure 5.16f. **h.** Blue on white liquor warmer and lid. No specimens known from a NZ context. The drawing is based on a photograph of a specimen in the Tucson Urban Renewal Project (TUR) collection, Arizona State Museum.

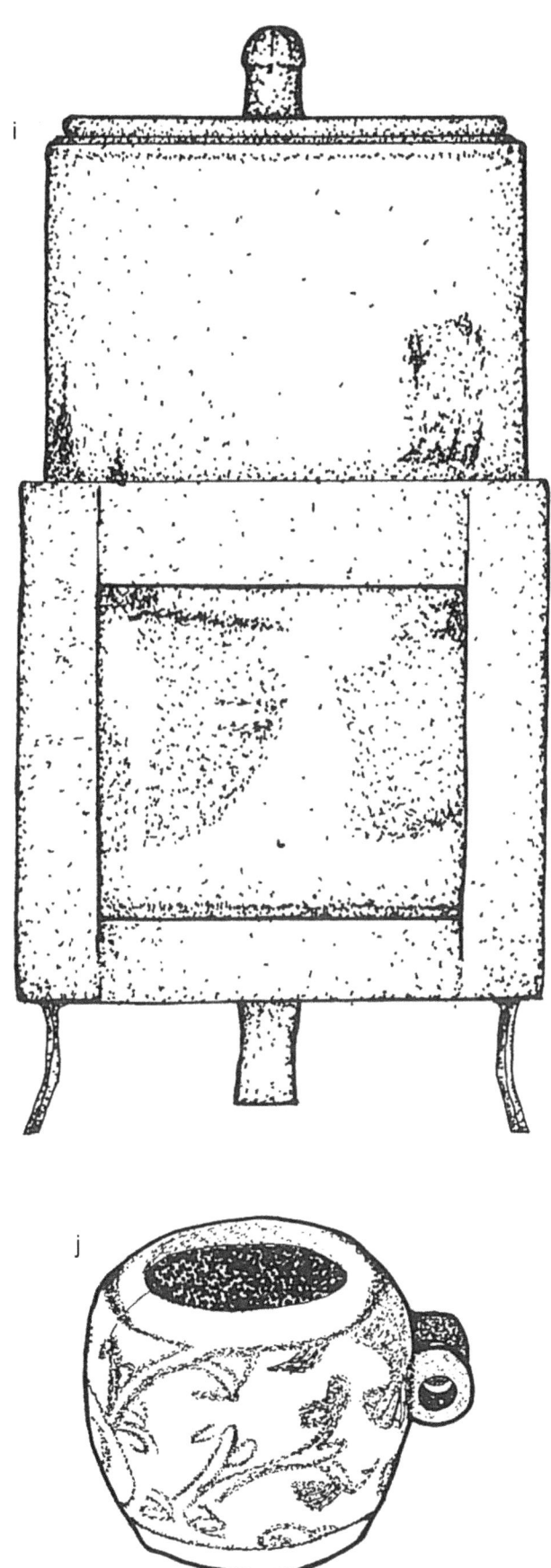

Figure 5.16. Miscellaneous Chinese tablewares (*continued*). **i.** Blue on white ginseng steamer. Drawing based on photograph of a specimen in the TUR collection, Arizona State Museum. No examples known from a NZ context. **j.** Blue on white bird feeder (see Section 5.2.1.6.4). Unprovenanced example from Cromwell Museum.

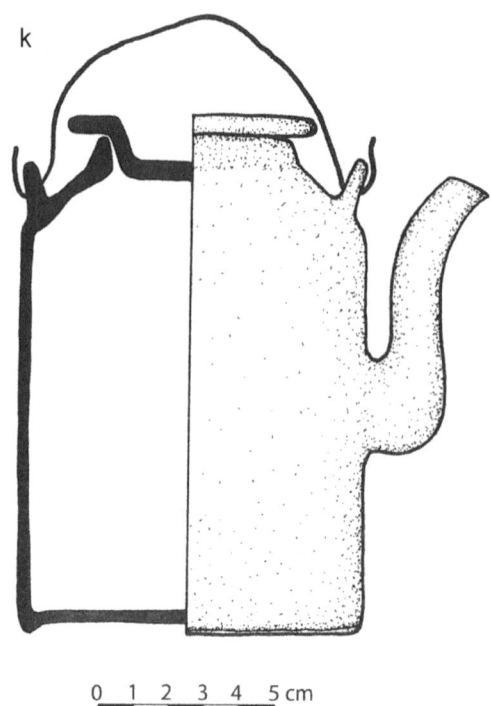

Figure 5.16. Miscellaneous Chinese tablewares (*continued*). **k.** Plain white teapot found at QB2 (C4 Ly.1).

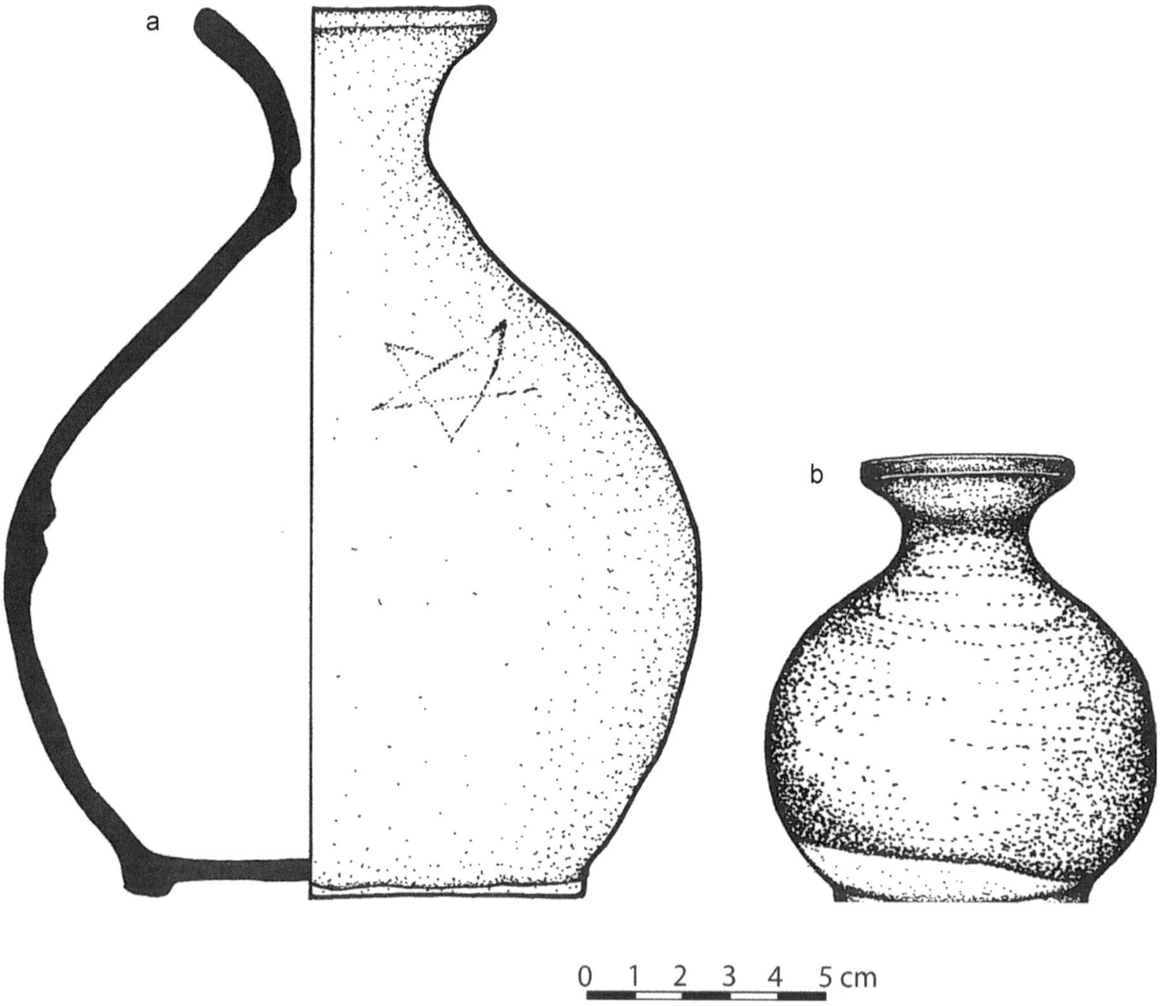

Figure 5.17. Ng Ka Py bottles. See Table 5.12 for distribution. **a.** Brown-glazed Ng Ka Py bottle found at various sites. **b.** Small Ng Ka Py bottle. Non-excavated specimen from the Redmond collection.

5 The material culture of the Chinese in southern New Zealand

Figure 5.18. Spouted pots. See Table 5.12 for distribution. **a.** Brown-glazed spouted pot found at various sites. **b.** Small brown-glazed spouted pot. Unknown provenance (Redmond collection), see Section 5.2.2.1.2. **c.** Square soy pot. None known from a NZ context. The drawing is based on a photograph of one in the *AACC Newsletter* (1984, Vol. 1(4):84–52), see Section 5.2.2.1.2. **d.** Unglazed earthenware mushroom-shaped plug found in the neck of a spouted pot of the type depicted in Figure 5.18a at Ch/12 test pit.

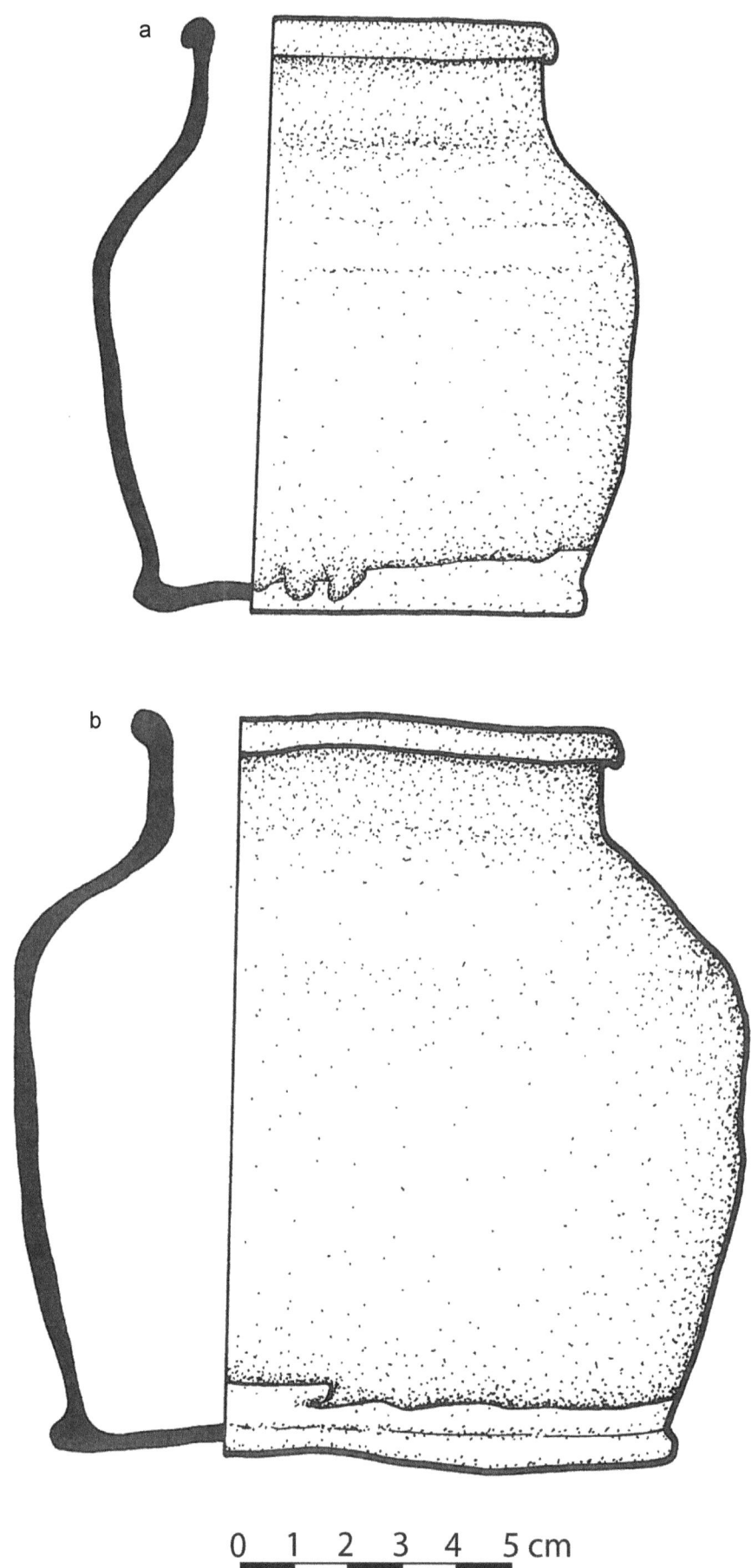

Figure 5.19. Brownware shouldered food jars. See Table 5.12 for distribution. **a.** Small size. **b.** Large size.

5 The material culture of the Chinese in southern New Zealand

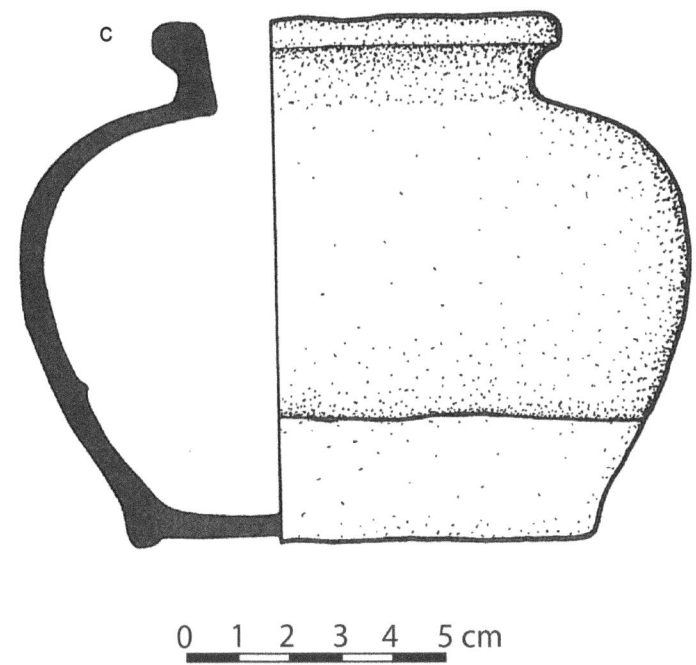

Figure 5.19c. Bulbous brown-glazed food jar, post-1920. See Table 5.12 for distribution and Section 5.2.2.1.4.

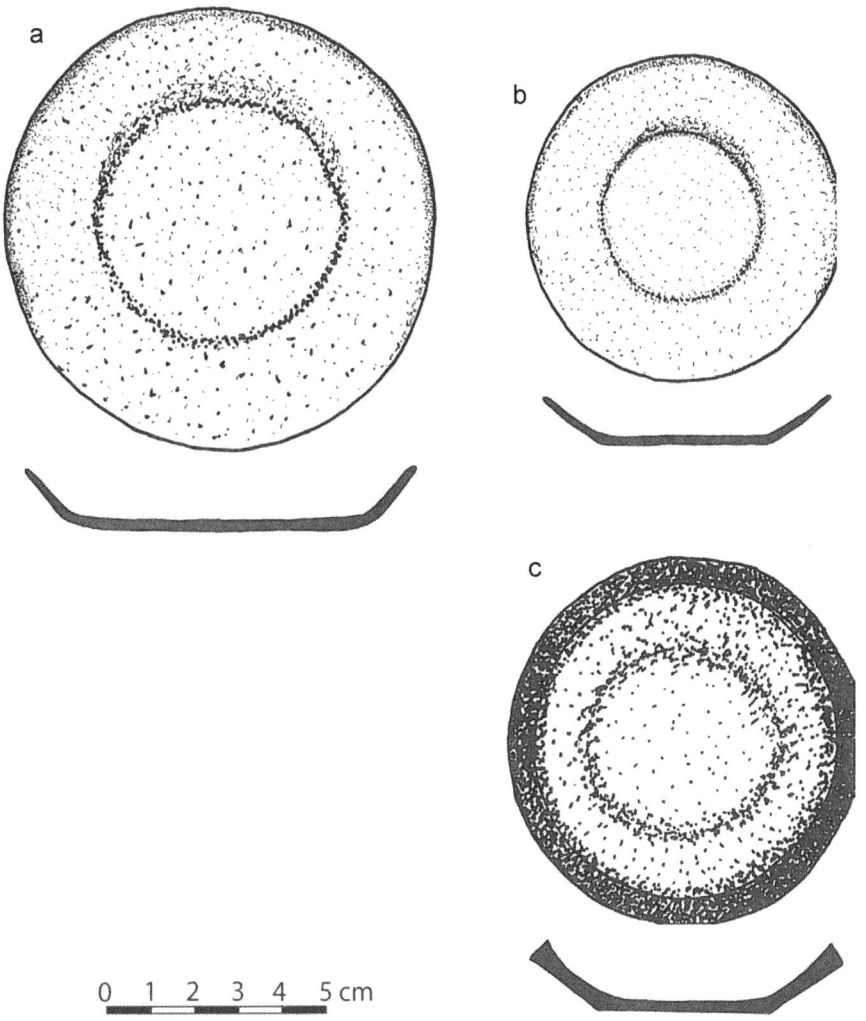

Figure 5.20. Shouldered food jar lids. See Table 5.12. for distribution and Section 5.2.2.1.3. **a.** Large, unglazed. **b.** Small, unglazed. **c.** Glazed on interior, distinct inward bevel on edges.

311

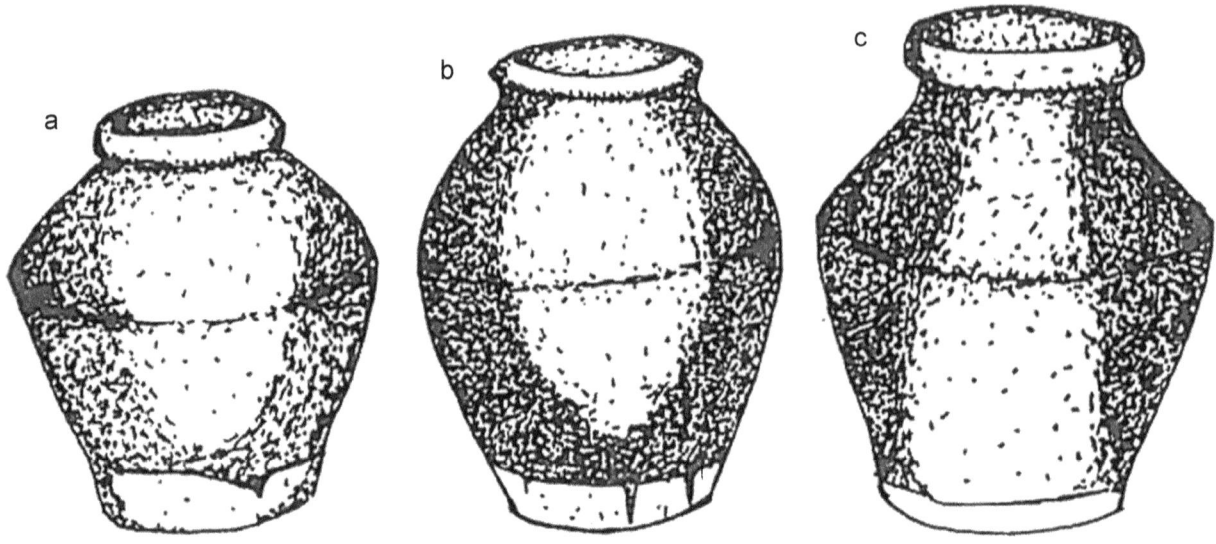

Figure. 5.21. Tall shouldered food jars. See Section 5.2.2.1.5.

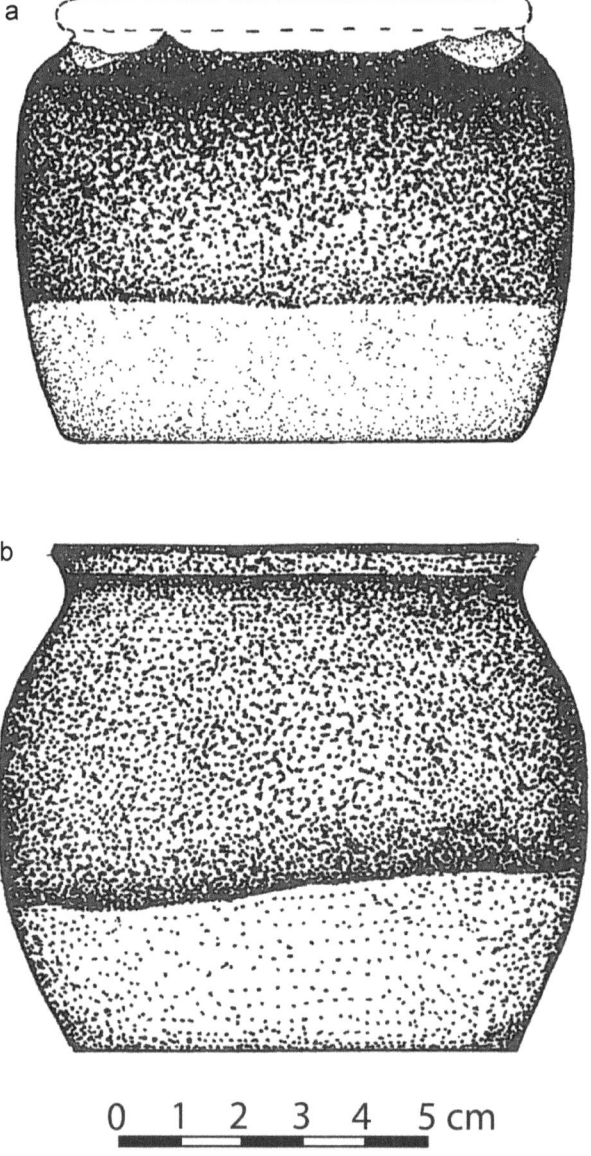

Figure 5.22. Brownware flat-rimmed food jars. **a.** Found at Ah Wee's (G8 Ly.1). **b.** Found at Ah Wee's (G8 Ly.2).

5 The material culture of the Chinese in southern New Zealand

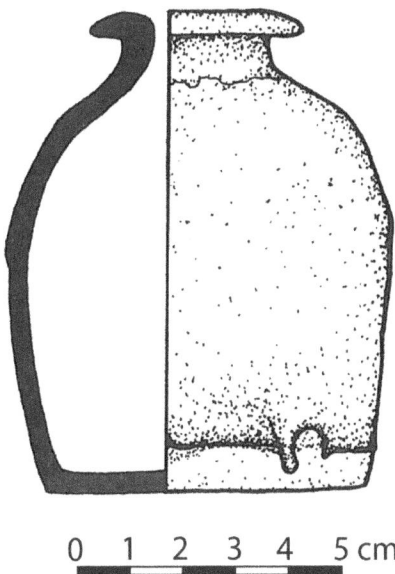

Figure 5.23. Brown-glazed jarlet (Mangos collection) found at upper Chinatown. See Table 5.12 for distribution.

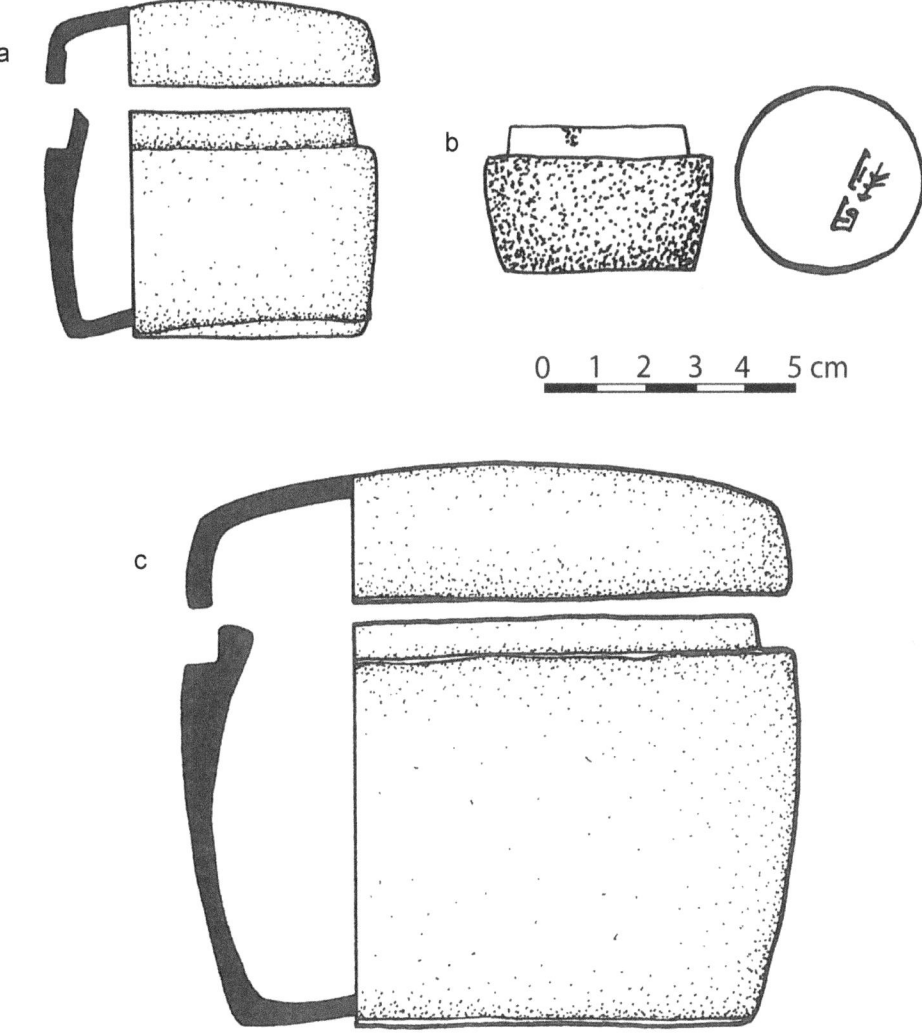

Figure 5.24. Brownware straight-sided jars and lids. See Tables 5.12 and 5.13 for distribution and sizes. **a.** Straight-sided pot and lid found at Ch/23 (J14 Ly.3). **b.** Straight-sided pot and base mark found during stump removal at ACS, August 1985. **c.** Straight-sided pot purchased in San Diego, California, 1981 (paper label reads "Tungoon Genuine Maltose – Packed in Kwangtung").

313

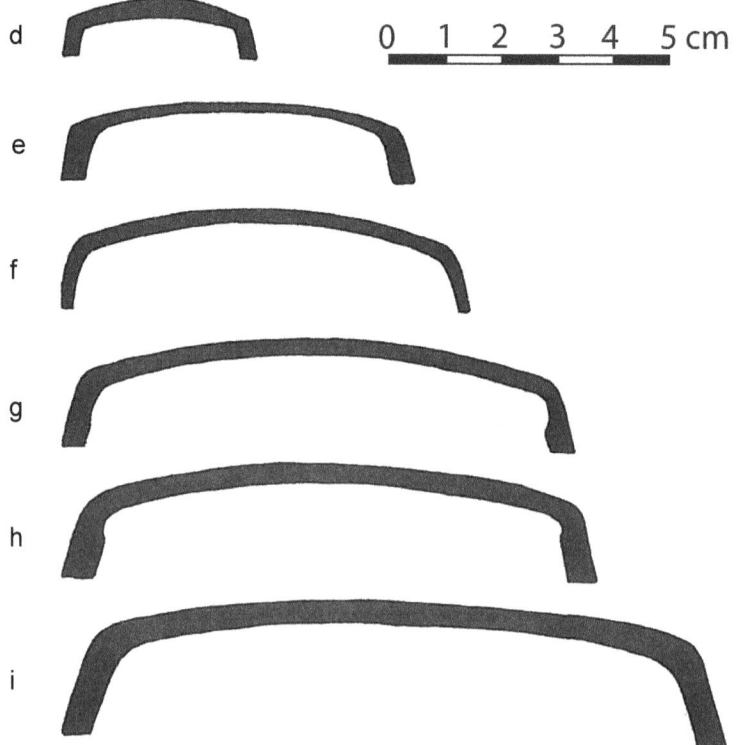

Figure 5.24. Brownware straight-sided jars and lids (*continued*). **d.** Found at Ch/26 (F14 Ly.2). **e.** Found at Ch/23 (K16 Ly.2). **f.** Found at Ch/23 (J15 Ly.3). **g.** Found at Ch/23 (J14 Ly.4). **h.** Found at Ch/21 (N11 Ly.3). **i.** Malted sugar container lid from Figure 5.24c.

Figure 5.25a. Brownware barrel jar uncovered behind Ah Lum's store (base punched out).

5 The material culture of the Chinese in southern New Zealand

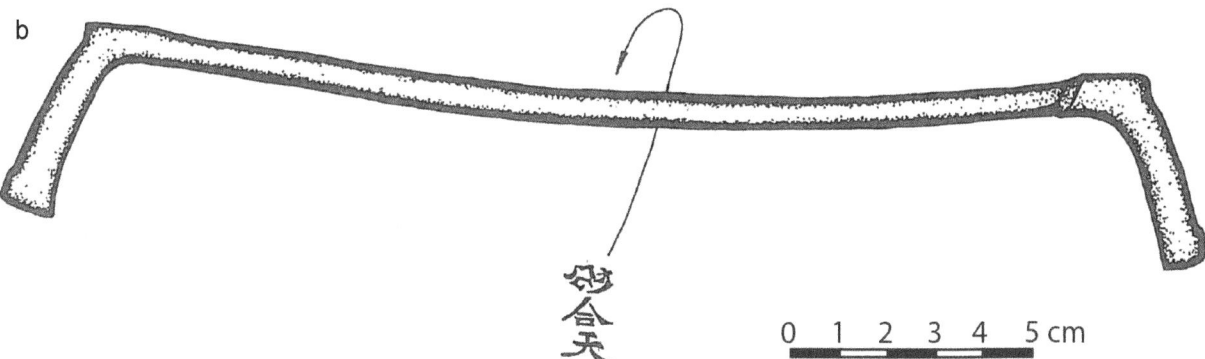

Figure 5.25b. Brown-slipped large-size barrel jar lid in profile. See Section 5.2.2.1.9. Max. dm. 36.6 cm. Max. ht. 4.8 cm. Found on Ch/34 surface pre-excavation. Untranslated characters impressed in centre of top surface.

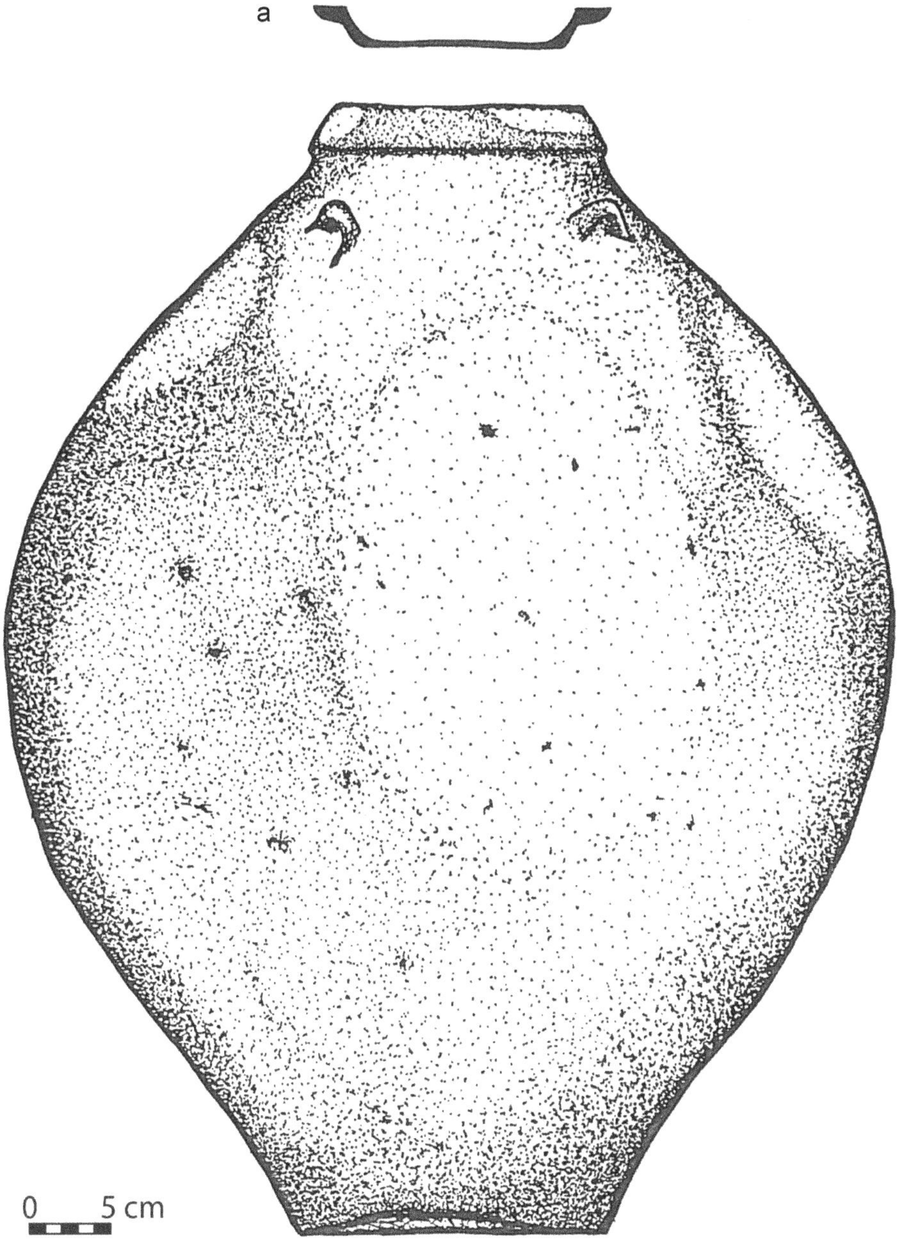

Figure 5.26. Globular jar. **a.** Unglazed earthenware lid believed to be associated with these vessels. **b.** Brown glazed globular storage jar from Chinese hut in Cardrona Valley (Dennison collection).

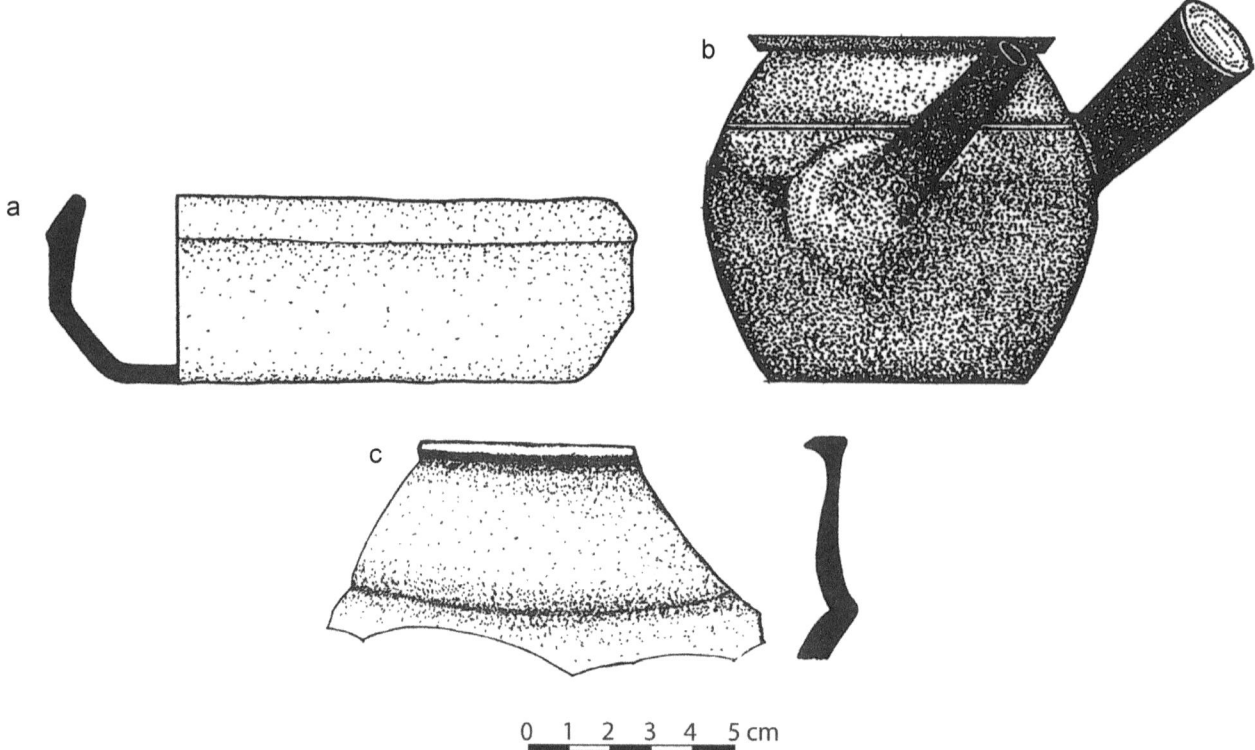

Figure 5.27. Miscellaneous Chinese ceramic cooking vessels. **a.** Brown-glazed pan. None known from a NZ context, see Section 5.2.2.6.1. **b.** Medicinal tea pot. Reproduced and enlarged from a photograph in Tomlin (1978) see Section 5.2.2.6.3. **c.** Rim fragment and profile of unglazed earthenware cooking pot found at a Chinese hut surface at Lion race, Nokomai, see Section 5.2.2.6.5.

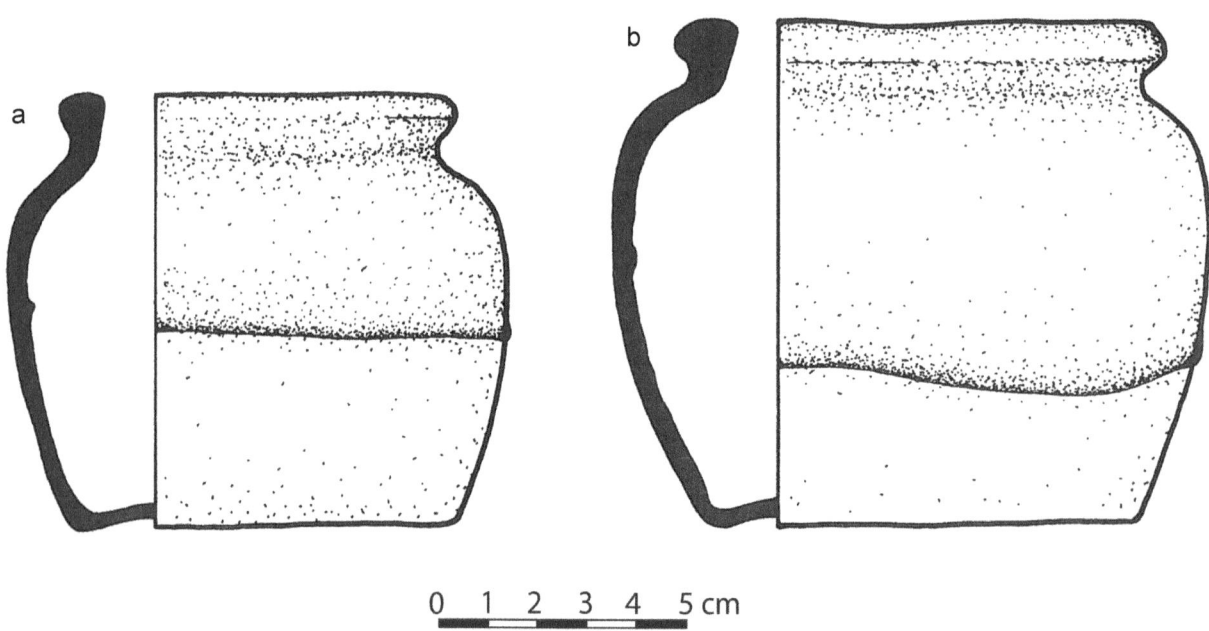

Figure 5.28. Green-glazed ginger jars. **a.** Standard size, found at various sites. **b.** Large size, limited distribution: see Table 5.14 for distribution.

5 The material culture of the Chinese in southern New Zealand

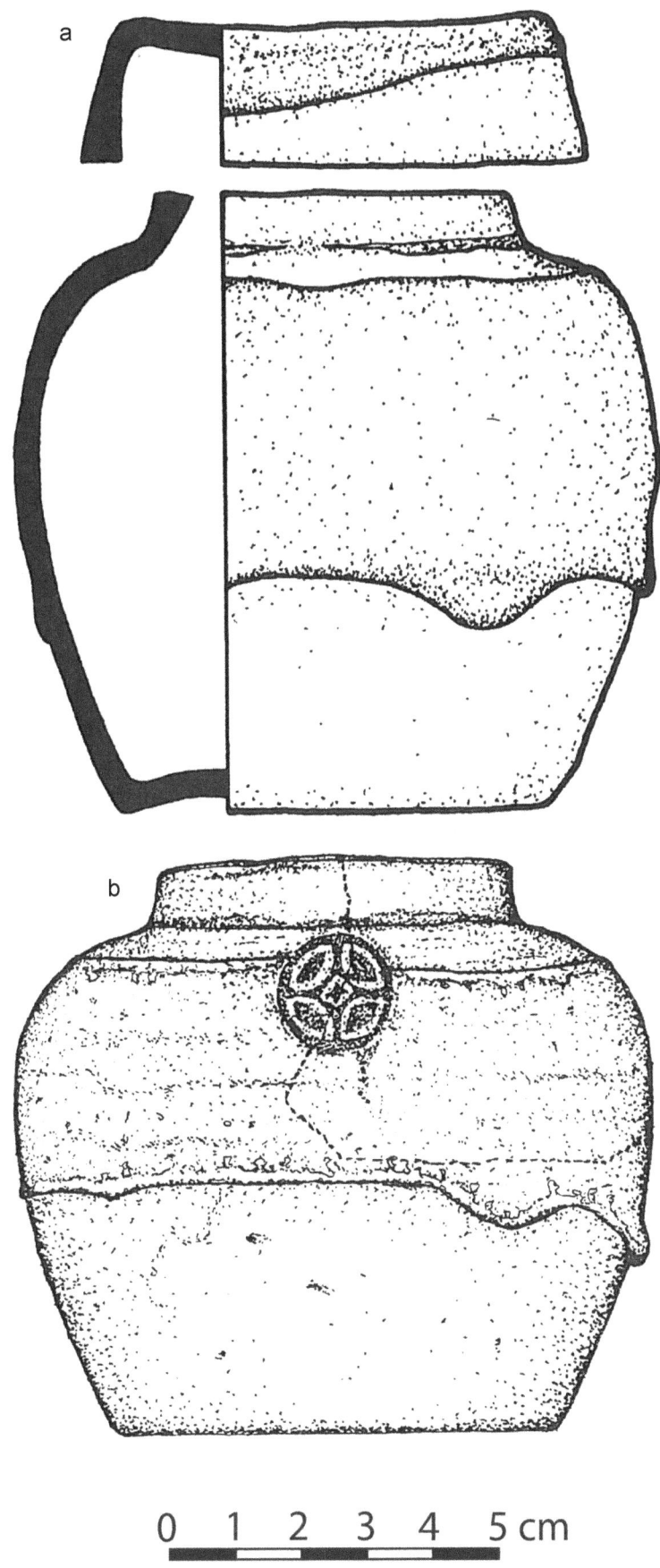

Figure 5.29. Green-glazed narrow-necked ginger jars. **a.** Narrow-necked ginger jar with flanged-lid bearing "quarters" design (see Figure 5.36b), found at upper Chinatown (Thomson collection). **b.** Narrow-necked ginger jar with embossed "quarters" design on shoulder found at Logan Park dump, Dunedin.

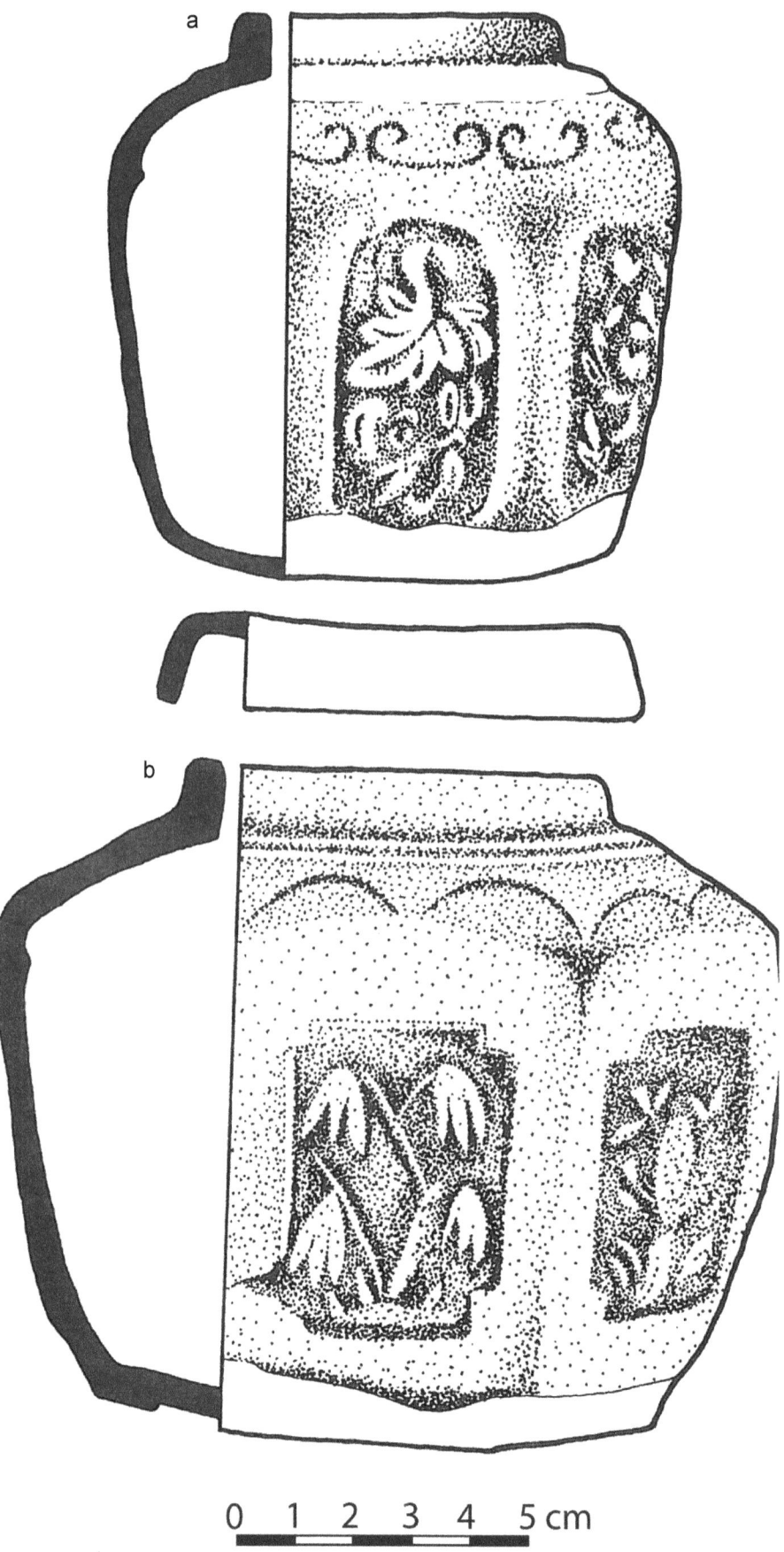

Figure 5.30. Green-glazed hexagon-sided ginger jars. See Section 5.2.2.3.3. **a.** Small size. Unprovenanced, purchased in antique shop. **b.** Large size. Unprovenanced, purchased in antique shop. These jars almost certainly postdate 1920.

5 The material culture of the Chinese in southern New Zealand

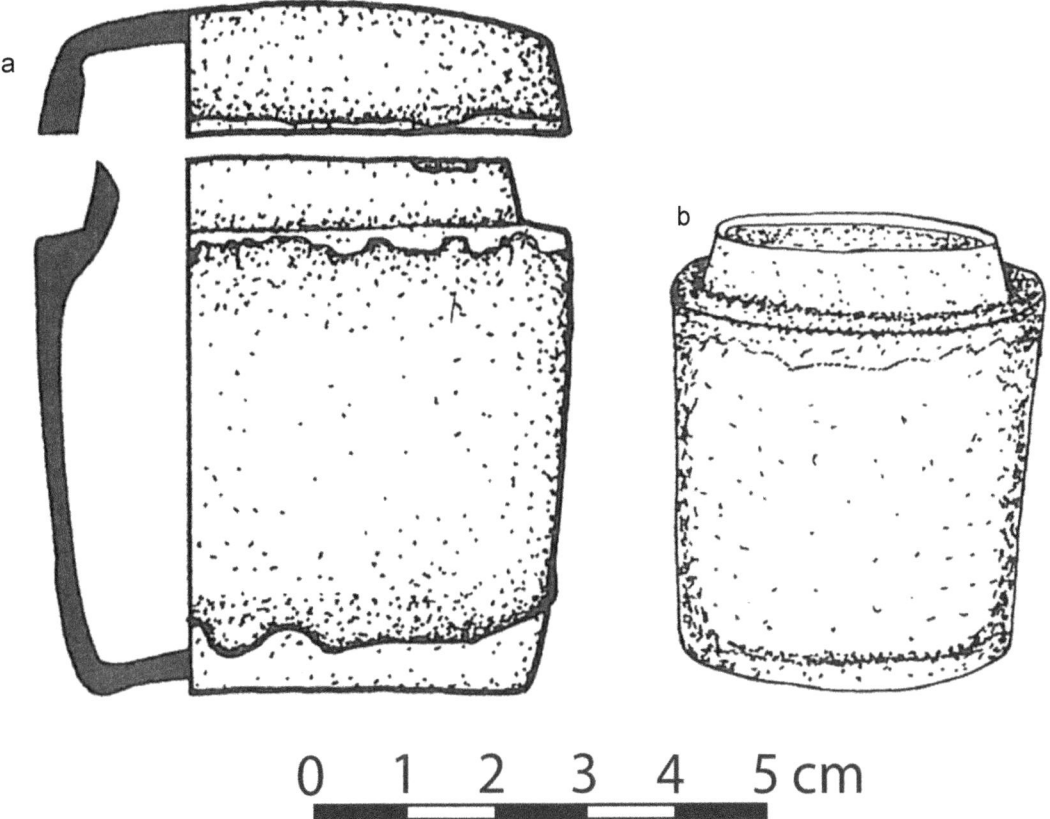

Figure 5.31. Green-glazed straight-sided pots. See Table 5.15 for dimensions. **a.** Found at upper Chinatown (Mangos collection). **b.** Found at Chinatown hut 23 (K16 Ly.2).

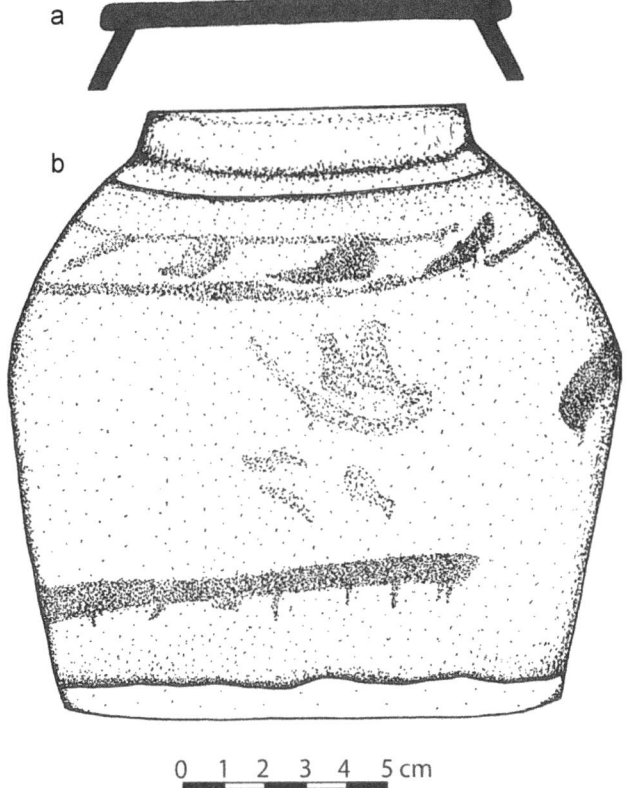

Figure 5.32. Type A blue-beige ginger jar. See Section 5.2.2.5.1. **a.** Beige-coloured flanged lid of ginger jar in profile. **b.** Jar body has smudgy blue underglaze surmounted by lustrous creamy-beige overglaze. The depicted specimen is from a Chinese camp in the Motatapu Valley (Aspinall collection).

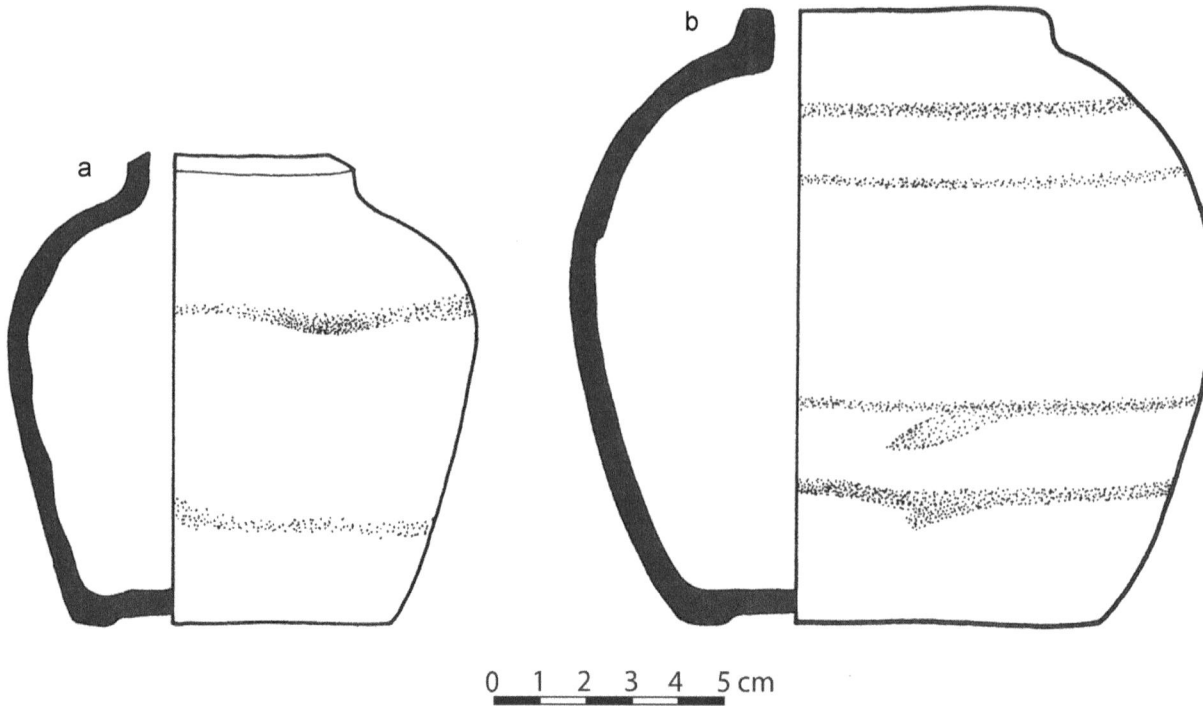

Figure 5.33. Type B blue-beige ginger jars with "muslin texture" on surface. **a.** Small size. **b.** Large size. None found in immediate study area (see Section 5.2.2.5.1.).

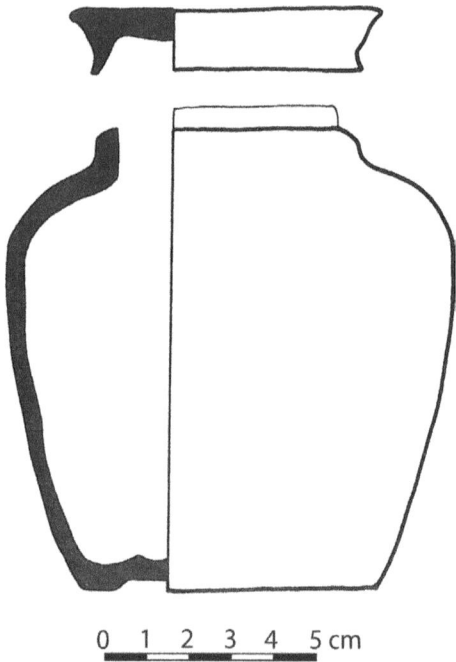

Figure 5.34. Type C blue-beige ginger jar. Jar has blue swirl underglaze with translucent clear overglaze. Donated – provenance unknown. Not known from a NZ archaeological context, but refer to the lid depicted in Figure 5.36c. Probably postdates 1920. Paper label on lid reads "Tung Fong, 'Lion Brand', Trade Mark, Finest Preserved Ginger, Made in Hong Kong". Possibly a successor to the smaller Type B ginger jar (Figure 5.33a).

5 The material culture of the Chinese in southern New Zealand

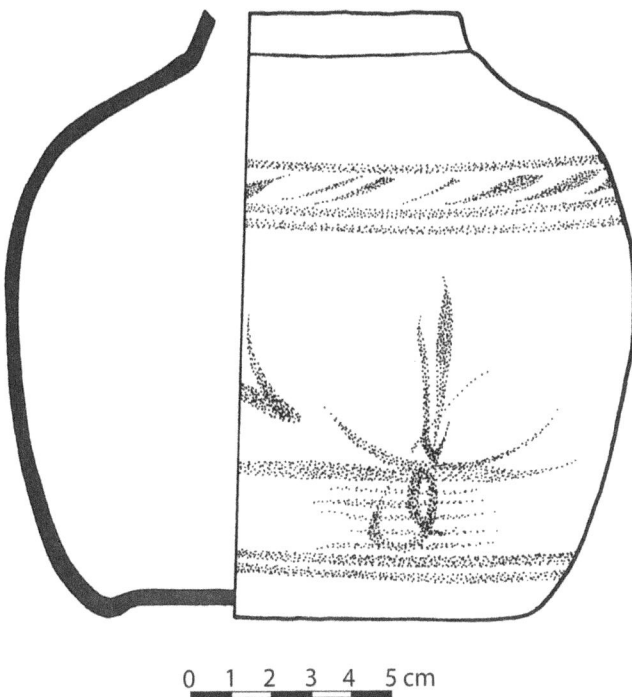

Figure 5.35. Blue-grey ginger jar with lustrous grey glaze and pictorial scenes in blue underglaze. Unprovenanced specimen purchased in a second-hand store on the West Coast (private collection).

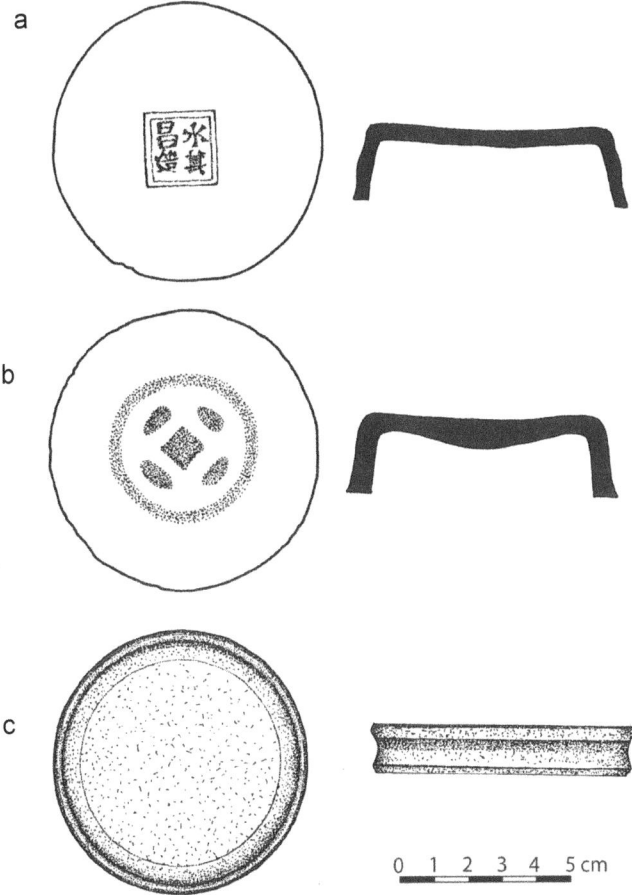

Figure 5.36. Flanged ginger jar lids. **a.** Unglazed flanged lid with impressed square containing four Chinese characters (untranslated), found in upper Chinatown (Thomson collection). **b.** Flanged lid with impressed "quarters" design and green glaze on top, found in upper Chinatown (Thomson collection). There is also an unglazed variant. **c.** Grey-glazed lid (refer to lid on specimen depicted in Figure 5.34) found at Chinatown hut 26 (N15 Ly.2).

Figure 5.37. Wing Lee Wai medicinal wine bottle. Unprovenanced specimen (Redmond collection). Almost certainly postdates 1920.

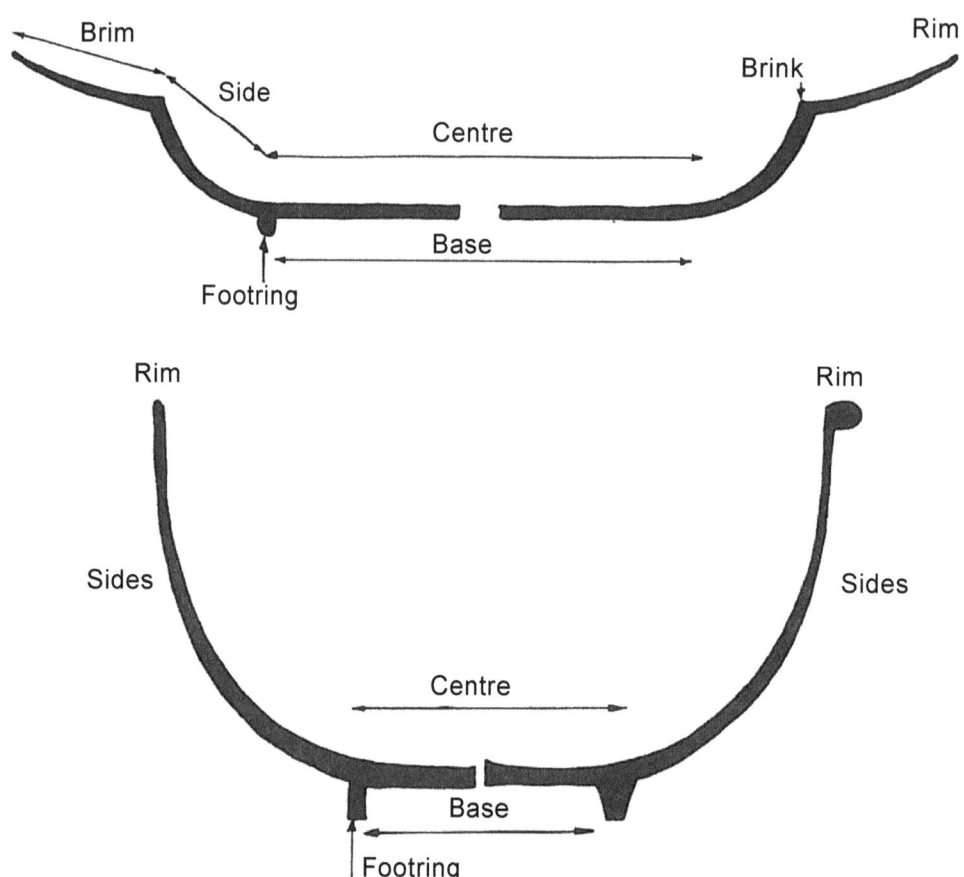

Figure 5.38. Ceramic terminology. Adapted from illustrations in Griffiths (1978:69–70).

5 The material culture of the Chinese in southern New Zealand

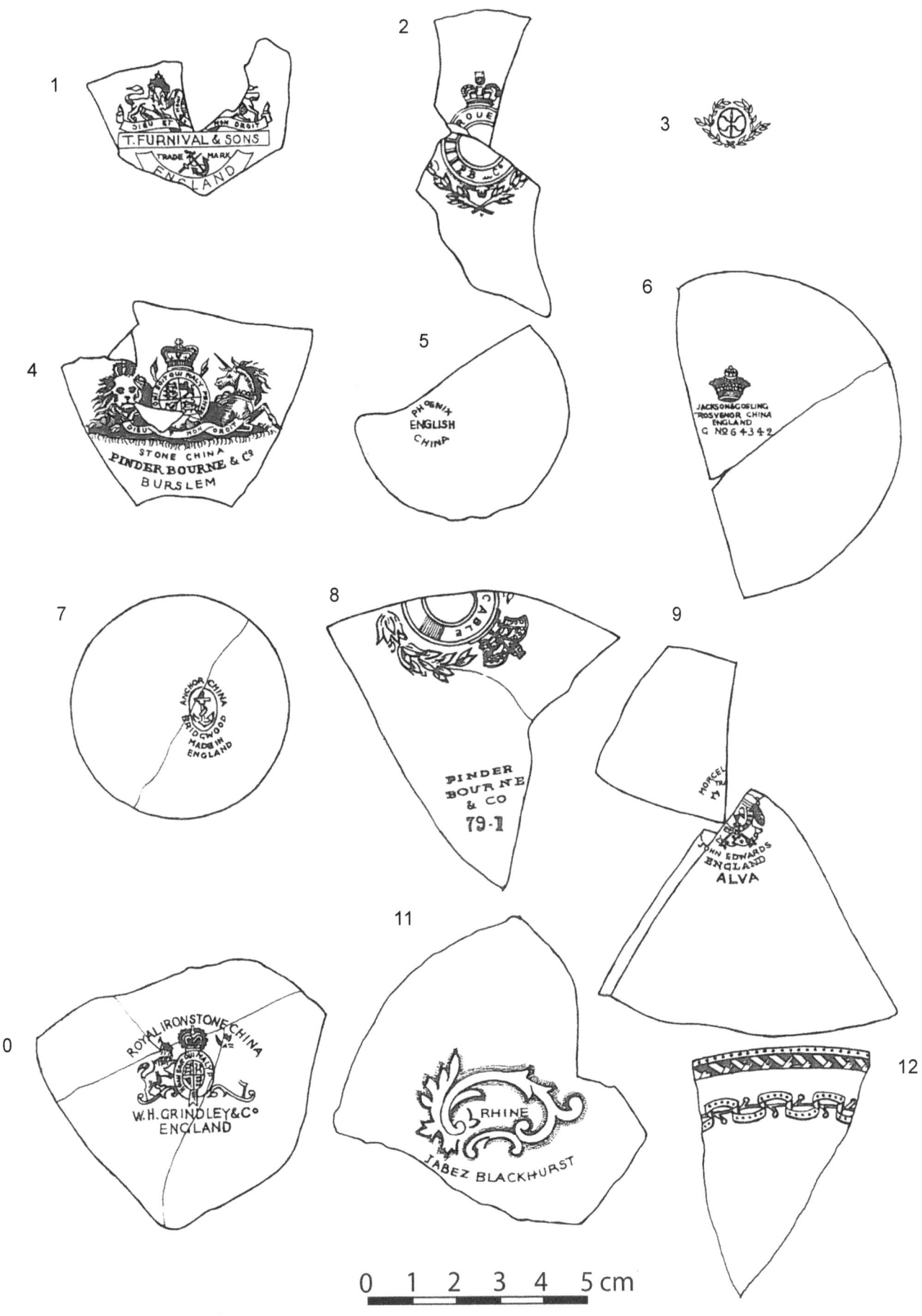

Figure 5.39. Manufacturer's marks. See Table 5.17 for details.

Figure 5.40. The common pale blue "Asiatic Pheasant" motif and base mark. This motif was used by several British manufacturers. It was also used during the latter period of the Milton Otago Potteries' operation (Lambert 1985:22).

5 The material culture of the Chinese in southern New Zealand

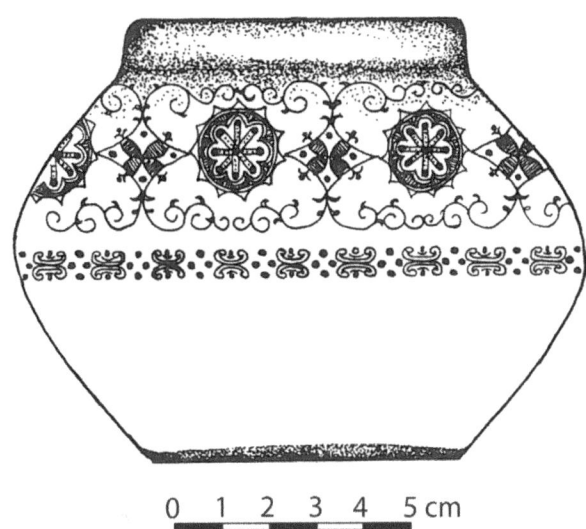

Figure 5.41. Japanese teapot with coralene beading found at ACS/2 (E11). Reconstructed from fragments, the spout and handle portions are missing.

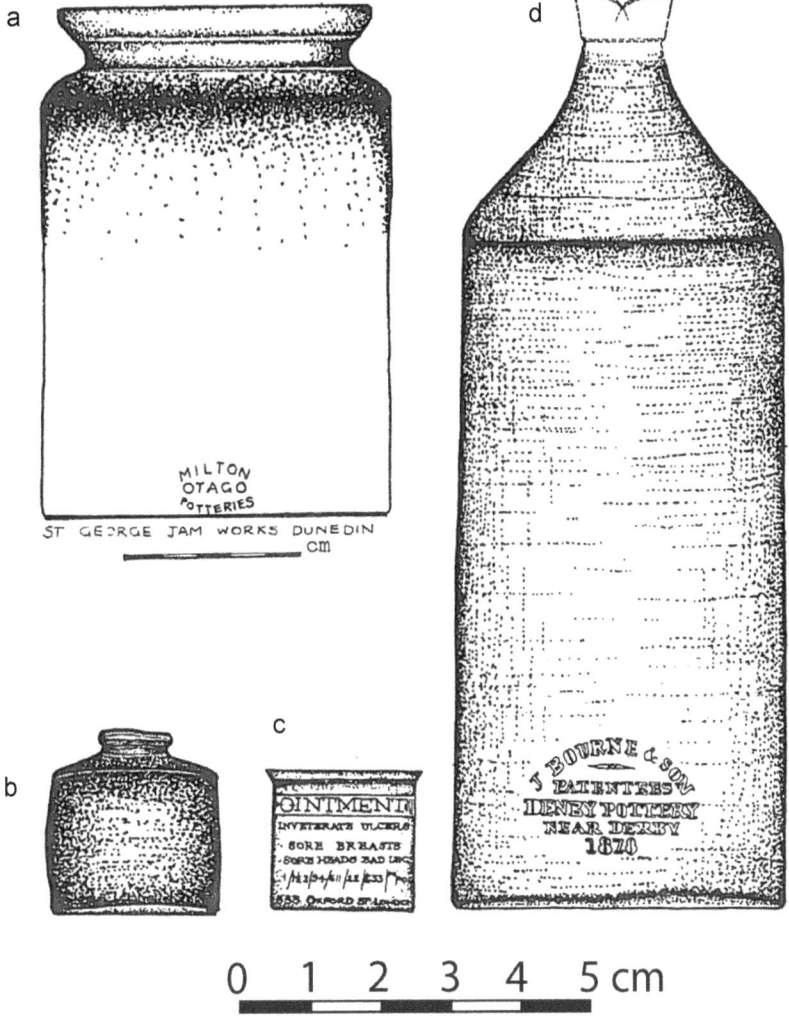

Figure 5.42. Euro-ceramic containers. See Table 5.17. **a.** Earthenware jam jar with cream glaze, "Milton Otago Potteries" impressed on one side. The other side is impressed "St George Jam Works, Dunedin". Date: 1900–15. Found at ACS/5 (P13 Ly.2). **b.** Penny ink bottle found at ACS/6 (K13 Ly.2). **c.** "Holloway's Ointment" pot. Date: post-1867. Found at QB2 (C5 Ly.1). **d.** Light brown-slipped stoneware ink bottle. Impressed "J Bourne & Sons, Patentees, Denby Pottery near Derby, 1878". Found at ACS/2 (F12 Ly.2).

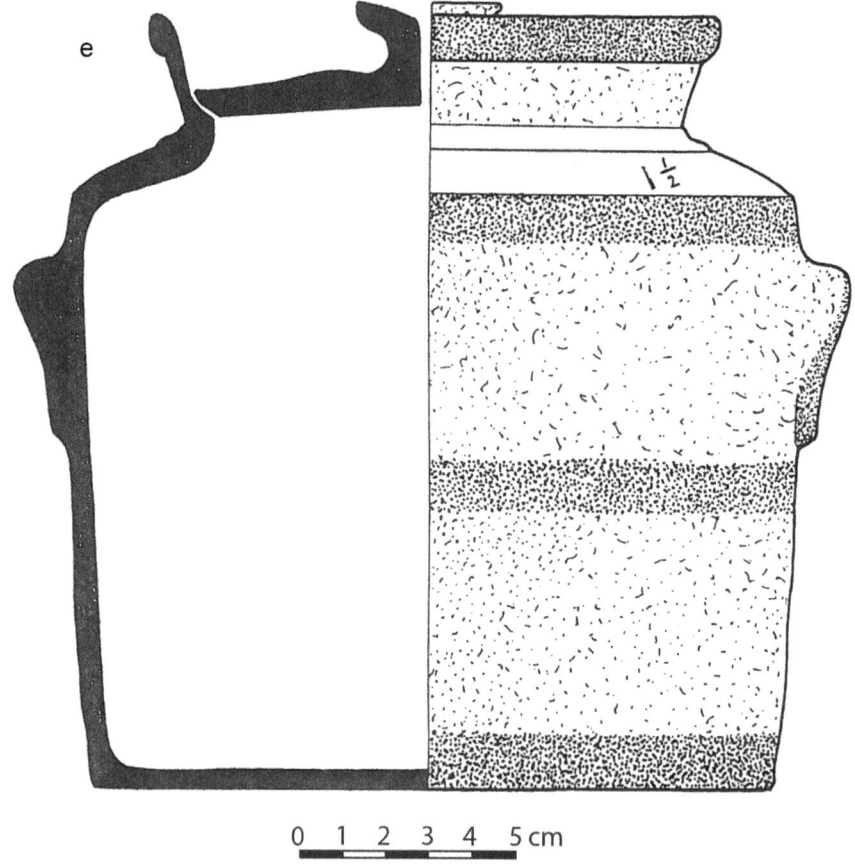

Figure 5.42e. Bristol-glazed crock found at Ch/26 (C3 Ly.2). This crock appears to be virtually identical to a type made by P. Hutson & Co., Newtown, Wellington (No. 14), depicted in a photograph in Lambert (1985:82).

5 The material culture of the Chinese in southern New Zealand

Figure 5.43. Can types. See Table 5.27 for distribution. **a.** "Hole-and-cap" can (note soldered seams). **b.** "Sanitary" can (also known as open-top or "packers" can). **c.** Sardine can. **d.** Oval fish can. **e.** Tapered meat can. **f.** Rectangular hole-and-cap meat can. **g.** Squat cylindrical hole-and-cap meat can. **h.** Key-opening meat can. **i.** Rectangular flanged-lid can.

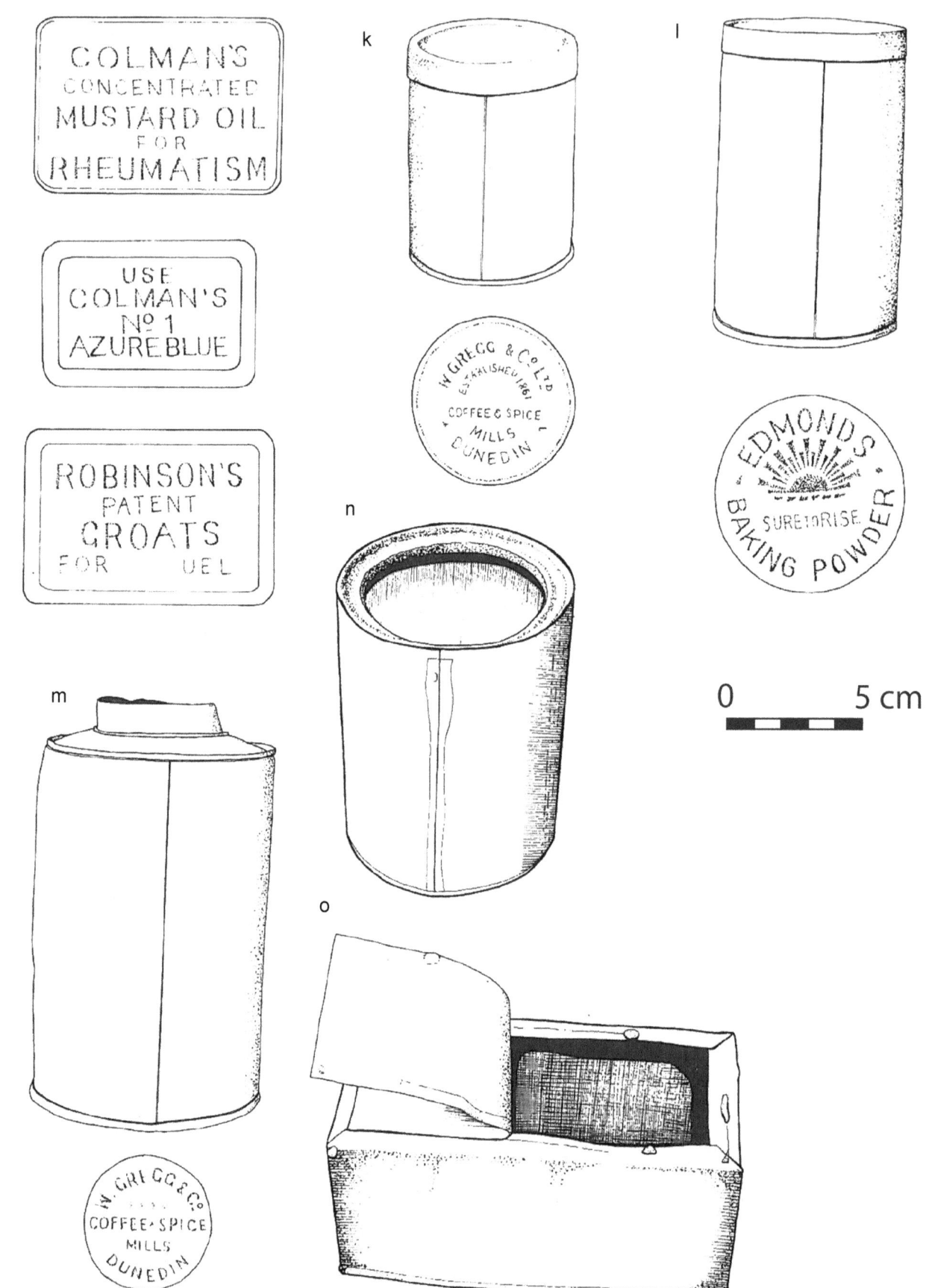

Figure 5.43. Can types (*continued*). See Table 5.27 for distribution. **j.** Embossed lids from rectangular flanged-lid cans. **k.** Circular flanged-lid spice tin with embossed lid. **l.** Circular flanged-lid can with embossed lid. **m.** Circular flanged-lid can with "Club Coffee" embossed on base (not shown). **n.** Lever-lid or press-top can. **o.** Soldered-top box.

5 The material culture of the Chinese in southern New Zealand

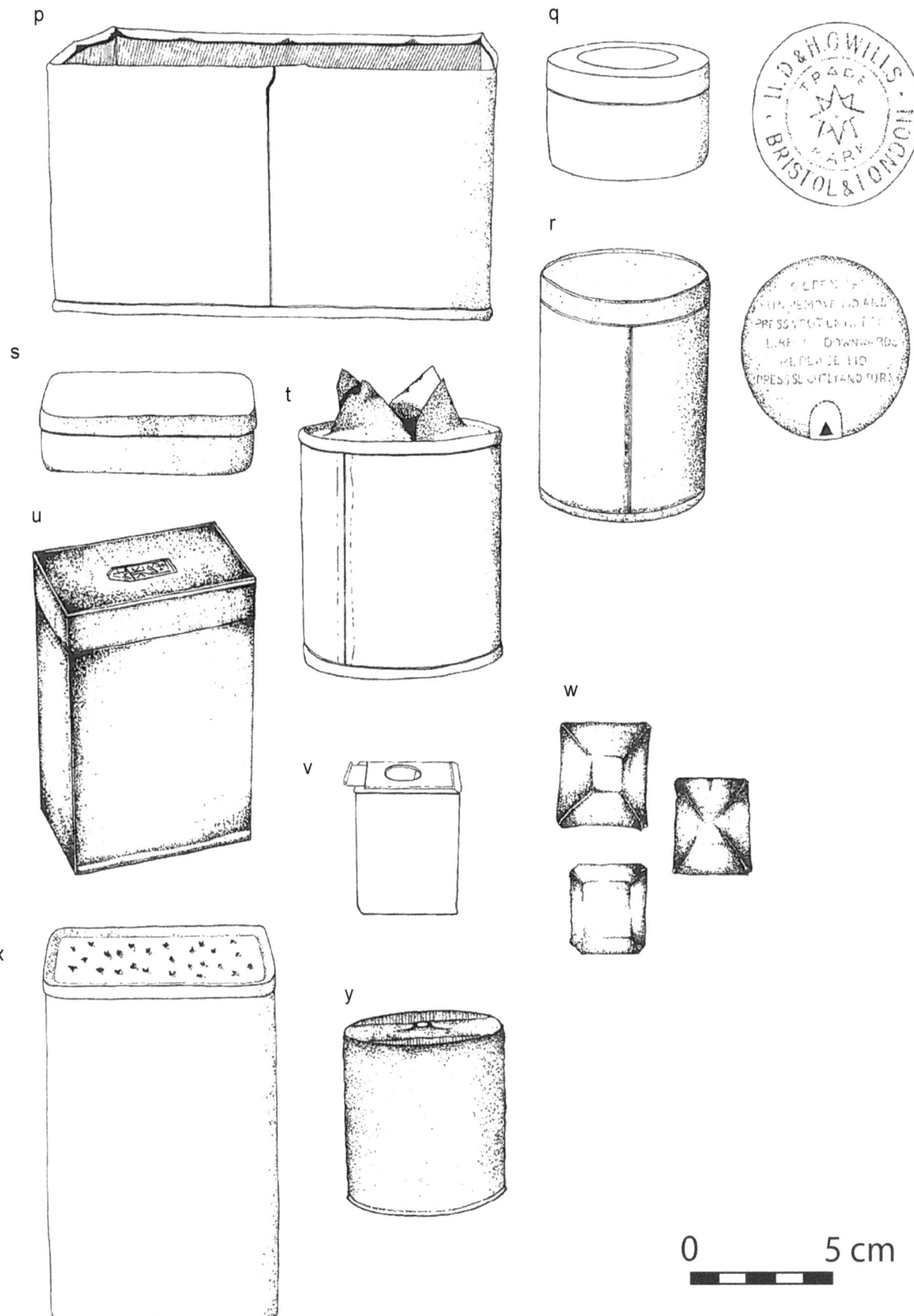

Figure 5.43. Can types (*continued*). See Table 5.27 for distribution. **p.** Tea box. **q.** Circular flanged-lid tobacco tin with embossed lid. **r.** Slip-lid cigarette tin with cutter. **s.** Pocket tobacco tin. **t.** Condensed milk can showing common method of opening. **u.** Brass opium can. **v.** Opium antidote(?) can.
w. "Funs trays" made from opium can metal. **x.** Rectangular flanged-lid can with perforated base.
y. Jam tin modified into opium lamp base.

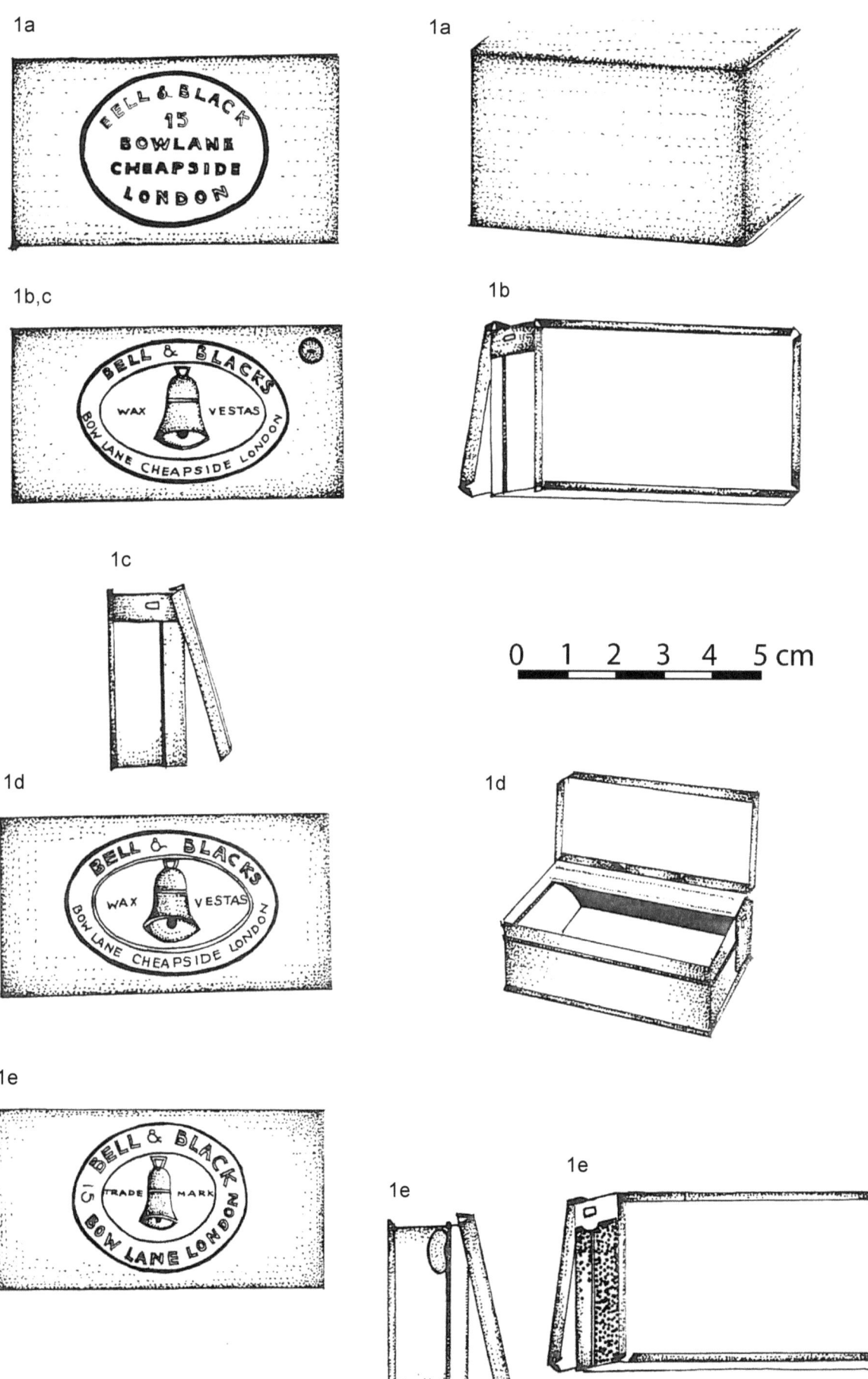

Figure 5.44. Wax vesta boxes. Reproduced from Bedford (1985a). See Table 5.30 for distribution.

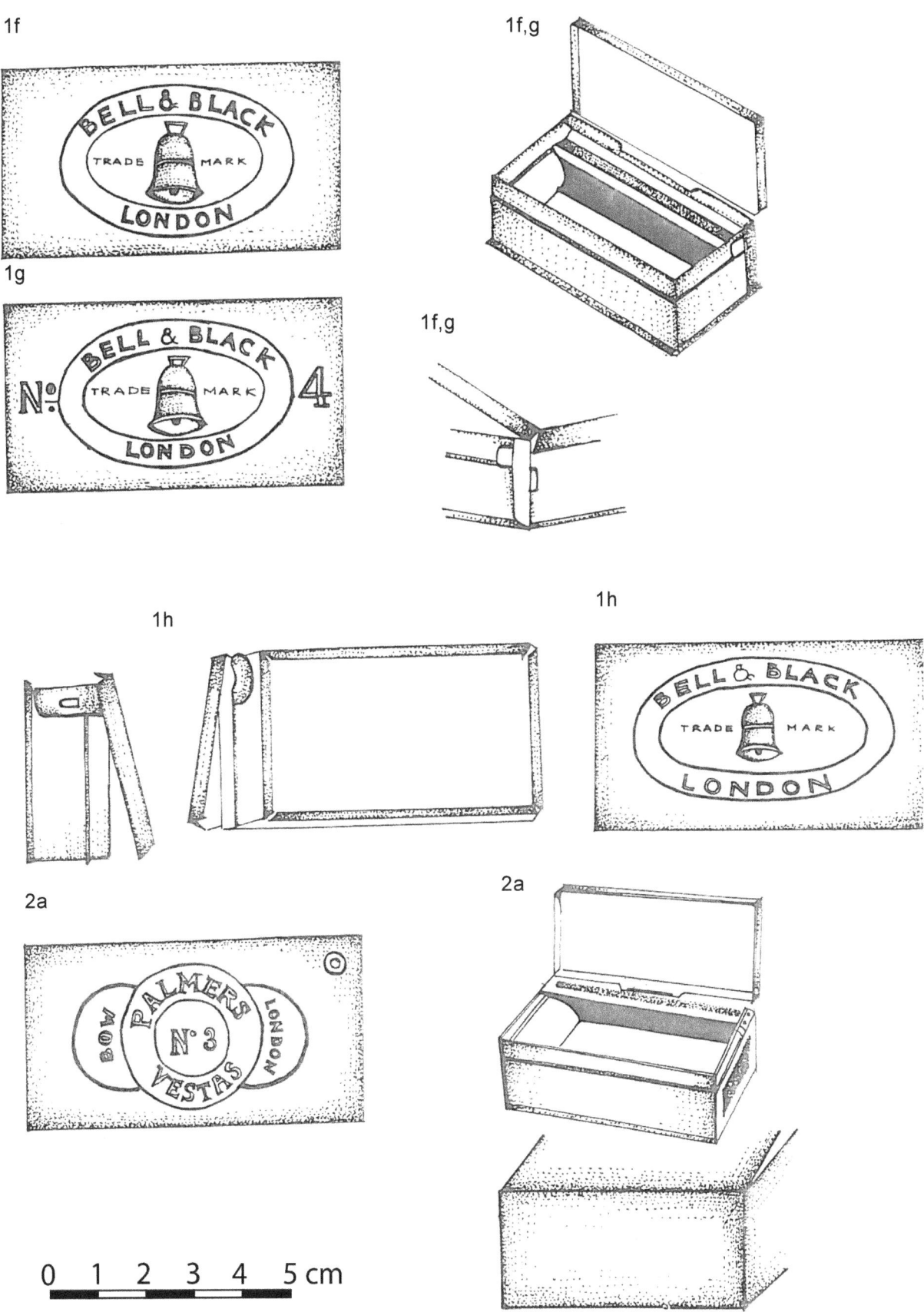

Figure 5.44. Wax vesta boxes (*continued*). Reproduced from Bedford (1985a). See Table 5.30 for distribution.

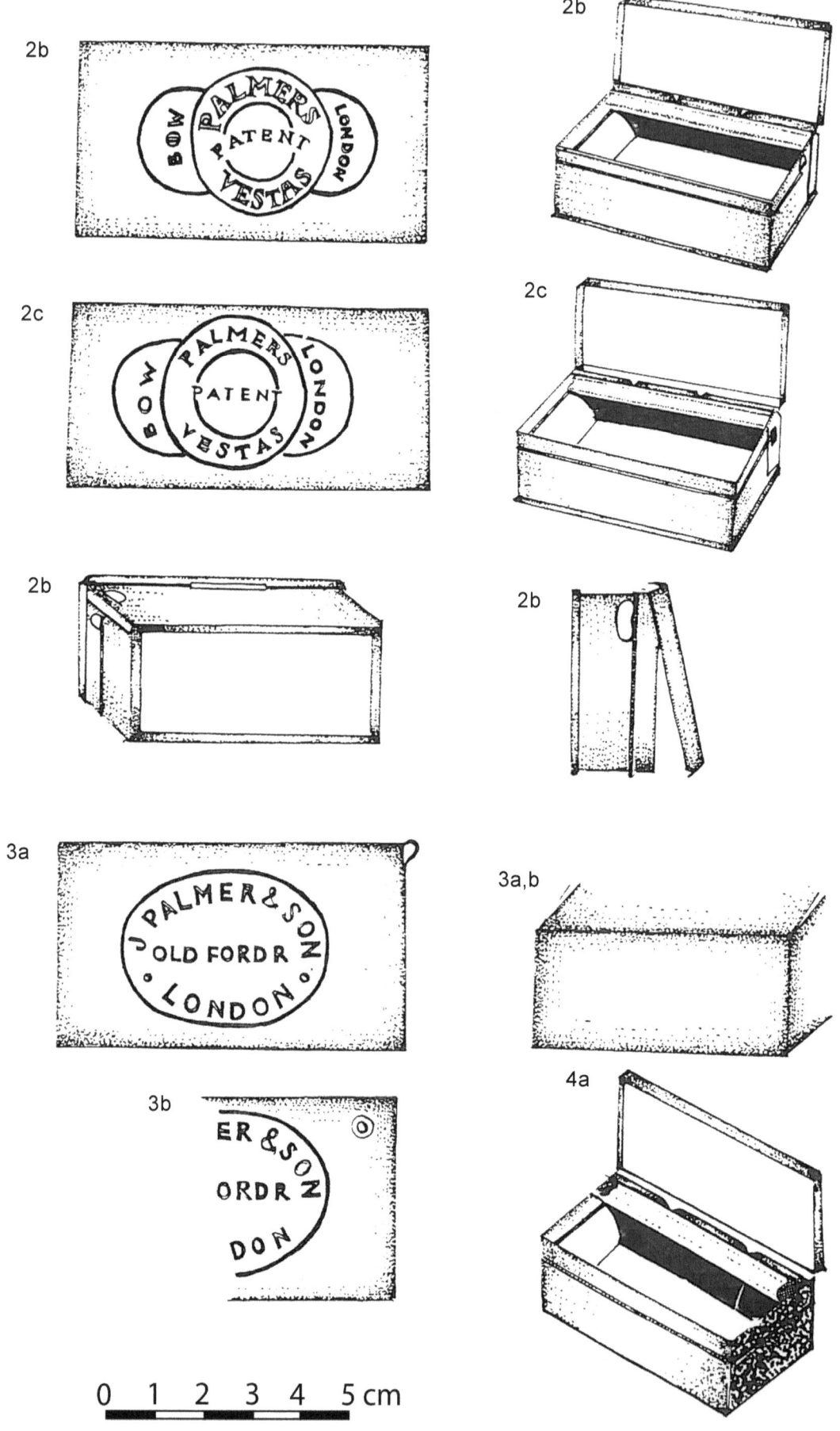

Figure 5.44. Wax vesta boxes (*continued*). Reproduced from Bedford (1985a). See Table 5.30 for distribution.

5 The material culture of the Chinese in southern New Zealand

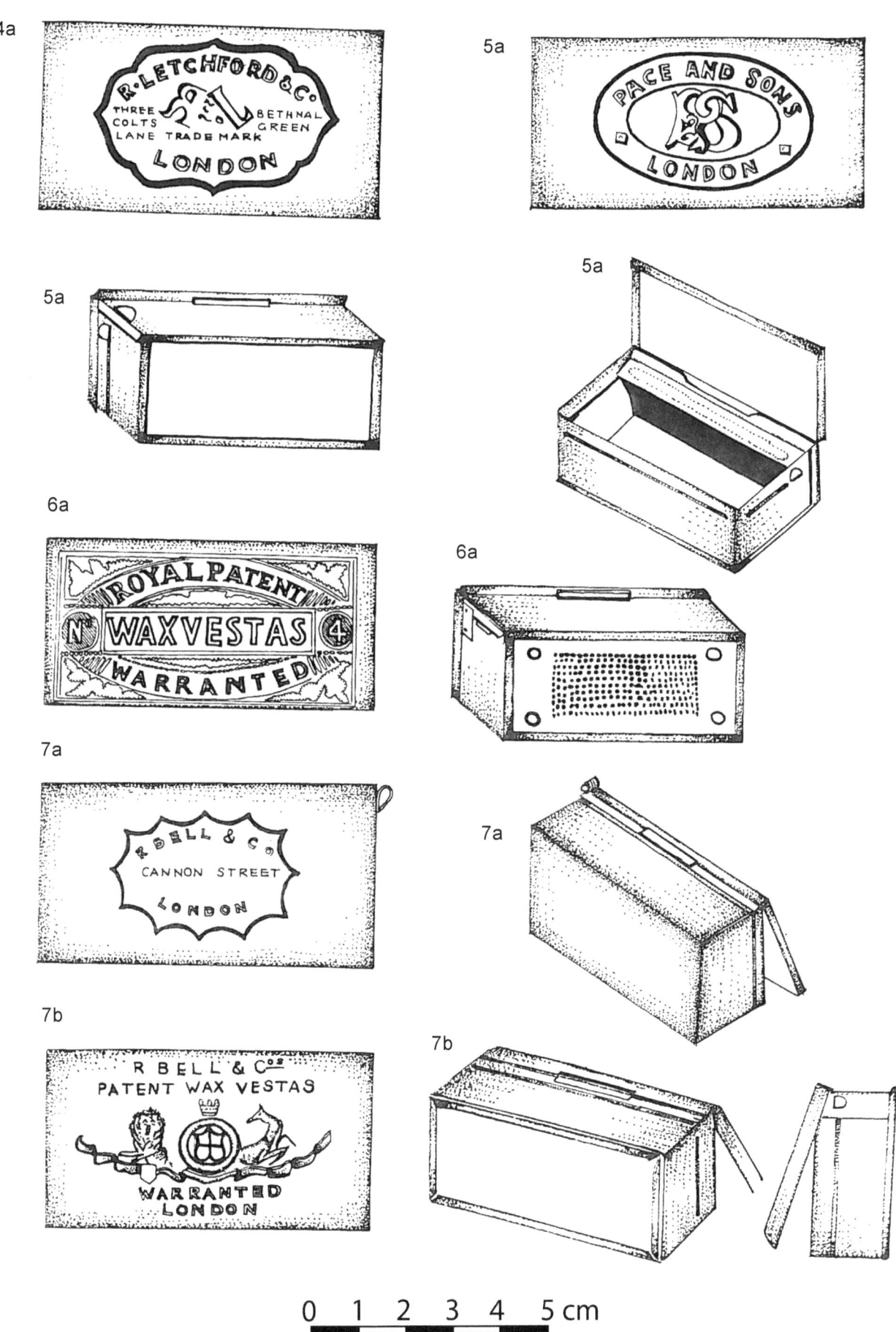

Figure 5.44. Wax vesta boxes (*continued*). Reproduced from Bedford (1985a). See Table 5.30 for distribution.

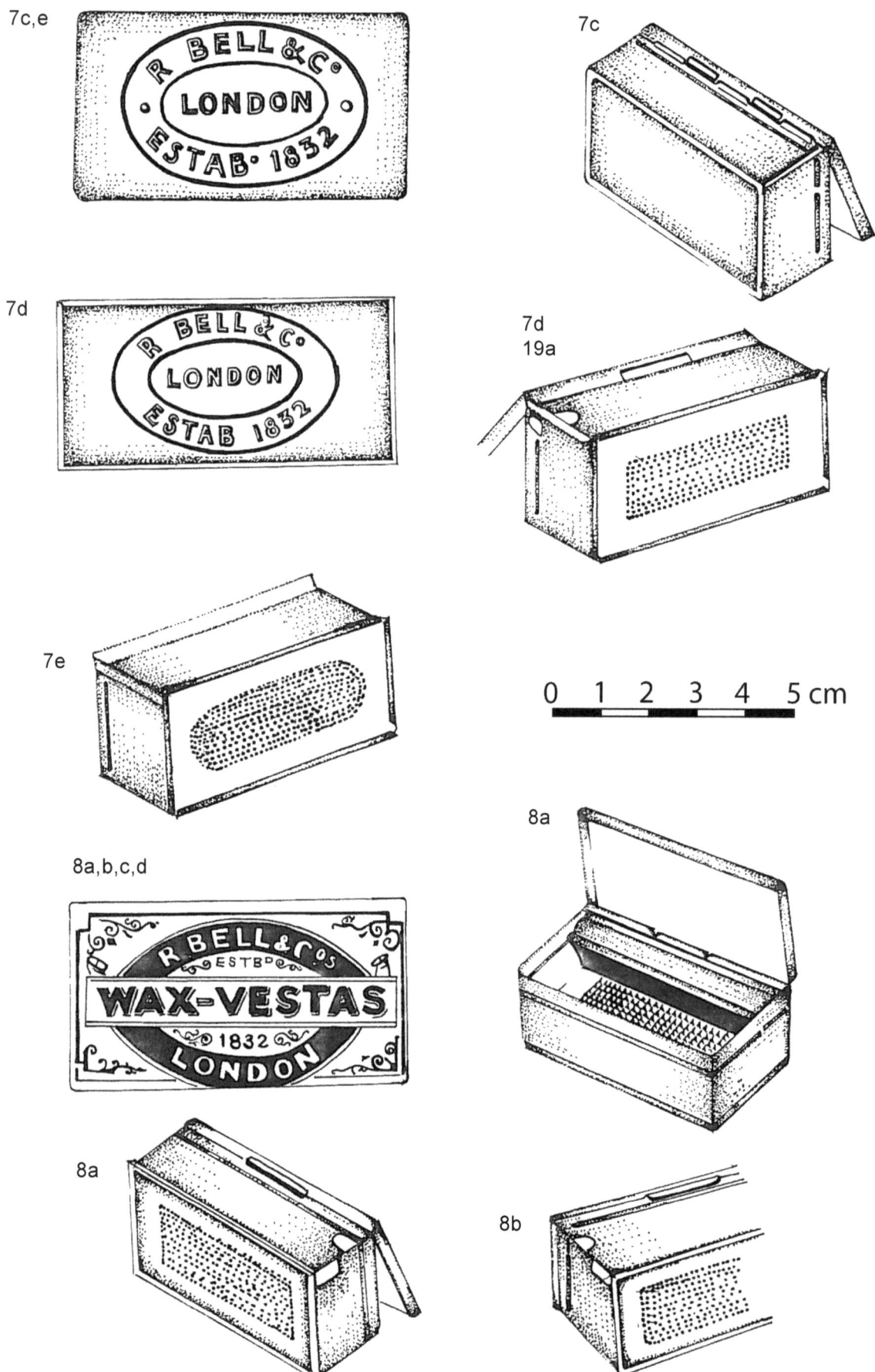

Figure 5.44. Wax vesta boxes (*continued*). Reproduced from Bedford (1985a). See Table 5.30 for distribution.

5 The material culture of the Chinese in southern New Zealand

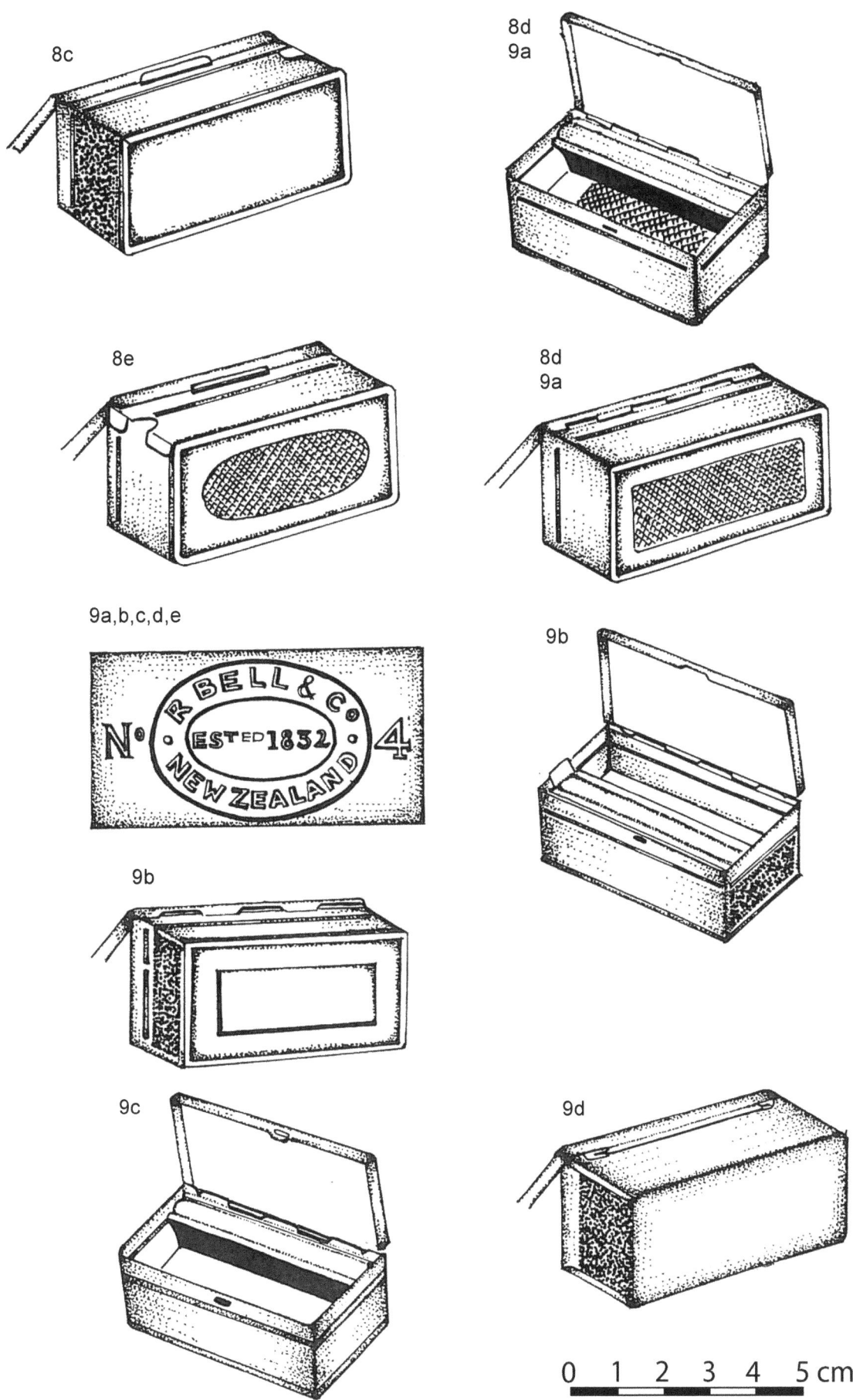

Figure 5.44. Wax vesta boxes (*continued*). Reproduced from Bedford (1985a). See Table 5.30 for distribution.

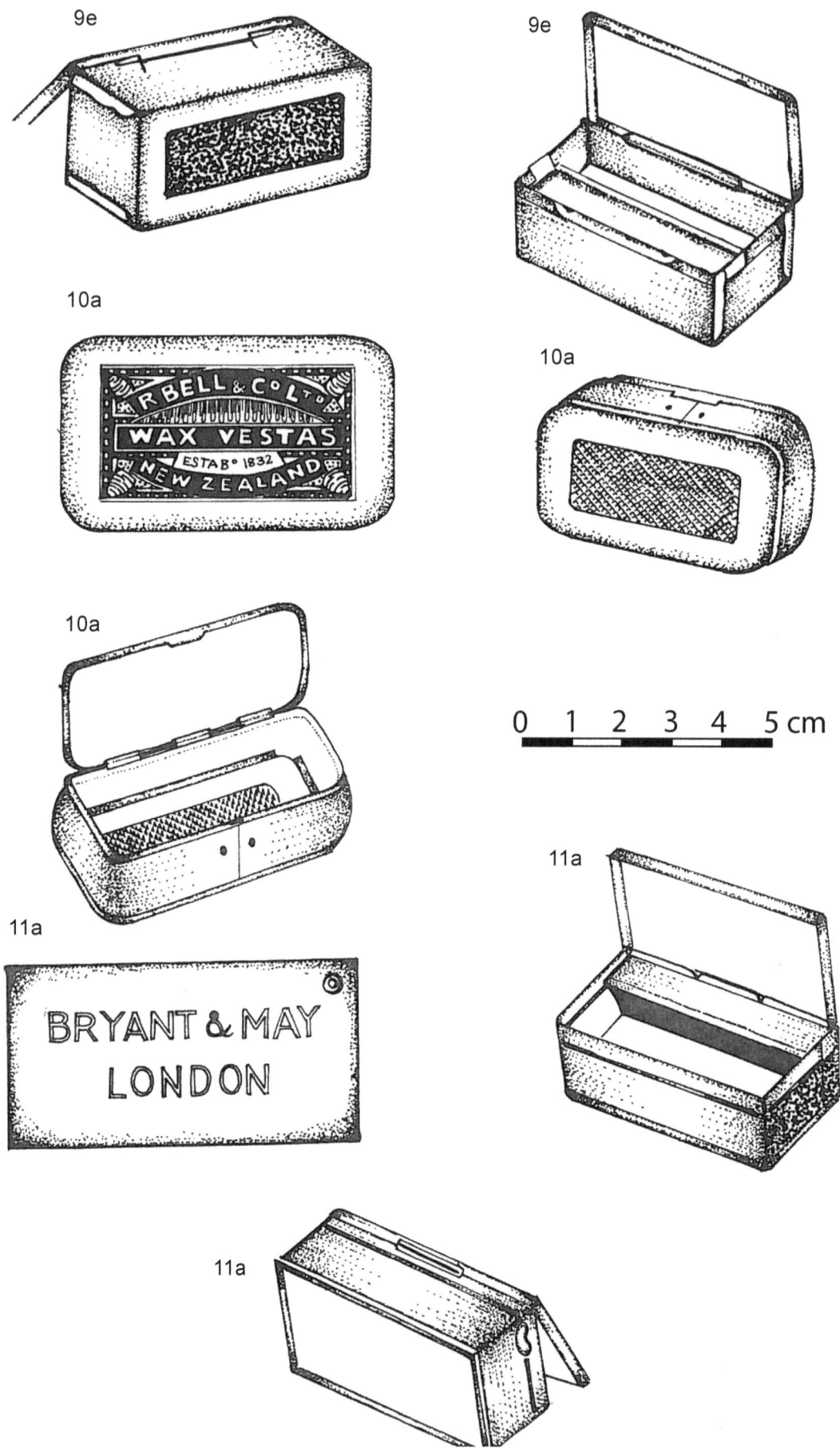

Figure 5.44. Wax vesta boxes (*continued*). Reproduced from Bedford (1985a). See Table 5.30 for distribution.

5 The material culture of the Chinese in southern New Zealand

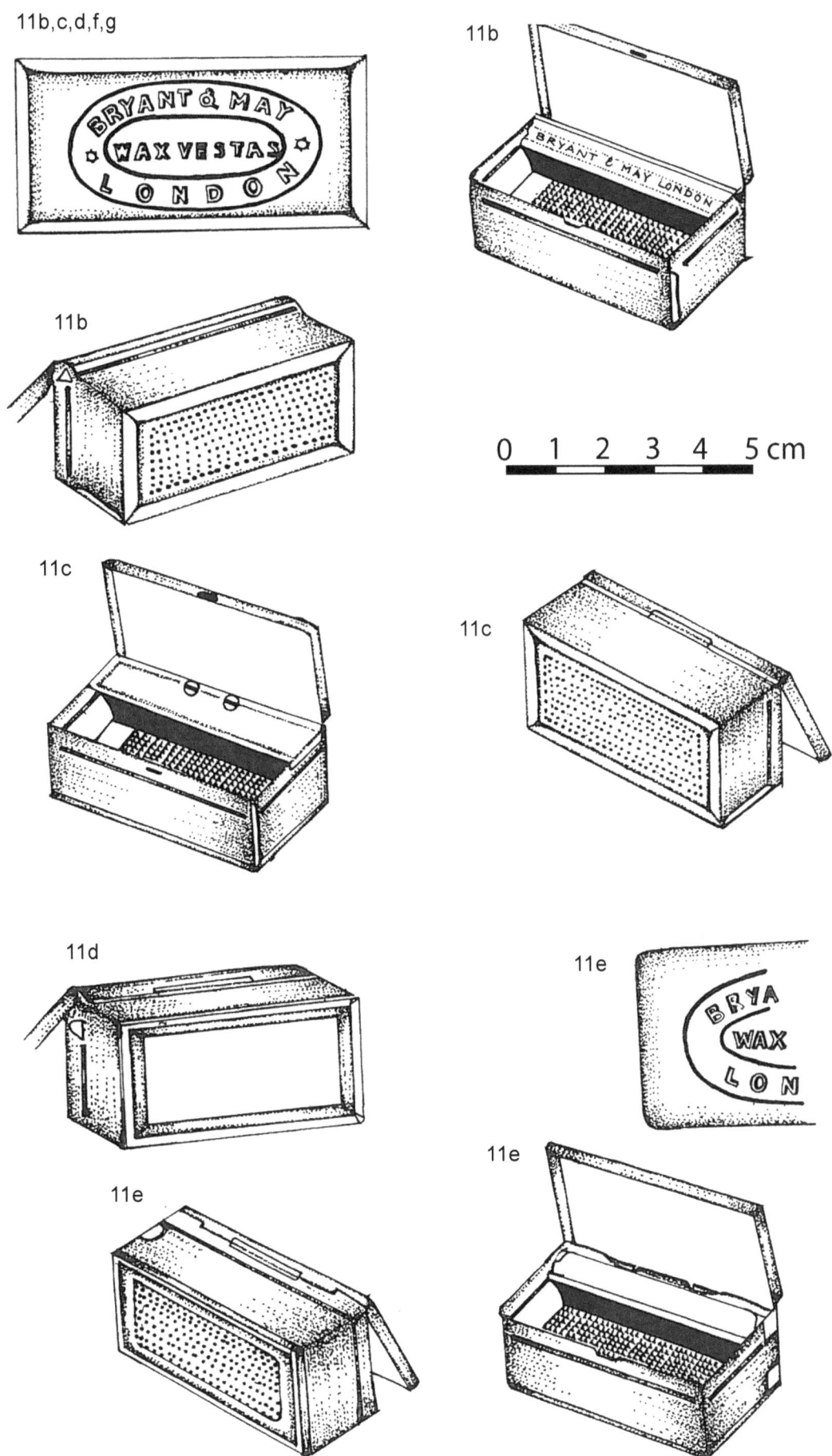

Figure 5.44. Wax vesta boxes (*continued*). Reproduced from Bedford (1985a). See Table 5.30 for distribution.

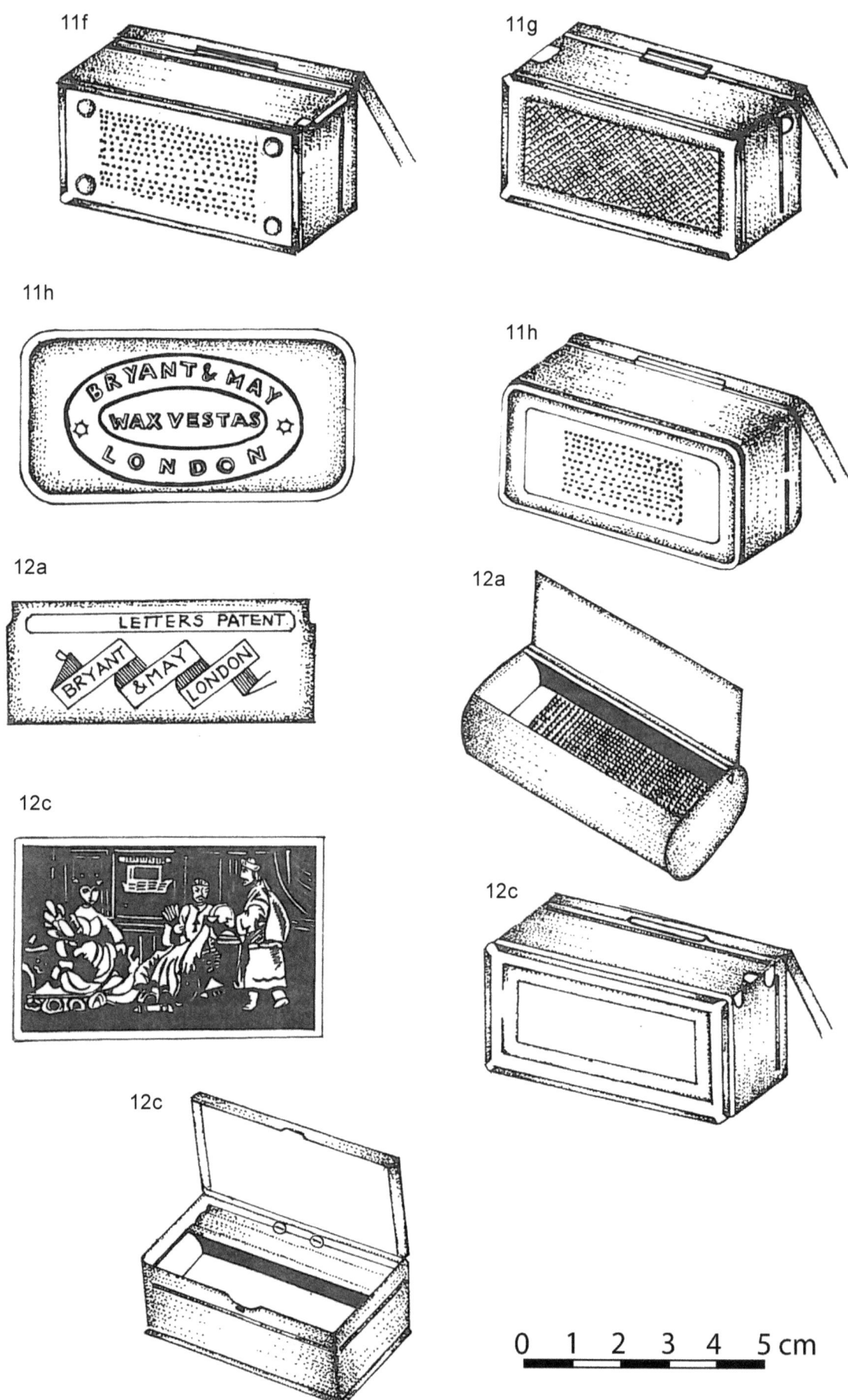

Figure 5.44. Wax vesta boxes (*continued*). Reproduced from Bedford (1985a). See Table 5.30 for distribution.

5 The material culture of the Chinese in southern New Zealand

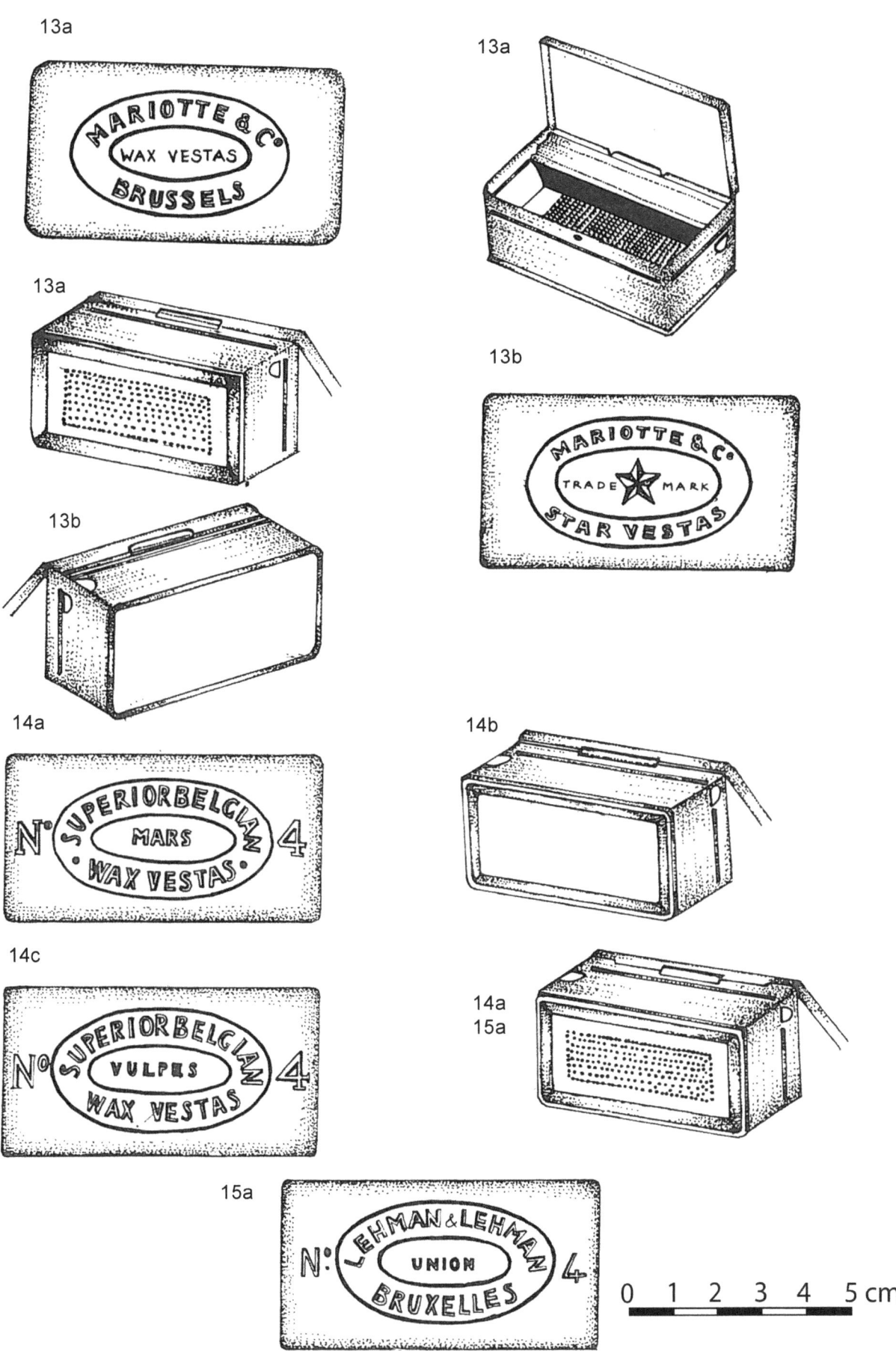

Figure 5.44. Wax vesta boxes (*continued*). Reproduced from Bedford (1985a). See Table 5.30 for distribution.

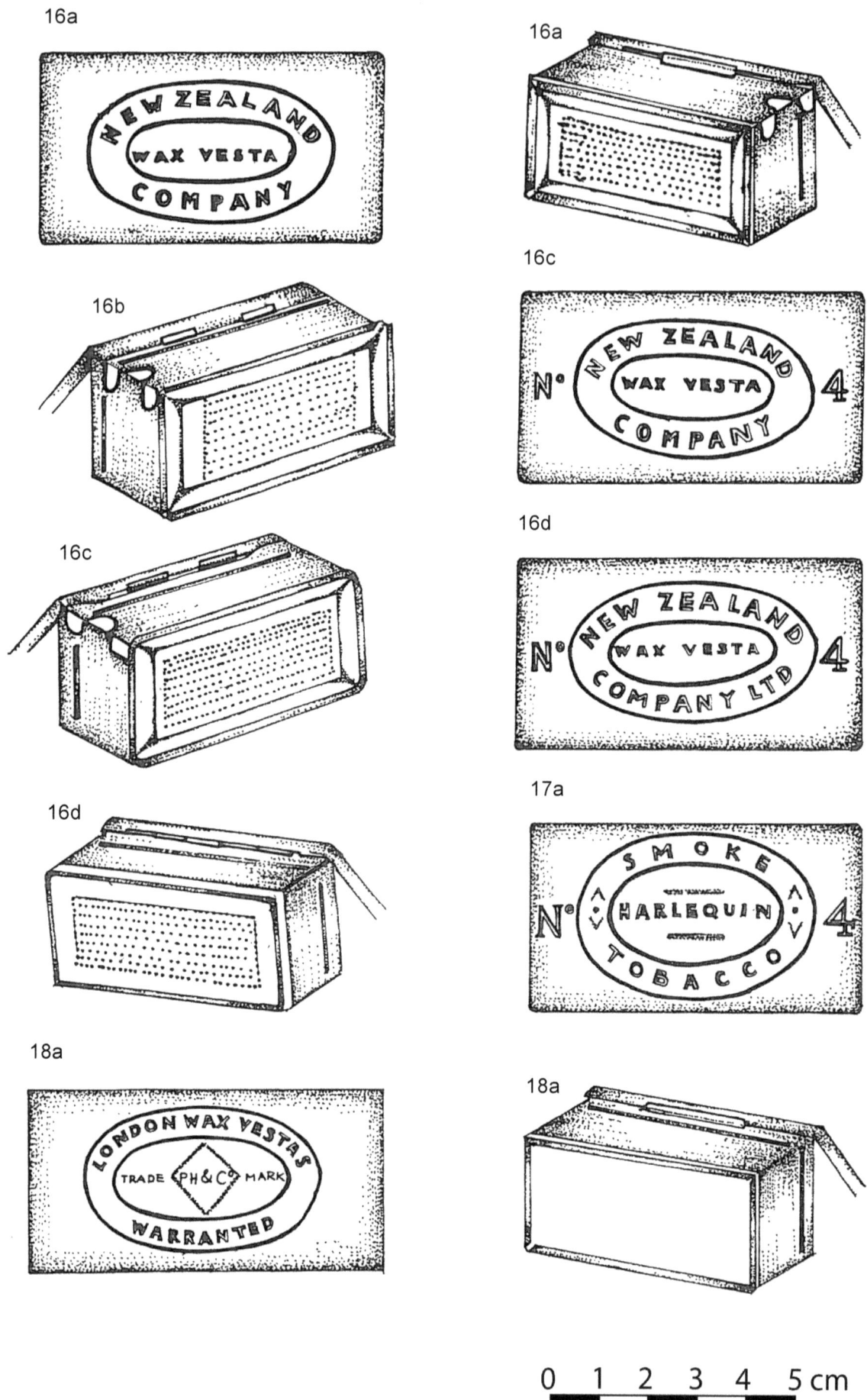

Figure 5.44. Wax vesta boxes (*continued*). Reproduced from Bedford (1985a). See Table 5.30 for distribution.

5 The material culture of the Chinese in southern New Zealand

19a

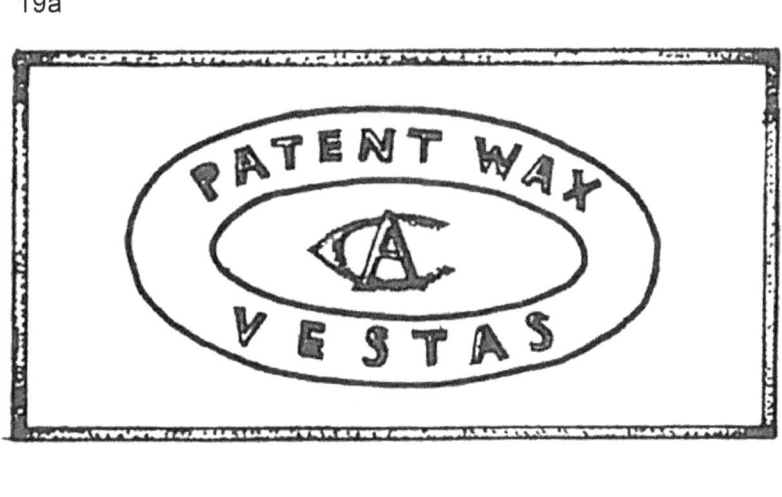

Figure 5.44. Wax vesta boxes (*continued*). Reproduced from Bedford (1985a). See Table 5.30 for distribution.

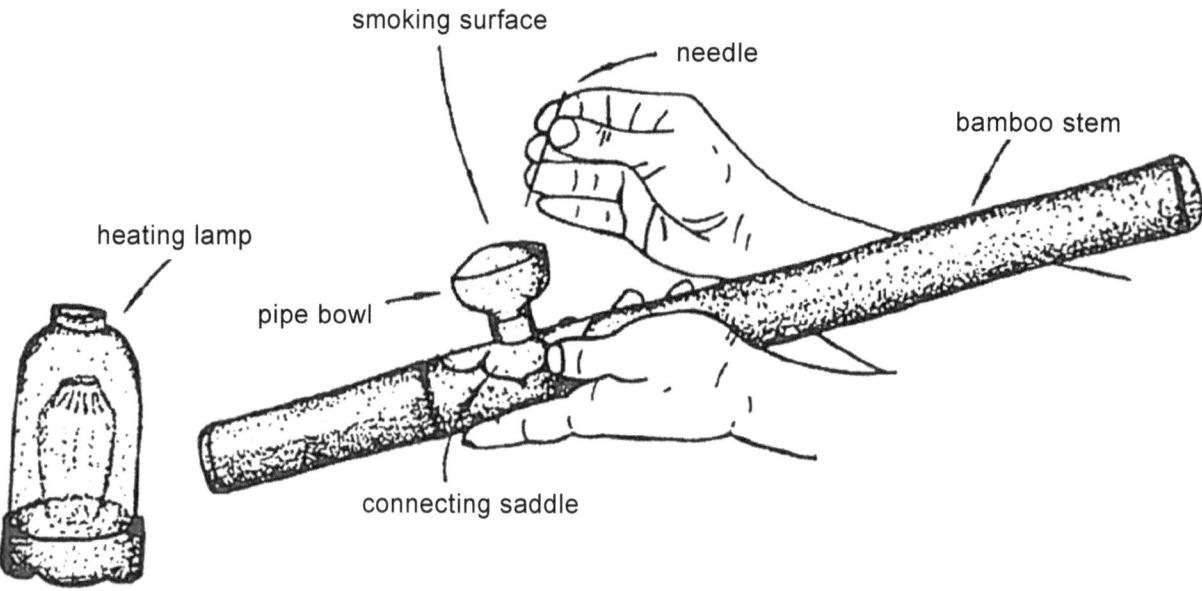

Figure 5.45. Opium pipe terminology.

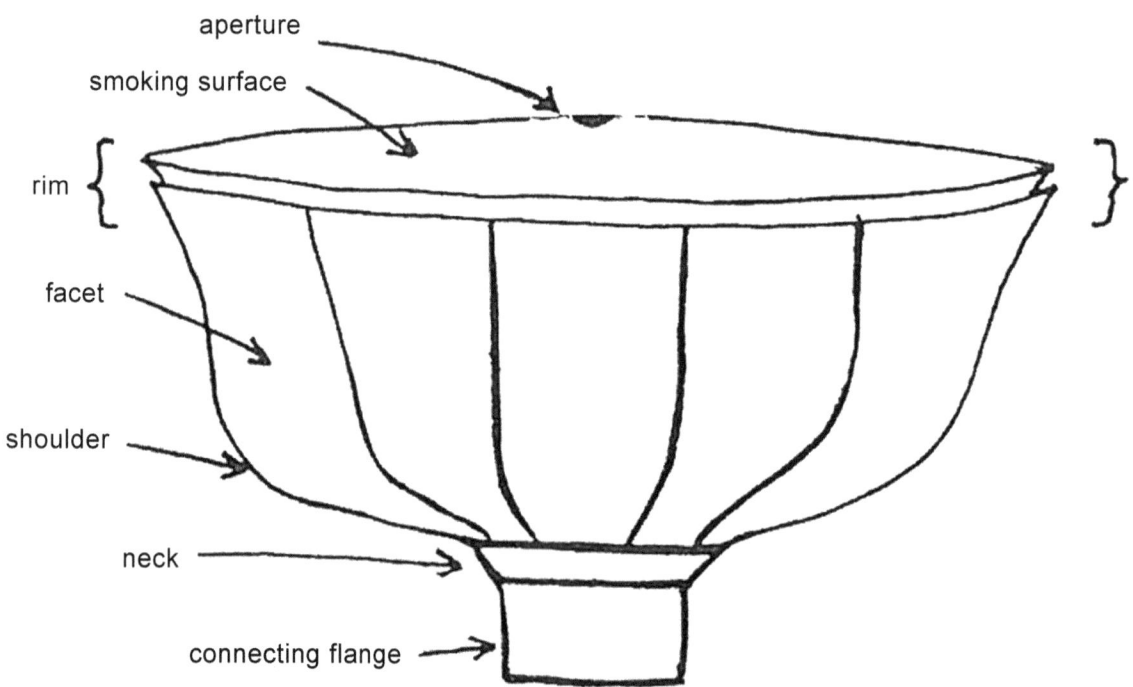

Figure 5.46. Opium pipe bowl terminology.

5 The material culture of the Chinese in southern New Zealand

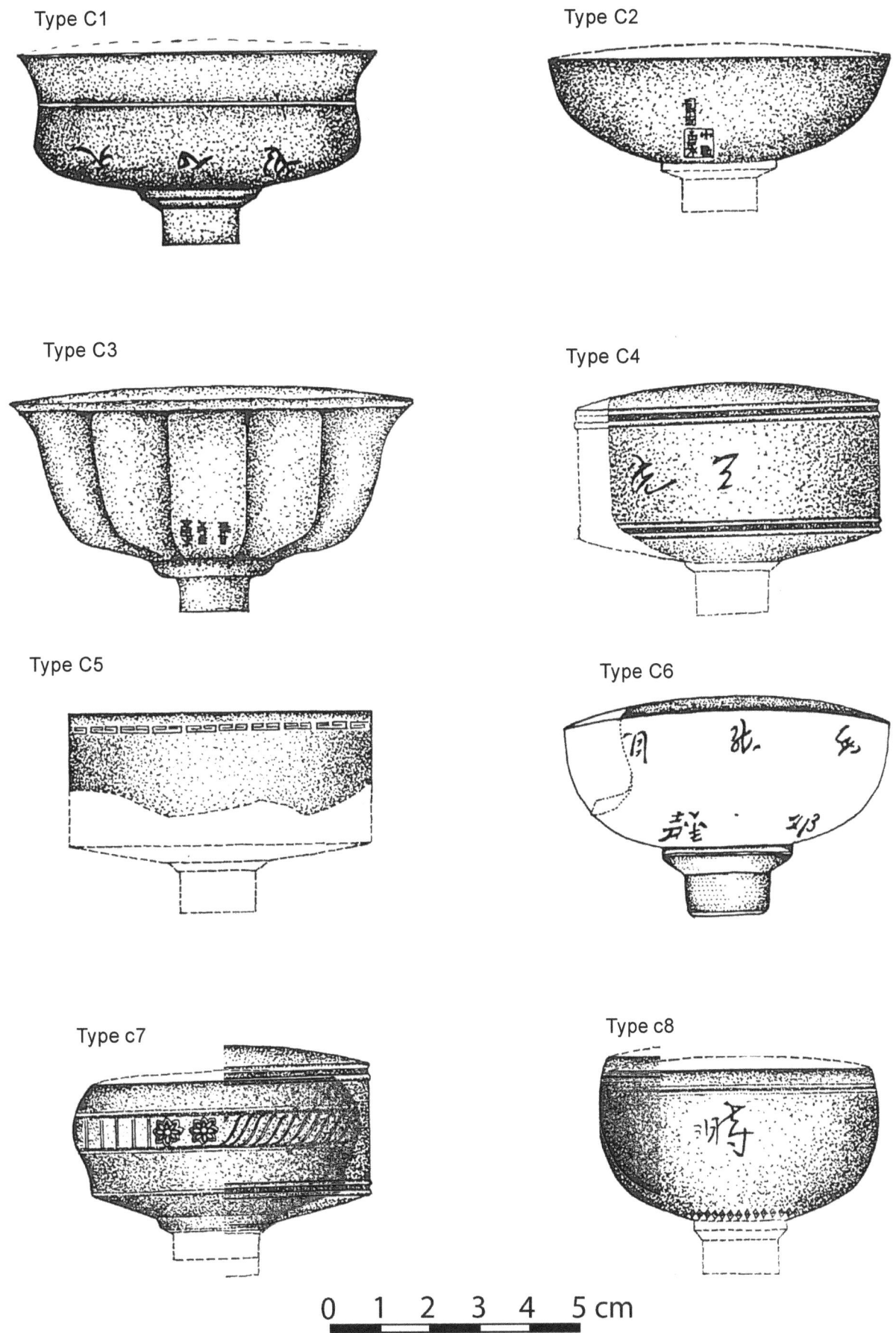

Figure 5.47. Opium pipe bowls from Central Otago sites. See Table 5.31.

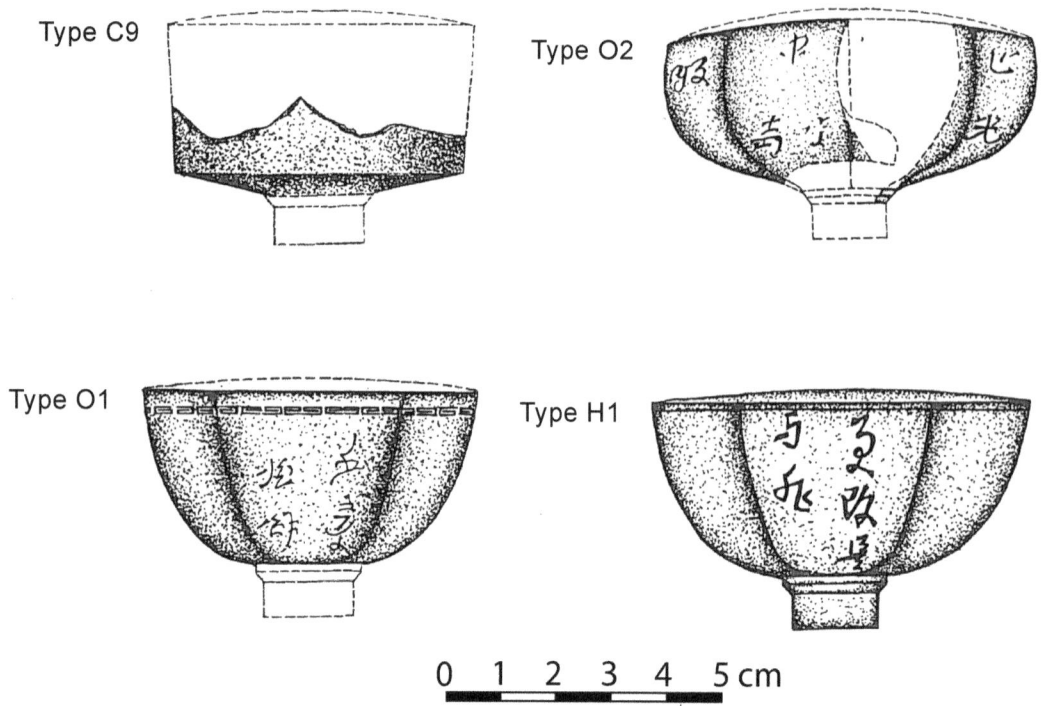

Figure 5.47. Opium pipe bowls from Central Otago sites. See Table 5.31 (*continued*).

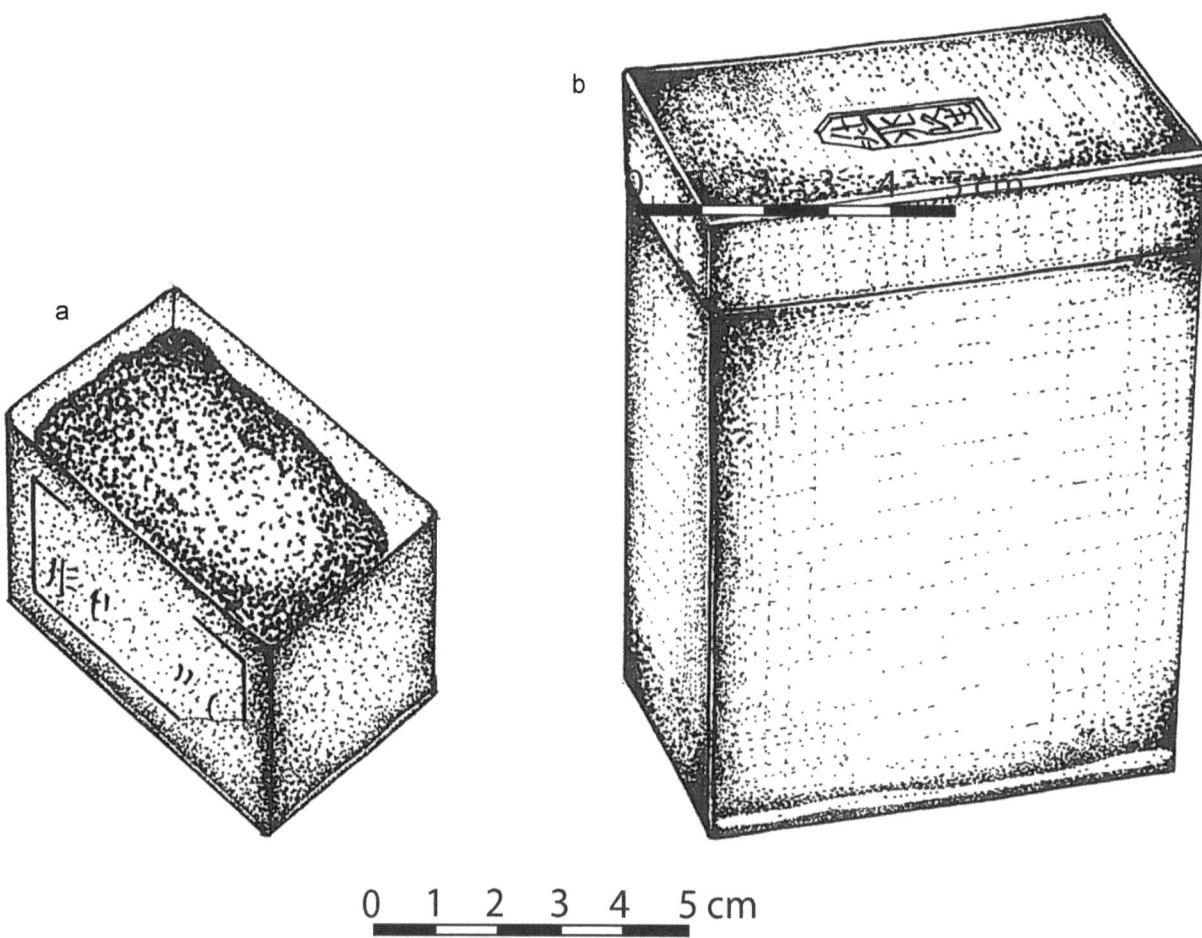

Figure 5.48. Opium cans. **a.** "cut-down" opium can with suspected opium residue found at Ch/6 (J20 Ly.3). **b.** Intact brass opium can showing lid strip and cartouche (Short collection).

5 The material culture of the Chinese in southern New Zealand

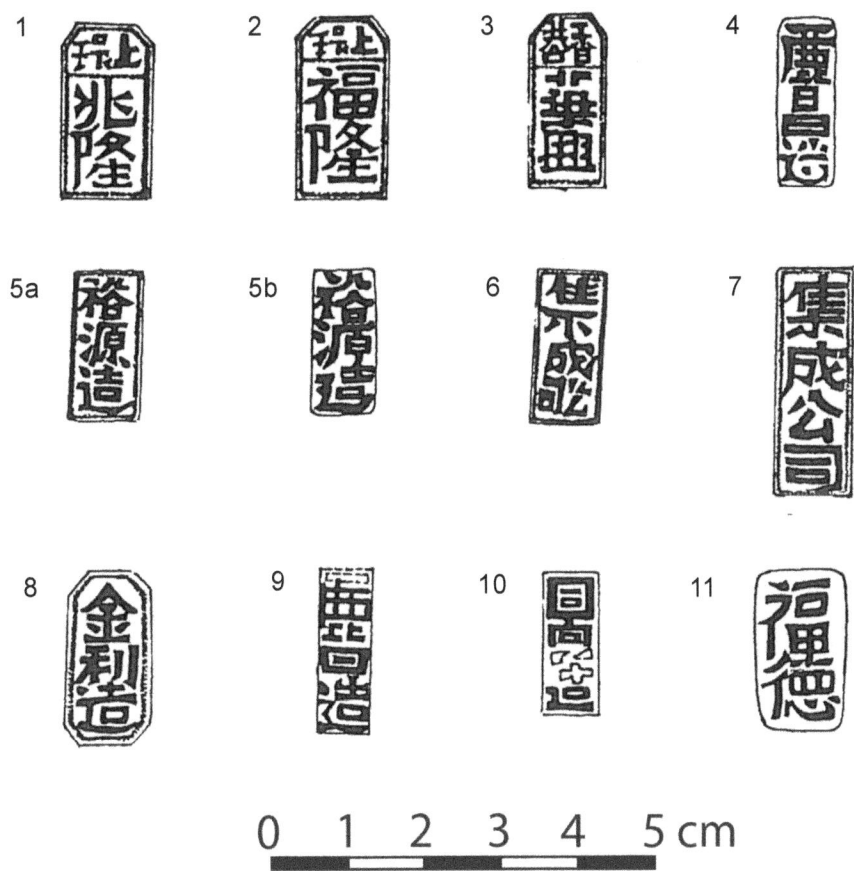

Figure 5.49. Opium can cartouche types.

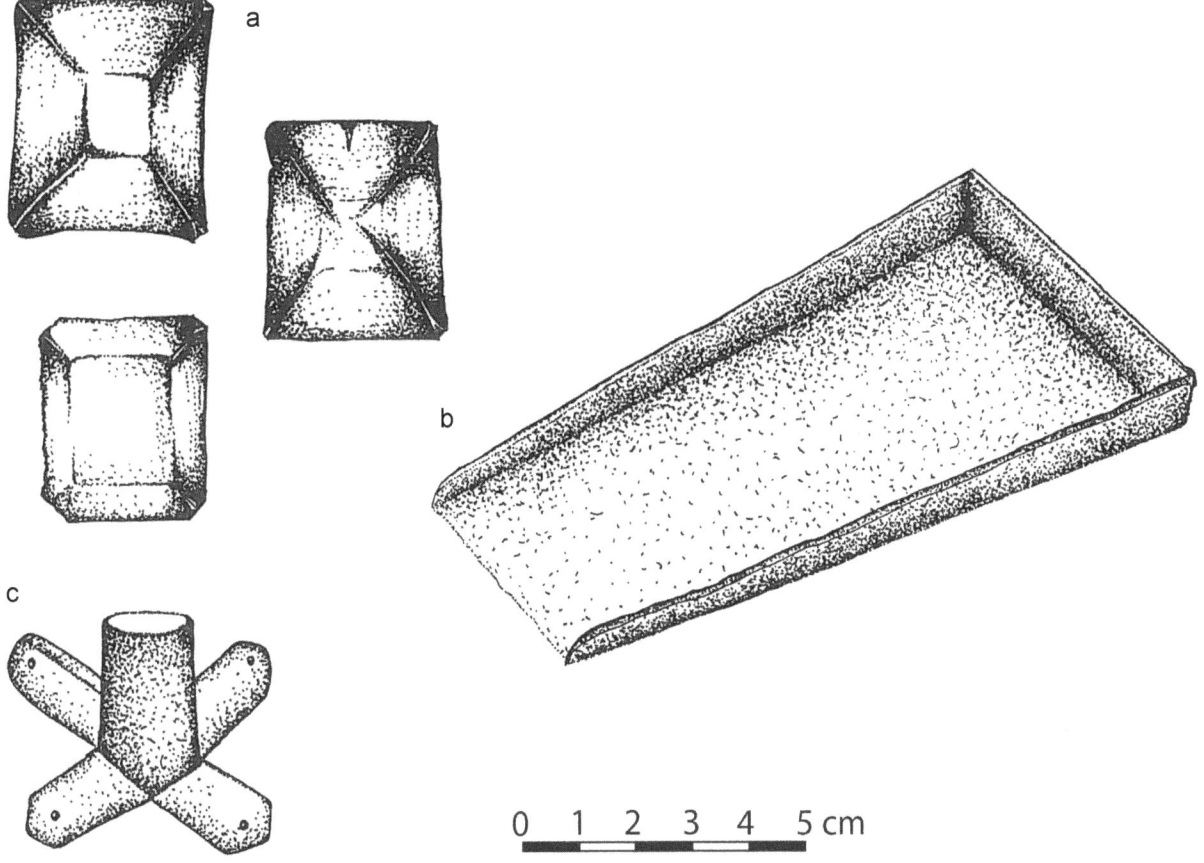

Figure 5.50. Artefacts made from opium can metal. See Table 5.36 for distribution. **a.** Three "funs trays" (see Section 5.4.4.6.) made from opium can metal, found at various sites. **b.** Small gold blowing tray found at Riverside site (A1 Ly.2). **c.** Candleholder made from opium can metal found at QB1 (D7 Ly.2).

345

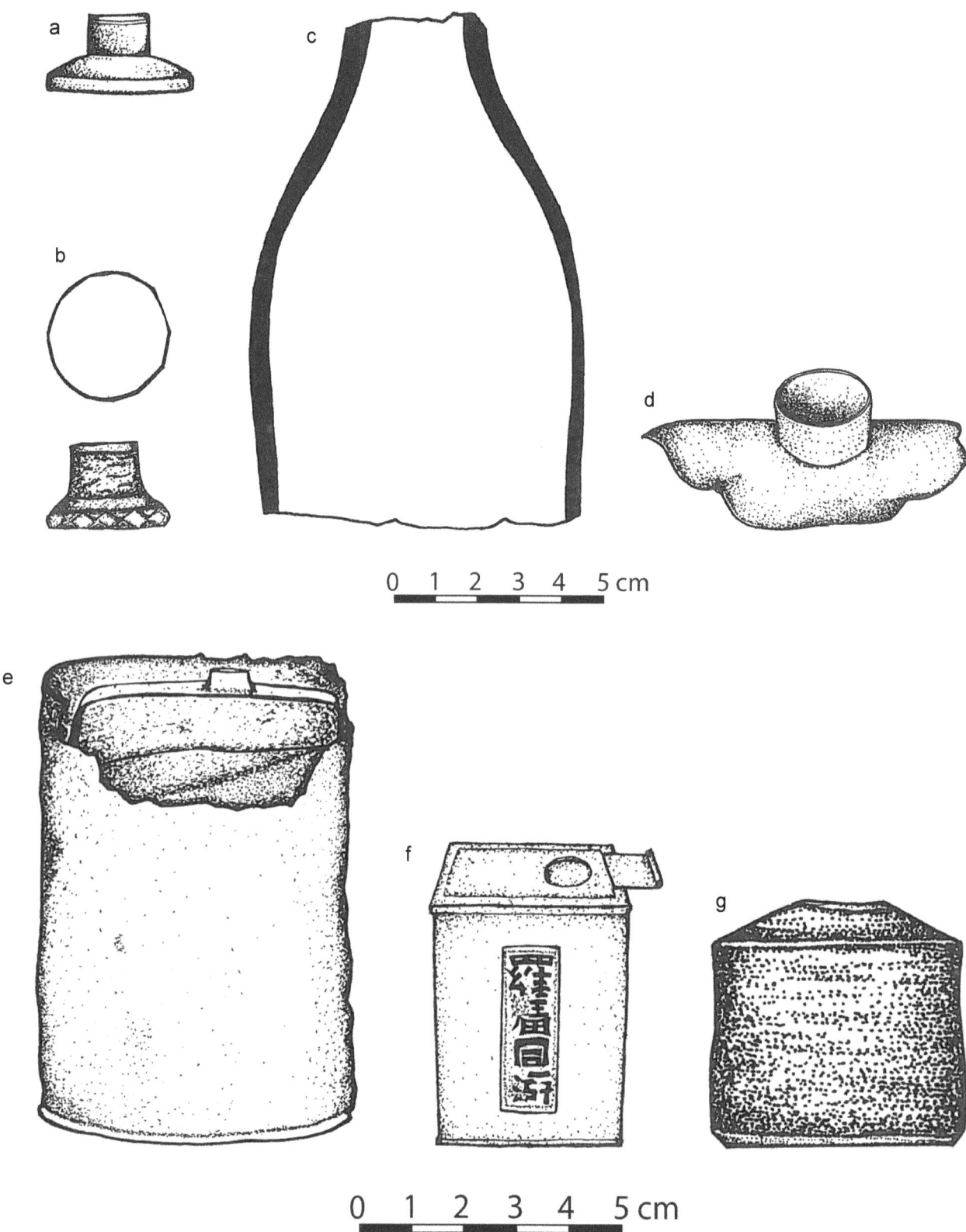

Figure 5.51. Artefacts associated with opium smoking. See Table 5.37 for site distribution. **a.** Brass circular connecting flange. **b.** Brass faceted connecting flange, and plan view. **c.** Light green brandy bottle modified into opium heating lamp. **d.** Brass connecting saddle. **e.** Opium lamp reservoir made from a tin can. The wickholder is made from an opium can reinforcing strip. found at QB2 (C4 Ly.2). **f.** Reputed opium antidote(?) tin with sliding closure. Recovered specimens from Chinatown and Arrowtown. The depicted example is an unprovenanced specimen in the Cromwell Museum (CR 77795C). **g.** Penny ink bottle modified into an opium pipe bowl(?). The neck has been removed and a small hole drilled in the base, found at ACS/6 (J8 Ly.1).

5 The material culture of the Chinese in southern New Zealand

Figure 5.52. A lustrous dark brown-glazed opium pipe bowl reputed to have been made by the Christchurch pottery of Luke Adams (Redmond pers. comm.).

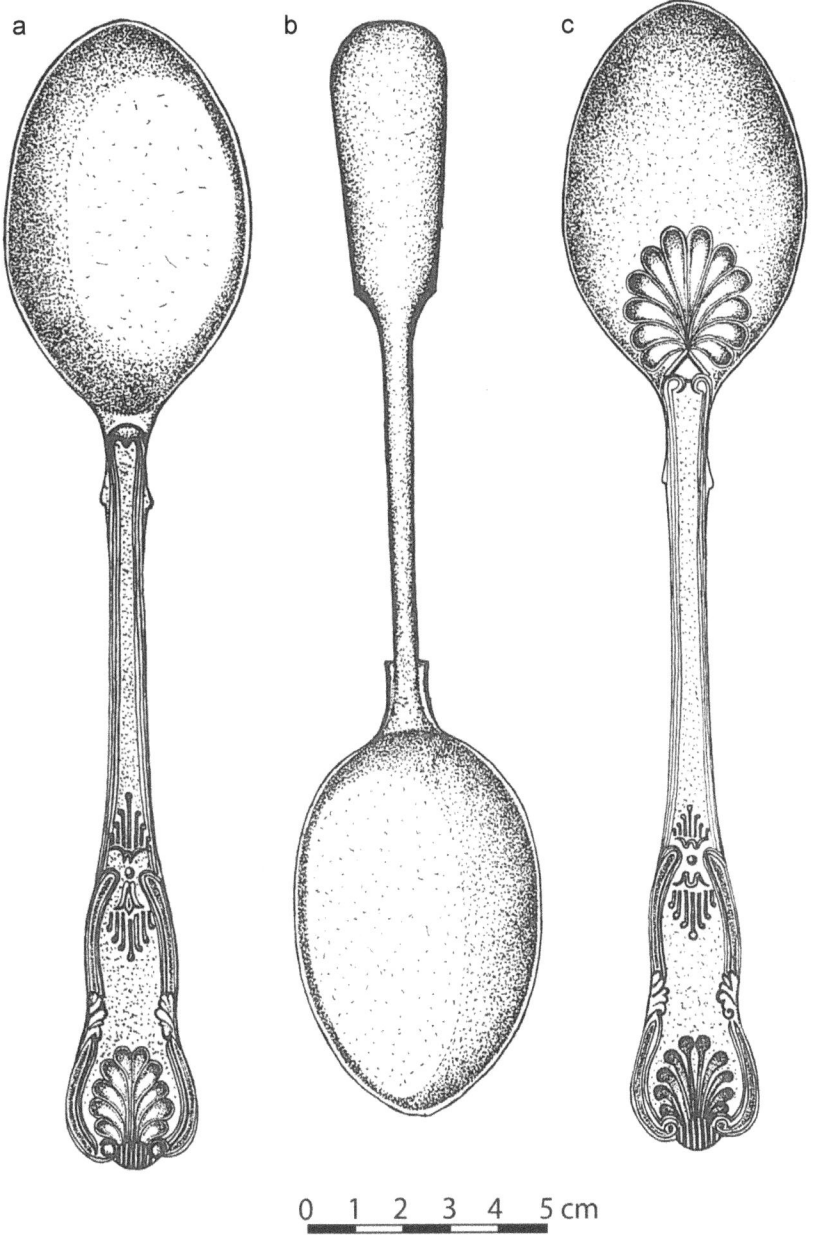

Figure 5.53. Tablespoons. **a.** Found at Ch/27 (L12) surface. **b.** Found at Ch/24 (P11 Ly.2). **c.** Found at Ch/23 (J16 Ly.2).

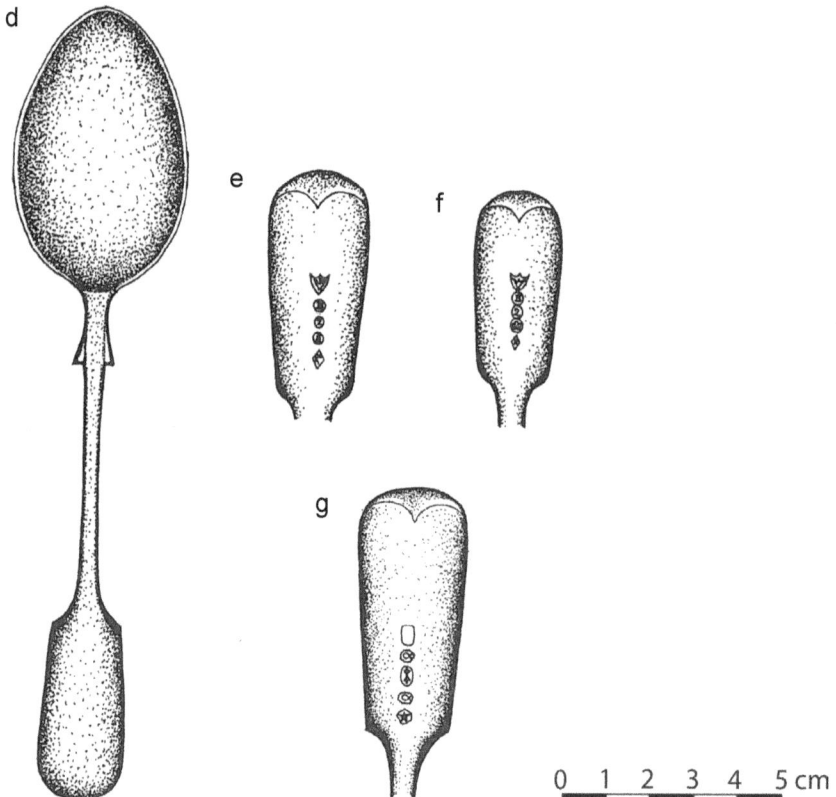

Figure 5.53. Tablespoons (*continued*). **d.** Found at ACS/5 (Q12 Ly.2). **e.** Found at Ch/9 (J20 Ly.1). **f.** Found at ACS/5 (Q15 Ly.1). **g.** Found at Ch/24 (P11 Ly.2). Reverse side of specimen depicted in Figure 5.53b.

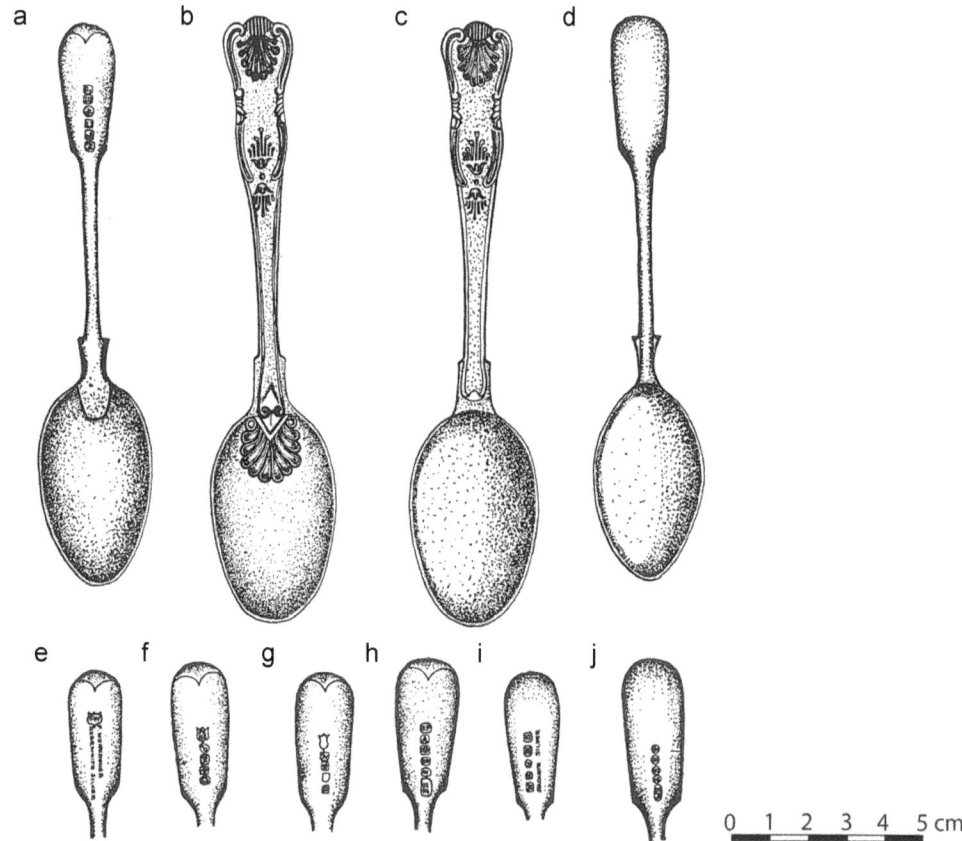

Figure 5.54. Teaspoons. **a.** Found at Ch/23 (J14 Ly.1). **b.** Found at Ch/34 (N14 Ly.2). **c.** Found at Ch/34 (M14 Ly.2). **d.** Found at Ch/33 (L18 Ly.1). **e.** Found at Ch/23 (T13 Ly.2.) **f.** Found at ACS/8 (H14 Ly.2). **g.** Found at ACS/5 rock infill. **h.** Found at Ch/33 (L18 Ly.1). Reverse side of Figure 5.54d. **i.** Found at ACS/5 (Q11 Ly.1). **j.** Found at Ch/27 (A12 Lv.2).

5 The material culture of the Chinese in southern New Zealand

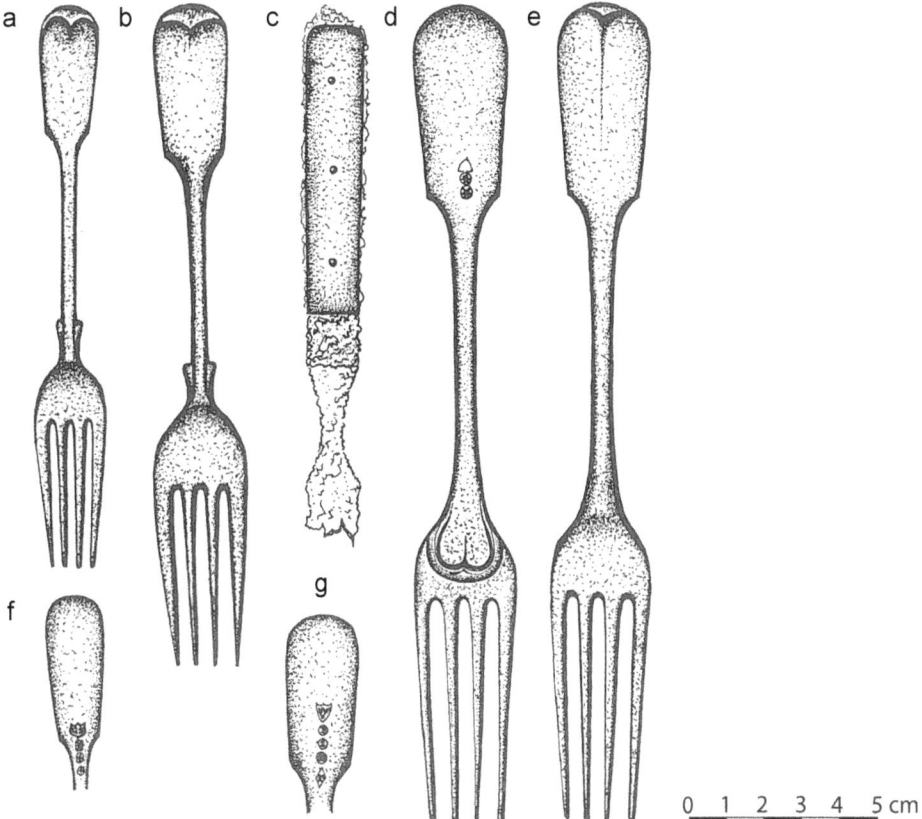

Figure 5.55. Table forks. **a.** Found at Ch/23 (J15 Ly.4). **b.** Found at Ch/18 (N2 Ly.2). **c.** Bone-handle fork found at Ch/16 (K16 Ly.2). **d.** Found at Ch/12 (Area A) surface. **e.** Found at Ch/12 (Area A) surface. **f.** Found at Ch/23 (J15 Ly.4), reverse of Figure 5.55a. **g.** Found at Ch/16 (N2 Ly.2).

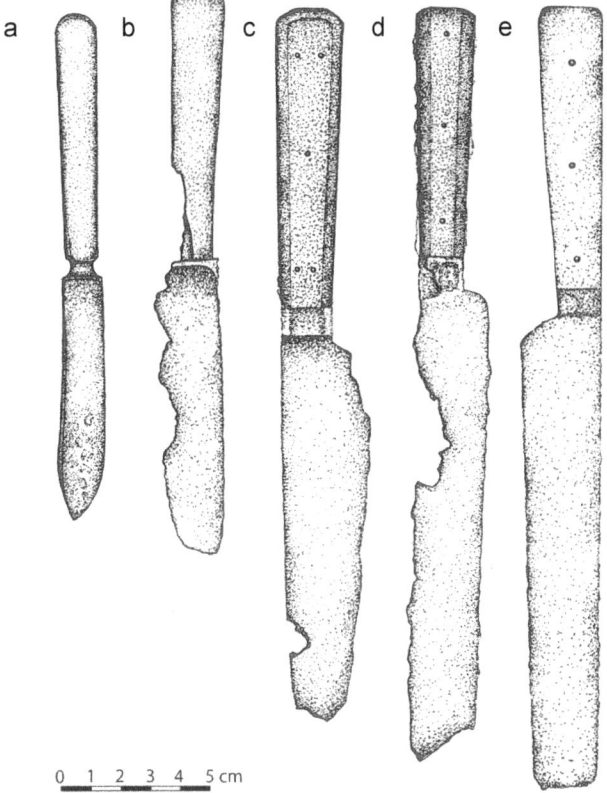

Figure 5.56. Knives. **a.** Silver-plated knife found at ACS/4 (I13 Ly.2). **b.** Bone-handled knife found at Ch/16 (L16 Ly.2). **c.** Bone-handled knife found at ACS/8 (F14 Ly.1). **d.** Bone-handled knife found at ACS/10 (G5 Ly.1). **e.** Bone-handled(?) knife found at ACS/6 (F7 Ly .1).

349

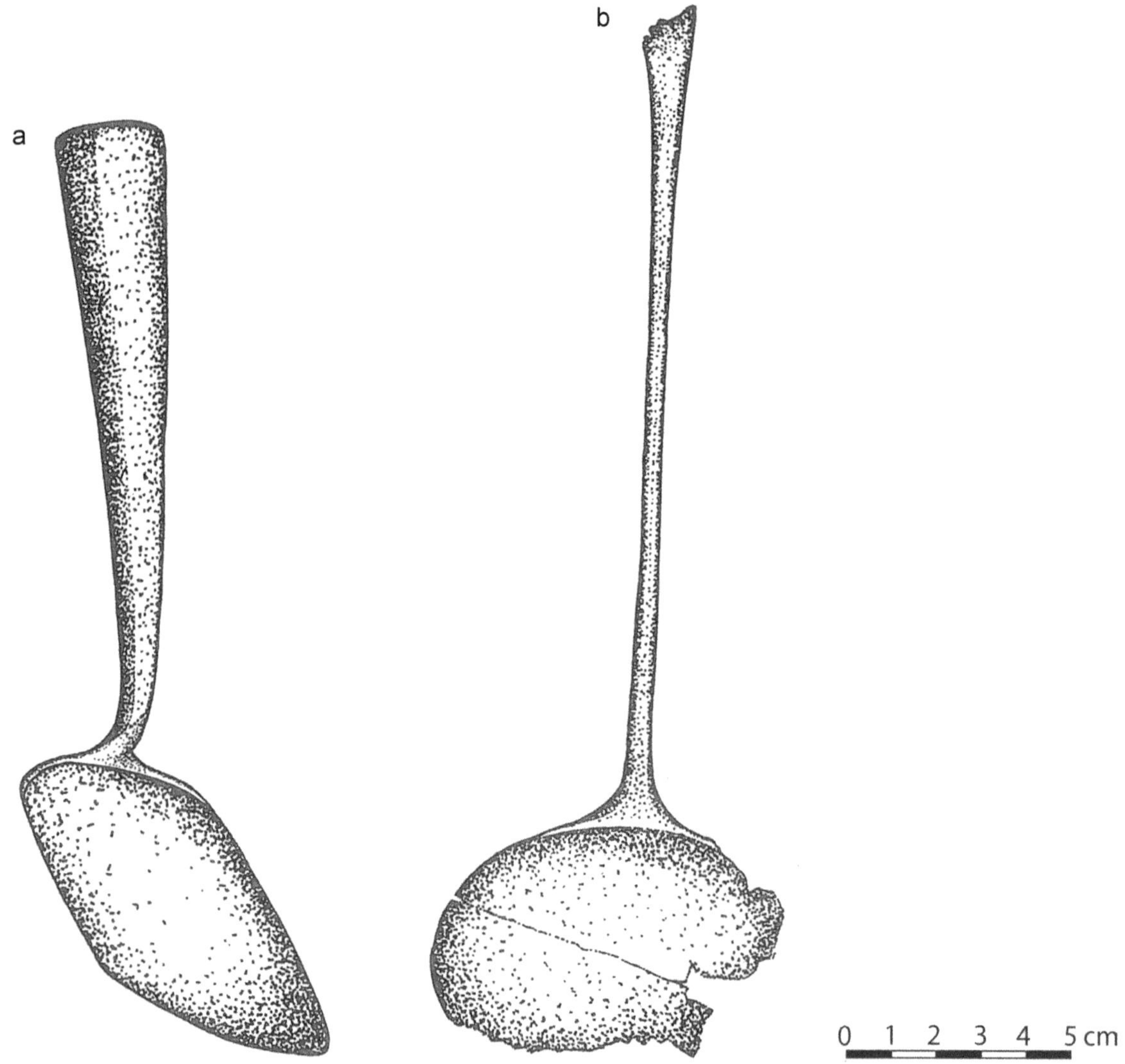

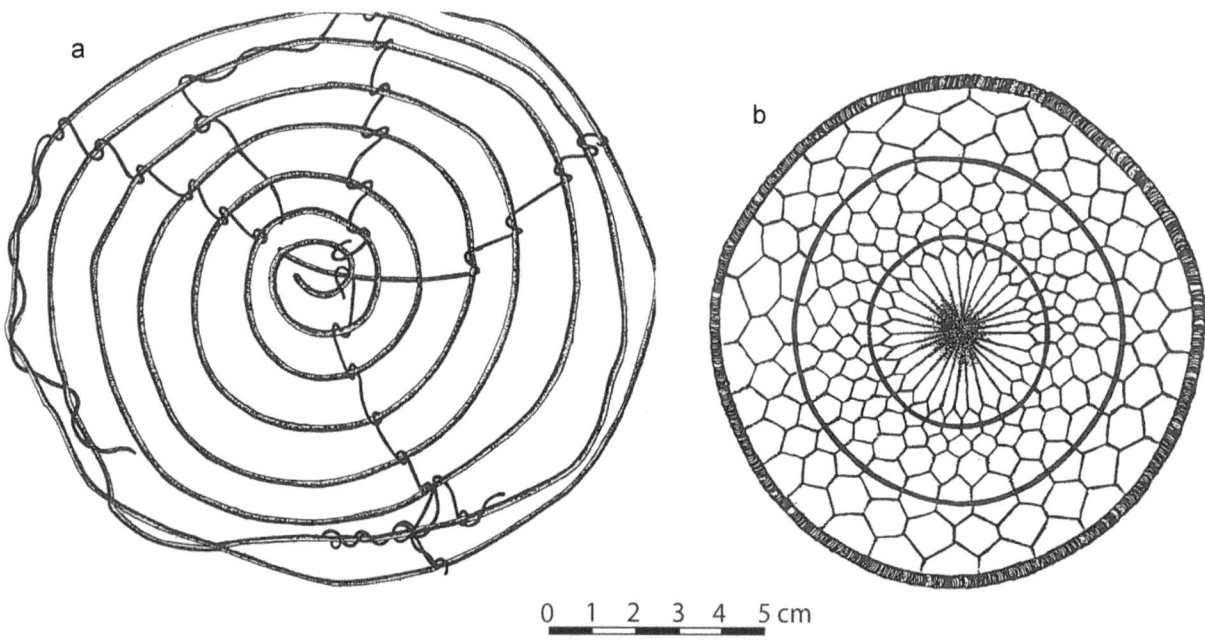

Figure 5.57. Wok spoons. **a.** Found at QB2 (C4 Ly.2). **b.** Found at Kawarau shelter (S133/72).

Figure 5.58. Strainers. **a.** Found at Caliche (G3 Ly.3). **b.** Found at Ch/23 (K19 Ly.2).

5 The material culture of the Chinese in southern New Zealand

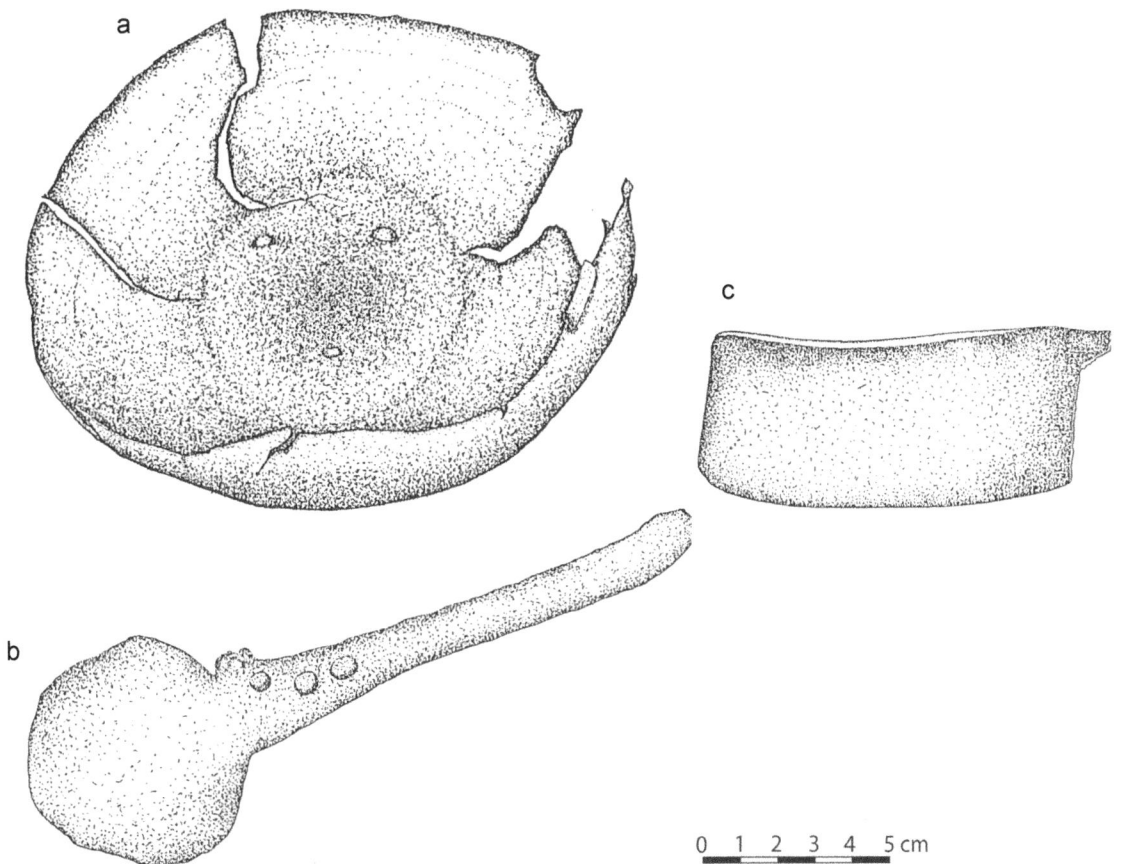

Figure 5.59. Wok, spoon and cleaver. See Table 5.38 for distribution. **a.** Improvised copper wok (burnt undersurface), found at Ch/26 (E11 Ly.2). **b.** Improvised rivetted wok spoon(?) found at Poplars site (G9 Ly.1). **c.** Cleaver blade found at ACS/2 (I11 Ly.2).

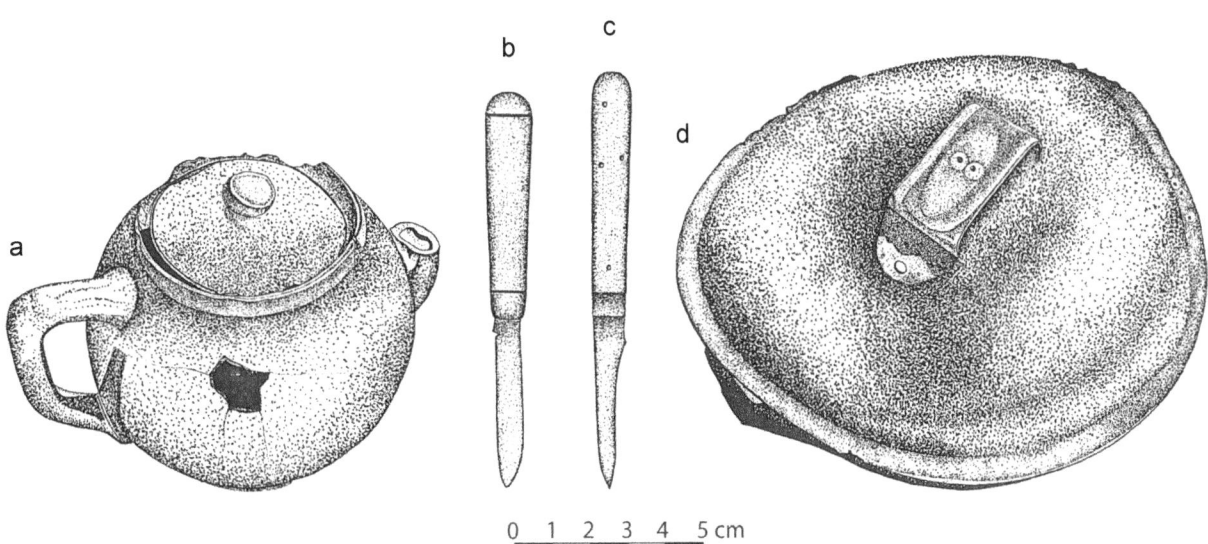

Figure 5.60. Miscellaneous European utensils. See Table 5.38 for distribution. **a.** Brown-glazed teapot found at ACS/3 (G9 Ly.2). **b.** Wooden-handled pocket knife found at Ch/24 (N16) surface. **c.** Pocket knife found at Ch/23 (D4 Ly.2). **d.** Billy lid with rivetted handle found at ACS/2 (K11 Ly.2).

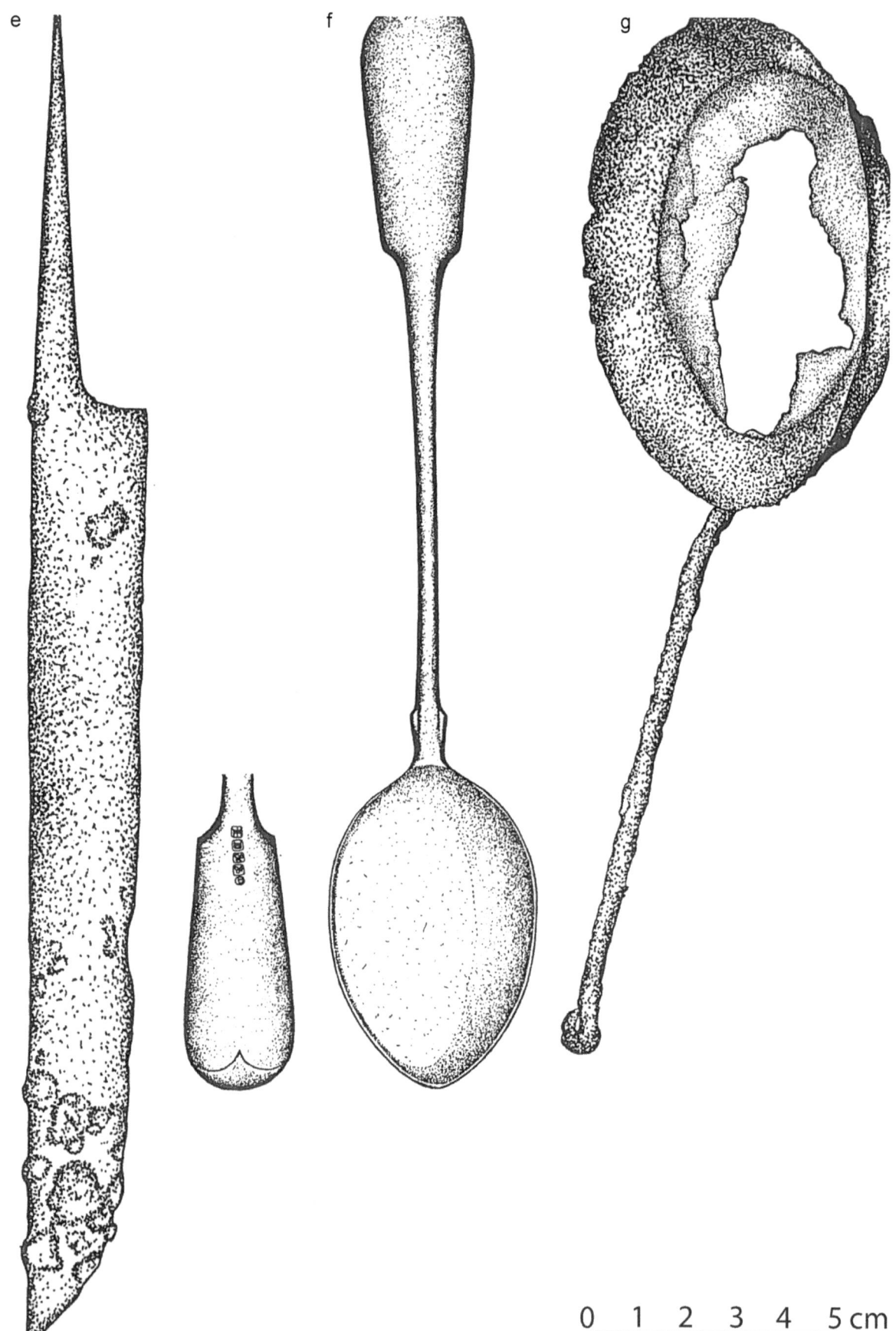

Figure 5.60. Miscellaneous European utensils (*continued*). See Table 5.38 for distribution. **e.** Long-bladed carving knife. found at ACS/3 (G8 Ly.2). **f.** Large tablespoon with hallmark found at ACS/3 (E5 Ly.2). **g.** "Typical" frying pan with distinctive long flat hook-ended handle.

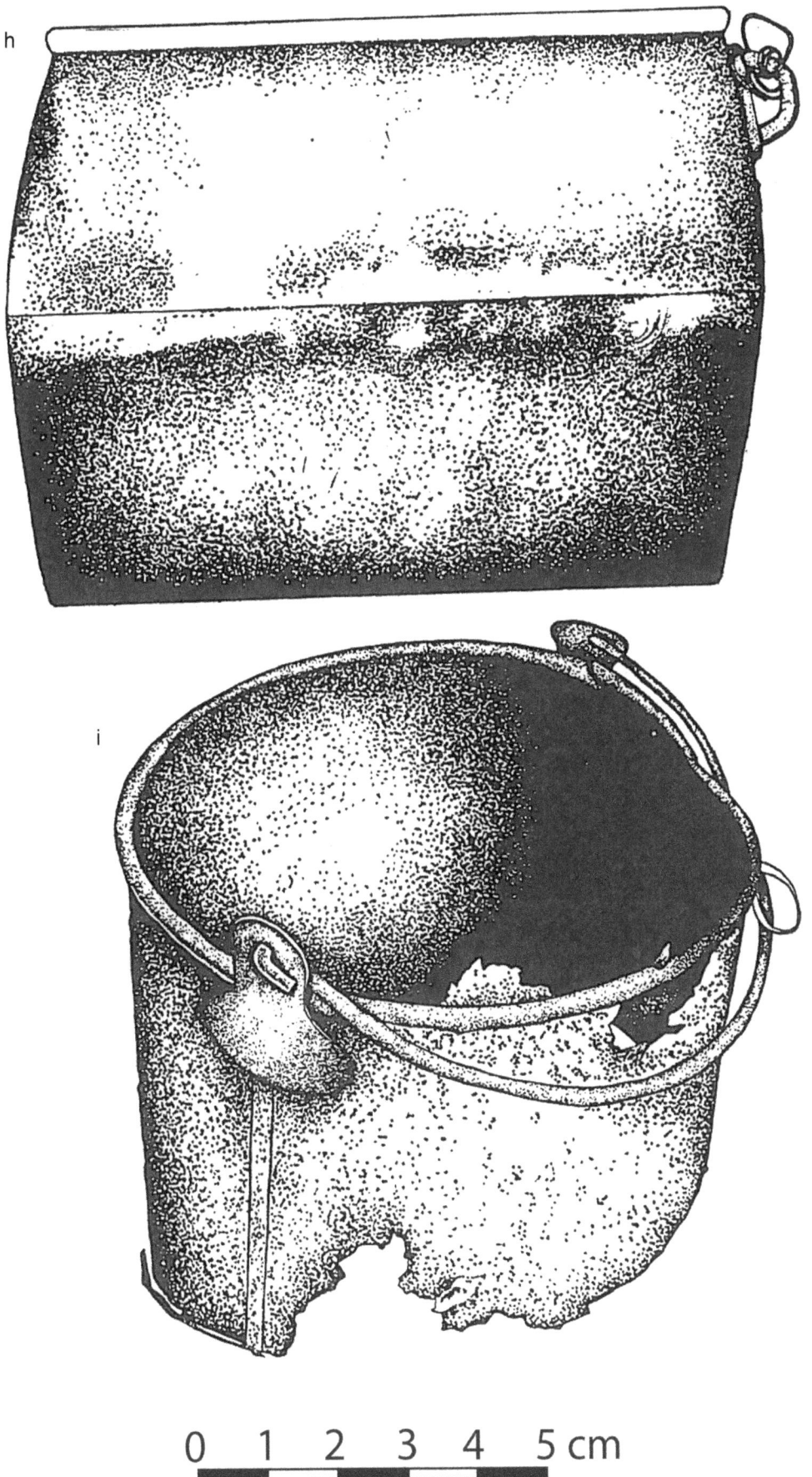

Figure 5.60. Miscellaneous European utensils (*continued*). See Table 5.38 for distribution. **h.** Cast iron pot found at Apple Tree (D9) surface. **i.** Typical tin billy with rivetted handle lugs.

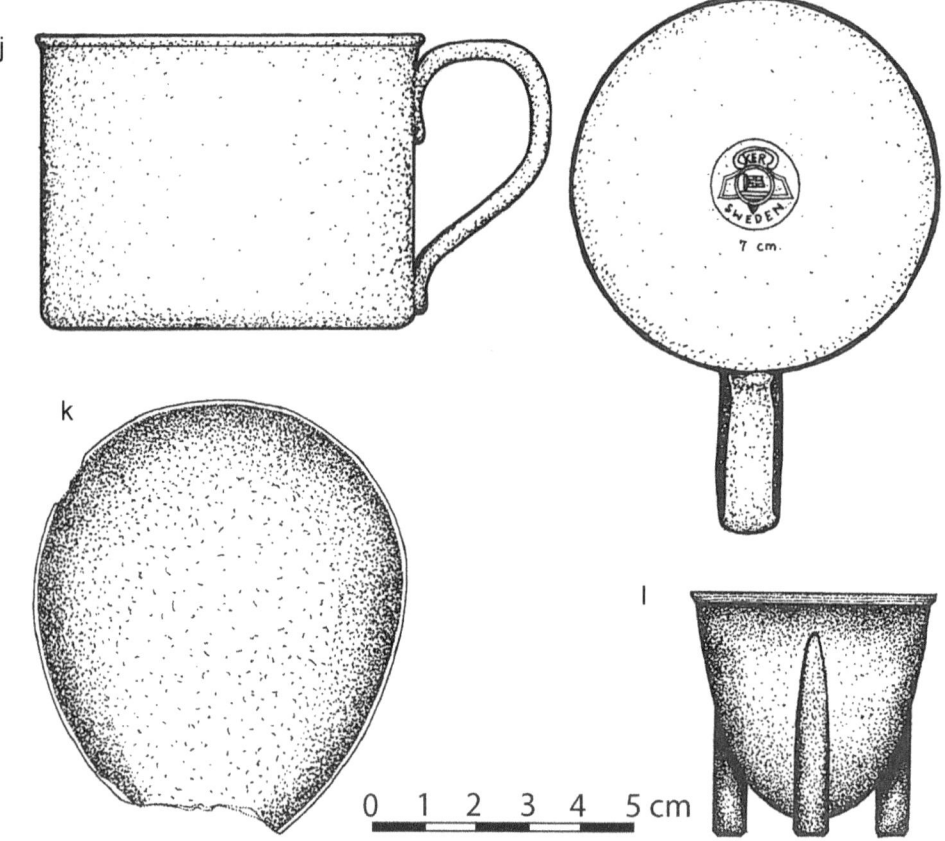

Figure 5.60. Miscellaneous European utensils (*continued*). See Table 5.38 for distribution. **j.** White enamelled mug with "KER Sweden" stamped on base, found at Ch/24 (M15 Ly.2). **k.** Wooden spoon found at Ch/21 (L5 Ly.2). **l.** Plastic eggcup found at Caliche (Y4 Ly.1).

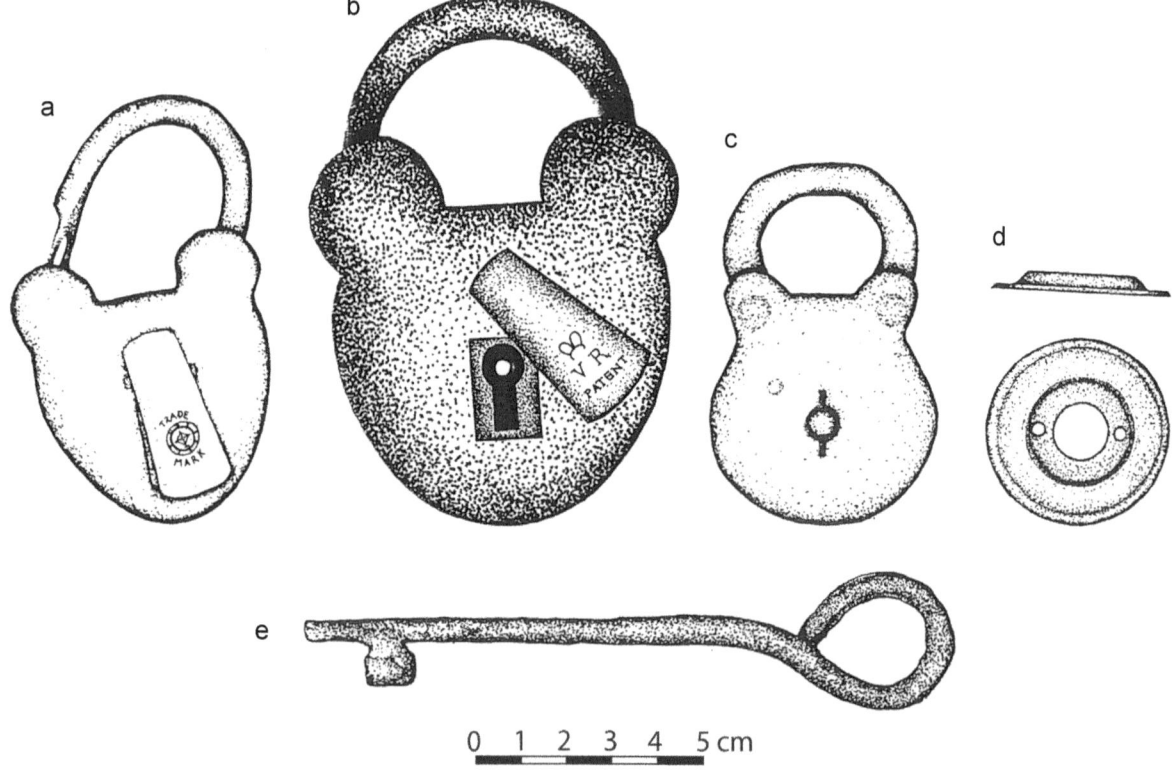

Figure 5.61. Security artefacts. **a.** Padlock found at Ch/7 surface, exterior. **b.** Padlock found at Apple Tree (G5 Ly.1). **c.** Padlock found at Ch/23 (J15 Ly.3). **d.** Door knob faceplate found at Ch/34 (K16 Ly.3). **e.** Improvised key found at Ah Wee's (H7 Ly.1).

5 The material culture of the Chinese in southern New Zealand

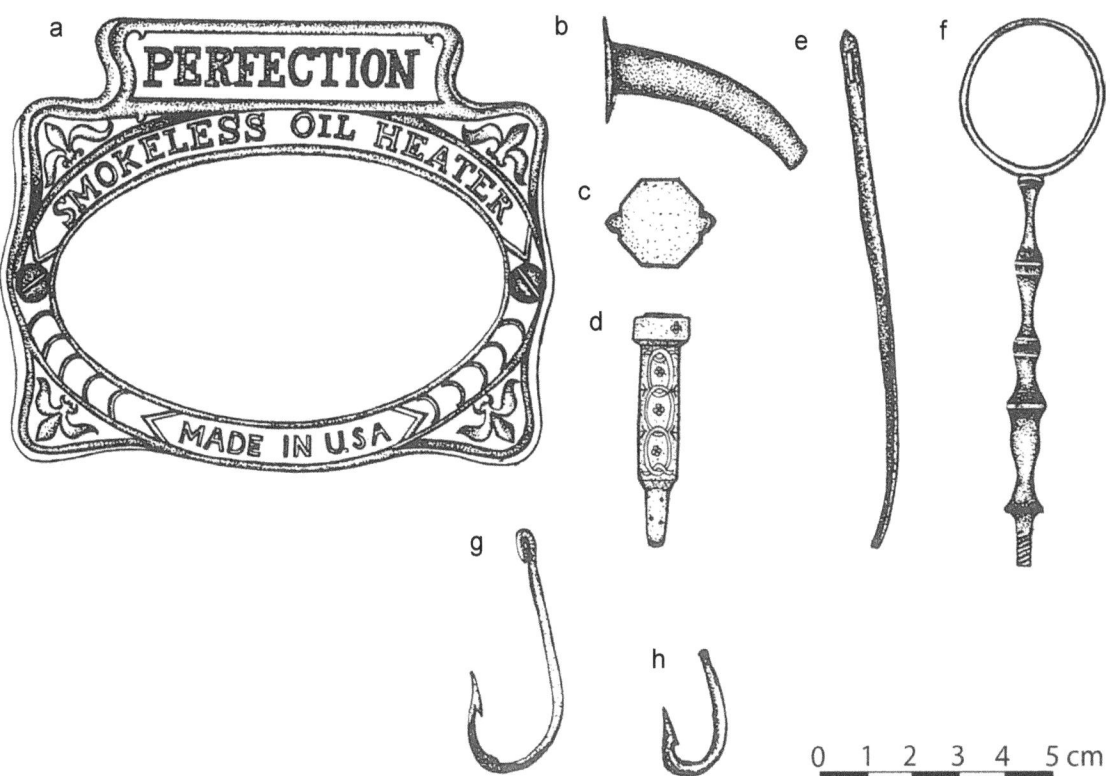

Figure 5.62. Miscellaneous metal artefacts. a. Aluminium "Perfection Smokeless Oil Heater" crest found at Ch/26 (M14 Ly.2). b. Iron spout found at ACS/6 (G9 Ly.2). c. Tin tobacco tag found at Apple Tree (E4 Ly.1). d. Small ointment(?) syringe made of lead alloy, found at Ch/23 (J14 Ly.4). e. Sack needle found at ACS/6 (E8 Ly.3). f. Threaded brass handle (use unknown) found at Caliche (Z4 Ly.2). g. Fishhook found at Flax Grove (G7 Ly.2). h. Fishhook found at Flax Grove (G5 Ly.1).

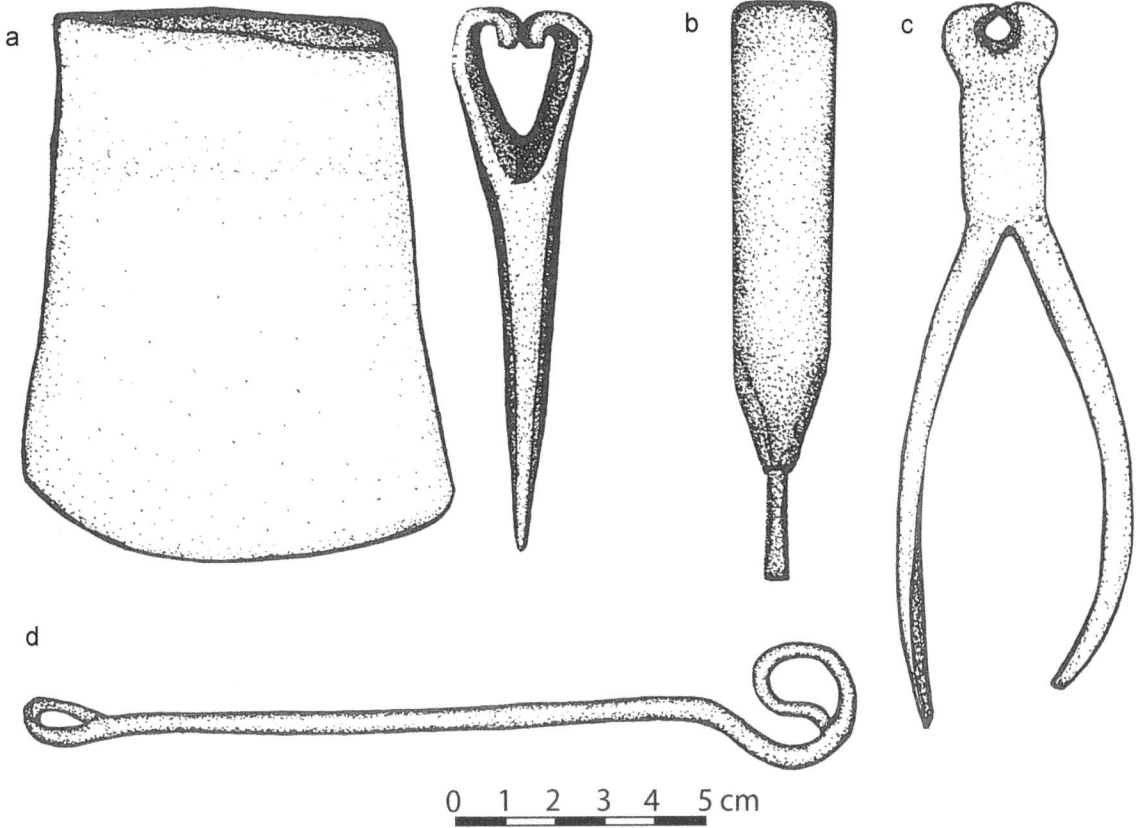

Figure 5.63. Tools. a. Axehead, side and end views. Found at Sheung Fong (X2 Ly.2). b. Screwdriver made from bone-handle knife. Found at ACS/2 (J15 Ly.2). c. Pliers found at Sheung Fong (V22 Ly.2). d. Threader(?) found at Ch/23 (J16 Ly.4).

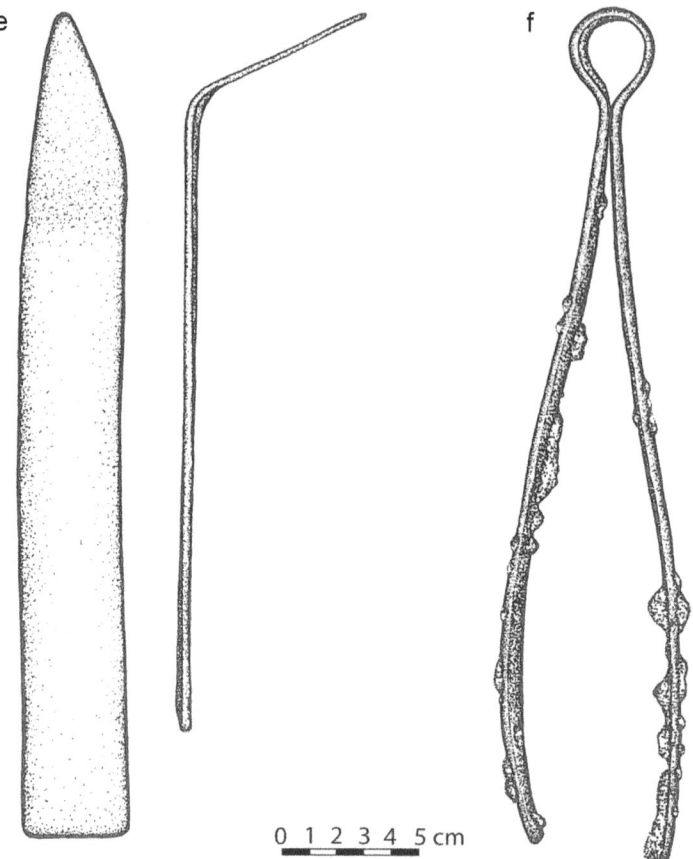

Figure 5.63. Tools (*continued*). **e.** Seed planting tool(?) found at Ha Fong (M16 Ly.4). **f.** Tongs found at ACS/2 surface.

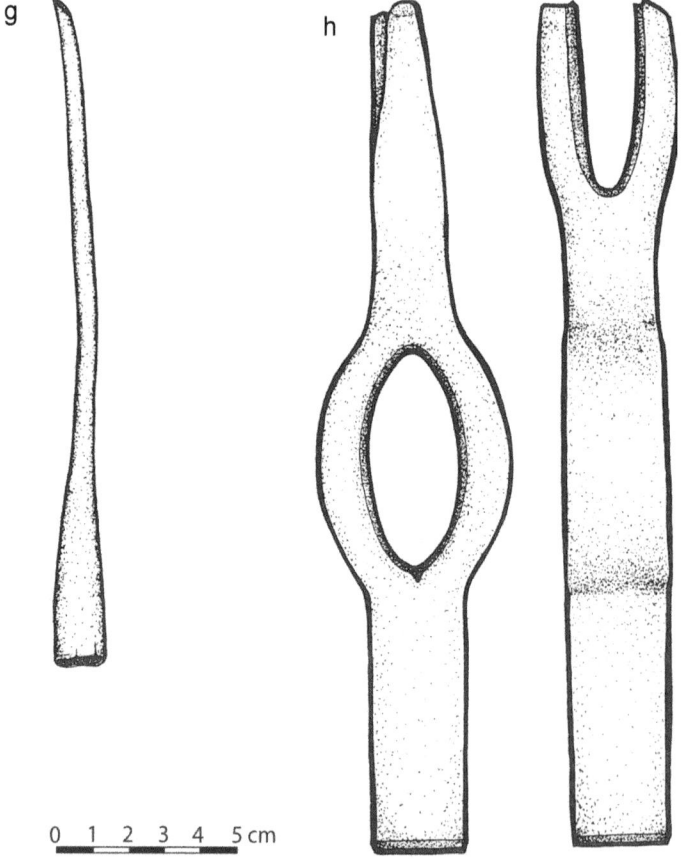

Figure 5.63. Tools (*continued*). **g.** Metal spike (use unknown) found at Ch/23 J16 Ly.1. **h.** Unusual hammerhead, top and side views. Found at Ch/33 (J14 Ly.1).

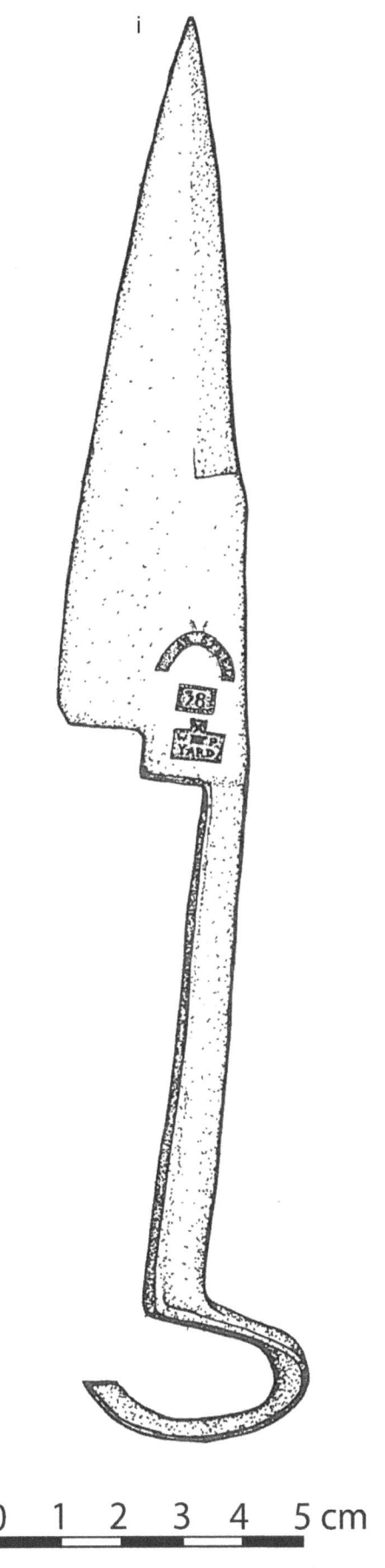

Figure 5.63i. Handshear blade (half) impressed with US(?) manufacturer's mark. The numerous "half blades" were possibly used as knives. ACS/2 E11 Ly.1.

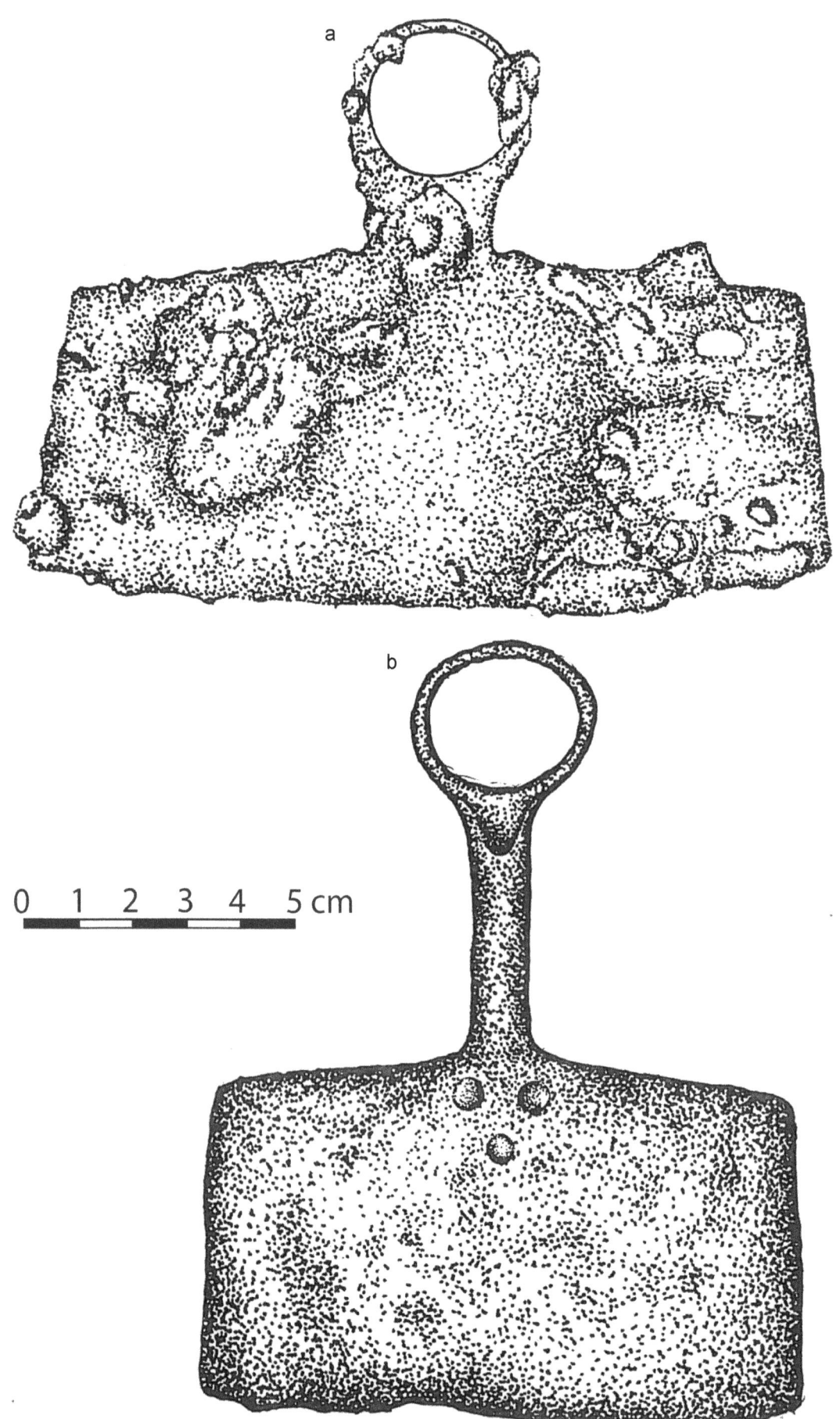

Figure 5.64. Gardening Tools. **a.** Hoe blade found at ACS/5, north-east corner of hut, exterior. **b.** Hoe blade found at Ch/6 (J20 Ly.3).

5 The material culture of the Chinese in southern New Zealand

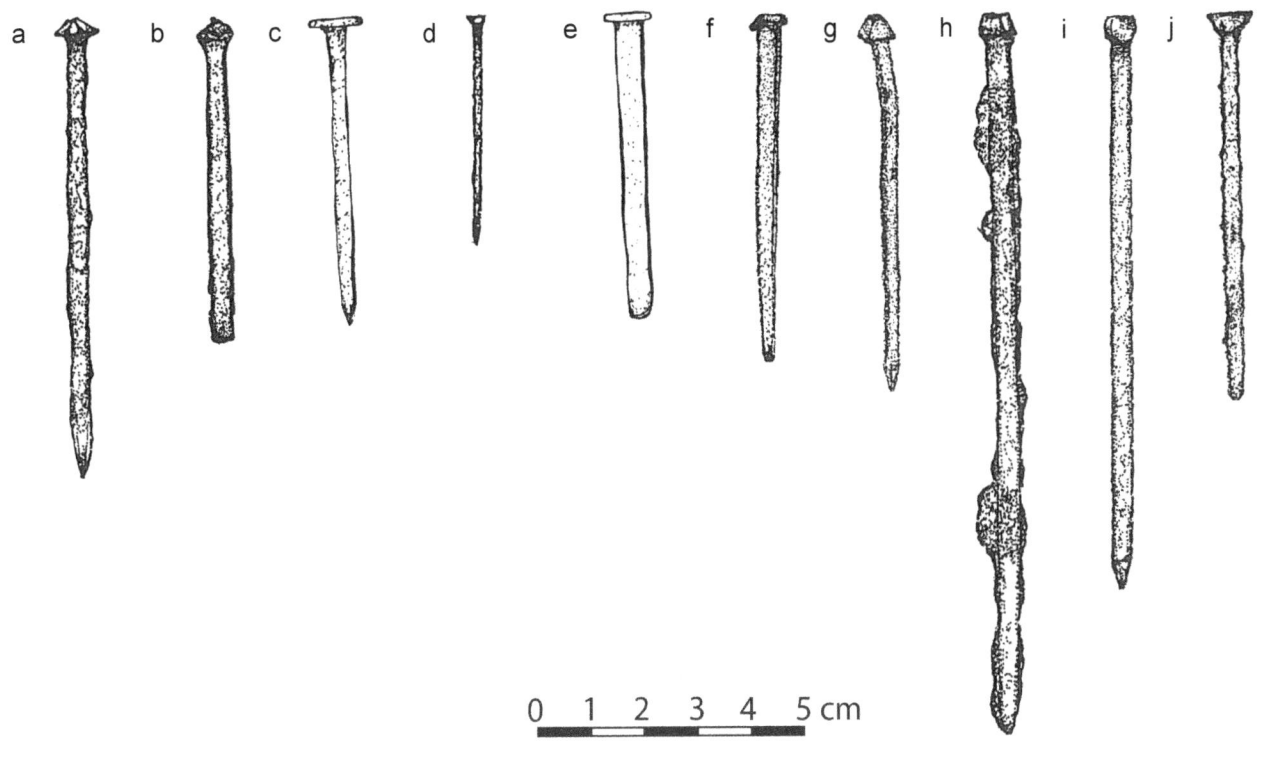

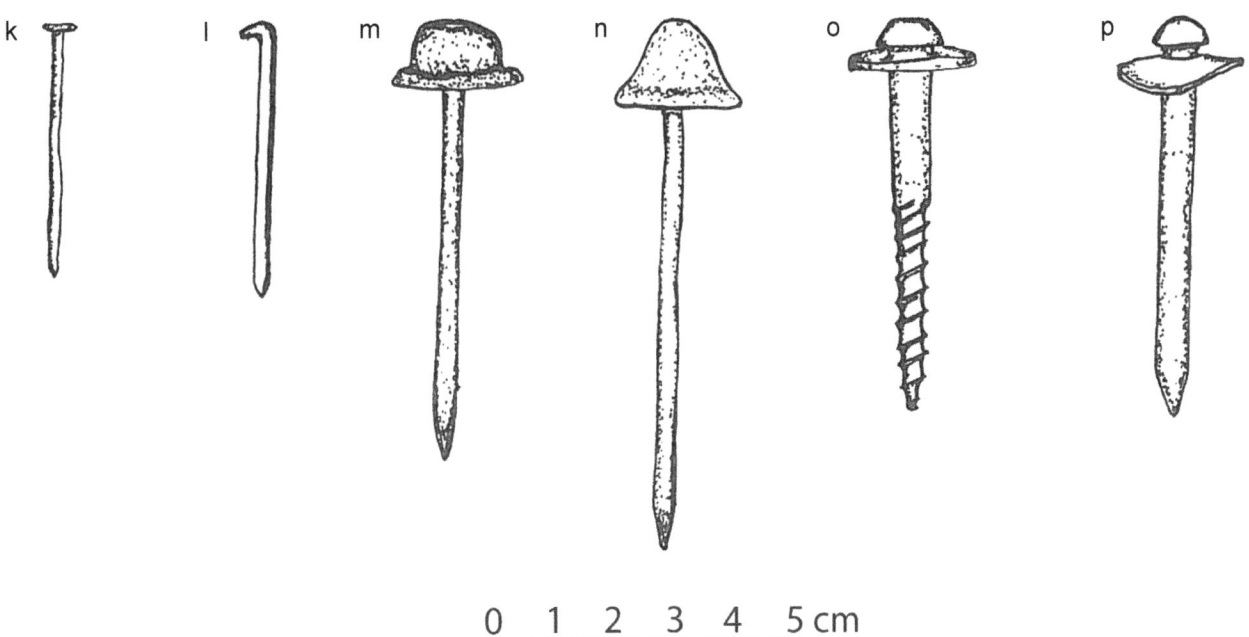

Figure 5.65. Nail types. **a.** Rosehead nail. **b.** Rosehead spike. **c.** Flathead. **d.** Small flathead. **e.** Flathead spike. **f.** Square-section flathead spike. **g.** Rhomboid head. **h.** Proto jolthead. **i.** Jolthead. **j.** Flarehead. **k.** Case nail. **l.** Offset head (Chinese?). **m.** Flat-top leadhead (roofing nail). **n.** Bell-top leadhead (roofing nail). **o.** Roofing screw (roofing nail). **p.** Disc-head roofing nail (roofing nail).

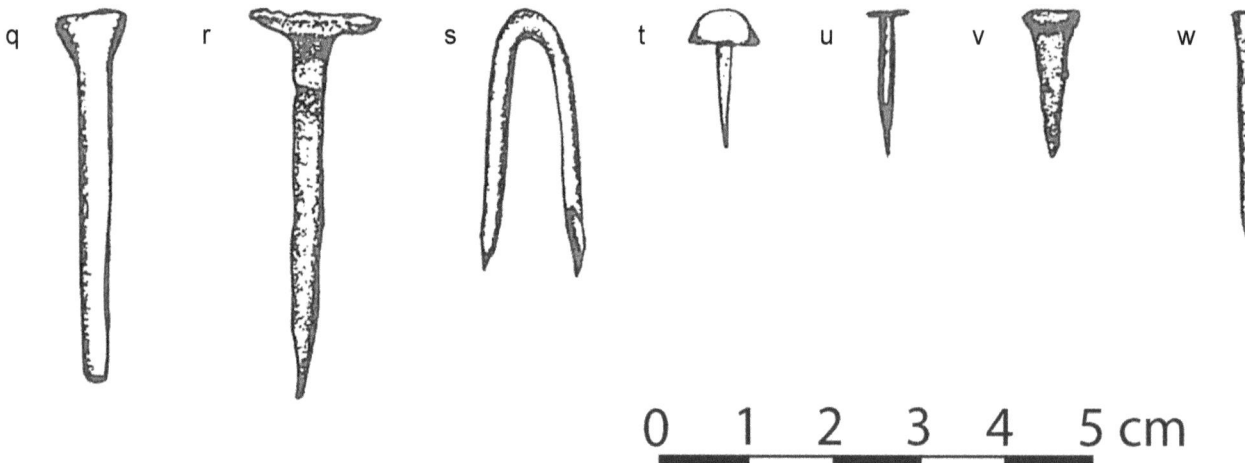

Figure 5.65q–w. Special purpose nails, see Section 5.5.4.1.4.

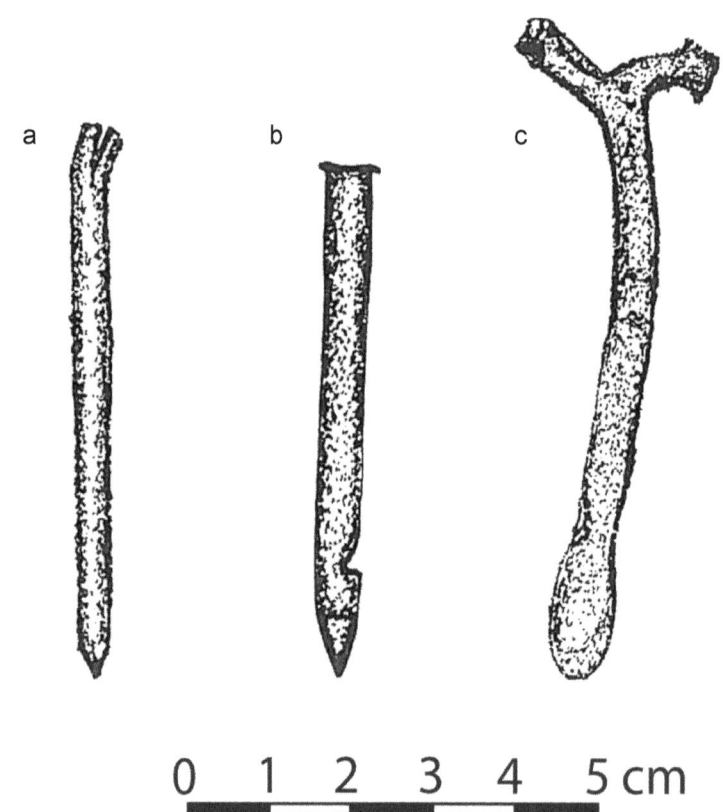

Figure 5.66. Modified nails. **a.** Notched nail found at Ah Wee's (F10 Ly.2). **b.** Nail or wire with barb found at ACS/1 (H13 Ly.1). **c.** Nail with split head and "screwdriver tip" found at Poplars site (J9 Ly.1).

5 The material culture of the Chinese in southern New Zealand

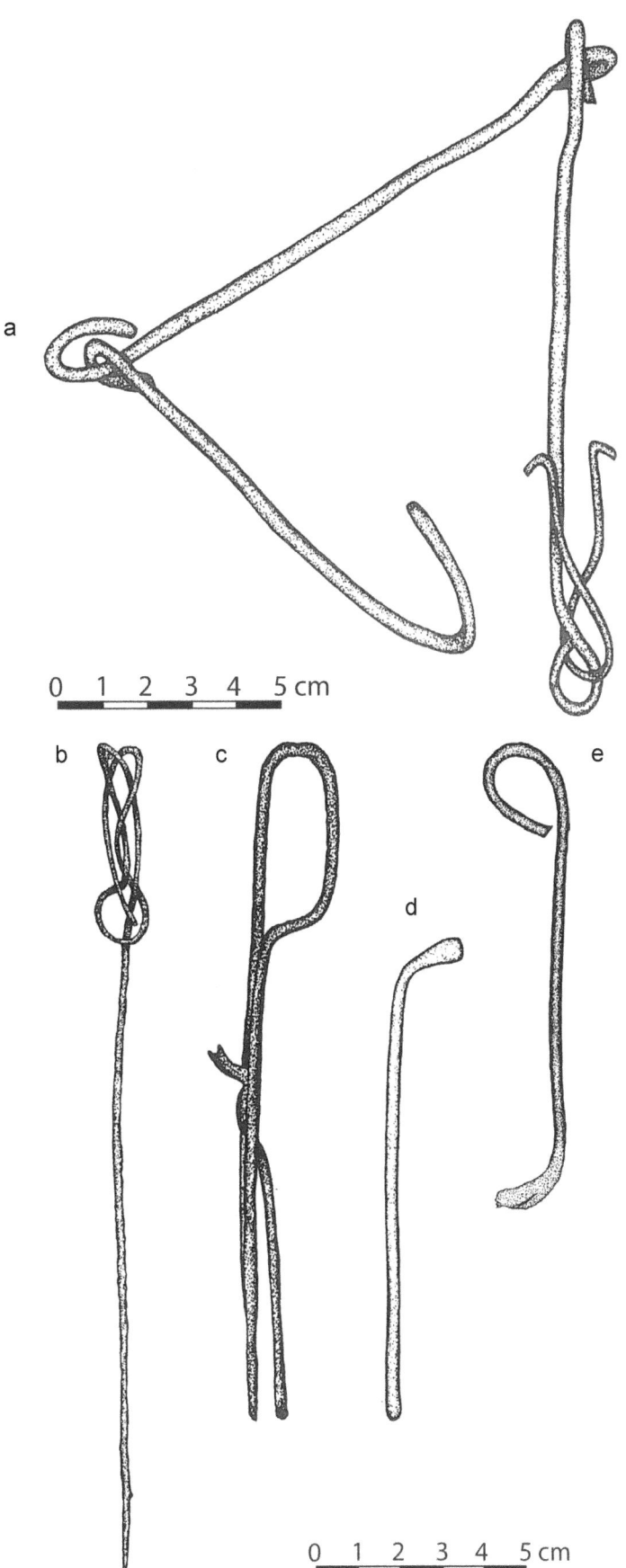

Figure 5.67. Wire artefacts. **a.** Billy hook(?) found at Ah Wee's (J9 Ly.1). **b.** Wire skewer(?) found at Sheung Fong (R21 Ly.2). **c.** Wire tongs found at Ch/12 (E8 Ly.1). **d.** Wire with modified screwdriver-like tip found at Ch/15 (N17 Ly.1). **e.** Wire with modified screwdriver-like tip found at Caliche (X4 Ly.1).

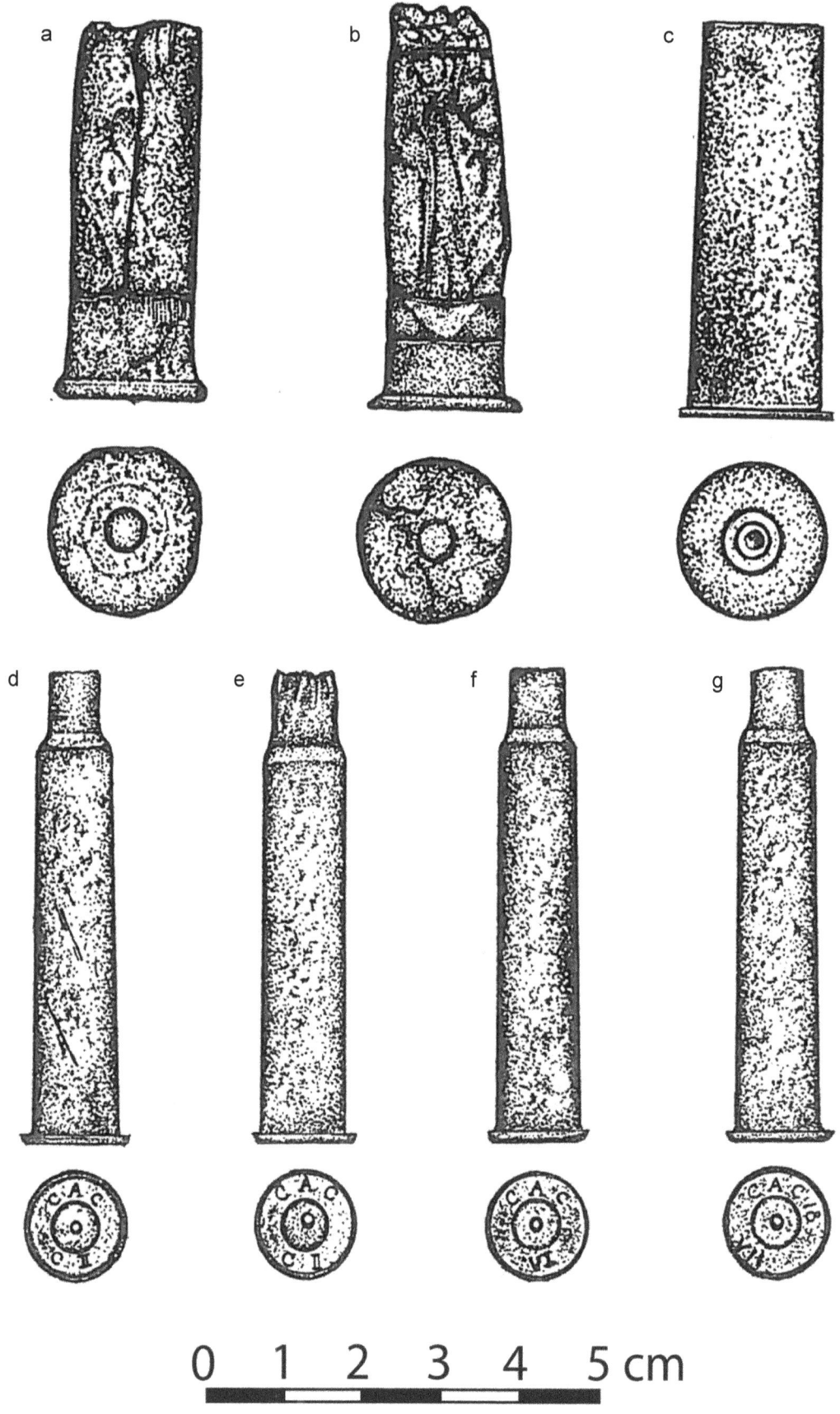

Figure 5.68. Cartridges. **a.** Snider .577 Mk 9 brass foil cartridge found at Ch/34 (L13 Ly.2). **b.** Snider .577 brass foil cartridge, boxer primer found at ACS/15 (L2 Ly.1). **c.** Snider .577 brass cartridge found at ACS/4 (E12 Ly.2). **d.** CAC .303 Mk II C2 cartridge found at CH/26 (F13 Ly.2). **e.** CAC .303 Mk II C2 cartridge (blank) found at ACS/5 (K12 Ly.2). **f.** CAC .303 Mk VI found at Ha Fong (J16 Ly.2). **g.** CAC .303 Mk VII found at Ha Fong (K17 Ly.1).

5 The material culture of the Chinese in southern New Zealand

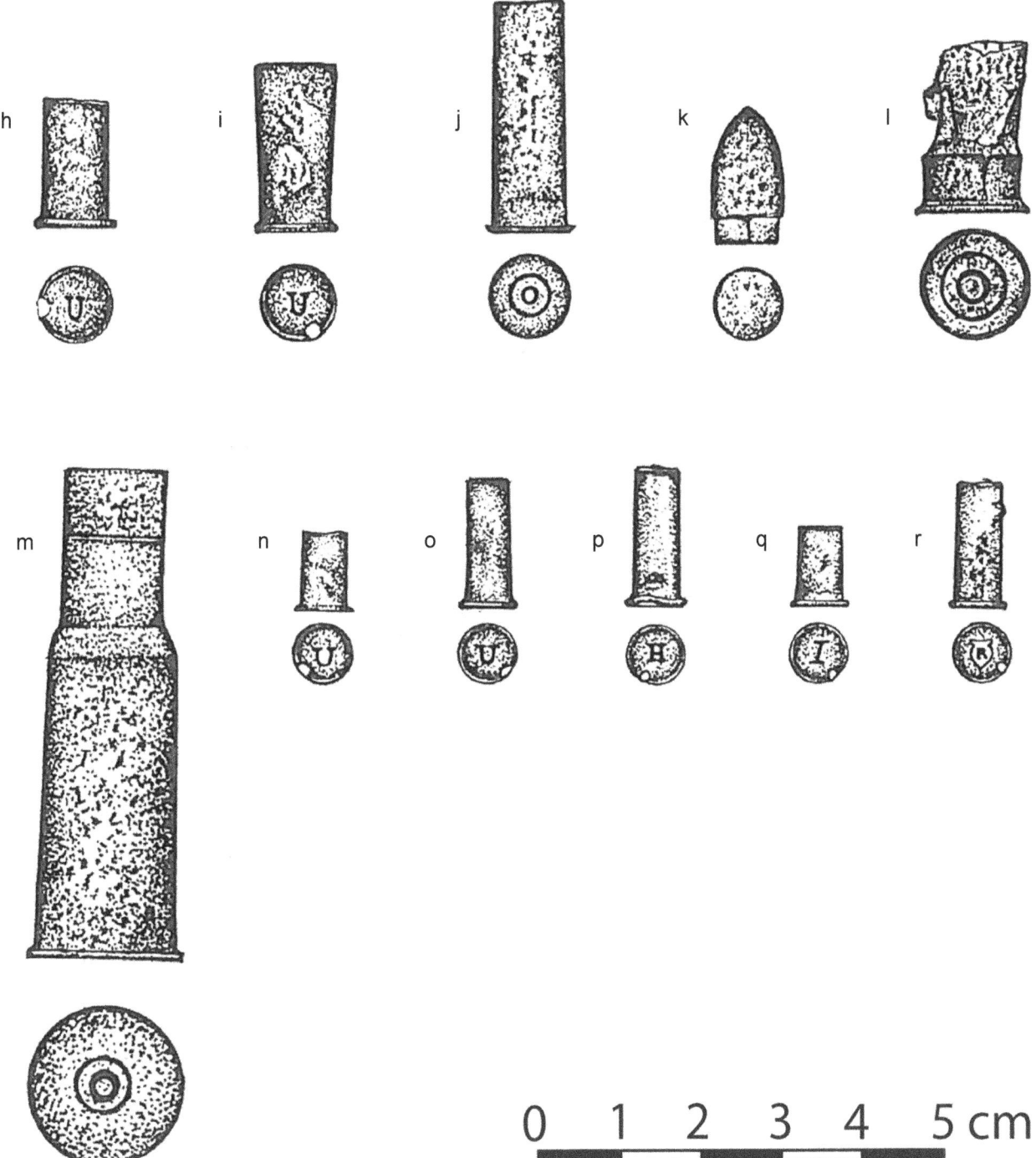

Figure 5.68. Cartridges (*continued*). **h.** .32 drawn brass, short rifle cartridge (Remington UMC) found at Ch/19 (M2 Ly.2). **i.** .32 drawn brass, long rifle cartridge (Remington UMC) found at Ch/1 (M6 Ly.1). **j.** .310 drawn brass, cadet rifle cartridge (possibly Kynock) found at ACS/6 (E7 Ly.2). **k.** .366 lead projectile found at Ch/33 (L17) surface. **l.** .410 brass foil cartridge found at Caliche (Z4 Ly.2). **m.** .450/577 drawn brass, Martini–Henry "bottleneck" cartridge found at Ch/6 (I20 Ly.3). **n.** .22 brass, short rifle cartridge (Remington UMC) found at Ch/24 (C5 Ly.2). **o.** .22 brass, short rifle cartridge (Remington UMC) found at Rapids site (G7 Ly.2). **p.** .22 brass, long rifle cartridge (Winchester) found at Ch/22 (E12 Ly.2). **q.** .22 brass, short rifle cartridge (ICI) found at Ha Fong (J19 Ly.1). **r.** .22 nickel – alloy, long rifle cartridge (RWS).found at Ha Fong (M15 Ly.1).

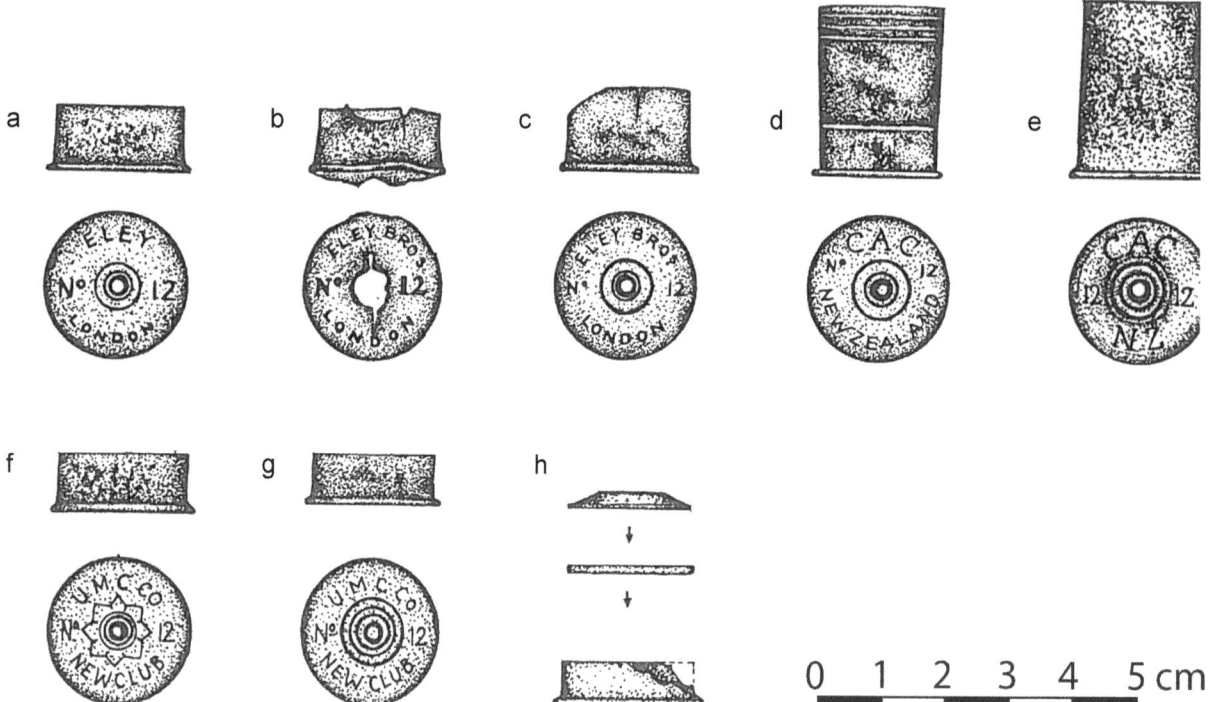

Figure 5.69. 12-gauge cartridges. **a.** "Eley No.12 London" found at Ch/34 (E12 Ly.1). **b.** "Eley Bros No.12 London" found at Firewood Creek (B12 Ly.1). **c.** "Eley Bros No.12 London" found at Ha Fong (A23 Ly.1). **d.** "CAC No.12 New Zealand" found at Ha Fong (F12 Ly.2). **e.** "CAC 12, 12 NZ" found at ACS/6 (H10 Ly.1). **f.** "UMC Co. No.12 New Club" with star pattern found at Ha Fong (T20 Ly.2). **g.** "UMC Co. No.12 New Club" found at Ah Wee's (P6 Ly.2). **h.** Wei-qi (go) counters(?) in 12-gauge cartridge base, found at Firewood Creek, see Section 5.5.6.5.

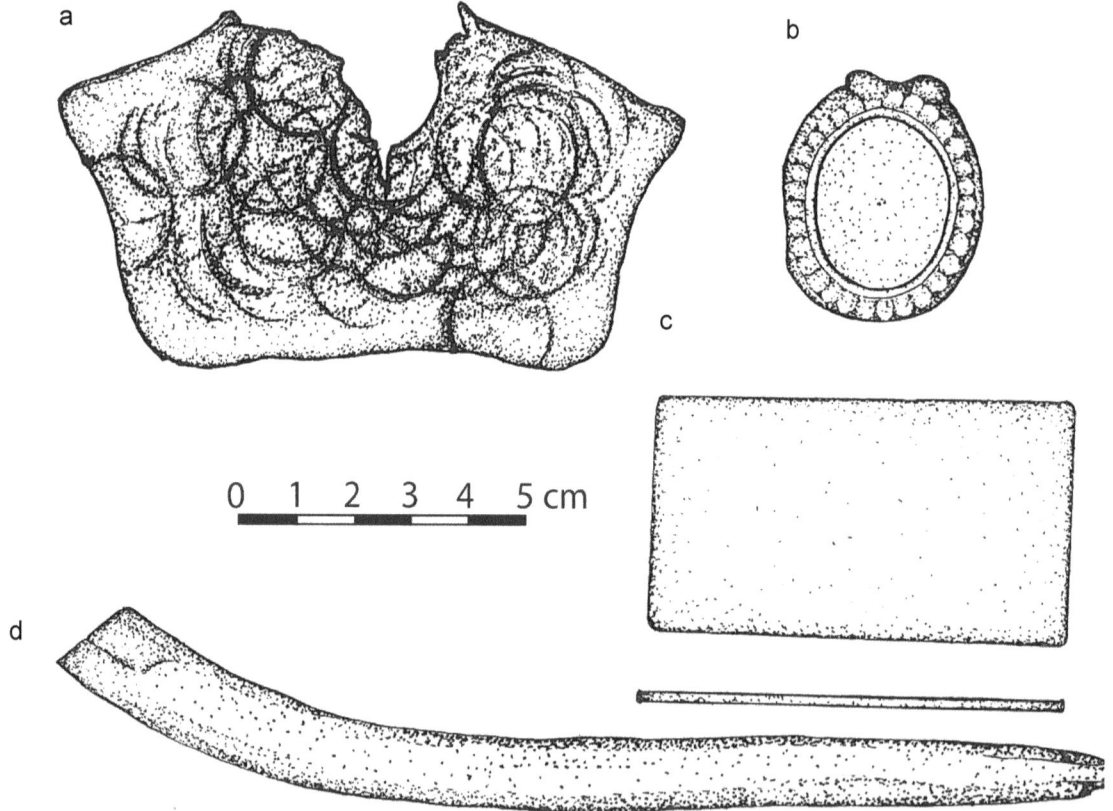

Figure 5.70. Lead artefacts. **a.** Piece of lead with punched impressions (from wadding punch?) found at Hanging Rock (J8 Ly.1). **b.** Harness rosette found at Ch/33 (L18 Ly.3). **c.** Cast lead slab in plan and section view, found at Ah Lum's, main room (B5 Ly.1). **d.** Cast lead "stick" found at Ch/4 (K12) surface.

5 The material culture of the Chinese in southern New Zealand

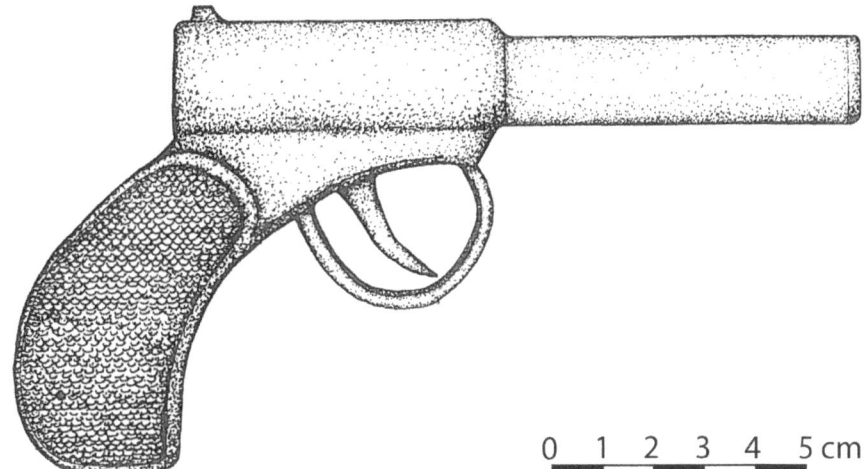

Figure 5.71. Eisenwerke Air Pistol (see Section 5.5.6.5) found at Ch/34 (M17 Ly.2).

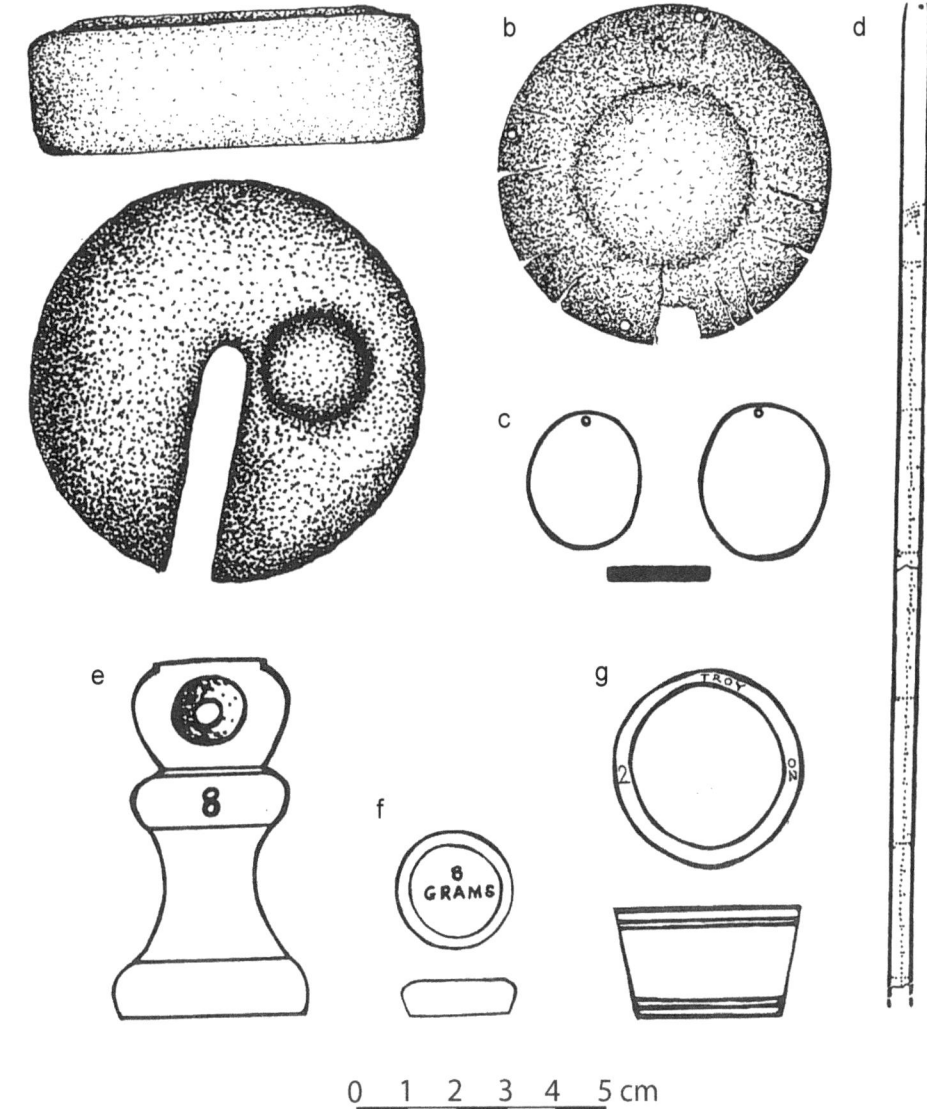

Figure 5.72. Scales and weights. **a.** Cast iron weight in plan and profile view, found at Ah Lum's store, main room (E7 Ly.1). **b.** Copper pan from rule scale found at Ch/18 (N17 Ly.2). **c.** Brass counterweights from rule scale. Left found at ACS/6 (D7 Ly.1), right found at Ch/23 (K15 Ly.2). **d.** Ivory balance arm from rule scale found at Ch/23 (K16 Ly.1). **e.** Brass 8 oz "standing" weight found at Ch/23 (K15 Ly.4). **f.** Brass 8 g "disc" weight, plan and profile view. Found at Ch/23 (J15 Ly.4). **g.** Brass 2 troy oz, container weight, plan and profile view. Found at Ch/14 (L7) surface.

365

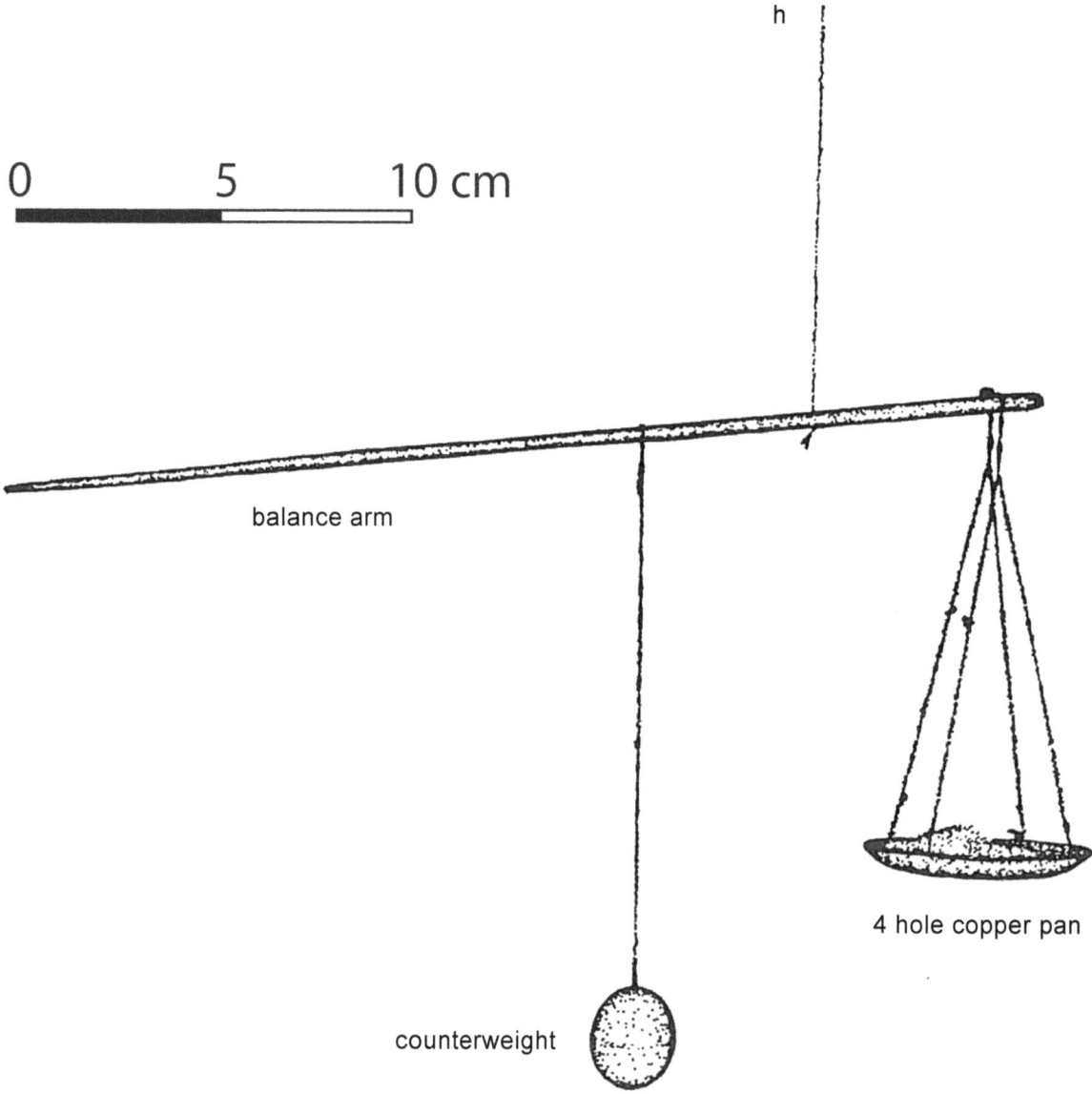

Figure 5.72h. Chinese rule scale.

5 The material culture of the Chinese in southern New Zealand

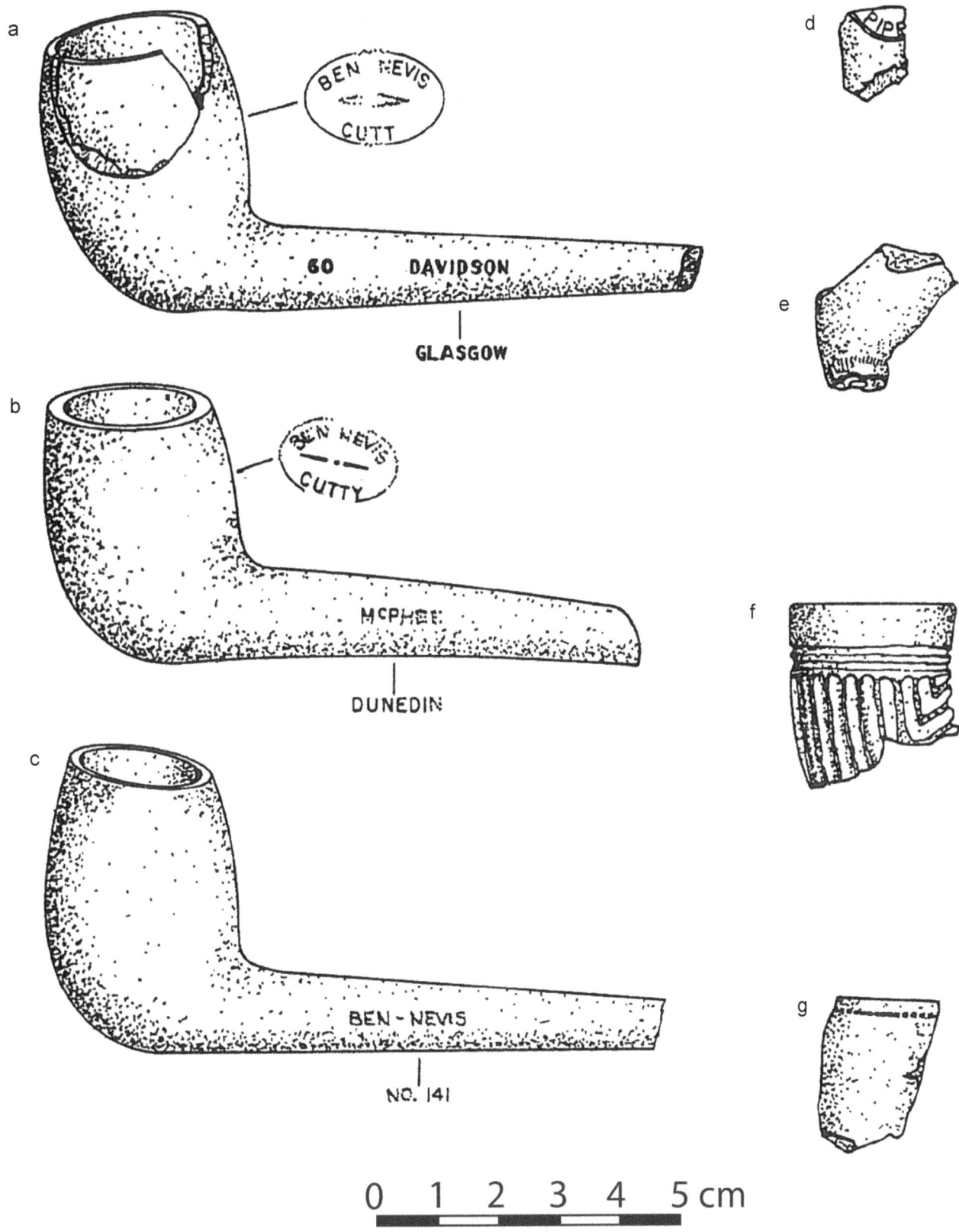

Figure 5.73. Clay tobacco pipes. **a.** Impressed "Davidson, Glasgow, 60, Ben Nevis Cutty", found at ACS/3 (G11 Ly.3). **b.** Impressed "McPhee, Dunedin", a Dunedin shopkeeper(?), found at ACS/3 (F12 Ly.3). **c.** Impressed "Ben Nevis, No. 141", found at Ah Lum's store, main room (D7 Ly.1). **d.** Impressed "-PIP[E]-" on bowl, found at Ah Lum's store, main room (D7 Ly.1). **e.** Modified shank found at ACS/7, trench B. **f.** Ribbed terracotta bowl (Pamplin pipe) found at ACS/6 (H6 Ly.1). **g.** Rouletted bowl found at ACS/4 (J10 Ly.1).

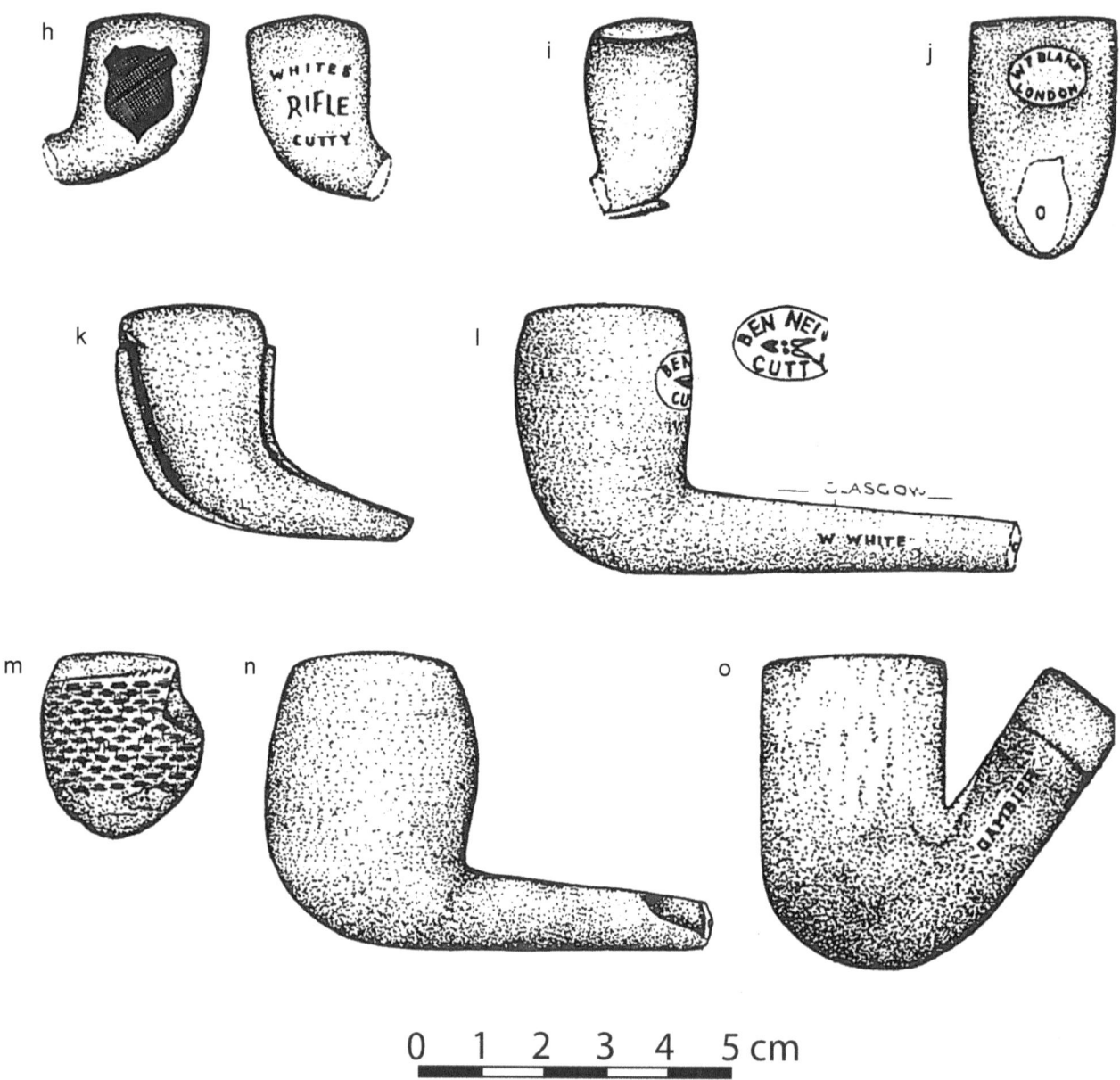

Figure 5.73. Clay tobacco pipes (*continued*). **h.** Impressed "White's Rifle Cutty" on bowl with a shield on the other side, found at Apple Tree site (S124/212; D5 Ly.1). **i.** Small plain bowl found at Sheung Fong (S133/21; T20 Ly.3). **j.** Impressed "W.T. Blake, London" on bowl, found at Rockfall 1 site (S133/121) surface. **k.** Plain bowl with ridges on upper and lower surfaces, found at Rockfall 2 site (S133/169; E5 Ly.1). **l.** Impressed "W White, Glasgow" on stem, "Ben Nevis Cutty" on bowl. Found at Sandy Point (H7 Ly.1) outside door. **m.** Bowl with raised ridge pattern found at Sandy Point (S124/231; F3 Ly.1). **n.** Large plain bowl found at Ch/23 (J14 Ly.4). **o.** Bowl impressed "A Tabis[?], Gambier" found at Chinatown hut 26 (M13 Ly.2).

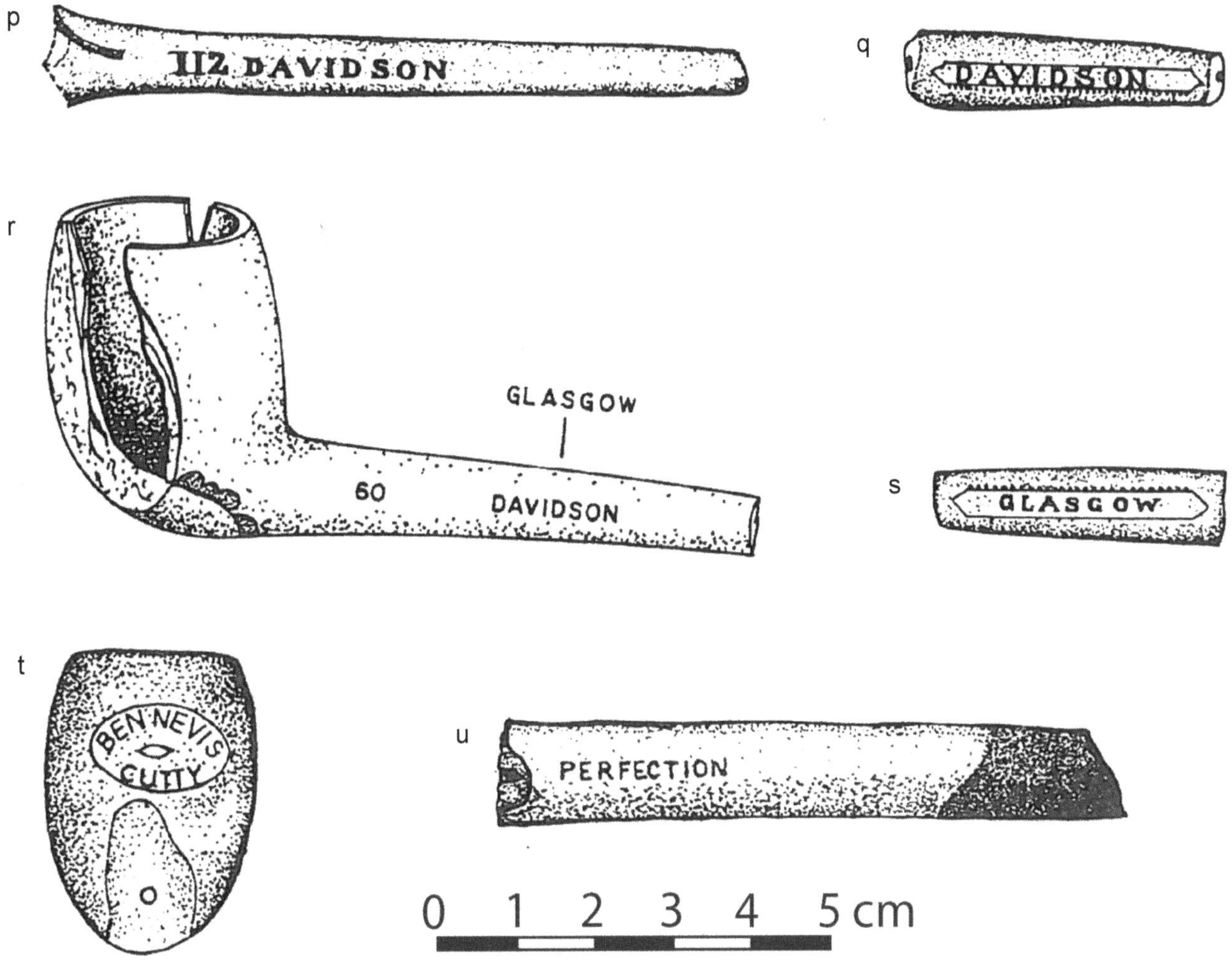

5 The material culture of the Chinese in southern New Zealand

Figure 5.73. Clay tobacco pipes (*continued*). **p.** Stem impressed "112 Davidson" found at Carricktown hut site surface. **q.** Stem section impressed "Davidson" found at Caliche shelter (C4 Ly. 2). **r.** Impressed "Davidson, Glasgow, 60", with plain bowl. Found at ACS/3 (G13) humus. **s.** Stem section impressed "Davidson" with dot pattern above the lettering, found at Caliche shelter (S133/223; C4 Ly.2). **t.** Bowl impressed "Ben Nevis Cutty" found at Firewood Creek (A10 Ly.1). **u.** Flat stem section with green-glazed mouth end, impressed "Perfection". Found at Chinatown horticultural terrace, trench B. See Section 5.6.1.1 for discussion on manufacturers.

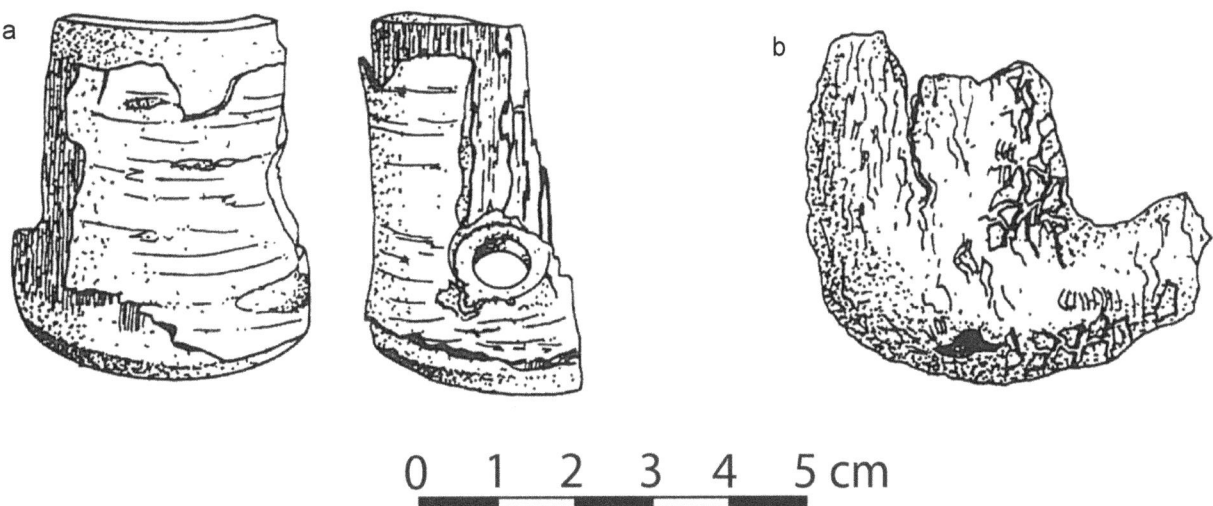

Figure 5.74. Wooden tobacco pipes. **a.** Left and rear view of cherrywood pipe bowl found at Ah Lum's store, kitchen surface. **b.** Briar tobacco pipe, half-bent billiard shape found at ACS/6 (I19 Ly.1). After Pfeiffer (1984:7).

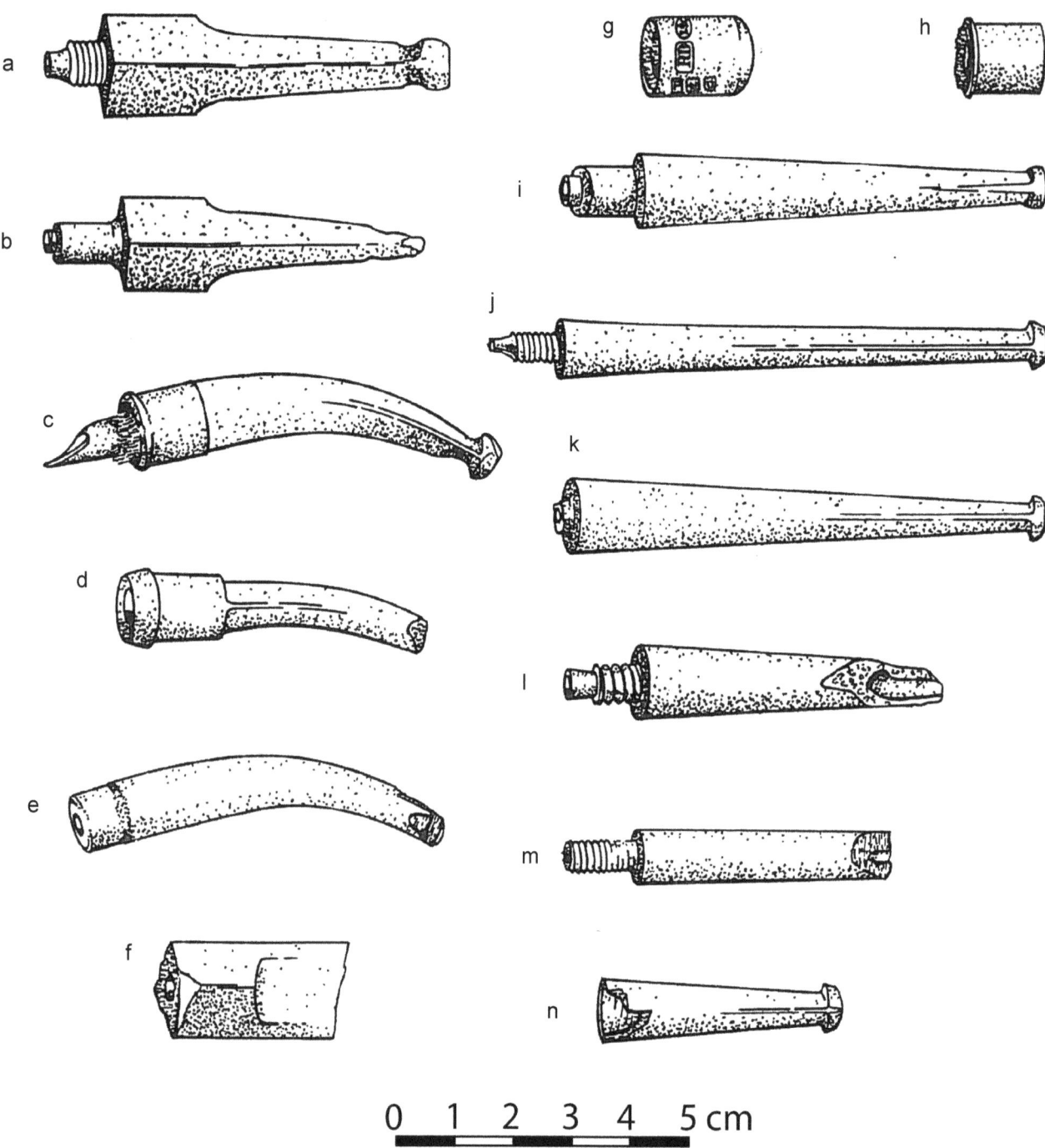

Figure 5.75. Vulcanite pipe stems and shank bands. See Table 5.61 for distribution. **a.** Vulcanite stem, straight bulldog shape. Found at ACS/2 (G9 Ly.1). **b.** Vulcanite stem, straight bulldog shape. Found at Ah Lum's store, mainroom surface. **c.** Vulcanite stem, tapered half-bent shape with brass shank band. Found at Ah Lum's store, bedroom surface. **d.** Vulcanite stem, half-bent saddle shape. Found at ACS/4 (I10 Ly.1). **e.** Vulcanite stem, tapered half-bent shape. Found at Ah Lum's store, bedroom surface. **f.** One of two amber-coloured stem fragments in straight bulldog shape found at Ah Lum's store, mainroom (B5) surface. **g.** Silver shank band marked with "P", "M" and a shield along the stem axis and "RD" and "L&Co" at 90° to the long axis. Found at ACS/8 (H12) rock infill. **h.** Copper shank band found at ACS/8 (F14 Ly.1). **i.** Vulcanite stem, tapered shape found at ACS, Feature No. 13 (D11), humus. **j.** Vulcanite stem, elongated tapered shape. A long thin stem usually indicates a "Prince" style pipe bowl. Found at ACS/6 (J9 Ly.1). **k.** Vulcanite stem, tapered shape, found at ACS/6 (J8), humus. **l.** Vulcanite stem, tapered shape, found at ACS/4 (H12 Ly.2). **m.** Vulcanite stem fragment in "Prince" style. Found at ACS/4 (F10, Ly.2). **n.** Vulcanite stem, tapered shape, found at Ah Lum's store, main room (B5 Ly.1).

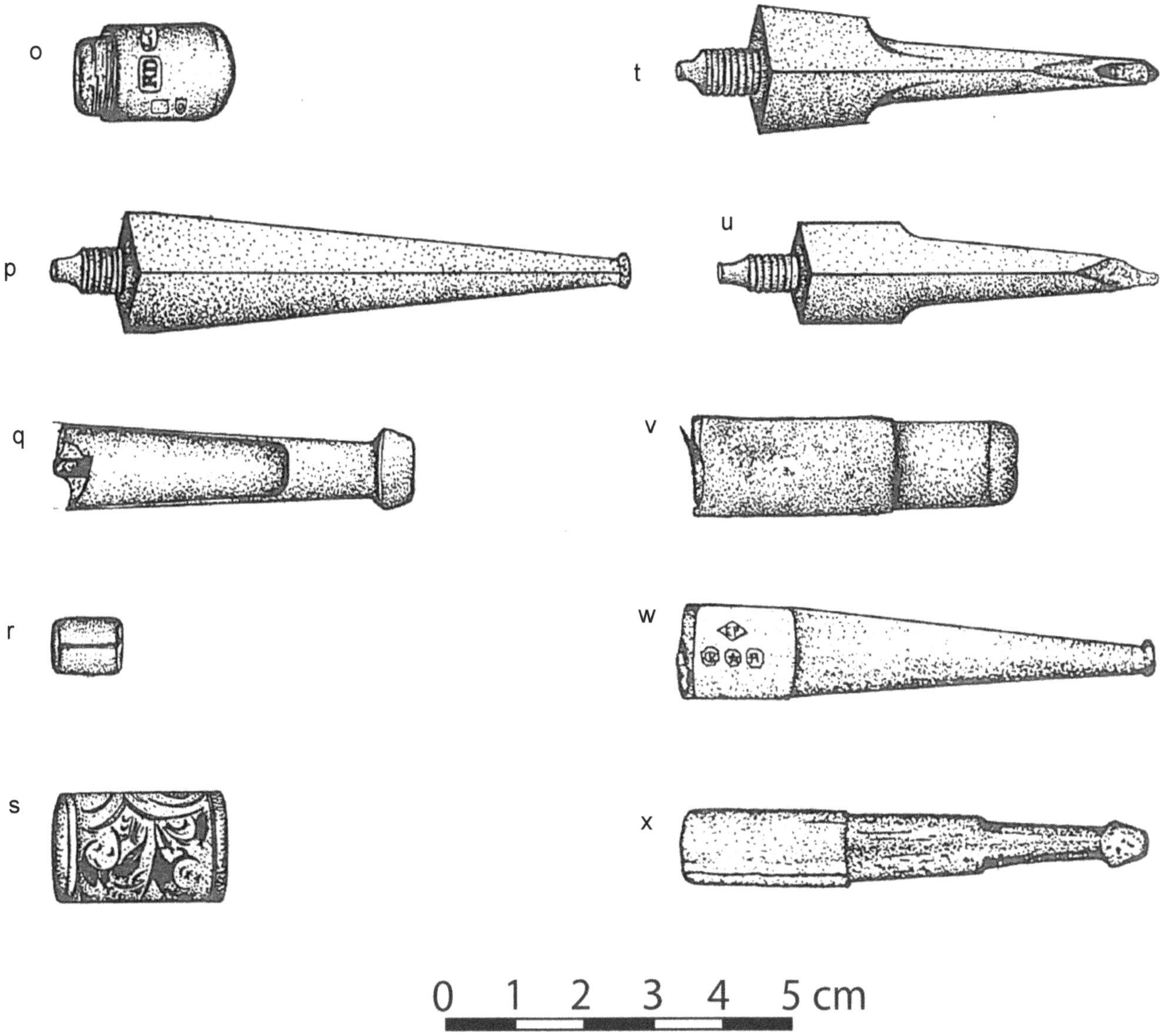

Figure 5.75. Vulcanite pipe stems and shank bands (*continued*). See Table 5.61 for distribution. **o.** Silver-plated brass shank band marked "RD" and "L&Co" at 90° to the stem axis, and "P", "M" and a shield along the stem axis. Found at ACS/8 (H12), rock infill. It has the same marks as the specimen depicted in Figure 5.75g. Containing remnant of wooden pipe stem. **p.** Vulcanite stem, tapered shape, found at ACS/4 (H11 Ly.3). **q.** Vulcanite stem, tapered shape, square section. Found at ACS/4. **r.** Small brass shank band(?) found at ACS/4 (L15 Ly.2). **s.** Brass shank band(?) with ornate impressed branch design. Found at Ch/12, Area 1 (Ly.1). **t.** Vulcanite stem, straight bulldog shape, found at Flax Grove (G6 Ly.1). **u.** Vulcanite stem, straight bulldog shape, found at Flax Grove (F6 Ly.1). **v.** Vulcanite stem, ovoid section, found at Flax Grove (F6 Ly.1). **w.** Vulcanite stem, tapered shape, with brass shank band marked (at 90° to the long axis) "EP" in a horizontal diamond over "?", a star and "ER[?]". Still attached to the mouthpiece and has a remnant of briar stem inside shank band. Found at Flax Grove (F6, Ly.1). **x.** Bone stem, faceted at mouth end with cylindrical brass shank band. Found at Sheung Fong (T22 Ly.6).

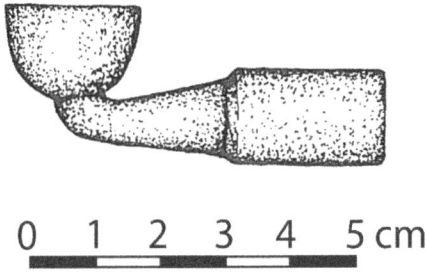

Figure 5.76. Chinese brass tobacco pipe bowl found in a Chinese hut, Cardrona Valley (Dennison pers. comm.).

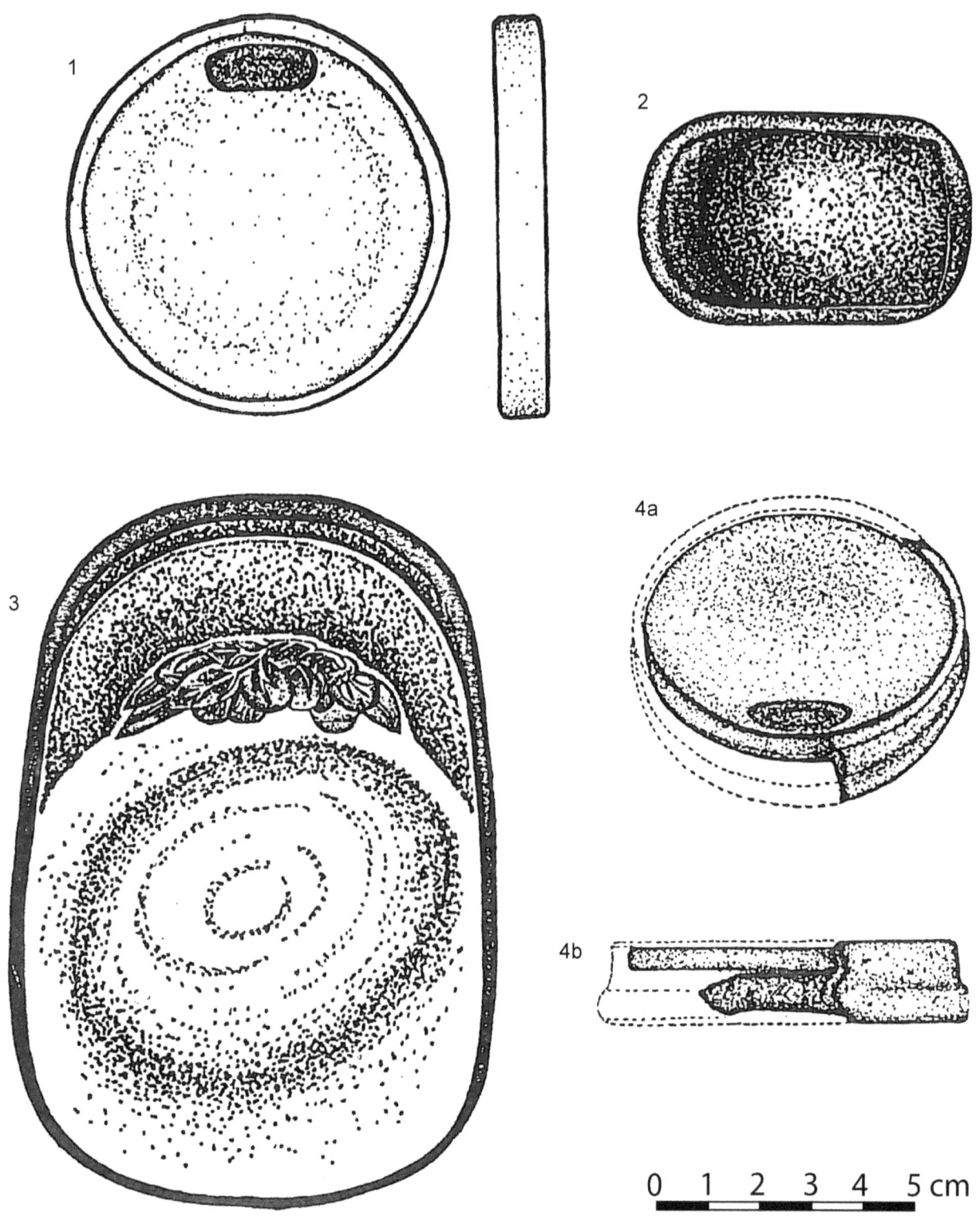

Figure 5.77. Chinese inkstones and writing brush, see Table 5.62 for provenance and descriptions of Figures 5.77-1–4b.

5 The material culture of the Chinese in southern New Zealand

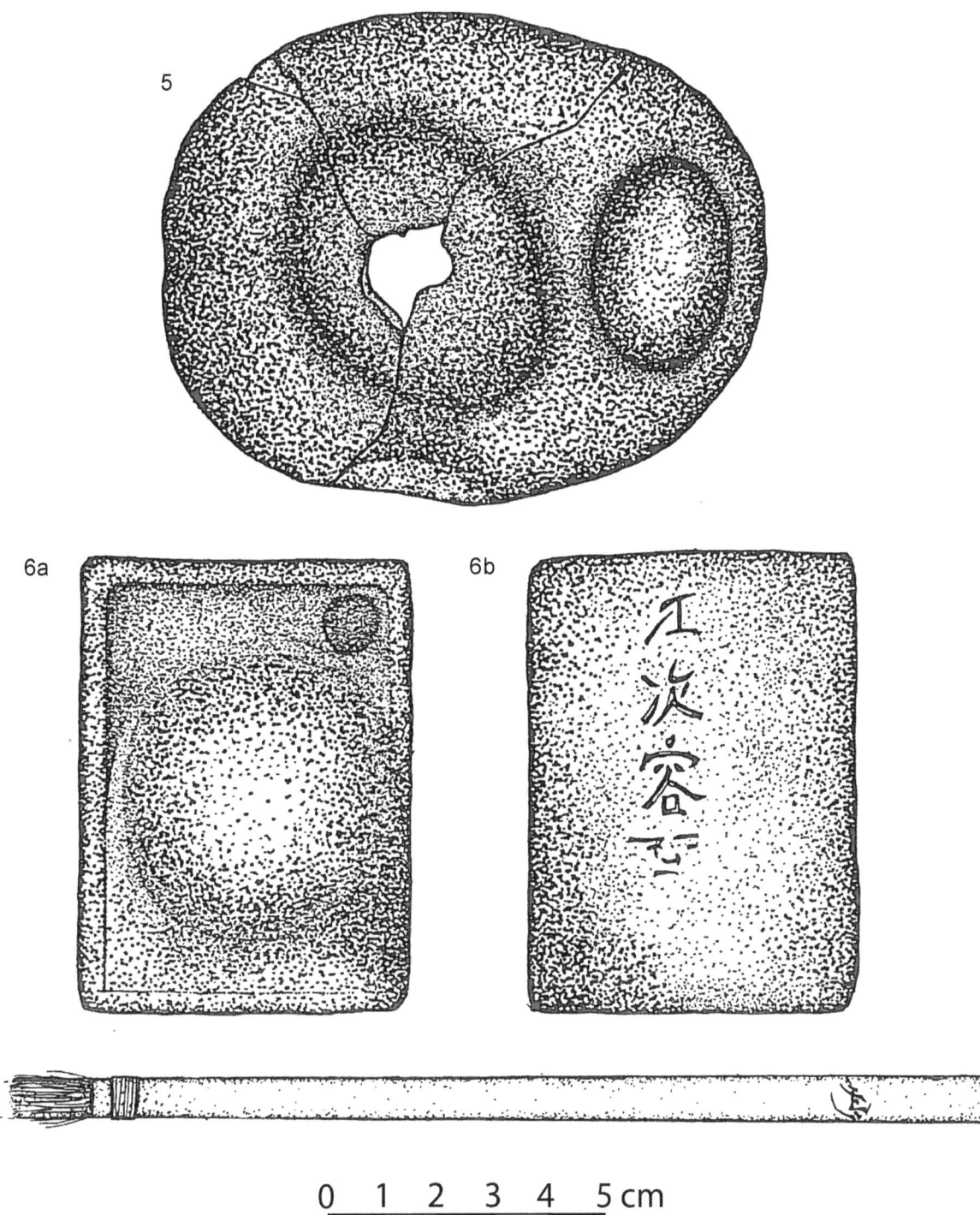

Figure 5.77. Chinese inkstones and writing brush (*continued*). see Table 5.62 for provenance and descriptions of Figures 5.77-5–6b. **7.** Unprovenanced Chinese writing brush held at Cromwell Museum (CR 77779B).

Archaeology and history of the Chinese in southern New Zealand during the nineteenth century

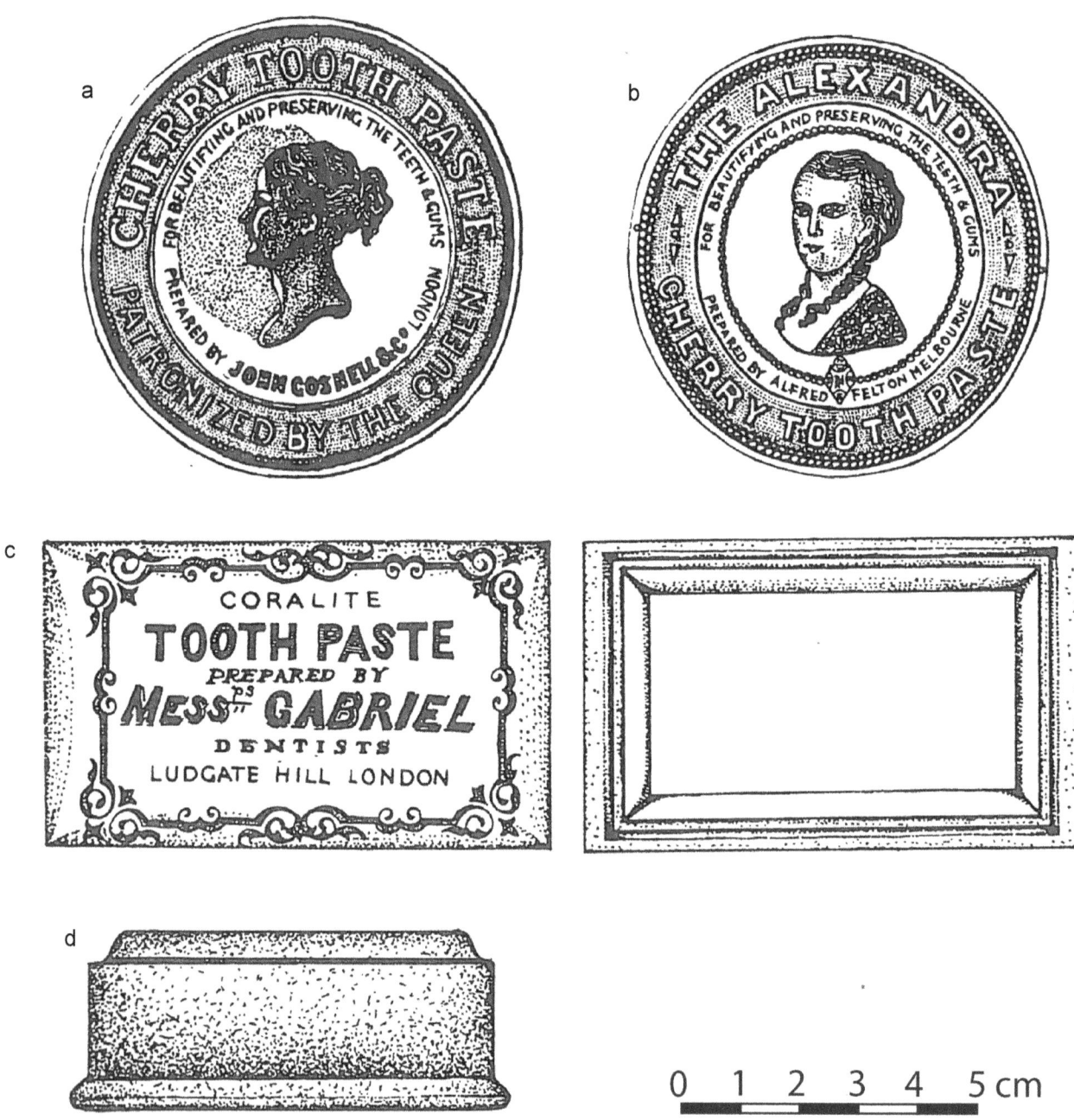

Figure 5.78. Ceramic toothpaste pots and bases. See Table 5.64 for further details.

5 The material culture of the Chinese in southern New Zealand

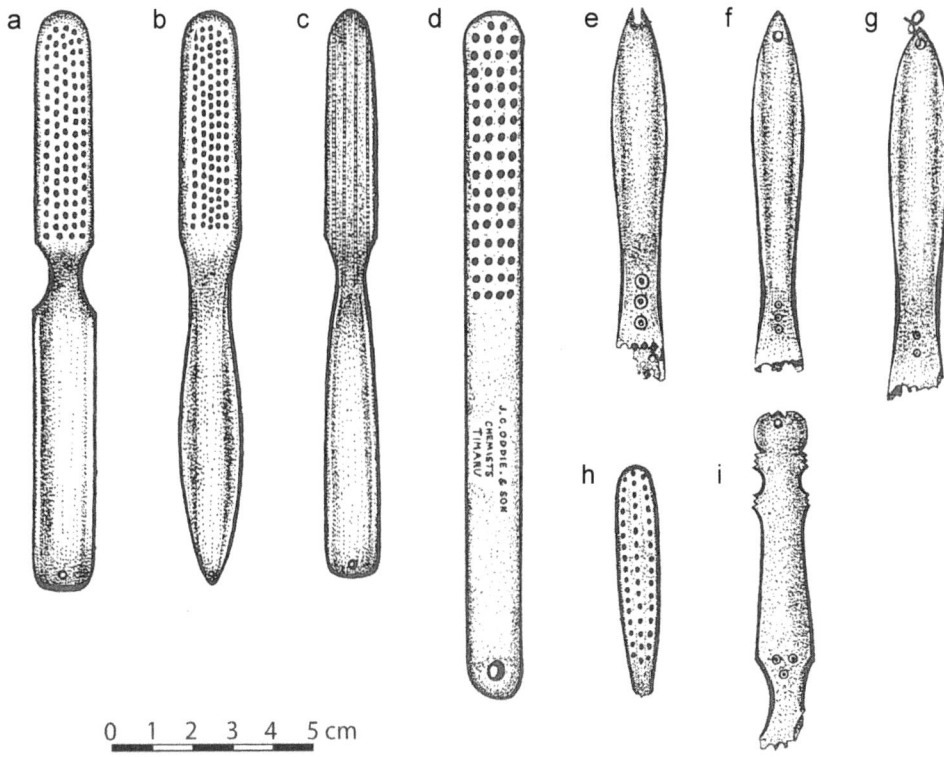

Figure 5.79. Bone toothbrushes. See Table 5.65 for further details and distribution.

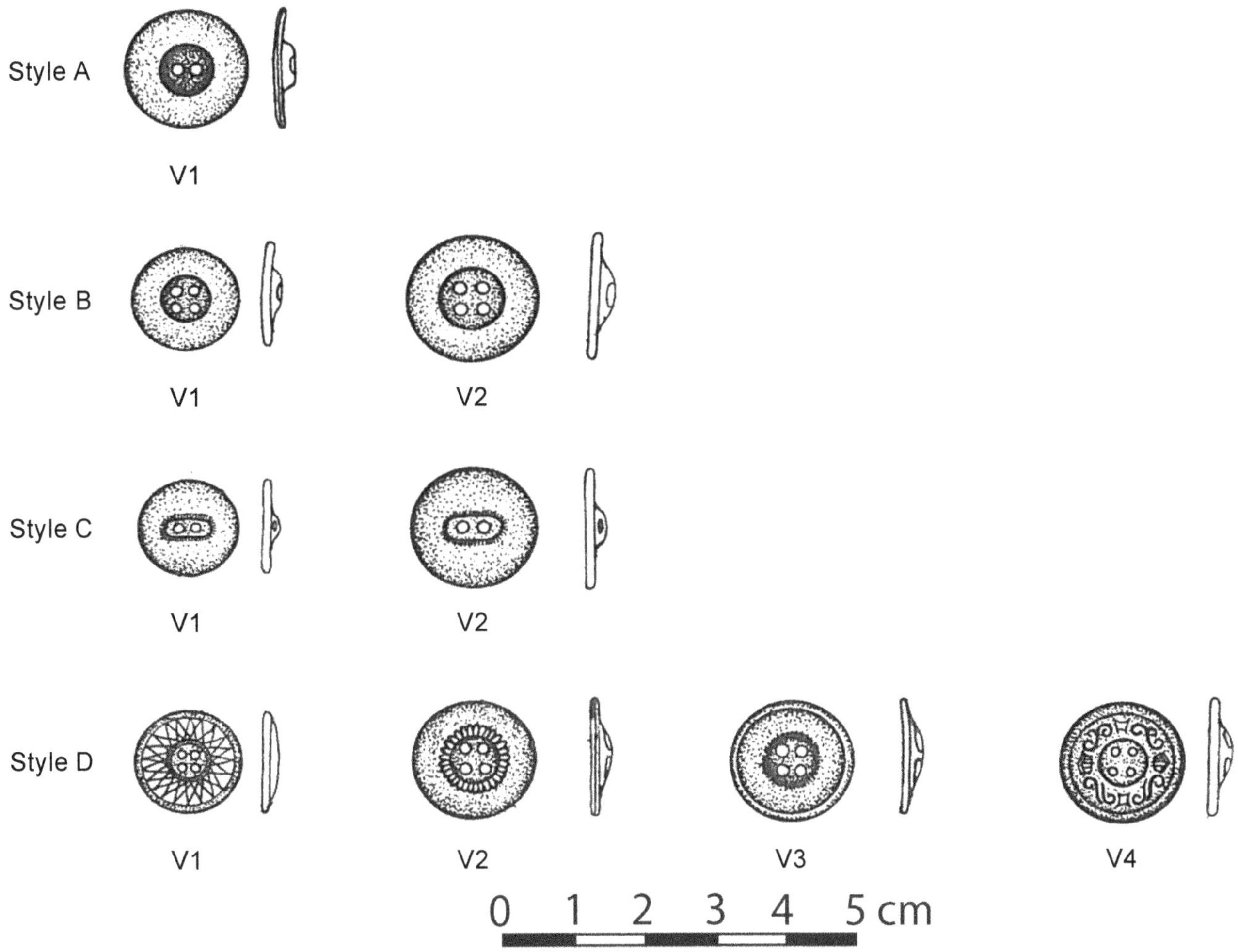

Figure 5.80. Metal buttons: one-piece construction. Reproduced from Cameron (1985).

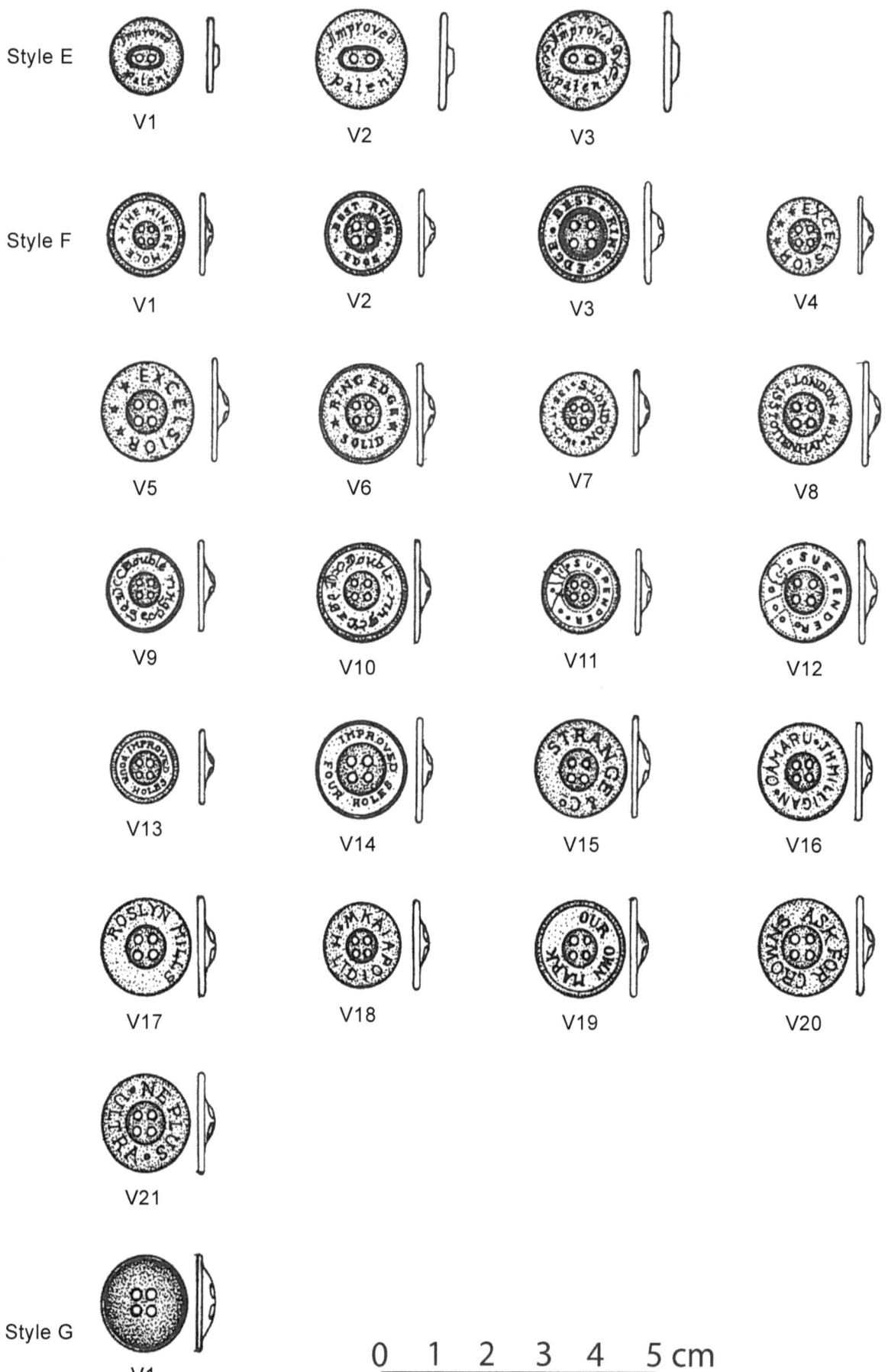

Figure 5.80. Metal buttons: one-piece construction (*continued*). Reproduced from Cameron (1985).

5 The material culture of the Chinese in southern New Zealand

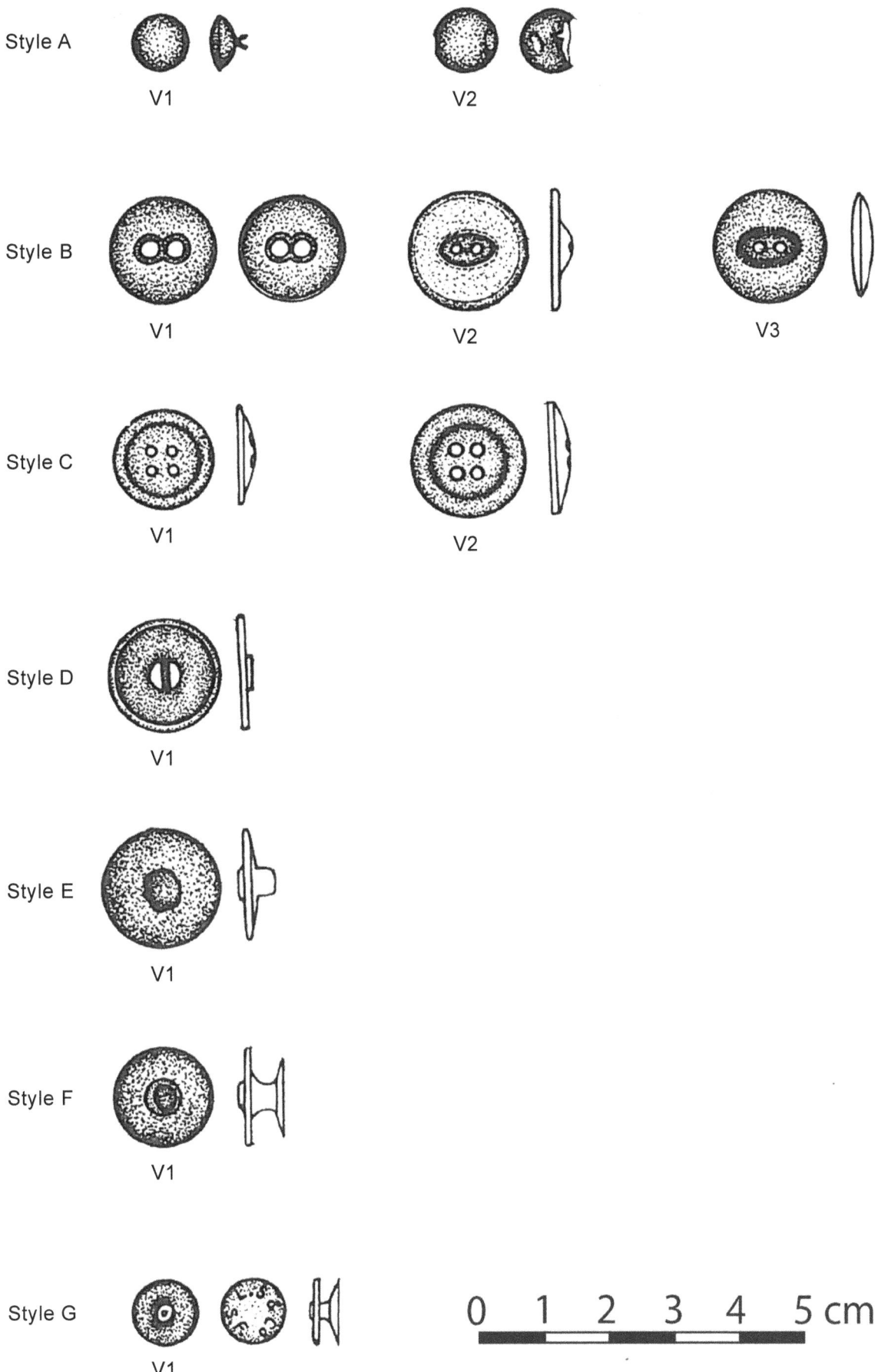

Figure 5.81. Metal buttons: two-piece construction. Reproduced from Cameron (1985).

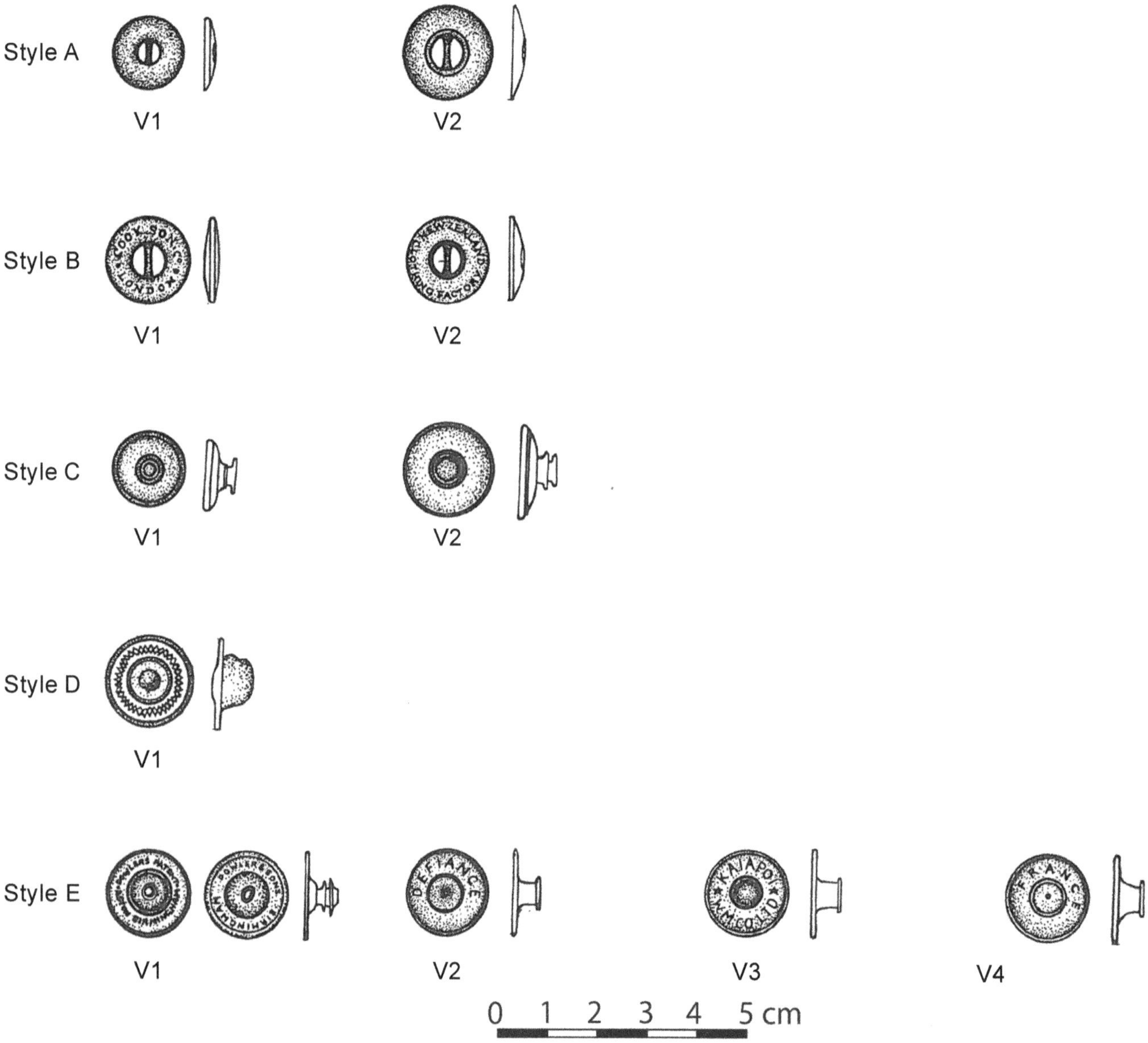

Style A
V1
V2
Style B
V1
V2
Style C
V1
V2
Style D
V1
Style E
V1
V2
V3
V4
0 1 2 3 4 5 cm

Figure 5.82. Metal buttons: three-piece construction. Reproduced from Cameron (1985).

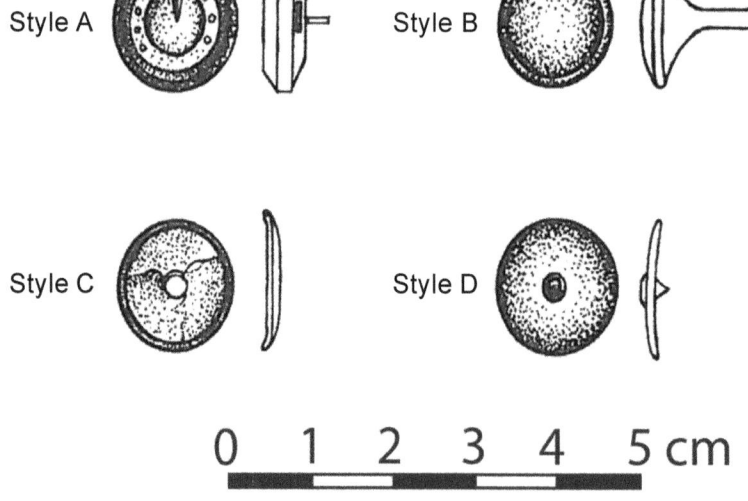

Style A
Style B
Style C
Style D
0 1 2 3 4 5 cm

Figure 5.83. Metal–non-metal composite buttons. Reproduced from Cameron (1985).

5 The material culture of the Chinese in southern New Zealand

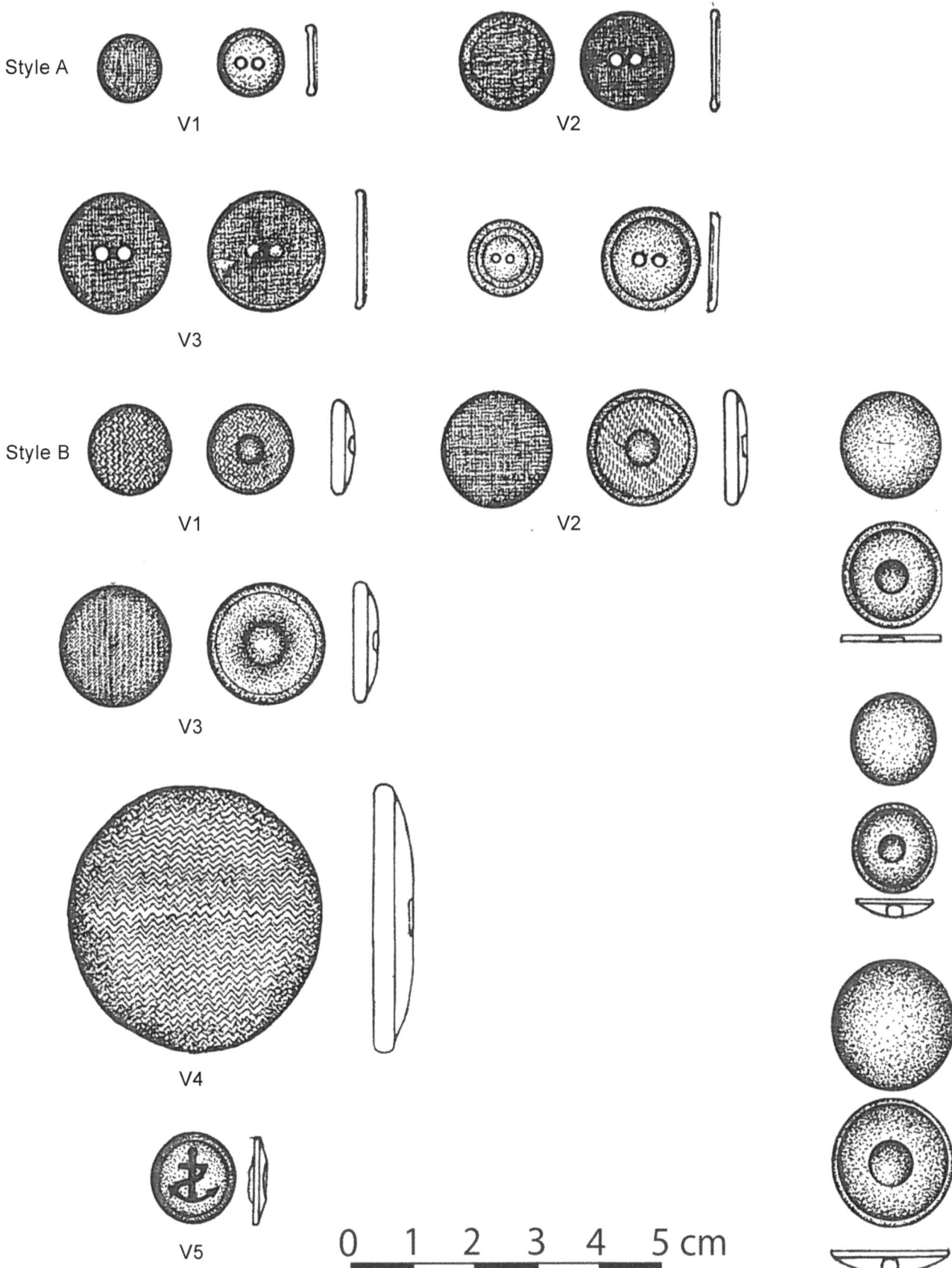

Figure 5.84. Fabric-covered buttons. Reproduced from Cameron (1985).

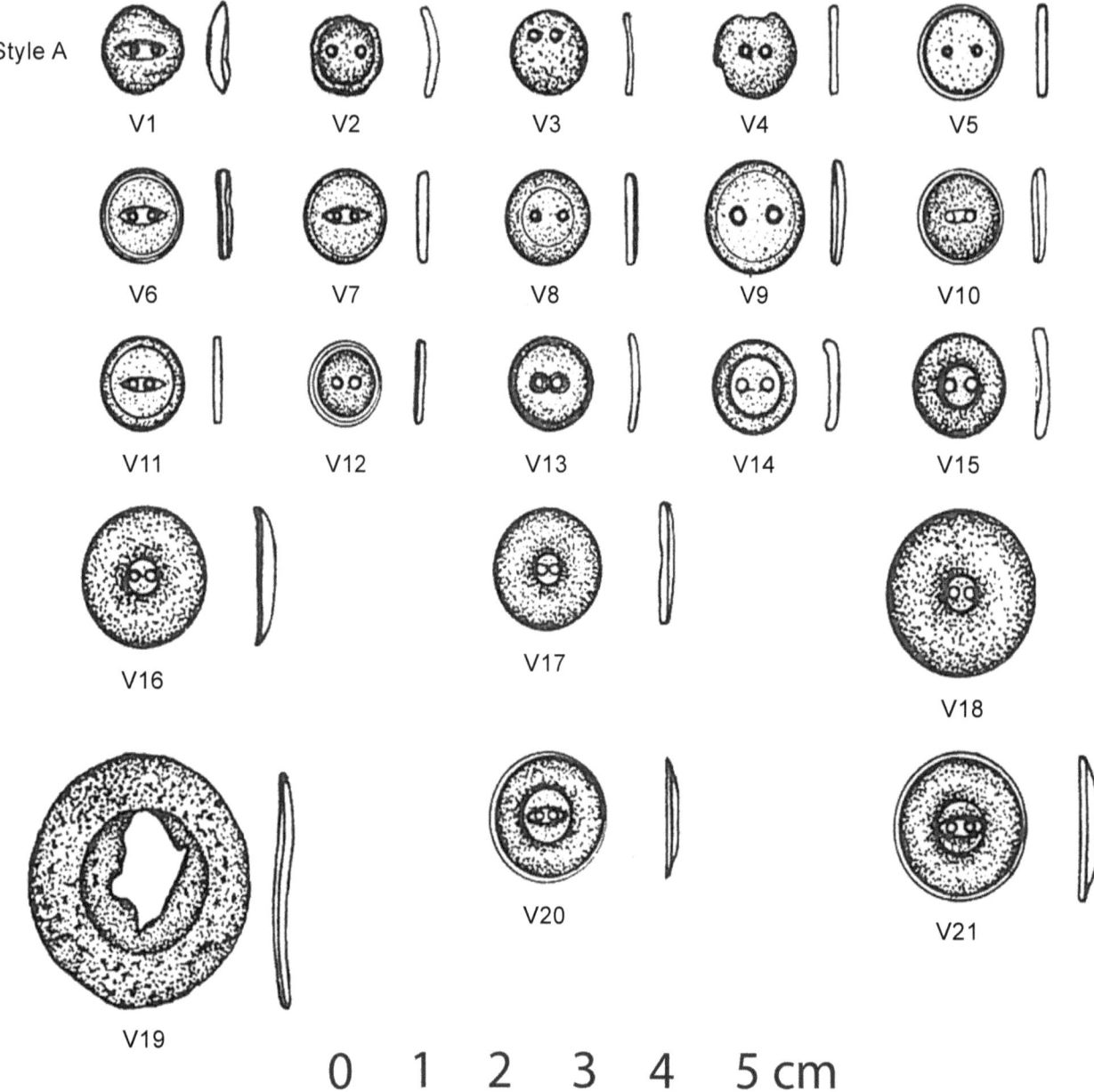

Figure 5.85. Shell buttons. Reproduced from Cameron (1985).

5 The material culture of the Chinese in southern New Zealand

Style B

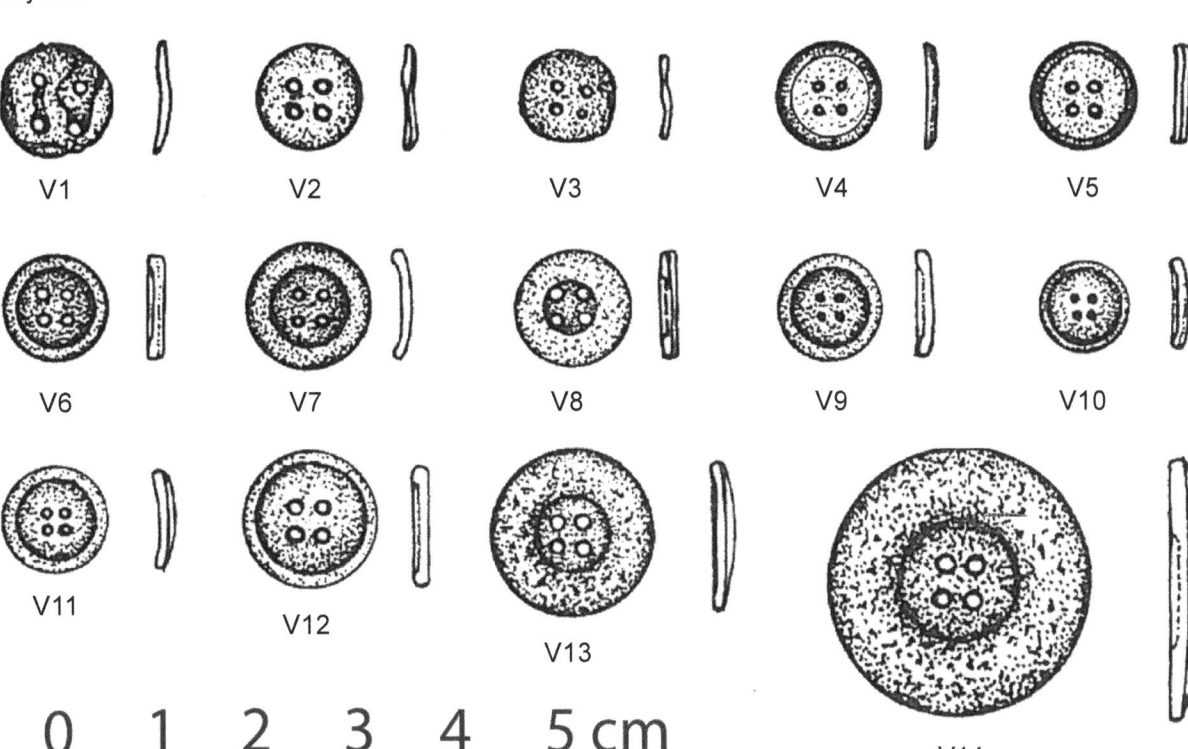

Figure 5.85. Shell buttons (*continued*). Reproduced from Cameron (1985).

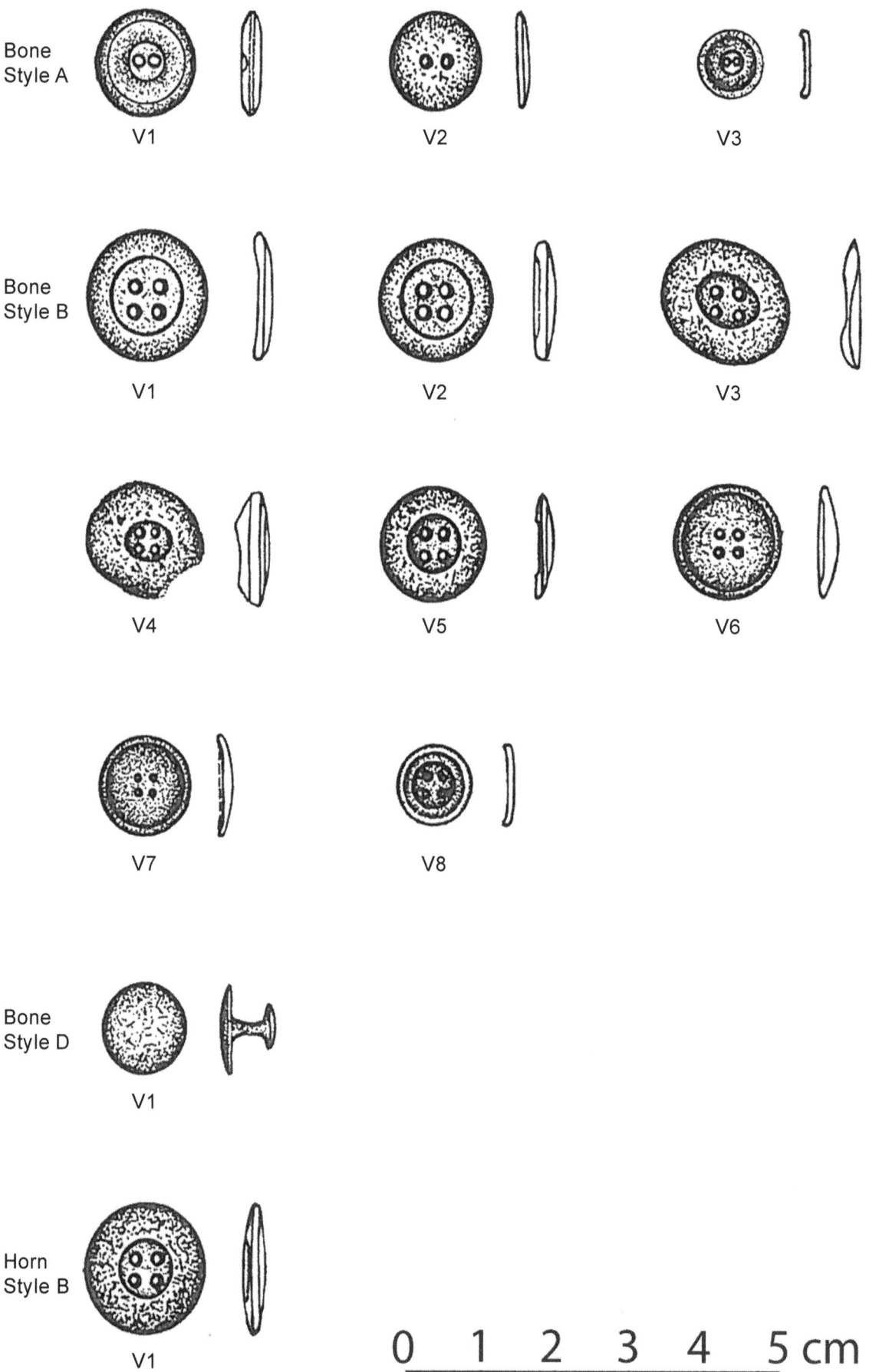

Figure 5.86. Bone and horn buttons. Reproduced from Cameron (1985).

5 The material culture of the Chinese in southern New Zealand

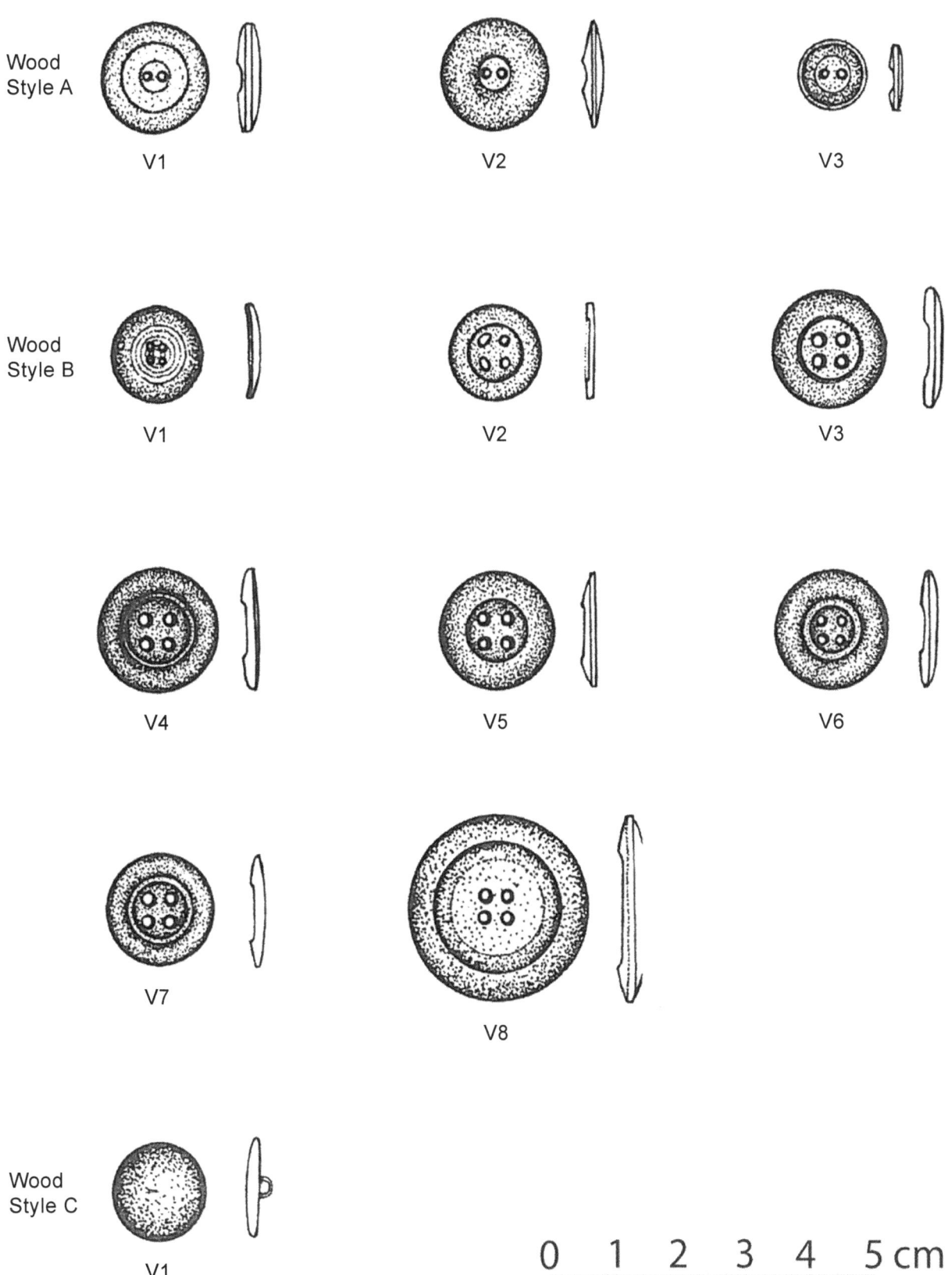

Figure 5.87. Wooden buttons. Reproduced from Cameron (1985).

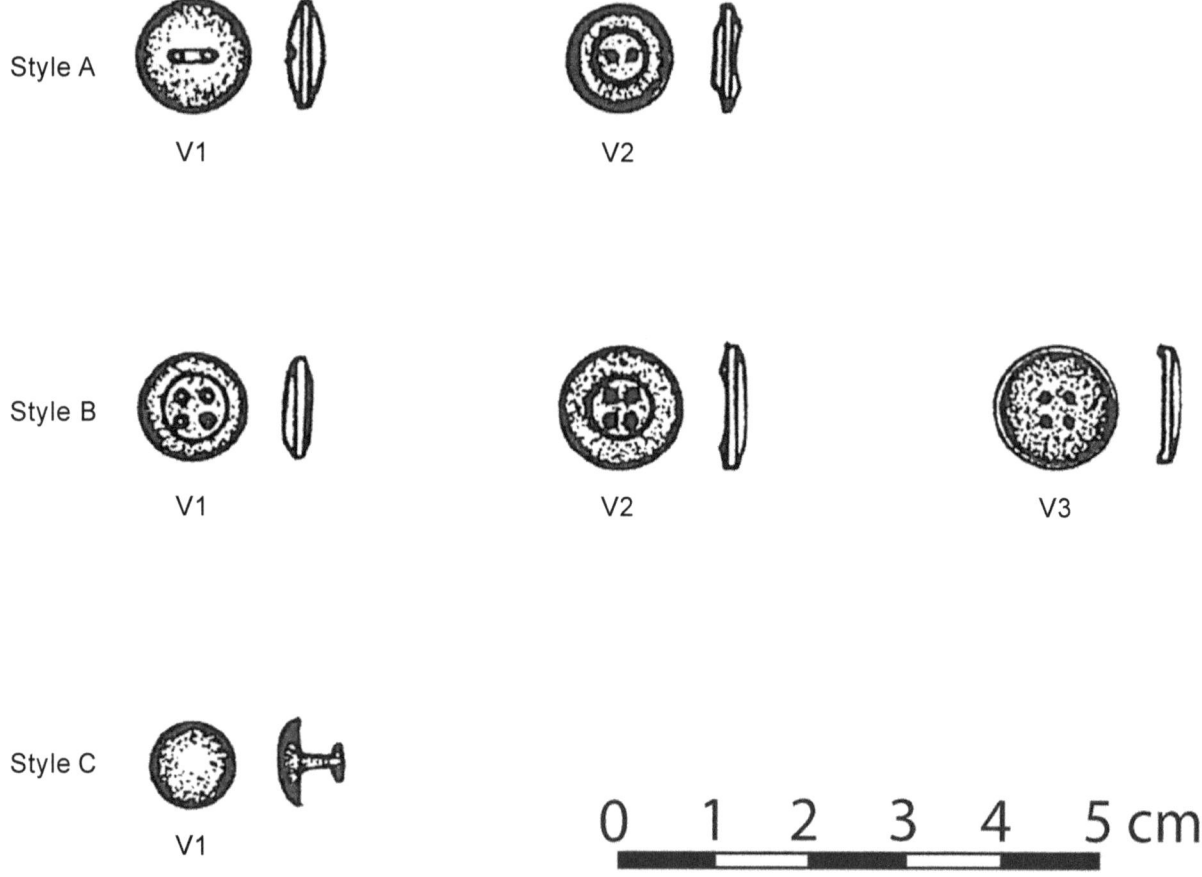

Figure 5.88. Glass buttons. Reproduced from Cameron (1985).

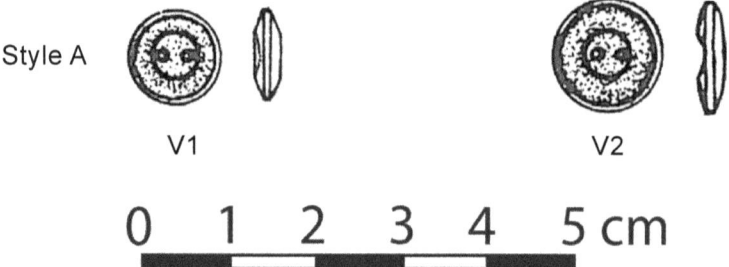

Figure 5.89. Porcelain/ceramic buttons. Reproduced from Cameron (1985).

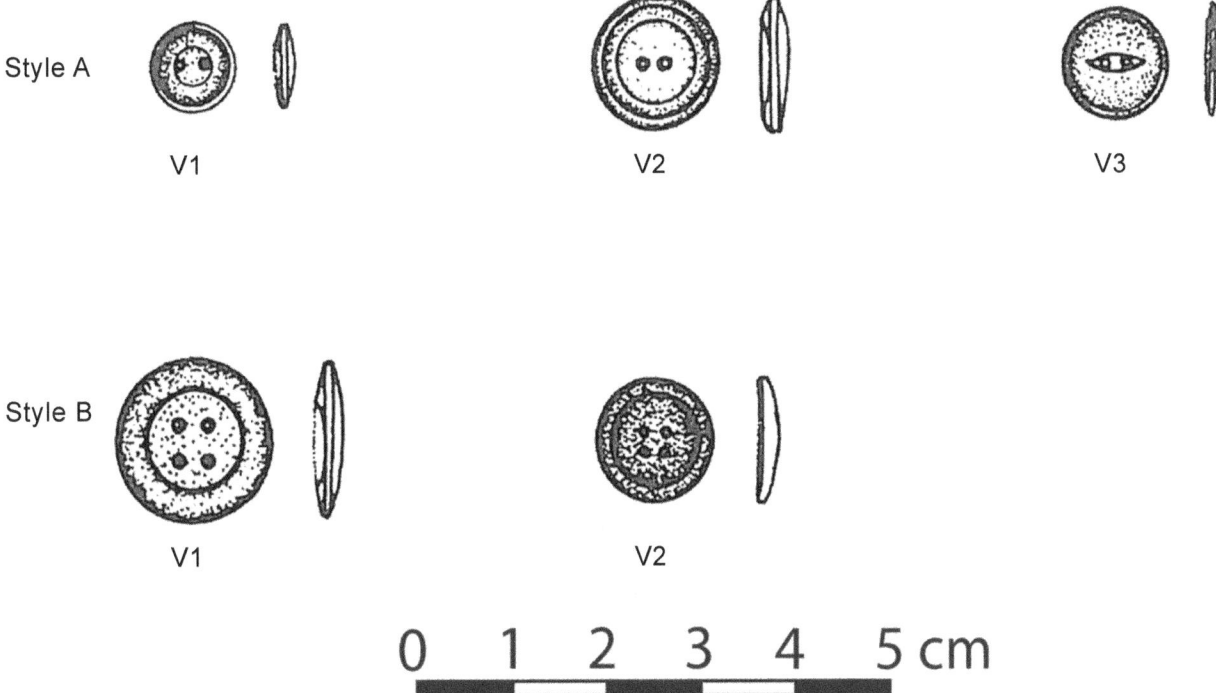

Figure 5.90. Plastic synthetic buttons. Reproduced from Cameron (1985).

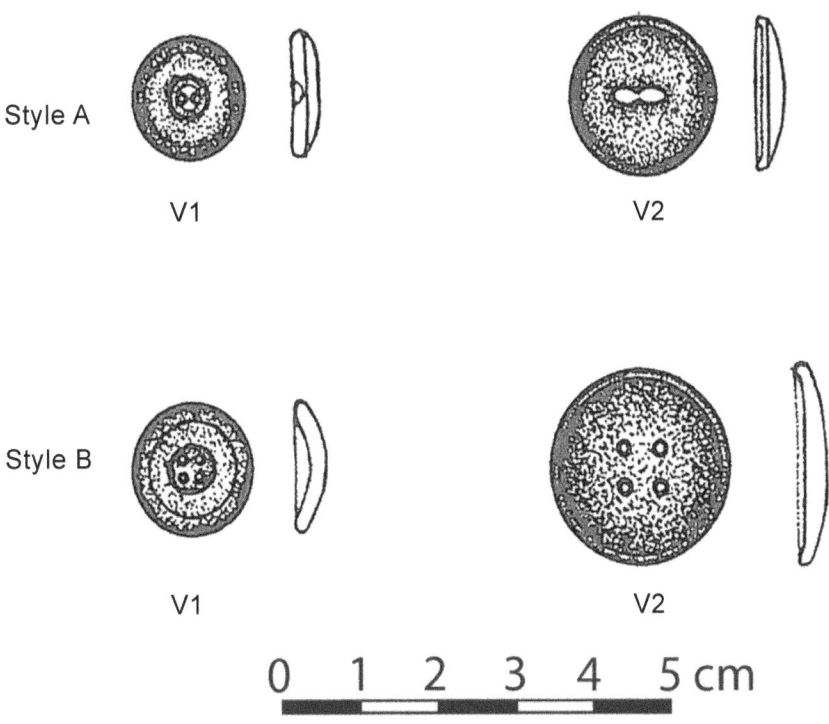

Figure 5.91. Rubber buttons. Reproduced from Cameron (1985).

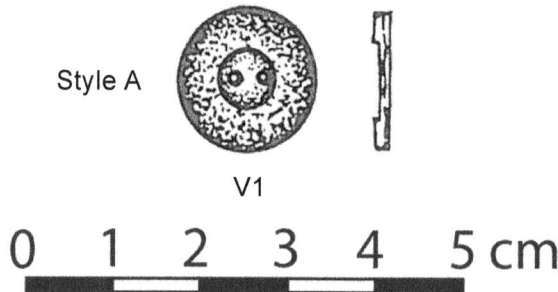

Figure 5.92. Slate button. Reproduced from Cameron (1985).

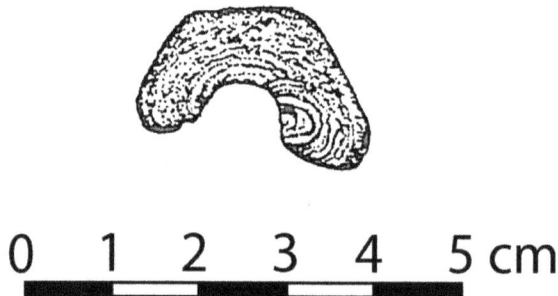

Figure 5.93. Worked shell toggle(?). Reproduced from Cameron (1985).

5 The material culture of the Chinese in southern New Zealand

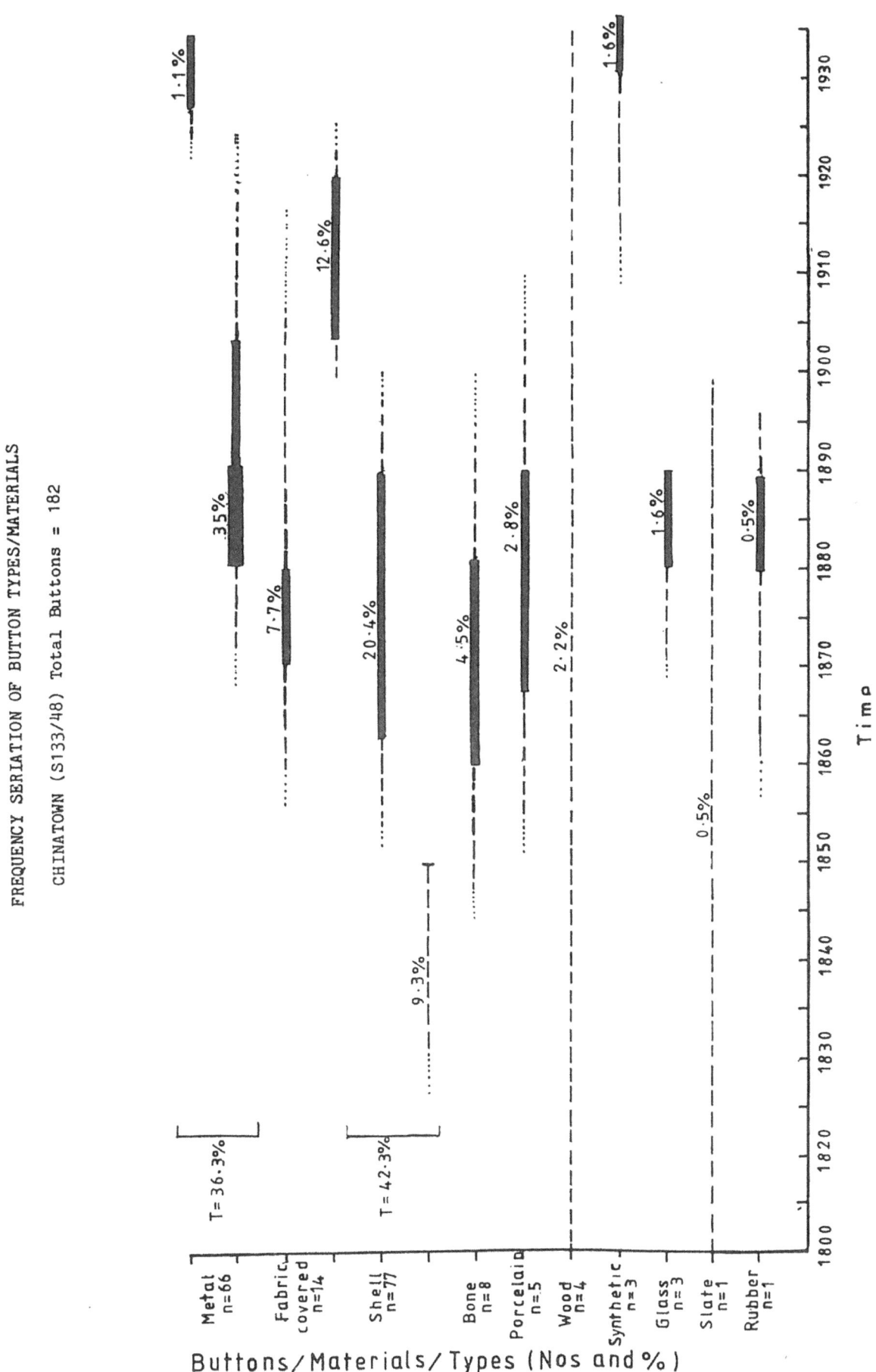

Figure 5.94. Frequency seriation of button types/materials: Cromwell's Chinatown. Reproduced from Cameron (1985:142).

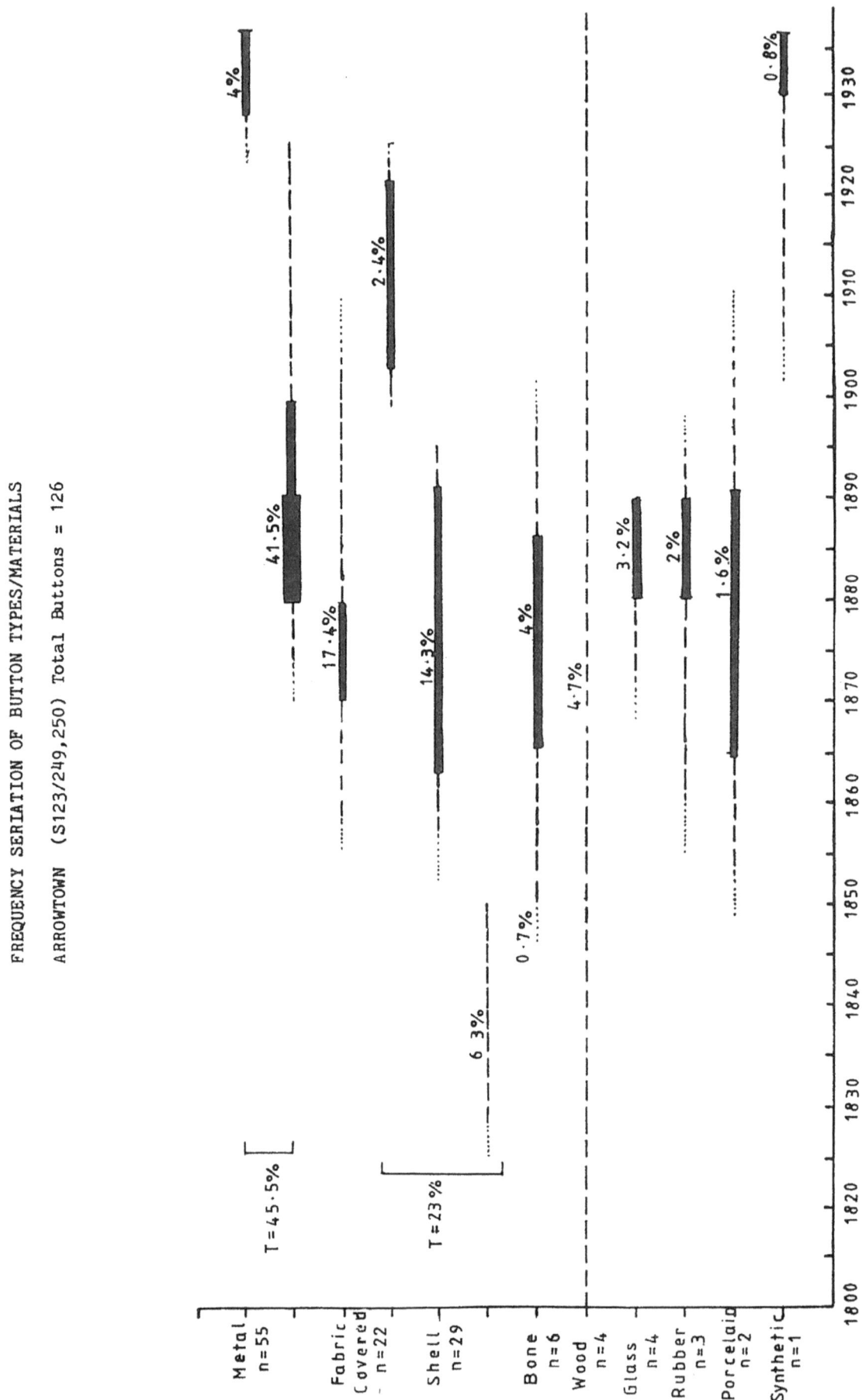

Figure 5.95. Frequency seriation of button types/materials: Arrowtown Chinese Camp. Reproduced from Cameron (1985:144).

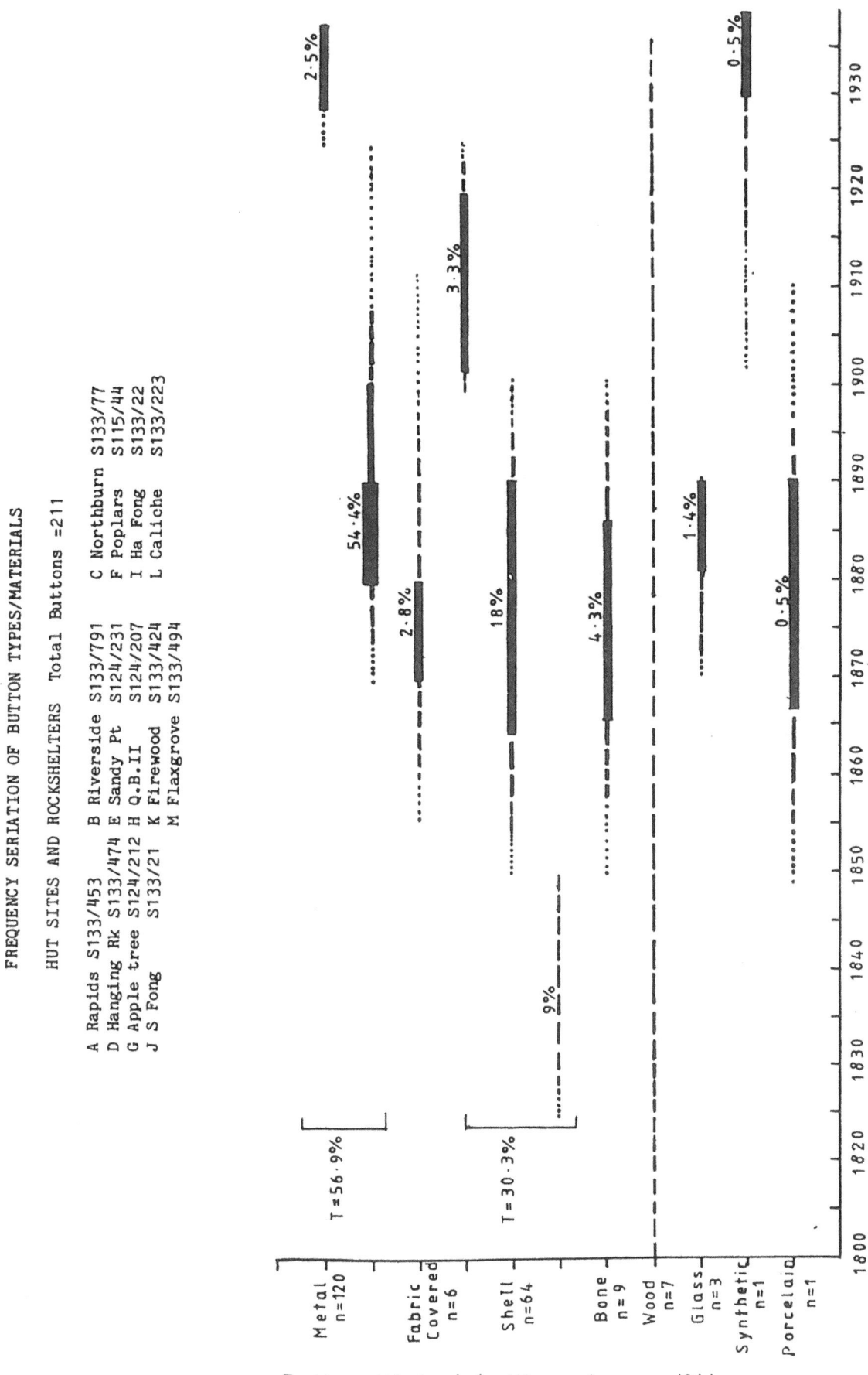

Figure 5.96. Frequency seriation of button types/materials: rural sites. Reproduced from Cameron (1985:145).

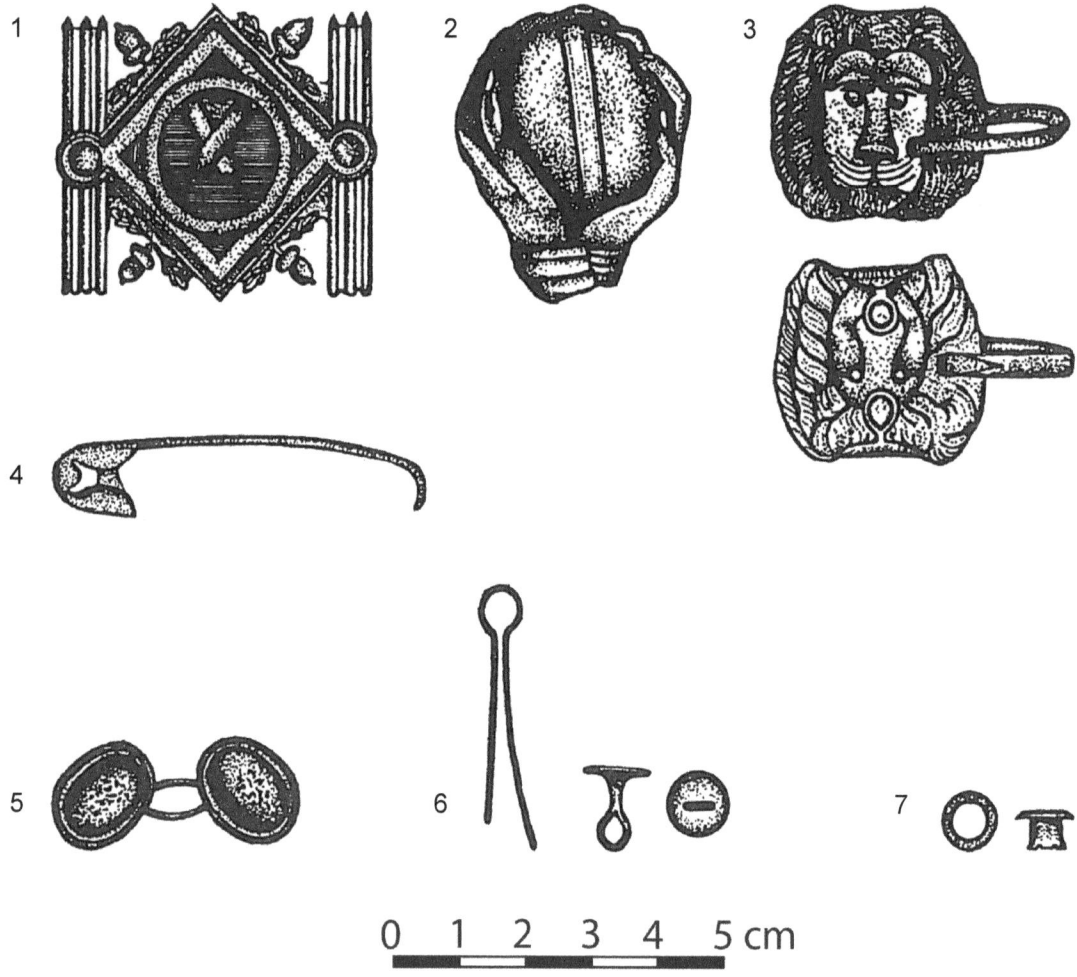

Figure 5.97. Miscellaneous clothing fasteners. Reproduced from Cameron (1985).

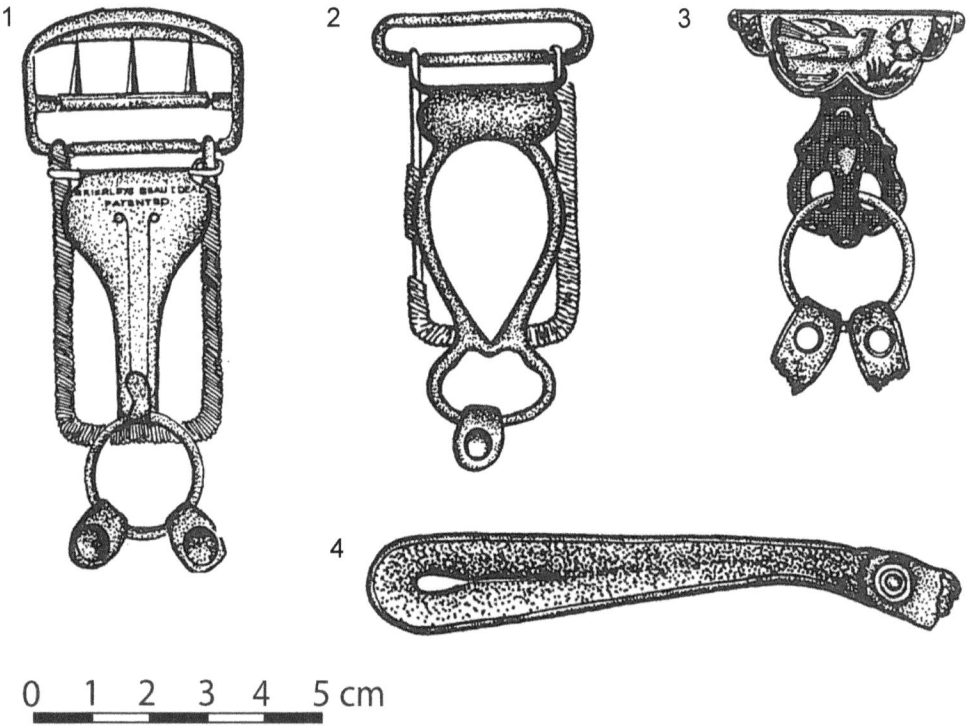

Figure 5.98. Clothing hardware: braces, suspenders, etc. Reproduced from Cameron (1985).

5 The material culture of the Chinese in southern New Zealand

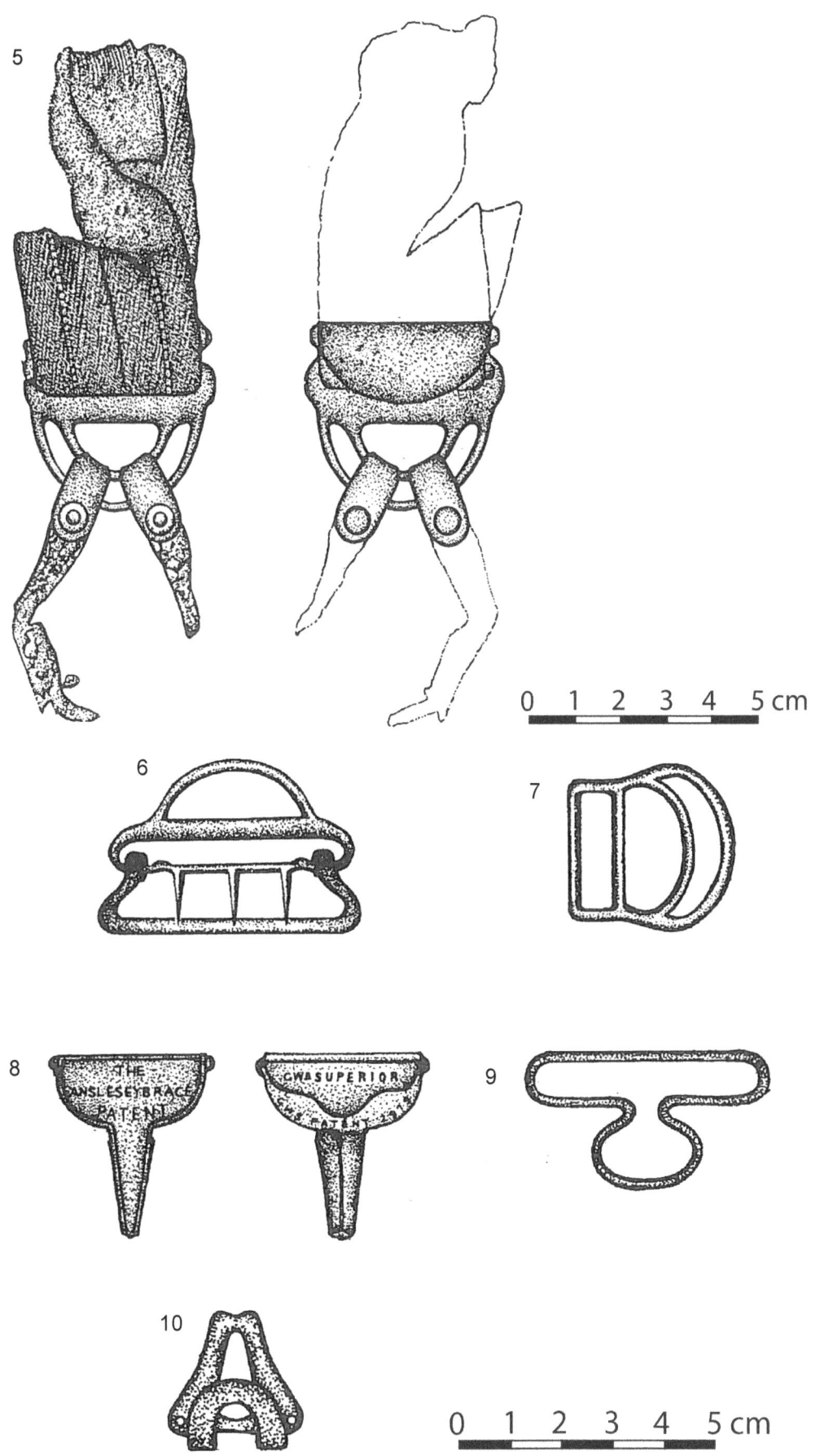

Figure 5.98. Clothing hardware: braces, suspenders, etc. (*continued*). Reproduced from Cameron (1985).

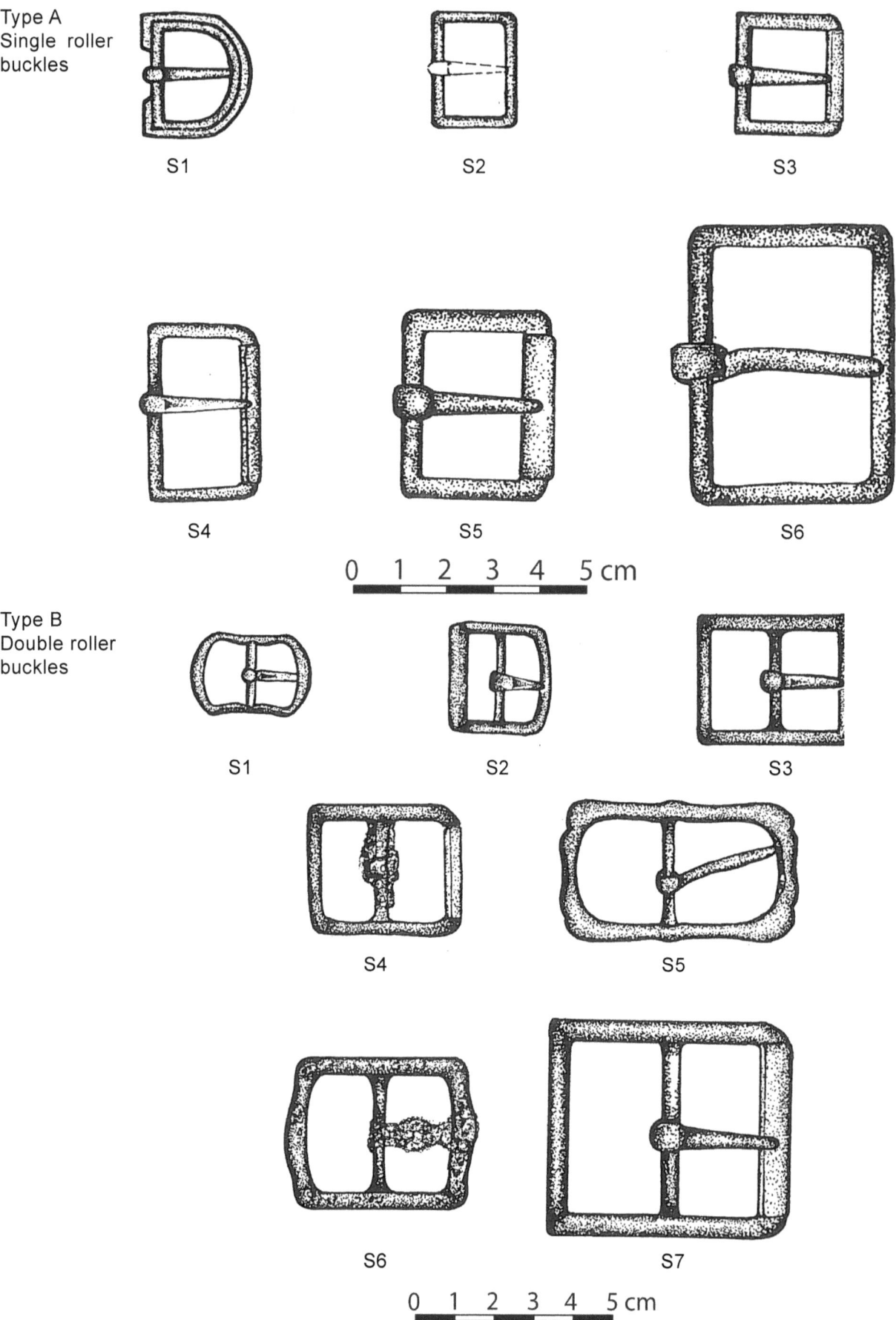

Figure 5.99. Buckles. Reproduced from Cameron (1985). See Cameron (1985) for further details.

5 The material culture of the Chinese in southern New Zealand

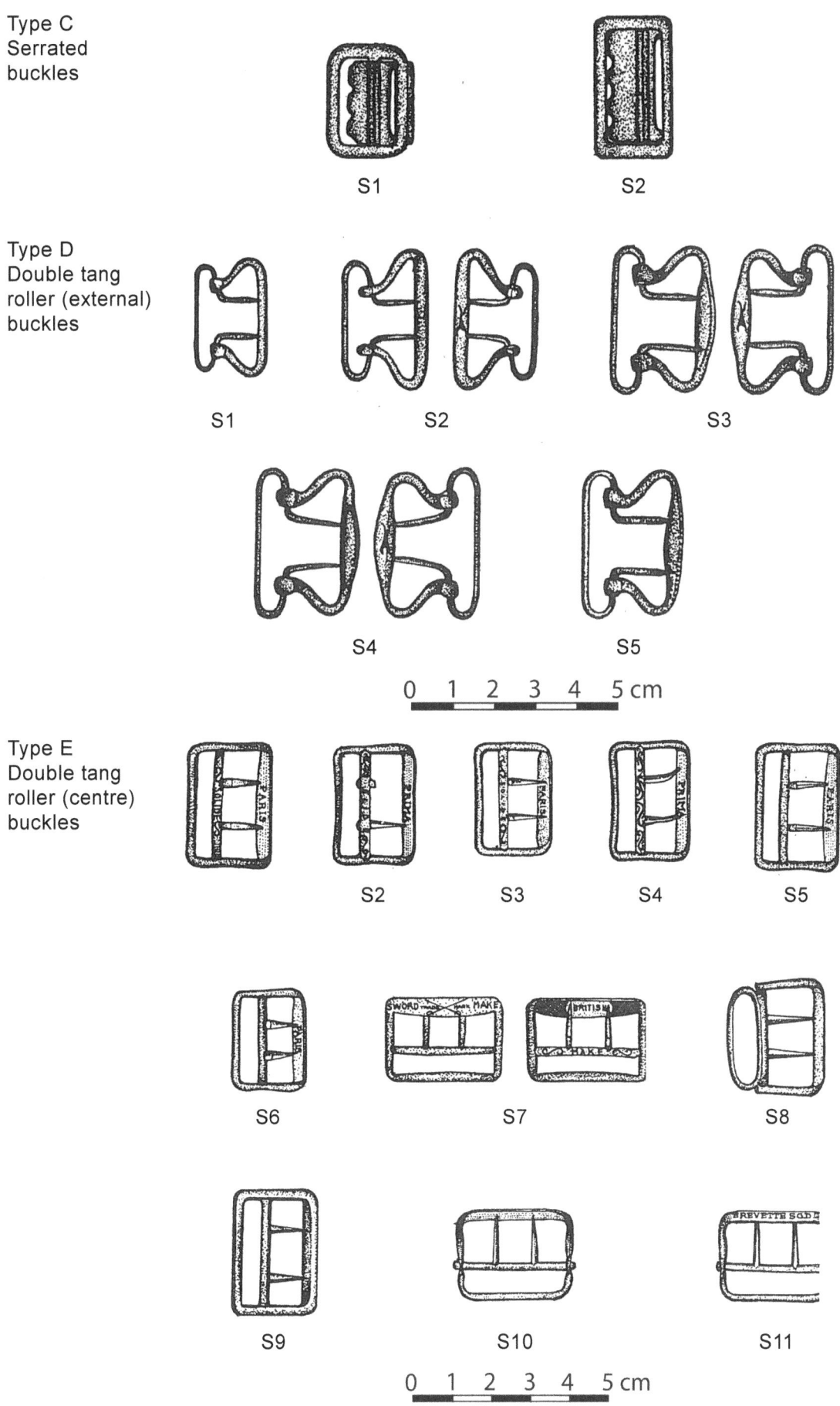

Figure 5.99. Buckles (*continued*). Reproduced from Cameron (1985). See Cameron (1985) for further details.

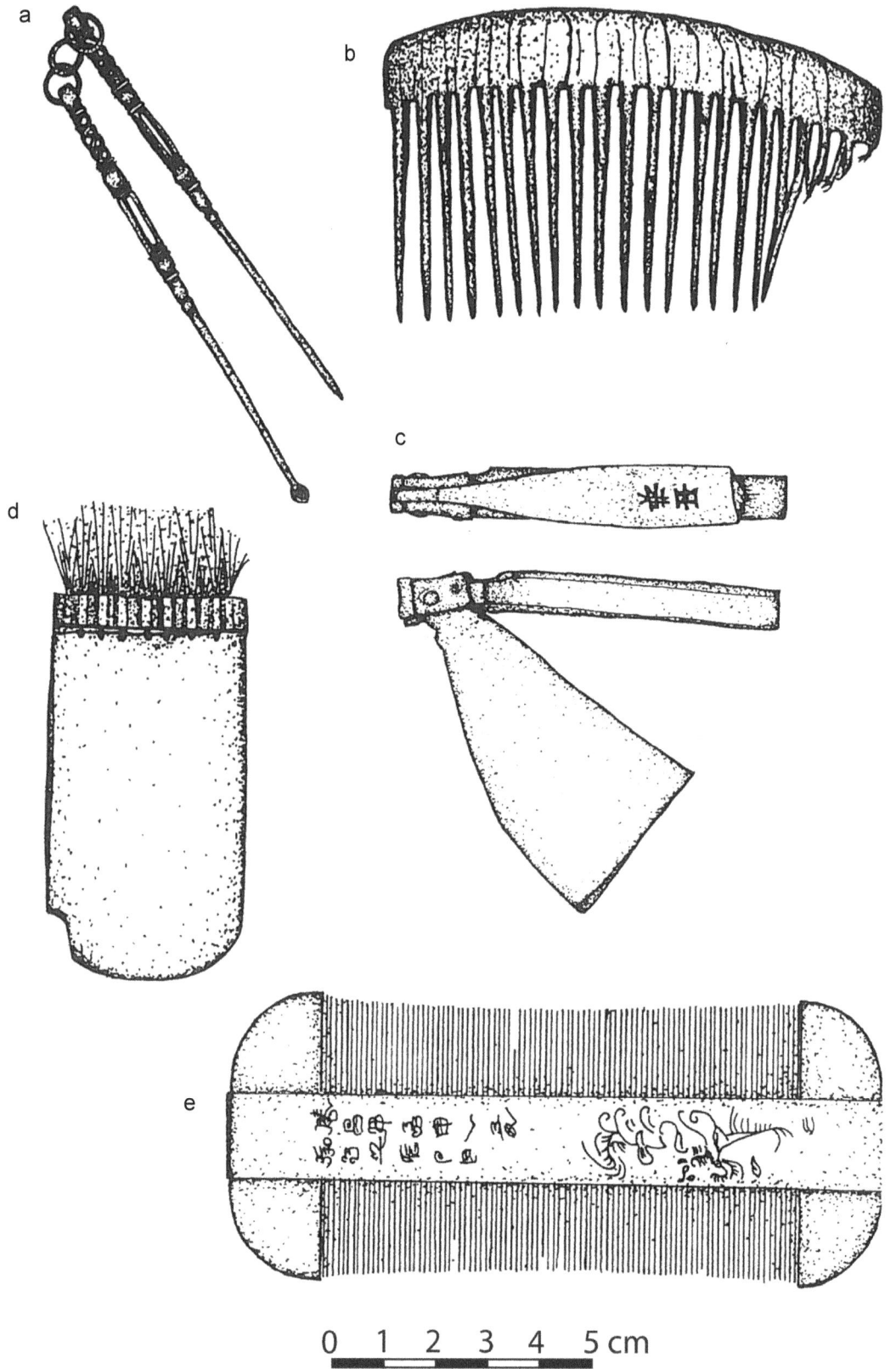

Figure 5.100. Chinese artefacts associated with grooming and personal hygiene. See Table 5.77 for distribution. **a.** Brass manicuring tools found at Sheung Fong (H6 Ly.2). **b.** Wooden comb found in Chinese hut in the Nevis Valley. **c.** Chinese razor, side and end view. Has a steel blade with wooden handle and two Chinese characters impressed into back of blade. Unprovenanced, held at Cromwell Museum (CR 77783). **d.** Small brush with curved horn handle (exact use unknown). Unprovenanced, held at Cromwell Museum (CR 77781). **e.** Double-sided wooden comb with stylised Chinese characters etched into centre section. Unprovenanced, held at Cromwell Museum (CR 77782).
Note. The specimens depicted in Figures 5.100c–e are believed to be of local origin (i.e. Cromwell Chinatown).

5 The material culture of the Chinese in southern New Zealand

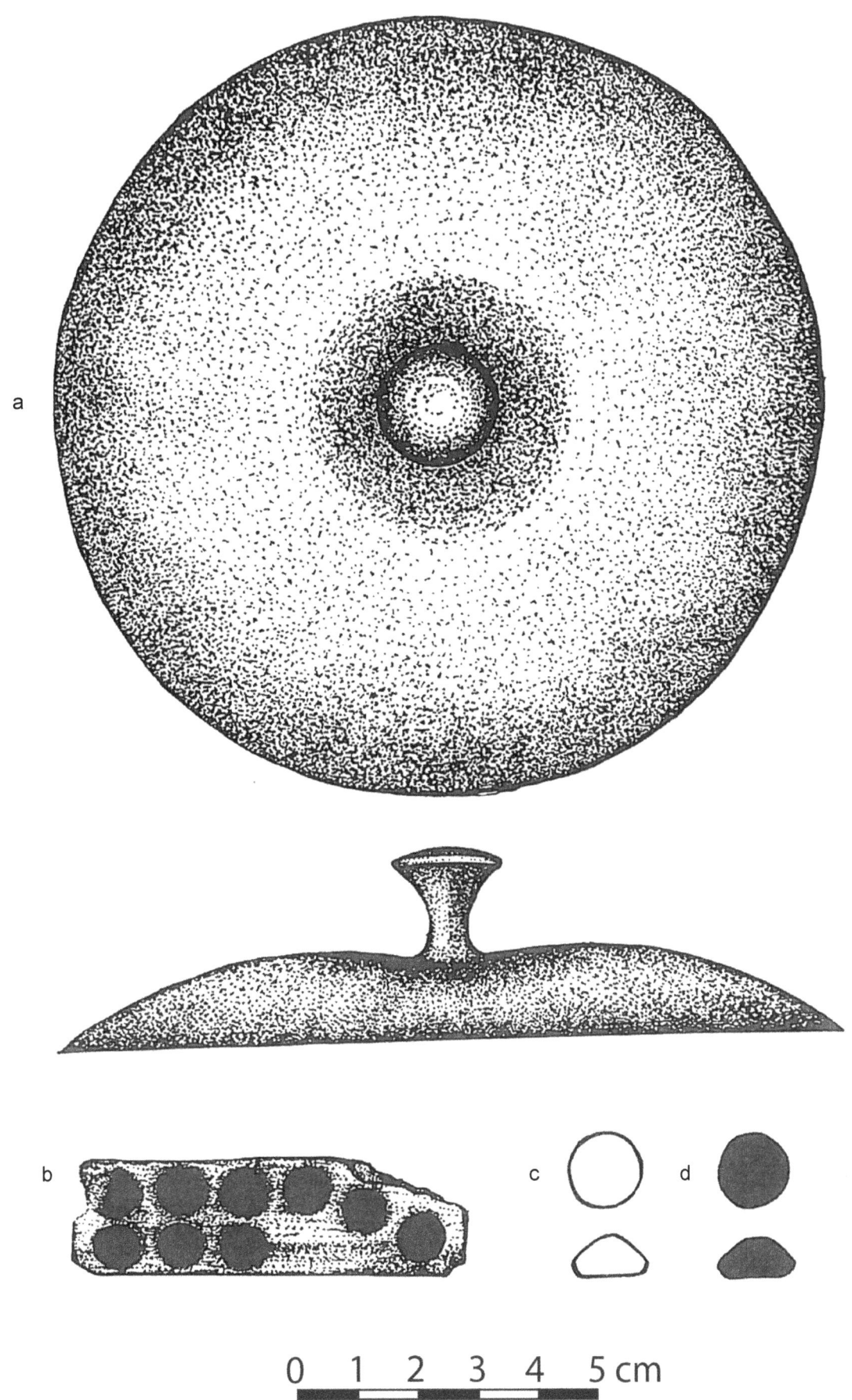

Figure 5.101. Artefacts associated with gambling and recreation. See Table 5.78 for distribution. **a.** Brass fantan cover(?) found at Rapids site (B5 Ly.1). **b.** Wooden domino found at Ah Lum's store, main room (B7 Ly.1). **c.** White glass counter (see Section 5.6.6.1). **d.** Black glass counter (see Section 5.6.6.1).

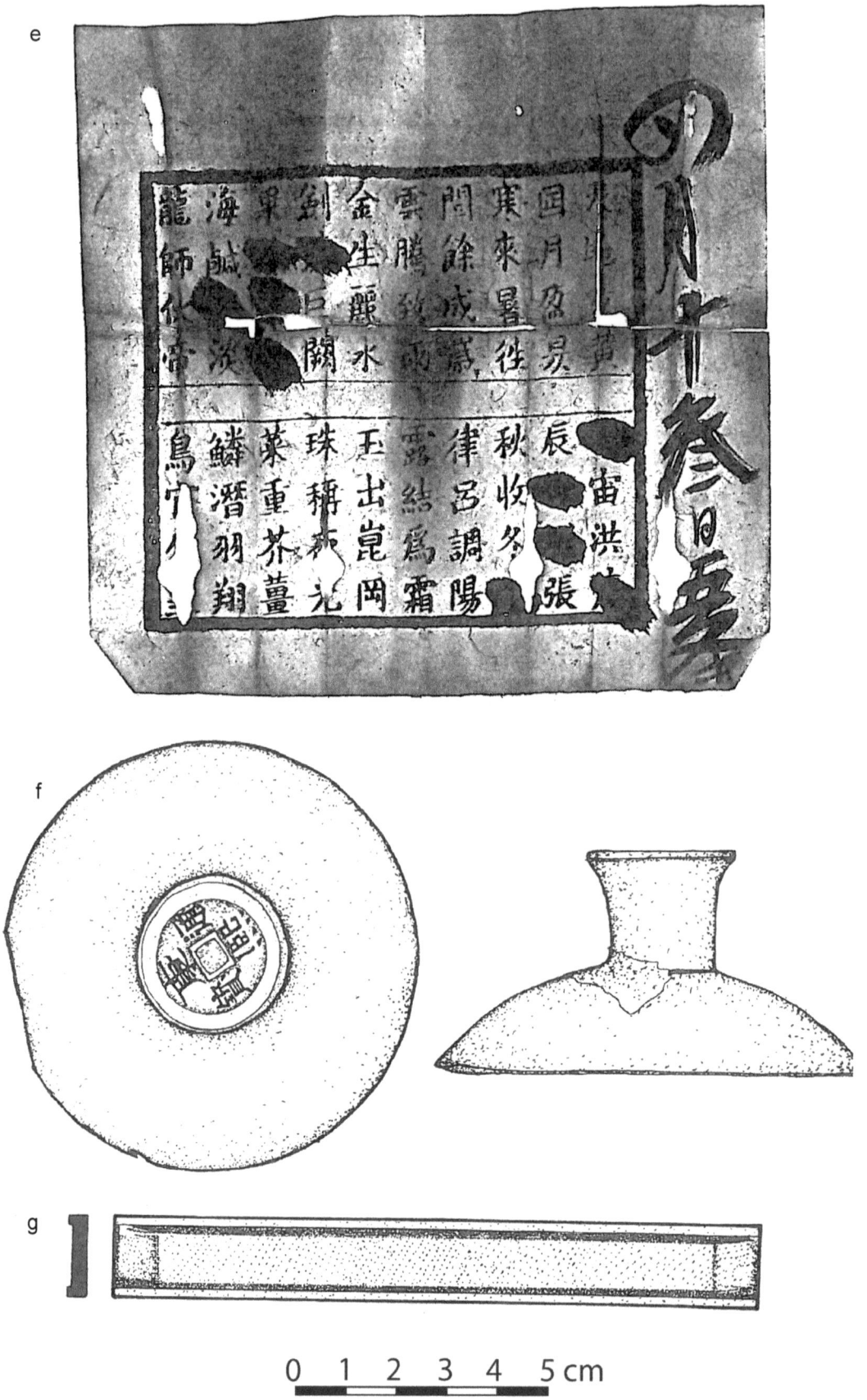

Figure 5.101. Artefacts associated with gambling and recreation (*continued*). See Table 5.78 for distribution. **e.** *Paak kop piu* ticket found at Flax Grove shelter in crevice in wall. **f.** Lead fantan cover(?) with Chinese coin inset in handle. Unprovenanced, held at Cromwell Museum (CR 77788). **g.** Wooden side of domino box(?) found at Ah Lum's store, main room (E7 Ly.1).

5 The material culture of the Chinese in southern New Zealand

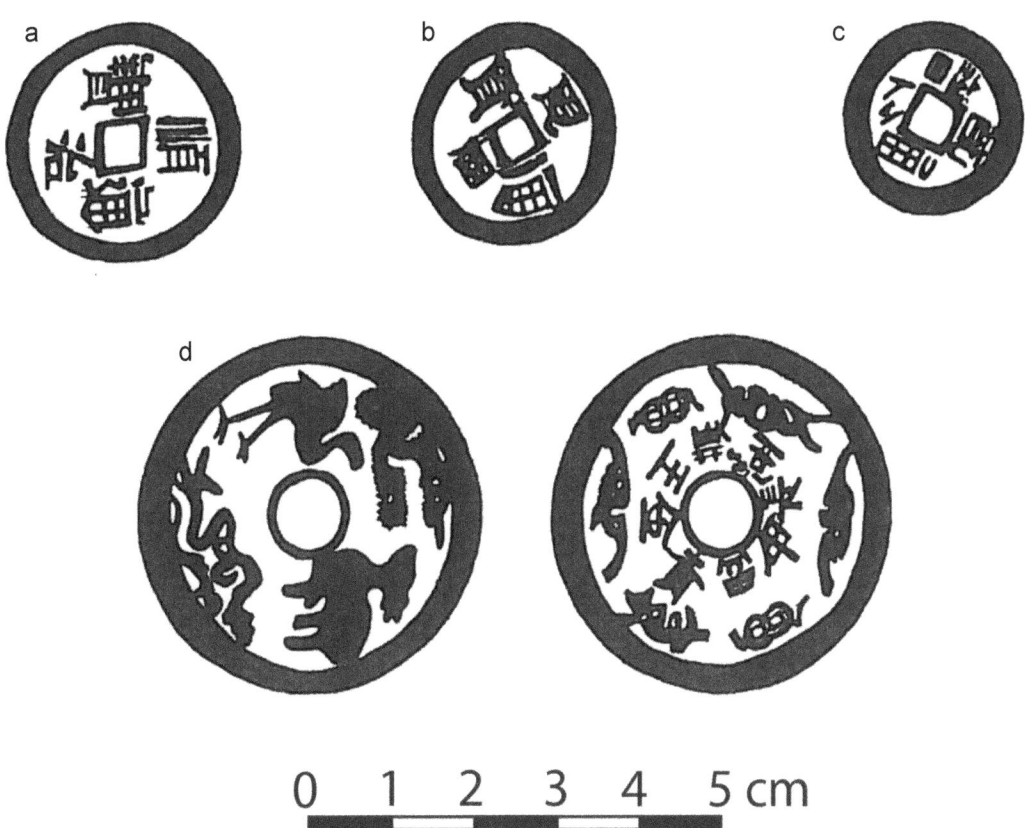

Figure 5.102. Chinese coins and amulet (see Appendix 8 for full listing). **a.** Found at Ch/26 (M12 Ly.2). **b.** Found at Ch/26 (M13 Ly.1). **c.** Found at Ch/26 (L13 Ly.1). **d.** Ya Sheng amulet, both sides. Found at Ch/34 (F9 Ly.2).

Figure 5.103. Medallion. Brass medallion embossed "New Theatre Covent Garden 1809". Found at Ch/34 (H5 Ly.2). The date on this medallion pre-dates Chinese settlement in the area by 50 years. Note hole drilled in top for attachment.

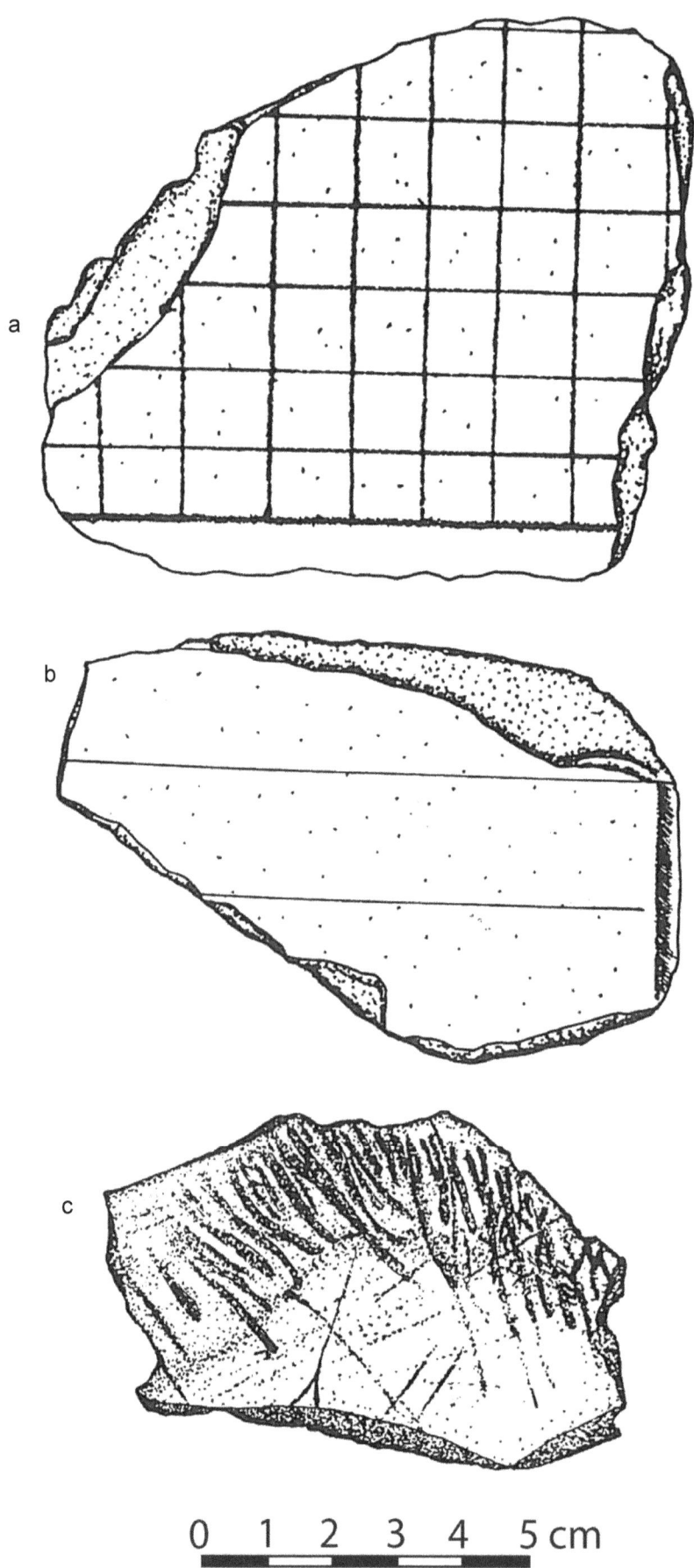

Figure 5.104. Slate artefacts. **a.** Fragment of gridded slate found at Ch/19 (F12 Ly.2). **b.** Scored slate found at Firewood Creek (A11 Ly.2). **c.** Incised slate found at Firewood Creek (A9 Ly.2).

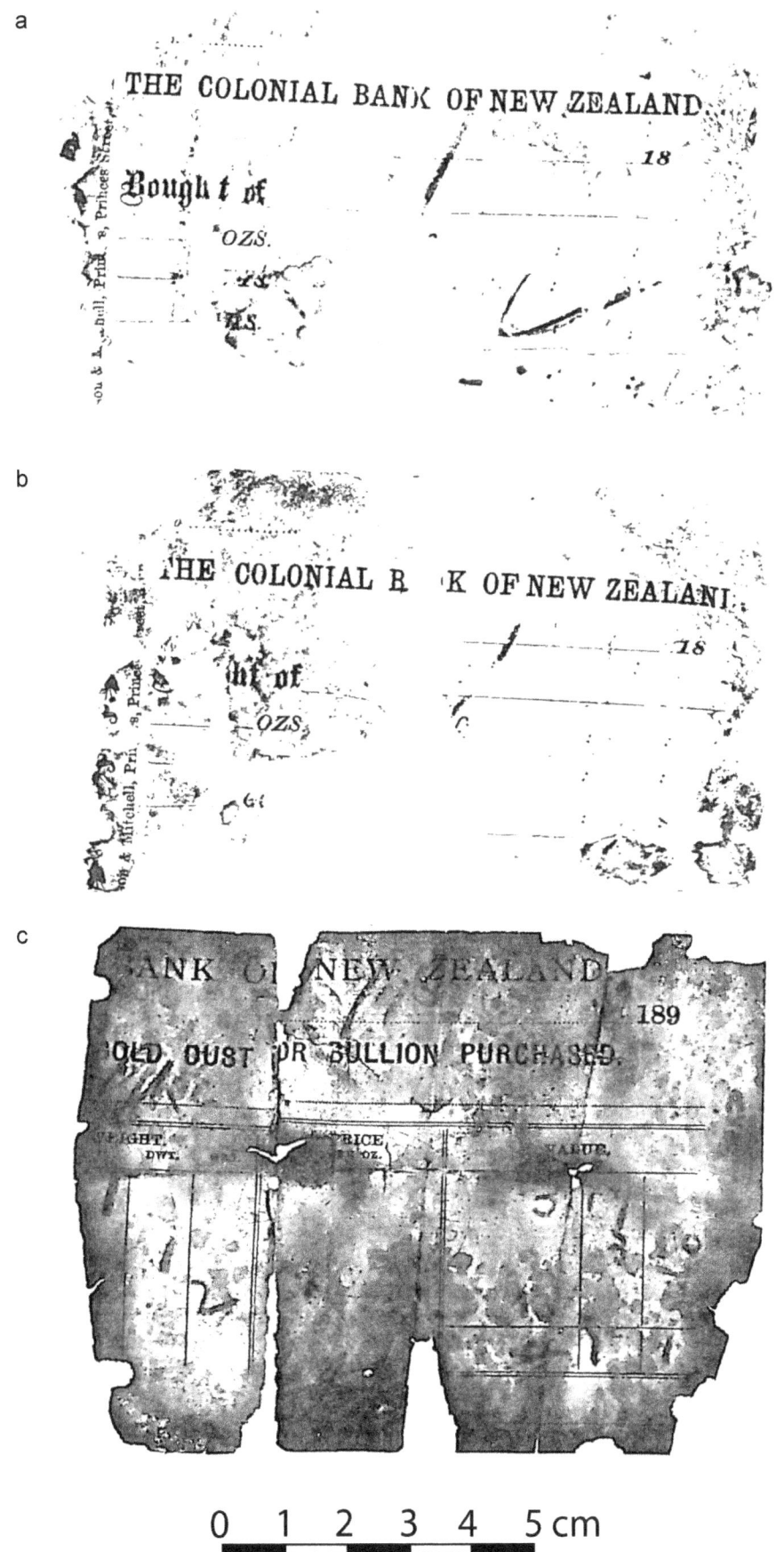

Figure 5.105. Bank receipts for gold deposits and other paper artefacts. **a. and b.** Colonial Bank of New Zealand gold receipts found at Rockfall I shelter (S133/121) in crevice in stonework **c.** Bank of New Zealand gold dust receipt dated "1896" in blue pencil. Found at Flax Grove shelter in crevice in stonework.

Figure 5.105. Bank receipts for gold deposits and other paper artefacts (*continued*). **d.** Page from the Bible written in Chinese on rice paper, possibly printed at a Mission Press in China. Found at Rockfall I site (S133/121) in crevice in stone wall. **e.** "R. Bell & Co., London" cylindical cardboard wax vesta box post-1900 found at Rockfall I site surface.

Chapter 6
DIETARY ANALYSIS

6.1 INTRODUCTION

This study of the diet of the Chinese miners is divided into three parts, beginning with faunal analyses, followed by discussion of the role of imported, preserved and locally-grown foods. In the final section, the subsistence pattern is examined to determine whether it reflects adaptative, acculturative or forced changes in the foods consumed. The study is based on three main data sources: comparative analysis of the faunal assemblages from the study sites; ethno-historical records and observations; and comparison with overseas studies.

Between 1970 and 1980, a considerable amount of research was undertaken, particularly in the United States, on bone material from historic sites, such as the work of Losey (1973), Clonts (1975), Cumbaa (1975) and Fradkin (1980). The primary objectives of these investigations were element and taxonomic identifications and the study of butchering techniques. In most instances, their findings were compared between two or more contemporary groups, e.g. the differences between the faunal remains of officers and enlisted men in military sites (Lyman 1977; Dansie 1979). Walker and Long (1977) examined various aspects of butchering, while Rosen (1978), Schulz (1979) and Langenwalter (1980) proposed "ethnic indicators" based on faunal studies. Lyman (1979) critically examined various quantification methods for assessing meat weights from assemblages of butchered domestic animal bones (sheep, beef and pig).

One of the more explicit published studies of the socio-economic implications of a 19th-century faunal assemblage is Schulz's (1979) investigation of the beef bones recovered from a mining camp in Panamint City, California. He compared the frequencies of beef cuts at Panamint City with those recovered from two other sites and used the abundance of meat cuts of different values to determine the economic status of the depositing population. Schulz and Gust (1983) took the process a step further. They postulated that the frequency of consumption of differently priced meat cuts can be expected to vary with the socio-economic status of the consumers. They demonstrated this by comparison of the faunal remains from four different social "contexts" within Old Sacramento; namely, the City Jail, a "middle class" saloon, an upmarket saloon and a "highly regarded" hotel.

Faunal remains, particularly butchered domestic animal bones, often constitute a large proportion of the recovered materials from Chinese sites in Central Otago. Although the vegetable food component is largely lost from the archaeological record, bones not only survive but also contain a considerable amount of cultural information that can be deciphered through analysis. Bones have an advantage too, in that they are of little interest to fossickers.

The assemblages used in this study were mainly from 10 sites: the Cromwell and Arrowtown Chinese urban settlements; Ah Lum's store at Arrowtown; and the following rural huts and rockshelters – Firewood Creek, QB2, the Poplars, Ah Wee's, the Rapids, Hanging Rock and Riverside shelters (the other study sites contained negligible amounts of cattle, sheep and pig bone). The number and percentage composition of faunal elements of the predominant species (sheep, pig and cattle) from each site are listed in Table 6.1.

Each of the sites had only one detectable "Chinese layer", although they varied considerably in depth and composition. The sites span the period from about 1870 until 1920. In each instance the faunal remains were derived from excavations in and around habitations or adjacent midden scatters. Despite considerable searching, no concentrated "bone pits" were located.

The following reasons can be advanced to account for the suspected low retention of faunal remains in some of the study sites:

1. Wastes were disposed of into adjacent creeks or rivers.
2. The bones or shells were softened in the cooking process, which would accelerate their decomposition.
3. The bones were consumed by other animals such as pigs, cats and rodents.
4. Faunal wastes were discarded into fireplaces and burnt (burning is evident on many of the animal bones from some of the sites).

6.2 THE OBJECTIVES

The objectives of the study were:

1. to determine which species were exploited;
2. to determine which meat cuts were represented and explain apparent preferences;
3. to examine butchering techniques and, if possible, determine if the animals were butchered by the Chinese or acquired from Europeans;
4. examine differences between the site assemblages and assess their socio-economic significance;

5. elucidate information on Chinese subsistence strategies, forced or acculturative changes, and their social implications.

6.3 METHODOLOGY

During the excavations, bones were bagged separately. In the lab, after cleaning, the contents of each bag were laid out and similar elements grouped. The taxon, element, side (if determinable), butchering marks, meat cut and other noteworthy observations (e.g. sex and maturity) were then recorded for each piece of identifiable bone on a prepared form (Figure 6.1). These were collated into volumes for each species. The data was then tabulated (Tables 6.2–6.7 and 6.10–6.12).

All the bones were identified and speciated by the author, assisted by Stuart Bedford, except for those from the Rapids site, which were speciated by Andrew Piper (Piper 1984). Species were determined by visual comparison of excavated bones with comparative specimens. Lists of distinguishing criteria were drawn up for the bones of each of the major species – *Bos*, *Sus* and *Ovis*. All bones were determined to be from immature or mature animals depending on the degree of fusion of the epiphyses. Estimates were made of the minimum number of elements (MNE), the minimum number of individuals (MNI) and the minimum number of particular meat cuts (MNMC). The latter is considered the most useful and accurate indicator of real consumption patterns. The recovery of 12 butchered pig right femora does not prove that a site's occupants consumed 12 pigs, only that they probably consumed 12 hams.

Mammalian meat cuts were determined by comparison of the cut locations on butchered bones with those depicted on meat cut diagrams, notably those published in Fitzgibbon (1976), Froud and Turgeon (1966, i.e. the *Larousse Gastronomique*) and meat cut charts obtained from the Dunedin Master Butcher's Association. Information on early 20th century European butchering practices was also obtained from two retired butchers now resident in Cromwell, Messrs. S. Summers and G. Bell. The latter is particularly notable because in the 1920s he lived opposite the Chinese Camp at Lawrence and sold meat to the Chinese there; consequently, he obtained first-hand knowledge of their meat preferences and methods of cooking.

General butchering patterns and inferred meat cuts were identified for each of the three dominant meat species – cattle (*Bos taurus*), pig (*Sus scrofa*) and sheep (*Ovis aries*). The cuts are described by their anatomical position, e.g. the shoulder or hind shank, and in terms familiar to most New Zealanders. Primal quartering cuts were distinguished from retail (secondary) and pre-cooking (tertiary) cuts where possible. Tables 6.2–6.12 list the minimum numbers of meat cuts for each species. The meat weights represented by the beef, pig and sheep meat cuts were calculated to assess their relative contribution to the diet of the Chinese who occupied the study sites. This discussion (Table 6.14) is titled "meat preferences" and follows the individual discourses on the cattle, pig and sheep bone assemblages.

A small portion (generally less than 50) of the sheep- and pig-size bones could not be accurately identified to either species specifically. Two bones presented problems in this area – "chopped up" or burnt ribs and vertebrae and occasionally phalanges or metapodials. These bones were recorded as "sheep/pig" and tabulated but omitted from further consideration.

Following the discussion on the main meat species, the butchering patterns evident on the remains of the smaller mammals such as rabbits and cats are outlined and their dietary contribution evaluated. The bird bones were speciated by R. McGovern-Wilson. The role of bird meat in the Chinese subsistence pattern was addressed by Ritchie and McGovern-Wilson (1986). The bird data, as well as the relatively scant aquatic food remains, are described separately in the later discussion. Before the final conclusions are presented, the contribution of imported, preserved and locally grown products is assessed.

6.4 MAIN MEAT SPECIES

6.4.1 CATTLE (*BOS TAURUS*)

Cattle were represented by a total of 393 bone portions (complete or cut portions of bone), the breakdown being: Chinatown 139; ACS 86; Ah Lum's 30; and the rural sites 138.

The following primary and secondary cuts were defined from study of the positions of saw cuts on the bones:

1. Removal of the head: evidenced by transverse saw and cleaver marks on the axis and atlas vertebrae. Head bones were uncommon in the combined assemblage, being restricted to two mandibular fragments in total. These may have been acquired as soup bones.
2. Sawing the carcass in half lengthways: This action is reflected in the fact that most of the recovered vertebrae are sawn in half longitudinally.
3. Quartering the beast: evidenced by transverse saw cuts through thoracic vertebrae.

Secondary breaking down of the beef carcasses is evidenced in the cuts depicted in Figures 6.2–6.13. The cuts are named in Tables 6.2–6.7 and 6.10–6.12:

1. Severing the shoulder: reflected in transverse saw cuts across the shoulder blade, generally towards the proximal end of the scapulae.
2. Transverse cuts across the proximal and distal ends of the humeri (particularly the distal ends).
3. Transverse cuts across the proximal and distal ends of the radiae and ulnae.
4. Transverse cuts across the lumbar vertebrae and pelvic ilium and ascetabulum.
5. Transverse cuts across the ribs about 15 cm apart.

6. Transverse cuts across the proximal and distal ends of the femora and tibiae.

These bone cuts are consistent with the European manner of breaking down a cattle beast for sale, with the notable exception of the "double cuts" on many of the long bones. These have both the proximal and distal ends sawn off leaving just the central shaft section, which is often further processed by being split longitudinally. This was not characteristic of European butchery practices of the time and was probably done to extract the marrow. Piper (1984:20) suggested that the ends were possibly sawn off by European butchers on request. It is also possible that the Chinese asked for short hind-shank cuts because they were cheaper or considered better value. Other evidence supports the contention that the cattle consumed by the Chinese were killed and dismembered by European butchers. The cuts conform to those depicted in contemporary English cookery and household guides, e.g. Beeton (1899) and Beeton (n.d.); they broadly conform to cuts depicted in American studies of faunal remains (e.g. Dansie 1979); they were familiar to Messrs. Summers and Bell, retired butchers of Cromwell; and there are no records that the Chinese raised or kept cattle in New Zealand.

According to Langenwalter (1980:105), the use of handsaws in butchering is an English trait that has no parallels in (traditional) Chinese butchering practices. Thus, he argued saw cuts on bones obtained from 19th-century Chinese sites were positive evidence of European butchering. While not disputing his contention, there are, as depicted in Table 6.8, considerably fewer saw marks than cleave/chop cuts on the beef bones from the study sites. This may reflect additional breaking down of carcasses by Chinese butchers or customers (discussion continues after Tables and Figures).

The represented beef cuts are, except for a few cuts from the rump area, either middle range or cheap cuts (Beeton 1899:384), with the emphasis being on the cheapest cuts such as the leg and shin. The latter cuts when cooked by Europeans are generally stewed or boiled (Beeton 1899:382). The meat from these areas is also recognised for its leanness, a factor that the Chinese sought after (Bell pers. comm.). Mr Bell recalled that the Chinese in Lawrence (a town about 100 km southeast of Cromwell) would buy any cut of meat that was available, but they had a definite preference for lean meat. Even when they bought a "roast" (e.g. sirloin or rump), they would cook the meat by "cutting it into small pieces and stewing it" (Bell pers. comm.).

Approximately 15% of the cattle bones were derived from immature specimens. The butchery of vealers follows a similar pattern to that of mature cattle. As indicated in Tables 6.2–6.4, the most preferred cuts were the fore and hind knuckles. These cuts were relatively cheap compared with other cuts of veal (Beeton 1899:25, 432–3) and were well suited for "stewing".

6.4.2 PIG (*SUS SCROFA*)

The meat-weight contribution of beef to the Chinese diet is compared to that of pig and sheep, following the discussions on the latter. Pig meat (*Sus scrofa*), poultry and fish are the traditional main sources of protein in southern China, pig meat being the most important (Anderson and Anderson 1977:336). Pig and fowl raising was popular because they could be kept in house yards or pens, would eat just about anything, reached maturity in a year and are prolific breeders (Lee and Lee 1979:25).

The Chinese who sought their fortune in New Zealand would have been well versed in pig husbandry and contemporary observations confirm that some raised pigs for their own consumption and sale (Don 1/3/1888:7.65; *Otago Daily Times* 14/1/1885:17). Don noted that a party (in the Moonlight Valley) "who acted as pig butchers for their fellow-Chinese were doing well", and consequently "they got unlimited credit from a European storekeeper" (Don 1895:16). At least four Chinese butcher shops operated on the Central Otago goldfields (Parcell 1976:150; Appendix 5), but it is uncertain whether they raised their own stock or acquired it from others.

Pig meat was represented by a total of 959 bone portions, the breakdown being: Chinatown 131; the ACS 336; Ah Lum's store 95; and the rural sites 397. The elements and meat units are listed in Tables 6.5–6.7.

The following butchering cuts were evident in the pig bone assemblages:

1. Crania are commonly split down the middle, presumably for brain extraction.
2. Mandibles were cut or pulled away from the crania and split longitudinally, to facilitate removal of the tongue. Secondary processing of both crania and mandibles involved a series of transverse cleaver blows resulting in the production of a lot of chunky dentary pieces that were probably boiled to produce brawn or soup stock.
3. The atlas and axis vertebrae are commonly cut into halves or quarters – the result of transverse cuts to sever the head from the body and the longitudinal cut made when a beast was halved.
4. The scapula bones bear two breakage patterns – seemingly erratic "dicing up" into small pieces or c. 2 cm wide strips made by a series of transverse cuts across the bone.
5. Butchers in Canton customarily remove all the meat from the ribs and backbone. The bones are then cut into small parts and prepared with a sweet dressing (Levine 1921:13). This butchering and cooking treatment is evident on many of the rib and vertebral fragments. Three distinctive rib cuts were defined:
    a. pieces of rib were cut into lengths between 2 and 4 cm long (described as "diced rib" in the tables);
    b. pieces of rib were cut into lengths between 6 and 9 cm long (described as "short ribs"). Chopping ribs into lengths up to c. 10 cm is the traditional

manner of cooking "spare ribs", either by grilling or roasting (Lee and Lee 1979:206);

c. proximal ends of ribs were found in about equal numbers, either "diced" or in the form of "short ribs". These bone cuts are possibly the result of cutting racks of pork chops into two portions, resulting in the creation of the aforementioned units.

6. The cut locations on humeri vary considerably but are predominantly towards the proximal end. These cuts appear to be primal cuts for separating the shoulder from the foreleg.
7. There was no consistent pattern in the cut locations on ulnae and radiae.
8. The pelvic bones were cut in the process of breaking down a carcass and, in particular, separating off the hams. The cut generally goes through the ascetabulum or the posterior end of the ilium, and frequently severs the ball of the femur. Chunky cut fragments of pelvic bone suggest these bones were often used as soup bones.
9. Distal and proximal end cuts occur on femora and tibiae in approximately equal numbers, suggesting that the hams were often divided into smaller portions – perhaps halves or thirds. As with *Bos* bones, many of the pig long bones have both ends cut off or have been split, again probably for marrow extraction.
10. Feet bones (carpals, tarsals and metapodials) are a common element in the assemblages. About 20% have cleaver marks. According to Levine (1921:14), the small amount of meat on the feet was considered a delicacy and was either cooked for immediate consumption or pickled.

After examining the pig bone assemblage (n=89) from the Rapids, one of the 15 study sites, Piper (1984:21) concluded that meat was commonly carved off joints, evidenced by multiple knife marks on some long bones. However, his conclusion is contrary to the cut-mark evidence on the pig bones (n=870) from the other study sites where less than 80 had positive knife marks and less than 2% had multiple knife marks (see Table 6.8).

Pig meat has traditionally been expensive in New Zealand and was certainly so in the 19th century (Beeton 1899:25, 532–3). Despite its cost, the fact that butchered pig bones are found in quantity in most of the study sites (Tables 6.5–6.7) indicates that pig meat was readily available and was widely consumed by the Chinese. On one occasion when Don was visiting the Chinese miners in Moke Creek, he expressed surprise that they had not killed a pig for over a week (Don 1895:28). Fresh pork was considered an essential on special occasions such as celebrating good fortune or festival feasts (Don 1908:16, 1/11/1884:85, 1/5/1885:204, 1/8/1885:27).

If saw cuts are a reliable indicator of non-Chinese butchering, it can be deduced that butchered pigs were occasionally acquired from European butchers or farmers. However, only 3% (26) of the pig bones have saw cuts (see Tables 6.8 and 6.9). The vast majority (92%, 812) bear cleaver cuts only and were presumably butchered by Chinese pig raisers or butchers. In southern China, pork was preserved by the farmers using a variety of drying, pressing and smoking techniques (Spence 1977:265). Similar methods were probably used to preserve meat on the goldfields. Immature bones, identified primarily by whether the epiphyses were fused or not, comprised between 33% and 64% of each site's pig bone assemblage. Unfused metapodials indicate that many of the pigs were butchered when less than two years old (Bull and Payne 1982:66). According to Levine (1921:6), the most profitable age at which to slaughter pigs is from eight to 10 months and it is not advisable to keep them longer than 12 months, unless feed is very cheap.

6.4.3 SHEEP (*OVIS ARIES*)

Sheep were represented by a total of 1,271 whole or part bones, the breakdown being: Chinatown 497; ACS 439; Ah Lum's 37; and the rural sites 298. Even though sheep meat was not a major traditional Chinese protein source, more sheep bones were recovered from the study sites than those of any other species. They are statistically dominant in two assemblages, those from Chinatown and the QB2 site, and there were approximately equal ratios of pig and sheep bones in the Arrowtown, Ah Wee's and Riverside sites. But, as is shown in the subsequent discussion in terms of "meat weight consumed", they represent considerably less meat than that derived from either cattle or pigs.

As was done in the course of speciating the cattle and pig bones, the sheep bones were divided into "mature" and "immature" (lamb) based on whether the epiphyses were fused and their size. The bone portions and inferred meat cuts are detailed in Tables 6.10–6.12.

The following primary and secondary cuts were defined from study of the positions of the saw or cleaver/knife cuts on the bones:

1. Cranial fragments are rare, being present only at the Rapids site (a sawn left mandible) and at Ah Lum's (a fragment containing the foramen magna). This suggests that sheep heads were removed at the butchering site and were generally not obtained by the Chinese. The sawn mandible from the Rapids may reflect the extraction of a sheep's tongue or possibly the use of butchered waste bone for soup stock (Piper 1984:22).
2. Axis and atlas vertebrae are commonly cut into "halves" or "quarters", reflecting the severing of an animal's head from the body and "halving" the carcass.
3. Scapulae fragments are relatively common. Most were cleaved rather than sawn. Three cut patterns were defined:
   a. saw cuts across the proximal ends of the bone, attributed to severing the head from the body;

b. roughly cleaved fragments, which were possibly used as stock or reflect breaking down the neck-chuck meat into traditional small portions;

c. about 2 cm wide transverse slices of scapula bone, both sawn and cleaved. These would result from systematic "slicing" of the blade meat into small portions.

4. Shoulder (proximal humerus), foreleg (distal humerus, ulnae and radii) and hind-shank cuts (femora, tibiae and calcaneum) occurred in approximately equal numbers (see Tables 6.10–6.12), with bones from immature specimens constituting around 30% of the total. No consistent pattern in the butchering of the hind and forequarters was apparent, severing cuts being evenly distributed on the proximal and distal ends and central shaft sections of the long bones. Most of the recovered sheep calcaneum were unmodified. A common site for the quartering cut to sever the hindquarters was across the ilium–ascetabulum area and through the femoral head. This is reflected in the recovery of several fragments of femoral "balls" and femora with the proximal condyles chopped off.

5. Marrow bones. Several headless shafts (mainly off tibiae and femora) were recovered, suggesting that marrow recovery was a common practice.

6. Cervical, thoracic and lumbar vertebrae. Most of the recovered vertebrae were split longitudinally, the result of halving carcasses. Over 50% of the recovered vertebrae are "diced"; that is, chopped up into small fragments. These were probably stewed or used in soup stock.

7. Pelvic bones. All the pelvic bone consisted of cut-up fragments. They appear to have been chopped up into small pieces that could be cooked and handled with chopsticks or used for stock.

8. Metapodials, tarsals and carpals. These bones have little meat value and are normally discarded by European butchers. Almost all the recovered metapodials have a single severing cut across the proximal end. Virtually all the carpals/tarsals were unmodified.

Approximately 85% of the sheep bones in the assemblages from Chinatown, Arrowtown, Ah Lum's and the rural sites have cleaver/chop marks rather than saw cuts (Tables 6.8 and 6.9). Sawn bones (scapulae, sterna, vertebrae and long bones) accounted for only 1% to 6% of each assemblage. From the high incidence of cleaving, it is inferred that most of the sheep meat was broken down by Chinese, but the animals were probably slaughtered by European farmers and acquired from European butchers.

Despite a virtual dearth of contemporary references about sheep meat consumption by the Chinese on the goldfields, it was a significant dietary component, as evidenced by the substantial faunal remains and the following quotation: "It is simply a mistake to suppose that the Chinese live on rice…when getting gold…they live as extravagantly as the barbarian digger, consuming sardines, bread, bottled fruits, pork and even the plebian mutton chops, with Old Tom [brandy] to wash it down" (Butler 1977:17). Don (1/12/1884:104) listed "mutton" among a range of foods that were used by the miners as accompaniments with rice during "big meals" (dinner).

Some of the Chinese may have kept sheep, but it is unlikely to have been a common practice because of the miners' mobility, lack of land tenure and access to grazing. The archaeological evidence indicates that individuals or groups of Chinese occasionally acquired whole carcasses or sides and took them home where they carried out further processing. The recovery of relatively large numbers of unmodified foot bones (which are usually discarded) suggests that they may have occasionally acquired sheep on the hoof as well and kept them until they decided to slaughter the animals.

6.5 MEAT PREFERENCES

Table 6.14 outlines the number of bone portions (pieces) of cattle, pig and sheep bone from each of the study sites. As Lyman (1979) and others have demonstrated, a direct comparison of numbers or weights of bone portions/elements can give an inaccurate or misleading impression of the comparative importance of various species in an assemblage. In particular, discrepancies are likely to occur in situations where the numbers of cattle (or other large animal) bones are compared with the numbers of sheep or pig (or other smaller animal) bones from a site(s), because of the much larger volume of meat represented by *Bos* meat cuts compared with that from the equivalent cuts of smaller animals.

Lyman (1979:542), who compared different techniques of calculating meat weights (including bone counts, bone weight, MNI, and counts of "skeletal portions" and "butchering units") on cattle, pig and sheep bones from the same assemblage from a military fort, concluded that "butchering unit" meat weights (see Table 6.16) are probably the most accurate indicator of the amount of consumed meat "because the analytical unit is cultural, and comparable to a consumption unit" (Lyman 1979:542). While on both logical and practical grounds the determination of meat weights by tallying the meat weights of individual butchering units appears to be the most accurate technique, it is a particularly time-consuming process if large numbers of butchering units from several sites are involved and is complicated if, as in the case of much of the bone from the Chinese sites, it is cut into relatively small portions. Furthermore, as Lyman (1979:542) commented, butchering units are not necessarily cross-cultural. The division of a carcass usually reflects ethnic preferences and although butchering units can be determined by analysis of bone assemblages, meat weights/units are generally only available from Anglo-American meat-weight studies. In short, there is no infallible meat-weight estimating system, and the role of some potential "meat products" such as fat, viscera, offal, brains, marrow and blood, can only be estimated using ethno-historical and archaeological evidence (for marrow consumption).

To circumvent the onerous task of calculating and tallying all the meat weights represented by the butchering units from the study sites, a simplified "meat-weight factor" was developed using the meat weight per "skeletal portion" data presented by Lyman (1979:543). His data indicates that the forequarters, hindquarters and ribs-vertebrae of cattle, pigs and sheep vary in terms of their meat weights by an average ratio of 5:2:1. To illustrate by means of an example, the bones of the hindquarters (pelvis, sacrum, tibia, femur, patella and tarsals) of a cattle beast constitute five times the weight of meat represented by the equivalent bones from sheep, and two and a half times that represented by the equivalent bones from pigs. The means by which these meat ratios were calculated is outlined in Table 6.13. While there is some inherent variation in the comparative meat weights of the three skeletal portions, it is contended that the 5:2:1 ratio provides a reasonable estimate of the meat volumes derived from the three animals, and certainly produces estimates that are nearer the mark than would be obtained by bone/element counts or weighing the bones of each species.

However, after an attempt to work out the minimum number of "skeletal portions" of cattle, pig and sheep "failed" because of the amount of finely chopped up bone (particularly ribs and vertebras, burnt bones and long bone shaft fragments), it was decided to apply the weighting factor directly to the numbers of bone portions/species from each site. This increases the margin of error, but only an indication of the relative dietary contribution of the various animal meats was sought. The calculations assume relatively equal numbers of the different skeletal portions from each animal (see Tables 6.14–6.16) and make no allowance for intra-species size differences.

The beef/pig/sheep meat weights of each site assemblage, as determined by using the method outlined above, are summarised in Table 6.15. As can be seen by comparison with Table 6.1, they present a completely different picture from that obtained by direct comparison of bone/species numbers (which ranked sheep and pig meat about equal in popularity, with beef consumption in third place). Using estimated meat weights, beef is predominant in five sites (and represents 44.9% of the total meat weight of all species); pig meat was predominant in the other five (33.8% of the total). In terms of "total meat consumed", sheep meat (21.3%) ranks third after beef and pig meat, although it was the second most popular meat in five sites, including Chinatown (see Table 6.15).

The meat-weight estimates indicate beef consumption was notably higher in the three urban sites – Chinatown, Arrowtown and Ah Lum's store – and was the main meat consumed in the Rapids and Firewood Creek sites, although cattle bones (by count and meat weight represented) were predominant in only one site – the Rapids. Piper (1984:29), who specifically studied the Rapids faunal assemblage, concluded that beef was more important than pork (the other major source of meat) because of the prevailing supply and price situation. Beef and especially mutton were by far the dominant meats sold by European butchers at this time (Bell pers. comm.; and contemporary store invoices), while pork was less readily available and likely to have been more expensive. But, notwithstanding the high cost of pork (from European butchers; see Beeton 1899:25, 532–3), it is apparent from ethno-historical records (documented earlier), and the substantial numbers of pig bones (n=959) recovered from the study sites, that the Chinese miners raised or acquired and consumed large volumes of pig meat (possibly pork obtained from their countrymen was cheaper than that available from European butchers).

The predominance of beef represented in the urban site assemblages, in addition to favourable pricing, possibly reflects easier access to supplies from European butchers in the adjacent towns (Cromwell and Arrowtown), as opposed to a general or developing preference for beef over pork. The marked predominance of beef bones in the Rapids site may simply reflect an individual preference, but overall, the consumption of beef by the Chinese miners is likely to have been considerably greater than the amounts, if any, they consumed in China, where it was much more expensive than pig meat. Many of the long bone shafts were split, suggesting marrow extraction, a distinctly Chinese practice.

Considering the lack of sheep meats in the traditional Cantonese diet, it is no surprise that the estimated meat weights of mutton and lamb consumed are considerably less than those of beef and pork, but the presence of "sheep meat" (i.e. bones) in all of the study sites suggests some degree of substitution and/or acculturation. The relatively higher proportion of sheep meat represented in the rural site assemblages may be attributable to easier access to free or cheap mutton from European farmers in the mining areas (see Don 1911:24). Leg meat cuts predominate. Although hind-leg cuts were expensive, they are relatively economical (Beeton 1899:25, 482–3). They are much less fatty than forequarters and can be cut into virtually fat free slices by boning them across the muscle.

Mr G. Bell (recorded interview, 1984), a retired butcher of Cromwell who sold meat to the remaining Chinese in the Lawrence Chinese settlement, told me "the Chinese preferred beef and pork over mutton, because the latter was too fatty". They only purchased pork and lean beef from him. He recalled that the belly was the preferred pork cut, "but they weren't fussy so long as it was lean". Stewing steak was the preferred beef cut, but other cuts such as corn roll or a flat rib of boiling beef were also purchased regularly. They also occasionally purchased mince, but not sausages. Unfortunately, these cuts or meat products would leave no archaeological record. Mr Bell stated that they "never went in for big joints because of the way they cooked their meat", which he described as follows: "they chopped it up into bite size pieces, then stewed it in small cast iron billies". Their method of cooking was to slowly stew or simmer meat until it could be "mushed up" into what he called a "stoup", a cross between a soup and a stew. Mr Bell's descriptions of the cooking techniques at Lawrence suggest that by then (c.1920), the remaining and now elderly Chinese inhabitants of the camp had simplified their cooking techniques, but they still maintained their cultural preference for beef and pork. He was unsure whether they fried meat, but he was adamant they never roasted it like Europeans.

The figures for pig meat consumption reflect an interesting inversion on the pattern of pig meat usage illustrated in an American study by Gust (1984:188). A table she presented shows the percentage of pig elements compared with those of beef and mutton from six urban Chinese site assemblages in the United States. The pork percentages vary from 57% to 99% of each site assemblage, whereas in the sites studied in this research, the pig element percentage varied from 17% to 76% of each assemblage. The discrepancy may reflect greater access to cheaper sheep meat and beef in New Zealand and conversely pricing or availability factors working against a higher level of pork consumption. According to Mr Bell (above), "when a Chinese miner was doing well, he always ate pork". With the course of time, one might have expected the gradual adoption or substitution of non-traditional meats (particularly increased consumption of mutton/lamb) by the Chinese in New Zealand, but such a change is not evident today (Chinese restaurant menus in New Zealand offer relatively few mutton/lamb dishes).

6.6 MEAT SUPPLIES

As outlined in the preceding discussion, most of the beef and sheep meat consumed by the Chinese appears to have been obtained in the form of traditional (English) meat cuts, but almost without exception they were further processed by the Chinese (mainly using cleavers) into small pieces that could be stewed or stir-fried and handled with chopsticks or European forks and knifes (see Section 5.5.1).

The situation regarding pig butchering is less clear-cut. Most of the primary pig meat cuts (as evident on the recovered bones) are indistinguishable from European cuts, but there are several ethno-historical records (cited earlier) of Chinese raising and butchering pigs for meat on the goldfields. The evidence suggests there was a dual supply situation and whether a miner obtained pig meat from a Chinese or European source was probably largely dependent on locally available supplies and factors such as competitive pricing. There is no evidence that the Chinese preferred to buy from their countrymen or that there was any form of collective resistance against buying from European traders. Although Chinese and European butchers almost certainly divided pig carcasses into slightly different meat units (i.e. primary cuts that should be apparent through study of cleaver/saw cuts and their locations on bones), no distinctive differences were apparent in the pig bone assemblages from the study sites (see Tables 6.5–6.7). The difficulty of recognising distinct ethnic-based butchery cuts is compounded because of the Chinese penchant for chopping up their meat into bite size portions; consequently, it is often difficult to distinguish primary from secondary and tertiary cuts.

Supplies of meat from Europeans could have been obtained from two sources – town-based butchers or directly from local farmers. There is little doubt that the Chinese obtained most of their beef supplies from European butchers, who were among the first businessmen to establish in the goldfield towns. The situation at Cromwell is used as an illustration. According to Parcell (1976:48), there was no butchery in Cromwell prior to the August 1862 goldrush, but when Captain Jackson Barry established his "Free Trade and No Monopoly" butchery in February 1863, there was already another butcher in business (Parcell 1976:51). By August 1866, Barry had bought a farm 3.2 km from Cromwell (Parcell 1976:213) and was raising fat wethers and pigs for sale and "a splendid breed of swine in 1864" (Barry 1897:157). In November 1866, he sold the butchery to a man named Dawkins (Parcell 1976:53). In 1869, Barry was running the Smithfield Butchery in competition with Dawkins' Free Trade Butchery (Parcell 1976:54). By 1871, due to financial difficulties, Barry no longer ran the shop but was in business as a carcass butcher (Parcell 1976:54). A slaughter yard was established near the Kawarau River in 1873, if not a few years earlier. By the mid-1880s, there were three European butchers operating in Cromwell (Parcell 1976:62). Mr G. Bell (pers. comm.) said in the early days the carcasses were broken down into butchering units in the butcher shops, but most of the meat was sold by hawking it around the goldfields as described by Barry:

> There were about 5,000 diggers and others working in and around Cromwell at this time [1863], and to the many stores in the outlying gullies or the diggings I dispatched packhorse loads of meat daily, besides keeping the carts constantly carrying the meat far and near without a shade of profit. (Barry 1897:153)

The important point here is that the butchers hawked meat around the goldfields, initially using packhorses, but as communications improved, enclosed carts (hawker's carts) were used. Advertisements for the Free Trade Butchery state that meat was "delivered at town prices throughout the district". This method of selling meat was used by butchers in Cromwell until after the Second World War (Bell pers. comm.). The early Cromwell butchers went on the rounds with their carts twice weekly, serving up to 120 customers per day and often travelling 32 km away from Cromwell (Bell pers. comm.). Chinese miners purchased meat regularly from the European butcher-hawkers (Bell pers. comm.), usually amicably, but occasionally there were disputes. Butler (1977:23) cites an instance where a brawl occurred between Chinese and Europeans in Tinkers Gully after a Chinese customer alleged that a European butcher had given him less pork than he had paid for (the Chinese man had reweighed the meat in his tent).

There were also a few Chinese butchers who operated stores on the southern goldfields, although only that of Ah Chong, who secured a slaughter yard licence and established a butchery at Bannockburn in 1871, was in the immediate study area. He sold the business to another Chinese, We Lee, in 1876 (Parcell 1976:149). Despite considerable effort to find the site of this butchery, with a view to excavating it, it has not been found. In 1869, there were two Chinese butchers and three storekeepers at the Nevis, serving a population of 250 (Parcell 1976:149). A new butcher's shop was opened at Round Hill in 1885 (Don l/8/1885:26), and there was a Chinese butcher resident at Ida Valley (Don 1906:33) and another had a hawker's round near Ophir. Overall, however, Chinese owned and operated butcheries do not appear to have been as numerous as those run by Europeans. Those mentioned above probably supplied local needs for various periods, but in other areas the Chinese were dependent on European butchers. Cured meat products such as bacon were also available from the general stores.

The acquisition of meat directly from farmers is a difficult question to evaluate because there are no written records. On probability grounds, it would seem unlikely that a European farmer would slaughter a cattle beast to supply individuals or small groups of Chinese miners, but the lesser amount of meat on a pig, lamb or mutton carcass would have facilitated their butchering and sale to potential customers. But unless there were very real advantages (like wholesale instead of retail prices), the Chinese are unlikely to have foregone the convenience of being able to buy small amounts of meat of their choice from the travelling butchers. The most likely exceptions are those who were working in remote gullies that were seldom, if ever visited by the butcher-hawkers, or when a Chinese community bought meat in bulk (especially pork) to celebrate a festival or some other special occasion. I have found no records of Chinese stealing or illicitly obtaining sheep or pigs (or other foods) for sustenance even when they were down on their luck.

6.7 BUTCHERING PATTERNS AND DIETARY CONTRIBUTION OF SMALLER MAMMALS

6.7.1 GOATS *(CAPRA HIRCUS)*

Goat bones were only positively identified from the Rapids site, and here only three bones from one individual were recovered (Piper 1984:57). The source of the goat meat is unlikely to have been a European butcher, leaving two other possibilities – acquisition from a European inhabitant or the hunting/trapping of the goat by the Chinese inhabitant of the site.

Very little is known about the early spread of goats in New Zealand (Wodzicki 1950:155), but it is known that they were sometimes kept by European prospectors and goldminers in their camps (Wodzicki 1950:154). When the beasts were accidentally or deliberately liberated, it led to the eventual formation of wild goat herds. Some European miners also kept milking goats (Bell pers. comm.). At the time of this research, feral goats in the Cromwell area were restricted to the south side of the Kawarau River, where the Rapids site is located. This distribution is believed to have existed in the 19th century too. Obviously, goat meat was not a major protein source for the Chinese miners around Cromwell, but they may have acquired it occasionally as circumstances permitted. According to Harry Helms, Ching Ching, who worked in the left-hand branch of the Skippers Stream (in the Shotover) c.1900, shot goats for food (Chandler pers. comm.).

6.7.2 CAT *(FELIS CATUS)*

Cat bones were found in huts 1, 7, 15 and 16 at Chinatown and huts 5, 10 and 15 at Arrowtown. According to Don (1901:18), some of the Chinese kept cats as pets, but most of the excavated bones were found on or near the surface and are almost certainly derived from cats that died there after the sites were abandoned. A left maxilla and an axis vertebra found in hut 16 at Chinatown had been cut longitudinally down the middle to divide the skull in half. An unspecified butchered cat bone was also uncovered in the Rapids site (Piper 1984:26). This suggests that, on occasion, some Chinese consumed the odd cat, but it is not certain how they were obtained or killed. The use of domestic cats as food was an acceptable practice in southeastern China according to Ball (1906), but possibly because of European aversion to the practice, it does not appear to have been a regular practice in overseas situations. Gust (1984:167–92) documented two instances where limited numbers of butchered cat bones were found in Chinese sites (Woodlands and Tucson) in the United States.

Wild cats are likely to have been particularly abundant in the Cromwell area during the latter part of the 19th century, because prior to the introduction of mustelids, sheep farmers in Central Otago purchased and released large numbers of cats as a means of controlling rabbits (Wodzicki 1950: 82–3). Piper (1984:26) suggested that the presence of butchered cat bones does not necessarily imply deliberate trapping of cats. They may have been caught occasionally in traps set for rabbits. It would be easier to kill a wild cat caught in a trap than attempt to release it. In view of the small numbers of butchered cat bones, this seems a reasonable explanation.

6 Dietary analysis

6.7.3 POSSUM (TRICHOSURUS VULPECULA)

Possum bones were found in two sites (huts 3 and 5 at Arrowtown) and the Rapids site (Piper 1984:26). There was no evidence of butchering on any of the bones and their position in the sites suggests post-abandonment deposition. According to one report, possums were liberated in Otago (place unspecified) in 1891 (Otago Acclimatisation Society 1891:7), but Wodzicki (1950:26) states possums were absent from Central Otago until at least 1948. This being so, there is no possibility of their exploitation by the Chinese.

6.7.4 RABBITS (ORYCTOLAGUS CUNICULIS)

Rabbits were liberated in Otago shortly after the establishment of the Otago settlement in 1848. At this time liberations were made at Queenstown, and more were liberated by the Otago Acclimatisation Society in the late 1860s. Gold prospectors often contributed to their spread by taking rabbits with them. By 1876, north and Central Otago were heavily infested (Wodzicki 1950:107–9).

Ethno-historic observations attest to the high rabbit populations. For example, Don (1908:17) writes of a Chinese man who told him that "unlike the situation in China one could never starve in New Zealand because you could live on potatoes and rabbits". The rabbit remains found in the study sites (Table 6.17) indicate that rabbits became an increasingly abundant resource, and the Chinese took advantage of that. The trapping of rabbits by some of the remaining Chinese in Chinatown was observed post-1900 (Scott pers. comm.), and the last Chinese inhabitant of the Apple Tree site is known to have gratefully accepted gifts of rabbits from Mr M. Lawless when he was a young boy c.1910 (Lawless pers. comm. 1981).

Analysis of rabbit bones to determine meat cuts is complicated for a number of reasons:

1. The leg bones are often broken while skinning a rabbit, so it is often difficult to distinguish butchering and/or skinning breaks from natural breaks.
2. Rabbits are still very abundant in Central Otago. As a result, those which have died naturally or from poisoning or gun shots frequently become integrated into archaeological deposits. Although they are easily identified if the skeletons are in situ, it is much more difficult once the bones have become scattered across several excavation units by scuffage, trampling and stratigraphically repositioned by rabbit burrowing.
3. Rabbit meat can be cooked and consumed with a minimal number of skeletal cuts or breaks, leaving little archaeological evidence that a rabbit has been butchered.

Although the minimum number of positively butchered rabbit bones only totalled 69 (11% of the total recovered: n=624; Table 6.17), it was apparent from study of the bones that the legs (especially the hind legs) were often removed from the carcass and chopped into small pieces using a cleaver, presumably to facilitate handling with chopsticks. The prepared meat was probably stewed and consumed with rice.

As far as I can ascertain, the consumption of rabbit meat by the peasantry in southern China was not a regular practice. Rabbit meat, along with venison and pheasant, was highly prized game meat, which was obtained by hunters who supplied the markets (Mote 1977:242). By comparison, their abundance in Central Otago in the late 19th century must have been a welcome and virtually free food resource that most of the remaining Chinese exploited. This is reflected not only in the skeletal remains but also the numerous traps (European-style gin traps) and associated components found in the sites (see Section 5.5.3). There have been no studies of the longevity of cooked rabbit bones in archaeological contexts. It is likely that the consumption of rabbit meat is grossly underrepresented in the study sites if the bones decompose rapidly.

6.7.5 RAT (RATTUS NORVEGICUS)

About 50 of the recovered bones (all species) bear evidence of rat gnawing, but rat bones were found in only two sites – the Hanging Rock shelter (a cranium) and huts 7 (lateral humerus) and 18 (tibia and fibula) at Chinatown. All the bones were intact and unmarked and presumably are derived from house rats that died in or around the miners' habitations.

6.7.6 DOG (CANIS DOMESTICUS)

Dog bones were found in only one site. A virtually complete skeleton of a medium-sized dog was uncovered in the fireplace of hut 5 at Arrowtown. It appears to have curled up and died there long after the site's abandonment.

6.8 AVIAN REMAINS

The diversity of the avifaunal remains afforded an opportunity for a specialised study on the exploitation of bird species and their socio-economic significance to the Chinese (Ritchie and McGovern-Wilson 1986). Consequently, only summary details are presented here.

The objectives of the study were to:

1. define minimum numbers and species and account for their presence;
2. determine butchering techniques, meat cut preferences and the significance of bird meat in the local Chinese subsistence pattern;
3. examine husbandry, hunting or collecting strategies.

The total avifaunal assemblage was not large (118 individuals; see Table 6.18), but it was substantial enough to reveal trends and indicate the main species that were exploited. The following reasons can be advanced to account for a suspected low retention of bird remains in the sites:

1. Wastes were disposed of into adjacent creeks or rivers.
2. The bones were softened and chopped up in the cooking process, which would accelerate their decomposition.
3. The bones were consumed by other animals such as pigs, cats and rodents.
4. They were discarded into fireplaces and burnt (burning is evident on many of the animal bones from some of the sites).

Of the total of 118 birds, 95 bear evidence of butchering in the form of breakage and cut marks. The method and forms devised by Leach (1979:103–6) were used for assessing and maximising minimum numbers.

The domestic hen (*Gallus domesticus*) was the most common species in every site, both rural and urban. Hens made up 61% of the total MNI. At Chinatown, hen bones were associated with all but three of the huts. Two of the 18 specimens were juvenile/immature birds. These were identified by unfused epiphyses on the long bones and the rougher texture of the bones.

The Chinatown bones were originally examined by Ron Scarlett (then osteologist, Canterbury Museum), who identified a few bones as belonging to "very large specimens of domestic chicken". However, McGovern-Wilson, who was responsible for speciating all the bird bones from the sites, believes their size and physical characteristics more closely resemble those of the domestic turkey (*Meleagris gallopavo*) and concluded that five specimens were represented (McGovern-Wilson n.d.a:1). Similarly, most of the bird remains at Arrowtown were either those of domesticated hens (23 specimens, 6 immature) or turkeys (3). Eight of the Arrowtown hens were found in or near Ah Lum's store.

Skeletal evidence of domestic hens (MNI=23) was recovered from all the rural sites. Again, the presence of sub-adult and immature specimens indicates that young birds were frequently eaten. Among the hen bones (MNI=2) from Sheung Fong shelter in the Cromwell Gorge, one set could be described as "normal", while the other (8 bones) are only half the normal size in linear terms. McGovern-Wilson (n.d.b:2) suggested they are possibly the remains of a bantam or a Chinese species such as a silky, which are both small birds in comparison to the domestic fowl. Spurs on some of the tarsometatarsi indicate the presence of roosters and suggest the breeding of domestic fowl. One was recovered from Chinatown (Ch/7), two from Arrowtown (ACS/4 and 6) and one from the Poplars. The Chinatown specimen had an arthritic growth on the distal side of the spur.

Sparse eggshell, believed to be hens', was found in four huts at Chinatown (Ch/16, 21, 24 and 26), two at Arrowtown (ACS/8 and 10), in five rural hut sites (the Poplars, the Willows, QB2, the Rapids and Ah Wee's) and in five rockshelters (Hanging Rock, Northburn, Ha Fong, Sheung Fong and Firewood Creek). The presence of single egg cups in two huts at Chinatown (Ch/7 and Ch/23), in the Caliche shelter, and outside Ah Lum's store suggests that some of the Chinese had adopted the European practice of boiling eggs and eating them out of the shell in an egg cup.

The other main feature of the assemblages is the presence of several wild birds, notably black swans (*Cygnus atratus*), grey and paradise ducks (*Anas superciliosa, Tadorna variegata*) and weka (*Gallirallus australis*). At Chinatown, 5 paradise and 3 grey ducks, 5 black swans and a single mute swan (*Cygnus alors*) are represented (the latter speciated on the strut formation on the dorsal side of an anterior fragment of a sternum), and at Arrowtown, the remains of 5 paradise ducks were recovered. These indicate that the Chinese supplemented their food or meat supplies (although possibly for feasts only) by exploiting wild species. The means of trapping or killing the wild birds was not readily apparent from the skeletal remains.

The unbutchered remains of a New Zealand quail (*Coturnix novaezealandiae*) were recovered from hut 18 in Chinatown. These birds, together with weka, were once common in the Upper Clutha area. Although Oliver thought the native quail still existed in small numbers in some areas of the South Island in 1872, there had been no reliable sightings in the preceding five years (Oliver 1974:438). Weka became locally extinct c.1900, succumbing to poisonous baits laid for rabbits (Ritchie 1980:45). Interestingly, weka remains were only found in the rural sites. Possibly there was no suitable habitat left in the vicinity of the established mining towns or they had already disappeared through over-exploitation or poisoning in those areas.

A harrier hawk (*Circus approximans*) found in ACS/1 was a surprise inclusion in the Arrowtown bird list. McGovern-Wilson concluded the single bone, a humerus, belonged to a sub-adult specimen, a nestling, which would have been taken in the period between January and late March (Oliver 1974:430–1).

The bones of several small, introduced birds found principally within the huts of the urban sites bear no definitive evidence of butchering. They include house sparrows, thrushes/blackbirds and single specimens of bellbird and tom tit. The high incidence of immature specimens among these tree-nesting species is attributed to their falling out of nests above the sites.

From study of the butchered bones, it appears all parts of the exploited species were consumed, although cranial bones are only represented by sparse fragments. Few intact bones were recovered. Most of the butchered bones bear "chop" marks, indicating they were cut with a cleaver or knife. In most instances, the distal or proximal ends of long bones have been detached from the shaft with a single cut/chop. Examination of the butchered sterna and pelvic fragments indicates that they were produced by transverse slicing at about 3 cm intervals across the carcass. McGovern-Wilson (n.d.a:4) concluded that most of the sterna fragments are probably from domestic chickens, but only those with part of the rostrum, which allows positive identification, have been included in the MNI calculations. This cutting pattern is consistent with traditional Chinese cooking procedures where meats and other foods are usually cut into portions small enough to be easily handled with chopsticks. Dicing foodstuffs also makes them suitable for stir-frying or stewing and minimises cooking time, the latter being an important consideration when firewood is in short supply.

Some bones (mostly fowl or duck) bear "snap-break marks". These present a problem because it is difficult to tell whether the breaks were deliberate or are the result of post-deposition damage. The Chinese often break bones in the process of boning or portioning a chicken (Lee and Lee 1979:189–90). Comparative counts were made of the proximal and distal portions of all the butchered fowl wing (carpometacarpi, humeri, ulnae and radii) and leg (femora, tibiae and tarsometatarsi) bones to determine if there was any consistent patterning in the cut locations on the wing and leg portions of the birds. This study proved inconclusive, although the ratio of distal to proximal ends varied by as much as 50% or more (see Table 6.19). Diced or broken central shaft portions were not included because of the difficulty of accurately speciating these fragments. It appears that the location of cuts on the limb bones was not critical and merely a function of where the cleaver happened to land during "dicing up" a chicken carcass. Counts of complete bones revealed there were twice as many complete leg bones as wing bones, suggesting the "meatier" leg portions were more frequently deboned.

The avian remains indicate that many of the Chinese miners in Central Otago not only kept domestic poultry (fowl, and possibly ducks and turkeys) but also supplemented their diet with birds from the local environment. These included waterbirds such as swans, grey and paradise ducks, and ground dwellers such as the weka, and perhaps the native quail during the earliest years of settlement. Small arboreal birds such as bellbirds, thrushes and blackbirds may have been consumed occasionally, but the recovered bones of these species bear no evidence of exploitation.

The keeping of fowl in the goldfields settlements and camps follows a long-established tradition of poultry raising in South China, the consumption of fowl meat being considered an essential part of festive occasions and a desirable dietary component (for eggs and meat) at other times. Don made numerous references to their consumption (e.g. Don 1/9/1882:44, 1/3/1883:164, 1/11/1884:85). Although there is less definitive evidence of duck raising by the Chinese on the Central Otago goldfields, they obtained ducks and they were on the menu of most celebration feasts (Don 1/11/1884:85, 1/8/1885:27). Ducks cost 2/- each in the 1890s (Chandler pers. comm.; see Table 6.20). Comparison of poultry husbandry and cooking practices in South China with the avian remains from the study sites shows that the miners essentially transplanted their indigenous husbandry and cooking methods into their new situation with minimal modification. Most of the recovered bones bear one or more clean knife or cleaver cuts consistent with accounts of traditional poultry butchering and meat preparation procedures as documented by Yee (1975) and the authors of many other Chinese cookbooks. No clear changes in bird meat butchery or acquisition practices were determined between the earliest sites and the later ones.

The presence of several turkeys in the Arrowtown (MNI=3) and Chinatown (MNI=5) assemblages is somewhat surprising. These birds were not a significant meat source in southern China and their consumption by Europeans in New Zealand has largely been restricted to Christmas and other celebrations. Their presence in both urban sites most likely reflects acquisition from local European farmers or suppliers rather than turkey raising by the Chinese, but the latter possibility cannot be ruled out. They were probably raised or acquired to supplement festal supplies. Wild turkeys is another possibility, but wild turkeys are uncommon in Central Otago.

The assemblages clearly show that the Chinese took advantage of "free resources" such as wild ducks, swans and weka. Interestingly, none of the sites contained exclusively wild or domesticated species. Similar patterns of subsistence, i.e. supplementing domestic poultry with wild birds, have been documented at the Sacramento "Chinatown" (Praetzellis and Praetzellis 1982:73) and the Woodland Chinese site (Simons 1984:168) in California.

6.9 AQUATIC SPECIES

Fish were and still are a major source of protein in southern China. According to Anderson and Anderson (1977:334), many hundreds of species of fish (both wild and pond-raised) and shellfish were consumed. Sea fish and oversupplies of freshwater species were usually dried or salted for preservation and transportation (Anderson and Anderson (1977:335) or made into fish pastes. Compared with the wide range of seafoods and freshwater species available in South China, the Chinese miners must have found the aquatic food resources of Central Otago very limited.

Sparse amounts of only four types of aquatic food refuse were found in the study sites: fish bones (mainly vertebrae); marine oyster shell; cuttlefish and freshwater mussel shells.

6.9.1 FISH

Fish bones were recovered from three sites: Chinatown (in six huts: nos 7, 16, 21, 22, 33 and 34), Arrowtown (in ACS/9 a midden) and in the Rapids site (3 bones). A single fish scale was found in the Caliche shelter. Some fish bones found in the Rockfall 1 site (S133/37), a pre-European shelter (which also contained evidence of Chinese occupation), are probably associated with the Chinese occupation there. They were compared by Graeme Mason against the extensive comparative collection of New Zealand and Oceanic fish species held in the University of Otago Anthropology Department's laboratory. He concluded that the bones may have been those of a dried fish, possibly some form of oriental carp, brought to the site by the Chinese miners (Mason pers. comm. 1978). Two large metal fish hooks were found in the Flax Grove shelter in the Kawarau Gorge.

Most of the 36 fish bones are vertebrae, which are difficult to speciate unequivocally. They were examined by Dr A.J. Anderson (Anthropology Department, University of Otago) and Dr C. Paulin (National Museum). Both concluded that the few diagnostic cranial bones were unlike any in the comparative collections in their respective institutions and suggested they are probably derived from imported dried fish. Paulin (pers. comm.) believes some of the bones are of a serranid fish, something like a sea perch or groper but definitely not of a type found in local waters. Paulin sent the fish bones to the British Museum for identification. The museum was unable to positively speciate them but suggested they were probably the bones of fish from tropical waters. Piper (1984:44) noted a possible snapper bone was found in the Rapids site. If his identification is correct, the bone is more likely to be derived from a dried imported specimen as the species does not frequent the waters of southern New Zealand.

Despite the significance of fresh fish and other aquatic species in the traditional Chinese diet, such foods would have been relatively hard to obtain in Central Otago during the 19th century. This is reflected in the relatively small fish bone assemblages. Several reasons can be advanced to explain this situation:

1. Before the introduction and establishment of European fish species such as brown and rainbow trout, fish life in the rivers of Central Otago was limited to eels and a few small and relatively rare native trout species.
2. Mining detritus, which was liberally discharged into the Clutha–Kawarau river system until after the turn of the century, is likely to have eliminated or markedly reduced fish life in the rivers.
3. Before the advent of refrigeration, it was difficult to obtain coastal marine fish in Central Otago.
4. Differential survival of fishbone cannot be overlooked. Cooking softens fishbone and it is likely to have decomposed faster than the more robust mammalian bones.

Given this situation, the Chinese in Central Otago would have been obliged to largely forego fresh fish in their diet, although it may have been obtainable occasionally. Don (1897:59) recorded an instance where he was offered an evening meal by a group of Chinese miners in the Upper Nevis Valley consisting of "a tender young chicken and two sweet fish accompanying the bowl of pearly grains". The archaeological evidence clearly indicates that they substituted canned fish, as demonstrated by the large numbers of sardine and other fish cans found in the Chinese sites (Ritchie and Bedford 1985; Section 5.3). Although canned fish often contains bones, they tend to be softened by the cooking process, decreasing the likelihood of their retention in sites. Furthermore, the softened bones are often eaten.

In addition to canned fish, dried fish (either imported or dried on the Otago/Southland coast) and Chinese fish pastes were available through some of the Chinese stores on the goldfields. Don's records contain two pertinent references. On one of his visits to the Round Hill goldfield (in June 1882), he was "offered a kind of preserved fish in a black pot". He implied it was imported from China (Don 2/10/1882:66). He also mentioned that a local Chinese man who earned a living by drying and selling fish was giving up until the return of the warmer weather (Don 2/10/1882:67). Although this man probably sold his fish locally, some may have been sold in the interior.

A few of the "fish" bones found in the Chinese sites may be eel bones. Some of the last Chinese in Cromwell's Chinatown trapped eels in the adjacent Kawarau River in the period between 1910 and 1920 (Scott pers. comm.), while Ah Luey (a.k.a. Ah Nuey), one of the last Chinese miners in the Bendigo area (c.1910), trapped eels that he kept alive in a small pond, thus having a supply of fresh fish on hand (Duff 1980:191). Ah Luey fed the eels on rabbit carcasses (Duff pers. comm. 1980). Further evidence that the Chinese consumed eels was recorded by Don (1891:15) when he noted an instance when he was given breakfast consisting of a piece of fried eel meat and potatoes by a Chinese miner who was working on the Molyneux (Clutha) River below Roxburgh. It is likely "fish meat" is considerably underrepresented in the study sites because of the poor survivability of cooked freshwater fish bones.

6.9.2 CUTTLEFISH *(SEPIA)*

The drying and distribution of seafoods, including cuttlefish, was a big business in China during the Qing dynasty (Spence 1977:228). Although dried cuttlefish could not be described as a staple, it was a commonly consumed food. Pieces of cuttlebone were found in hut 6 and Ah Lum's store at Arrowtown, in huts 17, 18, 23 and 34 at Chinatown, and in the Rapids site. As the species does not frequent New Zealand waters, the excavated specimens represent the remains of imported fish. It sold for 3/- a pound (Don 1895:59). In one instance, Don noted cuttlefish was on the menu of a festival feast (Don 1/5/1885:204).

6.9.3 SHELLFISH

Two types of shellfish were found in the sites: the southern marine oyster (*Ostrea*) and the freshwater mussel (*Hydridella menziesii*). Most of the oyster shells were found in the urban sites – at Chinatown (in huts 1, 7, 8, 12, 14, 25, 29 and 33) and at the Arrowtown settlement (in huts 3, 4, 5, 10, 11, 13 and 15), as well as in Ah Lum's store. A minimum number of 27 were uncovered in Chinatown, the Arrowtown assemblage totalled 34, and a single valve was found in the Caliche shelter.

Even though they do not keep well, and despite the long distances they would have had to have been conveyed, marine oyster shells from the Foveaux Strait beds (200 km to the south), are a common feature of late 19th century European mining sites in Central Otago. After the turn of the 19th century they were railed overnight to inland destinations, but it is not clear how they were transported or sold before c.1900, other than that they appear to have been conveyed and sold in the shell. They were probably transported as live shells in salt water. The Chinese probably acquired them occasionally from European oyster merchants.

Fragments of single valves of the freshwater mussel were found in two of the huts at Chinatown (Ch/22 and Ch/33). The species is locally available, although none of the present known colonies are less than a kilometre from Cromwell (Ritchie n.d.a.). They prefer slow, sluggish water in river backwaters and lakes. Possibly freshwater mussel beds were discovered during prospecting and occasionally exploited. Mussell shells decompose very rapidly in damp ground conditions, so it is possible that considerably larger numbers were consumed.

6.10 OTHER FOODS

The foods that have been discussed thus far are those that leave durable residues and consequently are amenable to systematic archaeological analyses. However, before an assessment can be made of their role in the diet of the Chinese miners, it is necessary to consider other foods the Chinese imported, grew or acquired from local sources.

6.10.1 IMPORTED AND PRESERVED FOODS

Of the imported foods, rice was undoubtedly the most important, as it was in southern China. Don's observations confirm that rice was eaten at most meal times and that "taking rice" was synonymous with "having a meal". He made frequent references to taking "morning", "noon" or "evening rice" with various groups of Chinese during his missionising travels (e.g. Don 1894–95:22). However, he was quick to try and put to rest the common European misconception that the Chinese "lived on rice". He agreed that rice was their "staff of life and occupied greater prominence than any single food eaten by Europeans, but it usually only amounted to 1/3 of their cost of living" (Don 1/12/1882:104). He went on to say that "a Chinese 'big meal' [dinner] usually always had two to five 'accompaniments', such as pork, cabbage, mutton, celery, onions, fish (fresh and preserved), pickles, turnips, fowl, potatoes, duck etc.". At a "small meal", sometimes only pastry was eaten (Don 1/12/1882:104). He considered that if "the Chinese were making wages" they normally spent about 15/- each on food per week but cited two instances where the weekly rate per man was 10/- for rice and pork alone (Don 2/7/1883:4).

Rice was imported in sacks. Although some of it came from China, much of the rice consumed by the New Zealand Chinese was imported from India and Java (Don 1/12/1882:104). The rice sacks were often used for roofing (Don 197.1:2) or as doors (hanging flaps) in their dwellings (Don 1901:26). Although rice continued to be a major dietary component, e.g. its purchase by Chinese customers is mentioned frequently in the accounts of a European storekeeper at Roxburgh in the late 1890s (Kinaston ledger), its overall proportion of the Chinese miners' diet probably decreased with time. After about the turn of the century, foods they could grow themselves or acquire cheaply, such as potatoes, were becoming increasingly important for many of the remaining miners.

Next to rice, tea was also a significant imported dietary component. It was drunk during most social occasions, as it was in China. Again, Don provides insights into its usage and social role. It was considered rude not to offer a visitor or guest a cup of tea (Don 1896:50), yet offering someone a second cup was a polite way of telling them that they had overstayed their welcome (Don 1891:12). Sometimes roasted rice was used as a tea substitute (Don 1906:36).

This writer is unaware of any 19th century New Zealand Chinese merchants shipping manifestos or price lists that are available for research in New Zealand. Overseas researchers (e.g. Spier 1958; Evans 1980) have found such documents contain a wealth of information, particularly regarding the importation of less durable products. In the absence of such documentation, archaeology provides an alternative source of such information by means of specialised studies of discarded containers (principally ceramic pots, glass bottles and jars, and tin cans). These affirm (see Sections 5.1–5.3) that the Chinese consumed many preserved products, both imports and New Zealand produce.

The Chinese ceramic container remains reflect a continued reliance on imported foods such as dried vegetables, soy sauce, preserved ginger, black vinegar, fish pastes, bean curd, piquant sauces and peanut oil. The latter was used for cooking. The Chinese never used beef suet or butter for cooking (Don 1/8/1886:22). The recovery of a small piece of coconut shell in hut 2 at Arrowtown suggests another imported food product. They also adopted many European foodstuffs that were packaged in glass. Foremost among these products were pickles, jams, Worcestershire sauce, vegetable oils and white vinegar. The role of bottled products was discussed in Section 5.1. Canned foods were also an important dietary component. The Chinese miners acquired and regularly consumed many canned foods such as vegetables (beans, tomatoes and jams), soups, meats and fish, as well as dried products such as coffee, spices and baking powder. The role of canned foods in the miners' diet was discussed in Section 5.3 and by Ritchie and Bedford (1985).

Traditionally, the Chinese were not great consumers of milk-based products (Hsu and Hsu 1977:302). According to Don, they disparagingly referred to butter as "cow's milk grease" (Don 1/10/1886:61) and considered its odour somewhat disagreeable (Don 2/8/1886:22). The low incidence of condensed milk cans in Chinese sites (compared to European sites of the same period) suggests that milk was a minor dietary component, although an 1890s Roxburgh store ledger (Kinaston 1896:532) cites several purchases of milk, butter and cheese by Chinese customers, indicating that some had developed a taste for these products as the years passed.

6.10.2 LOCALLY-GROWN FOODS

6.10.2.1 Vegetables and cereals

The keeping of vegetable gardens was much more common among the Chinese than their European counterparts. Three types can be defined:

a. **House gardens.** Many of the Chinese miners had small garden plots around their dwellings. They are evident in the numerous photographs taken by Don of Chinese miner's huts in many localities (some were reproduced in Butler 1977) and his recorded observations (e.g. Don 1901:55). They grew many European vegetables including peas, cabbages, celery, onions, pumpkins, turnips and potatoes, as well as Chinese cabbage, the seed of which was imported from China. It appears other seed stock was obtained from China too, as evidenced by an incident when Don met a Chinese man en route to the Round Hill goldfield from Riverton. The man was carrying a sack of turnip seed. He told Don he had imported the seed from China because he considered it was superior (Don 1/1/1883:126). Pumpkin seeds found in huts 26 and 33 at Chinatown and in hut 3 at Arrowtown were the only vegetable seeds recovered.

b. **Settlement gardens.** Large garden areas were established adjacent to many of the Chinese settlements, such as those at Arrowtown, Cromwell and Lawrence. Some may have been communally owned or worked, but in most instances, they were either owned by one reasonably affluent person, such as a storekeeper, who employed others to assist with the gardening work when necessary, or they were aggregations of individual miner's private plots. It is believed such a garden system is depicted in an 1887 photograph of the Arrowtown Chinese Settlement (Arrowtown Museum EL 286; Ritchie 1984:43; see Plate 9). The produce was sold, often via licensed hawkers, to both European and Chinese customers (Ritchie 1984:14, 16; Arrowtown Borough rate books; Butler 1977:59), but unlike the Chinese market gardening operation on the Palmer River goldfield, Queensland, documented by Jack, Holmes and Kerr (1984), the European miners in Central Otago were not totally reliant on Chinese garden produce. Large multi-terraced Chinese horticultural sites, such as those in southern Idaho (Fee pers. comm.), do not appear to be a feature of Chinese gardening in Central Otago, although small two-tier garden terraces were located on the slopes behind both the Arrowtown and Cromwell Chinese settlements (see Chapter 4).

c. **Market gardens.** From the time of their initial settlement in New Zealand in the mid-1860s, some of the Chinese became involved in full-time market gardening both in Dunedin and on the goldfields. The *Otago Witness* (7/9/1867) reported that five Chinese had leased an area of swampy land in Great King Street, Dunedin, to establish a garden. After 1878, "gardeners" constituted the second-largest Chinese occupation group after miners (NZ Census 1871, 1874, 1878, 1881, 1886, 1891, 1901; data summarised in Section 3.4).

Shortly after 1900, the number of Chinese involved in market gardening (791) exceeded, for the first time, the number involved in mining (612) (NZ Census 1906). By the late 1880s, there were some 80 Chinese gardeners in Dunedin (Don 1/6/1889:222) and Don mentions that Chinese gardens existed on the goldfields at Blacks (Ophir: 1/3/1887:164), Māori Point and Big Beach (on the Shotover: 1/3/1888:165, 1894:14), Conroy's (1/3/1888:167), Tinkers (2/4/1888:185, 1/5/1889:205), Māori Gully (Ida Valley: 2/4/1888:185), Matakanui (1911:16, 41), Clyde (1894:21) and Cromwell (1911:37), as well as large market gardens at Palmerston (1894:43), Milton (1895:65, 1911:41), Gore (2/4/1888:185, 1895:71), Oamaru (2/4/1888:184, 1/3/1889:166), Waikiwi (near Invercargill: 1/3/1888:165) and at Anderson's Bay, Dunedin (1909–11:23). There were also Chinese gardens at Waitahuna and Waitahuna Gully (Mayhew 1949:90) and one is depicted on Riddiford's (1890) map of the Bannockburn area. By the early 20th century, Chinese market gardens were established in every district in New Zealand.

Don made many observations about the Chinese miners' consumption of potatoes and items made of flour (see below). Neither product represents a significant departure from the Cantonese diet of the mid-19th century, although they appear to have accepted some European methods of cooking the foods. By the turn of the century, the cultivation of many traditional root crops in China was declining in Guangdong in the face of the growing acceptance of New World potatoes and the European carrot, with only taro (*Colocasia antiquorum*) retaining much importance (Anderson and Anderson 1977:329–30). Sweet potatoes had become a staple food for the poor in the southeastern provinces of China by the early 1700s (Spence 1977:263). Potatoes were usually grown by the miners in small fenced plots near their huts (Don 1/10/1887:64, 1908:9 and 16, 1911:39). Like

Europeans, they often boiled them (Don 1895:17), but potato fritters made from grated potato and flour were also popular (Don 1906:31). In the cited instance, the Chinese miner cooked the potato fritters for Don because he had exhausted his supplies of rice and flour (Don 1906:31). On other occasions Don was offered potato soup (Don 1/3/1888:165) and snacks made from grated potatoes, peanuts and sugar (Don 1/9/1889:46). The utility of potatoes (and rabbits) to the Chinese miners is demonstrated in these recorded comments of an old man who was comparing the difference between the food situations in New Zealand and China: "Here... even a poor man can plant a few potatoes and catch a rabbit or two but in China it is very different. At my village if the taro or the sweet potato crop failed, then we know well what it means to eat without being filled" (Don 1908:17).

It is evident from Don's records that many Chinese used flour regularly. Hand-milled wheat, corn and bean flour were significant traditional Chinese dietary components (Spence 1977:270). The use of flour by the Chinese in New Zealand probably increased with time and to some extent at the expense of rice. That it was used in considerable quantities by some of the miners is suggested by an occasion when Don met a man who had carried a 100 lb sack of flour 56 miles to his new diggings (Don 1911:30). Pancakes appear to have been the main product made from flour. These were simple affairs, usually just flour and water (Don 1908:21), but they were made appetising with fillings such as roasted peanuts and sugar (Don 1908:21), and probably jam, as well as cooked foods such as pork (Don 1891:11). Flour was also used for making dampers (Don 1897:22) and pastry (Don 1/12/1882:104, 1/2/1883:147).

According to a Mrs Moore (McNeur 1930:40), the Chinese miners sometimes ate bread and biscuits; that is, traditional European foods made from flour. The consumption of bread is attested by numerous entries indicating the purchase of "loaves" by Chinese customers in the ledger of R. Kinaston, a baker who operated in Roxburgh in the 1890s (e.g. Kinaston 1896:532). Other commonly cited products included rice, bacon, tea, sugar, cocoa, soap, matches, tobacco and candles (see Table 6.20 for contemporary food prices). Although biscuit tins were found in only two of the sites, their presence does not automatically indicate that biscuits had been consumed. The hinged biscuit tins would have made useful rodent-proof storage containers and empty ones may have been obtained from grocers or scavenged for such purposes.

6.10.2.2 Fruits and berries

Fresh fruit would have been difficult to obtain during the first decade or so of the goldrushes in Central Otago. To get around this deficiency, many of the Chinese planted fruit trees near their huts or settlements soon after they arrived. The remnants of small plum orchards that were planted by the Chinese still exist near the settlements at Cromwell and Arrowtown, while a lone plum tree stands near the Rapids site. Plum stones were found in the Ha Fong shelter in the Cromwell Gorge and in hut 33 at Chinatown. Apples were another favourite. One of two apple trees, noted by a European informant c.1920, still existed at the Cromwell Chinatown site at the time of the excavations in 1980. The Apple Tree site (S124/212) was so named because of the presence of an old apple tree beside the hut.

Peach kernels were found in four sites: huts 6 and 33 at Chinatown, and in Ah Wee's, the Rapids and Riverside sites. Don's notes contain several references about the growing of fruit trees. For example, he met a Chinese miner at Bendigo Gully "under his fruit trees" (Don 1911:13), and he mentioned that there were orchards run by Chinese at Speargrass Flat not far from the Arrowtown Chinese Camp (Don 1891:16) and at Conroy's Gully. In the latter instance, he sampled pears from the orchard (Don 1901:29). Mayhew (1949:90) recorded that there was a Chinese garden and orchard in Waitahuna Gully run by "Jimmy the Chinaman", who made regular trips with his produce to Waipori. On one occasion when Don visited the "Virtuous Peace" restaurant in the Round Hill Chinese settlement, he noted that the proprietor "was making jam because the fruit was spoiling" (Don 1/12/1882:104). An advertisement in the *Arrow Observer* (23/2/1882:2) stated that the Wong Yew store (Arrowtown) and orchard were for sale.

Strawberries and European gooseberries were also crops grown by the Chinese. Tangled remnants of old gooseberry bushes were a feature of many of the Chinese sites investigated during this study. It was often necessary to cut them back to enable the excavations to proceed. The evidence of strawberry raising is entirely dependent on Don's records. He mentioned in one instance being offered "strawberries and a cup of tea" (Don 1911:23). Elsewhere he noted that the strawberries grown by Ah Lok, a gardener at Thompson Creek, surpassed any he had seen elsewhere in Otago. The sign on Ah Lok's gate read: "One hour strawberries for 1/- cash. No Tick" (Don 1897:11).

6.11 DISCUSSION AND CONCLUSIONS

Useful faunal assemblages were recovered from nine of the 15 major study sites. The main meat species (cattle, pigs and sheep), their butchering treatments, sources of supply, Chinese meat preferences and relevant ethno-historical information have been outlined and are only briefly discussed further.

Although cattle were represented by the least number of bones (393), beef, in terms of meat weight (see Table 6.15, and note the calculations are likely to be conservative estimates), was the main meat consumed by the Chinese. The primary meat cuts are entirely consistent with 19th-century European beef butchering practices, indicating acquisition from European butchers.

Consumption was notably highest in the three urban sites – Chinatown, Arrowtown and Ah Lum's – although beef constituted 73% of the meat weight represented in the assemblage from the Rapids. Although they were, of course, larger settlements, it would seem that the urban dwellers took advantage of their more ready access to butcher shops and bought a wider variety of meats (both species and cuts).

The reason for the high incidence of beef bones in the Rapids site is not fully understood. Piper (1984:29), who analysed the faunal remains, argued that beef was predominant because it was more readily available than pork, but this seems only a partial explanation given the high pig and sheep bone ratios from the other sites. Two other explanations are advanced: the Chinese inhabitant(s) may have preferred beef, in which case the high incidence of beef bones reflects idiosyncratic behaviour; or the site was occupied at some stage by a European and his refuse was not distinguished from that of the Chinese. The first suggestion is supported by the fact that many of the cattle tibia have both ends sawn off and the central shaft sections are split, presumably to recover the marrow. This was not a European practice.

Pig bones, both numerically (n=959) and in terms of meat weight (Table 6.15), constituted the next largest category. They represented the most meat weight in the assemblages from five rural sites – QB2, Ah Wee's, Poplars, Hanging Rock and Riverside. Pig meat was clearly a favoured meat: evidenced by the high incidence of pig bones in all 10 of the studied assemblages (Table 6.1) and the numerous documented accounts of the predilection for pork in the Chinese diet. Over 90% of the pig bones bore cleaver cuts alone, which some (e.g. Langenwalter 1980:105) contend is a reliable indicator of Chinese butchering; however, as demonstrated earlier, the Chinese in some parts of Central Otago obtained much of their pork from European sources. A similar high incidence of pork bones is a feature of Chinese sites in the western United States, while contemporary European sites have a relatively low incidence (Gust 1984:188).

But an interesting difference is apparent. While pork and beef were the main meats consumed by the overseas Chinese in both New Zealand and the United States, the beef-weight predominance in the urban sites here differs from the situation in the American sites where pork predominates (Gust 1984:188). Although beef and pork form most of the meat component of the traditional Cantonese diet, clearly much more of both was eaten in New Zealand. The Chinese here were able to afford what they could only desire at home, where beef especially was particularly expensive.

Considering the fact that sheep were not a major traditional southern Chinese protein source, it is perhaps surprising that more whole and part sheep bones (1,271) were recovered than those of any other species (see Table 6.1). Sheep bones were numerically predominant in three sites (Cromwell's Chinatown, QB2 and Ah Wee's) and approximately equal to the number of pig bones in two others (the Arrowtown settlement and the Riverside site), but overall they represented the least meat weight (see Table 6.15). However, the archaeological evidence clearly shows that sheep meat was a significant source of protein and its consumption increased with time. This can be regarded as an acculturative change, probably influenced by its ready availability and favourable cost. Sheep meat has traditionally been the cheapest meat in New Zealand and is likely to have been more readily available than both pork and beef (Bell pers. comm.; c.1900 local store receipts).

The percentage of sheep bones (>80%) bearing cleaver cuts was nearly as high as that on the pig bones (c.85%; see Table 6.8). However, the meat appears to have been obtained in the form of traditional English cuts (Tables 6.10–6.12), which were further broken down by the Chinese miners (using cleavers) to suit their cooking styles (see the discussion on utensils and cooking methods, Section 5.5.1). Langenwalter (1980:107) contended that it is possible to distinguish between the cleaver cuts made with the narrow-bladed Chinese cleaver and those made by the wide-bevelled blade of European cleavers, and consequently use the information as an ethnic indicator. This distinction was sought by careful visual examination of the cleaved bones in the studied assemblages, but any differences were not readily apparent.

The obviously marginal role of goat and cat meat in the Chinese goldfields' economy needs no further discussion.

Although only 11% of the recovered rabbit bones had positive butchering marks, their presence, together with the contemporary observations documented earlier, suggests that rabbits, an essentially free resource, were consumed frequently, especially in the declining years of the Chinese sojourn, and they are likely to be well underrepresented in the recovered faunal assemblages.

The diversity of the avian remains afforded an opportunity for a specialised study on the Chinese exploitation of bird species. Their role is discussed at length in the main body of the text and needs no further elaboration here.

Aquatic foods were represented by sparse remains identified only to taxa level – unspecified fish species (including eels), cuttlebone, marine oysters and freshwater mussels. Although fish and shellfish constituted major sources of protein in southern China (see Chang 1977), they had limited availability in 19th-century Central Otago and this is reflected in the small assemblages. The numerous fish cans found in the Chinese sites indicate that the miners substituted canned fish to some extent.

From study of the distinctive ceramic containers frequently found in the sites (see Section 5.2.1), it is evident that there was a continuing reliance on many food products imported from China, including soy sauce, peanut oil, salted vegetables, preserved ginger and fish pastes, as well as rice and tea and other products that have left little tangible residue. In addition, the Chinese substituted or adopted many European provisions (packaged in glass and cans) such as jams, pickles, Worcestershire sauce, cooking oils and vinegar, and preserved fruits, vegetables, fish and meat. Since Worcestershire sauce is primarily soy sauce and vinegar (Lee and Lee 1979:179), its acceptance by the Chinese can be readily understood.

Keeping gardens was a much more common practice among the Chinese than their European counterparts on the goldfields. Gardening was significant not only because of its valuable contribution to the diet of the Chinese but also because it became another way of earning a living as mining waned.

To conclude, the ethno-historic record and the archaeological assemblages from the study sites provide complementary data. The archaeological evidence reaffirms many ethno-historical observations and the interplay of the two largely independent data sources serves to "fill in gaps" in the overall record. The archaeological evidence demonstrates that the basic Chinese subsistence pattern underwent only a few modifications that could be considered acculturative changes. Although several departures from traditional patterns are apparent, most can be regarded as replacements rather than adaptive changes. For the most part, there was a continuing reliance on traditional Chinese foods, butchering methods and culinary practices.

The main changes that have been defined or documented are:

1. the adoption of sheep meat with a trend towards increasing consumption over time and probably at the expense of pork;
2. the adoption of the potato, possibly as a substitute for the sweet potato;
3. the substitution of canned fish for (imported) dried or fresh fish;
4. the adoption of many European packaged foods including Worcestershire sauce, jams, pickles and canned provisions such as vegetables, soups and meat;
5. increased consumption of flour-based products, possibly at the expense of rice to some extent;
6. increased consumption of milk-based products.

While the dietary modifications are notable, there is little evidence (during the sojourn period) of cognitive changes or modifications to the basic culture pattern; that is, real evidence of acculturation (Herskovitz 1964:169–81). However, the fact that the Chinese dietary pattern maintained strong traditional links is useful; subsistence refuse can be used as an ethnic indicator, and coupled with historic data, can be used as a temporal marker. Acculturation and adaptive changes in the southern Chinese communities are examined further in the concluding chapter.

Table 6.1. Numerical predominance and ratios of pork/beef/sheep elements (meat cuts).

Site Name	No. of pig elements	% of total	No. of sheep elements	% of total	No. of beef elements	% of total	Total elements	Numerically Predominant
Firewood Creek	25	42.4	21	35.6	13	22	59	pig
(diced rib)	0							
Chinatown	131	17.1	497	64.8	139	18.1	767	sheep
(diced rib)	18		123					
QB2	78	34.2	144	63.1	6	2.6	228	sheep
(diced rib)	38							
Ah Wee's	13	35.1	23	62.1	1	2.7	37	sheep
(diced rib)	5							
Poplars	166	70.9	67	28.6	1	0.4	234	pig
(diced rib)	31							
Hanging Rock	45	76.3	13	22	1	1.7	59	pig
(diced rib)	12							
Riverside	2	50	2	50	0	0	4	sheep/pig
Arrowtown	336	39	439	51	86	10	861	sheep/pig
(diced rib)	176		230					
Rapids	89	39.2	28	12.3	110	48.5	227	beef
(diced rib)	2							
Ah Lum's store	95	58.6	37	22.8	30	18.5	162	pig
(diced rib)	73							
Total	990		1,271		387		2,638	

Notes

a. "Diced rib" fragments are included in the species subtotals.

b. Sheep/pig= means there were approximately equal numbers of sheep and pig bones.

c. Compare against Table 6.15 Estimated meat weights of pig, sheep and beef.

Table 6.2. Cattle (*Bos taurus*) elements (meat cuts) at the Chinatown (Cromwell Chinese Camp) huts.

Key		* immature specimen (veal)														
		p. proximal end d. distal end														

		Hut #														
Element	Meat Unit	1	6	7	12	14	16	17	18	19	21	22	23	25	26	27	33	Total
scapula p.	neck																1*	1
humerus p.	neck												1				1	2
humerus d.	arm	1*				1												2
radius p.	foreshank								1									1
radius d.	foreshank								2				1				1	4
ulna p.	foreshank	1*				2*		1	2				2*					8
atlas	neck						12											12
cervicals	neck												1					1
thoracics	neck	2						2					1	1	1		2	9
lumbars	loin	1		2		1							2					6
sacrals	loin			1									1		1			3
vert. fragments		1	2	2				1	1									7
ribs, whole		5																5
ribs, p. end		1	1					1	1	2			1		1			8
ribs, m	short rib	3	3		1	1			1	2							2	13
ilium	loin		1										1					2
ischium	rump												1					1
femur, p.	rump	1*															1	2
femur, d.	hindshank				1*								1				1	3
tibia, p.	hindshank			1						1					1	1*	1*	5
tibia, d	hindshank						1			1	1							3
shaft sections	marrow		4						1									5
patella	hindshank			1					1									2
calcaneum	hindshank												1	1				2
carpals	fore foot	1	1	6						2			4					14
tarsals	hind foot	2	2	8		1	4			2	1						1	21
phalanges	toe bones			1									1					2
Total		19	14	21	2	6	18	4	9	8	6	2	15	4	3	2	11	144

Table 6.3a. Cattle (*Bos taurus*) elements (meat cuts) at the Arrowtown Chinese Camp huts.

Key	* immature specimen (veal)												
	p. proximal end d. distal end												
		Hut #											
Element	Meat Unit	1	2	3	4	5	6	7	8	9	10	13	15	Total
mandible frags.					1									1
scapula p.	neck				1									1
scapula c/sect.							1	1						2
humerus d.	arm/bolar				1							1*		2
radius p.	foreshank			1	2		1						1	5
radius d.	foreshank			2								1		3
ulna p.	foreshank			2	2	1							1	6
ulna d,	foreshank						1							1
ulna c/sect										1				1
axis vert.	neck						1				1			2
thoracics		1		1			2			1				5
lumbars	loin	1												1
ribs p.				1			1		1	2				5
ribs m.	short rib		1	4	2		3				1		1	12
ilium	sirloin			1							1	1	1	4
ischium	rump			1							1		1	3
femur p.	rump		1*					1*						2
femur d.	hindshank												1	1
tibia p.	hindshank			2	1							1		4
tibia d.	hindshank			1	1						1	1		4
shaft section	marrow				1			1			1			3
calcaneum	hindshank					1								1
carpals	fore foot			1	1		4			1	2		1	10
tarsals	hind foot				2		1	1				2		6
phalanges	toe bones									1				1
Total		2	2	17	14	3	15	4	3	4	7	8	7	86

Table 6.3b. Cattle (*Bos taurus*) elements (meat cuts) at Ah Lum's store, Arrowtown.

Key	* immature (veal)					
	p. proximal end d. distal end					
Element	Meat Unit	Main room	Kitchen	Bank room	Outside building	Total
mandible fragment		1				1
scapula mid section			1	1	1	2
radius d.	shin bone			2*	2	2
ulna p.	foreshank			3	3	3
thoracics				1	1	1
ribs, whole				1	1	1
ribs, m.	short rib		1		3	4
ilium	loin			1	1	1
femur p.	rump			1	1	1
femur d.	hindshank			1*	1*	1*
tibia p.	hindshank			1*	1*	1*
shaft section	marrow	1				1
carpals			1	10	10	11
phalanges				1	1	1
Total		**2**	**1**	**2**	**26**	**31**

Table 6.4. Cattle (*Bos taurus*) elements (meat cuts) at the rural sites.

Key	* immature specimen (veal)							
	p. proximal end d. distal end							
Element	Meat Unit	Hanging Rock	Rapids	Ah Wee's	Poplars	QB2	Firewood Creek	Total
scapula mid sect.			4					4
humerus mid sect.			7					7
radius end unspecfied			8					8
ulna p.	foreshank	1						1
ulna end unspecified			7					7
thoracics			2		1	2		5
lumbars	loin		1					1
unidentified vertebrae			4					4
ribs p.	ribs		11		1			12
ribs mid section	short ribs		2*	1	3	4	1	11
pelvic fragments							1	1
femur end unspecified			2					2
tibia p.	hindshank						1*	1
tibia end unspecified			8					8
fibula					1*			1
shaft section	marrow		4		1		7	12
calcaneum	hindshank		3					3
carpals			1				2	3
tarsals			8				1	9
burnt bone fragments			14					14
veal bones			25					25
Total		**1**	**111**	**1**	**7**	**6**	**13**	**139**
Notes								
a. burnt bone fragments weighed 325 g								
b. Rapids site data from Piper (1984)								

6 Dietary analysis

Table 6.5. Pig (*Sus scrofa*) elements (meat cuts) at the Chinatown (Cromwell Chinese Camp) huts.

Key:
- * immature specimen
- f fragments
- R right hand side
- L left hand side
- p. proximal end
- d. distal end

Element	Meat Unit	1	4	6	7	14	16	17	18	19	21	22	23	24	26	27	33	34	Total
cranium	brain/soup	1f	2f		1f				1f	1f	1f	2L,3f		1f			2f		15
mandible	tongue/soup											1L							1
cervicals	shoulder											1							1
scapula p.	shoulder	1f					2f				2f	1f	1f		2f		1		10
atlas								1	1		1		1						5
humerus p.	arm																		1
humerus d.					2														2
radius p.	foreshank				1*								2						3
ulna p.	foreshank												1						1
ulna d.	foreshank				1														1
tarsals	trotters	1					1										1		3
metapodials	trotters		1*							1			1*	1*	4		2		6
phalanges	trotters	1											2*						3
thoracics	chine	1	1		1		1		3										7
lumbars	chine				1		1												2
vertebrae fragments		6					2												10
ilium		1			1				1		2f								5
sternum															1*				1
rib central section	"diced"		1			4	2	1	1		4	1	1		4	1	1	4	19
rib central section	spare rib	1		1						1	1	1	2	1		1	2		12
rib p. end	"diced"						1		3							1			9
ascetabulum	ham				1	2f			1								1		4
ischium/pubis	ham																2		2
pelvic fragments																	1		1
femur d.	ham										1*								1
femur p.	ham											1*							1
tibia p.	ham				1*	2*									1				4
tibia central section						1*													2
long bone fragments															3				3
fibula															1*				1
Total		13	5	1	10	9	10	2	12	3	12	11	13	2	12	3	15	4	137

423

Table 6.6a. Pig (*Sus scrofa*) elements (meat cuts) at the Arrowtown Camp huts.

Key	* immature specimen f fragments p. proximal end d. distal end											
		Hut #										
Element	Meat Unit	1	3	4	5	6	7	8	9	10	13	15	Total
cranium	brain/soup		1	1		4f	1		3				10
mandible	tongue			1		4f		1	4	1		1	12
scapula p.	shoulder			1		1			2		1	1	6
scapula mid						1							1
scapula d.			1	1		2							4
atlas/axis	neck											1	1
humerus p.	arm/bolar			1*					1		1	1	4
humerus p.					1	1*							2
humerus mid				1						1			2
radius p.	foreshank								1*				1
radius d.	foreshank			1*						1			2
ulna p.	foreshank								1*				1
lumbars	chine			1						1	1		3
vertebrae	"diced"				1	1							2
ilium				1	1								2
rib central section	"diced"		2	176	4	7		4	1	4		1	199
rib central section	spare rib			2		2			3*	10	1		18
ascetabulum	ham					1							1
ischium	ham			1									1
femur	ham			1*									1
tibia p.	ham								1				1
tibia d.	hindshank								1	1			2
carpals	trotters	1		3								1	5
tarsals	trotters								3				3
metapodials	trotters			6		6			1				13
phalanges	trotters			14		17			4				35
Total		1	4	212	7	47	1	5	26	19	4	6	332

Table 6.6b. Pig (*Sus scrofa*) elements (meat cuts) at Ah Lum's store.

Key	* immature specimen	**p.** proximal end	**d.** distal end					
Element	Meat Unit	Main room	Kitchen	Bank room	Bedroom	Strong room	Outside south end	Total
mandible	tongue						1	**1**
scapula p.	shoulder			2			1	**3**
humerus p.	arm						2*	**2**
humerus d.				1	2			**3**
radius p.	foreshank		2*				1*	**3**
radius mid sect.							1	**1**
ulna p.	foreshank						1	**1**
rib central section	"diced"	34	12	10	3	15	1	**75**
ribs central section	spare rib		1	2				**3**
ascetabulum	ham	1			1			**2**
femur	ham	1						**1**
Total		**36**	**15**	**15**	**6**	**15**	**8**	**95**

Table 6.7. Pig (*Sus scrofa*) elements (meat cuts) and minimum numbers (MNE) at the rural sites.

Sites	A Hanging Rock B Rapids			C Riverside D Ah Wee's		E Poplars F QB2		G Firewood Creek		
Element	Meat Unit	A	B	C	D	E	F	G	Frag.	MNE
cranium	brain/soup		5f			20f	20		27	4
cranium	brain/soup					1L			1	1
mandible frags.	tongue				1f	2f			3	2
mandible halves	tongue		4			2			6	6
axis	neck	1				2			3	3
atlas 1/4 cut	neck					2	1	2	5	5
cervicals	shoulder	3				1			4	4
scapula p.	shoulder	1			1	2	1		5	5
scapula mid			10			7f	2f	1f	20	15
sternum			1						1	1
humerus p.	arm/hock	1				2*	2	1	6	6
humerus mid sect.			8	1	1	1	1		12	12
humerus d.					1	4	3	1	9	9
radius p.	foreshank	1							1	1
radius d.	foreshank					2	4		6	6
radius mid sects			3						3	3
radius, whole	foreshank				1*	1*			2	2
ulna p.	foreshank					2*	1		3	3
ulna, whole	foreshank		7		1e	1*			9	9
thoracics/lumbars	loin	4				7		1	12	19
vertebrae fragments	diced'					19	15		34	34
ilium						3			3	3
ribs central sect	diced'	12	2	1	5	31	38		89	89
ribs mid section	spare ribs	11			1	2	2	5	21	21
ribs, prox. ends						3	3	5	11	11
ascetabulum	ham					6			6	6
ischium	ham					2			2	2
pelvic fragments		8	3			10			21	21
femur d.	ham					5	2		7	7
femur p.	ham		2		1*	3			6	6
femur, whole						1			1	1
tibia p.	ham					3	1	1	5	5
tibia d.						2e			2	2
tibia mid sect.			1						1	1
fibula						1*			1	1
long bone shafts			4			6	2		12	12
calcaneum						1			1	1
carpals	trotters		2			3		1	6	6
tarsals	trotters	2	1			5		1	9	9
metapodials	trotters					3		1	4	4
phalanges	trotters		5			8		5	18	18
immature/teeth (4)			31						31	376
Total		45	90	2	13	175	79	25	429	407

6 Dietary analysis

Table 6.8. Comparison of saw and cleaver chop cuts on bones.

Site Name	cleaved		sawn		cleaved and sawn		unmarked and intact		
Beef	#	%	#	%	#	%	#	%	Total
Chinatown	59	39.1	43	28.5	8	5.3	41	27.1	151
Arrowtown	43	39.1	40	36.4	4	3.6	17	15.4	104
Ah Lum's store	4	16.7	14	58.3	1	4.1	5	20.8	24
Rural sites	116	78.4	27	18.2	3	2	2	1.4	148
Total	222		124		16		65		427
Pig	#	%	#	%	#	%	#	%	Total
Chinatown	119	86.2	16	11.6	0	0	3	2.2	138
Arrowtown	377	92.2	4	1	2	0.5	26	6.4	409
Ah Lum's store	84	98.8	1	1.2	0	0	0	0	85
Rural sites	232	94.3	5	2	0	0	9	3.7	246
Total	812		26		2		38		878
Sheep	#	%	#	%	#	%	#	%	Total
Chinatown	406	85	27	5.6	5	1,0	40	8.4	478
Arrowtown	372	86.3	10	2.3	2	0.5	47	10.9	431
Ah Lum's store	25	75.8	2	6.1	0	0	6	18.2	33
Rural sites	231	86.8	2	0.7	2	0.7	31	11.6	266
Total	1,034		41		9		124		1,208

Notes

a. Some bones have multiple chop/saw marks.

b. Unfused epiphyses were not included in the intact/unmarked tallies.

Table 6.9. Cut-type distribution on bones.

chopped/cleaved	saw cuts	both	intact/unmarked
Beef			
long bones	long bones	vertebrae	toe bones
vertebrae	ribs	ribs	patallas
foot bones	pelvis	scapula	immature foreshank bones
scapulae	scapulae		
	vertebrae		
Pig			
all bones cleaved/chopped			
saw cuts restricted to scapulae, pelvis, vertebrae and crania			
intact bones restricted to feet and toe bones (trotters) – 80% were intact			
Sheep			
all bones cleaved/chopped			
saw cuts (all sites) restricted to sternum (3), pelvis (3), radius (6), ulna (3), humerus (3), tibia (5), scapulae (4), ribs (39), vertebrae (13), crania (2)			
intact bones largely restricted to foot bones and calcaneum			

Table 6.10. Sheep (*Ovis aries*) elements (meat cuts) at the Chinatown (Cromwell Chinese Camp) huts.

Key: (#) or * bone from immature specimen   f fragments   p. proximal end   d. distal end

Element	Meat Unit	1	4	6	7	12	14	15	16	17	18	19	21	22	23	24	25	26	27	33	34	MN Total
scapula p.	neck			1											1			1				4
scapula d.	chuck					1f	1f		2f				3f	3f	1					5f	1f	19
humerus p.	neck				1*	1	1					3f			1*					1		5
humerus, whole																	1					1
humerus d.	arm			1	1				1				2		2		1			1		9
radius p.	foreshank								2						1*							3
radius, whole	foreshank	1*													1		1					3
radius d.	foreshank		1		1	1			1						1							5
ulna p.	foreshank			1					1						2							4
ulna d.	foreshank				1																	1
atlas/axis	neck			1						1					1		1					4
cervicals	neck					1									1							2
thoracics									5	1				1	2				1			10
lumbars	loin	2				1						1		2	2					4		12
sacrum	loin					2								1	1							4
vert. frags.	"diced"	1		4		2			10			2	6	3	9			1		7	1	43
ribs p.	"chops"	5		2	4		1		7		1		14	3	9			5	2	7	4	64
ribs, c/sect.	"diced"		1		4	1	3		19	1	5	1	17	2	22	2		46	5	6	1	136
ribs, c/sect.	short rib	1	4	2	5				5		2	2	21		15			1	1	4		63
sternum	brisket								2	1*												3
ilium	loin	0						1				2f	2f	1f								5
ascetabulum					1			1					3f		1							5
ischium	rump											2f										2
femur p.	rump		1		2	1		1			1		3	1f	3*				1			13
femur d.	hindshank	2		1		1									3							8
tibia p.	hindshank				2	1*	1		2						2				1			9
tibia d.	hindshank	1		1*		1*	1				1*			1					1			7
shaft cent.	hindshank			3				1							2					3		10
calcaneum	hindshank	1		1			2	1								1						5
carpals		1										3			1		2			1		13
tarsals		4		1	5	2	2	1		2		5		1	4		2			1		23
phalanges				1																		1
Total		19	7	20	27	14	12	4	57	6	10	21	71	16	88	3	8	54	12	40	7	496

428

6 Dietary analysis

Table 6.11. Sheep (*Ovis aries*) elements (meat cuts) at the Arrowtown Chinese Camp huts.

Key: p. proximal end   d. distal end

Element	End	Meat Unit	1	2	3	4	5	6	7	8	9	10	11	13	15	Total
scapula	p.	neck/chuck		2		6	1									9
scapula	fragments			2	1	15	2	3						1	1	25
humerus	p.	neck						1								1
humerus	c/sect.			1								1				2
humerus	d.	foreshank		1		2		1			1					5
radius	p.	foreshank		2		1				1	1	2		1	1	9
radius	c/sect.	foreshank						1								1
radius	d.	foreshank			1	2		1				1				5
ulna	p.	foreshank		1	1	1		2				2				7
atlas/axis		neck				2										2
cervicals		neck			1	1										2
thoracics				1	1	15		1								18
lumbars		loin				1		1								2
vert. frags.		"diced"						3		2						5
ribs	p.	"chops"			4	15	4	2								25
ribs	c/sect.	short rib	4		9	203		2	1	1		8				228
sternum		brisket		1		4		1			1					7
ilium		loin				1		3	1			1				6
ischium		rump				2		1								3
femur	p.	rump		1							1					2
femur	d.	hindshank				1			1	1*						3
tibia	p.	hindshank				2			2							4
tibia	c/sect.	hindshank		1												1
tibia	d.	hindshank						1	1		1			1	1	5
shaft sect.		short "roast"				2						2				4
calcaneum		hindshank		2					1		1					4
metacarpals						4	1	2		1		1			2	11
metatarsals						2		7								9
phalanges			1		1	1		26		1						33
Total			5	18	19	283	8	59	7	7	6	18	0	3	5	438

Table 6.12. Sheep (*Ovis aries*) elements (meat cuts) at Ah Lum's store.

Key	p. proximal end d. distal end								
Element	End	Meat Unit	Main room	Kitchen	Bankroom	Strong room	Outside slope	Outside, south wall side	Total
crania	fragments							1	1
scapula	p.	neck/chuck						2	2
scapula	central sect.		1					2	3
humerus	p.	shoulder					1		1
humerus	d.	foreshank						3	3
radius	p.	foreshank				1		1	2
radius	d.	foreshank		1					1
ulna	p.	foreshank						2	2
atlas/axis		neck		2					2
thoracics			2	2					4
lumbars		loin	1						1
ribs	central sect.	short rib			1			1	2
sternum		brisket	1	1	1				3
ilium		loin						1	1
tibia	p.	hindshank					1		1
tibia	central sect.	hindshank	1						1
phalanges						1			1
Total			6	5	2	3	2	13	31

6 Dietary analysis

Table 6.13. Sheep (*Ovis aries*) elements (meat cuts) at the rural sites.

Key		(#) or * immature specimen p. proximal end d. distal end							
			Site						
Element	End	Meat Unit	Hanging Rock	Rapids	Riverside	Ah Wee's	Poplars	QB2	Firewood Creek	Total
mandible				1						1
atlas/axis		neck		1		2	1	4		8
scapula	p.	neck/chuck				2	3	3		8
scapula	central sect.					2	3			5
humerus	p.	shoulder		2				1f		3
humerus	d.	shoulder				2	1	3	1	7
radius	p.	foreshank	1			1	2	5	1	10
radius	d.	foreshank					2 (2)	1 (1)		6
radius	c/sect.	foreshank				1				1
radius	whole			1		3	1	1		6
ulna	p.	foreshank	2	2		2	4	7		17
cervicals		neck			1	3	4			8
sacrum		loin				1				1
vert. frags.		diced'					7	40	1	48
ribs	whole					1				1
ribs	p.	chops'	1					1		2
ribs	central sect.	short rib								
ribs	"diced"		8			18	53	7		86
ilium	fragments	loin						1f	1f	2
ischium		rump					1	2f		3
ascetabulum							4	3	1	8
pelvic	fragments			3		2	2	1		8
femur	p.	rump					1		1*	2
femur	d.	hindshank	1				2			3
tibia	p.	hindshank			1*		2 (1)			4
tibia	d.	hindshank	1				2			3
tibia	central sect.	hindshank		2						2
tibia	whole							1		1
femur/tibia		short 'roast'		8*						8
shaft sects.		marrow				1		1	1	3
patella		hindshank	1							1
calcaneum		hindshank				1	1	1		3
metapodials						1*	3	1		5
metacarpals							1	8		9
metatarsals							3	9	1	13
phalanges						1		2	2	5
Total			15	20	2	26	71	149	18	301
Note Rapids site data from Piper (1984:56).										

Table 6.14. Skeletal portion meat weights (adapted from Lyman 1979).

Skeletal portion	Components			
forequarters	radius-ulna, humerus, scapula, carpals			
ribs-vertebrae	thoracic, lumbar and cervical vertebrae, ribs			
hindquarters	pelvis, sacrum, tibia, femur, patella, calcaneum, tarsals			
	Meat weights (kg)			
	Beef	Pig	Sheep	Lamb
forequarters	28.51	5.67	4.49	2.58
ribs-vertebrae	34.68	20.06	7.17	2.63
hindquarters	17.52	3.35	4.54	2.04
Total	80.71	29.08	16.2	7.25
Difference Ratio	4.98	1.79	1	0.72
Rounded to	5	2	1	not used

Table 6.15. Estimated meat weights of pig, sheep and beef.

Key	* predominant species in terms of meat weight									
Site	Pig			Sheep			Beef			Total (kg)
	kg	x 2	%	kg	x 1	%	kg	x 5	%	all meats
Firewood Creek	25	50	36.8	21	21	15.5	13	65*	47.8	136
Chinatown	131	262	9.2	374	374	13.1	139	695*	52.2	1331
QB2	78	156*	47.3	144	144	43.6	6	30	9.1	330
Ah Wee's	13	26*	48.1	23	23	42.6	1	5	9.3	54
Poplars	166	332*	82.2	67	67	16.6	1	1	1.2	404
Hanging Rock	45	90*	83.3	13	13	12	1	5	4,7	108
Riverside	2	4*	66.6	2	2	33.3	0	0	0	6
Arrowtown	160	320	33.4	209	209	21.8	86	430*	44.8	959
Rapids	87	174	23.1	28	28	3.7	110	550*	73.2	752
Ah Lum's store	22	44	19	37	37	16	30	150*	65	231
Total (kg)		1,458			918			1,935		4,311
% of total		33.8			21.3			44.9		

Note
The meat weights are based on the 5:2:1 weighting formula discussed in the text. The formula is intended to give relative estimates only.

6 Dietary analysis

Table 6.16. Butchering unit definitions (adapted from Lyman 1979:542 and Piper 1984:50).

Butchering unit	Skeletal components	Meat weight per unit (kg)
Beef		
hindshank or leg	tibia, d. femur, patella	3.58
round and buttock	femur shaft	11.61
rump	p.femur, ischium, pubis, ascetabulum	2.33
sirloin	ilium, lumbar vertebrae, sacrum	14.53
flank	no bones (assume same weight as sirloin)	2.56
brisket	rib cartilage, sternum, ventral rib	9.59
ribs	dorsal ribs 6–12, thoracic vertebrae 6–12	9.26
shin	radius-ulna, d. humerus	3.13
neck	cervical vertebrae, p. humerus, d. scapula	0.52
chuck/blade	dorsal ribs 1–5, thoracic vertebrae 1–5	22.84
Veal (No meat weight data available for veal)		
hind knuckle	tibia, d. femur, patella	
fillet	femur shaft	
chump end of loin	p.femur, ischium, pubis, ascetabulum	
loin	ilium, lumbar vertebrae, sacrum	
flank	no bones (assume same weight as loin)	
breast	rib cartilage, sternum, ventral rib	
ribs	dorsal ribs 6–12, thoracic vertebrae 6–12	
fore knuckle	radius-ulna, d. humerus	
shoulder/blade	cervical vertebrae, p. humerus, d. scapula, dorsal ribs 1–5, thoracic vertebrae 1–5, p. humerus, humerus shaft, d scapula, scapula blade	
Pig		
heads	crania, mandible	1.45
neck butt	cervical vertebrae, scapula blade	1.36
shoulder	d. scapula, humerus, radius-ulna	1.67
loin	thoracic and lumbar vertbrae, dorsal ribs, ilium, sacrum	10.71
belly	mid and ventral ribs	9.48
leg/ham	femur, p. tibia and shaft	2.99
trotters	carpals, tarsals, metapodials, phalanges	0.27
Sheep/Lamb		
shoulder	cervical and thoracic vertebrae and ribs 1–5, scapula, p. humerus and shaft	1.63
foreshank	d. humerus, radius-ulna, metacafrpals	0.36
breast/brisket	sternum, rib carilage, ventral ribs 1–12	0.4
saddle	thoracic vertebrae and dorsal ribs 6–12	1.13
loin	lumbar vertbrae	1.31
chump/flank	no bones (assume same weight as loin)	0.36
leg	pelvis, sacrum, femur, tibia, metatarsals, patella, tarsals	2.27

Table 6.17. Rabbit bones at all sites.

Key		nc	no cutmarks		c	cutmarks		I	bone from immature specimen			
		L	left hand side		R	right hand side						

Element	Side	Chinatown			Arrowtown			Ah Lum's			Rural sites			Total
		nc	c	I	nc	c	I	nc	c	I	nc	c	I	
crania		9			5			3			3			**20**
mandibles	L	10			8			2			4			**24**
mandibles	R	7			1						5			**13**
scapula	L	4			6	1		1			4			**16**
scapula	R	2			5			1			5			**13**
humerus	L	6	2		5	1		1	1		9	2	1	**28**
humerus	R	12			10	2		1	1		7	1		**34**
radius	L	3			4						4			**11**
radius	R	1			3	1					5			**10**
ulna	L	6			4	1			1		9			**21**
ulna	R	4			6	1		2			6			**19**
vertebrae		23			28	1		2	1		29			**84**
ribs					6						19			**25**
sternum		4			3	1		1	1		1			**11**
pelvis	L	9			6				1		5			**21**
pelvis	R	10		1	6	1		1			7			**26**
pelvic fragments						1			3					**4**
femur	L	11			14	3		1			12	1		**42**
femur	R	8	1		11	2	1	2		1	10	1		**37**
tibia	L	9	4		15	7	3	4	3		9	4		**58**
tibia	R	10	5	3	19	6		3	3		9	1		**59**
tibia shaft					1	1			1					**3**
fibula	R	6												**6**
feet/toe bones		13			16	1		1	1		15			**47**
Subtotal		**167**	**12**	**4**	**182**	**31**	**4**	**26**	**17**	**1**	**177**	**10**	**1**	**631**

Summary	
no cut marks	552
cut marks	70
immature	10

Note The table does not include the bones from numerous complete rabbit skeletons, which were assumed to postdate the occupation of the sites and discarded.

6 Dietary analysis

Table 6.18. Bird remains: minimum number of individuals (MNI).

Species Code	A	Domestic Fowl	B	Domestic Turkey	C	Black Swan	D	Mute Swan
	E	Grey Duck	F	Paradise Duck	G	Mallard Duck	H	Weka
	I	House Sparrow	J	Thrush/Blackbird	K	Bellbird	L	South Island Tomtit
	M	Harrier Hawk	N	Shag	O	NZ Quail?		

Site or Hut #	A	B	C	D	E	F	G	H	I	J	K	L	M	N	O	Total
Chinatown 1	1	1														2
Chinatown 2	1															1
Chinatown 4	1															1
Chinatown 6	1			1?												2
Chinatown 7	2									1						3
Chinatown 12	1															1
Chinatown 14					1											1
Chinatown 16	1	1	1		1	1			1							6
Chinatown 18	1								2(1)		1					4
Chinatown 19	2 (1)									1						3
Chinatown 21	1					1				1?						3
Chinatown 22	1															1
Chinatown 23	2 (1)	2	3 (1)			1				1						9
Chinatown 25	1															1
Chinatown 26	1				1											2
Chinatown 27	1					1				(1)						2
Chinatown 33												1				1
Chinatown 34		1	(1)		1											3
Sub Total	18 (2)	5	4 (2)	1?	3	5	0	0	3 (1)	4 (1)	1	1	0	0	0	46
Arrowtown 1	1												1			2
Arrowtown 3	1															1
Arrowtown 4	5 (1)	1				1				1						8
Arrowtown 5	1															1
Arrowtown 6	3 (1)					1	1		1							6
Arrowtown 9	1															1
Arrowtown 10	2 (1)	1								1						4
Arrowtown 11										1						1
Arrowtown 15	1															1
Sub Total	15 (3)	2	0	0	0	2	1	0	1	3	0	0	1	0	0	25
Ah Lum's store	8 (3)	1				3	1									13
Poplars	5 (2)					1		1						1		8
QB2	4 (2)						1									5
Apple Tree	4 (2)						2									6
Sandy Point	1															1
Sheung Fong	2					1	1	1								5
Caliche	1															1
Hanging Rock	1							1								2
Riverside	2															2
Rapids	3 (1)+															3
Sub Total	31 (10)	1	0	0	0	4	2	6	0	0	0	0	0	1	0	39
Grand Total	64 (15)	8	4 (2)	1	3	11	3	6	4	8	1	1	1	1	1	118

Note The numbers in brackets are the numbers of immature and sub-adult specimens.
? there is some doubt about the identity of the species

Table 6.19. Fowl bones distribution.

Wing bones	complete	proximal end	distal end
Chinatown	2	18	7
Arrowtown	1	14	22
Ah Lums' store	0	10	15
All other sites	3	9	16
Leg bones	**complete**	**proximal end**	**distal end**
Chinatown	6	16	7
Arrowtown	0	5	10
Ah Lum's store	1	14	16
All other sites	4	5	3

Table 6.20. Commodity prices in the nineteenth century.

	1863		1894	
Product	Price	Quantity	Price	Quantity
flour	4 1/2d	lb.		
sugar	1/-	lb.	3d	lb.
coffee	2/3d	lb.		
tea		lb.	2-3/-	lb.
butter	2/-	lb.	1/3d	lb.
soap	10d-1/-	lb.		
jams	20–22/-	doz.		
pickles	24–26/-	doz.		
salmon	28–30/-	doz.		
rice			2–3/-	lb.
tobacco	7–8/-	lb.	6/-	lb.
bread			2d	lb.
mutton			6d	lb.
pork			7d	lb.
bacon and hams	2/2d	lb		
milk			6d	qt.
cheese			8d	lb.
eggs			8–10d	doz.
ducks			2/-	each
pigeons			6d	each*
pigs			35/-	each*

Sources

1863 data "Queenstown Prices Current" *Lake Wakatipu Mail* 16/5/1864:4; 23/12/1863 supp.

1894 data AJHR C–3A:62 "Price of Provisions".

* information from Peter Chandler

Note Generally the price of provisions on the goldfields dropped as transport improved, more commodities were produced locally, and competion increased.

Example only

BUTCHERING ANALYSIS

Site Firewood Creek   Site No. S133/424   Hut –   Bag No 16

Level 2   Unit G4

Species fowl (rooster)   Bone/Element tarso-metatarsus   Side R

Bone Identification Feature

MNI/MNE 1   Criteria

Probable Meat Cut discarded foot   Bone Portion distal 3/4

Age mature   Criteria spur   Sex M   Criteria spur

Burning Location –   Gnawing: XXXXX rodent   Extent: minor

Fragments 1   Total Weight (gms)

Cut Marks

1. Type of Cut: cleaver XXXXX XXXXX
   Direction: longitudinal transverse diagonal
   Cut Location: at proximal end

2. Type of Cut: cleaver sawn knife
   Direction: longitudinal transverse diagonal
   Cut location:

3. Type of Cut: cleaver sawn knife
   Direction: longitudinal transverse diagonal
   Cut location:

Additional Comments

Figure 6.1. Example of butchering analysis form.

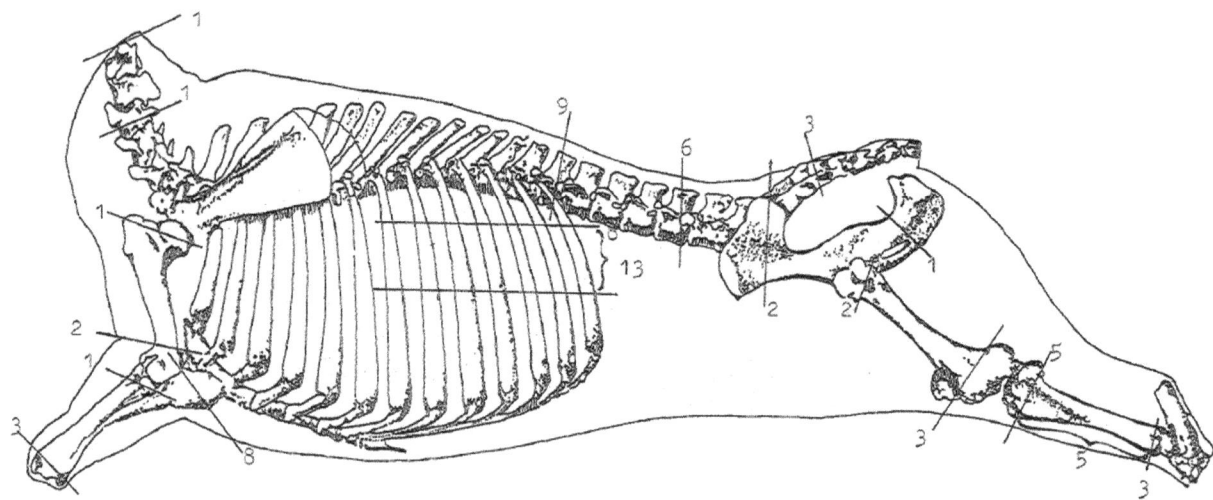

Figure 6.2. Chinatown beef meat cuts.

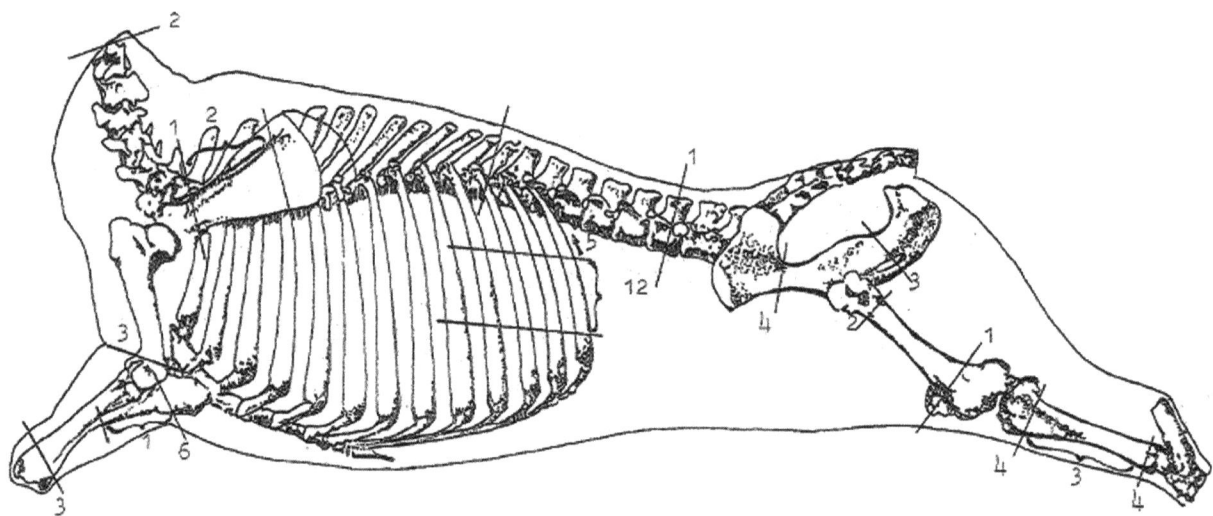

Figure 6.3. Arrowtown beef meat cuts.

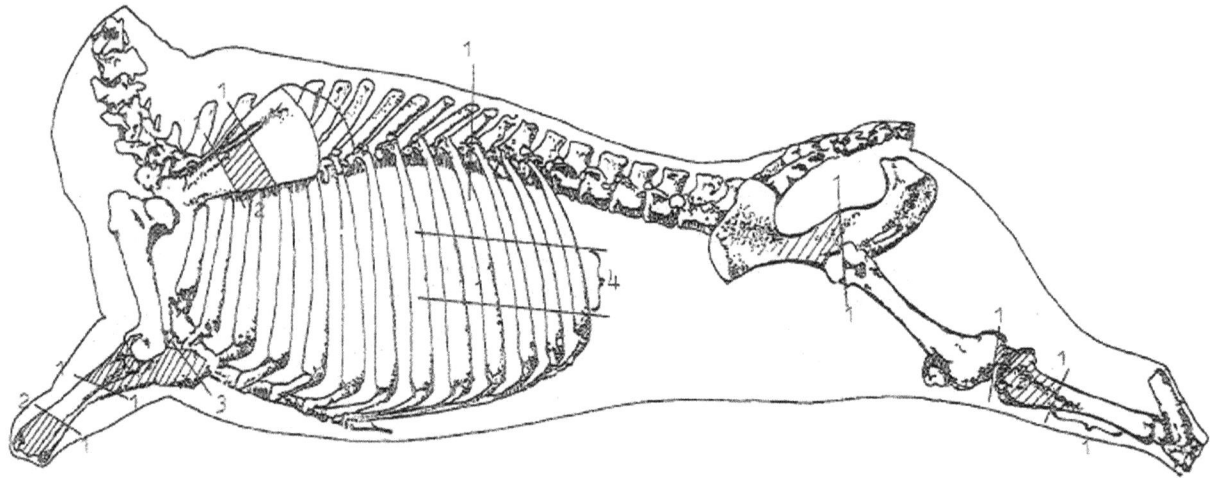

Figure 6.4. Ah Lum's store beef meat cuts.

6 Dietary analysis

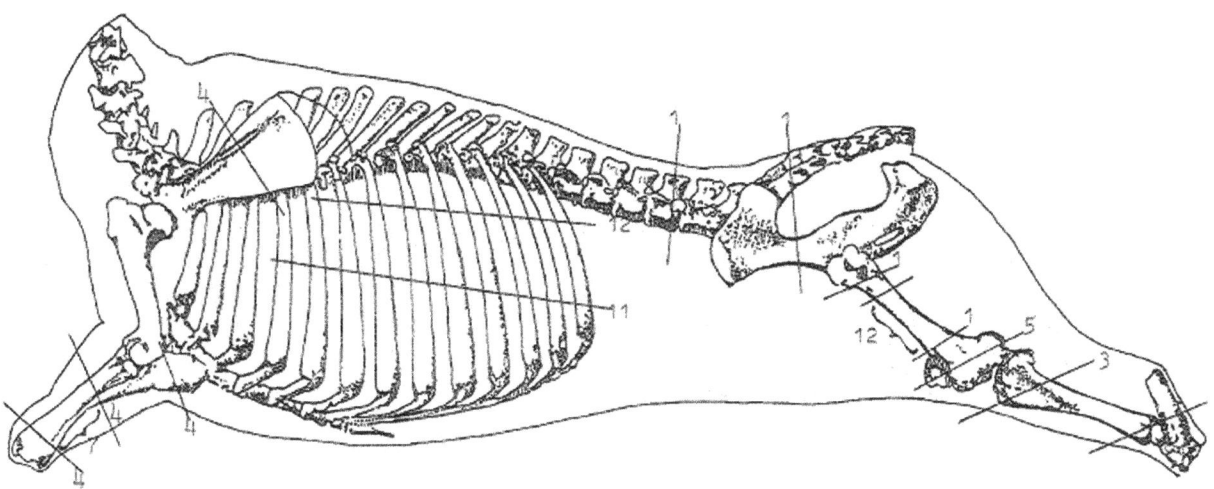

Figure 6.5. Rural sites beef meat cuts.

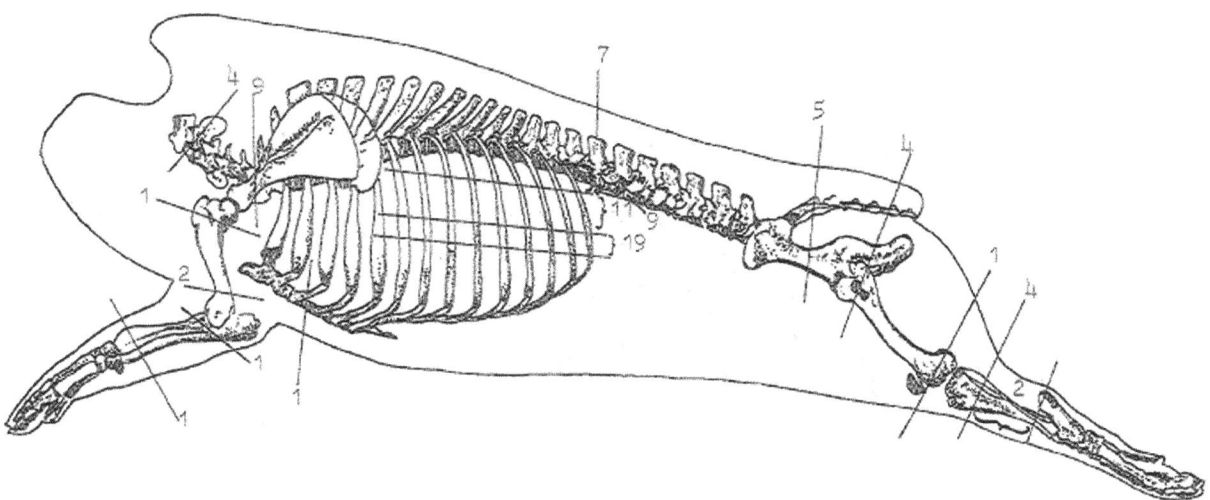

Figure 6.6. Chinatown (Cromwell Chinese Camp) pig meat cuts.

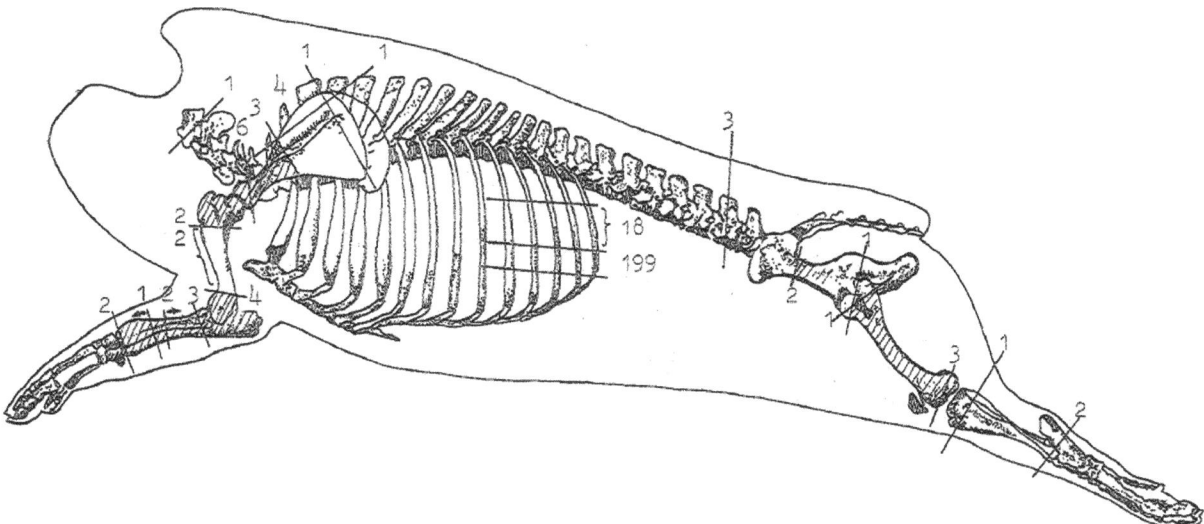

Figure 6.7. Arrowtown pig meat cuts.

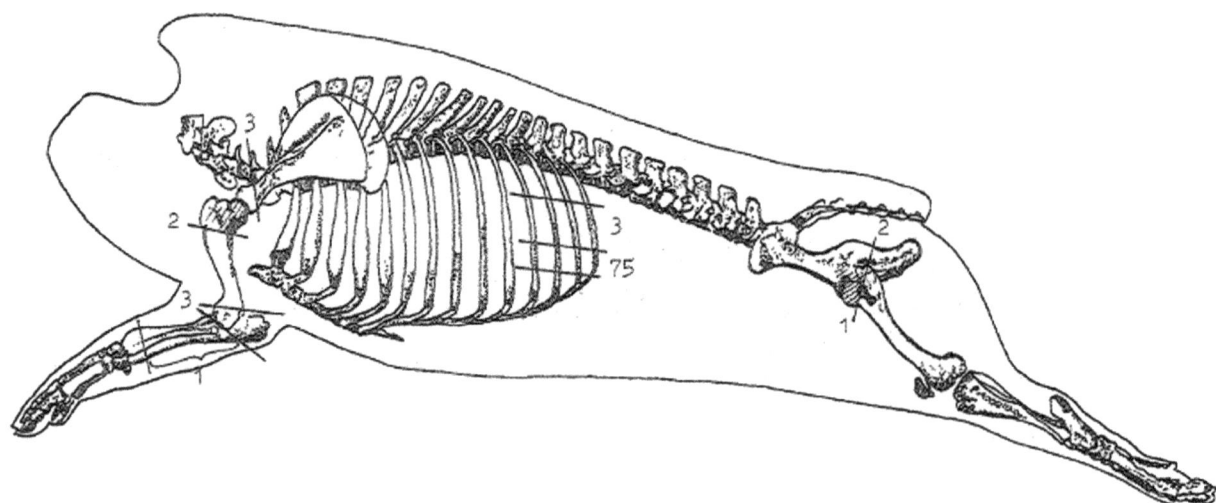

Figure 6.8. Ah Lum's store pig meat cuts.

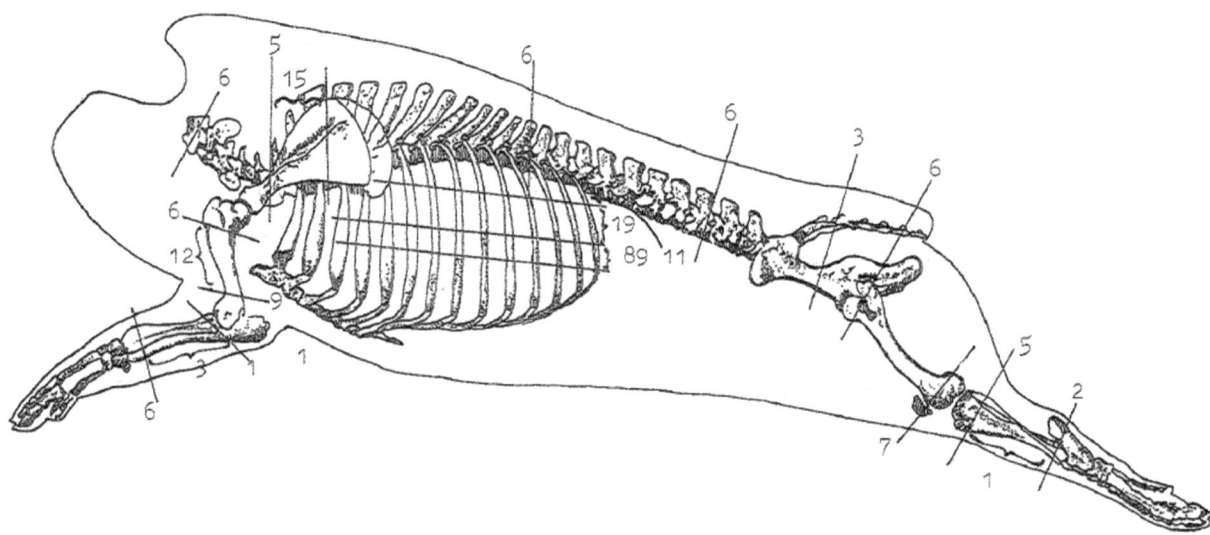

Figure 6.9. Rural sites pig meat cuts.

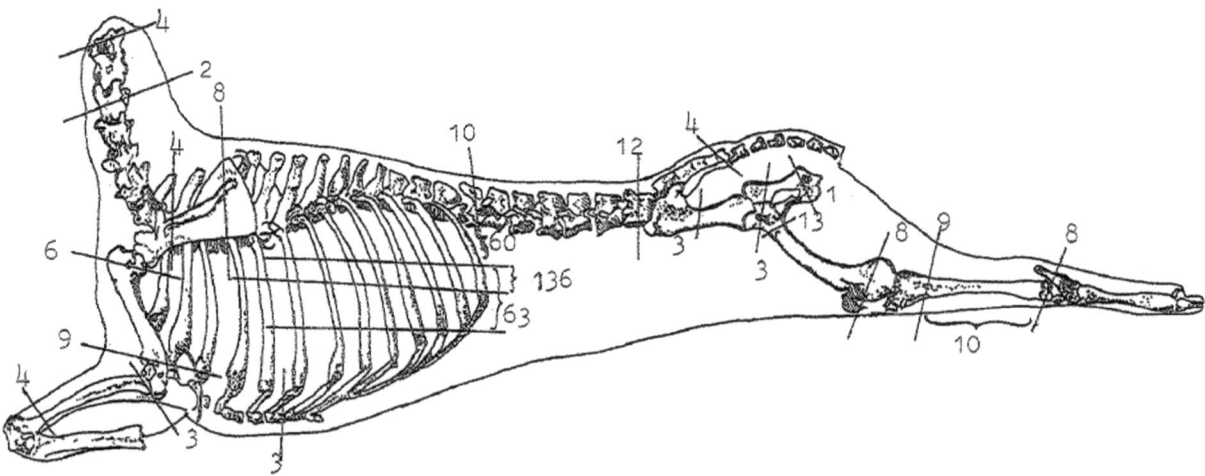

Figure 6.10. Chinatown (Cromwell Chinese Camp) sheep meat cuts.

6 Dietary analysis

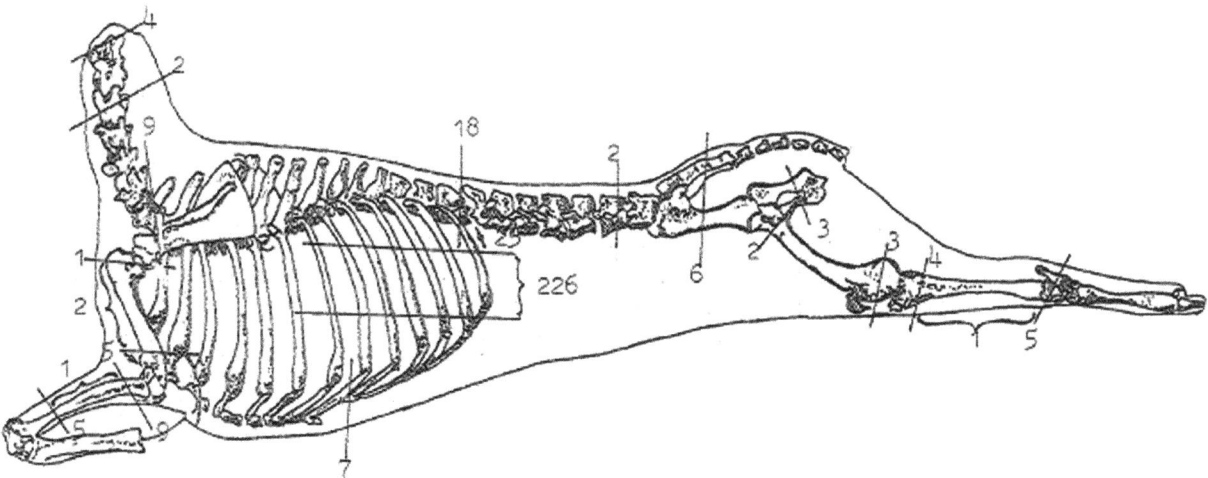

Figure 6.11. Arrowtown sheep meat cuts.

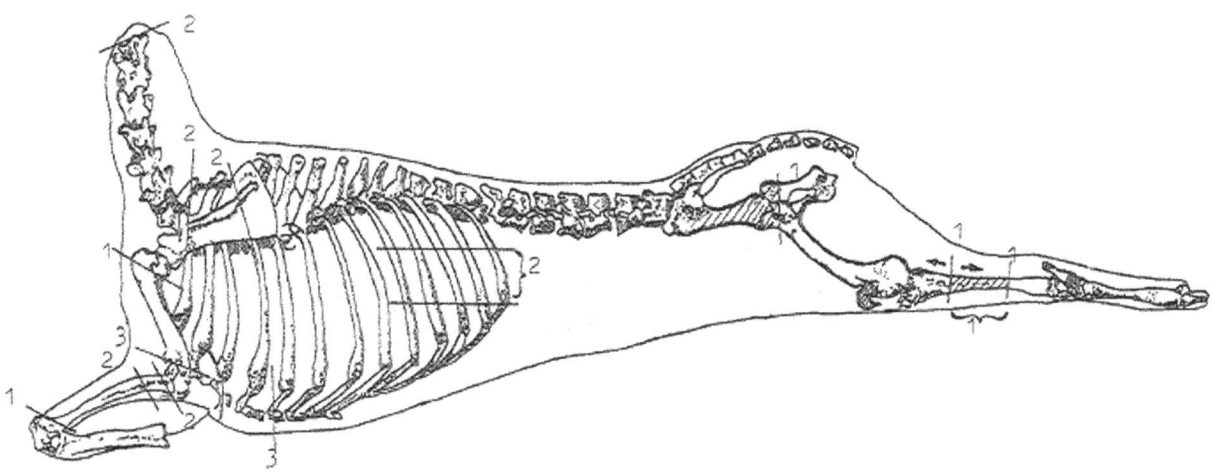

Figure 6.12. Ah Lum's store sheep meat cuts.

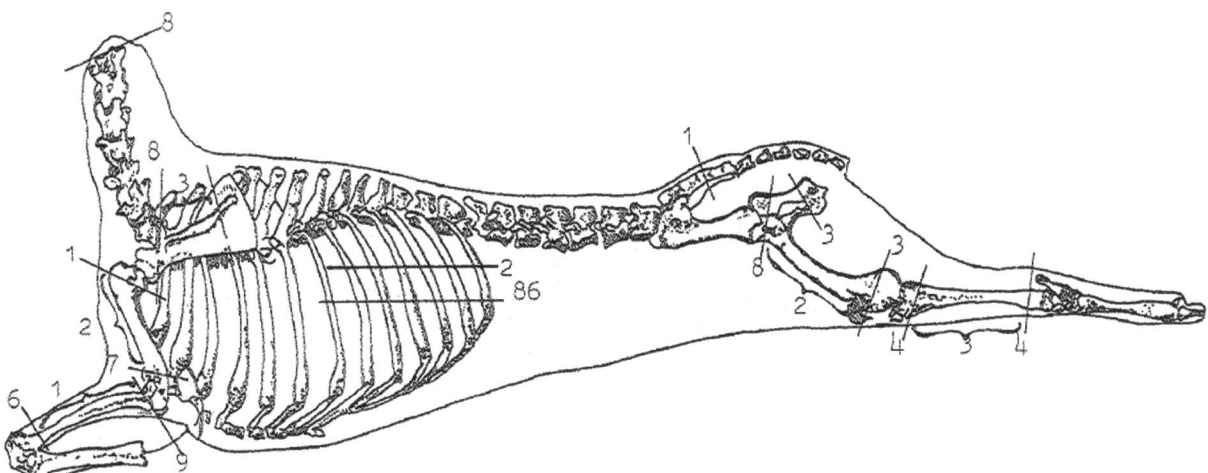

Figure 6.13. Rural sites sheep meat cuts.

Chapter 7
SUMMARY AND CONCLUSIONS

This research, by means of a series of interrelated historical and material culture studies, has provided a different perspective on the "way of life" of the Chinese miners who sojourned in New Zealand in the 19th century.

The strong maintenance of traditional lifeways by the Chinese migrants is well known and documented; indeed, "their inability to acculturate" was often cited by Europeans as a justification for not allowing Chinese immigration (see Sections 2.2, 2.3 and 3.9.1 for historical background). But many changes did occur, both voluntary and involuntary, because it is difficult for a minority ethnic group to maintain complete independence and traditional ways within a dominant host society for very long. From the outset, the Chinese were in an involuntary acculturation situation. Most left China because their families were under economic stress, but almost without exception, it was their intention and heartfelt desire to return, financially enriched, and slot back into traditional society, preferably at a higher level, e.g. as merchants rather than peasants. Most did not intend to settle permanently in New Zealand or adopt what many considered were inferior "Barbarian" practices (see Don 1891:17, 1901:39). While these factors set them aside from other nationalities among the goldseekers, most of the early goldrush miners were young adventurers. They came for the chance to make a fortune and set themselves up for life. When they came to New Zealand, they probably gave little thought to whether it was for a sojourn or permanent settlement.

The discussion now is directed towards an assessment of the changes in the New Zealand Chinese mining "community" in the 19th century. The following areas are examined, by comparison of traditional strategies and apparent "New Zealand modifications", to gauge the degree of change or stability: subsistence-related; dress and personal grooming; gambling; opium smoking; tobacco and alcohol use; mining technology; and habitations (shelter).

7.1 SUBSISTENCE-RELATED

Of the many ethnic groups represented among the thousands of goldseekers who landed in Otago, the Chinese were undoubtedly the most resistant to acculturation. This is reflected in virtually all aspects of life, but it is particularly obvious around subsistence. Although Chinese cuisine exhibits great regional diversity, it is grounded in a unified food tradition that has a long history. Chang (1977:11) summed up the situation nicely: "the preparation and consumption of food has occupied a remarkably central position within the broader Chinese scheme of things". An attempt is made here to measure the resistance to, or degree of, change by comparison of traditional consumption patterns with those of the sojourners. As the Chinese miners were virtually all from the same area in China (Guangdong province, which has its own food tradition – Cantonese), the documentation of changes is simplified.

The underlying principles of Chinese cooking are based on the complementary concepts of yin and yang – the all embracing duality of oriental thought (Chang 1977:10). One of the ways this holistic dualism manifests itself is in the distinction between *fan* dishes (grains and other cereal foods) and *cai* dishes (vegetables and meat foods). A balanced meal must have the appropriate amount of both *fan* and *cai* (Chang 1977:7). Grains, cooked whole or in the form of flour (e.g. noodles, pancakes), comprise the *fan* part of meals. Vegetables and meats cut up and mixed in various ways and combinations constitute the *cai* half of meals. This "opposition" includes not only foods but also the utensils used in their preparation and cooking, and is often incorporated into their names, e.g. in the modern kitchen, *fan guo* ("rice cooker") and *cai kuo* (wok) are very different and as a rule not interchangeable utensils. Cleavers and chopping anvils perhaps best typify *cai* utensils (Chang 1977:8). Another significant aspect of Chinese cuisine is the method of cooking *cai* dishes – stir-frying, which offers economy in cooking time and fuel consumption, requires few utensils and maximises the calorific value of foods.

The typical 19th-century Chinese peasant's diet was nutritionally adequate, if somewhat monotonous (Spence 1977:267). "Flesh foods" were usually eaten only on special occasions. Pork was by far the most important, but fowl (chickens, ducks and geese) and fish constituted significant secondary sources of protein. Beef cattle and sheep were rarely raised in South China, and dairy products such as milk, butter and cheese were virtually absent from the diet. The latter were replaced by soybean curd and other protein-rich vegetable by-products.

The *fan* dishes of South China were largely based on rice or noodles (wheat and millet were predominant in the north), topped with sauce-rich *cai* dishes. Typical features of Cantonese cooking are stir-fried dishes, often flavoured with black beans (salted and fermented soybeans); seafoods, often combined with meat in the same dish; a marked preference for vegetable oil rather than lard in cooking; and the use of a wide variety of finely cut vegetables:

> A huge bowl of rice, a good deal of bean curd, and a dish of cabbage – fresh in season, otherwise pickled – is the classic fare of the everyday south Chinese world. A little chili or preserved soybean for flavour, some *B. campestris* oil to stir-fry the greens… produces a perfectly adequate, nutritionally excellent meal, without the use of animal products or any plant that takes much land or effort. (Anderson and Anderson 1977:328)

Despite their long-established food traditions, the Chinese rapidly adopted many New World vegetables after trading contact was established with the Western world post-1650 AD, including white potatoes, sweet potatoes, corn, tomatoes and peppers (Anderson and Anderson 1977:328). The poor in 19th-century Guangdong often depended on a successful taro and sweet potato crop to ward off starvation (Don 1908:16). However, a diet of white potatoes was considered a mark of extreme poverty and they were never served on special occasions (Mote 1977:198).

7.1.1 THE SOJOURNER DIET

Compared with that of contemporary Guangdong, the diet of the Chinese in Otago had more similarities than differences; however, given the distance from their homeland and the difficulties associated with food transport and preservation, some dietary changes had to be made. The diet of the miners, as evidenced by ethno-historical accounts and archaeological remains, was described in Chapter 6. Discussion here is limited to general observations and elaboration of apparent changes. Although no Chinese shipment or store stock manifestos are known from New Zealand, the large numbers of imported food containers found in Chinese sites indicates that many traditional foods were readily available and they were consumed in substantial amounts.

Within the two years following the first influxes of Chinese miners into the Otago goldfields, Chinese merchant-entrepreneurs had established large stores in Dunedin, and branches and other privately owned stores were established in the mining areas (Section 3.2). They sold imported European and Chinese foods and goods. One of the reasons it was possible to stock a wide range of traditional foods was because over the centuries the Chinese have perfected many food preservation techniques. These include smoking, salting, sugaring, steeping, pickling, drying and marinating food in many kinds of soy-based sauces (Chang 1977:9).

Although much of the food consumed by the Chinese miners was traditional fare, they also acquired many products of European origin (see Chapter 6). Tables 7.1 and 7.2 were compiled from the recorded observations of the Rev. Don, contemporary newspaper accounts, invoices from a European store that detail purchases made by Chinese customers in the 1890s (Kinaston 1896) and the large volume of evidence derived from the analysis of food refuse from the study sites.

Spier (1958:80) listed over 40 imported items recorded on invoices from Chinese merchant stores in San Francisco, including salt beans, macaroni (noodles?), vinegar, oranges, pumeloes, dried oysters, shrimp, cuttlefish*, mushrooms, dry bean curd, bamboo shoots, narrow leaved greens, yams, ginger*, sugar, rice*, sweetmeats, sausage, dry duck, eggs, dried fruit, salt ginger, salted eggs, tea*, dried and minced turnips, bettlenut, orange skins, kumquat, duck livers, flour, birds' nests, fish fins, arrowroot, shrimp soy, chestnut flour, tamarind, dried persimmons, dried guts, bean sauce, lily seeds, beche de mer, Salisburia seeds, taro and seaweed. To Spier's list can be added the following products purchased by Chinese from a European store on the Oregon, USA, goldfields: soy sauce*, cinnamon, red peppers, sesame seeds, malt sugar, black beans, nuts (lychees?), bamboo (bamboo shoots?), melon seeds, dried cabbage, dried vegetables and salted radish (LaLande 1982:34). While definitive evidence of importation into New Zealand from China is limited to those products marked with asterisks, it is likely that virtually all those listed above were imported by Chinese merchants and available in Chinese stores in southern New Zealand too, especially in the heyday of Chinese mining in the 1870s.

In terms of the production and distribution of food, there was a notable difference between that of the Chinese miners' homeland and the situation on the New Zealand goldfields. Here there was no substitute for or re-establishment of the traditional "market day" system; days when food surpluses were taken to central locations and sold or traded. Because most of the population on the goldfields were concerned with mining rather than food production, the system that prevailed here involved the establishment of a network of stores (both Chinese and European) that bought local and imported supplies and sold them with high mark-ups to the miners. Some Chinese stores "packed out" supplies to customers (i.e. goods were transported on packhorses). In addition, individual Chinese earned a living or supplemented their income by hawking supplies for stores or personal food surpluses, especially vegetables (for which they required a hawker's licence; see Chapter 6).

The success of the Chinese merchant stores clearly points to a desire by the Chinese miners to eat foods they were familiar with, if not maintain their traditional lifestyle. Although the range of oriental foods stocked by the stores is likely to have been considerably less than that available in China, a wide variety and all the staples were available in New Zealand; and judging from the discarded food containers in the former habitation sites, considerable quantities were consumed.

Little information is available as to whether the people of Guangdong had adopted European manufactured/preserved foods prior to the large-scale emigrations to the North American and Australasian goldfields, but the archaeological evidence affirms that the Chinese miners consumed large quantities of several European preserved/manufactured foods such as jams, pickles, relishes, vinegar and Worcestershire sauce. However, except for jams, these foods were largely substitutes for traditional foods.

Chinese sites often contain large numbers of discarded hermetically-sealed tin cans. Although most of the cans are likely to have contained familiar products such as fruit, vegetables, meat and fish (albeit mostly of European/New Zealand origin), their high incidence in the Chinese sites suggests they weren't averse to these new Western "convenience foods". A stock of canned food also ensured that a rodent-proof supply was to hand and would have given them more food security during the winter months.

The keeping of gardens and fruit trees was much more common among the Chinese than their European counterparts (Chapter 6). These activities merely carried on long-established traditional horticultural practices (see the numerous references in Chang 1977 on Chinese fruit and vegetable production and consumption). But because of the cooler climate of southern New Zealand, many traditional cultigens, such as the sweet potato and rice, could not be grown here and substitutes had to be accepted. Perhaps the most notable was the substitution of the Irish potato in lieu of the sweet potato, despite the former's low standing as a food plant in southern China.

The consumption of meat per capita undoubtedly increased in New Zealand, but this is not really a divergence from the Cantonese pattern. The miners, especially in the early days, were able to afford meat in much greater quantities than they could in China. The two dominant meats in New Zealand, pork and beef, were the main meat components of the Cantonese diet, but whereas pork consumption was predominant in Canton, they appear (from the archaeological evidence) to have had roughly equal popularity in New Zealand. While sheep meat was of lesser importance in the traditional Cantonese diet (see Chang 1977, several references), its consumption appears to have increased over time in New Zealand, probably because of its relative cheapness and ready availability.

Fish represent another example of substitution. Here the Chinese attempted to maintain their traditional diet by importing dried fish (evidenced archaeologically by non-New Zealand fish bones in the sites) and by substituting canned fish for fresh fish, which other than eel meat had limited availability in Central Otago.

Historical records such as the 1890s Kinaston store ledger show that the sojourners' consumption of bread and milk-based products increased with time. The use of baking powder (evidenced by baking powder cans in the sites) also appears to have been a new feature. These can be considered minor acculturative changes. Two researchers who studied 19th-century American Chinese diets/sites have also noted the apparent adoption of baking powder (Langenwalter 1980; LaLande 1982). Langenwalter (1980:108) contended the presence of baking powder cans was evidence that leavened bread had been introduced into the diet.

In addition to those outlined, as the years passed there were other modifications to the diet, and the means of cooking food. Some, such as the consumption of rabbits and eel meat (discussed in Chapter 6), were not only used as substitutes but also reflect the Chinese miners' situation – a declining population of ageing males making do with whatever they could grow, catch or acquire. Ethno-historical observations indicate they increasingly simplified cooking procedures by resorting virtually to "one-pot stews". But these were forced acculturative changes, because there was still a marked preference for traditional foods if they were available or affordable.

The diet of the Chinese miners in New Zealand included a wide range of oriental and occidental foods, belying the popular misconception that "they lived on rice". Purchases recorded in European store ledgers indicate that Europeans on the goldfields lived on a diet dominated by mutton, potatoes, flour, bread, butter, jam and sugar, supplemented with tea, coffee, cocoa, condensed milk, relishes and pickles, eggs, bacon, canned meat, fish and vegetables, cheese, salt, rice and currants (plus tobacco and alcohol). By comparison, the diet of the Chinese seems better balanced both in terms of nutrition and variety. However, there was certainly no rush to add to the traditional range of foodstuffs. The apparent changes – the use of European preserved foods, rising agents in baking, the gradual acceptance of butter and other dairy products, notably increased meat consumption, the use of canned foods and acceptance of the white potato – were all pragmatic responses. Most were mere substitutions. Overall, the modest changes in the diet of the Chinese miners reflect little sign of acculturation. They attempted to maintain their traditional diet, only modifying it substantially or accepting new foods when forced to by circumstances such as climatic limitations, poverty, the closing of local Chinese stores, and the increasing non-availability of traditional foods as importations decreased.

Despite the limited changes in the types of food consumed, it is apparent from the archaeological assemblages (Section 5.2.3) that many of the Chinese miners regularly used Euro-ceramic tablewares. They were present in 13 of the 15 study sites and totalled 264 units, compared with 141 units of Chinese tableware (see Table 5.22). The considerably higher ratio of Euro-ceramics in the urban camp sites (plates predominating) possibly reflects a greater level of acculturation of the Chinese who lived in or near the established towns. Possible reasons were outlined in Section 5.2.3. Similarly, although the Chinese acquired and used many European utensils and cooking vessels such as knives, forks, spoons and billies, they maintained the basic culinary practices of their homeland, as evidenced by artefacts such as wok spoons, cleavers and imported food containers, and the meat butchering data (Chapter 6).

7.2 DRESS AND PERSONAL GROOMING

Acceptance of a host nation's "dress code" is regarded as one of the first phases of acculturation. Contemporary reports (e.g. *Otago Witness* 8/5/1869:5) indicate that most of the Chinese who landed in New Zealand directly from China wore traditional clothing (in the instance quoted, "traditional raincoats and slippers"), but from the outset they adopted Western work clothes on the goldfields. Many, if not most, also appear to have adopted Western clothes in non-work situations, even though Chinese garments were available (Section 5.6.4). The numerous photographs of Chinese miners taken by the Rev. Alexander Don almost invariably depict them wearing Western jackets, trousers and waistcoats. Although some may have been wearing their "Sunday best", it is notable that they are not wearing traditional Chinese garments. Conversely, the major Chinese merchant-entrepreneurs were invariably photographed in "expensive-looking" Chinese attire. They used traditional clothing as a status symbol.

Wearing Western clothes, like some of the dietary changes, was another pragmatic and essential response to their situation. Western clothing and footwear were warmer, more durable and better suited in mining environments than their traditional lightweight cotton attire. But it is notable that during the All Souls festival when it was customary to "feed and clothe the unfriended dead", in part by burning clothes, the Chinese purchased and burnt new Chinese clothes rather than European clothing (Don 1/4/1884:184, 1895:4). This suggests they had not rejected traditional clothing and would have adopted it anew upon their return to China. The Chinese were, of course, powerless to change their skin colour or physical appearance, but they may have found that wearing European clothes reduced any extra attention they received and that the Western clothes served to some extent as a symbol that they "were not different". The wearing of Western clothing on the goldfields probably hastened the complete acceptance of Western clothes by the Chinese who came to New Zealand later.

Grooming is another aspect of appearance. The study sites produced few artefacts associated with grooming, and the documentary records include few references about grooming at a personal level (see Section 5.6.5, Table 5.77), but some changes are evident. Regarding acceptance of new things, the adoption of European teeth-cleaning technology (Section 5.6.3) is perhaps the most notable. They also adopted the European "safety razor" for shaving, in preference to the traditional broad-bladed razor.

Judging from historic photographs, many of the miners appear to have dispensed with the traditional queue and wore their hair relatively close-cropped. Outwardly, this appears to be a significant acculturative change, rather than merely an act of convenience, but some may have hidden their queue under their miner's hat. According to LaLande (1982:41), a sojourner could not re-enter China without one. Even if his contention is totally or partially incorrect, the "cutting off" of a queue was an emotive act, and almost certainly reflects a sense of separation from their homeland and an identification with their situation in New Zealand. There is another possible reason for dispensing with queues. Some of the Chinese may have felt they would be more acceptable and less likely to attract the attention of louts if they looked more like Europeans (i.e. stopped maintaining their hair in a queue).

7.3 GAMBLING

The Chinese miners were avid gamblers and brought several traditional games of chance with them, including *pat kow* (dominoes), *fan-tan, paak kop piu* and probably *wei-qi* (go). Gambling was an important form of relaxation for the Chinese on the goldfields (Sections 3.3 and 5.6.6). Typical game pieces found in Chinese sites include wooden dominoes, black and white glass counters, paper *paak kop piu* tickets and brass "cash" (coins; Tables 5.83 and 5.84).

Although gambling artefacts were not restricted to any particular Chinese locale, they are much more common in the urban camps and, conversely, less common in remote rural mining sites. Most urban Chinese settlements had at least one gambling venue. Their socio-economic significance and close links with opium-smoking venues and Chinese merchandising were discussed in Section 3.3.

Judging from both the ethno-historic and archaeological evidence, little acculturation took place regarding gambling activities. Gambling venues offering the traditional games of chance flourished so long as the miners in the area were doing well and declined and closed when they were no longer economically viable. Although some miners indulged in European forms of gambling, notably card playing and betting on racehorses, such behaviour was idiosyncratic and "small time" compared with the time and money invested in the traditional Chinese games of chance. Traditional dice games were also played by the miners, but judging from the limited number of references to them, they were a less popular mode of gambling (see Culin 1893:491–537).

7.4 OPIUM SMOKING

Among men, opium smoking became an established part of life in Guangdong during the mid-19th century. Many of the sojourners brought the habit with them to New Zealand and others adopted the practice here. Although no figures are available, Don's records and the archaeological evidence (especially) suggest that a significant proportion of the Chinese miners smoked opium, at least on a casual basis. Opium paraphernalia such as opium pipe bowls and fittings, opium cans and heating lamps are among the most common "Chinese artefacts" in Chinese sites. While their presence in virtually every Chinese site clearly indicates that opium smoking was a widespread and regular practice among the Chinese on the goldfields, it is equally apparent (because of the amount of work and energy they expended collectively) that opium smoking could not have been too debilitating for moderate or casual users. An elderly Chinese American said this about regular opium users:

> I remember some of the older ones smoked opium… It seemed like nothing to them. They didn't get crazy or that kind of thing. I used to watch them every day, you know, and they could climb a tree as well as I could. (Nee and Nee 1973:24)

Both the archaeological evidence and historical records (notably Don's observations and the opium importation figures – Appendix 6) illustrate the persistence of this established cultural trait (smoking solid opium) by the sojourners in New Zealand. Although there is some evidence that Chinese consumption of liquid opiates such as laudanum (which formed the base of many medicines and was widely consumed by Europeans) may have increased after sales of solid opium to Chinese were banned in 1901, the use of liquid opiates was a response by individual Chinese to the lack of availability of solid opium rather than a preference for the liquid form. Physical dependency was obviously a contributing factor in the maintenance of the practice, but opium smoking also had important socio-economic and recreational roles. For merchants, not only was it a highly profitable commodity, it also attracted custom for other products and services. For the miners, it was an important form of socialising because it was seldom smoked without company. It may also have served to reinforce intra-group bonds, like the "going to the pub after work" ritual of modern New Zealand culture.

7.5 TOBACCO AND ALCOHOL USE

Tobacco smoking was a well-established habit among the Chinese long before the 19th-century diaspora from southern China. Long, thin-stemmed bamboo pipes with small brass bowls and ivory mouthpieces were the usual equipment employed, although metal water pipes were preferred by the affluent (Laufer 1924).

No traditional tobacco pipes (or components) were found in the study sites and only one is known from Central Otago. It was found in a Chinese hut in the Cardrona Valley and is now part of a private collection (Dennison pers. comm.). Instead, the Chinese bought and used European clay and briar pipes. European pipes were more compact, probably more readily available, likely to have been cheaper and their greater capacity possibly appealed too because they would have required less cleaning and refilling.

There is the abundant archaeological evidence – tobacco cans, matchboxes and remains of tobacco pipes, which are found in most Chinese sites. Overall the evidence shows that, although the Chinese adopted European smoking technology, the established practice of tobacco smoking persisted and probably grew in popularity among the Chinese on the goldfields.

Alcohol consumption has been an integral part of Chinese culture for several thousand years (Chang 1977). The traditional alcoholic drinks (Cantonese *chau*) of Guangdong were either undistilled alcohols made from grain (i.e. beers) or distilled, un-aged beverages made from starch bases. Generally, they were much stronger than their occidental equivalents. *Chau* were used extensively to infuse medicines and produce herbal tinctures (Anderson and Anderson 1977:342).

In contrast to the often sensational and derogatory descriptions by European observers of the Chinese mining settlements and opium dens (e.g. *West Coast Times* 29/7/1874; *Tuapeka Times* 11/3/1885:2), comments on alcohol usage by the Chinese stress their moderation and orderly behaviour compared to that of their European counterparts (see Buckingham 1974). A similar pattern has been documented in the United States (LaLande 1982:44–5). However, despite all the testimonials to their sobriety, large volumes of alcohol were consumed by the general populace in New Zealand in the 19th century (Eldred-Grigg 1984:206–14), and the Chinese were no exception. There is considerable archaeological and archival evidence (Section 5.1) that the Chinese consumed considerable quantities of alcohol per capita, albeit with less disturbance of the peace. Their more private and less obstreperous drinking behaviour appears to have created an impression that "the Chinese did not drink much".

Only one traditional Chinese alcohol "samshoo" (a.k.a. Ng Ka Py/Mui Kwe Lu; imported and sold in distinctive bulbous ceramic bottles; see Section 5.2.1) appears to have been consumed in quantity on the southern goldfields (Section 5.1). The remains of European alcohol bottles in the sites (particularly brandy/cognac, gin and beer bottles, and to a lesser extent whisky) indicate that many Chinese developed a liking for the main Western alcohols; a similar pattern has been documented in the United States (LaLande 1982). The drinking of European alcohols appears to have been more than just an act of substitution or making up for a shortfall in the supply of oriental liquors. The evidence (Don's observations and the archaeological remains) suggest that European alcohols were consumed in considerably greater quantities than oriental imports. Furthermore, they taste so different from the predominant oriental alcohols that their consumption constitutes the acceptance of new tastes and products and shows that some acculturation had occurred in their drinking habits.

7.6 MINING TECHNOLOGY

The archival, ethno-historical and archaeological records of Chinese mining in New Zealand were discussed in Section 3.7. Although the Chinese miners were of peasant stock, they were heirs to at least a 4,000-year legacy of knowledge about mining and related technology, such as dam and race construction, waterwheels and manually-operated pumps. The Chinese also have a long history of civil engineering knowledge based on simple labour-intensive technologies. They applied this collective knowledge successfully in New Zealand and made substantial returns from ground that had often already been worked over by Europeans.

They continued to use traditional mining techniques such as working in groups, wing damming and the use of waterwheels and pumps, but the Chinese were not slow to appreciate the benefits of Western technological innovations such as hydraulic sluicing and mercury amalgamation (possibly from earlier experience with these techniques in Australia); in fact, since the first Chinese miners who came to New Zealand came from the Victorian goldfields, they would have gained many insights into Western mining techniques, the nature of auriferous deposits and where gold was likely to be found there. The absence of recognisable Chinese mining equipment in contemporary photographs and in museum collections, and the lack of comments on same by contemporary observers, also point to the adoption of Western mining techniques.

While the use of Euro-American mining techniques can be considered acculturative changes, they also represent further practical responses by the Chinese, i.e. the adoption of methods that had been proven by the European miners to be successful and economical ways of recovering gold from the auriferous gravels in the southern New Zealand goldfields. Conversely, the Chinese largely stayed clear of technologies that required considerable capital and expertise, such as reef mining and dredging (but, as noted in Section 3.7, there were some notable exceptions).

7.7 HABITATIONS

The habitations of the Chinese miners differed markedly from those of their homeland. The accounts of Mawson et al. (1926) and others indicate that sun-dried and baked earth constituted the main construction material used in the houses in the nucleated villages around Guangzhou (Canton) and that most Chinese males knew the basics of house construction using these materials. As few of the Chinese miners were accompanied by family members, there was little need or desire to try and re-create replicas of contemporary Chinese villages in New Zealand. But from the outset they exhibited a remarkable adaptability and versatility about "house" construction using the materials to hand. Although they shunned tents, archival, photographic and archaeological evidence indicates that they built houses of turf, adobe, pungas (tree fern trunks), timber offcuts, canvas, cobblestones, schist slabs, corrugated iron, sheet metal and various combinations of the above, depending on local circumstances. In addition, in the Central Otago river gorges, where suitable sites abound, they formed comfortable homes by walling up the front of natural overhangs.

Again, the Chinese responded in practical ways to their situation. The habitations were generally one-roomed structures shared with one or more clansmen and afforded basic shelter. In Sections 4.5–4.6, several characteristic features of the Chinese miners' dwellings in Central Otago were identified. Although the miners' houses obviously differed from the family homes of Guangdong, they appear to have retained some characteristic Chinese features in many instances, e.g. many were windowless, a common feature of the houses in contemporary Guangdong (Mawson et al. 1926). Traditional features such as inscriptions on doors and walls and hut "shrines" were also common (Section 3.6), and the huts invariably had a chopping block outside, which according to Don (1/2/1883:147), who spent some time in China, is a positive indication of Chinese occupancy. Again, the evidence suggests the Chinese adopted a pragmatic response to housing on the goldfields (using free materials to hand), but traits such as those listed above reflected their ethnicity.

7.8 CONCLUDING DISCUSSION

The archaeological evidence and ethno-historical records used in this research revealed variable changes in the lifestyle of the Chinese miners in southern New Zealand compared with that of their homeland. Many of the findings are in themselves not revolutionary or unexpected, but the combination of archaeological and ethno-historical evidence has enabled some measure of the changes and a more specific understanding of their nature. The main conclusion is that it is clear the Chinese did not readily acculturate with the dominant Anglo-European population of New Zealand and strongly maintained their traditional lifeways where possible. Consequently, they differed from the goldseekers of other nationalities. When they did make or accept changes, these tended to be in areas of extrinsic behaviour such as clothing and housing. Intrinsic beliefs such as religious preferences, philosophical attitudes, kinship patterns, the belief in the superiority of "things Chinese" and the fact that most considered themselves sojourners rather than settlers seem to have remained essentially unchanged.

Acculturation can be categorised as either voluntary or involuntary. Voluntary acculturative behaviour involves a freely made choice for change or adopting new ways, even if limited, as opposed to the maintenance of traditional ways. Involuntary acculturation obviously denotes changes that were compelled by circumstances and there was little choice in the matter. The range between the two extremes represents a continuum of possible responses, from outright rejection to total acceptance. In the case of the Chinese, their choice was often governed by the availability or otherwise of desired oriental goods.

Food preparation and consumption habits show relatively little evidence of significant acculturation. There were involuntary changes in the methods of food production and distribution of surpluses, but the success of the Chinese stores clearly attests to the strong desire to maintain their traditional lifestyle. Most of the European foods the Chinese adopted were simply substitutes for similar Chinese products. The use of canned provisions by the Chinese argues more for convenience than acculturation. The consumption of beef and sheep meat and to a lesser extent pig meat clearly increased over traditional levels of consumption. In New Zealand they exploited wild birds, rabbits and eels, but hunter-gathering was also used to supplement food supplies in Guangdong. The consumption of dairy products and the use of baking powder to create leavened bread appear to be small but significant acculturative changes. They also adopted European-style plates and cutlery (especially in the urban sites), although rice bowls and other Chinese food preparation, cooking and consumption utensils were not forsaken. Overall, the food habits of the Chinese miners remained well within the traditional sphere, and the evidence suggests that adopted European food items were still cooked in "Chinese ways".

The adoption of Western style clothing probably represents the most voluntary acculturative response of the Chinese miners in New Zealand. It was one of several pragmatic responses they made to their situation.

Traditional Chinese forms of relaxation and opium and alcohol use persisted, but the adoption and predominant consumption of several European alcohols, notably brandy/cognac, gin and beer, is another significant change. It is uncertain whether they drank more than was the norm in China, but it is likely they did, especially in the early days when the men were young, gold was relatively plentiful and they were away for the first time from the strict social mores of their homeland and exposed to the "free-drinking" environment of the goldfields.

In closing, it is evident that the Chinese miners in New Zealand attempted to maintain their traditional material culture and lifestyle with as few changes as possible. Similar patterns of resistance to acculturation have been documented by North American archaeologists (e.g. Langenwalter 1980; LaLande 1982). Even when they adopted the extrinsic trappings of the Anglo-European majority in New Zealand, they maintained their "Chinese-ness" where it mattered most to them in social behaviour, religious beliefs and philosophy. Although as a group they did not make the cognitive changes identified with full acculturation (Herskovitz 1964:169–81), they were flexible in outlook, and readily adopted things that they considered useful or advantageous such as technological innovations in mining, European work clothes, canned food and new and unfamiliar materials for housing.

In effect, they "selectively acculturated". They were extremely practical and self-reliant, "specialised" in re-using items and adopting European substitutes for Chinese items that were unavailable. However, in the final analysis it could be argued that their general resistance to acculturation and their sojourner outlook was their downfall. Time and time again, throughout the 19th century, anti-Chinese agitators used their apparent inability to integrate as an argument for banning Chinese immigration. Of course, the problem was not that simple. Those of Chinese origin were "obviously different" and no amount of desire by the Chinese to integrate would have overcome ingrained European prejudices and fears in the prevailing social climate.

7.9 POSTSCRIPT

This writer's thesis was the major output of the Clutha Valley Archaeological Project although there were many more papers and reports by this author and others. These have been cited in this book. From the outset the project was relatively well resourced. During the 10 years of the project, I was able to employ approximately 150 students, mostly from the University of Otago but also a few from Auckland, for survey work during the May and August university holidays and for two stints of excavation work over the summer holidays (six weeks either side of Christmas–New Year). Some worked on the project several times, and it became a training ground for a generation of Otago archaeology students. Some 40 years later, at least 10 of the students who worked on the project are still working as professional archaeologists or in related occupations, including four in academic positions in Australia. A dozen or so overseas archaeologists on working holidays worked on the project too, but because they were not New Zealanders (and on tourist visas), they did not get paid.

The project made major contributions to typology and the analysis of European-era artefacts, but undoubtedly the two things for which it gained international recognition were the work on Chinese miners' sites and tailings analysis. The focus on the Chinese sites came about when I realised they constituted around 60% of the sites that were going to be inundated by the Clyde Dam, and they were easily recognisable by the distinctive artefacts of Chinese origin. At the time there was growing interest in ethnic archaeology, particularly in the USA and Australia, but I had about a four-year head start and they seemed to think I was some sort of expert on the subject, particularly after the excavation of the Cromwell Chinese miners' camp (locally known as Chinatown), and I began to produce papers on the Chinese sites and artefacts. I started getting regular requests from overseas archaeologists for copies of my Chinese site papers (all by letter, no email in those days). I knew little about Chinese artefacts when I started, but I learned fast, especially from bottle diggers who had been looting Chinese (and other) sites for years. By talking with them and studying their collections, I learned a lot about the types of Chinese artefacts we might encounter. The excavation of the Cromwell Chinese Camp (summer 1981–82) attracted a lot of interest, which led me to think about excavating and restoring another Chinese camp. This led to the excavation of the Arrowtown Chinese Camp over the summer of 1982–83, but the plan from the outset was to go far beyond the archaeology. It was to faithfully restore the structures and create the much-visited cultural heritage attraction it is today.

What would I have done differently with hindsight? The resources we had were pretty phenomenal at the time, but it's what we didn't have that would have made a huge difference. Back then (1977–1986) there was no email, personal computers were very expensive (I bought my first second-hand one for $4,000 in 1982), reports were typed either by myself or by a typing pool, no digital photography or Photoshop, no GPS, GIS, CAD or other drawing programs, no total stations for mapping, no Google Earth, no drones, and no online access to mining and historical records, historic maps and comparative collections. There was no Papers Past, the NZ online historic newspaper portal (like the Australian Trove), which now provides easy access to references about the Chinese in all the historic newspapers in New Zealand. It has revolutionised historic research. What I did have was a lot of operational freedom, and the Central Otago weather was great for fieldwork all year round. Since the completion of the Clutha Project, work on Chinese sites in New Zealand has been fairly limited, the main work being a major excavation on a Chinese market garden at the former Carlaw Park, Auckland (Bader and Adamson 2011; Adamson and Bader 2013), four seasons of archaeological work on the Lawrence Chinese Camp (a major report is in progress; Walters in prep.) and two significant historical studies of Chinese market gardening in Australasia (Lee and Lam 2012; Boileau 2017). In a subsequent paper, "Opening wealth's door", Boileau specifically describes Chinese market gardening on the New Zealand goldfields (Boileau 2016). A small but useful assemblage from a house site, Wakefield Street in Auckland, was reported in 2005 (Turner, Hill and Clough 2005). *Rushing for Gold: Life and Commerce on the Goldfields in New Zealand and Australia*, an edited volume, contains several papers about the arrival of the Chinese miners in New Zealand and their contribution (Carpenter and Fraser 2016). *Golden Prospects* is a notable historical work about the Chinese on the West Coast of the South Island (Bradshaw 2009). The most recent significant historical work is *Merchant, Miner, Mandarin: The Life and Times of the Remarkable Choie Sew Hoy*, undoubtedly the premier Chinese mining entrepreneur in New Zealand (Agnew and Agnew 2020).

Several significant Chinese sites in New Zealand have been registered by Heritage New Zealand in recent years. They include the Arrowtown Chinese Camp, the Lawrence Chinese Camp, Chinese graves, Wong Gong's Terrace in the Shotover Valley, Ly Bow's garden, the Golden Cross restaurant and the Ng King Brothers Chinese Market Garden Settlement in Hakatere (Ashburton), a rare example in New Zealand of a Chinese market garden settlement with most of the original buildings and a pig oven intact. The property is still owned by descendants of the original Chinese owners.

Bell (1996) reviewed the status of the archaeology of the Chinese in Australia. He concluded then that much of it was "ad hoc in design, hasty in execution and the product is poorly disseminated". Bell followed this up with *A History of the Chinese in Australia* (1997). Lindsay Smith's 1998 PhD, "Cold hard cash: a study of Chinese ethnicity in archaeology at Kiandra, New South Wales", evaluated how Chinese ethnicity could be identified in the archaeological resources of a remote colonial Australian goldmine. In 1999, Jane Lydon produced the groundbreaking *"Many Inventions": The Chinese in the Rocks, Sydney 1890–1930* (Lydon 1999). By 2003, when this author co-edited the 21st volume of *Australasian Historical Archaeology*, some real progress had been made. The volume includes Barry McGowan's groundbreaking contribution on the archaeology of Chinese alluvial mining in Australia (McGowan 2003), Kevin Rains' interpretation of the Chinese at Cooktown (Rains 2003), Anne-Louise Muir's very useful account of the Chinese ceramics in the Museum of Chinese Australian History (Muir 2003) and Gordon Grimwade's investigation of Chinese temples in far north Queensland (Grimwade 2003). The entire volume is devoted to good research on Chinese sites in Australia to that date with some useful North American comparisons. A few years later, *An Archaeology of Australia Since 1788* was published – the first volume in 10 years to cover the whole of Australian historical archaeology, with several sections on the Chinese experience in Australia (Lawrence and Davies 2011). Alister M. Bowen's monograph *Archaeology of the Chinese Fishing Industry in Colonial Victoria*, published by ASHA in 2012 and based on his 2008 PhD research, provided a refreshing focus on a specialised aspect of Chinese innovation (Bowen 2008, 2012). Other important contributions include Rains (2005), Dunk (2010, 2015) and Burke and Grimwade (2013). Recent work includes "Palmer River goldfield Chinese coin hoard: new evidence challenging its authenticity" (Zhu and Ritchie 2019) and "Pigs, temples and feasts: Australian Chinese pig ovens, a summation of knowledge on these peculiarly Chinese features" (Grimwade, in press).

A notable recent US initiative is the *Qiaoxiang* (Chinese homeland villages) project initially centred on the Pearl River Delta village of Cangdong. Here surveys and excavations around the village have revealed many of the ceramic types (and other artefacts) found in the USA, Australian and New Zealand sites such as celadon (wintergreen), Double Happiness and Bamboo.

Neville Ritchie, July 2023

7 Summary and conclusions

Table 7.1. Foods and beverages imported from China and consumed by the Chinese on the southern goldfields.

Key	D Don's records	K Kinaston store ledger
	A remains from archaeological contexts	
Product Type	**Container Type**	**Evidence/Documentation**
rice	sacks	D K
tea	wooden chests?	inferred
tea	paper packets, cans	A
black vinegar	ceramic pots	A D
soy sauce	ceramic pots	A D
ginger	ceramic pots	A
fish pastes	ceramic pots	A D
vegetable oil	ceramic pots	A D (Don 1/8/1866:22)
Ng Ka Py (samshoo)	ceramic pots	A D
preserved fish		D (Don 2/10/1882:66)
dried fish		A
turnip seed		D (Don 1/1/1883:126)
cabbage seed		D (Don 1906:26)
dolichos root		D (Don 1/6/1883:225)
cuttlefish		A (Don 1895:59)
coconut		A
Products almost certainly imported from China but lacking definitive archaeological or ethnohistorical evidence		
dried shellfish	dried shrimp	spices
sesame seeds	malt sugar	bean curd
lychees	dried mushrooms	noodles
salted radish	dried cabbage	sugar
dried seaweeds	soy beans	peppers
preserved eggs	black beans	bamboo shoots

Table 7.2. Foods/beverages/products of European/New Zealand origin definitely consumed/used by the Chinese on the southern goldfields.

Key		D Don's records	K Kinaston store ledger		
		A remains from archaeological contexts			
Product Type	**Container Type**	**Evidence/ Documentation**	**Product Type**	**Container Type**	**Evidence/ Documentation**
gin	bottles	A	baking powder	cans	A
whisky	bottles	A	butter	paper wrappers	K
brandy/cognac	bottles	A D	cheese	paper wrappers	K
beer	bottles	A	bacon	paper wrappers	K
aerated waters	bottles	A	bread		K (Butler 1977:17)
jam	cans, bottles	A D	matches/vestas	tin boxes	A K
Worcestershire sauce	bottles	A	cocoa	cans	A K
pickles	bottles	A	sugar	paper bags?	K
vinegar	bottles	A	candles	paper-wrapped	A K
magnesia	bottles	A	milk		K
emulsion	bottles	A	eggs		A D K
leather dressings	bottles	A	potatoes		D K
preserved fruit	bottles	A (Butler 1977:17)	chocolate	only recorded once	K
sardines	cans	A (Butler 1977:17)	soap		K
herrings	cans	A	peanuts		D K
salmon	cans	A	gooseberries		A
meat	cans	A	strawberries		D K
coffee essence	bottles	A	apricots		A D
spices	cans		peaches		A D
flour	sacks?	D	pears		A D
peas		D	plums		A D
onions		D	apples		A
pumpkins		A	pork		A D K
celery		D	beef		A D
turnips		D	sheep meat		A D
Chinese cabbage		D K	rabbits		A D
oysters		A (Butler 1977:17)	fish		A D
freshwater mussels		A	eels		A D
Probables					
beans	cans	A			
soups	cans	A			
tomatoes	cans	A			

REFERENCES

NEWSPAPERS

Arrow Observer (Arrowtown)
Bruce Herald (Milton)
Cromwell Argus (Cromwell)
Daily Telegraph (Dunedin)
Dunstan Times (Clyde-Alexandra)
Lake County Press (Queenstown)
Lake Wakatip Mail (Queenstown)
Mt Ida Chronicle (Naseby)
Nelson Examiner (Nelson)
New Zealand Herald (Auckland)
Otago Daily Times (Dunedin)
Otago Witness (Dunedin)
The Australian (Sydney)
Tuapeka Times (Lawrence)
West Coast Times (Greymouth)

ARCHIVAL SOURCES

AJHR	Appendices to the Journal of the House of Representatives, Hocken Library, Dunedin
DS	Dept of Statistics, Christchurch and Wellington
NZG	New Zealand Gazette
NZGC	New Zealand Government Census
NZHRS	New Zealand Health Report Series, Board of Health, Wellington
NZP	New Zealand Presbyterian, Hocken Library
NZPD	New Zealand Parliamentary Debates
NZPO	New Zealand Post Office
OPG	Otago Provincial Gazette, Hocken Library
V & P	Votes and Proceedings, Otago Provincial Gazette

Asian Artefact Inventory (AAI) data, Asian American Comparative Collection, University of Idaho, Laboratory of Anthropology, Moscow, Idaho, USA.

Asian American Comparative Collection Newsletter, (AACC Newsletter). P. Wegars (ed.), Laboratory of Anthropology, University of Idaho, Moscow, Idaho, USA.

Adams, William H. and Linda P. Gaw (1977). A model for determining time lag of ceramic artefacts. *Northwest Archaeological Research Notes* 11(2): 218–31.

Adamson, Janet and Hans-Dieter Bader (2013). Gardening to prosperity: the history and archaeology of Chan Dah Chee and the Chinese market garden at Carlaw Park, Auckland. In M. Campbell, S. Holdaway and S. Macready, eds. *Finding our Recent Past: Historical Archaeology in New Zealand*, 143–66. New Zealand Archaeological Association Monograph 29. Auckland: New Zealand Archaeological Association.

Aero, Rita (1980). *Things Chinese*. New York: Dolphin Books, Doubleday & Co.

Agnew, Jenny Sew Hoy and Agnew, Trevor (2020) *Merchant, Miner, Mandarin: The Life and Times of the Remarkable Choie Sew Hoy*. Christchurch: Canterbury University Press.

Albert, L.S. and K. Kent (1949). *The Complete Button Book*. New York: Doubleday & Co.

Aldridge, T. and C. Aldridge (1978). *New Zealand Antique Bottles Price Guide*. Wellington: John Milne Ltd.

Allen, F.J. (1969). Archaeology and the history of Port Essington. Unpublished PhD thesis, Australian National University, Canberra.

Anderson, A. (1968) The archaeology of mass-produced footwear. *Historical Archaeology* 2: 56–65.

Anderson, A.J., ed. (1979). *Birds of a Feather.* New Zealand Archaeological Association Monograph 11, British Archaeological Records International Series 62. Auckland: New Zealand Archaeological Association.

Anderson E.J. Jr, and M.L. Anderson (1977). Modern China: South. In K.C. Chang, ed. *Food in Chinese Culture: Anthropological and Historical Perspectives.* New Haven: Yale University Press.

Anson, D. (1983). Typology and seriation of tin wax vesta matchboxes from Central Otago: a new method of dating historic sites in New Zealand. *New Zealand Journal of Archaeology* 5: 115–38.

Armstrong, J. (1979). The Lovelock bottles. In Eugene M. Hattori, M.K. Rusco and D.R. Tuohy, eds. *Archaeological and Historical Studies at Ninth and Amherst, Lovelock, Nevada*, 199–250. Carson City, NV: Nevada State Museum Archaeological Services.

Arrowtown Borough rate books, held by the Lakes District Museum, Arrowtown.

Bader, H. and Adamson, J. (2011). *Kong Foong Yuen – The Gardens of Prosperity: Final Report on the Archaeological Excavations at Carlaw Park, Auckland, Authority #2007-48.* Auckland: Archaeology Solutions.

Ball, J.D. (1906). *Things Chinese; Or, Notes connected with China.* New York: Charles Scribner's Sons. 1st ed. Hong Kong: Kelly & Walsh. revised 5th ed. (1925).

Barnes, F.C. (1972). *Cartridges of the World.* Northfield, Illinois: Digest Books Inc.

Barry, W. (1897). *Past and Present, and Men of the Times.* Wellington: McKee & Gamble, printers.

Bartlett, M. (1971). Gold scales. *Antiques Journal*, January 1971: 22–3.

Beals, H.K. (1980). Chinese coins in six northwestern aboriginal sites. *Historical Archaeology* 14: 58–72.

Beaver, P. (1980). *Addis 1780–1980: All About the Home – The History of Addis Ltd.* London: Publications for Companies.

Bedford, S.H. (1985a). A simplified classification system for tin wax vesta matchboxes. *New Zealand Archaeological Association Newsletter* 28(1): 44–64.

Bedford, S.H. (1985b). *Alpine Archaeology 2: The First Ball Hut Site, Tasman Valley.* Cromwell: NZ Historic Places Trust.

Bedford, S.H. (1985c). For beautifying and preserving the teeth and gums: bone toothbrushes and ceramic toothpaste pots from historic sites in the Cromwell district. *New Zealand Archaeological Association Newsletter* 28(3): 172–82.

Bedford, S.H. (1986). *The Final Report on the Excavation of the Halfway House Hotel Site, Cromwell Gorge.* Cromwell: NZ Historic Places Trust.

Bedford, S.H. (n.d.) Domestic utensils used by the Chinese in Central Otago. Unpublished manuscript. Cromwell: NZ Historic Places Trust.

Beeton, I. (1899). *The Book of Household Management.* London: Ward, Lock & Co., Ltd.

Beeton, I. (n.d.). *Mrs Beeton's Family Cookery.* London: Ward, Lock & Co., Ltd.

Bell, G. (pers. comm.). Retired butcher of Cromwell. Sold meat to the Chinese at Lawrence c.1920. Informal discussions and a recorded interview.

Bell, Peter (1996). The archaeology of the Chinese in Australia. *Australasian Historical Archaeology* 14: 13–18.

Bente, V.G. (1976). Good luck, long life. In Roberta S. Greenwood, ed. *The Changing Faces of Main Street: Ventura Archaeological Project*, 457–95. Ventura, CA: Ventura Redevelopment Agency.

Berge, D.I. (1980). *Simpson Springs Station: Historical Archaeology in Western Utah, 1974–75.* Salt Lake City: Utah State Office, Bureau of Land Management.

Bernard, N. and S. Tamatsu (1975). *Metallurgical Remains of Ancient China.* Tokyo: Nichiosa.

Borrie, W.D. (1939). Immigration to New Zealand since 1854. Unpublished Master's thesis, University of Otago, Dunedin.

Boileau, J. (2016). Opening wealth's door: Chinese market gardening on the goldfields. In L. Carpenter and L. Fraser, eds. *Rushing for Gold: Life and Commerce on the Goldfields of New Zealand and Australia*, 122–32. Dunedin: Otago University Press.

Boileau, J. (2017). *Chinese Market Gardening in Australia and New Zealand: Gardens of Prosperity.* Cham, Switzerland: Palgrave Macmillan.

Bowen, A. (2008). "A power of money": The Chinese involvement in Victoria's early fishing industry. PhD thesis, La Trobe University, Melbourne.

Bowen, A.M. (2012). *Archaeology of the Chinese Fishing Industry in Colonial Victoria.* Studies in Australasian Archaeology 3, Australasian Society for Historical Archaeology. Sydney: Sydney University Press.

Bradshaw, Julia (2009) *Golden Prospects: Chinese on the West Coast of New Zealand.* Greymouth: Shantytown West Coast Historical and Mechanical Society Inc.

References

Bressie, W. and R. Bressie (1972). *Ghost Town Bottle Price Guide: With an Expanded Section on Oriental Ceramics*. Caldwell: Caxton Printers.

Brott, C.W. (1982). *Moon Lee One: Life in Old Chinatown, Weaverville, California*. Redding, CA: Great Basin Foundation.

Brown, B. and M.K. Rusco (1979). The laundry at Ninth and Amherst. In Eugene M. Hattori, M.K. Rusco and D.R. Tuohy, eds. *Archaeological Studies at Ninth and Amherst, Lovelock, Nevada*, 614–34. Carson City, NV: Nevada State Museum Archaeological Services.

Buckingham, P.D. (1974). *The Report of the Chinese Immigration Committee 1871: With respect to some aspects of public opinion in Otago Province*. Postgraduate diploma in Arts, University of Otago, Dunedin.

Bull, G. and S. Payne (1982). Tooth eruption and epiphysial fusion in pigs and wild boar. In R. Wilson, C. Grigson and S Payne, eds. *Ageing and Sexing Animal Bones from Archaeological Sites*. Oxford: British Archaeological Reports Series 109: 55–71.

Burke, H and Grimwade. G. (2013). The historical archaeology of the Chinese in Far North Queensland. *Queensland Archaeological Record* 16:121–39.

Busch, J. (1981). An introduction to the tin can. *Historical Archaeology* 15(1): 95–104.

Bushell, S.W. (1880). Coins of the present dynasty of China. *Journal of the North China Branch, Royal Asiatic Society*, New Series 15: 195–308.

Butler, P. (1977). *Opium and Gold: A History of the Chinese Miners in New Zealand*. Martinborough: Alistair Taylor.

Cameron, F.R. (1985). An analysis of buttons, clothing hardware and textiles of the nineteenth century Chinese goldminers of Central Otago. Unpublished BA Hons. dissertation, Anthropology Department, University of Otago, Dunedin.

Can Manufacturers Institute (1978). *The Can: Yesterday, Today and Tomorrow*. Washington, D.C.

Carpenter, L. and Fraser L., eds. (2016). *Rushing for Gold: Life and Commerce on the Goldfields of New Zealand and Australia*. Dunedin: Otago University Press.

Chace, P.G. (1976) Overseas Chinese ceramics. In Roberta S. Greenwood, ed. *The Changing Faces of Main Street*, 509–30. Ventura, CA: Ventura Redevelopment Agency.

Chace, Paul G. and William S. Evans, Jr. (1969). Celestial sojourners in the High Sierras: The ethno-archaeology of Chinese railroad workers (1865–1868). Presentation to Annual Meeting of the Society for Historical Archaeology, Tucson, Arizona, January 1969.

Chandler, Peter M. (pers. comm.). Historian, Ettrick, Central Otago.

Chang, K.C. (1977). *Food in Chinese Culture: Anthropological and Historical Perspectives*. New Haven: Yale University Press.

Chang, Raymond and Margaret S. Chang (1980). *Speaking of Chinese*. London: Andre Deutsch.

Chao, B.Y. (1972) *How to Cook and Eat in Chinese*. New York: Vintage Books.

Chapple, G., J. Maynard, D. Mitchell and W. Viscoe (1983). *Corrugated Iron in New Zealand*. Wellington: Reed.

Chappel, N.M. (1961). *New Zealand Banker's Hundred: A History of the Bank of New Zealand, 1861–1961*. Wellington: Bank of New Zealand.

Charteris, R.L. (1973). The lost Chinaman joke. *Southland Times* 11/1/1973.

Chinn, Thomas W., ed. (1969) *A History of the Chinese in California: A Syllabus*. San Francisco: Chinese Historical Society of America.

Choi, C.Y. (1975). *Chinese Migration and Settlement in Australia*. Sydney: Sydney University Press.

Clark, H.M. (1977). *The Tin Can Book: The Can as Collectible Art, Advertising Art and High Art*. New York: North American Library.

Clark, W.A.V. (1961). The Slums of Dunedin 1900–1910. *Proceedings of the Third Geography Conference*, 85–92. Palmerston North: New Zealand Geographical Society.

Clarke, H.G. (1970). *Underglaze Colour Picture Prints on Staffordshire Pottery: The Pictorial Pot Lid Book*. London: Courier Press.

Clerico, Sheryl (1979). The Lovelock buttons. In Eugene M. Hattori, M.K. Rusco and D.R. Tuohy, eds. *Archaeological and Historical Studies at Ninth and Amherst, Lovelock, Nevada*, 438–94. Carson City, NV: Nevada State Museum Archaeological Services.

Clonts, John B. (1975). Butchered faunal remains: an overview. In R.M. Herskovitz, *Identification and Analysis of Material Culture from Fort Bowie Historic Site, Arizona*, 303–15. Manuscript on file, US National Park Service, Western Archaeological Center Library, Tucson, Arizona.

Collis, M. (1941) *Foreign Mud*. London: Faber and Faber.

Coole, Arthur B. (1965). *Coins in China's History*. Kansas: privately published.

Courtenay, Keith (1982) signed letter on behalf of the Palmer River Historic Preservation Society, Queensland, Australia, giving details of the sale of Chinese coins found in a cache (30,000) on the Palmer River goldfield.

Courtwright, David (1982). Opiate addiction in the American West. *Journal of the West* XXI(3): 23–31.
Craig, Muriel (pers. comm.). Elder citizen of Cromwell, lived on terrace above the eastern end of Cromwell's Chinatown. She recalled the last Chinese there.
Cross, Nelson L. (pers. comm.). Gun collector of Alexandra. Identifications and comments on role of ammunition found in Chinese sites.
Cuffley, P. (1973). *A Complete Catalogue and History of Oil and Kerosene Lamps in Australia.* Yarra Glen: Pioneer.
Culin, Stewart (1887). China in America: A study in the social life of the Chinese in the eastern cities of the United States. Paper read before the American Association for the Advancement of Science (Section of Anthropology), at the Thirty-Sixth Meeting, New York.
Culin, Stewart (1891a). Opium smoking by the Chinese in Philadelphia. *American Journal of Pharmacy*, October 63 (10): 497–502.
Culin, Stewart (1891b). The gambling games of the Chinese in America. *Series in Philology, Literature and Archaeology* 1(4). Publications of the University of Pennsylvania. Reproduced by the Gamblers Book Club, Las Vegas, Nevada, 1972.
Culin, Stewart (1893). Chinese games with dice and dominoes. *Annual Report of the Board of Regents of the Smithsonian Institution 1893*, Washington, 491–537. Reprinted by the Shorey Bookstore, Seattle, 1972.
Cumbaa, Stephen L. (1975). Patterns of resource use and cross-cultural dietary change in the Spanish colonial period. Unpublished PhD thesis, University of Florida, Gainesville, Florida.
Cyclopedia of New Zealand 1897–1908. Cyclopedia Company, Limited:
    Vol. 1 Wellington Provincial District, Wellington, 1897
    Vol. 2 Auckland Provincial District, Christchurch, 1902
    Vol. 3 Canterbury Provincial District, Christchurch, 1903
    Vol. 4 Otago and Southland Provincial District, Christchurch, 1905
    Vol. 5 Nelson, Marlborough and Westland Provincial District, Christchurch 1906
    Vol. 6 Taranaki, Hawke's Bay and Wellington Provincial District, Christchurch, 1908.
Dane, A. and R. Morrison (1979). *Clay Pipes from Port Arthur 1830–1877.* Technical Bulletin No. 2, Department of Prehistory, Canberra: Research School of Pacific Studies, Australian National University.
Dansie, Amy (1979). Beef, bobcat and other beast bones: faunal remains from Lovelock's Chinatown. In Eugene M. Hattori, M.K. Rusco and D.R. Tuohy, eds. *Archaeological and Historical Studies at Nineth and Amherst, Lovelock, Nevada*, 348–410. Carson City, NV: Nevada State Museum Archaeological Services.
Davey, Peter, ed. (1979). *The Archaeology of the Clay Tobacco Pipe 1: Britain, the Midlands and Eastern England.* British Archaeological Reports Series 63. Oxford, England: B.A.R.
Davey, Peter, ed. (1980). *The Archaeology of the Clay Tobacco Pipe 3: Britain, the North and West.* British Archaeological Reports Series 78. Oxford: B.A.R.
Davis, A. (1967). *Package and Print: The Development of Container and Label Design.* London: Faber and Faber.
Davis, Herbert (1916). *The Canton Villages Mission of the Presbyterian Church of New Zealand, Dunedin.* Dunedin: Foreign Missions Committee.
Demuth, William (c1875) William Demuth Company (WDC), New York. pipe catalogue.
Dennison, Raymond (pers. comm.). Of Arrowtown. Has a small private collection of Chinese artefacts.
Dobie, Charles C. (1936). *San Francisco's Chinatown.* New York and London: D Appleton-Century Co. Inc.
Don, Rev. Alexander (1879–1911). Presbyterian Missioner to the Chinese on the southern goldfields (1882–1911). "Our Chinese Mission", in the *New Zealand Presbyterian*, various issues between 1879 and 1889, cited e.g. thus (Don 3/12/1887:156). References from Don's "Annual Inland Tour" reports (1891–1911) cited e.g. thus (Don 1896:13), Repository, Hocken Library, Dunedin.
Don, Rev. Alexander (1896) Diary. Ng collection, Alexander Turnbull Library, Wellington.
Don, Rev. Alexander (1936), edited, with a memoir of Alexander Don, by William J. Bennett. *Memories of the Golden Road: A History of the Presbyterian Church in Central Otago.* Reeds, Wellington.
Doo, Gretyl (pers. comm.). Dunedin potter. Comments on Chinese ceramic composition.
Dudley, Austin (pers. comm. 1983). Of Arrowtown (now deceased). Personal observations on the Arrowtown Chinese c.1915–1925.
Duff, Geoffrey (1980) *Sheep May Safely Graze: A History of the Tarras-Bendigo Area, Central Otago*. Tarras. privately published.
Duff, Geoffrey (pers. comm.). Discussions on Chinese in the Bendigo area.
Dunedin Master Butcher's Association (1984). *Meat Cut Charts for Mutton, Beef and Pork.* Dunedin: Dunedin Master Butcher's Association.
Dunk, Melissa, (2010) Made in China: An Analysis of the Artifact Assemblage from Atherton Chinatown, North Queensland, Unpublished BA Hons thesis, Department of Archaeology, La Trobe University, Melbourne.

Dunk, Melissa (2015) Overseas Chinese Ceramics in Nineteenth Century Australia: The Dennis O'Hoy collection. In *Angel by the Water: Essays in Honour of Dennis Reginal O'Hoy*. Kennington: Holland House.

Dunhill, Alfred (1969). *The Pipe Book*. London: Arthur Baker Ltd.

Ebbett, E. (1979) *In True Colonial Fashion*. Wellington: A.H. & A.W. Reed.

Edsall, Michael A. 1981 The New Zealand Public Schools Cadets "Model Rifle" of 1902. *New Zealand Antique Arms Journal* November 1981: 227–8.

Eldred-Grigg, Stevan (1984). *Pleasures of the Flesh: Sex and Drugs in Colonial New Zealand 1840–1915*. Wellington: A.H. & A.W. Reed.

Encyclopedia Britannica (1911). *A Dictionary of Arts, Sciences, Literature and General information*. 11th edition, Vol. XX. Cambridge: Cambridge University Press.

Encyclopedia Britannica (1979). *Micropaedia* 3: ceramic definitions; *Micropaedia* 5: history of opium usage.

Epstein, D. (1968) *Buttons*. New York: Walker & Co.

Etter, Patricia A. (1980). The West Coast Chinese and opium smoking. In Robert L. Schuyler, ed. *Archaeological Perspectives on Ethnicity in America*, 97–101. Farmingdale, New York: Baywood Publishing Co.

Evans, William S., Jr (1980). Food and fantasy: material culture of the Chinese in California and the West, circa. 1850–1900. In Robert L. Schuyler, ed. *Archaeological Perspectives on Ethnicity in America*, 89–96. Farmingdale, New York: Baywood Publishing Co.

Facey, Albert B. (1984). *A Fortunate Life: The Autobiography of Albert Facey*. Sydney: Reader's Digest Condensed Books.

Farris, Glenn J. (1979). "Cash" as currency: coins and tokens from Yreka Chinatown. *Historical Archaeology* 13: 48–52.

Farris, Glenn J. (1980). Coins and tokens of Old Sacramento. *California Archaeological Reports* 19: 23–44. Sacramento, CA: Cultural Resource Management Unit, Department of Parks and Recreation.

Farris, Glenn J. (1984). Chinese and Annamese coins found at the Woodland Opera House site. In *The Chinese Laundry on Second Street: Papers on Archaeology at the Woodland Opera House Site*. Sacramento, CA: California Archaeological Reports 24: 147–50. Department of Parks and Recreation.

Fee, Jeff (pers. comm.). Archaeologist, US Forest Service, McCall, Idaho.

Felton, David L., Frank Lortie and Peter D. Schulz (1984). Opium smoking in the nineteenth century. In *The Chinese Laundry on Second Street: Papers on Archaeology at the Woodland Opera House Site*. California Archaeological Reports 24:98–106. Sacramento, CA: Department of Parks and Recreation.

Fenstermaker, G.B. and Alice T. Williams (1979) *The Chinese Glass Bead and the Romance of the Bead Jewellery Trail*. Archaeological Research Booklets No. 15. Lancaster, PA: Fenstermaker.

Fitzgibbon, Theodora (1976). *The Food of the Western World: An Encyclopedia of Food from North America and Europe*. New York: Quadrangle/New York Times Book Co.

Fletcher, Edward (1972). *Bottle Collecting*. Dorset: Blandford Press.

Fletcher, Edward (1975). *Collecting Pot Lids*. London: Pitman.

Fong, Ng Bickleen (1959a). *The Chinese in New Zealand: A Study of Assimilation*. Hong Kong: Hong Kong University Press.

Fong, Ng Bickleen (1959b). The Chinese in New Zealand. *Journal of Human Relations* 7(3): 290–9.

Fontana, Bernard L. and L.J. Greenleaf (1962). Johnny Ward's ranch: a study in historic archaeology. *The Kiva* 28: 1–2.

Forrest, James (1961). Population and settlement on the Otago goldfields, 1861–1870. *New Zealand Geographer* 17(1): 64–8.

Foster, Debbie (1983) Clay pipes from the Cromwell area, Central Otago. *New Zealand Archaeological Association Newsletter* 26(2): 94–101.

Fradkin, Arlene (1980). Hog jowls and coon meat: an analysis of faunal remains from the Hampton Plantation, St Simons Island, Georgia. *Southeastern Archaeological Conference Bulletin* 22: 57–9.

Frond, N. and C. Turgeon, eds (1966). *Larousse Gastronomique: The Encyclopedia of Food, Wine and Cooking*. London: Hamlyn.

Fyfe, Frances (1948). Chinese Immigration to New Zealand in the Nineteenth Century. Unpublished Master's history thesis, University of New Zealand, Victoria.

Gaw, Linda P. (1975). The availability and selection of ceramics in Silcott, Washington 1900–1930. *Northwest Anthropological Research Notes* 9(1): 166–79.

Gilbart, Dr Joseph S.E. (1979). Air pistols and pellets part 3. *Guns Review*, September 19(9): 612–15.

Gilkinson, R. (1978). *Early Days in Central Otago*. Christchurch: Whitcouls.

Gittins, Jean (1981). *The Diggers from China: The Story of the Chinese on the (Australian) Goldfields*. Melbourne: Quartet Books.

Godden, Geoffrey A. (1964). *Encyclopedia of British Pottery and Porcelain Marks*. London: Barry and Jenkins.
Goldman, L.M. (1958). *The History of the Jews in New Zealand*. Wellington: A.H. & A.W. Reed.
Greenwood, Roberta S., ed. (1975). *3500 Years on One City Block: San Buenaventura Mission Plaza Archaeological Report, 1974*. Ventura, CA: Ventura Redevelopment Agency.
Greif, Stuart W. (1974). *The Overseas Chinese in New Zealand*. Singapore: Asia Pacific Press.
Griffiths, D.M. (1978). Use-Marks on Historic Ceramics: a preliminary study. *Historical Archaeology* 12: 68–81.
Grimwade, G. (2003). Gold, gardens, temples and feasts: Chinese Temple, Croydon, Qld. *Australasian Historical Archaeology* 21: 50–7.
Grimwade, Gordon (in press). Pigs, temples and feasts: Australian Chinese pig ovens. Part of an edited volume, *Archaeologies of Food in Australia*. Sydney: Sydney University Press.
Gust, Sherri M. (1984). Mammalian fauna from the Woodland Opera House site. In *The Chinese Laundry on Second Street: Papers on Archaeology at the Woodland Opera House Site*. Sacramento, CA: California Archaeological Reports 24: 167–92. Department of Parks and Recreation, .
Hall, T.D.H. and G.H. Scholefield (1937). Asiatic immigration to New Zealand: its history and legislation. In N. McKenzie, ed. *The Legal Status of Aliens in Pacific Countries*. Oxford: Oxford University Press.
Hall-Jones, John (1982). *Goldfields of the South*. Invercargill: Craig Printing Co Ltd.
Hamilton collection. Owned by Alan Hamilton, Arrowtown.
Hangar, Mark. (pers. comm.). Historical researcher.
Hardesty, Donald L. and Eugene M. Hattori (1983). *Archaeological studies in the Cortez Mining District, 1982*. In Bureau of Land Management, Nevada, *Contributions to the Study of Cultural Resources*, Technical Report No. 12.
Hardingham, M. (1978). *The Illustrated Dictionary of Fabrics*. London: Studio Vista.
Hargreaves, R.P. (1972). *From Beads to Banknotes*. Dunedin: McIndoe.
Harnett & Co (1863). *Harnett & Co.'s Dunedin Directory*. Dunedin: Harnett & Co.
Harney, Malachi L. and John C. Cross (1973) *The Narcotic Officer's Notebook* (section on opiates 48–93). Springfield, IL: Charles C. Thomas.
Harris, Lynn H. (1980). *The Military .303 Cartridge: Its History and Variations*. Wellington. self-published.
Harrison, Ann P. (1982). *Lake Roxburgh Archaeological Survey*. Cromwell: New Zealand Historic Places Trust.
Hart, Phillip D. (1979). The Chinese community in Lovelock, Nevada, 1870–1940. In Eugene M. Hattori, M.K. Rusco and D.R. Tuohy, eds. *Archaeological and Historical Studies at Ninth and Amherst, Lovelock, Nevada*, 11–56. Carson City, NV: Nevada State Museum Archaeological Services.
Hattori, Eugene M. (1979). The Lovelock coins: analysis of coins from the Lovelock Chinatown site. In Eugene M. Hattori, M.K. Rusco and D.R. Tuohy, eds. *Archaeological and Historical Studies at Ninth and Amherst, Lovelock, Nevada*, 411–35. Carson City, NV: Nevada State Museum Archaeological Services.
Hattori, Eugene M., Mary K. Rusco and Donald R. Tuohy (1979). *Archaeological and Historical Studies at Ninth and Amherst, Lovelock, Nevada*, 2 vols. Carson City, NV: Nevada State Museum Archaeological Services.
Hayward, Bruce W. and J.T. Diamond (1979). Archaeological evidence for the design of kauri driving dams in New Zealand. *New Zealand Journal of Archaeology* 1: 153–69.
Hayward, Bruce W. and J.T. Diamond (1980). Early earth driving dams in New Zealand. *Records of the New Zealand Historic Places Trust* 3: 8–17.
Hayward, Bruce W. and J.T. Diamond (1982). Excavation of a nineteenth century kauri bushmen's hut site, Waitakere Ranges, West Auckland. *New Zealand Archaeological Association Newsletter* 25(3): 171–9.
Hearn, T.J and R.P. Hargreaves (1985). *The Speculator's Dream: Gold Dredging in Southern New Zealand*. Dunedin: Allied Press.
Helvey, Pamela and David L. Felton (1979). The archaeology of Yreka Chinatown. Manuscript on file. Sacramento, CA: Cultural Resource Management Unit, Department of Parks and Recreation.
Herskovits, M.J. (1964). *Cultural Dynamics*. New York: Knopf.
Herskovitz, Robert M. (1978). *Fort Bowie Material Culture*. Anthropological Papers of the University of Arizona 31. Tucson, AZ: University of Arizona Press.
Higham, C.F.W., G.M. Mason and S.J.E. Moore (1976). Upper Clutha Valley: An Archaeological Survey. *Studies in Prehistoric Anthropology* 8.
Holmes, Edward M. (1911). Opium. In *The Encyclopedia Britannica: A Dictionary of Arts, Sciences, Literature and General Information*, 130–7. Cambridge: Cambridge University Press.
Hommel, Rudolf P. (1969). *China at Work: An Illustrated Record of the Primitive Industries of China's Masses*. Cambridge, MA: Massachusetts Institute of Technology Press. Originally published by the John Day Co, New York, 1937.
Hubbard, Clarence T. (1968). Tin tobacco tags. *The Antiques Journal*, June (2): 7–30.
Hunt, C.B. (1959). Dating of mining camps with tin cans and bottles. *Geo Times* 3(1): 8–10, 34.

Ingram, C.W.N. and P.O. Wheatley (1977). *New Zealand Shipwrecks, 1795–1975*. Wellington: Reed.
Israel, Fred L., ed. (1968). *1897 Sears Roebuck Catalogue, No. 104 1968* (edited reprint). New York: Chelsea House Publishers.
Jack, Ian (1982). (pers. comm.). Letter giving details of a large cache (30,000) of Chinese coins found on the Palmer River goldfield and being sold off (in 1982).
Jack, Ian, Kate Holmes and Ruth Kerr (1984). Ah Toy's garden: a Chinese market garden on the Palmer River Goldfield, North Queensland. *Australian Journal of Historical Archaeology* 2: 51–8.
Jeffrey, G.N. (pers. comm.). Retired chemist of Roxburgh. Provided information about the "Sunday trade" in opium to the Chinese.
Jenyns, R. Soame (1982). *Chinese Art III*. New York: Rizolli.
Johnson, Graham E. (1982). *Peasants and Rural Development in the 1970s: A South China Case. Regional Development and Regional Policy*. Nagoya: United Nations Center for Regional Development, R.P. Mishra, ed.
Jones, Kevin L., ed. (1981). *Proceedings of the Goldfields Seminar, Cromwell, October 1981*. Wellington: New Zealand Historic Places Trust.
Jones, Timothy W. (1980). *Archaeological Test Excavations in the Boise Redevelopment Project Area, Boise, Idaho*. University of Idaho Anthropological Research Manuscript Series 59. Moscow: Laboratory of Anthropology, University of Idaho.
Jones, Timothy W. (n.d.). A 3 page chronological listing of main developments in the canning industry. Moscow: Laboratory of Anthropology, University of Idaho.
Jones, Timothy W., Mary Anne Davis and George Ling (1979). *Idaho City: An Overview and Report on the Excavation*. University of Idaho Anthropological Research Manuscript Series 50. Moscow: Laboratory of Anthropology, University of Idaho.
Kamm, Minnie W. (1951). *Old China*. Grosse Pointe Farms, MI: privately published.
Kane, Harry H. (1882). *Opium Smoking in America and China*. Reprint of the edition published by G.P. Putnam's Sons, New York.
Kane, Stan (pers. comm.). Retired farmer, Wanaka.
Kang, Jye (1985). *Guests of the New Gold Hill*. Auckland: Hodder and Stoughton.
Kildare, M. (1972). Chinese Goldcamp weaponry. *Relics* 6(2): 12–15, 28, Austin.
Kinaston, R. (1893–96). Roxburgh grocer. His store ledger, in the possession of Mr G. Jeffery of Roxburgh, lists purchases by Chinese customers.
King, Frank H.H. (1965). *Money and Monetary Policy in China 1845–1895*. Cambridge, MA: Harvard University Press.
Kinsky, F.C. (1970). *Annotated Checklist of the Birds of New Zealand*. Wellington: A.H. and A.W. Reed.
Kirk, M.A. (1975). Buttons from the San Buenaventura Mission site, 1974. In Roberta S. Greenwood, ed. *3500 Years on One City Block: San Buenaventura Archaeological Report, 1974*. Ventura, CA: Ventura Redevelopment Agency.
Kirk, M A. (1976). Buttons from the San Buenaventura site, 1975. In Roberta S. Greenwood, ed. *The Changing Faces of Main Street*, Ventura, CA: Ventura Redevelopment Agency.
Kleeb, Gerald N. (1976). Analysis of the coins from a Chinese trash pit in Ventura. In Roberta S. Greenwood, ed. *The Changing Faces of Main Street*, 497–508. Ventura, California: San Buenaventura Redevelopment Agency.
Knowles, Russell (pers. comm.). Member, Otago Bottle Collectors Club.
Kooyman, Brian (pers. comm.). PhD student, Anthropology Department, University of Otago, Dunedin.
Kulp, Daniel Harrison (1972). *Country Life in China: The Sociology of Familism*. Reprint by Ch'eng Wen Publishing Co., Taipei, Taiwan.
LaLande, Jeffrey M. (1981). Sojourners in the Oregon Siskiyous: adaptation and acculturation of the Chinese miners in the Applegate Valley, ca. 1855–1900. Unpublished Master of Disciplinary Studies thesis, Oregon State University, Oregon.
LaLande, Jeffrey M. (1982). "Celestials" in the Oregon Siskiyous: diet, dress and drug use of the Chinese miners in Jackson County, ca. 1860–1900. *Northwest Anthropological Research Notes*, Spring 16(1): 1–61.
Lambert, Gail (1985). *Pottery in New Zealand: Commercial and Collectible*. Auckland: Heinemann Publishers.
Langenwalter II, Paul E. (1980). The archaeology of 19th century Chinese subsistence at the Lower China Store, Madera County, California. In Robert L. Schuyler, ed. *Archaeological Perspectives on Ethnicity*, 102–13, Farmingdale, NY: Baywood Publishing Co.
Laufer, Berthold (1924). Tobacco and its use in Asia. *Field Museum of Natural History, Chicago, Anthropology Leaflet* 1: 21–5.
Lawless, Murray (pers. comm.) Old identity of Queensberry who could recall last Chinese miner in the area.

Lawrence, George (c.1926). *Catalogue of the George Lawrence Co. (Shoe Repairers and Shoe Store Suppliers), of Portland, Oregon.*

Lawrence, Susan and Peter Davies (2011). *An Archaeology of Australia since 1788*. New York: Springer.

Leach, B. Foss (1979). Maximising minimum numbers: avian remains from the Washpool Midden site. In A.J. Anderson, ed. *Birds of a Feather*. British Archaeological Records International Series 62: 103–22.

Lee, Calvin B.T. and Audrey E. Lee (1979). *The Gourmet Chinese Regional Cookbook*. Secaucus, NJ: Castle Books.

Lee, Lily and Ruth Lam (2012). *Sons of the Soil: Chinese Market Gardening in New Zealand*. Pukekohe, Dominion Federation of NZ Chinese Commercial Growers.

Levine, Carl O. (1921). Butchering and curing meats in China. *Canton Christian College Bulletin* 27:1–41.

Levy, Howard S. (1967). *Chinese Footbinding: The History of a Curious Erotic Custom*. New York: Bell Publishing Co.

Losey, Timothy C. (1973). The relationship of faunal remains to social dynamics at Fort Enterprise, N.W.T. In R.M. Getty and K.R. Fladmark, eds. *Historical Archaeology in Northwestern North America*, 133–43. Calgary: University of Calgary Archaeological Association.

Luscomb, S.C. (1968). *The Collector's Encyclopedia of Buttons*. New York: Crown Publishers Inc.

Lydon, Jane (1999) "Many Inventions": The Chinese in the Rocks, Sydney 1890–1930. Monash Publications in History, Dept of History. Monash University, Victoria.

Lyman, R. Lee (1977). Analysis of historic faunal remains. *Historical Archaeology* 11: 67–73.

Lyman, R. Lee (1979). Available meat from faunal remains: a consideration of techniques. *American Antiquity* 44(3): 536–46.

Lyon, Rosemary (1972). Chew Chong and the butter trade. *New Zealand Heritage*, Vol. 4 Part 51.

Mason, Graeme (pers. comm.). Senior technician, Anthropology Department, University of Otago, Dunedin.

Mathews, Philip (1947) Chinese New Zealand, an unpublished study in rough draft only. Hocken Library, Dunedin.

Mawson, Rev. William et al. (1926). *The Story of the Canton Villages Mission of the Presbyterian Church of New Zealand*. Dunedin: Foreign Missions Committee.

Mayhew, W.R. (1949). *Tuapeka, The Land end the People: A Social History of Lawrence and Surrounding Districts*. Dunedin: Otago Centennial Historical Publications.

McArthur, John (1945). *The Narrative of John McArthur, written by McArthur in March 1945 (recalling 1870s–1880s)*. Copy in possession of the late P. Chandler, Ettrick.

McDonald, K.C. (1962). *White Stone Country*. Oamaru. North Otago Centennial Committee.

McGill, David (1982). *The Other New Zealanders*. Wellington: Mallinson Rendell Publishers Ltd.

McGovern-Wilson, Rick (1984a). Report on the bird bones from Chinese sites at Cromwell and Arrowtown. Unpublished manuscript, 7p. August 1984.

McGovern-Wilson, Rick (1984b) Report on bones (avian) from various Chinese/Historic sites in the Clutha Valley. Unpublished manuscript, 5p. October 1984.

McGowan, B. (2003). The archaeology of Chinese alluvial mining in Australia. *Australasian Historical Archaeology* 21: 11–17.

McKee & Co (1902). *Trade and Commerce and Industries of New Zealand, and Glimpses of Australia*. Christchurch: McKee & Co, printer and publisher.

McNeur, Margaret J. (Mrs Moore). (1930). The Chinese in New Zealand. Unpublished Master's thesis, Department of History, University of Otago, Dunedin.

McNeur, Rev. G.H. (1951). *The Church and Chinese in New Zealand* (pamphlet). Dunedin: Presbyterian Bookroom.

Millar, R.D. (1972). Early Reactions and Attitudes to Chinese Immigrants in Otago 1866–1870. Essay submitted in partial fulfilment of requirements for Honour's degree, Post-graduate Diploma in History, University of Otago, Dunedin.

Miller, George (1983). Wild horses, water barons, and Chinese sojourners: archaeology of Yema-Po, a Chinese construction camp in San Francisco's East Bay Hills. *C.E. Smith Museum Bulletin* 1(2): 2–8. Hayward, California: California State University.

Miller, J. Jefferson, and Lyle M. Stone (1970). Eighteenth century ceramics from Fort Michilimackinac. *Smithsonian Studies in History and Technology* 4. Washington, D.C.: Smithsonian Institution Press.

Miller, Martin and Judith Miller (1983). *Miller's Antique Price Guide* Vol. 4. The Grange, Beneden, Kent: MJM Publications.

Mitchell, John (1983). The history and archaeology of the armed constabulary archaeological sites along the Napier-Taupo road, 1869–1885. Unpublished research essay, Anthropology Department, University of Auckland, Auckland.

Morgan, R. (1974). *Mainly Codd's Wallop: The Story of the Great British Pop Bottle*. Wellingborough: Kollectorama.

Morse, H.B. (1966). *The Trade and Administration of the Chinese Empire*. Reprint of the 1907 original, Chong Wen, Taipei, Taiwan.

Mote, Frederick W. (1979). Yuan and Ming. In K.C. Chang, ed. *Food in Chinese Culture: Anthropological and Historical Perspectives*, 193–258. New Haven: Yale University Press.

Murray, Ron (pers. comm.). Historian of Cromwell who also has an extensive local photograph collection.

National Canners Association (1963). *The Canning Industry: Its History, Importance, Organization, Methods and the Public Service Value of its Products*. Washington, D.C.: National Canners Association.

Nichol, Reginald 1979 *Preliminary Report. on the Excavation of a Well in Albert Barracks, Auckland. New Zealand Archaeological Association Newsletter* 22 (3): 97–104.

New Zealand Antique Bottle Collector, Antique Publications, Auckland, 1970, and other issues.

New Zealand Board of Health (1970). *Drug Dependency and Drug Abuse in New Zealand*, New Zealand Board of Health Report Series No. 14.Wellington. New Zealand Board of Health.

Nee, Victor G. and Brett de Barry Nee (1973). *Longtime Californ': A Documentary Study of an American Chinatown*. New York: Pantheon Books.

Newman, Mary (1977) An archaeological survey of the new Cromwell Gorge highway. Unpublished paper for New Zealand Historic Places Trust.

Ng, James (1972a). Who are the New Zealand Chinese? *Otago Daily Times*, 22/7/1972 and 29/7/1972.

Ng, James (1972b). Chinese goldminers in Otago. *The Courier*, 9: 5–14. November 1973, Queenstown and District Historical Society.

Ng, James (1981). Perspectives in the history of the New Zealand-Chinese goldseekers. In *Sources and Methods of Writing Goldfields History*. Ex ARANZ conference, Dunedin.

Ng, James (1984a). One man's vision: the Canton Village Mission. *Otago Daily Times* "Weekend Magazine", 1/2/1984:17.

Ng, James (1984b). Choie Sew Hoy: pioneer from China. *Otago Daily Times* "Weekend Magazine", 29/9/1984:21.

Ng, James (1993–1999). *Windows on a Chinese Past* (4 volumes). Dunedin: Otago Heritage Books.

Ng, James (2016). The Otago Chinese goldminers: factors that helped them survive. In L. Carpenter and L. Fraser, eds. *Rushing for Gold: Life and Commerce on the Goldfields of New Zealand and Australia*, 101–21. Dunedin: Otago University Press.

O'Dell, Shannon (1982). *Domestic Metal Utensils from the Jose Trestle Construction Camp, 45-Fr-51, Lower Monumental Project*. Report for Anthro 502, Artefact Analysis, University of Idaho.

Oliver, W.R.B. (1974). *New Zealand Birds*. Wellington: Reed.

Olsen, John W. (1978). A study of Chinese ceramics excavated in Tucson. *The Kiva* 44(1): 1–50. Tucson, Arizona: published for the Arizona Archaeological and Historical Society.

Olsen, John W. (1983). An analysis of East-Asian coins excavated in Tucson, Arizona. *Historical Archaeology* 17(2): 41–55.

Oswald, A. (1975). *Clay Pipes for the Archaeologist*. British Archaeological Reports Series 14. Oxford, England: B.A.R.

Otago Acclimatisation Society (1891). *Annual Report of the Society*. Dunedin: J Wilkie & Co.

Otago Goldfields Park (1984). Provisional management plan for Arrowtown Chinese Settlement, Lands & Survey Department, Dunedin.

Parcell, J.C. (1976). *Heart of the Desert: A History of the Cromwell and Bannockburn Districts of Central Otago*. First published in 1951 as part of Otago Centennial Historical Publication Series, 2nd edition. Christchurch: Whitcouls.

Park, G. Stuart (1978). *An introduction to New Zealand Commercial Ceramics*. Published in conjunction with an exhibition in the Otago Museum, Dunedin.

Park, G. Stuart (1980). Chinese coins in New Zealand. *New Zealand Numismatic Journal* 15(2): 55–61.

Passmore, Jacki and Daniel P. Reid (1982). *The Complete Chinese Cookbook: Over 500 Authentic Recipes from China*. New York: Exeter Books.

Pastron, Allen G., R. Gross and Donna Garaventa (1981). Ceramics from Chinatown's tables: an historical archaeological approach to ethnicity, Appendix C: Chinese ceramic ware collected at N-5. In Pastron, Prichett and Ziebarth (eds). *Behind the Seawall: Historical Archaeology along the San Francisco Waterfront*, 365–469 and 653–82. San Francisco: San Francisco Clean Water program.

Pastron, Allen G., Jack Prichett and Marilyn Ziebarth (1981). *Behind the Seawall: Historical Archaeology along the San Francisco Waterfront* (3 volumes). San Francisco: San Francisco Clean Water Program.

Paulin, Christopher (pers. comm.). Fish specialist, National Museum, Wellington.

Peacock, P. (1972). *Buttons for the Collector.* Newton Abbot: David and Charles.

Pearce, G.L. (1976). *The Scots of New Zealand*. Auckland: Collins.

Pearce, G.L. (1982). *The Pioneer Craftsmen of New Zealand*. Auckland: Collins.

Perriam, Charles (pers. comm.). Farmer of Lowburn, information about the Lowburn Chinese Camp.

Peters, Frank (1981). *Fruit Jar Manual and Price Guide* (revised edition). Maverick Publications. Original 1973 edition published by *Old Bottle Magazine*, Bend, Oregon.

Pfeiffer, Michael A. (1985). Tobacco pipes from the Arrowtown Chinese Settlement, Central Otago, New Zealand. Unpublished manuscript.

Petersen, G.C. 1956 *Forest Homes: The Story of the Scandinavian Settlements in the Forty Mile Bush, New Zealand.* A H and A W Reed, Wellington.

Piper, Andrew (1984). Nineteenth century Chinese goldminers of Central Otago: a study of the interplay between cultural conservatism and acculturation through an analysis of changing diet. Unpublished BA Hons dissertation, Anthropology Department, University of Otago, Dunedin.

Piper, Andrew (1988). Chinese diet and cultural conservatism in nineteenth-century Southern New Zealand. *Australasian Historical Archaeology* 6: 34–42.

Pope, Marjorie (1984). *Textiles Recovered from the Woodland Opera House Site.* California Archaeological Reports 24: 139–46.

Potter, H.W. (1890). *Westward Ho! A Trip through the Western District of Southland, its Goldfields, Coal Measures and Agricultural Resources.* Invercargill: Phoenix Printing Co.

Praetzellis, Adrian and Mary Praetzellis (1979). The Lovelock ceramics. In Eugene M. Hattori, M.K. Rusco and D.R. Tuohy, eds. *Archaeological and Historical Studies at Ninth and Amherst, Lovelock, Nevada*, 140–98. Carson City, NV: Nevada State Museum Archaeological Services.

Praetzellis, Mary and Adrian Praetzellis (1982). *Archaeological and Historical Studies of the IJ56 Block, Sacramento, California: An Early Chinese Community.* Cultural Resources Facility, Anthropological Studies Center, Sonoma State University.

Prazniak, Roxann (1984). The Chinese in Woodland. In *The Chinese Laundry on Second Street: Papers on Archaeology at the Woodland Opera House Site.* California Archaeological Reports 24: 121–38. Department of Parks and Recreation, Sacramento, California.

Preshaw, G.O. (1888). *Banking Under Difficulties or Life on the Goldfields.* Sydney: Edwards, Dunlop & Co. Capper Press reprint 1977, Christchurch, NZ.

Price, C.A. 1974 *The Great White Walls are Built: Restrictive immigration to North America and Australasia 1836–1888.* Canberra: Australian Institute of International Affairs.

Prickett, Nigel (1981). The archaeology of a military frontier, Taranaki, New Zealand, 1860–1881. Unpublished PhD thesis, Anthropology Department, University of Auckland, 2 volumes.

Quellmalz, Carl Robert (1972). Chinese porcelain excavated from North American Pacific Coast sites. *Oriental Art* 18(2): 148–54.

Quellmalz, Carl Robert (1976). Late Chinese provincial export wares. *Oriental Art* 22(3): 289–98.

Rains, K. (2003). Rice bowls and beer bottles: interpreting evidence of overseas Chinese at Cooktown dumpsite. *Australasian Historical Archaeology* 21: 30–41.

Reader, W.J. (1976). *Metal Box: A History.* London: Heinemann.

Redmond, Doug (1983 pers. comm.). Bottle collector, Christchurch. Owner of the Redmond Collection.

Riddiford, Andrew (1890). Map of Bannockburn and environs. Hocken Library, Dunedin.

Ritchie, Neville A. (1978). The Archaeological Considerations of the Clutha Valley Development Project. In *Papers Presented to the Engineering Seminar, Cromwell, October 1978.* NZ Institute of Engineering Technicians.

Ritchie, Neville A. (1979a). The Clutha Valley Development Project: Archaeological and Cultural Resource Management. In J. McKinlay and K.L. Jones, eds. *Archaeological Resource Management in Australia and Oceania. Papers from the 49th ANZASS Congress*, Auckland Jan. 1979, N.Z.H.P.T., Wellington.

Ritchie, Neville A. (1979b). The Clutha Valley Development. Archaeological Programme. *New Zealand Archaeological Association Newsletter* 22(4): 162–72.

Ritchie, Neville A. (1980a). The Excavation of a Nineteenth Century Chinese Mining Settlement: Cromwell's Chinatown. *New Zealand Archaeological Association Newsletter* 23(4): 69–85.

Ritchie, Neville A. (1980b). Luggate-Upper Clutha Archaeological Survey. New Zealand Historic Places Trust, Cromwell.

Ritchie, Neville A. (1980c). Queensberry Archaeological Survey. New Zealand Historic Trust, Cromwell.

Ritchie, Neville A. (1981). Archaeological Interpretation of Alluvial Gold Tailing Sites, Central Otago, New Zealand. *New Zealand Journal of Archaeology* 3: 51–69.

Ritchie, Neville A. (1982a). Bobs Cove-12 Mile Creek Archaeological and Historic Sites Survey. For Lands and Survey Dept, Dunedin.

Ritchie, Neville A. (1982b). The Prehistoric Role of the Cromwell Gorge. *New Zealand Journal of Archaeology* 4: 21–43.

References

Ritchie, Neville A (1983a). Archaeological Research on Nineteenth Century Chinese Settlement in the Cromwell Area. *The Courier* 29: 2–18. May 1983. Bulletin of the Queenstown and District Historical Society.

Ritchie, Neville A. (1983b). Kawarau Valley Archaeological Survey Report. New Zealand Historic Places Trust, Cromwell.

Ritchie, Neville A. (1984). The Arrowtown Chinese Settlement: An Interim Report on the Excavation. Lands and Survey Dept, Dunedin.

Ritchie, Neville A. (1985). Alpine Archaeology I: The First Hermitage Site, Mt Cook. New Zealand. Historic Places Trust, Cromwell.

Ritchie, Neville A. (1986). The written word: writing equipment from Chinese sites in Central Otago. *New Zealand Archaeological Association Newsletter* 29(1): 41–51.

Ritchie, Neville, A. (1992). Form and adaptation: nineteenth century Chinese miners dwellings in Southern New Zealand. In P. Wegars, ed. *Hidden Heritage: Historical Archaeology of the Overseas Chinese*, 335–74. New York: Baywood Publishing Company.

Ritchie, Neville A. (2003). Taking stock: 20 years of Australasian Chinese archaeology. *Australasian Historical Archaeology* 21: 4–10.

Ritchie, Neville A. (2021). Looking back on the Clutha Valley Archaeology Project 1977–1986. Paper presented to the Clutha Archaeology Seminar organised by the Otago Anthropological Society, University of Otago, Dunedin, September 2021.

Ritchie, Neville A. (n.d.a) The Excavation of a Maori Camp Site, Italian Creek, Central Otago. New Zealand Historic Places Trust, Cromwell, unpublished manuscript.

Ritchie, Neville A. (n.d.b). The Role of Euro-ceramics in Nineteenth Century Chinese Mining settlements in Central Otago. New Zealand Historic Places Trust, Cromwell, unpublished manuscript.

Ritchie, Neville A. (n.d.c). From Bullets to Solder: Chinese Lead Salvage. New Zealand Historic Places Trust, Cromwell, unpublished manuscript.

Ritchie, Neville A. and Stuart H. Bedford (1983). Analysis of the glass containers and bottles from Cromwell's Chinatown. *New Zealand Archaeological Association Newsletter* 26(4): 235–58.

Ritchie, Neville A. and Stuart H. Bedford (1985). Analysis of the metal containers from Chinese sites in the Cromwell area. *New Zealand Journal of Archaeology* 7: 95–116.

Ritchie, Neville A. and Ann P. Harrison (1982). An Archaeological Analysis of Opium Smoking and Associated Artefacts from Chinese Sites in Central Otago. New Zealand Historic Places Trust, Cromwell. 46pp draft for comment. (much of the quantitative data in this paper is now out of date; the thesis contains the up-to-date data).

Ritchie, Neville A. and R. McGovern-Wilson (1986). A study of avifaunal remains from Chinese sites in Central Otago, New Zealand. *New Zealand Journal of Archaeology* 8: 61–71.

Ritchie, Neville A. and Stuart Park (1988). Chinese coins Down Under: their role on the New Zealand goldfields. *Australian Journal of Historical Archaeology* 5: 41–8.

Ritchie, Neville A. and Mary Casey, eds (2003). Taking Stock: 20 years of Australasian "Overseas Chinese archaeology" *Australasian Historical Archaeology* 21. contains 8 papers on Chinese site work mainly in Australia.

Roebuck, Lou (pers. comm. 1981–84). Former resident of Clyde who lived with some ex-Central Otago Chinese in Dunedin c.1920. Tape-recorded discussions re the Chinese.

Roop, William and Katherine Flynn (pers. comm. 1986). Consulting Archaeologists, Archaeological Resource Service, Novato, California. At the time writing up an urban Chinese site excavation in San Jose, California.

Rosen, Martin D. (1978). Faunal remains as indicators of acculturation in the Great Basin. *University of California, Los Angeles, Institute of Archaeology, Monograph* 7: 35–82.

Rossbach, S. (1985). *Feng Shui: ancient Chinese wisdom on arranging a harmonious living environment*, First published 1983. Rider imprint of the Hutchinson Publishing Group, London. 1985.

Roxburgh, Irvine (1957). *Wanaka Story: A History of the Wanaka, Tarras, Hawea and Surrounding Districts.* Christchurch: Otago Centennial Publications.

Rusden, Keith G. (1979). *Aerated Water Manufacturers of Eden Crescent 1845–1964.* Auckland: Elliot Stationery Limited.

Rusden, Keith G. (1982). *Clay Pipes. Their History and Varieties Found in New Zealand.* Auckland: privately published.

Salmon, J.H.M. (1963). *History of Goldmining in New Zealand.* Wellington: R.E. Owens, Government Printer.

Sanders, Charlie (pers. comm.). Retired butcher of Cromwell.

Sando, Ruth Ann and David L. Felton (1984). Inventory records of ceramics and opium from a nineteenth-century overseas Chinese store. Preliminary draft. Department of Parks and Recreation, Sacramento, California.

Savage, George and Harold Newman (1976). *An Illustrated Dictionary of Ceramics.* New York: Van Nostrum Reinhold Co.

Schild, Gary (1972). *Tobacco Tin Tags: A Listing of Over 3,000 Tags with 200 Illustrations.* Westbrook, CT: John L. Prentis (printer).

Schroeder, Joseph J., Jr, ed. (1970). *Montgomery Ward & Co. 1894–95 Catalogue and Buyers Guide.* Reprint published by Gun Digest Co, Northfield, Illinois.

Schulz, Peter D. (1979). Historical faunal remains from Panamint City: notes on diet and status in a California boom town. *Pacific Coast Archaeological Society Quarterly* 15(4): 55–63.

Schulz, Peter D. and Sherri Gust (1983). Faunal remains and social status in 19th century Sacramento. *Historical Archaeology* 17(1): 44–53.

Schulz, P.D. and B.J Rivers, M.M. Hales, C. A Litzinger, E.A. McKee. (1980). The bottles of Old Sacramento: a study of nineteenth century glass and ceramic retail containers. Part 1. California Archaeological Reports 20. Sacramento, CA: Department of Parks and Recreation.

Schuyler, Robert, L., ed. (1980). Archaeological Perspectives on Ethnicity in America. Farmingdale, NY: Baywood Publishing Company.

Scott, Issie (pers. comm. 1980). Elder citizen of Cromwell who worked in Jolly's store, Cromwell, c.1910–20. Sold products to the Chinese.

Scurrah, Vernon H.H. (1950). Asiatic immigration into New Zealand 1870–1920. Unpublished Master's thesis, History, University of Auckland, Auckland.

Seaby, Peter and P Frank Purvey, eds. (1981). Standard Catalogue of British Coins. Vol.1 Coins of England and the United Kingdom 8th edn. London: Seaby Publications Ltd.

Sedgewick, Charles P. (1982). The politics of survival: a social history of the Chinese in New Zealand. Unpublished PhD thesis, University of Canterbury, Christchurch.

Sellari, Carlo, and Dot Sellari (1975). *The Illustrated Price Guide of Antique Bottles.* Waukesha, WI: Country Beautiful.

Sharp, A. (1984). The clay tobacco pipe collection in the National Museum. *Review of Scottish Culture* 1: 34–42.

Sherriff, Grant (1983). The Volunteer Movement. *Otago Early Settlers Museum Newsletter* No. 23, July 1983: 73–4.

Sherriff, Grant (pers. comm.). Numerous discussions on cartridges recovered from the study sites.

Short, Alan (pers. comm.). Of Queenstown. Discussions about his private Chinese artefact collection, much of which was acquired in the Nokomai area.

Simons, Dwight D. (1984). Avifaunal remains from the Woodland Opera House site. In *The Chinese Laundry on Second Street: Papers on Archaeology at the Woodland Opera House Site.* California Archaeological Reports 24: 167–80. Sacramento, CA: Department of Parks and Recreation, Sacramento, California.

Skennerton, I.D. (1975). *Australian Service Longarms.* Margate, Qld: Skennerton.

Skinner, J.D. (pers. comm. 1982). Letter with illustrations showing opium pipe bowls he had collected on the Palmer River goldfield, Queensland, Australia.

Smith, Lindsay (1998). Cold hard cash: a study of Chinese ethnicity in archaeology at Kiandra, NSW. Unpublished PhD thesis, Australia National University, Canberra.

Smith, Lindsay (2003). Identifying Chinese ethnicity through material culture: archaeological excavations at Kiandra, NSW. *Australasian Historical Archaeology* 21:18–29.

South, Stanley (1977) *Methods and Theory in Historical Archaeology.* New York. Academic Press

Spence, Jonathan (1977). The Ch'ing dynasty. In K.C. Chang, ed. *Food in Chinese Culture: Anthropological and Historical Perspectives*, 259–94. New Haven: Yale University Press.

Spier, Robert F.G. (1958). Food habits of nineteenth-century California Chinese. *California Historical Quarterly* 37: 79–84 and 129–36.

Spring-Rice, Wynn (1982). A dated collection of matchboxes from Fort Galatea historic reserve, Bay of Plenty. *New Zealand Archaeological Association Newsletter* 25: 103–12.

Spring-Rice, Wynn (1983). The history and archaeology of Fort Galatea, Bay of Plenty, New Zealand, 1869–1969. Unpublished Master's thesis, University of Auckland.

Stanford University. Cangdong Village Project (*Qiaoxiang* project). https://cangdong.stanford.edu/.

Stanford University Museum (1979). *Opium Pipes, Prints and Paraphernalia.* A catalogue produced for a display of these artefacts at the Stanford University Museum of Art.

Stapp, Darby and Julia Longenecker (1984). *Test Excavations at 10-CW-159, The Pierce Chinese Mining Site.* University of Idaho Anthropological Research Manuscript Series 80. Moscow: Laboratory of Anthropology, University of Idaho.

Steeves, Richard Laban (1984). Chinese gold miners of northeastern Oregon, 1862–1900. Unpublished Master's thesis presented to the Interdisciplinary Studies Program, University of Oregon, Eugene, Oregon.

Stitt, Irene (1974). *Japanese Ceramics of the Last 100 Years.* New York: Crown Publishers.

Stone's Directories (1887–1920). Otago-Southland editions, Hocken Library.

Sudbury, Byron (1977). History of the Pamplin area tobacco pipe industry. *Quarterly Bulletin of the Archaeological Society of Virginia* 32(2): 1–35.

Sudbury, Byron (1979). Historic Clay Tobacco Pipemakers in the United States of America. The Archaeology of the Clay Tobacco Pipe 11: 151–341. *British Archaeological Reports Series* 60. Oxford: B.A.R.

Sudbury, Byron (1980). *Historic Clay Tobacco Pipe Studies No.1.* Privately published, Byron Sudbury, Ponca City, OK.

Sullivan, Catherine (1984). Perry Davis Pain Killer. *Canadian Collector* 19(2): 45–8.

Summers, Sandy (pers. comm.). Retired butcher of Cromwell. Information on meat-cutting techniques.

Tchen, John Kuo Wei (1984). *Genthe's Photographs of San Francisco's Old Chinatown.* New York: Dover Publications Inc.

Temple, B.A. (1977). *The Boxer Cartridge in British Service.* Wynnum Central, Qld: B.A. Temple.

Thornton, Geoffrey (1982). *New Zealand's Industrial Heritage.* Wellington: Reed.

Tjio, Soen-Hong (1973). *The Study of Wan-Yiu (kiln, Hong Kong): History and Ceramic Art.* Monograph 2. Association of Research, Institute of Literature and History, The Chu Hai College, Hong Kong. In Chinese with brief English summary and photographs of the ceramics produced there.

Tomlin, S. (1978). Sham Wan, Lamma Island: an archaeological site study. *Journal Monograph III, Hong Kong Archaeological Society*, April 1978.

Toulouse, J.H. (1971). *Bottle Makers and their Marks.* New York: Thomas Nelson Inc.

Triestman, Judith M. (1972). *The Prehistory of China: An Archaeological Exploration.* Garden City, NY: Double Day & Co.

Trlin, Andrew D. (1979). *Now Respected, Once Despised: Yugoslavs in New Zealand.* Palmerston North: Dunmore Press.

Trotter, M. (1973). *Early Woodlands: A Local History.* Invercargill: Southland Printing and Publishing Co.

Tunnel, Curtis (1970). Texas: railroad construction camps. "Current research". *Society for Historical. Archaeology Newsletter* (2): 15–16. Also see *S.H.A. Newsletter* 5 (2):10.

Turner, M., Hill, K. and Clough, R. (2005). Chinese artefacts from a site in Wakefield St, Auckland. *Archaeology in New Zealand* 48(3): 260–78.

Twain, Mark (1972). *Roughing It: The Works of Mark Twain,* with an Introduction by F.R. Rogers and P. Baender. Published for Iowa Center for Textual Studies by the University of California Press, Berkeley.

Twohill, Nicholas (1984). Industrial archaeology of the Mt Zeehan goldmining property. Unpublished Master's thesis, Anthropology Department, University of Auckland, Auckland.

Umberger, Art and Jewel Berger (1971). The tobacco tag, an historical accident. *Western Collector* 9(5): 24–7.

Vader, J. and B. Murray (1975). *Antique Bottle Collecting in Australia.* Sydney: Ure Smith.

Wakeman, F., Jr (1966). *Strangers at the Gate.* Berkeley: University of California Press.

Walker, Iain C. (1971). Nineteenth-century clay tobacco pipes in Canada. *Ontario Archaeology* 16: 19–35.

Walker, Iain C. (1977). Clay tobacco pipes with particular reference to the Bristol Industry. *History and Archaeology* 11 A–D. Ottawa: Parks Canada.

Walker, P.L. and J.C. Long (1977). An experimental study of the morphological characteristics of tool marks. *American Antiquity* 42(4): 605–16.

Walters, Richard (in prep.). A major volume on four seasons of excavations at the Lawrence Chinese Camp, Central Otago, New Zealand.

Wegars, Priscilla (1981). *Ceramic Wares: Nez Perce National Park Archaeological Excavations, 1979–1980.* University of Idaho Anthropological Research Manuscript Series 70:115–42. Moscow, Idaho: Laboratory of Anthropology, University of Idaho.

Wegars, Priscilla (1983). Comprehending the inscrutable: unusual artefacts of Chinese manufacture. Paper presented at the 16th Annual Meeting of the Society for Historical Archaeology, Denver, Colorado.

Wegars, Priscilla (1985). The history of Chinese settlement in Moscow, Idaho and its relationship to railroads on the Palouse, 1885–1890. Paper prepared for History 523 class, University of Idaho.

Wegars, Priscilla (pers. comm.). Numerous helpful discussions. Research Associate, Laboratory of Anthropology, University of Idaho, Moscow, Idaho. Curator of the Asian American Comparative Collection, and Editor of the *AACC Newsletter*, based at the above institution.

White, D.P. (1977). The Birmingham button industry. *Journal of Post Medieval Archaeology* 11: 67–79.

White, Henry P. and Burton D. Munhall (1977). *Cartridge Headstamp Guide – First Revision.* H.P. White Laboratory, 3114 Scarboro Road, Street, Maryland, USA.

White, James S. (1979). *Diving for Northwest Relics: Identification and Dating, Bottles, Pottery and Marine Hardware.* Portland, OR: Binford & Mort.

White, Susie (2016). The McPhees: New Zealand's first pipe makers. *Archaeology in New Zealand* 59(3): 10–28.

Whitlow, Janice I. (1981). Soya sauce, bean cake, and ginger ale: Chinese material culture and an anthropological approach to historic sites archaeology. Unpublished Senior Honours thesis, Anthropology 180H, San Jose State University.

Willetts, William and Lim Suan Poh (1981). *Nonya Ware and Kitchen Ch'ing: Ceremonial and Domestic Pottery of the 19th–20th Centuries Commonly Found in Malaysia.* Selangor, Malaysia: Southeast Asian Ceramic Society, West Malaysian Chapter: Oxford University Press.

Willmott, W.E. (1964). Chinese clan associations in Vancouver, *Man* LXIV (49): 33–7.

Willmott, W.E. (1969). Some aspects of Chinese communities in British Columbia towns. *British Columbia Studies* 1: 27–36.

Wise's Directories. All editions between 1872–1920.

Wishart, D. (pers. comm.). Long-time citizen of Cromwell. Personal observations of the last residents in Chinatown c.1915.

Wodzicki, K.A. (1950). *Introduced Mammals of New Zealand: An Ecological and Economic Survey.* New Zealand Dept of Scientific and Industrial Research Bulletin 98. Wellington: D.S.I.R.

Wylie, Jerry (1980). Opium pipes and other Chinese artefacts from Boise Basin, Idaho. Review draft, USDA Forest Service, Intermountain Region, Idaho Zone. Boise, Idaho: *Idaho Cultural Resource Notebook.*

Wylie, Jerry and Richard Fike (1985). Overseas Chinese opium smoking material culture survey: preliminary results and request for assistance. Ogden, Utah: USDA Forest Service.

Yee, Rhoda (1975). *Chinese Village Cookbook: A Practical Guide to Cantonese Country Cooking.* San Francisco: Yerba Buena Press.

Yee, S.T. and Jean Martin (1978). *Chinese Blue & White Ceramics.* Southeast Asian Ceramics Society in conjunction with the National Museum, Singapore. Singapore: Arts Orientalis.

Yong, C.F. (1977). *The New Gold Mountain: The Chinese in Australia, 1901–1921.* Richmond, SA: Raphael Arts.

Yu, Leslie Tseng-tseng (1981). *Chinese Painting in Four Seasons: A Manual of Aesthetic Techniques.* Englewood Cliffs, NJ: Prentice-Hall.

Zhu, Ron and Ritchie, Neville (2019). Palmer River goldfield Chinese coin hoard: new evidence challenging its authenticity. *Chinese Southern Diaspora Studies* 8: 190–224.

INDEX

abbreviations and acronyms xv
acculturation
    definition 2
    effects over time 2–3
    voluntary and involuntary 2–3
archaeological excavations on Chinese sites, summary 55–62, 68–69, 74–106

background to the Clutha Archaeological Project xxi
bottled products (glass containers)
    alcohol consumption 110–12
    alcohol prices on the goldfields 198
    Chinese foods and non-foods (pharmaceuticals) 112–13, 195
    European foods and non-foods 108–12, 191–94, 196–97
    re-use/repurposing of bottles and glass containers 114

Chinese ceramics *see also* ceramics
    containers typology 121–30, 201–03
    frequency of Chinese ceramic types in New Zealand 132–33, 204–05
    measurements of Chinese ceramic containers Appendix 4
    measurements of Chinese tablewares Appendix 3
    missing Chinese ceramic links 130–31
    sources and types 114–15, 131
    tablewares typology 115–20, 199–200
ceramics
    see also Chinese ceramics, Euro-ceramics
    ceramic bowl terminology 322
    discussion and conclusions 136–38
    distribution and types 210–18
    predominant ceramics (Euro or Chinese) by site types 210
Chinese
    decline years post-1900 44, 47–48
    diaspora 5
    estimated costs of living 25, 49
    exhumation of *sin yan* (former men), return to China 45–47, 53
    filial obligations 25, 37, 44, 182
    getting established on the Otago goldfields 10, 22
    habitation types
        on the goldfields 30–23, 63–68, 70–72
        traditional 29–30
    homeland counties in Guangdong 5, 15, 42
    inherent beliefs 34, 43
    invitation to come from Victoria to the Otago goldfields 8
    labour contracts (road and rail construction) 15
    locations of upcountry Chinese stores Appendix 5
    mining
        earnings 37, 49, 52
        locations 32, 54
        methods, preferences and skills 33–37
        numbers involved in different types of mining over time 51
        offences and crimes 37, 42
        technology, traditional and adopted 33
    occupation trends in the 19th century 50
        other occupations 28, 49
    populations
        in New Zealand 14, 16
        on the goldfields 15, 18, 51
    phases of settlement in New Zealand 6
    recreation activities 26, 111, 186–68, 276, 395
    settlements, contemporary descriptions 28–32, 51
    social and religious events and festivals 38–40
    sojourners 7, 29, 186
    supply network, merchants and stores 23–35
    traditional medicine versus western medicine and doctors 43
cartridges and bullets
    lead salvage from bullets 168–69
    sources of cartridges 168
    types and dates 169–70
clothing
    buttons
        classified by garment 270
        distribution 266–68
        embossed with maker's names 269
        types 180–82
    Chinese glass beads 270
    European/western 182, 185, 446
    fittings (buckles, braces adjusters, etc.) 271–72
    footwear 183–85
    textiles 273
    traditional Chinese 10, 182
coins
    Chinese 187–89, 276, 397, Appendix 8
    English and New Zealand coins 277

discrimination against the Chinese 40
    1871 Commission on "the Chinese Question" 12
    certificates of exemption from poll tax 19
    forms of harassment 40

discrimination against the Chinese *(cont.)*
    imposition of poll tax and further restrictions 13–14
    successive anti-Chinese legislation 13
domestic utensils, types and distribution 234–40
Don, Rev. Alexander, biography 21
dynasties and dynastic marks xxiv

Euro-ceramics *see also* ceramics
    decorative styles 134
    manufacturer's marks and dates 135, 206–09
    tablewares and containers 133–34
    three main types 133
evidence of earlier Māori occupation in rockshelters 190

field surveys 55
foods and dietary analysis
    beef 402–03, 418–22
    birds
        domesticated 409, 435–36
        wild 410, 435–36
    butchering units for beef, sheep and pig 433
    canned foods, contribution to diet 144
    Chinese butchering methods 403–04, 416
    Chinese hawkers 23, 49, 407–08, 444
    cleaved versus sawn cuts 427
    cuttlefish 412
    eels 412
    faunal analysis procedures 437
    fish, obtained locally and imported 411–12
    foods and beverages imported from China 121–30, 413–16
    foods/products of European/New Zealand origin adopted by the Chinese miners 444–45
    fruits and berries 415
    house gardens 414
    importance in Chinese culture 443
    inferences on diet from faunal analyses 415–17
    locally grown or wild foods 415, 452
    market gardens 414
    meat cut diagrams 438–41
    meat preferences 405–06
    minor animal foods/non-foods 408–09
    pork 403–04, 418, 423–26
    potatoes 415
    prices on the goldfields in the nineteenth century 436
    rabbit meat 409, 434
    settlement gardens 414
    sheep meat 404–04, 418, 428–31
    shellfish, including dried 411–12, 416, 451
    skeletal portion meat weights 432
    sources of beef, pork and sheep meats 407
    traditional diet in Guangdong 443
fossil fuels (coal and lignite) 189
framework, method and focus of book 1–3

gambling
    artefacts 276, 395–96
    role of Chinese coins (cash) in gambling 187–88
    social role, Chinese "love" of gambling 26
    types of gambling, games of chance 186–87
    venues 26

Historical Archaeology: introduction and role 1–2
horses, owned by Chinese 167
household and domestic artefacts 234–40

intermarriages (Chinese miners and Europeans) 29

Japanese ceramics 121, 208, 325

maps
    Canton Villages Mission, Guangdong 17
    Central Otago goldfields 54
    Chinese Mission map, Otago goldfields 18
    Clutha Valley Archaeological Project area 73
metal containers 138
    cans, discussion and insights 143–44
    historical background 138–40, 145
    metal boxes and cans, types and distribution 140–42, 219–20
    re-use, modification and repurposing 144
    wax vesta boxes
        origins, types and distribution 222–25
        use for dating 146–48
metals
    mercury, used for gold amalgamation 36, 114, 169, 193, 254, 297
    salvage and recycling of lead 169–71
musical instruments 164

nails
    analysis, Ah Lum's store 167, 244
    types and uses 165–67, 245–47, 359–60
New Zealand manufacturers 111–13, 133, 139–42, 158, 170, 183, 193–94, 196, 222, 261, 269, 288, 291–92, 295–97, 323, 335, 340, 347
nineteenth century commodity prices 436
numbers of Chinese in New Zealand: 1867–1981 Appendix 1

opium
    acquisition, smoking venues and use in NZ 28, 150, 154
    antidote cans (purported) 157
    archaeological evidence of opium smoking 152
    artefacts imported from China, Hong Kong 152
    artefacts made from copper opium can metal 155, 232
    cartouches 230–31
    containers 155
    discussion and conclusions on opium usage 150–68
    imports 148
    methodology 151

New Zealand-made opium pipe 158
Opium Prohibition Act 1901 28, 150
opium-related artefacts in study sites 227–28, 233
opium smoking artefacts, improvised 157
pipe bowl typology 226
prevalence in China 27
quantities and revenue from duty on opium imports Appendix 6
recreational usage and affects 151, 160
tincture of opium (laudanum), availability and use 160

paper artefacts 61, 176, 190
    container labels and wrappers 282
    cylindrical cardboard matchboxes (R. Bell and Co.) 282
    gold deposit receipts 282
    notes with Chinese writing (e.g. shopping lists) 61, 263
    of Chinese origin 263
    of European origin 282
    Paak kop piu gaming tickets 26, 176, 186, 263, 396
    pages from Bible written in Chinese 187, 263, 282, 400
patent and proprietary medicines 43, 109
    imported 43, 194, 291–93
    New Zealand-made 43, 194, 291–93
personal hygiene and grooming 275, 394
    combs 185, 275, 394
    manicuring tools 275, 394
    razors 185, 275, 394
    scissors 24, 152, 157, 163, 185, 236–68
    toothbrushes and toothpastes 177, 264–65, 374–75

recorded Chinese sites in Central Otago (in 1986) Appendix 2

scales and weights
    scale components 172
    types of scales 171–72
    weights 172
security-related artefacts 163, 354
Sew Hoy, dredging pioneer and mining entrepreneur 7, 10, 23, 36, 41, 46, 132
stone artefacts 190, 281
    inkstones 175, 177, 190, 281
    marble slabs 190, 281
    red ochre 190, 281
    slate (gridded) 190, 281, 398
study sites
    Ah Lum's store, Arrowtown 61
    Arrowtown Chinese camp 60–61
    architectural features and dimensions 63–67
    Cromwell Chinese camp (Chinatown) 57
    dates of occupation 62–63
    influence of feng shui 67–68
    internal layout and fittings 63–67

riverine rockshelters 56–57
rural sites 58, 60, 62
secondary sites 62
site plans 74–104
structural materials 190

tailings, mining xxii, 33–36, 56, 58–60, 62, 64, 69, 71, 107, 449
tobacco pipes 172
    brands, origins and dates 173
    McPhee, Dunedin pipe maker 173
    pipe components in sites 173
    types (clay, wood, vulcanite) 173–75
    ubiquity of tobacco smoking 175
tools
    carpentry 164
    distribution and types 241–43
    gardening 164
    mining 164
    rabbiting 165
    wood cutting 164
typologies (main ones) and associated descriptions
    Chinese opium can cartouches 229–30, 345
    Chinese opium pipe bowls 226, 343–44
    Chinese tablewares and containers 115–33, 199–205, 298–322
    European canned products 219–20, 327–29
    European buttons based on research by F. Cameron 375–86
    European wax vesta (match)boxes 330–41

weapon 171
    Eisenwerke air pistol 171
White Race League 42
women 28–29
writing and communications
    abacus beads 176
    accounting artefacts 176
    historical background, "the 4 precious things" 175
    inkstones 175, 177
    writing artefacts 175

www.ingramcontent.com/pod-product-compliance
Lightning Source LLC
Chambersburg PA
CBHW061538010526
44111CB00025B/2960